Psychology

Twelfth Edition

Carole Wade
Dominican University of California

Carol Tavris

Alan Swinkels, Contributor
St. Edward's University

PEARSON

Boston Columbus Indianapolis New York City San Francisco

Amsterdam Cape Town Dubai London Madrid Milan Munich Paris Montréal Toronto

Delhi Mexico City São Paulo Sydney Hong Kong Seoul Singapore Taipei Tokyo

VP, Product Development: *Dickson Musslewhite*
Executive Editor: *Erin Mitchell*
Editorial Assistant: *Danique Robinson*
Director, Content Strategy and Development: *Brita Nordin*
Development Editor: *Shannon LeMay-Finn*
VP Marketing: *Maggie Moylan*
Director, Project Management Services: *Lisa Iarkowski*
Project Team Lead: *Denise Forlow*
Project Manager: *Sherry Lewis*
Program Team Lead: *Amber Mackey*
Program Manager: *Reena Dalal*
Director of Field Marketing: *Jonathan Cottrell*
Senior Product Marketing Manager: *Lindsey Prudhomme Gill*
Executive Field Marketing Manager: *Kate Stewart*
Marketing Assistant, Field Marketing: *Amy Pfund*

Marketing Assistant, Product Marketing: *Frank Alarcon*
Operations Manager: *Mary Fischer*
Senior Operations Specialist: *Diane Peirano*
Associate Director of Design: *Blair Brown*
Interior Design: *Kathryn Foot*
Cover Art Director: *Maria Lange*
Cover Design: *Lumina Datamatics*
Cover Art: *Comstock Images/Stockbyte/Getty Images 98276187*
Digital Studio Product Manager: *Caroline Fenton*
Digital Studio Project Manager: *Pamela Weldin*
Digital Studio Team Lead: *Peggy Bliss*
**Full-Service Project Management
and Composition:** *SPi Global, Patty Donovan*
Printer/Binder: *RR Donnelley/Kendallville*
Cover Printer: *Phoenix Color/Hagerstown*

Acknowledgements of third party content appear on page 689, which constitutes an extension of this copyright page.

Library of Congress Cataloging-in-Publication Data
Names: Wade, Carole (Professor of psychology), author. | Tavris, Carol,
  author. | Swinkels, Alan, author.
Title: Psychology / Carole Wade, Carol Tavris, Alan Swinkels.
Description: Twelfth edition. | Upper Saddle River, NJ : Pearson Education,
  [2017]
Identifiers: LCCN 2015041762| ISBN 9780134240831 | ISBN 0134240839
Subjects: LCSH: Psychology.
Classification: LCC BF121 .W27 2017 | DDC 150--dc23 LC record available at
http://lccn.loc.gov/2015041762

10 9 8 7 6 5 4 3 2 1

Student Edition
ISBN-10:   0-13-424083-9
ISBN-13: 978-0-13-424083-1

Books a la Carte
ISBN-10:   0-13-437779-6
ISBN-13: 978-0-13-437779-7

To Howard, whose support has made it all possible.

Carole Wade

For Ronan, in loving memory.

Carol Tavris

Brief Contents

Contents

From the Authors

From the very first edition of our book, our primary goal has been the integration of critical and scientific thinking into the fabric of our writing, a goal that we believe is more important now than ever. A textbook is not a laundry list of items, and its writers are not simply reporters. For us, the most important job of an introductory textbook in psychology is to help students learn to think like a psychologist, and to understand why scientific and critical thinking is so important to the decisions they make in their own lives. Today, for example, the public in general, and students in particular, need to learn about the astonishing new developments in neuroscience, but they also need to learn to think intelligently about them. Not all of these developments are as dramatic or applicable as they are often made to appear in the popular press. Not all of the findings that are reported are based on good science, no matter how fancy the tools that produced them.

Changes in the 12th Edition

In this 12th edition of *Psychology*, we have retained the core concepts that characterized previous editions—an emphasis on critical thinking, applications to culture and human diversity, insights from research in biology and neuroscience—and added opportunities for students to test themselves on the material as they're learning it. In contrast to the usual "read and cram before tests" approach that students often rely on, we prompt students to read the material and challenge themselves to demonstrate their mastery of a section to make sure they understood it correctly.

At the end of Chapter 1, "Taking Psychology with You" is devoted to **The Nine Secrets of Learning**, a special feature directed to helping students understand and apply effective techniques for studying and mastering the material throughout the textbook. In this feature, we reassure students that they need not worry about their particular "learning style," whether visual or auditory; visualizing material helps everybody, and so does plain old active listening.

As always, in every chapter, we have updated the research to reflect progress in the field and cutting-edge discoveries. Here are a few highlights:

- Emerging techniques for mapping the brain, such as transcranial direct current stimulation (tDCS) and event-related potentials (ERP).
- New findings from the exciting field of epigenetics and genetic research in general.
- Revised sleep guidelines from the American Academy of Sleep Medicine.

- The new movement in psychological research to incorporate confidence intervals and Bayesian statistics to improve judgments about a finding's strength, reliability, and importance.
- Integration of DSM-5 terminology and classification systems.
- New findings on how self-confidence and grit contribute to achievement motivation.
- New chapter-opening vignettes that draw on recent real-world events to illustrate psychological principles and spark students' curiosity.

In addition, all chapter content is mapped to revised **learning objectives**, which highlight the major concepts throughout each chapter. The complete list of learning objectives for each chapter can be found in the *Instructor's Resource Manual*. The Test Bank items are also keyed to these learning objectives.

Goals and Principles

From the first edition of this book, five goals and principles have guided our writing. Here they are.

1. Thinking Critically about Critical Thinking

In a textbook, true critical thinking cannot be reduced to a set of rhetorical questions, a short boxed feature, or a formula for analyzing studies; it is a process that must be woven seamlessly into the narrative. The primary way we "do" critical and creative thinking is by applying a three-pronged approach: We *define* it, we *model* it, and we give students a chance to *practice* it.

The first step is to define what critical thinking is and what it is not. Chapter 1 introduces **Eight Guidelines to Critical Thinking**, which we draw on throughout the text as we evaluate research and popular ideas.

The second step is to model these guidelines in our evaluations of research and popular ideas. Throughout the textbook you'll find discussions of these critical thinking guidelines as we challenge the reader to evaluate what the evidence reveals—and importantly, does not reveal—about a particular phenomenon. Photo captions, writing prompts, and of course the narrative itself offer opportunities for students to sharpen their critical thinking skills to become active readers (and active learners) of psychology.

The third step is to give students opportunities to practice what we've preached. We have changed the Quick Quiz feature that was in previous editions to incorporate new end of module and end of chapter assessment. These tests require more than memorization of definitions; they help students check their progress, measure their understanding of the material, and encourage them to go back and review what they don't recall or comprehend. Many quiz questions include critical-thinking items that invite the students to reflect on the implications of findings and consider how psychological principles might illuminate real-life issues.

2. Exploring New Research in Biology and Neuroscience

Findings from the Human Genome Project, studies of behavioral genetics and epigenetics, discoveries about the brain, technologies such as fMRI, and the proliferation of medications for psychological disorders—all have had a profound influence on our understanding of human behavior and on interventions to help people with chronic problems. This work cannot be confined to a single chapter. Accordingly, we report new findings from biology and neuroscience wherever they are relevant throughout the book: in discussions of neurogenesis in the brain, memory, emotion, stress, child development, aging, mental illness, personality, and many other topics.

To further emphasize the integration of biology with other areas of research in understanding human problems, many chapters also have a feature called **Biology and . . .**—for example, "Biology and Hypnosis," "Biology and Beliefs," "Biology and Economic Choice," and "Biology and the Adolescent Brain." Although we caution students about the dangers of ignoring biological research, we also caution them about the dangers of reducing complex behaviors solely to biology by overgeneralizing from limited data, failing to consider other explanations, and oversimplifying solutions. Our goal is to provide students with a structure for interpreting research they will hear or read about in the future.

3. Mainstreaming Culture and Gender

At the time of our first edition, some considered our goal of incorporating research on gender and culture into introductory psychology to be quite radical, either a sop to political correctness or a fluffy and superficial fad. Today, the issue is no longer whether to include these topics, but how best to do it. From the beginning, our own answer has been to include studies of gender and culture in the main body of the text, wherever they are relevant to the larger discussion, rather than relegating these studies to an intellectual ghetto of separate chapters or boxed features. We discuss gender differences—and similarities—in many areas, from the brain, emotion, and motivation to heroism, sexuality, love, and eating disorders.

Over the years, most psychologists have come to appreciate the influence of culture on all aspects of life, from nonverbal behavior to the deepest attitudes about how the world should be. We present empirical findings about culture and ethnicity as topics warrant throughout the book. In addition, Chapter 8 highlights the sociocultural perspective in psychology and includes extended discussions of ethnocentrism, prejudice, and cross-cultural relations. However, the scientific study of cultural diversity is not synonymous with the popular movement called multiculturalism. The study of culture, in our view, should increase students' understanding of what culture means, how and why ethnic and national groups differ, and why no group is inherently better, kinder, or more moral than another. Thus, we try to apply critical thinking to our own coverage of culture, avoiding the twin temptations of ethnocentrism and stereotyping.

To highlight the importance of culture, many chapters contain a feature (comparable to "Biology and . . .") called **Culture and . . .**—for example, "Culture and the Brain," "Culture and Psychotherapy," "Culture and the Ideal Body," and "Culture and Mental Disorder."

4. Facing the Controversies

Psychology has always been full of lively, sometimes angry, debates, and we feel that students should not be sheltered from them. They are what make psychology so interesting! In this book, we candidly address controversies in the field of psychology, try to show why they are occurring, and suggest the kinds of questions that might lead to useful answers in each case. For example, we discuss the controversies about evolutionary psychology's explanations of human dating and mating practices (Chapter 3); limitations and the oversimplification of brain-scan technology (Chapter 4); the disease versus learning models of addiction (Chapter 15); the extent of parents' influence on their children's personality development (Chapters 13 and 14); conflicts of interest in research on medication for psychological disorders (Chapter 16); and the scientist-practitioner gap in psychotherapy (Chapter 16).

5. Applications and Active Learning

Finally, throughout this book, we have kept in mind one of the soundest findings about learning: It requires the active encoding of material. Several pedagogical features in particular encourage students to become actively involved in what they are reading.

You Are about to Learn . . . consists of a set of learning objectives that cover each major section within a chapter.

Other pedagogical features designed to help students study and learn better include **review tables**; a **running glossary** that defines boldfaced technical terms on the pages where they occur for handy reference and study; a **cumulative glossary** at the back of the book; a list of **key terms** at the end of each chapter that includes page numbers so that students can find the sections where the terms are covered; **chapter outlines**; and **chapter summaries** in paragraph form to help students review.

Taking Psychology with You, a feature that concludes each chapter, illustrates the practical implications of psychological research for individuals, groups, institutions, and society. This feature tackles topics of personal interest and relevance to many students: Does watching media violence or playing violent video games increase violence? How much control do we have over our emotions and our health? How can we motivate ourselves to reach our goals? How can we avoid being suckered by the "Barnum Effect"?

At the very end of the book, an epilogue called "Taking This Book with You" wraps up the text's major themes and suggests ways that students can apply what they have learned to ongoing concerns in their lives.

The Importance of Testing Yourself on What You've Studied

In our years of teaching, we have found that certain study strategies can greatly improve learning, and so we'd like to offer you, our reader, the following suggestions. Do not try to read this textbook the way you might read a novel, taking in large chunks at a sitting. If you are like most students, your favorite strategy is to read the textbook and your notes, and then simply read them again, but this is not really the best way to learn.

If you could do just one thing that would improve your learning and improve your grades it is this: Test yourself on what you've studied early, often, and repeatedly. Ask yourself questions, answer them, and then go back and restudy what you didn't know. Test yourself again and again until you learn the material. Even when you have learned it, you need to keep testing yourself regularly over the semester so that what you've learned stays learned. At the end of Chapter 1, we provide you with some other proven techniques to help you learn.

To get the most from your studying we recommend that you read only a part of each chapter at a time. Instead of simply reading silently, nodding along saying "hmmmmm" to yourself, try to restate what you have read in your own words at the end of each section. As specific points in each chapter, you will find several **Journal Writing Prompts** that challenge you to not just recall what you've learned, but actively develop your understanding of the material. These exercises will help you to discover what you know or still don't understand.

We have never gotten over our own initial excitement about psychology, and we have done everything we can think of to make the field as lively and absorbing for you as it is for us. However, what you bring to your studies is as important as what we have written. This text will remain only a collection of pages unless you choose to read actively, using the many active-learning and critical-thinking features we have provided.

Psychology can make a real difference in your own life, and we hope you will enjoy studying about it in this book. Welcome to psychology!

Carole Wade
Carol Tavris

Overview of Critical Thinking

One of the greatest benefits of studying psychology is that you learn not only about the findings of the field but also how to think critically. The following eight guidelines, which are emphasized throughout this book, will help you separate good psychology from pseudoscience. (For a full description, see Chapter 1.)

Eight Essential Guidelines to Critical and Creative Thinking

1   Ask questions; be willing to wonder.

- Why has obesity reached epidemic proportions all over the world? (Chapter 12)
- Do most adolescents really go through adolescent turmoil? (Chapter 13)

2   Define your terms.

- How should we define "prejudice"? Is feeling uncomfortable around unfamiliar members of another group the same as being prejudiced toward them? Is having an unconscious negative association with a stereotyped group the same as being overtly bigoted? (Chapter 8)
- In general, it's good to feel "in control" of your life, but what does control mean, exactly? Is it good to believe that you can control everything? (Chapter 11)

3   Examine the evidence.

- After disasters such as hurricanes and acts of terrorism, survivors are often offered "posttraumatic therapy" sessions. Do these interventions help, make no difference, or sometimes make matters worse? (Chapter 16)
- Under hypnosis, Jim remembers that he was a fourteenth-century French prince in a former life. Does the evidence support his memory? Can Jim speak fourteenth-century French and report accurate details of a life in a Parisian palace? (Chapter 5)

4   Analyze assumptions and biases.

- How do psychological scientists and psychotherapists differ in their assumptions about the relevance of research to clinical practice? (Chapter 16)
- Many people assume that women are the more "emotional" sex. Are they right? (Chapter 11)

5   Avoid emotional reasoning.

- Most people have strong beliefs about religious and political issues. How might their emotions and differing values affect their ability to assess the evidence for or against those beliefs? (Chapter 8))
- Many people are emotionally committed to their beliefs in psychic powers and ESP. Are they kidding themselves? (Chapter 6)

6   Don't oversimplify.

- Many people are enthusiastic about using brain scans as windows into the brain's workings. But if a scan shows that a brain area is active when a person is doodling, does that mean we've found the brain's "doodling center"? (Chapter 4)

- What's wrong with asking "Do children always lie (or always tell the truth) about sexual abuse?" (Chapter 10)

7 Consider other interpretations.

- Many people believe that brain abnormalities cause alcoholism. But might excessive alcohol cause brain abnormalities? (Chapter 15)

- Does watching TV make kids aggressive, or do aggressive kids watch more TV? Or could a third factor be involved? (Chapters 2 and 7)

8 Tolerate uncertainty.

- What do dreams mean? Do they have deep hidden meanings or are they random signals of a sleeping brain? At present, science doesn't have an answer everyone agrees on. (Chapter 5)

- If you think you remember your fourth birthday party perfectly, can you ever really be sure your memory is right? (Chapter 10)

From the Publisher

Teaching and Learning:

Integrated, Meaningful, Easy-to-Use Activities

As valuable as a good textbook is, it is one element of a comprehensive learning package. We at Pearson Publishers have made every effort to provide high-quality instructor and student supplements that will save you preparation time and will enhance the classroom experience.

For access to all instructor supplements for Wade and Tavris' *Psychology*, 12th edition, simply go to **www.pearsonhighered.com/irc** and follow the directions to register (or log in if you already have a Pearson user name and password). After you have registered and your status as an instructor is verified, you will be emailed a login name and password. Use your login name and password to access the catalogue. Click on *online catalog* and then > Psychology > General Psychology > Introductory Psychology > Wade/Tavris/Psychology, 12th edition. Under the description of each supplement is a link that allows you to download and save it to your computer.

You can request hard copies of the supplements through your Pearson sales representative. If you do not know your sales representative, go to http://www .pearsonhighered.com/replocator/ and follow the directions. For technical support for any of your Pearson products, you and your students can contact **247.pearsoned.com**.

Wade/Tavris/*Psychology*, 12th edition, is available in these formats:

- Paperback: 0-13-424083-9
- Revel: 0-13-432028-X
- Books a la Carte: 0-13-437779-6

REVEL™

Educational Technology Designed for the Way Today's Students Read, Think, and Learn

When students are engaged deeply, they learn more effectively and perform better in their courses. This simple fact inspired the creation of REVEL: an immersive learning experience designed for the way today's students read, think, and learn. Built in collaboration with educators and students nationwide, REVEL is the newest, fully digital way to deliver respected Pearson content.

REVEL enlivens course content with media interactives and assessments—integrated directly within the authors' narrative—that provide opportunities for students to read about and practice course material in tandem. This immersive educational technology boosts student engagement, which leads to better understanding of concepts and improved performance throughout the course.

Learn more about REVEL
http://www.pearsonhighered.com/revel/

Supplements for Instructors

The Instructor's Resource Center (**www.pearsonhighered.com/irc**) provides information and the following downloadable supplements:

Test Bank:

This test bank contains over 3,000 multiple choice, true/false, matching, short-answer, and essay questions, each referenced to the relevant page in the textbook. An additional feature for the test bank is the inclusion of *rationales for the conceptual and applied multiple-choice questions*. The rationales help instructors to evaluate the questions they are choosing for their tests and give instructors the option to use the rationales as an answer key for their students.

A Total Assessment Guide chapter overview makes creating tests easier by listing all of the test items in an easy-to-reference grid. All multiple-choice questions are categorized as factual, conceptual, or applied, and are correlated to each of the chapter's **learning objectives**. The Test Bank is available for download from the Instructor's Resource Center at www.pearsonhighered.com/irc.

MyTest:

The 12th edition test bank is also available through Pearson MyTest (**www.pearsonmytest.com**), a powerful assessment-generation program that helps instructors easily create and print quizzes and exams. Instructors can write questions and tests online, allowing them flexibility and the ability to efficiently manage assessments at any time, anywhere. Instructors can easily access existing questions and edit, create, and store using simple drag-and-drop and Word-like controls. Data on each question provide answers, textbook page number, and question types, mapped to the appropriate learning objective.

BlackBoard Test Item File and WebCT Test Item File:

For instructors who only need the test item file, we offer the complete test item file in BlackBoard and WebCT format. Go to Instructor's Resource Center at **www.pearsonhighered.com/irc**.

Writing Space

Writing Space Better writers make great learners—who perform better in their courses. To help you develop and assess concept mastery and critical thinking through writing, we created Writing Space. It's a single place to create, track, and grade writing assignments, provide writing resources, and exchange meaningful, personalized feedback with students, quickly and easily, including auto-scoring for practice writing prompts. Plus, Writing Space has integrated access to Turnitin, the global leader in plagiarism prevention.

Learning Catalytics

Learning Catalytics is a "bring your own device" student engagement, assessment, and classroom intelligence system. It allows instructors to engage students in class with real-time diagnostics. Students can use any modern, web-enabled device (smartphone, tablet, or laptop) to access it.

Standard Lecture PowerPoint Slides:

These slides, with **lecture notes, photos, and figures** are available online at **www.pearsonhighered.com/irc**.

Instructor's Resource Manual:

The Instructor's Resource Manual includes a detailed Chapter Lecture Outline, Lecture Launcher suggestions that draw on classic and current research findings, classroom-tested Student Activities, learning objectives for each chapter, and more resources to improve your classroom presentations.

Psychobabble and Biobunk: Using psychological science to think critically about popular psychology, 3ʳᵈ edition (ISBN 978-0-205-01591-7)

By Carol Tavris: This updated collection of book reviews and essays is tailored to the critical-thinking guidelines described in the 12th edition.

About the Authors

Carole Wade earned her Ph.D. in cognitive psychology at Stanford University. She began her academic career at the University of New Mexico, where she taught courses in psycholinguistics and developed the first course at the university on the psychology of gender. She was professor of psychology for 10 years at San Diego Mesa College and then taught at College of Marin and Dominican University of California. Dr. Wade has written and lectured widely on critical thinking and the enhancement of psychology education. In addition to this text, she and Carol Tavris have written *Psychology*; *Psychology in Perspective*; and *The Longest War: Sex Differences in Perspective*.

Carol Tavris earned her Ph.D. in the interdisciplinary program in social psychology at the University of Michigan. She writes and lectures extensively on diverse topics in psychological science and critical thinking. In addition to working with Carole Wade, Dr. Tavris is coauthor with Elliot Aronson of *Mistakes Were Made (But Not by Me): Why We Justify Foolish Beliefs, Bad Decisions, and Hurtful Acts*. She is also author of *The Mismeasure of Woman* and *Anger: The Misunderstood Emotion*. Many of her book reviews and opinion essays have been collected in *Psychobabble and Biobunk: Using Psychology to Think Critically About Issues in the News*.

Contributor Alan Swinkels is Professor and Chair of Psychology at St. Edward's University in Austin, Texas. He has received numerous research, advising, and teaching awards throughout his career, including being recognized as a Texas State Professor of the Year by the Carnegie Foundation and the Council for the Advancement and Support of Education.

Authors' Acknowledgments

Like any other cooperative effort, writing a book requires a support team. We are indebted to the following reviewers for their many insightful and substantive suggestions during the development of this edition of *Psychology* and for their work on supplements.

Pam Ansburg, Metropolitan State College of Denver
Joy Berrenberg, University of Colorado, Denver
Larry Cahill, University of California, Irvine
David Calhoun, Columbia College
Eve Clark, Stanford University
Paul Chance, Tokyo, Japan
Anne Coglianese, Ivy Tech Community College
Katherine Demitrakis, Central New Mexico
    Community College
William Domhoff, *University of California, Santa Cruz*
Michael Domjan, University of Texas
Kari Dudley, University of New Hampshire
Bart Ellenbroek, Victoria University of Wellington
Phoebe Ellsworth, University of Michigan
Kathleen Gerbasi, Niagara County Community College
Susan Gray, Barry University
Gina Grimshaw, Victoria University of Wellington
David Harper, Victoria University of Wellington
David Healy, Cardiff University
Diana Hingson, Florida Gateway College
Sheneice Hughes, Eastfield Community College

Fiona Jack, University of Otago
Lisa Jackson, Schoolcraft College
Robert Johnson, Arkansas State University
William Kimberlin, Lorain County Community College
Irving Kirsch, University of Plymouth and Harvard Medical
    School
Jennifer Lee, Cabrillo College
Geoff Loftus, University of Washington
Martha Low, WInston-Salem State University
Steven Jay Lynn, Binghamton University
Dorothy Marsil, Kennesaw State University
Jessica Maryott, Brandeis University
David McAllister, Salem State University
Kasey Melvin, Pamlico Community College
Diana Milillo, Nassau Community College
Bradley Mitchell, Ivy Tech State College
Robert Plomin, *Institute of Psychiatry, King's College, London*
Devon Polaschek, *Victoria University of Wellington*
Mark Rittman, Cuyahoga Community College
Susan Schenk, Victoria University of Wellington
Suzanne Schultz, Umpqua Community College
Lori Sheppard, Winston-Salem State University
Alan Swinkels, St. Edward's University
Nancy Voorhees, Ivy Tech Community College
Eric Weiser, Curry College
Christine Williams, Salem State University
Rachel Zajac, University of Otago

Chapter 1
What Is Psychology?

◀ Listen to the Audio

Learning Objectives

LO 1.1.A Define psychology, and describe how it addresses topics from a scientific perspective.

LO 1.1.B Provide examples of pseudoscience, psychobabble, popular opinion, and "plain old common sense" related to psychological topics, and describe how scientific psychology would address such claims.

LO 1.2.A Explain why critical thinking applies to all scientific pursuits, and also why it should guide everyday judgments and decision making.

LO 1.2.B List eight important critical-thinking guidelines and give an example of how each applies to the science of psychology.

LO 1.3.A Discuss some of the pre-psychological approaches to explaining psychological topics, from ancient times through the early 1800s.

LO 1.3.B Explain Wilhelm Wundt's contributions to the birth of modern psychology.

LO 1.3.C Compare the three early psychologies of structuralism, functionalism, and psychoanalysis, and identify the major thinkers who promoted each of these schools of thought.

LO 1.4.A List and describe the four major perspectives in psychology.

LO 1.4.B Describe how feminism influenced psychology.

LO 1.5.A Distinguish basic psychology and applied psychology, and summarize the kinds of research that various psychologists might conduct.

LO 1.5.B Compare the training and work settings of different psychological practitioners,

such as counselors, clinical psychologists, psychotherapists, psychoanalysts, and psychiatrists.

LO 1.5.C Give examples of three ways in which psychologists contribute to their communities.

Ask questions . . . be willing to wonder

How does "pop psych" on the Internet and TV differ from the psychology in this book?

If you want to think critically, must you always be critical?

If you call yourself a psychotherapist, will you be breaking the law?

What's the difference between a psychologist, a clinical psychologist, and a psychiatrist?

Every April Fools' Day, the James Randi Educational Foundation announces its "Pigasus" Awards for the year's worst "charlatans, swindlers, psychics, pseudo-scientists, and faith healers." James Randi is a professional magician who, years ago, became outraged to see charlatans and scammers use plain old magic tricks as evidence of their "psychic powers" and to prey on unsuspecting victims to make money. Randi made it his cause to educate the public by exposing their fraudulent methods. (The awards are named for the mythical flying horse Pegasus and for Randi's habit of saying, "such and such a belief will come true when pigs fly.") The awards and some recent "winners" include:

- The *Funder Pigasus Award*: The Pumpkin Hollow Retreat Center, for offering workshops and training on therapeutic touch (TT) as a method of healing. Practitioners of TT (which involves no touching and has shown no evidence of therapeutic powers) move their hands over a patient's body to realign the "human energy field" and redirect "healing energy" to afflicted areas. Interestingly, 9-year-old Emily Rosa executed a simple but elegant experiment for her fourth-grade science fair project demonstrating that TT therapists could not detect energy fields at levels better than chance, which suggests they'd have a hard time using that energy for any kind of

healing. Her publication in the *Journal of the American Medical Association* was by the youngest contributor ever (L. Rosa et al., 1998). By the way, Emily Rosa graduated from college with a degree in psychology.

- The *Refusal to Face Reality Award*: Mehmet Oz, a cardiac surgeon who has also promoted over the years faith healing, psychic communication with the dead, homeopathic medicines, and questionable weight loss schemes. "Dr. Oz," as he is known to fans of Oprah Winfrey (and from his own television and radio shows), holds an appointment at Columbia University and received his undergraduate degree from Harvard, yet he was recognized by the Randi Foundation for "his continued promotion of quack medical practices, paranormal belief, and pseudoscience." Dr. Oz also has the dubious distinction of winning the Pigasus Award more times than anyone else over the years.

How can you protect yourself from false claims and scammers? How can you tell the difference between treatments that work and save lives (such as vaccines) and those that are useless (such as therapeutic touch)? How are you supposed to distinguish useful information on the Internet from worthless opinions, marketing ploys, and downright rubbish?

Psychology, Pseudoscience, and Popular Opinion

Fortunately for you, you are taking an introductory psychology course, and by the time you finish it, you will have some good answers about how you can sift through the onslaught of claims competing for your attention, and decide what to ignore and what's important. To get a clear picture of this field, you need to know about its methods, its findings, and its ways of interpreting information. But first, let's look more closely at what psychology is, and equally importantly, what it is *not*.

What Psychology Is

LO 1.1.A **Define psychology, and describe how it addresses topics from a scientific perspective.**

In recent decades, the public's appetite for psychological and medical information has created a huge market for the kind of outlandish advice and products we just described to you: pseudoscience and quackery covered by a veneer of scientific-sounding language. Pseudoscience promises easy fixes to life's problems and challenges, such as resolving your unhappiness as an adult by "reliving" the supposed trauma of your birth, or becoming more creative on the job by "reprogramming" your brain. It often plays on the appeal of technology. All sorts of gizmos have been marketed with the promise that they will get both halves of your brain working at their peak: the Graham Potentializer, the Tranquilite, the Floatarium, the Transcutaneous Electro-Neural Stimulator, the Brain Supercharger, and the Whole Brain Wave Form Synchro-Energizer. (We are not making these up.)

The psychology you are about to study—*real* psychology—bears little relation to the popular psychology ("pop psych") and its pseudoscientific relatives (jokingly called "psychobabble") found on the Internet, on television, and in thousands of self-help books. **Psychology** can be defined generally as the discipline concerned with behavior and mental processes and how they are affected by an organism's physical state, mental state, and external environment. Unlike pop psychology, scientific psychology is based on research and **empirical** evidence, which is gathered by careful observation, experimentation, and measurement. It is therefore more complex, more informative, and far more helpful in its explanations than is popular psychology. Learn more about the many ways psychology impacts our daily lives in the video *Asking the Tough Questions 1*.

psychology
The discipline concerned with behavior and mental processes and how they are affected by an organism's physical state, mental state, and external environment; the term is often represented by Ψ, the Greek letter psi (usually pronounced "sy").

empirical
Relying on or derived from observation, experimentation, or measurement.

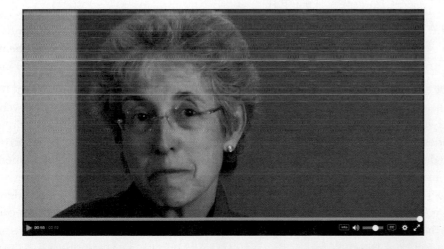

Psychologists use scientific methods to study many aspects of human behavior.

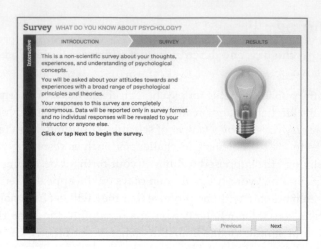

Scientific psychology also addresses a far broader range of issues than does popular psychology. When people think of psychology, they usually think of mental and emotional disorders, personal problems, and psychotherapy. But psychologists take as their subject the entire spectrum of brave and cowardly, intelligent and foolish, beautiful and brutish things that people do. They want to know how ordinary human beings (and other animals as well) learn, remember, solve problems, perceive, feel, and get along or fail to get along with others. They are therefore as likely to study commonplace experiences—rearing children, gossiping, remembering a shopping list, daydreaming, making love, and making a living—as exceptional ones.

What Psychology Is Not

LO 1.1.B Provide examples of pseudoscience, psychobabble, popular opinion, and "plain old common sense" related to psychological topics, and describe how scientific psychology would address such claims.

Because so many pop-psych ideas have filtered into the media, education, and even the law, we all need to develop an ability to distinguish between psychobabble and serious psychology, and between unsupported *popular opinion* and findings based on *research evidence*. Are unhappy memories "repressed" and then accurately recalled years later, as if they had been recorded in perfect detail in the brain? Do most women suffer from emotional symptoms of premenstrual syndrome (PMS)? Do policies of abstinence from alcohol reduce rates of alcoholism? If you play Beethoven to your infant, will your child become smarter? These beliefs are widely held, but as you will learn, they are wrong. Watch *Debunking Myths 1* to see some other common beliefs that people mistakenly hold.

At the start of an introductory psychology course, many students hold beliefs that have been promoted in the popular culture, or are based on personal experience or "common sense," but that are not scientifically supported. When two instructors gave their 90 introductory psychology students a true/false "Psychological Information" questionnaire on the first day of class—a questionnaire consisting entirely of false statements—the students were accurate only 38.5 percent of the time, which is actually worse than chance (Taylor & Kowalski, 2004). By the last week of class, however, when the students took a test containing all of the earlier items, their overall accuracy was much better: 66.3 percent (see Figure 1.1). Although there was still room for improvement, the students had lost confidence in their remaining misconceptions, suggesting that they were on the way to giving them up. If so, they had learned one of the most important lessons in science: Uncertainty about untested assumptions and beliefs can be a good thing.

Some people are influenced by psychology's many nonscientific competitors: palm-reading, graphology, fortune-telling, numerology, and the most popular, astrology. Like psychologists, promoters of these systems try to explain people's problems and predict their behavior. If you are having romantic difficulties, an astrologer may advise you to choose an Aries instead of an Aquarius as your next love, and a "past-lives channeler" may say it's because you were jilted in a former life. Belief in these unscientific approaches is widespread, even in scientifically advanced countries.

Yet, whenever the claims of psychics and astrologers are put to the test, those claims turn out to be so vague as to be meaningless ("Spirituality will increase next year") or just plain wrong—as in the case of all the doomsday predictions that have occurred for centuries, especially during times of great social change and anxiety (Radford, 2010; Shaffer & Jadwiszczok, 2010). Moreover, contrary to what you might think from watching TV shows that feature lead characters with psychic abilities or from reading claims on psychic websites, no psychic has ever found a missing child, identified a serial killer, or helped police solve any other crime by using "psychic powers" (Radford, 2011). Their "help" merely adds to the heartbreak the victim's family feels.

So why does belief in psychic abilities and other forms of pseudoscience persist? For one thing, it gives people a sense of control and predictability in a confusing world; indeed, our brains are probably wired to look for patterns in events, even when no patterns exist (Hood, 2009). Pseudoscience also confirms our existing beliefs and prejudices, whereas scientific psychology often challenges them. You do not have to be a psychologist to know that people do not always take kindly to having their beliefs challenged. You rarely hear someone cheerfully say, "Oh, thank you for explaining to me why my irrational beliefs are mistaken!" The person is more likely to say, "Oh, buzz off, and take your stupid ideas with you."

Psychological findings need not be surprising or counterintuitive, however, to be important. Sometimes they validate common beliefs and then explain or extend them. Like scientists in other fields, psychological researchers strive not only to discover new phenomena and correct mistaken ideas but also to deepen our understanding of an already familiar world—for example, by identifying the varieties of love, the origins of violence, or the reasons that a great song can lift our hearts. Fully understanding basic human processes that most people take for granted often involves examining them in a new light; turning common wisdom on its head for a different perspective, or shaking up cherished beliefs to see why and when they hold true. This kind of critical and creative thinking takes practice, and in the next section we'll suggest some guidelines that will allow you to adopt this same approach to understanding the psychological world around you.

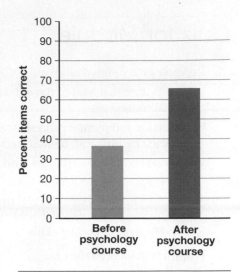

Figure 1.1 Psychology: It's Not Just "Common Sense"

On the first day of class, students in an introductory psychology course actually did worse than chance on a true–false psychological information questionnaire. But by the end of the semester, after they had learned to examine the scientific evidence for their beliefs, their performance had greatly improved.

JOURNAL PROMPT 1.1

Thinking Critically—Don't Oversimplify: Recall the last time you heard a claim that sounded too good to be true. Perhaps it had something to do with psychology ("Improve your memory in just 20 minutes"), health and fitness ("Get all the benefits of a complete workout in only 8 minutes a day"), or even a product promising to make your life easier ("One drop of Whizzo cleans your entire house!"). Describe the pseudoscience underlying the claim, and distinguish it from the real science that would be necessary to legitimately support the assertions. For example, the toned people shown exercising for 8 minutes a day can probably get away with it because they're already in shape to begin with. Hard data showing that sedentary people can achieve that same look in the same amount of time would be much more scientifically convincing.

Quiz for Module 1.1

1. Psychology is defined as an area of study concerned with:
   a. The factors that lead to flawed decision making in a social context
   b. Behavior and mental processes, and how these are affected by physical, mental, and environmental states
   c. The development, structure, and functioning of human society
   d. The biological bases of mental disorders and the interpersonal problems of adjustment faced by people who have poor coping skills

2. Empirical evidence refers to:
   a. Information that was gathered or derived from observation, experimentation, or measurement.
   b. The majority opinion adopted by most people when considering an issue.
   c. The opinions of experts that are believed by nonexperts for a given issue.
   d. The most straightforward explanation that can be offered for a particular phenomenon

3. "Getting poor grades in college is a result of students being lazy" is an example of _____. "Students who participated in a 6-week study skills course improved their grades by 15% by the end of the term" is an example of

   _____.

   a. Empirical evidence / empirical bias
   b. An opinion / research bias

   c. Research evidence / an opinion
   d. An opinion / empirical evidence

4. In one study you read about, a group of introductory psychology students completed a test of "psychological information" on the first day of class. What was the general result of that initial survey?
   a. Students were quite accurate in distinguishing factual statements about psychology from incorrect ones.
   b. Students believed that many false statements regarding psychology were actually true.
   c. Students performed better than chance at identifying correct findings from the psychological research literature.
   d. Students showed a bias to believe that all statements on the survey were false.

5. One reason why beliefs in pseudoscience and psychic abilities persist is that:
   a. They give people a sense of predictability in a confusing world
   b. Pseudoscience is still a type of science, and science is based on facts
   c. Psychic predictions have been shown to be accurate the majority of the time
   d. They challenge our existing beliefs, and humans like uncertainty

Thinking Critically and Creatively About Psychology

Throughout this book, you will gain practice in distinguishing scientific psychology from pseudoscience by thinking critically. As an approach to science, critical thinking forms the basis for all research methodologies. It can also serve as an excellent starting point for the way you approach the world in general. Separating fact from fiction, knowing what to believe and what to discard, and understanding how to evaluate evidence are important skills to have handy in your mental toolkit. But what does it mean to think critically, and how can you become skilled at it?

What Is Critical Thinking?

LO 1.2.A Explain why critical thinking applies to all scientific pursuits, and also why it should guide everyday judgments and decision making.

Critical thinking is the ability and willingness to assess claims and make objective judgments on the basis of well-supported reasons and evidence rather than emotion or anecdote. Critical thinkers are able to look for flaws in arguments and to resist claims that have no support. They realize that criticizing an argument is not the same as criticizing the person making it. Critical thinking, however, is not merely negative thinking. It includes the ability to be creative and constructive—the ability to come up with alternative explanations for events,

critical thinking

The ability and willingness to assess claims and make judgments on the basis of well-supported reasons and evidence rather than emotion or anecdote.

think of implications of research findings, and apply new knowledge to social and personal problems. Critical thinking is indispensable in ordinary life. Without it, people cannot formulate a rational argument or see through misleading ads that play on their emotions. They may have trouble assessing a political proposal or candidate, deciding whether or when to have children, or making medical decisions.

Most people know that you have to exercise the body to keep it in shape, but they may not realize that clear thinking also requires effort and practice. All around us, we can see examples of flabby thinking. Sometimes people justify their mental laziness by proudly telling you they are open-minded. Many scientists have observed that it's good to be open-minded, but open-mindedness does not mean that all opinions are created equal and that everybody's beliefs are as good as anyone else's (Hare, 2009). On matters of personal preference, that is true; if you prefer the look of a Chevy truck to the look of a Honda Accord, no one can argue with you. But if you say, "The Chevy truck is more reliable than a Honda and gets better mileage besides," you have uttered more than mere opinion. Now you have to support your belief with evidence of the car's reliability, mileage, and safety record (Ruggiero, 2011). And if you say, "Chevy trucks are the best in the world and Hondas do not exist; they are a conspiracy of the Japanese government," you forfeit the right to have your opinion taken seriously. Your opinion, if it ignores reality, is *not* equal to any other.

Critical thinking is fundamental to all science, including psychological science. It will also improve your life in countless ways, including helping you learn better: In the study of introductory students' misconceptions described earlier (Figure 1.1), students who did well on a critical-thinking test early in the course showed the greatest improvement over the semester. It will help you use the Internet better, too. You may pride yourself on being skilled at getting info with your favorite search engine, but a team of researchers found that most college students are easily tricked (Pan et al., 2007; Thompson, 2011). They tend to rely on the material that comes up at the top of the results list, without assessing its credibility: Was that profile of Martin Luther King, Jr. written by a scholar or by white supremacists? Is that article really a paid advertisement for some product? The researchers found that the average high school and college student is unable to detect hidden agendas in what they read; they need, in the words of Internet pioneer and critic Howard Rheingold, a course in "crap detection 101."

Will a baby become smarter by listening to classical music? Critical thinkers would insist on empirical evidence to answer this question.

Guidelines for Critical Thinking

LO 1.2.B List eight important critical-thinking guidelines, and give an example of how each applies to the science of psychology.

Critical thinking requires logical skills, but other skills and dispositions are also important (Anderson, 2005; Halpern, 2014; Levy, 2010; Stanovich, 2010). Here are eight essential critical-thinking guidelines that we will emphasize throughout this book.

ASK QUESTIONS; BE WILLING TO WONDER   What is one kind of question that parents of young children often hear? "Why" questions: "Why is the sky blue, Mommy?" "Why doesn't the plane fall?" "Why don't pigs have wings?" Unfortunately, as children grow up, they tend to stop asking "why" questions. (Why do you think this is?)

"The trigger mechanism for creative thinking is the disposition to be curious, to wonder, to inquire," observed Vincent Ruggiero (1988). "Asking 'What's wrong here?' and/or 'Why is this the way it is, and how did it come to be that way?' leads to the identification of problems and challenges." This educational program isn't working; why not? I want to stop smoking and improve my grades; why can't I seem to do it? Is my way of doing things the best way, or just the most familiar way? Critical thinkers are willing to question received wisdom—"We do it this way because this is the way we have always done things around here"—and ask, in essence, "Oh, yeah? Why?"

In psychological science, knowledge advances by asking questions. What is the biological basis of consciousness? How are memories stored and retrieved? Why do we sleep and dream? What causes schizophrenia? Critical thinkers are not discouraged by the fact that questions like these have not yet been fully answered; they see them as an exciting challenge. And they even enjoy thinking critically about poorly phrased questions, which can lead us to wrong answers. Consider the matter of homework. The questions have usually been: "Are American children doing too much homework or too little?" But as one observer wrote, "The question should be 'how effectively do children's after-school assignments advance learning?'" (Paul, 2011). As you probably know from experience, spending hours studying won't help you learn if you are not studying effectively—as you will see at the end of this chapter.

DEFINE YOUR TERMS   After you have raised a general question, the next step is to frame it in clear and concrete terms. "What makes people happy?" is a fine question for midnight reveries, but it will not lead to answers until you have defined what you mean by "happy." Do you mean being in a state of euphoria most of the time? Do you mean feeling pleasantly contented with life? Do you mean being free of serious problems or pain?

Vague or poorly defined terms in a question can lead to misleading or incomplete answers, or cause misunderstandings. For example, are people becoming less prejudiced against other groups? The answer may depend in part on how you define "prejudice." Everyone might agree that a conscious dislike of another group qualifies as a prejudice. But what if a person feels uncomfortable with another group because he or she is unfamiliar with its rules and beliefs; is that person bigoted or just uninformed? What if a person blurts out an insulting remark while drunk; is that person prejudiced or just drunk? What if a person is unaware of having any prejudiced beliefs or feelings, yet a test suggests that he or she has an unconscious prejudice; what does that mean? Psychologists have defined and measured this phenomenon, and they have obtained different results depending on how they define prejudice.

EXAMINE THE EVIDENCE   Have you ever heard someone in the heat of an argument exclaim, "I just know it's true, no matter what you say"? Have you ever made such a statement yourself? Accepting a claim or conclusion without evidence is a sure sign of lazy thinking. A critical thinker asks, "What evidence supports or refutes this argument and its opposition? How reliable is the evidence?" Have you ever received some dire warning or funny "I swear it's true!" story from a friend, and then posted it on your Facebook page, only to learn later that it was a hoax or an urban legend? A critical thinker would ask, "Is this story something I'd better check out on *snopes.com* before I tell my closest 90,000 friends?"

Sometimes, of course, checking the reliability of the evidence for a claim is not practical. In those cases, critical thinkers consider whether the evidence comes from a reliable source (Lipps, 2004). Sources who are reliable exercise critical thinking themselves. They have education or experience in the field in which they claim expertise. They do not pressure people to agree with them. They are trusted by other experts in the field. They share their evidence openly. In psychology, they draw on research conducted according to certain rules and procedures. For more tips on distinguishing reliable from less-reliable information, watch the video *Debunking Myths 2.*

ANALYZE ASSUMPTIONS AND BIASES   *Assumptions* are beliefs that are taken for granted. Critical thinkers try to identify and evaluate the unspoken assumptions on which claims and arguments may rest—in the books they read, the political speeches they hear, and the ads that bombard them daily. The assumption might be "All Democrats (or Republicans) are idiots,"

or "You need the product we are selling," or "People have free will and are entirely responsible for any crimes they commit" (or, conversely, "People's criminal behavior is a result of their biology or horrible childhood, so they aren't responsible for their acts"). Everyone, of course, makes assumptions about how the world works; we could not function otherwise. But if we do not recognize our own assumptions and those of other people, our ability to judge an argument's merits may be impaired.

When an assumption or belief keeps us from considering the evidence fairly, it becomes a *bias*. A bias often remains hidden until someone challenges our belief and we get defensive and angry. For instance, most people, psychologists included, believe that parents are the most important influence in shaping a child's personality. It's obvious, isn't it? In her book *The Nurture Assumption*, Judith Rich Harris (2009) dared to question that assumption. Genes and peers, she argued, are more important influences on a child's personality and behavior than how the parents raise the child. Because this idea challenged a widespread bias, it immediately provoked a storm of disbelief, outrage, and scorn. Some critics focused on Harris's lack of credentials instead of her facts or her logic (although she wrote a successful developmental psychology text, she does not have a PhD), and many attacked the book without even bothering to read it. That is the nature of a bias: It creates intellectual blinders.

Although parents can contribute in many ways to a child's development, is their influence of the greatest importance in a child's life? By analyzing assumptions and practicing critical thinking we can address such questions.

AVOID EMOTIONAL REASONING   Emotion has a place in critical thinking. Passionate commitment to a belief motivates people to think boldly, defend unpopular ideas, and seek evidence for creative new theories. But when gut feelings replace clear thinking, the results can be dangerous. "Persecutions and wars and lynchings," observed Edward de Bono (1985), "are all a result of gut feeling."

Because our emotional reactions and cherished beliefs feel so *right*, so natural, we may not realize that people who hold an opposing viewpoint feel just as strongly as we do. But they usually do, which means that emotional conviction alone cannot settle arguments; in fact, it often makes them worse. The fact that you *really, really* feel strongly that something is true—or want it to be—doesn't make it so.

All of us are apt to feel threatened and get defensive whenever our most cherished beliefs, or commitment to a course of action, are challenged by empirical evidence (Tavris & Aronson, 2007). At such times, it is especially important to separate the data from emotional reasoning. In a 2011 judicial ruling that vaccines do not cause autism, one of the judges expressed sympathy for parents coping with their children's disorder, but added, "I must decide this case not on sentiment, but by analyzing the evidence." You probably hold strong feelings about many topics of psychological interest, such as drug use, racism, sexual orientation, the origins of intelligence, and what makes people fat or thin. As you read this book, you may find yourself quarreling with findings that you dislike. Disagreement is fine; it means that you are reading actively and are engaged with the material. All we ask is that you think about why you are disagreeing: Is it because the evidence is unpersuasive or because the results make you feel anxious or annoyed?

DON'T OVERSIMPLIFY   Critical thinkers look beyond the obvious, resist easy generalizations, and reject either–or thinking. For instance, is it better to feel you have control over everything that happens to you or to accept with tranquility whatever life serves up? Either position oversimplifies. A sense of control has many important benefits, but sometimes it is best to go with the flow.

A common form of oversimplification is *argument by anecdote*—generalizing from a personal experience or from a few examples to everyone: One crime committed by a paroled ex-convict means that parole should be abolished; one friend who hates her school means that everybody who goes there hates it. Anecdotes are often the source of stereotyping as well: One dishonest mother on public assistance means everyone on welfare is dishonest; one encounter with an unconventional Californian means they are all flaky. Critical thinkers want more evidence than one or two stories before drawing such sweeping conclusions. Sharpen your critical thinking skills by watching the video *Debunking Myths 3*.

CONSIDER OTHER INTERPRETATIONS Critical thinkers creatively generate as many reasonable explanations of the topic at hand as possible before settling on the most likely one. Suppose a news magazine reports that people with chronic depression are more likely than nondepressed people to develop cancer. Before concluding that depression causes cancer, you would need to consider some other possibilities. Perhaps depressed people are more likely to smoke and to drink excessively, and those unhealthful habits increase their cancer risk. Or perhaps early, as yet undetected cancers produce biochemical changes that create the physical and emotional symptoms of depression. Alternative explanations such as these must be ruled out by further investigation before we can conclude that depression is a direct cause of cancer. (It's not, by the way.)

After several explanations of a phenomenon have been generated, a critical thinker chooses the one that accounts for the most evidence while making the fewest unverified assumptions. This principle is known as *Occam's razor*, after the 14th-century philosopher who first formulated it. Thus, if a fortune-teller reads your palm and predicts that you will meet the love of your life on a subway in London, that you will make a fortune with an Internet enterprise, and that you will have red-haired twins, then one of two things must be true (Steiner, 1989):

- The fortune-teller can actually sort out the infinite number of interactions among people, animals, events, objects, and circumstances that could affect your life and can know for sure the outcome. Moreover, this fortune-teller is able to alter all the known laws of physics and defy the hundreds of studies showing that no one, under proper procedures for validating psychic predictions, has been able to predict the future for any given individual.

  OR

- The fortune-teller is faking it.

A critical thinker would prefer the second alternative because it requires fewer assumptions and has the most supporting evidence.

TOLERATE UNCERTAINTY Ultimately, learning to think critically teaches us one of the hardest lessons of life: how to live with uncertainty. Sometimes there is little or no evidence available to examine. Sometimes the evidence permits only tentative conclusions. Sometimes the evidence seems strong enough to permit conclusions until, exasperatingly, new evidence throws our beliefs into disarray. Critical thinkers are willing to accept this state of uncertainty. They are not afraid to say, "I don't know" or "I'm not sure."

This admission is not an evasion but a spur to further creative inquiry. Critical thinkers know that the more important the question, the less likely it is to have a single simple answer. The need to accept a certain amount of uncertainty does not mean that we must abandon all of the beliefs and convictions that motivate and inspire us. It means only that we must hold them lightly enough to change our minds when we need to.

Fancy illustrations and spooky predictions might capture your imagination, but you should apply critical thinking guidelines to determine the validity of this approach to making life decisions.

Thinking Critically and Creatively about Psychological Issues

These eight critical-thinking guidelines will help you evaluate psychological findings, claims in the media, and problems that you encounter in your own life.

DEFINE YOUR TERMS
People refer to intelligence all the time, but what is it exactly? Does the musical genius of a world-class cellist like Yo-Yo Ma count as intelligence? Is intelligence captured by an IQ score, or does it also include wisdom and practical "smarts"?

ASK QUESTIONS; BE WILLING TO WONDER
Why do some people bravely come to the aid of their fellow human beings, even when it's not their official job? And, on the other hand, why do people often behave in ways that are selfish, cruel, or violent?

EXAMINE THE EVIDENCE
When demonstrating supposedly magical phenomena, fortune tellers such as this one exploit people's tendency to not engage in a full examination of evidence.

ANALYZE ASSUMPTIONS AND BIASES
People often assume that drug effects are purely biological, and many Americans also share a cultural bias that all psychoactive drugs are inevitably harmful. The Rastafarian church, however, regards marijuana as a "wisdom weed." Will these young Jamaican members react to the drug in the same way as someone who buys it on the street and smokes it alone or at a party?

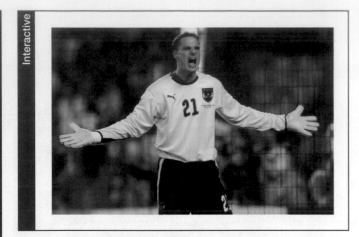

DON'T OVERSIMPLIFY

When you're feeling angry, is it better to "let it out" or keep it "bottled up"? Either answer oversimplifies. Depending on the circumstances, sometimes it is helpful to express your feelings, but sometimes venting your anger makes everything worse.

AVOID EMOTIONAL REASONING

Intense feelings about controversial issues such as gay marriage can keep us from considering other viewpoints. The resolution of differences requires that we move beyond emotional reasoning and instead weigh point and counterpoint.

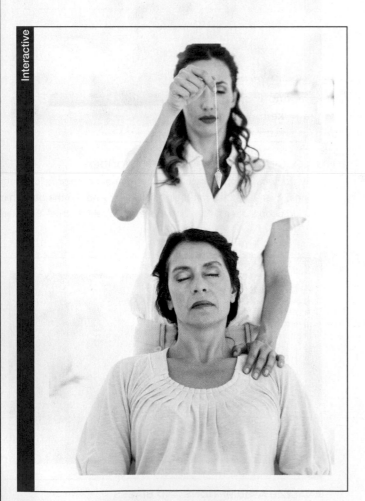

CONSIDER OTHER INTERPRETATIONS

Hypnosis has traditionally been considered a trance state in which people involuntarily do things they ordinarily could not or would not do. But might there be another interpretation of the surprising things that hypnotized people often do?

TOLERATE UNCERTAINTY

Many parents, because they naturally want their children to turn out well, have trouble accepting uncertainty about how to raise them. For example, should they let their baby sleep with them, or will that make the baby too dependent and clingy?

Review 1.1

Guidelines for Thinking Critically about Psychological Issues

Guideline	Example
Ask questions; be willing to wonder	"Can I recall events from my childhood accurately?"
Define your terms	"By 'childhood,' I mean ages 3 to 12; by 'events,' I mean things that happened to me personally, like a trip to the zoo or a stay in the hospital; by 'accurately,' I mean the event basically happened the way I think it did."
Examine the evidence	"I *feel* I recall my fifth birthday party perfectly, but studies show that people often reconstruct past events inaccurately."
Analyze assumptions and biases	"I've always assumed that memory is like a tape recorder—perfectly accurate for every moment of my life—but maybe this is just a bias because it's so reassuring."
Avoid emotional reasoning	"I really *want* to believe this memory is true, but that doesn't mean it *is*."
Don't oversimplify	"Some of my childhood memories could be accurate, others mistaken, and some partly right and partly wrong."
Consider other interpretations	"Some 'memories' could be based on what my parents told me later, not on my own recall."
Tolerate uncertainty	"I may never know for sure whether some of my childhood memories are real or accurate."

Critical thinking is a process, not a once-and-for-all accomplishment. No one ever becomes a perfect critical thinker, entirely unaffected by emotional reasoning and wishful thinking. We are all less open-minded than we think; it is always easier to poke holes in another person's argument than to critically examine our own position. Yet we think the journey is well worth the mental effort because the ability to think critically can help people in countless ways, from saving them money to improving their relationships.

As you read this text, keep in mind the eight guidelines we have described, which are summarized in Review 1.1. You can get practice applying these critical thinking guidelines by completing the journal writing prompts you'll find throughout this book.

JOURNAL PROMPT 1.2

Thinking Critically—Analyze Assumptions and Biases: Whether you've consciously recognized it or not, chances are you've already practiced the eight critical-thinking guidelines discussed in this section to a greater or lesser extent. Any time you've watched an infomercial and exclaimed, "That's too good to be true!" you've called out for an examination of the evidence. When your roommate claims to be smarter than you, you've probably insisted on defining terms such as "smart" or "smarter." Think about the eight critical-thinking guidelines. Which ones do you have the most trouble applying in your daily life? Which ones come more naturally to you?

Quiz for Module 1.2

1. Reggie tells his parents, "I read online that fast-food cooks make more money than college graduates. I'm dropping out and getting me a paper chef's hat!" Which one question should Reggie's parents ask to demonstrate their critical-thinking skills and show Reggie the error of his ways?

   a. "Will you be making dinner tonight?

   b. "How many nuggets does an average chicken yield?"

   c. "What's the salary breakdown per fiscal quarter?"

   d. "What was the source of the information?"

2. Luisa listened in amazement as she overheard her psychology professors design a new experiment. "We should be sure to measure this factor, to rule out a competing explanation for the results," said Professor Paskos. "Yes, and also allow for idiosyncratic responses in case anyone doesn't speak English as a first language," added Professor Green. "Let's not forget to have the results double-checked and interpreted by a qualified colleague," Professor Yufik chimed in. Although Luisa was amazed, to the professors this was second nature. Why?

   a. The professors were well versed in critical-thinking skills and were simply applying those principles to the scientific task at hand.

   b. The professors knew Luisa was listening, so they were showing off a little in order to impress her.

   c. The professors had already collected the data and were covering their tracks in case any of the results didn't precisely confirm their preconceptions.

   d. The professors knew that science often results from luck and guessing, so they simply repeated phrases people expect scientists to say.

3. Gary asked his psychology professor, "Why is the brain located in the head?" His professor replied, "That's a really good question. Although there are probably lots of reasons, I'm not sure of the one best answer. Let's find out together this semester." Which principle of critical thinking was Gary practicing?

   a. Examining the evidence

   b. Defining his terms

   c. Being willing to wonder about things

   d. Avoiding emotional reasoning

4. Gary asked his psychology professor, "Why is the brain located in the head?" His professor replied, "That's a really good question. Although there are probably lots of reasons, I'm not sure of the one best answer. Let's find out together this semester." Which principle of critical thinking was the professor practicing?

   a. Oversimplifying

   b. Defining his terms

   c. Tolerating uncertainty

   d. Avoiding emotional reasoning

5. Laurie told her friend Sandi about an amazing video she saw on YouTube. "It was incredible. This guy levitated a miniature poodle for 25 seconds using psychic energy. He channels a star-force through a time continuum, and that allows him to unleash the hidden powers of his mind. It's totally legit; he's got a website and everything." Sandi replied, "Maybe he's just making it up." Which principle of critical thinking is Sandi practicing?

   a. Sandi is reducing uncertainty

   b. Sandi is defining her terms

   c. Sandi is refining her biases

   d. Sandi is considering other interpretations

Psychology's Past: From the Armchair to the Laboratory

Now that you know what psychology is and what it isn't, and why studying it requires critical thinking, let's see how psychology developed into a modern science.

The Forerunners of Modern Psychology

LO 1.3.A Discuss some of the pre-psychological approaches to explaining psychological topics, from ancient times through the early 1800s.

Until the 19th century, psychology was not a formal discipline. Of course, many of the great thinkers of history, from Aristotle to Zoroaster, raised questions that today would be called psychological. They wanted to know how people take in information through their senses, use information to solve problems, and become motivated to act in brave or villainous ways. They wondered about the elusive nature of emotion, and whether it controls us or is something we can control. Like today's psychologists, they wanted to *describe*, *predict*, *understand*, and *modify* behavior in order to add to human knowledge and increase human happiness. But unlike modern psychologists, scholars of the past did not rely heavily on empirical evidence. Often their observations were based simply on anecdotes or descriptions of individual cases.

This does not mean that the forerunners of modern psychology were always wrong. On the contrary, they often had insights and made observations that were verified by later work. Hippocrates (c. 460 B.C.–c. 377 B.C.), the Greek physician known as the founder of modern medicine, observed patients with head injuries and inferred that the brain must be the ultimate source of "our pleasures, joys, laughter, and jests as well as our sorrows, pains, griefs, and tears." And so it is. In the first century A.D., the Stoic philosophers observed that people do not become angry, sad, or anxious because of actual events but because of their explanations of those events. And so they do. In the 16th century, English philosopher John Locke (1643–1704) argued that the mind works by associating ideas arising from experience, and this notion continues to influence many psychologists today.

But without empirical methods, the forerunners of psychology also committed terrible blunders. One was the theory of **phrenology** (Greek for "study of the mind"), which became wildly popular in Europe and the United States in the early 1800s. Phrenologists argued that different brain areas accounted for specific character and personality traits, such as "stinginess" and "religiosity." Moreover, they said, such traits could be "read" from bumps on the skull. Thieves supposedly had large bumps above the ears. When phrenologists examined people with "stealing bumps" who were *not* thieves, they explained away this counterevidence by saying that other bumps on the skull represented positive traits that must be holding the person's thieving impulses in check.

In the United States, all sorts of people eagerly sought the services of phrenologists. Parents used them to make decisions about childrearing; schools used them to decide which teachers to hire; and businesses used them to find out which employees were likely to be loyal and honest (Benjamin, 1998). Some phrenologists offered classes or self-study programs for people who wanted to overcome their deficiencies; these were the forerunners of today's many self-improvement programs and seminars. Enthusiasm for phrenology did not disappear until well into the 20th century, even though phrenology was a classic pseudoscience—sheer nonsense.

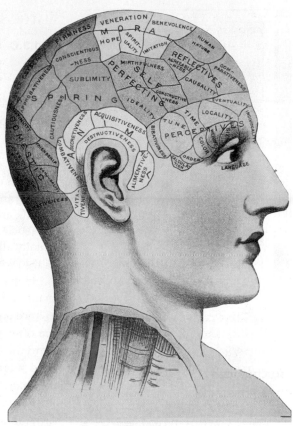

What stands out to you about this 19th-century phrenology "map"?

Credit: Classic Image / Alamy

The Birth of Modern Psychology

LO 1.3.B Explain Wilhelm Wundt's contributions to the birth of modern psychology.

At about the time that phrenology was peaking in popularity, several pioneering men and women were starting to study psychological issues using scientific methods. In 1879, the first psychological laboratory was officially established in Leipzig, Germany, by Wilhelm Wundt [VIL-helm Voont]. Wundt (1832–1920), who was trained in medicine and philosophy, wrote many volumes on psychology, physiology, natural history, ethics, and logic. But psychologists especially revere him because he was the first person to announce (in 1873) that he intended to make psychology a science and because his laboratory was the first to have its results published in a scholarly journal. Although it started out as just a few rooms in an old building, the Leipzig laboratory soon became the go-to place for anyone who wanted to become a psychologist.

One of Wundt's favorite research methods was called trained *introspection*—training volunteers to carefully observe, analyze, and describe their own sensations, mental images, and emotional reactions. This was not as easy as it sounds. Wundt's volunteers had to make 10,000 practice observations before they were allowed to participate in an actual study. Once trained, they might take as long as 20 minutes to report their inner experiences during a 1.5-second experiment. The goal was to break down behavior into its most basic elements, much as a chemist might break down water into hydrogen plus oxygen. Most psychologists eventually rejected trained introspection as being too subjective, but Wundt is still usually credited with formally initiating the movement to make psychology a science.

phrenology
The now-discredited theory that different brain areas account for specific character and personality traits, which can be "read" from bumps on the skull.

Wilhelm Wundt (1832–1920).

structuralism

An early psychological approach that emphasized the analysis of immediate experience into basic elements.

functionalism

An early psychological approach that emphasized the function or purpose of behavior and consciousness.

William James (1842–1910).

Three Early Psychologies

LO 1.3.C Compare the three early psychologies of structuralism, functionalism, and psychoanalysis, and identify the major thinkers who promoted each of these schools of thought.

During the early decades of psychology's existence as a formal discipline, three schools of psychological thought became popular: *structuralism*, *functionalism*, and *psychoanalysis*.

STRUCTURALISM   In the United States, Wundt's ideas were popularized in somewhat modified form by one of his students, E. B. Titchener (1867–1927), who gave Wundt's approach the name **structuralism**. Like Wundt, structuralists hoped to analyze sensations, images, and feelings into basic elements. A person might be asked to listen to a metronome clicking and to report exactly what he or she heard. Most people said they perceived a pattern (such as CLICK click click CLICK click click), even though the clicks of a metronome are actually all the same. Or a person might be asked to break down all the different components of taste when biting into an orange (sweet, tart, wet, and so on).

However, after you have discovered the building blocks of a particular sensation or image and how they link up, then what? The structuralists did not have an answer. And their reliance on introspection also got them into trouble, because despite their training, introspectors often produced conflicting reports. When asked what image came to mind when they heard the word *triangle*, most respondents said they imagined a visual image of a form with three sides and three corners. But one person might report a flashing red form with equal angles, whereas another reported a revolving colorless form with one angle larger than the other two. Some people even claimed they could think about a triangle without forming any visual image at all (Boring, 1953). It was hard, therefore, to know what mental attributes of a triangle were basic.

And so, despite its ability to generate an intensive program of research, structuralism soon lost favor. Years after its demise, Wolfgang Köhler (1959) recalled how he and his colleagues had responded to it as students: "What had disturbed us was . . . the implication that human life, apparently so colorful and so intensely dynamic, is actually a frightful bore."

FUNCTIONALISM   Another early approach to scientific psychology, called **functionalism**, emphasized the function or purpose of behavior, as opposed to its analysis and description. One of functionalism's leaders was William James (1842–1910), an American philosopher, physician, and psychologist who argued that searching for building blocks of experience, as Wundt and Titchener tried to do, was a waste of time because the brain and the mind are constantly changing. Attempting to grasp the nature of the mind through introspection, wrote James (1890/1950), is "like seizing a spinning top to catch its motion, or trying to turn up the gas quickly enough to see how the darkness looks." (James was a great writer.)

Where the structuralists asked *what* happens when an organism does something, the functionalists asked *how* and *why*. They were inspired in part by the evolutionary theories of British naturalist Charles Darwin (1809–1882). Darwin had argued that a biologist's job is not merely to describe, say, the puffed-out chest of a pigeon or the drab markings of a lizard, but also to figure out how these attributes enhance survival. Do they help the animal attract a mate or hide from its enemies? Similarly, the functionalists wanted to know how specific behaviors and mental processes help a person or animal adapt to the environment, so they looked for underlying causes and practical consequences of these behaviors and processes. Unlike the structuralists, they felt free to pick and choose among many methods, and they broadened the field of psychology to include the study of children, animals, religious experiences, and what James called the "stream of consciousness"—a term still used because it so beautifully describes the way thoughts flow like a river, tumbling over each other in waves, sometimes placid, sometimes turbulent.

As a school of psychology, functionalism, like structuralism, was short-lived. Yet the functionalists' emphasis on the causes and consequences of behavior was to set the course of psychological science.

PSYCHOANALYSIS   The 19th century also saw the development of psychological therapies. In the United States, the wildly popular Mind Cure movement lasted from 1830 to 1900; "mind cures" were efforts to correct the false ideas that were said to make people anxious, depressed, and unhappy. The Mind Cure movement was the forerunner of modern cognitive therapies.

Sigmund Freud (1856–1939).

However, the form of therapy that would have the greatest impact worldwide for much of the 20th century had its roots in Vienna, Austria. While researchers were working in their laboratories, struggling to establish psychology as a science, Sigmund Freud (1856–1939) was in his office, listening to his patients' reports of depression, nervousness, and obsessive habits. Freud became convinced that many of his patients' symptoms had mental, not physical, causes. Their distress, he concluded, was due to conflicts and emotional traumas that had occurred in early childhood and that were too threatening to be remembered consciously, such as forbidden sexual feelings for a parent.

Freud argued that conscious awareness is merely the tip of a mental iceberg. Beneath the visible tip, he said, lies the unconscious part of the mind, containing unrevealed wishes, passions, guilty secrets, unspeakable yearnings, and conflicts between desire and duty. Many of these urges and thoughts are sexual or aggressive in nature. We are not aware of them as we go blithely about our daily business, yet they make themselves known in dreams, slips of the tongue, apparent accidents, and even jokes. Freud (1905a) wrote, "No mortal can keep a secret. If the lips are silent, he chatters with his fingertips; betrayal oozes out of him at every pore."

Freud's ideas were not exactly an overnight sensation; his first book, *The Interpretation of Dreams* (1900/1953), managed to sell only 600 copies in the 8 years following its publication. Eventually, however, his ideas evolved into a broad theory of personality and a method of psychotherapy, both of which became known as **psychoanalysis**. Most Freudian concepts were, and still are, rejected by a majority of empirically oriented psychologists, but they had a profound influence on the philosophy, literature, and art of the twentieth century, and Freud's name is now as much a household word as Einstein's. Today, some schools of psychotherapy draw on psychoanalytic ideas, emphasizing unconscious forces and conflicts within the individual.

From these early beginnings in philosophy, natural science, and medicine, psychology has grown into a complex discipline encompassing many specialties, perspectives, and methods. Today the field is like a large, sprawling family. The members of this family share common great-grandparents; many of the cousins have formed alliances, but some are quarreling, and a few are barely speaking to one another.

psychoanalysis

A theory of personality and a method of psychotherapy, originally formulated by Sigmund Freud, that emphasizes unconscious motives and conflicts.

JOURNAL PROMPT 1.3

Thinking Critically—Consider Other Interpretations: Picture an apple in your mind's eye. From a structuralist's perspective, what would be important to know and understand about the concept of the apple that you're imagining? With the same image in your mind, now describe what would be important to know and understand about an apple from a functionalist's point of view. If you can, also discuss how a psychoanalyst would interpret the meaning of an apple to a patient with obsessive habits.

Quiz for Module 1.3

1. "The study of bumps on the head," a discredited approach to psychology, is also known as:
   a. Psychoanalysis
   b. Bumpology
   c. The theory of humors
   d. Phrenology

2. Trained introspection is a methodology that asks research participants to:
   a. Demonstrate the utility of their thoughts and feelings in observable behaviors
   b. Carefully observe and describe their own sensations, mental images, and emotional states
   c. Revisit earlier stages of their conscious development using hypnosis
   d. Respond quickly and accurately to changing external stimuli

3. With which school of thought is William James most closely associated?
   a. Functionalism
   b. Structuralism
   c. Psychoanalysis
   d. Behaviorism

4. Two psychologists, Eddie and Bill, walk into a bar, and each orders a beer. Eddie says, "Look at that golden nectar . . . the bubbles, the foam, the slight fruit notes on my tongue, the amber color; man, that's a beer!" Bill says, "This'll get me drunk." Eddie most likely endorses _____, whereas Bill most likely favors _____.
   a. Structuralism / psychoanalysis
   b. Structuralism / functionalism
   c. Functionalism / structuralism
   d. Structuralism / behaviorism

5. The idea that emotional problems spring from unconscious conflicts originated with:
   a. Psychoanalysis
   b. The mind cure
   c. Structuralism
   d. Functionalism

Psychology's Present: The Four Perspectives of Psychological Science

If you had a noisy, rude, surly neighbor, and you asked a group of psychologists to explain why this guy was such a miserable jerk, you would probably get different answers: It's because of his biological makeup, his belligerent attitude toward the world, the way he has learned to use his nasty temper to get his way, an unhappy family situation, or the customs of his culture. Modern psychological scientists typically approach their investigations from one of four different, although overlapping, approaches: *biological*, *learning*, *cognitive*, and *sociocultural*. Each perspective reflects different questions about human behavior, different assumptions about how the mind works, and, most important, different ways of explaining why people do what they do. In addition to these perspectives, various movements, such as *feminist psychology*, have emerged that don't fit neatly into one of these perspectives.

The Major Perspectives in Psychology

LO 1.4.A List and describe the four major perspectives in psychology.

Let's look at the four major perspectives in psychology. You can also get more information in the video *Diverse Perspectives*.

biological perspective

A psychological approach that emphasizes bodily events and changes associated with actions, feelings, and thoughts.

THE BIOLOGICAL PERSPECTIVE   The **biological perspective** focuses on how bodily events affect behavior, feelings, and thoughts. Electrical impulses shoot along the intricate pathways of the nervous system. Hormones course through the bloodstream, telling internal organs to slow down or speed up. Chemical substances flow across the tiny gaps that separate

Sociocultural Perspective:
Behavior results from
the social environment
and cultural pressures.

one microscopic brain cell from another. Biological psychologists study how these physical events interact with events in the external environment to produce perceptions, memories, and behavior.

Researchers adopting this perspective study how biology affects learning and performance, perceptions of reality, the experience of emotion, and vulnerability to disorders. They study how the mind and body interact in illness and health. They investigate the contributions of genes in the development of abilities and personality traits. One popular specialty, **evolutionary psychology**, follows in the footsteps of functionalism by focusing on how genetically influenced behavior that was functional or adaptive during our evolutionary past may be reflected in many of our present behaviors, mental processes, and traits. The message of the biological approach is that we cannot really know ourselves if we do not know our bodies.

THE LEARNING PERSPECTIVE   The **learning perspective** is concerned with how the environment and experience affect the behavior of human beings (and other animals). Within this perspective, *behaviorists* focus on the environmental rewards and punishers that maintain or discourage specific behaviors. Behaviorists do not invoke the mind or mental states to explain behavior. They prefer to stick to what they can observe and measure directly: acts and events taking place in the environment. For example, do you have trouble sticking to a schedule? A behaviorist would identify the environmental distractions that could help account for this common problem. Behaviorism was the dominant school of scientific psychology in North America for nearly 50 years, through the 1960s.

Today, *social-cognitive learning theorists* combine elements of behaviorism with research on thoughts, values, expectations, and intentions. They believe that people learn not only by adapting their behavior to the environment, but also by observing and imitating others and by thinking about the events happening around them. As we will see, the learning perspective has many practical applications. Historically, the behaviorists' insistence on precision and objectivity has done much to advance psychology as a science, and learning research in general has given psychology some of its most reliable findings.

THE COGNITIVE PERSPECTIVE   The **cognitive perspective** emphasizes what goes on in people's heads—how people reason, remember, understand language, solve problems, explain experiences, acquire moral standards, and form beliefs. (The word *cognitive* comes from the Latin for "to know.") One of its most important contributions has been to show how people's thoughts and explanations affect their actions, feelings, and choices. Using clever methods to infer mental processes from observable behavior, cognitive researchers have been able to study phenomena that were previously only the stuff of speculation, such as emotions, motivations, insight, and the kind of "thinking" that goes on without awareness. They are

evolutionary psychology

A field of psychology emphasizing evolutionary mechanisms that may help explain human commonalities in cognition, development, emotion, social practices, and other areas of behavior.

learning perspective

A psychological approach that emphasizes how the environment and experience affect a person's or animal's actions; it includes *behaviorism* and *social-cognitive learning theories*.

cognitive perspective

A psychological approach that emphasizes mental processes in perception, memory, language, problem solving, and other areas of behavior.

sociocultural perspective

A psychological approach that emphasizes social and cultural influences on behavior.

feminist psychology

A psychological approach that analyzes the influence of social inequities on gender relations and on the behavior of the two sexes.

designing computer programs that model how humans perform complex tasks, discovering what goes on in the mind of an infant, and identifying types of intelligence not measured by conventional IQ tests. The cognitive approach is one of the strongest forces in psychology and has inspired an explosion of research on the intricate workings of the mind.

THE SOCIOCULTURAL PERSPECTIVE   The **sociocultural perspective** focuses on social and cultural forces outside the individual, forces that shape every aspect of behavior, from how we kiss to what and where we eat. Most of us underestimate the impact of other people, the social context, and cultural rules on nearly everything we do. We are like fish that are unaware they live in water, so obvious is water in their lives. Sociocultural psychologists study the water—the social and cultural environment that we "swim" in every day.

Within this perspective, *social psychologists* focus on social rules and roles, how groups affect attitudes and behavior, why people obey authority, and how each of us is affected by other people—spouses, lovers, friends, bosses, parents, and strangers. *Cultural psychologists* examine how cultural rules and values, both explicit and unspoken, affect people's development, behavior, and feelings. They might study how culture influences people's willingness to help a stranger in distress or what they do when they are angry. American researchers still focus mainly on Americans, who comprise less than 5 percent of the world's population (Arnett, 2008). However, in this text we have made a concerted effort to cite studies that include other nationalities as well. Because human beings are social animals who are profoundly affected by their different cultural worlds, the sociocultural perspective is making psychology a more representative and rigorous discipline.

Review 1.2 summarizes these four perspectives and shows how they might be applied to a concrete issue, the problem of violence. See if you can apply these perspectives to another issue of your choosing.

Feminist Psychology

LO 1.4.B Describe how feminism influenced psychology.

Throughout psychology's history, various movements and intellectual trends have emerged that do not fit neatly into any of the major perspectives but that have had an impact on all of them. One is **feminist psychology**. As women began to enter psychology in greater numbers in the 1970s, they documented evidence of a pervasive bias in the research methods used and in the very questions that researchers had been asking (Crawford & Marecek, 1989; Eagly et al., 2012; Shields & Dicicco, 2011). They noted that many studies had used

Review 1.2

The Four Major Perspectives in Psychological Science

Perspective	Major Topics of Study	Sample Finding on Violence
Biological	The nervous system, hormones, brain chemistry, heredity, evolutionary influences	Brain damage caused by birth complications or child abuse might incline some people toward violence.
Learning	Environment and experience	
Behavioral	Environmental determinants of observable behavior	Violence increases when it pays off.
Social-Cognitive	Environmental influences, observation and imitation, beliefs and values	Violent role models can influence some children to behave aggressively.
Cognitive	Thinking, memory, language, problem solving, perceptions	Violent people are often quick to perceive provocation and insult.
Sociocultural	Social and cultural contexts	
Social Psychology	Social rules and roles, groups, relationships	People are often more aggressive in a crowd than they would be on their own.
Cultural Psychology	Cultural norms, values, and expectations	Cultures based on herding rather than agriculture tend to train boys to be aggressive.

only men as subjects—and usually only young, white, middle-class men at that—and they showed why it was often inappropriate to generalize to everyone else from such a narrow research base. They spurred the growth of research on topics that had long been ignored in psychology, including menstruation, motherhood, rape and domestic violence, the dynamics of power and sexuality in relationships, definitions of masculinity and femininity, gender roles, and sexist attitudes. They critically examined the male bias in psychotherapy, starting with Freud's own case studies. And they analyzed the social consequences of psychological findings, showing how research has often been used to justify the lower status of women and other disadvantaged groups. Feminist psychology has even influenced the study of men. In recent years, the field of men's studies and the psychology of men has been gaining prominence, focusing on such diverse topics as men's health, emotions, and the ways that culture shapes notions of "masculinity" (Vandello & Bosson, 2013).

Feminist psychology greatly advanced efforts to make psychology the study of all human beings, of all cultures and ethnicities, and other groups have made similar contributions. In 1976, black psychologist Robert Guthrie, in *Even the Rat Was White*, wrote a searing and influential indictment of racism in psychological research. Since the 1970s, African American, Latino, and Asian psychologists, gay and lesbian psychologists, and disabled psychologists have greatly expanded the theoretical and empirical vistas of psychology, as we will see throughout this book.

JOURNAL PROMPT 1.4

Thinking Critically—Ask Questions; Be Willing to Wonder: What makes us who we are? Psychological scientists often approach this question differently, depending on whether they take a biological, learning, cognitive, or sociocultural perspective. How do these influences interact to make us who we are?

Quiz for Module 1.4

1. Which of the following is *not* one of the major current perspectives on psychological science?
   a. Biological perspective
   b. Learning perspective
   c. Symbolic-interactionist perspective
   d. Sociocultural perspective

2. The dominant school of scientific psychology most closely associated with the learning perspective is:
   a. Feminist psychology
   b. Evolutionary psychology
   c. Behaviorism
   d. Socialism

3. Sid wants help dealing with his lack of motivation in school, so he enlists his roommate George, who's taking an introductory psychology course, to offer advice. "The problem is all in your brain," George suggests. "You've got an imbalance of chemicals and hormones, which is causing you to feel lackluster and unfocused." Which perspective on psychological science is George adopting?
   a. Learning perspective
   b. Biological perspective
   c. Psychoanalytic perspective
   d. Cognitive perspective

4. Maria's been feeling a lot of pressure lately. She wants to fit in with her peer group, so she started dressing as her friends do. She wants to be accepted by her family, so she's paid more attention to their traditions and customs lately. She also wants to fit in at school, so she's mindful of the implicit and explicit rules that students follow in that environment. Which type of psychological scientist would be most interested in explaining Maria's behaviors?
   a. Sociocultural psychologist
   b. Behaviorist
   c. Learning theorist
   d. Biological psychologist

5. Psychological science has increasingly embraced a diversity of viewpoints, research topics, and explanations for behavior. Which cross-cutting emphasis played a role in bringing about that kind of increased inclusiveness?
   a. Social-cognitive learning theory
   b. Behaviorism
   c. Feminist psychology
   d. Psychoanalysis

What Psychologists Do

Now you know the main viewpoints that guide psychologists in their work. But what do psychologists actually do with their time between breakfast and dinner?

To most people, the word *psychologist* conjures up an image of a therapist listening intently while a client pours forth his or her troubles. Many psychologists do in fact fit this image, but others do not. The professional activities of psychologists generally fall into three broad categories: (1) teaching and doing research in colleges and universities; (2) providing health or mental health services, often referred to as *psychological practice*; and (3) conducting research or applying its findings in nonacademic settings, such as business, sports, government, law, and the military (see Review 1.3). Some psychologists move flexibly across these areas. A researcher might also provide counseling services in a mental health setting, such as a clinic or a hospital; a university professor might teach, do research, and serve as a consultant in legal cases.

Psychological Research

LO 1.5.A Distinguish basic psychology and applied psychology, and summarize the kinds of research that various psychologists might conduct.

Most psychologists who do research have doctoral degrees (PhDs) or doctorates in education (EdDs). Some, seeking knowledge for its own sake, work in **basic psychology**, doing "pure" research. Others, concerned with the practical uses of knowledge, work in **applied psychology**. The two approaches are complementary: Applied psychology has direct relevance to human problems, but without basic psychology, there would be little knowledge to apply. A psychologist doing basic research might ask, "How does peer pressure influence people's attitudes and behavior?" An applied psychologist might ask, "How can knowledge about peer pressure be used to get college students to quit binge drinking?"

Research psychology is the aspect of psychology least recognized and understood by the public. Psychology has never had a U.S. postage stamp commemorating the discipline or its founders, unlike dozens of other fields, including poultry farming and truck driving.

basic psychology

The study of psychological issues for the sake of knowledge rather than for its practical application.

applied psychology

The study of psychological issues that have direct practical significance; also, the application of psychological findings.

Review 1.3

What Is a Psychologist?

Not all psychologists do clinical work. Many do research, teach, work in business, or consult. The professional activities of psychologists with doctorates fall into three general categories:

Academic/Research Psychologists	Clinical Psychologists	Psychologists in Industry, Law, or Other Settings
Specialize in areas of pure or applied research, such as:	Do psychotherapy and sometimes research; may work in any of these settings:	Do research or serve as consultants to institutions on such issues as:
Human development	Private practice	Sports
Psychometrics (testing)	Mental health clinics	Consumer issues
Health	General hospitals	Advertising
Education	Mental hospitals	Organizational problems
Industrial/organizational psychology	Research laboratories	Environmental issues
Physiological psychology	Colleges and universities	Public policy
Sensation and perception		Opinion polls
Design and use of technology		Military training
		Animal behavior
		Legal issues

Bemoaning this fact, Ludy Benjamin (2003) argued that it was evidence that the public "has minimal understanding of psychology as a science and even less appreciation for what psychological scientists do" or how psychological research contributes to human welfare. We hope that by the time you finish this text, you will have a greater appreciation for what research psychologists do and for their contributions to human welfare. Here are just a few of the major nonclinical specialties in psychology:

- *Experimental psychologists* conduct laboratory studies of learning, motivation, emotion, sensation and perception, physiology, and cognition. Do not be misled by the term *experimental*, though; other psychologists also do experiments.

- *Educational psychologists* study psychological principles that explain learning and search for ways to improve educational systems. Their interests range from the application of findings on memory and thinking to the use of rewards to encourage achievement.

Educational psychologists investigate ways to improve the educational system, such as incorporating technology in the learning process.

- *Developmental psychologists* study how people change and grow over time physically, mentally, and socially. Some specialize in childhood issues; others study adolescence, young adulthood, the middle years, or old age.

- *Industrial/organizational psychologists* study behavior in the workplace. They are concerned with group decision making, employee morale, work motivation, productivity, job stress, personnel selection, marketing strategies, equipment design, and many other issues.

- *Psychometric psychologists* design and evaluate tests of mental abilities, aptitudes, interests, and personality. Nearly all of us have had firsthand experience with one or more of these tests in school, at work, or in the military. The video *Asking the Tough Questions 2* will help you appreciate the broad range of interests and applications psychologists pursue.

Psychological Practice

LO 1.5.B Compare the training and work settings of different psychological practitioners, such as counselors, clinical psychologists, psychotherapists, psychoanalysts, and psychiatrists.

Psychological practitioners, whose goal is to understand and improve people's physical and mental health, work in mental hospitals, general hospitals, clinics, schools, counseling centers, and private practice. Since the late 1970s, the proportion of psychologists who are practitioners has steadily increased. Practitioners now account for over two-thirds of new psychology doctorates and members of the American Psychological Association (APA), which is international despite its name, and is the largest association of professional psychologists in the world.

Psychological practitioners typically work closely with an individual to address physical or mental health needs.

Some practitioners are *counseling psychologists*, who generally help people deal with problems of everyday life, such as test anxiety, family conflicts, or low job motivation. Others are *school psychologists*, who work with parents, teachers, and students to enhance students' performance and resolve emotional difficulties. The majority, however, are *clinical psychologists*, who diagnose, treat, and study mental or emotional problems. Clinical psychologists are trained to do psychotherapy with severely disturbed people, as well as with those who are simply troubled or unhappy or who want to learn to handle their problems better.

In almost all states, a license to practice clinical psychology requires a doctorate. Most clinical psychologists have a PhD, some have an EdD, and some have a PsyD (doctorate in psychology, pronounced "sy-dee"). Clinical psychologists typically complete 4 or 5 years of graduate work in psychology, plus at least a year's internship under the direction of a licensed psychologist. Clinical programs leading to a PhD or EdD are usually designed to prepare a person both as a scientist and as a clinical practitioner; they require completion of a *dissertation*, a research project that contributes to knowledge in the field. Programs leading to a PsyD do not usually require a dissertation, although they typically require the student to complete an extensive study, theoretical paper, or literature review.

People often confuse *clinical psychologist* with three other terms: *psychotherapist*, *psychoanalyst*, and *psychiatrist*. But these terms mean different things:

- A *psychotherapist* is simply anyone who does any kind of psychotherapy. The term is not legally regulated; in fact, in most states, anyone can say that he or she is a "therapist" of one sort or another without having any training at all.

- A *psychoanalyst* is a person who practices one particular form of therapy: psychoanalysis. To call yourself a psychoanalyst, you must have specialized training from a psychoanalytic institute and undergo extensive psychoanalysis yourself. At one time, admission to a psychoanalytic institute required an MD or a PhD, but this is no longer true; clinical social workers with master's degrees, and even interested laypeople, are often now admitted.

- A *psychiatrist* is a medical doctor (MD) who has completed a 3-year residency in psychiatry to learn how to diagnose and treat mental disorders. Like some clinical psychologists, some psychiatrists do research on mental problems instead of, or in addition to, working with patients. In private practice, psychiatrists may treat any kind of emotional disorder; in hospitals, they treat the most severe disorders, such as major depression and schizophrenia. Although psychiatrists and clinical psychologists often do similar work, psychiatrists, because of their medical training, are more likely to focus on possible biological causes of mental disorders and to treat these problems with medication. Unlike psychiatrists, most clinical psychologists cannot write prescriptions at present. (In the United States, only a select number of states have given prescription privileges to psychologists who receive special training.) Psychiatrists, however, are often uneducated in current psychological theories and methods and are unfamiliar with current research in psychology (Luhrmann, 2000).

Other mental health professionals include licensed clinical social workers (LCSWs) and marriage, family, and child counselors (MFCCs). These professionals ordinarily treat general problems in adjustment and family conflicts rather than severe mental disturbance, although their work may also bring them into contact with people who have serious problems—violent delinquents, people with drug addictions, sex offenders, individuals involved in domestic violence or child abuse. Licensing requirements vary from state to state but usually include

Review 1.4

Types of Psychotherapists

Just as not all psychologists are psychotherapists, not all psychotherapists are clinical psychologists. Here are the major terms used to refer to mental health professionals:

Psychotherapist	A person who does psychotherapy; may have anything from no degree to an advanced professional degree; the term is unregulated.
Clinical psychologist	Diagnoses, treats, and/or studies mental and emotional problems, both mild and severe; has a PhD, an EdD, or a PsyD.
Psychoanalyst	Practices psychoanalysis; has specific training in this approach after an advanced degree (usually, but not always, an MD or a PhD); may treat any kind of emotional disorder or pathology.
Psychiatrist	Does work similar to that of a clinical psychologist, but is likely to take a more biological approach; has a medical degree (MD) with a specialty in psychiatry.
Licensed clinical social worker (LCSW); marriage, family, and child counselor (MFCC)	Typically treats common individual and family problems, but may also deal with more serious problems such as addiction or abuse. Licensing requirements vary, but generally has at least an MA in psychology or social work.

a master's degree in psychology or social work and 1 or 2 years of supervised experience. (For a summary of the various types of psychotherapists and the training they receive, see Review 1.4.) As if this weren't complicated enough, thousands of people claim to be specialists in treating all kinds of problems, from sexual abuse to alcoholism; no uniform set of standards regulates their training. Some may have taken nothing more than a brief "certification" course.

Many research psychologists, and some practitioners, are worried about the increase in the number of counselors and psychotherapists who are unschooled in research methods and the empirical findings of psychology, and who use untested or ineffective therapy techniques (Baker, McFall, & Shoham, 2008; Lilienfeld, Lynn, & Lohr, 2014). Many therapists have been trained in freestanding professional schools that are unconnected to university psychology departments. Some of these schools offer a quality education, but others are designed to produce mental health professionals who may or may not know much about psychological research or its importance to sound clinical practice. These poorer quality programs are turning out increasing numbers of ill-prepared graduates (Peterson, 2003).

Many practitioners, for their part, argue that psychotherapy is an art and that training in research methods is largely irrelevant to the work they do with clients. There are differences in training and attitudes between scientists and many therapists. These differences contributed to the formation of the Association for Psychological Science (APS). The widening gap between scientists and practitioners, along with increased demands by insurers for evidence that psychotherapy is demonstrably effective, has motivated several prominent clinical psychologists to call for evidence-based treatment and collaboration between researchers and clinicians, in hopes of bridging the gap and improving patient care (Kazdin, 2008).

Psychology in the Community

LO 1.5.C Give examples of three ways in which psychologists contribute to their communities.

Psychology has expanded so rapidly that the American Psychological Association now has more than 50 divisions. Some represent major fields such as developmental psychology or physiological psychology. Others represent specific research or professional interests, such as the psychology of women, the psychology of men, ethnic minority issues, sports, the arts, environmental concerns, gay and lesbian issues, peace, psychology and the law, and health.

Psychologists work in all sorts of settings with all sorts of clients.

Today, psychologists contribute to their communities in about as many areas as you can think of. They advise utility companies on ways to get customers to conserve energy. They consult with companies to improve worker satisfaction and productivity. They establish programs to improve race relations. They do basic and applied research on ways of reducing conflict, locally and internationally. They strive to understand and prevent acts of terrorism. They advise commissions on how pollution and noise affect mental health. They do rehabilitation training for people with physical or mental disabilities. They educate judges and juries about eyewitness testimony and false confessions. They assist the police in emergencies involving hostages or disturbed people. They conduct public opinion surveys. They run suicide-prevention hotlines. They advise zoos on the care and training of animals. They help coaches improve the athletic performance of their teams. And those are just for starters. Is it any wonder that people are a little fuzzy about what a psychologist is?

BIOLOGY, CULTURE, and *Psychology*

The differences we have described among psychological perspectives and specialties have produced many passionate arguments. Not all psychologists, however, feel they must swear allegiance to one approach or another. Indeed, many are crossing the borders that have traditionally divided one specialty from another.

This trend has been fueled by two developments. The first is a revolution in our understanding of biology's influence on behavior. Neuropsychologists are now studying the workings of the brain and its influence on emotions and behavior. Cognitive psychologists are looking at the neurological aspects of thinking, decision making, and problem solving. Social psychologists have taken an interest in the brain and have even developed a new specialty called "social-cognitive neuroscience." Clinical scientists are examining the separate and combined effects of medication and psychotherapy in the treatment of psychological disorders. Behavioral geneticists are documenting the contributions of genetics to everything from the origins of personality to the origins of mental illness. Researchers who study almost any important phenomenon—aggression, anger, love, sexuality, child development, aging, prejudice, war—often now do so by combining psychological findings and biological ones.

The second major development is that psychologists are increasingly looking outward to culture as well as inward to biology (Ambady, 2011). They are documenting the many ways in which culture and ethnicity shape and influence much of what we do. Developmental psychologists are looking at culture's impact on mental, social, and linguistic development. Cognitive psychologists are studying cultural influences on achievement, problem solving, and test performance. Social psychologists are looking at how a culture's norms and history affect rates of aggression and cooperation, and even at how culture shapes the brain. Clinical researchers are exploring how the cultural backgrounds of therapists and clients affect the bond between them and the ultimate success of psychotherapy. Psychologists studying sensation are discovering how culture affects which tastes and smells

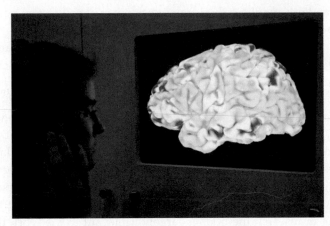

Psychologists increasingly adopt a biological perspective in understanding behavior, drawing on tools that provide a glimpse into the human body.

delight or disgust us. Accordingly, throughout this text you will find a heading called "Culture and . . . ," which will alert you to some of the most exciting results from research incorporating this perspective.

The modern field of psychology is like a giant mosaic made up of many fragments, yielding a rich, multicolored, psychological portrait. Psychologists may argue about which part of the portrait is most important, but they also have much in common. All psychological scientists, whatever their specialty, believe in the importance of gathering empirical evidence instead of relying on hunches. And one thing will always unite psychologists: a fascination with the unending mysteries of human behavior and the human mind. If you too have wondered what makes people tick; if you love a mystery and want to know not only who did it but also why they did it; if you are willing to reconsider what you think you think . . . then you are in the right course.

We invite you now to step into the world of psychology, the discipline that dares to explore the most complex topic on earth: *you*.

Thinking Critically—Ask Questions; Be Willing to Wonder: Now that you've read about the great variety of work that psychologists do, engage in a little introspection: If you chose a career in psychology, what type of work would interest you? Basic research? If so, what topic area or what type of specialization? Psychological practice? Would you prefer the emphases of a clinical psychologist, a psychiatrist, or some other kind of practitioner? Would you be interested in contributing to your larger community in some way? Think about how and where you might see yourself in this field someday.

Quiz for Module 1.5

1. Dr. Lifeson has taken a job consulting with Omega, Inc. The managers at Omega want to know why employee morale is so low in their manufacturing division, and they want Dr. Lifeson to design the appropriate studies and collect the necessary data to answer that question. Dr. Lifeson most likely is a specialist in:
    a. Industrial/organizational psychology
    b. Experimental psychology
    c. Human development
    d. Educational psychology

2. Which of the following academic psychologists would most likely be involved in constructing a personality test to measure introversion?
    a. Educational psychologist
    b. Developmental psychologist
    c. Health psychologist
    d. Psychometric psychologist

3. Which of the following specialists was specifically trained in a therapeutic approach started by Sigmund Freud?
    a. Psychiatrist
    b. Psychoanalyst
    c. Clinical psychologist
    d. Psychiatric social worker

4. Which of the following specialists has an MD and tends to take a medical approach to mental health problems?
    a. Clinical psychologist
    b. Psychoanalyst
    c. Psychiatrist
    d. Counseling psychologist

5. Which of the following would be an example of a psychologist contributing to the community at large?
    a. A social psychologist works with a local youth organization to implement ways of reducing prejudice and hostility between rival inner-city gangs.
    b. A biological psychologist conducts basic research into the origins of mental illness by conducting experiments on mice.
    c. A clinical psychologist expands her practice to include treating three more clients each week.
    d. A psychiatrist uses his prescription privileges to increase the dosage of depression-relieving drugs for all the residents of a hospital ward.

Taking Psychology with You

The Nine Secrets of Learning

How do you study? If you are like most students, your favorite strategy is to read the textbook and your notes, and then read them again (Karpicke, Butler, & Roediger, 2009). You may think that reading and rereading is the best way to learn. It is not.

Psychological research has uncovered many secrets to learning. What we're about to tell you is the real deal, proven to work in scientific laboratories and in schools from junior high to the university level (Brown et al., 2014; McDaniel et al., 2011; Roediger, Putnam, & Smith, 2011). If we had only one sentence to tell you the secret, it would be this: The secret to doing well is testing yourself on what you've studied—asking yourself questions, retrieving the answers, going back and restudying what you didn't know, and testing yourself

again and again until you learn the material. And even when you learn it, you need to keep testing yourself regularly over the semester so that what you've learned stays learned.

Okay, that's two sentences, but these secrets are so important, we snuck in an extra one. Here, in more detail, are the secrets to learning and doing well in your courses.

What to Do Before Class

Your instructor has encouraged you to explore the interactive features of this text and challenge yourself with quizzes and reviews. How will you learn all of this information?

Secret #1: Use the 3R technique: Read, Recite, Review.

Let's say you're supposed to read this chapter by your next class. Use these three basic steps:

- *Read* a section of the chapter. Then put aside the text and hide your notes.
- *Recite* (speak aloud) everything you can remember about what you've just read. You don't need fancy equipment. You can recite to yourself, to a friend, to your cat, or even to your coffee mug or a plant in your room.
- *Review* the section by reading it again to correct anything you got wrong, or to revisit important information that you overlooked, when you recited.

In one study comparing the effectiveness of various study techniques, students in three groups read long, technical encyclopedia entries (McDaniel, Howard, & Einstein, 2009). One group used the 3R technique; a second read the articles twice and did nothing else; a third read the articles once but took notes while reading. A week later, everyone took the same test. The students who had used the 3R technique did much better on the test than students who used the other techniques. What's more, it took students *less time* to use the 3R technique than reading and taking notes.

One reason that this method works so well is that when you practice the second R, you see immediately what you had trouble understanding, learning, and remembering, so you know what to concentrate on when you do the third R: review.

Secret #2: Dig deep.

You can't read your textbook the same way you check your Facebook page, at a quick, superficial level. Many students assume that the mind is a bin or a sponge; you just pour information into it and it stays there. Sorry. For the information to stay there, you have to *process* it until you *get it*. When you put in effort to understand something, you are signaling your brain that the "something" is worth remembering. An excellent way to do this, as you read, is to try to connect the new information to information you already know. For instance, in this chapter, you read about the four basic perspectives of psychological science. Taking each one, you could think of examples you have read about or that apply to your own life: *Many of my friends take medication to manage their depression or anxiety; that would follow from the biological perspective's approach.*

Secret #3: Use your imagination.

Students who visualize ideas remember them better than students who don't. Despite what you might read on all those "Train your brain!" websites, you don't need to conjure up bizarre images; you just need to make those images interact (Wollen, Weber, & Lowry, 1972). When reading that *glia cells* (from the Greek word for "glue") play an important role in brain function by holding neurons in place, you could visualize squirting a big bottle of glue labeled "glia" under neurons.

Secret #4: Test yourself.

Suppose you've just read the material in the first section of this chapter, and it's time for you to begin the recite phase. Start by trying to remember everything you can. Then check that you can define the bolded key terms in the chapter in your own words. As you go along, make a note about anything you can't remember, but don't look up the answers yet. When you're done, go back and see how well you knew the terms.

Now you're ready to review. Go back to the beginning of your section in the chapter, and read again. Keep in mind the parts that tripped you up as you're reading; when you finish, make sure you can answer the questions you couldn't last time.

What to Do During Class
Secret #5: Keep your head up and your pen down.

A lecture is not like a DVD. For one thing, you can't hit the pause button. For another thing, If you're not giving the lecture your full attention, you will miss something important and not even realize it. So when you're in class, don't talk to your friends, send text messages, or search the Web for pictures of adorable kittens doing adorable things.

It's crucial that you take good notes in class. There's a balance to note-taking: On the one hand, you want your notes to be accurate and complete; on the other hand, you don't want them to be a transcript because then the really important things are hard to find. Elliot Aronson (2010), who became one of the greatest social psychologists in the field, wrote this about his first term in college: "I discovered that I had never learned how to be a student. I didn't even know the first thing about taking notes. I would sit in class, listening to the lecture, scribbling furiously. By the time mid-semester exams came around, I pulled out my lecture notes and found they were virtually unintelligible."

While you're listening to your instructor, think about how what you're hearing is connected to what you already know. Write down key words and phrases, not full sentences and paragraphs the way a court reporter would. The act of sifting through what you're hearing and distilling it into its important components will help make that information more meaningful.

You may be thinking that if instructors let you record their lectures or post their slides online, you don't have to do any note-taking. But recordings and slides won't do your thinking for you, and they don't have to take the exams, either.

What to Do After Class
Secret #6: Process your notes.

As soon as you can after class, do what Elliot Aronson (2010) did. Having done poorly on his midterms, thanks to his lousy note-taking, he came up with a new strategy: "At the end of every class, I would find a little nook—sometimes even the nearest stairwell—read over my scribbled notes, and neatly summarize them in a page or two.

At the end of the semester, when it was time to prepare for the final, my notes described the heart of the course. More than that: They revealed the scope and pattern of the professor's thinking and the way the lectures dovetailed with the readings. I had taken the first step toward mastering the art of getting to the essence of a topic. . . . I found I was also learning to love to learn, and, perhaps most important, I was learning to think critically and challenge unsubstantiated assertions. For the first time in my life I understood what it was to be a student."

That "aha!" experience can strike you too. When you review your notes, zero in on the information from class. If your notes are dotted with doodles, arrows and asterisks, missing definitions, and phrases that just don't make sense, organize and rewrite them. Fill in the missing definitions or other information by consulting your text, your friends' notes, or asking a teaching assistant or instructor. These activities are another way of testing yourself and filling the gaps in what you don't know.

Studying for Exams

Secret #7: After you learn it, don't drop it.

You might be tempted to skip the parts of a chapter that you feel sure you know. Don't do it. Instead, take advantage of a powerful research finding: Students who retest themselves by recalling information they could remember earlier do twice as well on an exam as students who skipped retesting themselves on familiar material (Karpicke & Roediger, 2007).

Secret #8: Forget about cramming!

Somewhere along the line, many students come to the conclusion that studying for exams means staying up all night, drinking coffee by the gallon, and rereading their textbook and notes so many times that their eyeballs bleed. Indeed, most students decide what to study next based on whatever is due next (or overdue). Few students make a study schedule ahead of time and then stick to it (Kornell & Bjork, 2007).

The problem with cramming is that it gives you a misplaced sense of confidence that you know the material. In fact, although you will probably remember some of it for a while, you won't remember it for long. That's because you have not taken the time to repeatedly organize the information in your memory, connect it to what you already know, and pave the new mental roads that will help you retrieve information later, as on the exam. That's one of the reasons many students "blank out" when they actually take the test.

There is an alternative to those painful all-nighters. Rather than cramming all your attempts to test yourself into one giant awful block of time, test yourself regularly throughout the semester, say once a week (Bjork & Bjork, 2011), and be sure to include material you already know in your regular testing sessions. The secrets to doing well on a test tomorrow aren't different from the secrets to doing well all semester.

Secret #9: Forget about your "learning style."

If you've ever taken a test that tells you you're a "visual" learner, does that mean you'll have trouble taking in information in your lecture, especially compared to your classmates who have been told they are "auditory" learners? Happily, the answer is no. There is no evidence that people learn better when the method matches their preferences, and no evidence that using methods that don't match their preferences are ineffective (Pashler et al., 2008). Visualizing material helps everybody, and so does plain old active listening. In fact, learning-style tests do not seem to do much of anything except make the companies that own them a lot of money. The nine secrets to learning work equally well for all kinds of students. This means you.

In this course, you'll satisfy your curiosity about human nature, gain insights into political and social issues, and learn techniques that you can use to manage your emotions, improve your memory, and reduce unwanted habits. We hope you will enjoy and remember what you read. But ultimately, a tenth secret of learning is this: No matter how good they are, no course and no text can do your work for you.

Shared Writing Prompt

Think about what will be your most challenging course during this academic term (it might even be introductory psychology). You've probably already received a syllabus, reviewed the course requirements, and maybe been to a lecture or two. Now think about that course in terms of the nine secrets of learning you just read. Construct a brief essay outlining how you could effectively apply each of the principles to the course you have in mind. For example, if you're concerned that the material in your biology course might be too much to keep up with, write a short paragraph detailing how you'd use Secret #4 and Secret #6 to your advantage ("I'll set aside 15 minutes after my 11:00 class to review my notes, and I'll test myself with a five-item quiz at noon every Friday"), then flesh out the details for those and the remaining secrets. What you should have when you're finished is a coherent essay addressing each of the learning secrets, but also an effective plan that you can stick with to help you through the course.

Summary

Psychology, Pseudoscience, and Popular Opinion

LO 1.1.A   Define psychology, and describe how it addresses topics from a scientific perspective.

Psychology is the discipline concerned with behavior and mental processes and how they are affected by an organism's external and internal environment. An introductory psychology course can correct many misconceptions about human behavior.

LO 1.1.B   Provide examples of pseudoscience, psychobabble, popular opinion, and "plain old common sense" related to psychological topics, and describe how scientific psychology would address such claims.

Psychologists have many pseudoscientific competitors, such as astrologers and psychics. Psychology's methods and reliance on *empirical evidence* distinguish it from pseudoscience and "psychobabble." Psychobabble is appealing because it confirms our beliefs and prejudices; in contrast, psychology often challenges them.

Thinking Critically and Creatively about Psychology

LO 1.2.A   Explain why critical-thinking applies to all scientific pursuits, and also why it should guide everyday judgments and decision making.

One benefit of studying psychology is the development of *critical-thinking* skills and attitudes. Critical thinking helps people evaluate competing findings on psychological issues that are personally and socially important.

LO 1.2.B   List eight important critical thinking guidelines, and give an example of how each applies to the science of psychology.

Critical thinkers ask questions, define terms clearly, examine the evidence, analyze assumptions and biases, avoid emotional reasoning, avoid oversimplification, consider alternative interpretations, and tolerate uncertainty. Critical thinking is an evolving process rather than a once-and-for-all accomplishment.

Psychology's Past: From the Armchair to the Laboratory

LO 1.3.A   Discuss some of the pre-psychological approaches to explaining psychological topics, from ancient times through the early 1800s.

Psychology's forerunners made some valid observations and had useful insights, but without rigorous empirical methods, they also made serious errors in the description and explanation of behavior, as in the case of *phrenology*.

LO 1.3.B   Explain Wilhelm Wundt's contributions to the birth of modern psychology.

The official founder of scientific psychology was Wilhelm Wundt, who formally established the first psychological laboratory in 1879, in Leipzig, Germany. His technique of trained introspection, although too subjective for a reliable methodology, illustrated the movement toward making psychology a science.

LO 1.3.C   Compare the three early psychologies of structuralism, functionalism, and psychoanalysis, and identify the major thinkers who promoted each of these schools of thought.

Structuralism emphasized the analysis of immediate experience into basic elements. It was soon abandoned, in part because of its reliance on introspection. *Functionalism* was inspired in part by the evolutionary theories of Charles Darwin; it emphasized the purpose of behavior. One of its leading proponents was William James. Sigmund Freud's theory of *psychoanalysis* emphasized unconscious causes of mental and emotional problems.

Psychology's Present: The Four Perspectives of Psychological Science

LO 1.4.A   List and describe the four major perspectives in psychology.

Four points of view predominate today in psychological science. The *biological perspective* emphasizes bodily events associated with actions, thoughts, and feelings, as well as genetic contributions to behavior. Within this perspective, a popular specialty, *evolutionary psychology*, is following in the footsteps of functionalism. The *learning perspective* emphasizes how the environment and a person's history affect behavior; within this perspective, *behaviorists* reject mentalistic explanations and *social-cognitive learning theorists* combine elements of behaviorism with the study of thoughts, values, and intentions. The *cognitive perspective* emphasizes mental processes in perception, problem solving, belief formation, and other human activities. The *sociocultural perspective* explores how social contexts and cultural rules affect an individual's beliefs and behavior.

LO 1.4.B   Describe how feminism influenced psychology.

Feminist psychology has influenced the questions researchers ask, the methods they use, and their awareness of sexist biases in the field. As members of minority groups entered psychology, they too raised awareness of issues specific to different groups by virtue of their ethnicity, culture, and sexual orientation. The result has been to make psychology more representative of all human beings.

What Psychologists Do

LO 1.5.A **Distinguish basic psychology and applied psychology, and summarize the kinds of research that various psychologists might conduct.**

Many psychologists conduct research and teach in colleges and universities, where they investigate a broad range of topics. Among the many psychological specialties are experimental, educational, developmental, industrial/organizational, psychometric, counseling, school, and clinical psychology.

LO 1.5.B **Compare the training and work settings of different psychological practitioners, such as counselors, clinical psychologists, psychotherapists, psychoanalysts, and psychiatrists.**

Other psychologists provide mental health services (*psychological practice*). *Psychotherapist* is an unregulated term for anyone who does therapy, including people who have no credentials or

training at all. Licensed therapists differ according to their training and approach. *Clinical psychologists* have a PhD, an EdD, or a PsyD; *psychiatrists* have an MD; *psychoanalysts* are trained in psychoanalytic institutes; and licensed clinical social workers (LCSWs) and marriage, family, and child counselors (MFCCs) may have various postgraduate degrees.

LO 1.5.C **Give examples of three ways in which psychologists contribute to their communities.**

Some psychologists conduct research and apply findings in a variety of nonacademic settings. These professionals work to make their communities a better place to live, and to contribute to the mental, social, and physical health of people in those communities.

Chapter 1 Quiz

1. What distinguishes scientific psychology from pseudoscience and popular opinion?
   a. Popular ideas always take time to filter into the scientific literature, whereas scientific findings are immediately embraced by the scientific community.
   b. Scientific psychology relies on empirical evidence for its conclusions.
   c. Scientific psychology only studies topics that can't be explained through common sense.
   d. Evidence from a carefully controlled experiment isn't as compelling as people's long-held beliefs.

2. Which of the following statements is true regarding how scientific psychology differs from the popular psychology found on television shows, the Internet, or in self-help books?
   a. Scientific psychology addresses a much broader range of issues and topics than popular psychology typically does.
   b. Scientific psychology is only conducted in laboratories, whereas popular psychology is studied in a variety of settings.
   c. Popular psychology offers experience-based explanations for behavior, whereas scientific psychology detaches itself from everyday experience.
   d. Popular psychology produces testable predictions, whereas scientific psychology deals only with theories.

3. Daniela and her friend visit a psychic who tells her "you will experience great change in the coming year" and "you'll need to act fast to seize a new opportunity that awaits you." As they leave the session, Daniela chuckles quietly while her friend seems shocked and amazed. "That was awesome; that psychic really predicted some heavy stuff for you!" "Oh, it's just for laughs" replied Daniela. "I don't believe a word of it." Why is Daniela correct to be skeptical?
   a. Daniela experienced great change and seized a new opportunity during the previous year, so she knew those predictions couldn't come true again.
   b. Daniela thought the psychic was actually making predictions about her friend.
   c. Psychics practice a type of science that most people can't understand.
   d. Psychic predictions are typically so vague that they're essentially meaningless.

4. What's the most appropriate way to characterize critical thinking?
   a. Critical thinking is a process, rather than a once-and-for-all accomplishment.
   b. Critical thinking should be practiced by scientists, but not necessarily ordinary people.
   c. Critical thinking always starts with rejecting some commonsense explanation.
   d. Critical thinking skills are something you're born with, rather than something you learn.

5. Which of the following is *not* one of the eight critical-thinking guidelines discussed in this chapter?

   a. Tolerate uncertainty

   b. Avoid evidentiary confirmation

   c. Define your terms

   d. Examine the evidence

6. Beliefs that are taken for granted are called:

   a. Attitudes

   b. Assumptions

   c. Hypotheses

   d. Opinions

7. What characterized the thinking of pre-psychological approaches to psychology from ancient times through the early 1800s?

   a. Pre-psychological approaches all focused on explaining human actions as the result of spiritual forces; "religion" and "psychology" were seen as interchangeable terms.

   b. Conclusions were based on the opinions of medical doctors because they were the closest practitioners to "psychologists"; these conclusions were all biologically based.

   c. Without an empirical methodology, conclusions were based on opinion and casual observations; sometimes these conclusions were right, but many times they were wrong.

   d. Before it became a science, psychology was viewed as a type of witchcraft; therefore, any conclusions reached were contaminated by bias and prejudice.

8. The first psychological laboratory was officially established in:

   a. Leipzig, Germany

   b. Boston, Massachusetts

   c. Paris, France

   d. London, England

9. Psychoanalysis, a type of early psychology, was originated by:

   a. John Watson

   b. Wilhelm Wundt

   c. William James

   d. Sigmund Freud

10. Humans can accurately recognize a smile from a greater distance than they can other facial expressions of emotion. One explanation for this finding is that being able to predict, accurately and quickly, that an approaching stranger had good intentions contributed to the development of cooperation among humans, which in turn helped form societies. Upon which perspective on psychological science is this explanation based?

    a. Evolutionary psychology

    b. Social-cognitive learning

    c. Behaviorism

    d. Structuralism

11. Little Arnold screams and throws a fit whenever he doesn't get what he wants. When this happens, his parents rush to his side and soothe him, often fulfilling whatever wants or demands he has at the moment. Which perspective on psychological science would argue that Arnold has been rewarded for his behavior?

    a. The cognitive perspective

    b. The biological perspective

    c. The sociocultural perspective

    d. The learning perspective

12. Which cross-cutting influence helped to focus psychology on the study of *all* humans, rather than just culturally dominant or readily available humans?

    a. Feminism

    b. Humanism

    c. Inclusionism

    d. The "new spirituality" movement

13. Dr. Allanson studies mood awareness, individual differences in how people monitor and label their mood states. His interest is in knowing how the process works, what its limits are, and the mechanisms that cause it to happen. Dr. Martin wants to know whether people who are higher in mood awareness are better able to control and regulate their mood states, and therefore might experience better outcomes during therapy. Dr. Allanson's interests are in _____, whereas Dr. Martin's interests are in _____.

    a. Biological psychology / psychometrics

    b. Learning theory / sociocultural psychology

    c. Basic psychology / applied psychology

    d. Counseling psychology / clinical psychology

14. Beatrice decides she wants to "help people," so she rents an office, advertises her services, and has business cards printed. Which mental health term would Beatrice be allowed to use, despite not having a scrap of psychological training?

    a. Psychiatrist

    b. Psychoanalyst

    c. Marriage, family, and child counselor

    d. Psychotherapist

15. Which of the following would be an example of a psychologist contributing to the community at large?

  a. A clinical psychologist volunteers her services at an inner-city halfway house for recovering methamphetamine addicts.

  b. An industrial/organizational psychologist switches from consulting with a nonprofit group to consulting with a Fortune 500 corporation.

  c. A psychotherapist enrolls in continuing education workshops to obtain a legitimate degree, thereby expanding his clientele.

  d. A neuropsychologist studies the brain mechanisms involved in the regulation of hunger and thirst.

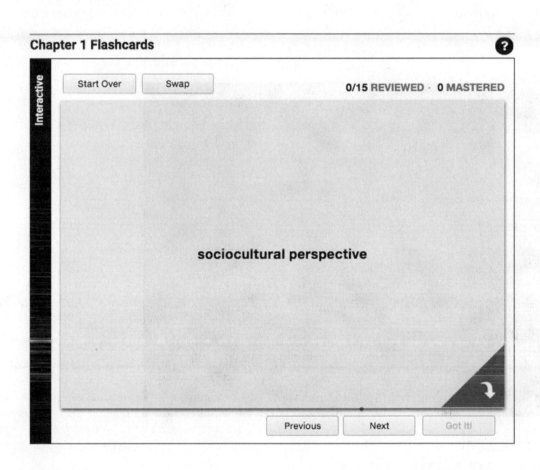

Chapter 1 Flashcards

Interactive

Start Over   Swap

0/15 REVIEWED · 0 MASTERED

sociocultural perspective

Previous   Next   Got It!

Chapter 2
How Psychologists Do Research

 Listen to the Audio

Learning Objectives

LO 2.1.A Distinguish between a theory, a hypothesis, and an operational definition.

LO 2.1.B Explain why skepticism in science involves more than just disbelief.

LO 2.1.C Explain why falsifiability is an important component of scientific research.

LO 2.1.D Describe why openness and replication are important qualities of the scientific enterprise.

LO 2.2.A Describe the major ways participants are selected for psychological studies, and why the method of selection might influence interpretations of a study's outcomes.

LO 2.2.B Discuss the advantages and disadvantages of using case studies as a means of data collection.

LO 2.2.C Discuss the advantages and disadvantages of using observational methods as a means of data collection.

LO 2.2.D Explain why norms, reliability, and validity are the three key hallmarks of any standardized psychological test.

LO 2.2.E Describe the advantages and limitations of using surveys in data collection.

LO 2.3.A Illustrate with an example how a correlation coefficient gives both the size and direction of the relationship between two variables.

LO 2.3.B Explain why a correlation between two variables does not establish a causal relationship between those variables.

LO 2.4.A Contrast an independent variable from a dependent variable and give an example of each concept in a psychology experiment.

LO 2.4.B Explain the difference between an experimental group and a control group, and discuss how random assignment helps create these two groups.

LO 2.4.C Explain why single-blind and double-blind procedures are crucial to establishing the soundness of an experiment.

LO 2.5.A Provide an example of how the arithmetic mean and standard deviation could be used to compare the performance of two groups of research participants.

LO 2.5.B Explain what a statistically significant research result means to an experimenter.

LO 2.5.C Compare cross-sectional and longitudinal studies, and discuss how effect size, meta-analysis, and Bayesian statistics allow us to judge the importance of a research outcome.

LO 2.6.A Discuss why the principles of informed consent and debriefing are two key characteristics of a researcher's code of ethics.

LO 2.6.B List and discuss four reasons why psychologists might use animals in research.

Ask questions . . . be willing to wonder

If you want to be a psychologist so that you can help people, why in the world do you need to study statistics and research methods?

If you hear that TV watching is linked to hyperactivity, can you say which causes which?

How could you find out whether driving while talking on a cell phone is dangerous?

Why do psychologists study animals—the nonhuman kind?

Here are four words that make many people nervous: *research*, *statistics*, *methods*, and *math*. "What do we have to learn this stuff for?" our students have often lamented. "I'm never going to need it anyway. Let's just cut straight to the findings." In this chapter, we hope to persuade you that of all the stuff you are going to learn in psychology, the information in this chapter may be the most important for protecting yourself from making wrong choices, adopting mistaken beliefs, or coming to wrong conclusions. Consider these claims:

- A study reports that testosterone, that famously male hormone, plummets after a man becomes a parent. And the more time he spends caring for his children, the lower his testosterone drops. Do men have to choose between manliness and dadliness?

- Various studies report that playing fast-paced video games such as *Medal of Honor* and *Grand Theft Auto* improves players' cognitive abilities, such as visual attention and speed of response. Moreover, these games have a "transfer effect," improving visual skills in other areas of life. Does this mean that college students now have a legitimate reason to spend more time playing video games?

- A paper in a major psychology journal claims that the results of nine experiments, involving 1,000 college students, found "statistically significant" evidence of extrasensory perception (ESP). The students had to choose which of two curtains on a computer screen had an erotic picture behind it, and they allegedly demonstrated ESP by doing this at a rate that was slightly above chance (Bem, 2011). Stephen Colbert had a lot of fun with this study, as you can imagine. But was it good evidence of ESP?

- Your 9-year-old brother is autistic. He lives in his own private world, cut off from normal social interaction. He does not speak, and he rarely looks you in the eye. He has never been able to function in a public school classroom. You hear about a technique called "facilitated communication" (FC), in which children with autism are placed in front of a keyboard while an adult "facilitator" gently places a hand over the child's hand or forearm. The method's proponents claim that children who have never used words before are able to peck out complete sentences, answer questions, and divulge their thoughts. Some children, through their facilitators, have supposedly mastered advanced subjects or have written poetry of astonishing beauty. Should your brother receive FC?

By the time you finish this chapter, you will know how to think about these questions and the many others you encounter. Research methods are the tools of the psychological scientist's trade, and understanding them is crucial for everyone who reads or hears about a new program or an "exciting finding" that is said to be based on psychological research. Trying to practice critical thinking or apply psychological findings to your own life without having these tools is like trying to dig a foundation for your house with teaspoons. You could do it, but it will take a *long* time and the result won't be very sturdy. Knowing the difference between claims based on good research and those based on sloppy research or anecdotes can help you make wiser psychological and medical decisions, prevent you from spending money on worthless programs, and sometimes even save lives.

What Makes Psychological Research Scientific?

When we say that psychologists are scientists, we do not mean they work with complicated gadgets and machines (although some do). The scientific enterprise has more to do with attitudes and procedures than with apparatus (Stanovich, 2010). Here are a few key characteristics of the ideal scientist.

Precision and Reliance on Empirical Evidence

LO 2.1.A Distinguish between a theory, a hypothesis, and an operational definition.

Scientists sometimes launch an investigation simply because of a hunch they have about some behavior. Often, however, they start out with a general **theory**, an organized system of assumptions and principles that purports to explain certain phenomena and how they are related. Many people misunderstand what scientists mean by a theory. A scientific theory is not just someone's personal opinion, as in "It's only a theory" or "I have a theory about why he told that lie." Many scientific theories are tentative, pending more research, but others, such as the theory of evolution, are accepted by nearly all scientists.

From a theory, a psychological scientist derives a **hypothesis**, a statement that attempts to describe or explain a given behavior. Initially, this statement may be quite general, as in, say, "Misery loves company." But before any research can be done, the hypothesis must be made more precise. "Misery loves company" might be rephrased as "People who are anxious about a threatening situation tend to seek out others facing the same threat."

A hypothesis, in turn, leads to predictions about what will happen in a particular situation. In a prediction, terms such as *anxiety* or *threatening situation* are given **operational definitions**, which specify how the phenomena in question are to be observed and measured. "Anxiety" might be defined operationally as a score on an anxiety questionnaire, and "threatening situation" as the threat of an electric shock. The prediction might be, "If you raise people's anxiety scores by telling them they are going to receive electric shocks, and then give them the choice of waiting alone or with others who are in the same situation, they will be more likely to choose to wait with others than they would be if they were not anxious." The prediction can then be tested using systematic methods.

Any theory, idea, or hunch may initially generate excitement because it is plausible or imaginative, but it must eventually be backed by *empirical evidence*—information that is observable and verifiable, gathered using the techniques of science. A collection of anecdotes or an appeal to authority will not do, nor will the intuitive appeal of the idea or its popularity. As Nobel Prize–winning scientist Peter Medawar (1979) once wrote, "The intensity of the conviction that a hypothesis is true has no bearing on whether it is true or not." In 2011, Richard Muller, a prominent physicist who had doubted that global warming was occurring, made headlines when he reported, after a 2-year investigation, that temperatures really are rising,

theory

An organized system of assumptions and principles that purports to explain a specified set of phenomena and their interrelationships.

hypothesis

A statement that attempts to predict or to account for a set of phenomena; scientific hypotheses specify relationships among events or variables and are empirically tested.

operational definition

A precise definition of a term in a hypothesis, which specifies the operations for observing and measuring the process or phenomenon being defined.

and the following year, that human beings are a large part of the reason. Muller had been funded in large measure by two conservative oil billionaires who did not welcome his results. But Muller let the evidence trump politics, as a scientist should.

Figure 2.1 illustrates the process of moving from a theory to evidence and back again, which is the central process of all sciences.

Skepticism

LO 2.1.B Explain why skepticism in science involves more than just disbelief.

Scientists do not accept ideas on faith or authority; their motto is "Show me!" Some of the greatest scientific advances have been made by those who dared to doubt what everyone else assumed to be true: that the sun revolves around the earth, that illness can be cured by applying leeches to the skin, that madness is a sign of demonic possession. In the world of science, skepticism means treating conclusions, both new and old, with caution. Don't take our word for it; the video *Thinking Critically 1* provides more insights about the value of being skeptical.

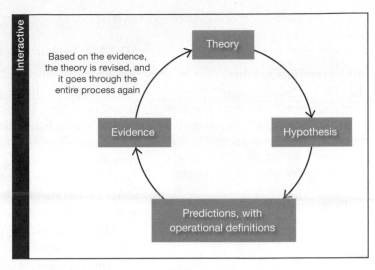

Figure 2.1 The Cycle of Scientific Research

"Doing science" involves many interactive elements. Theories allow a researcher to derive testable hypotheses, and make predictions about the pattern of results that should occur. Hypotheses are tested empirically by gathering data on operationally defined variables. By examining the evidence, modifications, extensions, and revisions to the theory can take place, thereby generating new hypotheses and continuing the cycle of research investigation.

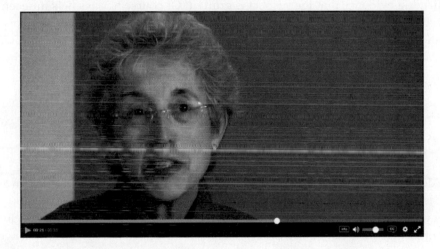

Thus, in the case of facilitated communication, psychological scientists did not simply say, "Wow, what an interesting way to help autistic kids." Rather than accept testimonials about the method's effectiveness, they have conducted experiments involving hundreds of autistic children and their facilitators (Romanczyk et al., 2003). Their techniques have been simple: They have the child identify a picture but show the facilitator a different picture or no picture at all; or they keep the facilitator from hearing the questions being put to the child. Under these conditions, the child types only what the facilitator sees or hears, not what the child sees or hears. This research shows that what happens in facilitated communication is exactly what happens when a medium guides a person's hand over a Ouija board to help the person receive "messages" from a "spirit": The person doing the "facilitating" unconsciously nudges the other person's hand in the desired direction, remaining unaware of having influenced the responses produced (Wegner, Fuller, & Sparrow, 2003). In other words, facilitated communication is really *facilitator* communication (Schlosser et al., 2014). This finding is vitally important because if parents waste their time and money on a treatment that doesn't work, they may never get genuine help for their children, and they will suffer when their false hopes are finally shattered by reality.

"Skepticism" is not simply about debunking some claim, but showing *why* the claim is invalid—so that better methods can replace it. Skepticism and caution, however, must be balanced by openness to new ideas and evidence. Otherwise, a scientist may wind up as shortsighted as the famous physicist Lord Kelvin, who reputedly declared with great confidence at the end of the 19th century that radio had no future, X-rays were a hoax, and "heavier-than-air flying machines" were impossible.

Willingness to Make "Risky Predictions"

LO 2.1.C Explain why falsifiability is an important component of scientific research.

principle of falsifiability

The principle that a scientific theory must make predictions that are specific enough to expose the theory to the possibility of disconfirmation; that is, the theory must predict not only what will happen but also what will *not* happen.

confirmation bias

The tendency to look for or pay attention only to information that confirms one's own belief.

A reliance on empirical evidence and a sense of skepticism are important characteristics of scientists. A related principle is that scientists must state an idea in such a way that it can be *refuted*, or disproved by counterevidence. This important rule, known as the **principle of falsifiability**, does not mean that the idea *will* be disproved, only that it could be if contrary evidence were to be discovered. In other words, a scientist must risk disconfirmation by predicting not only what will happen but also what will *not* happen. In the "misery loves company" study, the hypothesis would be supported if most anxious people sought each other out, but would be disconfirmed if most anxious people went off alone to sulk and worry, or if anxiety had no effect on their behavior (see Figure 2.2). A willingness to risk disconfirmation forces the scientist to take negative evidence seriously and to abandon mistaken hypotheses.

The principle of falsifiability is often violated in everyday life because all of us are vulnerable to the **confirmation bias**: the tendency to look for and accept evidence that supports our pet theories and assumptions and to ignore or reject evidence that contradicts our beliefs. If a police interrogator is convinced of a suspect's guilt, he or she may interpret anything the suspect says, even the person's maintenance of innocence, as confirming evidence that the suspect is guilty ("Of course he says he's innocent; he's a liar"). But what if the suspect *is* innocent? The principle of falsifiability compels scientists—and the rest of us—to resist the confirmation bias and to consider counterevidence. Learn more about the benefits of challenging your assumptions by watching the video *Thinking Critically 2*.

Openness

LO 2.1.D Describe why openness and replication are important qualities of the scientific enterprise.

Science depends on the free flow of ideas and full disclosure of the procedures used in a study. Secrecy is a big "no-no"; scientists must be willing to tell others where they got their ideas, how they tested them, and what the results were. They must do this clearly and in detail so that other scientists can repeat, or *replicate*, their studies and verify—or challenge—the

Figure 2.2 The Principle of Falsifiability

The scientific method requires researchers to expose their ideas to the possibility of counterevidence. Examining the outcomes of a simple study testing the idea that "misery loves company" would allow a researcher to either support or refute that hypothesis.

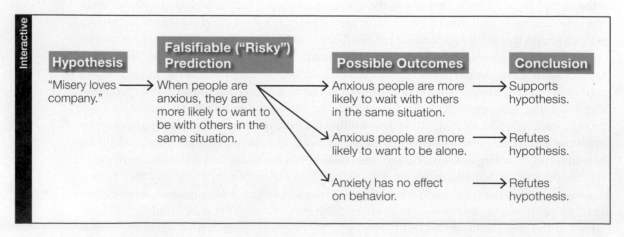

findings. Replication is an essential part of the scientific process because sometimes what seems to be a fabulous phenomenon turns out to be only a fluke.

If you think about it, you will see that these principles of good science correspond to critical thinking. Formulating a prediction with operational definitions corresponds to "define your terms." Reliance on empirical evidence helps scientists avoid the temptation to over-simplify. Openness to new ideas encourages scientists to "ask questions" and "consider other interpretations." The principle of falsifiability forces scientists to "analyze assumptions and biases" in a fair-minded fashion. And until their results have been replicated and verified, scientists must "tolerate uncertainty."

Do psychologists and other scientists always live up to these lofty standards? Not always. Being only human, they may put too much trust in their personal experiences, be biased by a conflict of interest when they are funded by private industry, or permit ambition to interfere with openness. Like everyone else, they may find it hard to admit that the evidence does not support their hypothesis; it is far easier to be skeptical about someone else's ideas than about your own (Tavris & Aronson, 2007).

Commitment to one's theories is not in itself a bad thing. Passion is the fuel of progress. It motivates researchers to think boldly and do the exhaustive testing that is often required to support an idea. But passion can also cloud perceptions, causing scientists to misinterpret their own data to confirm what they want to see. Other scientists, motivated by the desire for fame, discovery, or fortune, have even resorted to plagiarism, faking their data, and deceptive methods. That is why science is a communal activity. Scientists are expected to submit their results to professional journals, which send the findings to experts in the field for evaluation before deciding whether to publish them. This process, called *peer review*, is an effort to ensure that the work lives up to accepted scientific standards. Peer review and scientific publication are supposed to precede announcements to the public through press releases, Internet postings, or popular books. The research community acts as a jury, scrutinizing and sifting the evidence, judging its integrity, approving some viewpoints, and relegating others to the scientific scrap heap.

The peer-review process is not perfect, but it does give science a built-in system of checks and balances. Individuals are not necessarily objective, honest, or rational, but science forces them to subject their findings to scrutiny and to justify their claims.

JOURNAL PROMPT 2.1

Thinking Critically—Examine the Evidence: A lighthearted article in the *New England Journal of Medicine* noted that there is a strong relationship between the *per capita* consumption of chocolate in a given nation and the number of Nobel laureates produced by that nation (Messerli, 2012). One conclusion readily presents itself: People who consume more chocolate are smarter, and therefore national populations that consume more chocolate produce more Nobel laureates (who, by definition, need to be pretty smart). But how else could this relationship be interpreted? Be precise, be skeptical, look at the evidence, and offer some alternative interpretations.

Quiz for Module 2.1

1. An organized system of assumptions and principles that seeks to explain a phenomenon is known as a(n):
   a. Prediction
   b. Hypothesis
   c. Operational definition
   d. Theory

2. Natasha tells her psychology professor that she wants to study why similarity leads to attraction. "That's great," her professor replies. "But what do you mean, exactly, by 'similarity' and 'attraction'?" What is Natasha's professor urging her to do?
   a. Formulate a hypothesis about the relationship between her variables of interest.
   b. Create operational definitions of the variables she wants to study.
   c. Propose a theory to explain why similarity is correlated with attraction.
   d. Design a field experiment to test her hypothesis.

3. Luis tells his friend Meeta, "Since I've been wearing this copper bracelet, my joint pain has decreased. It must really work!" "Hmm . . . " replies Meeta. "I'm sure you believe that, and I'm glad you're feeling better. But I'd want to know how, when, and why copper would have that effect on pain." Which characteristic of being a good scientist is Meeta demonstrating?
   a. Skepticism
   b. Falsifiability
   c. Openness
   d. Argument from authority

4. "All swans are white" is a poor example of a scientific hypothesis. Gathering more and more examples of white swans would never really confirm the conclusion. However, finding a single *black* swan would be enough to disprove the hypothesis. Which scientific principle does this logic demonstrate?
   a. The code of Hammurabi
   b. The exception to the rule
   c. The principle of falsifiability
   d. The principle of precision

5. Winston wants to publish the results of his scientific study, but before he does so he collects more data using the same variables but with a new sample of research participants and a slightly different procedure. The results of the second study are consistent with those of the first, and Winston publishes both sets of results with greater confidence in his contribution to science. Which good scientific practice is Winston following?
   a. Replication
   b. Risky predictions
   c. Peer review
   d. Confirmation control

Descriptive Studies: Establishing the Facts

Psychologists gather evidence to support their hypotheses by using different methods, depending on the kinds of questions they want to answer. These methods are not mutually exclusive, however. Just as a police detective may rely on DNA samples, fingerprints, and interviews of suspects to figure out "who done it," psychological sleuths often draw on different techniques at different stages of an investigation. The video *How to Answer Psychological Questions* will help you sharpen your investigative skills.

Research Participants

LO 2.2.A Describe the major ways participants are selected for psychological studies and why the method of selection might influence interpretations of a study's outcomes.

representative sample

A group of individuals, selected from a population for study, which matches the population on important characteristics such as age and sex.

One of the first challenges facing any researcher, no matter what method is used, is to select the participants (sometimes called "subjects") for the study. Ideally, the researcher would prefer to get a **representative sample**, a group of participants that accurately represents the larger population that the researcher is interested in. Suppose you wanted to learn about drug use among first-year college students. Questioning or observing every first-year student in the

country would obviously not be practical; instead, you would need to recruit a sample. You could use special selection procedures to ensure that this sample contained the same proportion of women, men, blacks, whites, poor people, rich people, Catholics, Jews, and so on as in the general population of new college students. Even then, a sample drawn just from your own school or town might not produce results applicable to the entire country or even your state.

Plenty of studies are based on unrepresentative samples. The American Medical Association reported, based on a "random sample" of 664 women who were polled online, that binge drinking and unprotected sex were rampant among college women during spring break vacations. The media had a field day with this news. Yet the sample, it turned out, was not random at all. It included only women who volunteered to answer questions, and only a fourth of them had ever taken a spring break trip (Rosnow & Rosenthal, 2011).

A sample's size is less critical than its representativeness. A small but representative sample may yield accurate results, whereas a large study that fails to use proper sampling methods may yield questionable results. But in practice, psychologists and others who study human behavior must often settle for a sample of people who happen to be available—a "convenience" sample—and more often than not, this means undergraduate students. One group of researchers noted that most of these students are WEIRDos—from Western, educated, industrialized, rich, and democratic cultures—and thus hardly representative of humans as a whole. "WEIRD subjects are some of the most psychologically unusual people on the planet," said one of the investigators (Henrich, Heine, & Norenzayan, 2010).

College students, in addition, are younger than the general population. They are also more likely to be female and to have better cognitive skills. Does that matter? It depends. Many psychological processes, such as basic perceptual or memory processes, are likely to be the same in students as in anyone else; after all, students are not a separate species, no matter what they (or their professors) may sometimes think! When considering other topics, however, we may need to be cautious about drawing conclusions until the research can be replicated with nonstudents. Scientists are turning to technology to help them do this. Amazon runs a site called Mechanical Turk, where people across the world do online tasks that computers cannot do, typically for small rewards that they usually convert into Amazon vouchers. Many of the 500,000 registered Turk workers also participate in research, allowing scientists to quickly and cheaply recruit a diverse sample of thousands of people (Buhrmester, Kwang, & Gosling, 2011). One research team was able to analyze the patterns of moods in people's tweets worldwide (Golder & Macy, 2011).

We turn now to the specific methods used most commonly in psychological research. As you read about these methods, you may want to list their advantages and disadvantages so that you will remember them better. Then check your list against the one in Review 2.1. We begin with **descriptive methods**, which allow researchers to describe and predict behavior but not necessarily to choose one explanation over competing ones.

descriptive methods
Methods that yield descriptions of behavior but not necessarily causal explanations.

case study
A detailed description of a particular individual being studied or treated.

Case Studies

LO 2.2.B Discuss the advantages and disadvantages of using case studies as a means of data collection.

A **case study** (or *case history*) is a detailed description of a particular individual based on careful observation or formal psychological testing. It may include information about a person's childhood, dreams, fantasies, experiences, and relationships—anything that will provide insight into the person's behavior. Case studies are most commonly used by clinicians, but sometimes academic researchers use them as well, especially when they are just beginning to study a topic or when practical or ethical considerations prevent them from gathering information in other ways.

Suppose you want to know whether the first few years of life are critical for acquiring a first language. Can children who have missed out on hearing speech (or, in the case of deaf children, seeing signs) during their early years catch up later on? Obviously, psychologists cannot answer this question by isolating children and seeing what happens. So, instead, they have studied unusual cases of language deprivation.

One such case involved a 13-year-old girl who had been cruelly locked up in a small room since the age of 1½, strapped for hours to a potty chair. If she made the slightest sound, her severely disturbed father beat her with a large piece of wood. When she was finally rescued, "Genie," as researchers called her, did not know how to chew or stand erect and was not toilet-trained. Her only sounds were high-pitched whimpers. Eventually, she began to understand short sentences and to use words to convey her needs, but even after many years, Genie's grammar and pronunciation remained abnormal. She never learned to use pronouns correctly, ask questions, or use the little word endings that communicate tense, number, and possession (Curtiss, 1977, 1982; Rymer, 1993). This sad case, along with similar ones, suggests that a critical period exists for language development, with the likelihood of fully mastering a first language declining steadily after early childhood and falling off drastically at puberty (Pinker, 1994).

Case studies illustrate psychological principles in a way that abstract generalizations and cold statistics never can, and they produce a more detailed picture of an individual than other methods do. In biological research, cases of patients with brain damage have yielded important clues to how the brain is organized. But in most instances, case studies have serious drawbacks. Information is often missing or hard to interpret; no one knows what Genie's language development was like before she was locked up or whether she was born with mental deficits. The observer who writes up the case may have certain biases that influence which facts are noticed or overlooked. The person who is the focus of the study may have selective or inaccurate memories, making any conclusions unreliable (Loftus & Guyer, 2002). Most important, because that person may be unrepresentative of the group the researcher is interested in, this

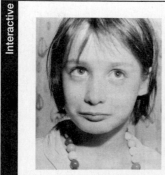

Case studies allow researchers to study rare events and unique individuals. Genie, a child who was raised in isolation, provided a glimpse into the workings of the mind and the process of language acquisition (left). Astronauts Scott and Mark Kelly, identical twins, have embarked on an unusual mission. Scott will spend one year living on the International Space Station to help NASA understand the effects of long-term space flight on the mind and body; Mark will spend the year being studied by NASA while he remains here on Earth. The photo on the right shows a Turkish woman whose family members walk on all fours. The genetic and environmental factors influencing this unusual behavior have captured the attention of scientists.

method has only limited usefulness for deriving general principles of behavior. For all these reasons, case studies are usually only sources, rather than tests, of hypotheses.

Many psychotherapists publish individual case studies of their clients in treatment. These can be informative, but they are not equivalent to scientific research and can sometimes be wrong or misleading. Consider the sensational story of "Sybil," whose account of her 16 personalities became a famous book and TV movie, eventually launching an epidemic of multiple personality disorder. Detective work by investigative journalists and other skeptics later revealed that Sybil was not a multiple personality after all; her diagnosis was created in collusion with her psychiatrist, Cornelia Wilbur, who hoped to profit professionally and financially from the story (Nathan, 2011). Wilbur omitted many facts from her case study of Sybil, such as the vitamin B_{12} deficiency that produced Sybil's emotional and physical problems. Wilbur did not disclose that she was administering massive amounts of heavy drugs to her patient, who became addicted to them. And she never informed her colleagues or the public that Sybil had written to her admitting that she did not have multiple personalities.

Be wary, then, of the compelling case histories reported in the media by individuals or by therapists. Often, these stories are only "arguing by anecdote," and they are not a basis for drawing firm conclusions about anything.

Observational Studies

LO 2.2.C Discuss the advantages and disadvantages of using observational methods as a means of data collection.

In **observational studies**, a researcher observes, measures, and records behavior, taking care to avoid intruding on the people (or animals) being observed. Unlike case studies, observational studies usually involve many participants. Often, an observational study is the first step in a program of research; it is helpful to have a good description of behavior before you try to explain it.

The primary purpose of *naturalistic observation* is to find out how people or animals act in their normal social environments. Psychologists use naturalistic observation wherever people happen to be—at home, on playgrounds or streets, in schoolrooms, or in offices. In one study, a social psychologist and his students ventured into a common human habitat: bars. They wanted to know whether people in bars drink more when they are in groups than when they are alone. They visited all 32 pubs in a midsized city, ordered beers, and recorded on napkins and pieces of newspaper how much the other patrons imbibed. They found that drinkers in groups consumed more than individuals who were alone. Those in groups did not drink any faster; they just lingered in the bar longer (Sommer, 1977).

Note that the students who did this study did not rely on their impressions or memories of how much people drank. In observational studies, researchers count, rate, or measure behavior in a systematic way, to guard against noticing only what they expect or want to see, and they keep careful records so that others can cross-check their observations. Observers must also take pains to avoid being obvious about what they are doing so that those who are being observed will behave naturally. If the students who studied drinking habits had marched into those bars with camcorders and announced their intentions to the customers, the results might have been quite different.

Sometimes psychologists prefer to make observations in a laboratory setting. In *laboratory observation*, researchers have more control over the situation. They can use sophisticated equipment, determine the number of people who will be observed, maintain a clear line of vision, and so forth. Say you wanted to know how infants of different ages respond when left with a stranger. You might have parents and their infants come to your laboratory, observe them playing together for a while through a one-way window, then have a stranger enter the room and, a few minutes later, have the parent leave. You could record signs of distress in the children, interactions with the stranger, and other behavior. If you did this, you would find that very young infants carry on cheerfully with whatever they are doing when the parent

observational study

A study in which a researcher carefully and systematically observes and records behavior without interfering with the behavior; it may involve either naturalistic or laboratory observation.

Try a little naturalistic observation of your own. Go to a public place where people voluntarily seat themselves near others, such as a movie theater or a cafeteria with large tables. If you choose a setting where many people enter at once, you might recruit some friends to help you; you can divide the area into sections and give each observer one section to observe. As individuals and groups sit down, note how many seats they leave between themselves and the next person. On average, how far do people tend to sit from strangers? After you have your results, see how many possible explanations you can come up with.

psychological tests

Procedures used to measure and evaluate personality traits, emotional states, aptitudes, interests, abilities, and values.

standardize

In test construction, to develop uniform procedures for giving and scoring a test.

norms

In test construction, established standards of performance.

reliability

In test construction, the consistency of scores derived from a test, from one time and place to another.

leaves. However, by the age of about 8 months, many children will burst into tears or show other signs of what child psychologists call "separation anxiety."

One shortcoming of laboratory observation is that the presence of researchers and special equipment may cause people to behave differently than they would in their usual surroundings. Furthermore, whether they are in natural or laboratory settings, observational studies, like other descriptive methods, are more useful for describing behavior than for explaining it. The barroom results we described do not necessarily mean that being in a group makes people drink a lot. People may join a group because they are already interested in drinking and find it more comfortable to hang around the bar if they are with others. Similarly, if we observe infants protesting whenever a parent leaves the room, is it because they have become attached to their parents and want them nearby, or have they simply learned from experience that crying brings an adult with a cookie and a cuddle? Observational studies alone cannot answer such questions.

Tests

LO 2.2.D Explain why norms, reliability, and validity are the three key hallmarks of any standardized psychological test.

Psychological tests, sometimes called *assessment instruments*, are procedures for measuring and evaluating personality traits, emotions, aptitudes, interests, abilities, and values. Typically, tests require people to answer a series of written or oral questions. The answers may then be totaled to yield a single numerical score, or a set of scores. *Objective tests*, also called *inventories*, measure beliefs, feelings, or behaviors of which an individual is aware; *projective tests* are designed to tap unconscious feelings or motives.

At one time or another, you no doubt have taken a personality test, an achievement test, or a vocational aptitude test. Hundreds of psychological tests are used in industry, education, the military, and the helping professions, and many tests are also used in research. Some tests are given to individuals, others to large groups. These measures help clarify differences among people, as well as differences in the reactions of the same person on different occasions or at different stages of life. Tests may be used to promote self-understanding, to evaluate psychological treatments and programs, or, in scientific research, to draw generalizations about human behavior. Well-constructed psychological tests are a great improvement over simple self-evaluation because many people have a distorted view of their own abilities and traits.

One test of a good test is whether it is **standardized**, having uniform procedures for giving and scoring the test. It would hardly be fair to give some people detailed instructions and plenty of time and others only vague instructions and limited time. Those who administer the test must know exactly how to explain the tasks involved, how much time to allow, and what materials to use. Scoring is usually done by referring to **norms**, or established standards of performance. The usual procedure for developing norms is to give the test to a large group of people who resemble those for whom the test is intended. Norms determine which scores can be considered high, low, or average.

Test construction presents many challenges. For one thing, the test must have **reliability**, producing the same results from one time and place to the next or from one scorer to another. A vocational interest test is not reliable if it says that Tom would make a wonderful engineer but a poor journalist, but then gives different results when Tom retakes the test a week later. Psychologists can measure *test–retest reliability* by giving the test twice to the same group of people and comparing the two sets of scores statistically. If the test is reliable, individuals' scores will be similar from one session to another. This method has a drawback, however: People tend to do better the second time they take a test, after they have become familiar with it. A solution is to compute *alternate-forms reliability* by giving different versions of the same test to the same group on two separate occasions (see Figure 2.3). The items on the

Figure 2.3 Consistency in the Measurement Process

Psychological tests, like all forms of scientific measurement, need to have the property of reliability. This means that a measuring instrument measures the same way each time someone uses it.

Reliability
How consistent are the test's results?

Test–Retest Reliability

Are scores similar from one session to another?

Alternate–Forms Reliability

Are scores similar on different versions of the test?

two forms are similar in format but are not identical in content. Performance cannot improve because of familiarity with the items, although people may still do somewhat better the second time around because they have learned the procedures expected of them.

To be useful, a test must also have **validity**, measuring what it sets out to measure. A creativity test is not valid if what it actually measures is verbal sophistication. If the items broadly represent the trait in question, the test is said to have *content validity*. If you were testing, say, employees' job satisfaction, and your test tapped a broad array of relevant beliefs and behaviors (e.g., "Do you feel you have reached a dead end at work?", "Are you bored with your assignments?"), it would have content validity. If the test asked only how workers felt about their salary level, it would lack content validity and would be of little use; after all, highly paid people are not always satisfied with their jobs, and people who earn low wages are not always dissatisfied.

Most tests are also judged on *criterion validity*, the ability to predict independent measures, or criteria, of the trait in question (see Figure 2.4). The criterion for a scholastic aptitude test might be college grades; the criterion for a test of shyness might be behavior in social situations. To find out whether your job satisfaction test had criterion validity, you might return a year later to see whether it correctly predicted absenteeism, resignations, or requests for job transfers.

Teachers, parents, and employers do not always stop to question a test's validity, especially when the results are summarized in a single, precise-sounding number, such as an IQ score of 115 or a job applicant's ranking of 5. Among psychologists and educators, however, controversy exists about the validity and usefulness of even some widely used tests, including mental tests like the Scholastic Assessment Test (SAT) and standardized IQ tests. A comprehensive review of the evidence from large studies and national samples concluded that mental tests do a good job of predicting intellectual performance (Sackett, Borneman, & Connelly, 2008). But not everyone has access to the opportunities that lead to strong test scores and strong real-world performance. Motivation, study skills, self-discipline, practical "smarts," and other traits not measured by IQ or other mental tests are major influences on success in school and on the job.

Criticisms and reevaluations of psychological tests keep psychological assessment honest and scientifically rigorous. In contrast, the pop-psych tests found in magazines, newspapers, and on the Internet usually have not been evaluated for either validity or reliability. These questionnaires have inviting headlines, such as "Which Breed of Dog Do You Most Resemble?" or "The Seven Types of Lovers," but they are merely lists of questions that someone thought sounded good.

Validity
Does the test measure what it was designed to measure?

Content Validity
Do items broadly represent the trait in question?

Criterion Validity
Do the test results predict other measures of the trait?

Behavior 1
Behavior 2
Behavior 3

Figure 2.4 Accuracy in the Measurement Process
Psychological tests, like all forms of scientific measurement, need to have the property of validity. This means that a measuring instrument actually measures what it was designed to measure.

validity
The ability of a test to measure what it was designed to measure.

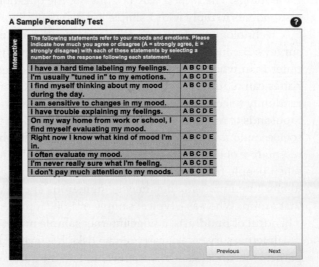

A Sample Personality Test

The following statements refer to your moods and emotions. Please indicate how much you agree or disagree (A = strongly agree, E = strongly disagree) with each of these statements by selecting a number from the response following each statement.

I have a hard time labeling my feelings.	A B C D E
I'm usually "tuned in" to my emotions.	A B C D E
I find myself thinking about my mood during the day.	A B C D E
I am sensitive to changes in my mood.	A B C D E
I have trouble explaining my feelings.	A B C D E
On my way home from work or school, I find myself evaluating my mood.	A B C D E
Right now I know what kind of mood I'm in.	A B C D E
I often evaluate my mood.	A B C D E
I'm never really sure what I'm feeling.	A B C D E
I don't pay much attention to my moods.	A B C D E

Previous   Next

By completing this survey, you would be able to gauge your level of mood awareness, which is the extent to which you monitor and label your own mood states. For more information on the Mood Awareness Scale, please consult the journal article found in the References.

surveys

Questionnaires and interviews that ask people directly about their experiences, attitudes, or opinions.

volunteer bias

A shortcoming of findings derived from a sample of volunteers instead of a representative sample; the volunteers may differ from those who did not volunteer.

Surveys

LO 2.2.E Describe the advantages and limitations of using surveys in data collection.

Everywhere you go, someone wants your opinion. Political polls want to know what you think of some candidate. Eat at a restaurant, get your car serviced, or stay at a hotel, and you'll get a satisfaction survey 5 minutes later. Online, readers and users of any product offer their rating. Whereas psychological tests usually generate information about people indirectly, **surveys** are questionnaires and interviews that gather information by asking people *directly* about their experiences, attitudes, or opinions. How reliable are all these surveys?

Surveys produce bushels of data, but they are not easy to do well. Sampling problems are often an issue. When a talk-radio host or TV personality invites people to send comments about a political matter, the results are not likely to generalize to the population as a whole, even if thousands of people respond. Why? As a group, people who listen to Rush Limbaugh are more conservative than fans of Jon Stewart. Popular polls and surveys (like the one about college women on spring break) also frequently suffer from a **volunteer bias**: People who are willing to volunteer their opinions may differ from those who decline to take part. When you read about a survey (or any other kind of study), always ask who participated. A nonrepresentative sample does not necessarily mean that a survey is worthless or uninteresting, but it does mean that the results may not hold true for other groups.

Yet another problem with surveys, and with self-reports in general, is that people sometimes lie, especially when the survey is about a touchy or embarrassing topic. ("What? Me do that disgusting/illegal/dishonest thing? Never!") In studies comparing self-reports of illicit drug use with urinalysis results from the same individuals, between 30 and 70 percent of those who test positive for cocaine or opiates deny having used drugs recently (Tourangeau & Yan, 2007). The likelihood of lying is reduced when respondents are guaranteed anonymity and allowed to respond in private. Researchers can also check for lying by asking the same question several times with different wording to see whether the answers are consistent. But not all surveys use these techniques, and even when respondents are trying to be truthful, they may misinterpret the survey questions, hold inaccurate perceptions of their own behavior, or misremember the past.

When you hear about the results of a survey or opinion poll, you also need to consider which questions were (and were not) asked and how the questions were phrased. These aspects of a survey's design may reflect assumptions about the topic or encourage certain responses—as political pollsters well know. Many years ago, famed sex researcher Alfred Kinsey, in his pioneering surveys of sexual behavior, made it his practice always to ask, "*How many times have you* (masturbated, had nonmarital sex, etc.)?" rather than "*Have you ever* (masturbated, had nonmarital sex, etc.)?" (Kinsey, Pomeroy, & Martin, 1948; Kinsey et al., 1953). The first way of phrasing the question tended to elicit more truthful responses than the second because it removed the respondent's self-consciousness about having done any of these things. The second way of phrasing the question would have permitted embarrassed respondents to reply with a simple but dishonest "no."

Technology can help researchers overcome some of the problems inherent in conducting surveys. Because many people feel more anonymous when they answer questions on a computer than when they complete a paper-and-pencil questionnaire, computerized questionnaires can reduce lying (Turner et al., 1998). Participants are usually volunteers and are not randomly selected, but because Web-based samples are often huge, consisting of hundreds of thousands of respondents, they are more diverse than traditional samples in terms of gender, socioeconomic status, geographic region, and age. In these respects, they tend to be more representative of the general population than traditional samples are (Gosling et al., 2004). Even when people from a particular group make up only a small proportion of the respondents, in absolute numbers, they may be numerous enough to provide useful information about that group. Whereas a typical sample of 1,000 representative Americans might include only a handful of Buddhists, a huge Internet sample might draw hundreds.

Internet surveys also carry certain risks, however. It is hard for researchers to know whether participants understand the instructions and the questions and are taking them seriously. Also, many tests and surveys on the Web have never been validated, which is why drawing conclusions from them about your personality or mental adjustment could be dangerous to your mental health! Always check the credentials of those designing the test or survey and be sure it is not just something someone made up at his or her computer in the middle of the night.

JOURNAL PROMPT 2.2

Thinking Critically—Don't Oversimplify: Case studies are often enormously compelling, which is why talk-show hosts love them. But often they are merely anecdotes. What are the dangers in using case studies to draw general conclusions about human nature?

Quiz for Module 2.2

1. Pedro wants to gauge the nation's attitudes toward handguns, so he polls a very large sample of National Rifle Association (NRA) members and asks them what they think. Despite having a lot of data, Pedro's conclusions are likely to be flawed. Why?

   a. He used a survey when he should have used an interview to collect the data.

   b. The sample he used wasn't representative of the population he's interested in learning about.

   c. Samples should always include about 13% of the population being studied.

   d. He didn't use alternate-forms reliability when constructing his measurements.

2. Trixie has been assigned to do a research project on human development for her Introductory Psychology course. She decides to conduct a case study of her Uncle Joe, and devises a days-long set of interview questions for him, ranging from his childhood experiences through the ensuing 60 years of his life. Although her intentions are admirable, Trixie might have spent the time more profitably by using a different methodology. Why?

   a. Case studies are of limited usefulness in deriving general conclusions about behavior.

   b. Case studies always produce biased and inaccurate results.

   c. By definition, case studies involve studying, and Trixie didn't devote enough time to this project.

   d. Case studies are a technique typically used by biologists, but not by psychologists.

3. Both Justine and Trish are interested in developmental psychology, specifically the types of play 5-year-olds engage in. Justine visits a local park and unobtrusively makes notes about the children she sees. Trish invites parents and their children to a specially designed room in the psychology building and watches the children through a one-way mirror. Both approaches are sensible. The difference is that Justine is using _____ whereas Trish is using

   _____.

   a. Laboratory observation / the case study method

   b. Naturalistic observation / laboratory observation

   c. The case study method / naturalistic observation

   d. Laboratory observation / naturalistic observation

4. Desmond administers a test of mathematical aptitude to a group of 25 incoming ninth graders, then inspects their final grades in their geometry class at the end of the school year. He finds that those students who were predicted to have high mathematical skills (based on the test) did well on their geometry class (based on their final grades), and that those who were predicted to do poorly did indeed do poorly. Desmond has collected some evidence for the _____ of his aptitude test.

   a. Projective content

   b. Test–retest reliability

   c. Content validity

   d. Criterion validity

5. Britt wants to know whether drug use is widespread on his college campus. He asks the members of his Chemical Dependency class if they'd be willing to respond to a short survey that he's constructed on this topic. Half the class agrees to participate. When Britt analyzes the data he concludes that drug use indeed takes place at a high rate. What's the flaw in this research process?

   a. Britt's sample was representative of his college population, but it may not have been representative of the average of college populations in his home state.

   b. Content validity is at issue; Britt's survey probably had little to do with drug-taking policies and more to do with drug-taking attitudes.

   c. Volunteer bias is probably at work; those students who agreed to participate might be quite different in their drug-taking attitudes or habits than those who chose not to participate.

   d. Britt relied on a standardized test; an assessment instrument should have been used instead, to assure that the confirmation effect was in place.

correlation

A measure of how strongly two variables are related to one another.

correlational study

A descriptive study that looks for a consistent relationship between two phenomena.

variables

Characteristics of behavior or experience that can be measured or described by a numeric scale.

positive correlation

An association between increases in one variable and increases in another—or between decreases in one and in another.

negative correlation

An association between increases in one variable and decreases in another.

Correlational Studies: Looking for Relationships

In descriptive research, psychologists often want to know whether two or more phenomena are related and, if so, how strongly. Are students' grade point averages related to the number of hours they spend watching television, playing video games, or texting? To find out, a psychologist would perform a *correlational study*.

Measuring Correlations

LO 2.3.A Illustrate with an example how the correlation coefficient gives both the size and direction of the relationship between two variables.

The word *correlation* is often used as a synonym for "relationship," which is why a **correlational study** examines the extent to which two things are related to one another. Technically, however, a correlation is a numerical measure of the *strength* of the relationship between two things. The "things" may be events, scores, or anything else that can be recorded and tallied. In psychological studies, such things are called **variables** because they can vary in quantifiable ways. Height, weight, age, income, IQ scores, number of items recalled on a memory test, number of smiles in a given time period—anything that can be measured, rated, or scored can serve as a variable.

A **positive correlation** means that high values of one variable are associated with high values of the other and that low values of one variable are associated with low values of the other. Height and weight are positively correlated; so are IQ scores and school grades. Rarely is a correlation perfect, however. Some tall people weigh less than some short ones; some people with average IQs are academic superstars and some with high IQs get poor grades. Figure 2.5a shows a positive correlation between scores on a psychology exam and the average number of boiled kumquats eaten per month by students. (Obviously, we made this up.) Each dot represents a student; you can find each student's score by drawing a horizontal line from the person's dot to the vertical axis. You can find the number of kumquats a student ate by drawing a vertical line from the student's dot to the horizontal axis. In general, the more kumquats, the higher the score.

A **negative correlation** means that high values of one variable are associated with *low* values of the other. Figure 2.5b shows a hypothetical negative correlation between scores on a psychology exam and number of *grilled* kumquats eaten per month. In general, the more

---

Figure 2.5 Correlations

Graph (a) shows a positive correlation between scores on a psychology test and number of boiled kumquats eaten per month: The higher the score, the higher the number of kumquats. Graph (b) shows a negative correlation between test scores and number of grilled kumquats eaten: The higher the scores, the lower the number of kumquats. Graph (c) shows the reality—a zero correlation between kumquat-eating and test scores.

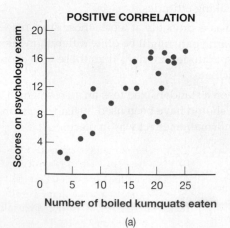

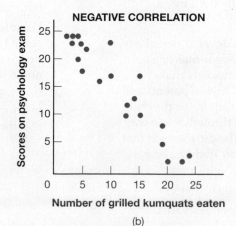

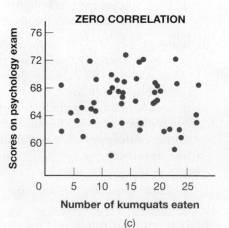

kumquats eaten, the lower the test score. Here's another more realistic example: In general, the older adults are, the fewer miles they can run. How about hours spent watching TV and grade point averages? You guessed it; they're negatively correlated: Spending lots of hours in front of the television is associated with lower grades (Ridley-Johnson, Cooper, & Chance, 1983). See whether you can think of other variables that are negatively correlated. Remember that a negative correlation tells you that the *more* of one thing, the *less* of another. If no relationship exists between two variables, we say that they are *uncorrelated* (see Figure 2.5c). Shoe size and IQ scores are uncorrelated.

The statistic used to express a correlation is called the **correlation coefficient**. This number conveys both the size of the correlation and its direction. A perfect positive correlation has a coefficient of +1.00, and a perfect negative correlation has a coefficient of 1.00. Suppose you weighed 10 people and listed them from lightest to heaviest, then measured their heights and listed them from shortest to tallest. If the names on the two lists were in exactly the same order, the correlation between weight and height would be +1.00. If the correlation between two variables is +.80, it means that they are strongly related. If the correlation is −.80, the relationship is just as strong, but it is negative. When there is no association between two variables, the coefficient is zero or close to zero.

Cautions about Correlations

LO 2.3.B Explain why a correlation between two variables does not establish a causal relationship between those variables.

Correlational findings are common in psychology and often make the news. But beware: Many supposed "correlations" reported in the media or on the Internet are based on rumor and anecdote, and turn out to be small or meaningless. Some are merely *illusory correlations*, apparent associations between two things that are not really related. Illusory correlations can create dangerous beliefs and cause great social harm. Claims of an association between autism and vaccination for childhood diseases have alarmed many parents. The supposed culprit was thimerosal, a preservative used in childhood vaccines until 1999, and now contained in trace amounts in only a few. However, no convincing evidence exists that thimerosal is involved in autism. After this preservative was removed from most vaccines, the incidence of autism did not decline, as it would have if thimerosal were to blame. And study after study has failed to find any connection whatsoever (Mnookin, 2011; Offit, 2008). In one major study of all children born in Denmark between 1991 and 1998 (over a half million children), the incidence of autism in vaccinated children was actually a bit *lower* than in unvaccinated children (Madsen et al., 2002). The apparent link between vaccination and autism is almost certainly a coincidence, an illusory correlation, arising from the fact that symptoms of childhood autism are often first recognized at about the same time that children are vaccinated.

You can see why an understanding of correlations matters. In 2009, a special court set up to rule on lawsuits filed by parents of autistic children ruled that the evidence overwhelmingly failed to support an autism–vaccination link. But unfortunately, some parents who believe that vaccines caused their children's autism are resorting to useless and potentially dangerous treatments, such as supplements that remove metals from the body—along with essential minerals necessary for physical and mental development. And rates of measles and whooping cough, which can be fatal, are rising in children whose parents have refused to have them vaccinated.

Even when correlations are meaningful, they can still be hard to interpret because *a correlation does not establish causation*. It is often easy to assume that if variable A predicts variable B, A must be causing B—that is, making B happen— but that is not necessarily so. A positive correlation has been found between the number of hours that children ages 1 to 3 watch television and their risk of hyperactivity (impulsivity, attention problems, difficulty concentrating) by age 7 (Christakis et al., 2004). Does this mean that watching TV *causes* hyperactivity? Maybe so, but it is also possible that children with a disposition to become hyperactive are more attracted to television than

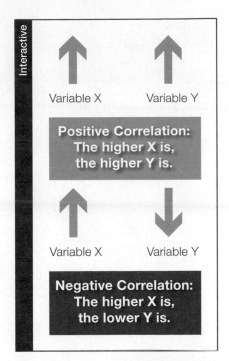

Correlations show the strength and direction of a relationship between two variables.

correlation coefficient

A measure of correlation that ranges in value from −1.00 to +1.00.

The number of hours toddlers spend watching TV is correlated with their risk of being hyperactive a few years later. Does that mean TV-watching causes hyperactivity? Are there other possible explanations for this finding?

those disposed to be calm. Or perhaps the harried parents of distractible children are more likely than other parents to rely on TV as a babysitter. It's also possible that neither variable causes the other directly: Perhaps parents who allow their young kids to watch a lot of TV have attention problems themselves and therefore create a home environment that fosters hyperactivity and inattentiveness. Likewise, the negative correlation between TV-watching and grades mentioned earlier might exist because heavy TV-watchers have less time to study because they have some personality trait that causes an attraction to TV *and* an aversion to studying because they use TV as an escape when their grades are low . . . you get the idea.

And remember the opening story about testosterone dropping in men who become involved fathers? Many commentators were quick to assume that there was some evolutionary reason for the hormonal decline; perhaps it equips men for bonding to infants. But we think a simpler explanation is in order: When men (and women) are tired because of having many demands on their time from childcare and housework, libido drops and sex life slows down. Accordingly, so do hormones. Fatherhood itself probably has little to do with hormones; fatigue does!

The moral: When two variables are associated, one variable may or may not be causing the other.

JOURNAL PROMPT 2.3

Thinking Critically—Consider Other Interpretations: Many studies have documented a positive correlation between temperature and temper: The hotter the weather, the higher the crime rate. Can you generate two or three possible explanations for this finding?

Quiz for Module 2.3

1. You notice a correlation coefficient of .02 between two variables you're studying. What conclusion should you reach about their relatedness?

   a. The two variables are pretty much unrelated to one another; scores on one variable show no consistent pattern with scores on the other variable.

   b. The two variables show a near-perfect positive correlation; .02 is close to ideal, and high scores on one variable are associated with high scores on the other.

   c. The two variables show a near-perfect negative correlation; .02 is close to ideal, and high scores on one variable are associated with low scores on the other.

   d. A correlation of .02 is under the ".10 threshold"; therefore, the data should be reexamined using a new group of research participants.

2. A negative correlation coefficient indicates that as scores on one variable _____, scores on the other variable _____.

   a. Increase / decrease

   b. Decrease / decrease

   c. Increase / increase

   d. Level out / decrease

3. Which of the following values for a correlation coefficient indicates the strongest degree of relationship?

   a. +.59

   b. −.35

   c. +.03

   d. −.69

4. Roya believes that every time the moon is full, her left knee feels shaky. "It's true," she insists. "My knee is shaky when the moon is full, and not shaky when the moon isn't full." Because there's probably not a reliable association between lunar phases and joint mobility, what does Roya's belief illustrate?

   a. A positive correlation coefficient

   b. A negative correlation coefficient

   c. Variable skew

   d. An illusory correlation

5. Variable A is strongly associated with Variable B. Therefore, it logically follows that:

   a. Variable A and Variable B are correlated with one another.

   b. Variable A causes Variable B to happen.

   c. Variable B causes Variable A to happen.

   d. Variable C causes both Variable A and Variable B to happen.

Experiments: Hunting for Causes

Researchers gain plenty of illuminating information from descriptive studies, but when they want to track down the causes of behavior, they rely heavily on the experimental method. An *experiment* allows a researcher to control and manipulate the situation being studied. Instead of being a passive recorder of behavior, the researcher actively does something that he or she believes will affect people's behavior and then observes what happens. These procedures allow the experimenter to draw conclusions about cause and effect—about what causes what. The basics of experimentation are reviewed in the video *Scientific Research Methods*.

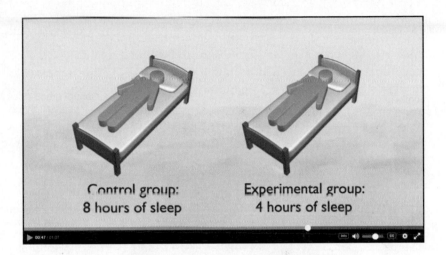

Experimental Variables

LO 2.4.A Contrast an independent variable from a dependent variable and give an example of each concept in a psychology experiment.

Imagine that you are a psychologist whose research interest is multitasking. Almost everyone multitasks these days, and you would like to know whether that's a good thing or a bad thing. Specifically, you would like to know whether or not using a handheld cell phone while driving is dangerous, an important question because most people have done so. Talking on a cell phone while driving is associated with an increase in accidents, but maybe that's just for people who are risk takers or lousy drivers to begin with. To pin down cause and effect, you decide to do an **experiment**.

In a laboratory, you ask participants to "drive" using a computerized driving simulator equipped with an automatic transmission, steering wheel, gas pedal, and brake pedal. The object, you tell them, is to maximize the distance covered by driving on a busy highway while avoiding collisions with other cars. Some of the participants talk on the phone for 15 minutes to a research assistant in the next room about a topic that interests them; others just drive. You are going to compare how many collisions the two groups have. The basic design of this experiment is illustrated in Figure 2.6, which you may want to refer to as you read the next few pages.

The aspect of an experimental situation manipulated or varied by the researcher is known as the **independent variable**. The reaction of the participants—the behavior that the researcher tries to predict—is the **dependent variable**. Every experiment has at least one independent and one dependent variable. In our example, the independent variable is cell phone use (use vs. nonuse). The dependent variable is the number of collisions.

Ideally, everything in the experimental situation except the independent variable is held constant, that is, kept the same for all participants. You would not have those in one group use a stick shift and those in the other group drive an automatic, unless shift type were an independent variable. Similarly, you would not have people in one group go through the experiment alone and those in the other perform in front of an audience.

experiment
A controlled test of a hypothesis in which the researcher manipulates one variable to discover its effect on another.

independent variable
A variable that an experimenter manipulates.

dependent variable
A variable that an experimenter predicts will be affected by manipulations of the independent variable.

Figure 2.6 Do Cell Phone Use and Driving Mix?

The text describes this experimental design to test the hypothesis that talking on a cell phone while driving impairs driving skills and leads to accidents.

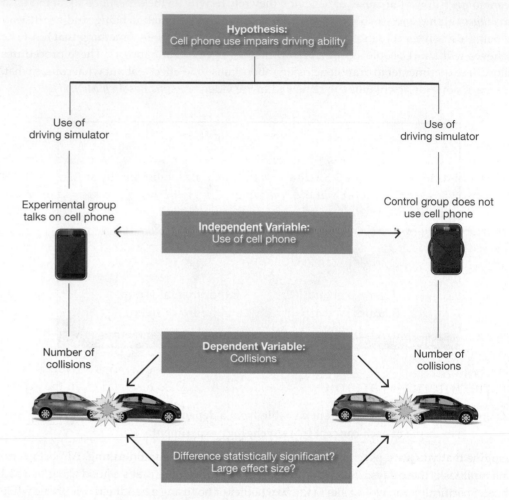

Holding everything but the independent variable constant ensures that whatever happens is due to the researcher's manipulation and no other factors. It allows you to rule out other interpretations.

Understandably, students often have trouble keeping independent and dependent variables straight. You might think of it this way: The dependent variable—the outcome of the study—*depends* on the independent variable. When psychologists set up an experiment, they

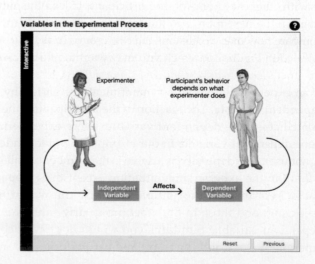

think, "If I do X, the people in my study will do Y." The "X" represents the independent variable; the "Y" represents the dependent variable.

Most variables may be either independent or dependent, depending on what the experimenter wishes to find out. If you want to know whether eating chocolate makes people nervous, then the amount of chocolate eaten is the independent variable. If you want to know whether feeling nervous makes people eat chocolate, then the amount of chocolate eaten is the dependent variable.

Experimental and Control Conditions

LO 2.4.B **Explain the difference between an experimental group and a control group, and discuss how random assignment helps create these two groups.**

Experiments usually require both an experimental condition and a comparison, or **control condition**. In the control condition, participants are treated exactly as they are in the experimental condition, except that they are not exposed to the same treatment or manipulation of the independent variable. Without a control condition, you cannot be sure that the behavior you are interested in would not have occurred anyway, even without your manipulation. In some studies, the same people can be used in both the control and the experimental conditions; they are said to serve as their own controls. In other studies, participants are assigned to either an *experimental group* or a *control group*.

In our cell phone study, we could have drivers serve as their own controls by having them drive once while using a cell phone and once without a phone. But for this illustration, we will use two different groups. Participants who talk on the phone while driving make up the experimental group, and those who just drive along silently make up the control group. We want these two groups to be roughly the same in terms of average driving skill. It would not do to start out with a bunch of reckless roadrunners in the experimental group and a bunch of tired tortoises in the control group. We also probably want the two groups to be similar in age, education, driving history, and other characteristics so that none of these variables will affect our results. One way to accomplish this is to use **random assignment** of people to one group or another, perhaps by randomly assigning them numbers and putting those with even numbers in one group and those with odd numbers in another. If we have enough participants in our study, individual characteristics that could possibly affect the results are likely to be roughly balanced in the two groups, so we can safely ignore them.

Sometimes researchers use different groups or conditions within their experiment. In our cell phone study, we might want to examine the effects of short versus long phone conversations, or conversations on different topics—say, work, personal matters, and *very* personal matters. In that case, we would have more than one experimental group to compare with the control group. In our hypothetical example, though, we just have one experimental group, and everyone in it will drive for 15 minutes while talking about whatever they wish.

This description does not cover all the procedures that psychological researchers use. In some kinds of studies, people in the control group get a **placebo**, a fake treatment or sugar pill that looks, tastes, or smells like the real treatment or medication, but is phony. If the placebo produces the same result as the real thing, the reason must be the participants' expectations rather than the treatment itself. Placebos are critical in testing new drugs because of the optimism that a potential "miracle cure" often brings with it. Medical placebos usually take the form of pills or injections that contain no active ingredients. (To see what placebos revealed in a study of Viagra for women's sexual problems, see Figure 2.7.)

Control groups, by the way, are also crucial in many nonexperimental studies. For example, some psychotherapists have published books arguing that girls develop problems with self-esteem and confidence as soon as they hit adolescence. But unless the writers have also tested or surveyed a comparable group of teenage boys, we cannot know whether low self-esteem is a problem unique to girls or is just as typical for boys.

control condition

In an experiment, a comparison condition in which participants are not exposed to the same treatment as in the experimental condition.

placebo

An inactive substance or fake treatment used as a control in an experiment or given by a medical practitioner to a patient.

Figure 2.7 Does Viagra Work for Women?

Placebos are essential to determine whether people taking a new drug improve because of the drug or because of their expectations about it. In one study, 41 percent of women taking Viagra said their sex lives had improved. That sounds impressive, but 43 percent taking a placebo pill also said their sex lives had improved (Basson et al., 2002).

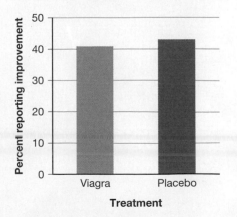

single-blind study

An experiment in which participants do not know whether they are in an experimental or a control group.

experimenter effects

Unintended changes in study participants' behavior due to cues that the experimenter inadvertently conveys.

double-blind study

An experiment in which neither the people being studied nor the individuals running the study know who is in the control group and who is in the experimental group until after the results are tallied.

field research

Descriptive or experimental research conducted in a natural setting outside the laboratory.

Experimenter Effects

LO 2.4.C Explain why single-blind and double-blind procedures are crucial to establishing the soundness of an experiment.

Because their expectations can influence the results of a study, participants should not know whether they are in an experimental or a control group. When this is so (as it usually is), the experiment is said to be a **single-blind study**. But participants are not the only ones who bring expectations to the laboratory; so do researchers. And researchers' expectations, biases, and hopes for a particular result may cause them to inadvertently influence the participants' responses through facial expressions, posture, tone of voice, or some other cue.

Many years ago, Robert Rosenthal (1966) demonstrated how powerful such **experimenter effects** can be. He had students teach rats to run a maze. Half of the students were told that their rats had been bred to be "maze bright," and half were told that their rats had been bred to be "maze dull." In reality, there were no genetic differences between the two groups of rats, yet the supposedly brainy rats actually did learn the maze more quickly, apparently because of the way the students were handling and treating them. If an experimenter's expectations can affect a rodent's behavior, reasoned Rosenthal, surely they can affect a human being's behavior, and he went on to demonstrate this point in many other studies (Rosenthal, 1994). Even an experimenter's friendly smile or cold demeanor can affect people's responses.

One solution to the problem of experimenter effects is to do a **double-blind study**. In such a study, the person running the experiment, the one having actual contact with the participants, also does not know who is in which group until the data have been gathered. Double-blind procedures are essential in drug research. Different doses of a drug (and whether it is the active drug or a placebo) are coded in some way, and the person administering the drug is kept in the dark about the code's meaning until after the experiment. To run our cell phone study in a double-blind fashion, we could use a simulator that automatically records collisions and have the experimenter give instructions through an intercom so he or she will not know which group a participant is in until after the results are tallied.

Think back now to the opening story on the alleged benefits of video games. Most of the studies that reported such benefits suffered from basic mistakes of experimental design. The experimental and control groups were not comparable: Often, the cognitive performances of expert gamers were compared with those of nongamers, who had no experience. The studies were not blind: Players knew they were chosen to participate precisely because they were expert gamers, an awareness that could have influenced their performance and motivation to do well. And the researchers knew which participants were in the experimental and control groups, knowledge that might have affected the participants' performance (Boot, Blakely, & Simons, 2011).

Because experiments allow conclusions about cause and effect, and because they permit researchers to distinguish real effects from placebo effects, they have long been the method of choice in psychology. However, like all methods, the experiment has its limitations. Just as in other kinds of studies, the participants are typically college students and may not always be representative of the larger population. Moreover, in an experiment, the researcher designs and sets up what is often a rather artificial situation, and the participants try to do as they are told. For this reason, many psychologists have called for more **field research**, the careful study of behavior in natural contexts such as schools and the workplace (Cialdini, 2009). Suppose you want to know whether women are more "talkative" than men. If you just ask people, most will say "sure women are!," as the stereotype suggests. A field study would be the best way to answer this question, and indeed such a study has been done. The participants wore an unobtrusive recording device as they went about their normal lives, and the researchers found no gender differences at all (Mehl et al., 2007).

Every research method has both its strengths and its weaknesses. Did you make a list of each method's advantages and disadvantages, as we suggested earlier? If so, compare it now with the one in Review 2.1.

Review 2.1

Research Methods in Psychology: Their Advantages and Disadvantages

Method	Advantages	Disadvantages
Case study	Good source of hypotheses. Provides in-depth information on individuals. Unusual examples can shed light on situations or problems that are unethical or impractical to study in other ways.	Vital information may be missing, making the example difficult to interpret. The person's memories may be selective or inaccurate. The individual may not be representative or typical.
Naturalistic observation	Allows description of behavior as it occurs in the environment. Often useful in first stages of a research program.	Allows researcher little or no control of the situation. Observations may be biased. Does not allow firm conclusions about cause and effect.
Laboratory observation	Allows more control than naturalistic observation. Allows use of sophisticated equipment.	Allows researcher only limited control of the situation. Observations may be biased. Does not allow firm conclusions about cause and effect. Behavior may differ from behavior in the natural environment.
Test	Yields information on personality traits, emotional states, aptitudes, and abilities.	Difficult to construct measures that are reliable and valid.
Survey	Provides a large amount of information on large numbers of people.	If sample is nonrepresentative or biased, it may be impossible to generalize from the results. Responses may be inaccurate or untrue.
Correlational study	Shows whether two or more variables are related. Allows general predictions.	Usually does not permit identification of cause and effect.
Experiment	Allows researcher to control the situation. Permits researcher to identify cause and effect and to distinguish placebo effects from treatment effects.	Situation is artificial, and results may not generalize well to the real world. Sometimes difficult to avoid experimenter effects.

CULTURE and *Research*

Doing good research is demanding enough, but the challenges are multiplied when psychologists venture into societies other than their own to learn which attitudes, behaviors, and traits are universal and which are specific to particular groups. Here are three major concerns that arise in cross-cultural research:

1. *Methods and sampling.* Right off the bat, researchers must worry about how one language translates into another. Speakers of English know that "Mary had a little lamb" means she owned one, not that she gave birth to it, ate it, or had an affair with it. But that's not clear from the words alone! Furthermore, sometimes the term for a concept or emotional experience that is central in one culture (say, the Chinese concept of "filial piety," honoring your ancestors) may have no exact linguistic equivalent in another. In doing cross-cultural research, scientists must also be sure that their samples are similar in all important ways except for ethnicity or nationality. Otherwise, what seems like a cultural difference may really be a difference in education, crowding, or some other noncultural factor.

2. *Stereotyping.* When researchers describe average differences across societies, they may be tempted to oversimplify their findings, which can lead to stereotyping. Of course, cultural rules do make Nigerians different, on average, from Australians and Cambodians different from Italians. Yet, within every society, individuals vary according to their temperaments, beliefs, and learning histories.

The challenge is to understand average cultural differences without implying that everyone in Culture A is as different from everyone in Culture B as chocolate is from cheese.

3. *Reification.* To *reify* means to regard an intangible process, such as a feeling, as if it were a literal object. When people say, "I have a lot of anger buried in me," they are treating anger as if it were a thing that sits inside them like a kidney, when in fact it is a cluster of mental and physical reactions that come and go. In cultural psychology, reification—treating "culture" as a thing instead of a collection of beliefs and traditions—can lead to circular reasoning, as in "Country A attacks its neighbors because it has a warlike culture, and we know it is a warlike culture because it attacks its neighbors." This is like telling a man with a leg injury that he can't walk because he's lame (Lonner & Malpass, 1994). Cultural psychologists must therefore identify not only the average differences in traits and behaviors across cultures but also the underlying mechanisms that account for them. They ask *why* Country A is "warlike," and why it changed from being peaceful (Matsumoto & Yoo, 2006).

Conducting good cross-cultural research is therefore difficult, requiring the right methods and the ability to interpret them critically. But the results are essential for a deeper, more accurate understanding of human behavior in all its rich variety.

JOURNAL PROMPT 2.4

Thinking Critically—Define Your Terms: Various groups of concerned citizens over the years have argued that listening to heavy metal music causes people to become more aggressive. Treat that hypothesis as a testable question. Identify the independent and dependent variables, describe what participants in the experimental and control groups would experience, and note any special considerations you would need to take into account, such as experimenter effects or single- or double-blind designs.

Quiz for Module 2.4

1. In a study where college students are pampered (given endless amounts of money, satellite TV, and spicy Chinese food) to see whether this will improve their scores in their psychology course, what is the *independent variable*?
   a. Students' scores on the next psychology midterm
   b. Whether students were pampered or not
   c. Students' previous scores (or baseline) on psychology midterms
   d. Students' scores on the next midterm minus the baseline score

2. Ingo is conducting a psychological experiment with the help of his professor. As research participants come to the laboratory, Ingo flips a coin. If the coin lands on heads, the participant takes part in the experimental group; if the coin lands on tails, the participant goes into the control group. What principle of experimental design is Ingo utilizing?
   a. Random assignment
   b. A double-blind procedure
   c. Controlling the dependent variable
   d. Placebo activation

3. Margo is studying people's moods during a stressful laboratory situation. Wanting to be nice, she smiles at each participant who enters the experimental condition (where they'll be stressed) and remains neutral toward participants in the control group. Surprisingly, she finds that participants in the stressful condition report being in better moods at the end of the experiment, compared to participants in the control group. Margo's professor is not so surprised, however, because she realizes the outcomes are plagued by:
   a. Placebo "bleed"
   b. Random assignment
   c. Regression toward the mean
   d. Experimenter effects

4. An experiment in which neither the participants nor the experimenter knows who is in the control group and who is in the experimental group is called:
   a. Single-blind
   b. Double-blind
   c. Omni-blind
   d. Placebo-neutral

5. _____ is a general term referring to studies that take place in a natural setting.
   a. Field research
   b. Reification
   c. Sampling expansion
   d. Dependent control

Evaluating the Findings

If you are a psychologist who has just conducted an observational study, a survey, or an experiment, your work has just begun. After you have some results in hand, you must do three things with them: (1) describe them, (2) assess how reliable and meaningful they are, and (3) figure out how to explain them.

Descriptive Statistics: Finding Out What's So

descriptive statistics

Statistical procedures that organize and summarize research data.

arithmetic mean

An average that is calculated by adding up a set of quantities and dividing the sum by the total number of quantities in the set.

LO 2.5.A Provide an example of how the arithmetic mean and standard deviation could be used to compare the performance of two groups of research participants.

Let's say that 30 people in the cell phone experiment talked on the phone, and 30 did not. We have recorded the number of collisions for each person on the driving simulator. Now we have 60 numbers. What can we do with them?

The first step is to summarize the data. The world does not want to hear how many collisions each person had. It wants to know how the cell phone group did as a whole compared to the control group. To provide this information, we need numbers that sum up our data. Such numbers, known as **descriptive statistics**, are often depicted in graphs and charts.

A good way to summarize the data is to compute group averages. The most commonly used type of average is the **arithmetic mean**, which is calculated by adding up all the individual scores and dividing the result by the number of scores. We can compute a mean for the cell phone group by adding up the 30 collision scores and dividing the sum by 30. Then we can do the same for the control group. Now our 60 numbers have been boiled down to two. For the sake of our example, let's assume that the cell phone group had an average of 10 collisions, whereas the control group's average was only seven.

We must be careful, however, about how we interpret these averages. It is possible that no one in our cell phone group actually had 10 collisions. Perhaps half the people in the group were motoring maniacs and had 15 collisions, whereas the others were more cautious and had only 5. Perhaps almost all the participants in the group had 9, 10, or 11 collisions. Perhaps the number of accidents ranged from 0 to 15. The mean does not tell us about such variability in the participants' responses. For that, we need other descriptive statistics. The **standard deviation** tells us how clustered or spread out the individual scores are around the mean; the more spread out they are, the less "typical" the mean is. (See Figure 2.8.) Unfortunately, when research is reported in the news, you usually hear only about the mean.

Inferential Statistics: Asking "So What?"

LO 2.5.B Explain what a statistically significant research result means to an experimenter.

At this point in our study, we have one group with an average of 10 collisions and another with an average of seven, a difference of three collisions. Should we break out the champagne? Hold a press conference? Call our mothers?

Better hold off. Perhaps if one group had an average of 15 collisions and the other an average of one, we might get excited. But rarely does a psychological study hit you between the eyes with a sensationally clear result. In most cases, the difference between the two groups is due simply to chance. Despite all our precautions, perhaps the people in the cell phone group just happened to be a little more accident-prone, and their extra three collisions had nothing to do with talking on the phone.

To find out how impressive the data are, psychologists use **inferential statistics**. These statistics do not merely describe or summarize the data; they permit a researcher to draw *inferences* (conclusions based on evidence) about how meaningful the findings are. Like descriptive statistics, inferential statistics involve the application of mathematical formulas to the data.

Historically, the most commonly used inferential statistics have been **significance tests**, which tell researchers how likely it is that their result occurred by chance. (We have given you the general meaning; statisticians use a more technical one.) Suppose that in the real world, people who talk on cell phones have no more collisions than people who do not. How likely, then, would you be to obtain the difference you found (or an even larger one) between the experimental group and the control group? If that likelihood is quite low, we reject the hypothesis that there is no difference in the real world, and we say that our result is *statistically significant*. This means there is a good probability that the difference we got in our study is real.

Psychologists consider a result to be significant if it would be expected to occur by chance only rarely, and "rarely" usually means five or fewer times in 100 repetitions of the study. We would then say that the result is significant at the .05 level, or $p < .05$, where p stands for probability and .05 is referred to as the *p value*. If, however, the significance test

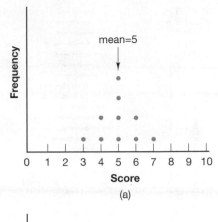

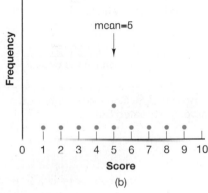

Figure 2.8 Same Mean, Different Meaning

In both distributions of scores, the mean is 5, but in (a), the scores are clustered around the mean, whereas in (b), they are widely dispersed, so the standard deviations for the distributions will be quite different. In which distribution is the mean more "typical" of all scores?

standard deviation

A commonly used measure of variability that indicates the average difference between scores in a distribution and their mean.

inferential statistics

Statistical procedures that allow researchers to draw inferences about how statistically meaningful a study's results are.

significance tests

Statistical tests that show how likely it is that a study's results occurred merely by chance.

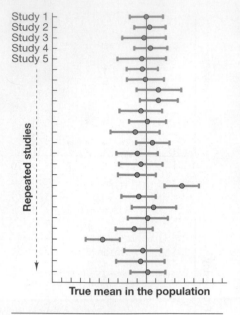

Figure 2.9 Confidence Intervals across Repeated Studies

shows that the *p* value is greater than .05, many researchers would have little confidence in the study's result, although they might still want to do further research to confirm their judgment.

Statistically significant results allow psychologists to make general predictions about human behavior: "Talking on a cell phone while driving increases people's risk of accidents." But these predictions do not tell us with any certainty what a *particular* person will do in a particular situation. Probabilistic results are typical in all of the sciences, not just psychology. Medical research can tell us that the odds are high that someone who smokes will get lung cancer, but because many variables interact to produce any particular case of cancer, research cannot tell us for sure whether Aunt Bessie, who smokes two packs a day, will come down with the disease.

Today, a growing number of psychologists and other researchers also report their results by using a statistical formula that creates a **confidence interval**. The mean from a particular sample will almost never be exactly the same value as the true mean in the population; instead, it will probably be a little higher or a little lower. A confidence interval draws a range a little higher and lower than the sample mean to help depict where the true mean probably lies (Fidler & Loftus, 2009). As Figure 2.9 shows, if you repeated your study over and over, you would produce a different sample mean and confidence interval each time. But notice something interesting: Although none of the means in each study (the green circles) is exactly the same as the population mean (the straight vertical line), most of the confidence intervals (CIs) contain the true mean. In fact, if you repeated your study over and over, 95 percent of the CIs would contain the true mean, although you would occasionally produce a rogue CI (the gray bars) (Cumming, 2014). So do you see the problem with drawing strong conclusions on the basis of any one study?

By the way, many studies similar to our hypothetical one have confirmed the dangers of talking on a cell phone while driving. In one study, cell phone users, whether their phones were hand-held or hands-free, were as impaired in their driving ability as intoxicated drivers were (Strayer, Drews, & Crouch, 2006). Because of such research, some states have made it illegal to drive while holding a cell phone to your ear. Others are considering making any cell phone use by a driver illegal.

Interpreting the Findings

LO 2.5.C Compare cross-sectional and longitudinal studies, and discuss how effect size, meta-analysis, and Bayesian statistics allow us to judge the importance of a research outcome.

The last step in any study is to figure out what the findings mean. Trying to understand behavior from uninterpreted findings is like trying to become fluent in Swedish by reading

confidence interval

A statistical measure that provides, with a specified probability, a range of values within which a population mean is likely to lie.

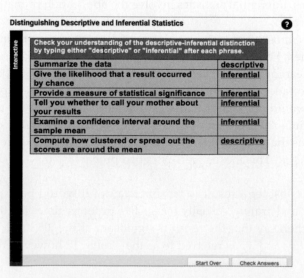

a Swedish–English dictionary. Just as you need the grammar of Swedish to tell you how the words fit together, psychologists need hypotheses and theories to explain how the facts that emerge from research fit together.

CHOOSING THE BEST EXPLANATION Sometimes it is hard to choose between competing explanations of a finding. Does cell phone use disrupt driving by impairing coordination, by increasing a driver's vulnerability to distraction, by interfering with the processing of information, by distorting the driver's perception of danger, or by some combination of these or other factors? Several explanations may fit the results equally well, which means that more research will be needed to determine the best one.

Sometimes the best interpretation of a finding does not emerge until a hypothesis has been tested in different ways. Although the methods we have described tend to be appropriate for different questions (see Review 2.2), sometimes one method can be used to confirm, disconfirm, or extend the results obtained with another. If the findings of studies using various methods converge, researchers have greater reason to be confident about them. If the findings conflict, researchers must modify their hypotheses or investigate further.

Here is an example. When psychologists compare the mental test scores of young people and old people, they usually find that younger people outscore older ones. This type of research, in which different groups are compared at the same time, is called a **cross-sectional study**.

Trying to operate a car and operate a cell phone simultaneously can be a recipe for disaster.

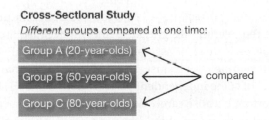

Cross-Sectional Study
Different groups compared at one time:

Group A (20-year-olds)
Group B (50-year-olds) → compared
Group C (80-year-olds)

But longitudinal studies can also be used to investigate mental abilities across the lifespan. In a **longitudinal study**, the same people are followed over a period of time and are reassessed at regular intervals.

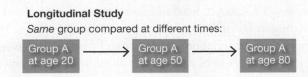

Longitudinal Study
Same group compared at different times:

Group A at age 20 → Group A at age 50 → Group A at age 80

cross-sectional study

A study in which people (or animals) of different ages are compared at a given time.

longitudinal study

A study in which people (or animals) are followed and periodically reassessed over a period of time.

In contrast to cross-sectional studies, longitudinal studies find that as people age, they sometimes perform as well as they ever did on certain mental tests. A *general* decline in ability may not occur until people reach their 70s or 80s. Why do results from the two types of studies conflict? Probably because cross-sectional studies measure generational differences; younger generations tend to outperform older ones in part because they are better educated or are

effect size

An objective, standardized way of describing the strength of the independent variable's influence on the dependent variable.

meta-analysis

A set of techniques for combining data from a number of related studies to determine the explanatory strength of a particular independent variable.

Bayesian statistics

Statistics that involve a formula for calculating the likelihood of a hypothesis being true and meaningful, taking into account relevant prior knowledge.

more familiar with the tests used. Without longitudinal studies, we might falsely conclude that all types of mental ability inevitably decline with advancing age.

JUDGING THE RESULT'S IMPORTANCE   Sometimes psychologists agree on the reliability and meaning of a finding but not on its ultimate relevance for theory or practice. Part of the problem is statistical. Traditional tests of significance continue to be used in the majority of psychological studies, which is why we have described them here, but these tests have important drawbacks (Cumming, 2014; Cumming et al., 2007; Erceg-Hurn & Mirosevich, 2008). A result may be statistically significant yet be small and of little consequence in everyday life because the independent variable does not explain most of the variation in people's behavior. Moreover, p values don't guarantee that other researchers (or even the same researchers) will be able to obtain a similar effect if they run their study again; in fact, p values can vary considerably from one replication to another (Cumming, 2014). That is why so many "findings" that make the news don't pan out in later studies. Remember the ESP study that we mentioned at the start of this chapter? Because the results were just barely statistically significant, the paper was published in an academic journal, which appalled many psychological scientists (Alcock, 2011). As one statistician noted, the article did not show that ESP exists; rather, it showed why a reliance on p values produces too many results that are just flukes (in Miller, 2011).

To gain better protection against spurious, unsubstantial results, many psychology journals now encourage or require the use of alternate methods and statistics. One is to use statistical procedures that reveal the **effect size**. Think of effect sizes as similar to measuring how much something weighs: Regardless of what you're weighing, 100 pounds is weightier than 10 pounds. Effect sizes, then, help us to understand how important—how weighty—an effect is. One such measure tells us how much of the variation in the data the independent variable accounts for. If it explains 5 percent of the variation, it's not very powerful, even if the result is statistically significant; if it explains 40 percent, it's very impressive.

A popular set of statistical techniques called **meta-analysis** provides an especially good way to measure the overall "weight" of a finding because it combines data from a number of related studies instead of assessing each study's results separately. A single result based on a small sample may be just a coincidence; meta-analysis comes to the rescue, assessing the effect of some independent variable across all the studies in the analysis. This approach is important because rarely does one study prove anything, in psychology or any other field. That is why you should be suspicious of headlines that announce a sudden major scientific breakthrough based on a single study. Breakthroughs do occur, but they are rare.

Consider the gender gap in math achievement, which persists in some nations but not in others. Is it largely due to a "natural" male superiority in math, or to gender differences in educational and professional opportunities in the sciences? A meta-analysis of studies across 69 nations, representing nearly 500,000 students ages 14–16, found that although boys have more positive attitudes toward math than girls do, average effect sizes in actual mathematics achievement are very small. Moreover, *national* effect sizes show considerable variability; that is, a male–female math gap is wider in some countries than in others. The most powerful predictors of that cross-national variation were whether boys and girls were equally likely to be enrolled in school; the percentage of women in research jobs; and women's representation in their nation's government (Else-Quest, Hyde, & Linn, 2010).

Another approach, growing in popularity among scientists in medicine and other fields as well as psychology, is based on **Bayesian statistics**, named for the 18th-century English minister who developed it (Dienes, 2011; McGrayne, 2011). Bayesian statistics involve a formula that takes prior knowledge into consideration when evaluating any finding. In the case of ESP, "prior knowledge" of physics and biology suggests no known or possible mechanism for this phenomenon. And in fact, when a team of mathematical psychologists reassessed the ESP paper using Bayes's formula, they concluded that the data actually support the hypothesis that ESP does *not* exist (Wagenmakers et al., 2011).

One writer nicely summarized the Bayesian approach as the "yeah, right" effect. If a study finds that eating blueberry muffins reduces the risk of heart disease by 90 percent or that a treatment cures drug addiction in a week, a Bayesian's reaction would be to evaluate that finding against what can be observed in the real world, and the result would have to pass the "yeah, right" test of plausibility (Carey, 2011). A team of researchers compared p values, effect sizes, and Bayes factors as measures of statistical evidence, using 855 published findings (Wetzels et al., 2011). They found that although p values and Bayes factors almost always agreed about which hypotheses were better supported by the data, the measures often disagreed about the strength of this support. In many cases, the Bayes analysis showed that the result was only anecdotal.

The Bayesian approach is still controversial, and arguments continue about how precisely to quantify "prior knowledge," which can vary from strong empirical evidence to more subjective estimates. But its importance is growing among the statistical methods of science.

Review 2.2 presents an overview of the various psychological research methods we have learned about in this chapter. In the next section, we'll look at ethical issues relating to psychological research.

Interactive

Review 2.2

Psychological Research Methods Contrasted

Psychologists may use different methods to answer different questions about a topic. This table shows some ways in which the methods described in this chapter can be used to study different questions about aggression. Sometimes, however, two or more methods can be used to investigate the same question, and findings based on one method may extend, support, or disconfirm findings based on another.

Method	Purpose	Example
Case study	To understand the development of aggressive behavior in a particular individual; to formulate research hypotheses about the origins of aggressiveness	Developmental history of a serial killer
Naturalistic observation	To describe the nature of aggressive acts in early childhood	Recording instances of hitting, kicking, etc., during free-play periods in a preschool
Laboratory observation	To find out whether aggressiveness in pairs of same-sex and different-sex children differs in frequency or intensity	Watching through a one-way window same-sex and different-sex pairs of preschoolers; pairs must negotiate who gets to play with an attractive toy that has been promised to each child
Test	To compare the personality traits of aggressive and nonaggressive people	Administration of personality scales to violent and nonviolent prisoners
Survey	To find out how common domestic violence is in the general population	Questionnaire asking anonymous respondents (in a sample representative of the population) about the occurrence of slapping, hitting, etc., in their homes
Correlational study	To examine the relationship between aggressiveness and television viewing	Administration to college students of a paper-and-pencil test of aggressiveness and a questionnaire on number of hours spent watching TV weekly; determining the extent to which those two variables go together
Experiment	To find out whether high air temperatures elicit aggressive behavior	Arrangement for individuals to "shock" a "learner" (actually a confederate of the experimenter) while seated in a room heated to either 72°F or 85°F

JOURNAL PROMPT 2.5

Thinking Critically—Ask Questions, Be Willing to Wonder: Imagine you and a friend are discussing the cognitive changes people go through between the ages of 18 and 22. Your friend proposes studying the question by testing groups of 18-, 20-, and 22-year-olds, and comparing their mean scores on a test of thinking skills. "It's the best way to do it," exclaims your friend. "In fact, it's about the only way to study this question." Can you propose a different research strategy that involves a single group but answers the same question? What other information would you examine beyond the arithmetic mean?

Quiz for Module 2.5

1. "I'm so confused!" sputters Henry. "I collected all this data for my research project, but I don't know which numbers to pay attention to. The highest values? The lowest values? The most common value? Argh!" "Why don't you look at the arithmetic mean of all the values?" suggests Raelynn. "Finding the average score would be a good indicator of what the values look like in general." How would you advise Henry to go about finding the arithmetic mean?

   a. Add up all the individual scores, then divide the result by the number of scores.

   b. Figure out how far away each score is from every other one.

   c. Subtract the lowest score from the highest score, then multiply the answer by 2.

   d. Add the five lowest scores to the five highest scores, then divide the result by 2.

2. Calculations that allow a researcher to draw conclusions about how meaningful a result is are collectively called:

   a. Qualitative statistics

   b. Descriptive statistics

   c. Inferential statistics

   d. Quantitative statistics

3. What threshold do psychological scientists usually adopt when deciding if a result is statistically significant?

   a. Whether the outcome would occur by chance alone less than 20 times out of 100.

   b. Whether the outcome would occur by chance alone less than 5 times out of 100.

   c. Whether the outcome matches what was predicted in the researcher's original hypothesis.

   d. Whether 60 percent of other researchers would reach the same conclusion when examining the data.

4. George and Eva are both interested in developmental psychology. George wants to compare a group of 5-year-olds to a group of 8-year-olds to see how their reasoning skills differ. Eva wants to study a group of 5-year-olds over the next 3 years to see how their reasoning skills change over time. Both designs have merit. The main difference is that George is proposing _____ whereas Eva wants to conduct _____.

   a. Cross-sectional research / cross-cultural research

   b. Cross-sectional research / a longitudinal study

   c. A longitudinal study / cross-sectional research

   d. A time-series design / a meta-analysis

5. Zoe reviewed the scientific literature on the effects of gum-chewing on attention among middle schoolers and found that 23 experiments had been conducted on this topic. She performed a series of statistical tests to reach an overall conclusion from these studies as a group. What technique was Zoe using?

   a. Confidence inference

   b. Cross-sectional encumbrance

   c. Bayesian sampling

   d. Meta-analysis

Keeping the Enterprise Ethical

Because rigorous research methods are the very heart of science, psychologists spend considerable time discussing and debating their procedures for collecting and evaluating data. And they are also concerned about the ethical principles governing research and practice. In colleges and universities, a review committee must approve all studies and be sure they conform to federal regulations. In addition, the American Psychological Association (APA) has a code of ethics that all members must follow. Even people who are not members of the APA, whether working in the United States or around the world, often follow the code in their research. The code of ethics is subject to frequent reexamination.

The Ethics of Studying Human Beings

LO 2.6.A Discuss why the principles of informed consent and debriefing are two key characteristics of a researcher's code of ethics.

The APA code calls on psychological scientists to respect the dignity and welfare of the people they study. Participants must enter a study voluntarily and must know enough about it to make an intelligent decision about taking part, a doctrine known as **informed consent**.

Researchers must also protect participants from physical and mental harm, and if any risk exists, they must warn them in advance and give them an opportunity to withdraw at any time.

The policy of informed consent sometimes clashes with an experimenter's need to disguise the true purpose of the study. In such cases, if the purpose were revealed in advance, the results would be ruined because the participants would not behave naturally. In social psychology especially, a study's design sometimes calls for an elaborate deception. For example, a confederate of the researcher might pretend to be having a seizure. The researcher can then find out whether bystanders—the uninformed participants—will respond to a person needing help. If the participants knew that the confederate was only acting, they would obviously not bother to intervene or call for assistance.

Sometimes people have been misled about procedures that are intentionally designed to make them angry, guilty, ashamed, or anxious so that researchers can learn what people do when they feel this way. In studies of embarrassment and anger, people have been made to look clumsy in front of others, have been called insulting names, or have been told they were incompetent. In studies of dishonesty, participants have been entrapped into cheating and have then been confronted with evidence of their guilt. The APA code requires that participants be thoroughly debriefed when the study is over and told why deception was necessary. In addition to debriefing, the APA's ethical guidelines require researchers to show that any deception is justified by a study's potential value and to consider alternative procedures.

The Ethics of Studying Animals

LO 2.6.B List and discuss four reasons why psychologists might use animals in research.

Ethical issues also arise in animal research. Animals are used in only a small percentage of psychological studies, but they play a crucial role in some areas. Usually they are not harmed (as in research on mating in hamsters, which is definitely fun for the hamsters), but sometimes they are (as when rats brought up in deprived or enriched environments are sacrificed so that their brains can be examined for any effects). Psychologists study animals for many reasons:

- *To conduct basic research on a particular species.* For example, researchers have learned a great deal about the unusually lusty and cooperative lives of bonobo apes.

- *To discover practical applications.* For example, behavioral studies have shown farmers how to reduce crop destruction by birds and deer without resorting to their traditional method—shooting the animals.

- *To clarify theoretical questions.* For example, we might not attribute the longer lifespans of women solely to lifestyle factors and health practices if we discover that a male–female difference exists in other mammals as well.

- *To improve human welfare.* For example, animal studies have helped researchers develop ways to reduce chronic pain, rehabilitate patients with neurological disorders, and understand the mechanisms underlying memory loss and senility.

In recent decades, some psychological and medical scientists have been trying to find ways to do their research without using animals at all, by using computer simulations or other new technologies. When animals are essential to research, the APA's ethical code includes comprehensive guidelines to ensure their humane treatment. Federal laws governing the housing and

informed consent

The doctrine that anyone who participates in human research must do so voluntarily and must know enough about the study to make an intelligent decision about whether to take part.

Psychologists sometimes use animals to study learning, memory, emotion, and social behavior. Here, Frans de Waal observes a group of chimpanzees socializing in an outdoor play area.

care of research animals—particularly our closest relatives, the great apes—are stronger than they used to be; no future research can be done on apes unless it is vital to human welfare and cannot be conducted with other methods. Moreover, thanks to a growing understanding of animals' instinctive, social, and cognitive needs—even in so-called "lower" species like the lab rat—many psychological scientists have changed the way they treat them, which improves their research as well as the animals' well-being (Patterson-Kane, Harper, & Hunt, 2001). The difficult task for scientists is to balance the benefits of animal research with an acknowledgment of past abuses and a compassionate concern for the welfare of species other than our own.

Now you are ready to explore more deeply what psychologists have learned about human psychology. The methods of psychological science, as we will see repeatedly in the remainder of the book, have overturned some deeply entrenched assumptions about the way people think, feel, act, and adapt, and have yielded information that greatly improves human well-being. These methods illuminate our human errors and biases and enable us to seek knowledge with an open mind. Biologist Thomas Huxley put it beautifully. The essence of science, he said, is "to sit down before fact as a little child, be prepared to give up every preconceived notion, follow humbly wherever and to whatever abyss nature leads, or you shall learn nothing."

JOURNAL PROMPT 2.6

Thinking Critically—Avoid Emotional Reasoning: Some people are concerned with maltreatment of animals used in medical, biological, or psychological research. Issues of unkempt living conditions, malnourishment, or impoverished environments often loom large in these arguments. What do you think? What would a researcher gain by keeping animal subjects in a substandard living environment? Would the validity of any research outcomes be questionable if the animals were mistreated prior to the start of an experiment? What would we learn by studying sickly, unrepresentative animals?

Quiz for Module 2.6

1. Guidelines for the ethical treatment of human and animal research participants have been established (and are updated) by:
   a. The Coalition for Psychological Justice (CPJ)
   b. The National Bureau of Standards (NBS)
   c. The International Federation of Psychological Scientists (IFPS)
   d. The American Psychological Association (APA)

2. The ethical principle of _____ means that research participants are given enough information about a study to make a reasonable decision about whether they will participate.
   a. Informed consent
   b. Debriefing
   c. Briefing
   d. Noblesse oblige

3. The ethical principle of _____ requires that researchers reveal the true nature and purpose of a psychological study to subjects at the conclusion of their participation, and explain any deception that was used during the study.
   a. Informed consent
   b. Briefing
   c. Debriefing
   d. Noblesse oblige

4. Which statement is true concerning the use of animals in psychological studies?
   a. Animals are used as research subjects when it is too expensive to recruit human participants.
   b. Animals are used in only a small percentage of psychological studies.
   c. Animal research has been banned in psychological science, although it is common in medical research.
   d. Animals are used in roughly 50 percent of all psychological research.

5. Which of the following is a reason why psychologists might study animals?
   a. To improve human welfare
   b. To avoid criticism from human subjects
   c. To take advantage of relaxed ethical standards
   d. To test vague hypotheses without ethical repercussions

Taking Psychology with You

Lying with Statistics

We have seen that statistical procedures are indispensable tools for assessing research. But in the real world, statistics can be manipulated, misrepresented, and even made up by people hoping to promote a particular political or social agenda. That is why an essential part of critical and scientific thinking is learning not only how to use statistics correctly but also how to identify their misuse.

A primary reason for the misuse of statistics is "innumeracy" (mathematical illiteracy). In *Damned Lies and Statistics*, Joel Best (2012) told of a graduate student who copied this figure from a professional journal: "Every year since 1950, the number of American children gunned down has doubled." Sounds scary, right? But if that claim were true, then by 1987, the number of children gunned down would have surpassed 137 billion, more than the total human population throughout history; and by 1995, the annual number of victims would have been 35 *trillion*!

Where did this wildly inaccurate number come from? The author of the original article misrepresented a statistic from the Children's Defense Fund (CDF), which in 1994 claimed that "The number of American children killed each year by guns has doubled since 1950." Notice the difference: The CDF was saying that there were twice as many deaths in 1994 as in 1950, not that the number had doubled every year.

We don't want you to distrust all statistics. Statistics don't lie; people do—or, more likely, they misrepresent or misinterpret what the numbers mean. When statistics are used correctly, they neither confuse nor mislead. On the contrary, they can expose unwarranted conclusions, promote clarity and precision, and protect us from our biases and blind spots. You need to be careful, though. Here are a few things you can do when you hear that "2 million people do this" or "one out of four people are that":

Ask how the number was computed. Suppose someone on your campus gives a talk about a hot social issue and cites some big number to show how serious and widespread the problem is. You should ask how the number was calculated. Was it based on government data, such as the census? Did it come from just one small study or from a meta-analysis of many studies? Or is it pure conjecture?

Ask about base rates and absolute numbers. If we tell you that the *relative risk* of getting ulcers is increased by 300 percent in college students who eat a bagel every morning (relax, it isn't!), that sounds pretty alarming, but it does not tell you much. You would need to know how many students get ulcers in the first place, and then how many bagel-eating students get ulcers. If the "300 percent increased risk" is a jump from 100 students in every thousand to 300 students, then you might reasonably be concerned. If the number shifts from one in every thousand to three in every thousand,

that is still a 300 percent increase, but the risk is very small and could even be a random fluke. Many health findings are presented in ways that increase worry and even panic, as an increased relative risk of this or that. What you want to know is the *absolute risk*, what the actual, absolute numbers show. They may be quite trivial (Bluming & Tavris, 2009; Gigerenzer et al., 2008).

Ask how terms were defined. If we hear that "one out of every four women" will be raped at some point in her life, we need to ask: How was rape defined? If women are asked if they have ever experienced any act of unwanted sex, the percentages are higher than if they are asked specifically whether they have been forced or coerced into intercourse. Similarly, although far more women are raped by men they know than by strangers, many women do not define acts of date rape or acquaintance rape as "rape."

Always, always look for the control group. If an experiment does not have a control group, then, as they say in New York, "fuhgedaboudit." The kinds of "findings" often reported without a control group tend to be those promoting a new herbal supplement, treatment, or self-improvement program. People are motivated to justify any program or treatment in which they have invested time, money, or effort. Furthermore, thanks to the placebo effect, people's expectations of success are often what helps them, not the treatment itself. This is why testimonials don't provide a full or accurate picture of a medication's or treatment's benefits or harms. It's like the bartender who says to the customer, "Why are you waving your arms around like that?" And the customer says, "It keeps the gerbils away." "But there aren't any gerbils here," the bartender says. "See?" says the customer, "It works!" All the arm-waving in the world won't substitute for a good study.

Be cautious about correlations. We said this before, but we'll say it again: With correlational findings, you usually cannot be sure what's causing what. A study reported that teenagers who listened to music 5 or more hours a day were eight times more likely to be depressed than those who didn't listen that often (Primack et al., 2011). Does listening to music make you depressed? A more likely explanation is that being depressed causes teenagers to tune out and listen to music, as they don't have the mental energy to do much else. "At this point, it is not clear whether depressed people begin to listen to more music to escape, or whether listening to large amounts of music can lead to depression, or both," said the lead researcher.

The statistics that most people like best are usually the ones that support their own opinions and prejudices. Unfortunately, bad statistics, repeated again and again, can infiltrate popular culture, spread like a virus on the Internet, and become difficult to eradicate. The information in this chapter gets you started on telling the difference between numbers that are helpful and those that mislead or deceive.

Summary

What Makes Psychological Research Scientific?

LO 2.1.A   Distinguish between a theory, a hypothesis, and an operational definition.

Theories are systems of assumptions and principles that try to explain a specified set of phenomena. *Hypotheses* are derived from a theory, and are precise statements that describe or explain a given behavior. *Operational definitions* summarize the way terms will be measured and studied in a particular research project.

Psychology, like all sciences, is empirical; this means psychologists rely on information gathered from studies using the scientific method as the basis for their evidence, rather than anecdotes, conjecture, or opinions.

LO 2.1.B   Explain why skepticism in science involves more than just disbelief.

Scientists practice skepticism as a way of treating claims and research findings with caution. Being skeptical means more than just doubting conclusions; it provokes an exploration of why a claim may or may not be valid.

LO 2.1.C   Explain why falsifiability is an important component of scientific research.

The *principle of falsifiability* instructs scientists to design studies in such a way that evidence can either confirm or disconfirm the existence of a phenomenon. As a general operating procedure, falsifiability also helps ward off the *confirmation bias*, the tendency to look for or only pay attention to information that confirms our beliefs.

LO 2.1.D   Describe why openness and replication are important qualities of the scientific enterprise.

Scientists must be willing to tell others where they got their ideas, how those ideas were tested, and what the results were, so that studies can be replicated and findings can be verified independently.

Descriptive Studies: Establishing the Facts

LO 2.2.A   Describe the major ways participants are selected for psychological studies, and why the method of selection might influence interpretations of a study's outcomes.

In any study, the researcher would ideally like to use a *representative sample*, one that is similar in composition to the larger population that the researcher wishes to describe. But in practice, researchers must often use "convenience" samples, which typically means college undergraduates. In the study of many topics, the consequences are minimal, but in other cases, conclusions about "people in general" must be interpreted with caution.

LO 2.2.B   Discuss the advantages and disadvantages of using case studies as a means of data collection.

Case studies are detailed descriptions of individuals. They are often used by clinicians and can also be valuable in exploring new research topics and addressing questions that would otherwise be difficult to study. But because the person under study may not be representative of people in general, case studies are typically sources rather than tests of hypotheses.

LO 2.2.C   Discuss the advantages and disadvantages of using observational methods as a means of data collection.

In *observational studies*, researchers systematically observe and record behavior without interfering in any way with the behavior. *Naturalistic observation* is used to find out how animals and people behave in their natural environments. *Laboratory observation* allows more control and the use of special equipment; behavior in the laboratory, however, may differ in certain ways from behavior in natural contexts.

LO 2.2.D   Explain why norms, reliability, and validity are the three key hallmarks of any standardized psychological test.

Psychological tests are used to measure and evaluate personality traits, emotional states, aptitudes, interests, abilities, and values. A good test is one that has been *standardized*, is scored using established *norms*, and is both *reliable* and *valid*. Critics have questioned the reliability and validity of even some widely used tests.

LO 2.2.E **Describe the advantages and limitations of using surveys in data collection.**

Surveys are questionnaires or interviews that ask people directly about their experiences, attitudes, and opinions. Unrepresentative samples and *volunteer bias* can influence the generalizability of survey results. Findings can also be affected by the fact that respondents sometimes lie, misremember, or misinterpret the questions. Technology and use of the Internet can help psychologists minimize some of these problems, but they also introduce some new methodological challenges. People should be cautious about tests they take on the Internet because not all of them meet scientific standards.

Correlational Studies: Looking for Relationships

LO 2.3.A **Illustrate with an example how a correlation coefficient gives both the size and direction of the relationship between two variables.**

In descriptive research, studies that look for relationships between phenomena are known as *correlational*. A *correlation* is a measure of the strength of a positive or negative relationship between two variables and is expressed by the *correlation coefficient*. Many correlations reported in the media or on the Internet are based on rumor and anecdote and are not supported by data.

LO 2.3.B **Explain why a correlation between two variables does not establish a causal relationship between those variables.**

A correlation between two variables does not necessarily demonstrate a causal relationship between the variables. The first variable could be causing the second to happen, the second variable could be causing the first to happen, or a third variable could be causing both of the other two to happen.

Experiments: Hunting for Causes

LO 2.4.A **Contrast an independent variable from a dependent variable and give an example of each concept in a psychology experiment.**

Experiments allow researchers to control the situation being studied, manipulate an *independent variable*, and assess the effects of the manipulation on a *dependent variable*.

LO 2.4.B **Explain the difference between an experimental group and a control group, and discuss why each one needs to be present in an experiment.**

Experimental studies require a comparison or control condition and often involve random assignment of participants to *experimental and control groups*. In some studies, those in the control group receive a *placebo*, or fake treatment.

LO 2.4.C **Explain why single-blind and double-blind procedures are crucial to establishing the soundness of an experiment.**

Single-blind and double-blind procedures can be used to prevent the expectations of the participants or the experimenter from affecting the results.

Evaluating the Findings

LO 2.5.A **Provide an example of how the arithmetic mean and standard deviation could be used to compare the performance of two groups of research participants.**

Psychologists use *descriptive statistics*, such as the *arithmetic mean* and the *standard deviation*, to summarize data. By finding the average score in a set of measurements and how clustered or spread out the scores are around that average, scientists get a good idea of what the measurements as a whole look like.

LO 2.5.B **Explain what a statistically significant research result means to an experimenter.**

Psychological scientists use *inferential statistics* to find out how impressive the data are. *Significance tests* tell the researchers how likely it is that the results of a study occurred merely by chance. The results are said to be *statistically significant* if this likelihood is very low.

LO 2.5.C **Compare cross-sectional and longitudinal studies, and discuss how effect size, meta-analysis, and Bayesian statistics allow us to judge the importance of a research outcome.**

Choosing among competing interpretations of a finding can be difficult, and care must be taken to avoid going beyond the facts. Sometimes the best interpretation does not emerge until a hypothesis has been tested in more than one way, as by using both *cross-sectional* and *longitudinal* methods. *Confidence intervals* help researchers evaluate where the real population mean is likely to be if they could repeat their study over and over. The *effect size* is an objective, standardized way of describing the strength of the independent variable's influence on the dependent variable. *Meta-analysis* is a procedure for combining data from many related studies to determine the overall strength of an independent variable. *Bayesian statistics* take prior knowledge into account in assessing the likelihood that a finding is true and meaningful.

Keeping the Enterprise Ethical

LO 2.6.A **Discuss why the principles of informed consent and debriefing are two key characteristics of a researcher's code of ethics.**

The APA's ethical code requires researchers to obtain the *informed consent* of anyone who is participating in a study or experiment, protect them from harm, and warn them in advance of any risks. Many studies require deceptive procedures. Concern about the morality of such procedures has led to guidelines to protect participants.

LO 2.6.B   List and discuss four reasons why psychologists might use animals in research.

Psychologists study animals to gain knowledge about particular species, discover practical applications of psychological principles, study issues that cannot be studied with human beings for practical or ethical reasons, clarify theoretical questions, and improve human welfare. Debate over the use of animals in research has led to more comprehensive regulations governing their treatment and care.

Chapter 2 Quiz

1. A statement that specifies the relationships among events and is derived from a theory is called:
   a. An extension
   b. An operational definition
   c. A predicate
   d. A hypothesis

2. Tammy believes everything she reads in her sociology textbook. Keiko disagrees with every point her political science professor makes. Peter listens to his astronomy professor but routinely asks "Why is that?" and "Could this also be true?" Which student is skeptical?
   a. All three students are practicing skepticism.
   b. Tammy
   c. Keiko
   d. Peter

3. Rocco argues that personality characteristics are fully formed prenatally, while babies are still in their mothers' wombs. Upon birth and exposure to the external environment, personality begins to change. Why is Rocco's hypothesis a poor one?
   a. It is a stage theory of development, but it needs more stages.
   b. It violates the principle of falsifiability; it can't be disconfirmed.
   c. It is based on a small sample of measurements; Rocco should collect more data.
   d. It is grounded in biological uncertainty; some mothers don't know the sex of their unborn child.

4. Under carefully controlled experimental conditions, Aldo finds that ninth graders who study an additional 2 hours raise their test scores by 5 percent. Before publicizing his results, he repeats the experiment with a different group of ninth graders, another group of ninth graders studying different material, and a group of 10th graders; in all cases the same pattern of results emerges. What important feature of the scientific process is Aldo demonstrating?
   a. Replication
   b. Falsifiability
   c. Operationalization
   d. Divergence

5. Connie administers a questionnaire on dating habits to the 35 students in her Introductory Psychology class. What type of sample do those participants constitute?
   a. A representative sample
   b. A convenience sample
   c. A population sample
   d. A dependent sample

6. Janelle wants to learn about the psychological impact of war on combat veterans, so she conducts an in-depth interview with her grandfather who served in the Vietnam War. What type of research approach is Janelle using?
   a. Experiment
   b. Observational study
   c. Survey
   d. Case study

7. A researcher wants to study whether people using laptop computers in a public setting are more likely to sit near one another or more likely to sit near someone not using a computer. She sits in a local coffee shop for 2 hours each day for a week and counts the number of other patrons with or without a laptop and whether they sit next to someone with or without a laptop. What type of research methodology is being used in this study?
   a. Survey
   b. Laboratory observation
   c. Naturalistic observation
   d. Case study

8. Compared to a group of 25,000 other test takers, Casey discovered she scored within the top 10% on an intelligence test. She was suitably proud and impressed with her achievement. What allowed her to interpret her score so readily?

   a. The intelligence test provided norms based on a large comparison group.

   b. She had been randomly assigned to the control condition of the intelligence experiment.

   c. The intelligence test had alternate-forms reliability.

   d. The other test takers formed the basis for test-retest reliability.

9. Florence is interested in college students' morality, so she administers a survey to 100 classmates asking how many times they've vandalized public property, shoplifted a small item, lied to a loved one, taken office supplies from a workplace, or kept miscounted change from a cashier. Florence was pleased to find that a staggering 92% of her participants reported little to none of these activities, and concluded that today's students are a highly moral bunch. Why might this conclusion not be entirely warranted?

   a. Interviews with those 100 participants would have been a more efficient methodology.

   b. Florence should have polled a more focused sample of known transgressors.

   c. People may not always respond accurately to self-report measures, such as surveys.

   d. She should have conducted case studies on the 8% of respondents who were immoral.

10. Which of the following values for a coefficient of correlation indicates the weakest degree of relationship?

    a. −.75

    b. −.29

    c. +.04

    d. +.42

11. Dr. Acula conducts a study and finds that worker satisfaction and worker productivity are highly positively correlated. What conclusion should she reach from her research?

    a. Greater satisfaction causes workers to be more productive.

    b. Higher levels of satisfaction are systematically related to higher levels of productivity.

    c. Higher productivity causes workers to be more satisfied with their jobs.

    d. Salary causes both increased productivity and increased satisfaction.

12. Carmen wants to test whether putting people in a good mood versus a bad mood affects the size of a donation they give to a homeless person. In this experiment, the dependent variable is:

    a. A person's mood state

    b. Being in a good mood

    c. Being in a bad mood

    d. The size of the donation

13. One group of research participants is given a new pain medication being tested by a pharmaceutical company. A second group of participants reports to the same study as the first group, goes through the same procedures, meets with the same researchers, but is given a sugar pill that has the same size, shape, and texture as the actual medication. What did this second group receive in this experiment?

    a. A placebo

    b. The dependent variable

    c. An agentic marker

    d. A baseline

14. When only the experimenter knows whether a given participant is in the experimental or control group (and the participants themselves do not), the study can be classified as:

    a. A single-blind experiment

    b. A double-blind experiment

    c. A repeated-measures design

    d. A failure

15. Hugo collects data on the number of hours college students study each day, and finds that his respondents typically study for 3 hours, give or take 1½ hours in either direction. "Typically" in this context refers to the _____, whereas "give or take" refers to the _____.

    a. Standard deviation / arithmetic mean

    b. Arithmetic mean / standard deviation

    c. Arithmetic mean / p value

    d. p value / standard deviation

16. "The arithmetic mean of the ratings in the experimental group was 45, although the mean could reasonably be as high as 52 or as low as 37 if the test were repeated with a new group of subjects." Which inferential statistic is being utilized in that statement?

    a. Effect size

    b. Confidence intervals

    c. Canonical correlation

    d. Significance testing

17. Bayesian statistics approaches the results of an experiment by:

    a. Taking into account relevant prior knowledge about the topic under study and the likelihood of a result's occurrence

    b. Assuming the result is incorrect, then reasoning backward to show how it could be accurate

    c. Setting a p value at 1 time out of 1,000

    d. Comparing the effect size if the result were correct to the effect size if the result were wrong

18. Anna reported to the Psychology Laboratory to participate in an experiment. Before she began, however, she was given a form to read and sign, outlining what her participation would require, detailing her options should she choose not to participate, and requesting her permission to take part in the study. Anna was given a(n):

   a. Debriefing form

   b. Consent form

   c. Indemnity form

   d. Issuance notice

19. Which of the following is a reason why psychologists might study animals?

   a. Because animals don't require payment, and human research subjects always get paid for their participation

   b. To test the limitations of new and dangerous equipment

   c. To avoid having to deal with APA ethical guidelines

   d. To conduct basic research on a particular species

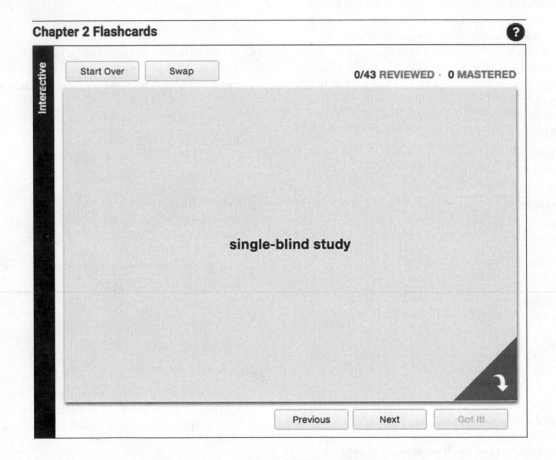

Chapter 3
Genes, Evolution, and Environment

◀ Listen to the Audio

Learning Objectives

LO 3.1.A Explain how genes, chromosomes, DNA, and genomes all relate to one another.

LO 3.1.B Explain why the study of epigenetics offers an important avenue for understanding the genetic components of thought and behavior.

LO 3.2.A Explain how natural selection contributes to changes in gene frequencies in a population.

LO 3.2.B List and describe five innate human characteristics.

LO 3.3.A Compare the sexual strategies of females and males, according to the sociobiological perspective.

LO 3.3.B Discuss four challenges to the evolutionary view of human mating strategies.

LO 3.4.A Explain what heritability refers to, and discuss three important facts about heritability that should be kept in mind when discussing genetic contributions to behavior.

LO 3.4.B Outline the basic design of a heritability study that involves twins and adoptees.

LO 3.5.A Discuss the extent to which intelligence may be heritable.

LO 3.5.B Explain why both between-group and within-group variability are important in arguments about group differences in intelligence.

LO 3.5.C List four ways that the environment nurtures or thwarts mental ability, and give an example of each.

LO 3.5.D Explain how both nurture and nature play an interactive role in shaping behavior.

Ask questions . . . be willing to wonder

If a trait is "genetic," is it inevitable?

Why do kittens, monkeys, toddlers, and grown-ups all love to play and "monkey around"?

Has evolution made men, but not women, naturally promiscuous?

To what extent is intellect "heritable"—and what exactly does that mean?

Think of all the ways human beings are alike. Everywhere, no matter what their backgrounds or where they live, people love, work, argue, dance, sing, complain, and gossip. They raise families, celebrate marriages, and mourn losses. They reminisce about the past and plan for the future. They help their friends and fight their enemies. They smile with amusement, frown with displeasure, and glare in anger. *Where do all these commonalities come from?*

Think of all the ways human beings differ. Some are extroverts, always ready to make new friends or speak up in a crowd; others are shy and introverted, preferring the safe and familiar. Some are ambitious and enterprising; others are placid, content with the way things are. Some take to book learning like a cat to catnip; others struggle in school but have plenty of street smarts

What will shape this baby's development? Edward L. Thorndike and John B. Watson were both prominent theorists in the early days of psychology, but they subscribed to vastly different views regarding human development. Thorndike was a nativist, emphasizing the important role of genetics in shaping an individual, whereas Watson was an empiricist, favoring the effects of nurture in shaping behavior. We now understand that both nature *and* nurture contribute to the development of a person.

and practical know-how. Some are overwhelmed by even petty problems; others remain calm and resilient in the face of severe difficulties. *Where do all these differences come from?*

Years ago, psychologists addressing these questions tended to fall into two camps: On one side were the *nativists*, who emphasized genes and inborn characteristics, or *nature*; on the other side were the *empiricists*, who focused on learning and experience, or *nurture*. Edward L. Thorndike (1903), one of the leading psychologists of the early 1900s, staked out the first position when he claimed that "in the actual race of life . . . the chief determining factor is heredity." But his contemporary, behaviorist John B. Watson (1925), insisted that experience could write virtually any message on the *tabula rasa*, the blank slate, of human nature: "Give me a dozen healthy infants, well-formed, and my own specified world to bring them up in and I'll guarantee to take any one at random and train him to become any type of specialist I might select—doctor, lawyer, artist, merchant-chief and yes, even beggar-man and thief, regardless of his talents, penchants, tendencies, abilities, vocations, and race of his ancestors."

In this chapter, we will examine the contributions of both nature and nurture in shaping our human commonalities and our individual differences. We will focus largely on findings from two related areas, *evolutionary psychology* and *behavioral genetics*. Scientists in these areas study much the same topics, including language learning, attention, perception, memory, sexual behavior, cooperation, helpfulness to others, emotion, reasoning, personality, and many other aspects of human psychology, but they emphasize different mechanisms to explain human differences.

Virtually no one, however, argues in terms of nature *versus* nurture anymore. Scientists today understand that heredity and environment constantly interact to produce our psychological traits and even most of our physical ones. This interaction works in two directions. First, genes affect the kinds of experiences we have. A teenager with a genetic aptitude for schoolwork may be more likely than other kids to join a chess team and get books and science kits as birthday presents. These experiences reward and encourage the development of academic skills, turning what began as a small intellectual advantage into a large one. Conversely, although most people don't realize it, experience affects our genes: Stress, diet, emotional events, and hormonal changes can all influence which genes are active ("expressed") over a person's lifetime (Fraga et al., 2005; Mischel, 2009). Try, then, as you read this chapter, to resist the temptation to think of nature and nurture in either–or terms.

Unlocking the Secrets of Genes

You might think the study of genetics is solely a matter of biology. Although it's true that biologists are keenly interested in understanding how information gets passed from one generation to the next at a cellular level, psychologists also want to know how genetic information influences what we think, how we feel, and how we act.

The Human Genome

LO 3.1.A Explain how genes, chromosomes, DNA, and genomes all relate to one another.

Researchers in **behavioral genetics** attempt to tease apart the relative contributions of heredity and environment to explain individual differences across people by adopting a nature *and* nurture approach in their investigations. Hereditary contributions originate in genetics, so let's begin by looking at what genes are and how they operate.

Genes, the basic units of heredity, are located on **chromosomes**, rod-shaped structures found in the center (nucleus) of every cell of the body. Each sperm cell and each egg cell (ovum) contains 23 chromosomes, so when a sperm and egg unite at conception, the fertilized egg and all the body cells that eventually develop from it (except for sperm cells and ova) contain 46 chromosomes, arranged in 23 pairs.

Chromosomes consist of threadlike strands of **DNA (deoxyribonucleic acid)** molecules, and genes consist of small segments of this DNA (see Figure 3.1). Each human chromosome contains thousands of genes. However, 98.8 percent of our total DNA, called *noncoding DNA*, lies *outside* the genes. This DNA used to be called "junk DNA" because scientists believed it was not important, but this belief is changing fast. Changes in this noncoding DNA may be associated with common diseases. Messages from noncoding DNA, along with random chemical events in cells, may also affect the expression of certain genes.

All of our genes, together with noncoding DNA, make up the human **genome**. Most genes in the human genome are found in other animals as well, but some are unique to our species, setting us apart from chimpanzees, mice, and wasps. Many genes contribute directly to a particular trait, but others work indirectly by switching other genes on or off. Many genes are inherited in the same form by everyone; others vary, contributing to our individuality.

behavioral genetics
An interdisciplinary field of study concerned with genetic contributions to individual differences in behavior and personality.

genes
The functional units of heredity; they are composed of DNA and specify the structure of proteins

chromosomes
Within every cell, rod-shaped structures that carry the genes.

DNA (deoxyribonucleic acid)
The chromosomal molecule that transfers genetic characteristics by way of coded instructions for the structure of proteins.

genome
The full set of genes in each cell of an organism (with the exception of sperm and egg cells), together with noncoding DNA located outside the genes.

Figure 3.1 Genes and Chromosomes
Genes are located on chromosomes, shown in the photo magnified almost 55,000 times.

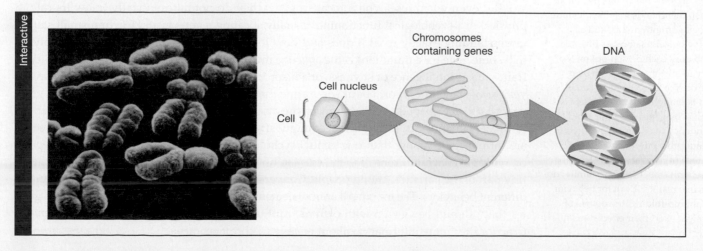

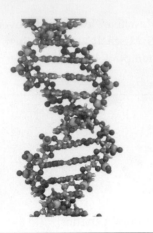

Figure 3.2 DNA Double Helix

A "helix" is an object with a three-dimensional twisting shape that looks like a wire wrapped around a cylinder. Crick and Watson's famous discovery was that DNA is always made up of two helixes, with the strands held together by four chemical elements called bases.

Ask members of your family, one person at a time, to clasp their hands together. Include aunts and uncles, grandparents, and as many other biological relatives as possible. Which thumb does each person put on top? The tendency to fold the left thumb over the right one or vice versa tends to run in families, and is thought by many geneticists to be influenced by genes. Do your relatives show one tendency over the other? (If your family is an adoptive one, of course, you have less chance of finding a trend.) Try the same exercise with someone else's family; do you get the same results? Even for behavior as simple as thumb-folding, the details of how genes might exert their effect remain uncertain.

Within each gene are four *bases*, the chemical elements that form DNA: adenine, thymine, cytosine, and guanine. These bases are identified by the letters A, T, C, and G and are arranged in a certain sequence, such as ACGTCTCTATA. In 1953, James Watson and Francis Crick made a groundbreaking discovery, which they published in a 985-word paper that revolutionized the field of genetics. They determined that DNA is always made up of two strands, with the bases in the middle holding the strands together in pairs—the famous double helix—as you can see in Figure 3.2.

Within a gene, a particular sequence may contain thousands or even millions of bases, which together constitute a code for the synthesis of one of the many proteins that affect virtually every aspect of the body, from its structure to the chemicals that keep it running. But this is a simplification; one small variation in the code can create a qualitatively different kind of protein. Also, many genes can make more than one protein, depending on when and where different segments of DNA on the gene are activated. In fact, our 22,000 or so genes can produce hundreds of thousands of different proteins. You might think that 22,000 is a lot of genes, but that's only about twice as many as a fruit fly has—and corn has about 32,000 (Schnable et al., 2009). The key is not how many genes you have, but what those genes can do.

In 2006, an international collaboration of 2,000 researchers working on the Human Genome Project announced that it had finished mapping the entire human genome. They had identified the sequence of nearly all 3 billion bases (those As, Cs, Ts, and Gs) and determined how the genes are arranged on the chromosomes. Lately, scientists have also begun using computers and new technologies to examine as many as a million DNA differences at once. Then they compare these DNA differences in people who share a particular disease or trait with those of people who do not have it. In these studies, called *genome-wide association studies*, researchers may have a candidate "culprit" gene in mind, but they do not need to do so because the approach is entirely statistical, based on correlations. The points where sequences differ in the two groups of people give researchers a clue to which sequences might be associated with a specific disease or trait (Hardy & Singleton, 2009). The latest big new development is *whole-genome sequencing*, sequencing the entire 3 *billion* base pairs of DNA (Plomin, 2012; Plomin, DeFries, & Knopik, 2013).

Scientists also sometimes use an older technique to carry out *linkage studies*, searching for the genes associated with rare disorders. Linkage studies take advantage of the tendency of genes lying close together on a chromosome to be inherited together across generations. The researchers start by looking for DNA differences called **genetic markers**, DNA segments that vary considerably among individuals and whose locations on the chromosomes are already known. They then look for patterns of inheritance of these markers in large families in which a condition—say, depression or impulsive violence—is common. If a marker tends to exist only in family members who have the condition, then it can be used as a genetic landmark. The gene involved in the condition is apt to be located nearby on the chromosome, so the researchers have some idea where to search for it.

But even when researchers locate a gene, they do not automatically know its role in physical or psychological functioning. Usually, locating a gene is just the first small step in understanding exactly what it does and how it works. Be wary of media reports implying that some gene (or a mutation) is the *only* one involved in a complex psychological ability or trait, such as intelligence or shyness, or a disorder, such as autism. It seems that nearly every year brings another report about some gene that supposedly explains a human trait. A few years back, newspapers even announced the discovery of a "worry gene." Don't worry about it! Most human traits, even such seemingly straightforward ones as height and eye color, are influenced by more than one gene. Psychological traits are especially likely to depend on multiple genes—dozens of them, or even hundreds—with each one accounting for just a tiny part of the variance among people. Conversely, any single gene is apt to influence many different behaviors. The moral: All announcements in the media of a "gene for this" or a "gene for that" should be viewed with extreme caution. Watch *Genetic Mechanisms and Behavioral Genetics 1* for more information about genes and chromosomes.

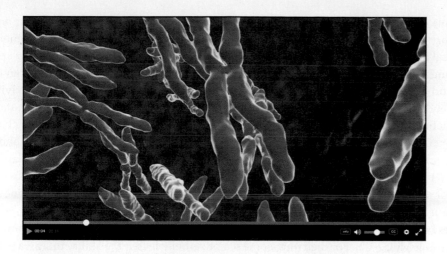

Epigenetics

LO 3.1.B Explain why the study of epigenetics offers an important avenue for understanding the genetic components of thought and behavior.

Many people think of the genome as a static blueprint, a set of coded messages that never changes over a person's lifetime. But this is a big misconception. One reason has to do with *mutations*, which produce variant forms of genes; these mutations may alter just one DNA base or, at the other extreme, a large part of a chromosome. Many mutations (gene variants) are inherited from our parents, but others are new ones that arise before or after birth. Mutations may occur because of a mistake made when DNA copies itself during cell division. Some occur because of environmental factors, such as ultraviolet radiation from the sun, which can cause mutations that lead to skin cancer.

Thus people differ in part because they carry different mutations in their genetic code. But they also differ for another reason: Scientists are learning that stable changes in gene (and therefore trait) expression can occur for a variety of reasons, without any changes in the sequence of bases in a gene's DNA. One of the most exciting developments in genetics is a specialty called **epigenetics**, which studies such changes (Berger et al., 2009). The mechanisms involve chemical molecules that regulate the activity of the genes. These changes are like software that tells your genome hardware to become active or inactive. Epigenetic changes affect behavior, learning and memory, and vulnerability to mental disorders (Zhang & Meaney, 2010). The video *Epigenetics* will tell you more about this fascinating area of investigation.

genetic marker

A segment of DNA that varies among individuals, has a known location on a chromosome, and can function as a genetic landmark for a gene involved in a physical or mental condition.

epigenetics

The study of stable changes in the expression of a particular gene that occur without changes in DNA base sequences; the Greek prefix *epi-* means "on top of" or "in addition to."

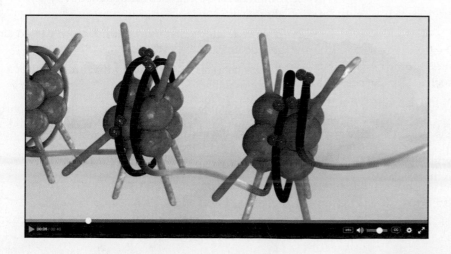

Epigenetic changes may help explain why one identical twin might get a disease and the other not get it. They can also help explain why identical twins and even cloned, genetically identical animals living in exactly the same environment may differ considerably in appearance and behavior (Raser & O'Shea, 2005). Yes, you read that right: Even clones can differ. The study of epigenetics is demonstrating that the timing and pattern of genetic activity are critical not only before birth but also throughout life (Feinberg, 2008). And just like mutations, epigenetic changes can be affected by environmental factors (Plomin et al., 2013; Zhang & Meaney, 2010). In coming years, you will be hearing a lot more about epigenetics, and how your own habits, activities, drug use, and stress level might affect the activity of your genes.

Scientists are understandably excited about these advances, but, as usual, we should be wary of oversimplification. Some popular writers get carried away. A news headline taken from a *preliminary* study suggesting that childhood poverty affects adult genetics blared: "Babies born into poverty are damaged forever before birth!" (reported in Davey Smith, 2012; Heijmans & Mill, 2012). For their part, some scientists believe that the ability to scan a person's unique genome will soon permit "personalized medicine," where your particular genetic pattern will determine the treatment you need for a given disease. Yet caution is called for here, too. Epidemiologist George Davey Smith (2011) explained how the hope for personalized medicine overlooks the powerful role of randomness and chance in human disease, and he calls epigenetic explanations "the currently fashionable response to any question to which you do not know the answer." Epigenetics and genetic testing will undoubtedly provide some fascinating discoveries about human behavior and health, but they will never provide the whole story—as we discuss further in "Taking Psychology with You" at the end of this chapter.

JOURNAL PROMPT 3.1

Thinking Critically—Tolerate Uncertainty: The Human Genome Project and the growing new field of epigenetics have excited the world about the promise of one day being able to tailor medical treatments to a person's specific genetic profile. Why might it be prudent to avoid getting too excited and to tolerate uncertainty before rushing out to get your own genome sequenced (after the price is right)?

Quiz for Module 3.1

1. The basic units of heredity are called

  a. RNA

  b. Chromosomes

  c. Genes

  d. Noncoding DNA

2. The four bases within each gene are identified by the letters:

  a. A – X – G – D

  b. A – E – I – O

  c. T – C – B – Y

  d. A – T – C – G

3. What does whole-genome sequencing involve?

  a. Sequencing the entire 3 billion base pairs of DNA that make up the human genome.

  b. Comparing DNA differences in people who share a particular trait with those of people who do not have that trait.

  c. Specifically targeting genes that are associated with rare medical disorders.

  d. Isolating individual genes that contribute uniquely to specific traits.

4. What do genetic mutations produce?

  a. Damaged genes that lead to illness or death

  b. Different forms of genes brought about by some type of alteration

  c. Inherited defects that will continue to be passed along genetic lines

  d. Abrupt changes in personality that are visible at a behavioral level

5. The study of stable changes in the expression of a particular gene that occur without changes in DNA is called

  a. Epigenetics

  b. Hereditarian bypass

  c. Linkage

  d. "Genome shift"

The Genetics of Similarity

What accounts for the similarities among all human beings, such as the universal capacity for language or loyalty to a family or clan? Evolutionary psychologists believe the answer lies partly in genetic dispositions that developed during the evolutionary history of our species.

Evolution and Natural Selection

LO 3.2.A Explain how natural selection contributes to changes in gene frequencies in a population.

Researchers in **evolutionary psychology** emphasize the evolutionary mechanisms that might help explain our human commonalities in a variety of areas, such as personality, emotion, sexual behavior, or reasoning. To read the messages from the past that are locked in our genes, we must first understand the nature of evolution itself. **Evolution** is basically a change in gene frequencies within a population, a change that typically takes place over many generations. As particular genes become more common or less common in the population, so do the characteristics they influence. These developments account for changes within a species. And when two populations within a species become geographically separated and must adapt to different conditions, eventually those two populations may evolve into two different species.

Why exactly do gene frequencies in a population change? During the division of the cells that produce sperm and eggs, if an error occurs in the copying of the original DNA sequence, genes can mutate. In addition, during the formation of a sperm or an egg, small segments of genetic material cross over from one member of a chromosome pair to another, exchanging places prior to the final cell division. As genes spontaneously mutate and recombine during the production of sperm and eggs, new genetic variations, and therefore potential new traits, keep arising.

But that is only part of the story. According to the principle of **natural selection**, first formulated in general terms by British naturalist Charles Darwin in *On the Origin of Species* (1859/1964), the fate of these genetic variations depends on the environment. Darwin did not actually know about genes, as their discovery had not yet been widely publicized, but he realized that a species' characteristics must somehow be transmitted biologically from one generation to the next.

The fundamental idea behind natural selection is this: In a given species living in a particular environment, some individuals with a genetically influenced trait tend to be more successful than others in finding food, surviving the elements, and fending off enemies—and are therefore better at staying alive long enough to produce offspring. As a result, their genes will become more and more common in the population, having been "selected" by reproductive success. Over many generations, these genes may even spread throughout the species. In contrast, those individuals whose traits are not as adaptive in the struggle for survival will not be as "reproductively fit": They will be more likely to die before reproducing, and their genes—and the traits influenced by those genes—will therefore become less and less common, and may possibly even disappear.

Scientists debate how gradually or abruptly evolutionary changes occur and whether competition for survival is always the primary mechanism of change, but they agree on the basic importance of evolution. During the past century and a half, Darwin's ideas have been resoundingly supported by findings in anthropology, botany, and molecular genetics (Ruse, 2010). Scientists have actually watched some organisms evolving, such as microbes, insects, and plants. Some rapid evolutionary changes, in mammals as well as microbes, are due to human activity. For example, the horns of bighorn rams have been getting smaller because of trophy hunting, which removes animals with larger horns from the breeding population (Coltman et al., 2003). Researchers have even identified specific genes that account for evolutionary changes that have occurred in animals in the wild, such as the transformation of mice

Evolutionary psychologists are interested in the origins of many human behaviors, such as smiling and laughter, which are universal among primates and are part of our shared evolutionary heritage.

evolutionary psychology

A field of psychology emphasizing evolutionary mechanisms that may help explain human commonalities in social practices, perception, emotional responses, and other areas of behavior.

evolution

A change in gene frequencies within a population over many generations; a mechanism by which genetically influenced characteristics of a population may change.

natural selection

The evolutionary process in which individuals with genetically influenced traits that are adaptive in a particular environment tend to survive and to reproduce in greater numbers than do other individuals; as a result, their traits become more common in the population.

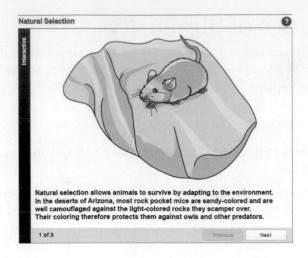

Natural Selection

Natural selection allows animals to survive by adapting to the environment. In the deserts of Arizona, most rock pocket mice are sandy-colored and are well camouflaged against the light-colored rocks they scamper over. Their coloring therefore protects them against owls and other predators.

1 of 3   Previous   Next

and lizards from light colored to dark colored (or vice versa) as the animals have migrated into different environments (Des Roches et al., 2013; Hoekstra et al., 2006). Evolutionary principles such as natural selection guide all of the biological sciences.

Although many evolutionary theorists have assumed that human evolution pretty much stopped thousands of years ago, scientists have found evidence of natural selection occurring occasionally in humans over just a few generations, in response to changing conditions. For instance, when Africans were brought to America as slaves, they had a genetic variation that protected them against malaria. Over time, as malaria became less of an environmental threat in the United States, natural selection slowly stopped favoring those with this genetic variation, and today it is less common among African Americans than it is among indigenous Africans (Jin et al., 2012). You can learn more about evolutionary psychology by watching the video *Evolutionary Psychology 1*.

TRAITS AND PREFERENCES Evolutionary biologists often start with an observation about some characteristic and then try to account for it in evolutionary terms. Why do male peacocks have such fabulous, flamboyant feathers, whereas females look so drab and dull? The evolutionary answer is that during the history of the species, males who could put on the flashiest display got the attention of females, and such males therefore had a better chance of reproducing. In contrast, all that females had to do was hang around and pick the guy with the fanciest feathers; they didn't even have to dress up.

Evolutionary psychologists work in the same way as biologists, but some take a slightly different tack: They start by asking what sorts of challenges human beings might have faced in their prehistoric past—say, having to decide which foods were safe to eat, or needing to size up a stranger's intentions quickly. Then they draw inferences about the behavioral tendencies that might have been selected because they helped our forebears solve these survival problems and enhanced their reproductive fitness. (They make no assumption about whether the behavior is adaptive or intelligent in the *present* environment.) Finally, they conduct research to see if those tendencies actually exist throughout the world.

Thus, our ancestors' need to avoid eating poisonous or rancid food might have led to an innate dislike for bitter tastes and rotten smells; those individuals who happened to be born with such dislikes would have stood a better chance of surviving long enough to reproduce. Similarly, it made good survival sense for our ancestors to develop an innate capacity for language and an ability to recognize faces and emotional expressions. But they would not have had much need for an innate ability to read or drive, inasmuch as books and cars had not yet been invented.

MENTAL MODULES Is the human mind like a general-purpose computer waiting to be programmed? Many evolutionary psychologists don't think so. Instead, they say, environment and genetics have combined to give us a collection of specialized and independent "mental modules" to handle specific survival problems (Buss, 1995, 1999; Cosmides, Tooby, & Barkow, 1992; Marcus, 2004; Pinker, 2002). A module does not have to correspond to one specific brain area; it may involve several dispersed but interconnected areas of the brain, just as a computer file can be fragmented on a hard drive.

Suppose that you are playing a game for money with a complete stranger whom you'll probably never see again. You can share your winnings with each other or just keep them all to yourselves. The smart thing to do is to keep all the money. Why would you give anything to a total stranger in a one-time interaction? Yet people do tend to share some of their winnings with strangers, just as they usually tip a waiter at a restaurant they won't go back to (Delton et al., 2011). Why? Evolutionary psychologists would say that the reason people are often generous, even when a generous act seems to hurt them, is that natural selection has shaped us to cooperate as a way of shoring up relationships. Social life is inherently uncertain; we cannot always predict who will be friend or foe in the future. So natural selection has produced something like a "cooperate because you might need this person later" module.

Critics are concerned that the notion of mental modules might lead to the misguided assumption that virtually every human activity and capacity, from cleanliness to cruelty, is innate. Frans de Waal (2002), a zoologist and evolutionary theorist, cautions against the impulse to assume that if a trait exists and has a genetic component, then it must be adaptive and be driven by a specialized module. After all, pimples and male-pattern baldness are not particularly adaptive, and neither one has a module associated with it! Many evolved and inherited traits are merely byproducts of other traits, and some are even dysfunctional—a fact you know if you have a bad back, which is one unfortunate consequence of our evolved ability to walk on two feet. To understand our evolutionary legacy, de Waal argues, we must consider not just individual traits in isolation but also the whole package of traits that characterizes the species. This is as true for psychological traits as for physical ones. A leading researcher explains more about the evolutionary perspective in the video *Evolutionary Psychology 2*.

The debate over modules will undoubtedly continue. But regardless of whether modules are the best way to describe traits that appear to be inherited, be careful to avoid the common error of assuming that if some behavior or trait exists, it must therefore be adaptive.

Innate Human Characteristics

LO 3.2.B List and describe five innate human characteristics.

Because of the way our species evolved, many abilities, tendencies, and characteristics are either present at birth in all human beings or develop rapidly as a child matures. These traits include not just the obvious ones, such as the ability to stand on two legs or to grasp objects with the forefinger and thumb, but also less obvious ones. Here are just a few examples:

1. **Infant reflexes.** Babies are born with a number of reflexes—simple, automatic responses to specific stimuli. For example, all infants will suck something put to their lips; this reflex enhances their chances of survival by aiding nursing.

2. **An interest in novelty.** Novelty is intriguing to human beings and many other species. If a rat has had its dinner, it will prefer to explore an unfamiliar wing of a maze rather than the familiar wing where food is. Human babies reveal a surprising interest in looking at and listening to unfamiliar things—which, of course, includes most of the world. A baby will even stop nursing momentarily if someone new enters his or her range of vision.

3. **A desire to explore and manipulate objects.** All birds and mammals have this innate inclination. Primates, especially, like to "monkey" with things, taking them apart and scrutinizing the pieces, apparently for the sheer pleasure of it (Harlow, Harlow, & Meyer, 1950). Human babies shake rattles, bang pots, and grasp whatever is put into their tiny hands. For human beings, the natural impulse to handle interesting objects can be overwhelming, which may be one reason that children, museumgoers, and shoppers so often ignore the command "Don't touch."

4. **An impulse to play and fool around.** Kittens and lion cubs, puppies and pandas, and all young primates play with and pounce on one another all day long. Animals sometimes play just for the reward of playing (Held & Spinka, 2011). But play and exploration may also be biologically adaptive because they help members of a species find food and other necessities of life and learn to cope with their environments. Indeed, the young of many species, including humans, enjoy *practice play*, behavior that will be used for serious purposes when they are adults (Vandenberg, 1985). A kitten will stalk and attack a ball of yarn, and human children at play are practicing their social, motor, and linguistic skills.

All primates, including human beings, are innately disposed to explore the environment, manipulate objects, play, and "monkey around."

5. **Basic cognitive abilities.** Many evolutionary psychologists believe that people are born with an ability to quickly and easily respond to the environment. Early in life, infants can interpret the expressions and gestures of others, identify faces, distinguish plants from animals, distinguish living from nonliving things, and acquire language. Young infants also appear to have a rudimentary understanding of number (Izard et al., 2009). Of course, tiny babies cannot count. However, by the age of only one week, they will spend more time looking at a new set of three items after getting used to a set of two, or vice versa, which means that they can recognize the difference. Other species, including chimpanzees and some birds, also have a basic sense of number.

Most psychologists accept that certain aspects of human behavior have been naturally selected. There are adaptive and evolutionary aspects of sensory and perceptual abilities, learning, ethnocentrism, cognitive biases, memory, emotions and emotional expressions, stress reactions, the tendency to gain weight when food is plentiful, and attachment to others. Let's look more closely at an area of particular interest to evolutionary psychologists: the nature of mating practices around the world.

JOURNAL PROMPT 3.2

Thinking Critically—Consider Other Interpretations: Think about a trait that would seem to be a hindrance to an individual. Shyness, for example, would tend to impede social interactions and therefore make it more difficult for a person to establish interpersonal bonds. Aggressiveness, as another example, might produce the same lack of social bonds but for a very different reason! Now consider why it is unwise to isolate any one trait or any single behavior and argue for its adaptiveness in the course of natural selection. With the trait you have in mind, discuss how and why it fits in to a larger pattern of human adaptive behavior.

Quiz for Module 3.2

1. Which statement correctly summarizes the nature of evolution?
   a. Evolution explains why species tend to remain stable across different environments.
   b. Evolution is the process by which an individual organism adapts to its environment.
   c. Evolution is the study of how one person's genes become more fit than another person's genes.
   d. Evolution is a change in gene frequencies in a population over many generations.

2. People all over the world display primary emotions using the same facial expressions: smiles for happiness, furrowed brows for anger, or curled upper lips for contempt. People all over the world are also quite accurate at decoding these emotional expressions. According to evolutionary psychologists, why is this?
   a. The ability to quickly signal and understand internal emotional states allowed early humans to anticipate the quality of their social interactions.
   b. All humans are genetically programmed to understand emotion because emotions are part of the genetic inheritance of our species.
   c. Environmental influences on a person's emotional state are not as pronounced as genetic influences on a person's tendency to feel happy or angry.
   d. Facial expressions are shaped by the environments humans find themselves in.

3. Carlos is pigeon-toed (his feet face inward rather than straight ahead). "It's great!" he argues. "I can shimmy down narrow stadium rows to get to my seat, and no one has to get up. My pigeon-toed feet sure are adaptive." Despite his optimism, why is Carlos misinformed about evolutionary psychology and the principles of inheritance?
   a. Carlos isn't misinformed; traits wouldn't exist in individuals if they weren't functional.
   b. Carlos's misshapen legs are the result of sleeping in peculiar positions as an infant rather than the product of heredity.
   c. Carlos assumes that if a trait exists, it must therefore be adaptive.
   d. Carlos assumes that his personal evolution has ended; in reality, people continue to change and grow throughout the lifespan.

4. Which of the following is *not* a well-documented innate human characteristic?
   a. An interest in novelty
   b. A preference for neutral colors
   c. An impulse to play
   d. A desire for exploration

5. Why would an impulse for play, exploration, and novelty be evolutionarily adaptive?

   a. Those characteristics would help an organism learn about an environment, find sources of food, and generally meet the challenges of daily living.

   b. Organisms who explore their environments would evolve at a faster rate than those who didn't.

   c. Those individuals who risked exploring their environment or trying novel activities would be more likely to die, and therefore eliminated from the gene pool.

   d. Novelty produces play, and play leads to exploration; therefore, organisms that follow that sequence will pass on their genes to their offspring.

Our Human Heritage: Courtship and Mating

Most psychologists agree that the evolutionary history of our species has made certain kinds of learning either difficult or easy. Most acknowledge that simple behaviors, such as smiling or preferring sweet tastes, resemble instincts (behaviors that are relatively uninfluenced by learning and that occur in all members of the species). And most agree that human beings inherit some of their cognitive, perceptual, and emotional capacities. But social scientists disagree heartily about whether biology and evolution can help account for complex social customs, such as warfare, cooperation, and marriage. Nowhere is this disagreement more apparent than in debates over the origins of male–female differences in sexual behavior, so we are going to focus here on that endlessly fascinating topic.

Evolution and Sexual Strategies

LO 3.3.A Compare the sexual strategies of females and males, according to the sociobiological perspective.

In 1975, one of the world's leading experts on ants, Edward O. Wilson, published a little book that had a big impact. It was titled *Sociobiology: The New Synthesis*, the "synthesis" being the application of biological principles to the social and sexual customs of both nonhuman animals and human beings. **Sociobiology** became a popular topic for researchers and the public, generating great controversy.

   Sociobiologists contend that evolution has bred into each of us a tendency to act in ways that maximize our chances of passing on our genes, and to help our close biological relatives, with whom we share many genes, do the same. In this view, just as nature has selected physical characteristics that have proved adaptive, it has selected psychological traits and social customs that aid individuals in propagating their genes. Customs that enhance the odds of such transmission survive in the form of kinship bonds, dominance arrangements, taboos against female adultery, and many other aspects of social life.

   In addition, sociobiologists believe that because the males and females of most species have faced different kinds of survival and mating problems, the sexes have evolved to differ profoundly in aggressiveness, dominance, and sexual strategies (Symons, 1979; Trivers, 1972). In many species, they argue, it is adaptive for males to compete with other males for access to young and fertile females, and to try to win and then inseminate as many females as possible. The more females a male mates with, the more genes he can pass along. But according to sociobiologists, females need to shop for the best genetic deal, as it were, because they can conceive and bear only a limited number of offspring. Having such a large biological investment in each pregnancy, females cannot afford to make mistakes. Besides, mating with a lot of different males would produce no more offspring than staying with just one. So females try to attach themselves to dominant males who have resources and status and are likely to have "superior" genes.

   In this view, the result of these two opposite sexual strategies is that males generally want sex more often than females do; males are often fickle and promiscuous, whereas females are usually devoted and faithful; males are drawn to sexual novelty, whereas females want stability and security; males are relatively undiscriminating in their choice of sexual partners, whereas females

sociobiology

An interdisciplinary field that emphasizes evolutionary explanations of social behavior in animals, including human beings.

are cautious and choosy; and males are competitive and concerned about dominance, whereas females are less so.

Evolutionary psychologists generally agree with these conclusions, but they rely less on comparisons with other species than sociobiologists do, focusing instead on commonalities in human mating and dating practices around the world. In one massive project, 50 scientists studied 10,000 people in 37 cultures located on six continents and five islands (Buss, 1994; Schmitt, 2003). Around the world, they found that men are more violent and more socially dominant than women. They are also more interested in the youth and beauty of their sexual partners, presumably because youth is associated with fertility (see Figure 3.3). According to their responses on questionnaires, they are more sexually jealous and possessive, presumably because if a man's mate had sex with other men, he could never be 100 percent sure that her children were also genetically his. They are quicker than women to have sex with partners they don't know well and more inclined toward polygamy and promiscuity, presumably so that their sperm will be distributed as widely as possible. In contrast, women tend to emphasize the financial resources or prospects of a potential mate, his status, and his willingness to commit to a relationship. On questionnaires, they say they would be more upset by a partner's emotional infidelity than by his sexual infidelity, presumably because abandonment by the partner might leave them without the support and resources needed to raise their offspring. Many studies have reported similar results (Buss & Schmitt, 2011).

The "Genetic Leash"

LO 3.3.B Discuss four challenges to the evolutionary view of human mating strategies.

Evolutionary views of sex differences in dating and mating have become enormously popular. Many academics and laypeople are persuaded that males have an evolutionary advantage in sowing their seeds far and wide, and females have an evolutionary advantage in finding a man with a good paycheck. But critics, including some evolutionary theorists, have challenged this conclusion on conceptual and methodological grounds:

1. **Stereotypes versus actual behavior.** In reality, the behavior of humans and other animals often fails to conform to the stereotyped images of sexually promiscuous males and coy, choosy females (Barash & Lipton, 2001; Birkhead, 2001; Fausto-Sterling, 1997; Hrdy, 1994; Roughgarden, 2004). In many species of birds, fish, and mammals, including human beings, females are sexually ardent and often have many male partners. The female's sexual behavior does not seem to depend only on the goal of being fertilized by the male: Females have sex when they are not ovulating and even when they are already pregnant. And in many species, from penguins to primates, males do not just mate and run. They stick around, feeding the infants, carrying them on their backs, and protecting them against predators (Hrdy, 2009; Snowdon, 1997).

     Human sexual behavior, especially, is amazingly varied and changeable across time and place. Cultures range from those in which women have many children to those in which they have very few; from those in which men are intimately involved in childrearing to those in which they take no part at all; and from those in which women may have many lovers to those in which women may be killed for having sex outside of marriage (Hatfield & Rapson, 1996/2005). In many places, the chastity of a potential mate is much more important to men than to women, but in other places, it is important to both sexes—or to neither one (see Figure 3.4). In some places, just as evolutionary theory predicts, a relatively few men—those with the greatest wealth and power—have a far greater number of offspring than other men do; but in many societies, including some

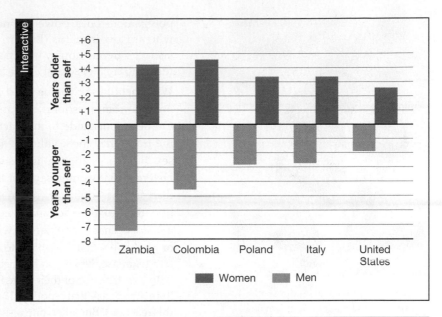

Figure 3.3 Preferred Age in a Mate

In most societies, men say they prefer to marry women younger than themselves, whereas women prefer men who are older (Buss, 1995). Evolutionary psychologists attribute these preferences to male concern with a partner's fertility and female concern with a partner's material resources and status. When the man is much older than the woman, people rarely comment, but when the woman is older, people take notice. Today, the gossip and jokes about women who are "cougars" reflect (1) the rising number of women who have male partners younger than they and (2) the ambivalence that many people feel about it. Do you think the word *cougar* is a compliment or an insult?

A basic assumption of evolutionary approaches to sexuality is that females across species have a greater involvement in childrearing than males do. But there are many exceptions. Female emperor penguins take off every winter, leaving behind males like this one to care for the kids. And among other species of penguins, males and females are equally likely to be providers (Saraux et al., 2011).

Figure 3.4 Attitudes toward Chastity

In many places, men care more about a partner's chastity than women do, as evolutionary psychologists would predict. But culture has a powerful impact on these attitudes, as this graph shows (from Buss, 1995). Notice that in China, both sexes prefer a partner who has not yet had intercourse, whereas in Sweden, chastity is a nonissue.

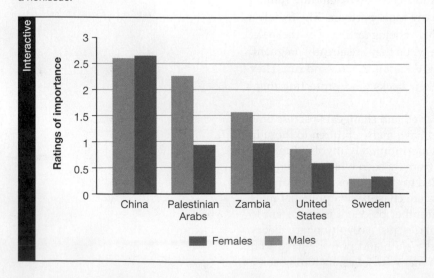

polygamous ones, powerful men do not have more children than men who are poor or who are low in status (Brown, Laland, & Mulder, 2009). Sexual attitudes and practices also vary tremendously within a culture, as is immediately apparent to anyone surveying the panorama of sexual attitudes and behaviors within the United States and Canada.

2. **What people say versus what they do.** Evolutionary psychologists have tended to rely on data from questionnaires and interviews, but critics observe that people's responses can be a poor guide to their actual choices and actions. When people are asked to rank the traits they most value in a sexual partner or someone they'd like to go out with, sex differences appear, just as evolutionary theory would predict (Kenrick et al., 2001): Heterosexual women say that they'd ideally like a man who is rich and handsome, and men say they'd like a woman who is good-looking and sexy. But those preferences are hypothetical; their actual choices about whom to date, love, and marry often tell a different story. That's why people who are plain, pudgy, smart, foolish, rich, poor, gorgeous, or goofy all usually manage to find partners.

Likewise, when you ask people which would upset them more, their mate having sex with someone else or their mate falling in love with someone else, women are usually likelier than men to say that emotional infidelity would be worse (although cultures vary widely on this reaction). But when one researcher asked people about their *actual* experiences with infidelity, men and women did not differ at all in the degree to which they had focused on the emotional or sexual aspects of their partner's behavior (C. Harris, 2003). In fact, men, supposedly the more sexually jealous sex, were significantly more likely than women to have tolerated their partner's sexual unfaithfulness, whereas women were more likely to have ended the relationship over it. As research continues to disentangle when and how evolutionary theory would predict sex differences in this area, the distinction between reported and actual behavior will be prominent (Kato, 2014; Sobraske, Boster, & Gaulin, 2013).

3. **Convenience versus representative samples.** "Convenience samples" of undergraduates sometimes produce results that do not apply to nonstudents, and this may well be the case in much of the evolutionary research on attitudes toward sex and marriage. In a national study, researchers at the Centers for Disease Control and Prevention (CDC) interviewed more than 22,000 American men and women ages 15 to 44 about sex, living together, marriage, divorce, and parenting (Groves et al., 2009). The agency had conducted similar surveys from 1973 to 2002, but only with women. Starting in 2002, the researchers asked a question that in retrospect seems obvious: What about men? Thus, more recent surveys were finally able to draw conclusions about male and female attitudes based on a sample that was far more representative of the general population than college students are. What the researchers found casts a different light on evolutionary notions of sex differences.

As we've seen, in the evolutionary view, women on the whole value commitment to a relationship more than men do and are more dedicated to parenting. Yet 66 percent of the men, compared to only 49 percent of the women, agreed that "It is better to get married than go through life being single." Furthermore, 68 percent of women and 75 percent of men agreed that "It is more important for a man to spend a lot of time with his family than be successful at his career." Among fathers living in the same household as their children, the majority spent considerable time feeding and bathing their kids, helping with homework, and taking them to activities. Some other results were in the stereotypical direction, but taken as a whole, the CDC findings suggest that American men today are just as interested in serious family relationships as women are (Jones & Mosher, 2013).

If you are thinking critically, you may be wondering whether these questionnaire results are any more reliable than those on dating preferences. Good question! The answer is yes. From studies that had people keep diaries of how they spend their time each day, we know that men's behavior has changed along with their attitudes. Women still do more housework and childcare than men do, but since the 1960s, the time men spend on housework has more than doubled, and since the 1980s, the time they spend on primary childcare has nearly tripled (Raley, Bianchi, & Wang, 2012; Wang & Bianchi, 2009).

4. **The Fred Flintstone problem.** Finally, some scientists have questioned evolutionary psychologists' emphasis on the Pleistocene Age, which extended from about 2 million years to about 11,000 years ago. Analysis of the human genome in Africans, East Asians, and Europeans suggests that during the past 10,000 to 15,000 years, natural selection has continued to influence genes associated with taste, smell, digestion, bone structure, skin color, fertility, and even brain function (Voight et al., 2006). Some of these changes may have begun when humans abandoned hunting and gathering in favor of agriculture, a switch that made certain genetic dispositions more adaptive and others less so. David Buller (2005), a philosopher who was captivated by evolutionary psychology until he took a closer look, concludes that "There is no reason to think that contemporary humans are, like Fred and Wilma Flintstone, just Pleistocene hunter-gatherers struggling to survive and reproduce in evolutionarily novel suburban habitats."

How large an influence does our Stone Age past have on our current courtship and mating customs?

Even if the Pleistocene period did strongly influence human mating preferences, those preferences may differ from the ones usually emphasized by evolutionary theory. Our prehistoric ancestors, unlike the undergraduates in many mate-preference studies, did not have 5,000 fellow students to choose from. They lived in small bands, and if they were lucky, they might get to choose between Urp and Ork, and that's about it; they could not hold out for some gorgeous babe or handsome millionaire down the road. Because they had only a small range of potential partners, there would have been no need for the kinds of sexual strategies described by most evolutionary theorists (Griskevicius, Haselton, & Ackerman, 2015). An alternative explanation is that evolution instilled in us a tendency to select a mate based on similarity (in looks, intelligence, and so forth) and proximity (the person is standing right there, available). And indeed the evidence supports this view.

Ultimately, what evolutionary scientists and their critics are quarreling about is the relative power of biology and culture. In *On Human Nature* (1978), Edward Wilson argued that genes hold culture on a leash. The big question, replied paleontologist Stephen Jay Gould (1987), is: How long and tight is that leash? Is it too short and tight to allow much change, or is it long and flexible enough to permit many possible customs? To sociobiologists, the leash is short and tight. To evolutionary psychologists, it is elastic enough to permit culture to modify evolved biological tendencies, although those tendencies can be pretty powerful (Kenrick & Trost, 1993). To critics of both sociobiology and evolutionary psychology, cultural variations mean that no single, genetically determined sexual strategy exists for human beings. What evolution *has* bestowed on us, they say, is an amazingly flexible brain. Therefore, in matters of sex and love, as in all other human behaviors, the leash is long and flexible. Learn more about the strengths and weaknesses of the evolutionary perspective in psychology by watching the video *Evolutionary Psychology 3*.

JOURNAL PROMPT 3.3

Thinking Critically—Examine the Evidence: A friend of yours tells you that men will always be more sexually promiscuous than women because, during evolution, the best reproductive strategy for a male primate has been to try to impregnate many females. What kind of evidence would you need to evaluate this claim?

Quiz for Module 3.3

1. What do sociobiologists focus on?
   a. Evolutionary explanations of social behaviors in animals and humans
   b. How animal societies develop over time
   c. Aggressive competition for resources between species occupying the same environment
   d. The communication patterns that develop within a species

2. Across a wide range of countries, what general trend do women and men report in their preference for a mate?
   a. Women report that they prefer men with financial resources, whereas men report that they prefer women with stable incomes.
   b. Men say they prefer to marry a woman younger than themselves, whereas women prefer men who are older than themselves.
   c. Both men and women report preferring romantic partners about the same age as themselves.
   d. Men prefer women who are financially solvent, whereas women prefer men who are physically attractive.

3. Which of the following is *not* a challenge to the evolutionary view of human mating strategies?
   a. Verbal claims versus behavioral actions
   b. The Fred Flintstone problem
   c. Sampling procedures used in data collection
   d. The universalist-drift hypothesis

4. What does a "genetic leash" refer to?
   a. The observation that genetics is tied to heredity, but culture can "roam free"
   b. The argument that genetic influences on behavior place a limit on the influence of culture
   c. The limited options that are available to women for mate selection, compared to the larger range of options available to men
   d. The ties that bind members of a genetically related group to a particular environment

5. What is the Fred Flintstone problem in interpreting the evolutionary perspective on human mating strategies?
   a. Humans living in the Pleistocene Age would have had a much larger pool of unattached mates to choose from compared to the limited selection available to modern humans.
   b. There has been a well-documented shift in mate preferences from the 1700s to the 1800s to the 1900s, demonstrating that social evolution has occurred.
   c. Strategies that may have been adaptive during the Pleistocene Age may have little relevance to humans living in a modern era.
   d. According to evolutionary theorists' own arguments, the Flintstones shouldn't have survived long enough to reproduce.

The Genetics of Difference

We have been focusing on the origins of human similarities. We turn now to the second great issue in debates about nature and nurture: the origins of the differences among us. We begin with a critical discussion of what it means to say that a trait is "heritable." Then, to illustrate how behavioral geneticists study differences that genes might influence, we will examine in detail a single, complex issue: the genetic and environmental contributions to intelligence. In other sections of this book, you will be reading about behavioral-genetic findings on many other topics, including weight and body shape, sexual orientation, personality and temperament, addiction, and mental disorders.

The Meaning of Heritability

LO 3.4.A Explain what heritability refers to, and discuss three important facts about heritability that should be kept in mind when discussing genetic contributions to behavior.

Suppose you want to measure flute-playing ability in a large group of music students, so you have some independent raters assign each student a score, from 1 to 20. When you plot the scores, you find that some people are what you might call melodically disadvantaged and should forget about a musical career, others are flute geniuses, and the rest fall somewhere in between. What causes the variation in this group of students? Why are some so musically talented and others so inept? Are these differences primarily genetic, or are they the result of experience and motivation?

To answer such questions, behavioral geneticists compute a statistic called **heritability**, which gives an estimate of the *proportion of the total variance in a trait that is attributable to genetic variation within a group*. Because the heritability of a trait is expressed as a proportion (such as .60), the maximum value it can have is 1.0 (equivalent to "100 percent of the variance"). Some traits, such as height, are highly heritable; that is, most of the differences in height within a group of equally well-nourished people will be accounted for by their genetic differences. In contrast, table manners have low heritability because most variation among individuals is accounted for by differences in upbringing. Our guess is that flute-playing ability, and indeed musical ability in general, falls somewhere in the middle.

Many people hold completely mistaken ideas about heritability. But as genetic findings pour in, the public will need to understand this concept more than ever. You cannot understand the nature–nurture issue without understanding the following important facts about heritability:

1. **An estimate of heritability applies only to a particular group living in a particular environment.** Heritability may be high in one group and low in another. Suppose that all of the children in Community A are affluent, eat plenty of high-quality food, have kind and attentive parents, and go to the same top-notch schools. Because their environments are similar, any intellectual differences among them will have to be due largely to their genetic differences. In other words, mental ability in this group will be highly heritable. In contrast, suppose the children in Community B are rich, poor, and in between. Some of them have healthy diets; others live on fatty foods or do not get enough to eat. Some attend good schools; others go to inadequate ones. Some have doting parents, and some have unloving and neglectful ones. These children's intellectual differences could be largely due to their environmental differences, and if that is so, the heritability of intelligence for this group will be low (Nisbett, 2009). Indeed, in a study that followed 48,000 American children from birth to age 7, heritability did depend greatly on family income. In impoverished families, 60 percent of the variance in IQ was accounted for by environmental factors shared by family members, and the contribution of genes was close to zero. In affluent families, in contrast, heritability was extremely high, and shared environment contributed hardly at all (Turkheimer & Horn, 2014).

2. **Heritability estimates do not apply to a specific person, only to variations within a group of people.** You inherited half of your genes from your mother and half from your father, but your combination of genes has never been seen before and will never be seen again, unless you have an identical twin. (And, as we will explain shortly, even identical twins are not 100 percent identical.) You also have a unique history of family relationships, intellectual training, and life experiences. It is impossible to know just how your genes and your personal history have interacted to produce the person you are today. If you are a great flute player, no one can say whether your ability is mainly a result of inherited musical talent, living all your life in a family of devoted flute players, a private obsession that you acquired at age 6 when you saw the opera *The Magic Flute*, or a combination of all of those influences. For one person, genes may make a tremendous difference in some aptitude or disposition; for another, the environment may be far more important. Scientists can study only the extent to which differences among people in general are explained by their genetic differences.

3. **Even highly heritable traits can be modified by the environment.** Behavioral geneticists have found many examples of how genes interact with the environment. Although height is highly heritable, malnourished children may not grow to be as tall as they would with sufficient food, and children who eat an extremely nutritious diet may grow to be taller than anyone thought they could. The same principle applies to psychological traits and skills.

heritability
A statistical estimate of the proportion of the total variance in some trait that is attributable to genetic differences among individuals within a group.

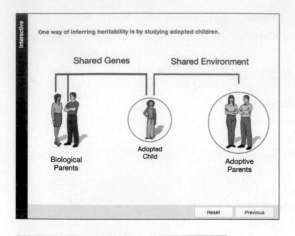

Figure 3.5 Heritability and Adoption

Biological and adoptive parents differ in the contributions they make to an adopted child. Biological parents contribute genetic influences but not an environmental setting, whereas adoptive parents contribute an environment in which the child grows and develops, but make no genetic contribution.

fraternal (dizygotic) twins

Twins that develop from two separate eggs fertilized by different sperm; they are no more alike genetically than are any other pair of siblings.

identical (monozygotic) twins

Twins that develop when a fertilized egg divides into two parts that develop into separate embryos.

Figure 3.6 Twins and Genetics

Genetic inheritance differs between fraternal and identical twins. Fraternal twins, which result from fertilization of separate eggs, share half their genes in common. Identical twins, which result when a single fertilized egg splits in two, share all of their genes in common.

Fraternal Twins

Separate eggs fertilized by separate sperm

Share only about half their genes

Identical Twins

Single egg fertilized by single sperm, then splits in two

Womb

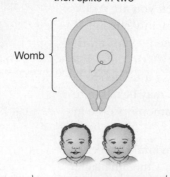

Share all of their genes

Computing Heritability

LO 3.4.B Outline the basic design of a heritability study that involves twins and adoptees.

Scientists currently have no way to estimate the heritability of a trait or behavior directly, so they must infer it by studying people whose degree of genetic similarity is known. You might think that the simplest approach would be to compare biological relatives within families; everyone knows about families that are famous for some talent or trait. But family traits do not tell us much because close relatives usually share environments as well as genes. If Carlo's parents and siblings all love lasagna, that does not mean a taste for lasagna is heritable. The same applies if everyone in Carlo's family has a high IQ, is mentally ill, or is moody.

One way of inferring heritability is by studying adopted children (e.g., Loehlin, Horn, & Willerman, 1996). Such children share half their genes with each birth parent, but they grow up in a different environment, apart from their birth parents. On the other hand, they share an environment with their adoptive parents and siblings but not their genes (see Figure 3.5). Researchers can compare correlations between the traits of adopted children and those of their biological and adoptive relatives and can use the results to compute an estimate of heritability.

Another approach is to compare identical twins with fraternal twins. **Fraternal (dizygotic) twins** develop when a woman's ovaries release two eggs instead of one, and each egg is fertilized by a different sperm. Fraternal twins are wombmates, but they are no more alike genetically than any two siblings (i.e., they share, on average, only half their genes), and they may be of different sexes. In contrast, **identical (monozygotic) twins** develop when a fertilized egg (zygote) divides into two parts that then develop as two separate embryos. Because identical twins come from the same fertilized egg, it has long been assumed that they share all their genes, and this is true for the vast majority of these twins. Some surprising evidence, however, suggests that duplicated blocks of DNA (sets of those As, Cs, Gs, and Ts discussed earlier) can sometimes exist in one identical twin but not in the other (Bruder et al., 2008). Also, prenatal accidents or illnesses can modify the genetic expression in only one twin (Plomin, 2011). Most identical twins, however, are genetically identical (see Figure 3.6).

Behavioral geneticists can estimate the heritability of a trait by comparing groups of same-sex fraternal twins with groups of identical twins. The assumption is that if identical twins are more alike than fraternal twins, then the increased similarity must be due to genetic influences.

If you are thinking critically, you might also suspect that identical twins are treated differently from fraternal twins. To avoid this problem, investigators have studied identical twins who were separated early in life and reared apart. (Decades ago, adoption policies and attitudes toward births out of wedlock permitted such separations to occur.) In theory, separated identical twins share virtually all their genes but not their environments, except, of course, for the environment they shared in their birth mother's womb. Any similarities between them should be primarily genetic and should permit an estimate of heritability.

Recently, scientists have become enthused about new methods, such as genome-wide association studies, for computing heritability directly rather than inferring it from twin studies. At present, however, much of our information comes from adoption and twin studies. The video *Genetic Mechanisms and Behavioral Genetics 2* provides more information about how heritability is studied.

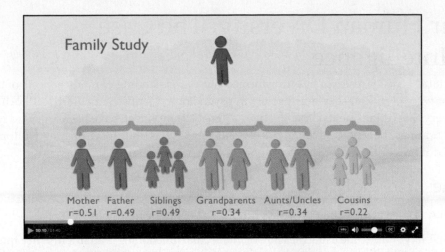

JOURNAL PROMPT 3.4

Thinking Critically—Don't Oversimplify: Consider these three cases, and point out the flaws in the arguments in each case:

1. Diane hears that basket-weaving ability is highly heritable. She assumes that her own poor performance in that area must therefore be due mostly to genes. What is wrong with her reasoning?

2. Bertram hears that basket-weaving ability is highly heritable. He concludes that schools should not bother trying to improve the skills of children who lack this talent. What is wrong with his reasoning?

3. Basket-weaving skills seem to run in Andy's family. Why shouldn't Andy conclude that his own talent is genetic?

Quiz for Module 3.4

1. The proportion of the total variance in a trait that is attributable to genetic variation within a group is also known as
   a. Genetic constancy
   b. Linkage
   c. Genetic shift
   d. Heritability

2. Wally is discussing his psychology class with Zanira. "We learned about the genetic influences on individual differences yesterday. My professor said that shoe size has a heritability estimate of .60. That means that my genes explain 60 percent of why my feet are so big," boasted Wally. "I'm pretty sure you've got that wrong," replied Zanira. "In fact, are you sure you were even in class yesterday?" Why is Zanira's snarky observation correct?
   a. Heritability is actually 100 percent minus a constant; in this case it would be 100% − 60% = 40%.
   b. Heritability is computed directly from genetic material rather than estimated; it's unlikely the professor collected a blood sample from Wally during class.
   c. Heritability estimates do not apply to a specific person but only to variations within a group of people.
   d. Zanira knows that Wally actually wears a size 6 narrow shoe, and no amount of genes could produce a foot that small on a 300-pound adult.

3. Which of the following is *not* a caution when interpreting heritability?
   a. Even highly heritable traits can be modified by the environment.

   b. Heritability estimates are likely to shift depending on the proportion of women to men tested in the environment.
   c. Heritability estimates do not apply to a specific person, only to variations within a group of people.
   d. An estimate of heritability applies only to a particular group living in a particular environment.

4. What percent of genes are shared in common by monozygotic twins?
   a. 100 percent
   b. 50 percent
   c. 25 percent
   d. 33 percent

5. How do adoption studies and twin studies shed light on heritability?
   a. Done correctly, they can help researchers estimate the relative contributions of genetics and environment when explaining differences in behavior.
   b. Fraternal twins are plentiful, whereas identical twins are rare; therefore comparing the two types allows researchers to compute the genetic inheritance of each.
   c. Fraternal twins tend to be adopted by different families, whereas identical twins tend to be raised in the same household.
   d. Compared to studies conducted using the general population, adoption and twin studies produce more reliable measurements.

intelligence quotient (IQ)
A measure of intelligence originally computed by dividing a person's mental age by his or her chronological age and multiplying the result by 100; it is now derived from norms provided for standardized intelligence tests.

Our Human Diversity: The Case of Intelligence

Behavioral-genetics research has transformed our understanding of many aspects of behavior that were previously explained solely in psychological terms. Some findings, such as the discovery that certain mental illnesses have a genetic component, have been accepted readily. Other findings, however, have inflamed political passions and upset people. No topic has aroused more controversy than the origins of human intelligence.

Genes and Individual Differences

LO 3.5.A Discuss the extent to which intelligence may be heritable.

In heritability studies, the usual measure of intellectual functioning is an **intelligence quotient**, or IQ score. Scores on an IQ test reflect how a child has performed compared with other children of the same age, or how an adult has performed compared with other adults. The average score for each age group is arbitrarily set at 100. The distribution of scores in the population approximates a normal (bell-shaped) curve, with scores near the average (mean) being most common, and very high or very low scores being rare. Two-thirds of all test takers score between 85 and 115.

Most psychologists believe that IQ tests measure a general quality that affects most aspects of mental ability, but the tests also have many critics. Some contend that intelligence comes in many varieties, more than a single score can capture. Others maintain that IQ tests are culturally biased, tapping mostly those abilities that depend on experiences in a middle-class environment and favoring white people over people of other ethnicities. Most heritability estimates apply only to those mental skills that affect IQ test scores, and that these estimates are likely to be more valid for some groups than for others.

Despite these important qualifications, it is clear that the kind of intelligence that produces high IQ scores is partly heritable, at least in the middle-class samples usually studied. For children and adolescents, heritability estimates average around .40 or .50; that is, genetic differences explain about half of the variance in IQ scores (Chipuer, Rovine, & Plomin, 1990; Devlin, Daniels, & Roeder, 1997). For adults, most estimates are even higher—in the .60 to .80 range (Bouchard, 1995; McClearn et al., 1997; McGue et al., 1993). These estimates show that the genetic contribution becomes relatively larger and the environmental one relatively smaller with age.

In studies of twins, the scores of identical twins are always much more highly correlated than those of fraternal twins, a difference that reflects the influence of genes. In fact, the scores of identical twins reared *apart* are more highly correlated than those of fraternal twins reared *together*, as you can see in Figure 3.7. In adoption studies, the scores of adopted children are

Figure 3.7 Correlations in Siblings' IQ Scores

The IQ scores of identical twins are highly correlated, even when they are reared apart. The figures represented in this graph are based on average correlations across many studies.

Credit: Graph based on data from Bouchard and McGue (1981).

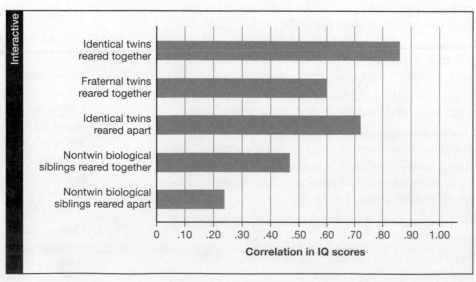

BIOLOGY and *Intellect*

How might genes affect intelligence? One possibility is by influencing the number of nerve cells in the brain or the number of connections among them, as reflected by the total volume of gray matter. Two brain-scan studies, conducted in Holland and Finland, have reported a moderately strong association between general intelligence and gray-matter volume. This research also found that the amount of gray matter was highly correlated in identical twins; the correlation was over 80 percent, compared to only about 50 percent in fraternal twins. The remarkably high correlation in the identical twins indicates that gray-matter volume is highly heritable (Posthuma et al., 2002; Thompson et al., 2001).

The timetable for the brain's development may also play a role. A longitudinal study used MRI scans to study the brains of 307 children from early childhood to the late teens. In the brightest children (as measured by IQ tests), the brain's outer covering, the cerebral cortex, which is involved in higher mental processes, started out thinner than in other kids, with *less* gray matter. But the cortex in the brightest children developed more rapidly and for a longer time, reaching its maximum thickness several years later than in other children (Shaw et al., 2006). In kids with average IQs, the peak occurred at age 7 or 8, but in those with the highest IQs, the peak did not occur until age 11 or 12. Children whose IQs were not quite as high fell in between. Genes may be responsible for these different developmental trajectories. But the results must be interpreted with caution because experience,

intellectual stimulation, and diet can also affect the number of connections among nerve cells in the brain and, thus, development of the brain's gray matter. As always with correlational studies, it is hard to know what is causing what.

Scientists are now looking for genes that might influence performance on IQ and other mental tests. They have identified some possible candidates, but progress has been much slower than anticipated. Far more genes are likely to be involved than was originally thought, and, just as with other traits, each of these genes is likely to contribute just a small piece to the puzzle of genetic variation in intelligence (Plomin et al., 2013; Rietveld et al., 2014). Furthermore, the genes that might be involved have been elusive. A genome-wide association study, which examined huge numbers of genes across more than 3,500 British and Norwegian adults, found that no one gene—nor even any particular group of genes—could account for IQ (Davies et al., 2011). In addition, when scientists attempted to replicate earlier studies that purportedly showed associations between a specific genetic variation and intelligence, they were in for a surprise. After examining the DNA of nearly 10,000 people and conducting 32 different, powerful statistical tests, they found only one significant correlation, even though they expected their sophisticated statistics to yield 10 to 15. They concluded that the earlier findings had been false positives—that any links between the genes in question and IQ were illusory (Chabris et al., 2012).

more highly correlated with those of their birth parents than with those of their biologically unrelated adoptive parents; the higher the birth parents' scores, the higher the child's score is likely to be. As adopted children grow into adolescence, the correlation between their IQ scores and those of their biologically unrelated family members diminishes, and in adulthood, the correlation falls to *zero* (Bouchard, 1997b; Scarr, 1993; Scarr & Weinberg, 1994). This does not mean that adoption has no positive effects; adopted children score higher on IQ tests than do birth siblings who were not adopted, probably because adoptees grow up in a more enriched environment (van IJzendoorn et al., 2005).

The Question of Group Differences

LO 3.5.B Explain why both between-group and within-group variability are important in arguments about group differences in intelligence.

If genes influence individual differences in intelligence, do they also help account for differences between groups, as many people assume? Unfortunately, the history of this issue has been marred by ethnic and class prejudice. Because this question has enormous political and social importance, we are going to examine it closely.

Most of the focus has been on black–white differences in IQ because African American children score lower, on average, than do white children. (The exact numbers are a matter of debate, but in any event, we are talking about *averages*, the distributions of scores for black children and white children overlap considerably.) A few researchers have proposed a genetic explanation of this difference and conclude that there is little point in spending money on programs that try to raise the IQs of low-scoring children, of whatever race (Murray, 2008; Rushton & Jensen, 2005).

Figure 3.8 The Tomato Plant Experiment

In the hypothetical experiment described in the text, even if the differences among plants within each pot were due entirely to genetics, the average differences between pots could be environmental. The same general principle applies to individual and group differences among human beings.

Genetic explanations, however, have a fatal flaw: They use heritability estimates based mainly on white samples to estimate the role of heredity in *group* differences, a procedure that is not valid. This problem sounds pretty technical, but it is really not too difficult to understand, so stay with us.

Consider, first, not people but tomatoes. (Figure 3.8 will help you visualize the following "thought experiment.") Suppose you have a bag of tomato seeds that vary genetically; all things being equal, some will produce tomatoes that are puny and tasteless, and some will produce tomatoes that are plump and delicious. Now you take a bunch of these seeds in your left hand and another bunch from the same bag in your right hand. Although one seed differs genetically from another, there is no *average* difference between the seeds in your left hand and those in your right. You plant the left hand's seeds in pot A, with some enriched soil that you have doctored with nitrogen and other nutrients, and you plant the right hand's seeds in pot B, with soil from which you have extracted nutrients. You sing to pot A and put it in the sun; you ignore pot B and leave it in a dark corner.

When the tomato plants grow, they will vary *within* each pot in terms of height, the number of tomatoes produced, and the size of the tomatoes, purely because of genetic differences. But there will also be an average difference between the plants in pot A and those in pot B: The plants in pot A will be healthier and bear more tomatoes. This difference *between* pots is due entirely to the different soils and the care that has been given to them, even though the heritability of the variation among the plants *within* each pot is 100 percent (Lewontin, 1970, 2001).

The principle is the same for people as it is for tomatoes. Although intellectual differences *within* groups are partly genetic in origin, that does not mean differences *between* groups are genetic. Blacks and whites do not grow up, on the average, in the same "pots" (environments). In fact, some scientists argue that in the United States, the long history of sexual relations between blacks and whites has virtually eliminated genetic differences between them, meaning that any remaining differences are almost exclusively the product of environment (Nisbett, 2009). Because of the legacy of racial discrimination and de facto segregation, black children, as well as Latino and other minority children, often receive far fewer nutrients—literally, in terms of food, and figuratively, in terms of education, encouragement by society, and intellectual opportunities. Ethnic groups also differ in countless cultural ways that affect their performance on IQ tests. And negative stereotypes about ethnic groups may cause members of these groups to doubt their own abilities, become anxious and self-conscious, and perform more poorly than they otherwise would on tests.

Conducting good research on the origins of group differences in IQ is extremely difficult in many countries, including the United States, where racism has affected the lives of even many affluent, successful African Americans. However, the few studies that have overcome past methodological problems fail to reveal any genetic differences between blacks and whites in whatever it is that IQ tests measure. One study found that children fathered by black or white American soldiers in Germany after World War II and reared in similar German communities by similar families did not differ significantly in IQ (Eyferth, 1961). Another showed that contrary to what a genetic theory would predict, degree of African ancestry (which can be roughly estimated from skin color, blood analysis, and genealogy) was not related to measured intelligence (Scarr et al., 1977).

Even among groups popularly thought to be high achievers, purely genetic explanations are unsatisfactory. For instance, although descendants of the Ashkenazi Jews of Europe tend to have higher IQ scores than their non-Jewish white counterparts, their accomplishments exceed what would be expected on the basis of their IQ scores alone (Nisbett et al., 2012). An intelligent reading of the research on intelligence, therefore, does not direct us to conclude that differences among cultural, ethnic, or national groups are permanent, genetically determined, or signs of any group's innate superiority. On the contrary, the research suggests that we should make sure that all children grow up in the best possible soil, with room for the smartest and the slowest to find a place in the sun.

The Environment and Intelligence

LO 3.5.C List four ways that the environment nurtures or thwarts mental ability, and give an example of each.

By now you may be wondering what kinds of environmental "nutrients" hinder intellectual development and what kinds of environmental "nutrients" promote it. Here are some environmental influences associated with reduced mental ability:

- *Poor prenatal care.* If a pregnant woman is malnourished, contracts infections, takes certain drugs, smokes, is exposed to secondhand smoke, or drinks alcohol regularly, her child is at risk of having learning disabilities and a lower IQ.

- *Malnutrition.* The average IQ gap between severely malnourished and well-nourished children can be as high as 20 points (Stoch et al., 1982; Winick, Meyer, & Harris, 1975).

- *Exposure to toxins.* Many children, especially poor and minority children, are exposed to dangerous levels of lead from dust, contaminated soil, lead paint, and old lead pipes, and lead can damage the brain and nervous system. Even children exposed to fairly low levels that are often believed to be "safe" develop attention problems, have lower IQ scores, and do worse in school (Hornung, Lanphear, & Dietrich, 2009; Koller et al., 2004). And children exposed in utero to high levels of pesticides (still legal for spraying on farm fields) later have an IQ that is 7 points lower than in children with the least exposure (Raloff, 2011).

- *Stressful family circumstances.* Factors that predict reduced intellectual competence include, among others, having a father who does not live with the family, a mother with a history of mental illness, parents with limited work skills, and a history of stressful events, such as domestic violence, early in life (Jeon, Buettner, & Hur, 2014; Sameroff et al., 1987). On average, each risk factor reduces a child's IQ score by 4 points. Children with seven risk factors score more than *30 points lower* than those with no risk factors. And when children live in severely disadvantaged neighborhoods, their verbal IQs decline over time, even after they have moved to better areas; the drop is comparable to that seen when a child misses a year of school (Sampson, Sharkey, & Raudenbush, 2008)

In contrast, a healthy and stimulating environment can raise IQ scores, as several intervention studies with at-risk children have shown. Attending a good-quality preschool increases the reading and math skills of children from racial and ethnic minorities, especially if they are not getting much cognitive stimulation elsewhere (Tucker-Drob, 2012). Two important longitudinal studies—the Abecedarian Project and the Child–Parent Center Education Program in Chicago—found that inner-city children who got lots of mental enrichment at home and in preschool showed significant IQ gains and had much better school achievement than did children in a control group (Campbell & Ramey, 1995; Reynolds et al., 2011). In another important study of abandoned children living in Romanian orphanages that provided little stimulation, researchers randomly assigned some children to remain in the orphanages and others to move to good foster homes. By age 4, the fostered children scored dramatically higher on IQ tests than did those left behind. Children who moved before age 2 showed the largest gains, almost 15 points on average. A comparison group of children reared in their biological homes did even better, with average test scores 10 to 20 points higher than those of the foster children (Nelson et al., 2007). (Since this study was done, Romania has stopped institutionalizing abandoned children younger than 2 unless they are seriously disabled.)

Severe poverty, exposure to toxic materials, run-down neighborhoods, and stressful family circumstances can all have a negative impact on children's cognitive development and IQ.

Environmental stimulation can contribute to intellectual development. Playing a musical instrument, taking acting classes, or joining a robotics league are activities that can stimulate attention, memory, and motor skills, which in turn can help sharpen intelligence.

Figure 3.9 Climbing IQ Scores

Raw scores on IQ tests have been rising in developed countries for many decades at a rate much too steep to be accounted for by genetic changes. Because test norms are periodically readjusted to set the average score at 100, most people are unaware of the increase. On this graph, average scores are calibrated according to 1989 norms. As you can see, performance was much lower in 1918 than in 1989.

Credit: Data from Horgan (1995).

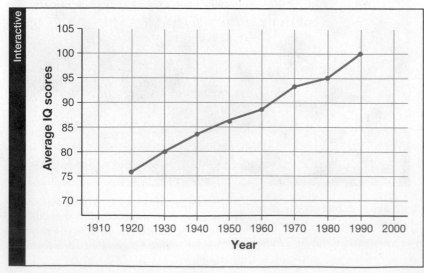

Although no single activity is going to turn anyone into a genius, certain experiences do appear to contribute to overall intelligence. In general, children's mental abilities improve when their parents talk to them about many topics and describe things accurately and fully, encourage them to think things through, read to them, and expect them to do well. A child's abilities also improve when the child's peers value and strive for intellectual achievement (Harris, 2009). Some kinds of enrichment classes may also help. When Canadian researchers randomly assigned first graders to weekly piano, singing, or drama lessons during the school year, or to a control group that received no extracurricular lessons, those children who learned to play the piano or sing showed an average IQ increase of 7 points by the end of the school year, compared to 4.3 points in the other groups. This difference was not large, but it was statistically significant (Schellenberg, 2004). The music lessons may have helped the children pay attention, use their memories, and hone their fine-motor skills, thus contributing to development of brain areas involved in intelligence.

Perhaps the best evidence for the importance of environmental influences on intelligence is the fact that in developed countries, IQ scores (as well as scores on related tests) have been climbing steadily for several generations (Flynn, 1987, 2013); genes cannot possibly have changed enough to account for these findings (see Figure 3.9). What, then, has caused this rise? One possibility is improvements in the education, health care, diets, and job opportunities of the poorest, lowest-scoring people, which increases the overall mean. If that is so, we would expect to see large and rapid increases in developing countries, and so we do: In Kenya, IQ scores of rural 6- to 8-year-old children jumped about 11 points between 1984 and 1998, the fastest rise in a group's average IQ scores ever reported (Daley et al., 2003). But even in a highly developed country such as the United States, the scores of children in the top 5 percent of achievement tests are still climbing (Wai & Putallaz, 2011).

We see, then, that although heredity may provide the range of a child's intellectual potential—a Homer Simpson can never become an Albert Einstein—many other factors affect where in that range the child will fall.

Beyond Nature versus Nurture

LO 3.5.D Explain how both nurture and nature play an interactive role in shaping behavior.

Throughout this chapter, we have seen that heredity and environment always interact to produce the qualities typical of human beings in general and the mix of qualities that makes each of us unique. Genetically influenced traits can affect how we respond to a specific environment and which environments we find most rewarding or compatible; the environment in turn influences the genome, through its effects on mutations and epigenetic changes. Human behavior is responsive to a constantly changing network of interlinked influences, both biological and environmental, plus the additional, unpredictable spice of chance and luck. The development of a human being (or other animal) is the result of a constant dialogue between the genome and its environment (Plomin et al., 2013; Zhang & Meaney, 2010).

The key lesson to be learned from this dynamic interaction is that we can no more speak of genes or the environment "causing" personality, intelligence, or behavior in a straightforward way than we can speak of butter, sugar, or flour individually causing the taste of a cake (Lewontin, Rose, & Kamin, 1984). Many people do speak that way, however, out of a desire to make things clearer than they actually are, and sometimes to justify prejudices about ethnicity, gender, or class.

An unstated assumption in many debates about nature and nurture is that the world would be a better place if certain kinds of genes prevailed. This assumption overlooks the fact that nature loves genetic diversity, not similarity. The ability of any species to survive depends on such diversity. If every penguin, porpoise, or person had exactly the same genetic strengths and weaknesses, these species could not survive major changes in the environment; a new virus or a change in climate would wipe out the entire group. With diversity, at least some penguins, porpoises, or people have a chance of making it.

Psychological diversity is adaptive, too. Each of us has something valuable to contribute, whether it is artistic talent, academic ability, creativity, social skill, athletic prowess, a sense of humor, mechanical aptitude, practical wisdom, a social conscience, or the energy to get things done. Our complicated, fast-moving world requires all of these qualities if we are to survive as communities and thrive as individuals.

JOURNAL PROMPT 3.5

Thinking Critically—Analyze Assumptions and Biases: Most behavioral-genetics studies show the heritability of intelligence to be high. A popular book argues that heredity must play a similarly large role in average IQ differences among ethnic groups. What's wrong with the assumption behind that reasoning?

Quiz for Module 3.5

1. A researcher interested in the heritability of intelligence would probably examine a group of people's IQ scores, or *intelligence quotients*. How are IQ scores distributed in the population?

    a. Scores average 400 on an 800-point scale, with most scores falling between 300 and 500.

    b. Scores typically range from 100 to 200, with scores below 100 indicating mental deficiencies.

    c. Scores near an average of 100 are most common, whereas very high or very low scores are rare.

    d. Scores near an average of 85 are most common, whereas scores higher than 85 are rare.

2. Which siblings show the highest degree of correlation in their IQ scores?

    a. Fraternal twins reared together in the same household

    b. Identical twins reared together in the same household

    c. Nontwin biological siblings reared together in the same household

    d. Identical twins reared apart in different households

3. Thinking critically about between-group and within-group differences in intelligence, and the hereditary and environmental influences that contribute to those differences, would lead to which conclusion?

    a. Intelligence test differences among cultural, ethnic, or national groups only reflect biases in the way the intelligence tests are constructed and administered.

    b. Intelligence tests measure innate abilities; therefore, any differences between groups must reflect differences in genetic inheritance between those groups.

    c. Intelligence is a result of a person's environment because genetic material is roughly the same across most groups of humans.

    d. Intelligence test differences among cultural, ethnic, or national groups are not permanent, genetically determined, or evidence of any group's innate superiority.

4. What conclusion can we reach about environmental hindrances to mental ability, such as poor prenatal care, exposure to toxins, or stressful family circumstances?

    a. Lack of environmental "nutrients" can lead to IQ score gaps of many points when comparing children raised in deprived environments to those who are not,

    b. Environmental hindrances affect intellectual development between the ages of birth and 5 years, but after that deprived children rebound quickly and resume normal intellectual functioning.

    c. The presence of even a single environmental hazard will decrease IQ scores by 12 points.

    d. Environmental hindrances have less of an impact on children with strong inherited mental agility, compared to children with weaker genetic material.

5. After reading this chapter, what's the correct conclusion to reach regarding the effects of heredity and the environment on shaping a human being?

    a. "Nature before nurture"

    b. "Nature versus nurture"

    c. "Nature or nurture"

    d. "Nature and nurture"

Taking Psychology with You

Should You Have Genetic Testing?

Imagine that you have been feeling depressed and you go to a clinical psychologist for help. The psychologist interviews you, gives you a battery of psychological tests, lets you talk about your problems—and then has your blood drawn to check your DNA, to find out if you have a genetic predisposition for depression.

You have your blood drawn? Right now, this scenario is hypothetical, but perhaps not for long. Genetic testing can already identify DNA markers that indicate an increased risk of developing many physical diseases. Eventually, the same may be true for learning disabilities and emotional disorders. Testing now relies on genome-wide associations, but many geneticists expect whole-genome mapping to become a standard tool in the coming years. Although it took the Human Genome Project several years and billions of dollars to produce the first map of the human genome, a map of an individual's genome can now be produced in hours for just several thousand dollars, and the price is expected to drop much further. Francis Collins (2010), former director of the Human Genome Project, believes that whole-genome mapping is likely to become part of newborn screening in just a few years.

The growing popularity of genetic testing raises many questions. Such testing is beginning to provide an invaluable tool for predicting how a person will respond to a particular medication, and can also help scientists hone in on the causes of specific medical conditions. But except for diseases like Huntington's, which is caused by a single variant, a genetic test cannot tell you that you *will* get a disease; it can only tell you your risk relative to that in the general population. You could have double the usual risk, yet that risk could still be quite low—a jump from 1.5 percent to 3 percent is "double" the risk, but still extremely rare.

Would you want to be tested for a gene that moderately increases the risk of developing Alzheimer's disease, which affects many people as they age and is currently not curable? What about a disorder that might or might not become symptomatic, or one that could be easily treated? What if the disorder in question were depression? And how would you feel about being tested for a gene that indicates a slight increase in the risk of dying early? Would you want to know so that you could plan accordingly or make lifestyle changes, or would you rather let life, and death, take their own course?

Consider, too, some questions raised by prenatal genetic screening. Pregnant women and their partners are often tested to determine whether they are carrying genes that are likely to condemn their child to a fatal or painful disease. When the test results are positive, many choose to abort the pregnancy. But what if you could be tested for a gene that slightly increases your future child's risk of developing schizophrenia, drug addiction, or autism? Or growing up gay? Or being short? Or having a reading disability? If you had that information, what would you do with it (Khan et al., 2014)?

In coming years, as noninvasive methods of genetic testing such as blood tests and saliva analysis become widespread, all of us are going to have to think long and hard about such questions. You can use information from this chapter to evaluate the pros and cons of such testing for yourself or a family member. Here are some things to keep in mind:

Genes are not destiny. You learned in this chapter that most human traits are influenced by many genes interacting with many environmental factors. As a result, genes do not *determine* most traits and diseases; they simply affect the probability of developing a particular trait or disease. That is why knowing that you have markers for one or two genes that may contribute slightly or moderately to a trait or disorder does not necessarily tell you much in practical terms.

Genetic information could be used to discriminate against you. Critics of genetic testing worry that insurance companies will refuse coverage to adults and children who are currently healthy but whose DNA reveals that they have some genetic predisposition for developing a physical or psychological disorder later in life. Employers may also be reluctant to hire them. Some countries—such as the United States, the United Kingdom, Finland, and New Zealand—have laws, codes, or other guidelines to protect the privacy of genetic information. But some bioethicists worry that these laws are not strong enough and are not keeping up with the rapid advances in genetic testing.

Knowing your genetic risk does not necessarily tell you what to do about it. If your child has a physical disorder called phenylketonuria (PKU), which prevents the body from assimilating protein and causes mental retardation, the solution is

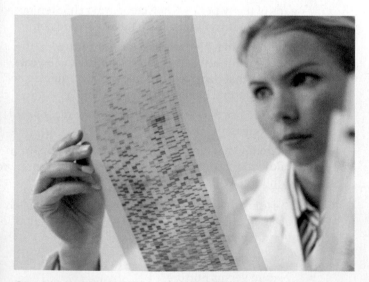

Genetic testing can reveal information that a person may or may not want to know. What's your view of the pros and cons of such testing?

obvious: Limit the intake of protein. (Children in most developed countries are screened for PKU at birth.) But in the case of behavioral, cognitive, or emotional problems, the answer may not be so straightforward. Often we simply don't yet know how to prevent problems that have a genetic component. Or many possible approaches exist and we don't know which one is best.

Genetic testing can be liberating or stigmatizing.   Knowing that a condition or trait is "not your fault" may help you live with it. On the positive side, knowing that your child's autism is genetic and not caused by bad parenting or vaccination can keep you from feeling unnecessary guilt. On the negative side, genetic testing can activate prejudices against anyone with "undesirable" looks or abilities. In the past, such prejudices led to horrifying efforts to "improve" the species through forced sterilization of low-IQ people—and not only in Nazi Germany. From the beginning of the 20th century until the mid-1960s, thousands of mentally ill and developmentally delayed Americans were sterilized against their will (Bruinius, 2006).

Defenders of genetic testing answer that the goal of prenatal screening is not to improve the human species; it is to relieve the suffering of parents and children, and therefore prospective parents should not feel guilty for taking advantage of this technology (Cowan, 2008). But to some social critics, prenatal testing for run-of-the-mill human qualities reflects a view of children as products to be perfected instead of as individuals to be appreciated for who they are (Sandel, 2007).

Knowing about a genetic disposition can create a premature diagnosis or a self-fulfilling prophecy.   If parents and school officials know that a child is at risk of developing a learning disorder, they may treat the child as cognitively impaired even though the child has not shown any signs of a problem. If they know that a child carries a gene associated with an increased risk of aggressiveness, they may come to think of the child as a "bad seed" even if the child has never had behavioral problems. If a person is aware of having a genetic predisposition toward depression, he or she may not develop the skills to cope with setbacks, deciding incorrectly that "There's nothing I can do."

We hope we have given you some things to think about. Under what circumstances, if any, would you want to undergo a genetic test, and why? And how might this information change your life?

Shared Writing Prompt

There are currently more than 2,000 genetic tests that can be performed, ranging from those that establish paternity to those that screen embryos for disease to those that help determine which type of medication might be best suited for an individual. Think about what you've learned about genetics and genetic testing, then answer this question: What are your own personal limits on what you'd find acceptable or unacceptable for genetic testing? For example, would you want to be tested only for a disorder that is currently known to be fatal if it develops, or would you scale the limits back a bit and be tested for a condition that might make life mildly unpleasant? Would you draw the line even earlier, and be tested for what are essentially lifestyle choices, such as the probability of your offspring having blue or brown eyes? Or would you reject gathering information about your genetic propensities altogether?

Summary

Unlocking the Secrets of Genes

LO 3.1.A   Explain how genes, chromosomes, DNA, and genomes all relate to one another.

In general, *behavioral geneticists* study our differences, such as those originating in heredity. *Genes*, the basic units of heredity, are located on *chromosomes*, which consist of strands of *DNA*. Our genes, together with noncoding DNA, make up the human *genome*. Most human traits depend on more than one gene pair, which makes tracking down the genetic contributions to a trait extremely difficult. However, advances in technology now permit scientists to carry out *genome-wide association studies*, examining variations in many DNA elements at once, and even *whole-genome sequencing*, which examines the entire 3 billion base pairs of DNA. But locating a gene does not automatically tell us what it does or how it does it, or how multiple genes interact and influence behavior.

LO 3.1.B   Explain why the study of epigenetics offers an important avenue for understanding the genetic components of thought and behavior.

The genome changes over time, because of *mutations* that arise before or after birth, and because of *epigenetic changes* that affect the expression (activity) of specific genes without altering the sequence of bases in those genes. Mutations and epigenetic changes can be affected by environmental factors.

The Genetics of Similarity

LO 3.2.A   Explain how natural selection contributes to changes in gene frequencies in a population.

In general, *evolutionary psychologists* study our commonalities and argue that many fundamental human similarities can be traced to the processes of *evolution*, especially the process of *natural selection*. They draw inferences about the behavioral tendencies that might have been selected because they helped our forebears solve survival problems and enhanced reproductive fitness; they then conduct research to see if such tendencies actually exist throughout the world.

LO 3.2.B   List and describe five innate human characteristics.

Many evolutionary psychologists believe that the mind is not a general-purpose computer, but instead evolved as a collection of specialized *mental modules* to handle specific survival problems. Among the candidates for such modules are inborn reflexes, an attraction to novelty, a motive to explore and manipulate objects, an impulse to play, and the capacity for certain basic cognitive skills, including a rudimentary understanding of number. However, because some behavior or trait exists does not necessarily mean that it is adaptive or the product of natural selection.

Our Human Heritage: Courtship and Mating

LO 3.3.A   Compare the sexual strategies of females and males, according to the sociobiological perspective.

Sociobiologists and evolutionary psychologists argue that males and females have evolved different sexual and courtship strategies in response to survival problems faced in the distant past. In this view, it has been adaptive for males to be promiscuous, to be attracted to young partners, and to want sexual novelty; and for females to be monogamous, to be choosy about partners, and to prefer security to novelty.

LO 3.3.B   Discuss four challenges to the evolutionary view of human mating strategies.

Critics argue that evolutionary explanations of infidelity and monogamy are based on simplistic stereotypes of gender differences; that they rely too heavily on answers to questionnaires, which often do not reflect real-life choices; that convenience samples used in questionnaire studies are not necessarily representative of people in general; and that the evolutionary emphasis on the Pleistocene Age may not be warranted. Moreover, our ancestors probably did not have a wide range of partners to choose from; evidence suggests that what may have evolved is mate selection based on similarity and proximity. The central issue dividing evolutionary theorists and their critics is the length of the "genetic leash."

The Genetics of Difference

LO 3.4.A   Explain what heritability refers to, and discuss three important facts about heritability that should be kept in mind when discussing genetic contributions to behavior.

Heritability refers to the extent to which differences in a trait or ability within a group of individuals are accounted for by genetic differences. Heritability estimates do not apply to specific individuals or to differences between groups. They apply only to differences within a particular group living in a particular environment; for example, heritability is higher for children in affluent families than in impoverished ones. And even highly heritable traits can often be modified by the environment.

LO 3.4.B   Outline the basic design of a heritability study that involves twins and adoptees.

Behavioral geneticists often study differences among individuals by using data from studies of adopted children and of *identical* and *fraternal twins*. By comparing the genetic and environmental "overlap" across these groups, researchers can estimate the heritability of a trait.

Our Human Diversity: The Case of Intelligence

LO 3.5.A   Discuss the extent to which intelligence may be heritable.

Heritability estimates for intelligence (as measured by tests of one's *intelligence quotient*, or IQ) average about .40 to .50 for children and adolescents and .60 to .80 for adults. Identical twins are more similar in IQ-test performance than fraternal twins, and adopted children's scores correlate more highly with those of their biological parents than with those of their nonbiological relatives. These results do not mean that genes determine intelligence; the remaining variance in IQ scores must be due largely to environmental influences.

LO 3.5.B   Explain why both between-group and within-group variability are important in arguments about group differences in intelligence.

It is a mistake to draw conclusions about *group* differences from heritability estimates based on differences *within* a group. The available evidence fails to support genetic explanations of black–white differences in performance on IQ tests.

LO 3.5.C   List four ways that the environment nurtures or thwarts mental ability, and give an example of each.

Environmental factors such as poor prenatal care, malnutrition, exposure to toxins, and stressful family circumstances are associated with lower performance on intelligence tests. Conversely, a healthy and stimulating environment, as well as certain kinds of enrichment activities, can improve performance. IQ scores have been rising in many countries for several generations, most likely because of improved education, better health, and the increase in jobs requiring abstract thought.

LO 3.5.D   Explain how both nurture and nature play an interactive role in shaping behavior.

The interaction between genes and environment is far more complex than anyone previously imagined. Genes influence which environments people find most congenial, and environmental factors influence the genome by their effects on mutations and epigenetic changes. Development of a person is the result of a dynamic dialogue between genes and the environment—plus the addition of chance events. Genetic and environmental influences blend and become indistinguishable in the development of any one person.

Chapter 3 Quiz

1. Chromosomes consist of threadlike strands of:

   a. CNA molecules

   b. RNA molecules

   c. DNA molecules

   d. Ribovax

2. A segment of DNA that varies across individuals, has a known location on a chromosome, and can function as a landmark for a gene implicated in a physical or mental condition is known as a:

   a. Genetic marker

   b. Part–whole genome

   c. Part–whole gene

   d. Genome

3. Epigenetics is an exciting new field of study that has vast implications for our understanding of how genetic information influences behavior. What is the process of epigenetics like?

   a. Genetic material is like a software program that needs an environmental setting to serve as a hardware platform; when the two combine, epigenesis takes place.

   b. "Epigenes" are a synonym for "mutations," and mutations cause genetic material to transform for a limited time and for a limited purpose.

   c. Segments of DNA get clipped from ribostatin molecules, and those segments get recombined to produce new genetic material.

   d. Chemical molecules that regulate the activity of genes act like software that instructs genetic hardware to become active or inactive.

4. _____ refers to a change in gene frequencies within a population, whereas _____ refers to a process by which some individuals with genetically influenced traits (that are adaptive to a particular environment) survive and reproduce in greater numbers.

   a. Evolution / natural selection

   b. Natural selection / evolution

   c. Evolution / modular punctuation

   d. Epigenesis / natural selection

5. What is an example of an innate reflex that infants are born with, and that contributes to survival?

   a. Crawling

   b. Cooing

   c. Sucking

   d. Pointing

6. Human babies can seem downright annoying at times. They grab at whatever is in reach, they bang on tables and chairs, and they're fascinated by shaking rattles or squeaking toys. Why are these behaviors to be expected, and in fact why are they adaptive?

   a. These behaviors signal distress to a caregiver, so that needy infants can stay alive.

   b. A desire to explore and manipulate objects is an innate human characteristic that contributes to mastering one's environment.

   c. Babies aren't socialized to the rules and expectations of the societies in which they live, therefore these actions allow parents to correct unwanted behaviors.

   d. Self-expression is a fundamental human drive, possibly genetic, so babies are just enacting a preprogrammed sequence of behaviors.

7. Why would men report desiring a younger female mate, according to sociobiological and evolutionary explanations?

   a. It is adaptive for males to seek females with material resources, and younger females generally have greater opportunities for that than do older females.

   b. Males want to know that a potential mate will stay with them to help with childrearing, and younger females would maximize that time span.

   c. It is adaptive for males to want young and fertile females, and to inseminate as many females as possible.

   d. Males know that a younger female will be closer in age to their offspring, and therefore be better caregivers because of those psychological and behavioral similarities.

8. In many societies men are expected to be promiscuous and aggressive, whereas women are thought to be choosy, chaste, and coy. How do these conceptions cloud our understanding of sex differences in dating and mating?

   a. Most women and men are equally promiscuous in the majority of societies.

   b. The genetic leash is actually the same length for both women and men.

   c. There's no evolutionary reason why women and men should act in these ways.

   d. Stereotypes and expectations for behavior are not always the same as actual behavior.

9. The study of sex differences in mating preferences and sexual behavior can be hampered by _____ samples and perhaps enhanced by _____ samples.

   a. Representative / convenience

   b. Convenience / representative

   c. Haphazard / convenience

   d. Unbiased / representative

10. When behavioral geneticists compute heritability, what does it refer to?

    a. An estimate of the contribution of genetic factors to a given trait divided by the contribution of environmental factors to that same trait.

    b. The extent to which a given individual's behaviors can be explained as being due to genetic factors.

    c. The proportion of the total variance in a trait that is attributable to genetic variation within a group.

    d. A baseline estimate of the percent of variance in a trait that is due to unchanging, genetically based, inherited factors.

11. How does the study of adopted children (and their biological and adoptive parents) shed light on heritability?

   a. Adopted children share genetics (but not environment) in common with their biological parents, but share environment (but not genetics) in common with their adoptive parents.

   b. Adopted children can be located easily through adoption services, so their biological lineage is easier to determine, which in turn allows a computation of heritability.

   c. Adopted children tend to be adopted by parents who share the same values, goals, and interests as the children; therefore, the similarity between parents and child can be estimated.

   d. Adopted children may or may not share both genetics and environment in common with their adoptive parents; by finding these special cases researchers can estimate heritability.

12. What evidence indicates that the kind of intellectual abilities measured on intelligence tests may be partly heritable?

   a. Common observation illustrates that smart parents generally have smart children.

   b. Correlations among intelligence test scores of people who share varying degrees of genetic overlap form a clear pattern.

   c. Intelligence tests measure innate abilities, and an innate ability would be produced by genetics rather than by the environment.

   d. The effects of the environment on intellectual abilities account for less than 5 percent of the total variance in intelligence test scores.

13. Joey, Janie, and Julie are members of the Tuff Darts, a local youth organization. Bobby, Betty, and Bernie are members of the Wild Bunch, a rival group. On average, the Tuff Darts are smarter than the Wild Bunch. However, Janie is smarter than Julie, and Bobby is smarter than either of them. It's therefore difficult to predict which group will excel at the upcoming Intellectual Decathlon. What general principle does this scenario illustrate?

   a. Between-group differences and within-group differences both need to be taken into account when explaining behavior.

   b. Within-group differences are generally smaller than between-group differences when explaining behavior.

   c. Between-group differences are generally larger than within-group differences when explaining behavior.

   d. Within-group differences are generally larger than between-group differences when explaining behavior.

14. Imagine that both Mick and Rusty each were born with 20 units of "genetic intelligence." Mick grows up in an environment full of books, stimulation, and parental attention. Rusty grows up in an environment full of monotony, malnutrition, and parental neglect. Despite their equivalence on "genetic intelligence," what would you predict about Mick and Rusty's intellectual development?

   a. Both Mick and Rusty are likely to show comparable performance on intelligence tests and other measures of mental ability.

   b. Rusty is likely to show better performance on intelligence tests and other measures of mental ability than is Mick.

   c. Mick is likely to show worse performance on intelligence tests and other measures of mental ability than is Rusty.

   d. Mick is likely to show better performance on intelligence tests and other measures of mental ability than is Rusty.

15. Genetics and the environment interact to produce behavior, although

   a. The environment always has a larger impact than genetics

   b. Genetics always has a larger impact than the environment

   c. Determining the relative contributions of each source can sometimes be difficult

   d. For some individuals one source explains behavior more completely than the other source.

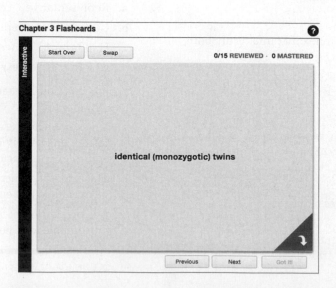

Chapter 4
The Brain and Nervous System

◀ Listen to the Audio

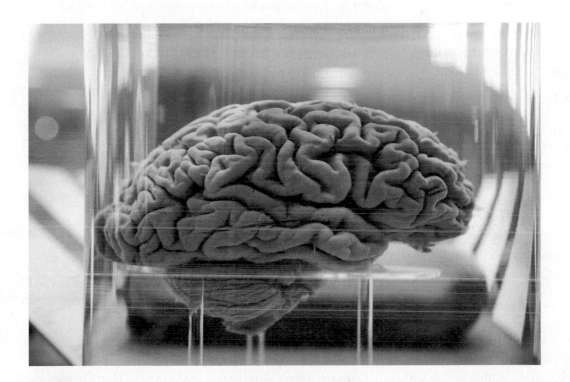

Learning Objectives

LO 4.1.A List the major structures of the central nervous system, and describe their primary functions.

LO 4.1.B List the major structures and major divisions of the peripheral nervous system, and describe their primary functions.

LO 4.2.A Compare the functions of neurons and glial cells in the nervous system.

LO 4.2.B Describe each of the three main parts of a neuron, and explain their functions.

LO 4.2.C Explain how stem cells contribute to the process of neurogenesis.

LO 4.2.D Outline the process by which neurons communicate with each other, and explain the basic functions of the synapse, action potential, synaptic vesicles, and neurotransmitters.

LO 4.2.E Summarize the effects of some of the main neurotransmitters in the brain, and list four hormones that influence behavior.

LO 4.3.A Describe three techniques researchers use for intervening in the brain and observing the behavior that results.

LO 4.3.B Describe five techniques researchers use for intervening in behavior and observing the effects on the brain.

LO 4.4.A List and describe three main structures in the brain stem, explain the primary functions each structure performs, and discuss the processes controlled by the cerebellum.

LO 4.4.B Describe the structure, function, and location of the thalamus.

LO 4.4.C Describe the structure, function, and location of the hypothalamus and pituitary gland.

LO 4.4.D Describe the structure, function, and location of the amygdala.

LO 4.4.E Describe the structure, function, and location of the hippocampus.

LO 4.4.F Describe the structure of the cerebrum, and explain the function of the corpus callosum.

LO 4.4.G Sketch the location of each of the lobes of the cerebral cortex, and explain the major functions each lobe performs, with particular reference to the prefrontal cortex.

LO 4.5.A Discuss the basic format of a split-brain experiment, and describe what the results of such experiments reveal about the functioning of the cerebral hemispheres.

LO 4.5.B Describe why the two hemispheres of the brain are allies rather than opposites.

LO 4.6.A Define neural plasticity, and summarize some of the main evidence that the brain has the ability to change in response to new experiences.

LO 4.6.B Summarize five cautions surrounding whether sex differences in anatomical brain size are linked to sex differences in behavior.

Ask questions . . . be willing to wonder

Can the experiences you have change your brain?

How can brain mapping mislead as well as inform?

Are people either "left-brained" or "right-brained"?

Are there "his" and "hers" brains?

After suffering damage to the right side of his brain, a Swiss stroke patient developed a puzzling symptom. Although the left side of his body was weak and he had trouble seeing objects in his left field of vision, what concerned him most was the blandness of the hospital food. The stroke had left the man obsessed with fine dining, a phenomenon later dubbed "gourmand syndrome." In his diary, the patient wrote, "It is time for . . . a good sausage with hash browns or some spaghetti Bolognese, or risotto and a breaded cutlet, nicely decorated, or a scallop of game in cream sauce with spaetzle." After recovering, he quit his job as a political journalist and became a food columnist (Regard & Landis, 1997).

Julie appears perfectly normal when you first meet her, but it soon becomes apparent that she lives in a bewildering place: the eternal present. Since suffering brain damage when a freight train hit her car, Julie has been unable to recall people and events from either the distant past or a few minutes ago. She cannot remember her daughter, who died in the accident. She knows she has a husband, but he must be reintroduced to her whenever she sees him.

She can cook or make a phone call, but when she tries to read, the words from the start of the paragraph vanish by the time she gets to the end. She keeps meticulous notes about her day, but she feels she is faking her way through life (Mason, 2008).

These cases, and thousands like them, teach us that the 3-pound organ inside our skulls provides the bedrock for everything we do and think. When injury or disease affects the brain's functioning, life is inevitably altered physically, emotionally, or mentally. Sometimes the changes are subtle and even benign, as in the case of "gourmand syndrome." All too often, as in Julie's case, they are not.

Meanwhile, discoveries about the brain constantly make headlines, as new research is announced and old puzzles begin to be solved. Consider these examples:

- A sleeping pill has restored awareness in some patients who spent several years in a "minimally conscious state" (which leaves the brain more intact than does a "persistent vegetative state," from which there is no recovery). In such patients, awareness often waxes and wanes. But with the drug zolpidem, some people recover much greater awareness over time. The pill would put a healthy person to sleep, but, surprisingly, it seems to arouse certain people with brain damage and help the brain to function more normally (Chatelle et al., 2014).

- A brain-monitoring technique has allowed researchers to recreate visual images based on brain-wave activity (Nishimoto et al., 2011). By measuring how the brain responds while watching hours and hours of YouTube videos, researchers were able to reverse the process, and use the pattern of brain activity to predict which new images a person was viewing—a sort of "mind reading" based on the electrochemical activity of the brain.

- Recently, scientists at the Johns Hopkins University Applied Physics Laboratory fitted a man who had both of his arms amputated at the shoulder with dual-arm robotic prosthetics.

Les Baugh had both of his arms amputated at the shoulder as a result of an electrical accident years ago. Working with researchers at Johns Hopkins University, he was able to control a pair of prosthetic arms using only his thoughts. Signals emanating from his brain allowed him to grasp and manipulate objects for the first time in 40 years.

The man could move his robotic prosthetic shoulders, elbows, and wrists and grasp objects, all through the use of signals emanating from his brain. This and other research raise hope that "neural prosthetics" will one day help paralyzed and incapacitated people.

Neuroscientists in psychology and other disciplines study the brain and the rest of the nervous system in hopes of gaining a better understanding of normal behavior and of the outer reaches of what is possible for this organ. *Cognitive neuroscientists* explore the biological foundations of consciousness, perception, memory, and language; *social neuroscientists* focus on processes such as attachment and attitudes; *affective neuroscientists* study the nervous system's involvement in emotion, motivation, and stress; and *behavioral neuroscientists* study the biology of such basic processes as learning, conditioning, eating, and sex. You can see that this list covers basically everything that human beings feel and do. In this chapter, we will examine the structure of the brain and the rest of the nervous system as background for our later discussions of these and other topics.

At this very moment, your own brain, assisted by other parts of your nervous system, is busily taking in these words. Whether you are excited, curious, or bored, your brain is registering some sort of emotional reaction. As you continue reading, your brain will (we hope) store away much of the information in this chapter. Later in the day, your brain may enable you to smell a flower, climb the stairs, greet a friend, solve a problem, or laugh at a joke. But the brain's most startling accomplishment is its knowledge that it is doing all these things. This self-awareness makes brain research different from the study of anything else in the universe. Scientists must use the cells, biochemistry, and circuitry of their own brains to understand the cells, biochemistry, and circuitry of brains in general.

William Shakespeare called the brain "the soul's frail dwelling house." Actually, this miraculous organ is more like the main room in a house filled with many alcoves and passageways—the "house" being the nervous system as a whole. Before we can understand the windows, walls, and furniture of this house, we need to become acquainted with the overall floor plan.

The Nervous System: A Basic Blueprint

The function of a nervous system is to gather and process information, produce responses to stimuli, and coordinate the workings of different cells. Even the lowly jellyfish and the humble earthworm have the beginnings of such a system. In very simple organisms that do little more than move, eat, and eliminate waste, the "system" may be no more than one or two nerve cells. In human beings, who do such complex things as dance, cook, and take psychology courses, the nervous system contains billions of cells. Scientists divide this intricate network into two main parts: the central nervous system and the peripheral (outlying) nervous system (see Figure 4.1). For additional information, watch the video *The Basics: How the Brain Works 1*.

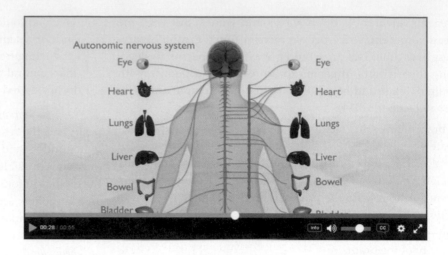

Figure 4.1 The Central and Peripheral Nervous Systems

The central nervous system includes the brain and the spinal cord. The peripheral nervous system consists of 43 pairs of nerves that transmit information to and from the central nervous system. Twelve pairs of cranial nerves in the head enter the brain directly; 31 pairs of spinal nerves enter the spinal cord at the spaces between the vertebrae.

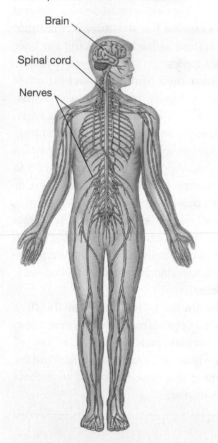

central nervous system (CNS)

The portion of the nervous system consisting of the brain and spinal cord.

spinal cord

A collection of neurons and supportive tissue running from the base of the brain down the center of the back, protected by a column of bones (the spinal column).

peripheral nervous system (PNS)

All portions of the nervous system outside the brain and spinal cord; it includes sensory and motor nerves.

The Central Nervous System

LO 4.1.A   List the major structures of the central nervous system, and describe their primary functions.

The **central nervous system (CNS)** receives, processes, interprets, and stores incoming sensory information—information about tastes, sounds, smells, colors, pressure on the skin, the state of internal organs, and so forth. It also sends out messages destined for muscles, glands, and internal organs. The CNS is usually conceptualized as having two components: the brain, which we will consider in detail later, and the **spinal cord**, which is an extension of the brain. The spinal cord runs from the base of the brain down the center of the back, protected by a column of bones (the spinal column), and it acts as a bridge between the brain and the parts of the body below the neck.

The spinal cord produces some behaviors on its own without any help from the brain. These *spinal reflexes* are automatic, requiring no conscious effort. If you accidentally touch a hot iron, you will immediately pull your hand away, even before your brain has had a chance to register what has happened. Nerve impulses bring a message to the spinal cord (hot!), and the spinal cord immediately sends out a command via other nerve impulses, telling muscles in your arm to contract and to pull your hand away from the iron. (Reflexes above the neck, such as sneezing and blinking, involve the lower part of the brain rather than the spinal cord.)

The neural circuits underlying many spinal reflexes are linked to neural pathways that run up and down the spinal cord, to and from the brain. Because of these connections, reflexes can sometimes be influenced by thoughts and emotions. An example is erection in men, a spinal reflex that can be inhibited by anxiety or distracting thoughts and initiated by erotic thoughts. Moreover, some reflexes can be brought under conscious control. If you concentrate, you may be able to keep your knee from jerking when it is tapped, as it normally would. Similarly, most men can learn to voluntarily delay ejaculation, another spinal reflex. (Yes, they can.)

The Peripheral Nervous System

LO 4.1.B   List the major structures and major divisions of the peripheral nervous system, and describe their primary functions.

The **peripheral nervous system (PNS)** handles the central nervous system's input and output. It contains all portions of the nervous system outside the brain and spinal cord, right down to the nerves in the tips of the fingers and toes. If your brain could not collect information about the world by means of a peripheral nervous system, it would be like a radio without a receiver. In the peripheral nervous system, *sensory nerves* carry messages from special receptors in the skin, muscles, and other internal and external sense organs to the spinal cord, which sends them along to the brain. These nerves put us in touch with both the outside world and the activities of our own bodies. *Motor nerves* carry orders from the central nervous system to muscles, glands, and internal organs. They enable us to move, and they cause glands to contract and to secrete substances, including chemical messengers called *hormones*.

Scientists further divide the peripheral nervous system into two parts: the somatic (bodily) nervous system and the autonomic (self-governing) nervous system. The **somatic nervous system**, sometimes called the *skeletal nervous system*, consists of nerves that are connected to sensory receptors—cells that enable you to sense the world—and also to the skeletal muscles that permit voluntary action. When you feel a bug on your arm, or when you turn off a light or write your name, your somatic system is active. The **autonomic nervous system** regulates the functioning of blood vessels, glands, and internal (visceral) organs such as the bladder, stomach, and heart. When you see someone you have a crush on and your heart pounds, your hands get sweaty, and your cheeks feel hot, you can blame your autonomic nervous system.

The autonomic nervous system is itself divided into two parts: the **sympathetic nervous system** and the **parasympathetic nervous system**. These two parts work together, but in opposing ways, to adjust the body to changing circumstances (see Figure 4.2). The sympathetic system acts like the accelerator of a car, mobilizing the body for action and an output of energy. It makes you blush, sweat, and breathe more deeply, and it pushes up your heart rate and blood pressure. When you are in a situation that requires you to fight, flee, or cope, the sympathetic nervous system whirls into action. The parasympathetic system is more like a brake: It does not stop the body, of course, but it does tend to slow things down and keep them running smoothly. It enables the body to conserve and store energy. If you have to jump out of the way of a speeding motorcyclist, sympathetic nerves increase your heart rate. Afterward, parasympathetic nerves slow it down again and keep its rhythm regular.

somatic nervous system

The subdivision of the peripheral nervous system that connects to sensory receptors and to skeletal muscles; sometimes called the *skeletal nervous system*.

autonomic nervous system

The subdivision of the peripheral nervous system that regulates the internal organs and glands.

sympathetic nervous system

The subdivision of the autonomic nervous system that mobilizes bodily resources and increases the output of energy during emotion and stress.

parasympathetic nervous system

The subdivision of the autonomic nervous system that operates during relaxed states and that conserves energy.

Figure 4.2 The Autonomic Nervous System

In general, the sympathetic division of the autonomic nervous system prepares the body to expend energy, and the parasympathetic division restores and conserves energy. Sympathetic nerve fibers exit from areas of the spinal cord shown in orange in this illustration; parasympathetic fibers exit from the base of the brain and from spinal-cord areas shown in blue.

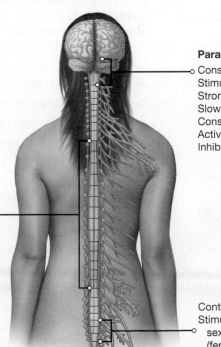

Parasympathetic Division
Constricts pupils
Stimulates tear glands
Strongly stimulates salivation
Slows heartbeat
Constricts bronchial tubes in lungs
Activates digestion
Inhibits glucose release by liver

Sympathetic Division
Dilates pupils
Weakly stimulates salivation
Stimulates sweat glands
Accelerates heartbeat
Dilates bronchial tubes in lungs
Inhibits digestion
Increases epinephrine,
  norepinephrine secretion
  by adrenal glands
Relaxes bladder wall
Decreases urine volume
Stimulates glucose release by liver
Stimulates ejaculation in males

Contracts bladder wall
Stimulates genital erection (both
  sexes) and vaginal lubrication
  (females)

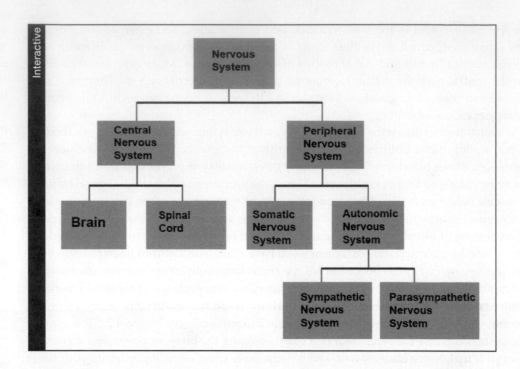

JOURNAL PROMPT 4.1

Thinking Critically—Don't Oversimplify: Although scientists separate the human nervous system into divisions and sub-divisions, in reality, all the parts are connected. It can be difficult to tell at a glance, for example, exactly where the spinal cord ends and the brain stem begins. Why is it helpful to make tidy divisions across systems, but why might that also blur our understanding of the overall functioning of the nervous system?

Quiz for Module 4.1

1. The central nervous system is composed of the
   a. Peripheral system and the lateral system
   b. Somatic system and the autonomic system
   c. Sympathetic system and the parasympathetic system
   d. Brain and spinal cord

2. Jimmy is camping with friends when he accidentally steps in the campfire and recoils his foot instantaneously. What produced this speedy foot-saving action?
   a. A pain signal sent from the brain to the foot
   b. The direct operation of the spinal cord
   c. A signal relayed from the foot to the brain to the spinal cord back to the foot
   d. The complex interplay of brain and spinal signals

3. Nerves that are connected to sensory receptors and to skeletal muscles are part of the
   a. Somatic nervous system
   b. Central nervous system
   c. Sympathetic nervous system
   d. Parasympathetic nervous system

4. As Keiko walked through a dark alley late at night, she heard a bottle break, a weird wheezing noise, and something rustling behind a dumpster. Her heart beat faster, she started to sweat, and she began to breathe more deeply. These physiological reactions were produced by Keiko's
   a. Somatic nervous system
   b. Parasympathetic nervous system
   c. Sympathetic nervous system
   d. Central nervous system

5. As Keiko continued down the alley she saw a mangy, asthmatic cat emerge from behind a dumpster. The cat yawned and hobbled away, as Keiko's heartbeat slowed and her breathing returned to normal. These physiological reactions were produced by Keiko's
   a. Central nervous system
   b. Sympathetic nervous system
   c. Parasympathetic nervous system
   d. Somatic nervous system

Communication in the Nervous System

The blueprint we just described provides only a general idea of the nervous system's structure. Now let's turn to the details.

Types of Cells

LO 4.2.A Compare the functions of neurons and glial cells in the nervous system.

Like the rest of your body, your brain is made of cells—two types of cells, in fact. **Neurons**, or *nerve cells*, are the brain's communication specialists, transmitting information to, from, and within the central nervous system. **Glia**, or *glial cells* (from the Greek for "glue"), hold the neurons in place.

Although glia used to get much less attention than neurons, we now know that these cells are much more than just "glue." They provide the neurons with nutrients, insulate them, help them grow, protect the brain from toxic agents, and remove cellular debris when neurons die. They also communicate chemically with each other and with neurons; without them, neurons could not function effectively. One kind of glial cell appears to give neurons the go-ahead to form connections and to start "talking" to each other (Ullian, Christopherson, & Barres, 2004). Another kind seems to act like the brain's electrician, identifying and trying to repair problems with the nerves' electrical systems (Graeber & Streit, 2010). And over time, glia help determine which neural connections get stronger or weaker, suggesting that they play a vital role in learning and memory (Fields, 2004).

It is the neurons, however, that are considered the building blocks of the nervous system, though in structure they are more like snowflakes than blocks, exquisitely delicate and differing from one another greatly in size and shape (see Figure 4.3). In the giraffe, a neuron that runs from the spinal cord down the animal's hind leg may be 9 feet long! In the human brain, neurons are microscopic. Scientists believed for many years that the brain contains about 100 billion neurons and 10 times as many glia. But recent advances, which allow researchers to count individual cells, put the numbers much lower. An adult brain contains about 171 billion cells, about evenly divided between neurons and glia (Herculano-Houzel, 2009; Lent et al., 2012).

The Structure of the Neuron

LO 4.2.B Describe each of the three main parts of a neuron, and explain their functions.

As you can see in Figure 4.4, a neuron has three main parts: *dendrites*, a *cell body*, and an *axon*. The **dendrites** look like the branches of a tree; indeed, the word *dendrite* means "little tree" in Greek. Dendrites act like antennas, receiving messages from as many as 10,000 other nerve

neuron
A cell that conducts electrochemical signals; the basic unit of the nervous system; also called a *nerve cell*.

glia [GLY-uh or GLEE-uh]
Cells that support, nurture, and insulate neurons, remove debris when neurons die, enhance the formation and maintenance of neural connections, and modify neuronal functioning.

dendrites
A neuron's branches that receive information from other neurons and transmit it toward the cell body.

Neurons in the outer layers of the brain.

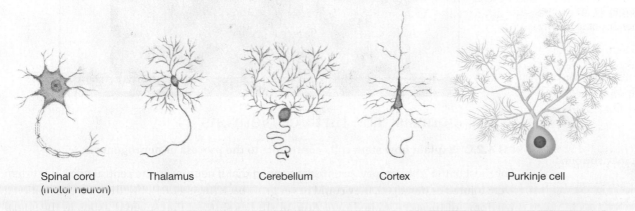

| Spinal cord (motor neuron) | Thalamus | Cerebellum | Cortex | Purkinje cell |

Figure 4.3 Different Kinds of Neurons
Neurons vary in size and shape, depending on their location and function. More than 200 types of neurons have been identified in mammals.

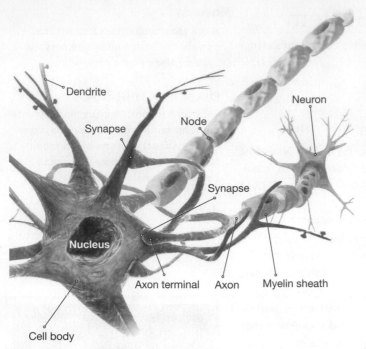

Figure 4.4 The Structure of a Neuron

Incoming neural impulses are received by the dendrites of a neuron and are transmitted to the cell body. Outgoing signals pass along the axon to terminal branches.

cell body

The part of the neuron that keeps it alive and determines whether or not it will fire.

axon

A neuron's extending fiber that conducts impulses away from the cell body and transmits them to other neurons.

myelin sheath

A fatty insulation that may surround the axon of a neuron.

nerve

A bundle of nerve fibers (axons and sometimes dendrites) in the peripheral nervous system.

cells and transmitting these messages toward the cell body. They also do some preliminary processing of those messages. The **cell body** is shaped roughly like a sphere or a pyramid; it includes the cell's nucleus, which contains genetic information (DNA) and controls the cell's growth and reproduction. The rest of the cell body contains the biochemical machinery for keeping the neuron alive and producing neurochemicals (which you will read about shortly). The **axon** (from the Greek for "axle") is attached to the cell body and transmits messages away from the cell body to other neurons or to muscle or gland cells. Axons commonly divide at the end into branches called *axon terminals*. In adult human beings, axons vary from only four thousandths of an inch to a few feet in length. Dendrites and axons give each neuron a double role: As one researcher put it, a neuron is first a catcher, then a batter (Gazzaniga, 1988).

Many axons, especially the larger ones, are insulated by a surrounding layer of fatty material called the **myelin sheath**, which in the central nervous system is made up of glial cells. Constrictions in this covering, called *nodes*, divide it into segments, which make it look a little like a string of link sausages (see Figure 4.4 again). One purpose of the myelin sheath is to prevent signals in adjacent cells from interfering with each other. Another purpose, as we will see shortly, is to speed up the conduction of neural impulses. In individuals with multiple sclerosis, loss of myelin causes erratic nerve signals, leading to loss of sensation, weakness or paralysis, lack of coordination, or vision problems (Czeipel, Boddeke, & Copray, 2015). To learn more about neurons and how they work, watch the video *The Basics: How the Brain Works 2*.

In the peripheral nervous system, the fibers of individual neurons (axons and sometimes dendrites) are collected together in bundles called **nerves**, rather like the lines in a telephone cable. The human body has 43 pairs of peripheral nerves; one nerve from each pair is on the left side of the body and the other is on the right. Most of these nerves enter or leave the spinal cord, but 12 pairs in the head, the *cranial nerves*, connect directly to the brain.

00:03 / 01:26

Neurogenesis: The Birth of Neurons

LO 4.2.C Explain how stem cells contribute to the process of neurogenesis.

For most of the 20th century, scientists assumed that if neurons in the central nervous system were injured or damaged, they could never grow back (regenerate). But then the conventional wisdom got turned upside down. Animal studies showed that severed axons in the spinal cord *can* regrow if you treat them with certain nervous system chemicals (Schnell & Schwab, 1990). Researchers are hopeful that regenerated axons will eventually enable people with spinal cord injuries to use their limbs again.

In the past two decades, scientists have also had to rethink another entrenched assumption: that mammals produce no new CNS cells after infancy. In the early 1990s, Canadian neuroscientists immersed immature cells from mice brains in a growth-promoting protein and showed that these cells could give birth to new neurons in a process called **neurogenesis**. Even more astonishing, the new neurons continued to divide and multiply (Reynolds & Weiss, 1992). Since then, scientists have discovered that the human brain and other body organs also contain such cells, which are now known as **stem cells**. Many of these cells, including those in brain areas involved in learning and memory, seem to divide and mature throughout adulthood (Qin, Zhang, & Yang, 2015). Animal studies suggest that physical exercise, effortful mental activity, and an enriched environment promote the production and survival of new cells, whereas aging and stress can inhibit their production and nicotine can kill them (Berger, Gage, & Vijayaraghavan, 1998; Wolf, Melnik, & Kempermann, 2011; Shors, 2009).

Stem-cell research is one of the hottest areas in biology and neuroscience because embryonic stem (ES) cells are *pluripotent*, a word that literally means "having many powers." Amazingly, ES cells can generate many types of specialist cells, from neurons to kidney cells (see Figure 4.5). Therefore, stem cells may be useful for treating damaged tissues. ES cells come from aborted fetuses and from embryos that are a few days old, which consist of just a few cells. (Fertility clinics store many such embryos because several "test tube" fertilizations are created for every patient who hopes to become pregnant; eventually, the extra embryos are destroyed.) In the United States, federal funding for basic stem cell research has faced strong resistance by antiabortion activists. In Europe, stem-cell research faced different problems, with the European Court of Justice ruling in 2011 that companies could not patent procedures involving human ES cells. This decision meant those companies had difficulty making money from their discoveries to pay their scientists, recover their costs, or invest in future research. The European Court lifted the ban in 2014, although the future status of ES cell research remains uncertain.

An alternative to the use of ES cells is to reprogram adult cells from certain organs to become stem cells (Takahashi et al., 2007; Yu et al., 2007). In one study, when stem cells derived from human nasal cells were transplanted into mice that had lesions in a part of the brain involved with memory, the mice performed better on learning and memory tasks (Nivet et al., 2011). Like ES cells, "induced pluripotent stem (iPS) cells" derived from adult tissues seem capable of giving rise to many types of cells. However, these cells are harder to keep alive than embryonic stem cells are, and it is still unclear whether they will prove to be as versatile.

Patient-advocacy groups hope that transplanted stem cells will eventually help people recover from diseases of the brain and from damage to the spinal cord and other parts of the body. Scientists have already had some success in animals. In one study, mice with recent spinal-cord injuries regained much of their ability to walk normally after being injected with stem cells derived from extracted human wisdom teeth (Sakai et al., 2012). Microscopic analysis showed that many of the cells had helped axons regenerate at the site of the spinal

neurogenesis

The production of new neurons from immature stem cells.

stem cells

Immature cells that renew themselves and have the potential to develop into mature cells; given encouraging environments, stem cells from early embryos can develop into any cell type.

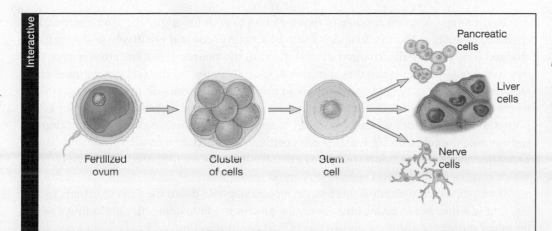

Figure 4.5 Stem Cell Production

Embryonic stem cells (ES) exhibit *pluripotency*, the capacity to develop into many types of mature cells. ES cells appear when an embryo is just a few days old, consisting of a cluster of approximately 100 cells.

Pancreatic cells

Liver cells

Nerve cells

Fertilized ovum

Cluster of cells

Stem cell

Interactive

These tiny embryonic stem cells, here greatly magnified, are *pluripotent*, meaning that they can generate many different kinds of cells in the body.

injury, by blocking substances that were inhibiting their growth. Findings such as these hold promise for treatments in humans, although scientists have found it frustratingly difficult to duplicate the findings from each other's laboratories. Perhaps successful approaches will have to be tailored to the unique circumstances of each patient (Noble et al., 2011).

A long road lies ahead, and many daunting technical hurdles remain to be overcome before stem cell research yields practical benefits for human patients. But exciting developments lie on the horizon, including ongoing clinical attempts to restore sight in legally blind people and heal damaged heart tissue. Each year brings more incredible findings about neurons, findings that only a short time ago would have seemed like science fiction.

How Neurons Communicate

LO 4.2.D Outline the process by which neurons communicate with each other, and explain the basic functions of the synapse, action potential, synaptic vesicles, and neurotransmitters.

Neurons do not directly touch each other, end to end. Instead, they are separated by a minuscule space called the *synaptic cleft*, where the axon terminal of one neuron nearly touches a dendrite or the cell body of another. The entire site—the axon terminal, the cleft, and the covering membrane of the receiving dendrite or cell body—is called a **synapse**. Because a neuron's axon may have hundreds or even thousands of terminals, a single neuron may have synaptic connections with a great many others. As a result, the number of communication links in the nervous system runs into the trillions or perhaps even the quadrillions. To learn more about how these connections change and multiply over time, watch the video *The Plastic Brain*.

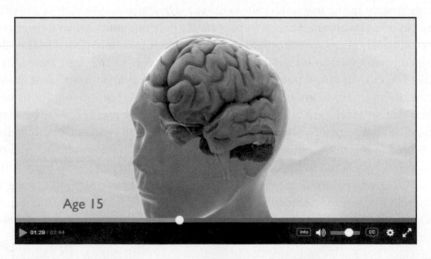

Age 15

▶ 01:29 / 03:44 　 info ◀) ━━●━━ CC ⚙ ⤢

synapse

The site where transmission of a nerve impulse from one nerve cell to another occurs; it includes the axon terminal, the synaptic cleft, and receptor sites in the membrane of the receiving cell.

action potential

A brief change in electrical voltage that occurs between the inside and the outside of an axon when a neuron is stimulated; it serves to produce an electrical impulse.

Neurons speak to one another, or in some cases to muscles or glands, in an electrical and chemical language. The inside and outside of a neuron contain positively and negatively charged ions (electrically charged atoms). At rest, the neuron has a negative charge relative to the outside. But when it is stimulated, special "gates" in the cell's membrane open, allowing positively charged sodium ions to move from the outside to the inside, making the neuron less negative. If this change reaches a critical level, it briefly triggers an **action potential**, during which gates in the axon membrane allow even more positively charged sodium into the cell, causing it to become positively charged; as a result, the neuron "fires." Then, positively charged potassium ions quickly move from within the axon to the outside, which returns the cell to its negatively charged resting state.

If an axon is unmyelinated, this process repeats stepwise down the axon like dominos falling over in a line. But in myelinated axons, the process is a little different. Conducting a neural impulse beneath the sheath is impossible, in part because sodium and potassium ions cannot cross the cell's membrane except at the breaks (nodes) between the myelin's "sausages." Instead, the action potential "hops" from one node to the next. (More precisely, positively charged ions flow down the axon at a fast rate, causing regeneration of the action potential at each node.) This arrangement allows the impulse to travel faster than it could if the action potential had to be regenerated at every point along the axon. Nerve impulses travel more slowly in babies than in older children and adults because when babies are born, the myelin sheaths on their axons are not yet fully developed.

When a neural impulse reaches the axon terminal's button-like tip, it must get its message across the synaptic cleft to another cell. At this point, *synaptic vesicles*, tiny sacs in the tip of the axon terminal, open and release a few thousand molecules of a chemical substance called a **neurotransmitter**. Like sailors carrying a message from one island to another, these molecules then diffuse across the synaptic cleft (see Figure 4.6).

When they reach the other side, the neurotransmitter molecules bind briefly with *receptor sites*, special molecules in the membrane of the receiving neuron's dendrites (or sometimes cell body), fitting these sites much as a key fits a lock. Remember: The receiving neuron will be negatively charged because it is still at rest. Some neurotransmitters will cause a decrease in the negative charge. When the charge reaches a critical level, the neuron will fire. This is called an *excitatory* effect. Other neurotransmitters will cause an increase in the negative charge, making the neuron less likely to fire. This is called an *inhibitory* effect. Inhibition in the nervous system is essential. Without it, we could not sleep or coordinate our movements. Excitation of the nervous system would be overwhelming, producing convulsions.

What any given neuron does at any given moment depends on the net effect of all the messages being received from other neurons. Only when the cell's voltage reaches a certain threshold will it fire. Thousands of messages, both excitatory and inhibitory, may be coming into the cell, and the receiving neuron must essentially average them. The message that reaches a final destination depends on the rate at which individual neurons are firing, how many are firing, what types of neurons are firing, where the neurons are located, and the degree of synchrony among different neurons. It does *not* depend on how strongly the individual neurons are firing, however, because a neuron always either fires or doesn't. The firing of a neuron is an all-or-none event, like turning on a light switch. For a better idea of how neurons communicate with one another, watch the video *The Basics: How the Brain Works 3*.

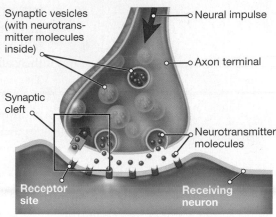

Synaptic vesicles (with neurotransmitter molecules inside)

Neural impulse

Axon terminal

Synaptic cleft

Neurotransmitter molecules

Receptor site

Receiving neuron

Figure 4.6 Neurotransmitter Crossing a Synapse

Neurotransmitter molecules are released into the synaptic cleft between two neurons from vesicles (chambers) in the transmitting neuron's axon terminal. The molecules then bind to receptor sites on the receiving neuron. As a result, the electrical state of the receiving neuron changes and the neuron becomes either more likely to fire an impulse or less so, depending on the type of neurotransmitter.

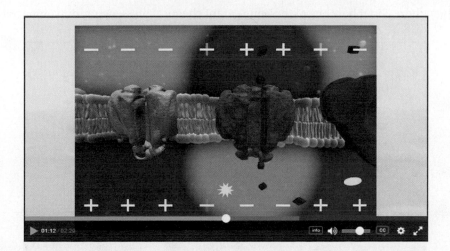

01:12 / 02:29

Chemical Messengers in the Nervous System

LO 4.2.E   Summarize the effects of some of the main neurotransmitters in the brain, and list four hormones that influence behavior.

The nervous system "house" would remain forever dark and lifeless without chemical couriers and helpers to carry messages from room to room. We will consider three classes of chemicals: neurotransmitters, hormones, and neuromodulators.

neurotransmitter

A chemical substance that is released by a transmitting neuron at the synapse and that alters the activity of a receiving neuron.

NEUROTRANSMITTERS: VERSATILE COURIERS   As we have seen, neurotransmitters make it possible for one neuron to excite or inhibit another. Neurotransmitters exist not only in the brain but also in the spinal cord, the peripheral nerves, and certain glands. Through their effects on specific nerve circuits, these substances control everything your brain does. The nature of the effect depends on the level of the neurotransmitter, its location, and the type of receptor it binds with. Here we will discuss just a few of the better-understood neurotransmitters and some of their known or suspected effects.

Four neurotransmitters each travel a particular path through parts of the brain, like following a bus route:

- *Serotonin* affects neurons involved in sleep, appetite, sensory perception, temperature regulation, pain suppression, and mood.
- *Dopamine* affects neurons involved in voluntary movement, attention, learning, memory, emotion, pleasure and reward, and possibly responses to novelty.
- *Acetylcholine* affects neurons involved in muscle action, arousal, vigilance, memory, and emotion.
- *Norepinephrine* affects neurons involved in increased heart rate and the slowing of intestinal activity during stress, and neurons involved in learning, memory, dreaming, waking from sleep, and emotion.

Two other common neurotransmitters are distributed throughout the entire brain:

- *GABA* (*gamma aminobutyric acid*) is the major inhibitory neurotransmitter in the brain.
- *Glutamate* is the major excitatory neurotransmitter in the brain; it is released by about 90 percent of the brain's neurons.

Harmful effects can occur when neurotransmitter levels are too high or too low. Abnormal GABA levels have been implicated in sleep and eating disorders and in convulsive disorders, including epilepsy. People with Alzheimer's disease lose brain cells responsible for producing acetylcholine and other neurotransmitters, and these deficits help account for their devastating memory problems. A loss of cells that produce dopamine is responsible for the tremors and rigidity of Parkinson's disease. In multiple sclerosis, immune cells overproduce glutamate, which damages or kills glial cells that normally make myelin. The video *Neurotransmitters* will show you more about how one of these important chemical messengers, dopamine, works.

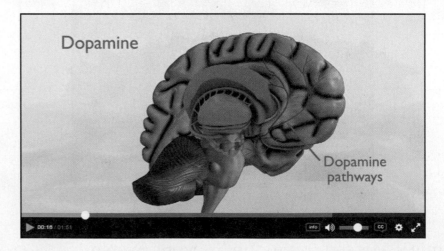

We want to warn you, however, that pinning down the relationship between neurotransmitter abnormalities and behavioral or physical abnormalities is extremely tricky. Each neurotransmitter plays multiple roles, and the functions of different substances often overlap. Furthermore, it is always possible that something about a disorder leads to abnormal neurotransmitter levels instead of the other way around. Correlation is not the same thing as causation. Finally, although drugs that boost or decrease levels of particular neurotransmitters are sometimes effective in treating certain mental disorders, this fact does not necessarily mean that abnormal neurotransmitter levels *cause* the disorders. After all, aspirin can relieve a headache, but headaches are not caused by a lack of aspirin!

Many of us regularly ingest things that affect our own neurotransmitters. Most recreational drugs produce their effects by blocking or enhancing the actions of neurotransmitters, and so do some herbal remedies. St. John's wort, which is often taken for depression, prevents the cells that release serotonin from reabsorbing excess molecules that have remained in the synaptic cleft; as a result, serotonin levels rise. Many people do not realize that such remedies, because they affect the nervous system's biochemistry, can interact with other medications and can be harmful in high doses. Even ordinary foods can influence the availability of neurotransmitters in the brain. Serotonin levels will decrease after a protein-rich meal (dairy products, meat, fish, and poultry) and increase after a high-carbohydrate, low-protein meal, which is why you may feel calm or lethargic after downing a big bowl of pasta (Spring, Chiodo, & Bowen, 1987). But the path between the bowl and the brain is complicated: If you're looking for brain food, you are most likely to find it in a well-balanced diet. Watch the video *Your Brain on Drugs* to learn more about how various substances can affect the brain.

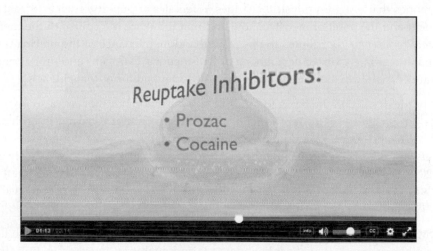

hormones

Chemical substances, secreted by organs called *glands*, that affect the functioning of other organs.

endocrine glands

Internal organs that produce hormones and release them into the bloodstream.

melatonin

A hormone, secreted by the pineal gland, that is involved in the regulation of daily biological rhythms.

oxytocin

A hormone, secreted by the pituitary gland, that stimulates uterine contractions during childbirth, facilitates the ejection of milk during nursing, and seems to promote, in both sexes, attachment and trust in relationships.

HORMONES: LONG-DISTANCE MESSENGERS **Hormones**, which make up the second class of chemical messengers, are produced primarily in **endocrine glands**, such as the pancreas, ovaries, testes, and adrenal glands. Hormones are released directly into the bloodstream, which carries them to organs and cells that may be far from their point of origin. Hormones have dozens of jobs, from promoting bodily growth to aiding digestion to regulating metabolism. Receptors for hormones exist throughout the body, including the brain. Because hormones are released into the bloodstream, their effects are widespread.

Neurotransmitters and hormones are not always chemically distinct because nature has been efficient, giving some substances more than one role. For instance, norepinephrine may be considered either a neurotransmitter or a hormone, depending on where it is located and what function it is performing.

The following hormones, among others, are of particular interest to research psychologists and neuroscientists:

1. **Melatonin**, which is secreted by the *pineal gland* deep within the brain, helps to regulate daily biological rhythms and promotes sleep.
2. **Oxytocin**, which is secreted by another small gland in the brain, the *pituitary gland*, enhances uterine contractions during childbirth and facilitates the ejection of milk during nursing. Along with another hormone, *vasopressin*, oxytocin contributes to relationships in both sexes by promoting attachment and trust.

adrenal hormones

Hormones that are produced by the adrenal glands and that are involved in emotion and stress.

sex hormones

Hormones that regulate the development and functioning of reproductive organs and that stimulate the development of male and female sexual characteristics; they include androgens, estrogens, and progesterone.

neuromodulators

Neurochemicals that modulate the functioning of neurons and neurotransmitters.

endorphins [en-DOR-fins]

Chemical substances in the nervous system that are similar in structure and action to opiates; they are involved in pain reduction, pleasure, and memory and are known technically as *endogenous opioid peptides*.

3. **Adrenal hormones**, which are produced by the *adrenal glands* (organs that are perched right above the kidneys), are involved in emotion and stress. These hormones also rise in response to other conditions, such as heat, cold, pain, injury, burns, and physical exercise, and in response to some drugs, such as caffeine and nicotine. The outer part of each adrenal gland produces *cortisol*, which increases blood sugar levels and boosts energy. The inner part produces *epinephrine* (commonly known as adrenaline) and *norepinephrine*. When adrenal hormones are released in your body, activated by the sympathetic nervous system, they increase your arousal level and prepare you for action. Adrenal hormones also enhance memory.

4. **Sex hormones**, which are secreted by tissue in the gonads (testes in men, ovaries in women) and also by the adrenal glands, include three main types, all occurring in both sexes but in differing amounts and proportions in males and females after puberty. *Androgens* (the most important of which is *testosterone*) are masculinizing hormones produced mainly in the testes but also in the ovaries and the adrenal glands. Androgens set in motion the physical changes males experience at puberty, including a deepened voice and facial and chest hair, and they cause pubic and underarm hair to develop in both sexes. Testosterone also influences sexual arousal in both sexes. *Estrogens* are feminizing hormones that bring on physical changes in females at puberty, such as breast development and the onset of menstruation, and that influence the course of the menstrual cycle. *Progesterone* contributes to the growth and maintenance of the uterine lining in preparation for a fertilized egg, among other functions. Estrogens and progesterone are produced mainly in the ovaries but also in the testes and the adrenal glands.

Sex hormones act on the brain to guide sexual behavior, but they are also involved in behavior not linked to sex or reproduction. The body's natural estrogen in both sexes is thought to enhance learning and memory by promoting the formation of synaptic connections in certain areas of the brain and by indirectly increasing the production of acetylcholine (Gibbs, 2010; Lee & McEwen, 2001; Sherwin, 1998). However, the common belief that fluctuating levels of estrogen and progesterone make most women "emotional" before menstruation has not been borne out by research.

NEUROMODULATORS: THE BRAIN'S VOLUME CONTROL   The brain is awash in thousands of other chemicals that affect how neurons and neurotransmitters function (Brezina, 2010). Because these chemicals modulate (vary the strength of) neural functions, they are called **neuromodulators**. One neuromodulator, the *serotonin transporter*, is a protein that acts like a garbage collector, picking up serotonin from the synaptic cleft after it has been released and transporting it back to the sending neuron for recycling. In that way, it controls the amount of serotonin that is available in the brain.

Endorphins are an intriguing group of chemicals known technically as *endogenous opioid peptides*. Endorphins have effects similar to those of natural opiates such as heroin; that is, they reduce pain and promote pleasure. They are also thought to play a role in appetite, sexual activity, blood pressure, mood, learning, and memory. Some endorphins function as neurotransmitters, but most of them act primarily as neuromodulators, by limiting or prolonging the effects of neurotransmitters.

Endorphin levels shoot up when an animal or a person is afraid or under stress. This is no accident; by making pain bearable in such situations, endorphins give a species an evolutionary advantage. When an organism is threatened, it needs to do something fast. But pain can interfere with action: A mouse that pauses to lick a wounded paw may become a cat's dinner; a soldier who is overcome by an injury may never get off the battlefield. Of course, the body's built-in system of counteracting pain is only partly successful, especially when painful stimulation is prolonged.

A link also exists between endorphins and human attachment. Research with animals suggests that in infancy, contact with the mother stimulates the flow of endorphins, which strengthens the infant's bond with her. Some researchers now think that this "endorphin rush" also occurs in the early stages of passionate love between adults, accounting for the feeling of euphoria that "falling" for someone creates (Diamond, 2004).

Thinking Critically—Ask Questions, Be Willing to Wonder: Imagine that someday scientists were able to pinpoint the exact action of specific neurotransmitters in affecting precise locations of particular cells in the brain. This discovery should make it possible to boost or inhibit levels of neurotransmitters to precisely regulate depression and anxiety, or even counteract conditions such as Parkinson's disease. If this day ever arrived, do you think it would be a good idea to regulate mental or physical states through skillful neurochemistry? Why or why not? What kinds of biological conditions should be candidates for this treatment, and who should decide?

Quiz for Module 4.2

1. Nerve cells found in the brain are called _____, whereas support cells found in the brain are called _____.
   a. Nerve cells / dendrites
   b. Neurons / glia
   c. Glia / axons
   d. Glia / neurons

2. In a typical neuron, information is received by _____ and transmitted to the next neuron by _____.
   a. Axons / dendrites
   b. Axons / glia
   c. Dendrites / glia
   d. Dendrites / an axon

3. Pluripotency is a property of embryonic stem cells. This means that these stem cells
   a. Will turn into neurons after a 1-year incubation period
   b. Can repair themselves without sending pain signals to the spinal cord
   c. Can divide four times, as opposed to most cells, which only divide twice
   d. Can generate many types of specialist cells, such as neurons or muscle cells

4. Rajiv was bragging to Chloe. "Man, I'm smart!" he crowed. "My brain cells are stitched so tightly together that there's no space between them. Information travels from neuron to neuron without a break!" "You can't be that smart," muttered Chloe, "if you don't even understand how misinformed you are." Why is Chloe correct?
   a. Myelin stimulates an action potential, and this sends a signal out through a dendrite; the strength of the signal is more important than the connection.
   b. Glial cells are responsible for transmitting information throughout the brain.
   c. Axons touch other axons, and dendrites touch other dendrites; the neuron itself doesn't matter.
   d. Neurons don't touch one another; there is a small gap between them called a synapse.

5. _____ is a neurotransmitter involved in voluntary movement, pleasure and reward, and attention.
   a. Dopamine
   b. GABA
   c. Serotonin
   d. Acetylcholine

Mapping the Brain

We come now to the main room of the nervous system "house": the brain. A disembodied brain stored in a formaldehyde-filled container is a putty-colored, wrinkled glob of tissue that looks a little like an oversized walnut. It takes an act of imagination to envision this modest-looking organ writing *Hamlet*, discovering radium, or inventing the telephone. In a living person, of course, this astonishing organ is encased in a thick protective vault of bone. How, then, can scientists study it?

One approach is to study patients who have had a part of their brain damaged or removed because of disease or injury. Another is to stimulate the brains of patients who are having brain surgery to try to identify the functions of various areas. But both of these methods rely on accidents of nature; for one reason or another, the brains of the people in these studies are not healthy. Fortunately, neuroscientists have a growing number of other tools that they can use to study healthy brains in action. We will discuss two broad approaches to mapping the brain. In the first, neuroscientists do something that temporarily affects particular brain areas and then observe the consequences for behavior; in the second, they manipulate behavior in some way and then record the effects in the brain.

lesion method

The removal or disabling of a brain structure to gain better understanding of its function; this method is used only in animals.

transcranial magnetic stimulation (TMS)

A method of stimulating brain cells, using a powerful magnetic field produced by a wire coil placed on a person's head; it can be used by researchers to temporarily inactivate neural circuits.

transcranial direct current stimulation (tDCS)

A technique that applies a very small electric current to stimulate or suppress activity in parts of the cortex; it enables researchers to identify the functions of a particular area.

Intervening in the Brain and Observing Behavior

LO 4.3.A Describe three techniques researchers use for intervening in the brain and observing the behavior that results.

When researchers work with animals, they sometimes surgically remove or disable a brain structure and then observe the effects on behavior. This approach is called the **lesion method**, and, unlike studies of patients with brain damage, it gives scientists a high level of control over the affected brain regions. Of course, the lesion method cannot be used on humans.

Transcranial magnetic stimulation (TMS) is a recent method that creates a "virtual" lesion—a temporary one that does not involve removing or permanently disabling brain tissue. It delivers a large current through a wire coil placed on a person's head. The current produces a magnetic field about 40,000 times greater than the earth's natural magnetic field, causing neurons under the coil to fire. Although TMS can be used to produce motor responses, such as a thumb twitch or a knee jerk, researchers can also use it to briefly inactivate an area and observe the effects on behavior. The drawback is that when neurons fire, they cause many other neurons to become active too, so it can be hard to tell which neurons are critical for a particular task. Still, TMS has been useful for examining the role of various brain regions in everything from vision to emotion to language (van deRuit, Perenboom, & Grey, 2015). As we will see, the left hemisphere of the brain plays a significant role in language, but TMS shows that the right side is important as well. TMS over the right hemisphere causes people to lose the ability to understand metaphors ("a blanket of snow"); although they still understand the individual words in the metaphor, they no longer can see the relationship between them (Pobric et al., 2008).

Transcranial direct current stimulation (tDCS) is an even newer way of studying brain function. The researcher applies a very small electric current to an area of the cortex, the outer surface of the brain (Cohen Kadosh, 2015). Depending on the direction of the current, brain activity in that area is either temporarily stimulated or suppressed. In one study, applying current in one direction increased activity, improving people's memory for the information they gained during one task while they focused on doing another. But applying the current in the other direction, which reduces activity, reduced their ability to do this task (Zaehle et al., 2011).

Intervening in Behavior and Observing the Brain

LO 4.3.B Describe five techniques researchers use for intervening in behavior and observing the effects on the brain.

The second general approach to mapping the brain is to do something that affects behavior and then record what happens in the brain. One recording method uses *electrodes*, devices pasted or taped onto the scalp to detect the simultaneous electrical activity of millions of neurons in particular brain regions. Wires from the electrodes are connected to a machine that translates the electrical energy from the brain into wavy lines on a moving piece of paper or a screen, which is why

Electrodes on the scalp (left) are used to produce an overall picture of electrical activity in different areas of the brain. Transcranial magnetic stimulation, or TMS (center), delivers a large current through a coil on a person's head, causing neurons under the coil to fire. It can be used to temporarily inactivate certain brain regions. Transcranial direct current stimulation, or tDCS (right), applies direct current to a specific area of the cortex, which either stimulates or suppresses activity in that area depending on the direction of the current.

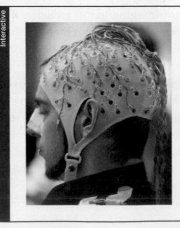  

electrical patterns in the brain are known as "brain waves." The brain-wave recording itself is called an **electroencephalogram (EEG)**. A standard EEG is useful but not very precise because it reflects the activities of so many cells at once. "Listening" to the brain with an EEG machine is like standing outside a sports stadium: You know when something is happening, but you can't be sure what it is or who is doing it.

One solution is a variation of EEG that uses statistical techniques to measure **event-related potentials (ERP)**, waves of electrical activity associated with particular stimuli ("events") such as seeing a picture or hearing a word. Any thought you have is made up of a series of different steps, and ERP allows scientists to see the neural activity associated with each step—in real time, as Figure 4.7 shows.

Even using ERP, scientists still cannot know exactly *where* in the brain the activity occurs, but they know *when* it occurred—much like knowing that one player has thrown a ball and another has caught it, but not precisely where they were when all the action happened. ERP is also useful in studying infants and other people who cannot follow instructions in an experiment. For example, scientists have used ERP to compare how infants exposed to one language differ from infants exposed to two languages. Monolingual infants raised in English-speaking households showed different ERPs for English and Spanish as early as 6 months old, suggesting they could distinguish the two languages and were more receptive to English. But bilingual infants did not show this ability to distinguish between languages until they were 10 to 12 months old, showing that their brains were equally receptive to both English and Spanish (GarciaSierra et al., 2011).

Yet another method, the **PET (positron emission tomography) scan**, records biochemical changes in the brain as they are happening. One type of PET scan takes advantage of the fact that nerve cells convert glucose, the body's main fuel, into energy. A researcher can inject a person with a glucose-like substance that contains a harmless radioactive element. This substance accumulates in brain areas that are particularly active and are therefore consuming glucose rapidly. The substance emits radiation, which is detected by a scanning device, and the result is a computer-processed picture of biochemical activity on a display screen (see Figure 4.8a). Other kinds of PET scans measure blood flow or oxygen consumption, which also reflect brain activity. Today PET scans are mostly used in medical research and diagnosis.

In psychological research, PET scans have largely been superseded by **magnetic resonance imaging (MRI)**, which uses powerful magnetic fields and radio frequencies to take highly detailed pictures of the brain. The magnets produce vibrations in the nuclei of atoms in the body's organs. The vibrations are then detected as signals by special receivers. A computer analyzes the signals, taking into account their strength and duration, and converts them into a high-contrast picture of whatever organ the scientist or physician is interested in, such as the brain. This is a *structural MRI* (see Figure 4.8b). It gives us a terrific picture of what the brain looks like, but not what it does. Another version of MRI, called **functional MRI (fMRI)**, allows us to see brain activity associated with specific thoughts or behaviors that last at least several seconds (see Figure 4.8c). In fMRI, the receivers detect levels of blood oxygen in different brain areas. Because neurons use oxygen as fuel, active brain areas produce a bigger signal.

Functional MRI can localize brain activity; it can tell where something is happening, but not when it is happening (just the opposite strengths and weaknesses of the EEG). Because all of your brain is active all of the time, scientists who use fMRI must compare the activity in the brain when people are engaged in control tasks and when they are engaged in experimental tasks. In one condition, people might read nonsense words (like "glorp") and in another condition real words. In both cases, people are seeing and identifying letters, but they are comprehending only the real words. By "subtracting" one brain image from the other, it is possible to identify the brain regions involved in comprehension. Researchers are using fMRI to study everything from racial attitudes to moral reasoning to spiritual meditation.

CONTROVERSIES AND CAUTIONS   Exciting though these developments and technologies are, we need to understand that technology cannot replace critical thinking (Legrenzi & Umiltà, 2011; Tallis, 2011; Wade, 2006). As one team of psychological scientists who use

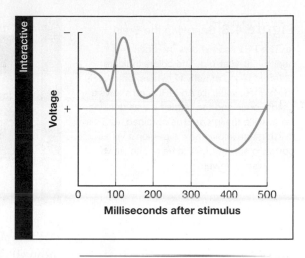

Figure 4.7 An Event-Related Potential

An ERP is the brain's response to a specific event—a wave of electrical activity detected on the scalp after a person encounters a stimulus, such as a picture or a word. The first parts of the wave show brain activity associated with encountering the stimulus; later parts show activity associated with understanding it.

electroencephalogram (EEG)

A recording of neural activity detected by electrodes.

event-related potentials (ERP)

A technique that isolates the neural activity associated with a specific stimulus ("event").

PET scan (positron-emission tomography)

A method for analyzing biochemical activity in the brain, for example by using injections of a glucose-like substance containing a radioactive element.

MRI (magnetic resonance imaging)

A method for studying body and brain tissue, using magnetic fields and special radio receivers.

fMRI (functional magnetic resonance imaging)

A type of magnetic resonance imaging used to study brain activity associated with specific thoughts and behaviors.

Figure 4.8 Scanning the Brain

(a) The PET scan shows the brain of a healthy 20-year-old. The colors indicate different levels of activity, where red reveals the highest level. (b) An MRI scan shows a child's brain and the bottle he was drinking from while the image was obtained. (c) This fMRI image shows how a person's visual cortex is activated while he or she views a red hibiscus flower.

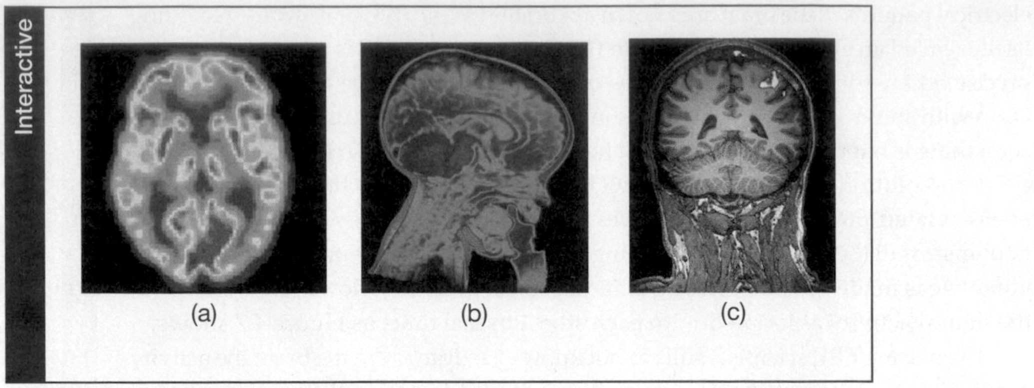

(a)   (b)   (c)

fMRIs to study cognition and emotion wrote, "Just because you're imaging the brain doesn't mean you can stop using your head" (Cacioppo et al., 2003). Because brain-scan images seem so "real" and scientific, many people fail to realize that these images can convey oversimplified and sometimes misleading impressions (see Figure 4.9). Simply by coloring various regions, researchers can make small contrasts look dramatic, and larger ones seem insignificant (Dumit, 2004). Combining individual brain scans into one average scan—a common practice—can mask significant variability among people's brains.

Furthermore, simply including an image of brain activity can be enough to make a study's conclusions seem more "scientifically reasoned" even when they are not. To illustrate this point, scientists asked people to read some scientific-sounding nonsense. For instance, one passage explained that because watching television and doing math problems both caused activation in the temporal lobe, watching television would improve math skills! (This conclusion is, of course, rubbish.) Some people read a version of the passage featuring no accompanying image, and others read the passage featuring either a bar graph of the results or an image of the brain, such as from an fMRI. People who read the version of the passage with the brain images thought it had much better scientific reasoning than did those who read the version with no images, or even the version with the graph (McCabe & Castell, 2008).

Research using fMRI has also sometimes suffered from questionable statistical procedures that have produced highly inflated correlations between brain activity and measures of personality and emotion (Vul et al., 2009). Yet the press usually reports these findings uncritically, giving the impression that psychological scientists know more about the relationship between the brain and psychological processes than they really do. One clever group of scientists made this point very well by doing an fMRI on a dead Atlantic salmon while asking it to view emotional images and determine what emotions the person in each photo was feeling (Bennett et al., 2010). We know what you're thinking: The salmon is dead, so why would the fMRI detect *any* brain activity? You're right. Why would it? But it did. The scan revealed that the salmon was "thinking" about the pictures and the people in them. That's because fMRI produces a mix of signal and noise, like trying to track a conversation in a crowded bar. Scientists have to use sophisticated techniques to "quiet" the noise and reveal the true signal. If they don't know what they are doing, they can make errors. In this case, the result is funny because we know the salmon is dead. But in real life, too, we may not know if the result is real . . . or another dead fish.

The problem is not with fMRI as a technology so much as it is with bad theories, poorly defined dependent measures, and inappropriate interpretations of results, all of which have produced a mountain of dubious findings. The enthusiasm for technology has generated the widespread belief that specific "brain centers" or "critical circuits" explain why you prefer Coke to Pepsi, why you identify as a liberal or a conservative, or what your brain is doing when you are in love. These beliefs are certainly appealing because they explain complicated behavior in simple terms (Beck, 2010). But the attempts to reduce complex behavior to single locations in the brain will almost certainly fail, just as phrenology failed (Gonsalves & Cohen, 2010; Tallis, 2011; Uttal, 2001). As clinical neuroscientist Raymond Tallis put it, "Love is not like a response to a single stimulus, such as a picture. It's not even a single enduring state, like being cold. It is a many splendored and many miseried thing" that includes jealousy,

Figure 4.9 Coloring the Brain

By altering the colors used in brain images, such as in this PET scan, researchers can create the appearance of dramatic brain differences. These scans are actually images of the same brain.

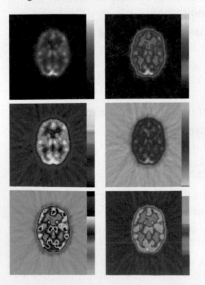

kindness, lust, guilt, happiness, fury, and moments of not feeling in love at all (quoted in Parry, 2011). So if you know that one part of the brain is activated when you are thinking hot thoughts of your beloved, what exactly do you know about love—or your brain? Is the same part activated when you are thinking about a luscious fudge brownie?

Regardless of whether neuroscientists manipulate different brain areas to determine how behavior is affected or manipulate behavior and then record the effects in the brain, their studies are just one step in understanding brain processes and must be interpreted with great caution. Nonetheless, when used appropriately, they do provide an illuminating look at the brain at work and play, and we will therefore report many findings from brain-scan research throughout this text. For scientists, the brain can no longer hide behind the thick fortress of the skull.

JOURNAL PROMPT 4.3

Thinking Critically—Don't Oversimplify: Brain scans provide us with fabulous windows on the brain. But if a scan shows that a brain area is active when you're doodling, does that mean the area is a "doodling center"?

Quiz for Module 4.3

1. Surgically removing brain structures from an animal to understand the effects on behavior is a technique for investigating brain function known as

   a. The lesion method
   b. PET scanning
   c. The LeMay technique
   d. The omega procedure

2. Although both techniques involve intervening in brain function, _____ employs a large electrical current whereas _____ uses a relatively small, focused current.

   a. MRI / TMS
   b. EEG / ERP
   c. tDCS / PET
   d. TMS / tDCS

3. When recording brainwaves, both _____ and _____ can provide a general record of electrical brain activity.

   a. EEG / ERP
   b. PET / MRI

   c. TMS / tDCS
   d. EOM / EOC

4. Biochemical activity in the brain can be recorded using

   a. EEG
   b. PET scans
   c. ERP
   d. TMS

5. Pierre and Solange were talking one day. "I'm a little nervous," confessed Pierre. "My doctor told me I should get a brain scan . . . M-R-something." "Oh!" Solange replied. "MRI, or fMRI?" "Hmmm, I'm not sure," replied Pierre. "What's the difference?" Can you answer Pierre's question?

   a. MRI is an intervention technique, whereas fMRI is simply a recording technique.
   b. MRI uses a pulsating electromagnetic current to stimulate the brain, whereas fMRI uses a low-voltage current.
   c. MRI records changes in blood glucose levels, whereas fMRI records generalized electrical activity.
   d. MRI records the structure of the brain, whereas fMRI records brain activity associated with specific thoughts or behaviors.

A Tour Through the Brain

Most modern brain theories assume that different brain parts perform different (though greatly overlapping) tasks. This concept, known as *localization of function*, goes back at least to Joseph Gall (1758–1828), an Austrian anatomist who thought that personality traits were reflected in the development of specific areas of the brain. Gall's theory of phrenology was completely wrongheaded (so to speak), but his general notion of specialization in the brain had merit.

To learn about what the major brain structures do, let's take an imaginary stroll through the brain. Pretend that you have shrunk to a microscopic size and that you are wending your way through the "soul's frail dwelling house," starting at the lower part, just above the spine. Figure 4.10 shows the major structures we will encounter along our tour; you may want to refer to it as we proceed. But keep in mind that any activity—feeling an emotion, having

brain stem

The part of the brain at the top of the spinal cord, consisting of the medulla and the pons.

pons

A structure in the brain stem involved in, among other things, sleeping, waking, and dreaming.

medulla [muh-DUL-uh]

A structure in the brain stem responsible for certain automatic functions, such as breathing and heart rate.

reticular activating system (RAS)

A dense network of neurons found in the core of the brain stem; it arouses the cortex and screens incoming information.

cerebellum

A brain structure that regulates movement and balance, is involved in remembering simple skills and acquired reflexes, and plays a role in cognitive and emotional learning.

Figure 4.10 Major Structures of the Human Brain

This cross section depicts the brain as if it were split down the middle and shows the structures described in the text.

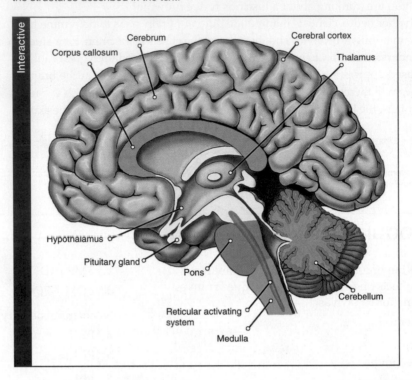

a thought, performing a task—involves many different structures working together. Our description, therefore, is a simplification.

The Brain Stem and Cerebellum

LO 4.4.A List and describe three main structures in the brain stem, explain the primary functions each structure performs, and discuss the processes controlled by the cerebellum.

We begin at the base of the skull with the **brain stem**, which began to evolve some 500 million years ago in segmented worms. The brain stem looks like a stalk rising out of the spinal cord. Pathways to and from upper areas of the brain pass through its two main structures: the medulla and the pons. The **pons** is involved in (among other things) sleeping, waking, and dreaming. The **medulla** is responsible for bodily functions that do not have to be consciously willed, such as breathing and heart rate. Hanging has long been used as a method of execution because when it breaks the neck, nerve pathways from the medulla are severed, stopping respiration.

Extending upward from the core of the brain stem is the **reticular activating system (RAS)**. This dense network of neurons, which extends above the brain stem into the center of the brain and has connections with areas that are higher up, screens incoming information and arouses the higher centers when something happens that demands their attention. Without the RAS, we could not be alert or perhaps even conscious.

Standing atop the brain stem and looking toward the back part of the brain, we see a structure about the size of a small fist. It is the **cerebellum**, or "lesser brain," which contributes to a sense of balance and coordinates the muscles so that movement is smooth and precise. If your cerebellum were damaged, you would probably become exceedingly clumsy and uncoordinated. You might have trouble using a pencil, threading a needle, or even walking. In addition, this structure is involved in remembering simple skills and acquired reflexes

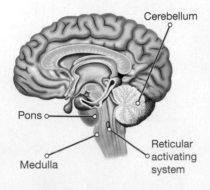

(Daum & Schugens, 1996; Krupa, Thompson, & Thompson, 1993). But the cerebellum, which was once considered just a motor center, is not as "lesser" as its name implies; it is involved in cognitive and emotional learning (Durisko & Fiez, 2010; Mariën et al., 2014).

The Thalamus

LO 4.4.B Describe the structure, function, and location of the thalamus.

Deep in the brain's interior, roughly at its center, we can see the **thalamus**, the sensory relay station of the brain. As sensory messages come into the brain—about the sight of a sunset, the sound of a siren, the feel of a fly landing on your arm—the thalamus directs them to higher areas in charge of vision, sound, or touch. The only sense that completely bypasses the thalamus is the sense of smell, which has its own private switching station, the *olfactory bulb*. The olfactory bulb lies near areas involved in emotion, which may be why particular odors, such as the smell of fresh laundry or a steaming bowl of chicken soup, often rekindle vivid memories.

The Hypothalamus and the Pituitary Gland

LO 4.4.C Describe the structure, function, and location of the hypothalamus and pituitary gland.

Beneath the thalamus sits a structure called the **hypothalamus** (*hypo* means "under"). It is the body's boss, constantly monitoring the body's current state and issuing instructions to help the body maintain a steady state called *homeostasis*. It is involved in basic survival drives associated with the "four Fs"—feeding, fighting, fleeing, and . . . sex. It regulates body temperature by triggering sweating or shivering, and it controls the complex operations of the autonomic nervous system. It also contains the biological clock that controls the body's daily rhythms.

Hanging down from the hypothalamus, connected to it by a short stalk, is a cherry-sized endocrine gland called the **pituitary gland**, mentioned earlier in our discussion of hormones. The pituitary is often called the body's "master gland" because the hormones it secretes affect many other endocrine glands. The master, however, is really only a supervisor. The true boss is the hypothalamus, which sends chemicals to the pituitary that tell it when to "talk" to the other endocrine glands. The pituitary, in turn, sends hormonal messages out to these glands.

The hypothalamus and several other loosely interconnected structures have often been considered part of the *limbic system*; the term is from the Latin for "border," and these structures were thought to form a border between the "higher" and "lower" parts of the brain. Structures in this region are heavily involved in emotions that we share with other animals, such as rage and fear, so the region is also sometimes called "the emotional brain." But researchers now know that these structures also have other functions, and that parts of the brain outside of the old limbic system are involved in emotion. As a result, the term *limbic system* has been going out of favor.

The Amygdala

LO 4.4.D Describe the structure, function, and location of the amygdala.

The **amygdala** (from the ancient Greek word for "almond") is responsible for evaluating sensory information, quickly determining its emotional importance, and contributing to the initial decision to approach or withdraw from a person or situation. Some people describe the amygdala as the brain's "fear center," but it is more than that. Your amygdala assesses stimuli for their fit with your current psychological state and even your core personality traits, responding to positive, negative, or even just plain interesting stimuli accordingly. It does so by working with higher brain areas to regulate your response. If you're extroverted, your amygdala responds more actively to photographs of happy people than it does if you are shy, and when you're hungry, your amygdala responds to food (Cunningham & Brosch, 2012). The amygdala also plays a role in mediating anxiety and depression and in forming and retrieving emotional memories.

thalamus
A brain structure that relays sensory messages to the cerebral cortex.

hypothalamus
A brain structure involved in emotions and drives vital to survival; it regulates the autonomic nervous system.

pituitary gland
A small endocrine gland at the base of the brain that releases many hormones and regulates other endocrine glands.

amygdala [uh-MIG-dul-uh]
A brain structure involved in the arousal and regulation of emotion and the initial emotional response to sensory information.

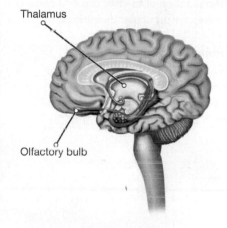

Thalamus

Olfactory bulb

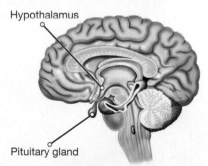

Hypothalamus

Pituitary gland

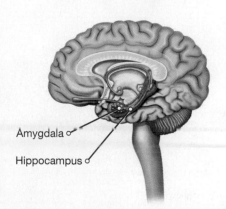

Amygdala

Hippocampus

hippocampus

A brain structure involved in the storage of new information in memory.

cerebrum [suh-REE-brum]

The largest brain structure, consisting of the upper part of the brain; divided into two hemispheres, it is in charge of most sensory, motor, and cognitive processes. From the Latin for "brain."

cerebral hemispheres

The two halves of the cerebrum.

corpus callosum

The bundle of nerve fibers connecting the two cerebral hemispheres.

lateralization

Specialization of the two cerebral hemispheres for particular operations.

cerebral cortex

A collection of several thin layers of cells covering the cerebrum; it is largely responsible for higher mental functions. *Cortex* is Latin for "bark" or "rind."

The Hippocampus

LO 4.4.E Describe the structure, function, and location of the hippocampus.

The shape of the **hippocampus** must have reminded someone of a sea horse, for in Latin that is what its name means. The structure compares sensory information with what the brain has learned about the world, and when a match occurs, the hippocampus tells the reticular activating system to "cool it." There's no need for neural alarm bells to go off every time a car goes by, a bird chirps, or you feel your saliva trickling down the back of your throat.

The hippocampus is also the brain's primary memory structure, and indeed has often been called the "gateway to memory." It enables us to take in and combine different components of experiences—sights, sounds, and feelings—and bind them together into one "memory," although the individual components may ultimately be stored in various parts of the cerebral cortex, which we will discuss shortly. When you recall meeting someone yesterday, various aspects of the memory—information about the person's greeting, tone of voice, appearance, and location—are probably stored in different locations in the cortex. But without the hippocampus, the information would never get to these destinations. This structure is also involved in the retrieval of information during recall.

We know about the central role the hippocampus plays in memory in part from research on patients whose brain damage produced severe memory problems. The most famous of these was Henry Molaison, known to the scientific community as H. M. When Henry was a child, he hit his head in a collision with a cyclist, and soon thereafter, possibly as a result, he began having seizures. By the time he was an adult, his blackouts and convulsions were preventing him from holding a job. He was referred to a surgeon who made the bold suggestion to remove Henry's hippocampus and some portion of his temporal lobes. Although the operation controlled Henry's epilepsy, it created a new problem for him: Henry could no longer form new memories for facts and events. He could remember his childhood, learn new skills, and carry on an intelligent conversation. But if you met him yesterday, he would not know you today. A lot of what psychological scientists know about the hippocampus and about memory is thanks to H. M.

The Cerebrum

LO 4.4.F Describe the structure of the cerebrum, and explain the function of the corpus callosum.

At this point in our tour, the largest part of the brain still looms above us. It is the cauliflower-like **cerebrum**, where the higher forms of thinking take place. The complexity of the human brain's circuitry far exceeds that of any computer in existence, and much of its most complicated wiring is packed into this structure. Compared to many other creatures, we humans may be ungainly, feeble, and thin-skinned, but our well-developed cerebrum enables us to overcome these limitations and creatively control our environment (and, some would say, to mess it up).

The cerebrum is divided into two separate halves, or **cerebral hemispheres**, connected by a large band of fibers called the **corpus callosum**. In general, the right hemisphere is in charge of the left side of the body, and the left hemisphere is in charge of the right side of the body. As we will see shortly, the two hemispheres also have somewhat different tasks and talents, a phenomenon known as **lateralization**.

The Cerebral Cortex

LO 4.4.G Sketch the location of each of the lobes of the cerebral cortex, and explain the major functions each lobe performs, with particular reference to the prefrontal cortex.

Working our way right up through the top of the brain, we find that the cerebrum is covered by several thin layers of densely packed cells known collectively as the **cerebral cortex**. Cell bodies in the cortex, as in many other parts of the brain, produce a grayish tissue, hence the

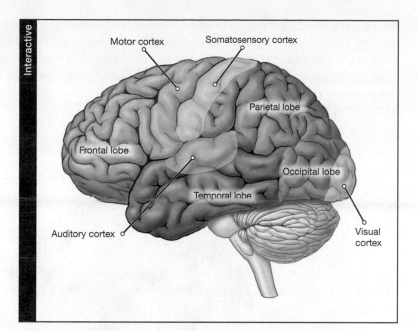

Figure 4.11 Lobes of the Cerebrum
Deep fissures divide the cortex of each cerebral hemisphere into four regions.

term *gray matter*. In other parts of the brain (and in the rest of the nervous system), long, myelin-covered axons prevail, providing the brain's *white matter*. Although the cortex is only about 3 millimeters (1/8 inch) thick, it contains almost three-fourths of all the cells in the human brain. The cortex has many deep crevasses and wrinkles, which enable it to contain its billions of neurons without requiring us to have the heads of giants—heads that would be too big to permit us to be born. In other mammals, which have fewer neurons, the cortex is less crumpled; in rats, it is quite smooth.

LOBES OF THE CORTEX In each cerebral hemisphere, deep fissures divide the cortex into four distinct regions, or lobes (see Figure 4.11):

- The **occipital lobes** (from the Latin for "in back of the head") are at the lower back part of the brain. Among other things, they contain the *visual cortex*, where visual signals are processed. Damage to the visual cortex can cause impaired visual recognition or blindness.

- The **parietal lobes** (from the Latin for "pertaining to walls") are at the top of the brain. They contain the *somatosensory cortex*, which receives information about pressure, pain, touch, and temperature from all over the body. The areas of the somatosensory cortex that receive signals from the hands and the face are disproportionately large because these body parts are particularly sensitive. Parts of the parietal lobes are also involved in attention and awareness of spatial relationships.

- The **temporal lobes** (from the Latin for "pertaining to the temples") are at the sides of the brain, just above the ears and behind the temples. They are involved in memory, perception, and emotion, and they contain the *auditory cortex*, which processes sounds. An area of the left temporal lobe known as *Wernicke's area* is involved in language comprehension.

- The **frontal lobes**, as their name indicates, are located toward the front of the brain, just under the skull in the area of the forehead. They contain the *motor cortex*, which issues orders to the 600 muscles of the body that produce voluntary movement. In the left frontal lobe, a region known as *Broca's area* handles speech production. During short-term memory tasks, areas in the frontal lobes are especially active. The frontal lobes are also involved in emotion and in the ability to make plans, think creatively, and take initiative.

Because the lobes of the cerebral cortex have different functions, they tend to respond differently when directly stimulated with tiny electrodes during brain surgery. (The brain does not feel anything when directly stimulated, so a patient can be awake during the operation.)

occipital |ahk-SIP-uh-tuhl| lobes

Lobes at the lower back part of the brain's cerebral cortex; they contain areas that receive visual information.

parietal [puh-RYE-uh-tuhl] lobes

Lobes at the top of the brain's cerebral cortex; they contain areas that receive information on pressure, pain, touch, and temperature as well as handle attention and awareness of spatial relationships.

temporal lobes

Lobes at the sides of the brain's cerebral cortex; they contain areas involved in hearing, memory, perception, emotion, and (in the left lobe, typically) language comprehension.

frontal lobes

Lobes at the front of the brain's cerebral cortex; they contain areas involved in short-term memory, higher-order thinking, initiative, social judgment, and (in the left lobe, typically) speech production.

If a surgeon touches the somatosensory cortex in the parietal lobes, a patient might feel a tingling in the skin or a sense of being gently touched. If the visual cortex in the occipital lobes were electrically stimulated, he or she might report a flash of light or swirls of color. And, eerily, many areas of the cortex, when stimulated, would produce no obvious response or sensation. These "silent" areas are sometimes called the *association cortex* because they are involved in higher mental processes. To review the major structures of the brain, watch the video *How the Brain Works Part 4.*

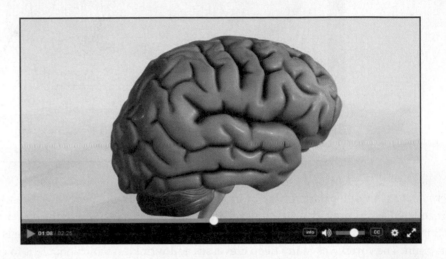

THE PREFRONTAL CORTEX   The most forward part of the frontal lobes is the *prefrontal cortex*. This area barely exists in mice and rats and takes up only 3.5 percent of the cerebral cortex in cats and about 7 percent in dogs, but it accounts for approximately one-third of the entire cortex in human beings. It is the most recently evolved part of our brains, and is associated with such complex abilities as reasoning, decision making, and planning.

Scientists have long known that the frontal lobes, and the prefrontal cortex in particular, must also have something to do with personality. The first clue appeared in 1848, when a bizarre accident drove an inch-thick, 3½-foot-long iron rod clear through the head of a young railroad worker named Phineas Gage. The rod (which is still on display at the Harvard University Medical School library, along with Gage's skull) entered beneath the left eye and exited through the top of the head, destroying much of the prefrontal cortex (H. Damasio et al., 1994; Van Horn et al., 2012). Miraculously, Gage survived this trauma and, by most accounts, he retained the ability to speak, think, and remember. But his friends complained that he was "no longer Gage." In a sort of Jekyll-and-Hyde transformation, he had changed from a mild-mannered, friendly, efficient worker into a foul-mouthed, ill-tempered, undependable lout who could not hold a steady job or stick to a plan. His employers had to let him go, and he was reduced to exhibiting himself as a circus attraction.

There is some controversy about the details of this sad incident, but many other cases of brain injury, whether from stroke or trauma, support the conclusion that most scientists draw from the Gage case: Parts of the frontal lobes are involved in social judgment, rational decision making, and the ability to set goals and to make and carry through plans. Like Gage, people with damage in these areas sometimes mismanage their finances, lose their jobs, and abandon their friends. Interestingly, the mental deficits that characterize damage to these areas are accompanied by a flattening-out of emotion and feeling, which suggests that normal emotions are necessary for everyday reasoning and the ability to learn from mistakes (A. Damasio, 2003; H. Damasio et al., 1994).

The frontal lobes also govern the ability to do a series of tasks in the proper sequence and to stop doing them at the proper time. Pioneering Soviet psychologist Alexander Luria (1980) studied many cases in which damage to the frontal lobes disrupted these abilities. One man kept trying to light a match after it was already lit. Another planed a piece of wood in the hospital carpentry shop until it was gone and then went on to plane the workbench! Watch *The Prefrontal Cortex* to learn more about how this important area of the brain influences behavior.

Review 4.1 summarizes the major parts of the brain that we have discussed and their primary functions.

JOURNAL PROMPT 4.4

Thinking Critically—Avoid Emotional Reasoning: Suppose it could be determined that 50 percent of hardened criminals had damage to areas of their prefrontal cortex (this is a hypothetical situation; just a thought exercise). Learning this, a lawmaker proposes that all current detainees in the juvenile justice center be screened for abnormalities in their frontal lobes, "to ward off the possibility of their committing serious future crimes." Would you support this proposal? Why or why not? What other evidence would you want to examine before jumping to an emotional conclusion?

Quiz for Module 4.4

1. Which of the following is *not* a main structure found in the brain stem?
   a. Reticular activating system
   b. Medulla
   c. Hypothalamus
   d. Pons

2. Which brain structure acts as a sensory relay station, directing visual or auditory sensations to other parts of the brain?
   a. Corpus callosum
   b. Hippocampus
   c. Pons
   d. Thalamus

3. If you had severe difficulty forming memories, what part of your brain might be damaged?
   a. Hippocampus
   b. Hypothalamus

   c. Cerebellum
   d. Pons

4. The thick band of fibers that connects the two hemispheres of the brain is called the
   a. Basal ganglia
   b. Cerebral cortex
   c. Thalamic extension
   d. Corpus callosum

5. The visual cortex is located in the
   a. Occipital lobe
   b. Parietal lobe
   c. Frontal lobe
   d. Temporal lobe

Review 4.1

Functions Associated with the Major Brain Structures

The functions listed here are just some of those that have been linked with these structures:	
Structure	**Functions**
Brain stem Pons Medulla Reticular activating system (RAS) (extends into center of the brain)	Sleeping, waking, dreaming Automatic functions such as breathing, heart rate Screening of incoming information, arousal of higher centers, consciousness
Cerebellum	Balance, muscular coordination, memory for simple skills and learned reflexes, involvement in cognitive and emotional learning
Thalamus	Relay of impulses from higher centers to the spinal cord and of incoming sensory information (except for olfactory sensations) to other brain centers
Hypothalamus	Behaviors necessary for survival, such as hunger, thirst, emotion, reproduction; regulation of body temperature; control of autonomic nervous system
Pituitary gland	Under direction of the hypothalamus, secretion of hormones that affect other glands
Amygdala	Initial evaluation of sensory information to determine its importance; mediation of anxiety and depression; formation and retrieval of emotional memories
Hippocampus	Comparison of new sensory information with existing knowledge in order to regulate the RAS; formation of new memories about facts and events, as well as other aspects of memory
Cerebrum (including cerebral cortex) Occipital lobes Parietal lobes Temporal lobes Frontal lobes	Higher forms of thinking Visual processing Processing of pressure, pain, touch, temperature Memory, perception, emotion, hearing, language comprehension Movement, short-term memory, planning, setting goals, creative thinking, initiative, social judgment, rational decision making, speech production

The Two Hemispheres of the Brain

We have seen that the cerebrum is divided into two hemispheres that control opposite sides of the body. Although similar in structure, these hemispheres have somewhat separate talents, or areas of specialization. Hemispheric specialization is especially apparent in patients who have suffered brain damage, usually as a result of a stroke. Those with left-hemisphere damage may lose the ability to speak or understand language, whereas those with right-hemisphere damage rarely do. A French neurologist named Paul Broca (whose name lives on in the term *Broca's area*) first made this observation in 1861, and many behavioral and cognitive difficulties associated with left- or right-hemisphere damage have been documented since then. Patients with left-hemisphere damage may have difficulties with reading, identifying objects, making symbolic gestures or pantomimes, and describing events in the correct order. For their part, patients with right-hemisphere damage may have difficulty identifying faces, interpreting emotional expressions in a face or voice, or understanding music or art. They may get lost easily, even in their own homes.

Split Brains: A House Divided

LO 4.5.A   Discuss the basic format of a split-brain experiment, and describe what the results of such experiments reveal about the functioning of the cerebral hemispheres.

Some of the most interesting findings about hemispheric specialization come from people known as "split-brain patients." In a normal brain, the two hemispheres of the cortex communicate with one another across the corpus callosum, the bundle of fibers that

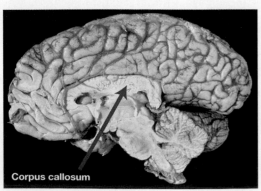

Corpus callosum

A cross section of a human brain, showing the corpus callosum.

connects them. Whatever happens in one side of the brain is instantly transferred to the other side. What would happen, though, if the two sides were cut off from one another?

In 1953, Ronald E. Myers and Roger W. Sperry took the first step toward answering this question by severing the corpus callosum in cats. They also cut parts of the nerves leading from the eyes to the brain. Normally, each eye transmits messages to both sides of the brain. After this procedure, a cat's left eye sent information only to the left hemisphere and its right eye sent information only to the right hemisphere.

At first, the cats did not seem to be affected much by this drastic operation. But Myers and Sperry showed that something profound had happened. They trained the cats to perform tasks with one eye blindfolded; a cat might learn to push a panel with a square on it to get food but ignore a panel with a circle. Then the researchers switched the blindfold to the cat's other eye and tested the animal again. Now the cats behaved as if they had never learned the trick. Apparently, one side of the brain did not know what the other side was doing; it was as if the animals had two brains in one body. Later studies confirmed this result with other species, including monkeys (Sperry, 1964).

In the animal studies, ordinary behavior, such as eating and walking, remained normal. In the early 1960s, a team of surgeons decided to try cutting the corpus callosum in patients with debilitating, uncontrollable epilepsy. In severe forms of this disease, disorganized electrical activity spreads from an injured area to other parts of the brain. The surgeons reasoned that cutting the connection between the two halves of the brain might stop the spread of electrical activity from one side to the other. The surgery was done, of course, for the sake of the patients, who were desperate. But there was a bonus for scientists, who would be able to find out what each cerebral hemisphere can do when it is quite literally cut off from the other.

The results of this *split-brain surgery* generally proved successful. Seizures were reduced and sometimes disappeared completely. In their daily lives, split-brain patients did not seem much affected by the fact that the two hemispheres were incommunicado. Their personalities and intelligence remained intact; they could walk, talk, and lead fairly normal lives. Apparently, connections in the undivided deeper parts of the brain kept body movements and other functions normal. The two functioning hemispheres were each doing their own job; they just couldn't communicate with each other. But in a series of ingenious studies, Sperry and his colleagues (and later other researchers) showed that perception and memory had been affected, just as they had been in the earlier animal research. Sperry won a Nobel Prize for his work.

To understand this research, you must know how nerves connect the eyes to the brain. (The human patients, unlike Myers and Sperry's cats, did not have these nerves cut.) If you look straight ahead, everything in the left side of the scene before you—the *visual field*—goes to the right half of your brain, and everything in the right side of the scene goes to the left half of your brain. This is true for both eyes (see Figure 4.12).

The procedure was to present information only to one or the other side of the patients' brains. In one early study, the researchers took photographs of different faces, cut them in two, and pasted different halves together (Levy, Trevarthen, & Sperry, 1972). The reconstructed photographs were then presented on slides. The person was told to stare at a dot in the middle of the screen, so that half of the image fell to the left of this point and half to the right. Each image was flashed so quickly that the person had no time to move his or her eyes.

Figure 4.12 Visual Pathways

Each cerebral hemisphere receives information from the eyes about the opposite side of the visual field. Thus, if you stare directly at the corner of a room, everything to the left of the juncture is represented in your right hemisphere, and vice versa. This is so because half the axons in each optic nerve cross over (at the optic chiasm) to the opposite side of the brain. Normally, each hemisphere immediately shares its information with the other one, but in split-brain patients, severing the corpus callosum prevents such communication.

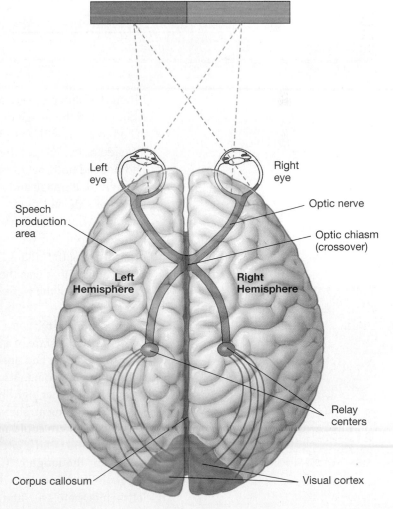

Figure 4.13 Divided View

Split-brain patients were shown composite photographs (a) and were then asked to pick out the face they had seen from a series of intact photographs (b). They said they had seen the face on the right side of the composite, yet they pointed with their left hands to the face that had been on the left. Because the two cerebral hemispheres could not communicate, the verbal left hemisphere was aware of only the right half of the picture, and the relatively mute right hemisphere was aware of only the left half (c).

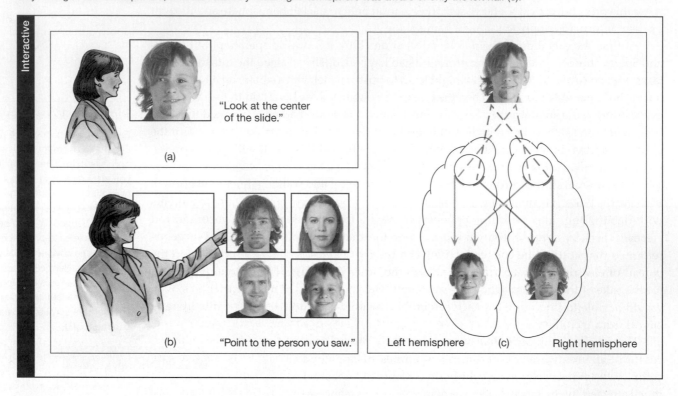

When the patients were asked to say what they had seen, they named the person in the right part of the image (which would be the little boy in Figure 4.13). But when they were asked to point with their left hands to the face they had seen, they chose the person in the left side of the image (the mustached man in the figure). Furthermore, they claimed they had noticed nothing unusual about the original photographs! Each side of the brain saw a different half image and automatically filled in the missing part. Neither side knew what the other side had seen.

Why did the patients name one side of the picture but point to the other? When the patient responded with speech, it was the left side of the brain, which usually controls speech, doing the talking. And because the left side of the brain had only seen the right side of the image, that was the face it saw. When the person pointed with the left hand, which is controlled by the right side of the brain, the right hemisphere was giving its version of what it had seen.

In another study, the researchers presented slides of ordinary objects and then suddenly flashed a slide of a nude woman. Both sides of the brain were amused, but because only the left side had speech, the two sides responded differently. When the picture was flashed to one woman's left hemisphere, she laughed and identified it as a nude. When it was flashed to her right hemisphere, she said nothing but began to chuckle. Asked what she was laughing at, she said, "I don't know . . . nothing . . . oh—that funny machine." The right hemisphere could not describe what it had seen, but it reacted emotionally just the same, and the talking left hemisphere was compelled to come up with a reasonable explanation for the laughter (Gazzaniga, 1967). Indeed, Michael Gazzaniga (1989), a leading psychological scientist who conducted this and other split-brain research, has called the left hemisphere an "interpreter" because one of its major roles is to continually provide a reasonable (though not always accurate) story to explain our thoughts, feelings, and behaviors. As another neuroscientist put it, the left hemisphere is the brain's "spin doctor" (Broks, 2004).

The Two Hemispheres: Allies or Opposites?

LO 4.5.B Describe why the two hemispheres of the brain are allies rather than opposites.

The split-brain operation is still being performed, although more rarely, now that better medications are available to treat epilepsy. However, there is a limit to the conclusions we can draw from split-brain patients. The fact that their seizures were severe enough to warrant such dramatic surgery indicates that they probably suffered neurological damage at some point, which could have affected the results.

Fortunately, research on left–right differences has also been done with people whose brains are intact (Hugdahl & Westerhausen, 2010; Prete et al., 2015). If a researcher flashes an image very quickly to the right side of your visual field, it will arrive first in your left visual cortex. Thanks to your corpus callosum, the image will then quickly transfer over to your right visual cortex. But your left visual areas will have had a small head start, and the difference in timing gives the investigator critical information. People read words faster if the words are flashed to the right visual field because those words go directly to the left hemisphere, which is specialized for reading. In contrast, people are better at identifying facial expressions that are flashed to the left visual field because those faces go directly to the right hemisphere, which typically shows an advantage for processing facial emotion (Abbott et al., 2014). Similarly, researchers can present different sounds to your two ears, the one in the left ear going to your right auditory cortex and the one in the right ear going to the left auditory cortex. These studies show that although the left hemisphere is specialized for processing words, the right hemisphere is specialized for processing the tone of voice in which the words are spoken (Grimshaw et al., 2003).

Although early researchers often spoke of the left hemisphere as dominant, especially because of its linguistic and analytic talents, over the years it has become clear that the right hemisphere is far from stupid or passive. It is superior not only at recognizing facial expressions but also at handling problems requiring spatial–visual ability, the ability you use to read a map or follow a dress pattern. It is active during the creation and appreciation of art and music. It recognizes nonverbal sounds, such as a dog's barking. It also has some language ability. Typically, it can read a word briefly flashed to it and can understand an experimenter's instructions.

Some researchers have also credited the right hemisphere with having a cognitive style that is intuitive and holistic, in contrast to the left hemisphere's more rational and analytic mode. This is a great oversimplification, one that has been promoted by books and programs that promise to make people more creative by making them more "right brained." In reality, the differences between the two hemispheres are relative, not absolute—a matter of degree. And in most real-life activities, the two sides cooperate naturally, with each making a valuable contribution. In visual perception, the left hemisphere generally "sees" the details, while the right hemisphere "sees" how they fit together (Robertson, Lamb, & Knight, 1988). In speech perception, the left hemisphere "hears" the individual sounds that make up the words, but the right hemisphere "hears" the intonation that tells us if the speaker is happy, sad, or sarcastic. In emotion, the left hemisphere "feels" emotions that lead us to approach situations or people, whereas the right hemisphere "feels" emotions that lead us to withdraw to safety (Davidson, 1992). Most thoughts and behaviors require the left and right hemispheres to work together. This is why it is wrong to think of a person as "left brained" or "right brained" and why we must be cautious about thinking of the two sides as two "minds." As Roger Sperry (1982) himself noted long ago, "The left–right dichotomy . . . is an idea with which it is very easy to run wild."

Have a righthanded friend tap on a sheet of paper with a pencil held in the right hand for 1 minute. Then have the person do the same with the left hand, using a fresh sheet of paper. Finally, repeat the procedure, having the person talk at the same time as tapping. For most people, talking will decrease the rate of tapping—but more for the right hand than for the left, probably because both activities involve the same hemisphere (the left one), and there is competition between them. (Lefthanded people vary more in terms of which hemisphere is dominant for language, so the results for them will be more variable.)

JOURNAL PROMPT 4.5

Thinking Critically—Define Your Terms: The left hemisphere is sometimes called the "interpreter" of our thoughts, feelings, and behaviors. What does that mean, exactly? What are some circumstances under which the left hemisphere—with its specializations for verbal skills and logical reasoning—might be called upon to interpret other actions of the brain? How do you define "interpret" in this context?

Quiz for Module 4.5

1. Imagine that an image of a cat was received by a split-brain patient's left hemisphere, and an image of a dog was received by that same patient's right hemisphere. If prompted for a verbal response, what would the patient say?

   a. "I saw a cat."

   b. "I saw a dog."

   c. "I saw a cat and a dog."

   d. The patient would be unable to verbalize anything.

2. Imagine that an image of a cat was received by a split-brain patient's left hemisphere, and an image of a dog was received by that same patient's right hemisphere. If the patient was prompted to point at an image using her or his *left* hand, what image would that be?

   a. The patient would be unable to point at anything.

   b. The cat

   c. Equally likely to be either the dog or the cat

   d. The dog

3. Imagine that an image of a cat was received by a split-brain patient's left hemisphere, and an image of a dog was received by that same patient's right hemisphere. If the patient was prompted to point at an image using her or his *right* hand, what image would that be?

   a. The cat

   b. The dog

   c. Equally likely to be either the dog or the cat

   d. The patient would be unable to point at anything.

4. If words were presented to one cerebral hemisphere or the other, which hemisphere would show an advantage in reading the words faster?

   a. The right hemisphere

   b. The left hemisphere

   c. There should be no difference between the reading speed of the two hemispheres

   d. The left hemisphere for short words, but the right hemisphere for longer words

5. What is the most reasonable conclusion to reach about the operation of the cerebral hemispheres, based on all we know from the available research?

   a. Some people are "left-brained" whereas others are "right-brained," and determining which is which can make life a lot easier for an individual.

   b. The two cerebral hemispheres are cooperative partners, each contributing to tasks that benefit the owner of that brain.

   c. The two cerebral hemispheres work in opposition to one another, each vying for supremacy on various kinds of tasks.

   d. Thinking that people have one brain is incorrect; people actually have "two brains" that operate independently of one another.

The Flexible Brain

Until this point, we have discussed the brain as if it were some fixed and unchanging organ, the same in everyone and essentially the same organ at birth as at age 8, 18, 28, or 98. Indeed, because we are all human and most of us share common early experiences—learning to walk, talk, deal with school and family members—our brains are fundamentally similar in their basic organization. Yet, we also have differing experiences as a result of growing up rich or poor, male or female, nurtured or neglected, and these experiences take place within a particular culture that shapes our values, skills, and opportunities. Such differences can affect the brain's wiring and how it is used.

Experience and the Brain

LO 4.6.A Define neural plasticity, and summarize some of the main evidence that the brain has the ability to change in response to new experiences.

Our brains are not fully formed at birth. During infancy, synapses proliferate at a great rate (see Figure 4.14). Neurons sprout new dendrites, creating new synapses and producing more complex connections among the brain's nerve cells (Bock et al., 2014; Greenough & Black, 1992; Kostović & Judaš, 2009; Rosenzweig, 1984). New learning and stimulating environments promote this increase in complexity. Then, during childhood, synaptic connections that are useful for helping the child respond to the environment survive and are strengthened whereas those that are not useful wither away, leaving behind a more efficient neural network. In this way, each brain is optimized for its environment. This **plasticity**, the brain's ability to change in response to new experiences, is most pronounced during infancy and early childhood, and has a resurgence in adolescence, but it continues throughout life.

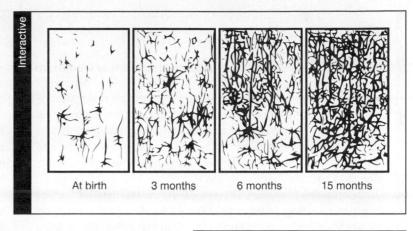

At birth | 3 months | 6 months | 15 months

Figure 4.14 Getting Connected

Neurons in a newborn's brain are widely spaced, but they immediately begin to form new connections. These drawings show the marked increase in the number of connections from birth to age 15 months.

plasticity

The brain's ability to change and adapt in response to experience, through neurogenesis, or by reorganizing or growing new neural connections.

The brain's plasticity may help explain why some people who cannot recall simple words after a stroke may be speaking almost normally within months, and why some who cannot move an arm after a head injury may regain full use of the limb after physical therapy. Their brains have apparently rewired themselves to adapt to the damage (Liepert et al., 2000). Plasticity is also apparent in some people who have been blind or deaf from birth or early childhood. In the period of rapid development after birth, connections form between the eyes and the visual cortex, and between the ears and the auditory cortex—but also between the eyes and the auditory cortex, and the ears and the visual cortex. (How this might affect the infant's perception, if it does, is a mystery.) Typically, experience strengthens connections between the eyes and the visual cortex, and between the ears and auditory cortex, and prunes away the other two types (Innocenti & Price, 2005). The intriguing question, therefore, is what happens in the visual cortex of blind people? Is it able to respond to sound because it is not receiving sight?

To answer this question, researchers used PET scans to examine the brains of people as they localized sounds heard through speakers (Gougoux et al., 2005). Some people were sighted but others had been blind from early in life. When they heard sounds through both ears, activity in the occipital cortex (an area associated with vision) decreased in the sighted people but *not* in the blind ones. When one ear was plugged, the blind people who did especially well at localizing sounds showed activation in two areas of the occipital cortex; neither sighted people nor blind people with ordinary ability showed that activation. What's more, the degree of activation in these regions was correlated with the blind people's accuracy on the task (see Figure 4.15). The brains of those with the best performance had apparently adapted to blindness by recruiting visual areas to take part in activities involving hearing—a dramatic example of plasticity.

In sighted people, the visual areas in the brain are quiet during tasks requiring hearing or touch (such as touching Braille letters). But researchers wondered what would happen to those visual areas if the volunteers were blindfolded for 5 days. The answer was that by day 5, those visual areas had become active during the tasks, and after the blindfolds were removed, the visual centers once again quieted down (Pascual-Leone et al., 2005). The visual areas of the brain apparently possess the computational machinery necessary for processing nonvisual information, but this machinery remains dormant until circumstances require its activation (Amedi et al., 2005). When people have been blind for most of their lives, new connections may form, permitting lasting structural changes in the brain's wiring. The opposite is true of deaf people. When neuroscientists asked deaf and hearing people to study sets of moving dots, the brains of deaf people showed activity in the auditory cortex, but the brains of hearing people did not (Finney, Fine, & Dobkins, 2001).

This research teaches us that the brain is a dynamic organ: Its circuits are continually being modified in response to information, challenges, and changes in the environment. As scientists come to understand this process better, they may be able to apply their knowledge by designing improved rehabilitation programs for people with sensory impairments, developmental disabilities, and brain injuries.

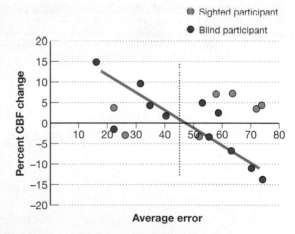

Figure 4.15 Adapting to Blindness

In some blind people, brain areas usually associated with vision may become active in tasks requiring hearing. The purple circles to the left of the dotted line represent blind individuals with low error rates in a sound-localization task; those to the right represent blind individuals with high error rates. The graph shows that error rates for blind people—but not sighted ones—were correlated with changes in cerebral blood flow (CBF), and thus neural activity, in a *visual* area of the brain. The more accurate blind people were, the greater the activity in this region. (Adapted from Gougoux et al., 2005.)

CULTURE and *the Brain*

We have just seen that the structure and function of the human brain is shaped by the environment throughout life. A big part of that environment is *culture*, a program of shared rules, values, symbols, communication systems, and conventions that governs the behavior of members of a community. The emerging field of *cultural neuroscience* examines how the links between neural and cultural forces can create different patterns of behavior, perception, and cognition (Ambady, 2011).

Consider bilingualism. Do bilingual people use different parts of their brains for their two languages? Evidence on this question has been mixed, but some intriguing findings suggest that different brain areas are involved in a first language versus a second language. One way to answer this question is to observe what happens when a surgeon stimulates different areas. The patient is usually awake and talking, but will stop when the surgeon stimulates brain areas that are critical for language. Studies using this approach show that a bilingual person's second language relies on a broader network of brain areas than the person's first language (Cervenka et al., 2011). This sort of information is surely crucial for brain surgeons to know.

Another cultural factor that may affect brain organization is literacy. Compared with literate people, illiterate individuals tend to have less white matter in a part of the parietal cortex associated with reading and verbal memory and in several other areas (de Schotten et al., 2014). Technological literacy may also affect brain activity. Some scientists speculate that Internet searching, text messaging, and social networking may strengthen the neural circuits involved in filtering information and making quick decisions, while possibly weakening others, such as those involved in sustained attention (Small, 2008).

When two cultures value different skills among their members, or when they emphasize different approaches to acquiring certain skills, people's brains may reflect those differences. The patterns of brain activity during mathematical processing are different in native Chinese speakers than in native English speakers. Both groups can learn that 2 + 2 = 4, but their brains will take different routes to get there because of the different ways that the Chinese and English languages process letters and sounds (Tang et al., 2006). In addition, brain activation in Westerners and Asians during a simple visual–spatial task depends on whether the task requires a person to attend to the visual context (a strategy emphasized in Asian cultures) or to ignore the visual context (which is encouraged in Western cultures). In both groups, fMRI scans show activation in frontal and parietal regions associated with attentional control to be greater when people are making judgments not typical for their cultural background (Hedden et al., 2008). This makes sense because those judgments require more attention and effort.

Cultures have a profound influence on their members' symbols, attitudes, and ways of navigating the world. Studies from cultural neuroscience are tracking that influence into the brain, where it shows up in fMRI studies of perception, problem solving, language, and thinking. Many people might be inclined to jump to the conclusion that our brains make us different, overlooking the equally powerful inference that our differences shape our brains. In the words of one researcher, "Much like the changing tide can erode a footprint in the sand, so too can changed experience over time reshape brain activations. In this sense, the brain can be seen as a 'cultural sponge' of sorts, absorbing the regularities of our surrounding physical and social environments" (Ambady, 2011).

Are There "His" and "Hers" Brains?

LO 4.6.B Summarize five cautions surrounding whether sex differences in anatomical brain size are linked to sex differences in behavior.

Many best-selling books today claim that men and women have different brains. *The Female Brain* was so successful that it inspired a sequel, *The Male Brain*. *It's a Baby Girl!* claims that "Without testosterone interfering, your daughter develops not only female genitalia but a decidedly female brain . . . [one] that will direct her female approach to the world" (quoted in Fine, 2010). (Critical thinkers might wonder what a "female approach to the world" is, that is, one unaffected by a woman's religion, culture, social class, age, generation, occupation, nationality, or education.) Popular books about leadership, marital problems, parenting, and education likewise claim that males and females have hardwired brain differences that explain, among other things, women's allegedly superior intuition and empathy, women's love of talking about feelings and men's love of talking about sports, women's greater verbal ability, men's greater math ability, and why men won't ask for directions when they're lost. Some writers call upon brain science to argue that the sexes are so different that they should be segregated into different schools.

What is a layperson to make of these arguments, which are often presented with lots of fMRI images and other pictures of the brain? Of course there are innumerable average differences in men's and women's experiences and behavior. Unfortunately, as a panel of eminent neuroscientists and other psychological scientists discussed at a professional meeting, ideology often gets in the way of interpreting research on sex differences and the brain: Some people worry that the research can be used to justify sexism (a legitimate concern, given those oversimplified pop-psych books), and others argue, just as legitimately, that ignoring the evidence is antiscientific and an impediment to improving the lives and health of both women and men (Saletan, 2011).

To evaluate this issue intelligently, we need to ask two separate questions: Do the brains of males and females differ, on average, in structure or function? And if so, what, if anything, do those differences have to do with men's and women's behavior, abilities, ways of solving problems, or anything else that matters in real life?

The answer to the first question is yes. Many anatomical and biochemical sex differences have been found in animal and human brains, in both their structure and function (Cahill, 2012; Luders et al., 2004). Some appear to be universal: A study combining fMRI data from 24 laboratories and more than 1,000 people worldwide—in Australia, China, England, Finland, Germany, the United States, and Wales—showed that when their brains are at rest (i.e., not engaged in doing any specific mental work), men and women have different patterns of activity across the brain as a whole (Biswal et al., 2010). Using fMRI, scientists can infer that two regions are connected if they become active at the same time and also inactive at the same time. In this huge international study, people of all ages, both sexes, and from all cultures showed remarkably similar patterns of connectivity. But there were also significant differences between the patterns seen in men and women, such as in connections between the cortex and the amygdala.

In addition, parts of the frontal lobes are larger in women, relative to the overall size of their brains, whereas parts of the parietal cortex and the amygdala are larger in men (Goldstein et al., 2001; Gur et al., 2002; Kim et al., 2012). Women also have more cortical folds in the frontal and parietal lobes (Luders et al., 2004). On average, men have more neurons than women do in the cortex, and some researchers speculate that this difference contributes to the sex difference in spatial abilities, such as skill at mentally rotating objects (Burgaleta et al., 2012). Finally, the amygdala appears to be lateralized according to sex. In men, the right amygdala keeps getting input from the rest of the brain; in women, the left amygdala gets that input. This lateralization seems to predispose men and women to encode and remember emotional information differently. In men, better memory is associated with greater activity in the right-hemisphere amygdala, but in women, better memory is associated with the left-hemisphere amygdala (Cahill et al., 2004).

Is your own male or female brain spinning yet? The bottom line is that average sex differences in the brain do exist. But we are still left with our second question: Overall, what do the differences mean for the behavior or personality traits of men and women in ordinary life? When you hear or read popular accounts of "sex and the brain," keep these cautions in mind:

1. **Many supposed differences between men and women in intuition, abilities, and traits are stereotypes**; they mislead because the overlap between the sexes is often greater than the difference between them. Even when gender differences are statistically significant, they are often quite small in practical terms. And national differences may be greater than sex differences. Thus, boys are somewhat better than girls in math in the United States, Taiwan, and Japan, but the bigger difference is between countries, with Taiwanese and Japanese girls outscoring American boys (Else-Quest, Hyde, & Linn, 2010). Some supposed differences, on closer inspection, even disappear. Are women more talkative than men, as many pop-psych books about the sexes assert? To test this assumption, psychologists wired up a sample of men and women with voice recorders that tracked their conversations while they went about their daily lives. The sexes did not differ in the number of words spoken; women and men alike used about

16,000 words per day on average, with large individual differences among the participants (Mehl et al., 2007).

2. **A brain difference does not necessarily produce a difference in behavior or performance.** In many studies, males and females have shown different patterns of brain activity while they are doing something or while an ability is being tested, but they have not differed in the behavior or ability in question. The different patterns of activity are of great interest to scientists, who, after all, want to understand the mechanisms that produce behavior. If six routes lead to Rome, they want to know all six; laypeople just want to get there in time for lunch. The problem occurs when laypeople wrongly infer that a brain difference is the reason for a behavioral difference—one that doesn't exist! (Fine, 2010). Researchers used MRI to examine the brains of men and women who had equivalent IQ scores. They found some differences, such as that women's brains had more white-matter areas related to intelligence, whereas men's brains had more gray-matter areas related to intelligence (Haier et al., 2005). That is interesting, yet the sexes do not differ in overall intelligence. The researchers concluded that brains may be organized differently yet produce the same intellectual abilities.

3. **Differences in the brain do not account for differences in behavior across situations.** Consider the example of empathy, a skill central to the female stereotype. Most people will tell you that women in some generic way are better than men at empathy and intuition, and on self-report questionnaires, women are more likely than men to describe themselves as being high in empathy. Unfortunately, what people say about themselves, on any trait or behavior from kindness and altruism to obedience and cruelty, is typically unrelated to how they actually behave in various situations. When we hear that women are hardwired to be empathic, therefore, we need to ask, which women? Under what circumstances? Empathy toward whom? Women are not more empathic toward their enemies, familial or national, than men are. Over and over, if you watch what people do rather than what they say they would do, and vary the situations in which they do it, gender differences fade (Fine, 2010; Jordan-Young, 2010).

4. **The eternal problem of cause and effect: Some male–female differences in the brain can be the result rather than the cause of behavioral differences.** As we have seen, experiences and cultural influences are constantly sculpting the circuitry of the brain, affecting the way brains are organized and how they function. Women and men, of course, often have different experiences in childhood and throughout their lives. Thus, when researchers find a sex difference in brain structure or function, they cannot automatically assume that the difference is innate or unchangeable.

5. **The elusive brain difference: Now you see it, now you don't.** People have an understandable tendency to think that if a study of a dozen men's and women's brains finds an average difference, that result is generalizable to everyone. After all, a brain is a brain, isn't it? But research on brains, as on anything else, must be replicated, and sometimes the results are surprising. Researchers once were convinced that the corpus callosum of men and women differed in size, but early findings were not replicated. Researchers once thought the amygdala was the "anger center"; then they thought it was the "fear center"; now, as you read earlier in this chapter, they understand its more varied functions. Researchers once were convinced that men's brains were less lateralized than women's brains, especially in tasks involving language, meaning that women use both sides of the brain when they are doing a task and men only one side. But meta-analyses and large-scale studies have failed to confirm what "everyone knew" about lateralization (Chiarello et al., 2009; Sommer et al., 2004, 2008).

One reason that scientists differ in their interpretation of the research is that some are focusing on the differences between the sexes and others are focusing on the similarities. Both sides may be right. Yet both would agree that we all should avoid oversimplifying, jumping to conclusions, and thinking in either–or terms (*either* men and women have "different" brains *or* we are all exactly alike). Critical thinking skills are something both sexes can learn.

We think you'll agree that findings about the brain are pretty fascinating, and we will discuss many others in the rest of this book. However, these findings should not deflect attention from all the other influences that make us who we are, for better or worse: our relationships, our experiences, our standing in society, our culture. Keep in mind (as well as in your brain) that analyzing a human being in terms of physiology alone is like analyzing the Eiffel Tower solely in terms of the rivets that were used to build it. Even if we could monitor every cell and circuit of the brain, we would still need to understand the circumstances, thoughts, and cultural rules that affect whether we are gripped by hatred, consumed by grief, lifted by love, or transported by joy.

JOURNAL PROMPT 4.6

Thinking Critically—Ask Questions: The study of the brain raises many challenging scientific and philosophical questions. Why can a small glitch in the brain's circuits be devastating to some people, whereas others can function with major damage? How do experiences in life alter our brains?

Quiz for Module 4.6

1. Although people typically think of the brain as fully formed or "static" by adulthood, it actually has the ability to change in response to new experiences, by strengthening some neural connections, pruning others, or reorganizing itself. This property is called
   a. Generativity
   b. Plasticity
   c. Reformation
   d. Reformulation

2. Which statement is correct regarding synaptic connections in the brain?
   a. Useful connections are strengthened by learning and experience, whereas connections that aren't useful tend to wither away, leaving an efficient network of interconnected neurons.
   b. With proper stimulation, all neural connections continue to expand and multiply in scale as a person ages.
   c. The number of synaptic connections reaches its peak by age 12, then slowly but steadily begins to decrease from that point through the remainder of a person's lifespan.
   d. Newborns have approximately 10 trillion synaptic connections at birth, but this number dwindles to approximately 250,000 by age 25.

3. Which of the following is a reliable sex difference in the brains of women and men that has been documented?
   a. Men tend to be "left-brained," whereas women tend to be "right-brained."
   b. The hypothalamus is generally more developed among women, whereas the thalamus is generally more developed among men.

   c. The occipital lobe is generally larger in men than it is in women, relative to an individual's body size.
   d. Parts of the parietal lobe are larger in men, whereas parts of the frontal lobes are larger in women, relative to the overall size of their brains.

4. Which of the following is *not* a caution to bear in mind when interpreting research findings regarding sex differences in the brains of women and men?
   a. Sex differences in the brain could be the result, rather than the cause, of differences in behavior.
   b. Anatomical and biochemical sex differences in the brain have not been documented by researchers.
   c. Differences in the brain do not account for differences in behavior across situations.
   d. A brain difference does not necessarily produce a difference in behavior or performance.

5. Stevie reads that women's and men's brains are organized differently, and therefore concludes that this organization produces sex differences in behavior. What is wrong about Stevie's logic?
   a. Sex differences in behavior are actually due to sex differences in brain *development* rather than sex differences in brain *organization*.
   b. Relatively small differences in brain organization—a few hundred neural connections or so—are sufficient to impact behavior; overall organization is beside the point.
   c. The causal arrow is reversed; well-documented sex differences in behavior cause differences in brain organization to develop.
   d. A brain difference does not necessarily produce a behavioral difference; different brain organizations can produce the same behavioral outcomes.

Taking Psychology with You

Cosmetic Neurology: Tinkering with the Brain

Should healthy people be permitted, even encouraged, to take "brain boosters" or "neuroenhancers," drugs that will sharpen concentration and memory? What about a pill that could erase a traumatic memory? If having cosmetic surgery can change parts of your body that you don't like, what's wrong with allowing "cosmetic neurology" to tinker with parts of your brain that you don't like?

For centuries, people have been seeking ways to stimulate their brains to work more efficiently, with caffeine being an especially popular drug of choice. But people who dislike coffee don't talk about the unfair advantage that coffee drinkers have. Likewise, no one objects to the finding that omega-3s, found in some kinds of fish, may help protect university students against the sudden increases in blood pressure that mental stress causes (Ginty & Conklin, 2012). But when it comes to prescription medications that increase alertness or appear to enhance memory and other cognitive functions, it's another kettle of fish oil, so to speak. What questions should you ask and what kind of evidence would you need to make wise decisions about using these medications? A new interdisciplinary specialty, *neuroethics,* has been formed to address the many legal, ethical, and scientific questions raised by brain research, including those raised by the development of neuroenhancing drugs (Gazzaniga, 2005).

Much of the buzz has focused on Provigil (modafinil), a drug approved for treating narcolepsy and other sleep disorders, and the amphetamines Ritalin and Adderall, approved for attention-deficit disorders. Some students, pilots, business executives, and jetlagged travelers are taking one or another of these drugs, either obtaining them illegally from friends or the Internet, or getting their own prescriptions. Most of these users claim the drugs help them learn better and stay alert. And one review of the literature concluded that Provigil can indeed improve memory for studied material (Smith & Farah, 2011), although the boost the medications deliver is less than what people expect (Repantis et al., 2010).

But the downside to these drugs rarely makes the news. Adderall, like all amphetamines, can cause nervousness, headaches, sleeplessness, allergic rashes, and loss of appetite, and, as the label says, it has "a high potential for abuse." Provigil, too, is habit-forming. Another memory-enhancing drug being studied targets a type of glutamate receptor in the brain. The drug apparently improves short-term memory, but at the price of impairing long-term memory (Talbot, 2009).

Even when a drug is benign for most of its users, there may be surprising and unexpected consequences. For example, the better able that people are to focus and concentrate on a task—the reason for taking stimulants in the first place—the less *creative* they often are. Creativity, after all, comes from being able to let our minds roam freely, at leisure. One neurologist therefore worries that the routine use of mind-enhancing drugs among students could create "a generation of very focused accountants" (quoted in Talbot, 2009).

Some bioethicists and neuroscientists think that the desire for cosmetic neurology is just part of human nature, a way for people to adapt to their environments and achieve goals that they could not achieve without the drugs (Müller & Schumann, 2011). After all, we use eyeglasses to improve vision and hearing aids to improve hearing; why not use pills to improve our memories and other mental skills? One team of scientists has argued that improving brain function with pills is no more objectionable than eating right or getting a good night's sleep. "In a world in which human work spans and life spans are increasing," they wrote, cognitive enhancement tools "will be increasingly useful for improved quality of life and extended work productivity, as well as to stave off normal and pathological age-related cognitive declines" (Greely et al., 2008).

Other scientists and social critics, however, consider cosmetic neurology to be a form of cheating that will give those who can afford the drugs an unfair advantage and increase socioeconomic inequalities. They think the issue is no different from the (prohibited) use of performance-enhancing steroids in athletics. And yes, they say, people wear glasses and hearing aids, but glasses and hearing aids do not have side effects or interact negatively with other treatments. Many neuroethicists also worry that ambitious parents will start giving these medications to their children to try to boost the child's academic performance, despite possible hazards for the child's developing brain. One reporter covering the pros and cons of neuroenhancers concluded that she's not sure she wants to live in a world where we are all worked so hard that we have to take drugs simply to keep up (Talbot, 2009).

And what if cognitive enhancement involved not pills but electrical stimulation of your brain? In 2012, neuroscientists at the University of Oxford reported that transcranial direct current stimulation (tDCS) might soon be used with healthy people to improve their math skills, memory, problem solving, and other mental abilities. One said, "I can see a time when people plug a simple device into an iPad so that their brain is stimulated when they are doing their homework, learning French, or taking up the piano." And, he added, tDCS would be a great educational aid for children.

Should you get in line to buy your own tDCS machine? Best to wait. As a critical thinker, you would want to ask how much research on tDCS has been done. (Answer: Most is preliminary laboratory work that has been done only on a small scale.) Has research determined whether there are better or worse ways of using tDCS for different mental abilities? (Not yet.) Has the method been tested on children, whose brains are still developing? (Not yet.) Is it known whether boosting ability in one area might affect abilities in other areas? (Not yet.) Has research determined whether the use of tDCS in the lab can improve people's abilities in everyday life? (Not yet.) Finally, critical thinkers should be wary of the entrepreneurs who won't want to wait for the answers to these questions before they start trying to market tDCS to parents, patients, and students.

Shared Writing Prompt

Imagine this scenario: In 5 years' time, scientists have amassed enough evidence to demonstrate that using tDCS in healthy people can improve their problem-solving skills by 20 percent over their current baseline. The equipment and the supervised application don't come cheap, however.

Coincidentally, imagine you've also been given $50,000 that you simply don't know what to do with. How much of the $50,000 would you be willing to spend to achieve the outcomes promised by tDCS? Can you defend your answer on ethical, logical, and/or scientific grounds?

Summary

The Nervous System: A Basic Blueprint

LO 4.1.A   List the major structures of the central nervous system, and describe their primary functions.

Scientists divide the nervous system into the *central nervous system* (CNS) and the *peripheral nervous system* (PNS). The CNS, which includes the brain and *spinal cord*, receives, processes, interprets, and stores information and sends out messages destined for muscles, glands, and organs.

LO 4.1.B   List the major structures and major divisions of the peripheral nervous system, and describe their primary functions.

The peripheral nervous system consists of the *somatic nervous system*, which permits sensation and voluntary actions, and the *autonomic nervous system*, which regulates blood vessels, glands, and internal (visceral) organs. The autonomic system usually functions without conscious control. The autonomic nervous system is further divided into the *sympathetic nervous system*, which mobilizes the body for action, and the *parasympathetic nervous system*, which conserves energy.

Communication in the Nervous System

LO 4.2.A   Compare the functions of neurons and glial cells in the nervous system.

Neurons are the basic units of the nervous system. They are held in place by *glial cells*, which nourish, insulate, protect, and repair neurons.

LO 4.2.B   Describe each of the three main parts of a neuron, and explain their functions.

Each neuron consists of *dendrites*, a *cell body*, and an *axon*. In the peripheral nervous system, axons (and sometimes dendrites) are collected together in bundles called *nerves*. Many axons are insulated by a *myelin sheath* that speeds up the conduction of neural impulses and prevents signals in adjacent cells from interfering with one another.

LO 4.2.C   Explain how stem cells contribute to the process of neurogenesis.

Research has disproven two old assumptions: that neurons in the human central nervous system cannot be induced to regenerate

and that no new neurons form after early infancy. Embryonic *stem cells* are pluripotent, meaning that they can generate many different kinds of cells in the body. These stem cells in various organs, including in brain areas associated with learning and memory, continue to divide and mature throughout adulthood, giving rise to new neurons. A stimulating environment seems to enhance this process of *neurogenesis*.

LO 4.2.D   Outline the process by which neurons communicate with each other, and explain the basic functions of the synapse, action potential, synaptic vesicles, and neurotransmitters.

Communication between two neurons occurs at the *synapse*. When a wave of electrical voltage (*action potential*) reaches the end of a transmitting axon, *neurotransmitter* molecules are released into the *synaptic cleft*. When these molecules bind to *receptor sites* on the receiving neuron, that neuron becomes either more or less likely to fire.

LO 4.2.E   Summarize the effects of some of the main neurotransmitters in the brain, and list four hormones that influence behavior.

Neurotransmitters play a critical role in mood, memory, and psychological well-being. *Serotonin*, *dopamine*, *acetylcholine*, and *norepinephrine* systems travel different paths through the brain; *GABA* and *glutamate* are distributed through the entire brain. *Hormones*, produced mainly by the *endocrine glands*, affect and are affected by the nervous system. Neuroscientists are especially interested in *melatonin*, which promotes sleep and helps regulate bodily rhythms; *oxytocin* and *vasopressin*, which play a role in attachment and trust; *adrenal hormones* such as *epinephrine* and *norepinephrine*, which are involved in emotions and stress; and the *sex hormones*, which are involved in the physical changes of puberty, the menstrual cycle (*estrogens* and *progesterone*), sexual arousal (*testosterone*), and some nonreproductive functions, including mental functioning.

Mapping the Brain

LO 4.3.A   Describe three techniques researchers use for intervening in the brain and observing the behavior that results.

Researchers study the brain by observing patients with brain damage; by using the *lesion method* with animals; and by using recent techniques such as *transcranial magnetic stimulation* (TMS) and *transcranial direct current stimulation* (tDCS).

LO 4.3.B Describe five techniques researchers use for intervening in behavior and observing the effects on the brain.

Tools such as *electroencephalograms*(EEGs), *event-related potentials* (ERP), *PET (positron emission tomography) scans*, *magnetic resonance imaging* (MRI), and *functional MRI* (fMRI) allow researchers to investigate the structure and function of the brain. These tools reveal which parts of the brain are active during different tasks, but they do not reveal discrete "centers" for particular functions.

A Tour through the Brain

LO 4.4.A List and describe three main structures in the brain stem, explain the primary functions each structure performs, and discuss the processes controlled by the cerebellum.

In the lower part of the brain, in the *brain stem*, the *medulla* controls automatic functions such as heartbeat and breathing, and the *pons* is involved in sleeping, waking, and dreaming. The *reticular activating system* (RAS) screens incoming information and is responsible for alertness. The *cerebellum* contributes to balance and muscle coordination, and plays a role in cognitive and emotional learning.

LO 4.4.B Describe the structure, function, and location of the thalamus.

The *thalamus* directs sensory messages to appropriate higher centers in the brain. Smell is the only sense that bypasses the thalamus, with specialized cells located instead in the *olfactory bulb*.

LO 4.4.C Describe the structure, function, and location of the hypothalamus and pituitary gland.

The *hypothalamus* is involved in emotion and in drives associated with survival. It also controls the operations of the autonomic nervous system and sends out chemicals that tell the *pituitary gland* when to "talk" to other endocrine glands.

LO 4.4.D Describe the structure, function, and location of the amygdala.

The *amygdala* is responsible for evaluating sensory information and quickly determining its importance, and thus your initial decision to approach or withdraw from a person or situation. It is also involved in forming and retrieving emotional memories.

LO 4.4.E Describe the structure, function, and location of the hippocampus.

The *hippocampus* moderates the reticular activating system. It has also been called the "gateway to memory" because it plays a critical role in the formation of long-term memories for facts and events and other aspects of memory.

LO 4.4.F Describe the structure of the cerebrum, and explain the function of the corpus callosum.

Much of the brain's circuitry is packed into the *cerebrum*, which is divided into two *hemispheres* (connected by the *corpus callosum*) and is covered by thin layers of cells known collectively as the *cerebral cortex*.

LO 4.4.G Sketch the location of each of the lobes of the cerebral cortex, and explain the major functions each lobe performs, with particular reference to the prefrontal cortex.

The *occipital*, *parietal*, *temporal*, and *frontal lobes* of the cortex have specialized (but partially overlapping) functions. The *association cortex* appears to be responsible for higher mental processes. The frontal lobes, particularly areas in the *prefrontal cortex*, are involved in social judgment, making and carrying out plans, and decision making.

The Two Hemispheres of the Brain

LO 4.5.A Discuss the basic format of a split-brain experiment, and describe what the results of such experiments reveal about the functioning of the cerebral hemispheres.

Studies of patients who have had *split-brain surgery* (a severing of the corpus callosum) show that the two cerebral hemispheres have somewhat different talents. In most people, language is processed mainly in the left hemisphere, which generally is specialized for logical, symbolic, and sequential tasks. The right hemisphere is associated with visual–spatial tasks, facial recognition, and the creation and appreciation of art and music.

LO 4.5.B Describe why the two hemispheres of the brain are allies rather than opposites.

In most mental activities the two hemispheres cooperate as partners, with each making a valuable contribution. The brain is more like an interactive federation than a house divided.

The Flexible Brain

LO 4.6.A Define neural plasticity, and summarize some of the main evidence that the brain has the ability to change in response to new experiences.

The brain's circuits are not fixed and immutable but are continually changing in response to information, challenges, and changes in the environment, a phenomenon known as *plasticity*. In some people who have been blind from an early age, brain regions usually devoted to vision are activated by sound—a dramatic example of plasticity.

LO 4.6.B Summarize five cautions surrounding whether sex differences in anatomical brain size are linked to sex differences in behavior.

Brain scans and other techniques have revealed many male–female differences in brain anatomy and function. Controversy exists, however, about what such differences mean in real life. Some of the brain research has focused on behavioral or cognitive differences that are small and insignificant. Some findings have been widely accepted but then have failed to replicate. Some male–female brain differences may be related to differences in behavior or performance, whereas others may not. Finally, sex differences in experience could affect brain organization and function rather than the other way around.

Chapter 4 Quiz

1. Which part of the central nervous system acts reflexively, sending and receiving signals with little to no conscious effort?

   a. The parasympathetic system

   b. The brain

   c. The spinal column

   d. The spinal cord

2. The two subdivisions of the autonomic nervous system are the _____ and the _____.

   a. Central nervous system / peripheral nervous system

   b. Sympathetic nervous system / parasympathetic nervous system

   c. Somatic nervous system / sympathetic nervous system

   d. Parasympathetic nervous system / peripheral nervous system

3. What is the distribution between neurons and glial cells in a typical human brain?

   a. There are approximately 1 trillion neurons and 4 billion glial cells in a typical brain.

   b. There are 12 times as many glial cells as there are neurons in the brain.

   c. Neurons and glia have a 3:1 ratio; for every three neurons, there is one glial cell.

   d. Neurons and glia are about evenly divided across the 171 billion cells that make up a typical brain.

4. The three main parts of a neuron are

   a. Dendrites, cell body, axon

   b. Axon, myelin, synapse

   c. Cell body, soma, dendrites

   d. Myelin, sclera, axon terminals

5. The production of new neurons from immature stem cells is a process known as

   a. Neuromimetics

   b. Neural spread

   c. Neurogenesis

   d. Ontogenesis

6. "Argh!" cried Jerry. "I can feel sodium and potassium ions moving across the cell membranes of my neurons! It's so distracting!" Two conclusions are correct regarding Jerry's statements. First, he can't really feel ions moving across his cell membranes. Second, but if he could, he'd be describing

   a. An action potential

   b. Reuptake

   c. Channelization

   d. The process of neurogenesis

7. Three primary types of sex hormones are _____, _____, and _____.

   a. Androgens / testosterone / protosterone

   b. Androgens / estrogens / progesterone

   c. Estrogens / gestrogens / testosterone

   d. Cortisol / epinephrine / norepinephrine

8. How does transcranial magnetic stimulation (TMS) help researchers to understand functioning in the brain?

   a. TMS can temporarily inactivate neural circuits, allowing researchers to observe the effects on behavior.

   b. TMS measures changes in blood glucose levels in the brain, which are correlated with different types of information-processing tasks.

   c. TMS provides a record of brain-wave activity, which allows researchers to predict where future patterns of thoughts are likely to occur.

   d. TMS detects differences in blood oxygen absorption in the brain, providing a kind of "map" of brain functions that researchers can inspect.

9. Why should scientists and the public at large be cautious when interpreting the results of an fMRI study claiming to have found a "brain center" for a particular behavior?

   a. EEG provides a better mechanism for pinpointing brain-based behavioral changes.

   b. fMRI is still an experimental technique that hasn't been used much in research.

   c. Brain scan images can often convey misleading or oversimplified conclusions.

   d. Neurogenesis makes isolating brain functions to a particular region impossible.

10. The brain stem structure involved in sleeping, waking, and dreaming is the

    a. Pons

    b. Medulla oblongata

    c. Reticular activating system

    d. Hypothalamic projection

11. Where is the thalamus located in the human brain?

    a. Below the cerebellum, but above the medulla oblongata

    b. Next to the pons on the brain stem

    c. Deep inside the brain's interior, almost at the center of the brain

    d. Above the pituitary gland and below the hypothalamus

12. Why is the pituitary gland often called the body's "master gland"?

    a. It secretes hormones that affect other endocrine glands.

    b. It controls the functions of the hypothalamus.

    c. It is located in the exact center of the human brain.

    d. It secretes chemicals that affect the prefrontal cortex.

13. Participants in an experiment are shown facial expressions of various emotions. Expressions of fear, sadness, anger, and happiness flash on a screen at a rapid rate. Although many parts of the brain are activated in response to these images, which of the following brain structures would play a particularly important role in processing this emotional content?

    a. The cerebellum
    b. The olfactory bulb
    c. The hippocampus
    d. The amygdala

14. Jeannie and Belinda were discussing cosmetic surgery one day. "I'm thinking of having my hippocampus removed," said Jeannie. "It's so tiny, and I just think my brain would look more streamlined without it." "Yeah . . . why don't you look into that," Belinda replied in sarcastic disbelief. Why does Belinda think Jeannie is pursuing a dramatically foolish idea?

    a. Jeannie would be unable to recognize threatening stimuli in her environment.
    b. Jeannie would lose her senses of smell and taste.
    c. Jeannie would be unable to form new memories.
    d. Jeannie would become partially deaf.

15. Why does the human cerebral cortex have so many deep crevasses and wrinkles in it?

    a. So that billions of neurons can fit in a relatively compact area.
    b. Because a cell's axons need to extend in multiple directions at once.
    c. Because evolutionary pressures caused many "restarts" to brain development.
    d. So that dendrites can coexist on multiple geometric planes across the cortex.

16. Where is the occipital lobe of the human cerebral cortex located?

    a. Below the frontal lobe
    b. At the front of the head
    c. Above the parietal lobe
    d. At the back of the head

17. Why would surgeons sever the corpus callosum in the human brain to create a split-brain patient?

    a. For the greater benefit of science
    b. As a means of studying how the corpus callosum works
    c. In order to relieve the consequences of debilitating epileptic seizures

    d. To gain access to brain structures such as the thalamus, hypothalamus, and hippocampus

18. Why is it incorrect to think of people as being "left-brained" or "right-brained"?

    a. There are no identifiable functions associated with one hemisphere or the other; talk of being "left-brained" is a stereotype.
    b. Information received in one hemisphere travels to the other hemisphere via the corpus callosum, so the "whole brain" is always engaged.
    c. The division between "lower" and "upper" brain structures is more important, such that some people are "low-brained" and others are "high-brained."
    d. "Left-brain" tasks are complex, whereas "right-brain" tasks deal with basic survival; therefore, we are all right-brained as long as we're alive and breathing.

19. Which statement best summarizes our current state of knowledge about the brain?

    a. The human brain is a dynamic organ capable of modifying its circuits in response to experience and changes in the environment.
    b. The human brain is fully formed in most humans by the age of 20 and undergoes relatively minor modifications after that.
    c. The human brain is a static organ that executes information-processing routines that are shaped by natural selection.
    d. The human brain shows explosive growth between birth and 5 years of age, then rapid decline after the age of 70.

20. Why should we be cautious in interpreting research on sex differences in the human brain?

    a. MRI scans are notoriously inconclusive evidence for structural differences in the brain.
    b. Promoting sex differences is a sociocultural means of creating divisions that don't exist.
    c. No documented sex difference in brain structures or functions has been confirmed by the Moser-O'Keefe standard.
    d. Findings that demonstrate a sex difference may not be replicated with new evidence and better techniques.

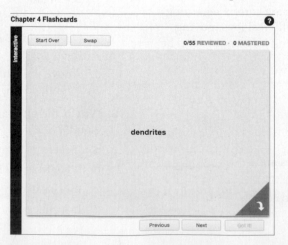

Chapter 4 Flashcards

Interactive

Start Over   Swap

0/55 REVIEWED · 0 MASTERED

dendrites

Previous   Next   Got It!

Chapter 5
Body Rhythms and Mental States

 Listen to the Audio

Learning Objectives

LO 5.1.A Define circadian rhythms, and explain how the body's "biological clock" works (and what happens when it doesn't).

LO 5.1.B Explain why seasonal affective disorder and premenstrual syndrome are examples of long-term biological rhythms, and summarize the evidence regarding the existence of both phenomena.

LO 5.2.A Describe the four stages of sleep, and explain the primary features of each stage.

LO 5.2.B List the mental consequences of sleeplessness and the mental benefits of a good night's sleep.

LO 5.3.A Discuss explanations for why we dream.

LO 5.3.B Summarize the strengths and weaknesses of each major dream theory.

LO 5.4.A Summarize six established facts about hypnosis, and outline the truth and misconceptions associated with each.

LO 5.4.B Contrast the dissociation theory of hypnosis from the sociocognitive approach, noting how each accounts for aspects of hypnotized behavior.

LO 5.5.A List the four main categories of psychoactive drugs, and summarize the main effects of each.

LO 5.5.B Outline the physiology of drug effects, and explain the process by which biochemical changes take place.

LO 5.5.C Summarize four psychological aspects of drug effects, and comment on how each one might moderate physiological drug effects.

Ask questions . . . be willing to wonder

If you didn't know what time it was, would your body?

Why do we need to sleep—and dream?

Can hypnotized people be made to do things against their will?

Why can a glass of wine make a person feel happy and excited on one occasion but tired and depressed on another?

In Lewis Carroll's classic story *Alice's Adventures in Wonderland*, the ordinary rules of everyday life keep dissolving in a sea of logical contradictions. First, Alice shrinks to within only a few inches of the ground; then she shoots up taller than the treetops. The strange antics of Wonderland's inhabitants make her smile one moment and shed a pool of tears the next. "Dear dear!" muses the harried heroine. "How queer everything is today! . . . I wonder if I've been changed in the night? Let me think: *Was* I the same when I got up this morning? I almost think I can remember feeling a little different. But if I'm not the same, the *next* question is, 'Who in the world am I?' Ah, *that's* the great puzzle!"

In a way, we all live in a sort of Wonderland. For much of our lives, we reside in a realm where the ordinary rules of logic and experience are often suspended: the dream world of sleep. Throughout the day, mood, alertness, efficiency, and *consciousness* itself—our awareness of ourselves and the environment—are in perpetual flux, sometimes shifting as dramatically as Alice's height. Sometimes we are hyperalert and attentive to our own feelings and everything around us; at other times, we daydream or go on "autopilot." Sometimes we speak as though our minds are separate from us; we say, "My mind is playing tricks on me," but who is the "me" watching your mind play those tricks, and who

is it that's being tricked? If you say that your brain stores events or registers emotions, who is the "you" that is "using" that brain?

One way to understand consciousness is to study how it changes over time. Starting from the assumption that mental and physical states are as intertwined as sunshine and shadow, psychologists, along with other scientists, are exploring the links between fluctuations in subjective experience and changes in brain activity and hormone levels. They have come to view changing states of consciousness as part of the rhythmic ebb and flow of experience over time. Dreaming, traditionally classified as a state of consciousness, is also related to a 90-minute cycle of brain activity.

Examining a person's ongoing rhythmic cycles is like watching a video of consciousness. Studying the person's distinct states of consciousness is more like looking at separate photos. In this chapter, we will first run the video, to see how functioning and consciousness vary predictably over time. Then we will zoom in on one specific snapshot, the world of dreams, and examine it in some detail. Finally, we will turn to two techniques that "retouch" or alter the video: hypnosis and the use of recreational drugs. Watch the *actual* video *States of Consciousness* to see how people much like yourself think of consciousness.

Biological Rhythms: The Tides of Experience

Are you an "early bird" or a "night owl"? Do you feel more energized at 5:00 in the morning or at 5:00 at night? Do you have a hard time revving up in the morning or winding down at night? Your answers to these questions may reflect how you respond to the complex interplay of your bodily systems' ups and downs as you progress through the day. In this section, we will take a look at the internal tempos and natural cycles our bodies regularly go through.

Circadian Rhythms

LO 5.1.A Define circadian rhythms, and explain how the body's "biological clock" works (and what happens when it doesn't).

The human body goes through dozens of ups and downs in physiological functioning over the course of a day, a week, and a year, changes that are known as **biological rhythms**. A biological clock in our brains governs the waxing and waning of hormone levels, urine volume, blood pressure, and even the responsiveness of brain cells to stimulation. Biological rhythms are typically in tune with external time cues, such as changes in clock time, temperature, and daylight, but many rhythms continue to occur even in the absence of such cues; they are **endogenous**, or generated from within.

Circadian rhythms are biological rhythms that occur approximately every 24 hours. They evolved in plants, animals, insects, and human beings as an adaptation to the many changes associated with the rotation of Earth on its axis, such as changes in light, air pressure, and temperature. The best-known circadian rhythm is the sleep–wake cycle, but hundreds of others affect physiology and performance. Body temperature fluctuates about 1 degree centigrade each day, peaking, on average, in the late afternoon and hitting a low point, or trough, in the wee hours of the morning. Other rhythms occur less frequently than once a day—say, once a month or once a season. In the animal world, seasonal rhythms are common. Birds migrate south in the fall, bears hibernate in the winter, and marine animals become active or inactive, depending on bimonthly changes in the tides. Some seasonal and monthly rhythms also occur in humans. In both men and women, testosterone peaks in the autumn and dips in the spring (Stanton, Mullette-Gillman, & Huettel, 2011), and in women, the menstrual cycle occurs roughly every 28 days. Other rhythms occur more frequently than once a day, many of them on about a 90-minute cycle. In humans, these include physiological changes during sleep, and (unless social customs intervene) stomach contractions, hormone levels, susceptibility to visual illusions, verbal and spatial performance, brain-wave responses during cognitive tasks, and daydreaming (Blumberg, Gall, & Todd, 2014; Escera, Cilveti, & Grau, 1992; Klein & Armitage, 1979; Lavie, 1976).

In most societies, clocks and other external time cues abound, and people's circadian rhythms become tied to them, following a strict 24-hour schedule. Therefore, to identify endogenous rhythms, scientists isolate volunteers from sunlight, clocks, environmental sounds, and all other cues to time. Some hardy souls have spent weeks isolated in underground caves; usually, however, participants live in specially designed rooms equipped with audio systems, comfortable furniture, and temperature controls. Free of the tyranny of a timepiece, a few of these people have lived a "day" that is much shorter or longer than 24 hours. If allowed to take daytime naps, however, most soon settle

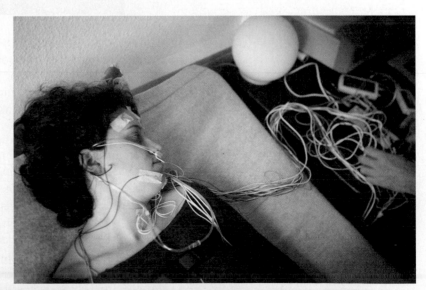

A person participating in a sleep study will be asked to spend a night in a sleep laboratory, often attached to various recording devices that measure physiological and brain activity throughout the night. After a period of adjustment, most people find they can drift off for the night despite these unusual circumstances.

biological rhythm

A periodic, more or less regular fluctuation in a biological system; it may or may not have psychological implications.

endogenous

Generated from within rather than by external cues.

circadian [sur-CAY-dee-un] rhythm

A biological rhythm with a period (from peak to peak or trough to trough) of about 24 hours; from the Latin *circa*, "about," and *dies*, "a day."

suprachiasmatic [soo-pruh-kye-az-MAT-ick] nucleus (SCN)

An area of the brain containing a biological clock that governs circadian rhythms.

melatonin

A hormone secreted by the pineal gland; it is involved in the regulation of circadian rhythms.

internal desynchronization

A state in which biological rhythms are not in phase with one another.

into a day that averages 5 to 10 minutes longer than 24 hours (Duffy et al., 2011). For many people, alertness, like temperature, peaks in the late afternoon and falls to a low point in the very early morning (Lavie, 2001).

THE BODY'S CLOCK Circadian rhythms are controlled by a biological clock, or overall coordinator, located in a tiny cluster of cells in the hypothalamus called the **suprachiasmatic nucleus (SCN)**. Neural pathways from special receptors in the back of the eye transmit information to the SCN and allow it to respond to changes in light and dark. The SCN then sends out messages that cause the brain and body to adapt to these changes. Other clocks also exist, scattered around the body, but for most circadian rhythms, the SCN is regarded as the master pacemaker.

The SCN regulates fluctuating levels of hormones and neurotransmitters, and they in turn provide feedback that affects the SCN's functioning. During the dark hours, one hormone regulated by the SCN, **melatonin**, is secreted by the pineal gland, deep within the brain. Melatonin induces sleep. When you go to bed in a darkened room, your melatonin level rises; when light fills your room in the morning, it falls. Melatonin, in turn, appears to help keep the biological clock in phase with the light–dark cycle (Haimov & Lavie, 1996; Houdek et al., 2015). What's more, melatonin treatments have been used to regulate the disturbed sleep–wake cycles of blind people who lack light perception and whose melatonin production does not cycle normally (Flynn-Evans et al., 2014). The video *Rhythms of Consciousness* provides more information on how the brain regulates sleep-wake cycles.

WHEN THE CLOCK IS OUT OF SYNC Under normal conditions, the rhythms governed by the SCN are in phase with one another. Their peaks may occur at different times, but if you know when one rhythm peaks, you can predict fairly well when another will. It's a little like knowing the time in London if you know the time in New York. But when your normal routine changes, your circadian rhythms may be thrown out of phase. Such **internal desynchronization** often occurs when people take airplane flights across several time zones. Sleep and wake patterns usually adjust quickly, but temperature and hormone cycles can take several days to return to normal. The resulting jet lag affects energy level, mental skills, and motor coordination (Sack, 2010).

Internal desynchronization also occurs when workers must adjust to a new shift. Efficiency drops, the person feels tired and irritable, accidents become more likely, and sleep disturbances and digestive disorders may occur. For police officers, emergency-room personnel, airline pilots, truck drivers, and operators of nuclear power plants, the consequences can be a matter of life and death. Night work itself is not necessarily a problem: With a schedule that always stays the same, even on weekends, people often adapt. However, many swing and night-shift assignments are made on a rotating basis, so a worker's circadian rhythms never have a chance to resynchronize.

Some scientists hope eventually to help rotating-shift workers and travelers crossing time zones adjust more quickly by using melatonin, drugs, or other techniques to "reset the clock" (van de Werken et al., 2013), but so far these techniques do not seem ready for prime time. Giving shift workers melatonin sometimes helps and sometimes does not; stimulant drugs can improve attention but don't eliminate physical fatigue; and although short naps on the job increase alertness, many employers do not like the idea of paying people to sleep (Kolla & Auger, 2011). When a pilot in Nevada was unable to contact a napping air traffic controller at 2:00 A.M., scientists butted heads with government officials about who was to blame. "There should be sanctioned on-shift napping. That's the way to handle night-shift work," said one neuroscientist. But the Federal Aviation Administration bans the practice, while nonetheless calling for more data.

One reason a simple cure for desynchronization has so far eluded scientists may be that circadian rhythms can be affected by illness, stress, exercise, drugs, mealtimes, and many other factors. Also, circadian rhythms differ greatly from person to person. There truly are morning people ("larks") and evening people ("owls"). Scientists call your identity as a lark or owl your "chronotype." Genetic influences may contribute to chronotypes, although early attempts to find "chronotype genes" have proven difficult to replicate (Chang et al., 2011, Osland et al., 2011). Moreover, your chronotype may change as you age: Adolescents are more likely than children and older adults to be owlish (Biss & Hasher, 2012), which may be why many teenagers have trouble adjusting to school schedules. You may be able to learn about your own personal pulses through careful self-observation, and you may want to try putting that information to use when planning your daily schedule.

Moods and Long-Term Rhythms

LO 5.1.B Explain why seasonal affective disorder and premenstrual syndrome are examples of long-term biological rhythms, and summarize the evidence regarding the existence of both phenomena.

According to Ecclesiastes, "To every thing there is a season, and a time for every purpose under heaven." Modern science agrees: Long-term cycles have been observed in everything from the threshold for tooth pain to conception rates. Folklore holds that our

For at least 3 days, except when you are sleeping, keep an hourly record of your mental alertness level, using this five-point scale: 1, extremely drowsy or mentally lethargic; 2, somewhat drowsy or mentally lethargic; 3, moderately alert; 4, alert and efficient; and 5, extremely alert and efficient. Does your alertness level appear to follow a circadian rhythm, reaching a high point and a low point once every 24 hours? Or does it follow a shorter rhythm, rising and falling several times during the day? Are your cycles the same on weekends as during the week? Most important, how well does your schedule mesh with your natural fluctuations in alertness?

Bright light therapy is often used in the treatment of seasonal affective disorder (SAD). Thirty minutes in front of a lamp such as this one may produce benefits for some people with this uncommon diagnosis.

seasonal affective disorder (SAD)

A controversial disorder in which a person experiences depression during the winter and an improvement of mood in the spring.

moods follow similar rhythms, particularly in response to seasonal changes and, in women, menstrual changes. But do they?

DOES THE SEASON AFFECT MOODS? Clinicians report that some people become depressed during particular seasons, typically winter, when periods of daylight are short, a phenomenon that has come to be known as **seasonal affective disorder (SAD)**. This condition is relatively uncommon and is not recognized as an official disorder in the leading diagnostic manual used by clinicians (American Psychiatric Association, 2013). During the winter months, SAD patients report feelings of sadness, lethargy, drowsiness, and a craving for carbohydrates. To counteract the effects of sunless days, physicians and therapists often treat SAD patients with phototherapy, having them sit in front of bright fluorescent lights at specific times of the day, usually early in the morning. In some cases, they have also begun prescribing antidepressants and other drugs.

Unfortunately, much of the research on the effectiveness of light treatments has been flawed; a review of 173 published studies found that only 20 had a proper design and suitable controls (Golden et al., 2005). But a meta-analysis of the data from those 20 studies did throw some light on the subject, so to speak. When people with SAD were exposed to either a brief period (e.g., 30 minutes) of bright light after waking or to light that slowly became brighter, simulating the dawn, their symptoms were in fact reduced. Light therapy even helped people with mild to moderate *non*seasonal depression (Pail et al., 2011).

SAD may occur in people whose circadian rhythms are out of sync; in essence, they have a chronic form of jet lag (Lewy et al., 2006). Or they may also have some abnormality in the way they produce or respond to melatonin (Wehr et al., 2001). They may produce too much daytime melatonin in the winter, or their morning levels may not fall as quickly as other people's. However, it is not clear why light therapy also appears to help some people with nonseasonal depression. True cases of SAD may have a biological basis, but if so, the mechanism remains uncertain. Keep in mind, too, that for many people who get the winter blues, the reason could be that they hate cold weather, are physically inactive, do not get outside much, or feel lonely during the winter holidays.

DOES THE MENSTRUAL CYCLE AFFECT MOODS? Controversy has persisted about another long-term rhythm, the female menstrual cycle, which occurs, on average, every 28 days. During the first half of this cycle an increase in the hormone estrogen causes the lining of the uterus to thicken in preparation for a possible pregnancy. At midcycle, the ovaries release a mature egg, or ovum. Afterward, the ovarian sac that contained the egg begins to produce progesterone, which helps prepare the uterine lining to receive the egg. Then, if conception does not occur, estrogen and progesterone levels fall, the uterine lining sloughs off as the menstrual flow, and the cycle begins again. The interesting question for psychologists is whether these physical changes cause emotional or intellectual changes, as folklore and tradition would have us believe.

Most people nowadays seem to think so. They are often surprised to learn that it was not until the 1970s that a vague cluster of physical and emotional symptoms associated with the days preceding menstruation—including fatigue, headache, irritability, and depression—was packaged together and given a label: *premenstrual syndrome (PMS)* (Parlee, 1994). Since then, most laypeople, doctors, and psychiatrists have assumed, uncritically, that many women "suffer" from PMS or from its supposedly more extreme and debilitating version, "premenstrual dysphoric disorder" (PMDD). What does the evidence actually show?

CULTURE and *PMS*

The story of PMS illustrates the close interconnection between bodily changes and cultural norms, which help determine how a person's bodily symptoms are labeled and interpreted (Chrisler & Caplan, 2002). PMS symptoms have been reported most often in North America, western Europe, and Australia. But with the rise of globalization and the influence of worldwide drug marketing, reports of such symptoms are increasing in places where they were previously not reported, from Mexico (Marvan, Diaz-Erosa, & Montesinos, 1998) to Saudi Arabia (Rasheed & Al-Sowielem, 2003). In most tribal cultures, however, PMS is virtually unknown; the concern has been with menstruation itself, which is often considered "unclean." And in some cultures, women say they have physical symptoms but not emotional symptoms: Women in China report fatigue, water retention, pain, and cold (American women rarely report cold), but not depression or irritability (Yu et al., 1996).

Hormones do influence all of us, of course, as do many other internal processes. In some cases, hormonal abnormalities or sudden hormonal changes can make women *and* men feel depressed, listless, irritable, or "not themselves." Yet even in cultures where PMS symptoms are most commonly reported, few women are likely to undergo personality shifts solely because of their hormones. And testosterone doesn't make men violent.

Many women do have *physical* symptoms associated with menstruation, including cramps, breast tenderness, and water retention. Naturally, these physical symptoms can make some women feel grumpy, just as pain or discomfort can make men feel grumpy. But *emotional* symptoms such as irritability and depression are quite rare, affecting fewer than 5 percent of women predictably over their cycles (Brooks-Gunn, 1986; Romans et al., 2012; Walker, 1994).

Then why do so many women think they have PMS? One possibility is that they tend to notice feelings of depression or irritability when these moods happen to occur premenstrually but overlook times when such moods are *absent* premenstrually. Or they may label symptoms that occur before a period as PMS ("I am irritable and cranky; I must be getting my period") and attribute the same symptoms at other times of the month to a stressful day or a low grade on an English paper ("No wonder I'm irritable and cranky; I worked really hard on that paper and only got a C"). A woman's perceptions and recall of her own emotional ups and downs can also be influenced by cultural attitudes and myths about menstruation. Yet most clinicians diagnose PMS on the basis of women's retrospective reports, and some studies have encouraged biases in the reporting of premenstrual and menstrual symptoms by using questionnaires with gloomy titles such as "Menstrual Distress Questionnaire."

To get around these problems, some psychologists have polled women about their psychological and physical well-being without revealing the true purpose of the study (e.g., AuBuchon & Calhoun, 1985; Chrisler, 2000; Gallant et al., 1991; Hardie, 1997; Parlee, 1982; Slade, 1984; Walker, 1994). Using double-blind procedures, they have had women report symptoms for a single day and have then gone back to see what phase of the menstrual cycle the women were in; or they have had women keep daily records over an extended period of time. Some studies have also included a control group that is usually excluded from research on hormones and moods: men!

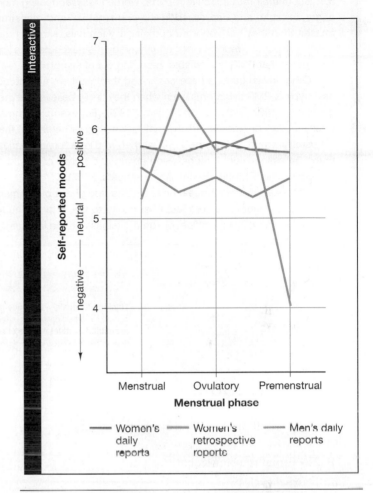

Figure 5.1 Mood Changes in Men and Women

In a study that challenged popular stereotypes about premenstrual syndrome, college women and men recorded their moods daily for 70 days without knowing the purpose of the study. At the end of the study, the women thought their moods had been more negative premenstrually than during the rest of the month (green line), but their daily diaries showed otherwise (blue line). Both sexes experienced only moderate mood changes, and there were no significant differences between women and men at any time of the month (McFarlane, Martin, & Williams, 1988).

In one such study, men and women completed a symptom questionnaire that made no mention of menstruation (Callaghan et al., 2009). The proportion of men who met the criteria for "premenstrual dysphoric disorder," a presumably more extreme version of PMS, did not differ significantly from the proportion of women who did so! In another study, women and men rated their moods every day for 70 days for what they thought was a straightforward study of mood and health (McFarlane, Martin, & Williams, 1988). After the 70 days were up, the women then recalled their average moods for each week and phase of their menstrual cycle. In their daily reports, women's moods fluctuated less over the menstrual cycle than over days of the week. (Mondays, it seems, are tough for most of us.) Moreover, women and men reported similar emotional symptoms and number of mood swings at any time of the month, as you can see in Figure 5.1. But in their retrospective reports, women *recalled* feeling more angry, irritable, and depressed in the premenstrual and menstrual phases than they had reported in their daily journals, showing that their retrospective reports were influenced by their expectations and their belief that PMS is a reliable, recurring set of symptoms.

Other investigations have confirmed that most women do not have typical PMS symptoms even when they firmly believe that they do (Hardie, 1997; McFarlane & Williams, 1994). For example, women often say they cry more premenstrually than at other times, but they are usually wrong. A study of Dutch women who kept "crying diaries" found no association at all between crying and phase of the menstrual cycle (van Tilburg, Becht, & Vingerhoets, 2003).

The really important question is whether the phase of the menstrual cycle a woman is in affects her ability to work, think, study, do brain surgery, run for office, or run a business. In the laboratory, women tend to be faster on tasks such as reciting words quickly or sorting objects manually before and after ovulation, when their estrogen is high (e.g., Saucier & Kimura, 1998). But phase of the menstrual cycle is unrelated to work efficiency, problem solving, grades, college exam scores, creativity, or any other behavior that matters in real life (Earl-Novell & Jessop, 2005; Golub, 1992; Richardson, 1992). In the workplace, men and women report similar levels of stress, well-being, and ability to do the work required of them—and it doesn't matter whether the women are premenstrual, menstrual, postmenstrual, or nonmenstrual (Hardie, 1997).

In sum, the body provides only the clay for our symptoms and feelings. Learning and culture mold that clay by teaching us which symptoms are important or worrisome, and which are not. Whether we are male or female, the impact of most of the changes associated with our biological rhythms depends on how we interpret and respond to them.

JOURNAL PROMPT 5.1

Thinking Critically—Examine the Evidence: Many women say they become more irritable or depressed premenstrually, and PMS remedies line the shelves of drugstores. But what does the evidence show about PMS? How might attitudes and expectations affect reports of emotional symptoms? What happens when women report their daily moods and feelings to researchers without knowing that menstruation is being studied?

Quiz for Module 5.1

1. Biological rhythms that occur roughly every 24 hours are called
   a. Nocturnal transmissions
   b. Diurnal cycles
   c. Circadian rhythms
   d. Synchronous cycles

2. The functioning of the biological clock governing circadian rhythms is affected by the hormone
   a. Melatonin
   b. Dexatronin
   c. Serotonin
   d. Dormitronin

3. Jet lag occurs because of
   a. Chronotypic variability
   b. Internal desynchronization
   c. Suprachiasmatic degeneration
   d. Incremental subduction

4. What do researchers know about seasonal affective disorder (SAD)?
   a. Although light therapy helps alleviate symptoms, the biological mechanisms that might cause SAD to occur are uncertain.
   b. SAD is a culturally generated myth because there is no reliable evidence that people affected by it respond well to light therapy.
   c. The treatment of SAD is unique to the disorder, suggesting its symptoms and biological underpinnings are distinct from other forms of depression.
   d. Light therapy effectively alleviates SAD symptoms because it causes the hypothalamus to produce decreased levels of dormitronin.

5. Emotional symptoms associated with menstruation, such as irritability and depression, affect approximately no more than _____ of women over their cycles.
   a. 50 percent
   b. 15 percent
   c. 25 percent
   d. 5 percent

The Rhythms of Sleep

Perhaps the most perplexing of all our biological rhythms is the one governing sleep and wakefulness. Sleep, after all, puts us at risk: Muscles that are usually ready to respond to danger relax, and senses grow dull. As British psychologist Christopher Evans (1984) once noted, "The behavior patterns involved in sleep are glaringly, almost insanely, at odds with common sense." Then why is sleep such a profound necessity?

The Realms of Sleep

LO 5.2.A Describe the four stages of sleep, and explain the primary features of each stage.

Let's start with some of the changes that occur in the brain during sleep. Until the early 1950s, little was known about these changes. Then a breakthrough occurred in the laboratory of physiologist Nathaniel Kleitman, who at the time was the only person in the world who had spent his entire career studying sleep. Kleitman had given one of his graduate students, Eugene Aserinsky, the tedious task of finding out whether the slow, rolling eye movements that characterize the onset of sleep continue throughout the night. To both men's surprise, eye movements did occur but they were rapid, not slow (Aserinsky & Kleitman, 1955). Using the electroencephalograph (EEG) to measure the brain's electrical activity, these researchers, along with another of Kleitman's students, William Dement, were able to correlate the rapid eye movements with changes in sleepers' brain-wave patterns (Dement, 1992, 2005). Adult volunteers were soon spending their nights sleeping in laboratories, while scientists measured changes in their brain activity, muscle tension, breathing, and other physiological responses.

As a result of this research, today we know that during sleep, periods of **rapid eye movement (REM)** alternate with periods of fewer eye movements, or *non REM (NREM) sleep*, in a cycle that recurs every 90 minutes or so (Iber et al., 2007). The REM periods last from a few minutes to as long as an hour, averaging about 20 minutes in length. Whenever they begin, the pattern of electrical activity from the sleeper's brain changes to resemble that of alert wakefulness. Non-REM periods are themselves divided into stages, each associated with a particular brain-wave pattern (see Figure 5.2).

When you first climb into bed, close your eyes, and relax, your brain emits bursts of *alpha waves*. Compared to brain waves during alert wakefulness, on an EEG recording alpha waves have a somewhat slower rhythm (fewer cycles per second) and a somewhat higher amplitude (height). Gradually, these waves slow down even further, and you drift into the Land of Nod, passing through three stages, each deeper than the previous one:

- *Stage NREM-1.* Your brain waves become small and irregular, and you feel yourself drifting on the edge of consciousness, in a state of light sleep. If awakened, you may recall fantasies or a few visual images.

- *Stage NREM-2.* Your brain emits occasional short bursts of rapid, high-peaking waves called *sleep spindles*. Minor noises probably won't disturb you.

- *Stage NREM-3.* Your brain emits *delta waves*, very slow waves with very high peaks, and you are in deep sleep. Your breathing and pulse have slowed down, your muscles are relaxed, and it will probably take vigorous shaking or a loud noise to awaken you. Oddly, though, if you walk in your sleep, this is when you are likely to do so. No one yet knows what causes sleepwalking, which occurs more often in children than adults, but it seems to involve unusual patterns of delta-wave activity (Zadra et al., 2013).

This sequence of stages takes about 30 to 45 minutes. Then you move back up the ladder from Stage 3 to 2 to 1. At that point, about 70 to 90 minutes after the onset of sleep, something peculiar happens. Stage 1 does not turn into drowsy wakefulness, as one might expect. Instead, your brain begins to emit long bursts of very rapid, somewhat irregular waves. Your heart rate increases, your blood pressure rises, and your breathing gets faster and more irregular. Small twitches in your face and fingers may occur. In men, the penis may become

rapid eye movement (REM) sleep
Sleep periods characterized by eye movement, loss of muscle tone, and vivid dreams.

Figure 5.2 Brain-Wave Patterns during Wakefulness and Sleep

Most types of brain waves are present throughout sleep, but different ones predominate at different stages.

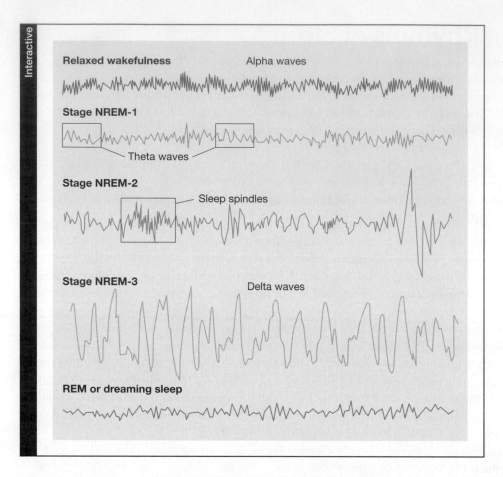

somewhat erect as vascular tissue relaxes and blood fills the genital area faster than it exits. In women, the clitoris may enlarge and vaginal lubrication may increase. At the same time, most skeletal muscles go limp, preventing your aroused brain from producing physical movement. You have entered the realm of REM.

Because the brain is extremely active while the body is entirely inactive, REM sleep has also been called "paradoxical sleep." It is during these periods that vivid dreams are most likely to occur. People report dreams when they are awakened from non-REM sleep, too; in one study, dream reports occurred 82 percent of the time when sleepers were awakened during REM sleep, but they also occurred 51 percent of the time when people were awakened during non-REM sleep (Foulkes, 1962). Non-REM dreams, however, tend to be shorter, less vivid, and more realistic than REM dreams, except in the hour or so before a person wakes up in the morning.

Occasionally, as the sleeper wakes up, a curious phenomenon occurs. The person emerges from REM sleep before the muscle paralysis characteristic of that stage has entirely disappeared, and becomes aware of an inability to move. About 30 percent of the general population has experienced at least one such episode, and about 5 percent have had a "waking

Because cats sleep up to 80 percent of the time, it is easy to catch them in the various stages of slumber. A cat in non-REM sleep (left) remains upright, but during the REM phase (right), its muscles go limp and it flops onto its side.

dream" in this state. Their eyes are open, but what they "see" are dreamlike hallucinations, most often shadowy figures. They may even "see" a ghost or space alien sitting on their bed or hovering in a hallway, a scary image that they would regard as perfectly normal it if were part of a midnight nightmare. Instead of saying, "Ah! How interesting! I am having a waking dream!" some people interpret this experience literally and come to believe they have been visited by aliens or are being haunted by ghosts (Clancy, 2005; McNally, 2003).

REM and non-REM sleep continue to alternate throughout the night. As the hours pass, Stage 3 tends to become shorter or even disappear, and REM periods tend to get longer and closer together (see Figure 5.3). This pattern may explain why you are likely to be dreaming when the alarm clock goes off in the morning. But the cycles are far from regular. An individual may bounce directly from Stage 3 back to Stage 2 or go from REM to Stage 2 and then back to REM. Also, the time between REM and non-REM is highly variable, differing from person to person and also within any given individual.

If you wake people up every time they lapse into REM sleep, nothing dramatic will happen. When finally allowed to sleep normally, however, they will spend a longer time than usual in the REM phase, and it will be hard to rouse them. Electrical brain activity associated with REM may burst through into non-REM sleep and even into wakefulness, as if the person is making up for something he or she had been deprived of. Some researchers have proposed that this "something" is connected with dreaming, but that idea has problems. For one thing, in rare cases, patients with brain damage have lost the capacity to dream, yet they continue to show the normal sleep stages, including REM (Bischof & Bassetti, 2004). Moreover, nearly all mammals experience REM sleep, but many theorists doubt that rats or moles have the cognitive abilities required to construct what we think of as dreams. REM is clearly important, but it must be for reasons other than dreaming, as we will see. (Table 5.1 lists the sleep stages we have discussed.)

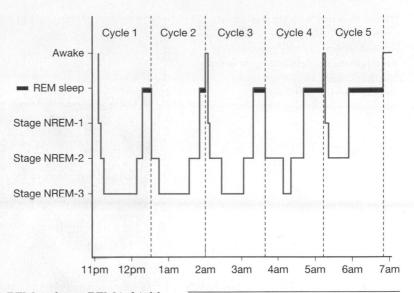

Figure 5.3 A Typical Night's Sleep for a Young Adult

In this graph, the thin horizontal red bars represent time spent in REM sleep. REM periods tend to lengthen as the night wears on, but Stage 3, which dominates during non-REM sleep early in the night, may disappear as morning approaches.

Why We Sleep

LO 5.2.B List the mental consequences of sleeplessness and the mental benefits of a good night's sleep.

Generally speaking, sleep appears to provide a time-out period, so that the body can eliminate waste products from muscles, repair cells, conserve or replenish energy stores, strengthen the immune system, and recover abilities lost during the day. When we do not get enough sleep, our bodies operate abnormally. Hormone levels necessary for normal muscle development and immune system functioning decline (Leproult, Van Reeth, et al., 1997).

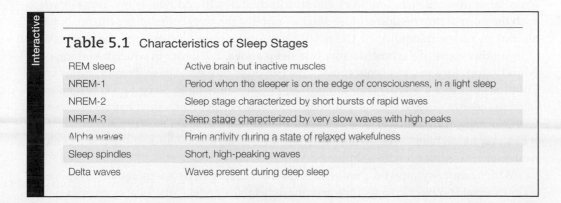

Table 5.1 Characteristics of Sleep Stages

REM sleep	Active brain but inactive muscles
NREM-1	Period when the sleeper is on the edge of consciousness, in a light sleep
NREM-2	Sleep stage characterized by short bursts of rapid waves
NREM-3	Sleep stage characterized by very slow waves with high peaks
Alpha waves	Brain activity during a state of relaxed wakefulness
Sleep spindles	Short, high-peaking waves
Delta waves	Waves present during deep sleep

The driver of this truck crashed when he apparently fell asleep at the wheel. Thousands of serious and fatal motor vehicle accidents occur each year because of driver fatigue.

Although most people can still get along reasonably well after a day or two of sleeplessness, sleep deprivation that lasts for four days or longer becomes uncomfortable and soon becomes unbearable. In animals, forced sleeplessness leads to infections and eventually to death, and the same seems to be true for people. In one tragic case, a 51-year-old man abruptly began to lose sleep. After sinking deeper and deeper into an exhausted stupor, he developed a lung infection and died. An autopsy showed that he had lost almost all the large neurons in two areas of the thalamus that have been linked to sleep and hormonal circadian rhythms (Lugaresi et al., 1986).

THE MENTAL CONSEQUENCES OF SLEEPLESSNESS   Sleep is also necessary for normal mental functioning. Chronic sleep deprivation increases levels of the stress hormone cortisol, which may damage or impair brain cells that are necessary for learning and memory (Minkel et al., 2014). Also, new brain cells may either fail to develop or may mature abnormally (Guzman-Marin et al., 2005). Perhaps in part because of such damage, after the loss of even a single night's sleep, mental flexibility, attention, and creativity all suffer. After several days of staying awake, people may even begin to have hallucinations and delusions (Dement, 1978).

Of course, sleep deprivation rarely reaches that point, but people do frequently suffer from milder sleep problems. According to the National Sleep Foundation, about 10 percent of adults are plagued by difficulty in falling or staying asleep. The causes of their insomnia include worry and anxiety, psychological problems, physical problems such as arthritis, and irregular or overly demanding work and study schedules. In addition, many drugs interfere with the normal progression of sleep stages—not just the ones containing caffeine, but also alcohol and some tranquilizers. The result can be grogginess and lethargy the next day.

Another cause of daytime sleepiness is **sleep apnea**, a disorder in which breathing periodically stops for a few moments, causing the person to choke and gasp. Breathing may cease hundreds of times a night, often without the person knowing it. Sleep apnea is seen most often in older males and overweight people but also occurs in others. It has several causes, from blockage of air passages to failure of the brain to control respiration correctly. Over time, it can cause high blood pressure and irregular heartbeat; it may gradually erode a person's health and is associated with a shortened life expectancy (Young et al., 2008).

With **narcolepsy**, an even more serious disorder that often develops in the teenage years, an individual is subject to irresistible and unpredictable daytime attacks of sleepiness lasting

sleep apnea

A disorder in which breathing briefly stops during sleep, causing the person to choke and gasp and momentarily awaken.

narcolepsy

A disorder involving sudden and unpredictable daytime attacks of sleepiness or lapses into REM sleep.

from 5 to 30 minutes. The cause is not well understood, but the disorder has been associated with reduced amounts of a particular brain protein, possibly brought on by an autoimmune problem, a viral infection, or genetic abnormalities (Baumann et al., 2014; Kornum, Faraco, & Mignot, 2011; Mieda et al., 2004). When the person lapses into sleep, he or she is likely to fall immediately into the REM stage. Some people with narcolepsy experience an unusual symptom called *cataplexy*, which brings on the paralysis of REM sleep although they are still awake; as a result, they may suddenly drop to the floor. Cataplexy is often triggered by laughing excitedly, but it can sometimes be induced by telling a joke or even having an orgasm (Overeem et al., 2011). You can learn more about these conditions by watching the video *Sleep Disorders*.

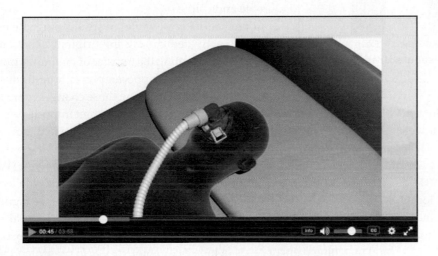

Other disorders also disrupt sleep, including some that cause odd or dangerous behavior. In **REM behavior disorder**, the muscle paralysis associated with REM sleep does not occur, and the sleeper (usually an older male) becomes physically active, often acting out a dream without any awareness of what he is doing (Randall, 2012; Schenck & Mahowald, 2002). If he is dreaming about football, he may try to "tackle" a piece of furniture; if he is dreaming about a kitten, he may try to pet it. Other people may consider this disorder amusing, but it is no joke; sufferers may hurt themselves or others, and they have an increased risk of later developing Parkinson's disease and dementia (Mariotti et al., 2015).

However, the most common cause of daytime sleepiness is the most obvious one: simply not getting enough sleep. Some people do fine on relatively few hours, but most adults need more than 6 hours for optimal performance, and many adolescents need 10. In the United States, drowsiness is involved in 100,000 vehicle accidents a year, causing 1,500 road deaths and 71,000 injuries. Sleep deprivation also leads to accidents and errors in the workplace, a concern especially for first-year doctors doing their medical residency. Although federal law limits work hours for airline pilots, truck drivers, and nuclear-plant operators, in many states, medical residents often still work 24- to 30-hour shifts (Landrigan et al., 2008).

Don't doze off as we tell you this, but lack of sleep has also been linked to reduced alertness in school and lower grades. In 1997, a high school in Minneapolis changed its start time from 7:20 A.M. to 8:30 A.M. Teachers watched in surprise as students became more alert and—according to their parents—"easier to live with" (Wahlstrom, 2010). Since then, many other school districts in the United States and other countries have followed suit by starting school later in the morning (Vedaa et al., 2012). Children and teenagers who start school later sleep more, have improved mood, are able to pay more attention in class, and get better test scores; teenage drivers even have fewer car accidents (Fallone et al., 2005; Vorona et al., 2011).

REM behavior disorder
A disorder in which the muscle paralysis that normally occurs during REM sleep is absent or incomplete, and the sleeper is able to act out his or her dreams.

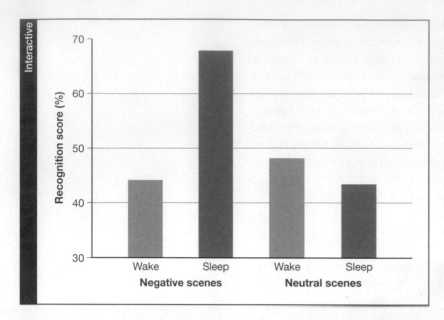

Figure 5.4 Sleep and Consolidation in Memory

When college students studied neutral scenes (e.g., an ordinary car) and emotionally negative scenes (e.g., a car totaled in an accident), sleep affected how well they later recognized the objects in the scenes. Students who studied the scenes in the evening and then got a night's sleep before being tested did better at recognizing emotional objects than did those who studied the scenes in the morning and were tested after 12 hours of daytime wakefulness (Payne et al., 2008).

consolidation

The process by which a memory becomes durable and stable.

THE MENTAL BENEFITS OF SLEEP Just as sleepiness can interfere with good mental functioning, a good night's sleep can promote it, and not just because you are well rested. In a classic study conducted nearly a century ago, students who slept for 8 hours after learning lists of nonsense syllables retained them better than students who went about their usual business (Jenkins & Dallenbach, 1924). For years, researchers attributed this result to the lack of new information coming into the brain during sleep, information that could interfere with already-established memories. Today, however, most believe that sleep is a crucial time for **consolidation**, in which synaptic changes associated with recently stored memories become durable and stable.

One theory is that while we are sleeping, the neurons that were activated during the original experience are reactivated, promoting the transfer of memories from temporary storage in the hippocampus to long-term storage in the cortex and thus making those changes more permanent (Born & Wilhelm, 2012). During sleep, consolidation seems to target important information that we know we might need later. When researchers had people learn new information and then let them sleep, those who were told before sleeping that they would later be taking a memory test did better on it than those who did not know about the upcoming test (Wilhelm et al., 2011). Sleep seems to strengthen many kinds of memories, including the recollection of events, locations, facts, and emotional experiences, especially negative ones (see Figure 5.4).

Memory consolidation is most closely associated with the slow waves of neural activity that occur during Stage N-REM 3 of sleep. In one study, while scientists taught people the locations of several matching pairs of cards (a memory game), they also presented the scent of roses. Later, some people were exposed to the smell of roses again during slow-wave sleep, REM sleep, or when they were awake. Exposure to the smell during slow-wave sleep, but not REM or wakefulness, improved people's memories for the card locations (Rasch et al., 2007). But REM sleep does seem to be related to some improvements in learning and memory (Mednick et al., 2011). When people or animals learned a perceptual task and were allowed to get normal REM sleep, their memory for the task was better the next day, even when they had been awakened during non-REM periods. When they were deprived of REM sleep, however, their memories were impaired (Karni et al., 1994). Thus, both periods of sleep seem to be important for consolidation, and scientists are now trying to determine their respective roles (Born & Wilhelm, 2012). To find out more about how sleep deprivation affects cognitive functioning, watch the video *Sleep, Memory, and Learning.*

If sleep enhances memory, perhaps it also enhances problem solving, which relies on information stored in memory. To find out, German researchers gave volunteers a math test that required them to use two mathematical rules to generate one string of numbers from another and to deduce the final digit in the new sequence as quickly as possible. The volunteers were not told about a hidden shortcut that would enable them to calculate the final digit almost immediately. One group was trained in the evening and then got to snooze for 8 hours before returning to the problem. Another group was also trained in the evening but then stayed awake for 8 hours before coming back to the problem. A third group was trained in the morning and stayed awake all day, as they normally would, before taking the test. Those people who got the nighttime sleep were nearly three times likelier to discover the hidden shortcut as those in the other two groups (Wagner et al., 2004).

Sleep, then, seems essential in memory and problem solving. The underlying biology appears to involve not only the formation of new synaptic connections in the brain but also the weakening of connections that are no longer needed (Donlea, Ramanan, & Shaw, 2009; Gilestro, Tononi, & Cirelli, 2009; Michel & Lyons, 2014). In other words, we sleep to remember, but we also sleep to forget, so that the brain will have space and energy for new learning. Remember that the next time you are tempted to pull an all-nighter. Even a quick nap may help your mental functioning and increase your ability to put together separately learned facts in new ways (Lau, Alger, & Fishbein, 2011; Mednick et al., 2002). Sleep on it.

JOURNAL PROMPT 5.2

Thinking Critically—Consider Other Interpretations: In a state between sleeping and waking, some people have thought they've seen a ghost or a visitor from space in their bedroom—a pretty scary experience. What other explanation is possible?

Quiz for Module 5.2

1. Short bursts of rapid, high-peaking brain waves (called sleep spindles) are characteristic of _____ sleep.
   a. Stage 3
   b. Stage 1
   c. Stage 2
   d. REM

2. During a night's sleep, when do REM periods tend to get longer and occur closer together?
   a. As the night progresses and the person spends a longer time asleep
   b. At the start of the sleep cycle, when the person first drifts off to sleep
   c. During the middle of the sleep cycle, about midway between first falling asleep and waking
   d. During the "hypnogogic gap" that occurs between Stage 1 and Stage 2 sleep

3. Ian is enjoying a good time with friends, telling stories and laughing heartily at their jokes. Out of the blue, he suddenly slumps on the couch, fast asleep in a REM state. Ian's friends aren't alarmed because they know he suffers from a sleep disorder. Which disorder is Ian most likely to have?
   a. Sleep apnea
   b. Narcolepsy
   c. REM behavior disorder
   d. Insomnia

4. The most common cause of daytime sleepiness is
   a. Narcolepsy
   b. Not getting enough sleep
   c. REM disruption
   d. Sleep apnea

5. Researchers believe that an important function of sleep is that it contributes to the process by which memories become durable and stable in the brain's circuitry. What is the name researchers give to this process?
   a. Neuronal drift
   b. Axonation
   c. Amelioration
   d. Consolidation

Exploring the Dream World

Every culture has its theories about dreams. In some cultures, dreams are believed to occur when the spirit leaves the body to wander the world or speak to the gods. In others, dreams are thought to reveal the future. A Chinese Taoist of the third century B.C. pondered the possible reality of the dream world. He told of dreaming that he was a butterfly flitting about. "Suddenly I woke up and I was indeed Chuang Tzu. Did Chuang Tzu dream he was a butterfly, or did the butterfly dream he was Chuang Tzu?"

For years, researchers believed that everyone dreams, and indeed most people who claim they never have dreams will report them if they are awakened during REM sleep. However, as we noted earlier, a few rare individuals apparently do not dream at all (Pagel, 2003; Solms, 1997). Most but not all of them have suffered some brain injury. In this section, we will explore the dream world, beginning with explanations of why people dream.

Explanations of Dreaming

LO 5.3.A Discuss explanations for why we dream.

In dreaming, the focus of attention is inward, though occasionally an external event, such as a wailing siren, can influence the dream's content. While a dream is in progress, it may be vivid or vague, terrifying or peaceful. It may also seem to make perfect sense—until you wake up and recall it as illogical, bizarre, and disjointed. Although most of us are unaware of our bodies or where we are while we are dreaming, some people say that they occasionally have **lucid dreams**, in which they know they are dreaming and feel as though they are conscious (LaBerge, 2014). A few even claim that they can control the action in these dreams, much as a scriptwriter decides what will happen in a movie.

Why do the images in dreams arise at all? Why doesn't the brain just rest, switching off all thoughts and images and launching us into a coma? Why, instead, do we spend our nights taking a chemistry exam, reliving an old love affair, flying through the air, or fleeing from dangerous strangers or animals in the fantasy world of our dreams?

In popular culture, many people still hold to Freudian psychoanalytic notions of dreaming. Freud (1900/1953) claimed that dreams are "the royal road to the unconscious" because our dreams reflect unconscious conflicts and wishes, often sexual or violent in nature. The thoughts and objects in these dreams, he said, are disguised symbolically to make them less threatening: Your father might appear as your brother, a penis might be disguised as a snake or a cigar, or intercourse with a forbidden partner might be expressed as a train entering a tunnel.

Most psychologists today accept Freud's notion that dreams are more than incoherent ramblings of the mind and that they can have psychological meaning, but they also consider psychoanalytic interpretations of dreams to be far-fetched. No reliable rules exist for interpreting the unconscious meaning of dreams, and there is no objective way to know whether a particular interpretation is correct. Nor is there any convincing empirical support for most of Freud's claims. Psychoanalytic interpretations are common in popular books and on the Internet, but they are only the writers' personal hunches. Even Freud warned against simplified, "this symbol means that" interpretations; each dream, said Freud, must be analyzed in the context of the dreamer's waking life. Not everything in a dream is symbolic; sometimes, he cautioned, "A cigar is only a cigar." Let's examine some explanations for why we dream.

DREAMS AS EFFORTS TO DEAL WITH PROBLEMS   One modern explanation of dreams holds that they reflect the ongoing *conscious* preoccupations of waking life, such as concerns over relationships, work, sex, or health (Cartwright, 1977; Hall, 1953a, 1953b). In this *problem-focused approach* to dreaming, the symbols and metaphors in a dream do not disguise its true meaning; they convey it. Psychologist Gayle Delaney told of a woman who dreamed she was swimming underwater. The woman's 8-year-old son was on her back, his head above the water. Her husband was supposed to take a picture of them, but for some reason he wasn't doing it, and she was starting to feel as if she were going to drown. To Delaney, the message

---

lucid dreams

Dreams in which the dreamer is aware of dreaming.

was obvious: The woman was "drowning" under the responsibilities of childcare and her husband wasn't "getting the picture" (in Dolnick, 1990).

The problem-focused explanation of dreaming is supported by findings that dreams are more likely to contain material related to a person's current concerns than chance would predict (Domhoff, 1996). Among college students, who are often worried about grades and tests, test-anxiety dreams are common: The dreamer is unprepared for or unable to finish an exam, or shows up for the wrong exam, or can't find the room where the exam is being given. Traumatic experiences can also affect people's dreams. In a cross-cultural study in which children kept dream diaries for a week, Palestinian children living in neighborhoods under threat of violence reported more themes of persecution and violence than did Finnish or Palestinian children living in peaceful environments (Punamaeki & Joustie, 1998).

Some psychologists believe that dreams not only reflect our waking concerns but also provide us with an opportunity to resolve them. According to Rosalind Cartwright (2010), in people suffering from the grief of divorce, recovery is related to a particular pattern of dreaming: The first dream of the night often comes sooner than it ordinarily would, lasts longer, and is more emotional and story-like. Depressed people's dreams tend to become less negative and more positive as the night wears on, and this pattern, too, predicts recovery (Cartwright et al., 1998). Cartwright concluded that getting through a crisis or a rough period in life takes "time, good friends, good genes, good luck, and a good dream system."

DREAMS AS THINKING   Like the problem-focused approach, the *cognitive approach* to dreaming emphasizes current concerns, but it makes no claims about problem solving during sleep. In this view, dreaming is simply a modification of the cognitive activity that goes on when we are awake. In dreams, we construct reasonable simulations of the real world, drawing on the same kinds of memories, knowledge, metaphors, and assumptions about the world that we do when we are not sleeping (Antrobus, 1991, 2000; Foulkes & Domhoff, 2014). Thus, the content of our dreams may include thoughts, concepts, and scenarios that may or may not be related to our daily problems. We are most likely to dream about our families, friends, studies, jobs, worries, or recreational interests—topics that also occupy our waking thoughts.

In the cognitive view, the brain is doing the same kind of work during dreams as it does when we are awake; indeed, parts of the cerebral cortex involved in perceptual and cognitive processing during the waking hours are highly active during dreaming. The difference is that when we are asleep we are cut off from sensory input and feedback from the world and our bodily movements; the only input to the brain is its own output. Therefore, our dreaming thoughts tend to be more unfocused and diffuse than our waking ones—unless we're daydreaming. Our brains show similar patterns of activity when we are night dreaming as when we are daydreaming—a finding that suggests that nighttime dreaming, like daydreaming, might be a mechanism for simulating events that we think (or fear) might occur in the future (Domhoff, 2011).

The cognitive view predicts that if a person could be totally cut off from all external stimulation while awake, mental activity would be much like that during dreaming, with the same hallucinatory quality. The cognitive approach also predicts that as cognitive abilities and brain connections mature during childhood, dreams should change in nature, and they do. Toddlers may not dream at all in the sense that adults do. And although young children may experience visual images during sleep, their cognitive limitations keep them from creating true narratives until age 7 or 8 (Foulkes, 1999). Their dreams are infrequent and tend to be bland and static, and are often about everyday things ("I saw a dog; I was sitting"). But as they grow up, their dreams gradually become more and more intricate and story-like.

DREAMS AS INTERPRETED BRAIN ACTIVITY   A third modern approach to dreaming, the **activation–synthesis theory**, draws heavily on physiological research and aims to explain not why you might dream about a test when you are about to take one, but why you might dream about being a cat that turns into a hippo that plays in a rock band. Often dreams just don't

activation–synthesis theory
The theory that dreaming results from the cortical synthesis and interpretation of neural signals triggered by activity in the lower part of the brain.

(a) These drawings from dream journals show that the images in dreams can be either abstract or literal. In either case, the dream may reflect a person's concerns, problems, and interests. The two fanciful paintings here represent the dreams of a person who worked all day long with brain tissue, which the drawings rather resemble. (b) This desk was sketched in 1939 by a scientist to illustrate his dream about a mechanical device for instantly retrieving quotations—an early desktop computer! (c) It can be fun to record your dreams. Keep a notebook or a recorder by your bedside. As soon as you wake up, record everything you can remember about your dreams. Do your dreams contain any recurring themes? Do you think they provide any clues to your current problems, activities, or concerns?

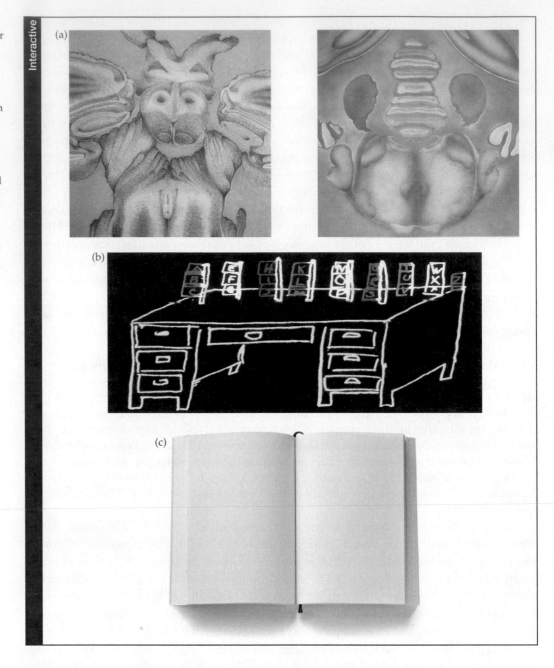

make sense; indeed, most are bizarre, illogical, or both. According to the activation–synthesis explanation, first proposed by psychiatrist J. Allan Hobson (1988, 1990), these dreams are not "children of an idle brain," as Shakespeare called them. They are largely the result of neurons firing spontaneously in the pons (in the lower part of the brain) during REM sleep. These neurons control eye movement, gaze, balance, and posture, and they send messages to sensory and motor areas of the cortex responsible during wakefulness for visual processing and voluntary action.

According to this view, the signals originating in the pons have no psychological meaning in themselves. But the cortex tries to make sense of them by *synthesizing*, or integrating, them with existing knowledge and memories to produce some sort of coherent interpretation. This is just what the cortex does when signals come from sense organs during ordinary wakefulness. The idea that one part of the brain interprets what has gone on in other parts, whether you are awake or asleep, is consistent with many modern theories of how the brain works.

When neurons fire in the part of the brain that handles balance, for instance, the cortex may generate a dream about falling. When signals occur that would ordinarily produce running, the cortex may manufacture a dream about being chased. Because the signals from the pons occur randomly, the cortex's interpretation—the dream—is likely to be incoherent and confusing. And because the cortical neurons that control the initial storage of new memories are turned off during sleep, we typically forget our dreams upon waking unless we write them down or immediately recount them to someone else.

Since Hobson's original formulation, he and his colleagues have refined and modified this theory (Hobson, Pace-Schott, & Stickgold, 2000; Hobson et al., 2011; Tranquillo, 2014). The brain stem, they say, sets off responses in emotional and visual parts of the brain. At the same time, brain regions that handle logical thought and sensations from the external world shut down. These changes could further account for the fact that dreams are often emotionally charged, hallucinatory, and illogical.

In sum, in this view, wishes do not cause dreams; brain mechanisms do. Dream content, says Hobson (2002), may be "as much dross as gold, as much cognitive trash as treasure, and as much informational noise as a signal of something." But that does not mean dreams are *always* meaningless. Hobson (1988) has argued that the brain "is so inexorably bent upon the quest for meaning that it attributes and even creates meaning when there is little or none to be found in the data it is asked to process." By studying these attributed meanings, you can learn about your unique perceptions, conflicts, and concerns—not by trying to dig below the surface of the dream, as Freud would, but by examining the surface itself. Or you can relax and enjoy the nightly entertainment that dreams provide.

Evaluating Dream Theories

LO 5.3.B Summarize the strengths and weaknesses of each major dream theory.

How are we to evaluate these attempts to explain dreaming? All three modern approaches account for some of the evidence, but each one also has its drawbacks.

Are dreams a way to solve problems? It seems pretty clear that some dreams are related to current worries and concerns, but skeptics doubt that people can actually solve problems or resolve conflicts while sound asleep (Blagrove, 1996; Squier & Domhoff, 1998). Dreams, they say, merely give *expression* to our problems. The insights into those problems that people attribute to dreaming could be occurring after they wake up and have a chance to think about what is troubling them.

The activation–synthesis theory has also come in for criticism (Domhoff, 2003). Not all dreams are as disjointed or as bizarre as the theory predicts; in fact, many tell a coherent, if fanciful, story. Moreover, the activation–synthesis approach does not account well for dreaming that goes on outside of REM sleep. Some neuropsychologists emphasize different brain mechanisms involved in dreams, and many believe that dreams do reflect a person's goals and desires.

Finally, the cognitive approach to dreams is promising, but some of its claims remain to be tested against neurological and cognitive evidence. At present, however, it is a leading contender because it incorporates many elements of other theories and fits what we currently know about waking cognition and cognitive development.

Perhaps it will turn out that different kinds of dreams have different purposes and origins. We all know from experience that some of our dreams seem to be related to daily problems, some are vague and incoherent, and some are anxiety dreams that occur when we are worried or depressed. But whatever the source of the images in our sleeping brains may be, we need to be cautious about interpreting our own dreams or anyone else's. A study of people in India, South Korea, and the United States showed that individuals are biased and self-serving in their dream interpretations, accepting those that fit in with their preexisting beliefs or needs, and rejecting those that do not. For example, they will give more weight to a

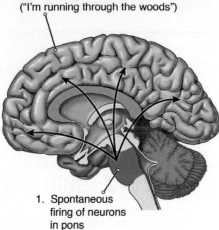

ACTIVATION–SYNTHESIS THEORY OF DREAMS

2. Cerebral cortex synthesizes signals, tries to interpret them ("I'm running through the woods")

1. Spontaneous firing of neurons in pons

dream in which God commands them to take a year off to travel the world than one in which God commands them to take a year off to work in a leper colony. And they are more likely to see meaning in a dream in which a friend protects them from attackers than one in which their romantic partner is caught kissing that same friend (Morewedge & Norton, 2009). Our biased interpretations may tell us more about ourselves than do our actual dreams.

JOURNAL PROMPT 5.3

Thinking Critically—Tolerate Uncertainty: There are many research-based explanations for dreams, and even more pseudoscientific ones. But at present, we cannot be sure about the function and meaning of dreams. Do all dreams have hidden meanings? Are all dreams due to random firing of brain cells? Is dreaming all that different from our waking thoughts? What makes this topic particularly difficult to study, and what forms of evidence would you seek to disentangle competing explanations?

Quiz for Module 5.3

1. In his dreams, Andy is a child crawling through a dark tunnel looking for something he has lost. Hearing about this, a psychologist remarks, "Clearly Andy has repressed an early sexual attraction to his mother, and the tunnel symbolizes her vagina." Which theory of dreams does the psychologist likely subscribe to?

   a. The cognitive approach

   b. Activation–synthesis theory

   c. The problem-focused approach

   d. Psychoanalytic theory

2. In his dreams, Andy is a child crawling through a dark tunnel looking for something he has lost. Hearing about this, a psychologist remarks, "While Andy was sleeping, neurons in his pons that would ordinarily stimulate parts of the brain involved in leg-muscle movements were active." Which theory of dreams does the psychologist likely subscribe to?

   a. Psychoanalytic theory

   b. Activation–synthesis theory

   c. The problem-focused approach

   d. The cognitive approach

3. In his dreams, Andy is a child crawling through a dark tunnel looking for something he has lost. Hearing about

this, a psychologist remarks, "Andy has broken up with his lover and is working through the emotional loss." Which theory of dreams does the psychologist likely subscribe to?

   a. Psychoanalytic theory

   b. The problem-focused approach

   c. Activation–synthesis theory

   d. The cognitive approach

4. Of the major scientific theories of dreaming, which one has a difficult time accounting for dreams that follow a logical, linear, coherent story line?

   a. Activation–synthesis theory

   b. Diathesis–stress theory

   c. The problem-focused approach

   d. The cognitive approach

5. Of the current explanations for dreaming, which theory shows the most promise?

   a. Activation–synthesis theory

   b. Psychoanalytic theory

   c. The problem-focused approach

   d. The cognitive approach

The Riddle of Hypnosis

For many years, stage hypnotists, "past-lives channelers," and some psychotherapists have been reporting that they can "age-regress" hypnotized people to earlier years or even earlier centuries. Some therapists claim that hypnosis helps their patients accurately retrieve long-buried memories, and a few even claim that hypnosis has helped their patients recall alleged abductions by extraterrestrials. What are we to make of all this? Because hypnosis has been used for everything from parlor tricks and stage shows to medical and psychological treatments, it is important to understand just what this procedure can and cannot achieve. In this section, we will begin with a general look at the major findings on hypnosis; then we will consider two leading explanations of hypnotic effects. But first, take this short quiz to see how much you know about hypnosis.

Interactive

True or False?

1. A hypnotized person is usually aware of what is going on and remembers the experience later.

2. Hypnosis gives us special powers that we do not ordinarily have.

3. Hypnosis reduces errors in memory.

4. Hypnotized people play no active part in controlling their behavior and thoughts.

5. Hypnosis can help people recall events that happened to them in infancy.

6. Hypnosis can be a helpful tool for pain management.

Answers: 1. True 2. False 3. False 4. False 5. False 6. True

The Nature of Hypnosis

LO 5.4.A Summarize six established facts about hypnosis, and outline the truth and misconceptions associated with each.

Hypnosis is a procedure in which a practitioner suggests changes in the sensations, perceptions, thoughts, feelings, or behavior of the subject (Lynn & Kirsch, 2015). The hypnotized person, in turn, tries to alter his or her cognitive processes in accordance with the hypnotist's suggestions (Nash & Nadon, 1997). Hypnotic suggestions typically involve performance of an action ("Your arm will slowly rise"), an inability to perform an act ("You will be unable to bend your arm"), or a distortion of normal perception or memory ("You will feel no pain," "You will forget being hypnotized until I give you a signal"). People usually report that their response to a suggestion feels involuntary, as if it happened without their willing it. Learn more about the scientific basis of hypnosis by watching the video *The Uses and Limitations of Hypnosis 1*.

hypnosis
A procedure in which the practitioner suggests changes in a subject's sensations, perceptions, thoughts, feelings, or behavior.

To induce hypnosis, the hypnotist typically suggests that the person being hypnotized feels relaxed, is getting sleepy, and feels the eyelids getting heavier and heavier. In a singsong or monotonous voice, the hypnotist assures the subject that he or she is sinking "deeper and deeper." Sometimes the hypnotist has the person concentrate on a color or a small object, or on certain bodily sensations. People who have been hypnotized report that the focus of attention turns outward, toward the hypnotist's voice. They sometimes compare the experience to being totally absorbed in a good movie or favorite piece of music. The hypnotized person almost always remains fully aware of what is happening and remembers the experience later unless explicitly instructed to forget it. Even then, the memory can be restored by a prearranged signal.

Since the late 1960s, thousands of articles on hypnosis have appeared. Based on controlled laboratory and clinical studies, most psychological scientists agree that hypnosis is not a mystical trance or strange state of consciousness. Indeed, some worry that thinking of hypnosis in those ways, as a kind of dark art, has interfered with our understanding of it (Posner & Rothbart, 2011). Although scientists disagree about what exactly hypnosis is, they generally agree on the following points (Kirsch & Lynn, 1995; Nash, 2001; Nash & Nadon, 1997):

1. **Hypnotic responsiveness depends more on the efforts and qualities of the person being hypnotized than on the skill of the hypnotist.** Some people are more responsive to hypnosis than others, but why they are is unknown (Barnier, Cox, & McConkey, 2014). Surprisingly, such susceptibility is unrelated to general personality traits such as gullibility, trust, submissiveness, or conformity (Nash & Nadon, 1997). And it is only weakly related to the ability to become easily absorbed in activities and the world of imagination (Council, Kirsch, & Grant, 1996; Green & Lynn, 2010; Nash & Nadon, 1997).

2. **Hypnotized people cannot be forced to do things against their will.** Like drunkenness, hypnosis can be used to justify letting go of inhibitions ("I know this looks silly, but after all, I'm hypnotized"). Hypnotized individuals may even comply with a suggestion to do something that looks embarrassing or dangerous. But the person is choosing to turn responsibility over to the hypnotist and to cooperate with the hypnotist's suggestions (Lynn, Rhue, & Weekes, 1990). Hypnotized people will not do anything that actually violates their morals or constitutes a real danger to themselves or others.

3. **Feats performed under hypnosis can be performed by motivated people without hypnosis.** Hypnotized subjects sometimes perform what seem like extraordinary mental or physical feats, but hypnosis does not actually enable people to do things that would otherwise be impossible. With proper motivation, support, and encouragement, the same people could do the same things even without being hypnotized (Chaves, 1989; Spanos, Stenstrom, & Johnson, 1988).

4. **Hypnosis does not increase the accuracy of memory.** In rare cases, hypnosis has been used successfully to jog the memories of crime victims, but usually the memories of hypnotized witnesses have been completely mistaken. Although hypnosis does sometimes boost the amount of information recalled, it also increases *errors*, perhaps because hypnotized people are more willing than others to guess, or because they mistake vividly imagined possibilities for actual memories (Dinges et al., 1992; Kihlstrom, 1994). Because pseudomemories and errors are so common in hypnotically induced recall, many scientific societies around the world oppose the use of "hypnotically refreshed" testimony in courts of law. The video *The Uses and Limitations of Hypnosis 2* shows you more about the legitimate uses of hypnosis.

5. **Hypnosis does not produce a literal re-experiencing of long-ago events.** Many people believe that hypnosis can be used to recover memories from as far back as birth. When one clinical psychologist who uses hypnosis in his own practice surveyed over 800 marriage and family therapists, he was dismayed to find that more than half agreed with this common belief (Yapko, 1994). But it is just plain wrong. When people are regressed to an earlier age, their mental and moral performance remains adultlike (Nash, 1987). Their brain-wave patterns and reflexes do not become childish; they do not reason as children do or show child-sized IQs. They may use baby talk or report that they feel 4 years old again, but the reason is not that they are actually reliving the experience of being 4; they are just willing to play the role.

Is it hypnosis that enables the man stretched out between two chairs to hold the weight of the man standing on him, without flinching? This audience assumes so, but the only way to find out whether hypnosis produces unique abilities is to do research with control groups. It turns out that people can do the same thing even when they are not hypnotized.

6. **Hypnotic suggestions have been used effectively for many medical and psychological purposes.** Although hypnosis is not of much use for finding out what happened in the past, it can be useful in the treatment of psychological and medical problems. Its greatest success is in pain management; some people experience dramatic relief of pain resulting from conditions as diverse as burns, cancer, and childbirth, and others have learned to cope better emotionally with chronic pain. Hypnotic suggestions have also been used in the treatment of stress, anxiety, obesity, asthma, irritable bowel syndrome, chemotherapy-induced nausea, and even skin disorders (Nash & Barnier, 2007; Patterson & Jensen, 2003).

dissociation
A split in consciousness in which one part of the mind operates independently of others.

Theories of Hypnosis

LO 5.4.B Contrast the dissociation theory of hypnosis from the sociocognitive approach, noting how each accounts for aspects of hypnotized behavior.

Over the years, people have proposed many explanations of what hypnosis is and how it produces its effects. Today, two competing theories predominate.

DISSOCIATION THEORIES One leading approach was originally proposed by Ernest Hilgard (1977, 1986), who argued that hypnosis, like lucid dreaming and even simple distraction, involves **dissociation**, a split in consciousness in which one part of the mind operates independently of the rest of consciousness. In many hypnotized people, said Hilgard, most of the mind is subject to hypnotic suggestion, but one part is a *hidden observer*, watching but not participating. Unless given special instructions, the hypnotized part remains unaware of the observer.

Hilgard attempted to question the hidden observer directly. In one procedure, hypnotized volunteers had to submerge an arm in ice water for several seconds, an experience that is normally excruciating. They were told that they would feel no pain, but that the unsubmerged hand would be able to signal the level of any hidden pain by pressing a key. In this situation, many people said they felt little or no pain—yet at the same time, their free hand was busily pressing the key. After the session, these people continued to insist that they had been pain-free unless the hypnotist asked the hidden observer to issue a separate report.

A contemporary version of this theory holds that during hypnosis, a dissociation occurs between two systems in the brain: the system that processes incoming information about the world, and an "executive" system that controls how we use that information. In hypnosis, the executive system turns off and hands its function over to the hypnotist. That leaves the hypnotist able to suggest how we should interpret the world and act in it (Woody & Bowers, 1994; Woody & Sadler, 2012) (see Figure 5.5).

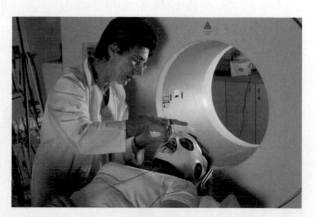

Ernest Hilgard, a pioneer in hypnosis research, discovered that when hypnotized people are told the pain will be minimal, they report little or no discomfort and seem unperturbed. Hypnosis has subsequently been used effectively for many medical purposes.

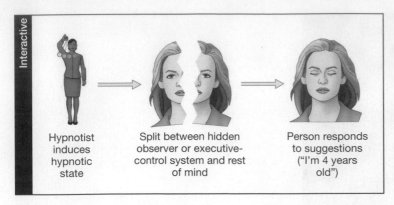

Figure 5.5 Dissociation Theories of Hypnosis

THE SOCIOCOGNITIVE APPROACH The second major approach to hypnosis, the *sociocognitive explanation*, holds that the effects of hypnosis result from an interaction between the social influence of the hypnotist (the "socio" part) and the abilities, beliefs, and expectations of the subject (the "cognitive" part) (see Figure 5.6) (Kirsch, 1997; Sarbin, 1991; Spanos, 1991). The hypnotized person is basically enacting a role. This role has analogies in ordinary life, where we willingly submit to the suggestions of parents, teachers, doctors, therapists, and television commercials. In this view, even the "hidden observer" is simply a reaction to the social demands of the situation and the suggestions of the hypnotist (Lynn & Green, 2011).

The hypnotized person is not merely faking or playacting, however. A person who has been instructed to fool an observer by faking a hypnotic state will tend to overplay the role and will stop playing it as soon as the other person leaves the room. In contrast, hypnotized subjects continue to follow the hypnotic suggestions even when they think they are not being watched (Kirsch et al., 1989; Spanos et al., 1993). Like many social roles, the role of "hypnotized person" is so engrossing and involving that actions required by the role may occur without the person's conscious intent.

Sociocognitive views explain why some people under hypnosis have reported spirit possession or "memories" of alien abductions (Clancy, 2005; Spanos, 1996). Suppose a young woman goes to a therapist or hypnotist seeking an explanation for her loneliness, unhappiness, nightmares, puzzling symptoms (such as waking up in the middle of the night in a cold sweat), or the waking dreams we described earlier. A therapist who already believes in alien abduction may use hypnosis, along with subtle and not-so-subtle cues about UFOs, to shape the way the client interprets her symptoms.

The sociocognitive view can also explain apparent cases of past-life regression. In a fascinating program of research, Nicholas Spanos and his colleagues (1991) directed hypnotized Canadian university students to regress past their own births to previous lives. About a third of the students (who already believed in reincarnation) reported being able to do so. But when they were asked, while supposedly reliving a past life, to name the leader of their country, say whether the country was at peace or at war, or describe the money used in their community, the students could not do it. (One young man, who thought he was Julius Caesar, said the year was 50 A.D. and he was emperor of Rome. But Caesar died in 44 B.C. and was never crowned emperor, and dating years as A.D. or B.C. did not begin until several centuries later.) Not knowing anything about the language, dates, customs, and events of their "previous life" did not deter the students from constructing a story about it, however. They tried to fulfill the requirements of the role by weaving events, places, and people from their *present* lives into their accounts, and by picking up cues from the experimenter.

Figure 5.6 Sociocognitive Theories of Hypnosis

The researchers concluded that the act of "remembering" another self involves the construction of a fantasy that accords with the rememberer's own beliefs and also the beliefs of others—in this case, those of the authoritative hypnotist.

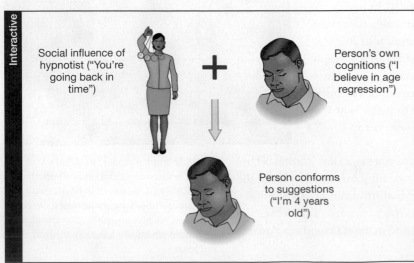

JOURNAL PROMPT 5.4

Thinking Critically—Examine the Evidence: Imagine that a hypnotherapist told you that, while under hypnosis, you revealed that in a past life you were a member of 12th-century Polish royalty, and that you described the palace and all its inhabitants fully and accurately. What are some questions you would ask to challenge the hypnotist's dubious claim? For example, if the therapist said you described the palace and its grounds from a bird's-eye view, wouldn't you be a little suspicious? The ability to get a bird's-eye view would be tough in the 12th century (without the invention of the airplane), and wouldn't a speaker describe what she or he saw from her own point of view (e.g., at eye level, while interacting with others)?

BIOLOGY and *Hypnosis*

Debates over what hypnosis really is and how it works have intensified as scientists have begun using technology to study this mysterious phenomenon. We have known for some time from EEG studies that alpha waves are common when a person is in a relaxed hypnotic state. This is not surprising because alpha waves are associated with relaxed wakefulness. Brain scans, however, permit a more detailed and useful picture of what is going on in the brain of a hypnotized person.

One study that used both fMRI and event-related potentials (ERP) showed that hypnosis can reduce conflict between two mental tasks (Raz, Fan, & Posner, 2005). The researchers gave participants the Stroop Test, which is often used to study what happens when color perception conflicts with reading. You look at words denoting colors (*blue*, *red*, *green*, *yellow*, etc.), with some of the letters printed in the corresponding color (e.g., *red* printed in red) and others in a different color (e.g., *red* printed in blue). It is a lot harder to identify the color of the ink a word is printed in when the word's meaning and its color are different. To see what we mean, try identifying as quickly as you can the color of the words in the illustration below. It's pretty hard, right?

In the study, hypnotized participants were told that later, after they were no longer hypnotized, they would see words from the Stroop Test on a computer screen but the words would seem like strings of meaningless symbols—like "characters in a foreign language that you do not know." During the test, highly suggestible people were faster and better at identifying the clashing colors the words were printed in than people who were less suggestible; in fact, the "Stroop effect" virtually disappeared. Apparently, the easily hypnotized people were literally not seeing the color words; they were seeing only gibberish. Moreover, during the task, they had reduced activity in a brain area that decodes written words and in another area toward the front of the brain that monitors conflicting thoughts. Because of the suggestions made during hypnosis, they were able to pay less attention to the words themselves during the task and thus were able to avoid reading them. They could focus solely on the color of the ink.

red
yellow
green
blue
red
blue
yellow
green
blue
red

Various regions of the brain also change when people are hypnotized and lying in a PET scanner. In one study, highly hypnotizable people, under hypnosis, were able to visually drain color from a drawing of red, blue, green, and yellow rectangles, or to see color when the same drawing was presented in gray tones. When they were told to see color in the gray drawing, their brains showed activation in areas associated with color perception; when they were told to see gray in the colored drawing, the same areas had decreased activation (Kosslyn et al., 2000).

What do findings like these mean for theories of hypnosis? The fact that hypnosis can affect patterns of activity in the brain gives encouragement to those who believe that hypnosis is a special state, different from elaborate role-playing or extreme concentration. Others feel that it is too soon to draw any conclusions from this research about the mechanisms or nature of hypnosis. *Every* experience alters the brain in some way; hypnosis is no exception, however it may work. Moreover, suggestion can reduce the Stroop effect in highly suggestible people even *without* hypnosis (Raz et al., 2006). In fact, highly suggestible people can even hallucinate color without hypnosis (McGeown et al., 2012).

Further work may tell us whether or not there is something special about hypnosis. But whatever the outcome of this debate, all hypnosis researchers agree that hypnosis does not cause memories to become sharper or allow early experiences to be replayed with perfect accuracy. The study of hypnosis is teaching us much about human suggestibility, the power of imagination, and the way we perceive the present and remember the past.

Quiz for Module 5.4

1. In which of these domains has hypnotism shown the most effectiveness?

   a. Producing re-experiences of past lives

   b. Increasing memory accuracy

   c. Pain management

   d. Giving people uncanny strength

2. Kristin was telling her friends Ana and Kathy about the hypnotist show she attended the night before. "It was really wild," said Kristin. "I volunteered to be hypnotized, and when I was up on stage, the hypnotist put me in a trance and commanded me to make out with random people and dance onstage. I've never done that before! I would never do that in real life! That hypnotist really had some weird mojo power over me." Ana whispered to Kathy, "I'll bet you a dollar she's made out with random people before, and she'll probably do it again within the next few months." How can Ana be so bold in her pronouncements and predictions?

   a. Ana knows that hypnotized people can't be forced to do things against their will; despite her protestations, Kristin was probably acting within the bounds of her normal range of behaviors.

   b. Ana knows that hypnotic suggestions can have powerful, lasting effects; when the implanted trigger word is mentioned again in a few months, Kristin will revert to her unusual behavior.

c. Ana knows that there is no scientific evidence for the existence of hypnotism; therefore, Kristin is fabricating a story to account for her questionable behavior.

d. Ana knows that hypnotized people are usually induced to commit malicious acts (such as harming another person) rather than lighthearted ones (such as dancing onstage).

3. In the year 2040, Keith is talking to his friends Arnie and Karl about his recent visit to a hypnotherapist. "Man, it was wild," said Keith. "The hypnotist brought back a memory of a stage show I went to 25 years ago. There was a girl named Kristin who was dancing onstage and acting all wild, and then she jumped into the audience and started making out with me. I'd forgotten all about that experience! I didn't even remember that I was there! My hypnotherapist really had some weird mojo power to improve my memory for that long-ago event." Arnie whispered to Karl, "I'll bet you a dollar he was never at that show 25 years ago; he probably just read about those events in some psychology textbook and thought he actually experienced them." How can Arnie be so bold in his pronouncements and predictions?

a. Arnie knows that therapists take a solemn oath to not use their hypnotic powers to coax hidden memories from clients.

b. Arnie knows that hypnotism can only bring back vivid repressed memories from the past 5 years, but not from periods longer ago than that.

c. Arnie knows that hypnotism can only bring back vivid repressed memories from at least 30 years ago, but not from periods more recent than that.

d. Arnie knows that hypnotism does not increase the accuracy of memory, and in fact can increase memory errors along with any actual information.

4. Which of the following is a dissociation theory of hypnosis?
   a. The hidden observer explanation
   b. The sociocultural explanation
   c. The Spanos-McGillicuddy hypothesis
   d. The dichromatic theory

5. Which theory of hypnosis highlights the interplay of the hypnotist's influence and the subject's expectations about being hypnotized?
   a. The executive-control approach
   b. The hidden observer approach
   c. The dissociation approach
   d. The sociocognitive approach

Consciousness-Altering Drugs

In Jerusalem, hundreds of Hasidic men celebrate the completion of the annual reading of the holy Torah by dancing for hours in the streets. For them, dancing is not a diversion; it is a path to religious ecstasy. In South Dakota, several Lakota (Sioux) adults sit naked in the darkness and crushing heat of a sweat lodge; their goal is euphoria, the transcendence of pain, and connection with the Great Spirit of the Universe. In the Amazon jungle, a young man training to be a shaman, a religious leader, takes a whiff of hallucinogenic snuff made from the bark of the virola tree; his goal is to enter a trance and communicate with animals, spirits, and supernatural forces. And some people simply sit quietly, focused intently on the private world of their innermost thoughts, absorbed in meditation as a means of enlightenment and expanded awareness. Some common alterations of consciousness are discussed more fully in the video *Altered States of Consciousness.*

These rituals, seemingly quite different, are all aimed at release from the confines of ordinary consciousness. Because cultures around the world have devised such practices, some writers believe they reflect a human need, one as basic as the need for food and water (Siegel, 1989). William James (1902/1936), who was fascinated by alterations in consciousness, would have agreed. After inhaling nitrous oxide ("laughing gas"), he wrote, "Our normal waking consciousness, rational consciousness as we call it, is but one special type of consciousness, whilst all about it, parted from it by the filmiest of screens, there lie potential forms of consciousness entirely different." But it was not until the 1960s, as millions of people began to seek ways to deliberately produce *altered states of consciousness,* that researchers became

interested in the psychology, as well as the physiology, of psychoactive drugs. The filmy screen described by James finally began to lift.

Classifying Drugs

LO 5.5.A **List the four main categories of psychoactive drugs, and summarize the main effects of each.**

A **psychoactive drug** is a substance that alters perception, mood, thinking, memory, or behavior by interacting with the biochemistry of brain and body. Around the world and throughout history, the most common ones have been nicotine, alcohol, marijuana, mescaline, opium, cocaine, peyote—and, of course, caffeine. The reasons for taking psychoactive drugs have varied: to alter consciousness, as part of a religious ritual, for recreation, to decrease physical pain or discomfort, and for psychological escape.

In Western societies, a whole pharmacopeia of recreational drugs exists, and new ones, both natural and synthetic, emerge every few years. Most of these drugs can be classified as **stimulants**, **depressants**, **opiates**, or **psychedelics**, depending on their effects on the central nervous system and their impact on behavior and mood (see Review 5.1). Here we describe their physiological and psychological effects.

psychoactive drugs
Drugs capable of influencing perception, mood, cognition, or behavior.

stimulants
Drugs that speed up activity in the central nervous system.

depressants
Drugs that slow activity in the central nervous system.

opiates
Drugs, derived from the opium poppy, that relieve pain and commonly produce euphoria.

psychedelic drugs
Consciousness-altering drugs that produce hallucinations, change thought processes, or disrupt the normal perception of time and space.

Interactive

All cultures have found ways to alter consciousness. The Mevlevis of Turkey (left), the famous whirling dervishes, spin in an energetic but controlled manner to achieve religious rapture. People in many cultures meditate (center) as a way to quiet the mind and achieve spiritual enlightenment. And in some cultures, psychoactive drugs are used for religious or artistic inspiration, as in the case of the Huichol Indians of western Mexico, one of whom is shown here harvesting hallucinogenic mushrooms.

Review 5.1

Some Psychoactive Drugs and Their Effects

Class of Drug	Type	Common Effects	Some Results of Abuse/Addiction
Amphetamines; methamphetamine (MDMA) (Ecstasy)*	Stimulants	Wakefulness, alertness, raised metabolism, elevated mood	Nervousness, headaches, loss of appetite, high blood pressure, delusions, psychosis, heart damage, convulsions, death
Cocaine	Stimulant	Euphoria, excitation, feelings of energy, suppressed appetite	Excitability, sleeplessness, sweating, paranoia, anxiety, panic, depression, heart damage, heart failure, injury to nose if sniffed
Nicotine (tobacco)	Stimulant	Varies from alertness to calmness, depending on mental set, setting, and prior arousal; decreases appetite for carbohydrates	*Nicotine:* heart disease, high blood pressure, impaired circulation, erectile problems in men, damage throughout the body due to lowering of a key enzyme *Tar (residue from smoking cigarettes):* lung cancer, emphysema, mouth and throat cancer, many other health risks
Caffeine	Stimulant	Wakefulness, alertness, shortened reaction time	Restlessness, insomnia, muscle tension, heartbeat irregularities, high blood pressure
Alcohol (several/many drinks)	Depressant	Slowed reaction time, tension, depression, reduced ability to store new memories or to retrieve old ones, poor coordination	Blackouts, cirrhosis of the liver, other organ damage, mental and neurological impairment, psychosis, death with very large amounts
Tranquilizers (e.g., Valium); barbiturates (e.g., phenobarbital)	Depressants	Reduced anxiety and tension, sedation	Increased dosage needed for effects; impaired motor and sensory functions, impaired permanent storage of new information, withdrawal symptoms; possibly convulsions, coma, death (especially when taken with other drugs)
Opium, heroin, morphine, codeine, codone-based pain relievers	Opiates	Euphoria, relief of pain	Loss of appetite, nausea, constipation, withdrawal symptoms, convulsions, coma, possibly death
LSD, psilocybin, mescaline, *Salvia divinorum*	Psychedelics	Depending on the drug: Exhilaration, visions and hallucinations, insightful experiences	Psychosis, paranoia, panic reactions
Marijuana	Mild psychedelic (classification controversial)	Relaxation, euphoria, increased appetite, reduced ability to store new memories, other effects depending on mental set and setting	Throat and lung irritation, possible lung damage if smoked heavily

*Ecstasy also has psychedelic properties.

1. *Stimulants* **speed up activity in the central nervous system.** They include nicotine, caffeine, cocaine, amphetamines, methamphetamine (meth), and MDMA (Ecstasy, which also has psychedelic properties). In moderate amounts, stimulants produce feelings of excitement, confidence, and well-being or euphoria. In large amounts, they can make a person anxious, jittery, and hyperalert. In very large doses, they may cause convulsions, heart failure, and death.

   Amphetamines are synthetic drugs taken in pill form, injected, smoked, or inhaled. Methamphetamine is structurally similar to amphetamine and is used in the same ways; it comes in two forms, as a powder or in a freebase (purified) form, as a crystalline solid. Cocaine is a natural drug, derived from the leaves of the coca plant. Rural workers in Bolivia and Peru chew coca leaf every day without apparent ill effects. In North America, the drug is usually inhaled, injected, or smoked in the freebase form known as *crack* (because of the cracking sound it makes when smoked). These methods provide more rapid access to the blood and therefore the brain, giving the drug a more immediate, powerful, and dangerous effect than when coca leaf is chewed. Amphetamines, methamphetamine, and cocaine make users feel charged up but do not actually increase energy reserves. Fatigue, irritability, and depression may occur when the effects of these drugs wear off.

2. *Depressants* **slow down activity in the central nervous system.** They include alcohol, tranquilizers, barbiturates, and most of the common chemicals that some people inhale to try to get high. Depressants usually make a person feel calm or drowsy, and they may

reduce anxiety, guilt, tension, and inhibitions. These drugs enhance the activity of GABA, the neurotransmitter that inhibits the ability of neurons to communicate with each other. In large amounts, depressants may produce insensitivity to pain and other sensations. Like stimulants, in very large doses they can cause irregular heartbeats, convulsions, and death.

People are often surprised to learn that alcohol is a central nervous system depressant. In small amounts, alcohol has some of the effects of a stimulant because it suppresses activity in parts of the brain that normally inhibit impulsive behavior, such as loud laughter and clowning around. In the long run, however, it slows down nervous system activity. Like barbiturates and opiates, alcohol can produce anesthesia, which is why people may pass out (if they don't throw up first) when they drink excessively. Over time, alcohol damages the liver, heart, and brain. Extremely large amounts of alcohol can kill by inhibiting the nerve cells in brain areas that control breathing and heartbeat. Every so often, a news report announces the death of a college student who had large amounts of alcohol "funneled" into him as part of an initiation or drinking competition. On the other hand, *moderate* drinking—an occasional drink or two of wine, beer, or liquor—is associated with a variety of health benefits, including a reduced risk of heart attack and stroke, and antidiabetic effects (Brand-Miller et al., 2007; Mukamal et al., 2003; Reynolds et al., 2003).

3. *Opiates* **relieve pain.** They include opium, derived from the opium poppy; morphine, a derivative of opium; heroin, a derivative of morphine; synthetic drugs such as methadone; and codeine and codone-based pain relievers such as oxycodone and hydrocodone. These drugs work on some of the same brain systems as endorphins do, and some have a powerful effect on the emotions. When injected, opiates can enhance the transmission of dopamine, and so produce a *rush*, a sudden feeling of euphoria. They may also decrease anxiety and motivation. Opiates are highly addictive and in large amounts can cause coma and even death.

4. *Psychedelic drugs* **disrupt normal thought processes**, such as the perception of time and space. Sometimes they produce hallucinations, especially visual ones. Some psychedelics, such as lysergic acid diethylamide (LSD), are made in a laboratory. Others, such as mescaline (from the peyote cactus), *Salvia divinorum* (from an herb native to Mexico), and psilocybin (from certain species of mushrooms), are natural substances. Emotional reactions to psychedelics vary from person to person and from one time to another for any individual. A "trip" may be mildly pleasant or unpleasant, a mystical revelation or a nightmare. For decades, research on psychedelics languished because of a lack of funding, but a few clinical researchers are now exploring their potential usefulness in psychotherapy, the relief of psychological distress, the treatment of anxiety disorders, and end-of-life distress (Gasser, Kirchner, & Passie, 2015; Griffiths et al., 2008). In a pilot study in which moderate doses of psilocybin were administered to 12 patients facing death from advanced-stage cancer, the drug significantly reduced their anxiety and despair (Grob et al., 2011).

Marijuana was once regarded as a mild and harmless sedative, but its image changed in the 1930s, when books and movies began to warn about the dire consequences of "reefer madness."

Some commonly used drugs fall outside these four classifications, combine elements of more than one category, or have uncertain effects. One is *marijuana*, which is smoked or, less commonly, eaten in foods such as brownies; it is the most widely used illicit drug in North America and Europe. Some researchers classify it as a psychedelic, but others feel that its chemical makeup and its psychological effects place it outside the major classifications. The main active ingredient in marijuana is tetrahydrocannabinol (THC), derived from the hemp plant, *Cannabis sativa*. In some respects, THC appears to be a mild stimulant, increasing heart rate and making tastes, sounds, and colors seem more intense. But users often report reactions ranging from mild euphoria to relaxation or even sleepiness.

Some researchers believe that heavy smoking of the drug (which is high in tar) may increase the risk of lung damage (Barsky et al., 1998; Zhu et al., 2000). In moderate doses, it can interfere with the transfer of information to long-term memory and impair coordination and reaction times, characteristics it shares with alcohol. In large doses, it can cause hallucinations and a sense of unreality. However, a meta-analysis found only a small impairment in memory and learning among long-term users versus nonusers, less than what typically occurs in users of alcohol and other drugs (Grant et al., 2003). And there have been zero deaths reported from the use of marijuana.

Cannabis has been used therapeutically for nearly 3,000 years and is one of the fundamental herbs of traditional Chinese medicine. Its benefits have been affirmed in contemporary medicine as well. It reduces the nausea and vomiting that often accompany chemotherapy treatment for cancer and AIDS treatments; it reduces the physical tremors, loss of appetite, and other symptoms caused by multiple sclerosis; it reduces pain; it helps reduce the frequency of seizures in some patients with epilepsy; it helps clear arteries; and it alleviates the retinal swelling caused by glaucoma (Aggarwal et al., 2009; Ben Amar, 2006; Grinspoon & Bakalar, 1993; Steffens et al., 2005).

The Physiology of Drug Effects

LO 5.5.B Outline the physiology of drug effects, and explain the process by which biochemical changes take place.

Psychoactive drugs produce their effects by acting on brain neurotransmitters, the chemical substances that carry messages from one nerve cell to another. A drug may increase or decrease the release of neurotransmitters at the synapse; prevent the reuptake (reabsorption) of excess neurotransmitter molecules by the cells that have released them; or interfere with the receptors that a neurotransmitter normally binds to. Figure 5.7 shows how one drug, cocaine, increases the amount of norepinephrine and dopamine in the synapse by blocking the reuptake of these neurotransmitters following their release. Cocaine, like other drugs, also increases the availability of serotonin (Müller & Homberg, 2015).

These biochemical changes affect cognitive and emotional functioning. Alcohol activates the receptor for GABA, the inhibitory neurotransmitter found in virtually all parts of the brain. Because GABA is so prevalent and modulates the activity of other neurotransmitter systems, alcohol can affect many behaviors. Just a couple of drinks can affect perception, response time, coordination, and balance, despite the drinker's own impression of unchanged or even improved performance. Alcohol also affects memory, possibly by interfering with the work of serotonin. Information stored before a drinking session remains intact during the session but is retrieved more slowly (Haut et al., 1989). Consuming small amounts does not seem to affect *sober* mental performance, but even occasional binge drinking—usually defined as five or more drinks on a single occasion—impairs later abstract thought. Binge-drinking college students often have impaired executive functioning: They are less able to hold on to, and work with, verbal information (Parada et al., 2012). In other words, a Saturday night binge is potentially more disabling than a daily drink.

As for other recreational drugs, there is little evidence that *light* or *moderate* use can damage the human brain enough to affect cognitive functioning, but nearly all researchers agree that heavy or frequent use is another matter. In one study, heavy users of methamphetamine had damage to dopamine cells and performed more poorly than other people on tests of memory, attention, and movement, even though they had not used the drug for at least 11 months (Volkow et al., 2001).

Figure 5.7 Cocaine's Effect on the Brain

Cocaine blocks the brain's reuptake of dopamine and norepinephrine so that synaptic levels of these neurotransmitters rise. The result is overstimulation of certain brain receptors and a brief euphoric high. Then, when the drug wears off, a depletion of dopamine may cause the user to "crash" and become sleepy and depressed.

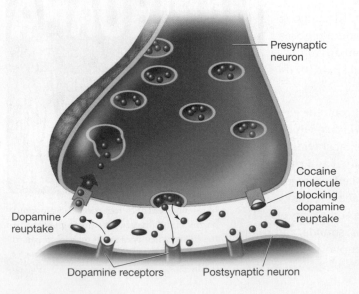

Presynaptic neuron

Cocaine molecule blocking dopamine reuptake

Dopamine reuptake

Dopamine receptors

Postsynaptic neuron

Under some conditions, the repeated use of some psychoactive drugs can lead to **tolerance**: Over time, more and more of the drug is needed to produce the same effect. When habitual heavy users stop taking a drug, they may suffer severe physical **withdrawal** symptoms, which, depending on the drug, may include nausea, abdominal cramps, sweating, muscle spasms, depression, disturbed sleep, and intense craving for more of the drug.

tolerance

Increased resistance to a drug's effects accompanying continued use.

withdrawal

Physical and psychological symptoms that occur when someone addicted to a drug stops taking it.

The Psychology of Drug Effects

LO 5.5.C Summarize four psychological aspects of drug effects, and comment on how each one might moderate physiological drug effects.

People often assume that the effects of a drug are automatic, the inevitable result of the drug's chemistry. But reactions to a psychoactive drug involve more than the drug's chemical properties. They also depend on a person's experience with the drug, individual characteristics, environmental setting, and mental set:

1. **Experience with the drug refers to the number of times a person has taken it.** When people try a drug—a cigarette, an alcoholic drink, a stimulant—for the first time, their reactions vary markedly, from unpleasant to neutral to enjoyable. Reactions to a drug may become increasingly positive after a person has used a drug for a while and has become familiar with its effects.

2. **Individual characteristics include body weight, metabolism, initial state of emotional arousal, personality characteristics, and physical tolerance for the drug.** Women generally get drunker than men on the same amount of alcohol because women are smaller, on average, so they get a higher proportionate dose of alcohol in each drink; their bodies also metabolize alcohol differently (Fuchs et al., 1995). Asians are more likely than Anglos to have a genetic variation that prevents alcohol from being metabolized normally and leads to the accumulation of a toxic substance, acetaldehyde. As a result, they tend to have adverse reactions to even small amounts of alcohol, which can cause severe headaches, facial flushing, and diarrhea (Cloninger, 1990). For individuals, a drug may have one effect after a tiring day and a different one after a rousing quarrel, or the effect may vary with the time of day because of circadian rhythms that affect various neurotransmitters. And some differences among individuals in their responses to a drug may be due to their personality traits. When people who are prone to anger and irritability wear nicotine patches, dramatic bursts of activity occur in the brain while they are working on competitive or aggressive tasks. These changes do not occur, however, in more relaxed and cheerful people (Fallon et al., 2004).

3. **"Environmental setting" refers to the context in which a person takes the drug.** A person might have one glass of wine at home alone and feel sleepy, but have three glasses of wine at a party and feel full of energy. Someone might feel happy and calm drinking with good friends, but fearful and nervous drinking with strangers. In an early study of reactions to alcohol, most of the drinkers became depressed, angry, confused, and

The motives for using a drug, expectations about its effects, and the setting in which it is used all contribute to a person's reactions to the drug. That is why drinking alone to drown your sorrows is likely to produce a different reaction than bingeing during a competitive game of beer pong.

unfriendly. Then it dawned on the researchers that anyone might become depressed, angry, confused, and unfriendly if asked to drink bourbon at 9:00 A.M. in a bleak hospital room, which was the setting for the experiment (Warren & Raynes, 1972).

4. **"Mental set" refers to a person's expectations about the drug's effects and reasons for taking it.** Some people drink to become more sociable, friendly, or seductive; some drink to try to reduce feelings of anxiety or depression; and some drink to have an excuse for abusiveness or violence. Addicts abuse drugs to escape from the real world; people living with chronic pain may use the same drugs to function in the real world. The motives for taking a drug greatly influence its effects.

Expectations can sometimes have a more powerful effect than the chemical properties of the drug itself. In several imaginative studies, researchers compared people who were drinking liquor (vodka and tonic) with those who *thought* they were drinking liquor but were actually getting only tonic and lime juice. (Vodka has a subtle taste, and most people could not tell the real and phony drinks apart.) The experimenters found a *"think–drink" effect*: Men behaved more belligerently when they thought they were drinking vodka than when they thought they were drinking plain tonic water, regardless of the actual content of the drinks. And both sexes reported feeling sexually aroused when they thought they were drinking vodka, whether or not they actually got vodka (Abrams & Wilson, 1983; Marlatt & Rohsenow, 1980).

None of this means that alcohol and other drugs are merely placebos. Psychoactive drugs, as we have seen, have physiological effects, many of them extremely potent. But by understanding the psychological factors involved in drug use, we can think more critically about the ongoing national debate over which drugs, if any, should be legal. In "Taking Psychology with You," we discuss some points to consider as you decide what your own position is on this issue.

JOURNAL PROMPT 5.5

Thinking Critically—Consider Other Interpretations: One person takes a drink and flies into a rage. Another has a drink and mellows out. What qualities of the user rather than the drug might account for this difference?

Quiz for Module 5.5

1. Which of these psychoactive drugs is classified as a stimulant?

   a. Mescaline

   b. Opium

   c. Heroin

   d. Nicotine

2. Barbiturates are a type of psychoactive drug that fall under the category of

   a. Stimulants

   b. Depressants

   c. Psychedelics

   d. Opiates

3. Which of the following drugs is *not* a psychedelic?

   a. Psilocybin

   b. LSD

   c. Codeine

   d. Mescaline

4. Repeatedly using psychoactive drugs can lead a person to need more and more of the substance over time to produce the same effects. This phenomenon is known as

   a. Lenience

   b. Withdrawal

   c. Tolerance

   d. Retraction

5. Harvey is given a shotglass full of straight tonic water, although he is told the glass contains vodka and tonic. He takes another shot just like the first, and then one more shot of straight tonic, still believing he is getting vodka mixed in. What is Harvey's subsequent behavior likely to be?

   a. He should act in a manner consistent with someone who took three shots of vodka.

   b. He should act in a manner consistent with someone who took three shots of tonic water.

   c. He should act in a manner consistent with his predrinking behavior.

   d. He should act in a manner consistent with a nondrinker.

Taking Psychology with You

The Drug Debate

Because the consequences of drug *abuse* are so devastating to individuals and to society, people often have trouble thinking critically about drug laws and policies: Which drugs should be legal, which should be illegal, and which should be "decriminalized" (i.e., not made legal, but not used as a reason for arresting and jailing their users)? At one extreme, some people cannot accept evidence that their favorite drug—be it caffeine, nicotine, alcohol, or marijuana—might have harmful effects. At the other extreme, some cannot accept the evidence that their most hated drug—be it alcohol, morphine, marijuana, or the coca leaf—might not be dangerous in all forms or amounts and might even have some beneficial effects. Both sides often confuse potent drugs with others that have only subtle effects and confuse light or moderate use with heavy or excessive use.

After a drug is declared illegal, many people assume it is deadly, even though some legal drugs are more dangerous than illegal ones. Addiction to prescription painkillers and sedatives used for recreational rather than medical purposes has risen dramatically among teenagers and adults. Nicotine, which of course is legal, is as addictive as heroin and cocaine, which are illegal. No one has ever died from smoking marijuana, but tobacco use contributes to between 400,000 and 500,000 deaths in the United States every year, 24 times the number of deaths from all illegal forms of drug use combined, and worldwide it is the largest single cause of preventable deaths (WHO Report, 2011). Yet most people have a far more negative view of marijuana, heroin, and cocaine than of nicotine and prescription painkillers.

Emotions run especially high in debates over marijuana. Heavy use has some physical risks, just as heavy use of any drug does. However, a review of studies done between 1975 and 2003 failed to find any compelling evidence that marijuana causes chronic mental or behavioral problems in teenagers or young adults. The researchers observed that cause and effect could just as well work in the other direction; that is, people with problems could be more likely to abuse the drug (Macleod et al., 2004).

Because marijuana has medical benefits, Canada, Spain, Italy, Portugal, Israel, Austria, Finland, the Netherlands, and Belgium have either decriminalized it or made it legally available for patients who demonstrate a medical need for it. In the United States, 23 states and the District of Columbia (as of 2015) have approved the medical use of marijuana, and residents of Alaska, Colorado, Oregon, and Washington voted to legalize recreational marijuana for adults 21 and older. In other states, possession of any amount of pot remains illegal, and punishment for offenses range from a few years in prison to a felony conviction. In some states, a person who has been convicted of marijuana possession cannot later get food stamps or welfare, which even convicted rapists and murderers are entitled to.

At one end of the spectrum, many people remain committed to the eradication of all currently illegal drugs. At the other end, some people think that all recreational drugs should be legalized or decriminalized. In between lie a range of possible strategies. One is to develop programs to reduce or at least delay drug use by young teens because multiple drug use before age 15 increases the risk of drug dependence, criminal activity, and other problems in adulthood (Odgers et al., 2008). Another approach would legalize narcotics for people who are in chronic pain and marijuana for recreational and medicinal use, but would ban tobacco and most hard drugs. And in a third approach, instead of punishing or incarcerating people who use drugs, society would regulate where drugs are used (never at work or when driving, for example), provide treatment for addicts, and educate people about the benefits and hazards of particular drugs.

Where, given the research findings, do you stand on this debate? Which illegal psychoactive drugs, if any, do you think should be legalized? Can we create mental sets and environmental settings that promote safe recreational use of some drugs, minimize the likelihood of drug abuse, and permit the medicinal use of beneficial drugs? What do you think?

Shared Writing Prompt

Humans generally have the right to modify their bodies as they see fit. People grow mustaches, shave their heads, get tattoos and piercings, and even bifurcate their tongues or have horns implanted under their skin. Within certain restrictions (e.g., people shouldn't be forced to modify their bodies; children can't get tattooed) people are free to change the external aspects of themselves. Should people also be free to regulate their own consciousness? As an internal aspect of the self (so deeply private, in fact, that no one has direct access to it except the individual in question), do we have a right to do as we please with our own conscious states, such as altering them through the ingestion of drugs? Like body modification, should some restrictions apply? What would those restrictions be?

Summary

Biological Rhythms: The Tides of Experience

LO 5.1.A   Define circadian rhythms, and explain how the body's "biological clock" works (and what happens when it doesn't).

Consciousness is the awareness of oneself and the environment. Changing states of consciousness are often associated with *biological rhythms*—periodic fluctuations in physiological functioning. *Circadian* fluctuations occur about once a day and are governed by a biological clock in the *suprachiasmatic nucleus (SCN)* of the hypothalamus. The SCN regulates and, in turn, is affected by the hormone *melatonin*, which is responsive to changes in light and dark and which increases during the dark hours. When a person's normal routine changes, the person may experience *internal desynchronization*, in which the usual circadian rhythms are thrown out of phase with one another.

LO 5.1.B   Explain why seasonal affective disorder and premenstrual syndrome are examples of long-term biological rhythms, and summarize the evidence regarding the existence of both phenomena.

Some people experience depression every winter in a pattern that has been labeled *seasonal affective disorder (SAD)*. The causes of SAD, which is relatively uncommon, are not yet clear, although light treatments can be effective in alleviating symptoms. Another long-term rhythm is the menstrual cycle, during which various hormones rise and fall. Well-controlled, double-blind studies on *premenstrual syndrome* do not support claims that emotional symptoms are reliably and universally tied to the menstrual cycle. Expectations and learning affect how both sexes interpret bodily and emotional changes. Few people of either sex are likely to undergo dramatic monthly mood swings or personality changes because of hormones.

The Rhythms of Sleep

LO 5.2.A   Describe the four stages of sleep, and explain the primary features of each stage.

During sleep, periods of *rapid eye movement (REM)* alternate with *non-REM (NREM) sleep* in approximately a 90-minute rhythm. Non-REM sleep is divided into stages on the basis of characteristic brain-wave patterns. During REM sleep, the brain is active, and there are other signs of arousal, yet most of the skeletal muscles are limp; vivid dreams are reported most often during REM sleep.

LO 5.2.B   List the mental consequences of sleeplessness and the mental benefits of a good night's sleep.

Sleep is necessary not only for bodily restoration but also for normal mental functioning. Many people get less than the optimal amount of sleep, perhaps suffering from *insomnia, sleep apnea, narcolepsy,* or *REM behavior disorder,* but the most common reason for daytime sleepiness is probably a simple lack of sleep. Sleep may contribute to the consolidation of memories and subsequent problem solving. These benefits have been associated most closely with slow-wave sleep, but also with REM sleep.

Exploring the Dream World

LO 5.3.A   Discuss explanations for why we dream.

Freud thought that dreams allow us to express forbidden or unrealistic desires that have been forced into the unconscious part of the mind, but there is no objective way to verify Freudian interpretations of dreams and no convincing support for most of his claims. Three modern theories of dreaming emphasize the connections between dreams and waking thoughts. The *problem-focused approach* holds that dreams express current concerns and may even help us solve current problems. The *cognitive approach* holds that dreams are simply a modification of the cognitive activity that goes on when we are awake. The difference is that during sleep we are cut off from sensory input from the world, so our thoughts tend to be more diffuse and unfocused. The *activation–synthesis theory* holds that dreams occur when the cortex tries to make sense of, or interpret, spontaneous neural firing initiated in the pons. The resulting synthesis of these signals with existing knowledge and memories results in a dream.

LO 5.3.B   Summarize the strengths and weaknesses of each major dream theory.

All of the current theories of dreams have some support, and all have weaknesses. Some psychologists doubt that people can solve problems during sleep. The *activation–synthesis theory* does not seem to explain coherent, story-like dreams or non-REM dreams. The cognitive approach is now a leading contender, although some of its specific claims remain to be tested.

The Riddle of Hypnosis

LO 5.4.A   Summarize six established facts about hypnosis, and outline the truth and misconceptions associated with each.

Hypnosis is a procedure in which the practitioner suggests changes in a person's sensations, perceptions, thoughts, feelings, or behavior, and the person tries to comply. Although hypnosis has been used successfully for many medical and psychological purposes, people hold many misconceptions about what it can accomplish. It cannot force people to do things against their will, confer special abilities that are otherwise impossible, increase the accuracy of memory, or produce a literal re-experiencing of long-ago events.

LO 5.4.B Contrast the dissociation theory of hypnosis from the sociocognitive approach, noting how each accounts for aspects of hypnotized behavior.

A leading approach to understanding hypnosis is that it involves *dissociation*, a split in consciousness. In one version of this approach, the split is between a part of consciousness that is hypnotized and a *hidden observer* that watches but does not participate. In another version, the split is between an executive-control system in the brain and other brain systems responsible for thinking and acting. The *sociocognitive explanation* regards hypnosis as a product of normal social and cognitive processes in which the hypnotized person's expectations and beliefs combine with the desire to comply with the hypnotist's suggestions. In this view, hypnosis is a form of role-playing; the role is so engrossing that the person interprets it as real. Sociocognitive processes can account for the apparent age and past-life "regressions" of people under hypnosis and their reports of alien abductions.

Consciousness-Altering Drugs

LO 5.5.A List the four main categories of psychoactive drugs, and summarize the main effects of each.

In all cultures, people have found ways to produce *altered states of consciousness*. *Psychoactive drugs* alter cognition and emotion by acting on neurotransmitters in the brain. Most psychoactive drugs are classified as *stimulants*, *depressants*, *opiates*, or *psychedelics*, depending on their central nervous system effects and their impact on behavior and mood. However, some common drugs, such as marijuana, straddle or fall outside these categories.

LO 5.5.B Outline the physiology of drug effects, and explain the process by which biochemical changes take place.

When used frequently and in large amounts, some psychoactive drugs can damage neurons in the brain and impair learning and memory. Their use may lead to *tolerance*, in which increasing dosages are needed for the same effect, and *withdrawal* symptoms if a heavy user tries to quit. But certain drugs, such as alcohol and marijuana, are also associated with some health benefits when used in moderation.

LO 5.5.C Summarize four psychological aspects of drug effects, and comment on how each one might moderate physiological drug effects.

Reactions to a psychoactive drug are influenced not only by its chemical properties but also by the user's prior experience with the drug, individual characteristics, environmental setting, and mental set—the person's expectations and motives for taking the drug. Expectations can be even more powerful than the drug itself, as shown by the *"think–drink" effect*.

Chapter 5 Quiz

1. The body's biological clock is located in the
   a. Suprachiasmatic nucleus
   b. Pineal gland
   c. Pituitary gland
   d. Thalamus

2. Hector seems to get depressed each winter, when the days get shorter and the nights get long. When spring comes he generally rallies, noticing a substantial improvement in his mood. Although there are many possible explanations for Hector's behavior, he favors the controversial diagnosis of _____ to account for his moods.
   a. PTSD
   b. Clinical depression
   c. Bipolar syndrome
   d. SAD

3. When sleeping, delta waves are usually associated with
   a. Stage 1 sleep
   b. Stage 3 sleep
   c. Stage 2 sleep
   d. REM sleep

4. Why is REM sleep sometimes called "paradoxical sleep"?
   a. The brain is very active even though the body is very inactive.
   b. It is the first stage of sleep, occurring right after being awake.
   c. REM periods are always shorter than NREM periods of sleep.
   d. There are no measureable indications that the person is asleep during this period.

5. Marvin stops breathing for a few moments dozens of times during his night's sleep, although he isn't even aware of it. Which sleep disorder does Marvin have?
   a. Narcolepsy
   b. Sleep apnea
   c. REM behavior disorder
   d. Insomnia

6. Jimmy often shows odd behavior while he is asleep. By all appearances he seems to be acting out the behaviors in his dreams, such as playing the banjo or feeding an imaginary baby. Having ruled out other disorders, his physician concluded that Jimmy is suffering from
   a. Cataplexy
   b. Insomnia
   c. Narcolepsy
   d. REM behavior disorder

7. Which theory of dreaming specifically implicates the pons, sensory cortex, and motor cortex of the brain?
   a. Cognitive theory
   b. Activation–synthesis theory
   c. Problem-solving theory
   d. Haptic theory

8. What conclusion should we reach about the nature of dreaming, based on currently available theories and evidence?

   a. We still lack a comprehensive understanding of why dreams occur.

   b. Dreams are the result of random firing in the cerebral cortex.

   c. Dreams are an evolutionary mechanism that developed to allow us to solve problems.

   d. The bizarre nature of dreams indicates that they must be symbolic.

9. While hypnotized, Arcelia is able to reproduce elaborate birdcalls using a series of spits, whistles, and tongue clicks, much to the amazement of her friends. All are impressed, except Gina, who knows that hypnotism is the weak ingredient in this fanciful stew. What does Gina know that Arcelia and her friends do not?

   a. Arcelia was primed through hypnotic suggestion, and without that her melodic songs would sound more like annoying screeches.

   b. Hypnotism is a culturally agreed-upon phenomenon rather than a scientifically documented phenomenon.

   c. Arcelia's feats depend entirely on the skillfulness of her hypnotist; in lesser hands she wouldn't be able to reproduce the birdcalls.

   d. Motivated, encouraged people can perform the same astonishing tasks without hypnosis that they can while hypnotized.

10. "Memories" of alien abductions, reports of spirit possessions, or accounts of past-life regressions can be explained by the _____ theory of hypnosis.

    a. Sociocognitive
    b. Dissociation
    c. Hidden observer
    d. Executive control

11. Which of the following is *not* a major category of psychoactive drugs?

    a. Stimulants
    b. Agonists
    c. Opiates
    d. Depressants

12. Psychoactive drugs that disrupt normal thought processes are called

    a. Depressants
    b. Opiates
    c. Stimulants
    d. Psychedelics

13. Eric is trying to kick heroin "cold turkey," without medical supervision or assistance from others. He experiences waves of sweating, nausea, vomiting, and diarrhea. These symptoms are signs of

    a. Prolapse
    b. Tolerance
    c. Alleviation
    d. Withdrawal

14. Emily and Richard stop at their local bar for a drink after a hard day's work. Three drinks in, Emily is slurring her words and having a difficult time holding her head up, whereas Richard appears in control of his faculties and speaks coherently. Both Emily and Richard drank the same amount of alcohol; why are their reactions so different?

    a. Individual differences in body weight, physical tolerance, or metabolism can modulate the effects of alcohol on an individual.

    b. Emily is an alcoholic.

    c. The environmental setting differed across their drinking experiences, and therefore influences their reactions.

    d. Richard "preloaded" with an additional three drinks before they left the office.

15. Cassius has a few drinks with old friends in a bar on a Thursday night, and feels energized, talkative, and lively. The following Thursday Cassius has the same number of drinks with some new coworkers in the same bar, but feels anxious, tired, and "buzzed." Why would the same amount of alcohol produce such very different outcomes for Cassius?

    a. The rebound effect—ingestion of the same drug at different times—accounts for complementary reactions.

    b. Experience with the drug—one week to the next—predicted that reactions should be different each time alcohol is ingested.

    c. The context of ingestion—close friends versus new workmates—can influence a drug's effects.

    d. The physiology of ingestion—alcohol's effects in the bloodstream—is poorly understood.

Chapter 6
Sensation and Perception

 Listen to the Audio

Learning Objectives

LO 6.1.A Distinguish between the basic processes of sensation and perception, explain how the doctrine of specific nerve energies applies to perception, and discuss how synesthesia contributes to our understanding of sensory modalities.

LO 6.1.B Differentiate between absolute thresholds, difference thresholds, and signal detection.

LO 6.1.C Discuss why the principle of sensory adaptation helps us understand how the human perceptual system works.

LO 6.1.D Describe how selective attention and inattentional blindness are related.

LO 6.2.A Describe the three psychological dimensions of vision, and relate them to the three physical properties of light that produce them.

LO 6.2.B Locate the structures and cells of the human eye, tracing the path that light follows all the way from the cornea to the optic nerve.

LO 6.2.C Summarize the evidence indicating that the visual system is not simply a "camera."

LO 6.2.D Compare the strengths and weaknesses of the trichromatic and opponent-process theories of color vision.

LO 6.2.E Summarize the principles and processes that guide form perception, depth and distance perception, visual constancies, and visual illusions.

LO 6.3.A Describe the three psychological dimensions of hearing, and relate them to the three physical properties of sound that produce them.

LO 6.3.B Sketch the major structures of the human ear, and briefly describe the functions of each component.

LO 6.3.C List five Gestalt principles of perception that apply to constructing the auditory world, and give an example of each.

LO 6.4.A Identify the major structures of the human tongue, and list the five basic tastes perceived by humans.

LO 6.4.B Describe the basic pathway from smell receptors to the cerebral cortex.

LO 6.4.C List the four basic skin senses that humans perceive.

LO 6.4.D Describe the principles of gate-control theory, and explain what phantom pain is and a novel way to treat it.

LO 6.4.E Discuss the two senses that allow us to monitor our internal environment.

LO 6.5.A Summarize the evidence suggesting that our perceptual powers are both inborn and dependent on experience.

LO 6.5.B Discuss four psychological factors that influence how we perceive the world.

LO 6.5.C Summarize the evidence both for and against subliminal perception.

Ask questions . . . be willing to wonder

Why do some people see religious images in a tortilla or a grilled cheese sandwich?

Why does having a cold make it harder to taste the flavor of food?

Why does pain sometimes persist long after the reason for it is gone?

Can subliminal messages affect what you buy and believe?

A college student in Missouri reports spotting three triangular "UFOs" hovering over the highway during rush hour. An Australian man sees an image of Jesus burned into the surface of an ashtray. A photograph published shortly after September 11, 2001, appears to show a sinister face in smoke billowing from the doomed World Trade Center, which some people interpret as Osama bin Laden's.

We have all heard reports like these. Some of us scoff at them; others take them seriously. Are UFOs, visions of faces in everyday objects, and other strange sightings reported only by gullible people, or do smart, savvy people see them too? If such experiences are illusions, then why are they so frequent and so detailed, and why are those who have them so confident that what they saw was real?

In this chapter, we will try to answer these questions by exploring how our senses take in information from the environment and how our brains use this information to construct a model of the world. We will focus on two closely connected sets of processes that enable us to know what is happening both inside our bodies and in the world beyond our own skins. The first, *sensation*, produces an immediate awareness of sound, color, form, and other building blocks of consciousness. Without sensation, we would lose touch with reality. But to make sense of the world impinging on our senses, we also need *perception* to organize sensory information into meaningful patterns.

As an example of how the processes of sensation and perception are separable yet intertwined, consider an unusual condition called *prosopagnosia*. People with this disorder have an inability to perceive faces, due to deficits in a specific area of the brain called the fusiform gyrus. Their eyes work just fine; there's no problem with sensing visual information in the world. But their ability to perceive those sensory impulses as a human face is compromised. Although sensation and perception usually "feel" to us like one seamless process, we will learn in this chapter that they can be distinguished by where and how they occur, and by disruptions that might affect one process but not the other.

Sensation and perception are the foundation for learning, thinking, and acting. Findings about these processes can also be put to practical use, as in the design of industrial robots and in the training of pilots who must make crucial decisions based on what they sense and perceive. In addition, an understanding of sensation and perception helps us think more critically about our own experiences, and encourages in us a certain humility: Usually we are sure that what we sense and perceive must be true, yet sometimes we are just plain wrong.

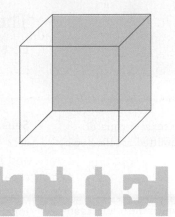

If you stare at the cube, the surface on the outside and front will suddenly be on the inside and back, or vice versa, because your brain can interpret the sensory image in two different ways. The other blue-and-white drawing can also be perceived in two ways. Do you see them?

Our Sensational Senses

At some point, you probably learned that we have five senses: vision, hearing, taste, touch, and smell. Actually, we have more than five senses. The skin, which is the organ of touch or pressure, also senses heat, cold, and pain, not to mention itching and tickling. The ear, which is the organ of hearing, also contains receptors that account for a sense of balance. The skeletal muscles contain receptors responsible for a sense of bodily movement.

All of our senses evolved to help us survive. Even pain, which causes so much human misery, is an indispensable part of our evolutionary heritage, for it alerts us to illness and injury. Some people are born with a rare condition that prevents them from feeling the usual hurts and aches of life, but you shouldn't envy them: They are susceptible to burns, bruises, and broken bones, and they often die at an early age because they can't take advantage of pain's warning signals. In this section we will examine the basics of how sensation takes place, from the painful jab of a wasp sting to the breathtaking vision of a glorious sunset. Before we get started, watch the video *Sensation and Perception* to learn more about how our senses allow us to experience the world.

The Riddle of Separate Sensations

LO 6.1.A Distinguish between the basic processes of sensation and perception, explain how the doctrine of specific nerve energies applies to perception, and discuss how synesthesia contributes to our understanding of sensory modalities.

sensation

The detection, by sense organs, of physical energy emitted or reflected by physical objects.

perception

The process by which the brain organizes and interprets sensory information.

sense receptors

Specialized cells that convert physical energy in the environment or the body to electrical energy that can be transmitted as nerve impulses to the brain.

doctrine of specific nerve energies

The principle that different sensory modalities exist because signals received by the sense organs stimulate different nerve pathways leading to different areas of the brain.

synesthesia

A condition in which stimulation of one sense also evokes another.

Figure 6.1 The General Process of Sensation

Although the individual senses respond to different kinds of energy in the world, the overall process of sensation is the same.

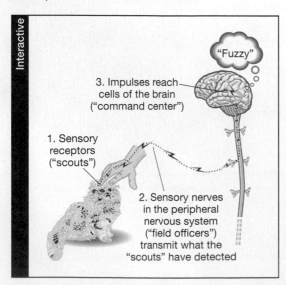

Sensation is the detection of physical energy emitted or reflected by physical objects. The cells that do the detecting are located in the *sense organs*—the eyes, ears, tongue, nose, skin, and internal body tissues. In contrast, **perception** refers to a set of mental operations that organizes sensory impulses into meaningful patterns.

Sensation begins with the **sense receptors**, cells located in the sense organs. The receptors for smell, pressure, pain, and temperature are extensions (dendrites) of sensory neurons. The receptors for vision, hearing, and taste are specialized cells separated from sensory neurons by synapses.

When the sense receptors detect an appropriate stimulus—light, mechanical pressure, or chemical molecules—they convert the energy of the stimulus into electrical impulses that travel along nerves to the brain. Sense receptors are like military scouts who scan the terrain for signs of activity. These scouts cannot make many decisions on their own: They must transmit what they learn to "field officers," sensory neurons in the nerves of the peripheral nervous system. The field officers in turn must report to generals at a command center, the cells of the brain. The generals are responsible for analyzing the reports, combining information brought in by different scouts, and deciding what it all means. Figure 6.1 illustrates this process.

The sensory-neuron "field officers" all use the same form of communication: a neural impulse. It is as if they must all send their messages on a bongo drum and can only go "boom." How, then, are we able to experience so many different kinds of sensations? The answer is that the nervous system *encodes* the messages. One kind of code, **anatomical** *code*, was first described in 1826 by German physiologist Johannes Müller in his **doctrine of specific nerve energies**. According to this doctrine, different sensory modalities (such as vision and hearing) exist because signals received by the sense organs stimulate different nerve pathways leading to different areas of the brain. Signals from the eye cause impulses to travel along the optic nerve to the visual cortex. Signals from the ear cause impulses to travel along the auditory nerve to the auditory cortex. Light and sound waves produce different sensations because of these anatomical differences.

The doctrine of specific nerve energies implies that what we know about the world ultimately reduces to what we know about the state of our own nervous system: We see with the brain, not the eyes, and we hear with the brain, not the ears. It follows that if sound waves could stimulate nerves that end in the visual part of the brain, we would "see" sound. In fact, a similar sort of crossover does occur if you close your right eye and press lightly on the right side of the lid: You will see a flash of light seemingly coming from the left. The pressure produces an impulse that travels up the optic nerve to the visual area in the right side of the brain, where it is interpreted as coming from the left side of the visual field. By taking advantage of such crossover from one sense to another, researchers hope to enable blind people to see by teaching them to interpret impulses from other senses that are then routed to the visual areas of the brain. Neuroscientists have developed a device that translates images from a camera into a pattern of electronic pulses that is sent to electrodes on the tongue, which in turn sends information about the pattern to visual areas of the brain that process images (Chebat et al., 2011; Proulx, Ptito, & Amedi, 2014). Using this device, congenitally blind people have been able to make out shapes, and their visual areas, long quiet, have suddenly become active.

Sensory crossover also occurs in a rare condition called **synesthesia**, in which the stimulation of one sense also consistently evokes a sensation in another. A person with synesthesia may say that the color purple smells like a rose, the aroma of cinnamon feels like velvet, or the sound of a note on a clarinet tastes like cherries. In its most common form, people experience certain colors when they see specific letters or numbers. Most synesthetes are born with the condition, but it can also result from damage to the brain. One woman who had recovered from a stroke experienced sounds as a tingling sensation on the left side of her body (Ro et al., 2007).

No one is certain yet about the neurological basis of synesthesia. A leading theory holds that synesthetes have a greater number of neural connections between different sensory brain areas than other people do (Bargary & Mitchell, 2008; Rouw & Scholte, 2007; Xu et al., 2015). Interestingly, areas associated with the "extra" sensations seem to be far more sensitive in synesthetes than in other people. Ordinary people tend to see brief flashes of light when their visual cortex is stimulated by transcranial magnetic stimulation, but synesthetes who see numbers or letters in color need only a third of the stimulation to see the flashes (Terhune et al., 2011). It may be that this greater neural responsiveness somehow helps to produce extra connections between brain areas. Yet another possibility is that the condition results from a lack of normal disinhibition in signals between different sensory areas (Hale et al., 2014).

Synesthesia, however, is an anomaly; for most of us, the senses remain separate. Anatomical encoding does not completely solve the riddle of why this is so, nor does it explain variations of experience *within* a particular sense—the sight of pink versus red, the sound of a piccolo versus the sound of a tuba, or the feel of a pinprick versus the feel of a kiss. An additional kind of code is therefore necessary. This second kind of code has been called *functional*. Functional codes rely on the fact that sensory receptors and neurons fire, or are inhibited from firing, only in the presence of specific sorts of stimuli. At any particular time, then, some cells in the nervous system are firing and some are not. Information about *which* cells are firing, *how many* cells are firing, the *rate* at which cells are firing, and the *patterning* of each cell's firing forms a functional code. Functional encoding may occur all along a sensory route, starting in the sense organs and ending in the brain.

Measuring the Senses

LO 6.1.B Differentiate between absolute thresholds, difference thresholds, and signal detection.

Just how sensitive are our senses? The answer comes from the field of *psychophysics*, which is concerned with how the physical properties of stimuli are related to our psychological experience of them. Drawing on principles from both physics and psychology, psychophysicists have studied how the strength or intensity of a stimulus affects the strength of sensation in an observer.

ABSOLUTE THRESHOLD   One way to find out how sensitive the senses are is to show people a series of signals that vary in intensity and ask them to say which signals they can detect. The smallest amount of energy that a person can detect reliably is known as the **absolute threshold**. However, the word *absolute* is a bit misleading because people detect borderline signals on some occasions and miss them on others. Reliable detection is said to occur when a person can detect a signal 50 percent of the time.

If your absolute threshold for brightness were being measured, you might be asked to sit in a dark room and look at a wall or screen. You would then be shown flashes of light varying in brightness, one flash at a time. Your task would be to say whether you noticed a flash. Some flashes you would never see. Some you would always see. And sometimes you would miss seeing a flash, even though you had noticed one of equal brightness on other trials. Such

This experimental device, which sends signals from the tongue to visual brain areas, has enabled blind people to make out some shapes—an example of sensory crossover applied to a real-life problem.

A popular "stumper" circulated on the Internet recently: What color is this dress? Some people saw it as white and gold, whereas others saw it as blue and brown. The amount and type of lighting available when we perceive this object can "fool" our visual system into believing one conclusion or the other. (The dress is actually blue and black, by the way.)

Figure 6.2 The Visible Spectrum of Electromagnetic Energy

Our visual system detects only a small fraction of the electromagnetic energy around us.

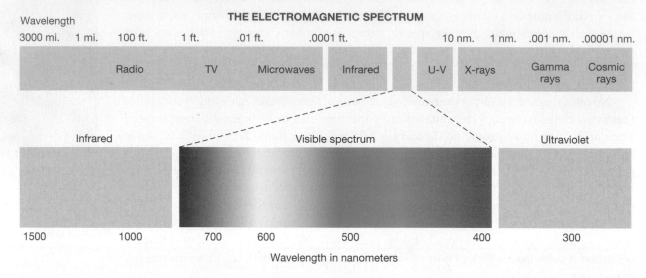

errors seem to occur in part because of random firing of cells in the nervous system, which produces fluctuating background noise, something like the static in a radio transmission that is slightly out of range.

By studying absolute thresholds, psychologists have found that our senses are very sharp indeed. If you have normal sensory abilities, you can see a candle flame on a clear, dark night from 30 miles away. You can also taste a teaspoon of sugar diluted in two gallons of water, smell a drop of perfume diffused through a three-room apartment, and feel the wing of a bee falling on your cheek from a height of only one centimeter (Galanter, 1962).

Despite these impressive skills, our senses are tuned in to only a narrow band of physical energies. We are visually sensitive to only a tiny fraction of the electromagnetic energy that surrounds us; we do not see radio waves, infrared waves, or microwaves (see Figure 6.2).

Many other species can pick up auditory and visual signals that we cannot. Dogs can detect high-frequency sound waves that are beyond our range, as you know if you have ever called yours with a "silent" doggie whistle. Bees can see ultraviolet light, which merely gives human beings a sunburn. Watch *The Visible Spectrum* to learn more about the energy our eyes detect.

Different species sense the world differently. The flower on the left was photographed under normal light. The one on the right, photographed under ultraviolet light, is what a butterfly might see because butterflies have ultraviolet receptors.

DIFFERENCE THRESHOLD   Suppose you're in the gym, pressing a barbell loaded with 100 pounds overhead, and one of your troublemaking friends adds weight to it when you are not looking. What is the smallest amount of weight she can add before you think to yourself, "Hey, wait a minute . . . this bar feels heavier"? If you and your friend tried to answer this question systematically, you would probably determine that the answer is another 2 pounds. In other words, 2 pounds is the smallest difference in the weight of the two barbells that you would reliably detect. (Again, "reliably" means half of the time.) Scientists call this point the **difference threshold** or *just noticeable difference (jnd)*.

Now suppose that after you lift a small 1-pound dumbbell overhead, your friend tries the same prank. Could she add 2 pounds to that little dumbbell before you would notice? Unlikely—that would triple the weight of the dumbbell. And here is where the interesting aspect of jnd comes in, thanks to 19th-century German scientist Ernst Weber. He determined that for people to detect a difference between two stimuli, such as two weights, those stimuli must differ by a certain fixed proportion (e.g., 2 percent), *not* a certain amount (e.g., 2 pounds or 2 ounces). Different properties of stimuli have their own constant percentage: For two weights, it is 2 percent; for the brightness of two lights or the saltiness of two liquids, it is 8 percent; and for the loudness of two noises, it is 5 percent.

difference threshold

The smallest difference in stimulation that can be reliably detected by an observer when two stimuli are compared; also called *just noticeable difference (jnd)*.

Experiment WEBER'S LAW

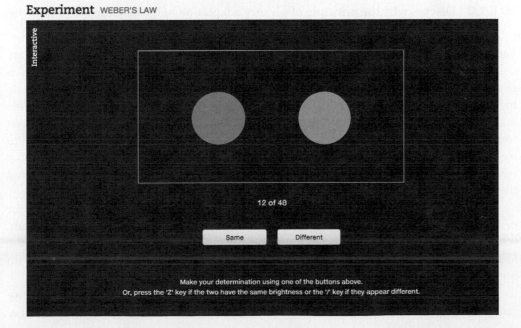

Interactive

12 of 48

Same   Different

Make your determination using one of the buttons above.
Or, press the 'Z' key if the two have the same brightness or the '/' key if they appear different.

signal-detection theory

A psychophysical theory that divides the detection of a sensory signal into a sensory process and a decision process.

sensory adaptation

The reduction or disappearance of sensory responsiveness when stimulation is unchanging or repetitious.

SIGNAL-DETECTION THEORY Despite their usefulness, the procedures we have described have a serious limitation. Measurements for any given person may be affected by that person's general tendency, when uncertain, to respond, "Yes, I noticed a signal (or a difference)" or "No, I didn't notice anything." Some people are habitual yea-sayers, willing to gamble that the signal was there. Others are habitual naysayers, cautious and conservative. In addition, alertness, motives, and expectations can influence how a person responds on any given occasion. If you are in the shower and you are expecting an important call, you may think you hear the telephone ring when it did not. In laboratory studies, when observers want to impress the experimenter, they may lean toward a positive response.

Fortunately, these problems of *response bias* are not insurmountable. According to **signal-detection theory**, an observer's response in a detection task can be divided into a *sensory process*, which depends on the intensity of the stimulus, and a *decision process*, which is influenced by the observer's response bias (Tanner & Swets, 1954). One way a researcher can separate these two components is by including some trials in which no stimulus is present and others in which a weak stimulus is present. Under these conditions, four kinds of responses are possible: The person (1) detects a signal that was present (a "hit"), (2) says the signal was there when it wasn't (a "false alarm"), (3) fails to detect the signal when it was present (a "miss"), or (4) correctly says that the signal was absent when it was absent (a "correct rejection").

Yea-sayers will have more hits than naysayers because they are quick to say "it was there" when it really was, but they will also have more false alarms because they are similarly quick to say "it was there" when it wasn't. Naysayers will have more correct rejections than yea-sayers, but they will also have more misses because they will often say "Nope, nothing was there" when in fact it was. This information can be fed into a mathematical formula that yields separate estimates of a person's response bias and sensory capacity. Each person's true sensitivity to a signal of any particular intensity can then be predicted.

The original method of measuring thresholds assumed that a person's ability to detect a stimulus depended solely on the stimulus. Signal-detection theory assumes that there is no single threshold because at any given moment a person's sensitivity to a stimulus depends on a decision that he or she actively makes. Signal-detection methods have many real-world applications, from screening applicants for jobs that require keen hearing to training air-traffic controllers, whose decisions about the presence or absence of a blip on a radar screen may mean the difference between life and death.

Sensory Adaptation

LO 6.1.C Discuss why the principle of sensory adaptation helps us understand how the human perceptual system works.

Variety, they say, is the spice of life. It is also the essence of sensation, for our senses are designed to respond to change and contrast in the environment. When a stimulus is unchanging or repetitious, sensation often fades or disappears. Receptors or nerve cells higher up in the sensory system get "tired" and fire less frequently. The resulting decline in sensory responsiveness is called **sensory adaptation**. Usually, such adaptation spares us from having to respond to unimportant information; most of the time, you have no need to feel your watch sitting on your wrist. Sometimes, however, adaptation can be hazardous, as when you no longer smell a gas leak that you thought you noticed when you first entered the kitchen.

We never completely adapt to extremely intense stimuli—a terrible toothache, the odor of ammonia, the heat of the desert sun. And we rarely adapt completely to visual stimuli, whether they are weak or intense. Eye movements, voluntary and involuntary, cause the location of an object's image on the back of the eye to keep changing, so visual receptors do not have a chance to "fatigue."

What would happen if our senses adapted to *most* incoming stimuli? Would we sense nothing, or would the brain substitute its own images for the sensory experiences no longer

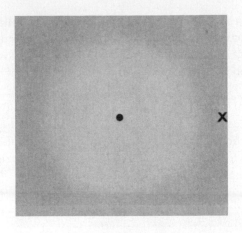 

Sensation depends on change and contrast in the environment. Hold your hand over one eye and stare at the dot in the middle of the circle on the right. You should have no trouble maintaining an image of the circle. However, if you do the same with the circle on the left, the image will fade. The gradual change from light to dark does not provide enough contrast to keep your visual receptors firing at a steady rate. The circle reappears only if you close and reopen your eye or shift your gaze to the X.

available by way of the sense organs? In early studies of **sensory deprivation**, researchers studied this question by isolating male volunteers from all patterned sight and sound. Vision was restricted by a translucent visor, hearing by a U-shaped pillow and noise from an air conditioner and fan, and touch by cotton gloves and cardboard cuffs. The volunteers took brief breaks to eat and use the bathroom, but otherwise they lay in bed, doing nothing. The results were dramatic. Within a few hours, many of the men felt edgy. Some were so disoriented that they quit the study the first day. Those who stayed longer became confused, restless, and grouchy. Many reported bizarre visions, such as a squadron of squirrels or a procession of marching eyeglasses. It was as though they were having waking dreams. Few people were willing to remain in the study for more than 2 or 3 days (Heron, 1957).

But the notion that sensory deprivation is unpleasant or even dangerous turned out to be an oversimplification (Suedfeld, 1975). Later research, using better methods, showed that hallucinations are less frequent and less disorienting than had first been thought. Many people enjoy limited periods of deprivation, and some perceptual and intellectual abilities actually improve. Your response to sensory deprivation depends on your expectations and interpretations of what is happening. Reduced sensation can be scary if you are locked in a room for an indefinite period, but relaxing if you have retreated to that room voluntarily for a little time out—at, say, a luxury spa or a monastery.

Nonetheless the human brain does require a minimum amount of sensory stimulation to function normally. This need may help explain why people who live alone often keep the radio or television on continuously, and why prolonged solitary confinement is used as a form of punishment or even torture.

Sensing without Perceiving

LO 6.1.D   Describe how selective attention and inattentional blindness are related.

If sensory deprivation can sometimes be upsetting, so can sensory overload. Fortunately, our capacity for **selective attention**—the ability to focus on some parts of the environment and block out others—protects us from being overwhelmed by the countless sensory signals that are constantly impinging on our sense receptors. Competing sensory messages all enter the nervous system, however, and they get some processing, enabling us to pick up anything important, such as our own name spoken by someone several yards away.

But our conscious awareness of the environment is much less complete than most people think. We may even fail to consciously register objects that we are looking straight at, a phenomenon known as **inattentional blindness**: We look, but we do not see (Mack, 2003). When people are shown a video of a ball-passing game and are asked to count up the passes, they may even miss something as seemingly obvious as a woman in a gorilla suit walking slowly among the players, thumping her chest (Chabris & Simons, 1999, 2009; Most et al., 2001). One team of researchers wondered which situation would be most likely to "blind"

sensory deprivation

The absence of normal levels of sensory stimulation.

selective attention

The focusing of attention on selected aspects of the environment and the blocking out of others.

inattentional blindness

Failure to consciously perceive something you are looking at because you are not attending to it.

Hard though it is to believe, even a woman in a gorilla suit may go unnoticed if people's attention is elsewhere.

people to the sight of a colorful clown riding on a unicycle: walking along while talking on a cell phone, walking while listening to music, walking alone, or strolling with one other person. The walkers who were least likely to notice the clown were those talking on their cell phones (Hyman et al., 2010).

Selective attention, then, is a mixed blessing. It protects us from overload and allows us to focus on what's important, but it also deprives us of sensory information that we may need. That could be disastrous if you are so focused on texting a friend that you walk right into a pothole or a street full of traffic.

> **JOURNAL PROMPT 6.1**
>
> Thinking Critically—Don't Oversimplify: Is sensory deprivation pleasant or unpleasant? Being isolated against your will can be terrifying, but many people have found meditating alone, away from all sights and sounds, to be calming and pleasant. How do you think environmental circumstances and individual differences both contribute to the experience of sensory deprivation?

Quiz for Module 6.1

1. The feeling of a needle piercing your skin is an act of _____, whereas your saying "Yowch! That hurts!" is an act of _____.
   a. Subduction / conduction
   b. Perception / sensation
   c. Sensation / perception
   d. Conduction / subduction

2. Klaus very clearly detects the number 6 as blue, the number 8 as orange, and the number 12 as magenta. Assuming Klaus is reporting his experiences accurately and honestly, which unusual sensory phenomenon is at work?
   a. Hypersensitivity
   b. Synesthesia
   c. Glossal retraction
   d. Inattentional deficit

3. Even on the clearest night, some stars cannot be seen by the naked eye because they are below the viewer's _____ threshold.
   a. Enaction-process

   b. Difference
   c. Decision-process
   d. Absolute

4. When you jump into a cold lake and the water no longer seems so cold moments later, sensory _____ has occurred.
   a. Adaptation
   b. Indifference
   c. Diffusion
   d. Equilibrium

5. During a break from her job in a restaurant, Anne gets so caught up in a book that she fails to notice the clattering of dishes or orders being yelled out to the cook. This is an example of
   a. Perceptual blunting
   b. Sensory deprivation
   c. Mindblindness
   d. Selective attention

Vision

Because we evolved to be most active in the daytime, we are equipped to take advantage of the sun's illumination. More information about the external world comes to us through our eyes than through any other sense organ. Get ready for an eye-opening look at how the process of vision works.

What We See

LO 6.2.A Describe the three psychological dimensions of vision, and relate them to the three physical properties of light that produce them.

The stimulus for vision is light; even cats, raccoons, and other creatures famous for their ability to get around in the dark need some light to see. Visible light comes from the sun and other stars and from lightbulbs, and it is also reflected off objects. The *physical* characteristics of light affect three *psychological* dimensions of our visual world: hue, brightness, and saturation (see Figure 6.3):

1. **Hue**, the dimension of visual experience specified by color names, is related to the *wavelength* of light—that is, to the distance between the crests of a light wave. Shorter waves tend to be seen as violet and blue, longer ones as orange and red. The sun produces white light, which is a mixture of all the visible wavelengths. Sometimes, drops of moisture in the air act like a prism: They separate the sun's white light into the colors of the visible spectrum, and we are treated to a rainbow.

2. **Brightness** is the dimension of visual experience related to the amount, or *intensity*, of the light an object emits or reflects, and corresponds to the amplitude (maximum height) of the light wave. Generally, the more light an object reflects, the brighter it appears. However, brightness is also affected by wavelength: Yellows appear brighter than reds and blues even when their physical intensities are equal.

3. **Saturation** (colorfulness) is the dimension of visual experience related to the *complexity* of light—that is, to how wide or narrow the range of wavelengths is. When light contains only a single wavelength, it is said to be pure, and the resulting color is completely saturated. White light, in contrast, contains all the wavelengths of visible light (corresponding to all the colors in the visible spectrum) and has zero saturation. Black is a lack of any light at all (has no color), and so is also completely unsaturated. In nature, pure light is extremely rare. We usually sense a mixture of wavelengths, and as a result we see colors that are duller and paler than completely saturated ones.

An Eye on the World

LO 6.2.B Locate the structures and cells of the human eye, tracing the path that light follows all the way from the cornea to the optic nerve.

Light enters the visual system through the eye, a wonderfully complex and delicate structure. As you read this section, examine Figure 6.4. Notice that the front part of the eye is covered by the transparent *cornea*. The cornea protects the eye and bends incoming light rays toward a *lens* located behind it. A camera lens focuses incoming light by moving closer to or farther from the shutter opening. However, the lens of the eye works by subtly changing its shape, becoming more or less curved to focus light from objects that are close by or far away. The amount of light that gets into the eye is controlled by muscles in the *iris*, the part of the eye

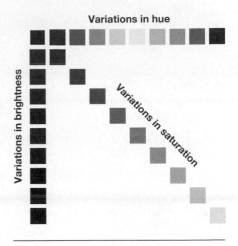

Variations in hue

Variations in brightness

Variations in saturation

Figure 6.3 Psychological Dimensions of the Visual World

Variations in brightness, hue, and saturation represent psychological dimensions of vision that correspond to the intensity, wavelength, and complexity of wavelengths of light.

hue

The dimension of visual experience specified by color names and related to the wavelength of light.

brightness

Lightness or luminance; the dimension of visual experience related to the amount (intensity) of light emitted from or reflected by an object.

saturation

Vividness or purity of color; the dimension of visual experience related to the complexity of light waves.

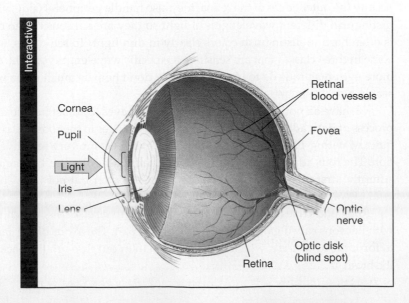

Interactive

Cornea
Pupil
Light
Iris
Lens
Retinal blood vessels
Fovea
Optic nerve
Optic disk (blind spot)
Retina

Figure 6.4 Major Structures of the Eye

Light passes through the pupil and lens and is focused on the retina at the back of the eye. The point of sharpest vision is at the fovea.

Figure 6.5 The Retinal Image

When we look at an object, the light pattern on the retina is upside down. René Descartes was probably the first person to demonstrate this fact. He cut a piece from the back of an ox's eye and replaced the piece with paper. When he held the eye up to the light, he saw an upside-down image of the room on the paper. You could take any ordinary lens and get the same result.

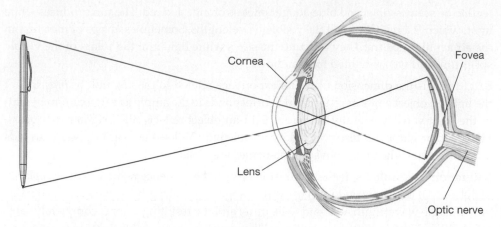

retina

Neural tissue lining the back of the eyeball's interior, which contains the receptors for vision.

rods

Visual receptors that respond to dim light.

cones

Visual receptors involved in color vision.

dark adaptation

A process by which visual receptors become maximally sensitive to dim light.

ganglion cells

Neurons in the retina of the eye, which gather information from receptor cells (by way of intermediate bipolar cells); their axons make up the optic nerve.

that gives it color. The iris surrounds the round opening, or *pupil*, of the eye. When you enter a dim room, the pupil widens, or dilates, to let more light in. When you emerge into bright sunlight, the pupil gets smaller, contracting to allow in less light.

The visual receptors are located in the back of the eye, or **retina**. In a developing embryo, the retina forms from tissue that projects out from the brain, not from tissue destined to form other parts of the eye; thus, the retina is actually an extension of the brain. As Figure 6.5 shows, when the lens of the eye focuses light on the retina, the result is an upside-down image, just as it is with any optical device. Light from the top of the visual field stimulates light-sensitive receptor cells in the bottom part of the retina, and vice versa. The brain interprets this upside-down pattern of stimulation as something that is right-side up.

About 120 to 125 million receptors in the retina are long and narrow, and are called **rods**. Another 7 or 8 million receptors are cone shaped, and are called, appropriately, **cones**. The center of the retina, or *fovea*, where vision is sharpest, contains only cones, clustered densely together. From the center to the periphery, the ratio of rods to cones increases, and the outer edges contain virtually no cones.

Rods are more sensitive to light than cones and thus enable us to see even in dim light. (Cats see well in dim light in part because they have a high proportion of rods.) Because rods occupy the outer edges of the retina, they also handle peripheral (side) vision. But rods cannot distinguish different wavelengths of light so they are not sensitive to color, which is why it is often hard to distinguish colors clearly in dim light. To see colors, we need cones, which come in three classes that are sensitive to specific wavelengths of light. But cones need much more light than rods do to respond, so they don't help us much when we are trying to find a seat in a darkened movie theater.

We have all noticed that it takes time for our eyes to adjust fully to dim illumination. This process of **dark adaptation** involves chemical changes in the rods and cones. The cones adapt quickly, within 10 minutes or so, but they never become very sensitive to the dim illumination. The rods adapt more slowly, taking 20 minutes or longer, but are much more sensitive. After the first phase of adaptation, you can see better but not well; after the second phase, your vision is as good as it will ever get.

Rods and cones are connected by synapses to *bipolar cells*, which in turn communicate with neurons called **ganglion cells** (see Figure 6.6). The axons of the ganglion cells converge to form the *optic nerve*, which carries information out through the back of the eye and on to the brain.

Figure 6.6 The Structures of the Retina

For clarity, all cells in this drawing are greatly exaggerated in size. To reach the receptors for vision (the rods and cones), light must pass through the ganglion and bipolar cells as well as the blood vessels that nourish them (not shown). Normally, we do not see the shadow cast by this network of cells and blood vessels because the shadow always falls on the same place on the retina, and such stabilized images are not sensed. But when an eye doctor shines a moving light into your eye, the treelike shadow of the blood vessels falls on different regions of the retina and you may see it—a rather eerie experience.

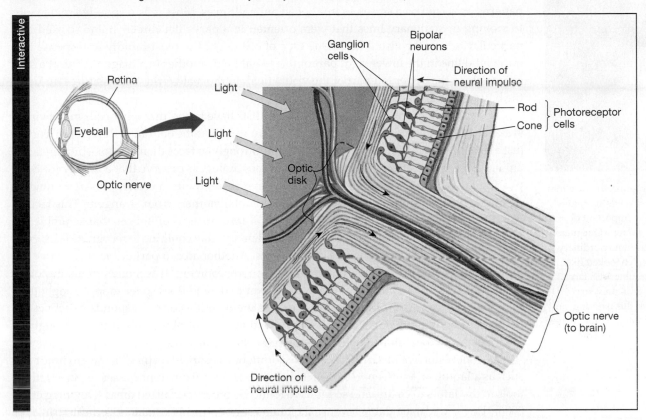

Where the optic nerve leaves the eye, at the *optic disk*, there are no rods or cones. The absence of receptors produces a blind spot in the field of vision. Normally, we are unaware of the blind spot because (1) the image projected on the spot is hitting a different, "nonblind" spot in the other eye; (2) our eyes move so fast that we can pick up the complete image; and (3) the brain fills in the gap. You can use Figure 6.7 to find your blind spot.

Why the Visual System Is Not a Camera

LO 6.2.C   Summarize the evidence indicating that the visual system is not simply a "camera."

Although the eye is often compared with a camera, the visual system, unlike a camera, is not a passive recorder of the external world. Neurons in the visual system actively build up a picture of the world by detecting its meaningful features.

Figure 6.7 Find Your Blind Spot

A blind spot exists where the optic nerve leaves the back of your eye. Find the blind spot in your left eye by closing your right eye and looking at the magician. Then slowly move the image toward and away from yourself. The rabbit should disappear when the image is between 9 and 12 inches from your eye.

Cases of brain damage support the idea that particular systems of brain cells are highly specialized for identifying important objects or visual patterns, such as faces. One man's injury left him unable to identify ordinary objects, which, he said, often looked like "blobs." Yet he had no trouble with faces, even when they were upside down or incomplete. When shown this painting, he could easily see the face but he could not see the vegetables comprising it (Moscovitch, Winocur, & Behrmann, 1997).

feature detectors

Cells in the visual cortex that are sensitive to specific features of the environment.

Ganglion cells and neurons in the thalamus of the brain respond to simple features in the environment, such as spots of light and dark. But in mammals, special **feature-detector cells** in the visual cortex respond to more complex features. This fact was first demonstrated by David Hubel and Torsten Wiesel (1962, 1968), who painstakingly recorded impulses from individual cells in the brains of cats and monkeys. In 1981, they were awarded a Nobel Prize for their work. Hubel and Wiesel found that different neurons were sensitive to different patterns projected on a screen in front of an animal's eyes. Most cells responded maximally to moving or stationary lines that were oriented in a particular direction and located in a particular part of the visual field. One type of cell might fire most rapidly in response to a horizontal line in the lower right part of the visual field, another to a diagonal line at a specific angle in the upper left part of the visual field. In the real world, such features make up the boundaries and edges of objects.

Since this pioneering work was done, scientists have found that other cells in the visual system have even more specialized roles. A group of cells at the bottom of the cerebral cortex, just above the cerebellum, responds much more strongly to faces than objects—human faces, animal faces, even cartoon faces. Evolutionary psychologists observe that a faculty for deciphering faces makes sense because it would have ensured our ancestors' ability to quickly distinguish friend from foe, or in the case of infants, mothers from strangers. This faculty could help explain why infants prefer looking at faces instead of images that scramble the features of a face, and why a person with brain damage may continue to recognize faces even after losing the ability to recognize other objects. Another area, a part of the cortex near the hippocampus, makes sure you understand your environment: It responds to images of all kinds of places, from your dorm room to an open park, and does so far more strongly than to objects or faces. And a third region, a part of the occipital cortex, responds selectively to bodies and body parts much more strongly than to faces or objects—and more strongly to other people's bodies than to a person's own (Pitcher et al., 2012).

Do other brain regions help us perceive additional important features of our environment, such as a laptop or a coffeepot? Researchers have studied 20 different classes of objects, from tools to predators to chairs, and so far have found no other specialized areas (Downing et al., 2006). This is understandable because the brain cannot possibly contain a dedicated area for every conceivable object. In general, the brain's job is to take fragmentary information about edges, angles, shapes, motion, brightness, texture, and patterns and figure out that a chair is a chair and the thing next to it is a dining room table. The perception of any given object probably depends on the activation of many cells in far-flung parts of the brain and on the overall pattern and rhythm of their activity. Keep in mind, too, that experiences change and shape the brain. Thus, some of the brain cells that are supposedly dedicated to face recognition respond to other things as well, depending on a person's experiences and interests. In one study, "face" cells fired when car buffs examined pictures of classic cars but not when they looked at pictures of exotic birds; the exact opposite was true for birdwatchers (Gauthier et al., 2000). You can learn more about face perception by watching the video *Recognizing Faces*.

How We See Colors

LO 6.2.D   Compare the strengths and weaknesses of the trichromatic and opponent-process theories of color vision.

For over 300 years, scientists have been trying to figure out why we see the world in living color. We now know that different processes explain different stages of color vision.

THE TRICHROMATIC THEORY   The **trichromatic theory** (also known as the *Young-Helmholtz theory*) applies to the first level of processing, which occurs in the retina of the eye. The retina contains three basic types of cones. One type responds maximally to blue, another to green, and a third to red. The thousands of colors we see result from the combined activity of these three types of cones.

Total color blindness is usually due to a genetic variation that causes cones of the retina to be absent or malfunction. The visual world then consists of black, white, and shades of gray. Many species of animals are totally color-blind, but the condition is extremely rare in human beings. Most "color-blind" people are actually *color deficient*, due to an absence of, or damage to, one or more types of cones. Usually, the person is unable to distinguish red and green; the world is painted in shades of blue, yellow, brown, and gray. In rarer instances, a person may be blind to blue and yellow and may see only reds, greens, and grays. Color deficiency is found in about 8 percent of white men, 5 percent of Asian men, and 3 percent of black men and Native American men (Sekuler & Blake, 1994). Because of the way the condition is inherited, it is rare in women.

THE OPPONENT-PROCESS THEORY   The **opponent-process theory** applies to the second stage of color processing, which occurs in ganglion cells in the retina and in neurons in the thalamus and visual cortex of the brain. These cells, known as *opponent-process cells*, either respond to short wavelengths but are inhibited from firing by long wavelengths, or vice versa (DeValois & DeValois, 1975). Some opponent-process cells respond in opposite fashion to red and green, or to blue and yellow; that is, they fire in response to one and turn off in response to the other. (A third system responds in opposite fashion to white and black and thus yields information about brightness.) The net result is a color code that is passed along to the higher visual centers. Because this code treats red and green, and also blue and yellow, as antagonistic, we can describe a color as bluish green or yellowish green but not as reddish green or yellowish blue.

Opponent-process cells that are *inhibited* by a particular color produce a burst of firing when the color is removed, just as they would if the opposing color were present. Similarly, cells that *fire* in response to a color stop firing when the color is removed, just as they would if the opposing color were present. These facts explain why we are susceptible to *negative afterimages* when we stare at a particular hue—why we see, for instance, red after staring at green. (To see this effect for yourself, see Figure 6.8.) A sort of neural rebound effect occurs: The cells that switch on or off to signal the presence of "green" send the opposite signal ("red") when the green is removed and vice versa.

Constructing the Visual World

LO 6.2.E   Summarize the principles and processes that guide form perception, depth and distance perception, visual constancies, and visual illusions.

We do not actually see a retinal image; the mind must actively interpret the image and construct the world from the often-fragmentary data of the senses. In the brain, sensory signals that give rise to vision, hearing, taste, smell, and touch are combined from moment to moment to produce a unified model of the world. This is the process of *perception*.

FORM PERCEPTION   To make sense of the world, we must know where one thing ends and another begins. In vision, we must separate the teacher from the lectern; in hearing, we must separate the piano solo from the orchestral accompaniment; in taste, we must separate

trichromatic theory

A theory of color perception that proposes three mechanisms in the visual system, each sensitive to a certain range of wavelengths; their interaction is assumed to produce all the different experiences of hue.

opponent-process theory

A theory of color perception that assumes that the visual system treats pairs of colors as opposing or antagonistic.

Figure 6.8 A Change of Heart

Opponent-process cells that switch on or off in response to green send an opposite message—"red"—when the green is removed, producing a negative afterimage. Stare at the black dot in the middle of this heart for at least 20 seconds. Then shift your gaze to a white piece of paper or a white wall. Do you get a "change of heart"? You should see an image of a red or pinkish heart with a blue border.

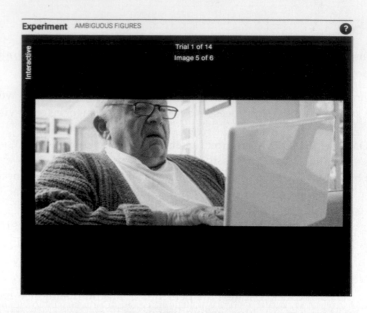

Experiment AMBIGUOUS FIGURES

Gestalt principles

Principles that describe the brain's organization of sensory information into meaningful units and patterns.

the marshmallow from the hot chocolate. This process of dividing up the world occurs so rapidly and effortlessly that we take it completely for granted, until we must make out objects in a heavy fog or words in the rapid-fire conversation of someone speaking a language we don't know.

Gestalt psychologists, who belonged to a movement that began in Germany and was influential in the 1920s and 1930s, were among the first to study how people organize the world visually into meaningful units and patterns. In German, *Gestalt* means "form" or "configuration." Gestalt psychologists' motto was "The whole is more than the sum of its parts." They observed that when we perceive something, properties emerge from the configuration as a whole that are not found in any particular component. A modern example of the Gestalt effect occurs when you watch a movie. The motion you see is nowhere in the film, which consists of separate frames projected at (usually) 24 frames per second.

Gestalt psychologists also noted that people organize the visual field into *figure* and *ground*. The figure stands out from the rest of the environment (see Figure 6.9). Some things stand out as figure by virtue of their intensity or size; it is hard to ignore the bright light of a flashlight at night or a tidal wave approaching your piece of beach. Unique objects also stand out, such as a banana in a bowl of oranges, and so do moving objects in an otherwise still environment, such as a shooting star. Indeed, it is hard to ignore a sudden change of any kind in the environment because our brains are geared to respond to change and contrast. However, selective attention—the ability to concentrate on some stimuli and to filter out others—gives us some control over what we perceive as figure and ground, and sometimes it blinds us to things we would otherwise interpret as figure, as we saw earlier.

Other **Gestalt principles** describe strategies used by the visual system to group sensory building blocks into perceptual units (Köhler, 1929; Wertheimer, 1923/1958). Gestalt psychologists believed that these strategies were present from birth or emerged early in infancy as a result of maturation. Modern research, however, suggests that at least some of them depend on experience (Quinn & Bhatt, 2012). Here are a few well-known Gestalt principles:

1. **Proximity.** Things that are near each other tend to be grouped together. Thus you perceive the dots on the left as three groups of dots, not as 12 separate, unrelated ones. Similarly, you perceive the pattern on the right as vertical columns of dots, not as horizontal rows:

Figure 6.9 Figure and Ground

Which do you notice first in this drawing— the white fish or the black fish?

2. **Closure.** The brain tends to fill in gaps to perceive complete forms. This is fortunate because we often need to decipher less-than-perfect images. The following figures are easily perceived as a triangle, a face, and the letter *e*, even though none of the figures is complete:

3. **Similarity.** Things that are alike in some way (such as in color, shape, or size) tend to be perceived as belonging together. In the figure on the left, you see the circles as forming an X. In the one on the right, you see horizontal bars rather than vertical columns because the horizontally aligned stars are either all red or all outlined in red:

4. **Continuity.** Lines and patterns tend to be perceived as continuing in time or space. You perceive the figure on the left as a single line partially covered by an oval rather than as two separate lines touching an oval. In the figure on the right, you see two lines, one curved and one straight, instead of two curved and two straight lines, touching at one focal point:

Unfortunately, consumer products are sometimes designed with little thought for Gestalt principles, which is why it can be a major challenge to, say, operate the correct dials on a new stovetop (Norman, 1988, 2004). Good design requires, among other things, that crucial distinctions be visually obvious. Watch the video *Perceptual Magic in Art 1* to learn more about how cues in the environment influence our perceptions.

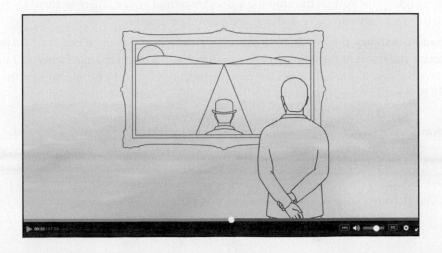

binocular cues

Visual cues to depth or distance requiring two eyes.

convergence

The turning inward of the eyes, which occurs when they focus on a nearby object.

retinal disparity

The slight difference in lateral separation between two objects as seen by the left eye and the right eye.

monocular cues

Visual cues to depth or distance, which can be used by one eye alone.

perceptual constancy

The accurate perception of objects as stable or unchanged despite changes in the sensory patterns they produce.

DEPTH AND DISTANCE PERCEPTION Ordinarily we need to know not only *what* something is but also *where* it is. Touch gives us this information directly, but vision does not, so we must infer an object's location by estimating its distance or depth.

To perform this remarkable feat, we rely in part on **binocular cues**, cues that require the use of two eyes. One such cue is **convergence**, the turning of the eyes inward, which occurs when they focus on a nearby object. The closer the object, the greater the convergence, as you know if you have ever tried to cross your eyes by looking at your own nose. As the angle of convergence changes, the corresponding muscular changes provide information to the brain about distance.

The two eyes also receive slightly different retinal images of the same object. You can prove this by holding a finger about 12 inches in front of your face and looking at it with only one eye at a time. Its position will appear to shift when you change eyes. Now hold up two fingers, one closer to your nose than the other. Notice that the amount of space between the two fingers appears to change when you switch eyes. The slight difference in lateral (sideways) separation between two objects as seen by the left eye and the right eye is called **retinal disparity**. Because retinal disparity decreases as the distance between two objects increases, the brain can use it to infer depth and calculate distance.

Binocular cues help us estimate distances up to about 50 feet. For objects farther away, we use only **monocular cues**, cues that do not depend on using both eyes. One such cue is *interposition*: When an object is interposed between the viewer and a second object, partly blocking the view of the second object, the first object is perceived as being closer. Another monocular cue is *linear perspective*: When two lines known to be parallel appear to be coming together or converging (say, railroad tracks), they imply the existence of depth. These and other monocular cues are illustrated on the following page.

VISUAL CONSTANCIES: WHEN SEEING IS BELIEVING Your perceptual world would be a confusing place without yet another important perceptual skill. Lighting conditions, viewing angles, and the distances of stationary objects are all continually changing as we move about, yet we rarely confuse these changes with changes in the objects themselves. This ability to perceive objects as stable or unchanging even though the sensory patterns they produce are constantly shifting is called **perceptual constancy**. The best-studied constancies are visual and include the following:

1. **Size constancy.** We see an object as having a constant size even when its retinal image becomes smaller or larger. A friend approaching on the street does not seem to be growing; a car pulling away from the curb does not seem to be shrinking. Size constancy depends in part on familiarity with objects; you know that people and cars do not change size from moment to moment. It also depends on the apparent distance of an object. An object that is close produces a larger retinal image than the same object farther away, and the brain takes this into account. When you move your hand toward your face, your brain registers the fact that the hand is getting closer, and you correctly perceive its unchanging size despite the growing size of its retinal image. There is, then, an intimate relationship between perceived size and perceived distance.

2. **Shape constancy.** We continue to perceive an object as having a constant shape even though the shape of the retinal image produced by the object changes when our point of view changes. If you hold a Frisbee directly in front of your face, its image on the retina will be round. When you set the Frisbee on a table, its image becomes elliptical, yet you continue to see it as round.

3. **Location constancy.** We perceive stationary objects as remaining in the same place even though the retinal image moves about as we move our eyes, head, and body. As you drive along the highway, telephone poles and trees fly by on your retina. But you know that these objects do not move on their own, and you also know that your body is moving, so you perceive the poles and trees as staying put.

Monocular Cues to Depth

Most cues to depth do not depend on having two eyes. Some monocular (one-eyed) cues are shown here.

LIGHT AND SHADOW
Both of these attributes give objects the appearance of three dimensions.

INTERPOSITION
An object that partly blocks or obscures another one must be in front of the other one, and is therefore seen as closer.

TEXTURE GRADIENTS
Distant parts of a uniform surface appear denser; that is, its elements seem spaced more closely together.

MOTION PARALLAX
When an observer is moving, objects appear to move at different speeds and in different directions. The closer an object, the faster it seems to move. Close objects appear to move backward, whereas distant ones seem to move forward.

RELATIVE SIZE
The smaller an object's image on the retina, the farther away the object appears.

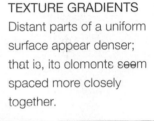

RELATIVE CLARITY
Because of particles in the air from dust, fog, or smog, distant objects tend to look hazier, duller, or less detailed.

LINEAR PERSPECTIVE
Parallel lines will appear to be converging in the distance; the greater the apparent convergence, the greater the perceived distance. Artists often exaggerate this cue to convey an impression of depth.

4. **Brightness constancy.** We see objects as having a relatively constant brightness even though the amount of light they reflect changes as the overall level of illumination changes. Snow remains white even on a cloudy day, and a black car remains black even on a sunny day. We are not fooled because the brain registers the total illumination in the scene and automatically adjusts for it.

5. **Color constancy.** We see an object as maintaining its hue despite the fact that the wavelength of light reaching our eyes from the object may change as the illumination changes. Outdoor light is "bluer" than indoor light, and objects outdoors therefore reflect more "blue" light than those indoors. Conversely, indoor light from incandescent lamps is rich in long wavelengths and is therefore "yellower." Yet an apple looks red whether you look at it in your kitchen or outside on the patio.

Part of the explanation involves sensory adaptation, which we discussed earlier. Outdoors, we quickly adapt to short-wavelength (bluish) light, and indoors, we adapt to long-wavelength light. As a result, our visual responses are similar in the two situations. Also, when computing the color of a particular object, the brain takes into account *all* the wavelengths in the visual field immediately around the object. If an apple is bathed in bluish light, so, usually, is everything else around it. The increase in blue light reflected by the apple is canceled in the visual cortex by the increase in blue light reflected by the apple's surroundings, and so the apple continues to look red. Color constancy is further aided by our knowledge of the world. We know that apples are usually red and bananas are usually yellow, and the brain uses that knowledge to recalibrate the colors in those objects when the lighting changes (Mitterer & de Ruiter, 2008).

VISUAL ILLUSIONS: WHEN SEEING IS MISLEADING   Perceptual constancies allow us to make sense of the world. Occasionally, however, we can be fooled, and the result is a *perceptual illusion*. For psychologists, illusions are valuable because they are systematic errors that provide us with hints about the perceptual strategies of the mind.

Although illusions can occur in any sensory modality, visual illusions have been the best studied. Visual illusions sometimes occur when the strategies that normally lead to accurate perception are overextended to situations where they do not apply. Compare the lengths of the two vertical lines in Figure 6.10a. You will probably perceive the line on the right as slightly longer than the one on the left, yet they are exactly the same. (Go ahead, measure them; everyone does.) This is the Müller-Lyer illusion, named after the German sociologist who first described it in 1889.

One explanation for the Müller-Lyer illusion is that the branches on the lines serve as perspective cues that normally suggest depth (Bulatov et al., 2015; Gregory, 1963). The line on the left is like the near edge of a building; the one on the right is like the far corner of a room (see Figure 6.10b). Although the two lines produce retinal images of the same size, the one with the outward-facing branches suggests greater distance. We are fooled into perceiving it as longer because we automatically apply a rule about the relationship between size and

Figure 6.10 The Müller-Lyer Illusion

The two lines in (a) are exactly the same length. We are probably fooled into perceiving them as different because the brain interprets the one with the outward-facing branches as farther away, as if it were the far corner of a room, and the one with the inward-facing branches as closer, as if it were the near edge of a building (b).

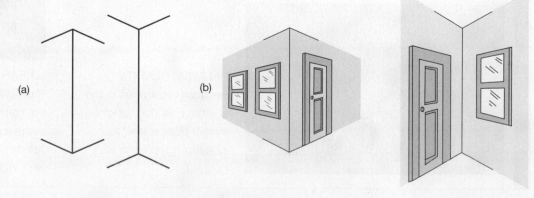

(a)   (b)

distance that is normally useful: When two objects produce the same-sized retinal image and one is farther away, the farther one is larger. The problem, in this case, is that the two lines do not actually differ in length, so the rule is inappropriate.

Just as there are size, shape, location, brightness, and color constancies, so there are size, shape, location, brightness, and color *in* constancies, resulting in illusions. The perceived color of an object depends on the wavelengths reflected by its immediate surroundings, a fact well known to artists and interior designers. Thus, you never see a good, strong red unless other objects in the surroundings reflect the blue and green part of the spectrum. When two objects that are the same color have different surroundings, you may mistakenly perceive them as different (see Figure 6.11).

Figure 6.11 Color in Context

The way you perceive a color depends on the color surrounding it. In this example, the small squares are exactly the same color and brightness.

Experiment THE MÜLLER-LYER ILLUSION

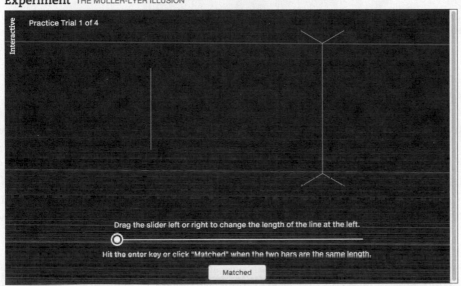

Some illusions are simply a matter of physics. Thus, a chopstick in a half-filled glass of water looks bent because water and air refract light differently. Other illusions occur due to misleading messages from the sense organs, as in sensory adaptation. Still others occur because the brain misinterprets sensory information, as in the Müller-Lyer illusion and the illusions in Figure 6.12.

Figure 6.12 Fooling the Eye

Although perception is usually accurate, we can be fooled. In (a), the cats as drawn are exactly the same size; in (b), the diagonal lines are all parallel. To see the illusion depicted in (c), hold your index fingers 5 to 10 inches in front of your eyes as shown and then focus straight ahead. Do you see a floating "fingertip frankfurter"? Can you make it shrink or expand?

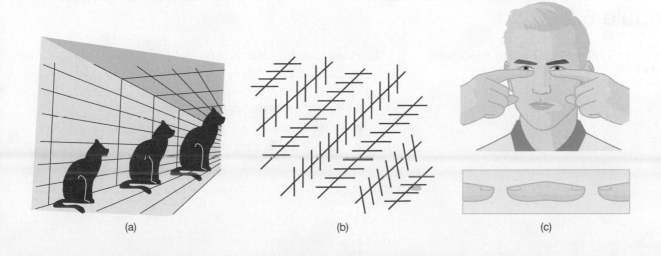

(a)   (b)   (c)

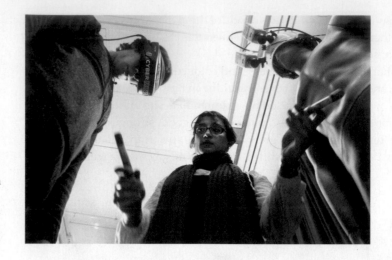

Talk about an illusion! The person on the left is wearing virtual-reality goggles, and the mannequin on the right is outfitted with a camera that feeds images to the goggles. As a result, the person quickly comes to feel as though he has swapped bodies with the mannequin.

Perhaps the ultimate perceptual illusion occurred when Swedish researchers tricked people into feeling that they were swapping bodies with another person or even a mannequin (Petkova & Ehrsson, 2008). The participants wore virtual-reality goggles connected to a camera on the other person's (or mannequin's) head. This allowed them to see the world from the other body's point of view as an experimenter simultaneously stroked both bodies with a rod. Most people soon had the weird sensation that the other body was actually their own; they even cringed when the other body was poked or threatened. The researchers speculate that the body-swapping illusion could some day be helpful in marital counseling, allowing each partner to *literally* see things from the other's point of view, or in therapy with people who have distorted body images (Ahn, Le, & Bailenson, 2013).

In everyday life, most illusions are harmless and entertaining. Occasionally, however, an illusion interferes with the performance of some task or skill, or may even cause an accident. For example, because large objects often appear to move more slowly than small ones, some drivers underestimate the speed of onrushing trains at railroad crossings. They think they can beat the train, with tragic results.

JOURNAL PROMPT 6.2

Thinking Critically—Examine the Evidence: Think about the last time your visual system was "tricked" in some way. Maybe you thought you saw something that turned out to be something else, or perhaps you misjudged the size or nearness of an object. Drawing on what researchers know about form perception, depth and distance perception, visual constancies, and the nature of visual illusions, explain the principles that were at work during your visual mishap.

Quiz for Module 6.2

1. The dimension of visual experience related to the *complexity* of light is called
   a. Hue
   b. Saturation
   c. Brightness
   d. Intensity

2. Visual receptors that respond to dim light are called _____, whereas receptors that are involved in color vision are called _____.
   a. Bipolar neurons / ganglion cells
   b. Cones / rods
   c. Ganglion cells / bipolar neurons
   d. Rods / cones

3. Taffi performs really well on her exams in almost all of her classes. Jealous and intrigued, her classmates want to know the secret of her success. "It's easy," replied Taffi. "I just stare at a page of notes or the information in a textbook until my eyes form a picture of what's there. It's like my eyes are a camera!" Despite her academic success, why is Taffi misled in this case?

   a. The visual system is not a passive receiver of information but instead actively constructs and detects meaningful features in the environment.

   b. Staring at a page of notes should lead to inattentional blindness, in which case Taffi would do poorly on her exams.

   c. Hearing is a more powerful sense than vision, so it's more likely that a teacher's words are causing Taffi's good grades than are images on a page.

   d. The visual system is prone to illusions, so Taffi couldn't be sure that what she was perceiving was accurate.

4. According to the trichromatic theory of color vision, the three basic types of cones in the retina respond maximally to blue, green, and

   a. Cyan

   b. Yellow

   c. White

   d. Red

5. Corrado perceives the red, yellow, and green lights on a traffic signal as belonging to a single unit rather than perceiving them as separate, individual lights. Which Gestalt principle of form perception accounts for this?

   a. Proximity

   b. Continuity

   c. Closure

   d. Convergence

Hearing

Like vision, the sense of hearing, or *audition*, provides a vital link with the world around us. Because social relationships rely so heavily on hearing, when people lose their hearing they sometimes come to feel socially isolated. That is why many people with a hearing impairment feel strongly about teaching deaf children American Sign Language (ASL) or other gestural systems, which allow them to communicate with other signers.

What We Hear

LO 6.3.A Describe the three psychological dimensions of hearing, and relate them to the three physical properties of sound that produce them.

The stimulus for sound is a wave of pressure created when an object vibrates (or when compressed air is released, as in a pipe organ). The vibration (or release of air) causes molecules in a transmitting substance to move together and apart. This movement produces variations in pressure that radiate in all directions. The transmitting substance is usually air, but sound waves can also travel through water and solids, as you know if you have ever put your ear to the wall to hear voices in the next room.

As with vision, *physical* characteristics of the stimulus—in this case, a sound wave—are related in a predictable way to *psychological* aspects of our experience:

1. **Loudness** is the psychological dimension of auditory experience related to the *intensity* of a wave's pressure. Intensity corresponds to the amplitude (maximum height) of the wave. The more energy contained in the wave, the higher it is at its peak. Perceived loudness is also affected by how high or low a sound is. If low and high sounds produce waves with equal amplitudes, the low sound may seem quieter.

   Sound intensity is measured in units called *decibels* (dB). A decibel is one-tenth of a *bel*, a unit named for Alexander Graham Bell, the inventor of the telephone. The average absolute threshold of hearing in human beings is zero decibels. Unlike inches on a rule, decibels are not equally distant; each 10 decibels denotes a 10-fold increase in sound

loudness

The dimension of auditory experience related to the intensity of a pressure wave.

pitch

The dimension of auditory experience related to the frequency of a pressure wave; the height or depth of a tone.

timbre

The distinguishing quality of a sound; the dimension of auditory experience related to the complexity of the pressure wave.

intensity. On the Internet, decibel estimates for various sounds vary a lot from site to site; this is because the intensity of a sound depends on things like how far away it is and the particular person or object producing the sound. The important thing to know is that a 60-decibel conversation is not twice as loud as a 30-decibel whisper; it is 1,000 times louder.

2. **Pitch** is the dimension of auditory experience related to the frequency of the sound wave and, to some extent, its intensity. *Frequency* refers to how rapidly the air (or other medium) vibrates—the number of times per second the wave cycles through a peak and a low point. One cycle per second is known as 1 *hertz* (Hz). The healthy ear of a young person normally detects frequencies in the range of 16 Hz (the lowest note on a pipe organ) to 20,000 Hz (the scraping of a grasshopper's legs).

3. **Timbre** is the distinguishing quality of a sound. It is the dimension of auditory experience related to the *complexity* of the sound wave, the relative breadth of the range of frequencies that make up the wave. A pure tone consists of only one frequency, but pure tones in nature are extremely rare. Usually what we hear is a complex wave consisting of several subwaves with different frequencies. Timbre is what makes a note played on a flute, which produces relatively pure tones, sound different from the same note played on an oboe, which produces complex sounds.

When many sound-wave frequencies are present but are not in harmony, we hear noise. When all the frequencies of the sound spectrum occur, they produce a hissing sound called *white noise*. Just as white light includes all wavelengths of the visible light spectrum, so does white noise include all frequencies of the audible sound spectrum. The video *Perceptual Magic in Art 2* will show you more about the complexity of sound.

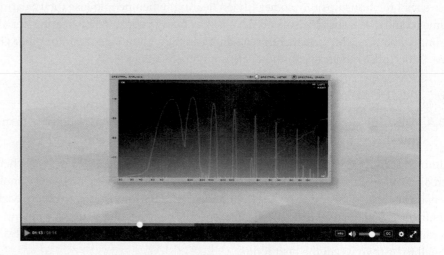

An Ear on the World

LO 6.3.B Sketch the major structures of the human ear, and briefly describe the functions of each component.

As Figure 6.13 shows, the ear has an outer, a middle, and an inner section. The soft, funnel-shaped outer ear is well designed to collect sound waves, but hearing would still be pretty good without it. The essential parts of the ear are hidden from view, inside the head.

A sound wave passes into the outer ear and through an inch-long canal to strike an oval-shaped membrane called the *eardrum*. The eardrum is so sensitive that it can respond to the movement of a single molecule! A sound wave causes it to vibrate with the same frequency and amplitude as the wave itself. This vibration is passed along to three tiny bones in the middle ear, the smallest bones in the human body. These bones, known informally as the hammer, the anvil, and the stirrup, move one after the other, which has the effect of intensifying the force of the vibration. The innermost bone, the stirrup, pushes on a membrane that opens into the inner ear.

Figure 6.13 Major Structures of the Ear

Sound waves collected by the outer ear are channeled down the auditory canal, causing the eardrum to vibrate. These vibrations are then passed along to the tiny bones of the middle ear. Movement of these bones intensifies the force of the vibrations separating the middle and inner ear. The receptor cells for hearing (hair cells), located in the organ of Corti (not shown) within the snail-shaped cochlea, initiate nerve impulses that travel along the auditory nerve to the brain.

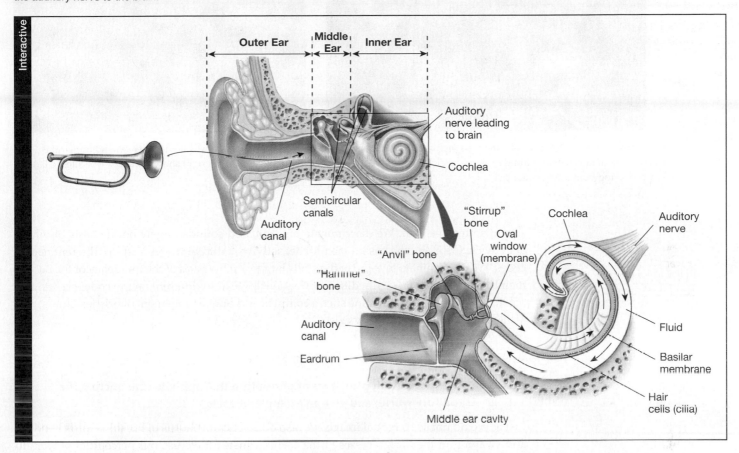

The actual organ of hearing, the **organ of Corti**, is a chamber inside the **cochlea**, a snail-shaped structure within the inner ear. The organ of Corti plays the same role in hearing that the retina plays in vision. It contains the all-important receptor cells, which in this case are called *hair cells* and are topped by tiny bristles, or *cilia*. Brief exposure to extremely loud noises, such as those from a gunshot or a jet airplane (140 dB), or sustained exposure to more moderate noises, such as those from shop tools or truck traffic (90 dB), can damage these fragile cells. The cilia flop over like broken blades of grass, and if the damage affects a critical number, hearing loss occurs. In modern societies, with their rock concerts, deafening bars and clubs, leaf blowers, jackhammers, and music players turned up to full blast, such damage is increasingly common, even among teenagers and young adults (Agrawal, Platz, & Niparko, 2008). Scientists are looking for ways to grow new, normally functioning hair cells, but hair-cell damage is currently irreversible (Liu et al., 2014).

The hair cells of the cochlea are embedded in the rubbery *basilar membrane*, which stretches across the interior of the cochlea. When pressure reaches the cochlea, it causes wavelike motions in fluid within the cochlea's interior. These waves of fluid push on the basilar membrane, causing it to move in a wavelike fashion, too. Just above the hair cells is yet another membrane. As the hair cells rise and fall, their tips brush against it, and they bend. This causes the hair cells to initiate a signal that is passed along to the *auditory nerve*, which then carries the message to the brain. The particular pattern of hair-cell movement is affected by the manner in which the basilar membrane moves. This pattern determines which neurons fire and how rapidly they fire, and the resulting code in turn helps determine the

organ of Corti [core-tee]

A structure in the cochlea containing hair cells that serve as the receptors for hearing.

cochlea [KOCK-lee-uh]

A snail-shaped, fluid-filled organ in the inner ear, containing the organ of Corti, where the receptors for hearing are located.

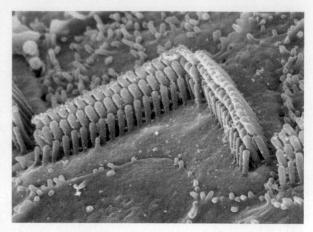

If prolonged, the 120-decibel music at a rock concert can damage or destroy the delicate hair cells of the inner ear and impair the hearing of fans that are sitting or standing close to the speakers. The microphotograph on the right shows minuscule bristles (cilia) projecting from a single hair cell.

sort of sound we hear. We discriminate high-pitched sounds largely on the basis of where activity occurs along the basilar membrane; activity at different sites leads to different neural codes. We discriminate low-pitched sounds largely on the basis of the frequency of the basilar membrane's vibration; again, different frequencies lead to different neural codes.

Could anyone ever imagine such a complex and odd arrangement of bristles, fluids, and snail shells if it did not already exist?

Constructing the Auditory World

LO 6.3.C List five Gestalt principles of perception that apply to constructing the auditory world, and give an example of each.

Just as we do not see a retinal image, we also do not hear a chorus of brushlike tufts bending and swaying in the dark recesses of the cochlea. Instead, we use our perceptual powers to organize patterns of sound and to construct a meaningful auditory world.

In your psychology class, your instructor hopes you will perceive his or her voice as *figure* and distant cheers from the athletic field as *ground*. Whether these hopes are realized will depend, of course, on where you choose to direct your attention. Other Gestalt principles also seem to apply to hearing. The *proximity* of notes in a melody tells you which notes go together to form phrases; *continuity* helps you follow a melody on one violin when another violin is playing a different melody; *similarity* in timbre and pitch helps you pick out the soprano voices in a chorus and hear them as a unit; *closure* helps you understand a cell phone caller's words even when interference makes some of the individual sounds unintelligible.

Besides needing to organize sounds, we also need to know where they are coming from. We can estimate the *distance* of a sound's source by using loudness as a cue: We know that a train sounds louder when it is 20 yards away than when it is a mile off. To locate the *direction* a sound is coming from, we depend in part on the fact that we have two ears. A sound arriving from the right reaches the right ear a fraction of a second sooner than it reaches the left ear, and vice versa. The sound may also provide a bit more energy to the right ear (depending on its frequency) because it has to get around the head to reach the left ear. It is hard to localize sounds that are coming from directly in back of you or from directly above your head because such sounds reach both ears at the same time. When you turn or cock your head, you are actively trying to overcome this problem. Horses, dogs, rabbits, deer, and many other animals do not need to do this because the lucky creatures can move their ears independently of their heads.

A few blind people have learned to harness the relationship between distance and sound to navigate their environment in astonishing ways—hiking, mountain biking, even golfing. They use their mouths to make clicking sounds and listen to the tiny echoes bouncing off objects, a process called *echolocation*, which is similar to what bats do when they fly around hunting for food. In blind human echolocators, the visual cortex responds to sounds that produce echoes—that is, sounds with information about the size and location of objects—but not to other sounds without echoes (Thaler, Arnott, & Goodale, 2011).

JOURNAL PROMPT 6.3

Thinking Critically—Define Your Terms: What do Neil Young, Pete Townshend, Chris Martin, and Dave Grohl all have in common? (Okay, besides being musicians.) They've all suffered a noticeable-to-substantial hearing loss as a consequence of their occupation. How are the cochlea, hair cells, and basilar membrane implicated in such hearing loss?

Quiz for Module 6.3

1. The psychological dimension of hearing that corresponds to the physical property of a sound wave's frequency is called
   a. Timbre
   b. Loudness
   c. Pitch
   d. Complexity

2. Neil's voice sounds nasally and Tom's voice sounds gravelly. Which psychological dimension of hearing describes the difference between the two?
   a. Pitch
   b. Timbre
   c. Frequency
   d. Intensity

3. Which of these structures is found in the inner ear?
   a. Pinna
   b. Eardrum
   c. Auditory canal
   d. Cochlea

4. The receptor cells for hearing, which can be irreversibly damaged in the presence of loud noise, are called
   a. Basila
   b. Hair cells
   c. Corti cells
   d. Cithia

5. Sound localization (determining the direction a sound wave is traveling from) is aided by the fact that humans typically have two ears. How does that process work?
   a. Sound waves coming from a particular direction are likely to reach one ear before the other, allowing us to determine the sound's relative location.
   b. Information from each ear travels up its respective auditory nerve to the brain, where specialized *location cells* decode the information.
   c. Having two ears allows humans to hear in stereo, and stereo sounds travel faster than monophonic sounds.
   d. Complex processing allows one ear to decode the timbre of a soundwave while the other ear decodes the intensity of the sound; this information gets recombined in the brain.

Other Senses

Psychological scientists have been particularly interested in vision and audition because of the importance of these senses to human survival. However, research on other senses is growing rapidly, as awareness of how they contribute to our lives increases and new ways are found to study them.

Taste: Savory Sensations

LO 6.4.A Identify the major structures of the human tongue, and list the five basic tastes perceived by humans.

Taste, or *gustation*, occurs because chemicals stimulate thousands of receptors in the mouth. These receptors are located primarily on the tongue, but some are also found in the throat, inside the cheeks, and on the roof of the mouth. If you look at your tongue in a mirror, you will notice many tiny bumps; they are called **papillae** (from the Latin for "pimples"), and they come in several forms. In all but one of these forms, the sides of each papilla are lined with **taste buds**, which up close look a little like segmented oranges (see Figure 6.14). Because of genetic differences, human tongues can have as few as 500 or as many as 10,000 taste buds (Miller & Reedy, 1990).

papillae [pa PILL ee]

Knoblike elevations on the tongue, containing the taste buds. (Singular: *papilla.*)

taste buds

Nests of taste receptor cells.

Figure 6.14 Taste Receptors

The illustration on the left shows taste buds lining the sides of a papilla on the tongue's surface. The illustration on the right shows an enlarged view of a single taste bud.

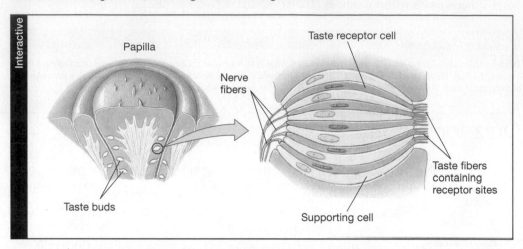

The taste buds are commonly referred to, mistakenly, as the receptors for taste. The actual receptor cells are *inside* the buds, 15 to 50 to a bud. These cells send tiny fibers out through an opening in the bud; the receptor sites are on these fibers. New receptor cells replace old ones about every 10 days. However, after age 40 or so, the total number of taste buds (and therefore receptors) declines. Interestingly, the center of the tongue contains no taste buds. However, as in the case of the eye's blind spot, you will not usually notice the lack of sensation because the brain fills in the gap.

Four basic tastes are part of our evolutionary heritage: *salty*, *sour*, *bitter*, and *sweet*, each produced by a different type of chemical. Their receptors are tuned to molecules that alert us to good or dangerous tastes: Bitter tastes help us detect poison; sweet tastes attract us to biologically useful sugars, such as those in fruit; salty tastes enable us to identify sodium, a mineral crucial to survival; and sour tastes permit us to avoid acids in concentrations that might injure tissue (Bartoshuk & Snyder, 2012). All of the basic tastes can be perceived at any spot on the tongue that has receptors, and differences among the areas are small. When you bite into an egg or a piece of bread or an orange, its unique flavor is composed of some combination of these tastes.

Some researchers believe that we have a fifth basic taste, *umami*, the taste of monosodium glutamate (MSG), which is said to permit us to detect protein-rich foods; they are searching for possible receptors on the tongue for it. Umami was identified by Japanese chemists in the early 1900s as a flavor enhancer. (The word has no exact English translation, but the closest is "delicious" or "savory.") However, findings on umami, which have largely been funded by the MSG industry, are controversial. In most foods containing protein, the umami taste is not perceptible, the way sugar is perceptible in the taste of a doughnut; and people differ widely in their responses to it (Bartoshuk, 2009).

The evidence that umami is probably not a hardwired fifth taste has led to another fascinating discovery: Taste receptors are found throughout the gastrointestinal tract and may have different functions in different locations. Protein molecules are too large to be sensed by taste or smell; but when they are eaten and digested, they are broken into their constituent amino acids, stimulating umami receptors in the gut, which in turn signal the brain that protein has been consumed, and creating a conditioned preference for the sensory properties of protein-rich foods such as bacon, roast beef, and cheese. The response to umami therefore occurs primarily in the gut, not the mouth, which would explain why a taste for protein is a learned preference rather than a universal one (Bartoshuk, 2009; Stratford & Finger, 2011).

Everyone knows that people live in what psychological scientist Linda Bartoshuk (1998) calls different "taste worlds." Some people love broccoli and others hate it. Some people can eat burning hot chili peppers and others cannot tolerate the mildest jalapeño. And perhaps no food divides people more than cilantro. Entire websites are devoted to complaints about those innocent-looking green leaves, whose detractors think taste like soap. What causes these taste differences?

According to Bartoshuk's research, about 25 percent of people live in a "neon" taste world. These *supertasters*, who are overrepresented among women, Asians, Hispanics, and blacks, have an unusually large number of small, densely packed papillae (Reedy et al., 1993). For them, bitter foods such as caffeine, quinine (the bitter ingredient in tonic water), and many vegetables are unpleasantly bitter—at least twice as bitter as they are for other people. Supertasters also perceive sweet tastes as sweeter and salty tastes as saltier than other people do, and they feel more "burn" from substances such as ginger, pepper, and hot chilies (Bartoshuk et al., 1998; Lucchina et al., 1998).

Taste differences, including those between supertasters and other people, are partly a matter of genetics, but culture and learning also play a role. Many Westerners who enjoy raw food such as oysters are put off by other forms of raw seafood that are popular in Asian countries, such as sea urchin. Even within a given culture, people have different taste preferences, some of which begin in the womb or shortly after birth. Flavors as diverse as vanilla, carrot, garlic, anise, hot spices, and mint can be transmitted to the fetus or newborn through amniotic fluid or breast milk, with long-lasting consequences (Beauchamp & Mennella, 2011; Mennella et al., 2011). Babies fed salty foods prefer salty foods when they become preschoolers (Stein, Cowart, & Beauchamp, 2012).

Even illnesses can affect taste. If you have ever had an ear infection, it has probably altered the activity of a nerve that runs through your tongue and changed your perception of taste. Your experience of taste, then, is not determined by just one factor, such as genes, but also by infections, cultural preferences, exposure to other cultures' foods, and what your parents taught you. That is why you *can* learn to like foods that you previously thought were unappealing or "dis-tasteful." Some former cilantro haters have learned to embrace their former herbal enemy simply by *trying* to like it (McGee, 2010)!

The attractiveness of a food can also be affected by its color, temperature, and texture. Even more important for taste is a food's odor. Much of what we call "flavor" is really the smell of gases released by the foods we put in our mouths. Indeed, subtle flavors such as chocolate and vanilla would have little taste if we could not smell them (see Figure 6.15). Smell's influence on flavor explains why you have trouble tasting your food when you have a stuffy nose. Most people who have chronic trouble detecting tastes have a problem with smell, not taste.

Smell: The Sense of Scents

LO 6.4.B Describe the basic pathway from smell receptors to the cerebral cortex.

The great author and educator Helen Keller, who became blind and deaf as a toddler, once called smell "the fallen angel of the senses." Yet our sense of smell, or *olfaction*, although seemingly crude when compared to a bloodhound's, is actually quite good; the human nose can detect aromas that sophisticated machines fail to detect.

The receptors for smell are specialized neurons embedded in a tiny patch of mucous membrane in the upper part of the nasal passage, just beneath the eyes (see Figure 6.16). Millions of receptors in each nasal cavity respond to chemical molecules (vapors) in the air. When you inhale, you pull these molecules into the nasal cavity, but they can also enter from the mouth, wafting up the throat like smoke up a chimney. These molecules trigger responses in the receptors that combine to yield the yeasty smell of freshly baked bread or the spicy smell of a curry. Signals from the receptors are carried to the brain's olfactory bulb by the

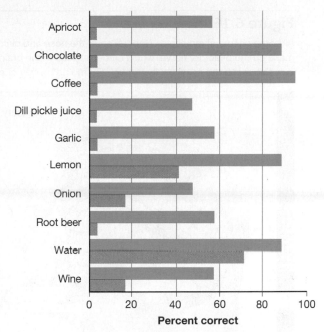

Figure 6.15 Taste Test

The turquoise bars show the percentages of people who could identify a substance dropped on the tongue when they were able to smell it. The orange bars show the percentage that could identify the substance when they were prevented from smelling it (Mozell et al., 1969).

Demonstrate for yourself that smell enhances the sense of taste. While holding your nose, take a bite of a slice of apple, and then do the same with a slice of raw potato. You may find that you cannot taste much difference. If you think you do taste a difference, perhaps your expectations are influencing your response. Try the same thing, but close your eyes this time and have someone else feed you the slices. Can you still tell them apart? It's also fun to do this little test with flavored jellybeans. They are still apt to taste sweet, but you may be unable to identify the separate flavors.

Figure 6.16 Receptors for Smell

Airborne chemical molecules (vapors) enter the nose and circulate through the nasal cavity, where the smell receptors are located. The receptors' axons make up the olfactory nerve, which carries signals to the brain. When you sniff, you draw more vapors into the nose and speed their circulation. Vapors can also reach the nasal cavity through the mouth by way of a passageway from the throat.

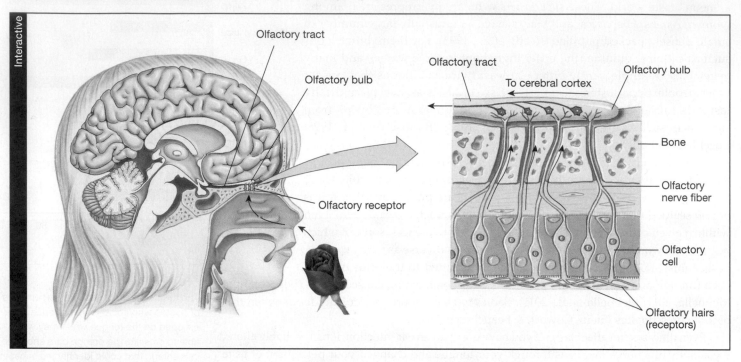

olfactory nerve, which is made up of the receptors' axons. From the olfactory bulb, they travel to a higher region of the brain.

Figuring out the neural code for smell has been a real challenge. Of the 10,000 or so smells we detect (rotten, burned, musky, fruity, fishy, spicy . . .), none seems to be more basic than any other. Moreover, roughly 1,000 kinds of receptors exist, each kind responding to a part of an odor molecule's structure (Axel, 1995; Buck & Axel, 1991; Nakamoto, 2015). Distinct odors activate unique combinations of receptors, and signals from different types of receptors are combined in individual neurons in the brain. Some neurons seem to respond only to particular mixtures of odors rather than the individual odors in a mixture, which may explain why a mixture of clove and rose may be perceived as carnation rather than as two separate smells (Zou & Buck, 2006).

Of course, some animals have a sense of smell that makes human beings seem truly impaired by comparison. At airports, dogs detect drugs, bombs, and contraband food in people's luggage; in clinics, they detect cancer simply by sniffing a person's breath (Sonoda et al., 2011). It's not just dogs that have amazingly helpful senses of smell; in Africa, rats are helping to detect people who have undiagnosed tuberculosis (Mgode et al., 2012). The olfactory talents of many nonhuman animals evolved because smell is so important to these animals' survival.

Although smell is less vital for human survival than for the survival of other animals, it is still important. We sniff out danger by smelling smoke, rotten food, and gas leaks, so a deficit in the sense of smell is nothing to turn up your nose at. Such a loss can result from infection, disease, injury to the olfactory nerve, or smoking. A person who has smoked two packs a day for 10 years must abstain from cigarettes for 10 more years before the sense of smell returns to normal (Frye, Schwartz, & Doty, 1990).

Odors can also have psychological effects on us, which is why we buy perfumes and sniff flowers. Perhaps because olfactory centers in the brain are linked to areas that process memories and emotions, specific smells often evoke vivid, emotionally colored memories (Herz & Cupchik, 1995; Vroon, 1997). Odors can also influence people's everyday behavior, which is why shopping malls and hotels often install aroma diffusers in hopes of putting you in a good mood.

Senses of the Skin

LO 6.4.C   List the four basic skin senses that humans perceive.

The skin's usefulness is more than just skin deep. Besides protecting our innards, our two square yards of skin help us identify objects and establish intimacy with others. By providing a boundary between ourselves and everything else, the skin also gives us a sense of ourselves as distinct from the environment.

The basic skin senses include *touch* (or pressure), *warmth*, *cold*, and *pain*. Within these four types are variations such as itch, tickle, and painful burning. Although certain spots on the skin are especially sensitive to the four basic skin sensations, for many years, scientists had difficulty finding distinct receptors and nerve fibers for these sensations, except in the case of pressure. But then Swedish researchers discovered a nerve fiber that seems responsible for the kind of itching caused by histamines (Schmelz et al., 1997). Another team has found that the same fibers that detect pain from a punch in the nose or a burn also seem to detect the kind of pathological itch that is unrelated to histamines and that cannot be relieved by antihistamine medications (Johanek et al., 2008). Scientists have also identified a possible cold receptor (McKemy, Neuhausser, & Julius, 2002; Peier et al., 2002).

Perhaps specialized fibers will be discovered for other skin sensations as well. In the meantime, many aspects of touch remain baffling, such as why gently touching adjacent pressure spots in rapid succession produces tickle and why scratching relieves (or sometimes worsens) an itch. Decoding the messages of the skin senses will eventually tell us how we are able to distinguish sandpaper from velvet and glue from grease.

The Mystery of Pain

LO 6.4.D   Describe the principles of gate-control theory, and explain what phantom pain is and a novel way to treat it.

Pain is a sensation most of us would prefer not to experience, as shown in the video *Managing Pain*.

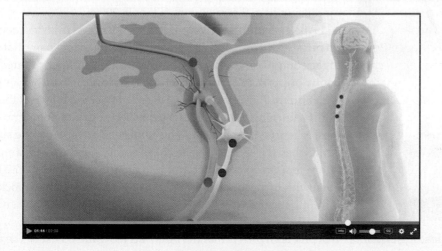

Pain, which is both a skin sense and an internal sense, has come under special scrutiny. Pain differs from other senses in an important way: Even when the stimulus producing it is removed, the sensation may continue, sometimes for years. Chronic pain disrupts and can wreck a person's life, putting stress on the body and causing depression and despair. Understanding the physiology of pain has been an enormous challenge because different types of pain (from, say, a thorn, a bruise, or a hot iron) involve different chemical changes and different changes in nerve-cell activity at the site of injury or disease, as well as in the spinal cord and brain. Several chemical substances are involved and so are glial cells, the cells that support nerve cells; they release inflammatory substances that can worsen the pain (Watkins

A nurse examines Ashlyn Blocker's feet for injuries. Because of a rare condition, Ashlyn cannot feel pain from scrapes and scratches. Severe, chronic pain causes terrible suffering for millions of people, but moderate, temporary pain is useful because it alerts us to injury.

gate-control theory
The theory that the experience of pain depends in part on whether pain impulses get past a neurological "gate" in the spinal cord and thus reach the brain.

phantom pain
The experience of pain in a missing limb or other body part.

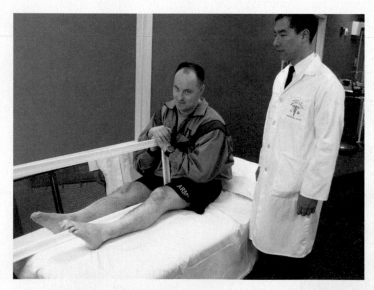

After his right leg was destroyed in an explosion while he was in Iraq, Army Sergeant Nicholas Paupore experienced excruciating phantom limb pain. Even morphine didn't help. Then he underwent a simple daily procedure. A mirror was placed at a strategic angle to reflect his intact leg, tricking his brain into registering two healthy legs. The pain almost immediately subsided. A year after therapy, he had only occasional, milder pain, and needed no medication. In some patients, mirror therapy has eliminated phantom pain entirely.

& Maier, 2003). Here, however, we focus on a general theory of pain and on the psychological factors that influence how pain is experienced.

For many years, the most influential theory of pain was the **gate-control theory**, which was first proposed by Canadian psychologist Ronald Melzack and British physiologist Patrick Wall (1965). According to this theory, pain impulses must get past a "gate" in the spinal cord. The gate is not an actual structure, but rather a pattern of neural activity that either blocks pain messages from the skin, muscles, and internal organs or lets those signals through. Normally, the gate is kept shut, either by impulses coming into the spinal cord from large fibers that respond to pressure and other kinds of stimulation or by signals coming down from the brain itself. But when body tissue is injured, the large fibers are damaged and smaller fibers open the gate, allowing pain messages to reach the brain unchecked. The gate-control theory correctly predicts that mild pressure, or other kinds of stimulation, can interfere with severe or protracted pain by closing the spinal gate. When we vigorously rub a banged elbow or apply ice packs, heat, or stimulating ointments to injuries, we are applying this principle.

In the gate-control theory, the brain not only responds to incoming signals from sensory nerves but is also capable of generating pain entirely on its own (Melzack, 1992, 1993). An extensive *matrix* (network) of neurons in the brain gives us a sense of our own bodies and body parts. When this matrix produces abnormal patterns of activity, the result is pain. The brain's ability to generate pain can help explain the many instances of severe, chronic pain that occur without any sign of injury or disease whatsoever.

Because technology now allows scientists to study pain at the molecular and cellular level, today we know that the gate-control theory, though useful, is incomplete (Mendell, 2014). Pain may also be caused by changes to the sensitivity of neurons in the central nervous system (CNS). For example, when bursts of heat are repeatedly applied to an animal's paw, pain receptors in the paw and skin are excited and remain sensitive for several hours. During that time, even a light, harmless touch will activate the pain receptors, and applying anesthetic at the site of injury will not make the pain receptors return to normal. This finding shows that changes at the CNS level can help explain how once-harmless stimuli can end up causing pain (Latremoliere & Woolf, 2009).

An extreme version of pain without injury occurs in **phantom pain**, in which a person continues to feel pain that seemingly comes from an arm or leg that has been amputated, or a bodily organ that has been surgically removed. Phantom limb pain afflicts up to 90 percent of amputees. The person may feel the same aching, burning, or sharp pain from sores, calf cramps, throbbing toes, or ingrown toenails that he or she endured before the surgery. Even when the spinal cord has been completely severed, amputees often continue to report phantom pain from areas below the break. Even with no nerve impulses for the spinal-cord gate to block or let through, the pain can be constant and excruciating; some sufferers commit suicide.

A leading explanation of phantom pain is that the brain has reorganized itself: The area in the sensory cortex that formerly corresponded to the missing body part has been "invaded" by neurons from another area, often one corresponding to the face. Higher brain centers then interpret messages from those neurons as coming from the nonexistent body part (Cruz et al., 2005; Ramachandran & Blakeslee, 1998). Even though the missing limb can no longer send signals through touch and internal sensations, memories of these signals remain in the nervous system, including memories of pain, paralysis, and cramping that occurred prior to amputation. The result is an inaccurate "body map" in the brain and pain signals that cannot be shut off.

Vilayanur Ramachandran, the neurologist who first proposed this theory, has developed an extraordinarily simple but effective treatment for phantom limb pain. Ramachandran wondered whether he could devise an illusion to trick the brain of an amputee with phantom arm pain into perceiving the missing limb as moving and pain-free. He placed a mirror upright and perpendicular to the sufferer's body, such that the amputee's intact arm was reflected in the mirror. From the amputee's perspective, the result was an illusion of two functioning arms. The amputee was then instructed to move both arms in synchrony while looking into the mirror. With this technique, which has now been used with many people, the brain is fooled into thinking its owner has two healthy arms or legs, resynchronizes the signals—and phantom pain vanishes (Ramachandran & Altschuler, 2009). Neurologists have tested this method with Iraq veterans, and are finding it to be more successful than control therapies in which patients just mentally visualize having two intact limbs (Anderson-Barnes et al., 2009; Chan et al., 2007).

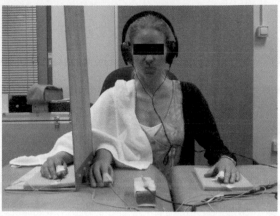

A demonstration of the rubber hand illusion.

Most of us can experience an illusion caused by a mechanism similar to the one Ramachandran set up. Imagine that you are sitting with your arms resting on a table. Between your arms is a screen, positioned so that you can see your left arm but not your right. But in front of the screen, also in your view, rests a full-sized right arm and hand made of rubber. You are asked to focus on the rubber hand while the experimenters take two small paintbrushes and gently stroke your left hand and the rubber hand simultaneously. Do you feel the touch of the paintbrush on the rubber hand?

Impossibly, the answer is yes! In this study of what has become known as "the rubber hand illusion," people reported that they felt the touch of the paintbrush on the artificial hand—which, in turn, felt as though it were their own (Botvinick & Cohen, 1998; Kammers et al., 2009). These people were not delusional. Usually, our abilities to see, feel, and know what our body parts are doing are all tightly coordinated. But in the rubber hand illusion, your brain tries to reconcile the unusual situation by "adopting" the rubber arm as its own, and "disowning" your real right arm. This fascinating phenomenon has been replicated in recent studies (Barnsley et al., 2011; Longo & Haggard, 2012; Ramachandran, Krause, & Case, 2011).

The Environment Within

LO 6.4.E Discuss the two senses that allow us to monitor our internal environment.

We usually think of our senses as pipelines to the world around us, but two senses keep us informed about the movements of our own bodies. **Kinesthesis** tells us where our bodily parts are located and lets us know when they move. This information is provided by pain and pressure receptors located in the muscles, joints, and tendons. Without kinesthesis, you would have trouble with any voluntary movement. Think of how hard it is to walk when your leg has "fallen asleep" or how awkward it is to chew when a dentist has numbed your jaw.

Equilibrium, or the sense of balance, gives us information about our bodies as a whole. Along with vision and touch, it lets us know whether we are standing upright or on our heads and tells us when we are falling or rotating. Equilibrium relies primarily on three **semicircular canals** in the inner ear (refer back to Figure 6.13). These thin tubes are filled with fluid that moves and presses on hairlike receptors whenever the head rotates. The receptors initiate messages that travel through a part of the auditory nerve that is not involved in hearing.

Normally, kinesthesis and equilibrium work together to give us a sense of our own physical reality, something we take utterly for granted but should not. Oliver Sacks (1985) told the heart-breaking story of Christina, a young British woman who suffered irreversible damage to her kinesthetic nerve fibers because of a mysterious inflammation. At first, Christina was as floppy as a rag doll; she could not sit up, walk, or stand. Then, slowly, she learned to do these things, relying on visual cues and sheer willpower. But her movements remained unnatural; she had to grasp a fork with painful force or she would drop it. More important, despite

kinesthesis [KIN-es-THEE-sis]

The sense of body position and movement of body parts; also called *kinesthesia*.

equilibrium

The sense of balance.

semicircular canals

Sense organs in the inner ear that contribute to equilibrium by responding to rotation of the head.

BIOLOGY and *the Power of Placebos*

One of the most powerful potential weapons in the treatment of pain and serious medical problems is the placebo (Benedetti et al., 2005; Rief, 2011). When fibromyalgia patients were given active medication or an inactive placebo and rated their pain before and after treatment, 45 percent of the improvement in the medication group was due to a placebo effect (as measured using advanced statistics for comparing the two groups). And for patients with painful nerve damage caused by diabetes, the figure was 62 percent (Häuser et al., 2011). The more expensive the placebo, the better it "works": Higher-priced placebos produce more relief than the same ones described as cheaper (Waber et al., 2008).

Whatever their cost, size, or color, placebos themselves cannot "do" anything to reduce pain; they're just inert substances, after all. Then why do they have an effect?

Expectations are an important factor. In one study, volunteers were trained to expect jolts of heat applied to their legs after a tone sounded. The intensity of the heat varied depending on the delay between the tone and the heat: The longer the delay, the stronger the heat. Functional MRI showed that the stronger the pain the participants *expected* to feel, the greater the activity in certain brain regions before actual delivery of the pain, and most of these regions overlapped with those that responded to the pain itself. But eventually the delay stopped being predictable. Sometimes a less severe jolt followed the longest delays, and sometimes a severe jolt followed the shortest delays. When the volunteers expected a moderate jolt and instead received a very painful one, their self-reported pain fell by 28 percent compared with when they expected the most painful jolt and actually got it (Koyama et al., 2005; see Figure 6.17). This decrease was equal to what they would have experienced had they received a shot of morphine!

Such findings suggest a mechanism for how placebos reduce pain. When placebos affect expectations ("I'm going to get relief"), they also seem to affect the brain mechanisms underlying pain. Indeed, when volunteers in another study had an "analgesic cream" (actually a placebo) rubbed on their skin before getting a painful shock to the wrist, MRI scans showed decreased activity in the pain matrix, the pain-sensitive areas of their brains (Wager et al., 2004).

Placebos may also promote the production of endorphins, the body's natural pain-relieving opiates. Researchers gave volunteers a slow, harmless injection of a pain-inducing solution in the jaw and had them rate their pain level (Zubieta et al., 2005). As the injection

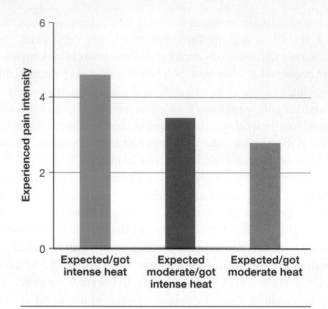

Figure 6.17 Expectations and Pain

When people expected moderate heat but got intense heat (blue bar), their self-reported pain was lower than it would have been had they expected the intense heat (green bar).

continued, the researchers told some of the participants (falsely) that a pain-relieving serum had been added and again asked all of the subjects to rank their discomfort. Throughout the procedure, PET scans tracked the activity of endorphins in the subjects' brains. Those who got the placebo produced endorphins in pain-control areas of the brain, which is just what would have happened had they taken a real painkiller.

Expectations about pain are affected not only by placebos but also by your environment (does it make you feel safe or apprehensive?), what your doctor tells you, psychological states such as general anxiety or depression, and cultural beliefs governing how appropriate it is for people to notice symptoms and express distress. These nonmedical influences on pain contribute to the rise and fall of pain epidemics, as in sudden, apparently mysterious outbreaks of back pain, whiplash, and repetitive-motion injuries (Gawande, 1998). People who suffer during such epidemics are not faking it, and their pain is not "just in their heads." But it may be in their brains.

her remaining sensitivity to light touch on the skin, she said she could no longer experience herself as physically embodied: "It's like something's been scooped right out of me," she told Sacks, "right at the center."

With equilibrium, we come, as it were, to the end of our senses. Every single second, millions of sensory signals reach the brain, which combines and integrates them to produce a model of reality. How does it know how to do this? Are our perceptual abilities inborn, or must we learn them? We turn next to this issue.

JOURNAL PROMPT 6.4

Thinking Critically—Ask Questions, Be Willing to Wonder: The U.S. military has spent some time and money looking into *nonlethal weapons development*, or what's also known as "stench warfare." Military scientists have sought a smell that would prove noxious, aversive, and perhaps incapacitating to an enemy, so as to render an advantage during military operations. (The clear winner in tests so far is the smell of human feces.) Why would smell have this kind of power? How do smell receptors and the process of smell perception differ from the other senses, and why might it predict an immediate, nearly universal response to some odors?

This person obviously has exceptional kinesthetic talents and equilibrium.

Quiz for Module 6.4

1. Which of the following is *not* one of the basic tastes detected by the tongue?

   a. Spicy

   b. Sweet

   c. Bitter

   d. Sour

2. The olfactory nerve is composed of

   a. Dendrites from the olfactory receptor cells

   b. Hair cells from the olfactory bulb

   c. Axons from the olfactory receptor cells

   d. A collection of olfactory bulbs

3. Compared to vision or hearing, how well do scientists understand the mechanisms that determine skin sensations?

   a. Poorly

   b. Very well

   c. Not at all

   d. We understand skin sensations better than we understand hearing, but not as well as we understand vision.

4. The leading theory that helps us understand pain is called

   a. Activation–synthesis model

   b. Gate-control theory

   c. Elaboration-likelihood model

   d. Receptor-damage theory

5. A person's sense of balance is called

   a. Exteroception

   b. Kinesthesis

   c. Vestibular sense

   d. Equilibrium

Perceptual Powers

What happens when babies first open their eyes? Do they see the same sights, hear the same sounds, and smell the same smells as an adult does? Or is an infant's world, as William James once suggested, only a "blooming, buzzing confusion," waiting to be organized by experience and learning? The truth lies somewhere between these two extremes.

Inborn Abilities and Critical Periods

LO 6.5.A   Summarize the evidence suggesting that our perceptual powers are both inborn and dependent on experience.

In human beings, most basic sensory abilities and many perceptual skills are inborn or develop very early. Infants can distinguish salty from sweet and can discriminate among odors. They can distinguish a human voice from other sounds. They will startle to a loud

Figure 6.18 A Cliff-Hanger

Infants as young as 6 months usually hesitate to crawl past the apparent edge of a visual cliff, which suggests that they are able to perceive depth.

noise and turn their heads toward its source, showing that they perceive sound as being localized in space. Many visual skills, too, are present at birth or develop shortly afterward. Human infants can discriminate sizes and colors very early, possibly even right away. They distinguish contrasts, shadows, and complex patterns after only a few weeks, and depth perception develops during the first few months.

Testing an infant's perception of depth requires considerable ingenuity. One classic procedure has been to place infants on a device called a *visual cliff* (Gibson & Walk, 1960). The "cliff" is a pane of glass covering a shallow surface and a deep one (see Figure 6.18). Both surfaces are covered by a checkerboard pattern. The infant is placed on a board in the middle, and the child's mother tries to lure the baby across either the shallow side or the deep side. Babies only 6 months of age will crawl across the shallow side but will hesitate to crawl out over the "cliff," suggesting that they have depth perception. Infants often spend a considerable amount of time at the edge of the "cliff," exploring their options and investigating the situation (Adolph, Kretch, & LoBue, 2014). This would suggest that it's not fear that's keeping them from the deep side, but rather a curiosity to explore coupled with a canny recognition that the circumstances are somehow not quite right for normal locomotion (Adolph, 2000; Adolph & Kretch, 2012).

Although many perceptual abilities are inborn, experience also plays a vital role. If an infant misses out on certain experiences during a crucial window of time called a *critical period*, perception will be impaired. Innate abilities may not survive because cells in the nervous system deteriorate, change, or fail to form appropriate neural pathways.

One way to study critical periods is to see what happens when the usual perceptual experiences of early life fail to take place. To do this, researchers have studied animals whose sensory and perceptual systems are similar to our own, such as kittens. Like human infants, kittens are born with the visual ability to detect horizontal and vertical lines and other spatial orientations; at birth, kittens' brains are equipped with the same kinds of feature-detector cells that adult cats have. But if they are deprived of normal visual experience, these cells deteriorate or change and perception suffers (Crair, Gillespie, & Stryker, 1998; Hirsch & Spinelli, 1970). In one classic study, kittens were reared in darkness for 5 months after birth, but for several hours each day, they were put into a special cylinder that permitted them to see only vertical or horizontal lines and nothing else. Later, cats that were exposed only to vertical lines had trouble perceiving horizontal ones; they would bump into horizontal obstacles. Those exposed only to horizontal lines had trouble perceiving vertical ones; they would run to play with horizontal bars but not vertical ones (Blakemore & Cooper, 1970).

What about human beings? Because of the brain's impressive plasticity, some people who are unable to see or hear until middle childhood or even adulthood can regain enough perceptual ability to get along fine in daily life (Ostrovsky, Andalman, & Sinha, 2006; Šikl et al., 2013). However, their perception is unlikely to fully recover. When adults who have been blind from infancy have their vision restored, most of them do not see well. Areas in the brain normally devoted to vision may have taken on different functions when these people were blind. As a result, their depth perception may be poor, causing them to trip constantly (Ostrovsky et al., 2009). They cannot always make sense of what they see; to identify objects, they may have to touch or smell them. They may have trouble recognizing faces and emotional expressions. They may even lack size constancy and need to remind themselves that people walking away from them are not shrinking in size (Fine et al., 2003). Generally, the best recoveries occur when an infant's congenital blindness is corrected early, probably because a critical period for visual development occurs in infancy or early childhood.

Similar findings apply to hearing. When adults who were born deaf, or who lost their hearing before learning to speak, receive cochlear implants (devices that stimulate the auditory nerve and allow auditory signals to travel to the brain), they tend to find sounds confusing. They are unable to learn to speak normally, and sometimes they ask to have the implants removed. But cochlear implants are more successful in children and in adults who became deaf late in life (Rauschecker, 1999). Young children presumably have not yet passed through the critical period for processing sounds, and older adults have already had years of auditory experience.

In sum, our perceptual powers are both inborn and dependent on experience. Because neurological connections in infants' brains and sensory systems are not completely formed, their senses are far less acute than an adult's. It takes time and experience for their sensory abilities to fully develop. But an infant's world is clearly not the blooming, buzzing confusion that William James took it to be.

Psychological and Cultural Influences

LO 6.5.B Discuss four psychological factors that influence how we perceive the world.

The fact that some perceptual processes appear to be innate does not mean that all people perceive the world in the same way. A camera doesn't care what it "sees." A digital recorder doesn't ponder what it "hears." But because we care about what we see, hear, taste, smell, and feel, psychological factors can influence what we perceive and how we perceive it. Here are a few of these factors:

1. **Needs.** When we need something, have an interest in it, or want it, we are especially likely to perceive it. That is why hungry people are faster than others at seeing words related to hunger when the words are flashed briefly on a screen (Radel & Clément-Guillotin, 2012; Wispé & Drambarean, 1953). People also tend to perceive objects that they want—a water bottle if they are thirsty, money they can win in a game, a personality test with favorable results—as being physically closer to them than objects they don't want or need. Some psychological scientists call these motivated misperceptions "wishful seeing" (Balcetis & Dunning, 2010).

2. **Beliefs.** What we hold to be true about the world can affect our interpretation of ambiguous sensory signals. Images that remind people of Jesus or Mary have been reported on walls, dishes, tortillas, and sandwiches; the Arabic script for "Allah" has been reported on fish scales, chicken eggs, and beans. Such images cause great excitement among those who believe that divine messages can be found on everyday objects. However, mundane events inevitably prove to be the explanation. An image of Jesus on a garage door in California attracted crowds until it turned out to be caused by two streetlights that merged the shadows of a bush and a "For Sale" sign in the yard.

People often see what they want to see. Diana Duyser, a cook at a Florida casino, took a bite out of a grilled cheese sandwich and believed she saw the image of the Virgin Mary in what remained of it. She preserved the sandwich in plastic for 10 years and then decided to sell it. An online casino bought it on eBay for $28,000, even with a bite of it missing!

3. **Emotions.** Emotions can also influence our interpretation of sensory information, as when a small child afraid of the dark sees a ghost instead of a robe hanging on the bedroom door. Pain, as we noted, is particularly intensified by negative emotions such as anxiety and sadness. Conversely, soldiers who are seriously wounded often deny being in much pain, even though they are alert and are not in shock. Their relief at being alive may offset the worry and fear that would otherwise make their pain worse (although the body's own pain-fighting mechanisms may also be involved). Interestingly, when people perceive their pain as resulting from another person's malicious intent (e.g., they think the other person intentionally stepped on their toe), they feel the hurt more than they would if they thought it was simply due to a clumsy accident (Gray & Wegner, 2008).

4. **Expectations.** Previous experiences affect how we perceive the world. The tendency to perceive things in a certain way based on your expectations is called a **perceptual set**. Such sets can come in handy, helping us fill in words in sentences when we haven't really heard every one. But perceptual sets can also cause misperceptions, as you can see in the illustration here.

Expectations can even reduce our reactions to stimuli that would otherwise be unpleasant, such as the universally obnoxious sound of fingernails scratching a chalkboard (human ears have a physiological sensitivity to sounds in that frequency range). In one study, people rated the unpleasantness of such sounds while they were wired up to devices that measured physiological markers of stress, including heart rate and sweating. Some people were told what the sounds really were; others were told that the sounds were from musical compositions. Those who thought the sounds were "music" found them less unpleasant than people who knew that the sounds were fingernails scraping, even though both groups showed similar stress responses (Reuter & Oehler, 2011).

Perception Without Awareness

LO 6.5.C Summarize the evidence both for and against subliminal perception.

As we saw earlier in our discussion of selective attention, even when people are oblivious to speech sounds, they are processing and recognizing those sounds at some level. Much of our perception occurs without our conscious awareness, and the things we see, hear, touch, or even smell without conscious awareness may nonetheless influence our behavior.

Behavior can be affected even by stimuli that are so weak or brief that they are below a person's absolute threshold for detecting them—that is, *subliminal*. People sometimes correctly sense a change in a scene (say, in the color or location of an object) even though the change took place too quickly to be consciously recognized and identified (Rensink, 2004). And when people are subliminally exposed to a face, they will later tend to prefer that face over one they did not "see" in this way (Bornstein, Leone, & Galley, 1987).

perceptual set

A habitual way of perceiving, based on expectations.

CULTURE and *Perception*

Our needs, beliefs, emotions, and expectations are all affected, in turn, by the culture we live in. Different cultures give people practice with different environments. In a classic study done in the 1960s, researchers found that members of some African tribes were much less likely to be fooled by the Müller-Lyer illusion (refer back to Figure 6.10) and other geometric illusions than were Westerners. In the West, the researchers observed, people live in a "carpentered" world, full of rectangular structures. Westerners are also used to interpreting two-dimensional photographs and perspective drawings as representations of a three-dimensional world. Therefore, they interpret the kinds of angles used in the Müller-Lyer illusion as right angles extended in space, a habit that increases susceptibility to the illusion. The rural Africans in the study, living in a less carpentered environment and in round huts, seemed more likely to take the lines in the figures literally, as two-dimensional, which could explain why they were less susceptible to the illusion (Segall, Campbell, & Herskovits, 1966; Segall et al., 1999).

Culture also affects perception by shaping our stereotypes, directing our attention, and telling us what to notice or ignore. Westerners tend to focus mostly on the figure when viewing a scene and much less on the ground. East Asians, in contrast, tend to pay attention to the overall context and the relationship between figure and ground. In a memory experiment, Japanese and Americans were shown animated underwater scenes containing brightly colored fish that were larger and moving faster than other objects in the scene. Afterward, both groups reported the same numbers of details about the fish, but the Japanese remembered more details about everything else in the background, such as rocks and plants (Masuda & Nisbett, 2001).

Why should the Japanese pay more attention to context than Americans? One possibility is that a greater concern with the social world directs the attention of the Japanese to contexts of all types. Another possibility is that in Japanese environments, specific objects really do stand out less than in comparable American environments, so living in Japan tends to direct a person's attention to the whole visual field. Indeed, when researchers randomly sampled pictures of hotels, elementary schools, and post offices from small, medium, and large cities in Japan and the United States, they found that the Japanese scenes were more ambiguous and contained more elements than comparable American scenes—just the kind of scenes that encourage attention to context (Miyamoto, Nisbett, & Masuda, 2006).

As you can see, what you see partly depends on the culture you live in. When travelers visit another culture and are surprised to find that its members "see things differently," they may be literally correct.

Thus, people often know more than they know they know. However, even in the laboratory, where researchers have considerable control, subliminal perception can be difficult to demonstrate and replicate. The strongest evidence for its existence comes from studies using simple stimuli (faces or single words such as *bread*) rather than complex stimuli such as sentences ("Eat whole-wheat bread, not white bread, if you know what's good for you").

If subliminal exposure to stimuli can affect judgments and preferences in the laboratory, you may be wondering whether it can be used to manipulate people's attitudes and behavior in ordinary life. In the 1950s an advertising executive claimed to have increased popcorn and Coke sales at a theater by secretly flashing the words EAT POPCORN and DRINK COKE on the movie screen. The claim turned out to be a hoax, devised to save the man's struggling advertising company.

Ever since, scientists have been skeptical, but that has not deterred people who market subliminal recordings that promise to help you lose weight, stop smoking, relieve stress, or boost your motivation, all without any effort on your part. Ah, if only those claims were true! But they are not. In study after study, placebo recordings, which do not contain the messages that participants think they do, have been just as "effective" as those containing the supposed subliminal messages (Eich & Hyman, 1992; Merikle & Skanes, 1992; Moore, 1992, 1995). In one typical experiment, people listened to recordings labeled "memory" or "self-esteem," but some heard recordings that were incorrectly labeled. About half showed improvement in the area specified by the label *whether or not it was correct*; the improvement was due to expectations alone (Greenwald et al., 1991).

However, previous efforts at subliminal persuasion may have left out an important ingredient: the person's motivation. A team of researchers used subliminal messages—the words *thirst* and *dry*—to make participants feel thirsty and incline them to drink. Later, when given a chance to drink, these people did in fact drink more than those in a control group did, though only if they had been moderately thirsty to begin with (Strahan, Spencer, & Zanna, 2002).

Does this mean that advertisers can seduce us into buying soft drinks or voting for political candidates by slipping subliminal slogans and images into what we watch and hear? Given the many studies that have found no evidence of subliminal persuasion in real life and the subtlety of the effects that occur in the laboratory (e.g., you have to be somewhat thirsty already to be influenced to drink more), we think there's little cause for worry about subliminal manipulation.

Quiz for Module 6.5

1. What does a *critical period* in perceptual development refer to?
   a. The 3 months immediately after birth, when a rotation of visual–auditory–tactile stimulation needs to be present for an infant to develop appropriate perceptual responses.
   b. The time period between 8 and 22 months of age when locomotion, language, and interpersonal perception all develop.
   c. The prenatal period when a physician can judge whether perceptual development is progressing as it should be.
   d. A period of time during which certain experiences need to be present for an individual to attain well-developed perceptual abilities.

2. Marcia's parents, both artists, had a unique nursery décor in mind. They painted Marcia's room with bold, black vertical lines running from floor to ceiling, broken only by the stark white vertical space in between. They proudly noted how this mimicked the slats on Marcia's crib, and spoke authoritatively about how the lamps, changing table, and rocking chair all carried this same black vertical theme. They were astonished, therefore, when Marcia either paused dumbfounded or stumbled directly into every horizontal surface she encountered after she learned to walk. How can you explain poor baby Marcia's predicament?
   a. Marcia's horizontal feature-detection cells were not stimulated during a critical period of development, and therefore her perceptual abilities were compromised.

b. Marcia's increased visual stimulation during infancy was at the expense of locomotor stimulation, which impaired her walking ability.

c. Marcia's parents should have continued the vertical theme throughout the rest of the house; as a young child, Marcia felt scared when she didn't see familiar vertical lines.

d. Marcia's interests were naturally drawn toward verticality, and as such she was bored and disinterested by horizontal surfaces.

3. You've probably heard the expression, "I'll believe it when I see it." But here's an expression that's equally true: "I'll see it when I believe it." What does this second expression illustrate?

a. People can suspend belief until sensory information guides them to a conclusion.

b. The human perceptual system is biased toward confirming our expectations.

c. Sensory systems respond best to constant input, such as results from core beliefs.

d. People's preexisting beliefs can influence how we perceive events and stimuli in the world.

4. Jooyoun made the mistake of taking too little water with her on a hot summer hike. As she descended the hiking trail and approached the parking area she was certain she saw a frosty bottle of water sitting on the curb. As she got closer she realized it was a shiny rock, and in fact it wasn't shaped at all like a water bottle. Why were Jooyoun's perceptions so mistaken?

a. Her belief that water should be present caused a hallucination.

b. Her need for water influenced her perceptual abilities.

c. Her delicate emotional state prompted her misperception.

d. Her semicircular canals were disrupted from the hike.

5. Stimuli that are below a person's threshold of detection are called

a. Supraliminal

b. Superliminal

c. Subliminal

d. Subthreshal

Taking Psychology with You

Extrasensory Perception: Reality or Illusion?

Eyes, ears, mouth, nose, skin: We rely on these organs for our experience of the external world. Some people, however, claim they can send and receive messages about the world without relying on the usual sensory channels, by using *extrasensory perception* (*ESP*). Reported ESP experiences involve things like telepathy, the direct communication of messages from one mind to another without the usual sensory signals, and precognition, the perception of an event that has not yet happened. How should critical thinkers respond to such claims? What questions should they ask, and what kind of evidence should they look for?

Evidence or Coincidence?

Much of the supposed evidence for ESP comes from anecdotal accounts. But people are not always reliable reporters of their own experiences. They often embellish and exaggerate, or they recall only part of what happened. They also tend to forget incidents that do not fit their beliefs, such as "premonitions" of events that fail to occur. Many ESP experiences could merely be unusual coincidences that are memorable because they are dramatic. What passes for telepathy or precognition could also be based on what a person knows or deduces through ordinary means. If Joanne's father has had two recent heart attacks, her premonition that her father will die shortly (followed, in fact, by her father's death) may not be so impressive.

The scientific way to establish a phenomenon is to produce it under controlled conditions. Unfortunately, most of the attempts to demonstrate ESP in the laboratory have been poorly designed, with inadequate precautions against fraud and improper statistical analysis (Alcock, 2011). As a result, the history of research on this subject has been one of initial enthusiasm because of apparently positive results (Bem & Honorton, 1994; Dalton et al., 1996), followed by disappointment when the results cannot be replicated (Milton & Wiseman, 1999, 2001). One researcher who tried for 30 years to establish the reality of psychic phenomena finally gave up in defeat. "I found no psychic phenomena," she wrote, "only wishful thinking, self-deception, experimental error, and even an occasional fraud. I became a skeptic" (Blackmore, 2001).

The issue has not gone away, however. Many people *really, really* want to believe that ESP exists. James Randi, a famous magician who is dedicated to educating the public about psychic deception, has for years offered a million dollars to anyone who can demonstrate ESP or other paranormal powers under close observation. Many have taken up the challenge; no one has succeeded. We think Randi's money is safe.

Lessons from a Magician

Despite the lack of evidence for ESP, many people say they believe in it. Perhaps you yourself have had an experience that seemed to involve ESP, or perhaps you have seen a convincing demonstration by someone else. Surely you can trust the evidence of your own eyes. Or can you? We will answer this question with a true story, one that contains an important lesson about why it's a good idea to think critically regarding ESP.

During the 1970s, Andrew Weil (now known for his efforts to promote alternative medicine) set out to investigate the claims of a self-proclaimed psychic named Uri Geller (Weil, 1974a, 1974b). Weil, who believed in telepathy, felt that ESP might be explained by principles of modern physics, and he was receptive to Geller's claims. When he met Geller at a private gathering, he was not disappointed. Geller correctly identified a cross and a Star of David sealed inside separate envelopes. He made a stopped watch start running and made a ring sag into an oval shape, apparently without touching

them. He made keys change shape. Weil came away a convert. What he had seen with his own eyes seemed impossible to deny . . . until he went to visit the Amazing Randi.

To Weil's astonishment, Randi was able to duplicate much of what Geller had done. He, too, could bend keys and guess the contents of sealed envelopes. But Randi's feats were tricks, and he was willing to show Weil exactly how they were done. Weil suddenly experienced "a sense of how strongly the mind can impose its own interpretations on perceptions; how it can see what it expects to see, but not see the unexpected."

Weil was disillusioned—literally. Even when he knew what to look for in a trick, he could not catch the Amazing Randi doing it. Weil learned that our sense impressions of reality are not the same as reality. Our eyes, our ears, and especially our brains can play tricks on us.

Shared Writing Prompt

Researchers might debate the evidence for and against ESP (although the overwhelming evidence falls in the "against" column), but many laypeople would like to believe that ESP exists. Even well-educated critical thinkers, who are presented with the flaws of ESP research and alternative explanations for seemingly spooky findings, occasionally like to chalk up an event to "weird coincidences" or extra-normal forces. Why do you think that is? Why do you think humans want to believe in ESP, or for that matter the existence of ghosts, pyramid power, telekinesis, or other wacky stuff? Is there something safe or comforting in believing in a world beyond our powers of perception?

Summary

Our Sensational Senses

LO 6.1.A Distinguish between the basic processes of sensation and perception, explain how the doctrine of specific nerve energies applies to perception, and discuss how synesthesia contributes to our understanding of sensory modalities.

Sensation is the detection and direct experience of physical energy as a result of environmental or internal events. *Perception* is the process by which sensory impulses are organized and interpreted. Sensation begins with the *sense receptors*, which convert the energy of a stimulus into electrical impulses that travel along nerves to the brain. Separate sensations can be accounted for by *anatomical codes* (as set forth by the *doctrine of specific nerve energies*) and *functional codes* in the nervous system. Sensory crossover from one modality to another can sometimes occur, and in *synesthesia*, sensation in one modality consistently evokes a sensation in another, but these experiences are rare.

LO 6.1.B Differentiate between absolute thresholds, difference thresholds, and signal detection.

Psychological scientists specializing in *psychophysics* have studied sensory sensitivity by measuring *absolute* and *difference thresholds*. *Signal-detection theory*, however, holds that responses in a detection task depend on both a sensory process and a decision process and will vary with the person's motivation, alertness, and expectations.

LO 6.1.C Discuss why the principle of sensory adaptation helps us understand how the human perceptual system works.

Our senses are designed to respond to change and contrast in the environment. When stimulation is unchanging, *sensory adaptation* occurs. Too little stimulation can cause *sensory deprivation*.

LO 6.1.D Describe how selective attention and inattentional blindness are related.

Selective attention prevents us from being overwhelmed by the countless stimuli impinging on our senses by allowing us to focus on what is important, but it also deprives us of sensory information we may need, as in *inattentional blindness*.

Vision

LO 6.2.A Describe the three psychological dimensions of vision, and relate them to the three physical properties of light that produce them.

The stimulus for vision is light, which is a form of electromagnetic radiation. Vision is affected by the wavelength, intensity, and complexity of light, which produce the psychological dimensions of visual experience—*hue*, *brightness*, and *saturation*.

LO 6.2.B Locate the structures and cells of the human eye, tracing the path that light follows all the way from the cornea to the optic nerve.

The visual receptors, *rods* and *cones*, are located in the *retina* of the eye. They send signals (via other cells) to the *ganglion cells* and ultimately to the *optic nerve*, which carries visual information to the brain. Rods are responsible for vision in dim light; cones are responsible for color vision.

LO 6.2.C Summarize the evidence indicating that the visual system is not simply a "camera."

Specific aspects of the visual world, such as lines at various orientations, are detected by *feature-detector cells* in the visual areas of the brain. Some of these cells respond maximally to complex patterns, and three separate groups of cells in the brain help us identify faces, places, and bodies.

LO 6.2.D Compare the strengths and weaknesses of the trichromatic and opponent-process theories of color vision.

The *trichromatic* and *opponent-process* theories of color vision apply to different stages of visual processing. In the first stage, three types of cones in the retina respond selectively to different wavelengths of light. In the second, *opponent-process cells* in the retina and the thalamus respond in opposite fashion to short and long wavelengths of light.

LO 6.2.E Summarize the principles and processes that guide form perception, depth and distance perception, visual constancies, and visual illusions.

Perception involves the active construction of a model of the world from moment to moment. The *Gestalt principles* (e.g., *figure and ground*, *proximity*, *closure*, *similarity*, and *continuity*) describe visual strategies used by the brain to perceive forms. We localize objects in visual space by using both *binocular* and *monocular* cues to depth. *Perceptual constancies* allow us to perceive objects as stable despite changes in the sensory patterns they produce. *Perceptual illusions* occur when sensory cues are misleading or when we misinterpret cues.

Hearing

LO 6.3.A Describe the three psychological dimensions of hearing, and relate them to the three physical properties of sound that produce them.

Hearing (*audition*) is affected by the intensity, frequency, and complexity of pressure waves in the air or other transmitting substance, corresponding to the experience of *loudness*, *pitch*, and *timbre* of the sound.

LO 6.3.B Sketch the major structures of the human ear, and briefly describe the functions of each component.

The receptors for hearing are *hair cells* (topped by *cilia*) embedded in the *basilar membrane*, located in the *organ of Corti* in the interior of the *cochlea*. These receptors pass signals along to the *auditory nerve*. The sounds we hear are determined by patterns of hair-cell movement, which produce different neural codes.

LO 6.3.C List five Gestalt principles of perception that apply to constructing the auditory world, and give an example of each.

Gestalt principles (such as proximity, figure/ground, continuity, or similarity) help us to make sense of our auditory world. When we localize sounds, we use as cues subtle differences in how pressure waves reach each of our ears. A few blind people are able to use *echolocation* to navigate.

Other Senses

LO 6.4.A Identify the major structures of the human tongue, and list the five basic tastes perceived by humans.

Taste (*gustation*) is a chemical sense. Elevations on the tongue, called *papillae*, contain many *taste buds*, which in turn contain the taste receptors. The basic tastes include salty, sour, bitter, and sweet. *Umami*, associated with the taste of protein, has also been proposed as a basic taste, but this is debatable. In most protein-rich foods, umami is not detectable; also, responses to umami vary among individuals, and the main role of umami appears to be in the gut, after protein is eaten and digested.

LO 6.4.B Describe the basic pathway from smell receptors to the cerebral cortex.

Smell (*olfaction*) is also a chemical sense. No basic odors have been identified, and up to a thousand different receptor types exist. But researchers have discovered that distinct odors activate unique combinations of receptor types, and they have identified some of those combinations.

LO 6.4.C List the four basic skin senses that humans perceive.

The skin senses include touch (pressure), warmth, cold, pain, and variations such as itch and tickle. Receptors for some types of itching and a possible receptor for cold have been discovered.

LO 6.4.D Describe the principles of gate-control theory, and explain what phantom pain is and a novel way to treat it.

Pain has proven to be physiologically complicated, involving the release of several different chemicals and changes in both neurons and glial cells. According to the *gate-control theory*, the experience of pain depends on whether neural impulses get past a "gate" in the spinal cord and reach the brain; in addition, a matrix of neurons in the brain can generate pain even in the absence of signals from sensory neurons. A leading theory of *phantom pain* holds that it occurs when the brain rewires itself after amputation of a limb or removal of a body organ.

LO 6.4.E Discuss the two senses that allow us to monitor our internal environment.

Kinesthesis tells us where our body parts are located and *equilibrium* tells us the orientation of the body as a whole. Together, these two senses provide us with a feeling of physical embodiment.

Perceptual Powers

LO 6.5.A   Summarize the evidence suggesting that our perceptual powers are both inborn and dependent on experience.

Many fundamental perceptual skills are inborn or acquired shortly after birth. However, without certain experiences during *critical periods* early in life, cells in the nervous system deteriorate, change, or fail to form appropriate neural pathways, and perception is impaired.

LO 6.5.B   Discuss four psychological factors that influence how we perceive the world.

Psychological influences on perception include needs, beliefs, emotions, and expectations (which produce *perceptual sets*).

LO 6.5.C   Summarize the evidence both for and against subliminal perception.

In the laboratory, simple visual subliminal messages can influence certain behaviors and judgments, depending on a person's motivational state (e.g., thirst). However, in everyday life complex behaviors cannot be altered by the many kinds of "subliminal-perception" recordings on the market.

Chapter 6 Quiz

1. What are the two kinds of codes the human nervous system uses to turn sensory information into perceptions?
   a. Central and peripheral
   b. Direct and indirect
   c. Anatomical and functional
   d. Cogent and plangent

2. According to signal-detection theory, there are several ways for a person to respond in the presence or absence of a stimulus. What is it called when a person says a signal was present when it really wasn't?
   a. False alarm
   b. Miss
   c. Hit
   d. Correct rejection

3. Think about how your tongue feels resting inside your mouth. Focus on it. Think about the slight pressure it exerts on your teeth. Think about its size and shape. Chances are you weren't thinking about your own tongue 5 minutes ago, and chances are you also won't still be focused on the sensation of your tongue in your mouth 5 minutes from now. Your decreased responsiveness to the constant stimulation of your tongue is called
   a. Stimulus constancy
   b. Sensory deprivation
   c. Sensory adaptation
   d. Stimulus generalization

4. Greta is absorbed in watching her favorite television show. She startles as her roommate appears right by her side, shouting, "Greta! Didn't you hear the phone ringing for the last 5 minutes?!" Why was Greta oblivious to both her roommate's shouts and the obvious noise of the telephone?
   a. She was devoting selective attention to her television program.
   b. She was in a state of sensory deprivation.
   c. She had active mindblindness.
   d. She had an inattentive deficit.

5. The psychological dimension of hue corresponds to the physical properties of a light's _____, just as the psychological dimension of _____ corresponds to the physical property of a light's complexity.
   a. Frequency / intensity
   b. Intensity / brightness
   c. Brightness / saturation
   d. Wavelength / saturation

6. The optic nerve is composed of bundles of axons from
   a. Ganglion cells
   b. Bipolar neurons
   c. Rods
   d. Cones

7. Specialized cells that respond selectively to horizontal lines, vertical lines, or faces in the environment are all examples of
   a. Bipolar neurons
   b. Feature-detector cells
   c. Purkinje cells
   d. Dendritic emanations

8. Opponent-process theory holds that some cells in the visual system respond to blue/yellow, light/dark, and _____ wavelengths of light.
   a. Red/blue
   b. Orange/purple
   c. Red/green
   d. Yellow/green

9. Convergence and retinal disparity are both examples of _____ in depth and distance perception.
   a. Monocular cues
   b. Binocular cues
   c. Gestalt principles
   d. Perceptual constancies

10. Decibels are a means of measuring a sound wave's
    a. Pitch
    b. Frequency
    c. Complexity
    d. Intensity

11. The three tiny bones in a human's middle ear are called
    a. Anvil, hammer, and stirrup
    b. Drum, mallet, and latch
    c. Cilia, basia, and ancira
    d. Pathos, ethos, and logos

12. Alex is playing a complicated riff on his guitar, while Gary joins in and plays an equally complicated riff on the bass. You're able to follow the stream of notes that Alex is playing, and appreciate the melody, due to the Gestalt principle of
    a. Good form
    c. Similarity
    b. Closure
    d. Continuity

13. _____ are tiny bumps on the tongue, and they are lined with _____.
    a. Marjoram / origana
    c. Taste buds / afria
    b. Bulbs / cilia
    d. Papillae / taste buds

14. About how many smells can humans detect?
    a. 1,000
    c. 50,000
    b. 10,000
    d. 5,000

15. Human skin senses warmth, cold, pain, and
    a. Heat
    c. Pressure
    b. Irritation
    d. Puncture

16. When Georgie returned from his tour of duty in Afghanistan 4 years ago, he regrettably came back without a right arm. Even now, though, he feels tingling sensations and throbbing where his right arm *ought* to be. This experience is called
    a. Phantom pain
    c. Gate control
    b. Synchronous loss
    d. Asynchronous loss

17. Even with her eyes closed, Wanda is able to sense that her hands are hanging limp at her sides, she is leaning forward a bit, and her legs are bent slightly at the knees. Which sensory system allows her to perceive all of this?
    a. Equilibrium
    c. Orthobulbar
    b. Kinesthesis
    d. Prioncepsis

18. Which of the following is an example of an inborn perceptual ability?
    a. Infants can distinguish a human voice from other sounds in their environment.
    b. Newborns can focus their eyes on a bright object 6 feet away from them.
    c. Newborns will rub their own cheeks for tactile stimulation.
    d. Infants can detect subsonic audio frequencies.

19. Practitioners of sadomasochism report feeling pleasure during the experience of pain. Objectively, whipping and constriction should hurt, yet subjectively, the recipients feel they do not. Why is that?
    a. Gate-control theory predicts that pain gates will open and close rapidly during instances of "sought pain," whereas they will remain closed during "accidental pain."
    b. The body's "psychic immune system" inhibits levels of painful stimulation from becoming great enough to cause psychological distress.
    c. External observers always overestimate the extent to which pain hurts, compared to the people actually experiencing the pain.
    d. Emotions can influence our interpretations of sensory information; even painful stimuli might not be experienced as such.

20. Rather than studying for your upcoming Introductory Psychology exam, you decide instead to record your own voice reciting key terms from the chapter. Placing your playback device under your pillow while you sleep, your goal is to subliminally master the material without direct conscious effort. What grade do you predict you'll get on the exam, if this is the only study method you use?
    a. F
    c. B+
    b. A
    d. A−

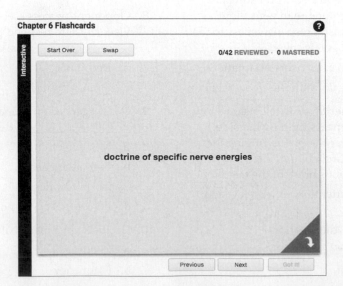

Chapter 7
Learning and Conditioning

 Listen to the Audio

Learning Objectives

LO 7.1.A List and explain each of the four key elements that make classical conditioning take place.

LO 7.1.B Discuss the basic principles of classical conditioning, including the extinction and recovery of a classically conditioned response, how higher-order conditioning takes place, and the process of stimulus generalization and discrimination.

LO 7.1.C Explain why the stimulus to be conditioned should precede the unconditioned stimulus in order for classical conditioning to take place.

LO 7.2.A Provide an example of how classical conditioning takes place in forming preferences.

221

LO 7.2.B Provide an example of how classical conditioning takes place in avoiding fearful stimuli, and describe how the process of counterconditioning takes place.

LO 7.2.C Describe how classical conditioning is involved in avoiding a food associated with aversive outcomes.

LO 7.2.D Describe how classical conditioning can affect reactions to medical treatments, including a patient's reaction to a placebo.

LO 7.3.A Discuss how Edward Thorndike's research served as the basis for operant conditioning.

LO 7.3.B Distinguish between reinforcement and punishment and between a positive and negative stimulus, and provide examples of positive and negative reinforcement and punishment and primary and secondary reinforcement and punishment.

LO 7.4.A Describe the basic principles of operant conditioning, including extinction and recovery, stimulus generalization and discrimination, schedules of learning and shaping, and some biological limits on learning.

LO 7.4.B Discuss some of the misconceptions surrounding the work and ideas of B. F. Skinner and, by extension, some of the misconceptions surrounding the general goals of operant conditioning.

LO 7.5.A List and discuss six reasons why punishment often fails to effectively change behavior.

LO 7.5.B Discuss reasons why rewards may backfire and not produce their intended results for behavior.

LO 7.6.A Define latent learning, and give an example of how it might work in the daily life of a college student.

LO 7.6.B Define observational learning, and give an example of how it might influence learning during childhood.

Ask questions . . . be willing to wonder

Why are so many people scared of snakes and spiders?

Why do efforts to crack down on wrongdoers often fail?

Is there anything wrong with paying kids to get good grades?

Why does playing violent video games make some people aggressive and others not?

It's January 1, a brand new year. The sins and lapses of the old year are behind you; the slate is clean and you're ready for a fresh start. Optimistically, you sit down to record your New Year's resolutions: to eat fewer sweets, study harder, control your temper, get more exercise, manage your spending, . . . (you can fill in the rest). How likely are you to achieve these goals? Within weeks, days, or even hours, many people find themselves reverting to their old habits ("Well, maybe just one *small* dish of double chocolate ice cream"). They may decide that trying to mend their ways is pointless because they lack the willpower, brains, or courage to do it. In this chapter, however, we will see that, in fact, willpower, brains, and courage often have little to do with the ability to change your ways.

People do not want to fix just their own behavior, of course; they are forever trying to improve or fix other people's behavior as well. We imprison criminals, spank children, shout at spouses, give the finger to a driver who cuts us off, and impose zero-tolerance policies for the slightest infraction of a rule. On the positive side, we give children gold stars for good work, give parents bumper stickers that praise their children's successes, give bonuses to employees, and give out trophies for top performance. Do any of these efforts get the results we hope for? Well, yes and no. After you understand the laws of *learning*, the topic of this chapter, you will realize that behavior, whether it's your own or other people's, *can* change for the better—and you will also understand why often it does not.

Research on learning has been heavily influenced by *behaviorism*, the school of psychology that accounts for behavior in terms of observable acts and events. Unlike the cognitive approach, a behavioral perspective emphasizes the influence of prior experience on current behavior, rather than thoughts or other aspects of the "mind." Behaviorists focus on *conditioning*, which involves associations among environmental stimuli and behavior. As we will see, they have shown that two types of conditioning, *classical conditioning* and *operant conditioning*, can explain a great deal of behavior both in animals and in people.

Classical Conditioning

We will begin our exploration of learning with a look at classical conditioning. Watch *Classical Conditioning: An Involuntary Response* to get an overview of the principles and applications we'll be discussing.

New Reflexes from Old

LO 7.1.A List and explain each of the four key elements that make classical conditioning take place.

At the turn of the 20th century, the great Russian physiologist Ivan Pavlov (1849–1936) was studying salivation in dogs as part of a research program on digestion. One of his procedures was to make a surgical opening in a dog's cheek and insert a tube that conducted saliva away from the animal's salivary gland so that the saliva could be measured. To stimulate the reflexive flow of saliva, Pavlov placed meat powder or other food in the dog's mouth (see Figure 7.1).

Pavlov was a truly dedicated scientific observer. Many years later, as he lay dying, he even dictated his sensations for posterity! And he instilled in his students and assistants the same passion for detail. During his salivation studies, one of the assistants noticed something that most people would have overlooked or dismissed as trivial. After a dog had been brought to the laboratory a few times, it would start to salivate *before* the food was placed in its mouth. The sight or smell of the food, the dish in which the food was kept, and even the sight of the person who delivered the food were enough to start the dog's mouth watering. These new salivary responses clearly were not inborn, so they must have been acquired through experience.

Figure 7.1 Pavlov's Method

The photo shows Ivan Pavlov (in the white beard), flanked by his students and a canine subject. The drawing depicts an apparatus similar to the one he used; saliva from a dog's cheek flowed down a tube and was measured by the movement of a needle on a revolving drum.

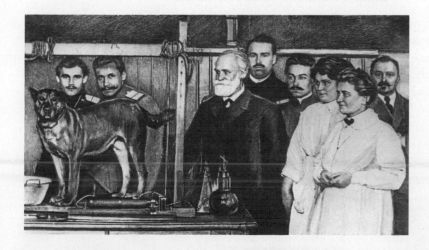

learning

A relatively permanent change in behavior (or behavioral potential) due to experience.

conditioning

A basic kind of learning that involves associations among environmental stimuli and an organism's behavior.

unconditioned stimulus (US)

The classical-conditioning term for a stimulus that already elicits a certain response without additional learning.

unconditioned response (UR)

The classical-conditioning term for a response elicited by an unconditioned stimulus.

conditioned stimulus (CS)

The classical-conditioning term for an initially neutral stimulus that comes to elicit a conditioned response after being associated with an unconditioned stimulus.

conditioned response (CR)

The classical-conditioning term for a response that is elicited by a conditioned stimulus; it occurs after the conditioned stimulus is associated with an unconditioned stimulus.

classical conditioning

The process by which a previously neutral stimulus becomes associated with a stimulus that already elicits a response and, in turn, acquires the capacity to elicit a similar or related response. Also called *Pavlovian* or *respondent conditioning*.

At first, Pavlov treated the dog's drooling as just an annoying secretion. But he quickly realized that his assistant had stumbled onto an important phenomenon, one that Pavlov came to believe was the basis of most **learning** in human beings and other animals (Pavlov, 1927). He called that phenomenon a "conditional" reflex because it depended on environmental conditions. Later, an error in the translation of his writings transformed "conditional" into "conditioned," the word most commonly used today. Such **conditioning** came to refer to a basic kind of learning based on association.

Pavlov soon dropped what he had been doing and turned to the study of conditioned reflexes, to which he devoted the last three decades of his life. Why were his dogs salivating to things other than food? Pavlov initially speculated about what his dogs might be thinking and feeling when they drooled before getting their food. Was the doggy equivalent of "Oh boy, this means chow time" going through their minds? He soon decided, however, that such speculation was pointless. Instead, he focused on analyzing the environment in which the conditioned reflex arose.

The original salivary reflex, according to Pavlov, consisted of an **unconditioned stimulus (US)**, food in the dog's mouth, and an **unconditioned response (UR)**, salivation. By an unconditioned stimulus, Pavlov meant a thing or event that already produces a certain response without additional learning. By an unconditioned response, he meant the response that is produced:

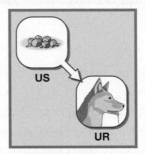

In Pavlov's lab, when some neutral stimulus such as the dish—a stimulus that did not typically cause the dog to salivate—was regularly paired with food, the dog learned to associate the dish and the food. As a result, the dish alone acquired the power to make the dog salivate:

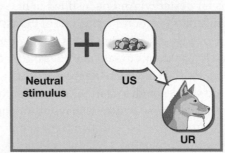

More generally, as a neutral stimulus and US become associated, the neutral stimulus becomes a **conditioned stimulus (CS)**. The CS then has the capacity to elicit a learned or **conditioned response (CR)** that is usually similar or related to the original, unlearned one. In Pavlov's laboratory, the sight of the food dish, which had not previously elicited salivation, became a CS for salivation:

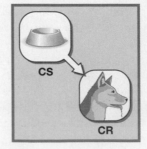

Review 7.1

Classical Conditioning Terms: Part 1

	Definition
Unconditioned stimulus (US)	A stimulus that already elicits a certain response without additional learning
Unconditioned response (UR)	A response elicited by an unconditioned stimulus
Conditioned stimulus (CS)	An initially neutral stimulus that comes to elicit a conditioned response after being associated with an unconditioned stimulus
Conditioned response (CR)	A response that is elicited by a conditioned stimulus; it occurs after the conditioned stimulus is associated with an unconditioned stimulus

The procedure by which a previously neutral stimulus becomes a conditioned stimulus eventually became known as **classical conditioning** and is sometimes also called *Pavlovian* or *respondent conditioning*. Pavlov and his students went on to show that all sorts of things can become conditioned stimuli for salivation if they are paired with food: the ticking of a metronome, the musical tone of a bell, the vibrating sound of a buzzer, a touch on the leg, even a pinprick or an electric shock.

Principles of Classical Conditioning

LO 7.1.B Discuss the basic principles of classical conditioning, including the extinction and recovery of a classically conditioned response, how higher-order conditioning takes place, and the process of stimulus generalization and discrimination.

Classical conditioning occurs in all species, from one-celled amoebas to *Homo sapiens*. Many responses besides salivation have been classically conditioned, including heartbeat, blood pressure, alertness, hunger, and sexual arousal. In the laboratory, the optimal interval between the presentation of the neutral stimulus and the presentation of the US is often quite short, sometimes less than a second. Let's look more closely at some of classical conditioning's other important features: extinction, higher-order conditioning, and stimulus generalization and discrimination.

EXTINCTION Conditioned responses can persist for months or years. But if a conditioned stimulus is repeatedly presented without the unconditioned stimulus, the conditioned response will weaken and may eventually disappear, a process known as **extinction** (see Figure 7.2). Suppose that you train your dog Milo to salivate to the sound of a bell, but then you ring the bell every 5 minutes and do *not* follow it with food. Milo will salivate less and less to the bell and will soon stop salivating altogether; salivation will have been extinguished. Extinction, however, is not the same as unlearning. If you come back the next day and ring the bell, Milo may salivate again for a few trials, although the response will probably be weaker. The reappearance of the response, called **spontaneous recovery**, explains why completely eliminating a conditioned response often requires more than one extinction session.

HIGHER-ORDER CONDITIONING Sometimes a neutral stimulus can become a conditioned stimulus by being paired with an already established CS, a procedure known as **higher-order conditioning**. Say Milo has learned to salivate to the sight of his food dish. Now you flash a bright light before presenting the dish. With repeated pairings of the light and the dish, Milo may learn to salivate to the light. The procedure for higher-order conditioning is illustrated in Figure 7.3.

extinction

The weakening and eventual disappearance of a learned response; in classical conditioning, it occurs when the conditioned stimulus is no longer paired with the unconditioned stimulus.

spontaneous recovery

The reappearance of a learned response after its apparent extinction.

higher-order conditioning

In classical conditioning, a procedure in which a neutral stimulus becomes a conditioned stimulus through association with an already established conditioned stimulus.

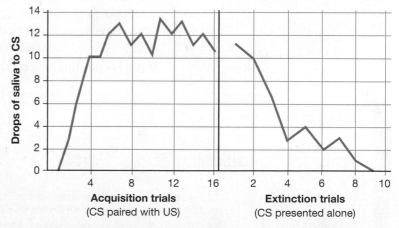

Figure 7.2 Acquisition and Extinction of a Salivary Response

A neutral stimulus that is consistently followed by an unconditioned stimulus for salivation will become a conditioned stimulus for salivation (left side of graph). But when this conditioned stimulus is then repeatedly presented without the unconditioned stimulus, the conditioned salivary response will weaken and eventually disappear; it has been extinguished.

Figure 7.3 Higher-Order Conditioning

In this illustration of higher-order conditioning, the food dish is a previously conditioned stimulus for salivation (left). When the light, a neutral stimulus, is paired with the dish (center), the light also becomes a conditioned stimulus for salivation (right).

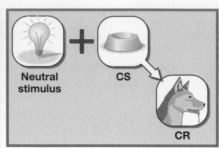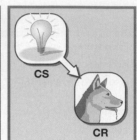

stimulus generalization

After conditioning, the tendency to respond to a stimulus that resembles one involved in the original conditioning; in classical conditioning, it occurs when a stimulus that resembles the CS elicits the CR.

stimulus discrimination

The tendency to respond differently to two or more similar stimuli; in classical conditioning, it occurs when a stimulus similar to the CS fails to evoke the CR.

Higher-order conditioning may explain why some words trigger emotional responses in us—why they can inflame us to anger or evoke warm, sentimental feelings. When words are paired with objects or other words that already elicit some emotional response, they too may come to elicit that response (Staats & Staats, 1957). A child may learn a positive response to the word *birthday* because of its association with gifts and attention. Conversely, the child may learn a negative response to ethnic or national labels if the labels are paired with words that the child has already learned are disagreeable, such as *dumb* or *dirty*. Higher-order conditioning, in other words, may contribute to the formation of prejudices.

STIMULUS GENERALIZATION AND DISCRIMINATION After a stimulus becomes a conditioned stimulus for some response, similar stimuli may produce a similar reaction, a phenomenon known as **stimulus generalization**. If you condition your patient pooch Milo to salivate to middle C on the piano, Milo may also salivate to D, which is one tone above C, even though you did not pair D with food. Stimulus generalization is described nicely by an old English proverb: "He who hath been bitten by a snake fears a rope."

The mirror image of stimulus generalization is **stimulus discrimination**, in which *different* responses are made to stimuli that resemble the conditioned stimulus in some way. Suppose that you have conditioned Milo to salivate to middle C on the piano by repeatedly pairing the sound with food. Now you play middle C on a guitar, *without* following it by food (but you continue to follow C on the piano by food). Eventually, Milo will learn to salivate to a C on the piano and not to salivate to the same note on the guitar; that is, he will discriminate between the two sounds. If you keep at this long enough, you could train Milo to be a pretty discriminating drooler!

Review 7.2

Classical Conditioning Terms: Part 2

Extinction	The weakening and eventual disappearance of a learned response; in classical conditioning, it occurs when the conditioned stimulus is no longer paired with the unconditioned stimulus.
Spontaneous recovery	The reappearance of a learned response after its apparent extinction
Higher-order conditioning	A procedure in which a neutral stimulus becomes a conditioned stimulus through association with an already established conditioned stimulus.
Stimulus generalization	After conditioning, the tendency to respond to a stimulus that resembles one involved in the original conditioning; in classical conditioning, it occurs when a stimulus that resembles the CS elicits the CR
Stimulus discrimination	The tendency to respond differently to two or more similar stimuli; in classical conditioning, it occurs when a stimulus similar to the CS fails to evoke the CR.

What Is Actually Learned in Classical Conditioning?

LO 7.1.C Explain why the stimulus to be conditioned should precede the unconditioned stimulus in order for classical conditioning to take place.

A critical feature of classical conditioning is that the animal or person learns to associate stimuli, rather than learning to associate a stimulus with a response. Milo will learn to salivate to the bell because he has learned to associate the bell with food, not (as is commonly thought) because he has learned to associate the bell with salivating. For classical conditioning to be most effective, the stimulus to be conditioned should *precede* the unconditioned stimulus rather than follow it or occur simultaneously with it. This makes sense because in classical conditioning the conditioned stimulus becomes a *signal* for the unconditioned stimulus. Classical conditioning is in fact an evolutionary adaptation, one that enables the organism to anticipate and prepare for a biologically important event that is about to happen. In Pavlov's studies, for instance, a bell, buzzer, or other stimulus was a signal that meat was coming, and the dog's salivation was preparation for digesting food. Today, therefore, many psychologists contend that what an animal or person actually learns in classical conditioning is not merely an association between two paired stimuli that occur close together in time, but rather *information* conveyed by one stimulus about another: "If a tone sounds, food is likely to follow."

This view is supported by the research of Robert Rescorla (1988, 2008), who showed, in a series of imaginative studies, that the mere pairing of an unconditioned stimulus and a neutral stimulus is not enough to produce learning. To become a conditioned stimulus, the neutral stimulus must reliably signal, or *predict*, the unconditioned stimulus. If food occurs just as often *without* a preceding tone as with it, the tone is unlikely to become a conditioned stimulus for salivation because the tone does not provide any information about the probability of getting food. Think of it this way: If every phone call you got brought bad news that made your heart race, your heart might soon start pounding every time the phone rang—a conditioned response. Ordinarily, though, upsetting calls occur randomly among a far greater number of routine ones. The ringtone may sometimes be paired with bad news, but it doesn't always signal disaster, so no conditioned heart-rate response occurs.

Rescorla concluded that "Pavlovian conditioning is not a stupid process by which the organism willy-nilly forms associations between any two stimuli that happen to co-occur. Rather, the organism is better seen as an information seeker using logical and perceptual relations among events, along with its own preconceptions, to form a sophisticated representation of its world." Not all learning theorists agree; an orthodox behaviorist would say that it is silly to talk about the preconceptions of a rat. The important point, however, is that concepts such as "information seeking," "preconceptions," and "representations of the world" open the door to a more cognitive view of classical conditioning.

Try out your behavioral skills by conditioning an eyeblink response in a willing friend, using classical-conditioning procedures. You will need a drinking straw and something to make a ringing sound; a spoon tapped on a water glass works well. Tell your friend that you are going to use the straw to blow air in his or her eye, but do not say why. Immediately before each puff of air, make the ringing sound. Repeat this procedure 10 times. Then make the ringing sound but *don't* puff. Your friend will probably blink anyway, and may continue to do so for one or two more repetitions of the sound before the response extinguishes. Can you identify the US, the UR, the CS, and the CR in this exercise?

JOURNAL PROMPT 7.1

Thinking Critically—Examine the Evidence: Think of a detrimental association you've learned through classical conditioning. For example, maybe you like to study while laying on your bed. However, your bed is associated with drowsiness and sleep, and therefore when you try to study, all that really happens is that you feel tired and doze off. Identify the US, UR, CS, and CR in your example, and describe how extinction might be used to "unlearn" that association.

Quiz for Module 7.1

1. Five-year-old Katrina is watching a storm from her window. A huge bolt of lightning is followed by a tremendous thunderclap, and Katrina jumps at the noise. In the language of classical conditioning, the sound of thunder is the

   a. UR
   b. US
   c. CS
   d. CR

2. Five-year-old Katrina is watching a storm from her window. A huge bolt of lightning is followed by a tremendous thunderclap, and Katrina jumps at the noise. This happens several more times. There is a brief lull and then another lightning bolt. Katrina jumps in response to the bolt. In classical conditioning terms, Katrina's reaction is the

   a. CS
   b. UR
   c. US
   d. CR

3. Five-year-old Katrina is watching a storm from her window. A huge bolt of lightning is followed by a tremendous thunderclap, and Katrina jumps at the noise. This happens several more times. There is a brief lull and then another lightning bolt. Katrina jumps in response to the bolt. In classical conditioning terms, the sight of the lightning bolt is the

   a. US
   b. UR

   c. CS
   d. CR

4. When a previously learned response reappears even after it was thought to have been distinguished, classical conditioning theorists say that _____ has occurred.

   a. De-extinction
   b. Unexpected regeneration
   c. Anomalous resurgence
   d. Spontaneous recovery

5. Why should a neutral stimulus precede an unconditioned stimulus in order for classical conditioning to be successful?

   a. The neutral stimulus signals that the unconditioned stimulus is coming; eventually the neutral stimulus becomes the conditioned stimulus.

   b. The neutral stimulus "wipes the learning slate clean," so to speak, making the impact of the unconditioned stimulus stronger.

   c. In order for a neutral stimulus to become paired with a conditioned stimulus, it must first be paired with an unconditioned stimulus.

   d. The neutral stimulus elicits the unconditioned response, but the unconditioned stimulus needs to be present at first.

Classical Conditioning in Real Life

If a dog can learn to salivate to the ringing of a bell, so can you. In fact, you probably have learned to salivate to the sound of a lunch bell, the phrase *hot fudge sundae*, and "mouth-watering" pictures of food. But classical conditioning affects us every day in many other ways.

Learning to Like

LO 7.2.A Provide an example of how classical conditioning takes place in forming preferences.

One of the first psychologists to recognize the real-life implications of Pavlovian theory was John B. Watson, who founded American **behaviorism** and enthusiastically promoted Pavlov's ideas. Watson believed that the whole rich array of human emotion and behavior could be accounted for by conditioning principles. He even went so far as to claim that we learn to love another person when that person is paired with stroking and cuddling. Most psychologists, and nonpsychologists too, think Watson was wrong about love, which is a lot more complicated than he thought. But he was right about the power of classical conditioning to affect our emotions, preferences, and tastes.

behaviorism

An approach to psychology that emphasizes the study of observable behavior and the role of the environment and prior experience as determinants of behavior.

Classical conditioning plays a big role in our emotional responses to objects, people, symbols, events, and places. It can explain why sentimental feelings sweep over us when we see a school mascot, a national flag, or the logo of the Olympic Games. These objects have been associated in the past with positive feelings:

 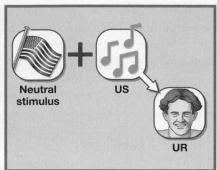 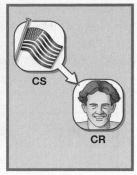

Many advertising techniques take advantage of classical conditioning's role in emotional responses. When you see ads, notice how many of them pair a product with music the advertiser thinks you'll like, with good-looking people, with idyllic scenery, or with celebrities you admire or think are funny. In classical-conditioning terms, the music, scenery, attractive person, or celebrity is an unconditioned stimulus for internal responses associated with pleasure, and the advertiser hopes that the product in the ad will become a conditioned stimulus, evoking similar responses in you.

Learning to Fear

LO 7.2.B Provide an example of how classical conditioning takes place in avoiding fearful stimuli, and describe how the process of counterconditioning takes place.

Positive emotions are not the only ones that can be classically conditioned; so can dislikes and fears. A person can learn to fear just about anything if it is paired with something that elicits pain, surprise, or embarrassment. Human beings, however, are biologically primed or "prepared" to acquire some kinds of fears more readily than others. It is far easier to establish a conditioned fear of spiders, snakes, and heights than of butterflies, flowers, and toasters. The former can be dangerous to your health, so in the process of evolution, human beings acquired a tendency to learn quickly to be wary of them and to retain this fear (LoBue & DeLoache, 2008, 2011; Öhman & Mineka, 2001). Evolution may also have instilled in humans a readiness to learn to fear unfamiliar members of groups other than their own, a tendency that could contribute to the emotional underpinnings of prejudice (Maia, 2009; Navarrete et al., 2009; Olsson et al., 2005).

When fear of an object or situation becomes irrational and interferes with normal activities, it qualifies as a *phobia*. To demonstrate how a phobia might be learned, John Watson and Rosalie Rayner (1920/2000) deliberately established a rat phobia in an 11-month-old boy named Albert. Their goal was to demonstrate how an inborn reaction of fear could transfer to a wide range of stimuli; today, we call this *stimulus generalization*. They also wanted to demonstrate that adult emotional responses, such as specific fears, could originate in early childhood. The research procedures used by Watson and Rayner had some flaws, and for ethical reasons, no psychologist today would attempt to do such a thing to a child. Nevertheless, the study's main conclusion, that fears can be conditioned, is still well accepted.

"Little Albert" was a placid child who rarely cried. (Watson and Rayner deliberately chose such a child because they thought their demonstration would do him relatively little harm.) When Watson and Rayner gave Albert a live, furry rat to play with, he showed no fear; in fact, he was delighted. The same was true when they showed him a variety of other objects, including a rabbit and some cotton wool. However, like most children, Albert was innately afraid of loud noises. When the researchers made a loud noise behind his head by striking a steel bar with a hammer, he would jump and fall sideways onto the mattress where he was sitting. The noise made by the hammer was an unconditioned stimulus for the unconditioned response of fear.

Having established that Albert liked rats, Watson and Rayner set about teaching him to fear them. Again they offered him a rat, but this time, as he reached for it, one of the researchers struck the steel bar. Startled, Albert fell onto the mattress. A week later, they repeated this procedure several times. Albert began to whimper and tremble. Finally, they held out the rat to him without making the noise. Albert fell over, cried, and crawled away so quickly that he almost reached the edge of the table he was sitting on before an adult caught him; the rat had become a conditioned stimulus for fear:

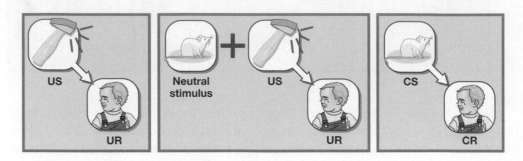

Tests done a few days later showed that Albert's fear had generalized to other hairy or furry objects, including a white rabbit, cotton wool, a Santa Claus mask, and even John Watson's hair.

Unfortunately, Watson and Rayner lost access to Little Albert, so we do not know how long the child's fears lasted. (Who Albert actually was has also been a matter of some debate, leading to a mix of speculation and investigation regarding his identity and ultimate fate [Beck & Irons, 2011; Fridlund et al., 2012; Powell et al., 2014].) Furthermore, because the study ended early, Watson and Rayner had no opportunity to reverse the conditioning.

However, Watson and Mary Cover Jones did reverse another child's conditioned fear—one that was, as Watson put it, "home grown" rather than psychologist-induced (Jones, 1924). A 3-year-old named Peter was deathly afraid of rabbits. To reverse Peter's fear, Watson and Jones used a method called **counterconditioning**, in which a conditioned stimulus is paired with some other stimulus that elicits a response incompatible with the unwanted response. Counterconditioning probably does not eliminate prior learning, but instead leads to new learning that supplants or overrides old learning. In this case, the rabbit (the CS) was paired with a snack of milk and crackers, and the snack produced pleasant feelings that were incompatible with the conditioned response of fear. At first, Watson and Jones kept the rabbit some distance from Peter, so that his fear would remain at a low level. Otherwise, Peter might have learned to fear milk and crackers! Then gradually, over several days, they brought the rabbit closer and closer. Eventually, Peter learned to like rabbits:

counterconditioning

In classical conditioning, the process of pairing a conditioned stimulus with a stimulus that elicits a response that is incompatible with an unwanted conditioned response.

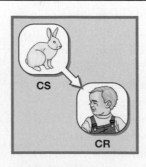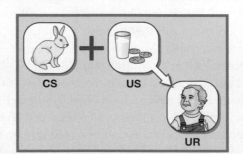

Peter was even able to sit with the rabbit in his lap, playing with it with one hand while he ate with the other. A variation of this procedure, called *systematic desensitization*, was later devised for treating phobias in adults.

Back when John Watson was using counterconditioning to help young Peter overcome his fear of rabbits, he focused on the observable associations between unconditioned and conditioned stimuli and responses. Techniques for understanding the biological basis of classical conditioning were limited. But today, technology and a better understanding of the brain are letting scientists explore methods for helping people overcome debilitating conditioned fears in ways that Watson could scarcely have imagined.

The amygdala plays a central role in the conditioning of fear, in part because of a receptor for the neurotransmitter glutamate. Giving rats a drug that blocks this receptor prevents extinction of a conditioned fear, whereas giving a drug that enhances the receptor's activity speeds up extinction (Schmidt et al., 2015; Walker et al., 2002). Inspired by these results, scientists set out to discover whether the same receptor-enhancing drug, which is safe in humans, could help people with a phobic fear of heights (Davis et al., 2005). Using a double-blind procedure, they gave the drug to 15 people with that phobia and a placebo to 15 others. All participants then underwent two therapy sessions in which they donned virtual-reality goggles and "rode" a glass elevator to progressively higher floors in a virtual hotel—an incredibly scary thing to do if you're terrified of heights. They could also "walk" out on a bridge and look down on a fountain in the hotel lobby. During each session, and again at 1-week and 3-month follow-up sessions, the participants rated their discomfort at each "floor." Combining the therapy with the drug reduced symptoms far more than combining it with the placebo. Furthermore, in their everyday lives, people who got the drug were less likely than the controls to avoid heights.

Such research helps us to understand the biological mechanisms that underlie our fears, and the principles of behaviorism that may help us control and even overcome them. Learn more about these important topics by watching the video *Learning to Overcome Phobias*.

Accounting for Taste

LO 7.2.C   Describe how classical conditioning is involved in avoiding a food associated with aversive outcomes.

Classical conditioning can also explain learned reactions to many foods and odors. In the laboratory, behavioral scientists have taught animals to dislike particular foods or odors by pairing them with drugs that cause nausea or other unpleasant symptoms. One team trained slugs to associate the smell of carrots, which slugs normally like, with a bitter-tasting chemical they detest. Soon the slugs were avoiding the smell of carrots. The researchers then demonstrated higher-order conditioning by pairing the smell of carrots with the smell of potato. Sure enough, the slugs began to avoid the smell of potato as well (Sahley, Rudy, & Gelperin, 1981).

Many people have learned to dislike a food after eating it and then falling ill, even when the two events were unrelated. The food, previously a neutral stimulus, becomes a conditioned stimulus for nausea or other symptoms produced by the illness. Psychologist

Whether we say "yuck" or "yum" to a food may depend on a past experience involving classical conditioning.

Martin Seligman once told how he himself was conditioned to hate béarnaise sauce. One night, shortly after he and his wife ate a delicious filet mignon with béarnaise sauce, he came down with the flu. Naturally, he felt wretched. His misery had nothing to do with the béarnaise sauce, of course, yet the next time he tried it, he found to his annoyance that he disliked the taste (Seligman & Hager, 1972).

Notice that unlike conditioning in the laboratory, Seligman's aversion to the sauce occurred after only one pairing of the sauce with illness and with a considerable delay between the conditioned and unconditioned stimuli. Moreover, Seligman's wife did not become a conditioned stimulus for nausea, and neither did his dinner plate or the waiter, even though they also had been paired with illness. Why? In earlier work with rats, John Garcia and Robert Koelling (1966) had provided the answer: the existence of a greater biological readiness to associate sickness with taste than with sights or sounds (the "Garcia effect"). Like the tendency to acquire certain fears, this biological tendency probably evolved because it enhanced survival: Eating bad food is more likely to be followed by illness and death than are particular sights or sounds.

Psychologists have taken advantage of this phenomenon to develop humane ways of discouraging predators from preying on livestock, using conditioned taste aversions instead of traps and poisons. In one classic approach, researchers laced sheep meat with a nausea-inducing chemical; after eating it just one or two times, coyotes and wolves still ran up to lambs, but instead of attacking, they retreated, hid, and vomited. They had developed a conditioned aversion to sheep (Dingfelder, 2010; Gustavson et al., 1974). Similar techniques have been used to control other predators—for example, to deter raccoons from killing chickens, and ravens and crows from eating crane eggs (Garcia & Gustavson, 1997).

Reacting to Medical Treatments

LO 7.2.D Describe how classical conditioning can affect reactions to medical treatments, including a patient's reaction to a placebo.

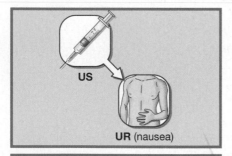

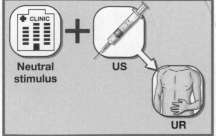

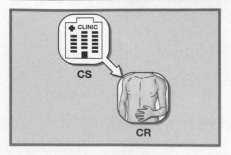

Because of classical conditioning, medical treatments can create unexpected misery or relief from symptoms for reasons that are entirely unrelated to the treatment itself. Many patients know that unpleasant reactions to a treatment can generalize to a wide range of other stimuli. This is a particular problem for cancer patients. The nausea and vomiting resulting from chemotherapy often generalize to the place where the therapy takes place, the waiting room, the sound of a nurse's voice, or the smell of rubbing alcohol. The drug treatment is an unconditioned stimulus for nausea and vomiting, and through association, the other previously neutral stimuli become conditioned stimuli for these responses. Even *mental images* of the sights and smells of the clinic can become conditioned stimuli for nausea (Dadds et al., 1997; Redd et al., 1993):

Some cancer patients also acquire a classically conditioned anxiety response to anything associated with their chemotherapy (Jacobsen et al., 1995). However, patients may have *reduced* pain and anxiety when they receive *placebos*, pills and injections that have no active ingredients or treatments that have no direct physical effect on the problem. Placebos can be amazingly powerful, especially when they take the form of an injection, a large pill, or a pill with a brand name (Benedetti & Levi-Montalcini, 2001). In fact, placebos can act on the same neural pathways in the brain that real medicines do (Price, Finniss, & Benedetti, 2008).

Why do placebos work? Cognitive psychologists emphasize the role of expectations, at least in humans; expectations of getting better may reduce anxiety, and that reduction may have a positive effect on the immune system. Such expectations may also cause us to act in ways that produce the outcome we hope for (Michael, Garry, & Kirsch, 2012). But behaviorists emphasize conditioning: The doctor's white coat, the doctor's office, and pills or injections all become conditioned stimuli for relief from symptoms because these stimuli have been associated in the past with *real* drugs (Ader, 2000). The real drugs are the unconditioned stimuli, and the relief they bring is the unconditioned response. Placebos acquire the ability to elicit similar reactions, thereby becoming conditioned stimuli.

The expectancy explanation of placebo effects and the classical-conditioning explanation are not mutually exclusive (Kirsch, 2004; Stewart-Williams & Podd, 2004). As we saw earlier, many behaviorists now accept the view that classical conditioning itself involves the expectation that the conditioned stimulus will be followed by the unconditioned stimulus. Thus, at least some classically conditioned placebo effects may involve the patient's expectations. In fact, the patient's previous conditioning history may be what created those expectations to begin with.

JOURNAL PROMPT 7.2

Thinking Critically—Ask Questions, Be Willing to Wonder: Associating a neutral stimulus with positive feelings capitalizes on the principles of classical conditioning. For example, a used-car lot may offer free hot dogs and balloons for kids during a weekend sales event, or an ad for toothpaste may show beautiful people with perfect teeth smiling widely. Think of three distinct examples in which an advertiser has used this technique in the hopes of increasing sales. Can you identify the classical conditioning principles at work in each of your examples?

Quiz for Module 7.2

1. Professor Sudovest brings a treat for her students every time she lectures; sometimes candy, sometimes cash, sometimes extra points on a quiz. Although she's a terrible lecturer, students always come to class and always give her high course evaluations. According to the principles of classical conditioning, why is that?

   a. The treats are a conditioned stimulus that leads to an unconditioned response; in this case, the favorable attitudes toward Professor Sudovest.

   b. Students have previously been conditioned to dislike their classes, so Professor Sudovest is extinguishing that behavior by providing treats.

   c. Students associate the presence of Professor Sudovest with the presence of treats; they like the treats, so by association they also like her.

   d. The treats are a conditioned stimulus that produces stimulus discrimination; in this case, responding to the favorability of the treats.

2. Little Amanda is afraid of the bath, so her father puts just a little water in the tub and gives Amanda a lollipop to suck on while she is being washed. Soon Amanda loses her fear of the bath. What classical conditioning technique has her father used?

   a. Counterconditioning

   b. Stimulus generalization

   c. Pre-extinction

   d. Spontaneous discrimination

3. Edgar wants his toddler son Craig to eat healthy foods and avoid junk food. Each time they're driving in the car and they pass a fast-food restaurant, Edgar screams at the top of his lungs in a short burst of terrible noise, startling Craig and making him cry. Not surprisingly, Craig grows up with an aversion to junk food. What is the conditioned stimulus in this example?

   a. Craig's avoidance of junk food

   b. Edgar's screams

   c. Craig's crying

   d. The presence of a fast-food restaurant

4. Barney eats at Shawarma Palace one night, and feasts on plates of pita, hummus, tahini, and tabouleh. Watching the news later that night, he sees that Shawarma Palace has been closed down by the health inspector, and Barney's violent episodes of gastric distress confirm the reasons why. Several months later, when friends invite him to Falafel Kingdom for dinner, Barney immediately declines the invitation. What has happened to poor Barney?

   a. Stimulus discrimination is at work; Barney has learned to discriminate against a particular type of cuisine.

   b. Barney showed evidence of spontaneous recovery after his food aversion had been extinguished.

   c. The gut-wracking outcomes of his illness were associated with a particular type of food, leading to a learned taste aversion for that food.

   d. Higher-order conditioning has made the sight of food become associated with a particular type of food, leading to an aversive reaction.

5. Chemotherapy often produces nausea and vomiting for cancer patients undergoing that treatment. Over time, patients associate the administration room, the sight of white uniforms, and the style of the waiting room chairs with that unpleasant experience. Just showing up for treatment and experiencing all those sensations can lead to the onset of nausea. In this example, the unconditioned stimulus is

   a. The chemicals used in chemotherapy

   b. The sight of the administration room and all the elements in it

   c. Feelings of nausea due to the environmental setting

   d. Feelings of nausea due to the chemotherapy

Operant Conditioning

Classical conditioning relies on the association between stimuli to form the basis of learning, and its applicability to both human and nonhuman learning situations is well documented. A different kind of association, however, forms the basis for a second type of learning; let's look at that approach now.

The Birth of Radical Behaviorism

operant conditioning

The process by which a response becomes more likely to occur or less so, depending on its consequences.

LO 7.3.A Discuss how Edward Thorndike's research served as the basis for operant conditioning.

At the end of the 19th century, in the first known scientific study of anger, G. Stanley Hall (1899) asked people to describe angry episodes they had experienced or observed. One person told of a 3-year-old girl who broke out in seemingly uncontrollable sobs when she was kept home from a ride. In the middle of her outburst, the child suddenly stopped and asked her nanny in a perfectly calm voice if her father was in. Told no, and realizing that he was not around to put a stop to her tantrum, she immediately resumed her sobbing.

Children, of course, cry for many valid reasons—pain, discomfort, fear, illness, fatigue—and these cries deserve our sympathy and attention. The child in Hall's study, however, was crying because she had learned from prior experience that an outburst of sobbing would pay off by bringing her attention and possibly the ride she wanted. Her tantrum illustrates one of the most basic laws of learning: *Behavior becomes more likely or less likely depending on its consequences.*

This principle is at the heart of **operant conditioning** (also called *instrumental conditioning*), the second type of conditioning studied by behaviorists. In classical conditioning, it does not matter whether an animal's or person's behavior has consequences. In Pavlov's procedure, the dog learned an association between two events that were not under its control (e.g., a tone and the delivery of food) and the animal got food regardless of whether it salivated. But in operant conditioning, the organism's response (such as the little girl's sobbing) *operates*—produces effects—on the environment. These effects, in turn, influence whether the response will occur again.

Thus, whereas the central feature of classical conditioning is an association between stimuli (the neutral stimulus and the unconditioned stimulus), in operant conditioning the central feature is an association between a stimulus (consequence) and a response. Classical conditioning and operant conditioning also tend to differ in the types of responses they involve. In classical conditioning, the response is typically reflexive, an automatic reaction to something happening in the environment, such as the sight of food or the sound of a bell. Generally, responses in operant conditioning are complex and are not reflexive—for instance, riding a bicycle, writing a letter, climbing a mountain, . . . or throwing a tantrum.

Edward Thorndike (1898) set the stage for operant conditioning research by observing cats as they tried to escape from a complex "puzzle box" to reach a scrap of fish located just outside the box. At first, the cat would scratch, bite, or swat at parts of the box in an unorganized way. Then, after a few minutes, it would chance on the successful response (loosening a bolt, pulling a string, or hitting a button) and rush out to get the reward. Placed in the box again, the cat now took a little less time to escape, and after several trials, the animal immediately made the correct response. According to Thorndike, this response had been "stamped in" by the satisfying result of getting the food. In contrast, annoying or unsatisfying results "stamped out" behavior. Behavior, said Thorndike, is controlled by its consequences.

This general principle was elaborated and extended to more complex forms of behavior by B. F. (Burrhus Frederic) Skinner. Skinner called his approach "radical behaviorism" to distinguish it from the behaviorism of John Watson, who emphasized classical conditioning. Skinner argued that to understand behavior, we should focus on the external causes of an action and the action's consequences. He avoided terms that Thorndike used, such as "satisfying" and "annoying," which reflect assumptions about what an organism internally feels and wants. To explain behavior, he said, we should look outside the animal or person, not inside.

The Consequences of Behavior

LO 7.3.B Distinguish between reinforcement and punishment and between a positive and negative stimulus, and provide examples of positive and negative reinforcement and punishment and primary and secondary reinforcement and punishment.

In Skinner's analysis, which has inspired an immense body of research, a response ("operant") can be influenced by two types of consequences:

1. **Reinforcement strengthens the response or makes it more likely to recur.** When your dog begs for food at the table, and you give her the lamb chop off your plate, her begging is likely to increase:

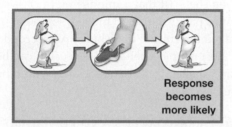

   Response becomes more likely

   Reinforcers are roughly equivalent to rewards, and many psychologists use *reward* and *reinforcer* as approximate synonyms. However, strict behaviorists avoid the word *reward* because it implies that something has been earned that results in happiness or satisfaction. To a behaviorist, a stimulus is a reinforcer if it strengthens the preceding behavior, whether or not the organism experiences pleasure or a positive emotion. Conversely, no matter how pleasurable a reward is, it is not a reinforcer if it does not increase the likelihood of a response. It's great to get a paycheck, but if you get paid regardless of the effort you put into your work, the money will not reinforce "hard-work behavior."

2. **Punishment weakens the response or makes it less likely to recur.** Any aversive (unpleasant) stimulus or event may be a **punisher**. If your dog begs for a lamb chop off your plate, and you lightly swat her nose and shout "No," her begging is likely to decrease—as long as you don't feel guilty and then give her the lamb chop anyway:

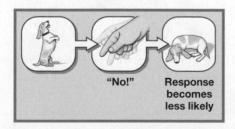

   "No!" Response becomes less likely

Parents, employers, and governments resort to reinforcers and punishers all the time—to get kids to behave well, employees to work hard, and taxpayers to pay up—but they do not always use them effectively. For one thing, they often wait too long to deliver the reinforcer or punisher. In general, the sooner a consequence follows a response, the greater its effect; you are likely to respond more reliably when you do not have to wait ages for a grade, a smile, or a compliment. When other responses occur during a delay, it may be difficult to learn the connection between the desired or undesired response and the consequence.

PRIMARY AND SECONDARY REINFORCERS AND PUNISHERS   Food, water, light stroking of the skin, and a comfortable air temperature are naturally reinforcing because they

reinforcement

The process by which a stimulus or event strengthens or increases the probability of the response that it follows.

punishment

The process by which a stimulus or event weakens or reduces the probability of the response that it follows.

primary reinforcer

A stimulus that is inherently reinforcing, typically satisfying a physiological need; an example is food.

primary punisher

A stimulus that is inherently punishing; an example is electric shock.

secondary reinforcer

A stimulus that has acquired reinforcing properties through association with other reinforcers.

secondary punisher

A stimulus that has acquired punishing properties through association with other punishers.

positive reinforcement

A reinforcement procedure in which a response is followed by the presentation of, or increase in intensity of, a reinforcing stimulus; as a result, the response becomes stronger or more likely to occur.

negative reinforcement

A reinforcement procedure in which a response is followed by the removal, delay, or decrease in intensity of an unpleasant stimulus; as a result, the response becomes stronger or more likely to occur.

satisfy biological needs. They are therefore known as **primary reinforcers**. Similarly, pain and extreme heat or cold are inherently punishing and are therefore known as **primary punishers**. Primary reinforcers and punishers can be powerful, but they have some drawbacks, both in real life and in research. For one thing, a primary reinforcer may be ineffective if an animal or person is not in a deprived state; a glass of water is not much of a reward if you just drank three glasses. Also, for obvious ethical reasons, scientists cannot go around using primary punishers (say, by punching their research participants) or taking away primary reinforcers (say, by starving their volunteers).

Fortunately, behavior can be controlled just as effectively by **secondary reinforcers** and **secondary punishers**, which are learned. Money, praise, applause, good grades, awards, and gold stars are common secondary reinforcers. Criticism, demerits, scolding, fines, and bad grades are common secondary punishers. Most behaviorists believe that secondary reinforcers and punishers acquire their ability to influence behavior by being paired with primary reinforcers and punishers. (If that reminds you of classical conditioning, reinforce your excellent thinking with a pat on the head! Indeed, secondary reinforcers and punishers are often called *conditioned* reinforcers and punishers.) As a secondary reinforcer, money has considerable power over most people's behavior because it can be exchanged for primary reinforcers such as food and shelter. It is also associated with other secondary reinforcers, such as praise and respect.

POSITIVE AND NEGATIVE REINFORCERS AND PUNISHERS   In our example of the begging dog, something pleasant (getting the lamb chop) followed the dog's begging response, so the response increased. Similarly, if you get a good grade after studying, your efforts to study are likely to continue or increase. This kind of process, in which a pleasant consequence makes a response more likely, is known as **positive reinforcement**. But another type of reinforcement, **negative reinforcement**, involves the *removal* of something *unpleasant*. Negative reinforcement occurs when you *escape* from something aversive or *avoid* it by preventing it from ever occurring. If someone nags you to study but stops nagging when you comply, your studying is likely to increase because you will then avoid the nagging:

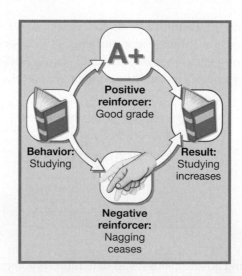

Likewise, negative reinforcement occurs when taking a pill eliminates your pain or when you take a certain route across campus to avoid a rude person.

The positive–negative distinction can also be applied to punishment: Something unpleasant may occur following some behavior (positive punishment), or something *pleasant* may be *removed* (negative punishment). If your friends tease you for studying (positive punishment) or if studying makes you lose time with your friends (negative punishment), you may stop studying:

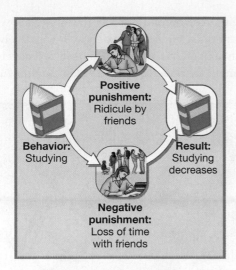

The distinction between positive and negative reinforcement and punishment has been a source of confusion for generations of students, turning many strong minds to mush. You will master these terms more quickly if you understand that "positive" and "negative" have nothing to do with "good" or "bad." They refer to whether something is given or taken away. In the case of reinforcement, think of a positive reinforcer as something that is added or obtained (imagine a plus sign) and a negative reinforcer as avoidance of, or escape from, something unpleasant (imagine a minus sign). *In either case, a response becomes more likely.* Do you recall what happened when Little Albert learned to fear rats through a process of classical conditioning? After he acquired this fear, crawling away was negatively reinforced by escape from the now-fearsome rodent. The negative reinforcement that results from escaping or avoiding something unpleasant explains why so many fears are long-lasting. When you avoid a feared object or situation, you also cut off all opportunities to extinguish your fear.

Understandably, people often confuse negative reinforcement with positive punishment because both involve an unpleasant stimulus. With punishment, you are subjected to the unpleasant stimulus; with negative reinforcement, you escape from it or avoid it. To keep these terms straight, remember that punishment, whether positive or negative, *decreases* the likelihood of a response; and reinforcement, whether positive or negative, *increases* it. In real life, punishment and negative reinforcement often go hand in hand. If you use a chain collar to teach your dog to heel, a brief tug on the collar punishes the act of walking; release of the collar negatively reinforces the act of standing by your side.

Review 7.3

Positive and Negative Reinforcers and Punishers

	Effect
Positive reinforcement	Increases likelihood of a response
Negative reinforcement	Increases likelihood of a response
Positive punishment	Decreases likelihood of a response
Negative punishment	Decreases likelihood of a response

Interactive

You can positively reinforce your studying of this material by taking a short break. As you master the material, a decrease in your anxiety will negatively reinforce studying. But we hope you won't punish your efforts by telling yourself "I'll never get it" or "It's too hard"! Applications of reinforcement are reviewed in the video *Learning from Consequences*.

JOURNAL PROMPT 7.3

Thinking Critically—Don't Oversimplify: Suppose you wanted to use operant conditioning to modify your own behavior, such as exercising more often, eating healthier foods, or cutting back the number of hours you spend watching television or playing video games. Describe how you might use positive reinforcement, negative reinforcement, positive punishment, and negative punishment to accomplish the goal you have in mind. Which of these would be most successful in modifying your behavior, and why?

Quiz for Module 7.3

1. Operant conditioning focuses on the association between _____, whereas classical conditioning focuses on the association between _____.

   a. Two stimuli / a stimulus and a response

   b. A stimulus and a response / two stimuli

   c. A response and its punishment / a response and its reinforcement

   d. A response and its reinforcement / a response and its punishment

2. Despite the many forms and varieties they might take, reinforcement _____, whereas punishment _____.

   a. Acts on an unconditioned response / acts on a conditioned response

   b. Makes a response more likely to occur / also makes a response more likely to occur

   c. Acts on an unconditioned stimulus / acts on a conditioned stimulus

   d. Makes a response more likely to occur / makes a response less likely to occur

3. Primary reinforcers are _____, whereas secondary reinforcers are _____.

   a. Capable of making a behavior occur again / unlikely to make a behavior occur again

   b. Rewarding / punishing

   c. Naturally reinforcing / learned

   d. Acquired through habit / acquired through reinforcement

4. Mauricio gives his daughter a piece of her favorite candy after she finishes cleaning her room. The candy is an example of a

   a. Positive reinforcer

   b. Negative reinforcer

   c. Conditioned stimulus

   d. Conditioned response

5. Natalie can be excused from the dinner table to go play after she eats three bites of the broccoli casserole she's not fond of. This is an example of

   a. Positive punishment

   b. Positive reinforcement

   c. Negative reinforcement

   d. Negative punishment

Principles of Operant Conditioning

Thousands of operant-conditioning studies have been conducted, many using animals. A favorite experimental tool is the *Skinner box*, a chamber equipped with a device that delivers a reinforcer, usually food, when an animal makes a desired response, or a punisher, such as a brief shock, when the animal makes an undesired response (see Figure 7.4). In modern versions, a computer records responses and charts the rate of responding and cumulative responses across time.

Early in his career, Skinner (1938) used the Skinner box for a classic demonstration of operant conditioning. A rat that had previously learned to eat from the pellet-releasing device was placed in the box. The animal proceeded to scurry about the box, sniffing here and there, and randomly touching parts of the floor and walls. Quite by accident, it happened to press a lever mounted on one wall, and immediately a pellet of tasty rat food fell into the food dish. The rat continued its movements and again happened to press the bar, causing another pellet to fall into the dish. With additional repetitions of bar-pressing followed by food, the animal began to behave less randomly and to press the bar more consistently. Eventually, Skinner had the rat pressing the bar as fast as it could.

The Importance of Responses

LO 74.A   Describe the basic principles of operant conditioning, including extinction and recovery, stimulus generalization and discrimination, schedules of learning and shaping, and some biological limits on learning.

Operant conditioning shares many terms in common with classical conditioning. Classical conditioning, however, places a premium on the association between two stimuli, whereas operant conditioning focuses on how responses to stimuli get reinforced. The centrality of responses is illustrated in the operant conditioning principles we now turn to.

EXTINCTION   In operant conditioning, as in classical conditioning, **extinction** is a procedure that causes a previously learned response to stop. In operant conditioning, however, extinction takes place when the reinforcer that maintained the response is withheld or is no longer available. At first, there may be a spurt of responding, but then the responses gradually taper off and eventually cease. Suppose you put a coin in a vending machine and get nothing back. You may throw in another coin, or perhaps even two, but then you will probably stop trying. The next day, you may put in yet another coin, an example of *spontaneous recovery*. Eventually, however, you will give up on that machine. Your response will have been extinguished.

STIMULUS GENERALIZATION AND DISCRIMINATION   In operant conditioning, as in classical conditioning, **stimulus generalization** may occur. That is, responses may generalize to stimuli that were not present during the original learning situation but resemble the original stimuli in some way. For example, a pigeon that has been trained to peck at a picture

extinction
The weakening and eventual disappearance of a learned response; in operant conditioning, it occurs when a response is no longer followed by a reinforcer.

stimulus generalization
In operant conditioning, the tendency for a response that has been reinforced (or punished) in the presence of one stimulus to occur (or be suppressed) in the presence of other similar stimuli.

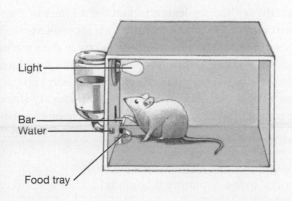

Light
Bar
Water
Food tray

Figure 7.4 The Skinner Box
When a rat in a Skinner box presses a bar, a food pellet or drop of water is automatically released. The photo shows Skinner training one of his subjects.

stimulus discrimination

In operant conditioning, the tendency of a response to occur in the presence of one stimulus but not in the presence of other similar stimuli that differ from it on some dimension.

discriminative stimulus

A stimulus that signals when a particular response is likely to be followed by a certain type of consequence.

continuous reinforcement

A reinforcement schedule in which a particular response is always reinforced.

intermittent (partial) schedule of reinforcement

A reinforcement schedule in which a particular response is sometimes but not always reinforced.

of a circle may also peck at a slightly oval figure. But if you wanted to train the bird to discriminate between the two shapes, you would present both the circle and the oval, giving reinforcers whenever the bird pecked at the circle and withholding reinforcers when it pecked at the oval. Eventually, **stimulus discrimination** would occur. Pigeons, in fact, have learned to make some extraordinary discriminations. They have learned to discriminate between two paintings by different artists, such as Vincent van Gogh and Marc Chagall (Watanabe, 2001). And then, when presented with a new pair of paintings by those same two artists, they have been able to tell the difference between them! Pigeons have even learned to discriminate beautiful paintings from ugly ones, a discrimination similar to what human beings would make (Watanabe, 2010).

Sometimes an animal or person learns to respond to a stimulus only when some other stimulus, called a **discriminative stimulus**, is present. The discriminative stimulus signals whether a response, if made, will pay off. In a Skinner box containing a pigeon, a light may serve as a discriminative stimulus for pecking at a circle. When the light is on, pecking brings a reward; when it is off, pecking is futile. Human behavior is controlled by many discriminative stimuli, both verbal ("Store hours are 9 to 5") and nonverbal (traffic lights, doorbells, the ring of your cell phone, other people's facial expressions). Learning to respond correctly when such stimuli are present allows us to get through the day efficiently and to get along with others.

LEARNING ON SCHEDULE When a response is first acquired, learning is usually most rapid if the response is reinforced each time it occurs; this procedure is called **continuous reinforcement**. However, after a response has become reliable, it will be more resistant to extinction if it is rewarded on an **intermittent (partial) schedule of reinforcement**, which involves reinforcing only some responses, not all of them. Skinner (1956) happened on this fact when he ran short of food pellets for his rats and was forced to deliver reinforcers less often. (Not all scientific discoveries are planned.) On intermittent schedules, a reinforcer is delivered only after a certain number of responses occur or after a certain amount of time has passed since a response was last reinforced; these patterns affect the rate, form, and timing of behavior. (The details are beyond the scope of this book.)

Intermittent reinforcement helps explain why people often get attached to "lucky" hats, charms, and rituals. A batter pulls his earlobe, gets a home run, and from then on always pulls his earlobe before each pitch. A student takes an exam with a purple pen and gets an A, and from then on will not take an exam without a purple pen. Such rituals persist because sometimes they are followed, purely coincidentally, by a reinforcer—a home run, a good grade—and so they become resistant to extinction.

Skinner (1948) once demonstrated this phenomenon by creating eight "superstitious" pigeons in his laboratory. He rigged the pigeons' cages so that food was delivered every 15 seconds, even if the birds didn't lift a feather. Pigeons are often in motion, so when the food came, each animal was likely to be doing something. That something was then reinforced by delivery of the food. The behavior, of course, was reinforced entirely by chance, but it still became more likely to occur and thus to be reinforced again. Within a short time, six of the pigeons were practicing some sort of consistent ritual: turning in counterclockwise circles, bobbing their heads up and down, or swinging their heads to and fro. None of these activities had the least effect on the delivery of the reinforcer; the birds were behaving "superstitiously," as if they thought their movements were responsible for bringing the food.

Now listen up, because here comes one of the most useful things to know about operant conditioning: If you want a response to persist after it has been learned, you should reinforce it *intermittently*, not continuously. If you are giving Harry, your hamster, a treat every time he pushes a ball with his nose, and then you suddenly stop the reinforcement, Harry will soon stop pushing that ball. Because the change in reinforcement is large, from continuous to none at all, Harry will easily discern the change. But if you have been reinforcing Harry's behavior only every so often, the change will not be so dramatic, and your hungry hamster will keep responding for quite a while. Pigeons, rats, and people on intermittent schedules of reinforcement have responded in the laboratory thousands of times without reinforcement before throwing in the towel, especially when the timing of the reinforcer varies. Animals will sometimes work so hard for an unpredictable, infrequent bit of food that the energy they expend is greater than that gained from the reward; theoretically, they could actually work themselves to death.

It follows that if you want to get rid of a response, whether it's your own or someone else's, you should be careful *not* to reinforce it intermittently. If you are going to extinguish undesirable behavior by ignoring it—a child's tantrums, a friend's midnight phone calls, a parent's unwanted advice—you must be absolutely consistent in withholding reinforcement (your attention). Otherwise, the other person will learn that if he or she keeps up the screaming, calling, or advice-giving long enough, it will eventually be rewarded. From a behavioral point of view, one of the most common errors people make is to reward intermittently the very responses that they would like to eliminate.

SHAPING For a response to be reinforced, it must first occur. But suppose you want to train cows to milk themselves, a child to use a knife and fork properly, or a friend to play terrific tennis. Such behaviors, and most others in everyday life, have almost no probability of appearing spontaneously. You could grow old and gray waiting for them to occur so that you could reinforce them. The operant solution is a procedure called **shaping**.

In shaping, you start by reinforcing a tendency in the right direction, and then you gradually require responses that are more and more similar to the final desired response. The responses that you reinforce on the way to the final one are called **successive approximations**. Take the problem of teaching cows to milk themselves. How can cows possibly do that when they have no hands? Ah, but cows *can* be trained to use a milking robot. In several countries, psychologists have done just that (Stiles, Murray, & Kentish-Barnes, 2011). First, they give the cow crushed barley (the cow equivalent of a chocolate treat) for simply standing on a platform connected to the robot. After that response is established, they give her barley for turning her body toward the spot where the robot attaches the milking cups. After that, they reward her for being in the exact spot the robot requires for attaching the cups, and so on until the cow finally learns to milk herself. The key is that as each approximation is achieved, the next one becomes more likely, making it available for reinforcement. Cows allowed to milk themselves do so three or four times a day instead of the traditional twice a day, and show fewer signs of stress than other cows. Farmers show less stress too because they no longer have to get up at 5:00 A.M. for the early-morning milking!

Using shaping and other techniques, Skinner was able to train pigeons to play table tennis with their beaks and to "bowl" in a miniature alley, complete with a wooden ball and tiny bowling pins. (Skinner had a great sense of humor.) Today, animal trainers routinely use shaping to teach animals their parts in movies and TV shows, and to act as the "eyes" of the blind and as the "limbs" of people with spinal cord injuries. These talented animal companions learn to turn on light switches, open refrigerator doors, and reach for boxes on shelves.

shaping
An operant-conditioning procedure in which successive approximations of a desired response are reinforced.

successive approximations
In the operant-conditioning procedure of shaping, behaviors that are ordered in terms of increasing similarity or closeness to the desired response.

Behavioral techniques such as shaping have many useful applications.

BIOLOGICAL LIMITS ON LEARNING All principles of operant conditioning, like those of classical conditioning, are limited by an animal's genetic dispositions and physical characteristics. If you try to teach a fish to dance the samba, you're going to get pretty frustrated (and wear out the fish). Operant-conditioning procedures always work best when they capitalize on inborn tendencies.

Decades ago, two psychologists who became animal trainers, Keller and Marian Breland (1961), learned what happens when you ignore biological constraints on learning. They found that their animals were having trouble learning tasks that should have been easy. One animal, a pig, was supposed to drop large wooden coins in a box. Instead, the animal would drop the coin, push at it with its snout, throw it in the air, and push at it some more. This odd behavior actually delayed delivery of the reinforcer (food, which is *very*

Review 7.4

Operant Conditioning Terms

	Definition
Extinction	The weakening and eventual disappearance of a learned response; in operant conditioning, it occurs when a response is no longer followed by a reinforcer.
Stimulus generalization	The tendency for a response that has been reinforced (or punished) in the presence of one stimulus to occur (or be suppressed) in the presence of other similar stimuli.
Stimulus discrimination	The tendency of a response to occur in the presence of one stimulus but not in the presence of other similar stimuli that differ from it on some dimension.
Discriminative stimulus	A stimulus that signals when a particular response is likely to be followed by a certain type of consequence.

instinctive drift

During operant learning, the tendency for an organism to revert to instinctive behavior.

reinforcing to a pig), so it was hard to explain in terms of operant principles. The Brelands finally realized that the pig's rooting instinct—using its snout to uncover and dig up edible roots—was keeping it from learning the task. They called such a reversion to instinctive behavior **instinctive drift**.

In human beings, too, operant learning is affected by genetics, biology, and the evolutionary history of our species. Human children are biologically disposed to learn language, and they may be disposed to learn some arithmetic operations as well. Furthermore, temperaments and other inborn dispositions may affect how a person responds to reinforcers and punishments. It will be easier to shape belly-dancing behavior if a person is temperamentally disposed to be outgoing and extroverted than if the person is by nature shy.

Skinner: The Man and the Myth

LO 7.4.B Discuss some of the misconceptions surrounding the work and ideas of B. F. Skinner and, by extension, some of the misconceptions surrounding the general goals of operant conditioning.

Because of his groundbreaking work on operant conditioning, B. F. Skinner is one of the best known of American psychologists. He is also one of the most misunderstood. Many people (even some psychologists) think that Skinner denied the existence of human consciousness and the value of studying it. In reality, Skinner (1972, 1990) maintained that private internal events—what we call perceptions, emotions, and thoughts—are as real as any others, and we can study them by examining our own sensory responses, the verbal reports of others, and the conditions under which such events occur. But he insisted that thoughts and feelings cannot *explain* behavior. These components of consciousness, he said, are themselves simply behaviors that occur because of reinforcement and punishment.

Skinner aroused strong passions in both his supporters and his detractors. Perhaps the issue that most provoked and angered people was his insistence that free will is an illusion. In contrast to humanist and some religious doctrines that human beings have the power to shape their own destinies, his philosophy promoted the *determinist view* that our actions are determined by our environments and our genetic heritage.

B. F. Skinner invented the Air Crib to provide a more comfortable, less restrictive infant bed than the traditional crib with its bars and blankets. Here the Skinners play with their 13-month-old daughter, Deborah.

Because Skinner thought the environment should be manipulated to alter behavior, some critics have portrayed him as cold-blooded. One famous controversy regarding Skinner occurred when he invented an enclosed "living space," the Air Crib, for his younger daughter Deborah when she was an infant. This "baby box," as it came to be known, had temperature and humidity controls to eliminate the usual discomforts that babies suffer: heat, cold, wetness, and confinement by blankets and clothing. Skinner believed that to reduce a baby's cries of discomfort and make infant care easier for the parents, you should fix the environment. But people imagined, incorrectly, that the Skinners were leaving their child in the baby box all the time without cuddling and holding her, and rumors circulated for years (and still do from time to time) that she had sued her father, gone insane, or killed herself. Actually, both of Skinner's daughters were cuddled and doted on, loved their parents deeply, and turned out to be successful, perfectly well-adjusted adults.

Skinner, who was a kind and mild-mannered man, felt that it would be unethical *not* to try to improve human behavior by applying behavioral principles. And he practiced what he preached, proposing many ways to improve society and reduce human suffering. At the height of public criticism of Skinner's supposedly cold and inhumane approach to understanding behavior, the American Humanist Association recognized his efforts on behalf of humanity by honoring him with its Humanist of the Year Award.

JOURNAL PROMPT 7.4

Thinking Critically—Consider Other Interpretations: People cling to superstitious rituals because they think they work. Could this "effectiveness" be an illusion, explainable in terms of operant principles? How would extinction, stimulus generalization, stimulus discrimination, or schedules of reinforcement be involved in maintaining a superstitious belief?

Quiz for Module 7.4

1. To extinguish a response that has been reinforced through operant conditioning, it is necessary to
   a. Associate the response with a different unconditioned stimulus.
   b. Countercondition the response with a different reinforcer.
   c. Withhold the reinforcer for a period of time.
   d. Replace the primary reinforcer with a secondary reinforcer.

2. Imani has a ringtone on her phone that identifies when her boyfriend calls her: "BbbrriiingBeepBeep." When she hears it she perks up because she knows it's her sweet snookums calling. One day in a coffee shop she hears a ringtone: "BbbrriiingBoopBoop." Grabbing her phone in delightful expectation, she's disappointed to see that no one has called, and that instead someone else's phone at a nearby table was ringing. Imani's response in the coffee shop is an example of
   a. Successive approximation
   b. Stimulus discrimination
   c. Spontaneous recovery
   d. Stimulus generalization

3. Marjoe trains his dog by giving a reward every time the dog sits up on his hind legs. Lowell trains his dog to do the same trick, but gives the animal a reward every once in a while. After a month Lowell's dog is still reliably performing the trick, whereas Marjoe's dog does so only

haphazardly. Why would there be a difference in these outcomes?
   a. Lowell used intermittent reinforcement, whereas Marjoe used continuous reinforcement.
   b. Marjoe used positive reinforcement, whereas Lowell used negative reinforcement.
   c. Lowell used a primary reinforcer, whereas Marjoe used a secondary reinforcer.
   d. Marjoe used a discriminative stimulus, whereas Lowell used a distributive stimulus.

4. According to the operant conditioning principle of shaping, if you want your parrot to ring a bell three times, what should you first do?
   a. Punish the bird for ringing the bell more than three times.
   b. Reinforce the bird for ringing the bell one time.
   c. Withhold reinforcement the first few times the bell is rung correctly.
   d. Reinforce the bird before putting it in its cage.

5. The main proponent of operant conditioning as a general explanatory system of behavior was
   a. E. B. Titchener
   b. Edward Lee Thorndike
   c. John Broaddus Watson
   d. B. F. Skinner

Operant Conditioning in Real Life

behavior modification

The application of operant-conditioning techniques to teach new responses or to reduce or eliminate maladaptive or problematic behavior; also called *applied behavior analysis*.

Operant principles can clear up many mysteries about why people behave as they do. They can also explain why people have trouble changing when they want to, in spite of all the motivational seminars they attend or resolutions they make. If life remains full of the same old reinforcers, punishers, and discriminative stimuli (a grumpy boss, an unresponsive roommate, a refrigerator stocked with junk food), any new responses that have been acquired may fail to generalize.

To help people change unwanted, dangerous, or self-defeating habits, behaviorists have carried operant principles out of the laboratory and into the wider world of the classroom, athletic field, prison, mental hospital, nursing home, rehabilitation ward, childcare center, factory, and office. The use of operant techniques in such real-world settings is called **behavior modification** (also known as *applied behavior analysis*).

Behavior modification has had some enormous successes (Kazdin, 2012; Martin & Pear, 2014). Behaviorists have taught parents how to toilet-train their children in only a few sessions. They have trained disturbed and intellectually impaired adults to communicate, dress themselves, mingle socially with others, and earn a living. They have taught patients with brain damage to control inappropriate behavior, focus their attention, and improve their language abilities. They have helped children with autism improve their social and language skills. And they have helped ordinary folk get rid of unwanted habits, such as smoking and nail-biting, or acquire desired ones, such as practicing the piano, exercising more, or studying. Yet when nonpsychologists try to apply the principles of conditioning to commonplace problems without thoroughly understanding those principles, their efforts sometimes miss the mark, as we are about to see. To find out how you can successfully apply these principles in your own life, watch the video *How to Make Healthier Choices*.

The Pros and Cons of Punishment

LO 7.5.A List and discuss six reasons why punishment often fails to effectively change behavior.

In a novel called *Walden Two* (1948/1976), Skinner imagined a utopia in which reinforcers were used so wisely that undesirable behavior was rare. Unfortunately, we do not live in a utopia; bad habits and antisocial acts abound.

Punishment might seem to be an obvious solution. Almost all Western countries have banned the physical punishment of schoolchildren by principals and teachers, but many American states still permit it for disruptiveness, vandalism, and other misbehavior. The United States is also far more likely than any other developed country to jail its citizens for nonviolent crimes such as drug use and to administer the death penalty for violent crimes.

And, of course, in their relationships, people punish one another frequently by yelling, scolding, and sulking. Does all this punishment work?

WHEN PUNISHMENT WORKS   Sometimes punishment is unquestionably effective. For example, punishment can deter some young criminals from repeating their offenses. A study of the criminal records of all Danish men born between 1944 and 1947 (nearly 29,000 men) examined repeat arrests (recidivism) through age 26 (Brennan & Mednick, 1994). After any given arrest, punishment reduced rates of subsequent arrests for both minor and serious crimes, though recidivism still remained fairly high. Contrary to expectation, however, the *severity* of punishment made no difference; fines and probation were about as effective as jail time. What mattered most was the *consistency* of the punishment. This is understandable in behavioral terms: When lawbreakers sometimes get away with their crimes, their behavior is intermittently reinforced and therefore becomes resistant to extinction.

Unfortunately, that is often the situation in the United States. Young offenders are punished less consistently than in Denmark, in part because prosecutors, juries, and judges do not want to condemn them to mandatory prison terms. This helps to explain why harsh sentencing laws and simplistic efforts to crack down on wrongdoers often fail or even backfire. Because many things influence crime rates—the proportion of young versus older people in the population, poverty levels, drug policies, discriminatory arrest patterns—the relationship between incarceration rates and crime rates in the United States varies considerably from state to state (King, Maurer, & Young, 2005). But international surveys find that, overall, the United States has a high rate of violent crime compared to many other industrialized countries, in spite of its extremely high incarceration rates.

WHEN PUNISHMENT FAILS   What about punishment that occurs every day in families, schools, and workplaces? Laboratory and field studies find that it, too, often fails, for several reasons:

1. **People often administer punishment inappropriately or mindlessly.** They swing in a blind rage or shout things they don't mean, use harsh methods with toddlers, apply punishment so broadly that it covers all sorts of irrelevant behaviors, or misunderstand the proper application of punishment.

2. **The recipient of harsh or frequent punishment often responds with anxiety, fear, or rage.** Through a process of classical conditioning, these emotional side effects may then generalize to the entire situation in which the punishment occurs—the place, the person

As we all know, people often do things that they're not supposed to. Have you ever wondered why so many people ignore warnings and threats of punishment?

delivering the punishment, and the circumstances. These negative emotional reactions can create more problems than the punishment solves. A teenager who has been severely punished may strike back or run away. A spouse who is constantly insulted, belittled, and criticized will feel bitter and resentful and is likely to retaliate with small acts of hostility. And extreme punishment—physical abuse—is a risk factor, especially in children, for the development of depression, low self-esteem, violent behavior, and many other problems (Fréchette, Zoratti, & Romano, 2015; Gershoff, 2002; Widom, DuMont, & Czaja, 2007).

3. **The effectiveness of punishment is often temporary, depending heavily on the presence of the punishing person or circumstances.** All of us can probably remember some transgressions of childhood that we never dared commit when our parents were around but that we promptly resumed as soon as they were gone and reinforcers were once again available. All we learned was not to get caught.

4. **Most misbehavior is hard to punish immediately.** Punishment, like reward, works best if it quickly follows a response. But outside the laboratory, rapid punishment is often hard to achieve, and during the delay, the behavior may be reinforced many times. If you punish your dog when you get home for getting into the doggie biscuits and eating them all up, the punishment will not do any good because you are too late. Your pet's misbehavior has already been reinforced by all those delicious treats.

5. **Punishment conveys little information.** It may tell the recipient what *not* to do, but it does not communicate what the person (or animal) *should* do. Spanking a toddler for messing in her pants will not teach her to use the potty chair, and scolding a student for learning slowly will not teach him to learn more quickly.

6. **An action intended to punish may instead be reinforcing because it brings attention.** Indeed, in some cases, angry attention may be just what the offender is after. If a mother yells at a child who is throwing a tantrum, the very act of yelling may give him what he wants: a reaction from her. In the schoolroom, teachers who scold children in front of other students, thus putting them in the limelight, may unwittingly reward the very misbehavior they are trying to eliminate.

Because of these drawbacks, most psychologists believe that punishment, especially when it's severe, is a poor way to eliminate unwanted behavior. Consider spanking. A Canadian review of two decades of research found that although spanking may put a halt to a child's annoying or dangerous behavior in the short term, it backfires in the long term because children who are physically punished tend to become more aggressive and antisocial over time (Durrant & Ensom, 2012). Spanking is also associated with later mental health problems and slower cognitive development. No study has ever established a link between physical discipline and any positive outcome. Parents are starting to get the message. Fifty years ago, in many parts of the world, most parents thought that hitting their children was a good approach to correcting bad behavior, but today roughly half hold that belief (Holden et al., 2014; Roberts, 2000; Straus, 2005). A judge in Texas, a state that generally approves of corporal punishment for children, beat his teenage daughter with a belt because she had downloaded video games. She videotaped the beating and posted it on YouTube, where over 100,000 people saw it. As a result, her father was removed from office. To date, 32 countries, including nations as different as Denmark, Israel, Tunisia, Costa Rica, and New Zealand, have outright bans on hitting children.

In special cases, as when children with mental disabilities are in immediate danger of seriously injuring themselves or a school bully is about to beat up a classmate, temporary physical restraint may be necessary. But even in these cases, alternatives are often available. School programs have successfully reduced school violence by teaching kids problem-solving skills, emotional control, and conflict resolution, and by rewarding good behavior (Hahn et al., 2008; Wilson & Lipsey, 2007). And in some cases, the best way to discourage a behavior—a child's nagging for a cookie before dinner, a roommate's interruptions when you're studying—is to extinguish it by ignoring it. Of course, ignoring a behavior requires patience and is not always feasible. If your dog barks all day and night, telling your neighbors that it's best to ignore the racket will not be a winning strategy for long, even if you explain that you learned all about the drawbacks of punishment in your psychology class.

Finally, when punishment must be applied, these guidelines should be kept in mind: (1) It should not involve physical abuse; instead, parents can use time-outs and loss of privileges (negative punishers); (2) it should be consistent; (3) it should be accompanied by information about the kind of behavior that would be appropriate; and (4) it should be followed, whenever possible, by the reinforcement of desirable behavior. Learn more about how reinforcement and punishment affect behavior in the video *Physical Punishment: You Decide.*

The Problems with Reward

LO 7.5.B Discuss reasons why rewards may backfire and not produce their intended results for behavior.

So far, we have been praising the virtues of praise and other reinforcers. But like punishers, rewards do not always work as expected. Let's look at two complications that arise when people try to use them.

MISUSE OF REWARDS For many years, teachers everywhere have been handing out lavish praise, happy-face stickers, and high grades, even if students don't deserve them, in hopes that students' performance will improve as they learn to "feel good about themselves." Scientifically speaking, however, this approach is misguided. Study after study finds that high self-esteem does not improve academic performance (Baumeister et al., 2003). Instead, academic achievement requires effort and persistence (Duckworth et al., 2011). It is nurtured not by undeserved rewards but by a teacher's honest appreciation of the content of a student's work, and specific constructive feedback on how to correct mistakes or fix weaknesses (Damon, 1995). These strong findings from psychological science have finally begun to influence some teachers, who are now shifting away from doling out unwarranted "self-esteem boosters" and focusing on helping students appreciate the benefits of effort and persistence.

One obvious result of the misuse of rewards in schools has been grade inflation at all levels of education. Grade inflation at universities began in the 1970s, during the Vietnam War, as a way to help many students avoid the draft. Since then, grades have risen steadily but graduation rates have not. Moreover, the literacy of graduates has declined, as have scores on entrance exams. And today, at many colleges and universities, Cs (which are supposed to mean average or satisfactory) are nearly extinct; in U.S. universities, 43 percent of grades are now As (Rojstaczer & Healy, 2012). One study found that a third of college students expected Bs just for showing up to class, and 40 percent felt they were entitled to a B merely for doing the required reading (Greenberger et al., 2008).

extrinsic reinforcers

Reinforcers that are not inherently related to the activity being reinforced.

intrinsic reinforcers

Reinforcers that are inherently related to the activity being reinforced.

We have talked to students who feel that hard work should even be enough for an A. If you yourself have benefited from grade inflation, you may feel good about it—but remember that critical thinking requires us to separate feelings from facts! The problem is that rewards, including grades, serve as effective reinforcers only when they are tied to the behavior one is trying to increase, not when they are dispensed indiscriminately. Getting a good grade for "showing-up-in-class behavior" reinforces going to class, but not necessarily for learning much after you are there. Would you want to be treated by a doctor, represented by a lawyer, or have your taxes done by an accountant who got through school just by showing up for class? Or who did all the required reading, but without understanding it?

WHY REWARDS CAN BACKFIRE   Most of our examples of operant conditioning have involved **extrinsic reinforcers**, which come from an outside source and are not inherently related to the activity being reinforced. Money, praise, gold stars, applause, and hugs are all extrinsic reinforcers. But people (and probably some other animals as well) also work for **intrinsic reinforcers**, such as enjoyment of the task and the satisfaction of accomplishment. In real-world settings, extrinsic reinforcement sometimes becomes too much of a good thing: If you focus on it exclusively, it can kill the pleasure of doing something for its own sake.

Consider what happened in a classic study of how praise affects children's intrinsic motivation (Lepper, Greene, & Nisbett, 1973). Nursery school children were given the chance to draw with felt-tipped pens during free play and observers recorded how long each child spontaneously played with the pens. The children clearly enjoyed this activity. Then the researchers told some of the children that if they would draw with felt-tipped pens they would get a prize, a "Good Player Award" complete with gold seal and red ribbon. After drawing for 6 minutes, each child got the award as promised. Other children did not expect an award and were not given one. A week later, during free play, those children who had expected and received an award spent much less time with the pens than they had before the start of the experiment. In contrast, children in a control group who had neither expected nor received an award continued to show as much interest in playing with the pens as they had initially, as you can see in Figure 7.5. Similar results have occurred in other studies when children have been offered a reward for doing something they already enjoy.

Why should extrinsic rewards undermine the pleasure of doing something for its own sake? The psychologists who did the pen study suggested that when we are paid for an activity, we interpret it as work instead of something we do because of our own interests, skills, and efforts. It is as if we say to ourselves, "Because I'm being paid, it must be something I wouldn't do if I didn't have to." Then, when the reward is withdrawn, we refuse to "work" any longer. Another possibility is that we tend to regard extrinsic rewards as controlling, so they make us feel pressured and reduce our sense of autonomy and choice ("I guess I have to do what I'm told to do—but *only* what I'm told to do") (Deci, Koestner, & Ryan, 1999). A third, more behavioral explanation is that extrinsic reinforcement sometimes raises the rate of responding above some optimal, enjoyable level, at which point the activity really does become work.

Findings on extrinsic versus intrinsic reinforcements have wide-ranging implications. Economists have shown that financial rewards can undermine ethical and moral norms such as honesty, hard work, and fairness toward others, and can decrease people's willingness to contribute to the common good (e.g., by paying taxes and giving to charity). In other words, an emphasis solely on money encourages selfishness (Bowles, 2008).

We must be careful, however, not to oversimplify this issue. The effects of extrinsic rewards depend on many factors, including a person's initial motivation, the context in which rewards are achieved, and in the case of praise, the sincerity of the praiser (Henderlong & Lepper, 2002). Sometimes extrinsic rewards can help boost achievement. When some U.S. high schools started offering large cash rewards to students who got high scores on Advanced Placement tests for

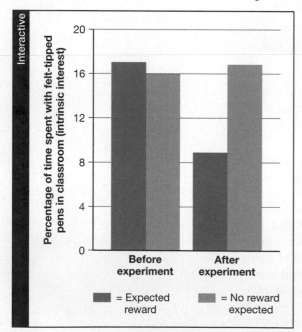

Figure 7.5 Turning Play into Work

Extrinsic rewards can sometimes reduce the intrinsic pleasure of an activity. When preschoolers were promised a prize for drawing with felt-tipped pens, the behavior temporarily increased. But after they got their prizes, they spent less time with the pens than they had before the study began (Lepper, Greene, & Nisbett, 1973).

college, achievement skyrocketed at inner-city schools. Suddenly, disadvantaged minority students were taking statistics classes on Saturdays and passing the placement tests in larger numbers. But these effects might be limited to a unique combination of already motivated teachers and students. In a study of more than 27,000 students in Dallas, New York City, and Chicago, students were paid to read books, to complete assignments, or for getting good grades. The financial incentives had no effect. Although the students were excited about the money, they did not have the basic study skills to build on in order to achieve the goals (Fryer, 2011).

As for the relationship between intrinsic and extrinsic reinforcement, in general, if you get praise, money, a high grade, or a trophy for doing a task *well*, for achieving a certain level of performance, or for improving your performance rather than for just doing the task, your intrinsic motivation is not likely to decline; in fact, it may increase (Cameron, Banko, & Pierce, 2001; Pierce et al., 2003). The rewards are apt to make you feel competent rather than controlled. And if you have always been crazy about reading or about playing the banjo, you will keep reading or playing even when you do not happen to be getting a grade or applause for doing so. In such cases, you will probably attribute your continued involvement in the activity to your own intrinsic interests and motivation rather than to the reward.

So, what is the take-home message about extrinsic rewards? First, they are often useful or necessary. Few people would trudge off to work every morning if they never got paid, and in the classroom, teachers may need to offer incentives to some students. But extrinsic rewards should be used carefully and should not be overdone, so that intrinsic pleasure in an activity can blossom. Educators, employers, and policymakers can avoid the trap of either–or thinking by recognizing that most people do their best when they get tangible rewards for real achievement *and* when they have interesting, challenging, and varied kinds of work to do.

JOURNAL PROMPT 7.5

Thinking Critically—Don't Oversimplify: Because reinforcers increase desirable behavior, some teachers give out high grades whether or not students deserve them. Does this practice improve the students' performance or self-esteem? What do these rewards actually reinforce? Can you think of an example from your own life where you were rewarded for something that wasn't really reward-worthy?

Quiz for Module 7.5

1. Which of the following factors is predictive of when punishment is effective in changing behavior?
   a. The authority of the punisher
   b. The severity of the punishment
   c. The publicness of the punishment
   d. The consistency of the punishment

2. "Just you wait 'til your father gets home tonight! When I tell him what you've done you'll be punished for sure!" Why is this often-heard strategy, unfortunately present in many households, generally ineffective in changing behavior?
   a. Punishment works best if it quickly follows the response-to-be-punished.
   b. Punishment is effective if it is administered by the same person every time.
   c. Severe punishments are more effective than less-severe punishments, and severity tends to decrease over time.
   d. Dad's arrival is pleasantly reinforcing, but Dad's punishment is harsh; counterconditioning will take place.

3. When Roscoe makes a mistake on a math problem in class, his teacher chides him and derides him, thinking that punishment will make him work harder and get the problem right next time. Instead, Roscoe is in a steady downward spiral, failing math and hating school. What could you tell Roscoe's teacher about the effectiveness of her punishment strategy?
   a. "Intermittent punishment is more effective than constant punishment; let a few of Roscoe's mistakes slide, but then pound him with a *bunch* of derision all at once."
   b. "Punishment needs to be consistent; you should deride Roscoe *every* time he makes a mistake so that he can learn from his mistakes more quickly."
   c. "Punishment might indicate what not to do, but it doesn't provide any information about what *should* be done instead; you're not really helping Roscoe to learn how to do math correctly."
   d. "Physical punishment is more effective than verbal punishment; Roscoe's not learning because you're chiding him rather than pinching him when he makes a mistake."

4. What effect does increasing self-esteem in students have on improving their academic performance?

   a. A moderate amount

   b. A great deal

   c. Virtually none

   d. A small but consistent amount

5. Mitzi loves to color and draw in the little sketchbook her Aunt Beatrice gave her. One day Aunt Bea tells her, "Mitzi, I'll give you 25 cents for any picture you draw for me." Soon Mitzi finds that her piggy bank is heavier, yet

her enthusiasm for drawing and coloring has drastically diminished. Why?

   a. Stimulus generalization has occurred, where drawing and cash have been associated over time.

   b. The intrinsic reinforcement of drawing for its own sake has shifted to an extrinsic reinforcement of drawing for money.

   c. Extinction has taken place, and Mitzi finds her drawing skills are not as strong as they used to be.

   d. Mitzi is in the "trough period" of operant conditioning, but eventually spontaneous recovery will cause her interest in drawing to return.

Learning and the Mind

latent learning

A form of learning that is not immediately expressed in an overt response; it occurs without obvious reinforcement.

For half a century, most American learning theories held that learning could be explained by specifying the behavioral "ABCs": *antecedents* (events preceding behavior), *behaviors*, and *consequences*. Behaviorists liked to compare the mind to an engineer's hypothetical "black box," a device whose workings must be inferred because they cannot be observed directly. To them, the box contained irrelevant wiring; it was enough to know that pushing a button on the box would produce a predictable response. But even as early as the 1930s, a few behaviorists could not resist peeking into that black box.

Latent Learning

LO 7.6.A Define latent learning and give an example of how it might work in the daily life of a college student.

Behaviorist Edward Tolman (1938) committed virtual heresy at the time by noting that his rats, when pausing at turning points in a maze, seemed to be *deciding* which way to go. Moreover, the animals sometimes seemed to be learning even without any reinforcement. What, he wondered, was going on in their little rat brains that might account for this puzzle?

In a classic experiment, Tolman and C. H. Honzik (1930) placed three groups of rats in mazes and observed their behavior daily for more than 2 weeks. The rats in Group 1 always found food at the end of the maze and quickly learned to find it without going down blind alleys. The rats in Group 2 never found food and, as you would expect, they followed no particular route. Group 3 was the interesting group. These rats found no food for 10 days and seemed to wander aimlessly, but on the 11th day they received food, and then they quickly learned to run to the end of the maze. By the following day, they were doing as well as Group 1, which had been rewarded from the beginning (see Figure 7.6).

Group 3 had demonstrated **latent learning**, learning that is not immediately expressed in performance. A great deal of human learning also remains latent until circumstances allow or require it to be expressed. A driver gets out of a traffic jam and finds her way to Fourth and Kumquat Streets using a route she has never used before (without GPS!). A little boy observes a parent setting the table or tightening a screw but does not act on this learning for years; then he finds he knows how to do these things.

Latent learning raises questions about what, exactly, is learned during operant learning. In the Tolman and Honzik study, the rats that did not get any food until the 11th day seemed to have acquired a mental representation of the maze. They had been learning the whole time; they simply had no reason to act on that learning until they began to find food. Similarly, the driver taking a new route can do so because she already knows how the city is laid out. What

Figure 7.6 Latent Learning

In a classic experiment, rats that always found food in a maze made fewer and fewer errors in reaching the food (blue curve). In contrast, rats that received no food showed little improvement (gold curve). But rats that got no food for 10 days and then found food on the 11th day showed rapid improvement from then on (red curve). This result suggests that learning involves cognitive changes that can occur in the absence of reinforcement and that may not be acted on until a reinforcer becomes available (Tolman & Honzik, 1930).

seems to be acquired in latent learning, therefore, is not a specific response, but *knowledge* about responses and their consequences. We learn how the world is organized, which paths lead to which places, and which actions can produce which payoffs. This knowledge permits us to be creative and flexible in reaching our goals.

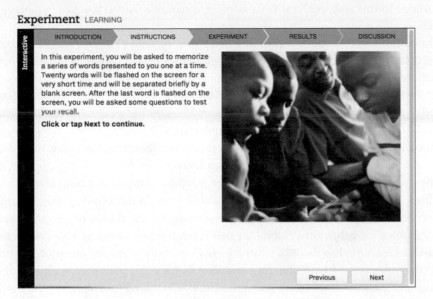

Social-Cognitive Learning Theories

LO 7.6.B Define observational learning and give an example of how it might influence learning during childhood.

During the 1960s and 1970s, many learning theorists concluded that human behavior could not be understood without taking into account the human capacity for higher-level cognitive processes. They agreed with behaviorists that human beings, along with the rat and the rabbit, are subject to the laws of operant and classical conditioning. But they added that human beings, unlike the rat or the rabbit, are full of attitudes, beliefs, and expectations that affect the way they acquire information, make decisions, reason, and solve problems. Today, this view has become very influential.

We will use the term **social-cognitive theory** for all theories that combine behavioral principles with cognitive ones to explain behavior (Bandura, 1986; Mischel, 1973; Mischel & Shoda, 1995). These theories share an emphasis on the importance of beliefs, perceptions, and observations of other peoples' behavior in determining what we learn, what we do at any given moment, and the personality traits we develop. To a social-cognitive theorist, differences in beliefs and perceptions help explain why two people who live through the same event may come away with entirely different lessons from it (Bandura, 2012). All siblings know this. One sibling may regard being grounded by their father as evidence of his all-around meanness, whereas another may see the same behavior as evidence of his care and concern for his children. For these siblings, being grounded is likely to affect their behavior differently.

LEARNING BY OBSERVING   Late one night, a friend living in a rural area was awakened by a loud clattering noise. A raccoon had knocked over a "raccoon-proof" garbage can and seemed to be demonstrating to an assembly of other raccoons how to open it: If you jump up and down on the can's side, the lid will pop off. According to our friend, the observing raccoons learned from this episode how to open stubborn garbage cans, and the observing humans learned how smart raccoons can be. In short, they all benefited from **observational learning**, learning by watching what others do and what happens to them for doing it.

The behavior learned by the raccoons through observation was an operant one, but observational learning also plays an important role in the acquisition of automatic, reflexive responses, such as fears and phobias (Mineka & Zinbarg, 2006; Olsson & Phelps, 2004). Thus, in addition to learning to be frightened of rats directly through classical conditioning, as

social-cognitive theories

Theories that emphasize how behavior is learned and maintained through observation and imitation of others, positive consequences, and cognitive processes such as plans, expectations, and beliefs.

observational learning

A process in which an individual learns new responses by observing the behavior of another (a model) rather than through direct experience; sometimes called *vicarious conditioning*.

Little Albert did, you might also learn to fear rats by observing the emotional expressions of other people when they see or touch one. The perception of someone else's reaction serves as an unconditioned stimulus for your own fear, and the learning that results may be as strong as it would be if you had had a direct encounter with the rat yourself. Children often learn to fear things in this way, perhaps by observing a parent's fearful reaction whenever a dog approaches.

Behaviorists refer to observational learning as *vicarious conditioning*, and believe it can be explained in stimulus–response terms. But social-cognitive theorists believe that observational learning in human beings cannot be fully understood without taking into account the thought processes of the learner (Meltzoff & Gopnik, 1993). They emphasize the knowledge that results when a person sees a *model*—another person—behaving in certain ways and experiencing the consequences (Bandura, 1977).

None of us would last long without observational learning. Learning would be both inefficient and dangerous. We would have to learn to avoid oncoming cars by walking into traffic and suffering the consequences, or learn to swim by jumping into a deep pool and flailing around. Parents and teachers would be busy 24 hours a day shaping children's behavior. Bosses would have to stand over their employees' desks, rewarding every little link in the complex behavioral chains we call typing, report writing, and accounting. But observational learning has its dark side as well: People often imitate antisocial or unethical actions (they observe a friend cheating and decide they can get away with it too) or self-defeating and harmful ones (they watch a film star smoking and take up the habit in an effort to look just as cool).

BANDURA'S CLASSIC RESEARCH   Many years ago, Albert Bandura and his colleagues showed just how important observational learning is for children who are learning the rules of social behavior (Bandura, Ross, & Ross, 1963). Nursery school children watched a short film of two men, Rocky and Johnny, playing with toys. (Apparently the children did not think this behavior was the least bit odd.) In the film, Johnny refuses to share his toys, and Rocky responds by clobbering him. Rocky's aggressive actions are rewarded because he winds up

In studies by Albert Bandura and his colleagues, children watched films of an adult kicking, punching, and hammering on a big rubber doll (top). Later, the children imitated the adult's behavior, some of them almost exactly.

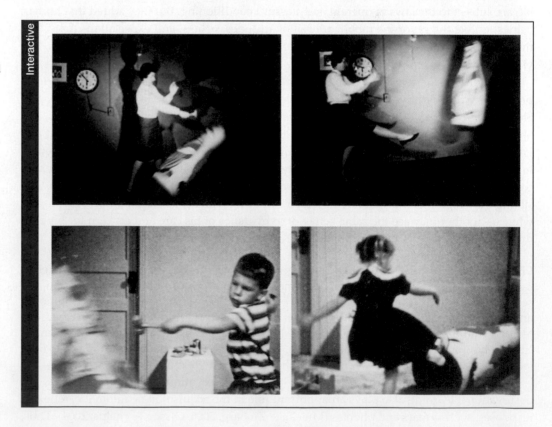

with all the toys. Poor Johnny sits dejectedly in the corner, while Rocky marches off with a sack full of loot and a hobbyhorse under his arm.

After viewing the film, each child was left alone for 20 minutes in a playroom full of toys, including some of the items shown in the film. Watching through a one-way mirror, the experimenters found that the children were much more aggressive in their play than a control group that had not seen the film. Some children imitated Rocky almost exactly. At the end of the session, one little girl even asked for a sack!

Findings on latent learning, observational learning, and the role of cognition in learning can help us evaluate arguments in the passionate debate about the effects of media violence. Children and teenagers in the United States and many other countries see countless acts of violence on television, in films, and in video games. Does all this mayhem of blood and guts affect them? Do you think it has affected *you*? In "Taking Psychology with You," we offer evidence that bears on these questions, and suggest ways of resolving them without over-simplifying the issues.

JOURNAL PROMPT 7.6

Thinking Critically—Define Your Terms: There are probably many horrible things you've learned to do just from observing someone else and without (hopefully) any direct reinforcement of your own behavior. For example, you could learn how to break into someone's home or car from watching a crime show on television. Yet you'll probably (again, hopefully!) never enact such a behavior, nor will the vast majority of other people who've observed the same thing. How does this conclusion illustrate the distinction between learning and performance? Can learning take place without the necessity of acting on that learning? If so, how would you know if the behavior was actually learned?

Quiz for Module 7.6

1. Murray rides with his carpool buddies to work each morning and always sits in the back seat while others drive. One day his friends' cars are all in the repair shop, and he unexpectedly has to drive the crew to work. Although he has never driven that route on his own, he navigates every twist and turn, and makes the journey flawlessly. Which principle of learning can account for Murray's performance?
   a. Latent learning
   b. Spontaneous recovery
   c. Shaping of successive approximations to an end goal
   d. Reinforcement

2. What seems to be acquired when latent learning takes place?
   a. Knowledge about responses and their consequences
   b. A specific response applicable to a specific situation
   c. A set of contingencies that applies to a range of reinforcers
   d. Discriminations among competing responses

3. Social-cognitive theories emphasize
   a. The interaction of behavioral and cognitive principles to explain behaviors
   b. Behavior taking place in a unique cultural context

   c. Reinforcement of social behavior
   d. The distinction between social learning and cognitive learning

4. Three-year-old Barry watches as his older brother Sid reaches up to put his hand on the hot burner of a stove. Barry sees Sid recoil in terror and hears his frightened screams as he plunges his injured hand into cold water. For the rest of his life, Barry never put his hand on a stovetop burner, never got reinforced for not doing so, and in fact never had any direct experience with singed flesh or dangerous kitchen equipment, yet clearly some learning had taken place. What kind of learning did Barry experience?
   a. Observational learning
   b. Classical conditioning
   c. Operant conditioning
   d. Discriminative learning

5. The researcher most clearly associated with social-cognitive learning theory, and observational learning in particular, is
   a. Albert Bandura
   b. B. F. Skinner
   c. J. B. Watson
   d. Arnold Layne

Taking Psychology with You

Does Media Violence Make You Violent?

In 2011, the U.S. Supreme Court overturned a 2005 California law that had banned shops from selling or renting violent video games to anyone under age 18. California argued that violence is as obscene as pornography, and if selling or renting porn to young people is illegal, surely selling or renting violent video games should be prohibited as well. The court thought otherwise, ruling that not only are violent video games not obscene, but many parents think they are harmless fun. Just look at what happens to Hansel and Gretel, or Cinderella, said one of the justices; "Grimm's Fairy Tales," he wrote, "are grim indeed." But other countries, such as Australia, New Zealand, and England, have concluded that violent video games can be dangerous enough to children to justify restrictions or even a complete ban. Which conclusion is right? Does violence depicted in films, on TV, and in video games lead to real violence?

Psychologists are strongly divided in their answers to this question. One group of investigators concluded, "Research on violent television and films, video games, and music reveals unequivocal evidence that media violence increases the likelihood of aggressive and violent behavior," both in the short term and long term (Anderson et al., 2003). Their meta-analyses find that the greater the exposure to violence in movies and on television, the stronger the likelihood of a person's behaving aggressively, and this correlation holds for both sexes and across cultures, from Japan to England (Anderson et al., 2010). Video games that directly reward violence, as by awarding points or moving the player to the next level after a "kill," increase feelings of hostility, aggressive thinking, and aggressive behavior (Carnagey & Anderson, 2005). Moreover, when grade school children cut back on time spent watching TV or playing violent video games, the children's aggressiveness declines (Robinson et al., 2001).

Violent media may also desensitize people to the pain or distress of others. In a field study, people who had just seen a violent movie took longer to come to the aid of a woman struggling to pick up her crutches than did people who had seen a nonviolent movie or people still waiting to see one of the two movies (Bushman & Anderson, 2009).

However, an opposing group of psychologists believes that the effects of video games have been exaggerated and sensationalized (Ferguson, 2013; Ferguson & Kilburn, 2010). The correlation between playing violent video games and behaving aggressively, they maintain, is too small to worry about (Ferguson, 2007; Sherry, 2001). Other factors that are correlated with violent criminality are far more powerful; they include genetic influences (.75), perceptions of criminal opportunity (.58), owning a gun (.35), poverty (.25), and childhood physical abuse (.22). In their calculations, watching violent video games has the lowest correlation, only .04 (Ferguson, 2009; Ferguson & Kilburn, 2010). Besides, they observe, rates of teenage violence declined significantly throughout the 1990s, a period in which the number of violent video games was increasing astronomically.

In the social-cognitive view, both conclusions about the relationship of media violence to violent behavior have merit. Repeated acts of aggression in the media do model behavior and responses to conflict that a few people may imitate, just as media ads influence what many people buy and what many people think the ideal male or female body should look like. However, children watch many different programs and movies and have many models to observe besides those they see in the media, including parents and peers. For every teenager who is obsessed with playing a video game that involves grim fantasies of blowing up the world, hundreds more think the game is just plain fun and then go off to do their homework.

Moreover, perceptions and interpretations of events, personality dispositions such as aggressiveness and sociability, and the social context in which the violence is viewed can all affect how a person responds (Feshbach & Tangney, 2008). One person may learn from seeing people being blown away in a film that violence is cool and masculine; another may decide that the violent images are ugly and stupid; a third may conclude that they don't mean anything at all, that they are just part of the story.

What should be done, if anything, about media violence? Even if only a small percentage of viewers learn to be aggressive from observing all that violence, the social consequences can be serious because the total audiences for TV, movies, and video games are immense. But censorship, which some people think is the answer, brings its own set of problems, quite apart from constitutional issues of free speech. Should we ban *Hamlet*? Bloody graphic comics? Films that truthfully depict the realities of war, murder, and torture?

Consider, too, that it's not just video games and other visual media that can increase aggression. In two studies, students read a violent passage from the Bible, with two sentences inserted in which God sanctions the violence. Later, in what they thought was a different study, they played a competitive reaction-time game with a partner. In the game, they were more willing to blast their competitor with a loud noise than were students who had been told the violent passage was from an ancient scroll or students who had read a passage that did not mention God (Bushman et al., 2007). Participants who believed in God were most affected by the passage in which God condones the violence, but many nonbelievers were affected too. Although the general message of the scriptures is one of peace and reconciliation, the Bible is also full of violence, some of it sanctioned by God. Yet few people would be willing to ban the Bible or censure its violent parts.

As you can see, determining a fair and equitable policy regarding media violence will not be easy. It will demand good evidence—and good thinking.

Summary

Classical Conditioning

LO 7.1.A   List and explain each of the four key elements that make classical conditioning take place.

Classical conditioning was first studied by Russian physiologist Ivan Pavlov. In this type of learning, when a neutral stimulus is paired with an *unconditioned stimulus* (US) that already elicits a certain *unconditioned response* (UR), the neutral stimulus becomes associated with the US. The neutral stimulus then becomes a *conditioned stimulus* (CS), and has the capacity to elicit a *conditioned response* (CR) that is similar or related to the UR.

LO 7.1.B   Discuss the basic principles of classical conditioning, including the extinction and recovery of a classically conditioned response, how higher-order conditioning takes place, and the process of stimulus generalization and discrimination.

In *extinction*, the conditioned stimulus is repeatedly presented without the unconditioned stimulus, and the conditioned response eventually disappears, although later it may reappear (*spontaneous recovery*). In *higher-order conditioning*, a neutral stimulus becomes a conditioned stimulus by being paired with an already-established conditioned stimulus. In *stimulus generalization*, after a stimulus becomes a conditioned stimulus for some response, other similar stimuli may produce the same or similar reaction. In *stimulus discrimination*, different responses are made to stimuli that resemble the conditioned stimulus in some way.

LO 7.1.C   Explain why the stimulus to be conditioned should precede the unconditioned stimulus in order for classical conditioning to take place.

Many theorists believe that what an animal or person learns in classical conditioning is not just an association between the unconditioned and conditioned stimulus, but also information conveyed by one stimulus about another. Indeed, classical conditioning appears to be an evolutionary adaptation that allows an organism to prepare for a biologically important event. Considerable evidence exists to show that a neutral stimulus does not become a CS unless it reliably signals or predicts the US.

Classical Conditioning in Real Life

LO 7.2.A   Provide an example of how classical conditioning takes place in forming preferences.

Classical conditioning helps account for positive emotional responses to particular objects and events, typically through the pairing of a neutral stimulus (a car, for example) with a pleasurable stimulus (an attractive spokesperson, free trinkets, or cold hard cash).

LO 7.2.B   Provide an example of how classical conditioning takes place in avoiding fearful stimuli, and describe how the process of counterconditioning takes place.

John Watson showed how fears may be learned and then may be unlearned through a process of *counterconditioning*. Work on classical conditioning is now integrating findings on fear, learning, and biology. Using a drug to enhance the activity of a certain receptor in the amygdala speeds up the extinction of a phobia (fear of heights) during virtual-reality treatments.

LO 7.2.C   Describe how classical conditioning is involved in avoiding a food associated with aversive outcomes.

Because of evolutionary adaptations, human beings (and many other species) are biologically primed to acquire some classically conditioned responses easily, such as conditioned taste aversions. Often a single trial pairing a stimulus with an unpleasant outcome (e.g., a desired meal followed by nausea) can produce aversive conditioning.

LO 7.2.D   Describe how classical conditioning can affect reactions to medical treatments, including a patient's reaction to a placebo.

Classical conditioning can also account for reactions to medical treatments. Associating neutral stimuli (the color of a waiting room, for example, or the smell of disinfectant) with an unpleasant outcome (nausea from chemotherapy, pain from an injection) can lead to the stimuli themselves eliciting an aversive response.

Operant Conditioning

LO 7.3.A   Discuss how Edward Thorndike's research served as the basis for operant conditioning.

In *operant conditioning*, behavior becomes more or less likely to occur depending on its consequences. Responses in operant conditioning are generally not reflexive and are more complex than in classical conditioning. Research in this area is closely associated with B. F. Skinner, who called his approach "radical behaviorism," although an early study conducted by Edward Thorndike (cats escaping a puzzle box) set the stage for some basic principles of operant conditioning.

LO 7.3.B   Distinguish between reinforcement and punishment and between a positive and negative stimulus, and provide examples of positive and negative reinforcement and punishment and primary and secondary reinforcement and punishment.

In the Skinnerian analysis, *reinforcement* strengçthens or increases the probability of a response, and *punishment* weakens or decreases the probability of a response. *Reinforcers* are called *primary* when they are naturally reinforcing because they satisfy a biological need, and are called *secondary* when they have acquired their ability to strengthen a response through association with other reinforcers. A similar distinction is made for *punishers*. In *positive reinforcement*, something pleasant follows a response; in *negative reinforcement*, something unpleasant is removed. In *positive punishment*, something unpleasant follows the response; in *negative punishment*, something pleasant is removed.

LO 7.4.A   Describe the basic principles of operant conditioning, including extinction and recovery, stimulus generalization and discrimination, schedules of learning and shaping, and some biological limits on learning.

Extinction, *stimulus generalization*, and *stimulus discrimination* occur in operant conditioning as well as in classical conditioning. A *discriminative stimulus* signals that a response is likely to be followed by a certain type of consequence. *Continuous reinforcement* leads to the most rapid learning. However, *intermittent* (*partial*) *reinforcement* makes a response resistant to extinction (and, therefore, helps account for the persistence of superstitious rituals). *Shaping* is used to train behaviors with a low probability of occurring spontaneously. Reinforcers are given for *successive approximations* to the desired response until the desired response is achieved. However, biology places limits on what an animal or person can learn through operant conditioning, or how easily it is learned. Animals sometimes have trouble learning a task because of *instinctive drift*.

7.4.B   Discuss some of the misconceptions surrounding the work and ideas of B. F. Skinner and, by extension, some of the misconceptions surrounding the general goals of operant conditioning.

Operant conditioning is one of the mainstays of learning theory, and its findings and conclusions have been demonstrated repeatedly. As the sole explanatory system for why organisms do what they do, however, it is incomplete. Skinner's radical behaviorism was often misinterpreted as a cold, mechanistic view of the human condition.

Operant Conditioning in Real Life

LO 7.5.A   List and discuss six reasons why punishment often fails to effectively change behavior.

Punishment, when used properly, can discourage undesirable behavior, including criminal behavior. But it is frequently misused and can have unintended consequences. It is often administered inappropriately because of the emotion of the moment; it may produce rage and fear; its effects are often only temporary; it is hard to administer immediately; it conveys little information about the kind of behavior that is desired; and it may provide attention that is rewarding. Extinction of undesirable behavior, combined with reinforcement of desired behavior, is generally preferable to the use of punishment.

LO 7.5.B   Discuss reasons why rewards may backfire and not produce their intended results for behavior.

Reinforcers can also be misused. Rewards that are given out indiscriminately, as in efforts to raise children's self-esteem, do not reinforce desirable behavior. An exclusive reliance on *extrinsic reinforcement* can sometimes undermine the power of *intrinsic reinforcement*. But money and praise do not usually interfere with intrinsic pleasure when a person is rewarded for succeeding or making progress rather than for merely participating in an activity, or when a person is already highly interested in the activity.

Learning and the Mind

LO 7.6.A   Define latent learning, and give an example of how it might work in the daily life of a college student.

Even during behaviorism's heyday, some researchers were probing the "black box" of the mind. In the 1930s, Edward Tolman studied *latent learning*, in which no obvious reinforcer is present during learning and a response is not expressed until later, when reinforcement does become available. What appears to be acquired in latent learning is not a specific response but rather knowledge about responses and their consequences.

LO 7.6.B   Define observational learning, and give an example of how it might influence learning during childhood.

The 1960s and 1970s saw the increased influence of *social-cognitive theories* of learning, which focus on *observational learning* and the role played by beliefs, interpretations of events, and other cognitions in determining behavior. Social-cognitive theorists argue that in observational learning, as in latent learning, what is acquired is knowledge rather than a specific response. Because people differ in their perceptions and beliefs, they may learn different lessons from the same event or situation.

Chapter 7 Quiz

1. Jack feeds his cat canned food every night. The ritual is always the same: Jack takes out the electric can opener, whirs the can around the blade to open it, scoops the food into a bowl, and presents it to Fluffikins. Jack has noticed, however, that Fluffikins will run into the kitchen in eager anticipation as soon as she hears the sound of the cabinet door open and hears the whir of the can opener in motion. According to the principles of classical conditioning, the sound of the can opener is the

   a. US
   b. CS
   c. CR
   d. UR

2. Shelly had trained her dog that whenever it saw a photo of the cat next door, it would receive a treat. Through multiple pairings of the photo and the treat, the dog came to salivate when the photo alone was presented. Shelly then extinguished the salivation behavior by presenting the photo but withholding the treat. She was surprised to find that, a week later, when she happened to hold up the photo of the cat, her dog started to salivate. What's going on here?

   a. Stimulus generalization; the dog had been salivating to lots of images of cats, and Shelly just happened to present the correct one.
   b. Stimulus discrimination; Shelly's dog was waiting for a specific photo to reappear in order to start salivating again.
   c. Spontaneous recovery; extinguishing a conditioned response doesn't necessarily mean that it is "unlearned" and gone forever.
   d. Higher-order conditioning; extinction of a conditioned response simply means that another, stronger response has taken its place.

3. Roland learned about classical conditioning in his psychology class, and he was eager to use it to train his dog. He presented a tasty morsel, rang a bell, then watched the animal drool as it ate. He repeated this multiple times: food, bell, response. Then he rang the bell all by itself—and nothing happened. No drooling, no response, just an indifferent look from a bored dog. Why had no learning taken place?

   a. The US and UR need to be established separately before being paired together.
   b. The US and the CR need to be established separately before being paired together.
   c. The CS needs to precede the US in order for conditioning to take place.
   d. Roland was actually extinguishing a UR using his technique.

4. Rosie wants to buy a new microwave oven. She looks at two models in the same store. Both models have identical features. Both models suit her needs. But one model has a sticker of a smiley face on it, whereas the other one does not. Rosie decides to buy the stickered microwave. According to the principles of classical conditioning, why is that?

   a. The microwave oven is the US, the smiley face is the CS, and the purchasing is the UR.
   b. Rosie knew that the store managers wouldn't put a happy face on a lousy oven, so she assumed that it had some unknown better quality to it.
   c. Rosie had an unconditioned response to react favorably to microwave ovens, since she associates them with yummy foods.
   d. Rosie associated the pleasant feelings produced by the smiley sticker with the qualities of the microwave oven.

5. Angelo is afraid of heights. A friend suggests that Angelo should take a ride in an elevator to the top floor of a downtown high-rise while listening to his favorite soothing music through headphones. Angelo finds the courage to do so, then does it again several more times. Eventually he finds that his fear of heights has greatly diminished. What classical conditioning principle has taken place?

   a. Stimulus retraction
   b. Spontaneous recovery
   c. Stimulus discrimination
   d. Counterconditioning

6. Reggie likes to eat chicken fingers dipped in honey mustard sauce. One night, just after eating at Chubby's Chicken Shack, he becomes painfully ill with stomach cramps and nausea due to the flu virus that had been percolating in his body the past few days. When his friends invite him back to Chubby's in a month, Reggie swiftly declines. What principle of classical conditioning is at work in Reggie's reaction?

   a. Stimulus discrimination
   b. Learned taste aversion
   c. Stimulus identification
   d. Learned taste discrimination

7. Maria's parents have really bad luck and show really poor planning. Each time they take Maria to the doctor for her immunizations, they dress her in the same red sweater. Without fail, Maria has her red sweater on when she gets an injection from the doctor. One day her mother pulled the sweater out of the closet and asked, "Would you like to wear this today, honey?" and couldn't understand why Maria burst into tears. Can you explain why?

   a. Maria showed spontaneous recovery of an extinguished response.
   b. Maria associated the sweater with both her mother and father, so she thought her father was gone.
   c. Maria learned that the sweater predicted a ride in the car.
   d. Maria had associated the presence of the sweater with a painful trip to the doctor.

8. Cats trapped in a puzzle box will at first make many random movements to try to get out, yet only one behavior trips the latch that opens the door that sets them free. Over time, random behaviors that don't produce that outcome will become less frequent, and the one behavior that does produce that outcome will become more frequent. In fact, eventually a cat put in such a box will immediately show that one effective behavior over and over. According to the principles of operant conditioning, why does this happen?

   a. When many behaviors get reinforced, eventually one behavior will rise above the others.

b. Random behaviors tend to get punished; ineffective strategies punish the animal by keeping it in the puzzle box.

c. Behaviors that get reinforced tend to occur again in the future; the one behavior that opens the latch is reinforced by the cat's freedom.

d. Organisms learn at their own pace; reinforcing several behaviors, then gradually reinforcing a single behavior, matched the pace of learning for these cats.

9. Praise, money, good grades, compliments, and applause are all examples of

a. Primitive reinforcers   c. Discriminative stimuli

b. Primary reinforcers   d. Secondary reinforcers

10. When trying to teach an animal to do something using operant conditioning, sometimes the animal will revert to performing behaviors that are characteristic of its species. This phenomenon is known as

a. Bioreversion   c. Instinctive drift

b. Species shift   d. Organismic tuning

11. What common misconception do many people hold about B. F. Skinner?

a. That he once won $250,000 in Las Vegas by applying behaviorist principles to the game of poker; in reality, he was a well-known blackjack player.

b. That he was a member of the Communist Party; in reality, he advocated a variant of totalitarianism as an effective form of self-government.

c. That he wanted to manipulate the environment in order to control people; in reality, he wanted to improve human behavior by applying operant conditioning principles.

d. That he started a self-sufficient commune based on operant conditioning principles; in reality, he was asked by the CIA to infiltrate and modify an existing commune.

12. When her child misbehaves, Honjoo uses several strategies to modify his behavior, such as placing him in time-out, redirecting him to another behavior, or ignoring the undesired behavior and reinforcing desired ones. She doesn't use physical punishment, because Honjoo knows that

a. Either punishment or reinforcement can effectively change behavior, but reinforcement is easier to enact.

b. Punishment is a poor way to eliminate unwanted behavior.

c. She can be charged as a criminal for threatening to spank her child.

d. Punishment can act as a primary reinforcer in these situations.

13. Ms. Schmidel is eager to start her first year as a kindergarten teacher. When students arrive to her classroom each morning, she gives each of them a Good Arriver sticker. When she asks them to open their picture books, she awards every student a Bravo Bookworm badge whether they have a book or not. And before the students go out to play at recess, they all get Righteous Runner medals to hang around their necks. What would you predict about Ms. Schmidel's students' intrinsic motivation to learn and achieve throughout the school year?

a. It would be moderately high.

b. It would be very high.

c. It would be high.

d. It would be pretty low.

14. Roddy spent his childhood watching his father fix cars. Roddy's father never actually let Roddy help, but he did agree to perch Roddy in a nearby chair so he could see what was going on. As a young adult, when Roddy purchased his first car, he was able to fix and maintain every aspect of it. What's going on here?

a. Roddy received tacit reinforcement while growing up.

b. Roddy knew his father would disapprove if he didn't know how to fix cars, so he secretly worked on junker cars while growing up.

c. Roddy acquired latent learning that was later enacted in performance.

d. Roddy knew he would be punished if he didn't follow in his father's footsteps, and the threat of punishment outweighed the benefits of reinforcement.

15. When Wanda rides in the car with her mother Gladys, she notices that each time her mom has to slam on the brakes, she slaps the steering wheel and yells, "You dirty creep!" A few months later, Gladys notices that while Wanda is pedaling along in her toy pushcar and her brother cuts her off, Wanda slaps the steering wheel and yells, "You dirty creep!" at her brother. Gladys is horrified, but you're not; what's going on with Wanda?

a. Observational learning   c. Spontaneous recovery

b. Operant conditioning   d. Higher-order conditioning

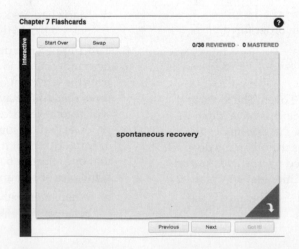

Chapter 8
Behavior in Social and Cultural Context

 Listen to the Audio

Learning Objectives

LO 8.1.A Compare social norms and social roles, and note how each contributes to the social rules that govern a culture.

LO 8.1.B Outline the basic procedures and findings of the Milgram obedience experiments, and discuss five conditions that make disobedience to authority more likely.

LO 8.1.C Outline the basic procedures and findings of the Zimbardo prison study.

LO 8.1.D Explain how feelings of entrapment contribute to destructive obedience.

LO 8.2.A Contrast situational and dispositional attributions, explain how and why the fundamental attribution error takes place, and describe three biases that people hold about themselves and others.

LO 8.2.B Outline the process of cognitive dissonance, and explain how the validity effect and the familiarity effect shape our attitudes.

LO 8.2.C Summarize four elements that contribute to indoctrination.

LO 8.3.A Outline the basic procedures and findings of the Asch line-judging study.

LO 8.3.B List four symptoms of groupthink.

LO 8.3.C Explain how diffusion of responsibility and deindividuation contribute to the madness of crowds.

LO 8.3.D Discuss four situational factors that increase one's likelihood to offer help to others.

LO 8.4.A Contrast social identity, ethnic identity, and acculturation, and offer examples of each concept.

LO 8.4.B Define ethnocentrism, and describe how it contributes to us–them dichotomies.

LO 8.4.C Define what a stereotype is, and discuss three ways in which stereotypes distort reality.

LO 8.5.A Describe four sources of prejudice.

LO 8.5.B Describe five ways of measuring prejudicial attitudes.

LO 8.5.C Describe four situations that can help reduce prejudice and intergroup conflict.

LO 8.5.D Explain the phrase "the banality of evil," and discuss how it contributes to otherwise-good people behaving badly.

Ask questions . . . be willing to wonder

Why do ordinary people sometimes do unspeakably evil things?

When people argue about political or social issues, how come so few ever change their views?

What enables some people to choose conscience over conformity?

What causes prejudice? What reduces it?

Brigadier General Sha'afiq Masa is the commander of Branch 215 of Syria's military intelligence division. Although that might sound like a benign information-gathering bureaucracy, the unit's nickname—"the Hell branch"—suggests otherwise. Masa's unit has the highest number of torture-related deaths in Syria: by most estimates, more than 3,000 people since 2011. According to Human Rights Watch, the victims were often arbitrarily arrested and detained, or were suspected of opposing the Syrian regime, perhaps solely in their thoughts. Human rights organizations have documented 45 different torture methods used by Masa and his squad, including electrocution, hanging by the wrists for days, or simply being beaten to death with clubs. The International Criminal Court and United Nations investigators are assembling evidence against Masa and Syrian President Bashar al-Assad for crimes against humanity.

In 1994 in Rwanda, members of the Hutu tribe shot or hacked to death nearly one million people from the minority Tutsi, a rival tribe. At one point, thousands of Tutsi took refuge in a Benedictine convent, believing the nuns there would shelter them. Instead, the mother superior, Sister Gertrude, and another nun, Sister Maria Kisito—both of them Hutu—reported the refugees to the Hutu militia. More than 7,000 Tutsi were killed in the ensuing massacre. When the two nuns were brought to trial in Belgium, where they had fled after the war, observers testified that when 500 Tutsi fled to the convent's garage, the two nuns brought the militiamen gasoline. The garage was set afire, and anyone trying to escape the flames was hacked to death. The women were sentenced to 15- and 12-year terms, respectively, for crimes against humanity.

In 1961, Adolf Eichmann, who had been a high-ranking officer of the Nazi elite, was sentenced to death for his part in the deportation and killing of millions of Jews during World War II. He was proud of his efficiency at his work and his ability to resist feeling pity for his victims. But when the Israelis captured him, he insisted that he was not anti-Semitic. Shortly before his execution, Eichmann said, "I am not the monster I am made out to be. I am the victim of a fallacy" (Brown, 1986).

The fallacy to which Eichmann referred was the widespread belief that a person who does monstrous deeds must be a monster. Sha'afiq Masa, Sisters Gertrude and Maria Kisito, and Adolf Eichmann all committed terrible deeds. Were they all deranged? Or evil? There does seem to be so much evil and cruelty in the world, and yet so much kindness, sacrifice, and heroism too. How can we even begin to explain either side of human nature?

The fields of *social psychology* and *cultural psychology* approach this question by examining the powerful influence of the social and cultural environment on the actions of individuals and

Syrian President Bassar al-Assad has overseen a regime that tortures its own people; Rwandan Hutu nuns Sister Gertrude and Sister Maria Kisito were charged with crimes against humanity for their role in Tutsi slaughter; Adolf Eichmann is shown during his trial in Israel. All of these people have been linked to crimes that horrified the world. Were they "monsters"?

groups. In this chapter, we will focus on the foundations of social psychology, basic principles that can help us understand why some people who are not "crazy" or "monstrous" nonetheless do unspeakably evil things, and, conversely, why otherwise ordinary people may reach heights of heroism when the occasion demands.

We will look at the influence of roles and attitudes, how people's behavior is affected by the groups and situations they are in, and the conditions under which people conform or dissent. Finally, we will consider some of the social and cultural reasons for prejudice and conflict between groups.

Social Forces

Imagine the life of a hermit. Completely cut off from society, you'd be able to do whatever you want whenever you want, not have to answer to anyone else, not have to meet anyone's expectations, and never have to interact with another human being. In some ways that might sound ideal, but in actuality you'd probably find that the absence of other people had a debilitating effect on you. Humans are social animals, and we pay a high price for loneliness, isolation, and social exclusion (Cacioppo et al., 2015; Freidler, Capser, & McCullough, 2015; Stillman & Baumeister, 2013). Yet sometimes it seems we pay an equally high price for social engagement. When humans agree to live in interactive social arrangements, a complex set of rules, expectations, and standards are an implicit part of the bargain.

Roles and Rules

LO 8.1.A Compare social norms and social roles, and note how each contributes to the social rules that govern a culture.

"We are all fragile creatures entwined in a cobweb of social constraints," social psychologist Stanley Milgram once said. The constraints he referred to are social **norms**, rules about how we are supposed to act, enforced by threats of punishment if we violate them and promises of reward if we follow them. Norms are the conventions of everyday life that make interactions with other people predictable and orderly; like a cobweb, they are often as invisible as they are strong. Every society has norms for just about everything in human experience: for conducting courtships, for raising children, for making decisions, for behavior in public places. Some norms are enshrined in law, such as "A person may not beat up another person, except in self-defense." Some are unspoken cultural understandings, such as "A man may beat up another man who insults his masculinity." And some are tiny, unspoken regulations

norms

Rules that regulate social life, including explicit laws and implicit cultural conventions.

that people follow unconsciously, such as "You may not sing at the top of your lungs on a public bus."

When people observe that "everyone else" seems to be violating a social norm, they are more likely to do so too—and this is the mechanism by which entire neighborhoods can deteriorate. In six natural field experiments conducted in the Netherlands, passersby were more likely to litter, to park illegally, and even to steal a five-euro bill from a mailbox if the sidewalks were dirty and unswept, if graffiti marked the walls, or if strangers were setting off illegal fireworks (Keizer, Linderberg, & Steg, 2008).

In every society, people also fill a variety of social **roles**, positions that are regulated by norms about how people in those positions should behave. Gender roles define the proper behavior for a man and a woman. Occupational roles determine the correct behavior for a manager and an employee, a professor and a student. Family roles set tasks for parent and child. Certain aspects of every role must be carried out or there will be penalties—emotional, financial, or professional. As a student, you know just what you have to do to pass your psychology course (or you should by now). How do you know what a role requirement is? You know when you violate it, intentionally or unintentionally, because you will probably feel uncomfortable, or other people will try to make you feel that way.

The requirements of a social role are in turn shaped by the culture you live in. **Culture** can be defined as a program of shared rules that govern the behavior of people in a community or society, and a set of values, beliefs, and customs shared by most members of that community and passed from one generation to another (Lonner, 1995). You learn most of your culture's rules and values the way you learn your culture's language: without thinking about it.

One cultural norm governs the rules for *conversational distance*: how close people normally stand to one another when they are speaking (Hall, 1959, 1976). In general, Arabs like to stand close enough to feel your breath, touch your arm, and see your eyes—a distance that makes most white Americans, Canadians, and northern Europeans uneasy, unless they are talking intimately with a lover. The English and the Swedes stand farthest apart when they converse; southern Europeans stand closer; and Latin Americans and Arabs stand the closest (Keating, 1994; Sommer, 1969). If you are talking to someone who has different cultural rules for distance from yours, you are likely to feel uncomfortable without knowing why. You may feel that the person is crowding you or being strangely distant. A student from Lebanon told us how relieved he was to learn this. "When Anglo students moved away from me, I thought they were prejudiced," he said. "Now I see why I was more comfortable talking with Latino students. They like to stand close, too."

Naturally, people bring their own personalities and interests to the roles they play. Just as two actors will play the same part differently even though they are reading from the same script, you will have your own reading of how to play the role of student, friend, parent, or employee. Nonetheless, the requirements of a social role are strong, so strong that they may even cause you to behave in ways that shatter your fundamental sense of the kind of person you are. We turn now to two classic studies that illuminate the power of social roles in our lives.

The Obedience Study

LO 8.1.B Outline the basic procedures and findings of the Milgram obedience experiments, and discuss five conditions that make disobedience to authority more likely.

In the early 1960s, Stanley Milgram (1963, 1974) designed a study that would become world famous. Milgram wanted to know how many people would obey an authority figure when directly ordered to violate their ethical standards. Participants in the study

Either alone or with a friend, try a mild form of norm violation (nothing alarming, obscene, dangerous, or offensive). You might stand backward in line at the grocery store or cafeteria; sit right next to a stranger in the library or at a movie, even when other seats are available; sing or hum loudly for a couple of minutes in a public place; or stand "too close" to a friend in conversation. Notice the reactions of onlookers, as well as your own feelings, while you violate this norm. If you do this exercise with someone else, one of you can be the "violator" and the other can write down the responses of others; then switch places. Was it easy to do this exercise? Why or why not?

role

A given social position that is governed by a set of norms for proper behavior.

Arabs stand much closer in conversation than Westerners do, close enough to feel one another's breath and "read" one another's eyes. Most Westerners would feel "crowded" standing so close, even when talking to a friend.

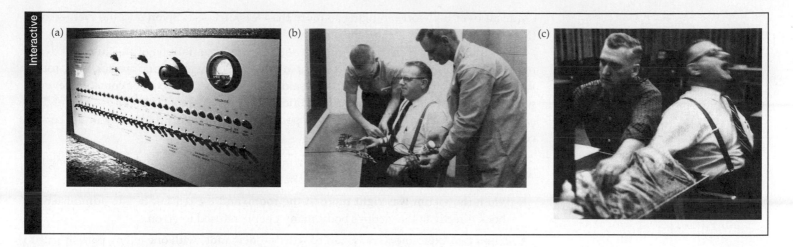

Figure 8.1 The Milgram Obedience Experiment

(a) Milgram's original shock machine; in 1963, it looked pretty ominous. (b) The "learner" is being strapped into his chair by the experimenter and the "teacher." (c) In Milgram's study, when the "teacher" had to administer shock directly to the learner, most subjects refused, but this one continued to obey.

Copyright 1965 by Stanley Milgram. From the film *Obedience*, distributed by Penn State Media Sales.

thought they were part of an experiment on the effects of punishment on learning. Each was assigned, apparently at random, to the role of "teacher." Another person, introduced as a fellow volunteer, was the "learner." Whenever the learner, seated in an adjoining room, made an error in reciting a list of word pairs he was supposed to have memorized, the teacher had to give him an electric shock by depressing a lever on a machine (see Figure 8.1). With each error, the voltage (marked from 0 to 450) was to be increased by another 15 volts. The shock levels on the machine were labeled from SLIGHT SHOCK to DANGER—SEVERE SHOCK and, finally, ominously, XXX. In reality, the learners were confederates of Milgram and did not receive any shocks, but none of the teachers ever realized this during the study. The actor-victims played their parts convincingly: As the study continued, they shouted in pain and pleaded to be released, all according to a pre-arranged script.

Before doing this study, Milgram asked a number of psychiatrists, students, and other adults how many people they thought would "go all the way" to XXX upon orders from the researcher. The psychiatrists predicted that most people would refuse to go beyond 150 volts, when the learner first demanded to be freed, and that only one person in a thousand, someone who was disturbed and sadistic, would administer the highest voltage. The nonprofessionals agreed with this prediction, and all of them said that they personally would disobey early in the procedure.

That is not, however, the way the results turned out. Every single person administered some shock to the learner, and about two-thirds of the participants, of all ages and from all walks of life, obeyed to the fullest extent. Many protested to the experimenter, but they backed down when he calmly asserted, "The experiment requires that you continue." They obeyed no matter how much the victim shouted for them to stop and no matter how painful the shocks seemed to be. They obeyed even when they themselves were anguished about the pain they believed they were causing. As Milgram (1974) noted, participants would "sweat, tremble, stutter, bite their lips, groan, and dig their fingernails into their flesh"—but still they obeyed.

Over the decades, more than 3,000 people of many different ethnicities have gone through replications of the Milgram study. Most of them, men and women equally, inflicted what they thought were dangerous amounts of shock to another person. High percentages of obedience

culture

A program of shared rules that govern the behavior of people in a community or society, and a set of values, beliefs, and customs shared by most members of that community.

occur all over the world, ranging to more than 90 percent in Spain and the Netherlands (Meeus & Raaijmakers, 1995; Smith & Bond, 1994).

Milgram and his team subsequently set up several variations of the study to determine the circumstances under which people might disobey the experimenter. They found that virtually nothing the victim did or said changed the likelihood of compliance, even when the victim said he had a heart condition, screamed in agony, or stopped responding entirely, as if he had collapsed. However, people *were* more likely to disobey under certain conditions:

- **When the experimenter left the room,** many people subverted authority by giving low levels of shock but reporting that they had followed orders.
- **When the victim was right there in the room,** and the teacher had to administer the shock directly to the victim's body, many people refused to go on.
- **When two experimenters issued conflicting demands,** with one telling participants to continue and another saying to stop at once, no one kept inflicting shock.
- **When the person ordering them to continue was an ordinary man,** apparently another volunteer instead of the authoritative experimenter, many participants disobeyed.
- **When the participant worked with peers who refused to go further,** he or she often gained the courage to disobey.

Obedience, Milgram concluded, was more a function of the *situation* than of the personalities of the participants. "The key to [their] behavior," Milgram (1974) summarized, "lies not in pent-up anger or aggression but in the nature of their relationship to authority. They have given themselves to the authority; they see themselves as instruments for the execution of his wishes; once so defined, they are unable to break free."

The Milgram study has had critics. Some consider it unethical because people were kept in the dark about what was really happening until the session was over (of course, telling them in advance would have invalidated the study) and because many suffered emotional pain (Milgram countered that they would not have felt pain if they had simply disobeyed instructions). The original study could never be repeated in the United States today because of these ethical concerns. However, a "softer" version of the experiment has been done, in which "teachers" who had not heard of the original Milgram study were asked to administer shocks only up to 150 volts, when they first heard the learner protest. That amount of shock had been a critical choice point in Milgram's study, and in the replication, nearly 80 percent of those who went past 150 ended up going all the way to the end (Packer, 2008). Overall obedience rates were only slightly lower than Milgram's, and once again, gender, education, age, and ethnicity had no effect on the likelihood of obeying (Burger, 2009). In another, rather eerie cyberversion replication of Milgram's study, participants had to shock a virtual woman on a computer screen. Even though they knew she wasn't real, their heart rates increased and they reported feeling bad about delivering the "shocks." Yet they kept doing it (Slater et al., 2006).

Some psychologists have questioned Milgram's conclusion that personality traits are virtually irrelevant to whether people obey an authority. Certain traits, they note, especially hostility, narcissism, and rigidity, do increase obedience and a willingness to inflict pain on others (Blass, 2000; Twenge, 2009). Others have objected to the parallel Milgram drew between the behavior of the study's participants and the brutality of the Nazis and others who have committed acts of barbarity in the name of duty (Darley, 1995). The people in Milgram's study typically obeyed only when the experimenter was hovering right there, and many of them felt enormous discomfort. In contrast, most Nazis acted without direct supervision by authorities, without external pressure, and without feelings of anguish.

Nevertheless, no one disputes that Milgram's compelling study has had a tremendous influence on public awareness of the dangers of uncritical obedience. As John Darley (1995) observed, "Milgram shows us the beginning of a path by means of which ordinary people, in the grip of social forces, become the origins of atrocities in the real world."

The Prison Study

LO 8.1.C Outline the basic procedures and findings of the Zimbardo prison study.

Another famous demonstration of the power of roles is known as the Stanford prison study. Its primary designer, Philip Zimbardo, wanted to know what would happen if ordinary college students were randomly assigned to the roles of prisoners and guards. And so he and his associates set up a serious-looking "prison" in the basement of a Stanford building, complete with individual cells, different uniforms for prisoners and guards, and nightsticks for the guards (Haney, Banks, & Zimbardo, 1973). The students agreed to live there for 2 weeks.

Within a short time, most of the prisoners became distressed and helpless. They developed emotional symptoms and physical ailments. Some became apathetic; others became rebellious. One panicked and broke down. The guards, however, began to enjoy their new power. Some tried to be nice, helping the prisoners and doing little favors for them. Some were "tough but fair," holding strictly to "the rules." But about a third became punitive and harsh, even when the prisoners were not resisting in any way. One guard became unusually sadistic, smacking his nightstick into his palm as he vowed to "get" the prisoners and instructing two of them to simulate sexual acts (they refused). Zimbardo, who had not expected such a speedy and alarming transformation of ordinary students, ended this study after only 6 days.

Generations of students and the general public have seen emotionally charged clips from videos of the study made at the time. To Zimbardo, the results demonstrated how roles affect behavior: The guards' aggression was entirely a result of wearing a guard's uniform and having the power conferred by a guard's authority (Haney & Zimbardo, 1998). Some social psychologists, however, have argued that the prison study is really another example of obedience to authority and of how willingly some people obey instructions, in this case from Zimbardo himself (Carnahan & McFarland, 2007; Haslam & Reicher, 2003). Consider the briefing that Zimbardo provided to the guards at the beginning of the study:

> You can create in the prisoners feelings of boredom, a sense of fear to some degree, you can create a notion of arbitrariness that their life is totally controlled by us, by the system, you, me, and they'll have no privacy . . . . We're going to take away their individuality in various ways. In general what all this leads to is a sense of powerlessness. That is, in this situation we'll have all the power and they'll have none. (*The Stanford Prison Study* video, quoted in Haslam & Reicher, 2003)

These are pretty powerful suggestions to the guards about how they would be permitted to behave, and they convey Zimbardo's personal encouragement ("*We'll* have all the power"), so perhaps it is not surprising that some took Zimbardo at his word and behaved quite brutally. The one sadistic guard later said he was just trying to play the role of the "worst S.O.B. guard" he'd seen in the movies. Even the investigators themselves noted at the time that the data were "subject to possible errors due to selective sampling. The video and audio recordings tended to be focused upon the more interesting, dramatic events which occurred" (Haney, Curtis, & Zimbardo, 1973).

Despite these flaws, the Stanford prison study remains a useful cautionary tale. In real prisons, guards do have tremendous power, and they too may be given permission to use that power harshly. Thus the prison study provides a good example of how the social situation affects behavior, causing some people to behave in ways that seem out of character.

Prisoners and guards quickly learn their respective roles, which often have more influence on their behavior than their personalities do.

Why People Obey

LO 8.1.D **Explain how feelings of entrapment contribute to destructive obedience.**

entrapment

A gradual process in which individuals escalate their commitment to a course of action to justify their investment of time, money, or effort.

Of course, obedience to authority or to the norms of a situation is not always harmful or bad. A certain amount of routine compliance with rules is necessary in any group, and obedience to authority has many benefits for individuals and society. A nation could not operate if all its citizens ignored traffic signals, cheated on their taxes, dumped garbage wherever they chose, or assaulted each other. A business organization could not function if its members came to work only when they felt like it. But obedience also has a darker aspect. Throughout history, the plea "I was only following orders" has been offered to excuse actions carried out on behalf of orders that were foolish, destructive, or criminal. Writer C. P. Snow observed that "more hideous crimes have been committed in the name of obedience than in the name of rebellion."

Most people follow orders because of the obvious consequences of disobedience: They can be suspended from school, fired from their jobs, or arrested. But they may also obey an authority because they hope to gain advantages or promotions or expect to learn from the authority's greater knowledge or experience. They obey because they are dependent on the authority and respect the authority's legitimacy (van der Toorn, Tyler, & Jost, 2011). And, most of all, they obey because they do not want to rock the boat, appear to doubt the experts, or be rude, fearing that they will be disliked or rejected for doing so (Collins & Brief, 1995). But what about all those people in Milgram's study who felt they were doing wrong and who wished they were free, but who could not untangle themselves from the "cobweb of social constraints"? How do people become morally disengaged from the consequences of their actions?

One answer is **entrapment**, a process in which individuals escalate their commitment to a course of action in order to justify their investment in it (Brockner & Rubin, 1985). The first stages of entrapment may pose no difficult choices, but as people take another step, or make a decision to continue, they will justify that action, which allows them to feel that it is the right one. Before long, the person has become committed to a course of action that is increasingly self-defeating, cruel, or foolhardy.

Thus, in the Milgram study, after participants had given a 15-volt shock, they had committed themselves to the experiment. The next level was "only" 30 volts. Because each increment was small, before they knew it most people were administering what they believed were dangerously strong shocks. At that point, it was difficult to justify a sudden decision to quit, especially after reaching 150 volts, the point at which the "learner" made his first verbal protests. Those who administered the highest levels of shock justified their actions by adopting the attitude of "It's his problem; I'm just following orders," handing over responsibility to the authority and absolving themselves of accountability for their own actions (Burger, 2014; Kelman & Hamilton, 1989; Modigliani & Rochat, 1995). In contrast, individuals who refused to give high levels of shock justified *their* decision by taking responsibility for their actions. "One of the things I think is very cowardly," said a 32-year-old engineer, "is to try to shove the responsibility onto someone else. See, if I now turned around and said, 'It's your fault . . . it's not mine,' I would call that cowardly" (Milgram, 1974).

A chilling study of entrapment was conducted with 25 men who had served in the Greek military police during the authoritarian regime that ended in 1974 (Haritos-Fatouros, 1988). A psychologist interviewed the men, identifying the steps used in training them to use torture in questioning prisoners. First, the men were ordered to stand guard outside the interrogation and torture cells. Then they stood guard inside the detention rooms, where they observed the torture of prisoners. Then they "helped" beat up prisoners. After they had obediently followed these orders and became actively involved, the torturers found their actions easier to carry out. Similar procedures have been used around the world to train military and police interrogators to use torture on political opponents and criminal suspects, although torture is expressly forbidden under international law (Conroy, 2000; Huggins, Haritos-Fatouros, & Zimbardo, 2003; Mayer, 2009).

From their standpoint, torturers justify their actions because they see themselves as "good guys" who are just "doing their jobs," especially in wartime. And perhaps they are—but such a justification overlooks entrapment. This prisoner might be a murderer or a terrorist, but what if this other one is completely innocent? Before long, the torturer has shifted his reasoning from "If this person is guilty, he deserves to be tortured" to "If I am torturing this person, he must be guilty—and besides, if I am doing it, it isn't torture." And so the abuse escalates (Tavris & Aronson, 2007).

This is a difficult concept for people who divide the world into "good guys" versus "bad guys" and cannot imagine that good guys might do brutal things; if the good guys are doing it, by definition, it's all right to do. Yet in everyday life, as in the Milgram study, people often set out on a path that is morally ambiguous, only to find that they have traveled a long way toward violating their own principles. From Greece's torturers to the African nuns, from Milgram's well-meaning volunteers to all of us in our everyday lives, from cheating on exams to cheating in business, people face the difficult task of drawing a line beyond which they will not go. For many, the demands of the role and the social pressures of the situation defeat the inner voice of conscience.

JOURNAL PROMPT 8.1

Thinking Critically—Define Your Terms: Think of three social norms that you regularly follow, and think of three social roles that you fill. Which of these are implicit and which are explicit? Now describe what you might do to violate one of those norms or roles. What kinds of reactions would come from the people around you, and what kinds of punishment might you experience because of that violation? Finally, discuss how the social situations you find yourself in maintain and define the norms and roles you subscribe to.

Quiz for Module 8.1

1. Rules that regulate social life, such as explicit laws and implicit cultural conventions, are referred to as

   a. Regulations

   b. Customs

   c. Norms

   d. Roles

2. Stanley Milgram's research on obedience found that "teachers" tended to deliver less shock to "learners" if

   a. The experiment took place in a prestigious setting.

   b. The experimenter was presented as a legitimate authority figure.

   c. The experimenter was not physically present.

   d. Milgram himself stood near the teacher and gave the orders.

3. About what proportion of the people in Milgram's obedience study administered the highest level of shock?

   a. One-half

   b. Two-thirds

   c. One-third

   d. One-tenth

4. What general conclusion can be reached from the Stanford prison study?

   a. Social situations can exert a strong influence on behavior.

   b. Sadistic people will behave sadistically when given the opportunity to do so.

   c. A powerful authority figure can use fear to decrease the amount of destructive obedience in a prison.

   d. Prisoners have either a genetic weakness or a personality weakness that makes them conform.

5. When people escalate their commitment to a course of action in order to justify their investment in that course of action—even if the actions are wrong or destructive—the process of _____ has taken place.

   a. Engagement

   b. Conformity

   c. Compliance

   d. Entrapment

Social Influences on Beliefs and Behavior

attribution theory

The theory that people are motivated to explain their own and other people's behavior by attributing causes of that behavior to a situation or a disposition.

fundamental attribution error

The tendency, in explaining other people's behavior, to overestimate personality factors and underestimate the influence of the situation.

Social psychologists are interested not only in what people do in social situations, but also in what is going on in their heads while they are doing it. Those who study *social cognition* examine how people's perceptions of themselves and others affect their relationships and also how the social environment influences their perceptions, beliefs, and values. Current approaches draw on evolutionary theory, neuroimaging studies, surveys, and experiments to identify universal themes in how human beings perceive and feel about one another. In this section, we will consider two important topics in social cognition: attributions and attitudes.

Attributions

LO 8.2.A **Contrast situational and dispositional attributions, explain how and why the fundamental attribution error takes place, and describe three biases that people hold about themselves and others.**

A detective's job is to find out *who* did the dirty deed, but most of us also want to know *why* people do bad things. Was it because of a terrible childhood, a mental illness, possession by a demon, or what? According to **attribution theory**, the explanations we make of our behavior and the behavior of others generally fall into two categories. When we make a *situational attribution*, we are identifying the cause of an action as something in the situation or environment: "Joe stole the money because his family is starving." When we make a *dispositional attribution*, we are identifying the cause of an action as something in the person: "Joe stole the money because he is a born thief."

When people are trying to explain someone else's behavior, they tend to overestimate personality traits and underestimate the influence of the situation (Forgas, 1998; Gilbert & Malone, 1995; Nisbett & Ross, 1980). In terms of attribution theory, they tend to ignore situational attributions in favor of dispositional ones. This tendency has been called the **fundamental attribution error** (Jones, 1990).

Were the hundreds of people who obeyed Milgram's experimenters sadistic by nature? Were the student guards in the prison study cruel and the prisoners cowardly by temperament? Were the individuals who pocketed the money from a mailbox on a dirty street "born thieves"? Those who think so are committing the fundamental attribution error. The impulse to explain other people's behavior in terms of their personalities is so strong that we do it even when we know that the other person was *required* to behave in a certain way (Yzerbyt et al., 2001).

The fundamental attribution error is especially prevalent in Western nations, where middle-class people tend to believe that individuals are responsible for their own actions and dislike the idea that the situation has much influence over them. Therefore, they prefer to explain behavior in terms of people's traits (Na & Kitayama, 2011). They think that *they* would have refused the experimenter's cruel orders and *they* would have treated fellow-students-temporarily-called-prisoners fairly. In contrast, in countries such as India, where everyone is embedded in caste and family networks, and in Japan, China, Korea, and Hong Kong, where people are more group oriented than in the West, people are more likely to be aware of situational constraints on behavior, including their own behavior (Balcetis, Dunning, & Miller, 2008; Choi et al., 2003). Thus, if someone is behaving oddly, makes a mistake,

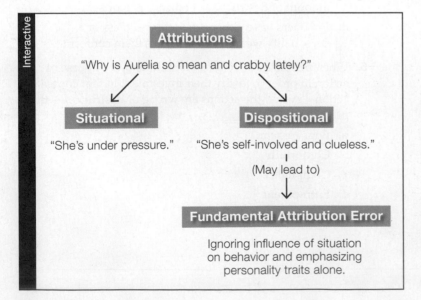

Attributions

"Why is Aurelia so mean and crabby lately?"

Situational

"She's under pressure."

Dispositional

"She's self-involved and clueless."

(May lead to)

Fundamental Attribution Error

Ignoring influence of situation on behavior and emphasizing personality traits alone.

or commits an ethical lapse, a person from India or China, unlike a Westerner, is more likely to make a situational attribution of the person's behavior ("He's under pressure") than a dispositional one ("He's incompetent").

A primary reason for the fundamental attribution error is that people rely on different sources of information to judge their own behavior and that of others. We know what we ourselves are thinking and feeling, but we can't always know the same of others. Thus, we assess our own actions by introspecting about our feelings and intentions, but when we observe the actions of others, we have only their behavior to guide our interpretations (Pronin, 2008; Pronin, Gilovich, & Ross, 2004). This basic asymmetry in social perception is further widened by *self-serving biases*, habits of thinking that make us feel good about ourselves, even (perhaps especially) when we shouldn't. Here are three types of self-serving biases that are especially relevant to the attributions that people often make:

1. **The bias to choose the most flattering and forgiving attributions of our own lapses.** When it comes to explaining their own behavior, people tend to choose attributions that are favorable to them, taking credit for their good actions (a dispositional attribution) but letting the situation account for their failures, embarrassing mistakes, or harmful actions (Mezulis et al., 2004). For instance, most North Americans, when angry, will say, "I am furious for good reason; this situation is intolerable." They are less likely to say, "I am furious because I am an ill-tempered grinch." On the other hand, if they do something admirable, such as donating to charity, they are likely to attribute their motives to a personal disposition ("I'm so generous") instead of the situation ("That guy on the phone pressured me into it").

2. **The bias that we are better, smarter, and kinder than others.** This one has been called the "self-enhancement" bias or the "better-than-average" effect. It describes the tendency of most people to think they are much better than their peers on many valued dimensions: more virtuous, honorable, and moral; more competent; more compassionate and generous (Balcetis, Dunning, & Miller, 2008; Brown, 2012; Dunning et al., 2003; Loughnan et al., 2011). They overestimate their willingness to do the right thing in a moral dilemma, give to a charity, cooperate with a stranger in trouble, and so on. But when they are actually in a situation that calls for generosity, compassion, or ethical action, most people fail to live up to their own inflated self-image because the demands of the situation have a stronger influence than good intentions. This bias even occurs among people who literally strive to be "holier than thou" and "humbler than thee" for religious reasons (Rowatt et al., 2002). In two studies conducted at fundamentalist Christian colleges, the greater the students' intrinsic religiosity and fundamentalism, the greater was their tendency to rate themselves as being more adherent to biblical commandments than other people—and more humble than other people, too!

3. **The bias to believe that the world is fair.** According to the **just-world hypothesis**, attributions are also affected by the need to believe that justice usually prevails, that good people are rewarded and bad guys punished (Lerner, 1980). When this belief is thrown into doubt—especially when bad things happen to "good people" who are just like us—we are motivated to restore it (Aguiar et al., 2008; Hafer & Rubel, 2015). Unfortunately, one common way of restoring the belief in a just world is to call upon a dispositional attribution called *blaming the victim*: Maybe that person wasn't so good after all; he or she must have done *something* to deserve what happened or to provoke it. Blaming the victim is virtually universal when people are ordered to harm others or find themselves entrapped into harming others (Bandura, 1999). In the Milgram study, some "teachers" made comments such as "[The learner] was so stupid and stubborn he deserved to get shocked" (Milgram, 1974).

It is good for our self-esteem to feel that we are kinder, more competent, and more moral than other people, and to believe that we are not influenced by external circumstances (except when they excuse our mistakes). But these flattering delusions can distort communication, impede the resolution of conflicts, and lead to serious misunderstandings.

just-world hypothesis
The notion that many people need to believe that the world is fair and that justice is served, that bad people are punished and good people are rewarded.

cognitive dissonance

A state of tension that occurs when a person simultaneously holds two cognitions that are psychologically inconsistent or when a person's belief is incongruent with his or her behavior.

Of course, sometimes dispositional attributions *do* explain a person's behavior. The point to remember is that the attributions you make can have huge consequences. For example, happy couples usually attribute their partners' occasional thoughtless lapses to something in the situation ("Poor guy is under a lot of stress") and their partners' loving actions to a stable, internal disposition ("He has the sweetest nature"). But unhappy couples do just the reverse. They attribute lapses to their partners' personalities ("He is totally selfish") and good behavior to the situation ("Yeah, he gave me a present, but only because his mother told him to") (Karney & Bradbury, 2000). You can see why the attributions you make about your partner, your parents, and your friends will affect how you get along with them—and how long you will put up with their failings.

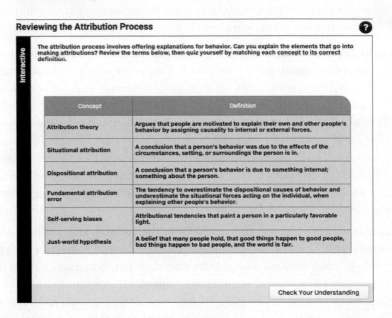

Reviewing the Attribution Process

The attribution process involves offering explanations for behavior. Can you explain the elements that go into making attributions? Review the terms below, then quiz yourself by matching each concept to its correct definition.

Concept	Definition
Attribution theory	Argues that people are motivated to explain their own and other people's behavior by assigning causality to internal or external forces.
Situational attribution	A conclusion that a person's behavior was due to the effects of the circumstances, setting, or surroundings the person is in.
Dispositional attribution	A conclusion that a person's behavior is due to something internal; something about the person.
Fundamental attribution error	The tendency to overestimate the dispositional causes of behavior and underestimate the situational forces acting on the individual, when explaining other people's behavior.
Self-serving biases	Attributional tendencies that paint a person in a particularly favorable light.
Just-world hypothesis	A belief that many people hold, that good things happen to good people, bad things happen to bad people, and the world is fair.

Check Your Understanding

Attitudes

LO 8.2.B Outline the process of cognitive dissonance, and explain how the validity effect and the familiarity effect shape our attitudes.

People hold attitudes about all sorts of things—politics, food, children, movies, sports heroes, you name it. An *attitude* is a belief about people, groups, ideas, or activities. Some attitudes are *explicit*: We are aware of them, they shape our conscious decisions and actions, and they can be measured on self-report questionnaires. Others are *implicit*: We are unaware of them, they may influence our behavior in ways we do not recognize, and they are measured in indirect ways (Stanley, Phelps, & Banaji, 2008).

COGNITIVE DISSONANCE Some of your attitudes change when you have new experiences, and on occasion they change because you rationally decide you were wrong about something. But attitudes also change because of the psychological need for consistency and the mind's normal biases in processing information. **Cognitive dissonance** is the uncomfortable feeling that occurs when two attitudes, or an attitude and a behavior, are in conflict (are dissonant). To resolve this dissonance, most people will change one of their attitudes. If a politician or celebrity you admire does something stupid, immoral, or illegal, you can restore consistency either by lowering your opinion of the person or by deciding that the person's behavior wasn't so stupid or immoral after all.

Here's an example closer to home: cheating. Let's say two students have the same general attitude toward it: It's not an ideal way to get ahead, but it's not the greatest crime, either (see Figure 8.2a). Now they take an important exam and freeze on a crucial question. They have a choice: Read their neighbor's answers and cheat (to get a better grade) or refrain from doing so (to maintain feelings of integrity). Impulsively, one cheats; the other doesn't (see Figure 8.2b). What happens now? The answer is illustrated in Figure 8.2c. To reduce dissonance, *each one will justify their action to make it consonant with their beliefs*. The one who refrained will begin to think that cheating is serious after all, that it harms everyone, and that cheaters should be punished ("Hey! Expel them!"). But the one who cheated will need to resolve the dissonance between "I am a fine, honest human being" and "I just cheated." He or she could say, "I guess I'm not an honest person after all," but it is more likely that the person will instead decide that cheating isn't very serious ("Hey! Everyone does it!").

Understanding how cognitive dissonance works to keep our beliefs and behavior in harmony is important because the way we reduce dissonance can have major, unexpected consequences. The student who cheated "just this once" will find it easier to cheat again on an assignment, and then again by turning in a term paper written by someone else, sliding down the slippery slope of entrapment. By the time the cheater has slid to the bottom, it will be extremely difficult to go back up because that would mean admitting "I was wrong; I did a bad thing." That is how a small act of dishonesty, corruption, or error—from cheating to staying in a bad relationship—can set a person on a course of action that becomes increasingly self-defeating, cruel, or foolhardy . . . and difficult to reverse (Tavris & Aronson, 2007).

Unfortunately for critical thinking, people often restore cognitive consistency by dismissing evidence that might otherwise throw their fundamental beliefs into question (Aronson, 2012). In fact, they often become even *more* committed to a discredited belief. In one study, when people were thrown into doubt about the rightness of a belief or their position on some issue that was very important to them—such as being a vegetarian or carnivore—they reduced dissonance by advocating their original position even more strongly. As the researchers summarized, "When in doubt, shout!" (Gal & Rucker, 2010). This mechanism explains why people in religious cults that have invested heavily in failed doomsday predictions rarely say, "What a relief that I was wrong." Instead, many become even more committed proselytizers (Festinger, Riecken, & Schachter, 1956). To learn more about the process of cognitive dissonance, watch the video *Changing Attitudes and Behavior 1*.

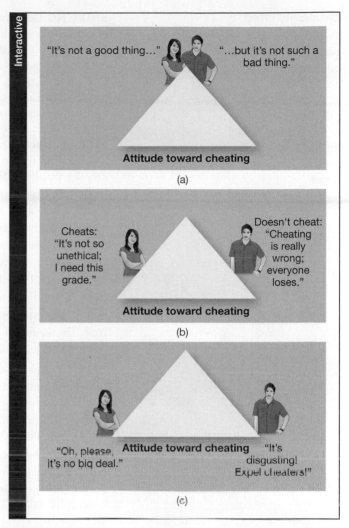

Figure 8.2 The Slippery Slope of Self-Justification

(a) Imagine two people with the same neutral attitude toward cheating. (b) Given an opportunity, one cheats and the other doesn't. (c) Because of the need to reduce cognitive dissonance, each will then justify the action they took so that their opinion about cheating is consonant with their behavior. Over time, they both will have moved a long way from their original attitude.

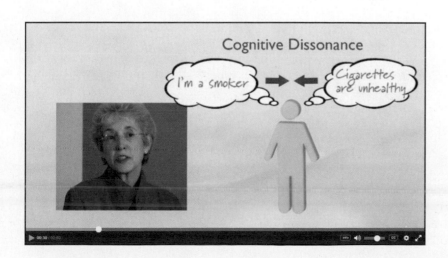

familiarity effect

The tendency of people to feel more positive toward a person, item, product, or other stimulus the more familiar they are with it.

validity effect

The tendency of people to believe that a statement is true or valid simply because it has been repeated many times.

SHIFTING OPINIONS AND BEDROCK BELIEFS   All around you, every day, advertisers, politicians, and friends are trying to influence your attitudes. One weapon they use is the drip, drip, drip of a repeated idea (Lee, Ahn, & Park, 2015). Repeated exposure even to a nonsense syllable such as *zug* is enough to make a person feel more positive toward it (Zajonc, 1968). The **familiarity effect**, the tendency to hold positive attitudes toward familiar people or things, has been demonstrated across cultures, across species, and across states of awareness, from alert to preoccupied. It works even for stimuli you aren't aware of seeing (Monahan, Murphy, & Zajonc, 2000). A related phenomenon is the **validity effect**, the tendency to believe that something is true simply because it has been repeated many times. Repeat something often enough, even the basest lie, and eventually the public will believe it. Hitler's propaganda minister, Joseph Goebbels, called this technique the "Big Lie."

In a series of experiments, Hal Arkes and his associates demonstrated how the validity effect operates (Arkes, 1993; Arkes, Boehm, & Xu, 1991). In a typical study, people read a list of statements, such as "Mercury has a higher boiling point than copper" or "Over 400 Hollywood films were produced in 1948." They had to rate each statement for its validity, on a scale of 1 (definitely false) to 7 (definitely true). A week or two later, they again rated the validity of some of these statements and also rated others that they had not seen previously. The result: Mere repetition increased the perception that the familiar statements were true. The same effect also occurred for other kinds of statements, including unverifiable opinions (e.g., "At least 75 percent of all politicians are basically dishonest"), opinions that subjects initially felt were true, and even opinions they initially felt were false. "Note that no attempt has been made to persuade," said Arkes (1993). "No supporting arguments are offered. We just have subjects rate the statements. Mere repetition seems to increase rated validity. This is scary."

On most everyday topics, such as movies, sports, and the boiling point of mercury, people's attitudes range from casual to committed. If your best friend is neutral about baseball whereas you are an insanely devoted fan, your friendship will probably survive. But when the subject is one involving beliefs that give meaning and purpose to a person's life—most notably, politics and religion—it's another ball game, so to speak. Wars have been fought, and are being fought as you read this, over people's most passionate convictions. Perhaps the attitude that causes the most controversy and bitterness around the world is the one toward religious diversity: accepting or intolerant. Some people of all religions accept a world of differing religious views and practices; they believe that church and state should be separate. But for many fundamentalists in any religion, religion and politics are inseparable; they believe that one religion should prevail (Jost et al., 2003). You can see, then, why these irreconcilable attitudes cause continuing conflict, and sometimes are used to justify terrorism and war. Why are people so different in these views? Watch *Changing Attitudes and Behavior 2* to learn what an expert in this field has to say about this issue.

BIOLOGY and *Beliefs*

Do you support or disapprove of the death penalty, a woman's right to choose an abortion, and same-sex marriage? Are you worried about environmental issues or health-care reform? Where did your attitudes on these issues come from?

Many attitudes result from learning and experience, of course. But research from behavioral genetics has found that some core attitudes stem from personality traits that are heritable. That is, the variation among people in these attitudes is due in part to their genetic differences. Two such traits are "openness to experience" and "conscientiousness." We would expect people who are open to new experiences to hold positive attitudes toward novelty and change in general—say, in religion, art, music, and social and political events in the larger culture. We would expect people who prefer the familiar and conventional, and who are conscientious about order and obligations, to be drawn to conservative politics, religious denominations, and philosophies. And that is what research finds. In a study of Protestant Christians, fundamentalist Christians scored much lower than liberal Christians on the dimension of openness to experience (Streyffeler & McNally, 1998). Conversely, conservatives score higher than liberals on conscientiousness (Jost, 2006).

Religious *affiliation*—whether a person is a Methodist, Muslim, Catholic, Jew, Hindu, and so on—is not heritable. Most people choose a religious group because of their parents, ethnicity, culture, and social class, and many Americans switch their religious affiliation at least once in their lives. Increasing numbers report having no religious affiliation or belief. But, as studies of twins reared apart have found, *religiosity*—a person's depth of religious feeling and adherence to a religion's rules—does have a genetic component. When religiosity combines with conservatism and authoritarianism (an unquestioning trust in authority), the result is a deeply ingrained acceptance of tradition and dislike of those who question it (Ludeke, Johnson, & Bouchard, 2013; Olson et al., 2001; Saucier, 2000).

Likewise, political affiliation is not heritable; it is largely related to your upbringing and to the friends you make in early adulthood, the key years for deciding which party you want to join. Nor do the casual political opinions held by many swing voters or people who are politically disengaged have a genetic component. But political conservatism has high heritability: 0.65 in men and 0.45 in women (Bouchard, 2004). Various political positions on emotionally hot topics that are associated with conservative or liberal views are also partly heritable. A team of researchers analyzed two large samples of more than 8,000 sets of twins who had been surveyed about their personality traits, religious beliefs, and political attitudes (Alford, Funk, & Hibbing, 2005). The researchers compared the opinions of fraternal twins (who share, on average, 50 percent of their genes) with those of identical twins (who share virtually all of their genes). They calculated

how often the identical twins agreed on each issue, subtracted the rate at which fraternal twins agreed, and ended up with a rough measure of heritability. As you can see in Figure 8.3, the attitudes showing the highest heritability were those toward school prayer and property taxes; attitudes showing the lowest influence of genes included those toward nuclear power, divorce, modern art, and abortion.

As a result of such evidence, some psychological scientists maintain that ideological belief systems may have evolved in human societies to be organized along a left–right dimension, consisting of two core sets of attitudes: (1) whether a person advocates social change or supports the system as it is, and (2) whether a person thinks inequality is a result of human policies and can be overcome, or is inevitable and should be accepted as part of the natural order (Graham, Haidt, & Nosek, 2009). Liberals tend to prefer the values of progress, rebelliousness, chaos, flexibility, feminism, and equality, whereas conservatives tend to prefer tradition, conformity, order, stability, traditional values, and hierarchy. Those two dimensions underlie a host of specific attitudes. A study of undergraduates at the University of Texas at Austin found that liberal students were more

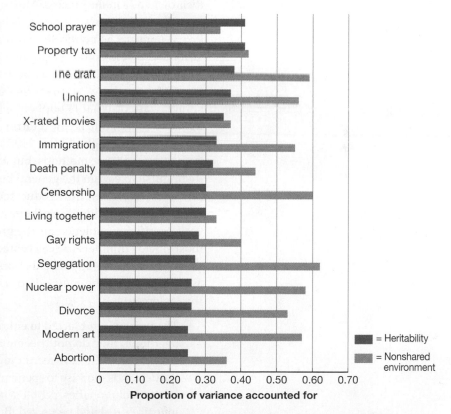

Figure 8.3 The Genetics of Belief

A study of thousands of identical and fraternal twins identified the approximate genetic contribution to the variation in attitudes about diverse topics. Heritability was greatest for school prayer and property tax, and lowest for divorce, modern art, and abortion. But notice that in almost all cases, a person's unique life experiences (the "nonshared environment") were far more influential than genes, especially on attitudes toward topics as unrelated as the draft, censorship, and segregation (Alford, Funk, & Hibbing, 2005).

likely than conservative students to have favorable attitudes toward atheists, poetry, Asian food, jazz, street people, tattoos, foreign films, erotica, big cities, recreational drugs, and foreign travel—all examples of "openness to experience" rather than preference for the familiar (Jost, Nosek, & Gosling, 2008).

You can see why liberals and conservatives argue so emotionally over issues such as gun control, social protest, and gay marriage. They are not only arguing about the specific issue, but also about each side's underlying assumptions and values that emerge from their personality traits. Evolutionary psychologists point out that both sets of attitudes would have had adaptive benefits over the centuries: Conservatism would have promoted stability, tradition, and order, whereas liberalism would have promoted flexibility and change (Graham, Haidt, & Nosek, 2009).

These findings are provocative, but let's not oversimplify by incorrectly assuming that everyone's political opinions are hard-wired and unaffected by events. In fact, the factor that accounts for even more of the variation in political attitudes than heritability is individual life experiences, or what behavioral geneticists call the *nonshared environment* (Alford, Funk, & Hibbing, 2005). What do you think might be the personality dispositions that underlie your own ideological commitments? What might be the experiences you have had, because of your family, gender, ethnicity, social class, or unique history, that have shaped your own political views?

Persuasion or "Brainwashing"? The Case of Suicide Bombers

LO 8.2.C Summarize four elements that contribute to indoctrination.

Let's now see how the social-psychological factors discussed thus far might help explain the disturbing phenomenon of suicide bombers. In many countries, young men and women have wired themselves with explosives and blown up soldiers, civilians, and children, sacrificing their own lives in the process. Although people on two sides of a war dispute the definition of terrorism—one side's "terrorist" is the other side's "freedom fighter"—most social scientists define *terrorism* as politically motivated violence specifically designed to instill feelings of terror and helplessness in a population (Moghaddam, 2005; Roberts, 2015). Are these perpetrators mentally ill? Have they been "brainwashed"?

"Brainwashing" implies that a person has had a sudden change of mind without being aware of what is happening; it sounds mysterious and strange. On the contrary, the methods used to create a terrorist suicide bomber are neither mysterious nor unusual (Bloom, 2005; Moghaddam, 2005). Some people may be more emotionally vulnerable than others to these methods, but most of the people who become terrorists are not easily distinguishable from the general population. Indeed, most of them had no psychopathology and were often quite educated and affluent (Krueger, 2007; Sageman, 2008; Silke, 2003). Rather than defining themselves as terrorists, they saw themselves as committing "self-sacrificing violence for the greater good"; and far from being seen as crazy loners, most suicide bombers are celebrated by their families and communities for their "martyrdom." This social support enhances their commitment to the cause (Bloom, 2005; Ginges & Atran, 2011). The methods of indoctrination that lead to that commitment include these elements:

- **The person is subjected to entrapment.** Just as ordinary people do not become torturers overnight, they do not become terrorists overnight either; the process proceeds step by step. At first, the new recruit to the cause agrees only to do small things, but gradually the demands increase to spend more time, spend more money, make more sacrifices. Like other revolutionaries, people who become suicide bombers are idealistic and angry about injustices, real and perceived. But some ultimately take extreme measures because, over time, they have become entrapped in closed groups led by strong or charismatic leaders (Moghaddam, 2005).

- **The person's problems, personal and political, are explained by one simple attribution,** repeatedly emphasized: "It's all the fault of those bad people; we have to eliminate them."

- **The person is offered a new identity and is promised salvation.** The recruit is told that he or she is part of the chosen, the elite, or the saved. In 1095, Pope Urban II launched a holy war against Muslims, assuring his forces that killing a Muslim was an act of Christian penance. Anyone killed in battle, the pope promised, would bypass thousands of years of torture in purgatory and go directly to heaven. This is what young Muslim terrorists are promised today for killing Western "infidels."

- **The person's access to disconfirming (dissonant) information is severely controlled.** As soon as a person is a committed believer, the leader limits the person's choices, denigrates critical thinking, and suppresses private doubts. Recruits may be physically isolated from the outside world and thus from antidotes to the leader's ideas. They are separated from their families, are indoctrinated and trained for 18 months or more, and eventually become emotionally bonded to the group and the leader (Atran, 2010).

More than 900 members of the People's Temple committed mass suicide at the instigation of their leader, Jim Jones.

These methods are similar to those that have been used to entice Americans into religious and other sects (Ofshe & Watters, 1994; Singer, 2003). In the 1970s, cult leader Jim Jones told the more than 900 members of his "People's Temple" that the time had come to die, and they dutifully lined up to drink a Kool-Aid-like drink mixed with cyanide; parents gave it first to their infants and children. (The legacy of that massacre is the term "drinking the Kool-Aid," which refers to a person or group's unquestioning belief in an ideology that could lead to their death.) In the 1990s, David Koresh, leader of the Branch Davidian cult near Waco, Texas, led his followers to a fiery death in a shootout with the FBI. In these groups, as in the case of terrorist cells, most recruits started out as ordinary people, but after being subjected to the techniques we have described, they ended up doing things that they previously would have found unimaginable. Social psychologists can explain the extremes of persuasion found in terrorism, "brainwashing," and cult activity. Fortunately, they can also explain the mechanisms at work during more mundane examples of persuasion. Watch the video *Persuasion* to learn more about attitude change tactics.

Peripheral route processing

Thinking Critically—Analyze Assumptions and Biases: Think about the last time you made an unfavorable dispositional attribution for someone's behavior ("That guy is such a jerk!"). What information did you have access to, and what information did that person have access to? That is, as an observer of the other person's behavior, what did you focus on, and how did that influence your conclusion about the cause of that behavior? Now imagine the other person's perspective: What did that person focus on, and how might it lead to that person reaching a different conclusion about the cause of her or his own behavior?

Quiz for Module 8.2

1. The fundamental attribution error occurs when

   a. Observers fail to discount the effects of dispositional qualities of the other person.

   b. Observers overestimate situational influences and underestimate dispositional influences on another person's behavior.

   c. Observers underestimate situational influences and overestimate dispositional influences on another person's behavior.

   d. We perceive others to be more similar to ourselves than they really are.

2. Blaming the victim is an example of

   a. Entrapment

   b. Making a situational attribution for someone's misfortune

   c. Restoring one's belief in a just world

   d. The false consensus effect

3. After getting the last several questions wrong on this quiz, you conclude that it simply must be "a bad test," and that you are certain of your superior intellectual abilities and knowledge of the material. Although this may be true, this may also illustrate which of the following?

   a. A bias to believe that good things happen to good people

   b. A bias to see greater amounts of consensus for an opinion than actually exists

   c. An attributional bias to paint ourselves in a flattering light

   d. The fundamental attribution error

4. Bobby told Annika that California has a population of 200 million people. Although dubious about this figure, Annika also heard the same thing from Randy and from Jerzy (both of whom had talked to Bobby previously). Bobby also talked to Sheila, and Sheila talked to Annika, and reiterated that the state of California has a population of 200 million people. Even though the actual population of California is a little less than 40 million people, Annika came to believe that it was five times that amount. What's going on here?

   a. The sleeper effect

   b. The familiarity effect

   c. The correspondence bias

   d. The validity effect

5. Which of the following is *not* an element identified with the process of indoctrination?

   a. A person's problems are explained by one simple attribution.

   b. A person has a sudden change of mind without being aware of what's happening.

   c. A person's access to disconfirming information is severely controlled.

   d. A person is subjected to entrapment.

Individuals in Groups

To see for yourself how "social" you are, try this simple experiment: Turn off your cell phone. *Off!* You may use your laptop to take notes in class, but no fair texting while you do. Now, how long can you go without checking Facebook, IMs, tweets, email, or the Web? Keep track of your feelings on a (written!) notepad as time passes. Are you feeling anxious? Nervous? How long can you remain "cut off" before you start to feel isolated from your friends and family?

The need to belong may be the most powerful of all human motivations. It makes good evolutionary sense because, like apes, bees, and elephants, human beings could never have survived without being a part of a tribe. The need for connection explains why sending a prisoner to solitary confinement is considered a form of torture: Its psychological consequences are even more devastating than physical abuse (Gawande, 2009). (And it's also why some parents use removal of their teenager's cell phone as a form of punishment!) In fact, the *social* pain of being excluded, rejected, or humiliated activates parts of the brain that are highly diagnostic of *physical* pain (Chen et al., 2008; DeWall & Bushman, 2011; Eisenberger, Lieberman, & Williams, 2003; Williams, 2009). Social rejection also impedes the ability to empathize, think critically, and solve problems and can lead to mental disorders, eating disorders, and attempted suicide. Conversely, social *acceptance*, a sense of belonging, can have many positive effects. For example, minority students who feel that they belong in school have better grades, health, and well-being (Walton & Cohen, 2011).

Of course, we belong to many different groups, which vary in their importance to us. But the point to underscore is that as soon as we join a bunch of other people, we act differently than we would on our own. This change occurs regardless of whether the group has convened to solve problems and make decisions, has gathered to have a party, consists of anonymous bystanders, or is a crowd of spectators. In this section, we will look at the many ways the presence of other people can affect our own behavior.

Conformity

LO 8.3.A Outline the basic procedures and findings of the Asch line-judging study.

Suppose that you are required to appear at a psychology laboratory for an experiment on perception. You join seven other students seated in a room. You are shown a 10-inch line and asked which of three other lines is identical to it. The correct answer, line A, is obvious, so you are amused when the first person in the group chooses line B. "Bad eyesight," you say to yourself. "He's off by 2 whole inches!" The second person also chooses line B. "What a dope," you think. But by the time the fifth person has chosen line B, you are beginning to doubt yourself. The sixth and seventh students also choose line B, and now you are worried about *your* eyesight. The experimenter looks at you. "Your turn," he says. Do you follow the evidence of your own eyes or the collective judgment of the group?

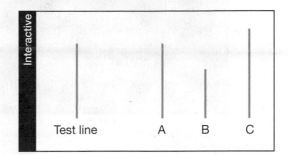

This was the design for a series of famous studies of conformity conducted by Solomon Asch (1952, 1965). The seven "nearsighted" students were actually Asch's confederates. Asch wanted to know what people would do when a group unanimously contradicted an obvious fact. He found that when people made the line comparisons on their own, they were almost always accurate. But in the group, only 20 percent of the students remained completely independent on every trial, and often they apologized for not agreeing with the others. One-third conformed to the group's incorrect decision more than half the time, and the rest conformed at least some of the time. Whether or not they conformed, the students often felt uncertain of their decision. As one participant later said, "I felt disturbed, puzzled, separated, like an outcast from the rest." Asch's experiment has been replicated many times and in many countries over the years (Bond & Smith, 1996).

There are two basic motives for conformity, and, remarkably, both motives appear in many other species, from rats to primates, suggesting that conformity has a powerful adaptive function (Claidière & Whiten, 2012). One is the *need for social acceptance*, which is the reason that people can end up doing all kinds of stupid things (or smart things!) simply because their friends are doing them. By understanding the power of this motive, social psychologists have designed interventions to rally people's peer groups to help them stop smoking and binge drinking, stay in school and improve their performance, and make many other beneficial changes they would not do on their own (Wilson, 2011).

The second reason for conformity is the *need for information* before deciding on the "right" thing to do (Cialdini, 2009). People often intuitively understand that sometimes the group knows more than they do, and this reliance on group judgment begins in very early childhood. When 3- and 4-year-old children were given a choice between relying on information provided by a three-adult majority or a single adult about the name of an unfamiliar object, they sided with the majority (Corriveau, Fusaro, & Harris, 2009). It works the same way with adults: The belief that "everyone else" is doing something must mean it is the wisest choice or course of action. Again, social psychologists have used this knowledge to induce people to make improvements. When hotels put notices in guest bathrooms saying that "the majority of guests in this room reuse their towels" (in contrast to simply requesting the guest to do the same because it's good for the environment), the number who participate in the reuse program rises markedly (Goldstein, Cialdini, & Griskevicius, 2008).

Like obedience, therefore, conformity has positive aspects. Society runs more smoothly when people feel that they belong, know how to behave in a given situation, and share the same norms. But also like obedience, conformity has negative consequences, notably its power to suppress critical thinking and creativity. In a group, many people will deny their private beliefs, agree with silly notions, and even repudiate their own values—just to be accepted.

Sometimes people like to conform to feel part of the group . . . and sometimes they like to assert their individuality.

groupthink

The tendency for all members of a group to think alike for the sake of harmony and to suppress disagreement.

Groupthink

LO 8.3.B List four symptoms of groupthink.

Close, friendly groups usually work well together. But they face the problem of getting the best ideas and efforts from their members while avoiding an extreme form of conformity called **groupthink**, the tendency to think alike and suppress dissent. According to Irving Janis (1982, 1989), groupthink occurs when a group's need for total agreement overwhelms its need to make the wisest decision. The symptoms of groupthink include the following:

- **An illusion of invulnerability.** The group believes it can do no wrong and is 100 percent correct in its decisions.
- **Self-censorship.** Dissenters decide to keep quiet rather than make trouble, offend their friends, or risk being ridiculed.
- **Pressure on dissenters to conform.** The leader teases or humiliates dissenters or otherwise pressures them to go along.
- **An illusion of unanimity.** By discouraging dissent and failing to consider alternative courses of action, leaders and group members create an illusion of consensus; they may even explicitly order suspected dissenters to keep quiet.

Throughout history, groupthink has led to disastrous decisions in military and civilian life. In 1961, President John F. Kennedy and his advisers approved a CIA plan to invade Cuba at the Bay of Pigs and try to overthrow the government of Fidel Castro; the invasion was a humiliating defeat. In 1986, NASA officials insulated themselves from the dissenting objections of engineers who warned them that the space shuttle *Challenger* was unsafe; NASA launched it anyway, and it exploded shortly after takeoff. And when, in 2003, President George W. Bush launched an invasion of Iraq, claiming the country had weapons of mass destruction and was allied with al-Qaeda, he and his team ignored dissenters and evidence from intelligence agencies that neither claim was true (Mayer, 2009). The agencies themselves later accused the Bush administration of "groupthink."

Fortunately, groupthink can be minimized if the leader rewards the expression of doubt and dissent, protects and encourages minority views, asks group members to generate as many alternative solutions to a problem as they can think of, and has everyone try to think of the risks and disadvantages of the preferred decision. Resistance to groupthink can also be fostered by creating a group identity that encourages members to think of themselves as open-minded problem solvers rather than invulnerable know-it-alls (Turner, Pratkanis, & Samuels, 2003). Leaders who encourage group members to identify strongly with the collective enterprise are also more likely to hear dissenting opinions because members will be less willing to support a decision they regard as harmful to the group's goal (Packer, 2009).

Not all leaders want to run their groups this way, of course. For many people in positions of power, from presidents to company executives to movie moguls, the temptation is great to surround themselves with others who agree with what they want to do, and to demote or fire those who disagree on the grounds that they are being "disloyal." Perhaps a key quality of great leaders is that they are able to rise above this temptation.

The Wisdom and Madness of Crowds

LO 8.3.C Explain how diffusion of responsibility and deindividuation contribute to the madness of crowds.

Many popular websites offer some variation on the "you might also like" theme. Whether you're downloading a book or buying a song, chances are you'll get a message highlighting the recommendations and preferences of other people who've purchased the same item. This strategy comes straight from a phenomenon known as the "wisdom of crowds": the fact that a crowd's judgment is often more accurate than that of its individual members—a reason for conformity, as we noted earlier (Surowiecki, 2004; Vul & Pashler, 2008). Just as neurons interconnect in networks that create thoughts and actions beyond the scope of any individual cell so does a crowd create a social network whose "behavior" is more than individual members may intend or even be aware of (Goldstone, Roberts, & Gureckis, 2008; Wegner, 1986). But crowds can create havoc, too. They can spread gossip, rumors, misinformation, and panic as fast as they can share recommendations for your Netflix queue. They can turn from joyful and peaceful to violent and destructive in a flash.

DIFFUSION OF RESPONSIBILITY Suppose you were in trouble on a city street or in another public place—say, being mugged or having a sudden appendicitis attack. Do you think you would be more likely to get help if (1) one other person was passing by, (2) several other people were in the area, or (3) dozens of people were in the area? Most people would choose the third answer, but that is not how human beings operate. On the contrary, the more people around you, the *less* likely that one of them will come to your aid. Why?

The answer has to do with a group process called the **diffusion of responsibility**, in which responsibility for an outcome is diffused, or spread, among many people, reducing each individual's personal sense of accountability. People are more likely to come to a stranger's aid if they are the only ones around to help because responsibility cannot be diffused. But one result of being in a crowd is the *bystander effect*: Individuals often fail to take action or call for help when they see someone in trouble because they assume that someone else will do so (Darley & Latané, 1968; Fischer et al., 2011). In New York City a homeless man pushed a stranger in front of an oncoming subway train in 2012 as a crowd of onlookers watched. Although there was time for someone to help the struggling man up from the tracks, no one did. In fact, a freelance news photographer took a photo of the victim.

A meta-analysis of the many studies conducted since the first identification of bystander apathy revealed some cause for optimism, though: In truly dangerous, *unambiguous* emergencies—a child drowning, or people are being shot by a deranged gunman in a school, movie theater, or street—people are more likely to rush to help, and in fact are often spurred to do so by the presence of others. One reason is that the person who intervenes counts on getting physical and psychological support from other observers. In addition,

diffusion of responsibility

In groups, the tendency of members to avoid taking action because they assume that others will.

dangerous emergencies are most effectively handled by cooperation among observers (Fischer et al., 2011; Greitmeyer, 2015). Watch the video *Under the Influence of Others 1* to review the processes at work in deciding to offer help to someone in need.

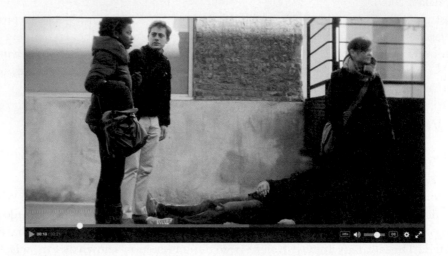

deindividuation

In groups or crowds, the loss of awareness of one's own individuality.

DEINDIVIDUATION   The most extreme instances of the diffusion of responsibility occur in large, anonymous mobs or crowds. The crowds may consist of cheerful sports spectators or angry rioters. Either way, people often lose awareness of their individuality and seem to hand themselves over to the mood and actions of the crowd, a state called **deindividuation** (Festinger, Pepitone, & Newcomb, 1952). You are more likely to feel deindividuated in a large city, where no one recognizes you, than in a small town, where it is hard to hide. (You are also more likely to feel deindividuated in large classes, where you might—mistakenly!—think you are invisible to the teacher, than in small ones.) Sometimes organizations actively promote the deindividuation of their members to enhance conformity and allegiance to the group. This is an important function of uniforms or masks, which eliminate each member's distinctive identity.

Deindividuation has long been considered a prime reason for mob violence. According to this explanation, because deindividuated people in crowds "forget themselves" and do not feel accountable for their actions, they are more likely to violate social norms and laws—breaking store windows, looting, getting into fights, or rioting at a sports event—than they would be on their own. But deindividuation does not always make people more combative. Sometimes it makes them more friendly; think of all the chatty, anonymous people on buses and planes who reveal things to their seatmates they would never tell anyone they knew.

What really seems to be happening when people are in large crowds or anonymous situations is not that they inevitably become mindless or aggressive. Rather, they become

People in crowds, feeling anonymous, may do destructive things they would never do on their own.

disinhibited, just as if they were intoxicated on alcohol. That disinhibition, in turn, makes them more likely to conform to the norms of the *specific situation*, which may be either antisocial or prosocial (Hirsh, Galinsky, & Zhong, 2011; Postmes & Spears, 1998). College students who go on wild sprees during spring break may be violating the local laws and norms not because their aggressiveness has been released but because they are conforming to the "Let's party!" norms of their fellow students. Crowd norms can also foster helpfulness, as they often do in the aftermath of disasters, when strangers come out to help victims and rescuers, leaving food, clothes, and tributes. And so, should the deindividuation excuse, like the "I was only following orders" excuse, exonerate a person of responsibility for looting, rape, or even murder? What do you think?

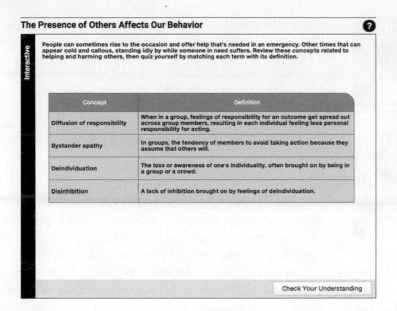

The Presence of Others Affects Our Behavior ❓

People can sometimes rise to the occasion and offer help that's needed in an emergency. Other times that can appear cold and callous, standing idly by while someone in need suffers. Review these concepts related to helping and harming others, then quiz yourself by matching each term with its definition.

Concept	Definition
Diffusion of responsibility	When in a group, feelings of responsibility for an outcome get spread out across group members, resulting in each individual feeling less personal responsibility for acting.
Bystander apathy	In groups, the tendency of members to avoid taking action because they assume that others will.
Deindividuation	The loss or awareness of one's individuality, often brought on by being in a group or a crowd.
Disinhibition	A lack of inhibition brought on by feelings of deindividuation.

Check Your Understanding

Altruism and Dissent

LO 8.3.D **Discuss four situational factors that increase one's likelihood to offer help to others.**

We have seen how roles, norms, and pressures to obey authority and conform to one's group can cause people to behave in ways they might not otherwise. Yet throughout history, men and women have disobeyed orders they believed to be wrong and have gone against prevailing cultural beliefs; their actions have sometimes changed the course of history. In 1955, in Montgomery, Alabama, a shy, quiet woman named Rosa Parks refused to give up her bus seat to a white passenger, and she was arrested for breaking the law. Her protest sparked a 381-day bus boycott and helped launch the modern civil rights movement.

Sadly, the costs of dissent, courage, and honesty are often high; remember that most groups do not welcome deviance, nonconformity, and disagreement. Most whistle-blowers, far from being rewarded for their bravery, are punished for it. Three women were named *Time* magazine's Persons of the Year for their courage in exposing wrongdoing in their respective organizations—Enron, WorldCom, and the FBI—yet all paid a steep professional price for doing so. In fact, studies of whistle-blowers find that half to two-thirds lose their jobs and have to leave their professions entirely. Many lose their homes and families (Andrade, 2015).

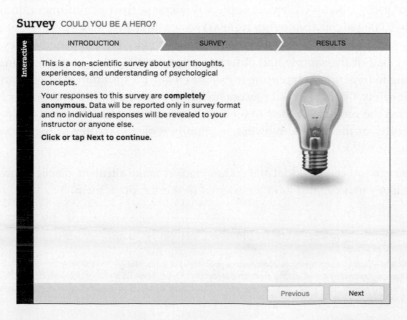

Survey COULD YOU BE A HERO?

INTRODUCTION   SURVEY   RESULTS

This is a non-scientific survey about your thoughts, experiences, and understanding of psychological concepts.

Your responses to this survey are **completely anonymous.** Data will be reported only in survey format and no individual responses will be revealed to your instructor or anyone else.

Click or tap Next to continue.

Previous   Next

Helping others doesn't always need to involve dramatic, heroic actions. These people have come together to help one another and improve their community.

Nonconformity, protest, and *altruism*, the willingness to take selfless or dangerous action on behalf of others, are in part a matter of personal convictions and conscience. However, just as there are situational reasons for obedience and conformity, there are external influences on a person's decision to state an unpopular opinion, choose conscience over conformity, or help a stranger in trouble. Here are some of the situational factors that can overcome bystander apathy and increase the likelihood of helping others or behaving courageously:

1. **You perceive the need for intervention or help.** It may seem obvious, but before you can take independent action, you must realize that such action is necessary. Sometimes people willfully blind themselves to wrongdoing to justify their own inaction ("I'm just minding my business"; "I have no idea what they're doing over there at that concentration camp"). But blindness to the need for action also occurs when a situation imposes too many demands on people's attention, as it often does for residents of densely populated cities.

2. **Cultural norms encourage you to take action.** Would you tell a passerby that he or she had dropped a pen? Offer to help a person with an injured leg who had dropped an armful of magazines? Assist a blind person across the street? An international field study investigated strangers' helpfulness to one another with those three nonemergency acts of kindness, in 23 U.S. cities and 22 cities in other countries. Cultural norms for helping were more important than population density in predicting levels of helpfulness: Pedestrians in busy Copenhagen and Vienna were kinder to strangers than were passersby in busy New York City. Helping rates ranged from 93 percent in Rio de Janeiro, Brazil, to 40 percent in Kuala Lumpur, Malaysia (R. Levine, 2003; Levine, Norenzayan, & Philbrick, 2001).

3. **You have an ally.** In Asch's conformity experiment, the presence of one other person who gave the correct answer was enough to overcome agreement with the majority. In Milgram's experiment, the presence of someone who disobeyed the experimenter's instruction to shock the learner sharply increased the number of people who also disobeyed. One dissenting member of a group may be viewed as a troublemaker, but two or three are a coalition. An ally reassures a person of the rightness of the protest, and their combined efforts may eventually persuade the majority (Wood et al., 1994).

4. **You become entrapped.** Does this sound familiar by now? Having taken the initial step of getting involved, most people will increase their commitment. In one study, nearly 9,000 federal employees were asked whether they had observed wrongdoing at work, whether they had told anyone about it, and what happened if they had told. Nearly half of the sample had observed some serious cases of wrongdoing, such as stealing federal funds, accepting bribes, or creating a situation that was dangerous to public safety. Of that half, 72 percent had done nothing at all, but the other 28 percent reported the problem to their immediate supervisors. After they had taken that step, a majority of the whistle-blowers eventually took the matter to higher authorities (Graham, 1986).

As you can see, certain social and cultural factors make altruism, disobedience, and dissent more likely to occur, just as other external factors suppress them.

JOURNAL PROMPT 8.3

Thinking Critically—Don't Oversimplify: Is conformity a good thing or a bad thing? That simple question turns out to be loaded with nuance. Describe two situations in which conformity makes sense, is a reasonable response, and is beneficial to a person, and two situations in which conformity can be disastrous, can lead to negative outcomes, or seems to be the completely wrong response to make.

Quiz for Module 8.3

1. The two motives for conformity are the need for
_____ and the need for _____.
   a. Information / justification
   b. Social approval / justification
   c. Social acceptance / social approval
   d. Social acceptance / information

2. Martin attended a cocktail party at a business conference, and he wasn't sure if he should tip the bartender or if gratuities were the responsibility of the event organizers. He asked a waiter for advice, who replied, "It is up to individual attendees to tip the bartender," so Marvin did. Which aspect of conformity do Marvin's actions illustrate?
   a. The need for equity
   b. The need for social acceptance
   c. The need for information
   d. The need for dissonance rebuttal

3. Which of the following is *not* a symptom of groupthink?
   a. Self-censorship
   b. An illusion of unanimity
   c. An illusion of invulnerability
   d. An inclusive leader

4. The violence instigated during a riot by otherwise-respectable citizens may best exemplify
   a. Acculturation and ethnocentrism
   b. Cross-cultural differences in leadership behavior
   c. Deindividuation felt by the participants
   d. The effects of social inhibition

5. You see a blind pedestrian starting to veer into a busy street. Although you could just as easily go about your business, you instead offer assistance and guide the person back to the safe and correct path. Why the sudden burst of helpfulness?
   a. Diffusion of responsibility took hold; although you felt little responsibility to take action, it was still more than the amount felt by other passersby.
   b. Cultural norms encouraged you to take action; in this case, a norm that holds "we should help those who need our help."
   c. Altruism is largely genetic; your hereditary tendencies overruled the situational impulse to ignore the person in need.
   d. The bystander effect was at work; as a bystander, you felt morally obligated to help.

Us Versus Them: Group Identity

Just who do you think you are? That's not a challenge or an insult, but rather a primary question that social psychologists address. Defining who we are is often an exercise in examining the people we associate with, how they define themselves, and what impact that process has on us. In this section, we will examine these issues, starting with our social and ethnic identities.

Ethnic Identity

LO 8.4.A Contrast social identity, ethnic identity, and acculturation, and offer examples of each concept.

Each of us develops a personal identity that is based on our particular traits and unique life history. But we also develop **social identities** based on the groups we belong to, including our national, religious, political, and occupational groups (Abrams, 2015; Tajfel & Turner, 1986). In multicultural societies such as the United States and Canada, different social identities sometimes collide. In particular, people often face the dilemma of balancing an **ethnic identity**, a close identification with a religious or ethnic group, and **acculturation**, identification with the dominant culture (Phinney, 2006). The hallmarks of having an ethnic identity are that you identify with the group, feel proud to be a member, feel emotionally attached to the group, and behave in ways that conform to the group's rules, values, and norms.

Many Americans today do not want to be pigeonholed into one ethnic or racial category. Some have created combination identities, such as Blaxican (African American and Mexican), Negripino (African American and Filipino), and Chino-Latino (Chinese and Hispanic). In the 2010 U.S. Census, nearly half of all Latinos identified themselves as belonging to an ethnic group but refused to respond to what "race" they belong to, saying

social identity

The part of a person's self-concept that is based on his or her identification with a nation, religious or political group, occupation, or other social affiliation.

ethnic identity

A person's identification with a racial or ethnic group.

acculturation

The process by which members of minority groups come to identify with and feel part of the mainstream culture.

Do you have an ethnic identity? If you are a member of an ethnic minority within your country, city, or college, how acculturated do you feel? Do you feel at ease in more than one culture, or only in your own? Does your comfort level depend on the situation you're in? Now ask five friends, relatives, or acquaintances, ideally from different ethnic groups, how they would answer these questions. If you feel that you do not have an ethnic heritage other than a national identity, why is that? Would your parents and grandparents feel the same as you do?

they are too mixed to choose one; Latinos are in fact overwhelmingly blended with Indian, European, African, and other racial categories. The blurring of traditional ethnic and racial boundaries is likely to continue: In 2010, nearly 15 percent of all new marriages in the United States were interracial, more than double what the number was in 1980 (6.7 percent).

Of course, most minorities remain identified with their ethnicity of origin, while picking and choosing among the values, foods, and customs of the mainstream culture. However, acculturation is not always easy, in any nation. Many immigrants arrive in their host country with every intention of becoming part of the mainstream culture. If they encounter discrimination or other setbacks, however, they may realize that acculturation is harder than they anticipated and that their original ethnic identity offers greater solace; this is why new immigrants often have poorer health in response to the stresses of trying to acculturate than their children do (Schwartz et al., 2010). There seems to be a critical period for successful acculturation: People become better able to identify with their host culture the longer they are exposed to it, but, as a study of Chinese immigrants in Canada found, often only if that exposure occurs when they are relatively young (Cheung, Chudek, & Heine, 2011).

Ethnocentrism

LO 8.4.B Define ethnocentrism, and describe how it contributes to us–them dichotomies.

Social identities give us a sense of place and position in the world. Without them, most of us would feel like loose marbles rolling around in an unconnected universe. It feels good to be part of an "us." But does that mean that we must automatically feel superior to "them"?

Ethnocentrism is the belief that your own culture, nation, or religion is superior to all others. Ethnocentrism is universal, probably because it aids survival by increasing people's attachment to their own group and their willingness to work on its behalf. It is even embedded in some languages: The Chinese word for China means "the center of the world" (consigning the other 6 billion people to the suburbs?) and the Navajo, the Kiowa, and the Inuit call themselves simply "The People." Social identities can exert a powerful influence on our lives, as the video *Under the Influence of Others 2* discusses.

ethnocentrism

The belief that one's own ethnic group, nation, or religion is superior to all others.

Ethnocentrism rests on a fundamental social identity: us. As soon as people have created a category called "us," however, they invariably perceive everybody else as "not-us." This in-group solidarity can be manufactured in a minute in a laboratory, as Henri Tajfel and his colleagues (1971) demonstrated in an experiment with British schoolboys. Tajfel showed the boys slides with varying numbers of dots on them and asked the boys to guess how many dots there were. The boys were arbitrarily told that they were "overestimators" or "underestimators" and were then asked to work on another task. In this phase, they had a chance to give points to other boys identified as overestimators or underestimators. Although each boy worked alone in his cubicle, almost every single one assigned far more points to boys he thought were like him, an overestimator or an underestimator. As the boys emerged from their rooms, they were asked, "Which were you?" The answers received either cheers or boos from the others.

Us–them social identities are strengthened when two groups compete with each other. Years ago, Muzafer Sherif and his colleagues used a natural setting, a Boy Scout camp called Robbers Cave, to demonstrate the effects of competition on hostility and conflict between groups (Sherif, 1958; Sherif et al., 1961). Sherif randomly assigned 11- and 12-year-old boys to two groups, the Eagles and the Rattlers. To build a sense of in-group identity and team spirit, he had each group work together on projects such as making a rope bridge and building a diving board. Sherif then put the Eagles and Rattlers in competition for prizes. During fierce games of football, baseball, and tug-of-war, the boys whipped up a competitive fever that soon spilled off the playing fields. They began to raid each other's cabins, call each other names, and start fistfights. No one dared to have a friend from the rival group. Before long, the Eagles and the Rattlers were as hostile toward each other as any two gangs fighting for turf. Their hostility continued even when they were just sitting around together watching movies.

Then Sherif decided to try to undo the hostility he had created and make peace between the Eagles and Rattlers. He and his associates set up a series of predicaments in which both groups needed to work together to reach a desired goal—for example, pooling their resources to get a movie they all wanted to see or pulling a staff truck up a hill on a camping trip. This policy of *interdependence in reaching mutual goals* was highly successful in reducing the boys' "ethnocentrism," competitiveness, and hostility; the boys eventually made friends with their former enemies (see Figure 8.4). Interdependence has a similar effect in adult groups (Gaertner et al., 1990). The reason, it seems, is that cooperation causes people to think of themselves as members of one big group instead of two opposed groups, us and them.

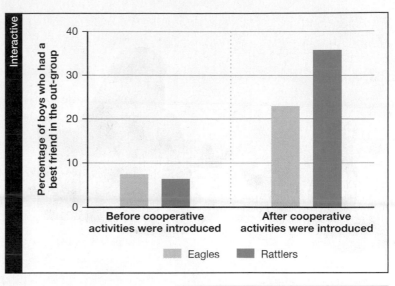

Figure 8.4 The Experiment at Robbers Cave

In this study, competitive games fostered hostility between the Rattlers and the Eagles. Few boys had a best friend from the other group (left). But after the teams had to cooperate to solve various problems, the percentage that made friends across "enemy lines" shot up (right) (Sherif et al., 1961).

Stereotypes

LO 8.4.C Define what a stereotype is, and discuss three ways in which stereotypes distort reality.

We're going to bet you don't have a lot of experience with people from Lichtenstein, a tiny nation located in the Alps between Switzerland and Austria. At only 62 square miles and populated by only 37,000 people, it's smaller than many cities in the United States. Yet knowing just this bit about it—it's probably like Switzerland, it most likely has wealthy inhabitants, probably a majority white population—you've no doubt already formed an opinion of what typical Lichtensteinians are like. A **stereotype** is a summary impression of a group of people in which all members of the group are viewed as sharing a common trait or traits. People have stereotypes of drivers of Ferraris or Hondas, of engineering students and art students, of feminists and fraternity men.

Stereotypes aren't necessarily bad and they are sometimes accurate (Lee, McCauley, & Jussim, 2013). They are, as some psychologists have called them, useful tools in the mental toolbox—energy-saving devices that allow us to make efficient decisions (Macrae & Bodenhausen, 2000). They help us quickly process new information and retrieve memories. They allow us to organize experience, make sense of differences among individuals and groups,

stereotype

A summary impression of a group, in which a person believes that all members of the group share a common trait or traits (positive, negative, or neutral).

What is this woman's occupation? Among non-Muslims in the West, the assumption is that Muslim women who wear the full-length black niqab must be repressed sexually as well as politically. But the answer shatters the stereotype. Wedad Lootah, a Muslim living in Dubai, United Arab Emirates, is a marriage counselor and sexual activist, author of a best-selling Arabic book, *Top Secret: Sexual Guidance for Married Couples*. She wrote it, she says, because of a 52-year-old client who had many children but had never experienced sexual pleasure with her husband. "Finally, she discovered orgasm!" Ms. Lootah reported. "Imagine, all that time she did not know."

and predict how people will behave. In fact, the brain automatically registers and encodes the basic categories of gender, ethnicity, and age, suggesting that there is a neurological basis for the cognitive efficiency of stereotyping (Ito & Urland, 2003).

However, although stereotypes reflect real differences among people, they also distort that reality in three ways (Judd et al., 1995). First, *they exaggerate differences between groups*, making the stereotyped group seem odd, unfamiliar, or dangerous, not like "us." Second, *they produce selective perception*; people tend to see only the evidence that fits the stereotype and reject any perceptions that do not fit. Third, *they underestimate differences within the stereotyped group*, creating the impression that all members of that group are the same.

Cultural values affect how people evaluate the actions of another group and whether a stereotype becomes positive or negative. Chinese students in Hong Kong, where communalism and respect for elders are valued, think that a student who comes late to class or argues with a parent about grades is being selfish and disrespectful of adults. But Australian students, who value individualism, think that the same behavior is perfectly appropriate (Forgas & Bond, 1985). You can see how the Chinese might form negative stereotypes of "disrespectful" Australians, and how the Australians might form negative stereotypes of the "spineless" Chinese. Unfortunately, it's a small step from stereotypical thinking to the formation of prejudicial attitudes to the enactment of discriminatory behavior. In the next section we will examine how prejudice develops, how scientists can measure it, and what can be done to reduce it. Before we address those topics, take a look at the video *Are Stereotypes and Prejudice Inevitable?* for perspectives on this aspect of social behavior.

JOURNAL PROMPT 8.4

Thinking Critically—Avoid Emotional Reasoning: Write down three stereotypes that you hold. (Don't say you don't have any because everyone does.) They don't necessarily have to be negative or denigrating to a particular group. Now write about how events in your own life experiences might have contributed to the formation of those stereotypes. For example, does your own ethnic identity play a role in how you see other people? Were you consciously taught to hold some stereotypes, or were they formed implicitly? Did a personal experience with one person lead you to conclude that all members of Group X behaved that way? Sometimes the act of thinking critically about where your attitudes come from can counteract the emotional or less-rational bases for those attitudes. Putting your thoughts into words can help you understand the basis of stereotype formation.

Quiz for Module 8.4

1. Frank, an African American college student, has to decide between living in a dorm with mostly white students who share his interest in science, or living in a dorm with other black students who are studying the history and contributions of African culture. The first choice values _____, whereas the second values _____.

   a. Ethnocentrism / ethnic identity
   b. Ethnic identity / acculturation
   c. Ethnocentrism / acculturation
   d. Acculturation / ethnic identity

2. Willie knows and likes the Chicano minority in his town, but he privately believes that his Anglo culture is superior to all others. His belief is evidence of his

   a. Cultural framing
   b. Correspondence bias
   c. Ethnocentrism
   d. Sociality

3. What strategy does the Robbers Cave study suggest for reducing "us–them" thinking and hostility between groups?

   a. Competition for scarce resources
   b. Interdependence in reaching mutual goals
   c. Dialogue and debate between representatives of each group
   d. "Time-sharing" of power positions

4. An Albanian family has moved to Barry's neighborhood. This group is particularly quiet, tidy, and keeps to themselves. When Barry and his next-door neighbor are talking over the fence one day, Barry remarks, "Yeah, all those Albanians are the same; real standoffish," even though Barry doesn't know any other Albanians, hasn't interacted with any Albanians, and can't even find Albania on a world map. What is Barry promoting with his viewpoint?

   a. Implicit egoism
   b. Acculturation
   c. An ethnic identity
   d. A stereotype

5. What conclusion can we reach about the nature of stereotypes?

   a. They are held about specific individuals, based on their membership in a particular group.
   b. They are always negative and demeaning to a group of people.
   c. They are mental tools that can allow us to efficiently process social information.
   d. They are based on racial and ethnic differences between groups.

Group Conflict and Prejudice

Here's a short thought exercise for you. Think about the year of your birth, and think about the current year. What's the longest period during that time span that the world has been free from intergroup conflict; one nation warring with another, one group fighting with another, or one ethnicity trying to vanquish another?

If your rough estimate is "zero," you're probably sadly correct. "World peace" is difficult to define—ideally it would be a period of no conflict between identifiable groups—and historically there have been some nations that have enjoyed some measure of harmony. Japan during the Edo Period (1603–1868) is often cited as a time of great peace for that country, and Sweden hasn't been a major presence in a conflict since 1814. But scattered examples are far outweighed by world wars, civil unrest, or seemingly never-ending conflicts over race, religion, or ideology.

Part of what fuels conflict is prejudice. One group's actions may be belligerent toward another, but those actions are often interpreted through a lens of preconceived notions and long-standing beliefs. In this section we examine the causes and consequences of prejudice, and consider ways that group conflict and hostility can be reduced.

prejudice

A strong, unreasonable dislike or hatred of a group, based on a negative stereotype.

The Origins of Prejudice

LO 8.5.A Describe four sources of prejudice.

A **prejudice** consists of a negative stereotype and a strong, unreasonable dislike or hatred of a group. Prejudice provides the fuel for ethnocentrism. Its targets change, but it persists everywhere in some form because it has so many sources and functions: psychological, social, economic, and cultural.

1. **Psychological causes.** Prejudice often serves to ward off feelings of doubt, fear, and insecurity. As research from many nations has confirmed, it is a tonic for low self-esteem: People puff up their own feelings of low self-worth by disliking or hating groups they see as inferior (Islam & Hewstone, 1993; Stephan et al., 1994). Prejudice also allows people to use the target group as a scapegoat ("Those people are the source of all my troubles"), to displace anger and cope with feelings of powerlessness. Immediately after 9/11, some white Americans took out their anger on fellow Americans who happened to be Arab, Sikh, Pakistani, Hindu, or Afghan. Two men in Chicago beat up an Arab-American taxi driver, yelling, "This is what you get, you mass murderer!"

2. **Social causes.** Not all prejudices, however, have deep-seated psychological roots. Some are acquired through pressure to conform to the views of friends, relatives, or associates; if you don't agree with a group's prejudices toward another group, you may be gently or abruptly asked to leave the group. Some are passed along mindlessly from one generation to another, as when parents communicate to their children, "We don't associate with people like that."

3. **Economic causes.** Prejudice makes official forms of discrimination seem legitimate, by justifying the majority group's dominance, status, or greater wealth. Wherever a majority group systematically discriminates against a minority to preserve its power—whites, blacks, Muslims, Hindus, Japanese, Hutu, Christians, Jews, you name it—they will claim that their actions are legitimate because the minority is so obviously inferior and incompetent (Islam & Hewstone, 1993; Jost et al., 2008; Morton et al., 2009; Sidanius, Pratto, & Bobo, 1996).

   You can see how prejudice rises and falls with changing economic conditions by observing what happens when two groups are in direct competition for jobs, or when people are worried about their incomes: Prejudice between them increases. Consider how white attitudes toward Chinese immigrants in the United States fluctuated during the 19th century, as reflected in newspapers of the time (Aronson, 2012). When the Chinese were working in the gold mines and potentially taking jobs from white laborers, the white-run newspapers described them as depraved, vicious, and bloodthirsty. Just a decade later, when the Chinese began working on the transcontinental railroad, doing difficult and dangerous jobs that few white men wanted, prejudice against them declined. Whites described them as hardworking, industrious, and law-abiding. Then, after the railroad was finished and the Chinese had to compete with Civil War veterans for scarce jobs, white attitudes changed again. Whites now thought the Chinese were "criminal," "crafty," "conniving," and "stupid." (The newspapers did not report the attitudes of the Chinese.)

   The oldest prejudice in the world may be sexism, and it, too, serves to legitimize existing sex roles and inequities in power. According to research with 15,000 men and women in 19 nations, *hostile sexism*, which reflects active dislike of women, is different from *benevolent sexism*, which puts women on a pedestal. The latter type of sexism is affectionate but patronizing, conveying the attitude that women are so wonderful, good, kind, and moral that they should stay at home, away from the rough-and-tumble (and power and income) of public life (Glick et al., 2000; Glick & Fiske, 2012). Because benevolent sexism lacks a tone of hostility to women, it doesn't seem like a prejudice to many people (Christopher & Wojda, 2008). But both forms of sexism—whether someone thinks women are too good for equality or not good enough—legitimize discrimination against women (Brandt, 2011).

   Perhaps you are thinking: "What about men? There are plenty of prejudices against men, too—that they are sexual predators, emotionally heartless, domineering, and arrogant." In fact, according to a 16-nation study of attitudes toward men, many people do believe that men are aggressive and predatory, and overall just not as warm and wonderful as women (Glick et al., 2004). This attitude seems hostile to men, the researchers found, but it also reflects and supports gender inequality by characterizing men as being designed for leadership, dominance, and high-paying jobs.

4. **Cultural and national causes.** Finally, prejudice bonds people to their own ethnic or national group and its ways; by disliking "them," we feel closer to our own group. That feeling, in turn, justifies whatever we do to "them" to preserve our customs and national policies. In fact, although many people assume that prejudice causes war, the reverse is far more often the case: War causes prejudice. When two nations declare war, when one country decides to invade another, or when a weak leader displaces the country's economic problems onto a minority scapegoat, the citizenry's prejudice against that enemy or scapegoat will be inflamed. Of course, sometimes anger at an enemy is justified, but war usually turns legitimate anger into blind prejudice: Those people are not only the enemy; they are less than human and deserve to be exterminated (Keen, 1986; Staub, 1999). That is why enemies are so often described as vermin, rats, mad dogs, heathens, baby killers, or monsters—anything but human beings like us.

Review 8.1 summarizes the causes of prejudice.

Defining and Measuring Prejudice

LO 8.5.B Describe five ways of measuring prejudicial attitudes.

With the historic election in 2008 of Barack Obama as the nation's first African American president, and with women increasingly attaining positions of status and authority in business and government, many people became hopeful that the worst forms of racism and sexism in the United States were ending. Indeed, on surveys in the United States and Canada throughout the 2000s, prejudice toward blacks, gays, and women declined, especially among young people (Weaver, 2008). But in 2012, an AP survey found that among white Americans, prejudice toward blacks and other minorities was rising significantly again. Recent racial tensions, fueled by high-profile cases involving police and minority group members, suggest that negative attitudes still exist.

The reason, as Gordon Allport (1954/1979) observed so long ago, is that "defeated intellectually, prejudice lingers emotionally." Attitudes may change and discriminatory behavior may be outlawed, but deep-seated negative feelings and bigotry may persist in subtle ways. As we just saw, prejudices may lie dormant during good times, only to be easily aroused during bad times.

That is why prejudice is like a weasel—hard to grasp and hold on to. Moreover, not all prejudiced people are prejudiced in the same way or to the same extent. Suppose that

Review 8.1

Sources of Prejudice

Psychological	Social	Economic	Cultural/National
Low self-esteem Anxiety Insecurity Powerlessness	Groupthink Conformity Parental messages	Majority's desire to preserve its status Competition for jobs, power, resources	Ethnocentrism Desire for group identity The justification of war

Examples of resulting prejudice:			
"Those people are not as moral and decent as we are."	"My parents taught me that those people are just no good."	"Those people are not smart enough to do this work."	"We have to protect our religion/country/government from those monsters."

The Many Targets of Prejudice

Prejudice has a long and universal history. Why do new prejudices keep emerging, others fade away, and some old ones persist?

Some prejudices rise and fall with historical events such as war or conquest. Anti-Japanese feelings in the United States ran high in the 1920s and again in the 1940s and 1990s; today, prejudice against the Japanese is virtually gone.

Some prejudices, such as that toward Native Americans, were widespread for three centuries but are fading.

Some hatreds, notably homophobia and anti-Semitism, reflect people's deeper anxieties and are therefore more persistent.

Prejudices toward African Americans and women have long been part of Western history. In the United States, women have been excluded from men's clubs and occupations, and segregation of blacks was legal until the 1950s.

Other prejudices emerge with changing economic concerns. Anti-immigrant prejudice always emerges when native-born citizens are worried about their jobs. In the aftermath of 9/11, hostility mounted toward Middle Easterners and Muslims.

Raymond wishes to be tolerant and open-minded, but he grew up in a small homogeneous community and feels uncomfortable with members of other cultural and religious groups. Should we put Raymond in the same category as Rupert, an outspoken bigot who detests all ethnic groups other than his own? Do good intentions count? What if Raymond knows nothing about Muslims and mindlessly blurts out a remark that reveals his ignorance? Is that prejudice or thoughtlessness? And what about people who say they are not prejudiced but then make remarks that suggest otherwise?

Although social psychologists welcome the evidence that *explicit*, conscious prejudices have declined and that it is no longer fashionable to admit one's prejudices, some have used various measures to see whether *implicit*, unconscious negative feelings between groups have also diminished. They maintain that implicit attitudes, being automatic and unintentional, reflect lingering negative feelings that keep prejudice alive below the surface (Cheon et al., 2015; Dovidio & Gaertner, 2008). They have developed several ways of measuring these feelings (Olson, 2009):

1. **Measures of social distance and "microaggressions."** *Social distance* is a possible behavioral expression of prejudice, a reluctance to get "too close" to another group. Does a straight man stand farther away from a gay man than from another heterosexual? Does a nondisabled woman move away from a woman in a wheelchair? Some psychologists call these subtle acts "microaggressions": the "slights, indignities, and put-downs" that many minorities and people with physical disabilities experience (Dovidio, Pagotto, & Hebl, 2011; Nadal et al., 2011). Derald Sue (2010) offers these examples: A white professor compliments an Asian American graduate student on his "excellent English," although the student has lived in the United States his whole life. A white woman leaving work starts to enter an elevator, sees a black man inside, covers her necklace with her hand, and "remembers" she left something at her desk, thereby conveying to her black coworker that she thinks he is a potential thief. Men in a discussion group ignore the contributions of the one female member, talking past her and paying attention to only one another.

2. **Measures of unequal treatment.** Most forms of explicit discrimination are now illegal in the United States, but prejudices can express themselves behaviorally in less obvious ways. Consider how blacks and whites are treated unequally in the "war against drugs" (Fellner, 2009). Across the country, relative to their numbers in the general population and among drug offenders, African Americans are disproportionately arrested, convicted, and incarcerated on drug charges. A study in Seattle, which is 70 percent white, found that the great majority of those who use or sell serious drugs are white, yet almost two-thirds of

those who are arrested are black. Whites constitute the majority of those who use or sell methamphetamine, Ecstasy, powder cocaine, and heroin; blacks are the majority of those who use or sell crack. But the police virtually ignore the white market and concentrate on crack arrests. The focus on crack offenders did not appear to be related to the frequency of crack transactions compared to other drugs, public safety or health concerns, crime rates, or citizen complaints. The researchers concluded that the police department's drug law enforcement reflects racial discrimination: the unconscious impact of race on official perceptions of who is causing the city's drug problem (Beckett, Nyrop, & Pfingst, 2006).

3. **Measures of what people do when they are stressed or angry.** Many people are willing to control their negative feelings under normal conditions, but as soon as they are angry, drunk, or frustrated, or get a jolt to their self-esteem, their unexpressed prejudice often reveals itself (Aronson, 2012). In one of the first experiments to demonstrate this phenomenon, white students were asked to administer shock to black or white confederates of the experimenter in what the students believed was a study of biofeedback. In the experimental condition, participants overheard the biofeedback "victim" (who actually received no shock) saying derogatory things about them. In the control condition, participants overheard no such nasty remarks. Then all the participants had another opportunity to shock the victims; their degree of aggression was defined as the amount of shock they administered. At first, white students actually showed *less* aggression toward blacks than toward whites. But as soon as the white students were angered by overhearing derogatory remarks about themselves, they showed *more* aggression toward blacks than toward whites (Rogers & Prentice-Dunn, 1981). The same pattern appeared in studies of how English-speaking Canadians behave toward French-speaking Canadians (Meindl & Lerner, 1985), straights toward gays, non-Jewish students toward Jews (Fein & Spencer, 1997), and men toward women (Maass et al., 2003).

4. **Measures of brain activity.** Social neuroscientists have been using fMRI to determine which parts of the brain are involved in forming stereotypes, holding prejudiced beliefs, and feeling disgust, anger, or anxiety about an ethnic or stigmatized group, such as addicts or the homeless (Cacioppo et al., 2003; Harris & Fiske, 2006; Stanley, Phelps, & Banaji, 2008). In one study, when African Americans and whites saw pictures of each other, activity in the amygdala (the brain structure associated with fear, anxiety, and other negative emotions) was elevated. But it was not elevated when people saw pictures of members of their own group (Hart et al., 2000). However, the fact that parts of the brain are activated under some conditions does not mean a person is "prejudiced." In a similar experiment, when participants were registering the faces as individuals or as part of a simple visual test rather than as members of the category "blacks," there was no increased activation in the amygdala. The brain may be designed to register differences, it appears, but any negative associations with those differences depend on context and learning (Wheeler & Fiske, 2005).

5. **Measures of implicit attitudes.** A final, controversial method of assessing prejudice is the *Implicit Association Test (IAT)*, which measures the speed of people's positive and negative associations to a target group (Greenwald, McGhee, & Schwartz, 1998; Greenwald et al., 2009). Its proponents have argued that if white students take longer to respond to black faces associated with positive words (e.g., *triumph, honest*) than to black faces associated with negative words (e.g., *devil, failure*), it must mean that white students have an unconscious prejudice toward blacks. Millions of people have taken the test online, and it has also been given to students, business managers, and many other groups to identify their alleged prejudices toward blacks, Asians, women, older adults, and other categories (Nosek, Greenwald, & Banaji, 2007).

We say "alleged" prejudices because other social psychologists believe that whatever the test measures, it is not a stable prejudice (De Houwer et al., 2009; Oswald et al., 2013). Two experimenters got an IAT effect by matching target faces with nonsense words and neutral words that had no evaluative connotations at all. They concluded that the IAT does not measure emotional evaluations of the target but rather the *salience* of the word associated with it—how much it stands out. (Negative words attract more attention in general.) When they corrected for these factors, the presumed unconscious prejudice faded away (Rothermund & Wentura, 2004). Moreover, as we saw earlier, people find familiar names, products, and even nonsense syllables to be more pleasant than unfamiliar ones. Some investigators argue that the IAT may simply be measuring, say, white subjects' unfamiliarity with African Americans and the greater salience of white faces to them, rather than a true prejudice (Kinoshita & Peek-O'Leary, 2005).

As you can see, defining and measuring prejudice are not easy tasks. To understand prejudice, we must distinguish explicit attitudes from unconscious ones, active hostility from simple discomfort, what people say from what they feel, and what people feel from how they actually behave.

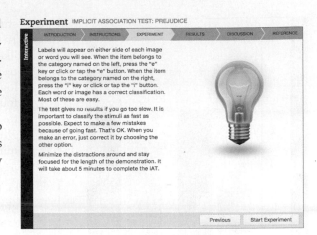

Experiment IMPLICIT ASSOCIATION TEST: PREJUDICE

Labels will appear on either side of each image or word you will see. When the item belongs to the category named on the left, press the "e" key or click or tap the "e" button. When the item belongs to the category named on the right, press the "i" key or click or tap the "i" button. Each word or image has a correct classification. Most of these are easy.

The test gives no results if you go too slow. It is important to classify the stimuli as fast as possible. Expect to make a few mistakes because of going fast. That's OK. When you make an error, just correct it by choosing the other option.

Minimize the distractions around and stay focused for the length of the demonstration. It will take about 5 minutes to complete the IAT.

Previous   Start Experiment

Reducing Conflict and Prejudice

LO 8.5.C Describe four situations that can help reduce prejudice and intergroup conflict.

The findings that emerge from the study of prejudice show us that efforts to reduce prejudice by appealing to moral or intellectual arguments are not enough. They must also touch people's deeper insecurities, fears, or negative associations with a group. Of course, given the many sources and functions of prejudice, no one method will work in all circumstances or for all prejudices. But just as social psychologists investigate the situations that increase prejudice and animosity between groups, they have also examined the situations that might reduce them. Here are four of them (Allport, 1954/1979; Dovidio & Gaertner, 2010; Pettigrew & Tropp, 2006):

1. **Both sides must have equal legal status, economic opportunities, and power.** This requirement is the spur behind efforts to change laws that permit discrimination. Integration of public facilities in the American South would never have occurred if civil rights advocates had waited for segregationists to have a change of heart. Women would never have gotten the right to vote, attend college, or do "men's work" (law, medicine, bartending . . .) without persistent challenges to the laws that permitted gender discrimination. But changing the law is not enough if two groups remain in competition for jobs or if one group retains power and dominance over the other.

2. **Authorities and community institutions must provide moral, legal, and economic support for both sides.** Society must establish norms of equality and support them in the actions of its officials—teachers, employers, the judicial system, government officials, and the police. Where segregation is official government policy or an unofficial but established practice, conflict and prejudice not only will continue but also will seem normal and justified.

3. **Both sides must have many opportunities to work and socialize together, formally and informally.** According to the *contact hypothesis*, prejudice declines when people have the chance to get used to another group's rules, food, customs, and attitudes, thereby discovering their shared interests and shared humanity and learning that "those people" aren't, in fact, "all alike." The contact hypothesis has been supported by many studies in the laboratory and in the real world: studies of newly integrated housing projects in the American South during the 1950s and 1960s; young people's attitudes toward older adults; healthy people's attitudes toward the mentally ill; nondisabled children's attitudes toward the disabled; and straight people's prejudices toward gay men and lesbians (Herek & Capitanio, 1996; Pettigrew & Tropp, 2006; Wilner, Walkley, & Cook, 1955). Remarkably, contact actually works best for the most intolerant and mentally rigid people, apparently because it reduces their feelings of threat and anxiety and increases feelings of empathy and trust (Hodson, 2011).

    Multiethnic college campuses are a living laboratory for testing the contact hypothesis. White students who have roommates, friends, and romantic relationships across ethnic lines tend to become less prejudiced and find commonalities (Van Laar, Levin, & Sidanius, 2008). Cross-group friendships benefit minorities and reduce their prejudices, too. Minority

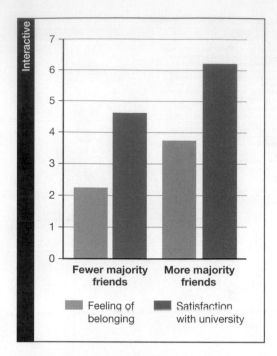

Figure 8.5 The Impact of Cross-Ethnic Friendships on Minority Students' Well-Being

Cross-ethnic friendships benefit both parties. In a longitudinal study of minority black students at a predominantly white university, many black students at first felt left out of school life and thus dissatisfied with their educational experience. But the more white friends they made, the higher their sense of belonging (orange bar) and satisfaction with the university (blue bar). This finding was particularly significant for minority students who initially had been the most sensitive to rejection and who had felt the most anxious and insecure about being in a largely white school. The study was later replicated with minority Latino students (Mendoza-Denton & Page-Gould, 2008).

students who join ethnic student organizations tend to develop, over time, not only an even stronger ethnic identity, but also an increased sense of victimization. Just like white students who live in white fraternities and sororities, they often come to feel they have less in common with other ethnic groups (Sidanius et al., 2004). But a longitudinal study of black and Latino students at a predominantly white university found that friendships with whites increased their feelings of belonging and reduced their feelings of dissatisfaction with the school. This was especially true for students who had been feeling insecure and sensitive about being rejected as members of a minority (Mendoza-Denton & Page-Gould, 2008). (See Figure 8.5.)

4. **Both sides must cooperate, working together for a common goal.** Although contact reduces prejudice, it is also true that prejudice reduces contact. And when groups don't like each other, forced contact just makes each side resentful and even more prejudiced, as a longitudinal field survey of students in Germany, Belgium, and England found (Binder et al., 2009). At many multiethnic high schools, ethnic groups form cliques and gangs, fighting one another and defending their own ways.

To reduce the intergroup tension and competition that exist in many schools, Elliot Aronson and his colleagues developed the "jigsaw" method of building cooperation. Students from different ethnic groups work together on a task that is broken up like a jigsaw puzzle; each person needs to cooperate with the others to put the assignment together. Students in such classes, from elementary school through college, tend to do better, like their classmates better, and become less stereotyped and prejudiced in their thinking than students in traditional classrooms (Aronson, 2000; J. Aronson, 2010; Slavin & Cooper, 1999). Cooperation and interdependence often reduce us–them thinking and prejudice by creating an encompassing social identity—the Eagles and Rattlers solution.

Each of these four approaches to creating greater harmony between groups is important, but none is sufficient on its own. Perhaps one reason that group conflicts and prejudice are so persistent is that all four conditions for reducing them are rarely met at the same time.

The Question of Human Nature

LO 8.5.D Explain the phrase "the banality of evil," and discuss how it contributes to otherwise-good people behaving badly.

The most difficult lesson from the study of social psychology, as we have seen throughout this chapter, is that human nature contains the potential for unspeakable acts of cruelty and inspiring acts of goodness. Most people believe that some cultures and individuals are inherently evil and therefore not fully human; if we can just get rid of them, everything will be fine. But from the standpoint of social and cultural psychology, all human beings, like all cultures, contain the potential for both good and evil.

That is why virtually no nation has bloodless hands. The Nazis systematically exterminated millions of Jews, Gypsies, homosexuals, disabled people, and anyone not of the "pure" Aryan "race." But they were not unique. Americans and Canadians slaughtered native peoples in North America, Turks slaughtered Armenians, the Khmer Rouge slaughtered millions of fellow Cambodians, the Spanish conquistadors slaughtered native peoples in Mexico and South America, Idi Amin waged a reign of terror against his own people in Uganda, the Japanese slaughtered Koreans and Chinese, despotic political regimes in Argentina and Chile killed thousands of dissidents and rebels, Bosnian Serbs massacred Bosnian Muslims in the name of "ethnic cleansing" . . . to say nothing of ongoing warfare in the Middle East and Africa today.

It's easy to conclude that outbreaks of violence like these are a result of inner aggressive drives, the sheer villainy of the perpetrators, or age-old tribal hatreds. But in the social-psychological view, they result from the all-too-normal processes we have discussed in this chapter, including mindless obedience to authority, conformity, groupthink, deindividuation, stereotyping, ethnocentrism, and prejudice. These processes are especially likely to be activated when a government feels weakened and vulnerable. By generating an outside enemy, rulers create us–them thinking to impose order and cohesion among their citizens and to create a scapegoat for the country's economic problems (Smith, 1998). The good news is that when circumstances change, societies can also change from being warlike to being peaceful.

Philosopher Hannah Arendt (1963), who covered the trial of Adolf Eichmann, used the phrase "the banality of evil" to describe how it was possible for Eichmann and other ordinary people in Nazi Germany to commit the monstrous acts they did. (*Banal* means "commonplace" or "unoriginal.") The compelling evidence for the banality of evil is difficult for many people to accept. Clearly, some people do stand out as being unusually heroic or unusually sadistic. But as we have seen, good people can do terribly disturbing things when their roles encourage or require them to do so, when the situation takes over and they do not stop to think critically.

The research discussed in this chapter suggests that ethnocentrism and prejudice are part of our human heritage, awaiting the conditions that will awaken them. But it can also help us formulate ways of living in a diverse world. By identifying the conditions that create the banality of evil, perhaps we can create other conditions that foster the "banality of virtue"—everyday acts of kindness, selflessness, and generosity.

JOURNAL PROMPT 8.5

Thinking Critically—Define Your Terms: What does it mean to be "prejudiced"? Is prejudice blatant hostility, or does it also include vague discomfort with another group, a patronizing attitude of superiority, or unconscious feelings of dislike? Does ignorance about an unfamiliar culture count as prejudice?

Quiz for Module 8.5

1. Which of the following is a *psychological* cause of prejudice?
   a. People increase their own sense of self-worth by seeing other groups as inferior.
   b. People derive a greater sense of national pride by actively combatting another group.
   c. People dislike members of a group because their parents and grandparents have also disliked that same group.
   d. People dislike members of a group because those members are seen as unfairly taking limited resources.

2. Paul calls women "gal" or "doll," applauds their efforts to become better homemakers, and generally views them as a rarefied, delicate sex. Although he might be well intentioned, Paul's attitudes have many of the markers of
   a. National sexism
   b. Hostile sexism
   c. Ascendant sexism
   d. Benevolent sexism

3. Arlo walks home from work every day. However, he opts for a longer route to avoid walking through what he describes as "a rough part of town." Police statistics show that the crime rate in the avoided area is no higher than in neighboring areas, but Arlo sticks to his principles. Arlo's behavior could be an example of

using _____ to measure prejudicial attitudes.
   a. Between-group variability
   b. Within-group variability
   c. Social distance
   d. Implicit contempt

4. According to the *contact hypothesis*, which of the following conditions must be present in order to reduce prejudice and intergroup hostility between two groups?
   a. Groups with a history of intergroup hostility should have limited contact with one another.
   b. Laws, mandates, or prohibitions should govern the behavior of both of the groups.
   c. Laws, mandates, or prohibitions should govern the behavior of one of the groups.
   d. There must be an opportunity to get to know rival group members as individuals.

5. Social psychologists recognize that humanity's potential for unbridled cruelty is matched by
   a. Humanity's potential for admirable goodness
   b. A demonstrated willingness to viciously act on those cruel intentions
   c. An indifference to the suffering of outgroup members
   d. Humanity's fervor for religious guidance

Taking Psychology with You

Dealing with Cultural Differences

A French salesman worked for a company that was bought by Americans. When the new American manager ordered him to step up his sales within the next 3 months, the employee quit in a huff, taking his customers with him. Why? In France, it takes years to develop customers; in family-owned businesses, relationships with customers may span generations. The American manager wanted instant results, as Americans often do, but the French salesperson knew this was impossible and quit. The American view was "He wasn't up to the job; he's lazy and disloyal, so he stole my customers." The French view was "There is no point in explaining anything to a person who is so stupid as to think you can acquire loyal customers in 3 months" (Hall & Hall, 1987).

Both men were committing the fundamental attribution error: assuming that the other person's behavior was due to personality rather than the situation, in this case a situation governed by cultural rules. Many corporations now realize that such rules are not trivial and that success in a global economy depends on understanding them. But you don't have to go to another country to encounter cultural differences; they are likely to exist in your own hometown.

If you find yourself getting angry over something a person from another culture is doing or not doing, use the skills of critical thinking to find out whether your expectations and perceptions of that person's behavior are appropriate. Take the time to examine your assumptions and biases, consider other explanations of the person's actions, and avoid emotional reasoning. For example, people who shake hands as a gesture of friendship and courtesy are likely to feel insulted if a person from a non-handshaking culture refuses to do the same, unless they have asked themselves the question, "Does everyone have the custom of shaking hands that my culture does?"

Similarly, people from Middle Eastern and Latin American cultures are used to bargaining for what they buy; Americans and northern Europeans are used to having a fixed price. People who do not know how to bargain, therefore, are likely to find bargaining an exercise in frustration because they will not know whether they got taken or got a great deal. In contrast, people from bargaining cultures will feel just as exasperated if a seller offers a flat price. "Where's the fun in this?" they'll say. "The whole human transaction of shopping is gone!"

Learning another culture's rule or custom is hard enough, but it is much more difficult to comprehend cultural differences that are deeply embedded in its language. In Iran, the social principle of *taarof* describes the practice of deliberate insincerity, such as giving false praise and making promises you have no intention of keeping. Iranians know that they are supposed to tell you what you want to hear to avoid conflict or to offer hope for a compromise. To Iranians, these practices are a part of good manners; they are not offended by them. But Americans and members of other English-speaking cultures are used to "straight talking," to saying directly and succinctly what they want. Therefore, they find *taarof* hard to learn, let alone to practice. As an Iranian social scientist told the *New York Times* (August 6, 2006), "Speech has a different function than it does in the West"—in the West, "yes" generally means yes; in Iran, "yes" can mean yes, but it often means maybe or no. "This creates a rich, poetic linguistic culture," he said. "It creates a multidimensional culture where people are adept at picking up on nuances. On the other hand, it makes for bad political discourse. In political discourse people don't know what to trust."

You can see why critical thinking can help people avoid the tendency to stereotype and to see cultural differences in communication solely in hostile, negative ways. "Why are the Iranians lying to me?" an American might ask. The answer is that they are not "lying" in Iranian terms; they are speaking in a way that is completely natural for them, according to their cultural rules for communication.

To learn the unspoken rules of a culture, you must look, listen, and observe. What is the pace of life like? Do people regard brash individuality and loud speech as admirable or embarrassing? When customers enter a shop, do they greet and chat with the shopkeeper or ignore the person as they browse? Are people expected to be direct in their speech or evasive? Sociocultural research enhances critical thinking by teaching us to appreciate the many cultural rules that govern people's behavior, values, attitudes, and ways of doing business. Before you write off someone from a culture different from your own as being rude, foolish, stubborn, or devious, consider other interpretations of that person's behavior—just as you would want that person to consider other, more forgiving, interpretations of yours.

Shared Writing Prompt

The world is becoming a much smaller place, with people traveling greater distances than ever before. In fact, the Internet has even rendered the notion of going to other places rather quaint; Skype, instant messaging, and YouTube have brought the exotic, far-away world to our computer screens. With this increasing understanding of and interaction with members of other cultures, what do you think are the greatest challenges faced by humans in an interactive environment? Are they issues of stereotypes, prejudice, and misattribution? Conversely, what do you think are some of the greatest points of opportunity that could result from increased cross-cultural awareness? Do you predict that misbegotten attitudes or stereotypical ways of thinking would decrease with greater exposure to different cultures?

Summary

Roles and Rules

LO 8.1.A   Compare social norms and social roles, and note how each contributes to the social rules that govern a culture.

Social psychologists study how social roles, attitudes, relationships, and groups influence individuals; *cultural psychologists* study the influence of culture on human behavior. Many cultural rules, such as those governing correct *conversational distance*, are unspoken but nonetheless powerful.

LO 8.1.B   Outline the basic procedures and findings of the Milgram obedience experiments, and discuss five conditions that make disobedience to authority more likely.

Milgram's obedience study illustrates the power of *norms* and *roles* to affect individual actions; most people in the role of "teacher" inflicted what they thought was extreme shock on another person because of the authority of the experimenter.

LO 8.1.C   Outline the basic procedures and findings of the Zimbardo prison study.

Similarly, in the Stanford prison study, college students tended to behave in accordance with the role of "prisoner" or "guard" that they had been assigned. The social situation exerted a powerful influence on individuals' behavior, often prompting them to behavior in uncharacteristic ways.

LO 8.1.D   Explain how feelings of entrapment contribute to destructive obedience.

Obedience to authority contributes to the smooth running of society, but obedience can also lead to actions that are deadly, foolish, or illegal. People obey orders because they can be punished if they do not, out of respect for authority, and to gain advantages. Even when they would rather not obey, they may do so because they have been *entrapped*, justifying each step and decision they make, and handing over responsibility for any harmful actions they commit to the authority.

Social Influences on Beliefs and Behavior

LO 8.2.A   Contrast situational and dispositional attributions, explain how and why the fundamental attribution error takes place, and describe three biases that people hold about themselves and others.

According to *attribution theory*, people are motivated to search for causes to which they can attribute their own and other people's behavior. Their attributions may be *situational* or *dispositional*. The *fundamental attribution error* occurs when people overestimate personality traits as a cause of behavior and underestimate the influence of the situation. Attributions are further influenced by three *self-serving biases*: the bias to choose the most flattering and forgiving explanations of our own behavior; the bias that we

are better, smarter, and kinder than others; and the bias that the world is fair (the *just-world hypothesis*).

LO 8.2.B   Outline the process of cognitive dissonance, and explain how the validity effect and the familiarity effect shape our attitudes.

People hold many *attitudes* about people, things, and ideas. Attitudes may be *explicit* (conscious) or *implicit* (unconscious). Attitudes may change through experience, conscious decision, or as an effort to reduce *cognitive dissonance*. One powerful way to influence attitudes is by taking advantage of the *familiarity effect* and the *validity effect*: Simply exposing people repeatedly to a name or product makes them like it more, and repeating a statement over and over again makes it seem more believable.

LO 8.2.C   Summarize four elements that contribute to indoctrination.

Suicide bombers and terrorists have not been "brainwashed" and most are not psychopaths or mentally ill. They have been entrapped into taking increasingly violent actions against real and perceived enemies; encouraged to attribute all problems to that one enemy; offered a new identity and salvation; and cut off from access to dissonant information.

Individuals in Groups

LO 8.3.A   Outline the basic procedures and findings of the Asch line-judging study.

In groups, individuals often behave differently than they would on their own. Conformity permits the smooth running of society and allows people to feel in harmony with others like them. Two basic, beneficial motives for conformity are the *need for social acceptance* and the *need for information*. But as the Asch experiment showed, most people will conform to the judgments of others even when the others are obviously wrong.

LO 8.3.B   List four symptoms of groupthink, and give an example from history, politics, or business to illustrate them.

Close-knit groups are vulnerable to *groupthink*, the tendency of group members to think alike, censor themselves, actively suppress disagreement, and feel that their decisions are invulnerable. Groupthink often produces faulty decisions because group members fail to seek disconfirming evidence for their ideas. However, groups can be structured to counteract groupthink.

LO 8.3.C   Explain how diffusion of responsibility and deindividuation contribute to the madness of crowds.

Sometimes a group's collective judgment is better than that of its individual members—the "wisdom of crowds." But crowds can also spread panic, rumor, and misinformation. *Diffusion of responsibility* in a group can lead to inaction on the part of individuals, as in *bystander apathy*. The diffusion of responsibility is likely to occur under conditions that promote *deindividuation*, the loss of awareness of one's individuality.

LO 8.3.D   Discuss four situational factors that increase one's likelihood to offer help to others.

In some situations, crowd norms lead deindividuated people to behave aggressively, but in others, crowd norms foster helpfulness. In truly dangerous, *unambiguous* emergencies people are more likely to help, and in fact are often spurred to do so by the presence of others. The willingness to speak up for an unpopular opinion, blow the whistle on illegal practices, or help a stranger in trouble and perform other acts of *altruism* is partly a matter of personal belief and conscience. But several situational factors are also important: The person perceives that help is needed; cultural norms support taking action; the person has an ally; and the person becomes entrapped in a commitment to help or dissent.

Us versus Them: Group Identity

LO 8.4.A   Contrast social identity, ethnic identity, and acculturation, and offer examples of each concept.

People develop *social identities* based on their ethnicity, including nationality, religion, occupation, and other social memberships. In culturally diverse societies, many people face the problem of balancing their *ethnic identity* with *acculturation* into the larger society.

LO 8.4.B   Define ethnocentrism and describe how it contributes to us–them dichotomies.

Ethnocentrism, the belief that one's own ethnic group or religion is superior to all others, promotes "us–them" thinking. One effective strategy for reducing us–them thinking and hostility between groups is *interdependence*, having both sides work together to reach a common goal.

LO 8.4.C   Define what a stereotype is, and discuss three ways in which stereotypes distort reality.

Stereotypes help people rapidly process new information, organize experience, and predict how others will behave. But they distort reality by exaggerating differences between groups, underestimating the differences within groups, and producing selective perception.

Group Conflict and Prejudice

LO 8.5.A   Describe four sources of prejudice.

A *prejudice* is an unreasonable negative feeling toward a category of people. Psychologically, prejudice wards off feelings of anxiety and doubt and bolsters self-esteem when a person feels threatened (by providing a scapegoat). Prejudice also has social causes: People acquire prejudices mindlessly, through conformity and parental lessons. Prejudice also serves to justify a majority group's economic interests and dominance. Finally, prejudice serves the cultural and national purpose of bonding people to their social groups and nations, and in extreme cases justifying war.

LO 8.5.B   Describe five ways of measuring prejudicial attitudes.

Psychologists disagree on whether racism and other prejudices are declining or have merely taken new forms. Some are trying to measure prejudice indirectly, by measuring *social distance* and instances of "microaggressions"; measuring unequal treatment by the police or other institutions; seeing whether people are more likely to behave aggressively toward a target when they are stressed or angry; observing changes in the brain; or assessing unconscious positive or negative associations with a group, as with the *Implicit Association Test (IAT)*. However, the IAT has many critics who claim it is not capturing true prejudice.

LO 8.5.C   Describe four situations that can help reduce prejudice and intergroup conflict.

Efforts to reduce prejudice need to target both the explicit and implicit attitudes that people have. Four conditions help to reduce two groups' mutual prejudices and conflicts: Both sides must have equal legal status, economic standing, and power; both sides must have the legal, moral, and economic support of authorities and cultural institutions; both sides must have opportunities to work and socialize together informally and formally (the *contact hypothesis*); and both sides must work together for a common goal.

LO 8.5.D   Explain the phrase "the banality of evil," and discuss how it contributes to otherwise-good people behaving badly.

Although many people believe that only bad people do bad deeds, the principles of social and cultural psychology show that under certain conditions, good people often can be induced to do bad things too. Everyone is influenced to one degree or another by the social processes of obedience, entrapment, conformity, persuasion, bystander apathy, groupthink, deindividuation, ethnocentrism, stereotyping, and prejudice.

Chapter 8 Quiz

1. When Abdallah met Aimee for the first time he was struck by three things: she was pretty, she was tall, and she kept backing away from him. Aimee also was struck by three things: Abdallah was handsome, he was tall, and he stood really, really close to her—uncomfortably close, as a matter of fact. Why would some of their initial impressions be so similar yet others be so different?

   a. Cultural rules modified the social roles that each person was required to "play."

   b. Making and holding eye contact is a social rule that each of them violated.

   c. Each of them adopted a social role that was incorrect for their interaction.

   d. Appropriate conversational distance is a norm that varies from culture to culture.

2. How much electrical shock was actually delivered to the "learners" in Milgram's obedience experiment?

   a. None

   b. 25 volts

   c. 150 volts

   d. 450 volts

3. Tomas is asked to play the role of a prison guard in a realistic simulation of an actual prison setting. Over time, what do you predict Tomas's behavior will be like in this environment?

   a. He will disobey the unreasonable requests of those in power over him.

   b. He will stay true to his own beliefs and personal values.

   c. He will adopt many of the mannerisms, attitudes, and behaviors of actual prison guards.

   d. He will start to act more like a prisoner than like a guard.

4. Gradual commitment to the requests of an authority figure can eventually lead to feelings of _____.

   a. Conformity

   b. Entrapment

   c. Resentment

   d. Resistance

5. The just-world hypothesis holds that:

   a. People will behave in response to the situation and downplay their dispositional tendencies.

   b. Good things happen to good people and bad things happen to bad people.

   c. Favorable outcomes are due to dispositional causes, whereas unfavorable outcomes are due to the effects of the situation.

   d. There is just this world, and no afterlife.

6. Keisha has announced to her friends that she wants to exercise more this semester. As her friends head off to the school gym, she flips on the television and settles in for a night of relaxed inactivity. Which of the following terms describes her mental state at the moment?

   a. Cognitive bias

   b. Cognitive consonance

   c. Implicit familiarity

   d. Cognitive dissonance

7. Marcie has been instructed by her Supreme Leader to assassinate the infidel Demi Lovato. She is convinced that this is the only means to bring about world peace and install the Supreme Leader in his rightful position of world domination. Marcie knows she will no doubt be shot on sight for her actions, but she looks forward to the eternal salvation and promised heavenly rewards for completing her mission. How likely will Marcie be to follow through on her assignment?

   a. Not very likely; she doesn't seem to believe in her own cause.

   b. Very likely; she shows many characteristics of being indoctrinated.

   c. Very likely; she has made a dispositional attribution to the effects of the situation.

   d. Not very likely; entrapment is easily overcome.

8. What did Solomon Asch discover in his famous experiment on judging the lengths of lines?

   a. Many people asserted their informational authority and swayed the group to their own beliefs.

   b. Most people dissented when the group's opinions were at odds with their own.

   c. Only "weak-willed" individuals, defined as such by their friends, conformed to the group's opinions.

   d. Many people conformed to the opinions of a group, despite those opinions being obviously wrong.

9. The tendency for group members to strive for consensus and agreement at the expense of realistically considering other viewpoints and relevant information is called:

   a. Social loafing

   b. Group mind

   c. Groupthink

   d. Group polarization

10. The more people who are around you in an emergency, the less likely it is that one of them will offer assistance. What produces this curious and disturbing finding?

   a. Allocentrism

   b. Groupthink

   c. Obedience

   d. Diffusion of responsibility

11. Helping can be increased by
    a. Increasing feelings of deindividuation among those present
    b. Increasing the number of people available to offer assistance
    c. The presence of an ally who holds the same opinions as you
    d. Waiting for a leader to emerge from the group of bystanders

12. Liudvika is proud of her Lithuanian heritage, and makes a point of cooking traditional bacon buns and borscht for her Milwaukee family, teaching her children the Lithuanian language, and actively contributing to the Lithuanians-in-America League. Social psychologists would conclude that Liudvika has a strong
    a. Acculturation tendency
    b. Ethnic identity
    c. Outgroup identity
    d. Situationist identity

13. Bronislav will tell anyone who listens that Lithuanian culture is superior to all others. He carries with him detailed charts outlining why Latvia, Poland, and Estonia are impoverished cultures; maintains a scrapbook of famous Lithuanian singers and actors; and he contributes regularly to the Only-Lithuanians-Are-Rockin'-Cool fund. Social psychologists would conclude that Bronislav shows strong
    a. Indemnified identity
    b. Acculturation
    c. Situationist identity
    d. Ethnocentrism

14. Mary believes that all Asian people excel at mathematics. Although that might be considered a complimentary view, it is also nonetheless
    a. Discriminatory
    b. Prejudicial
    c. A stereotype
    d. Acculturative

15. "No wonder I can't get a job!" grumbled Felipe. "All these immigrants flooding into this country are taking the jobs away from decent, hard-working citizens, and all we're getting is the shaft." Felipe's attitudes represent _____ causes for prejudice.
    a. Economic
    b. Social
    c. National
    d. Psychological

16. One behavioral measure of prejudice might be obtained by recording
    a. Brain-wave activity when people view photos of other races
    b. How people respond to questionnaires asking about their prejudicial attitudes
    c. What people do when they are angry or stressed
    d. How people respond to the Implicit Association Test

17. The Plain-Bellied Sneeches and the Star-Bellied Sneeches have a history of hostility and intergroup conflict. Which of the following events would have the greatest chance of reducing their conflicts?
    a. The central Sneechatorium (gym) burns down and the two groups cooperate to rebuild it.
    b. The local minister asks members of both groups to attend sermons on harmony and togetherness.
    c. The local neighborhood center sponsors a bocci ball competition between the two groups.
    d. The city builds a park for the Star-Bellied Sneeches.

18. Research on obedience, prejudice, helping others, ethnocentrism, groupthink, and conformity illustrates that sometimes people can do really bad things when norms, roles, and situations impact them. But the same research also points a way to understanding that
    a. Personality differences are a stronger predictor of behavior than are situational factors.
    b. People can do even more atrocious things when social pressures are lifted.
    c. People can also do really good things when norms, roles, and situations dictate.
    d. Humans are fundamentally good, and it is society that leads us to behave badly.

Chapter 8 Flashcards

familiarity effect

Chapter 9
Thinking and Intelligence

 Listen to the Audio

Learning Objectives

LO 9.1.A Distinguish between the various elements of cognition, such as concepts, prototypes, propositions, schemas, and mental images.

LO 9.1.B Distinguish between the varieties of conscious thought, such as subconscious thinking, nonconscious thinking, and implicit learning.

LO 9.1.C Contrast algorithms and heuristics as problem-solving strategies, and give an example of each.

LO 9.1.D Discuss the various types of reasoning, such as formal reasoning, informal reasoning, dialectical reasoning, and stages of reflective judgment, and note the defining characteristics of each.

LO 9.2.A Describe how the affect heuristic and the availability heuristic both illustrate the tendency to exaggerate the improbable.

LO 9.2.B Explain how the framing effect leads people to avoid loss in probabilistic judgments.

LO 9.2.C Summarize the mechanisms driving the fairness bias, hindsight bias, confirmation bias, and mental sets, and give an example of each.

LO 9.2.D Explain the process of cognitive dissonance, and describe three conditions under which feelings of cognitive dissonance are likely to occur.

LO 9.2.E Discuss the conditions under which cognitive biases can be detrimental to reasoning, and when they might be beneficial.

LO 9.3.A Outline the basic logic underlying factor analysis, and describe its use in measuring intelligence.

LO 9.3.B Summarize the original notion of IQ and some problems associated with it, and discuss how intelligence tests evolved during the early 1900s.

LO 9.4.A Describe how metacognition, the triarchic theory of intelligence, the theory of multiple intelligences, and emotional intelligence shed light on the diversity of what "intelligence" means.

LO 9.4.B Outline how longitudinal studies and cross-cultural studies shed light on the interplay of motivation, hard work, and intellectual achievement.

LO 9.5.A Summarize the evidence both supporting and refuting the concept of animal intelligence.

LO 9.5.B Summarize the evidence both supporting and refuting the concept of animal language use.

LO 9.5.C Explain why both anthropomorphism and anthropodenial are unwise approaches to understanding animal cognition.

Ask questions . . . be willing to wonder

Is all of our thinking conscious?

Why is it often so hard for people to reason rationally?

Does a high IQ guarantee success in school and in life?

Can animals think—and if so, what do they think about?

Each day, in the course of ordinary living, we all make decisions, draw up plans, draw inferences, construct explanations, and organize and reorganize the contents of our mental world. Descartes' famous declaration "I think, therefore I am" could just as well have been reversed: "I am, therefore I think." Our powers of thought and intelligence have inspired humans to immodestly call ourselves *Homo sapiens*, Latin for wise or rational man.

But just how "sapiens" are we, really? In Australia, a 23-year-old man put fireworks between his buttocks and set them off. This party trick backfired—literally. He was taken to the hospital with severe, painful burns on his backside and genitals. In Nottingham, England, the mayor decided to distribute flyers to visitors telling them that Robin Hood and his pals never actually lived in nearby Sherwood Forest, inasmuch as they were not real people; tourism plummeted. In Colorado, after daylight savings time began, a woman complained to a local newspaper that the "extra hour of sunlight" was burning up her front lawn.

We could go on.

Of course, our cognitive abilities are also pretty impressive. Think for a moment about what thinking does for you. It frees you from the confines of the immediate present: You can think about a trip taken 3 years ago, a party next Saturday, or the War of 1812. It carries you beyond the boundaries of reality: You can imagine unicorns and utopias, Martians and magic. You can make plans far into the future and judge the probability of events, both good and bad. Because you think, you do not need to grope your way blindly through your problems but can apply knowledge and reasoning to solve them intelligently and creatively.

Yes, the human mind—which has managed to come up with poetry, penicillin, and PCs—is a miraculous thing. But the human mind has also managed to come up with traffic jams, spam, and war. To better understand why the same species that figured out how to get to the moon is also capable of breathtaking bumbling here on Earth, we will examine in this chapter how people reason, solve problems, and grow in intelligence, as well as some sources of their mental shortcomings. These topics are the focus of *cognitive psychology*, the study of cognition (mental processes).

Thought: Using What We Know

In 2011, when an IBM computer named Watson defeated two very smart human beings on *Jeopardy*, the world was abuzz about whether that meant that machines would finally outthink people. But cognitive scientists were quick to point out that the human mind is actually far more complex than a computer; the machines have yet to learn to make puns and jokes, acquire an immediate insight into another person's feelings, or write a play or book.

Nonetheless, parallels between mind and machine can be useful guides to thinking about cognition because both actively process information by altering it, organizing it, and using it to make decisions. Just as computers internally manipulate representations of 0s and 1s to "think," so we *mentally* manipulate internal representations of objects, activities, and situations. For a preview of these processes, watch the video *I Am, Therefore I Think.*

The Elements of Cognition

LO 9.1.A   Distinguish between the various elements of cognition, such as concepts, prototypes, propositions, schemas, and mental images.

One type of mental representation is the **concept**, a mental category that groups objects, relations, activities, abstractions, or qualities having common properties. The instances of a concept are seen as roughly similar: *golden retriever, cocker spaniel,* and *border collie* are instances of the concept *dog*; and *anger, joy,* and *sadness* are instances of the concept *emotion.* Concepts simplify and summarize information about the world so that it is manageable and so that we can make decisions quickly and efficiently. You may never have seen a *basenji* or eaten *escargots*, but if you know that the first is an instance of *dog* and the second an instance of *food*, you will know, roughly, how to respond (unless you do not like to eat snails, which is what escargots are).

Basic concepts have a moderate number of instances and are easier to acquire than those having either few or many instances (Rosch, 1973). What is the object pictured here? You will probably call it an apple. The concept *apple* is more basic than *fruit*, which includes many more instances and is more abstract. It is also more basic than *Braeburn apple*, which is quite specific. Children seem to learn basic-level concepts earlier than other concepts, and adults use basic concepts more often than other concepts because basic concepts convey an optimal amount of information in most situations.

The qualities associated with a concept do not necessarily all apply to every instance: Some apples are not red; some dogs do not bark; some birds do not fly. But all the instances of a concept do share a family resemblance. When we need to decide whether something belongs to a concept, we are likely to compare it to a **prototype**, a representative instance of the concept (Rosch, 1973). Which dog is doggier, a golden retriever or a Chihuahua? Which fruit is more fruitlike, an apple or a pineapple? Which activity is more representative of sports, football or weightlifting? Most people within a culture can easily tell you which instances of a concept are most representative, or *prototypical*.

The words used to express concepts may influence or shape how we think about them. Many decades ago, Benjamin Lee Whorf, an insurance inspector by profession and a linguist and anthropologist by inclination, proposed that language molds cognition and perception. According to Whorf (1956), because English has only one word for snow and Eskimos (the Inuit) have many (for powdered snow, slushy snow, falling snow . . .), the Inuit notice differences in

What is this?

concept

A mental category that groups objects, relations, activities, abstractions, or qualities having common properties.

basic concepts

Concepts that have a moderate number of instances and that are easier to acquire than those having few or many instances.

prototype

An especially representative example of a concept.

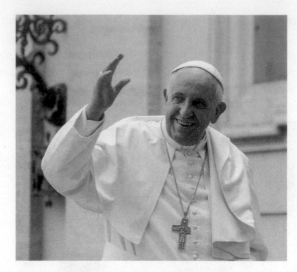

Some instances of a concept are more representative or prototypical than others. A "bachelor" is an unmarried man. Is John Mayer a bachelor, even though he is often romantically linked to different women for years at a time? Is the Pope a bachelor? What about Elton John, who married his long-time male partner David Furnish in Britain in 2014 but whose marriage would not have been recognized in some American states at the time?

How do you divide up these hues? People who speak a language that has only one word for blue and green, but separate words for shades of green, handle green contrasts better than the blue–green distinction. English speakers do the opposite.

snow that English speakers do not. He also argued that grammar—the way words are formed and arranged to convey tense and other concepts—affects how we think about the world.

Whorf's theory was popular for a while and then fell from favor. After all, English speakers can see all those Inuit kinds of snow and they have plenty of adjectives to describe the different varieties. But Whorf's ideas have once again gained attention. Vocabulary and grammar do affect how we perceive the location of objects, think about time, attend to shapes and colors, and remember events (Boroditsky, 2003; Gentner & Goldin-Meadow, 2003; Gentner, et al., 2013). A language spoken by a group in Papua, New Guinea, refers to blue and green with one word, but to distinct shades of green with two separate words. On perceptual discrimination tasks, New Guineans who speak this language handle green contrasts better than blue–green ones, whereas the reverse holds true for English speakers (Roberson, Davies, & Davidoff, 2000). Similar results on the way language affects color perception have been obtained in studies comparing English with certain African languages (Özgen, 2004; Roberson, Davidoff, Davies, & Shapiro, 2005).

Here's another example: In many languages, speakers must specify whether an object is linguistically masculine or feminine, as in Spanish, where *la cuenta*, the bill, is feminine but *el cuento*, the story, is masculine. It seems that labeling a concept as masculine or feminine affects the attributes that native speakers ascribe to it. Thus, a German speaker will describe a key (masculine in German) as hard, heavy, jagged, serrated, and useful, whereas a Spanish speaker is more likely to describe a key (feminine in Spanish) as golden, intricate, little, and lovely, shiny (Boroditsky, Schmidt, & Phillips, 2003). The video *The Mind Is What the Brain Does* reviews some of the elements of cognition.

Concepts are the building blocks of thought, but they would be of limited use if we merely stacked them up mentally. We must also represent their relationships to one another. One way we accomplish this may be by storing and using **propositions**, units of meaning that are made up of concepts and that express a unitary idea. A proposition can express nearly any sort of knowledge ("Rachael raises border collies") or belief ("Border collies are smart"). Propositions, in turn, are linked together in complicated networks of knowledge, associations, beliefs, and expectations. These networks, which psychologists call **cognitive schemas**, serve as mental frameworks for describing and thinking about various aspects of the world. Gender schemas represent a person's beliefs and expectations about what it means to be male or female, and people also have schemas about cultures, occupations, animals, geographical locations, and many other features of the social and natural environment.

Mental images—especially visual images, or pictures in the mind's eye—are also important in thinking and in constructing cognitive schemas. Although no one can directly see another person's visual images, psychologists are able to study them indirectly. One method is to measure how long it takes people to rotate an image in their imaginations, scan from one point to another in an image, or read off some detail from an image. The results suggest that visual images behave much like images on a computer screen: We can manipulate them, they occur in a mental space of a fixed size, and small ones contain less detail than larger ones (Kosslyn, 1980; Shepard & Metzler, 1971). People often rely on visual images when they solve spatial or mechanical puzzles (Hegarty & Waller, 2005). Most people also report auditory images (such as a song, slogan, or poem you can hear in your "mind's ear"), and many report images in other sensory modalities as well—touch, taste, smell, or pain. Some even report kinesthetic images, imagined sensations in the muscles and joints.

Figure 9.1 is a visual summary of the elements of cognition.

How Conscious Is Thought?

LO 9.1.B Distinguish between the varieties of conscious thought, such as subconscious thinking, nonconscious thinking, and implicit learning.

When we think about thinking, we usually have in mind those mental activities that are carried out in a deliberate way with a conscious goal in mind, such as solving a problem, drawing up plans, or making calculated decisions. However, much mental processing is not conscious.

SUBCONSCIOUS THINKING   Some cognitive processes lie outside of awareness but can be brought into consciousness with a little effort when necessary. These **subconscious processes** allow us to handle more information and to perform more complex tasks than if we depended entirely on conscious processing. Indeed, many automatic but complex routines are performed "without thinking," though they might previously have required careful, conscious attention: knitting, typing, driving a car, decoding the letters in a word in order to read it.

Because of the capacity for automatic processing, people can eat lunch while reading a book or drive a car while listening to music; in such cases, one of the tasks has become automatic. However, this does not mean you should go ahead and text your friends while driving. That's *multitasking*, and multitasking rarely works well. In fact, far from saving time, toggling between two or more tasks that require attention increases the time required to complete them (and in the case of driving and texting, is extremely dangerous). In addition, stress goes up, errors increase, reaction times lengthen, and memory suffers (Lien, Ruthruff, & Johnston, 2006). In one recent example, a commuter train's engineer violated company policy by texting while on the job, and he never saw an oncoming freight train. The resulting collision killed 25 people, including the engineer himself.

proposition

A unit of meaning that is made up of concepts and expresses a single idea.

cognitive schema

An integrated mental network of knowledge, beliefs, and expectations concerning a particular topic or aspect of the world.

mental image

A mental representation that mirrors or resembles the thing it represents; mental images occur in many and perhaps all sensory modalities.

subconscious processes

Mental processes occurring outside of conscious awareness but accessible to consciousness when necessary.

Figure 9.1 The Elements of Cognition

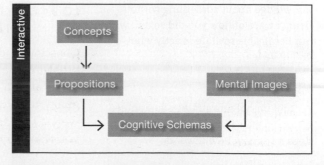

Some well-learned skills do not require much conscious thought and can be performed while doing other things, but multitasking can also get you into serious trouble. It's extremely dangerous to text and drive at the same time.

Even overhearing one side of someone else's cell phone conversation siphons your attention away from a task you are doing, possibly because of the effort required to make sense of just one half of a conversation. In one experiment, when people listened to a "halfalogue" while they were doing a visual task, they made more than six times as many errors on the task than when they listened to an ordinary two-person conversation (Emberson et al., 2010). As for multitasking when you are the person talking on the phone, that can be hazardous to your health. Cell phone use greatly impairs a person's ability to drive, whether the phone is hands-free or not; a driver's attention is diverted far more by a phone conversation than by listening to music (Briggs, Hole, & Land, 2011; Strayer & Drews, 2007). Other distractions are equally dangerous. Drivers have been caught on camera checking their stocks, applying makeup, flossing their teeth, and putting in contact lenses—all while hurtling down the highway at high speeds (Klauer et al., 2006). Although we'd like to believe we have the unlimited cognitive capacity to take on more and more tasks simultaneously, ample evidence suggests otherwise.

NONCONSCIOUS THINKING   Other kinds of thought processes, **nonconscious processes**, remain outside of awareness, even when you try to bring them back. As we will see shortly, people often find the solution to a problem when it suddenly pops into mind after they have given up trying to figure it out. And sometimes people learn a new skill without being able to explain how they perform it. For instance, they may discover the best strategy for winning at a card game without ever being able to consciously identify what they are doing (Bechara et al., 1997). With such **implicit learning**, you learn a rule or an adaptive behavior, either with or without a conscious intention to do so; but you don't know how you learned it, and you can't state, either to yourself or to others, exactly what it is you have learned (Frensch & Rünger, 2003; Lieberman, 2000). Many of our abilities, from speaking our native language properly to walking up a flight of stairs, are the result of implicit learning. But implicit learning is not always helpful because it can also generate biases and prejudices. We can learn an association between "stupidity" and "those people" without ever being aware of how we learned it or who taught it to us.

Even when our thinking is conscious, often we are not thinking very *hard*. We may act, speak, and make decisions out of habit, without stopping to analyze what we are doing or why we are doing it. *Mindlessness*—mental inflexibility, inertia, and obliviousness to the present context—keeps people from recognizing when a change in a situation requires a change in behavior. In a classic study of mindlessness, a psychologist approached people as they were about to use a photocopier and made one of three requests: "Excuse me, may I use the copy machine?" "Excuse me, may I use the copy machine, because I have to make copies?" or "Excuse me, may I use the copy machine, because I'm in a rush?" Normally, people will let someone go before them only if the person has a legitimate reason, as in the third request. In this study, however, people also complied when the reason sounded like an authentic explanation but was actually meaningless ("because I have to make copies"). They heard the form of the request but they did not hear its content, and they mindlessly stepped aside (Langer, Blank, & Chanowitz, 1978).

Problem Solving and Decision Making

LO 9.1.C Contrast algorithms and heuristics as problem-solving strategies, and give an example of each.

Conscious and nonconscious processes are both involved in solving problems. In well-defined problems, the nature of the problem is clear ("I need more cookies for the party tomorrow"). Often, all you need to do to solve the problem is apply the right **algorithm**, a set of procedures guaranteed to produce a correct (or a best) solution even if you do not understand why it works. To increase a cookie recipe, for example, you can simply multiply the number of cookies you want per person by the number of people you need to feed. If the original recipe produced

nonconscious processes

Mental processes occurring outside of and not available to conscious awareness.

implicit learning

Learning that occurs when you acquire knowledge about something without being aware of how you did so and without being able to state exactly what it is you have learned.

algorithm

A problem-solving strategy guaranteed to produce a solution even if the user does not know how it works.

10 cookies and you need 40, you can then multiply each ingredient by four. The recipe itself is also an algorithm (add flour, stir lightly, add raisins . . .), though you probably won't know the chemical changes involved when you combine the ingredients and heat the batter in an oven.

Other problems are fuzzier. There is no specific goal ("What should I have for dinner tomorrow?") and no clearly correct solution, so no algorithm applies. In such cases, you may resort to a **heuristic**, a rule of thumb that suggests a course of action without guaranteeing an optimal solution ("Maybe I'll browse through some recipes online, or go to the market and see what catches my eye"). Many heuristics, like those used when playing chess, help you limit your options to a manageable number of promising ones, reducing the cognitive effort it takes to arrive at a decision (Galotti, 2007; Galotti, Wiener, & Tandler, 2014). Heuristics are useful to a student trying to choose a major, an investor trying to predict the stock market, a doctor trying to determine the best treatment for a patient, and a factory owner trying to boost production. All of them are faced with incomplete information with which to reach a solution, and may therefore resort to rules of thumb that have proven effective in the past.

As useful as algorithms and heuristics are, sometimes the conscious effort to try to solve a problem seems to get you nowhere. Then, with insight, you suddenly see how to solve an equation or finish a puzzle without quite knowing how you found the solution. Insight probably involves different stages of mental processing (Bowers et al., 1990). First, clues in the problem automatically activate certain memories or knowledge. You begin to see a pattern or structure to the problem, although you cannot yet say what it is; possible solutions percolate in your mind. Although you are not aware of it, considerable mental work is guiding you toward a hypothesis, reflected in your brain as patterns of activity that differ from those associated with ordinary, methodical problem solving (Fields, 2011; Kounios & Beeman, 2009). Eventually, a solution springs to mind, seemingly from nowhere ("Aha, now I see!").

People also say they sometimes rely on intuition—hunches and gut feelings—rather than conscious thinking when they make judgments or solve problems. Why do we trust such feelings? One possibility is that changes in our bodies signal that we are close to success. Long before people can consciously identify the best strategy for winning a card game, their bodies already seem to "know" it: Changes in their sweat and heart rate occur as soon as they make a wrong move (Bechara et al., 1997). What's more, people who are better at paying attention to their heart rates tend to be better at figuring out the best strategy (Dunn et al., 2010).

Should you therefore go with your gut or take your pulse when answering questions or solving problems on your next test? Not necessarily. Daniel Kahneman's book *Thinking, Fast and Slow* (2011) explains why. "Fast" thinking applies to our rapid, intuitive, emotional, almost automatic decisions; "slow" thinking requires intellectual effort. Naturally, most people rely on fast thinking because it saves time and effort, but it is often wrong. Here is one of his examples: Suppose that a bat and ball together cost $1.10 and that the bat costs one dollar more than the ball. How much does the ball cost? Most people answer with fast thinking and say 10 cents. But the correct answer is five cents. Think (slowly) about it.

Jerome Kagan (1989) once likened consciousness to firefighters who are quietly playing cards at the station house until an alarm goes off, calling them into action. Much of the time we rely on automatic processes and unconscious impressions to guide us through our daily tasks. Usually that's a good thing. Walking around in a state of fully conscious awareness would be impossible, and undesirable as well; we would never get anything done if we had to examine "thoughtfully" every little thing we do, say, decide, or overhear. But multitasking, mindlessness, and operating on automatic pilot can also lead to errors and mishaps, ranging from the trivial (misplacing your keys) to the serious (walking into traffic because you're texting). Therefore, most of us would probably benefit if our mental firefighters paid a little more attention to their jobs. How can we improve our capacity to reason rationally and think critically? We turn to that question next.

heuristic
A rule of thumb that suggests a course of action or guides problem solving but does not guarantee an optimal solution.

Whether you are a chess grand master or just an ordinary person solving ordinary problems, you need to use heuristics, rules of thumb that help you decide on a strategy.

Reasoning Rationally

LO 9.1.D Discuss the various types of reasoning, such as formal reasoning, informal reasoning, dialectical reasoning, and stages of reflective judgment, and note the defining characteristics of each.

reasoning

The drawing of conclusions or inferences from observations, facts, or assumptions.

dialectical reasoning

A process in which opposing facts or ideas are weighed and compared, with a view to determining the best solution or resolving differences.

Reasoning is purposeful mental activity that involves operating on information to reach a conclusion. Unlike impulsive ("fast") or nonconscious responding, reasoning requires us to draw specific inferences from observations, facts, or assumptions. In *formal reasoning* problems—the kind you might find, say, on an intelligence test or a college entrance exam—the information needed for drawing a conclusion or reaching a solution is specified clearly, and there is a single right (or best) answer. In *informal reasoning* problems, there is often no clearly correct solution. Many approaches, viewpoints, or possible solutions may compete, and you may have to decide which one is most "reasonable."

To do this wisely, a person must be able to use **dialectical reasoning**, the process of comparing and evaluating opposing points of view to resolve differences. Philosopher Richard Paul (1984) once described dialectical reasoning as movement "up and back between contradictory lines of reasoning, using each to critically cross-examine the other." Dialectical reasoning is what juries are supposed to do to arrive at a verdict: consider arguments for and against the defendant's guilt, point and counterpoint. It is also what voters are supposed to do when thinking about whether the government should raise or lower taxes, or about the best way to improve public education.

However, many adults have trouble thinking dialectically; they take one position, and that's that. When do people develop the ability to think critically—to question assumptions, evaluate and integrate evidence, consider alternative interpretations, and reach conclusions that can be defended as most reasonable?

To find out, Patricia King and Karen Kitchener (1994, 2002, 2004) provided a large, diverse sample of adolescents and adults with statements describing opposing viewpoints on various topics. Each person then had to answer several questions, such as "What do you think about these statements?" "On what do you base your position?" and "Why do you suppose disagreement exists about this issue?" From the responses of thousands of participants, King and Kitchener identified several stations on the road to what they call *reflective judgment* and we have called critical thinking. At each one, people make different assumptions about how things are known and use different ways of justifying their beliefs.

In general, people who rely on *prereflective thinking* tend to assume that a correct answer always exists and that it can be obtained directly through the senses ("I know what I've seen") or from authorities ("They said so on the news"; "That's what I was brought up to believe"). If authorities do not yet have the truth, prereflective thinkers tend to reach conclusions on the basis of what "feels right" at the moment. They do not distinguish between knowledge and belief or between belief and evidence, and they see no reason to justify a belief. One respondent, when asked about evolution, said, "Well, some people believe that we evolved from apes and that's the way they want to believe. But I would never believe that way and nobody could talk me out of the way I believe because I believe the way that it's told in the Bible."

People who are *quasi-reflective thinkers* recognize that some things cannot be known with absolute certainty and that judgments should be supported by reasons, yet they pay attention only to evidence that fits what they already believe. They seem to think that because knowledge is uncertain, any judgment about the evidence is purely subjective. Quasi-reflective thinkers will defend a position by saying, "We all have a right to our own opinion," as if all opinions are created equal. One college student, when asked whether one opinion on the safety of food additives was right and others were wrong, answered, "No. I think it just depends on how you feel personally because people make their decisions based on how they feel and what research they've seen. So what one person thinks is right, another person might think is wrong. . . . If I feel that chemicals cause cancer and you feel that food is unsafe without them, your opinion might be right to you and my opinion is right to me."

One reason that Auguste Rodin's *The Thinker* became world famous and has been much imitated is that it captures so perfectly the experience of thinking reflectively.

Finally, some people become capable of *reflective judgment*. They understand that although some things can never be known with certainty, some judgments are more valid than others because of their coherence, their fit with the available evidence, their usefulness, and so on. They are willing to consider evidence from a variety of sources and to reason dialectically. Figure 9.2 shows an interview with a graduate student that illustrates reflective thinking.

Sometimes the types of judgments people make depend on the kind of problem or issue they are thinking about. They might be able to use reflective judgment for some issues yet be prereflective on others that hold deep emotional meaning for them (Haidt, 2012; King & Kitchener, 2004). But most people show no evidence of reflective judgment until their middle or late 20s, if ever. A longitudinal study found that many college students graduate without learning to distinguish fact from opinion, evaluate conflicting reports objectively, or resist emotional statements and political posturing (Arum & Roksa, 2011). Still, there's reason for hope. When college students get ample support for thinking reflectively, have opportunities to practice it in their courses, and apply themselves seriously to their studies, their thinking tends to become more complex, sophisticated, and well grounded (Kitchener et al., 1993). You can see why, in this book, we emphasize thinking about psychological findings, and not just memorizing them.

Q: Can you ever say you know for sure that your point of view on chemical additives is correct?

A: No, I don't think so . . . [but] I think that we can usually be reasonably certain, given the information we have now, and considering our methodologies. . . . [I]t might be that the research wasn't conducted rigorously enough. In other words, we might have flaws in our data or sample, things like that.

Q: How then would you identify the "better opinion"?

A: One that takes as many factors as possible into consideration. I mean one that uses the higher percentage of the data that we have, and perhaps that uses the methodology that has been most reliable.

Q: And how do you come to a conclusion about what the evidence suggests?

A: I think you have to take a look at the different opinions and studies that different groups offer. Maybe some studies offered by the chemical industry, some studies by the government, some private studies. . . . You have to try to interpret people's motives and that makes it a more complex soup to try to strain out.

Figure 9.2 Reflective Thinking

Here's an example of the process of reflective thinking. Notice how the discussants consider multiple perspectives and weigh the merits of the available evidence when reaching their conclusions.

JOURNAL PROMPT 9.1

Thinking Critically—Examine the Evidence: Think about the last time you found yourself mindlessly performing a task. Maybe you drifted off while driving to a place you drive to every day and missed your turnoff, perhaps you unthinkingly walked to the wrong classroom on the wrong day, or maybe you added the wrong ingredients to a recipe you thought you knew by heart. What types of information should you have paid attention to instead, and what kinds of cognitive processes should you have relied on to produce a more mindful result?

Quiz for Module 9.1

1. Which of the following concepts is the most basic?
   a. Recliner
   b. Chair
   c. Furniture
   d. High chair

2. Which example of the concept *chair* is prototypical?
   a. Beanbag chair
   b. High chair
   c. Rocking chair
   d. Dining room chair

3. Pedro intends to drive to the grocery store on Saturday morning. About 10 minutes into his journey, he notices that he's taken the wrong route and is in fact headed toward the office he drives to most days of the week. Pedro's error can be attributed to:
   a. Mindlessness
   b. Reinforcement
   c. Prototypical thinking
   d. Dialectical reasoning

4. Cindy is solving a long-division problem in her math class, so she follows the steps that her teacher showed her to accomplish that task. Cindy's problem-solving strategy is an example of:
   a. Heuristic reasoning
   b. An algorithm
   c. Best-case analysis
   d. Nonconscious processing

5. Mina thinks the media have a liberal political bias, and Sophie thinks they are too conservative. "Well," says Mina, "I have my truth and you have yours. It's purely subjective." Which of King and Kitchener's types of thinking describes Mina's statement?
   a. Quasi-reflective
   b. Prereflective
   c. Reflective
   d. Formal reasoning

Barriers to Reasoning Rationally

affect heuristic

The tendency to consult one's emotions instead of estimating probabilities objectively.

availability heuristic

The tendency to judge the probability of a type of event by how easy it is to think of examples or instances.

Although most people have the capacity to think logically, reason dialectically, and make judgments reflectively, it is clear that they do not always do so. One obstacle is the need to be right; if your self-esteem depends on winning arguments, you will find it hard to listen with an open mind to competing views. Other obstacles include limited information and a lack of time to reflect carefully. But human thought processes are also tripped up by many predictable, systematic biases and errors. Psychologists have studied dozens of them (Kahneman, 2003, 2011). Here we describe just a few.

Exaggerating the Improbable (and Minimizing the Probable)

LO 9.2.A Describe how the affect heuristic and the availability heuristic both illustrate the tendency to exaggerate the improbable.

One common bias is the inclination to exaggerate the probability of rare events. This bias helps to explain why so many people enter lotteries and buy disaster insurance, and why some irrational fears persist. Evolution has equipped us to fear certain natural dangers, such as snakes. However, in modern life, many of these dangers are no longer much of a threat; the risk of a renegade rattler sinking its fangs into you in Chicago or New York is very low! Yet the fear lingers on, so we overestimate the danger. Evolution has also given us brains that are terrific at responding to an immediate threat or to acts that provoke moral outrage even though they pose no threat to the survival of the species (e.g., flag burning). Unfortunately, our brains were not designed to become alarmed by serious *future* threats that do not seem to pose much danger right now, such as global warming (Gilbert, 2006).

When judging probabilities, people are strongly influenced by the **affect heuristic**, the tendency to consult their emotions (affect) to judge the "goodness" or "badness" of a situation instead of judging probabilities objectively (Slovic & Peters, 2006; Slovic et al., 2002; Västfäll, Peters, & Slovic, 2014). Emotions can often help us make decisions by narrowing our options or by allowing us to act quickly in an uncertain or dangerous situation. But emotions can also mislead us by preventing us from accurately assessing risk. One unusual field study looked at how people in France responded to the "mad cow" crisis that occurred several years ago. (Mad cow disease affects the brain and can be contracted by eating meat from contaminated cows.) Whenever many newspaper articles reported the dangers of "mad cow disease," beef consumption fell during the following month. But when news articles, reporting the same dangers, used the technical names of the disease—Creutzfeldt-Jakob disease and bovine spongiform encephalopathy—beef consumption stayed the same (Sinaceur, Heath, & Cole, 2005). The more alarming labels caused people to reason emotionally and to overestimate the danger. (During the entire period of the supposed crisis, only six people in France were diagnosed with the disease.)

Our judgments about risks are also influenced by the **availability heuristic**, the tendency to judge the probability of an event by how easy it is to think of instances of it (Tversky & Kahneman, 1973). The availability heuristic often works hand in hand with the affect heuristic. Catastrophes and shocking accidents evoke an especially strong emotional reaction in us, and thus stand out in our minds, becoming more available mentally than other kinds of negative events. (An image of a "mad cow"—that sweet, placid creature running amok!—is highly "available.") This is why people overestimate the frequency of deaths from tornadoes and underestimate the frequency of deaths from asthma, which occur dozens of times more often but

Because of the affect and availability heuristics, many of us overestimate the chances of suffering a shark attack. Shark attacks are extremely rare, but they are terrifying and easy to visualize.

do not make headlines. It is why news accounts of a couple of shark attacks make people fear that they are in the midst of a shark-attack epidemic, even though such attacks on humans are extremely rare.

Avoiding Loss

LO 9.2.B Explain how the framing effect leads people to avoid loss in probabilistic judgments.

In general, people try to avoid or minimize the risk of incurring losses when they make decisions. That strategy is rational enough, but people's perceptions of risk are subject to the **framing effect**, the tendency for choices to differ depending on how they are presented. When a choice is framed as the risk of losing something, people will respond more cautiously than when the very *same* choice is framed as a potential gain. They will choose a ticket that has a 1 percent chance of winning a raffle over one that has a 99 percent chance of losing. Or they will rate a condom as effective when they are told it has a 95 percent success rate in protecting against the AIDS virus but not when they are told it has a 5 percent failure rate—which of course is exactly the same thing (Linville, Fischer, & Fischhoff, 1992).

Suppose you had to choose between two health programs to combat a disease expected to kill 600 people. Which would you prefer: a program that will definitely save 200 people, or one with a one-third probability of saving all 600 people and a two-thirds probability of saving none? (Problem 1 in Figure 9.3 illustrates this choice.) When asked this question, most people, including physicians, say they would prefer the first program. In other words, they reject the riskier though potentially more rewarding solution in favor of a sure gain. However, people will take a risk if they see it as a way to *avoid loss*. Suppose now that you have to choose between a program in which 400 people will definitely die and a program in which there is a one-third probability of nobody dying and a two-thirds probability that all 600 will die. If you think about it, you will see that the alternatives are exactly the same as in the first problem; they are merely worded differently (see Problem 2 in Figure 9.3). Yet this time, most people choose the second solution. They reject risk when they think of the outcome in terms of lives saved, but they accept risk when they think of the outcome in terms of lives lost (Tversky & Kahneman, 1981).

Few of us will have to face a decision involving hundreds of lives, but we may have to choose between different medical treatments for ourselves or a relative. Our decision may be affected by whether the doctor frames the choice in terms of chances of surviving or chances of dying.

Biases and Mental Sets

LO 9.2.C Summarize the mechanisms driving the fairness bias, hindsight bias, confirmation bias, and mental sets, and give an example of each.

Relying on heuristics or being swayed by framing effects are just some of the barriers to reasoning rationally. Human thinkers also fall prey to a range of biases in the reasoning process. Let's look at some of these.

THE FAIRNESS BIAS Imagine that you are playing a two-person game called the *Ultimatum Game*, in which your partner gets $20 and must decide how much to share with you. You can choose to accept your partner's offer, in which case you both get to keep your respective portions, or you can reject the offer, in which case neither of you gets a penny. How low an offer would you accept?

Actually, it makes sense to accept any amount at all, no matter how paltry, because then at least you will get *something*. But that is not how people respond when playing the Ultimatum Game. If the

framing effect
The tendency for people's choices to be affected by how a choice is presented, or framed, such as whether it is worded in terms of potential losses or gains.

Figure 9.3 A Matter of Wording

The decisions we make can depend on how the alternatives are framed. When asked to choose between the two programs in Problem 1, which are described in terms of lives saved, most people choose the first program. When asked to choose between the programs in Problem 2, which are described in terms of lives lost, most people choose the second program. Yet the alternatives in the two problems are actually identical.

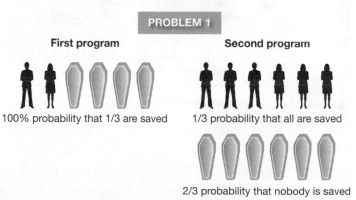

PROBLEM 1

First program · Second program

100% probability that 1/3 are saved · 1/3 probability that all are saved

2/3 probability that nobody is saved

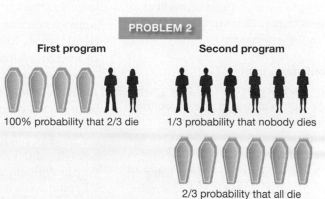

PROBLEM 2

First program · Second program

100% probability that 2/3 die · 1/3 probability that nobody dies

2/3 probability that all die

BIOLOGY and *Economic Choice*

Why does a desire for fair play sometimes outweigh the desire for economic gain? Evolutionary theorists suggest that cooperative tendencies and a desire for fairness and reciprocity evolved because they were beneficial to our forebears, ensuring teamwork and harmony among members of a group (Fehr & Fischbacher, 2003; Trivers, 2004). Different cultures develop their own rules to promote cooperation and punish cheaters, but a concern with fairness appears to be universal, part of our biological heritage.

The idea that the Golden Rule ("Treat others as you would like to be treated") has a basis in biology has gained support from studies of nonhuman primates and human babies. In one study, capuchin monkeys received a token that they could then exchange for a slice of cucumber. The monkeys regarded this exchange as a pretty good deal—until they saw a neighboring monkey exchanging tokens for

In this drawing, made from a video, the monkey on the right watches as the one on the left exchanges a token for a reward. Later, the observing monkey may refuse a lesser reward.

an even better reward, a grape. At that point, they began to refuse to exchange their tokens, even though they were then left with no reward at all (Brosnan & de Waal, 2003). Sometimes they even threw the cucumber slice on the ground in apparent disgust!

Human babies also have a sense of fairness. In ingenious studies with 19- and 21-month-old infants, researchers took advantage of the fact that infants will look longer at something when it violates their expectations. When the experimenter failed to distribute rewards equally to two adult women who were doing a chore, the infants' expectation of fair play was violated. But it was not violated when the experimenter simply opened a box to reveal the items rather than distributing them, or when the rewards were distributed by an inanimate object (Sloane, Baillargeon, & Premack, 2012). Although the experimenters noted that young children might be learning about fair play from early interactions with adults, the early age at which infants seem to know at least some rules of fairness suggests a biological predisposition to acquire such rules.

Some behavioral economists have studied fairness by using fMRI to examine brain activity when people play variations of the Ultimatum Game (Camerer, 2003; Haruno, Kimura, & Frith, 2014). Typically, while a person is deciding whether to accept a low or unfair offer, two brain areas are active: a part of the prefrontal cortex linked to rational problem solving, and an area called the *anterior insula*, which is associated with pain, disgust, and other unpleasant feelings. According to economist Colin Camerer (quoted in D'Antonio, 2004), "Basically the brain toggles between 'Yes, money is good' and 'Ugh, this guy is treating me like crap.'" People with greater activation of the prefrontal cortex are likely to accept low offers; they do the economically smart thing and let the insult slide. In contrast, those with greater activation of the anterior insula are likely to refuse. In fact, Camerer estimates that researchers can predict the outcome 70 percent of the time simply by looking at participants' brain scans.

Now, if only the apparently innate desire for fairness didn't lead human beings to inflict suffering so often on those whom they perceive as being unfair, and if only their ability to cooperate didn't lead so often to cooperation in waging war.

hindsight bias

The tendency to overestimate one's ability to have predicted an event after the outcome is known; the "I knew it all along" phenomenon.

confirmation bias

The tendency to look for or pay attention only to information that confirms one's own belief.

mental set

A tendency to solve problems using procedures that worked before on similar problems.

offer is too low, they are likely to reject it. In industrial societies, offers of 50 percent are typical and offers below 20 or 30 percent are commonly rejected, even when the absolute sums are large. In other societies, the amounts offered and accepted may be higher or lower, but there is always some amount that people consider unfair and refuse to accept (Güth & Kocher, 2014; Henrich et al., 2001). People may be competitive and love to win, but they are also powerfully swayed by a *fairness bias*, and motivated to see fairness prevail in these situations.

THE HINDSIGHT BIAS There is a reason for the saying that hindsight is 20/20. When people learn the outcome of an event or the answer to a question, they are often sure that they "knew it all along." Armed with the wisdom of hindsight, they see the outcome that actually occurred as inevitable, and they overestimate their ability to have predicted what happened beforehand (Fischhoff, 1975; Hawkins & Hastie, 1990). This **hindsight bias** shows up all the time in evaluating relationships ("I always knew they would break up"), medical judgments ("I could have told you that mole was cancerous"), and military opinions ("The generals should have known that the other side would attack").

Perhaps you feel that we are not telling you anything new because you have always known about the hindsight bias. But then, you may just have a hindsight bias about the hindsight bias.

THE CONFIRMATION BIAS   When people want to make the most accurate judgment possible, they usually try to consider all of the relevant information. But when they are thinking about an issue they already feel strongly about, they often succumb to the **confirmation bias**, paying attention only to evidence that confirms their belief and finding fault with evidence that points in a different direction (Edwards & Smith, 1996; Nickerson, 1998). You rarely hear someone say, "Oh, thank you for explaining to me why my lifelong philosophy of childrearing (or politics, or investing) is wrong. I'm so grateful for the facts!" The person is more likely to say, "Oh, get lost, and take your crazy ideas with you."

After you start looking for it, you will see the confirmation bias everywhere. Politicians brag about economic reports that confirm their party's position and dismiss counterevidence as biased or unimportant. Many jury members, instead of considering and weighing possible verdicts against the evidence, quickly construct a story about what happened and then consider only the trial evidence that supports their version of events. These same people are the most confident in their decisions and most likely to vote for an extreme verdict (Kuhn, Weinstock, & Flaton, 1994). We bet you can see the confirmation bias in your own reactions to what you are learning in psychology. In thinking critically, most of us apply a double standard; we think most critically about results we dislike. That is why the scientific method can be so difficult. It forces us to consider evidence that *disconfirms* our beliefs (see Figure 9.4).

MENTAL SETS   Another barrier to rational thinking is the development of a **mental set**, a tendency to try to solve new problems by using the same heuristics, strategies, and rules that worked in the past on similar problems (see Figure 9.5). Mental sets make human learning and problem solving efficient; because of them, we do not have to keep reinventing the wheel. But mental sets are not helpful when a problem calls for fresh insights and methods. They cause us to cling rigidly to the same old assumptions and approaches, blinding us to better or more rapid solutions.

One general mental set is the tendency to find patterns in events. This tendency is adaptive because it helps us understand and exert some control over what happens in our lives. But it also leads us to see meaningful patterns even when they do not exist. For example, many people with arthritis think that their symptoms follow a pattern dictated by the weather. They suffer more, they say, when the barometric pressure changes or when the weather is damp or humid. Yet when 18 arthritis patients were observed for 15 months, no association whatsoever emerged between weather conditions and the patients' self-reported pain levels, their ability to function in daily life, or a doctor's evaluation of their joint tenderness (Redelmeier & Tversky, 1996). Of course, because of the confirmation bias, the patients refused to believe the results.

The Need for Cognitive Consistency

LO 9.2.D   Explain the process of cognitive dissonance, and describe three conditions under which feelings of cognitive dissonance are likely to occur.

Mental sets and the confirmation bias cause us to avoid evidence that contradicts our beliefs. But what happens when disconfirming evidence finally smacks us in the face, and we cannot ignore or discount it any longer? As the 20th century rolled to an end, predictions of the end of the world escalated. Similar doomsday predictions have been made throughout history and continue today; after all, you are reading this despite the alleged Mayan prophecy that the world would end in December 2012. When these predictions fail, how come we never hear believers say, "Boy, what a fool I was"?

Figure 9.4 Confirming the Confirmation Bias

Suppose someone deals out four cards, each with a letter on one side and a number on the other. You can see only one side of each card, as shown here. Your task is to find out whether the following rule is true: "If a card has a vowel on one side, then it has an even number on the other side." Which two cards do you need to turn over to find out? The majority of people say they would turn over the E and the 6, but they are wrong. You do need to turn over the E (a vowel), because if the number on the other side is even, it confirms the rule, and if it is odd, the rule is false. However, the card with the 6 tells you nothing. The rule does not say that a card with an even number must always have a vowel on the other side. Therefore, it doesn't matter whether the 6 has a vowel or a consonant on the other side. The card you do need to turn over is the 7, because if it has a vowel on the other side, that fact disconfirms the rule. People do poorly on this problem because they are biased to look for confirming evidence and to ignore the possibility of disconfirming evidence.

Figure 9.5 Connect the Dots

Copy this figure, and try to connect the dots by using no more than four straight lines without lifting your pencil or pen. A line must pass through each point. Can you do it? Most people have difficulty with this problem because they have a mental set to interpret the arrangement of dots as a square. They then assume that they can't extend a line beyond the apparent boundaries of the square. Now that you know this, you might try again if you haven't yet solved the puzzle. Some solutions are given at the end of this chapter.

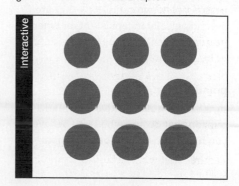

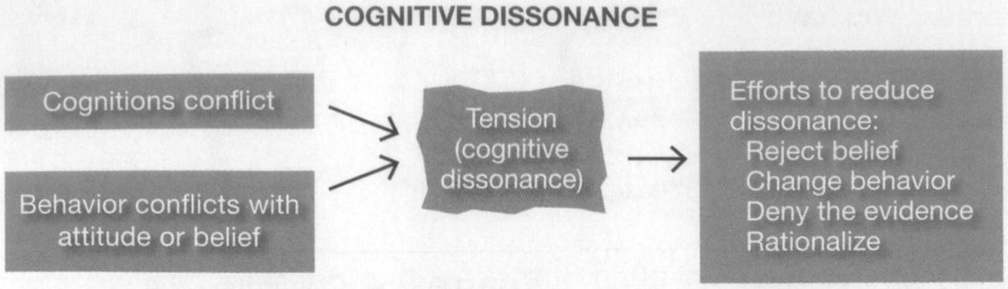

COGNITIVE DISSONANCE

Figure 9.6 The Process of Cognitive Dissonance

According to the theory of **cognitive dissonance**, people will resolve such conflicts in predictable, though not always obvious, ways (Festinger, 1957). *Dissonance*, the opposite of consistency (*consonance*), is a state of tension that occurs when you hold either two cognitions (beliefs, thoughts, attitudes) that are psychologically inconsistent with one another, or a belief that is incongruent with your behavior. This tension is psychologically uncomfortable, so you will be motivated to reduce it. You may do this by rejecting or modifying one of those inconsistent beliefs, changing your behavior, denying the evidence, or rationalizing, as shown in Figure 9.6.

Years ago, in a famous field study, Leon Festinger and two associates explored people's reactions to failed prophecies by infiltrating a group of people who thought the world would end on December 21 (Festinger, Riecken, & Schachter, 1956). The group's leader, whom the social psychologists called Marian Keech, promised that the faithful would be picked up by a flying saucer and whisked to safety at midnight on December 20. Many of her followers quit their jobs and spent all their savings, waiting for the end to come. What would they do or say, Festinger and his colleagues wondered, to reduce the dissonance between "The world is still muddling along on the 21st" and "I predicted the end of the world and sold off all my worldly possessions"?

Festinger predicted that believers who had made no public commitment to the prophecy, who awaited the end of the world by themselves at home, would simply lose their faith. However, those who had acted on their conviction by selling their property and waiting with Keech for the spaceship would be in a state of dissonance. They would have to *increase* their religious belief to avoid the intolerable realization that they had behaved foolishly and others knew it. That is just what happened. At 4:45 A.M., long past the appointed hour of the saucer's arrival, the leader had a new vision. The world had been spared, she said, because of the impressive faith of her little band.

Cognitive dissonance theory predicts that in more ordinary situations as well, people will resist or rationalize information that conflicts with their existing ideas, just as the people in the arthritis study did. For example, cigarette smokers are often in a state of dissonance because smoking is dissonant with the fact that smoking causes illness. Smokers may try to reduce the dissonance by trying to quit, by rejecting evidence that smoking is bad, by persuading themselves that they will quit later on, by emphasizing the benefits of smoking ("A cigarette helps me relax"), or by deciding that they don't want a long life, anyhow ("It will be shorter but sweeter").

You are particularly likely to reduce dissonance under three conditions (Aronson, 2012):

1. **When you need to justify a choice or decision that you made freely.** All car dealers know about buyer's remorse: The second that people buy a car, they worry that they made the wrong decision or spent too much, a phenomenon called **postdecision dissonance**. You may try to resolve this dissonance by deciding that the car you chose (or the toaster, or house, or spouse) is really, truly the best in the world. *Before* people make a decision, they can be open-minded, seeking information on the pros and cons of the choice at hand. *After* they make that choice, however, the confirmation bias will kick in, so that they will now notice all the good things about their decision and overlook or ignore evidence that they might have been wrong.

2. **When you need to justify behavior that conflicts with your view of yourself.** If you consider yourself to be honest, cheating will put you in a state of dissonance. To avoid feeling like a hypocrite, you will try to reduce the dissonance by justifying your behavior ("Everyone else does it"; "It's just this once"; "I had to do it to get into med school and learn to save lives"). Or if you see yourself as a kind person and you harm someone, you

cognitive dissonance

A state of tension that occurs when a person holds two cognitions that are psychologically inconsistent, or when a person's belief is incongruent with his or her behavior.

postdecision dissonance

In the theory of cognitive dissonance, tension that occurs when you believe you may have made a bad decision.

Figure 9.7 The Justification of Effort

The more effort you put into reaching a goal, the more highly you are likely to value it. As you can see in the graph on the left, after people listened to a boring group discussion, those who went through a severe initiation to join the group rated it most highly (Aronson & Mills, 1959). In the photo, soldiers undergo special and difficult training to join an elite unit. They will probably become extremely devoted members.

may reduce your dissonance by blaming the person you have victimized or by finding other self-justifying excuses.

3. **When you need to justify the effort put into a decision or choice.** The harder you work to reach a goal, or the more you suffer for it, the more you will try to convince yourself that you value the goal, even if the goal turns out to be not so great after all (Aronson & Mills, 1959). This explains why hazing, whether in social clubs, on athletic teams, or in the military, turns new recruits into loyal members (see Figure 9.7). The cognition "I went through a lot of awful stuff to join this group" is dissonant with the cognition "only to find I hate the group." Therefore, people must decide either that the hazing was not so bad or that they really like the group. This mental reevaluation is called the **justification of effort**, and it is one of the most popular methods of reducing dissonance.

Some people are secure enough to own up to their mistakes instead of justifying them, and individuals and cultures vary in the kinds of experiences that cause them to feel dissonance. However, the need for cognitive consistency in those beliefs that are most central to our sense of self and our values is universal (Tavris & Aronson, 2007).

Overcoming Our Cognitive Biases

LO 9.2.E Discuss the conditions under which cognitive biases can be detrimental to reasoning, and when they might be beneficial.

Sometimes our mental biases are a good thing. The ability to reduce cognitive dissonance helps us preserve our self-confidence and avoid sleepless nights second-guessing ourselves, and having a sense of fairness keeps us from behaving like self-centered louts. From this point of view, such biases are not so irrational after all. But our mental biases can also get us into trouble. The confirmation bias, the justification of effort, and a need to reduce postdecision dissonance permit people to stay stuck with decisions that eventually prove to be self-defeating, harmful, or incorrect. Physicians may continue using outdated methods, district attorneys may overlook evidence that a criminal suspect might be innocent, and managers may refuse to consider better business practices.

To make matters worse, most people have a "bias blind spot." They acknowledge that *other* people have biases that distort reality, but they think that they themselves are free of bias and see the world as it really is (Pronin, Gilovich, & Ross, 2004; Ross, 2010). This blind

justification of effort

The tendency of individuals to increase their liking for something that they have worked hard or suffered to attain; a common form of dissonance reduction.

spot is itself a bias, and it is a dangerous one because it can prevent individuals, nations, and ethnic or religious groups from resolving conflicts with others. Each side thinks that its own proposals for ending a conflict, or its own analyses of a problem, are reasonable and fair but the other side's are "biased."

Fortunately, the situation is not entirely hopeless. For one thing, people are not equally irrational in all circumstances. When they are doing things in which they have some expertise or are making decisions that have serious personal consequences, their cognitive biases often diminish (Smith & Kida, 1991). Furthermore, after we understand a bias, we may, with some effort, be able to reduce or eliminate it, especially if we make an active, mindful effort to do so and take time to think carefully (Kida, 2006).

Some people, of course, seem to think more rationally than others a great deal of the time; we call them "intelligent." Just what is intelligence, and how can we measure and improve it? We take up these questions next.

JOURNAL PROMPT 9.2

Critical Thinking—Ask Questions: Time and again, doomsday predictions fail. Why don't people who wrongly predict a devastating earthquake or the end of the world feel embarrassed when their forecasts flop?

Quiz for Module 9.2

1. In 2014, the Centers for Disease Control and Prevention reported four diagnoses of the Ebola virus in the United States. Three of the patients recovered, although one person unfortunately died from the disease. Nonetheless, people nationwide feared for their health and safety, although the probability of any one individual contracting the disease was extremely small. Which barriers to reasoning rationally help explain this panicked reaction?

  a. The availability heuristic and the hindsight bias

  b. The fairness bias and the hindsight bias

  c. The hindsight bias and the confirmation bias

  d. The affect heuristic and the availability heuristic

2. Jerry hears on a news broadcast that a proposed recycling program for his city will reclaim 80% of household waste. Dee Dee, watching a different news broadcast at the same time, learns that the same proposed program will send 20% of household waste to the local landfill. Jerry thinks the new program is great, but Dee Dee thinks it's horrible. What barrier to reasoning rationally could be affecting their conclusions?

  a. The framing effect

  b. The availability heuristic

  c. The affect heuristic

  d. The hindsight bias

3. Adnan meets a young woman at the gym. They hit it off and eventually get married. Says Adnan, "I knew when I woke up that morning that something special was going to happen." What cognitive bias is affecting his thinking, charmingly romantic though it is?

  a. The fairness bias

  b. The hindsight bias

  c. The confirmation bias

  d. The framing effect

4. Keisha has announced to her friends that she wants to lose weight this semester. As she pays for her meal at the cafeteria, she notices she has selected a double cheeseburger, French fries, and a jumbo soda. Which of the following terms describes her mental state at the moment?

  a. Cognitive consonance

  b. Cognitive dissonance

  c. Disrupted mental set

  d. Unfairness bias

5. Burt and Lana are having a heated discussion. "Burt, you are so biased! You only look at evidence that supports your beliefs and ignore information that doesn't. In my psychology class we call that the *confirmation bias*, and you do it all the time. You should be more open-minded, fair, and even-handed, like I am," decreed Lana. What makes both you and Burt think that Lana is incorrect in her assessment?

  a. Most people have a "bias blind spot"; they think other people are biased, but they themselves are not.

  b. People rarely fall prey to the confirmation bias; Lana has used an obscure example to make her case.

  c. Lana has proposed an unfalsifiable argument; Burt can't provide evidence for his biases one way or another.

  d. Lana isn't wrong in her assessment; there are some people who never resort to biased thinking, and Lana is likely to be one of them.

Measuring Intelligence: The Psychometric Approach

Intelligent people disagree on just what *intelligence* is. Some equate it with the ability to reason abstractly, others with the ability to learn and profit from experience in daily life. Some emphasize the ability to think rationally, others the ability to act purposefully. Part of the disagreement lies in the fact that the topic under discussion can't be directly observed.

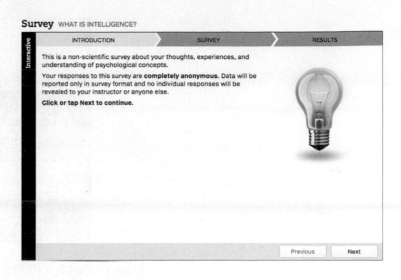

Measuring the Invisible

LO 9.3.A Outline the basic logic underlying factor analysis, and describe its use in measuring intelligence.

If a surgeon wanted to know how much a person's gall bladder weighed, the patient could be sliced open, the gall bladder removed and weighed, and the patient stitched back up again. If the surgeon wanted to know the weight of many people's gall bladders, that procedure could be repeated with as many patients as desired. Gall bladders are tangible parts of the human body, able to be observed and measured directly. **Intelligence**, on the other hand, has an invisible quality to it; no matter how much a surgeon prods, pokes, or hunts, intelligence can't be held in one's hands or weighed on a bathroom scale. Rather, we infer a certain degree of intelligence in a person based on characteristics we *can* see and measure directly, such as the outcomes of rational decisions, answers to standardized tests, or the purposefulness of behavior. These qualities are all part of what most people mean by intelligence, but theorists weigh them differently.

The traditional approach to intelligence, the **psychometric approach**, focuses on how well people perform on standardized aptitude tests, which are designed to measure the ability to acquire skills and knowledge. A typical intelligence test asks you to do several things: Provide a specific bit of information, notice similarities between objects, solve arithmetic problems, define words, fill in the missing parts of incomplete pictures, arrange pictures in a logical order, arrange blocks to resemble a design, assemble puzzles, use a coding scheme, or judge what behavior would be appropriate in a particular situation. A statistical method called **factor analysis** helps to identify which basic abilities underlie performance on the various items. This procedure identifies clusters of correlated items that seem to be measuring some common ability, or factor. For example, performance on vocabulary, spelling, and reading comprehension tests is typically correlated within an individual. The underlying intellectual factor that contributes to each of these specific skills might be identified as "verbal reasoning."

More than a century of research has convinced most psychometric psychologists that a general ability, or **g factor**, underlies the various abilities and talents measured by intelligence tests (Bouchard, 2014; Gottfredson, 2002; Jensen, 1998; Lubinski, 2004; Spearman, 1927; Wechsler, 1955). This general ability has two components. **Crystallized intelligence** refers to knowledge and skills, the kind that allow you to do arithmetic, define words, and make political decisions. **Fluid intelligence** refers to the capacity to reason and use information to solve new problems (Horn & Cattell, 1966). Crystallized *g* is heavily dependent on education and tends to remain stable or even increase over a lifetime, whereas fluid *g* is relatively independent of education and tends to decrease in old age. Tests of *g* do a good job of predicting academic achievement, occupational success, and eminence in many fields (Kuncel, Hezlett, & Ones, 2004; Schmidt & Hunter, 2004; Simonton & Song, 2009). But, as we will see, some scientists dispute the existence of a global quality called "intelligence," observing that a person can be smart in some areas and not in others (Gould, 1994; Guilford, 1988). For more perspectives on what intelligence is or how it should be defined, watch the video *What Is Intelligence?*

intelligence

An inferred characteristic of an individual, usually defined as the ability to profit from experience, acquire knowledge, think abstractly, act purposefully, or adapt to changes in the environment.

psychometrics

The measurement of mental abilities, traits, and processes.

factor analysis

A statistical method for analyzing the intercorrelations among various measures or test scores; clusters of measures or scores that are highly correlated are assumed to measure the same underlying trait, ability, or aptitude (factor).

***g* factor**

A general intellectual ability assumed by many theorists to underlie specific mental abilities and talents.

crystallized intelligence

Cognitive skills and specific knowledge acquired over a lifetime; it is heavily dependent on education and tends to remain stable over time.

fluid intelligence

The capacity to reason and use information to solve problems; it is relatively independent of education.

The Invention of IQ Tests

LO 9.3.B Summarize the original notion of IQ and some problems associated with it, and discuss how intelligence tests evolved during the early 1900s.

The first widely used intelligence test was devised in 1904, when the French Ministry of Education asked psychologist Alfred Binet (1857–1911) to find a way to identify children who were slow learners so they could be given remedial work. The ministry was reluctant to let teachers identify such children because the teachers might have prejudices about poor children, or might assume that shy or disruptive children were mentally impaired. The government wanted a more objective approach.

BINET'S BRAINSTORM   Wrestling with the problem, Binet had a great insight: In the classroom, the responses of "dull" children resembled those of ordinary children of younger ages. Bright children, in contrast, responded like children of older ages. The thing to measure, then, was a child's **mental age (MA)**, or level of intellectual development relative to that of other children. Then instruction could be tailored to the child's capabilities.

The test devised by Binet and his colleague, Théodore Simon, measured memory, vocabulary, and perceptual discrimination. Items ranged from those that most young children could do easily to those that only older children could handle, as determined by the testing of large numbers of children. A scoring system developed later by others used a formula in which a child's mental age was divided by the child's actual age to yield an **intelligence quotient (IQ)** (a quotient is the result of division). With this formula, all average children, regardless of their age, would have an IQ of 100 because their mental age and their actual age would be the same. But a child of 8 who performed like the average 10-year-old would have a mental age of 10 and an IQ of 125 (10 divided by 8, times 100). For a brief history of the development of intelligence testing, watch the video *Intelligence Testing, Then and Now 1*.

---

mental age (MA)

A measure of mental development expressed in terms of the average mental ability at a given age.

intelligence quotient (IQ)

A measure of intelligence originally computed by dividing a person's mental age by his or her chronological age and multiplying by 100; it is now derived from norms provided for standardized intelligence tests.

Unfortunately, this method of computing IQ had serious flaws. At one age, scores might cluster tightly around the average, whereas at another age they might be more dispersed. As a result, the score necessary to be in the top 10 or 20 or 30 percent of your age group varied, depending on your age. Also, the IQ formula did not make sense for adults; a 50-year-old who scores like a 30-year-old does not have low intelligence! Today, therefore, intelligence tests are scored differently. The mean (average) is usually set arbitrarily at 100; tests are constructed so that about two-thirds of all people score between 85 and 115; and individual scores are computed from tables based on established norms. These scores are still informally referred to as IQs, and they still reflect how a person compares with other people, either children of a particular age or adults in general. At all ages, the distribution of scores approximates a normal (bell-shaped) curve, with scores near the mean more common than high or low scores (see Figure 9.8).

THE IQ TEST COMES TO AMERICA In the United States, Stanford psychologist Lewis Terman revised Binet's test and established norms for American children. His version, the *Stanford–Binet Intelligence Scales*, was first published in 1916, and has been updated several times since. It can be given to children as young as age 2 or adults as old as age 85. The test asks a person to perform a variety of tasks—to fill in missing words in sentences, answer questions requiring general knowledge, predict how a folded paper will look when unfolded, measure a quantity of water using two containers of different sizes, and distinguish between concepts that are similar but not exactly the same (such as, say, *vigor* and *energy*). The older the test taker is, the more the test requires in the way of verbal comprehension and fluency, spatial ability, and reasoning.

Two decades later, David Wechsler designed another test expressly for adults, which became the *Wechsler Adult Intelligence Scale (WAIS)*; it was followed by the *Wechsler Intelligence Scale for Children (WISC)*. These tests, too, have been updated several times. They produce a general IQ score and also separate scores for verbal comprehension, perceptual reasoning, processing speed, and working memory (the ability to hold information in mind so that it can be used for a task). Items measure a range of abilities, including vocabulary, arithmetic abilities, the ability to recognize similarities (e.g., "How are books and movies alike?"), general knowledge and comprehension (e.g., "Who was Thomas Jefferson?" "Why do people who want a divorce have to go to court?"), and nonverbal skills, such as the ability to re-create a block design within a specified time limit or to identify a part missing from a picture. (See Figure 9.9 for some sample items.) More information on these types of tests is provided in the video *Intelligence Testing, Then and Now 2*.

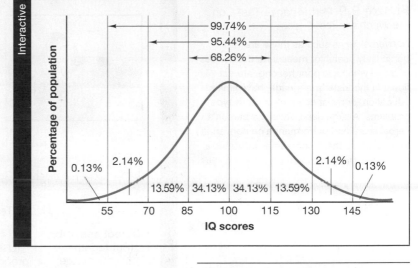

Figure 9.8 Expected Distribution of IQ Scores

In a large population, IQ scores tend to be distributed on a normal (bell-shaped) curve. On most tests, about 68 percent of all people will score between 85 and 115; about 95 percent will score between 70 and 130; and about 99.7 percent will score between 55 and 145. In any actual sample, however, the distribution will depart somewhat from the theoretical ideal.

Figure 9.9 Performance Tasks on the Wechsler Tests

Nonverbal items such as these are particularly useful for measuring the abilities of those who have poor hearing, are not fluent in the tester's language, have limited education, or resist doing classroom-type problems. A large gap between a person's verbal score and performance on nonverbal tasks such as these sometimes indicates a specific learning problem.

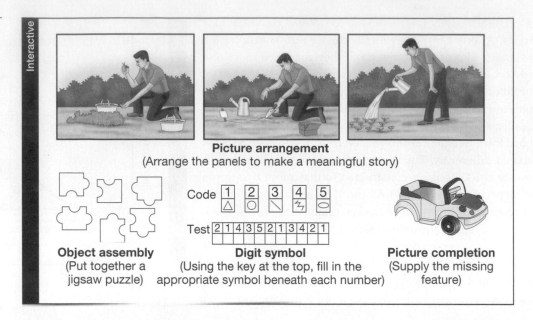

Picture arrangement
(Arrange the panels to make a meaningful story)

Object assembly
(Put together a jigsaw puzzle)

Digit symbol
(Using the key at the top, fill in the appropriate symbol beneath each number)

Picture completion
(Supply the missing feature)

stereotype threat

A burden of doubt a person feels about his or her performance, due to negative stereotypes about his or her group's abilities.

Binet had emphasized that his test merely *sampled* intelligence and did not measure everything covered by that term. A test score, he said, could be useful, along with other information, for predicting school performance, but it should not be confused with intelligence itself. The tests were designed to be given individually, so that the test giver could tell when a child was ill or nervous, had poor vision, or was unmotivated. The purpose was to identify children with learning problems, not to rank all children. But when intelligence testing was brought from France to the United States, its original purpose got lost at sea. IQ tests became widely used not to bring slow learners up to the average, but to categorize people in school and in the armed services according to their presumed "natural ability." The testers overlooked the fact that in America, with its many ethnic groups, people did not all share the same background and experience (Gould, 1996).

CULTURE and *Intelligence Testing*

Intelligence tests developed between World War I and the 1960s for use in schools favored urban children over rural ones, middle-class children over poor ones, and white children over nonwhite children. One item asked whether the Emperor Concerto was written by Beethoven, Mozart, Bach, Brahms, or Mahler. (The answer is Beethoven.) Critics complained that the tests did not measure the kinds of knowledge and skills that indicate intelligent behavior in a minority neighborhood or a remote rural community. They feared that because teachers thought IQ scores revealed the limits of a child's potential, low-scoring children would not get the educational attention or encouragement they needed. The video *Intelligence Tests and Stereotypes* explores these issues further.

Whether or not you feel "stereotype threat" depends on what category you are identifying with at the time. Asian women do worse on math tests when they see themselves as "women" (stereotype = poor at math) rather than as "Asians" (stereotype = good at math) (Shih, Pittinsky, & Ambady, 1999).

Test makers responded by trying to construct tests that were unaffected by culture or that incorporated knowledge and skills common to many different cultures. But these efforts were disappointing. One reason was that cultures differ in the problem-solving strategies they emphasize (Serpell & Haynes, 2004). In the West, white, middle-class children typically learn to classify things by category—to say that an apple and a peach are similar because they are both fruits, and that a saw and a rake are similar because they are both tools. But children who are not trained in middle-class ways of sorting things may classify objects according to their sensory qualities or functions; they may say that an apple and a peach are similar because they taste good. That may be a charming and innovative answer, but it is one that test givers have interpreted as less intelligent (Miller-Jones, 1989).

Testing experts also discovered that cultural values and experiences affect many things besides responses to specific test items. These include a person's general attitude toward exams, comfort in the settings required for testing, motivation, rapport with the test giver, competitiveness, comfort in solving problems independently rather than with others, and familiarity with the conventions for taking tests (Anastasi & Urbina, 1997; López, 1995; Sternberg, 2004).

Moreover, people's performance on IQ and other mental-ability tests depends in part on their own expectations about how they will do, and those expectations are affected by cultural stereotypes. Stereotypes that portray women or members of certain ethnic, age, or socioeconomic groups as unintelligent can actually depress the performance of people in those groups. You might think that a woman would say, "So, sexists think women are dumb at math? I'll show them!" or that an African American would say, "So racists believe that blacks aren't as smart as whites? Just give me that exam." But often that is not what happens.

On the contrary, such individuals commonly feel a burden of doubt about their abilities, creating an insecurity known as **stereotype threat** (Steele, 1992, 1997, 2010) (see Figure 9.10). The threat occurs when people believe that if they do not do well, they will confirm the stereotypes about their group. Negative thoughts intrude and disrupt their concentration ("I hate this test," "I'm no good at math") (Cadinu et al., 2005). The resulting anxiety may then worsen their performance or kill their motivation to even try to do well.

More than 300 studies have shown that stereotype threat can affect many African Americans, Latinos, low-income people, women, and older adults, all of whom perform better when they are not feeling self-conscious about themselves as members of negatively stereotyped groups (e.g., J. Aronson, 2010; Brown & Josephs, 1999; Inzlicht & Ben-Zeev, 2000; Lamont, Swift, & Abrams, electronic preview; Levy, 1996; Quinn & Spencer, 2001; Steele & Aronson, 1995; Thomas & Dubois, 2011). Anything that increases the salience of group stereotypes can increase stereotype threat and affect performance, including taking the test in a setting where you are the only member from your group, or being asked to state your race before taking the test. The media and even some scholars have sometimes misinterpreted these results to mean that stereotype threat is the *only* reason for group differences in test performance, which it is not (Sackett, Hardison, & Cullen, 2004). It is, however, an important contributing factor.

What can be done to reduce stereotype threat? One effective approach is to assure people that the test is fair; another is simply to tell people about the existence of stereotype threat (Good, Aronson, & Harder, 2008; Johns, Schmader, & Martens, 2005). But these solutions are unlikely to eliminate all group differences in test scores, and that fact points to a dilemma at the heart of intelligence and mental-ability testing. Intelligence and other mental-ability tests put some groups of people at a disadvantage, yet they also measure skills and knowledge useful in the classroom. How can psychologists and educators recognize and accept cultural differences and, at the same time, promote the mastery of the skills, knowledge, and attitudes that can help people succeed in school and in the larger society?

Figure 9.10 Stereotype Threat

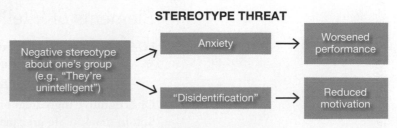

STEREOTYPE THREAT

Negative stereotype about one's group (e.g., "They're unintelligent") → Anxiety → Worsened performance

→ "Disidentification" → Reduced motivation

JOURNAL PROMPT 9.3

Critical Thinking—Consider Other Interpretations: When tests find IQ differences between groups of children from different cultures, many people assume that the children who score lower are inherently less intelligent. What other explanations are possible?

Quiz for Module 9.3

1. Lorsha takes a spelling test, grammar test, and vocabulary test as part of an overall intellectual assessment process. The examiner reports her individual scores on the tests but also derives a more general *verbal skills* score. What psychometric technique did the examiner use to produce this more general measurement?

   a. Path analysis

   b. The crystallization approach

   c. Fluid dynamics

   d. Factor analysis

2. The capacity to reason and use information to solve new problems is referred to as:

   a. Crystallized intelligence

   b. Fluid intelligence

   c. Adaptive insight

   d. Metacognition

3. The original calculation of an IQ score was produced by dividing a person's _____ by that same person's _____. This calculation often proved to be problematic.

   a. Verbal test score / performance test score

   b. Actual age / mental age

   c. Performance test score / verbal test score

   d. Mental age / actual age

4. The adult population of an entire city agrees to take the same standardized intelligence test. Even before the outcomes are known, what percentage of that population would you predict would have test scores above 130?

   a. About 2%

   b. About 16%

   c. About 50%

   d. About 68%

5. Which U.S. researcher modified Alfred Binet's original intelligence test and called it the Stanford–Binet test?

   a. Theodore Simon

   b. David Wechsler

   c. Lewis Terman

   d. Raymond Cattell

Dissecting Intelligence: The Cognitive Approach

Critics of standard intelligence tests point out that such tests tell us little about *how* a person goes about answering questions and solving problems. Nor do the tests explain why people with low scores often behave intelligently in real life, making smart consumer decisions, winning at the racetrack, and making wise choices in their relationships instead of repeating the same dumb patterns. Therefore, many scientists believe that the psychometric approach yields an incomplete picture of intelligence. Their aim is to identify the cognitive processes and strategies that people use when they are thinking and behaving intelligently.

Elements of Intelligence

LO 9.4.A **Describe how metacognition, the triarchic theory of intelligence, the theory of multiple intelligences, and emotional intelligence shed light on the diversity of what "intelligence" means.**

One cognitive ingredient of intelligence is *working memory*, a complex capacity that enables you to manipulate information retrieved from long-term memory and interpret it appropriately for a given task. It permits you to juggle your attention while you are working on a problem, shifting your attention from one piece of information to another while ignoring distracting or irrelevant information. People who do well on tests of working memory tend to be good at many complex real-life tasks requiring the control of attention, including reading comprehension, writing, and reasoning (Engle, 2002). In contrast, people with less working-memory capacity often have trouble keeping their minds on the job at hand and do not get better on a task, even with practice (Kane et al., 2007). Instead of trying to help people do better on individual tasks, therefore, might it be possible to improve their working memories, and thereby improve a crucial component of intelligence? Some scientists have reported success with working-memory training programs (Klingberg, 2010). Unfortunately, more rigorous recent research suggests that although people do get better, with practice, at specific working-memory tests, those gains do not translate to better performance on other tests of working memory or intelligence (Redick et al., 2012).

Another cognitive ingredient of intelligence is **metacognition**, the knowledge or awareness of your own cognitive processes and the ability to monitor and control those processes. Students who are weak in metacognition fail to notice when a passage in a textbook is difficult, and they do not always realize that they haven't understood what they've been reading. As a result, they spend too little time on difficult material and too much time on material they already know. They are overconfident about their comprehension and memory, and are surprised when they do poorly on exams (Dunlosky & Lipko, 2007). In contrast, students who are strong in metacognition check their comprehension by restating what they have read, testing themselves, backtracking when necessary, and questioning what they are reading. When time is limited, they tackle fairly easy material (where the payoff will be great), and then move on to more difficult material; as a result, they learn better (Metcalfe, 2009).

It works in the other direction, too: The kind of intelligence that enhances academic performance can also help you develop metacognitive skills. Students with poor academic skills typically fail to realize how little they know; they think they're doing fine (Dunning, 2005; Schlösser, Dunning, Johnson, & Kruger, 2013). The very weaknesses that keep them from doing well on tests or in their courses also keep them from realizing their weaknesses. In one study, students in a psychology course estimated how well they had just done on an exam relative to other students. As you can see in Figure 9.11, those who had performed in the bottom quartile greatly overestimated their own performance (Dunning et al., 2003). In contrast, people with strong academic skills tend to be more realistic. Often, they even underestimate slightly how their performance compares with the performance of others.

THE TRIARCHIC THEORY Having a good working memory and strong metacognitive skills, however, does not explain why some smart people keep making the same dumb choices in their relationships, or why people who don't seem especially bright are wildly successful in their jobs. That is why some psychological scientists reject the idea of a *g* factor as an adequate description of intelligence, and prefer to speak of different kinds of intelligence. To learn more about these differing perspectives, watch the video *Theories of Intelligence 1*.

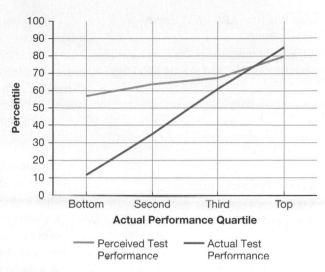

Figure 9.11 Ignorance Is Bliss

In school and in other settings, people who perform poorly often have poor metacognitive skills and therefore fail to recognize their own lack of competence. As you can see, the lower that students scored on an exam, the greater the gap between how they thought they had done and how they actually had done (Dunning et al., 2003).

metacognition

The knowledge or awareness of one's own cognitive processes, and the ability to monitor and control those processes.

triarchic [try-ARE-kick] theory of intelligence

A theory of intelligence that emphasizes analytic, creative, and practical abilities.

tacit knowledge

Strategies for success that are not explicitly taught but that instead must be inferred.

multiple intelligences theory

A theory of intelligence that emphasizes many different ways of processing information.

One is Robert Sternberg (1988, 2004, 2012), who has developed the **triarchic theory** of intelligence (*triarchic* means "three-part"). He generally defines intelligence as "the skills and knowledge needed for success in life, according to one's own definition of success, within one's sociocultural context." A guitar player, builder, scientist, and farmer can all be called successful if they make the most of their strengths, correct their weaknesses, and adapt to, select, and shape their environments to improve their lives. According to Sternberg, successfully intelligent people balance three kinds of intelligence: analytic, creative, and practical. If they are weak in one, they learn to work around that weakness:

1. **Componential or analytical intelligence** refers to the information-processing strategies you draw on when you are thinking intelligently about a problem: recognizing and defining the problem, comparing and contrasting, selecting a strategy for solving it, mastering and carrying out the strategy, and evaluating the result. Such abilities are required in every culture but are applied to different kinds of problems. One culture may emphasize the use of these components to solve abstract problems, whereas another may emphasize using the same components to maintain smooth relationships. In Western cultures, analytic intelligence is the kind that is most often measured on standardized tests and is associated with academic work.

2. **Experiential or creative intelligence** refers to your creativity in transferring skills to new situations. People with experiential intelligence cope well with novelty and learn quickly to make new tasks automatic. Those who are lacking in this area perform well only under a narrow set of circumstances. A student may do well in school, where assignments have specific due dates and feedback is immediate, but be less successful after graduation if her job requires her to set her own deadlines and her employer doesn't tell her how she is doing.

3. **Contextual or practical intelligence** refers to the practical application of intelligence, which requires you to take into account the different contexts in which you find yourself. If you are strong in contextual intelligence, you know when to adapt to the environment (you are in a dangerous neighborhood, so you become more vigilant). You know when to change environments (you had planned to be a teacher but discover that you dislike working with kids, so you switch to accounting). And you know when to fix the situation (your marriage is rocky, so you and your spouse go for counseling).

Contextual intelligence allows you to acquire **tacit knowledge**—practical, action-oriented strategies for achieving your goals that usually are not formally taught or even verbalized but must instead be inferred by observing others. College professors, business managers, and salespeople who have tacit knowledge and practical intelligence tend to be better than others at their jobs. Among college students, tacit knowledge about how to be a good student actually predicts academic success as well as entrance exams do (Sternberg et al., 2000).

MULTIPLE INTELLIGENCES   Howard Gardner has also argued for an expanded definition of intelligence. His **multiple intelligences theory** (Gardner, 1983, 2011) holds that an intelligence is best characterized as a capacity to process certain kinds of information. Just as bees,

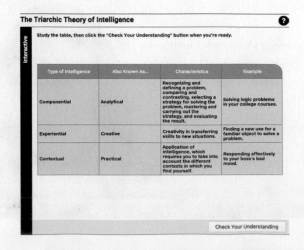

birds, and bears rely on the interplay of different biological and environmental mechanisms to navigate their cognitive worlds, so too do humans. Rather than spotlighting a single *g* factor, Gardner claims that the information-processing skills we possess can take many forms. A person with a great deal of *musical intelligence*, for example, might process information about pitch or rhythm more effectively than someone else, just as someone with a lot of *interpersonal intelligence* might be skilled at decoding the nonverbal behavior of others. This approach to defining intelligence is discussed in more detail in the video *Theories of Intelligence 2*.

EMOTIONAL INTELLIGENCE Other psychologists, too, are expanding the definition of intelligence. One of the most important kinds of nonintellectual "smarts" may be **emotional intelligence**, the ability to identify your own and other people's emotions accurately, express your emotions clearly, and manage emotions in yourself and others (Mayer & Salovey, 1997; Salovey & Grewal, 2005). People with high emotional intelligence, popularly known as "EQ," use their emotions to motivate themselves, to spur creative thinking, and to deal empathically with others. People who are lacking in emotional intelligence are often unable to identify their own emotions; they may insist that they are not depressed when a relationship ends, but meanwhile they start drinking too much, become extremely irritable, and stop going out with friends. They may express emotions inappropriately, perhaps by acting violently or impulsively when they are angry or worried. They often misread nonverbal signals from others; they will give a long-winded account of all their problems even when the listener is obviously bored.

Studies of adults with brain damage suggest a biological basis for emotional intelligence. Neuroscientist Antonio Damasio (2003) has studied patients with prefrontal-lobe damage that makes them incapable of experiencing strong feelings. Although they score in the normal range on conventional mental tests, these patients persistently make "dumb," irrational decisions because they cannot assign values to different options based on their own emotional reactions and cannot read emotional cues from others. Feeling and thinking are not always incompatible, as many people assume; in fact, one often requires the other.

Not everyone is enthusiastic about the proliferation of "intelligences" and their components. For example, some argue that emotional intelligence is not a special cognitive ability but a collection of ordinary personality traits, such as empathy and extroversion (Matthews, Zeidner, & Roberts, 2003, 2012). Nonetheless, broadening the notion of intelligence has been useful for several reasons. It has forced us to think more critically about what we mean by intelligence and to consider how different abilities help us function in our everyday lives. It has generated research on tests that provide ongoing feedback to the test taker so that the person can learn from the experience and improve his or her performance (Sternberg, 2004).

The cognitive approach has also led to a focus on teaching children strategies for improving their abilities in reading, writing, doing homework, and taking tests. Children have been taught to manage their time so they don't procrastinate and to study differently for multiple-choice exams than for essay exams (Sternberg et al., 1995). Most important, new approaches to intelligence encourage us to overcome the mental set of assuming that the only kind of abilities necessary for a successful life are the kind captured by IQ tests.

emotional intelligence
The ability to identify your own and other people's emotions accurately, express your emotions clearly, and regulate emotions in yourself and others.

Theorists who argue for an expanded definition of intelligence would say that Taylor Swift has musical intelligence, a surveyor has spatial intelligence, and a compassionate friend has emotional intelligence. Should the definition be broadened in this way? Or are these abilities better defined as talents?

Motivation, Hard Work, and Intellectual Success

LO 9.4.B Outline how longitudinal studies and cross-cultural studies shed light on the interplay of motivation, hard work, and intellectual achievement.

Even with a high IQ, emotional intelligence, and practical know-how, you still might get nowhere at all. Talent, unlike cream, does not inevitably rise to the top; success also depends on drive and determination.

Consider a finding from one of the longest-running psychological studies ever conducted. In 1921, Louis Terman and his associates began following more than 1,500 children with IQ scores in the top 1 percent of the distribution. These boys and girls, nicknamed Termites after Terman, started out bright, physically healthy, sociable, and well adjusted. As they entered adulthood, most became successful in the traditional ways of the times: Men went into careers and women became homemakers (Sears & Barbee, 1977; Terman & Oden, 1959). However, some gifted men failed to live up to their early promise, dropping out of school or drifting into low-level work. The 100 most successful men had been ambitious, were socially active, had many interests, and had been encouraged by their parents. The 100 least successful drifted casually through life. There was no average difference in IQ between the two groups.

After you are motivated to succeed intellectually, you need self-discipline to reach your goals. In a longitudinal study of ethnically diverse eighth graders attending a magnet school, students received a self-discipline score based on their self-reports, parents' reports, teachers' reports, and questionnaires (Duckworth & Seligman, 2005). Students were also scored on a behavioral measure of self-discipline—their ability to delay gratification. (The teens had to choose between keeping an envelope containing a dollar or returning it in exchange for getting two dollars a week later.) Self-discipline accounted for more than twice as much of the variance in the students' final grades and achievement-test scores as IQ did. As you can see in Figure 9.12, correlations between self-discipline and academic performance were much stronger than those between IQ and academic performance.

Self-discipline and motivation to work hard at intellectual tasks depend, in turn, on your attitudes about intelligence and achievement, which are strongly influenced by cultural values. For many years, Harold Stevenson and his colleagues studied attitudes toward achievement in Asia and the United States, comparing large samples of elementary school-age children, parents, and teachers in Minneapolis, Chicago, Sendai (Japan), Taipei (Taiwan), and Beijing (Stevenson, Chen, & Lee, 1993; Stevenson & Stigler, 1992). Their results have much to teach us about the cultivation of intellect.

In 1980, the Asian children far outperformed the American children on a broad battery of mathematical and reading tests. On computations and word problems, there was virtually no overlap between schools, with the lowest-scoring Beijing schools doing better than the highest-scoring Chicago schools. (A similar gap occurred in reading scores.) By 1990, the gulf between the Asian and American children had grown even greater. Only 4 percent of the Chinese children and 10 percent of the Japanese children had math scores as low as those

Figure 9.12 Grades, IQ, and Self-Discipline

Eighth-grade students were divided into five groups (quintiles) based on their IQ scores and then followed them for a year to test their academic achievement. Self-discipline was a stronger predictor of success than IQ was (Duckworth & Seligman, 2005).

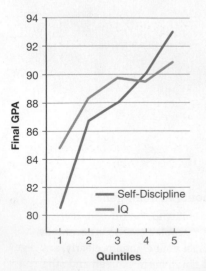

of the *average* American child. These differences could not be accounted for by educational resources: The Chinese had worse facilities and larger classes than the Americans, and on average, the Chinese parents were poorer and less educated than the American parents. Nor did it have anything to do with intellectual abilities in general; the American children were just as knowledgeable and capable as the Asian children on tests of general information.

But the Asians and Americans were worlds apart in several key ways:

- *Beliefs about intelligence.* American parents, teachers, and children were far more likely than Asians to believe that mathematical ability is innate (see Figure 9.13). They tended to think that if you have this ability, you don't have to work hard, and if you don't have it, there's no point in trying.

- *Standards.* American parents had far lower standards for their children's performance; they were satisfied with scores barely above average on a 100-point test. In contrast, Chinese and Japanese parents were happy only with very high scores.

- *Values.* American students did not value education as much as Asian students did, and they were more complacent about mediocre work. When asked what they would wish for if a wizard could give them anything they wanted, more than 60 percent of the Chinese fifth graders named something related to their education. Can you guess what the American children wanted? A majority said money or possessions.

When it comes to intellect, then, it's not just what you've got that counts, but what you do with it. Complacency, fatalism, low standards, and a desire for immediate gratification can prevent people from recognizing what they don't know and reduce their efforts to learn.

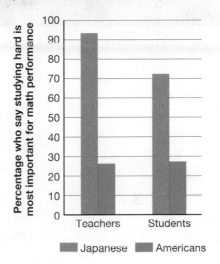

Figure 9.13 What's the Secret of Math Success?

Japanese schoolteachers and students are much more likely than their American counterparts to believe that the secret to doing well in math is working hard. Americans tend to think that you either have mathematical intelligence or you don't (Stevenson, Chen, & Lee, 1993).

JOURNAL PROMPT 9.4

Thinking Critically—Define Your Terms: Expanding the notion of intelligence to include different kinds of abilities allows us to recognize the strengths that people may have in nontraditional areas of thought and reasoning. However, there's a danger of taking that approach too far. Tying one's shoes very quickly does not necessarily represent being high in shoe-tying intelligence, for example. How would you strike a balance between recognizing a core set of intellectual capacities (as might be revealed through factor analysis) without creating an "intelligence" for every skill or ability?

Quiz for Module 9.4

1. Logan understands the material in his statistics class, but on tests he spends the entire period on the most difficult problems and never even gets to the problems he can solve easily. Which ingredient of intelligence does he need to improve?
   a. Triarchic skills
   b. Working memory
   c. Metacognition
   d. Creative intelligence

2. Which of the following is *not* an element of Sternberg's triarchic theory of intelligence?
   a. Contextual intelligence
   b. Componential intelligence
   c. Experiential intelligence
   d. Kinesthetic intelligence

3. Traci does not have an unusually high IQ, but at work she is quickly promoted because she knows how to set priorities, communicate with management, and make others

feel valued. Traci has _____ knowledge about how to succeed on the job.
   a. Tacit
   b. Componential
   c. Triarchic
   d. Analytical

4. How many varieties of intelligence did Howard Gardner propose in his *multiple intelligences* theory?
   a. 12
   b. 9
   c. 5
   d. 3

5. In a study of eighth graders, _____ was more strongly correlated with school performance than _____ was.
   a. Self-discipline / IQ
   b. IQ / self-discipline
   c. IQ / self-compassion
   d. Self-compassion / IQ

How smart is this otter?

Animal Minds

A green heron swipes some bread from a picnicker's table and scatters the crumbs on a nearby stream. When a minnow rises to the bait, the heron strikes, swallowing its prey before you can say "dinnertime." A sea otter, floating calmly on its back, bangs a mussel shell against a stone that is resting on its stomach. When the shell cracks apart, the otter devours the tasty morsel inside, tucks the stone under its flipper, and dives for another shell, which it will open in the same way. Incidents such as these and scores of others have convinced some biologists, psychologists, and ethologists that we are not the only animals with cognitive abilities—that "dumb beasts" are not so dumb after all. But how smart are they?

Animal Intelligence

LO 9.5.A Summarize the evidence both supporting and refuting the concept of animal intelligence.

In the 1920s, Wolfgang Köhler (1925) put chimpanzees in situations in which some tempting bananas were just out of reach and watched to see what the apes would do. Most did nothing, but a few turned out to be quite clever. If the bananas were outside the cage, the chimp might pull them in with a stick. If they were hanging overhead, and there were boxes in the cage, the chimp might pile up the boxes and climb on top of them to reach the fruit. Often the solution came after the chimp had been sitting quietly for a while. It appeared as though the animal had been thinking about the problem and was struck by a sudden insight.

Learning theorists felt that this seemingly impressive behavior could be accounted for perfectly well by the standard principles of operant learning, without resorting to mental explanations. Because of their influence, for years, any scientist who claimed that animals could think was likely to be ignored or laughed at. Today, however, the study of animal intelligence is booming, especially in the interdisciplinary field of **cognitive ethology**. (Ethology is the study of animal behavior, especially in natural environments.) Cognitive ethologists argue that some animals can anticipate future events, make plans, and coordinate their activities with those of their comrades (Griffin, 2001).

cognitive ethology

The study of cognitive processes in non-human animals.

In an early study of animal intelligence, Sultan, a talented chimpanzee studied by Wolfgang Köhler, was able to figure out how to reach a cluster of bananas by stacking some boxes and climbing on top of them.

When we think about animal intelligence, we must be careful because even complex behavior that appears to be purposeful might be genetically prewired and automatic, instead of requiring cognition (Wynne, 2004). The assassin bug of South America catches termites by gluing nest material on its back as camouflage, but it is hard to imagine how the bug's tiny dab of brain tissue could enable it to plan this strategy consciously. Yet explanations of animal behavior that leave out any sort of consciousness at all and that attribute animals' actions entirely to instinct do not seem to account for some of the amazing things that animals can do. Like the otter that uses a stone to crack mussel shells, many animals use objects in the natural environment as rudimentary tools, and in some nonhuman primates, the behavior is learned.

Thus, chimpanzee mothers occasionally show their young how to use stones to open hard nuts (Boesch, 1991). Orangutans in one particular Sumatran swamp have learned to use sticks as tools, held in their mouths, to pry insects from holes in tree trunks and to get seeds out of cracks in a bulblike fruit, whereas nearby groups of orangutans use only brute force to get to the delicacies (van Schaik, 2006). Even some nonprimates may have the capacity to learn to use tools, although the evidence remains controversial among ethologists. Female bottlenose dolphins off the coast of Australia attach sea sponges to their beaks while hunting for food, which protects them from sharp coral and stinging stonefish, and they seem to have acquired this unusual skill from their mothers (Krützen et al., 2005). Is this yet another case of mothers telling their daughters what to wear?

In the laboratory, nonhuman primates have accomplished even more surprising things; for example, chimpanzees have demonstrated that they have a rudimentary sense of number. In one study, chimps compared two pairs of food wells containing chocolate chips. One pair might contain, say, five chips and three chips, the other four chips and three chips. Allowed to choose which pair they wanted, the chimps almost always chose the one with the higher combined total, showing some sort of summing ability (Rumbaugh, Savage-Rumbaugh, & Pate, 1988). Chimpanzees can even remember over a period of 20 minutes which of two containers holds more bananas (e.g., five versus eight, or six versus 10), after watching the bananas being placed one at a time into the containers. In fact, they do as well as young children on this task (Beran & Beran, 2004; Parrish, Evans, & Beran, 2011).

One of the most controversial questions about animal cognition is whether any animals besides human beings have a **theory of mind**, a system of beliefs about the way one's own mind and the minds of others work, and an understanding of how thoughts and feelings affect behavior. A theory of mind enables you to draw conclusions about the intentions, feelings, and beliefs of others; empathize with others ("What would I experience if I were in the other person's position?"); deceive others; recognize when someone else is lying; recognize yourself in a mirror; and know when others can or cannot see you. In human beings, a theory of mind starts to develop in the second year and is clearly present by about age 3 or 4.

Some researchers believe that the great apes (chimpanzees, gorillas, and orangutans), dolphins, and elephants have certain abilities that reflect a theory of mind (de Waal, 2001; Plotnik, de Waal, & Reiss, 2006; Suddendorf & Whiten, 2001). When looking in a mirror, these animals may try to find marks on their bodies that are not directly visible, suggesting self-recognition, or at least bodily awareness. In addition, chimpanzees console other chimps who are in distress, use deceptive tactics when competing for food, and point to draw attention to objects, suggesting that they are able to grasp what is going on in another chimp's mind. In the wild, when one male African chimp makes an exaggerated scratching movement on part of its body during social grooming—say, on the forehead—a comrade will then groom the indicated spot, even if he was already grooming some other spot (Pika & Mitani, 2006). Chimps and even monkeys may also be capable of some metacognition, the ability to understand and monitor their own cognitive processes. When they are tested on a new task, they will sometimes avoid difficult trials in which they are likely to be wrong. And they will press an icon on a touch screen to request "hints" provided by their human observers when they are unsure of the correct response, even when seeking a hint means getting a lesser reward for a correct answer (Kornell, 2009). These findings suggest that the animals know what they know and don't know.

theory of mind
A system of beliefs about the way one's own mind and the minds of others work, and of how individuals are affected by their beliefs and feelings.

Animals and Language

LO 9.5.B Summarize the evidence both supporting and refuting the concept of animal language use.

A primary ingredient of human cognition is *language*, the ability to combine elements that are themselves meaningless into an infinite number of utterances that convey meaning. Do animals have anything comparable? Many people have wished they could ask their pet what it's like to be a dog, or a cat, or a horse. If only animals could speak!

To qualify as a language, a communication system must use combinations of sounds, gestures, or symbols that are *meaningful*, not random. It must permit *displacement*, communication about objects and events that are not present here and now but rather are displaced in time or space. And it must have a grammar (syntax) that permits *productivity*, the ability to produce and comprehend an infinite number of new utterances. By these criteria, no nonhuman species has its own language. Animals do communicate, of course, using gestures, body postures, facial expressions, vocalizations, and odors. Some of these signals have highly specific meanings: Vervet monkeys seem to have separate calls to warn about leopards versus eagles versus snakes (Cheney & Seyfarth, 1985). But vervets cannot combine these sounds to produce entirely novel utterances, as in "Look out, Harry, that eagle-eyed leopard is a real snake-in-the-grass."

Perhaps, however, some animals could acquire language if they got a little help from their human friends. Because the vocal tract of an ape does not permit speech, most investigators have used innovative approaches that rely on gestures or visual symbols. In one project, chimpanzees learned to use as words geometric plastic shapes arranged on a magnetic board (Premack & Premack, 1983). In another, they learned to punch symbols on a keyboard monitored by a computer (Rumbaugh, 1977). In yet another, they learned hundreds of signs in American Sign Language (Fouts & Rigby, 1977; Gardner & Gardner, 1969).

Animals in these studies learned to follow instructions, answer questions, and make requests. They even seemed to use their newfound skills to apologize for being disobedient, scold their trainers, and talk to themselves. Koko, a lowland gorilla, reportedly used signs to say that she felt happy or sad, to refer to past and future events, to mourn for her dead pet kitten, and to lie when she did something naughty (Patterson & Linden, 1981). Most important, the animals combined individual signs or symbols into longer utterances that they had never seen before.

Unfortunately, in their desire to talk to the animals and their affection for their primate friends, some early researchers overinterpreted the animals' utterances, reading all sorts of meanings and intentions into a single sign or symbol, ignoring scrambled word order ("banana eat me") and unwittingly giving nonverbal cues that might enable the apes to respond correctly. But over the past few decades, as researchers have improved their techniques, they have discovered that with careful training, chimps can indeed acquire some aspects of language, including the ability to use symbols to refer to objects. Some animals have also used signs spontaneously to converse with each other, suggesting that they are not merely imitating or trying to get a reward (Van Cantfort & Rimpau, 1982). Bonobos (a type of ape) are especially adept at language. One bonobo named Kanzi has learned to understand English words, short sentences, and keyboard symbols without formal training (Savage-Rumbaugh & Lewin, 1994; Savage-Rumbaugh, Shanker, & Taylor, 1998). Kanzi responds correctly to commands such as "Put the key in the refrigerator" and "Go get the ball that is outdoors," even when he has never heard the words combined in that particular way before. He picked up language as children do—by observing others using it and through normal social interaction. He has also learned, with training, to manipulate keyboard symbols to request favorite foods or activities (games, TV, visits to friends) and to announce his intentions.

Research on animal language and comprehension of symbols is altering our understanding of animal cognition, and not only of primates. Dolphins have learned to respond correctly to requests made in an artificial language consisting of either computer-generated whistles or hand and arm gestures (Herman, Kuczaj, & Holder, 1993; Herman & Morrel-Samuels, 1996). Taking the meaning of symbols and their order (syntax) into account, they were able to understand the difference between "To left Frisbee, right surfboard take" and "To right surfboard, left Frisbee take."

Kanzi, a bonobo who answers questions and makes requests by punching symbols on a specially designed computer keyboard, also understands short English sentences.

Some psychologists are calling border collies "the new chimps," ever since a border collie named Rico and another named Betsy acquired vocabularies of more than 200 words (Kaminski, Call, & Fisher, 2004; Morell, 2008). Since then, another border collie, Chaser, has stunned the public and psychologists alike by showing that she knows more than 1,100 words! (Pilley, 2013). When Chaser is asked to retrieve an object from another room, she can do it with astonishing accuracy. Even more impressive, when a new toy she had never seen (a Darwin doll) was placed among a dozen of her familiar toys and she was asked to fetch it, she did. She paused and walked among the toys, seemingly making an inference: Because none of the familiar toys matched the request, the new Darwin toy must be the one that was wanted.

Most amazingly, we now know that birds are not as birdbrained as previously assumed. Irene Pepperberg (2000, 2002, 2008) has been working since the late 1970s with African gray parrots. Her favorite, named Alex, could count, classify, and compare objects by vocalizing English words. When he was shown up to six items and was asked how many there were, he responded with spoken (squawked?) English phrases, such as "two cork(s)" or "four key(s)." He even responded correctly to questions about items specified on two or three dimensions, as in "How many blue key(s)?" or "What matter [material] is orange and three-cornered?" Alex also made requests ("Want pasta") and answered simple questions about objects ("What color [is this]?" "Which is bigger?"). When presented with a blue cork and a blue key and asked "What's the same?" he would correctly respond "color." He actually scored slightly better with new objects than with familiar ones, suggesting that he was not merely "parroting" a set of stock phrases. He could sum two small sets of objects, such as nuts or jelly beans, for amounts up to six (Pepperberg, 2006).

Alex was also able to say remarkably appropriate things in informal interactions. He would tell Pepperberg, "I love you," "I'm sorry," and, when she was feeling stressed out, "Calm down." One day, Alex asked Pepperberg's accountant, "Wanna nut?" "No," said the accountant. "Want some water?" "No," she said. "A banana?" "No." After making several other suggestions, Alex finally said, "What *do* you want?" (quoted in Talbot, 2008). To the sorrow of thousands of his admirers all over the world, Alex died suddenly in 2007. Pepperberg is continuing her work with other African grays.

Thinking about the Thinking of Animals

LO 9.5.C **Explain why both anthropomorphism and anthropodenial are unwise approaches to understanding animal cognition.**

These results on animal language and cognition are impressive, but scientists are still divided over just what the animals in these studies are doing. Do they have true language? Are they thinking, in human terms? How intelligent are they? Are Kanzi, Chaser, and Alex unusual, or are they typical of their species? In their efforts to correct the centuries-old *under estimation* of animal cognition, are modern researchers now reading too much into their data and *over estimating* animals' abilities?

On one side are those who worry about *anthropomorphism*, the tendency to falsely attribute human qualities to nonhuman beings without considering simpler explanations for the animals' behavior (Balter, 2012; Epley, Schroeder, & Waytz, 2013; Wynne, 2004). They like to tell the story of Clever Hans, a "wonder horse" at the turn of the century who was said to possess mathematical and other abilities (Spitz, 1997). Clever Hans would answer math problems by stamping his hoof the appropriate number of times. But a little careful experimentation by psychologist Oskar Pfungst (1911/1965) revealed that when Clever Hans was prevented from seeing his questioners, his powers left him. It seems that questioners were staring at the horse's feet and leaning forward expectantly after stating the problem, then lifting their eyes and relaxing as soon as he completed the right number of taps. Clever Hans was indeed clever, but not at math or other human skills. He was merely responding to nonverbal signals that people were inadvertently providing. (Perhaps he had a high EQ.)

Alex was a remarkably clever bird. His abilities have raised intriguing questions about the intelligence of animals and their capacity for specific aspects of language.

This old photo shows Clever Hans in action. His story has taught scientists to beware of anthropomorphism when they interpret findings on animal cognition.

On the other side are those who warn against *anthropodenial*, the tendency to think, mistakenly, that human beings have nothing in common with other animals, who are, after all, our evolutionary cousins (de Waal, 2001; Fouts, 1997). The need to see our own species as unique, they say, may keep us from recognizing that other species, too, have cognitive abilities, even if not as sophisticated as our own. Those who take this position point out that most modern researchers have gone to great lengths to avoid the Clever Hans problem.

The outcome of this debate is bound to affect the way we view ourselves and our place among other species. Perhaps we can find a way to study and think about animal abilities and emotions without assuming sentimentally that they are just like our own. There is no disputing, however, that scientific discoveries about the cognitive abilities of our animal relatives are teaching us to have greater respect for animal minds.

We human beings are used to thinking of ourselves as the smartest species around because of our astounding ability to adapt to change, find novel solutions to problems, invent endless new gizmos, and use language to create everything from puns to poetry. Yet, as this chapter has shown, we are not always as wise in our thinking as we might think. We can, however, boast of one crowning accomplishment: We are the only species that tries to understand its own misunderstandings and improve itself (Gazzaniga, 2008). We want to know what we don't know; we are motivated to overcome our mental shortcomings. This uniquely human capacity for self-examination is probably the best reason to remain optimistic about our cognitive abilities.

JOURNAL PROMPT 9.5

Thinking Critically—Analyze Assumptions: Elsewhere in this chapter you read about approaches that expand the definition of what it means to be "intelligent." Concepts such as emotional intelligence or the triarchic theory suggest that there are many ways of defining intelligent behavior. How would you apply that approach to the topic of animal cognition? Assuming a dolphin isn't going to compose an operetta anytime soon, what *would* qualify as intelligent animal behavior, how could you recognize it, and how would you measure it?

Quiz for Module 9.5

1. The study of cognitive processes in nonhuman animals is called:

   a. Cognitive ethology

   b. Tacit anthropomorphism

   c. Metacognition

   d. Preternaturalism

2. Which of the following animals has *not* been shown (so far) to have the ability to acquire language skills?

   a. Border collies

   b. Bonobos

   c. Mice

   d. African gray parrots

3. A honeybee performs a little dance that communicates to other bees the direction and distance of food. Because the bee can "talk" about something that is located elsewhere, its communication system shows _____. But because the bee can create only utterances that are genetically wired into its repertoire, its communication system lacks _____.

   a. Displacement / meaning

   b. Productivity / displacement

   c. Meaning / displacement

   d. Displacement / productivity

4. Barnaby thinks his pet snake Curly is harboring angry thoughts about him because Curly has been standoffish and won't curl around his neck anymore. What error is Barnaby making?

   a. Anthropodenial

   b. Anthropomorphism

   c. Anthropodiatry

   d. Anthropomordism

5. Humans share an evolutionary past with other animals; as such, it is unwise to assume that other animals possess no cognitive skills, and that humans are the only ones with such abilities. This position cautions against the notion of:

   a. Anthropodiatry

   b. Anthropomordism

   c. Anthropodenial

   d. Anthropomorphism

Taking Psychology with You

Becoming More Creative

Throughout this book, we emphasize the importance of asking questions, thinking of nonobvious explanations, and examining assumptions and biases. These critical-thinking guidelines involve creativity as much as they do reasoning.

Take a few moments to test your own creativity by answering these items based on the Remote Associates Test, a test of mental flexibility. Your task is to come up with a fourth word that is associated with each item in a set of three words (Mednick, 1962). For example, an appropriate answer for the set *news–clip–wall* is *paper*. Got the idea? Now try these (the answers are given at the end of this chapter):

1. piggy—green—lash
2. surprise—political—favor
3. mark—shelf—telephone
4. stick—maker—tennis
5. cream—cottage—cloth

Creative thinking requires you to associate elements of a problem in new ways by finding unexpected connections among them, as on the Remote Associates Test. People who are uncreative rely on *convergent thinking*, following a particular set of steps that they think will converge on one correct solution. Then, after they have solved a problem, they tend to develop a mental set and approach future problems the same way. Creative people, in contrast, exercise *divergent thinking*; instead of stubbornly sticking to one tried-and-true path, they explore side alleys and generate several possible solutions. They come up with new hypotheses, imagine other interpretations, and look for connections that might otherwise be overlooked. For artists and novelists, of course, creativity is a job requirement, but it also takes creativity to invent a tool, put together a recipe from leftovers, find ways to distribute unsold food to the needy, or decorate your room. Creative people tend to have three characteristics (Helson, Roberts, & Agronick, 1995; McCrae, 1987; Schank, 1988):

- **Nonconformity**. Creative individuals are not overly concerned about what others think of them. They are willing to risk ridicule by proposing ideas that may initially appear foolish or off the mark. Geneticist Barbara McClintock's research on transposons (genes that are able to "jump" from one chromosomal location to another) was ignored or belittled by many for nearly 30 years. But she was sure she could show how genes move around and produce sudden changes in heredity. In 1983, when McClintock won the Nobel Prize, the judges called her work the second greatest genetic discovery of our time, after the discovery of the structure of DNA.

- **Curiosity**. Creative people are open to new experiences; they notice when reality contradicts expectations, and they are curious about the reason. Wilhelm Roentgen, a German physicist, was studying cathode rays when he noticed a strange glow on one of his screens. Other people had seen the glow, but they ignored it because it didn't jibe with their understanding of cathode rays. Roentgen studied the glow, found it to be a new kind of radiation, and thus discovered X-rays.

- **Persistence**. After that imaginary lightbulb goes on over your head, you still have to work hard to make the illumination last. Or, as Thomas Edison, who invented the real lightbulb, reportedly put it, "Genius is 1 percent inspiration and 99 percent perspiration." No invention or work of art springs forth full-blown from a person's head. False starts and painful revisions occur along the way.

If you are thinking critically (and creatively!), you may wonder whether these qualities are enough. Do you recall the "Termites" who were the most successful? They were smart, but they also got plenty of encouragement for their efforts. Likewise, some individuals may be more creative than others, but *circumstances* can foster or inhibit creative accomplishment. Creativity is not just "in you"; it can be stimulated or suppressed by the situations in which you live and work. It flourishes when schools and employers encourage intrinsic motivation (a sense of accomplishment, intellectual curiosity, the sheer love of an activity) and not just extrinsic rewards such as gold stars and money. It thrives when you work with others who have different ideas, perspectives, and occupational training because they tend to jolt you out of your familiar way of seeing problems. But individual creativity often requires solitude—having "lazy" time to daydream productively—and the freedom to perform a task or solve a problem independently. "Brainstorming" sessions tend to produce more storm than brain (Amabile, 1983; Amabile & Khaire, 2008). Finally, organizations encourage creativity when they let people take risks, give them plenty of time to think about problems, and welcome innovation.

In sum, if you hope to become more creative, you can do two things. One is to cultivate your own talents and qualities of curiosity, intrinsic motivation, and self-discipline. The other is to seek out the kinds of situations that will permit you to express your abilities and experiment with new ideas.

Shared Writing Prompt

Think of the most creative person you know (it might even be yourself!), and describe where that person would fall on each of the dimensions of (1) nonconformity, (2) curiosity, and (3) persistence. Is your creative person high on all three dimensions? Provide an example to support your conclusions.

Summary

Thought: Using What We Know

LO 9.1.A Distinguish between the various elements of cognition, such as concepts, prototypes, propositions, schemas, and mental images.

A *concept* is a mental category that groups objects, relations, activities, abstractions, or qualities that share certain properties. *Basic concepts* have a moderate number of instances and are easier to acquire than concepts with few or many instances. *Prototypical* instances of a concept are more representative than others. *Propositions* are made up of concepts and express a unitary idea. They may be linked together to form *cognitive schemas*, which serve as mental frameworks for thinking about aspects of the world. *Mental images* also play a role in thinking.

LO 9.1.B Distinguish between the varieties of conscious thought, such as subconscious thinking, nonconscious thinking, and implicit learning.

Not all mental processing is conscious. *Subconscious processes* lie outside of awareness but can be brought into consciousness when necessary. They allow us to perform two or more actions at once when one action is highly automatic. But *multitasking*—toggling between tasks that are not automatic—is usually inefficient, introduces errors, and can even be dangerous. *Nonconscious processes* remain outside of awareness but nonetheless affect behavior; they are involved in *implicit learning*, when we learn something but don't know how we learned it and aren't able to state exactly what we've learned. Even conscious processing may be carried out in a *mindless* fashion if we overlook changes in context that call for a change in behavior.

LO 9.1.C Contrast algorithms and heuristics as problem-solving strategies, and give an example of each.

When problems are well defined, they can often be solved by applying an *algorithm*; when problems are fuzzier, however, people often must apply rules of thumb called *heuristics*. Some problems lend themselves to nonconscious processes such as *intuition* and *insight*. "Fast" thinking applies to rapid, intuitive, emotional, almost automatic decisions; "slow" thinking requires intellectual effort, which is why most people rely on the former—and make mistakes.

LO 9.1.D Discuss the various types of reasoning, such as formal reasoning, informal reasoning, dialectical reasoning, and stages of reflective judgment, and note the defining characteristics of each.

Reasoning is purposeful mental activity that involves drawing inferences and conclusions from observations, facts, or assumptions. *Formal reasoning problems* provide the information necessary to reach a conclusion or solution and permit a single correct or best answer; *informal reasoning problems* often have no clearly correct solution and thus require *dialectical thinking* about opposing points of view.

Studies of *reflective judgment* show that many people have trouble thinking dialectically. *Prereflective* thinkers do not distinguish between knowledge and belief or between belief and evidence. *Quasi-reflective* thinkers believe that because knowledge is sometimes uncertain, any judgment about the evidence is purely subjective. Those who think *reflectively* understand that although some things cannot be known with certainty, some judgments are more valid than others, depending on their coherence, fit with the evidence, and so on.

Barriers to Reasoning Rationally

LO 9.2.A Describe how the affect heuristic and the availability heuristic both illustrate the tendency to exaggerate the improbable.

People tend to exaggerate the likelihood of improbable events in part because of the *affect and availability heuristics*. Being able to easily think of instances of an event, especially one with a strong emotional component, sways us to believe the event is particularly likely to happen.

LO 9.2.B Explain how the framing effect leads people to avoid loss in probabilistic judgments.

We are swayed in our choices by the desire to *avoid loss* and by the *framing effect*—how the choice is presented. The same information can be evaluated quite differently if it is presented in either a positive or negative light.

LO 9.2.C **Summarize the mechanisms driving the fairness bias, hindsight bias, confirmation bias, and mental sets, and give an example of each.**

People often forgo economic gain because of a *fairness bias*, which appears to have evolutionary roots and is being studied in primates and human toddlers, and by using brain scans. People also often overestimate their ability to have made accurate predictions (the *hindsight bias*) and attend mostly to evidence that confirms what they want to believe (the *confirmation bias*). Another barrier to reasoning is that people tend to form *mental sets*, seeing patterns where none exist.

LO 9.2.D **Explain the process of cognitive dissonance, and describe three conditions under which feelings of cognitive dissonance are likely to occur.**

The theory of *cognitive dissonance* holds that people are motivated to reduce the tension that exists when two cognitions, or a cognition and a behavior, conflict. They can reduce dissonance by rejecting or changing a belief, changing their behavior, or rationalizing. Dissonance is most uncomfortable, thereby motivating efforts to reduce it, under three conditions: after a decision has been made (*postdecision dissonance*); when people's actions violate their concept of themselves as honest and kind; and when they have put hard work into an activity (the *justification of effort*).

LO 9.2.E **Discuss the conditions under which cognitive biases can be detrimental to reasoning, and when they might be beneficial.**

"Biases" sound like bad things, but they can sometimes be beneficial by speeding our mental processing of a complex world or smoothing our social interactions. Although we'd like to believe that other people are biased (but not ourselves), in fact most people can reduce their irrationality in many situations, such as when a decision is particularly important or personally meaningful.

Measuring Intelligence: The Psychometric Approach

LO 9.3.A **Outline the basic logic underlying factor analysis, and describe its use in measuring intelligence.**

Intelligence is difficult to define. The *psychometric approach* focuses on how well people perform on standardized aptitude tests. Most psychometric psychologists believe that a general ability, a *g factor*, underlies this performance, and that this general ability can be further described as either *crystallized* (reflecting accumulated knowledge) or *fluid* (reflecting the ability to reason and to use information to solve new problems).

LO 9.3.B **Summarize the original notion of IQ and some problems associated with it, and discuss how intelligence tests evolved during the early 1900s.**

The *intelligence quotient*, or *IQ*, represents how well a person has done on an intelligence test compared to other people. Alfred Binet designed the first widely used intelligence test to identify children who could benefit from remedial work. But in the United States, people assumed that intelligence tests revealed natural ability and used the tests to categorize people.

IQ tests have been criticized for being biased in favor of white, middle-class people, but efforts to construct tests that are free of cultural influence have been disappointing. Culture affects nearly everything to do with taking a test, from attitudes to problem-solving strategies. Stereotypes about a person's ethnicity, gender, or age may cause the person to feel *stereotype threat*, which can lead to anxiety that interferes with test performance (in the case of negative stereotypes) or enhanced performance (in the case of positive stereotypes).

Dissecting Intelligence: The Cognitive Approach

LO 9.4.A **Describe how metacognition, the triarchic theory of intelligence, the theory of multiple intelligences, and emotional intelligence shed light on the diversity of what "intelligence" means.**

Cognitive approaches to intelligence emphasize several kinds of intelligence and the strategies people use to solve problems. An important cognitive ingredient of intelligence is *metacognition*, the understanding and monitoring of your own cognitive processes.

Robert Sternberg's *triarchic theory* proposes three aspects of intelligence: *componential/analytic*, *experiential/creative*, and *contextual/practical*.

Gardner's *multiple intelligences theory* holds that an intelligence is best characterized as a capacity to process certain kinds of information.

Emotional intelligence is also important; the ability to identify your own and other people's emotions accurately, express emotions clearly, and regulate emotions in yourself and others can facilitate social interactions.

LO 9.4.B **Outline how longitudinal studies and cross-cultural studies shed light on the interplay of motivation, hard work, and intellectual achievement.**

Intellectual achievement also depends on motivation, hard work, and self-discipline. Cross-cultural work shows that beliefs about the origins of mental abilities, parental standards, and attitudes toward education play a big role in creating differences in academic performance.

Animal Minds

LO 9.5.A **Summarize the evidence both supporting and refuting the concept of animal intelligence.**

Some researchers, especially those in *cognitive ethology*, argue that nonhuman animals have greater cognitive abilities than has previously been thought. Some animals can use objects as simple tools, and chimpanzees and birds have shown evidence of a simple understanding of numbers. Some researchers argue that the great apes, dolphins, and elephants have aspects of a *theory of mind*, an understanding of how their own minds and the minds of others work.

LO 9.5.B Summarize the evidence both supporting and refuting the concept of animal language use.

In projects using visual symbol systems or American Sign Language, primates have acquired linguistic skills. Some animals (even nonprimates such as dolphins and African gray parrots) seem able to use simple grammatical ordering rules to convey or comprehend meaning.

LO 9.5.C Explain why both anthropomorphism and anthropodenial are unwise approaches to understanding animal cognition.

Scientists are divided about how to interpret the findings on animal cognition, with some worrying about *anthropomorphism* (falsely attributing human qualities to nonhuman beings) and others about *anthropodenial* (believing that human beings have nothing in common with other animals).

Chapter 9 Quiz

1. A representative instance of a concept is called a:
   a. Heuristic
   b. Basic concept
   c. Schema
   d. Prototype

2. Mental processes that occur outside of conscious awareness (but are accessible to consciousness when necessary) are called _____, whereas mental processes that occur outside of conscious awareness (but are not available to conscious awareness) are called _____.
   a. Subconscious processes / nonconscious processes
   b. Nonconscious processes / preconscious processes
   c. Preconscious processes / subconscious processes
   d. Nonconscious processes / subconscious processes

3. Manoosh wants to make a lot of money after she graduates from college. When deciding which major to pursue, she narrows her choices to pre-med, business, pre-law, engineering, and computer science. Although she's not sure exactly what she wants to study, nor which type of work will make her happiest, she at least narrowed the field of options considerably in solving her problem. What type of decision-making strategy did Manoosh rely on?
   a. Algorithms
   b. Heuristics
   c. Mental images
   d. Prereflective thinking

4. Gerald thinks politicians have too much influence on people's daily lives, and Edgar thinks they have too little. "Well," says Gerald, "I suppose there are many ways to look at this issue. The important thing is that we're both thinking it through and offering cohesive arguments for our points of view." Which of King and Kitchener's types of thinking describes Gerald's statement?
   a. Formal reasoning
   b. Prereflective
   c. Quasi-reflective
   d. Reflective

5. Jimmy is asked whether English words that end in *-ing* are more common than words that have *n* as the second-to-last letter. He mentally generates a long list of *-ing* words (*running, jumping, reading, laughing*) but can only think of a few that have *n* as the second-to-last letter (*drink, second*). He therefore incorrectly concludes that *-ing* endings are more common. Which barrier to rational reasoning did Jimmy fall prey to?
   a. The affect heuristic
   b. The availability heuristic
   c. The framing effect
   d. The hindsight bias

6. Inga listens intently as her economics professor describes the 4 percent unemployment rate in her county. Troubled by this statistic, she later talks with her friend Marlo, who is enrolled in a different section of the same economics course. "Unemployment in our county is horrible!" laments Inga. "What do you mean?" replied Marlo. "The professor clearly told us that 96 percent of people in our county have a job, which sounds pretty good to me." Which barrier to reasoning rationally could be affecting Inga and Marlo's conclusions?
   a. The affect heuristic
   b. The availability heuristic
   c. The framing effect
   d. The hindsight bias

7. Franco and Carla are walking down the street when they spy a paper bag. Carla is the first to pick it up, and discovers 20 one-dollar bills inside. "This is great!" says Carla. "Here; you take $5 and I'll keep $15." Franco indignantly huffs, "You're nuts! Either give me half or put the bag back down. I'd rather have nothing than take your lousy offer!" Which barrier to rational reasoning is Franco illustrating?

a. The fairness bias

b. The affect heuristic

c. The confirmation bias

d. Cognitive dissonance

8. Mitch has wanted to join an exclusive country club for years. He moved to a nicer neighborhood to impress the admissions committee, paid exorbitant application fees, and sent birthday cards to each board member for three years. He finally was accepted, only to discover the people around him were obnoxious boors who had nothing in common with him. Predictably, Mitch loved being a country club member. Which principle of cognitive dissonance theory explains Mitch's newfound love of his circumstances?

a. Self-justification

b. Justification of effort

c. Predecision dissonance reduction

d. Dissonance adherence

9. When is people's reliance on cognitive biases likely to diminish?

a. When they are doing things in which they have some expertise, or when the decisions being made have serious personal consequences.

b. When they are judging the behavior of others, but not when they are judging their own behavior.

c. When they are judging their own reasons for making a decision, but not when they try to understand the decision making of others.

d. When they are faced with a quantitative decision, but not when they are faced with a qualitative judgment.

10. The cognitive skills and specific knowledge that a person acquires over a lifetime is called:

a. Psychometrics

b. Fluid intelligence

c. Crystallized intelligence

d. Mental age

11. Which of the following statements best captures the spirit of what intelligence tests measure and how intelligence tests should be used?

a. Intelligence tests measure innate ability; their accuracy in predicting basic levels of inherited intellectual skills has been well documented.

b. Intelligence tests sample intelligence, but do not measure everything associated with that concept; as such, they should be used in conjunction with other forms of evidence when evaluating an individual.

c. Intelligence tests should be used primarily to categorize people along a dimension of "smartness."

d. Intelligence tests have demonstrated their applicability to testing people from all over the world; the long history of intelligence testing has shown uniformity in the way the tests measure innate abilities.

12. According to the triarchic theory of intelligence, which component refers to utilizing information-processing skills such as recognizing and defining a problem, comparing and contrasting solutions, and evaluating the results of a problem-solving strategy?

a. Contextual intelligence

b. Experiential intelligence

c. Analytical intelligence

d. Practical intelligence

13. Sara has slightly-above-average intelligence, but she sets and attains daily study goals for herself, is willing to work late into the night, and maintains a positive attitude about her progress in school. Which of the following statements, supported by research findings, best summarizes Sara's situation?

a. IQ is a useful measure of intellectual success, but hard work, motivation, and self-discipline also predict achievement.

b. Without a solid core component of raw intelligence, Sara is unlikely to achieve much success later in life.

c. Hard work makes people feel a sense of accomplishment, but it only leads to success when coupled with high intellect.

d. Sara is demonstrating all the components of emotional intelligence; as such, she is likely to be "people smart" but not "book smart."

14. A system of beliefs about the way one's own mind and the minds of others work is called:

a. Anthropomorphism

b. Contextual intelligence

c. Meta-belief

d. Theory of mind

15. The ability to communicate about objects that are not currently physically present, but rather are elsewhere in either space or time, is called:

a. Meta-language

b. Symbolic interactionism

c. Perspective taking

d. Displacement

Some solutions to the nine-dot problem in Figure 9.5 (from Adams, 2001):

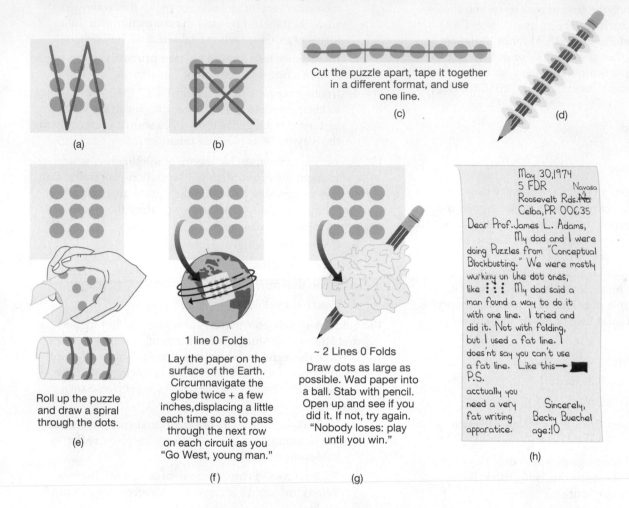

(a)

(b)

Cut the puzzle apart, tape it together in a different format, and use one line.

(c)

(d)

Roll up the puzzle and draw a spiral through the dots.

(e)

1 line 0 Folds

Lay the paper on the surface of the Earth. Circumnavigate the globe twice + a few inches, displacing a little each time so as to pass through the next row on each circuit as you "Go West, young man."

(f)

~ 2 Lines 0 Folds

Draw dots as large as possible. Wad paper into a ball. Stab with pencil. Open up and see if you did it. If not, try again. "Nobody loses: play until you win."

(g)

May 30, 1974
5 FDR   Navasa
Roosevelt Rds. Na
Celba, PR 00635
Dear Prof. James L. Adams,
    My dad and I were doing Puzzles from "Conceptual Blockbusting." We were mostly working on the dot ones, like ⋮⋮⋮ My dad said a man found a way to do it with one line. I tried and did it. Not with folding, but I used a fat line. I does'nt say you can't use a fat line. Like this→ ▬
P.S.
acctually you need a very fat writing apparatice.
                Sincerely,
                Becky Buechel
                age: 10

(h)

Answers to the creativity test in the Taking Psychology with You feature: back, party, book, match, cheese

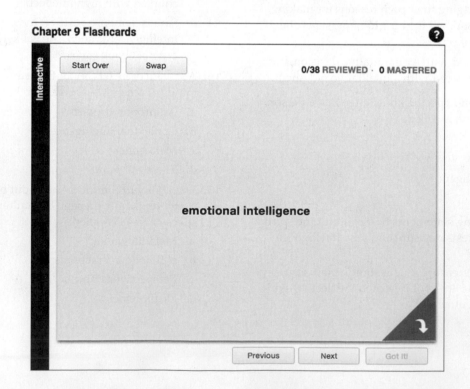

Chapter 10
Memory

◀ Listen to the Audio

Learning Objectives

LO 10.1.A Explain why the workings of memory are more reconstructive than people imagine them to be.

LO 10.1.B Describe three conditions under which confabulation is especially likely to occur.

LO 10.1.C Summarize the evidence indicating that eyewitness testimony can be susceptible to memory errors.

LO 10.1.D Explain the conditions under which children might provide reliable versus unreliable eyewitness testimony.

LO 10.2.A Distinguish between recall and recognition tasks in explicit memory, and distinguish between priming and relearning in implicit memory.

LO 10.2.B Describe the basic characteristics of three memory systems according to the information-processing model, and note the challenges to this view proposed by parallel distributed processing.

LO 10.3.A Explain the functions, duration, and location of the sensory registers in the three-box model of memory.

LO 10.3.B Explain the functions and duration of short-term memory, and contrast the *leaky bucket* and *working memory* approaches to understanding this "box" of memory.

LO 10.3.C Describe semantic categories and four forms of long-term memory, and explain how *primacy* and *recency* illustrate the serial-position effect in transferring information from short-term to long-term memory.

LO 10.4.A Outline the process of long-term potentiation in the formation of memories.

LO 10.4.B Evaluate the evidence that memories are not stored in any one "place" in the brain.

LO 10.4.C Summarize the evidence that memory can be influenced by emotion and hormonal levels.

LO 10.5.A Describe some major strategies that contribute to memory retention, and give an example of each.

LO 10.6.A Summarize the processes of decay, replacement, interference, and cue-dependent forgetting, and explain how each contributes to our understanding of forgetting.

LO 10.6.B Explain why claims of repressed memories should be greeted with a strong skeptical reaction.

LO 10.6.C Discuss three reasons why childhood amnesia is likely to take place.

Ask questions . . . be willing to wonder

Is everything that ever happened to us stored in the brain?

What strategies can help us remember better?

Why can't we remember events from our first two years of life?

Do people repress traumatic memories?

Have you ever, in the heat of some deliriously happy moment, said to yourself, "I'll never forget this, never, *never*, NEVER"? Do you find that you can more clearly remember saying those words than the deliriously happy moment itself? Is it any wonder that most of us have wished, at one time or another, for a perfect "photographic memory"?

Actually, having a perfect memory is not the blessing that you might suppose. Consider Brad Williams and Jill Price, who both have extraordinary memories and have offered scientists the opportunity to study their abilities. When given any date going back for decades, they are able to say instantly what they were doing, what day of the week it was, and whether anything of great importance happened on that date. Mention November 7, 1991, to Williams, and he says (correctly), "Let's see; that would be around when [basketball star] Magic Johnson announced he had HIV. Yes, a Thursday. There was a big snowstorm here the week before." Neither Williams nor Price can say where their accurate memories come from. Although Williams and his family regard his abilities as a source of amusement, Price describes her nonstop recollections as a mixed blessing (____ill, & McGaugh, 2006). The phenomenon of con____rollable recall, she wrote, is "totally exhausting.

Some have called it a gift, but I call it a burden. I run my entire life through my head every day and it drives me crazy!"

Memory refers to the capacity to retain and retrieve information, and also to the structures that account for this capacity. People like Brad Williams and Jill Price have extraordinary memory. Yet even average human beings are capable of astonishing feats of memory. Most of us can easily remember the tune of our national anthem, how to use an ATM, the most embarrassing experience we ever had, and hundreds of thousands of other bits of information. Memory confers competence; without it, we would be as helpless as newborns, unable to carry out even the most trivial of our daily tasks. Memory also gives us our sense of who we are, for if we are not the sum of our recollections, then who are we? Our very identity depends on our memories, which is why we feel so threatened when others challenge them. Individuals and cultures alike rely on a remembered history for a sense of coherence and meaning. Memory gives us our past and guides our future. In this chapter, we examine the many fascinating aspects of memory, as well as the importance of forgetting. But first, to learn more about Jill Price's extraordinary memory skills, watch the video *The Woman Who Cannot Forget*.

Reconstructing the Past

What would life be like if you could never form any new memories? That's what happens to older people who are suffering from dementia, and it also sometimes happens to younger people who have brain injuries or diseases. Henry Molaison's case is the most intensely studied in the annals of medicine (Corkin, 1984, 2013; Corkin et al., 1997; Hilts, 1995; Milner, 1970; Ogden & Corkin, 1991). In 1953, when Henry, known in the scientific literature as H. M., was 27 years old, surgeons made a last-ditch effort to cure his unrelenting, uncontrollable epileptic seizures by removing his hippocampus, most of his amygdala, and a portion of his temporal lobes. The operation did achieve its goal: Henry's seizures became milder and could be controlled by medication. But his memory had been affected profoundly: He could no longer remember new experiences for much longer than 15 minutes. Facts, songs, stories, and faces all vanished like water down a drain. He would read the same magazine over and over without realizing it; he could not recall the day of the week, the year, or even his most recent meal.

Henry still loved to do crossword puzzles and play bingo, skills he had learned long before the operation. And he remained cheerful, even though he knew he had memory problems. He would occasionally recall an unusually emotional event, such as the assassination of someone named Kennedy, and he sometimes remembered that both of his parents were dead. But according to Suzanne Corkin, who studied H. M. extensively, these "islands of remembering" were the exceptions in a vast sea of forgetfulness. This good-natured man felt sad that he could never make friends because he could never remember anyone, not even the scientists who studied him for decades. He always thought he was much younger than he really was, and he was unable to recognize a photograph of his own face; he was stuck in a time warp from the past.

After he died in 2008 at age 82, one neuroscientist said that H. M. gave science the ultimate gift: his memory (Ogden, 2012). He also taught neuroscientists a great deal about the biology of memory; before his surgery, scientists did not realize the important role played by the hippocampus. We will meet H. M. again at several points in this chapter, and you can learn more about his remarkable case in the video *When Memory Fails.* For now, let's consider the fragility of memory; how it's constructed, how it's susceptible to distortion, and how it might be manipulated.

The Manufacture of Memory

LO 10.1.A Explain why the workings of memory are more reconstructive than people imagine them to be.

People's descriptions of memory have always been influenced by the technology of their time. Ancient philosophers compared memory to a soft wax tablet that would preserve anything imprinted on it. Later, with the advent of the printing press, people began to describe memory as a gigantic library, storing specific events and facts for later retrieval. Today, many people compare memory to a digital recorder or video camera, automatically capturing every moment of their lives.

Popular and appealing though this belief about memory is, it is wrong. Unless you are someone like Brad Williams or Jill Price, who have extraordinary memory abilities, not everything that happens to you or impinges on your senses is tucked away for later use. Memory is selective. If it were not, our minds would be cluttered with mental junk: the temperature at noon on Thursday, the price of milk two years ago, a phone number needed only once. Moreover, remembering is not at all like replaying a recording of an event. It is more like watching a few unconnected clips and then figuring out what the rest of the recording must have been like.

One of the first scientists to make this point was British psychologist Sir Frederic Bartlett (1932). Bartlett asked people to read lengthy, unfamiliar stories from other cultures and then tell the stories back to him. As the volunteers tried to recall the stories, they made interesting errors: They often eliminated or changed details that did not make sense to them, and they added other details from their own culture—details that made the story more sensible to them. Memory, Bartlett concluded, must therefore be largely a *reconstructive* process. We may reproduce some kinds of simple information by rote, said Bartlett, but when we remember complex information, our memories are distorted by previous knowledge and beliefs. Since Bartlett's time, hundreds of studies have supported his original idea, showing that it applies to all sorts of memories.

In reconstructing their memories, people often draw on many sources. Suppose that someone asks you to describe one of your early birthday parties. You may have some direct memory of the event, but you may also incorporate information from family stories, photographs, or home videos, and even from accounts of other people's birthdays and reenactments of birthdays on television. You take all these bits and pieces and build one integrated account. Later, you may not be able to distinguish your actual memory from information you got elsewhere—a phenomenon known as **source misattribution**, or sometimes *source confusion* (Johnson, Hashtroudi, & Lindsay, 1993; Mitchell & Johnson, 2009).

A dramatic instance of reconstruction once occurred with H. M. (Ogden & Corkin, 1991). After eating a chocolate Valentine's Day heart, H. M. stuck the shiny red wrapping in his shirt pocket. Two hours later, while searching for his handkerchief, he pulled out the paper and looked at it in puzzlement. When a researcher asked why he had the paper in his pocket, he

source misattribution

The inability to distinguish an actual memory of an event from information you learned about the event elsewhere.

replied, "Well, it could have been wrapped around a big chocolate heart. It must be Valentine's Day!" But a short time later, when she asked him to take out the paper again and say why he had it in his pocket, he replied, "Well, it might have been wrapped around a big chocolate rabbit. It must be Easter!" Sadly, H. M. *had* to reconstruct the past; his damaged brain could not recall it in any other way. But those of us with normal memory abilities also reconstruct, far more often than we realize.

Of course, some shocking or tragic events—such as earthquakes, a mass killing, an assassination—do hold a special place in memory. So do some unusual, exhilaratingly happy events, such as learning that you just won a lottery. Years ago, these vivid recollections of emotional and important events were labeled *flashbulb memories*, to capture the surprise, illumination, and seemingly photographic detail that characterize them (Brown & Kulik, 1977). Some flashbulb memories can last for years. In a Danish study, older people who had lived through the Nazi occupation of their country in World War II retained accurate memories, for decades, of the day that the radio announced liberation (Berntsen & Thomsen, 2005). Sometimes, events that are unsurprising can also produce memories with the characteristics of flashbulbs—vivid, emotion-laden images—if they have significant personal or national consequences, such as a student's first day of college or an extraordinary national event (Talarico, 2009; Tinti et al., 2009).

Yet even flashbulb memories are not always complete or accurate. People typically remember the *gist* of a startling, emotional event they experienced or witnessed, but when researchers question them about their memories over time, errors creep into the details, and after a few years, some people even forget the gist (Neisser & Harsch, 1992; Talarico & Rubin, 2003). Just one day after the 2001 attacks on the World Trade Center and the Pentagon, researchers asked college students when they had first heard the news of the attacks, who had told them the news, and what they had been doing at the time. They also asked the students to report details about a mundane event from the days immediately before the attacks, to allow a comparison of ordinary memories with flashbulb ones. The students were retested at various intervals, up to eight months later. Over time, the vividness of the flashbulb memories and the students' confidence in these memories remained higher than for the everyday memories. Their confidence, however, was misplaced. The details the students reported became less and less consistent (and equally inconsistent) for *both* types of memories (Hirst et al., 2015; Talarico & Rubin, 2003).

If these happy children remember this birthday party later in life, their constructions may include information picked up from family photographs, videos, and stories. And they will probably be unable to distinguish their actual memories from information they got elsewhere.

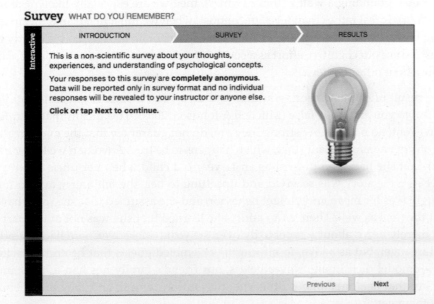

Survey WHAT DO YOU REMEMBER?

Interactive

| INTRODUCTION | SURVEY | RESULTS |

This is a non-scientific survey about your thoughts, experiences, and understanding of psychological concepts.

Your responses to this survey are **completely anonymous.** Data will be reported only in survey format and no individual responses will be revealed to your instructor or anyone else.

Click or tap Next to continue.

Previous   Next

confabulation

Confusion of an event that happened to someone else with one that happened to you, or a belief that you remember something when it never actually happened.

Even with flashbulb memories, then, facts tend to get mixed with fiction. Remembering is an active process, one that involves not only dredging up stored information but also putting two and two together to reconstruct the past. Sometimes, unfortunately, we put two and two together and get five.

The Conditions of Confabulation

LO 10.1.B Describe three conditions under which confabulation is especially likely to occur.

Because memory is reconstructive, it is subject to **confabulation**—confusing an event that happened to someone else with one that happened to you, or coming to believe that you remember something that never really happened. Such confabulations are especially likely under certain circumstances (Garry et al., 1996; Hyman & Pentland, 1996; Mitchell & Johnson, 2009):

1. **You have thought, heard, or told others about the imagined event many times.** Suppose that at family gatherings you keep hearing about the time that your uncle Sam got so angry at a party that he began pounding the wall with a hammer, with such force that the wall collapsed. The story is so colorful that you can practically see it unfold in your mind. The more you think about this event, the more likely you are to believe that you actually were there and that it happened as you "remember" it, even if you were sound asleep in another house. This process has been called *imagination inflation* because your own active imagination inflates your belief that the event really occurred as you assume it did (Garry & Polaschek, 2000). Even merely explaining how a hypothetical childhood experience *could* have happened inflates people's confidence that it really did. Explaining an event makes it seem more familiar and thus real (Sharman, Manning, & Garry, 2005).

2. **The image of the event contains lots of details that make it feel real.** Ordinarily, we can distinguish imagined events from real ones by the amount of detail we recall; memories of real events tend to contain more details. But the longer you think about an imagined event, the more likely you are to embroider those images with details—what your uncle was wearing, the crumbling plaster, the sound of the hammer—and these added details will persuade you that you really do remember the event and aren't just confusing other people's reports with your own experience (Johnson et al., 2011).

3. **The event is easy to imagine.** If imagining an event takes little effort (as does visualizing a man pounding a wall with a hammer), then we are especially likely to think that a memory is real rather than false. In contrast, when we must make an effort to form an image of an experience, a place we have never seen, or an activity that is utterly foreign to us, we use our cognitive effort as a cue that we are merely imagining the event or have heard about it from others.

As a result of confabulation, you may end up with a memory that feels emotionally, vividly real to you and yet is false (Mitchell & Johnson, 2009). This means that your feelings about an event, no matter how strong they are, do not guarantee that the event really took place. Consider again our Sam story, which happens to be true. A woman we know believed for years that she had been present as an 11-year-old child when her uncle destroyed the wall. Because the story was so vivid and upsetting to her, she felt angry at him for what she thought was his mean and violent behavior, and she assumed that she must have been angry at the time as well. Then, as an adult, she learned that she was not at the party at all but had merely heard about it repeatedly over the years. Moreover, Sam had not pounded the wall in anger, but as a joke, to inform the assembled guests that he and his wife were about to remodel their home. Nevertheless, our friend's family has had a hard time convincing her that her "memory" of this event is entirely wrong, and they are not sure she believes them yet.

Brian Williams is a familiar face to many U.S. television viewers. As the main news anchor at NBC since 2004, his nightly accounts of the day's events provided viewers with timely, reliable information. In 2015, however, he was suspended over an incident in which he misrepresented his involvement in a helicopter incident during the Iraq War in 2003. Was this a case of lying, embellishment, confabulation, or suggestion, or was it simply an example of faulty memory?

As the Sam story illustrates, and as laboratory research verifies, false memories can be as stable over time as true ones (Johnson, Mitchell, & Ankudowich, 2012). There's just no getting around it: Memory is reconstructive.

The Eyewitness on Trial

LO 10.1.C **Summarize the evidence indicating that eyewitness testimony can be susceptible to memory errors.**

As we've seen, the reconstructive nature of memory helps the mind work efficiently. Instead of cramming our brains with infinite details, we can store the essentials of an experience and then use our knowledge of the world to figure out the specifics when we need them. But precisely because memory is so often reconstructive, it is also vulnerable to suggestion—to ideas implanted in our minds after the event, which then become associated with it. This fact raises thorny problems in legal cases that involve eyewitness testimony or people's memories of what happened, when, and to whom.

Take, for example, the case of Jennifer Thompson and Ronald Cotton. After being raped, Thompson identified who she believed was her assailant from a book of mug shots, and later she identified the same man in a lineup. After a jury heard her eyewitness testimony, Cotton was convicted and sentenced to prison for two life terms. A few years later, evidence surfaced that the real rapist might have been another man, a convict named Bobby Poole. A judge ordered a new trial, where Jennifer Thompson looked at both men face to face and once again said that Ronald Cotton was the man who raped her. Cotton was sent back to prison. Eleven years later, DNA evidence completely exonerated Cotton and just as unequivocally implicated Poole, who confessed to the crime. As Thompson learned to her sorrow, eyewitness testimony is not always reliable. Lineups and photo arrays don't necessarily help because witnesses may simply identify the person who looks most like the perpetrator of the crime (Fitzgerald, Oriet, & Price, 2015; Wells & Olson, 2003). As a result, some convictions based on eyewitness testimony, like that of Ronald Cotton, turn out to be tragic mistakes.

Eyewitnesses are especially likely to make mistaken identifications when the suspect's ethnicity differs from their own. Because of unfamiliarity with other ethnic groups, the eyewitness may focus solely on the ethnicity of the person they see committing a crime ("He's black"; "She's white"; "He's an Arab") and ignore the distinctive features that would later make identification more accurate (Knuycky, Kleider, & Cavrak, 2014; Wilson, Hugenberg, & Bernstein, 2013).

In a program of research spanning more than four decades, Elizabeth Loftus and her colleagues have shown that memories are also influenced by the way in which questions are put to the eyewitness and by suggestive comments made during an interrogation or interview. In one classic study, the researchers showed how even subtle changes in the wording of questions can lead a witness to give different answers. Participants first watched short films depicting car collisions. Afterward, the researchers asked some of them, "About how fast were the cars going when they hit each other?" Other viewers were asked the same question, but with the verb changed to *smashed*, *collided*, *bumped*, or *contacted*. Estimates of how fast the cars were going varied, depending on which word was

Ronald Cotton (left) was convicted of rape solely on the basis of eyewitness testimony by Jennifer Thompson (right). He spent 11 years in prison until DNA evidence established that he could not have committed the crime and that the real rapist was another man. Cotton and Thompson became friends after his release. In thinking about cases in which an eyewitness provides the only evidence against a suspect, a critical thinker would ask: How accurate is eyewitness testimony, even when the witness is the victim? How trustworthy are our memories, even of traumatic events? Psychological scientists have learned some startling answers, as this chapter will show.

used. *Smashed* produced the highest average speed estimates (40.8 mph), followed by *collided* (39.3 mph), *bumped* (38.1 mph), *hit* (34.0 mph), and *contacted* (31.8 mph) (Loftus & Palmer, 1974).

Misleading information from other sources also can profoundly alter what witnesses report. Consider what happened when students were shown the face of a young man who had straight hair, then heard a description of the face supposedly written by another witness—a description that wrongly said the man had light, curly hair (see Figure 10.1). When the students reconstructed the face using a kit of facial features, a third of their reconstructions contained the misleading detail, whereas only 5 percent contained it when curly hair was not mentioned (Loftus & Greene, 1980). In real life, misleading information about a perpetrator's appearance can reduce an eyewitness's ability to identify the real perpetrator later in a lineup (Zajac & Henderson, 2009).

Does the number of eyewitnesses affect a person's susceptibility to misleading information? In a study of this question, people first watched a video of a simulated crime and later read three eyewitness reports about the crime, each report containing the same misleading claim—such as about the location of objects, the thief's actions, or the name on the side of the suspect van. One group was told that a single person wrote all three reports, whereas another group was told that each report was written by a different person. It made no difference; a single witness's report proved to be as influential as the reports of three different witnesses. Such is the power of a single witness's voice (Foster et al., 2012).

Leading questions, suggestive comments, and misleading information affect people's memories not only for events they have witnessed but also for their own experiences. Researchers have successfully used these techniques to induce people to believe they are recalling complicated events from early in life that never actually happened, such as getting lost in a shopping mall, being hospitalized for a high fever, being harassed by a bully, getting in trouble for playing a prank on a first-grade teacher, or spilling punch all over the mother of the bride at a wedding (Hyman & Pentland, 1996; Lindsay et al., 2004; Loftus & Pickrell, 1995; Mazzoni et al., 1999). When people were shown a phony Disneyland ad featuring Bugs Bunny, about 16 percent later recalled having met a Bugs character at Disneyland (Braun, Ellis, & Loftus, 2002). In later studies, the percentages were even higher. Some people even claimed to remember shaking hands with the character, hugging him, or seeing him in a parade. But these memories were impossible, because Bugs Bunny is a Warner Bros. creation and would definitely be *rabbit non grata* at Disneyland!

Figure 10.1 The Influence of Misleading Information

Students saw the face of a young man with straight hair and then had to reconstruct it from memory. On the left is one student's reconstruction in the absence of misleading information about the man's hair. On the right is another person's reconstruction of the same face after exposure to misleading information that mentioned curly hair (Loftus & Greene, 1980).

Children's Testimony

LO 10.1.D Explain the conditions under which children might provide reliable versus unreliable eyewitness testimony.

The power of suggestion can affect anyone, but its impact on children who are being questioned about possible sexual or physical abuse is especially worrisome. How can adults determine whether a young child has been sexually molested without influencing what the child says? The answer is crucial. Throughout the 1980s and 1990s, accusations of child abuse in daycare centers skyrocketed. After being interviewed by therapists and police investigators, children were claiming that their teachers had molested them in the most terrible ways: hanging them in trees, raping them, and even forcing them to eat feces. Although in no case had parents actually seen the daycare teachers treating the children badly, although none of the children had complained to their parents, and although none of the parents had noticed any symptoms or problems in their children, the accused teachers were often sentenced to many years in prison.

Thanks largely to research by psychological scientists, the hysteria eventually subsided and people were able to assess more clearly what had gone wrong in the way children had been interviewed in these cases. Today, we know that although children, like adults, can remember many things accurately, they can also be influenced by an interviewer's leading questions, suggestions, or pressure to report certain information (Ceci & Bruck, 1995). Moreover, in the courtroom, the style of questions put to children under cross-examination often leads them to be highly inaccurate (O'Neill & Zajac, 2012). The question to ask, therefore, is not "Can children's memories be trusted?" but "Under what conditions are children apt to be suggestible, and to report that something happened to them when in fact it did not?"

The answer, from many experimental studies, is that a child is more likely to give a false report when an interviewer strongly believes that the child has been molested and then uses suggestive techniques to get the child to reveal molestation (Bruck, 2003). Interviewers who are biased in this way seek only confirming evidence and ignore discrepant evidence and other explanations for a child's behavior. They reject a child's denial of having been molested and assume the child is "in denial." They use techniques that encourage imagination inflation ("Let's pretend it happened") and that blur reality and fantasy in the child's mind. They pressure or encourage the child to describe terrible events, badger the child with repeated questions, tell the child that "everyone else" said the events happened, or use bribes and threats (Poole & Lamb, 1998).

A team of researchers analyzed the actual transcripts of interrogations of children in the first highly publicized sexual abuse case in the United States, the McMartin preschool case (which ended in a hung jury). Then they applied the same suggestive techniques in an experiment with preschool children (Garven et al., 1998). A young man visited children at their preschool, read them a story, and handed out treats. The man did nothing aggressive, inappropriate, or surprising. A week later, an experimenter questioned the children individually about the man's visit. She asked children in one group leading questions ("Did he bump the teacher? Did he throw a crayon at a kid who was talking?" "Did he tell you a secret and tell you not to tell?"). She asked a second group the same questions but also applied influence techniques used by interrogators in the McMartin and other daycare cases: telling the children what "other kids" had supposedly said, expressing disappointment if answers were negative, and praising the children for making allegations.

In the first group, children said "Yes, it happened" to about 17 percent of the false allegations about the man's visit. And in the second group, they said "yes" to the false allegations suggested to them a whopping 58 percent of the time. As you can see in Figure 10.2, the 3-year-olds in this group, on average, said "yes" to over 80 percent of the false allegations,

Children's testimony is often crucial in child sexual abuse cases. Under what conditions do children make reliable or unreliable witnesses?

Figure 10.2 Social Pressure and Children's False Allegations

When researchers asked 3-year-olds leading questions about events that had not occurred—such as whether a previous visitor to their classroom had committed aggressive acts—nearly 30 percent said that yes, he had. This percentage declined among older children. But when the researchers used influence techniques taken from actual child-abuse investigations, most of the children agreed with the false allegation, regardless of their age (Garven et al., 1998).

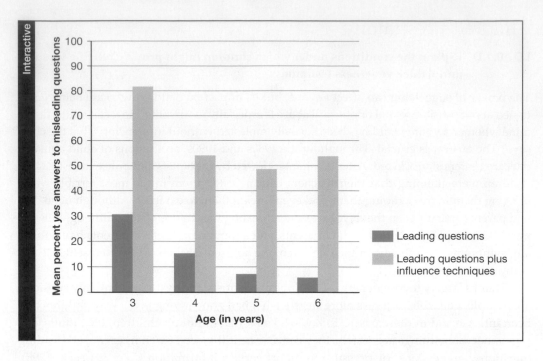

and the 4- to 6-year-olds said "yes" to over half of the allegations. Note that the interviews in this study lasted only 5 to 10 minutes, whereas in actual investigations, interviewers often question children repeatedly over many weeks or months.

Many people believe that children cannot be induced to make up experiences that are truly traumatic, but psychologists have shown that this assumption, too, is wrong. When schoolchildren were asked for their recollections of an actual sniper incident at their school, many of those who had been absent from school that day reported memories of hearing shots, seeing someone lying on the ground, and other details they could not possibly have experienced directly. Apparently, they had been influenced by the accounts of the children who had been there (Pynoos & Nader, 1989). Indeed, rumor and hearsay play a big role in promoting false beliefs and memories in children, just as they do in adults (Principe et al., 2006).

As a result of such findings, psychologists have been able to develop ways of interviewing children that reduce the chances of false reporting. If the interviewer says, "Tell me the reason you came to talk to me today," and nothing more, most actual victims will disclose what happened to them (Bruck, 2003). The interviewer must not assume that the child was molested, must avoid leading or suggestive questions, and must understand that children do not speak the way adults do. Young children often drift from topic to topic, and their words may not be the words adults would use (Poole & Lamb, 1998). One little girl being interviewed thought her "private parts" were her elbows!

In sum, children, like adults, can be accurate in what they report and, also like adults, they can distort, forget, fantasize, and be misled. As research shows, their memory processes are only human.

JOURNAL PROMPT 10.1

Thinking Critically—Ask Questions; Be Willing to Wonder: Have you ever played the "telephone game"? To refresh your memory, it's a game in which one person whispers a message directly into the ear of another person, who in turn whispers it to another person, and so on, and so on, until the last person announces the message to all assembled. By that point the message is usually far from what was originally whispered by the first person! Based on what you know about the reconstructive nature of memory, what can you suggest are some reasons why the message often changes so dramatically in this game?

Quiz for Module 10.1

1. What's the best way to think about memory?

   a. It's like a kaleidoscope, with an overall image assembled from bits and fragments of information.

   b. It's like a video camera, capturing information accurately until the video is deleted.

   c. It's like a strainer, where only the smallest pieces of information are retained.

   d. It like an engraved metal plate, where information is carved for posterity.

2. Becky fondly remembers seeing her favorite band in concert in the late 1990s. She was such a fan she collected newspaper clippings about the group, swapped stories with other fans about concerts they'd been to, and watched the band whenever it performed on television. As time passed it occurred to Becky that she had a hard time distinguishing her personal memories of a particular concert from other information she'd accumulated over the years. Becky is falling prey to

   a. Source misinference

   b. Source misattribution

   c. Source misidentity

   d. Conflagration

3. Marlo has heard many times about how, when she was 3 years old, she smashed both her hands into her chocolate birthday cake. It's a favorite family story, usually told whenever there's a gathering of relatives and especially at birthdays. One day Marlo is flipping through a scrapbook and finds photos of herself, clearly dated on her third birthday, with a pristine strawberry cake in front of her. Photo after photo shows the cake being sliced and distributed, with nary a smudge on her hands nor any chocolate in sight. Why did Marlo hold a false memory for so many years?

   a. Marlo enjoys being the center of attention, and the chocolate cake story makes that happen.

   b. Her parents created a second, undocumented birthday party that involved chocolate cake.

   c. False memories are especially likely to be created by loved ones and family members.

   d. Hearing a detailed story many times contributes to confabulation of memory.

4. Eyewitnesses are especially likely to make mistaken identifications when:

   a. The suspect's ethnicity is the same as their own.

   b. The suspect is the same sex as the witness.

   c. The suspect's ethnicity is different from their own.

   d. The suspect's age is at least 10 years older or younger than their own.

5. Which of the following statements would be the best one to ask when interviewing a child about an alleged victimization?

   a. "Tell me why you came to talk to me today."

   b. "Do you want to talk about the bad thing that happened at school?"

   c. "There must be something pretty serious going on, huh?"

   d. "You look like you're worried and nervous; why are you upset?"

In Pursuit of Memory

Now that we have seen how memory *doesn't* work—namely, like an infallible recording of everything that happens to you—we turn to studies of how it *does* work.

Measuring Memory

LO 10.2.A Distinguish between recall and recognition tasks in explicit memory, and distinguish between priming and relearning in implicit memory.

Conscious, intentional recollection of an event or an item of information is called **explicit memory**. It is usually measured using one of two methods. The first method tests for **recall**, the ability to retrieve and reproduce information encountered earlier. Essay and fill-in-the-blank exams require recall. The second method tests for **recognition**, the ability to identify information you have previously observed, read, or heard about. The information is given to you, and all you have to do is say whether it is old or new, or perhaps correct or incorrect, or pick it out of a set of alternatives. The task, in other words, is to compare the

Test Your Recall: You can try this test of recall if you are familiar with the poem that begins "'Twas the Night Before Christmas" or the song "Rudolph the Red-Nosed Reindeer." Rudolph had eight reindeer friends; name as many of them as you can. After you have done your best, turn to the next page for a recognition test on the same information.

explicit memory

Conscious, intentional recollection of an event or of an item of information.

recall

The ability to retrieve and reproduce from memory previously encountered material.

recognition

The ability to identify previously encountered material.

implicit memory

Unconscious retention in memory, as evidenced by the effect of a previous experience or previously encountered information on current thoughts or actions.

priming

A method for measuring implicit memory in which a person reads or listens to information and is later tested to see whether the information affects performance on another type of task.

Test Your Recognition: If you took the recall test on the previous page, now try a recognition test. From the following list, see whether you can identify the correct names of Rudolph the Red-Nosed Reindeer's eight reindeer friends. The answers are at the end of this chapter—but no fair peeking!

Blitzen	Dander	Dancer	Masher
Cupid	Dasher	Prancer	Comet
Kumquat	Donner	Flasher	Pixie
Bouncer	Blintzes	Trixie	Vixen

Which was easier, recall or recognition? Can you speculate on the reason?

information you are given with the information stored in your memory. True–false and multiple-choice tests call for recognition.

Recognition tests can be tricky, especially when false items closely resemble correct ones. Under most circumstances, however, recognition is easier than recall. Recognition for visual images is particularly impressive. If you show people 2,500 slides of faces and places, and later you ask them to identify which ones they saw out of a larger set, they will be able to identify more than 90 percent of the original slides accurately (Haber, 1970).

The superiority of recognition over recall was demonstrated in a study of people's memories of their high school classmates (Bahrick, Bahrick, & Wittlinger, 1975). The participants, ages 17 to 74, first wrote down the names of as many classmates as they could remember. Recall was poor; even when prompted with yearbook pictures, the youngest people failed to name almost a third of their classmates, and the oldest failed to name most of them. Recognition, however, was far better. When asked to look at a series of cards, each of which contained a set of five photographs, and to say which picture in each set showed a former classmate, recent graduates were right 90 percent of the time—and so were people who had graduated 35 years earlier. The ability to recognize names was nearly as impressive.

Sometimes, information encountered in the past affects our thoughts and actions even though we do not consciously or intentionally remember it, a phenomenon known as **implicit memory** (Schacter, Chiu, & Ochsner, 1993). To get at this subtle sort of memory, researchers must rely on indirect methods instead of the direct ones used to measure explicit memory. One common method, **priming**, asks you to read or listen to some information and then tests you later to see whether the information affects your performance on another type of task.

Suppose that you read a list of words, some of which began with the letters *def* (such as *define*, *defend*, or *deform*). Later, if you were asked to complete word fragments (such as *def-*) with the first word that came to mind, you would be more likely to complete the fragments so they turned into words from the list than if you had never seen the list—even if you could not remember the original words very well (Richardson-Klavehn & Bjork, 1988; Roediger, 1990). That is, the words on the list have "primed" (made more available) your responses on the word-completion task. Priming isn't limited to words; priming people with unusual sentence constructions causes them to adopt those constructions a week later (Kaschak et al., 2011). Fragments of pictures can also act as primes. In one study, people briefly saw fragments of drawings depicting objects and animals. Then, *17 years later,* they were mailed the same fragments and also fragments of new drawings, with a request to name what the fragments depicted. Even when people couldn't remember having been in the original experiment, they identified the primed objects much better than the new objects (Mitchell, 2006). These studies show that people know more than they think they know—and that they can know it for a very long time.

Another way to measure implicit memory, the **relearning method**, or *savings method,* was devised by Hermann Ebbinghaus (1885/1913) in the 19th century. The relearning method requires you to relearn information or a task that you learned earlier. If you master it more quickly the second time around, you must be remembering something from the first experience.

Models of Memory

LO 10.2.B Describe the basic characteristics of three memory systems according to the information-processing model, and note the challenges to this view proposed by parallel distributed processing.

Although people usually refer to memory as a single faculty, as in "I must be losing my memory" or "He has a memory like an elephant's," the term *memory* actually covers a complex collection of abilities and processes. If a video camera is not an accurate metaphor for capturing these diverse components of memory, what metaphor would be better?

Many cognitive psychologists liken the mind to an information processor, along the lines of a computer, though more complex. They have constructed *information-processing models* of cognitive processes, liberally borrowing computer-programming terms such as *input, output, accessing,* and *information retrieval*. When you type something on your computer's keyboard, a software program encodes the information into an electronic language, stores it on a hard drive, and retrieves it when you need to use it. Similarly, in information-processing models of memory, we *encode* information (convert it to a form that the brain can process and use), *store* the information (retain it over time), and *retrieve* the information (recover it for use). In storage, the information may be represented as concepts, propositions, images, or *cognitive schemas*, mental networks of knowledge, beliefs, and expectations concerning particular topics or aspects of the world.

In most information-processing models, storage takes place in three interacting memory systems. A *sensory register* retains incoming sensory information for a second or two, until it can be processed further. *Short-term memory (STM)* holds a limited amount of information for a brief period of time, perhaps up to 30 seconds or so, unless a conscious effort is made to keep it there longer. *Long-term memory (LTM)* accounts for longer storage, from a few minutes to decades (Atkinson & Shiffrin, 1968, 1971). Information can pass from the sensory register to short-term memory and in either direction between short-term and long-term memory, as illustrated in Figure 10.3.

This model, which is known informally as the *three-box model*, has dominated research on memory since the late 1960s. The problem is that the human brain does not operate like your average computer. Most computers process instructions and data sequentially, one item after another, and so the three-box model has emphasized sequential operations. In contrast, the brain performs many operations simultaneously, in parallel. It recognizes patterns all at once rather than as a sequence of information bits, and it perceives new information, produces speech, and searches memory all at the same time. It can do these things because millions of neurons are active at once, and each neuron communicates with thousands of others, which in turn communicate with millions more.

Because of these differences between human beings and machines, some cognitive scientists prefer a **parallel distributed processing (PDP) model** or *connectionist model*. Instead of representing information as flowing from one system to another, a PDP model represents the contents of memory as connections among a huge number of interacting processing units, distributed in a vast network and all operating in parallel—just like the neurons of the brain (McClelland, 1994, 2011; Rogers & McClelland, 2014; Rumelhart, McClelland, & the PDP Research Group, 1986). As information enters the system, the ability of these units to excite or inhibit each other is constantly adjusted to reflect new knowledge.

In this chapter, we emphasize the three-box model, but keep in mind that the computer metaphor that inspired it could one day be as outdated as the metaphor of memory as a camera.

relearning method

A method for measuring retention that compares the time required to relearn material with the time used in the initial learning of the material.

parallel distributed processing (PDP) model

A model of memory in which knowledge is represented as connections among thousands of interacting processing units, distributed in a vast network, and all operating in parallel. Also called a *connectionist model*.

Figure 10.3 Three Memory Systems

In the three-box model of memory, information that does not transfer out of the sensory register or short-term memory is assumed to be forgotten forever. Once in long-term memory, information can be retrieved for use in analyzing incoming sensory information or performing mental operations in short-term memory.

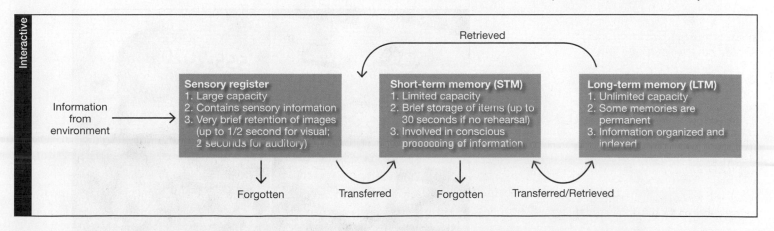

Interactive

Retrieved

Information from environment →

Sensory register
1. Large capacity
2. Contains sensory information
3. Very brief retention of images (up to 1/2 second for visual; 2 seconds for auditory)

Short-term memory (STM)
1. Limited capacity
2. Brief storage of items (up to 30 seconds if no rehearsal)
3. Involved in conscious processing of information

Long-term memory (LTM)
1. Unlimited capacity
2. Some memories are permanent
3. Information organized and indexed

Forgotten   Transferred   Forgotten   Transferred/Retrieved

Quiz for Module 10.2

1. The ability to retrieve information from memory and reproduce it is called
   a. Recognition
   b. Recall
   c. Priming
   d. Implicit memory

2. Claude is studying 100 terms and definitions for his upcoming chemistry test. It takes him 8 hours to rifle through the list on the first day, 4 hours to go through the list on the second day, and 2 hours to make it through the list on the third day. What method of measuring implicit memory is Claude using?
   a. The priming effect
   b. The Omega technique
   c. The primacy effect
   d. The relearning method

3. Alberta solved a crossword puzzle a few days ago. She no longer recalls the words in the puzzle, but while playing a game of Scrabble, she unconsciously tends to form words that were in the puzzle, showing that she has _____ memories of some of the words.
   a. Complicit
   b. Explicit
   c. Implicit
   d. Illicit

4. The three basic memory processes are _____, storage, and _____.
   a. Savings / recognition
   b. Subtyping / distribution
   c. Sensory / short-term
   d. Encoding / retrieval

5. The three memory systems in the three-box model of memory are _____, short-term memory, and _____.
   a. Sensory register / long-term memory
   b. Sensation / recall
   c. Sensory register / recognition
   d. Encoding / distribution

The Three-Box Model of Memory

The information-processing model of three separate memory systems—sensory, short-term, and long-term—remains a leading approach because it offers a convenient way to organize the major findings on memory, does a good job of accounting for these findings, and is consistent with the biological facts about memory. Let us now peer into each of the "boxes"; you can get a sneak peek by watching the video *Memory 1*.

The Sensory Register: Fleeting Impressions

LO 10.3.A Explain the functions, duration, and location of the sensory registers in the three-box model of memory.

In the three-box model, all incoming sensory information must make a brief stop in the **sensory register**, the entryway of memory. The sensory register includes a number of separate memory subsystems, as many as there are senses. Visual images remain in a visual subsystem for a maximum of a half second. Auditory images remain in an auditory subsystem for a slightly longer time, by most estimates up to two seconds or so.

The sensory register acts as a holding bin, retaining information in a highly accurate form until we can select items for attention from the stream of stimuli bombarding our senses. It gives us a moment to decide whether information is extraneous or important; not everything detected by our senses warrants our attention. And the identification of a stimulus on the basis of information already contained in long-term memory occurs during the transfer of information from the sensory register to short-term memory.

Information that does not quickly go on to short-term memory vanishes forever, like a message written in disappearing ink. That is why people who see an array of 12 letters for just a fraction of a second can only report four or five of them; by the time they answer, their sensory memories are already fading (Sperling, 1960). The fleeting nature of incoming sensations is actually beneficial; it prevents multiple sensory images—"double exposures"—that might interfere with the accurate perception and encoding of information.

In a dark room or closet, swing a flashlight rapidly in a circle. You will see an unbroken circle of light instead of a series of separate points. The reason: The successive images remain briefly in the sensory register.

Short-Term Memory: Memory's Notepad

LO 10.3.B Explain the functions and duration of short-term memory, and contrast the *leaky bucket* and *working memory* approaches to understanding this "box" of memory.

Like the sensory register, **short-term memory (STM)** retains information only temporarily—for up to about 30 seconds by many estimates, although some researchers think that the maximum interval may extend to a few minutes for certain tasks. In short-term memory, the material is no longer an exact sensory image but is an encoding of one, such as a word or a phrase. This material either transfers into long-term memory or decays and is lost forever.

Victims of brain injury demonstrate the importance of transferring new information from short-term memory into long-term memory. H. M. was able to store information on a short-term basis; he could hold a conversation and his behavior appeared normal when you first met him. Yet, for the most part, he could not retain explicit information about new facts and events for longer than a few minutes. His terrible memory deficits involved a problem in transferring explicit memories from short-term storage into long-term storage. With a great deal of repetition and drill, patients like H. M. can learn some new visual information, retain it in long-term memory, and recall it normally (McKee & Squire, 1992). But usually information does not get into long-term memory in the first place.

THE LEAKY BUCKET People such as H. M. fall at the extreme end on a continuum of forgetfulness, but even those of us with normal memories know from personal experience how frustratingly brief short-term retention can be. We look up a phone number, and before we can use it we find that the number has vanished from our minds. We meet someone at a party and two minutes later find ourselves groping for the person's name. Is it any wonder that short-term memory has been called a "leaky bucket"?

According to most memory models, if the bucket did not leak it would quickly overflow because at any given moment, short-term memory can hold only so many items. Years ago, George Miller (1956) estimated its capacity to be "the magical number 7 plus or minus 2." Conveniently, 5-digit zip codes and 7-digit phone numbers fall in this range (at least in the United States); 16-digit credit card numbers do not. Since then, estimates of STM's capacity

sensory register

A memory system that momentarily preserves extremely accurate images of sensory information.

short-term memory (STM)

In the three-box model of memory, a limited-capacity memory system involved in the retention of information for brief periods; it is also used to hold information retrieved from long-term memory for temporary use.

have ranged from 2 items to 20, with one estimate putting the "magical number" at 4 (Cowan, 2001; Cowan et al., 2008; Mathy & Feldman, 2012). Everyone agrees, however, that the number of items that short-term memory can handle at any one time is small.

Experiment DIGIT SPAN

| INTRODUCTION | INSTRUCTIONS | EXPERIMENT | RESULTS | DISCUSSION | REFERENCE |

Interactive

You can hardly walk across campus, eat in a restaurant, or ride on a bus, without seeing someone using their cell phone. With the explosion of cell phones on the market, phone companies have been pressed to support the ever-increasing use of all of the possible phone numbers available in any one state. As a result, many states have gone from a 7-digit dialing procedure to a 10-digit dialing procedure so they can add additional area codes to highly populated areas. While some people have adjusted to these changes with little effort, others have struggled. They find trying to remember 10 digits more difficult than remembering 7 digits.

Click or tap Next to continue.

Next

Given the limits on short-term memory, how do we remember the beginning of a spoken sentence until the speaker reaches the end? After all, most sentences are longer than just a few words. Most information-processing models of memory propose that we bind small bits of information into larger units, or **chunks**. The real capacity of STM, it turns out, is not a few bits of information but a few chunks (Gilchrist & Cowan, 2012). A chunk can be a word, a phrase, a sentence, or even an image, and it depends on previous experience. For most Americans, the number 1776 is one chunk, not four, but 1840 is probably four chunks—unless you're from New Zealand, in which case 1840 is one chunk. (In that year, the British Crown and native Maori chiefs signed a treaty that became New Zealand's founding document.) A chunk can be visual: If you know football, when you see a play unfolding, you might see a single chunk of information—say, a wishbone formation—and be able to remember it. If you do not know football, you will see only a field full of players, and you probably won't be able to remember their positions when you look away.

But even chunking cannot keep short-term memory from eventually filling up. Information that will be needed for longer periods must be transferred to long-term memory or it will be displaced by new information and spill out of the bucket. Particularly meaningful items may transfer quickly, but other information will usually require more processing—unless we do something to keep it in STM for a while, as we will discuss shortly.

WORKING MEMORY In the original three-box model, short-term memory functioned basically as a container for temporarily holding on to new information or information retrieved from long-term memory. But this view did not account for the sense of effort we feel when trying to solve a problem. Does $2 \times (3 + 5) / 4 = 4$? Solving that problem feels as though we are not simply holding on to information but also *working* with it, which is why psychologists today think that STM is really part of a **working memory** system. STM keeps its job as a temporary holding bin, but another more active part—an "executive"—controls attention, focusing it on the information we need for the task at hand and warding off distracting information (Baddeley, 1992, 2007; Ma, Husain, & Bays, 2014). In the previous algebra problem, your working memory must contain the numbers and instructions for operating on them, and also carry out those operations and retain the intermediate results from each step.

chunk
A meaningful unit of information; it may be composed of smaller units.

working memory
In many models of memory, a cognitively complex form of short-term memory; it involves active mental processes that control retrieval of information from long-term memory and interpret that information appropriately for a given task.

People who do well on tests of working memory tend to do well on intelligence tests and on tasks requiring complex cognition and the control of attention, such as understanding what you read, following directions, taking notes, playing bridge, learning new words, estimating how much time has elapsed, and many other real-life tasks (Broadway & Engle, 2011). When they are engrossed in challenging activities that require their concentration and effort, they stay on task longer, and their minds are less likely than other people's to wander (Kane et al., 2007).

The ability to bring information from long-term memory into short-term memory or to use working memory is not disrupted in patients like H. M. They can do arithmetic, relate events that predate their injury, and do anything else that requires retrieval of information from long-term into short-term memory. Their problem is with the flow of information in the other direction, from short-term to long-term memory.

These card players are having a great time using their working memories.

Long-Term Memory: Memory's Storage System

LO 10.3.C Describe semantic categories and four forms of long-term memory, and explain how *primacy* and *recency* illustrate the serial-position effect in transferring information from short-term to long-term memory.

The third box in the three-box model of memory is **long-term memory (LTM)**. The capacity of long-term memory seems to have no practical limits. The vast amount of information stored there enables us to learn, get around in the environment, and build a sense of identity and a personal history.

ORGANIZATION IN LONG-TERM MEMORY Because long-term memory contains so much information, it must be organized in some way, so that we can find the particular items we are looking for. One way to organize words (or the concepts they represent) is by the *semantic categories* to which they belong. *Chair*, for example, belongs to the category *furniture*. In a study done many years ago, people had to memorize 60 words that came from four semantic categories: animals, vegetables, names, and professions. The words were presented in random order, but when people were allowed to recall the items in any order they wished, they tended to recall them in clusters corresponding to the four categories (Bousfield, 1953). This finding has been replicated many times.

Evidence on the storage of information by semantic category also comes from cases of people with brain damage. In one such case, a patient called M. D. appeared to have made a complete recovery after suffering several strokes, with one odd exception: He had trouble remembering the names of fruits and vegetables. M. D. could easily name a picture of an abacus or a sphinx, but he drew a blank when he saw a picture of an orange or a carrot. He could sort pictures of animals, vehicles, and other objects into their appropriate categories, but did poorly with pictures of fruits and vegetables. On the other hand, when M. D. was *given* the names of fruits and vegetables, he immediately pointed to the corresponding pictures (Hart, Berndt, & Caramazza, 1985). Apparently, M. D. still had information about fruits and vegetables, but his brain lesion prevented him from using their names to get to the information when he needed it, unless someone else provided the names. This evidence suggests that information in memory about a particular concept (such as *orange*) is linked in some way to information about the concept's semantic category (such as *fruit*).

Indeed, many models of long-term memory represent its contents as a vast network of interrelated concepts and propositions (Anderson, 1990; Collins & Loftus, 1975). In these models, a small part of a conceptual network for *animals* might look something like the one in Figure 10.4. The way people use these networks, however, depends on experience and education. In rural Liberia, one study showed that the more schooling children had, the more likely they were to use semantic categories in recalling lists of objects (Cole & Scribner, 1974). This makes sense because in school, children must memorize a lot of information in a short

long-term memory (LTM)

In the three-box model of memory, the memory system involved in the long-term storage of information.

Figure 10.4 Part of a Conceptual Grid in Long-Term Memory

Many models of memory represent the contents of long-term semantic memory as an immense network or grid of concepts and the relationships among them. This illustration shows part of a hypothetical grid for *animals*.

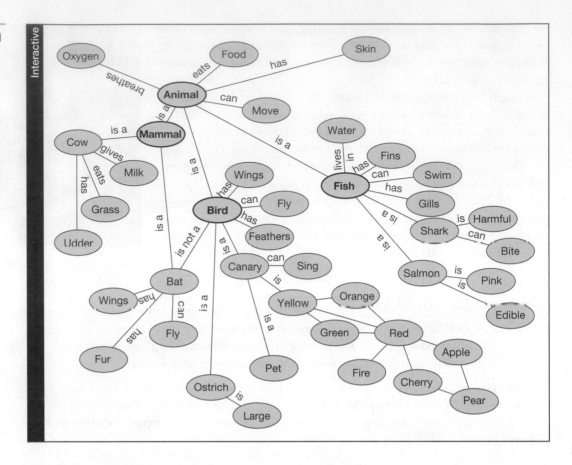

time, and semantic grouping can help. Unschooled children, having less need to memorize lists, do not cluster items and do not remember them as well. But this does not mean that unschooled children have poor memories. When the task is one that is meaningful to them, such as recalling objects that were in a story or a village scene, they remember extremely well (Mistry & Rogoff, 1994).

We organize information in long-term memory not only by semantic groupings but also in terms of the way words sound or look. Have you ever tried to recall some name, phrase, or word that just escaped you? Nearly everyone experiences these *tip-of-the-tongue (TOT) states*, which occur across many languages and cultures; users of sign language call them "tip of the finger" states (Thompson, Emmorey, & Gollan, 2005). Scientists value them as a sort of slow-motion video of memory processes (A. Brown, 2012; Resnik et al., 2014). People in a TOT state tend to come up with words that resemble the right one in sound, meaning, or form (e.g., number of syllables) before finally recalling the one they're searching for, which indicates that information in long-term memory is organized in those terms (R. Brown & McNeill, 1966). For the name *Kevin* they might say, "Wait, it starts with a K and has two syllables . . . Kenny? Kerran? . . . "

Information in long-term memory may also be organized by its familiarity, relevance, or association with other information. The method used in any given instance probably depends on the nature of the memory; you would no doubt store information about the major cities of Europe differently from information about your first date. To understand the organization of long-term memory, then, we must know what kinds of information can be stored there.

Culture affects the encoding, storage, and retrieval of information in long-term memory. Navajo healers, who use stylized, symbolic sand paintings in their rituals, must commit to memory dozens of intricate visual designs because no exact copies are made and the painting is destroyed after each ceremony.

THE CONTENTS OF LONG-TERM MEMORY. Most theories of memory distinguish skills or habits ("knowing how") from abstract or representational knowledge ("knowing that").

Procedural memories are memories of knowing how to do something—comb your hair, use a pencil, solve a jigsaw puzzle, knit a sweater, or swim. Many researchers consider procedural memories to be implicit, because after skills and habits are learned well, they do not require much conscious processing. **Declarative memories** involve knowing that something is true, as in knowing that Ottawa is the capital of Canada; they are usually assumed to be explicit.

Declarative memories come in two varieties: semantic memories and episodic memories (Tulving, 1985). **Semantic memories** are internal representations of the world, independent of any particular context. They include facts, rules, and concepts—items of general knowledge. On the basis of your semantic memory of the concept *cat*, you can describe a cat as a small, furry mammal that typically spends its time eating, sleeping, prowling, and staring into space, even though a cat may not be present when you give this description, and you probably won't know how or when you first learned it.

Episodic memories are internal representations of personally experienced events. When you remember how your cat once surprised you in the middle of the night by pouncing on you as you slept, you are retrieving an episodic memory. Figure 10.5 summarizes these kinds of memories.

Episodic memory allows us to travel not only backward in time, but also forward, to imagine possible future experiences (Schacter et al., 2015). We mine our episodic memories to construct scenarios of what might happen and then rehearse how we might behave. In fact, regions of the brain known to be involved when we retrieve personal memories, notably the hippocampus and parts of the prefrontal cortex and temporal lobe, are also activated when we imagine future events (Addis, Wong, & Schacter, 2007). Patients who cannot retrieve any episodic memories because of damage to the hippocampus often cannot envision future episodes either, even in response to such simple questions as "What will you do tomorrow?" (Hassabis & Maguire, 2007). The "time-travel" function of episodic memories is often beneficial and motivating because people tend to forget negative episodic memories

procedural memories

Memories for the performance of actions or skills ("knowing how").

declarative memories

Memories of facts, rules, concepts, and events ("knowing that"); they include semantic and episodic memories.

semantic memories

Memories of general knowledge, including facts, rules, concepts, and propositions.

episodic memories

Memories of personally experienced events and the contexts in which they occurred.

Figure 10.5 Types of Long-Term Memories

This diagram summarizes the distinctions among long-term memories. A procedural memory might be of learning how to ride a bike; a declarative memory might be knowing that Ottawa is the capital of Canada. Can you come up with your own examples of each memory type?

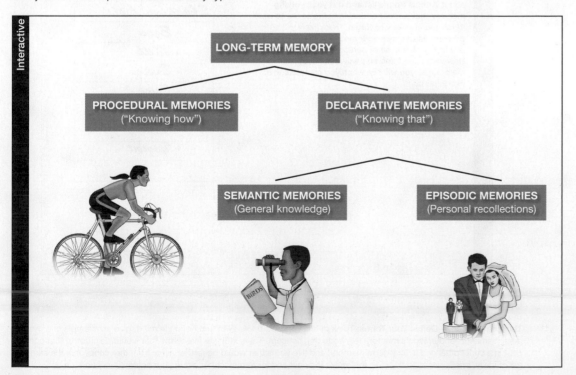

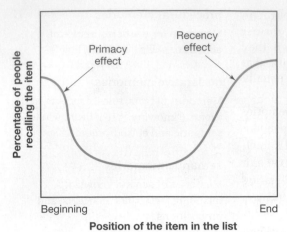

Figure 10.6 The Serial-Position Effect

When people try to recall a list of similar items immediately after learning it, they tend to remember the first and last items best and the ones in the middle worst.

serial-position effect

The tendency for recall of the first and last items on a list to surpass recall of items in the middle of the list.

faster than positive ones, leaving us with a forgiving past and rosy future (Szpunar, Addis, & Schacter, 2012).

FROM SHORT-TERM TO LONG-TERM MEMORY: A PUZZLE   The three-box model of memory is often invoked to explain an interesting phenomenon called the **serial-position effect**. If you are shown a list of items and are then asked immediately to recall them, your recall will be best for items at the beginning of the list (the *primacy effect*) and at the end of the list (the *recency effect*); the items in the middle of the list will tend to drop away (Bhatarah, Ward, & Tan, 2008; Johnson & Miles, 2009). If we plot the results, we see a U-shaped curve as shown in Figure 10.6. A serial-position effect occurs when you meet a lot of people at a party and find you can recall the names of the first few and the last few, but almost no one in between.

Primary and recency effects apparently occur for different reasons. Primacy effects happen because the first few items in a list are rehearsed many times and so are likely to make it to long-term memory and remain memorable. Recency effects occur because at the time of recall, they are plucked out of short-term memory, where they are still sitting. The items in the middle of a list are not so well retained because by the time they get into short-term memory, it is already crowded with the first few items. As a result, middle items often drop out of short-term memory before they can be stored in long-term memory. Indeed, a functional MRI (fMRI) study found that recognition memory for words early in a list activated areas in the hippocampus associated with retrieval from long-term memory, but recognition for words that came near the end of the list did not (Talmi et al., 2005).

The problem with this explanation is that the recency effect sometimes occurs even after a considerable delay, when the items at the end of a list should no longer be in short-term memory (Davelaar et al., 2004). Moreover, the serial-position effect can occur not just with semantic memories but also episodic ones—memories of past personal experiences, such as the soccer games you played in over the last season. The serial-position curve, therefore, remains something of a puzzle.

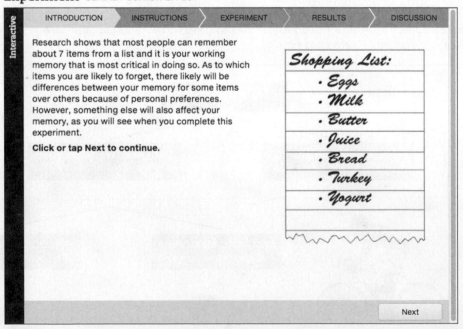

Experiment SERIAL POSITION EFFECT

JOURNAL PROMPT 10.3

Thinking Critically—Define Your Terms: Think of this concept: *book*. With that notion in mind, give an example of a procedural, semantic, and episodic memory related to that concept. Then, indicate five terms that would be close to that concept in a conceptual grid in long-term memory, and five terms that would be farther away from that concept in the same grid. Finally, briefly describe the links that make the near and far terms connected in your semantic network.

Quiz for Module 10.3

1. The _____ holds images for a fraction of a second.
   a. Working memory
   b. Leaky bucket
   c. Auditory sensory register
   d. Visual sensory register

2. Short-term memory can contain information for up to _____ by many estimates.
   a. 5 minutes
   b. 15 seconds
   c. 30 seconds
   d. 2 minutes

3. The most appropriate unit for measuring the capacity of short-term memory is
   a. Syllables
   b. Individual pieces of information
   c. Words
   d. Chunks

4. Your knowledge of how to dance the hokey-pokey is an example of
   a. Semantic memory
   b. Declarative memory
   c. Procedural memory
   d. Working memory

5. Ray is introduced to a bunch of people at a business meeting: Charles, Aldo, Mary, Frank, Candace, Aileen, Ronnie, Keith, Mark, Susanna, Jay, Sophie, Mario, and Rick. According to the primacy effect, whose names should he remember the easiest?
   a. Frank, Candace, and Aileen
   b. Charles, Aldo, and Mary
   c. Mark, Mary, and Mario
   d. Sophie, Mario, and Rick

The Biology of Memory

We have been discussing memory solely in terms of information processing, but what is happening in the brain while all of that processing is going on? For a preview of the answers, watch the video *Memory 2*.

Changes in Neurons and Synapses

LO 10.4.A   Outline the process of long-term potentiation in the formation of memories.

Forming a memory involves chemical and structural changes at the level of synapses, and these changes differ for short-term memory and long-term memory.

long-term potentiation

A long-lasting increase in the strength of synaptic responsiveness, thought to be a biological mechanism of long-term memory.

consolidation

The process by which a long-term memory becomes durable and relatively stable.

In short-term memory, changes within neurons temporarily alter their ability to release neurotransmitters, the chemicals that carry messages from one cell to another. Evidence comes from studies with sea snails, sea slugs, and other organisms that have small numbers of easily identifiable neurons (Kandel, 2001; Kandel & Schwartz, 1982). These primitive animals can be taught simple conditioned responses, such as withdrawing or not withdrawing parts of their bodies in response to a light touch. When the animal retains the skill for only the short term, the neuron or neurons involved temporarily show an increase or decrease in readiness to release neurotransmitter molecules into a synapse.

In contrast, long-term memory involves lasting structural changes in the brain. To mimic what they think happens during the formation of a long-term memory, researchers apply brief, high-frequency electrical stimulation to groups of neurons in the brains of animals or to brain cells in a laboratory culture. In various areas, especially the hippocampus, this stimulation increases the strength of synaptic responsiveness, a phenomenon known as **long-term potentiation** (Bliss & Collingridge, 1993; Whitlock et al., 2006). Certain receiving neurons become more responsive to transmitting neurons, making synaptic pathways more excitable.

Long-term potentiation probably underlies many and perhaps all forms of learning and memory. Both calcium and the neurotransmitter glutamate seem to play a key role in this process, causing receiving neurons in the hippocampus to become more receptive to the next signal that comes along (Lisman, Yasuda, & Raghavachari, 2012). It is a little like increasing the diameter of a funnel's neck to permit more flow through the funnel. In addition, during long-term potentiation, dendrites grow and branch out, and certain types of synapses increase in number (Greenough, 1984). At the same time, in another process, some neurons become *less* responsive than they were previously (Bolshakov & Siegelbaum, 1994).

Most of these changes take time, which probably explains why long-term memories remain vulnerable to disruption for a while after they are stored—why a blow to the head may disrupt new memories even though old ones are unaffected. Memories must therefore undergo a period of **consolidation**, or stabilization, before they "solidify." Consolidation can continue for weeks in animals and for several years in human beings. And memories probably never completely solidify. The very act of remembering previously stored memories can make them unstable again. A new round of consolidation often then sweeps up new information into the old memory, remolding it (Schiller & Phelps, 2011). Sleep plays a role in ensuring consolidation of new information.

Where Memories Are Made

LO 10.4.B   Evaluate the evidence that memories are not stored in any one "place" in the brain.

Scientists have used electrodes, brain-scan technology, and other techniques to identify the brain structures responsible for the formation and storage of specific types of memories (see Figure 10.7). The amygdala is involved in the formation, consolidation, and retrieval of memories of fearful and other emotional events (Buchanan, 2007). Areas in the frontal lobes of the brain are especially active during short-term and working-memory tasks (Goldman-Rakic, 1996; Mitchell & Johnson, 2009). The prefrontal cortex and areas adjacent to the hippocampus in the temporal lobe are also important for the efficient encoding of pictures and words.

But it is the hippocampus that has the starring role in many aspects of memory. It is critical to the formation of long-term declarative memories ("knowing that"); as we have seen in the case of H. M., damage to this structure can cause amnesia for new facts and events. The hippocampus is also critical in recalling past experiences (Pastalkova et al., 2008).

Figure 10.7 Brain Areas Involved in Memory

Different parts of the brain are involved in different aspects of memory. As you can see here, some centers deep within the brain (such as the amygdala and hippocampus) play an important role, but so too do "higher" centers of the brain in the cerebral cortex. Forming and storing a memory relies on many interacting processes.

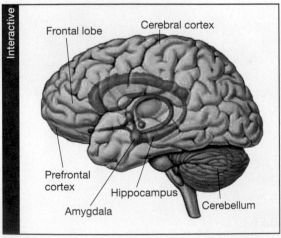

A team of researchers has identified how neurons in the hippocampus may become involved in specific memories. They implanted electrodes into the brains of 13 people about to undergo surgery for severe epilepsy. (This is standard procedure because it enables doctors to pinpoint the location of the brain activity causing the seizures.) As the patients were being prepped, they watched a series of 5- to 10-second film clips of TV shows or of animals and landmarks. The researchers recorded which neurons in the hippocampus were firing as the patients watched; for each patient, particular neurons might become highly active during particular videos and respond only weakly to others. After a few minutes, the patients were asked to recall what they had seen. They remembered almost all of the clips, and as they recalled each one, the very neurons that had been active when they first saw it were reignited (Gelbard-Sagiv et al., 2008).

The formation and retention of procedural memories (memory for skills and habits) seem to involve other brain structures and pathways. In work with rabbits, Richard Thompson (1983, 1986) showed that one kind of procedural memory—a simple, classically conditioned response to a stimulus, such as an eyeblink in response to a tone—depends on activity in the cerebellum. Human patients with damage in the cerebellum are incapable of this type of conditioning (Daum & Schugens, 1996).

The formation of declarative and procedural memories in different brain areas could explain a curious finding about patients like H. M. Despite their inability to form new declarative memories, with sufficient practice such patients can acquire new procedural memories that enable them to solve a puzzle, read mirror-reversed words, or play tennis—even though they do not recall the training sessions in which they learned these skills. Apparently, the parts of the brain involved in acquiring new procedural memories have remained intact. These patients also retain some implicit memory for verbal material, as measured by priming tasks, suggesting that the brain has separate systems for implicit and explicit tasks. This view has been bolstered by brain scans, which reveal differences in the location of brain activity when ordinary people perform explicit or implicit memory tasks (Reber, Stark, & Squire, 1998; Squire et al., 1992).

The brain circuits that take part in the *formation* and *retrieval* of long-term memories, however, are not the same as those involved in long-term *storage* of those memories. Although the hippocampus is vital for the formation and retrieval of memories, the storage of memories eventually becomes the responsibility of the cerebral cortex (Battaglia et al., 2011). In fact, memories may be stored in the same cortical areas that were involved in the original perception of the information. When people remember pictures, visual parts of the brain become active; when people remember sounds, auditory areas become active, just as they did when the information was first perceived (Nyberg et al., 2000; Thompson & Kosslyn, 2000).

The typical "memory" is a complex cluster of information. When you recall meeting a man yesterday, you remember his greeting, his tone of voice, how he looked, and where he was. Even a single concept, such as *shovel*, includes a lot of information about its length, what it's made of, and what it's used for. These different pieces of information are probably processed separately and stored at different locations that are distributed across wide areas of the brain, with all the sites participating in the representation of the event or concept as a whole. The hippocampus may somehow bind together the diverse aspects of a memory at the time it is formed, so that even though these aspects are stored in different cortical sites, the memory can later be retrieved as one coherent entity (Squire & Zola-Morgan, 1991).

Review 10.1 summarizes the structures that we have discussed and some of the memory-related functions associated with them. But we have given you just a few small nibbles from the smorgasbord of findings now available. Neuroscientists hope that someday they will be able to describe the entire stream of events in the brain that occur from the moment you say to yourself "I must remember this" to the moment you actually do remember—or find that you can't.

Review 10.1

Some Brain Areas Involved in Memory

No simple summary of brain areas associated with memory can do this complex topic justice. Here are just a few of the areas and functions that have been studied.

Brain Area	Associated Memory Function
Amygdala	Formation, consolidation, and retrieval of emotional memories
Frontal lobes	Short-term memory and working-memory tasks
Prefrontal cortex, parts of temporal lobes	Efficient encoding of words and pictures, working memory, source monitoring
Hippocampus	Formation of long-term declarative memories; aids in the retrieval of specific memories; may bind together diverse elements of a memory so it can be retrieved later as a coherent entity
Cerebellum	Formation and retention of simple classically conditioned responses
Cerebral cortex	Storage of long-term memories, possibly in areas involved in the original perception of the information

Hormones, Emotion, and Memory

LO 10.4.C Summarize the evidence that memory can be influenced by emotion and hormonal levels.

Have you ever smelled fresh cookies and recalled a tender scene from your childhood? Do you have a vivid memory of seeing a particularly horrifying horror movie? Emotional memories such as these are often especially intense, and the explanation resides partly in our hormones.

Hormones released by the adrenal glands during stress and emotional arousal, including epinephrine (adrenaline) and norepinephrine, can enhance memory. If you give people a drug that prevents their adrenal glands from producing these hormones, they will remember less about emotional stories they heard than a control group will (Cahill et al., 1994). Conversely, if you give animals norepinephrine right after learning, their memories will improve. The link between emotional arousal and memory makes evolutionary sense: Arousal tells the brain that an event or piece of information is important enough to encode and store for future use.

However, extreme arousal is not necessarily a good thing. When animals or people are given very high doses of stress hormones, their memories for learned tasks sometimes suffer instead of improving; a moderate dose may be optimal (Andreano & Cahill, 2006). Two psychologists demonstrated the perils of high stress and anxiety in a real-life setting: the Horror Labyrinth of the London Dungeon (Valentine & Mesout, 2009). The labyrinth is a maze of disorienting mirrored walls set in Gothic vaults. As visitors walk through it, they hear strange noises and screams, and various alarming things suddenly appear, including a "scary person"—an actor dressed in a dark robe, wearing makeup to appear scarred and bleeding. Volunteers wore a wireless heart-rate monitor as they walked through the labyrinth, so that their stress and anxiety levels could be recorded. The higher their stress and anxiety, the less able they were to accurately describe the "scary person" later, and the fewer correct identifications they made of him in a lineup.

Such effects on memory do not matter much at an amusement attraction, but they can have serious consequences when crime victims, police officers, and combat soldiers must recall details of a highly stressful experience, such as a shootout or the identity of an enemy interrogator. Even highly trained soldiers have great difficulty in correctly identifying their captors

(Morgan et al., 2007). The unintended effects of misleading suggestions, combined with the effects of extreme stress on memory, mean that we should be especially cautious about how investigators gather intelligence information from captured suspected terrorists (Loftus, 2011).

Assuming that adrenal hormones do not become *too* high, how might these hormones enhance storage of information in the brain? One possibility is that norepinephrine affects glutamate receptors on the surfaces of nerve cells, increasing the strength of incoming signals (Hu et al., 2007; McGaugh, 1990). Another is that adrenal hormones cause the level of glucose (a sugar) to rise in the bloodstream, and from there the glucose can readily enter the brain. In the brain, glucose may enhance memory either directly or by altering the effects of neurotransmitters. If so, increasing the amount of glucose available to the brain should enhance memory. Indeed, this "sweet memories" effect does occur both in aged rats and mice and in human beings. In one encouraging study, healthy older people fasted overnight, drank a glass of lemonade sweetened with either glucose or saccharin, and then took two memory tests. The saccharin-laced drink had no effect on their performance, but lemonade with glucose greatly boosted their ability to recall a taped passage 5 or 40 minutes after hearing it (Manning, Hall, & Gold, 1990).

Before you reach for a candy bar, you should know that the effective dose of glucose is narrow; too much can impair cognitive functioning instead of helping it. The "sweet memories" effect also depends on your metabolism, what you have eaten that day, and the level of glucose in your brain before you ingest it. In this area, as in others in the biology of memory, we have much to learn. No one knows yet exactly how the brain stores information, how different memory circuits link up with one another, or how a student is able to locate and retrieve information at the drop of a multiple-choice item.

JOURNAL PROMPT 10.4

Thinking Critically—Consider Other Interpretations: From an evolutionary, biological, and developmental perspective, why would it be a horrible idea if memories were all stored in a single location in the brain? On the one hand, it makes intuitive sense that there should be a "memory center," just as there are other identifiable brain structures with well-defined properties. On the other hand, what dangers would you predict if memories were stored in such a center?

Quiz for Module 10.4

1. Long-term potentiation is associated with
   a. Potassium–sodium ionization in dendritic cavities
   b. A decrease in receptors on certain receiving neurons
   c. Decreased responsiveness of certain receiving neurons to interneurons
   d. Increased responsiveness of certain receiving neurons to transmitting neurons

2. The process by which a long-term memory becomes durable and relatively stable is called
   a. Consolidation
   b. Determination
   c. Potentiation
   d. Concretization

3. The cerebellum has been associated with _____ memories; the hippocampus has been associated with _____ memories.
   a. Declarative / procedural
   b. Procedural / declarative

   c. Semantic / episodic
   d. Episodic / semantic

4. The frontal lobes seem to play a particular role in
   a. Short-term memory and working-memory tasks
   b. The retrieval of emotional memories
   c. The formation of classically conditioned responses
   d. The consolidation of sensory memories

5. How do hormone levels contribute to the retention of information?
   a. High hormone levels are optimal for learning new tasks.
   b. Moderate hormone levels are optimal for learning new tasks.
   c. Low hormone levels are optimal for learning new tasks.
   d. Low hormone levels are best for learning physical tasks, high hormone levels are best for learning cognitive tasks.

How We Remember

Some stage performers with amazing recall abilities rely on complicated schemes to keep track of information, such as associating a person's name with a common household object or visualizing a map of all the zip codes in the United States. We are not going to spend time discussing these strategies because for ordinary memory tasks, such tricks are often no more effective than rote repetition, and sometimes they are actually worse (Wang, Thomas, & Ouellette, 1992). Most memory researchers do not use such techniques themselves (Hébert, 2001); after all, why bother to memorize a grocery list using a fancy strategy when you can write down what you need to buy?

The Nine Secrets of Learning discussed elsewhere in the book are based on well-established principles of memory that help us keep track of information so that it sticks in our minds and will be there when we need it. In this section we'll dig into the science behind those secrets and examine the processes that contribute to making memories "stick." The video *Making It Stick* provides helpful hints on this topic from leading experts in memory research.

Encoding, Rehearsal, and Retrieval

LO 10.5.A Describe some major strategies that contribute to memory retention, and give an example of each.

People who want to give their powers of memory a boost sometimes use **mnemonics** [neh-MON-iks], formal strategies and tricks for improving memory. (Mnemosyne, pronounced neh-MOZ-eh-nee, was the ancient Greek goddess of memory.) Some mnemonics take the form of easily memorized rhymes (e.g., "Thirty days hath September/April, June, and November . . . "). Others use formulas (e.g., "**E**very **g**ood **b**oy **d**oes **f**ine" for remembering which notes are on the lines of the treble clef in musical notation). Still others use visual images or word associations. Mnemonics may also reduce the amount of information by chunking it, which is why many companies use words for their phone numbers instead of unmemorable numbers. In various ways, mnemonics contribute to the processes of encoding, storing, and retrieving information.

EFFECTIVE ENCODING   Our memories, as we have seen, are not exact replicas of experience. Sensory information is summarized and encoded as words or images almost as soon as it is detected. When you hear a lecture, you may hang on every word (we hope you do), but you do not memorize those words verbatim. You extract the main points and encode them.

To remember information well, you have to encode it accurately in the first place. With some kinds of information, accurate encoding takes place automatically, without effort. Think about where you usually sit in your psychology class. When were you last there? You can probably provide this information easily, even though you never made a deliberate effort to encode it. But many kinds of information require *effortful encoding*: the plot of a novel, the procedures

mnemonics

Strategies and tricks for improving memory, such as the use of a verse or a formula.

for assembling a cabinet, the arguments for and against a proposed law. To retain such information, you might have to select the main points, label concepts, or associate the information with personal experiences or with material you already know. Experienced students know that most of the information in a college course requires effortful encoding, otherwise known as studying. The mind does not gobble up information automatically; you must make the material digestible.

REHEARSAL   An important technique for keeping information in short-term memory and increasing the chances of long-term retention is *rehearsal*, the review or practice of material while you are learning it. When people are prevented from rehearsing, the contents of their short-term memories quickly fade (Peterson & Peterson, 1959). You are taking advantage of rehearsal when you look up a phone number and then repeat it over and over to keep it in short-term memory until you no longer need it. And when you can't remember a phone number because your phone always remembers it for you, you are learning what happens when you *don't* rehearse!

A poignant demonstration of the power of rehearsal occurred during a session with H. M. (Ogden & Corkin, 1991). The experimenter gave H. M. five digits to repeat and remember, but then she was unexpectedly called away. When she returned after more than an hour, H. M. was able to repeat the five digits correctly. He had been rehearsing them the entire time.

Short-term memory holds many kinds of information, including visual information and abstract meanings. But most people, or at least most hearing people, seem to favor speech for encoding and rehearsing the contents of short-term memory. The speech may be spoken aloud or to oneself. When people make errors on short-term memory tests that use letters or words, they often confuse items that sound the same or similar, such as *d* and *t*, or *bear* and *bare*. These errors suggest that they have been rehearsing verbally.

Some strategies for rehearsing are more effective than others. **Maintenance rehearsal** involves merely the rote repetition of the material. This kind of rehearsal is fine for keeping information in STM, but it will not always lead to long-term retention. A better strategy if you want to remember for the long haul is **elaborative rehearsal**, also called *elaboration of encoding* (Cermak & Craik, 1979; Craik & Tulving, 1975). Elaboration involves associating new items of information with material that has already been stored or with other new facts. It can also involve analyzing the physical, sensory, or semantic features of an item.

Suppose that you are studying the concept of working memory. Simply memorizing the definition is unlikely to help much. But if you can elaborate the concept, you are more likely to remember it. The word *working* should remind you that working memory is involved in tasks that require effort and attention. And what benefits do effort and attention bring? Yes, that is why working memory is related to the ability to concentrate, resist distraction, and solve problems. Many students try to pare down what they are learning to the bare essentials, but knowing more details about something makes it more memorable; that is what elaboration means.

A related strategy for prolonging retention is **deep processing**, or the processing of meaning (Craik & Lockhart, 1972). If you process only the physical or sensory features of a stimulus, such as how the word *hypothalamus* is spelled and how it sounds, your processing will be shallow even if it is elaborated. If you recognize patterns and assign labels to objects or events ("*Hypo* means 'below,' so the *hypo*thalamus must be *below* the thalamus"), your processing will be somewhat deeper. If you fully analyze the meaning of what you are trying to remember (perhaps by encoding the functions and importance of the hypothalamus), your processing will be deeper yet. *Shallow processing* is sometimes useful; when you memorize a poem, for instance, you will want to pay attention to (and elaborately encode) the sounds of the words and the patterns of rhythm in the poem and not just the poem's meaning. Usually, though, deep processing is more effective. That is why, if you try to memorize information that has little or no meaning for you, the information may not stick.

It seems obvious, but often we fail to remember because we never encoded the information in the first place. Which of these Lincoln pennies is the real one? (The answer is at the end of this chapter.) If you are an American, you have seen zillions of pennies, yet you will probably have trouble recognizing the real one because you have never paid close attention to and encoded the details of its design (Nickerson & Adams, 1979). If you are not an American, try drawing the front of one of your most common coins and then check to see how well you did. Again, you're likely to have trouble remembering the details.

maintenance rehearsal
Rote repetition of material in order to maintain its availability in memory.

elaborative rehearsal
Association of new information with already stored knowledge and analysis of the new information to make it memorable.

deep processing
In the encoding of information, the processing of meaning rather than simply the physical or sensory features of a stimulus.

When actors learn a script, they do not rely on maintenance rehearsal alone. They also use elaborative rehearsal and deep processing, analyzing the meaning of their lines and associating their lines with imagined information about the character they are playing.

RETRIEVAL PRACTICE Many students think that the way to remember course material is simply to study it once thoroughly, or maybe twice, so they can retrieve the correct answers on an exam. Unfortunately, within just a few weeks or months after the exam, some of those answers will have vanished like steam on a bathroom mirror. *Retrieval practice*, the repeated retrieval of an item of information from memory, is necessary if a memory is to undergo consolidation and remain available for a long time. After all, that's the goal of learning.

In a college course, a good way to ensure retrieval practice is to take short quizzes after you have learned some material but before the big exam. In a series of experiments in which students learned words in foreign languages, after a student had learned a word it was (1) repeatedly studied but dropped from further testing, (2) repeatedly tested but dropped from further studying, or (3) dropped from studying and testing. To the surprise of the students themselves, studying after learning had no effect on their subsequent ability to recall the foreign words. But repeated *testing*, which caused them to repeatedly retrieve the words from memory, had a large benefit (Karpicke, 2012; Karpicke & Roediger, 2008). So when your professors and your textbook authors want to keep quizzing you, it's only for your own good!

JOURNAL PROMPT 10.5

Thinking Critically—Define Your Terms: One way to improve your study skills is to practice deep processing of information. Rather than just memorizing a stock definition of a term from the margin of a textbook, challenge yourself to think of an example of the term. Generating an example requires more effort on your part—you're having to think more about the information—which should lead to better retention of the information. What are some other ways you could achieve deeper levels of processing? Think of three or four techniques and describe why they would lead to deep processing.

Quiz for Module 10.5

1. Dominique seems to be a memory whiz. When asked how she can remember the colors of the visible spectrum, she tells you her friend ROY G BIV helps her out. When asked about the order of mathematical operations (which she learned about in elementary school), she tells you her Dear Aunt Sally helps her keep track. Finally, she tells you that she has several HOMES on the Great Lakes. Dominique's memory success sounds like it's due to her effective use of

   a. Recall

   b. Short-term memory

   c. Recognition

   d. Mnemonics

2. Accurate _____ is the first step toward effective memory retention.

   a. Distribution

   b. Retrieval

   c. Storage

   d. Encoding

3. Information will rapidly fade from short-term memory unless we engage in

   a. Potentiality

   b. Rehearsal

   c. Retrieval

   d. Parallel distributed processing

4. _____ rehearsal involves the rote repetition of material, whereas _____ rehearsal involves associating new material with material that has already been learned.

   a. Maintenance / elaborative

   b. Elaborative / maintenance

   c. Recall / retrieval

   d. Recognition / retrieval

5. Rollie is trying to learn a list of terms for his upcoming anatomy exam. "Small intestine" he reads. "My Uncle Bob has had trouble with his small intestine; 'Bob's small intestine.' 'Transverse colon' . . . hmm, our neighbors are from the town of Colon, Panama, and they traversed their way here. 'Rectum'; I remember when we were kids, my little brother took my Hot Wheels cars and wrecked 'em." What information-processing strategy is Rollie using?

   a. Maintenance rehearsal

   b. Deep processing

   c. Automatic encoding

   d. Chunking

Why We Forget

It would seem that someone who followed the advice so far in this chapter would have a hard time forgetting things. Encoding information efficiently, practicing deep processing, relying on rehearsal strategies, and so on, should make memories resistant to fading. Of course many people do have excellent memories, and that can be a real advantage for them. But as it turns out, forgetting is also adaptive: We need to forget some things if we wish to remember efficiently. Piling up facts without distinguishing the important from the trivial is just confusing. Nonetheless, most of us forget more than we want to and would like to know why. Let's take a look at some of the reasons why information gets lost over time by focusing on the major explanations for forgetting.

Mechanisms of Forgetting

LO 10.6.A Summarize the processes of decay, replacement, interference, and cue-dependent forgetting, and explain how each contributes to our understanding of forgetting.

In the early days of psychology, in an effort to measure pure memory loss independent of personal experience, Hermann Ebbinghaus (1885/1913) memorized long lists of nonsense syllables—such as *bok*, *waf*, or *ged*—and then tested his retention over a period of several weeks. Most of his forgetting occurred soon after the initial learning and then leveled off (see Figure 10.8a). Generations of psychologists adopted Ebbinghaus's method of studying memory, but his method did not tell them much about the kinds of memories that people care about most.

A century later, Marigold Linton decided to find out how people forget real events rather than nonsense syllables. Like Ebbinghaus, she used herself as a subject, but she charted the curve of forgetting over years rather than days. Every day for 12 years she recorded on a 4- by 6-inch card two or more things that had happened to her that day. Eventually, she accumulated a catalog of thousands of discrete events, both trivial ("I have dinner at the Canton Kitchen: delicious lobster dish") and significant ("I land at Orly Airport in Paris"). Once a month, she took a random sampling of all the cards accumulated to that point, noted whether she could remember the events on them, and tried to date the events. Linton (1978) expected the kind of rapid forgetting reported by Ebbinghaus. Instead, as you can see in Figure 10.8b, she found that long-term forgetting was slower and proceeded at a much more constant pace, as details gradually dropped out of her memories.

Figure 10.8 Two Kinds of Forgetting Curves

Hermann Ebbinghaus, who tested his own memory for nonsense syllables, found that his forgetting was rapid at first and then tapered off (a). In contrast, when Marigold Linton tested her own memory for personal events over a period of several years, her retention was excellent at first, but then it fell off at a gradual but steady rate (b).

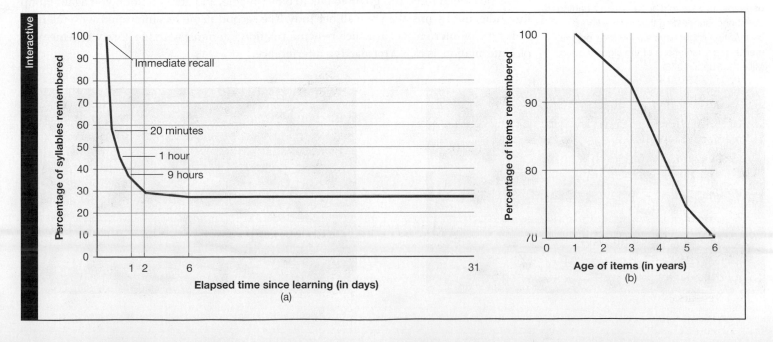

Motor skills, which are stored as procedural memories, can last a lifetime; they rarely decay.

decay theory

The theory that information in memory eventually disappears if it is not accessed; it applies better to short-term than to long-term memory.

retroactive interference

Forgetting that occurs when recently learned material interferes with the ability to remember similar material stored previously.

Figure 10.9 The Stop-Sign Study

When people who saw a car with a yield sign (left) were later asked if they had seen "the stop sign" (a misleading question), many said they had. Similarly, when those shown a stop sign were asked if they had seen "the yield sign," many said yes. These false memories persisted even after the participants were told about the misleading questions, suggesting that misleading information might have erased their original mental representations of the signs (Loftus, Miller, & Burns, 1978).

Of course, some memories, especially those that mark important transitions, are more memorable than others. But why did Marigold Linton, like the rest of us, forget so many details? Psychologists have proposed four mechanisms to account for forgetting: decay, replacement of old memories by new ones, interference, and cue-dependent forgetting.

DECAY   One commonsense view, the **decay theory**, holds that memories simply fade with time if they are not accessed now and then. We have already seen that decay occurs in sensory memory and that it occurs in short-term memory as well unless we keep rehearsing the material. However, the mere passage of time does not account so well for forgetting in long-term memory. People commonly forget things that happened only yesterday while remembering events from many years ago. Indeed, some memories, both procedural and declarative, can last a lifetime. If you learned to swim as a child, you will still know how to swim at age 30, even if you have not been in a pool or lake for 22 years. We are also happy to report that some school lessons have great staying power. In one study, people did well on a Spanish test some 50 years after taking Spanish in high school, even though most had hardly used Spanish at all in the intervening decades (Bahrick, 1984). Decay alone cannot entirely explain lapses in long-term memory.

REPLACEMENT   Another theory holds that new information entering memory can wipe out old information, just as writing over the contents of a hard drive will obliterate the original material. In a study supporting this view, researchers showed people slides of a traffic accident and used leading questions to get them to think that they had seen a stop sign when they had really seen a yield sign, or vice versa (see Figure 10.9). People in a control group who were not misled in this way were able to identify the sign they had actually seen. Later, all the participants were told the purpose of the study and were asked to guess whether they had been misled. Almost all of those who had been misled continued to insist that they had *really, truly* saw the sign whose existence had been planted in their minds (Loftus, Miller, & Burns, 1978). The researchers interpreted this finding to mean that the subjects had not just been trying to please them and that people's original perceptions had been erased by the misleading information.

INTERFERENCE   A third theory holds that forgetting occurs because similar items of information interfere with one another in either storage or retrieval; the information may get into memory and stay there, but it becomes confused with other information. Such interference, which occurs in both short- and long-term memory, is especially common when you have to recall isolated facts such as names, addresses, passwords, and area codes.

Suppose you are at a party and you meet someone named Julie. A little later you meet someone named Judy. You go on to talk to other people, and after an hour, you again bump into Julie, but by mistake you call her Judy. The second name has interfered with the first. This type of interference, in which new information interferes with the ability to remember old information, is called **retroactive interference**.

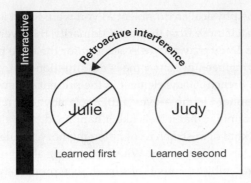

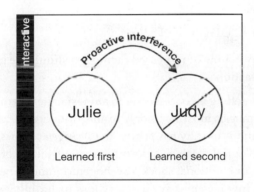

Because new information is constantly entering memory, we are all vulnerable to the effects of retroactive interference, or at least most of us are. H. M. was an exception; his memories of childhood and adolescence were unusually detailed, clear, and unchanging. H. M. could remember actors who were famous when he was a child, the films they were in, and who their costars had been. He also knew the names of friends from the second grade. Presumably, these early declarative memories were not subject to interference from memories acquired after the operation, for the simple reason that H. M. had not acquired any new memories.

Interference also works in the opposite direction. Old information (such as the foreign language you learned in high school) may interfere with the ability to remember current information (such as the new language you are trying to learn now). This type of interference is called **proactive interference**.

proactive interference
Forgetting that occurs when previously stored material interferes with the ability to remember similar, more recently learned material.

cue-dependent forgetting
The inability to retrieve information stored in memory because of insufficient cues for recall.

Over a period of weeks, months, and years, proactive interference may cause more forgetting than retroactive interference does because we have stored up so much information that can potentially interfere with anything new.

CUE-DEPENDENT FORGETTING   Often, when we need to remember, we rely on *retrieval cues*, items of information that can help us find the specific information we're looking for. If you are trying to remember the last name of an actor you saw in an old film, it might help to know the person's first name or a movie the actor starred in.

When we lack retrieval cues, we may feel as if we are lost in the mind's library. In long-term memory, this type of memory failure, called **cue-dependent forgetting**, may be the most common type of all. Willem Wagenaar (1986), who, like Marigold Linton, recorded critical details about events in his life, found that within a year he had forgotten 20 percent of those details; after 5 years, he had forgotten 60 percent. Yet when he gathered cues from witnesses about 10 events that he thought he had forgotten, he was able to recall something about all 10, which suggests that some of his forgetting was cue dependent.

Cues that were present when you learned a new fact or had an experience are apt to be especially useful later as retrieval aids. That may explain why remembering is often easier

state-dependent memory

The tendency to remember something when the rememberer is in the same physical or mental state as during the original learning or experience.

mood-congruent memory

The tendency to remember experiences that are consistent with one's current mood and overlook or forget experiences that are not.

amnesia

The partial or complete loss of memory for important personal information.

repression

In psychoanalytic theory, the selective, involuntary pushing of threatening or upsetting information into the unconscious.

when you are in the same physical environment as you were when an event occurred: Cues in the present context match those from the past. Ordinarily, this overlap helps us remember the past more accurately. But it may also help account for the eerie phenomenon of *déjà vu*, the fleeting sense of having been in *exactly* the same situation that you are in now (*déjà vu* means "already seen" in French). Some element in the present situation, familiar from some other context that you cannot identify—even a dream, a novel, or a movie—may make the entire situation seem so familiar that it feels like it happened before (Brown, 2004). In other words, déjà vu may be a kind of mistaken recognition memory. Similar feelings of familiarity can actually be produced in the laboratory. When something about newly presented words, shapes, or photographs resembles elements of stimuli seen previously, people report that the new words, shapes, or photographs seem familiar even though they can't recall the original ones (Cleary, 2008).

In everyday situations, your mental or physical state may act as a retrieval cue, evoking a **state-dependent memory**. If you were afraid or angry at the time of an event, you may remember that event best when you are once again in the same emotional state (Lang et al., 2001). Your memories can also be biased by whether or not your current mood is consistent with the emotional nature of the material you are trying to remember, a phenomenon known as **mood-congruent memory** (Bower & Forgas, 2000; Buchanan, 2007; Fitzgerald et al., 2011). You are more likely to remember happy events, and forget or ignore unhappy ones, when you are feeling happy than when you are feeling sad. Likewise, you are apt to remember unhappy events better and remember more of them when you are feeling unhappy, which in turn creates a vicious cycle. The more unhappy memories you recall, the more depressed you feel, and the more depressed you feel, the more unhappy memories you recall—so you stay stuck in your depression and make it even worse (Gaddy & Ingram, 2014; Joormann & Gotlib, 2007).

The Repression Controversy

LO 10.6.B Explain why claims of repressed memories should be greeted with a strong skeptical reaction.

A final perspective on forgetting is concerned with **amnesia**, the loss of memory for important personal information. Amnesia most commonly results from organic conditions such as brain disease or head injury, and is usually temporary. In *psychogenic amnesia*, however, the causes of forgetting are psychological, such as a need to escape feelings of embarrassment, guilt, shame, disappointment, or emotional shock. Psychogenic amnesia begins immediately after the precipitating event, involves massive memory loss including loss of personal identity, and usually ends suddenly, after just a few weeks. Despite its frequent portrayal in films and novels, it is quite rare in real life (McNally, 2003).

Psychologists generally accept the notion of psychogenic amnesia. *Traumatic amnesia*, however, is far more controversial. Traumatic amnesia allegedly involves the burying of specific traumatic events for a long period of time, often for many years. When the memory returns, it is supposedly immune to the usual processes of distortion and confabulation, and is recalled with perfect accuracy. The notion of traumatic amnesia originated with the psychoanalytic theory of Sigmund Freud, who argued that the mind defends itself from unwelcome and upsetting memories through the mechanism of **repression**, the involuntary pushing of threatening or upsetting information into the unconscious.

Most memory researchers reject the argument that a special unconscious mechanism called "repression" is necessary to explain either psychogenic or traumatic amnesia (Rofé, 2008). Richard McNally (2003) reviewed the experimental and clinical evidence and concluded, "The notion that the mind protects itself by repressing or dissociating memories of trauma, rendering them inaccessible to awareness, is a piece of psychiatric folklore devoid of convincing empirical support." The problem for most people who have suffered disturbing experiences is not that they cannot remember, but rather that they cannot forget: The memories keep intruding. There is no case on record of anyone who has repressed the memory of being in a concentration camp, being in combat, or being the victim of an earthquake or a terrorist attack, although details of even these horrible experiences are subject to distortion and fading over time, as are all memories.

Furthermore, repression is hard to distinguish from normal forgetting. People who seem to forget disturbing experiences could be intentionally keeping themselves from retrieving their painful memories by distracting themselves whenever a memory is reactivated. Or they may be focusing consciously on positive memories instead. Perhaps, understandably, they are not rehearsing unhappy memories, so those memories fade with time. Perhaps they are simply avoiding the retrieval cues that would evoke the memories. But a reluctance to think about an upsetting experience is not the same as an *inability* to remember it (McNally, 2003).

The debate over traumatic amnesia and repression erupted into the public arena in the 1990s, when claims of recovered memories of sexual abuse began to appear. Many women and some men came to believe, during psychotherapy, that they could recall long-buried memories of having been sexually victimized for many years, often in bizarre ways. For therapists who accepted the notion of repression, such claims were entirely believable (Brown, Scheflin, & Whitfield, 1999; Herman, 1992). But most researchers today believe that almost all of these memories were false, having been evoked by therapists who were unaware of the research we described earlier on the power of suggestion and the dangers of confabulation (Lindsay & Read, 1994; Lynn et al., 2015; McNally, 2003; Schacter, 2001). By asking leading questions, and by encouraging clients to construct vivid images of abuse, revisit those images frequently, and focus on emotional aspects of the images, such therapists unwittingly set up the very conditions that encourage confabulation and false memories.

Since the 1990s, accusations based on "recovered memories" have steadily declined and many accusers have reconciled with their families (McHugh et al., 2004). Yet the concept of repression lingers on. Many of its original proponents have turned to the term "dissociation" to account for memory failures in traumatized individuals, the idea being that upsetting memories are split off (dissociated) from everyday consciousness. But reviews of the research have found no good evidence that early trauma causes such dissociation (Giesbrecht et al., 2008; Huntjens, Verschuere, & McNally, 2012).

Of course, it is obviously possible for someone to forget a single unhappy or deeply unpleasant experience and not recall it for years, just as going back to your elementary school might trigger a memory of the time that you did something embarrassing in front of your whole class. How then should we respond to an individual's claim to have recovered memories of years of traumatic experiences that were previously "repressed"? How can we distinguish true memories from false ones?

Clearly, a person's recollections are likely to be trustworthy if corroborating evidence is available, such as medical records, police or school reports, or the accounts of other people who had been present at the time. But in the absence of supporting evidence, we may have to tolerate uncertainty because a person might have a detailed, emotionally rich "memory" that feels completely real but that has been unintentionally confabulated (Bernstein & Loftus, 2009). In such cases, it is important to consider the content of the recovered memory and how it was recovered.

Thus, given what we know about memory, we should be skeptical if the person says that he or she has memories from the first year or two of life; as we will see in the next section, this is not possible, physiologically or cognitively. We should be skeptical if, over time, the person's memories become more and more implausible; for instance, the person says that sexual abuse continued day and night for 15 years without ever being remembered and without anyone else in the household ever noticing anything amiss. We should also be skeptical if a person suddenly recovers a traumatic memory as a result of therapy or after hearing about supposed cases of recovered memory in the news or reading about one in a best-selling autobiography. And we should hear alarm bells go off if a therapist used suggestive techniques—such as hypnosis, dream analysis, "age regression," guided imagery, and leading questions—to "recover" the memories (Lynn et al., 2015) These techniques are all known to increase confabulation.

childhood amnesia

The inability to remember events and experiences that occurred during the first 2 or 3 years of life.

Childhood Amnesia: The Missing Years

LO 10.6.C   Discuss three reasons why childhood amnesia is likely to take place.

A curious aspect of autobiographical memory is that most adults cannot recall any events from earlier than age 2; and even after that, memories are sketchy at best until about age 6 (Jack & Hayne, 2010). A few people can vaguely recall significant events that occurred when they were as young as 2 years old, such as the birth of a sibling, but not earlier ones (Fivush & Nelson, 2004; Usher & Neisser, 1993). As adults, we cannot remember taking our first steps, or uttering our first halting sentences. We are victims of **childhood amnesia** (sometimes called *infantile amnesia*).

Childhood amnesia is disturbing to many people, so disturbing that some adamantly deny it, claiming to remember events from the second or even the first year of life. But like other false memories, these are merely reconstructions based on photographs, family stories, and imagination. The "remembered" event may not even have taken place. Swiss psychologist Jean Piaget (1952) once reported a memory of nearly being kidnapped at the age of 2. Piaget remembered sitting in his pram, watching his nurse as she bravely defended him from the kidnapper. He remembered the scratches she received on her face. He remembered a police officer with a short cloak and white baton who finally chased the kidnapper away. But when Piaget was 15, his nurse wrote to his parents confessing that she had made up the entire story. Piaget noted, "I therefore must have heard, as a child, the account of this story . . . and projected it into the past in the form of a visual memory, which was a memory of a memory, but false."

Of course, we all retain procedural memories from the toddler stage, when we first learned to use a fork, drink from a cup, and pull a wagon. We also retain semantic memories acquired early in life: the rules of counting, the names of people and things, knowledge about objects in the world, words and meanings. Moreover, toddlers who are only 1 to 2 years old often reveal nonverbally that they remember past experiences (e.g., by imitating something they saw earlier); and some 4-year-olds can remember experiences that occurred before age 2½ (Bauer, 2002; McDonough & Mandler, 1994; Tustin & Hayne, 2010). What young children do not do well is encode and retain their early episodic memories—memories of particular events—and carry them into later childhood or adulthood. They cannot start doing this consistently until about age 4½ (Fivush & Nelson, 2004).

Freud thought that childhood amnesia was a special case of repression, but memory researchers today think that repression has nothing to do with it, and they point to better explanations (Bauer, 2015):

1. **Brain development.** The prefrontal cortex, and other parts of the brain involved in the formation or storage of events, are not well developed until a few years after birth (McKee & Squire, 1993; Newcombe, Lloyd, & Balcomb, 2012). In addition, the brains of infants and toddlers are busily attending to all the new experiences of life, but this very fact makes it difficult for them to focus on just one event and shut out everything else that's going on—the kind of focus necessary for encoding and remembering (Gopnik, 2009).

2. **Cognitive development.** Before you can carry memories about yourself with you into adulthood, you have to have a self to remember. The emergence of a self-concept usually does not take place before age 2 (Howe, Courage, & Peterson, 1994). In addition, the cognitive schemas used by preschoolers are very different from those used by older children and adults. Only after acquiring language and starting school do children form schemas that contain the information and cues necessary for recalling earlier experiences (Howe, 2000). Young children's limited vocabularies and language skills also prevent them from narrating some aspects of an experience to themselves or others. Later, after their linguistic abilities have matured, they still cannot use those abilities to recall earlier,

This infant, whose leg is attached by a string to a colorful mobile, will learn within minutes to make the mobile move by kicking it. She may still remember the trick a week later, an example of procedural memory (Rovee-Collier, 1993). However, when she is older, she will not remember the experience itself; she will fall victim to childhood amnesia.

preverbal memories because those memories were not encoded linguistically (Simcock & Hayne, 2002).

3. **Social development.** Preschoolers have not yet mastered the social conventions for reporting events, nor have they learned what is important to others. As a result, they focus on the routine aspects of an experience rather than the distinctive ones that will provide retrieval cues later, and they encode their experiences far less elaborately than adults do. Instead, they tend to rely on adults' questions to provide retrieval cues ("Where did we go for breakfast?" or "Who did you go trick-or-treating with?"). This dependency on adults may prevent them from building up a stable core of remembered material that will be available later on (Fivush & Nelson, 2005). But as children get older, their conversations with parents help them develop their own autobiographical memories, and thus play an important role in ending childhood amnesia (Reese, Jack, & White, 2010).

Nonetheless, our first memories, even when they are not accurate, may provide useful insights into our personalities, current concerns, ambitions, and attitudes toward life. What are *your* first memories—or, at least, what do you think they are? What might they tell you about yourself?

JOURNAL PROMPT 10.6

Thinking Critically—Consider Other Interpretations: How should critical thinkers evaluate someone's claim that they repressed memories of bizarre, traumatic experiences that went on for years, and only remembered what happened decades later, in therapy? What other explanations can account for these apparent memories?

Quiz for Module 10.6

1. During the late 1800s Hermann Ebbinghaus memorized long lists of nonsense syllables (such as *gek, bof,* or *jeh*) and tested his recall over varying time delays. According to his results, when did the greatest amount of forgetting occur?

    a. Within the first 2 days after the initial learning took place.

    b. After 1 week had elapsed since the initial learning took place.

    c. After 3 weeks had elapsed since the initial learning took place.

    d. After 1 month had elapsed since the initial learning took place.

2. Alan learned to play the entire Led Zeppelin catalog on the guitar when he was in high school; pretty much every song, for better or worse, with fairly good results. As time passed and he pursued other musical interests, he stopped playing those songs. Decades later, when trying to recall how to play one of those tunes, he found that he was thoroughly stumped, and couldn't even remember where to begin. What theory of forgetting would predict this kind of outcome?

    a. Repression

    b. Decay

    c. Proactive interference

    d. Mood-congruent forgetting

3. When new information interferes with the ability to remember old information, _____ interference has taken place.

    a. Retrogressive

    b. Proactive

    c. Retroactive

    d. Progressive

4. Which of these notions would be greeted with the most skepticism by psychological scientists?

    a. Retroactive interference

    b. Psychogenic amnesia

    c. Traumatic amnesia

    d. Mood-congruent memory

5. Which type of memory is not encoded very well in children under the age of 4?

    a. Semantic memory

    b. Episodic memory

    c. Procedural memory

    d. Reactive memory

Taking Psychology with You

Memory and Narrative: The Stories of Our Lives

Communications researcher George Gerbner observed that human beings are unique because we are the only animal that tells stories—and lives by the stories we tell. This view of human beings as the "storytelling animal" has had a huge impact in cognitive psychology. The *narratives* we compose to simplify and make sense of our lives have a profound influence on our plans, memories, love affairs, hatreds, ambitions, and dreams.

Thus we say, "I have no academic motivation because I flunked the third grade." We say, "Let me tell you the story of how we fell in love." We say, "When you hear what happened, you'll understand why I felt entitled to take such cold-hearted revenge." These stories are not necessarily fictions; rather, they are attempts to organize and give meaning to the events of our lives. But because these narratives rely heavily on memory, and because memories are reconstructed and are constantly shifting in response to current needs, beliefs, and experiences, our autobiographies are also, to some degree, works of interpretation and imagination. Adult memories thus reveal as much about the present as they do about the past.

When you construct a narrative about an incident in your life, you have many choices about how to do it. The spin you put on a story depends on who the audience is; you are apt to put in, leave out, understate, and embellish different things depending on whether you are telling about an event in your life to a therapist, your boss, or friends on Facebook. Your story is also influenced by your purpose in relating it: to convey facts, entertain, or elicit sympathy. As a result of these influences, distortions are apt to creep in, even when you think you are being accurate. And after those distortions are part of

the story, they are likely to become part of your memory of the events themselves (Marsh & Tversky, 2004).

Your culture also affects how you encode and tell your story. American college students live in a culture that emphasizes individuality, personal feelings, and self-expression. Their earliest childhood memories reflect that fact: They tend to report lengthy, emotionally elaborate memories of events, memories that focus on—who else?—themselves. In contrast, Chinese students, who live in a culture that emphasizes group harmony, social roles, and personal humility, tend to report early memories of family or neighborhood activities, conflicts with friends or relatives that were resolved, and emotionally neutral events (Wang, 2008).

After you have formulated a story's central theme ("My father never liked us"; "My partner was always competing with me"), that theme may then serve as a cognitive schema that guides what you remember and what you forget (Mather, Shafir, & Johnson, 2000). Teenagers who have strong and secure attachments to their mothers remember previous quarrels with their moms as being less intense and conflicted than they reported at the time, whereas teenagers who have more ambivalent and insecure attachments remember such quarrels as being worse than they were (Feeney & Cassidy, 2003). A story's theme may also influence our judgments of events and people in the present. If you have a fight with your lover, the central theme in your story about the fight might be negative ("He was a jerk") or neutral ("It was a mutual misunderstanding"). This theme may bias you to blame or forgive your partner long after you have forgotten what the conflict was about (McGregor & Holmes, 1999). You can see that the spin you give a story is critical, so be careful about the stories you tell!

Shared Writing Prompt

What's your story? We don't mean that in a snotty, challenging sense, but rather in a literal (and literary) sense. Take some time to write no more than three paragraphs to construct the narrative of your life. A list of details is not what you're after. Instead, focus on identifying some major themes or major events that have shaped you into the person you are today.

Summary

Reconstructing the Past

LO 10.1.A   Explain why the workings of memory are more reconstructive than people imagine them to be.

Unlike a digital recorder or video camera, human memory is highly selective and is *reconstructive*: People add, delete, and change elements in ways that help them make sense of information and events. They often experience *source misattribution*, the

inability to distinguish information stored during an event from information added later. Even vivid *flashbulb memories* tend to become less accurate or complete over time.

LO 10.1.B   Describe three conditions under which confabulation is especially likely to occur.

Because memory is so often reconstructive, it is subject to *confabulation*, the confusion of imagined events with actual ones.

Confabulation is especially likely when people have thought, heard, or told others about the imagined event many times and thus experience *imagination inflation*, the image of the event contains many details, or the event is easy to imagine.

Memory and the Power of Suggestion

LO 10.1.C   Summarize the evidence indicating that eyewitness testimony can be susceptible to memory errors.

The reconstructive nature of memory also makes memory vulnerable to suggestion. Eyewitness testimony is especially vulnerable to error when the suspect's ethnicity differs from that of the witness, when leading questions are put to witnesses, or when witnesses are given misleading information.

LO 10.1.D   Explain the conditions under which children might provide reliable versus unreliable eyewitness testimony.

Like adults, children often remember the essential aspects of an event accurately but can also be suggestible, especially when responding to biased interviewing by adults—when they are asked questions that blur the line between fantasy and reality, are asked leading questions, are told what "other kids" had supposedly said, and are praised for making false allegations.

In Pursuit of Memory

LO 10.2.A   Distinguish between recall and recognition tasks in explicit memory, and distinguish between priming and relearning in implicit memory.

The ability to remember depends in part on the type of performance called for. In tests of *explicit memory* (conscious recollection), *recognition* is usually better than *recall*. In tests of *implicit memory*, which is measured by indirect methods such as *priming* and the *relearning method*, past experiences may affect current thoughts or actions even when these experiences are not consciously remembered.

LO 10.2.B   Describe the basic characteristics of three memory systems according to the information-processing model, and note the challenges to this view proposed by parallel distributed processing.

In *information-processing models*, memory involves the *encoding*, *storage*, and *retrieval* of information. The *three-box model* proposes three interacting systems: the sensory register, short-term memory, and long-term memory. Some cognitive scientists prefer a *parallel distributed processing (PDP)* or *connectionist* model, which represents knowledge as connections among numerous interacting processing units, distributed in a vast network and all operating in parallel.

The Three-Box Model of Memory

LO 10.3.A   Explain the functions, duration, and location of the sensory registers in the three-box model of memory.

In the three-box model, incoming sensory information makes a brief stop in the *sensory register*, which momentarily retains it in the form of sensory images.

LO 10.3.B   Explain the functions and duration of short-term memory, and contrast the *leaky bucket* and *working memory* approaches to understanding this "box" of memory.

Short-term memory (STM) retains new information for up to 30 seconds (unless rehearsal takes place). The capacity of STM is extremely limited but can be extended if information is organized into larger units by *chunking*. Early models of STM portrayed it mainly as a bin for the temporary storage of information, but many models now envision it as a part of a more general *working-memory* system. Working memory permits us to control attention, resist distraction, and therefore maintain information in an active, accessible state.

LO 10.3.C   Describe semantic categories and four forms of long-term memory, and explain how *primacy* and *recency* illustrate the serial-position effect in transferring information from short-term to long-term memory.

Long-term memory (LTM) contains an enormous amount of information that must be organized to make it manageable. Words (or the concepts they represent) are often organized by semantic categories. Research on *tip-of-the-tongue (TOT) states* shows that words are also indexed in terms of sound and form. Memories can take different forms, such as *procedural* or *declarative*, and within declarative memories, either *semantic* or *episodic*. The three-box model is often invoked to explain the *serial-position effect* in memory, but although it can explain the *primacy effect*, it cannot explain why a *recency effect* sometimes occurs after a considerable delay.

The Biology of Memory

LO 10.4.A   Outline the process of long-term potentiation in the formation of memories.

Short-term memory involves temporary changes within neurons that alter their ability to release neurotransmitters, whereas long-term memory involves lasting structural changes in neurons and synapses. *Long-term potentiation*, an increase in the strength of synaptic responsiveness, seems to be an important mechanism of long-term memory. Neural changes associated with long-term potentiation take time to develop, which helps explain why long-term memories require a period of *consolidation*.

LO 10.4.B   Evaluate the evidence that memories are not stored in any one "place" in the brain.

The amygdala is involved in the formation, consolidation, and retrieval of emotional memories. Areas of the frontal lobes are especially active during short-term and working-memory tasks. The prefrontal cortex and parts of the temporal lobes are involved in the efficient encoding of words and pictures. The hippocampus plays a critical role in the formation and retrieval of long-term declarative memories. Other areas, such as the cerebellum, are crucial for the formation of procedural memories. Studies of patients with amnesia suggest that different brain systems are active during explicit and implicit memory tasks. The long-term storage of declarative memories possibly takes place in cortical areas that were active during the original perception of the information or event. The various components of a memory are probably stored at different sites, with all of these sites participating in the representation of the event as a whole.

LO 10.4.C Summarize the evidence that memory can be influenced by emotion and hormonal levels.

Hormones released by the adrenal glands during stress or emotional arousal, including epinephrine and norepinephrine, enhance memory. These adrenal hormones cause the level of glucose to rise in the bloodstream, and glucose may enhance memory directly or by altering the effects of neurotransmitters.

How We Remember

LO 10.5.A Describe some major strategies that contribute to memory retention, and give an example of each.

Some kinds of information, such as material in a college course, require *effortful*, as opposed to automatic, encoding. Rehearsal of information keeps it in short-term memory and increases the chances of long-term retention. *Elaborative rehearsal* is more likely to result in transfer to long-term memory than is *maintenance rehearsal*, and *deep processing* is usually a more effective retention strategy than *shallow processing*. *Retrieval practice* is necessary if a memory is going to be consolidated, and therefore last and be available for a long time.

Why We Forget

LO 10.6.A Summarize the processes of decay, replacement, interference, and cue-dependent forgetting, and explain how each contributes to our understanding of forgetting.

Forgetting can occur for several reasons. Information in sensory and short-term memory appears to *decay* if it does not receive further processing. New information may erase and replace old information in long-term memory. *Proactive* and *retroactive interference* may take place. *Cue-dependent forgetting* may occur when *retrieval cues* are inadequate. The most effective retrieval cues are those that were present at the time of the initial experience. A person's mental or physical state may act as a retrieval cue, evoking a *state-dependent memory*. We tend to remember best those events that are congruent with our current mood (*mood-congruent memory*).

LO 10.6.B Explain why claims of repressed memories should be greeted with a strong skeptical reaction.

Amnesia, the forgetting of important personal information, usually occurs because of disease or injury to the brain. *Psychogenic amnesia*, which involves a loss of personal identity and has psychological causes, is rare. *Traumatic amnesia*, which allegedly involves the forgetting of specific traumatic events for long periods of time, is highly controversial, as is *repression*, the psychodynamic explanation of traumatic amnesia. Because these concepts lack good empirical support, psychological scientists are skeptical about their validity and about the accuracy of "recovered memories."

LO 10.6.C Discuss three reasons why childhood amnesia is likely to take place.

Most people cannot recall any events from earlier than the age of 2. The reasons for such *childhood amnesia* include the immaturity of certain brain structures, making it difficult for very young children to focus attention, encode, and remember; cognitive factors such as immature cognitive schemas, lack of linguistic skills, and lack of a self-concept; and lack of knowledge of social conventions for encoding and reporting events.

Chapter 10 Quiz

1. The inability to distinguish an actual memory from information gathered through other sources is called
   a. Persistent allocation
   b. Source confabulation
   c. Source disruption
   d. Source misattribution

2. Confabulated memories
   a. Are the result of motivated lying on the part of memory-implanters
   b. Are the result of motivated lying on the part of the memory-holder
   c. Can be just as strong, vivid, and retained for long periods of time as actual memories
   d. Decay swiftly over time, unlike actual memories, which decay slowly over time

3. The detective instructed the eyewitness, "Tell me which of the African American men you're about to see in the lineup stole your purse. They all have past criminal records for one offense or another." The witness recalled that the perpetrator had dark skin, but he might have been African American, Brazilian, Sri Lankan, or Haitian. Based on what you know about eyewitness identification, what is the witness likely to do?
   a. Tell the detective that her leading questions have tainted the identification process.
   b. Recognize that the men in the lineup might not have committed the crime.
   c. Ask the detective to display photographs of a much larger sample of suspects, one at a time.
   d. Misidentify one of the men in the lineup as the perpetrator.

4. A kindergartener is asked by a law-enforcement official, "Do you remember the time when your teacher slapped a student from another class because the boy walked into your room by accident and disrupted the lesson?" Although there is scant evidence that this event ever happened, what is the kindergartner likely to say in response?

   a. "Yes, I remember that."

   b. "That never happened."

   c. "That happened in my sister's class."

   d. "It was a girl, not a boy."

5. Under most circumstances, which is an easier memory-retrieval task to perform?

   a. Rehearsal

   b. Recall

   c. Encoding

   d. Recognition

6. Which of the following is a contemporary challenge to the three-box model of memory?

   a. Information-processing model

   b. Parallel distributed processing

   c. Mind-as-sieve hypothesis

   d. Ebbinghaus-Bartlett theory

7. Most estimates of the time information can stay in the auditory sensory register put the duration at about

   a. 1 minute

   b. 10 seconds

   c. 30 seconds

   d. 2 seconds

8. How does the concept of working memory differ from traditional views of short-term memory?

   a. The working-memory model addresses implicit forms of memory, whereas traditional models focus only on a hierarchy of retrieval cues.

   b. The working-memory model places primary importance on the value of chunking; traditional views of short-term memory do not consider this type of operation.

   c. The working-memory model includes short-term memory storage and the operations performed on information as it gets retrieved from long-term memory.

   d. The working-memory model uses a "leaky bucket" metaphor to describe short-term memory, whereas traditional notions think of it as a perforated box.

9. Carly remembers that St. Paul is the capital of Minnesota. Shannon remembers that she lived in St. Paul when she was 9 years old. Carly is demonstrating _____ memory, whereas Shannon is demonstrating _____ memory.

   a. Semantic / episodic

   b. Episodic / semantic

   c. Semantic / procedural

   d. Procedural / semantic

10. "Cells that fire together, wire together." This expression (not taken literally) might describe which process that takes place among hippocampal cells during learning and memory formation?

    a. Stochastic synchronization

    b. Refractory disinhibition

    c. Bilateral continuity

    d. Long-term potentiation

11. A kind of "memory filing cabinet," important for the formation and retrieval of memories that might be stored in various locations throughout the brain, is the

    a. Fissure of Rolando

    b. Hippocampus

    c. Parietal lobe

    d. Corpus callosum

12. Which hormones, released by the adrenal glands, can enhance memory during appropriate circumstances?

    a. Epinephrine and norepinephrine

    b. Glutamate and GABA

    c. Acetylcholine and testosterone

    d. Dopamine and serotonin

13. Madison wants to remember the telephone number of the man she just met, so she repeats it over and over to keep it in short-term memory: 555-3825 . . . 555-3825 . . . 555-3825. What rehearsal strategy is Madison using?

    a. Deep processing

    b. Elaborative rehearsal

    c. Maintenance rehearsal

    d. Effortful encoding

14. Cue-dependent forgetting occurs when

    a. We lack retrieval cues to call up appropriate information from memory

    b. Recognition memory is faster than recall memory

    c. Proactive interference is present, but not when retroactive interference is present

    d. Damage to the hippocampus makes memory storage difficult

15. The proposed mechanism that produces traumatic amnesia is _____; like the concept of traumatic amnesia itself, this mechanism is also controversial.

    a. Suppression

    b. Regression

    c. Projection

    d. Repression

16. Which of the following is *not* a compelling explanation for childhood amnesia?

   a. The amygdala and the hippocampus synchronize with one another to encode episodic memories, and both structures take approximately 3 years to develop to maturity.

   b. Social conventions for encoding, reporting, and retrieving information take time to develop; young children lack the social development necessary for effective memory development.

   c. Children lack a well-developed self-schema and other cognitive schemas through which to interpret, categorize, and mentally "file" events that happen in their early years.

   d. The prefrontal cortex is involved in memory formation and storage, but the prefrontal cortex takes years to develop.

Answers to the Get Involved exercises on pages 349 and 350: Rudolph's eight friends were Dasher, Dancer, Prancer, Vixen, Comet, Cupid, Donner, and Blitzen.

Answer to the Get Involved exercise on page 365: The real penny is the left one in the bottom row.

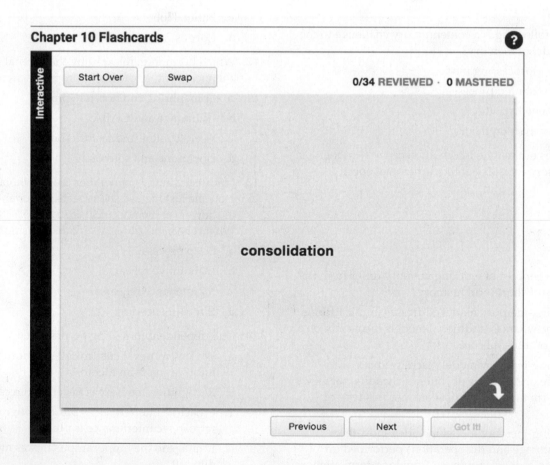

Chapter 11
Emotion, Stress, and Health

◀ Listen to the Audio

Learning Objectives

LO 11.1.A Explain the components that define an emotion, list the emotions that have a universal facial expression, and describe some of the limits affecting the ability to decode facial expressions of emotion.

LO 11.1.B Discuss the brain structures involved in the experience of emotions, explain what mirror neurons do, and describe the primary chemicals involved in emotional experience.

LO 11.1.C Summarize the basic research findings indicating that cognitive appraisal plays a role in emotional experience.

LO 11.2.A Describe the ways emotional experience can differ across cultures, in terms of concepts, language, and expectations.

LO 11.2.B Explain how display rules and emotion work influence the communication of emotion in a social and cultural context.

LO 11.2.C Explain sex differences that appear to exist in emotional experience, and comment on the complex reasons for these differences.

LO 11.3.A Describe the three phases of the general adaptation syndrome, and discuss how modern conceptualizations of the HPA axis and psychoneuroimmunology extend those ideas.

LO 11.3.B Describe some of the contributions to health that result from optimism, conscientiousness, and a sense of control.

LO 11.4.A Summarize the evidence that negative emotions (such as hostility and depression) detract from health.

LO 11.4.B Summarize the evidence that positive emotions contribute to health.

LO 11.4.C Discuss how confession, forgiveness, and other forms of "letting grievances go" contribute to health benefits.

LO 11.5.A Discuss how emotion-focused coping and problem-focused coping contribute to the problem-solving approach to dealing with stress.

LO 11.5.B Describe three effective coping strategies that rely on rethinking the stressful problem at hand, and give an example of each.

LO 11.5.C Discuss the ways in which friends can help or hinder successful coping efforts.

Ask questions . . . be willing to wonder

Do people everywhere in the world feel the same emotions?

Do we have any control over our emotions or do they just "come out of nowhere"?

Does stress increase your chances of getting sick?

When life hands you a lemon of a problem, how can you make lemonade?

"I think he should suffer."

"Without a doubt, this was what I was definitely hoping for."

"I wasn't disappointed either way."

"I just wish he'd showed some kind of emotion."

These comments were made by Boston residents in a recent *Boston Globe* article, reflecting on the fate of Dzhokhar Tsarnaev, who was sentenced to death in 2015 for planting bombs at the 2013 Boston Marathon. Aided by his brother Tamerlan, Tsarnaev was responsible for killing three people and wounding over 250 others. During the days in which they eluded capture, the brothers also murdered an MIT police officer, carjacked a Mercedes, and engaged law enforcement in a shootout that involved a wounded Dzhokhar running over Tamerlan with the stolen SUV. After a tense manhunt, Tsarnaev was eventually captured, tried, and convicted of conspiring to use a weapon of mass destruction.

This is a story that's defined by strong emotions. Think of how the brothers' actions were characterized: Terrorism. Few emotion terms carry as much weight as *terror*, and few among us would say we can't imagine what that feels like. The Tsarnaev brothers had anger and hatred in their hearts to guide their actions, and

Boston residents suffered fear and anxiety during the bombing and subsequent manhunt. The sadness and anguish felt by the wounded and the relatives of the victims will surely take time to diminish, yet for many, there was joy and satisfaction that justice was eventually served.

This is also a story of stress and coping. The thousands of law enforcement officials searching for the brothers were on high alert, not sure of who they were looking for or where they might find them. The citizens of Watertown, where Tsarnaev was eventually captured, dealt with curfews, flying bullets, and tremendous amounts of uncertainty. Coping with the loss of a loved one, regrouping after a serious injury, or simply moving ahead with life in the wake of tragedy may be the most stressful circumstances of all.

In this chapter, we will examine the physiology and psychology of emotions and stress. Prolonged negative emotions such as anger can certainly be stressful, and stress can certainly produce negative emotions. Both of these processes, however, are shaped by how we interpret the events that happen to us, by the demands of the situation we are in, and by the rules of our culture.

The Nature of Emotion

People often wish to be freed from painful feelings of anger, jealousy, shame, guilt, and grief. Yet imagine a life without emotions. You would be unmoved by the magic of music. You would never care about losing someone you love, not only because you would not know sadness but also because you would not know love. You would never laugh because nothing would strike you as funny. And you would be a social isolate because you would not be able to know what other people were feeling. You wouldn't do *anything* if you didn't have emotions because you wouldn't care.

Emotions evolved to help people meet the challenges of life (Nesse & Ellsworth, 2009). For example, disgust evolved as a mechanism that protects infants and adults from eating tainted or poisonous food (Stevenson et al., 2014). Embarrassment and blushing, so painful to an individual, serve an important function: appeasing others when you feel you have made a fool of yourself, broken a moral rule, or violated a social norm (Crozier & de Jong, 2013; Feinberg, Willer, & Keltner, 2012). And the positive emotions of joy, love, laughter, and playfulness do not appear to be simply selfish feelings of pleasure; their adaptive function may be to help increase mental flexibility and resilience, build bonds with others, and stimulate creativity (Baas, De Dreu, & Nijstad, 2008; Kok et al., 2013).

Let's begin with some findings from neuroscientists and other researchers who are studying the biological aspects of emotions: facial expressions, brain regions and circuits, and the autonomic nervous system.

Emotion and the Face

LO 11.1.A Explain the components that define an emotion, list the emotions that have a universal facial expression, and describe some of the limits affecting the ability to decode facial expressions of emotion.

The components of **emotion** are *physiological changes* in the face, brain, and body; *cognitive processes* such as appraisals and interpretations of events; *action tendencies* that spur us to fight or flee; and *subjective feeling*. In turn, *culture* and *social context* influence both the inner experience and the outward expression of emotion.

There are many channels of communication that humans use to express their thoughts and feelings, but the simplest dichotomy is between verbal and nonverbal channels. *Verbal communication* refers to a person's speech or writing; it's the words we use to send a message to another person. *Nonverbal* channels include all the other mechanisms used in communication: vocal channels (such as tone of voice, speech hesitations, or the rate of speech), body language (including posture, hand gestures, interpersonal distance, eye contact, gait), facial expressions, and even the clothes we wear or the way we maintain our environments (Gosling, 2009; Knapp, Hall, & Horgan, 2014).

Notice that there are many more forms of nonverbal communication than forms of verbal communication. Nonverbal channels can carry a great deal of information, especially when it comes to communicating emotion (Ekman & Friesen, 1969). But among nonverbal forms of communication, the face conveys the greatest degree of information about a person's emotional state. A stranger's crossed arms might signify a negative emotion, but is it anger, worry, defiance, or disgust? Arms, legs, and postures don't have a lot of variability to them, but the face, packed with a rich array of muscles, is capable of communicating a wide range of expressions with a great deal of specificity (Hwang & Matsumoto, 2015).

In 1872, Charles Darwin argued that human facial expressions—the smile, the frown, the grimace, the glare—are as innate as the wing flutter of a frightened bird, the purr of a contented cat, and the snarl of a threatened wolf (Darwin, 1872). Such expressions evolved, he said, because they allowed our ancestors to tell at a glance the difference between a friendly stranger and a hostile one. In addition, he argued, the evolutionary functions of emotion are

emotion

A state of arousal involving facial and bodily changes, brain activation, cognitive appraisals, subjective feelings, and tendencies toward action.

to prepare the organism to respond to challenges in the environment and to communicate important information to others, and modern research supports his ideas (Hess & Thibault, 2009; Shariff & Tracy, 2011).

Decades ago, Paul Ekman and his colleagues gathered abundant evidence for the universality of the facial expressions of seven emotions: anger, happiness, fear, surprise, disgust, sadness, and contempt (Ekman, 2003; Ekman et al., 1987). In every culture they studied—in Brazil, Chile, Estonia, Germany, Greece, Hong Kong, Italy, Japan, New Guinea, Scotland, Sumatra, Turkey, and the United States—a large majority of people recognized the emotional expressions portrayed by those in other cultures (see Figure 11.1). Even most members of isolated cultural groups who had never watched a movie or read *People* magazine, such as the Foré of New Guinea or the Minangkabau of West Sumatra, could recognize the emotions expressed in pictures of people who were entirely foreign to them, and Westerners could recognize theirs. Lately, some researchers have added pride to the list, arguing that its adaptive function is to motivate people to achieve and excel, and thereby to increase their attractiveness to others and to their groups (Williams & DeSteno, 2009). Children as young as 4 years old, and people from an isolated culture in Africa, can reliably identify facial and bodily expressions of pride (Tracy & Robins, 2007, 2008).

Ekman and his associates developed a coding system to identify and analyze each of the nearly 80 muscles of the face, as well as the combinations of muscles associated with various emotions (Ekman, 2003). When people try to hide their feelings and put on an emotion, they generally use different groups of muscles than they do for authentic ones. When people try to pretend that they feel sad, only 15 percent manage to get the eyebrows, eyelids, and forehead

Figure 11.1 Some Universal Expressions

Most people around the world can readily identify expressions of anger, happiness, disgust, surprise, contempt, sadness, and fear—no matter what the age, culture, sex, or historical era of the person conveying the emotion. Can you match the emotion to each face shown here?

wrinkle exactly right, mimicking the way true grief is expressed spontaneously. Authentic smiles last only 2 seconds; false smiles may last 10 seconds or more, and rarely involve the muscles around the eyes (Ekman, Friesen, & O'Sullivan, 1988).

THE FUNCTIONS OF FACIAL EXPRESSIONS   Interestingly, facial expressions not only reflect our internal feelings but also *influence* them. In the process of **facial feedback**, the facial muscles send messages to the brain about the basic emotion being expressed: A smile tells us that we're happy, a frown that we're angry or perplexed. When people are told to smile and look pleased or happy, their positive feelings increase; when they are told to look angry, displeased, or disgusted, positive feelings decrease (Kleinke, Peterson, & Rutledge, 1998; Strack, Martin, & Stepper, 1988). If you put on an angry face, your heart rate will rise faster than if you put on a happy face (Levenson, Ekman, & Friesen, 1990).

If facial feedback helps us process emotion, what happens when that feedback is blocked—say, because of the cosmetic use of botulinum toxin-A, otherwise known as Botox, which paralyzes the facial muscles used in frowning? Researchers recruited 40 women who were about to have Botox injections, and tested them before and after treatment by having them read sentences describing situations evoking sad, happy, and angry emotions. Botox hindered the women's ability to process the sentences evoking sadness and anger (Havas et al., 2010). Other research found that Botoxed women were significantly less accurate than other women at recognizing both positive and negative emotions in photographs of human eyes (Neal & Chartrand, 2011).

As Darwin suggested, facial expressions also probably evolved to help us communicate our emotional states to others and provoke a response from them—"Come help me!" "Get away!" (Fridlund, 1994; Hager & Ekman, 1979). This signaling function begins in infancy. A baby's expressions of misery or angry frustration are apparent to most parents, who respond by soothing an uncomfortable baby or feeding a grumpy one (Izard, 1994; Stenberg & Campos, 1990). And an infant's smile of joy usually melts the heart of the weariest parent, provoking a happy cuddle.

By the age of 6 to 7 months, babies reveal special sensitivity to adults' fearful expressions (Leppänen & Nelson, 2012) and soon begin to alter their own behavior in reaction to their parents' facial expressions of emotion. This ability, too, has survival value. If you have ever watched a toddler take a tumble and then look at his or her parent before deciding whether to cry or to forget it, you will understand the influence of parental facial expressions. And you can see why they have had such survival value for babies: An infant needs to be able to read the parent's facial signals of alarm because young children do not yet have the experience necessary for judging danger.

FACIAL EXPRESSIONS IN CONTEXT   However, there are important cultural and social limits to the universal *readability* of facial expressions. When you perceive another person's facial expression, you are being influenced by what else is happening in the situation, by your own emotional state, and by the cultural context (Barrett, Mesquita, & Gendron, 2011; Jack et al., 2012). People are better at identifying emotions expressed by others in their own ethnic, national, or regional group than they are at recognizing the emotions of foreigners (Elfenbein, 2013). Within a culture, facial expressions can have different meanings depending on the situation; a smile can mean "I'm happy!" or "I don't want to make you angry while I tell you this." Likewise, people often interpret identical facial expressions—even of universal emotions such as disgust, sadness, and anger—in very different ways, depending on what else they are observing in the social context. For example, almost all adults recognize the expression of disgust if that's all they see in a picture of a face. But when they see a picture of the same disgusted expression on a man with his arm raised as if to strike, they will say the expression is anger (Aviezer et al., 2008).

Moreover, although infants and young children can obviously *display* facial expressions of various emotions, they have to learn how to identify those expressions in adults. At first, they seem to have only two general categories: positive (happy) and negative (notably fear and

facial feedback

The process by which the facial muscles send messages to the brain about the basic emotion being expressed.

anger). They do not recognize adults' expressions of sadness until they are about age 3, and disgust at about age 5; until then, they will usually misinterpret these expressions as anger (Widen & Russell, 2010).

Finally, of course, facial expressions are only part of the emotional picture. Emotions exist without facial expressions, and facial expressions need not convey emotions. People can feel sad, anxious, or angry without letting it show—and, conversely, they can use facial expressions to lie about their feelings. In Shakespeare's play *Henry VI*, the villain who will become the evil King Richard III says:

> *Why, I can smile, and murder while I smile;*
> *And cry content to that which grieves my heart;*
> *And wet my cheeks with artificial tears,*
> *And frame my face to all occasions.*

Emotion and the Brain

LO 11.1.B   Discuss the brain structures involved in the experience of emotions, explain what mirror neurons do, and describe the primary chemicals involved in emotional experience.

Various parts of the brain are involved in the different components of emotional experience: recognizing another person's emotion, feeling a specific emotion, expressing an emotion, and acting on an emotion. People who have a stroke that affects brain areas involved in the experience of disgust are often unable to feel disgusted. One young man with stroke damage in these regions had little or no emotional response to images and ideas that would be disgusting to most people, such as feces-shaped chocolate (Calder et al., 2000). Are you making a disgusted expression as you read that? He couldn't.

Most emotions motivate a response (an *action tendency*) of some sort: to embrace or approach the person who instills joy in you, attack a person who makes you angry, withdraw from a food that disgusts you, or flee from a person or situation that frightens you (Frijda, Kuipers, & ter Schure, 1989). The prefrontal regions of the brain are involved in these impulses to approach or withdraw. Regions of the *right* prefrontal region are specialized for the impulse to withdraw or escape (as in disgust and fear). Regions of the *left* prefrontal cortex are specialized for the motivation to approach others (as in happiness, a positive emotion, and anger, a negative one) (Harmon-Jones & Harmon-Jones, 2015). People who have greater-than-average activation of the left areas, compared with the right, have more positive feelings, a quicker ability to recover from negative emotions, and a greater ability to suppress negative emotions (Urry et al., 2004). People with damage to this area often lose the capacity for joy.

Parts of the prefrontal cortex are also involved in the *regulation* of emotion, helping us modify and control our feelings, keeping us on an even keel and responding appropriately to others (Jackson et al., 2003). A degenerative disease that destroys cells in parts of the frontal lobes causes not only a loss of cells, say researchers, but a profound change in personality. It blunts the sufferer's ability to respond to the emotions of others, understand why they and others feel as they do, and adjust their own emotional responses appropriately: A loving mother becomes indifferent to her child's injury; a businessman does embarrassing things and doesn't notice the reaction of others (Levenson & Miller, 2007).

The amygdala plays a key role in emotion, especially anger and fear. It is responsible for evaluating sensory information, determining its emotional importance, and making the initial decision to approach or withdraw from a person or situation (LeDoux, 1996). The amygdala instantly assesses danger or threat, which is a good thing because otherwise you could be standing in the street asking, "Is it wise to cross now, while that very large truck is coming toward me?" The amygdala's initial response may then be overridden by a more accurate appraisal from the cortex. This is why you jump with fear when you suddenly feel a hand on

Facial expressions do not always convey the emotion being felt. True feelings of happiness may not be obvious at all. This athlete looks angry or in pain but is actually feeling joyful after winning a gold medal.

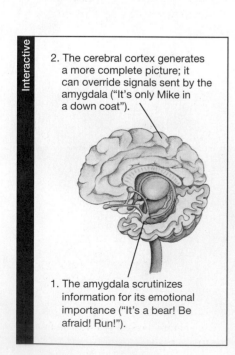

2. The cerebral cortex generates a more complete picture; it can override signals sent by the amygdala ("It's only Mike in a down coat").

1. The amygdala scrutinizes information for its emotional importance ("It's a bear! Be afraid! Run!").

your back in a dark alley, and why your fear evaporates when the cortex registers that the hand belongs to a friend whose lousy idea of humor is to scare you in a dark alley.

If either the amygdala or critical areas of the cortex are damaged, abnormalities result in the ability to experience fear or recognize it in others. A patient known as S. M. has a rare disease that destroyed her amygdala, and as a result she cannot feel fear—not toward snakes, not when watching scary movies, not even when she was attacked in a park by a man with a knife (Feinstein et al., 2011). Conversely, people with damage in the cortex may have difficulty turning off their own fear responses, causing anxiety and obsessive–compulsive disorders.

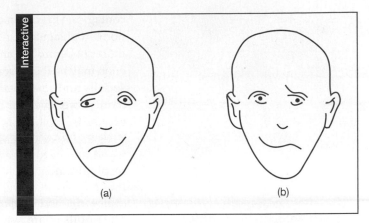

(a)   (b)

These faces have expressions of happiness on one side and sadness on the other. Look at the nose of each face; which face looks happier? Which face looks sadder?

You are likely to see face *b* as the happier one and face *a* as the sadder one. The reason is that in most people the left side of a picture is processed by the right side of the brain, where recognition of emotional expression primarily occurs (Oatley, Keltner, & Jenkins, 2006).

NEURONS FOR IMITATION AND EMPATHY   In 1992, a team of Italian neuroscientists accidentally made an astonishing discovery. They had implanted wires in the brains of macaque monkeys, in regions involved in planning and carrying out movement. Every time a monkey moved and grasped an object, the cells fired and the monitor registered a sound. One day, a graduate student heard the monitor go off when the monkey was simply observing him eating an ice cream cone. The neuroscientists looked more closely and found that certain neurons in the monkeys' brains were firing not only when the monkeys were picking up peanuts and eating them but also when the monkeys were merely observing their human caretakers doing exactly the same thing. These neurons responded only to very specific actions: A neuron that fired when a monkey grasped a peanut would also fire when the scientist grasped a peanut but not when the scientist grasped something else (Rizzolatti & Sinigaglia, 2010). The scientists called these cells **mirror neurons**.

Human beings also have mirror neurons that fire when we observe others doing something and mimic the action ourselves. The "mirror system," containing millions of neurons, is involved in helping us identify what others are feeling, understand other people's intentions, and imitate their actions and gestures (Ferri et al., 2015; Fogassi & Ferrari, 2007). When you see another person in pain, one reason you feel a jolt of empathy is that mirror neurons involved in pain are firing. When you watch a spider crawl up someone's leg, one reason you have a creepy sensation is that your mirror neurons are firing—the same ones that would fire if the spider were crawling up your own leg. And when you see another person's facial expression, your own facial muscles will often subtly mimic it, activating a similar emotional state (Dimberg, Thunberg, & Elmehed, 2000).

mirror neurons

Brain cells that fire when a person or animal observes another carrying out an action; these neurons appear to be involved in empathy, language comprehension, imitation, and reading emotions.

The discovery of mirror neurons is exciting, but some popular writers have exaggerated its implications, and scientists are still debating their function in human beings (Gallese et al., 2011). For example, these neurons seem strongly involved in empathy, but empathy has social limits: Mirror neurons go to sleep when people look at individuals they dislike or are prejudiced against. If you like a person, mimicking their facial movements and gestures will increase that liking, but if you dislike the person, trying to perk up your mirror neurons by mimicking won't improve matters at all (Stel et al., 2010; van Baaren et al., 2009).

Among people who do like each other or are in the same social or ethnic group, mirror neurons may be the underlying mechanism for *mood contagion*, the spreading of an emotion from one person to another. Have you ever been in a cheerful mood, had lunch with a depressed friend, and come away feeling vaguely depressed yourself? Have you ever stopped to have a chat with a friend who was nervous about an upcoming exam and ended up feeling edgy yourself? That's mood contagion at work. Mood

Mirror neurons are surely at work in this conversation.

contagion also occurs when two people feel rapport with one another's *positive* emotions, nonverbal signals, and posture: Their gestures become more synchronized, they behave more cooperatively, and they feel more cheerful (Wiltermuth & Heath, 2009). This phenomenon may be the reason that synchronized human activities—marches, bands, dancing—are socially and emotionally beneficial. And it means that our friends and neighbors may have more power over our moods than we realize.

THE ENERGY OF EMOTION   After the brain areas associated with emotion are activated, the next stage of the emotional relay is the release of hormones to enable you to respond quickly. When you are under stress or feeling an intense emotion, the sympathetic division of the autonomic nervous system spurs the adrenal glands to send out *epinephrine* and *norepinephrine*. These chemical messengers produce arousal and alertness. The pupils dilate, widening to allow in more light; the heart beats faster; blood pressure increases; breathing speeds up; and blood sugar rises. These changes provide the body with the energy needed to take action, whether you are happy and want to get close to someone you love or are scared and want to escape a person who is frightening you (Löw et al., 2008).

Epinephrine in particular provides the energy of an emotion, that familiar tingle of excitement. At high levels, it can create the sensation of being "seized" or "flooded" by an emotion that is out of your control. In a sense, you are out of control because you cannot consciously alter your heart rate and blood pressure. However, you can learn to control your actions when you are under the sway of an emotion. As arousal subsides, anger may pale into annoyance, ecstasy into contentment, fear into suspicion, past emotional whirlwinds into calm breezes.

In sum, the physiology of emotion involves characteristic facial expressions; activity in specific parts of the brain, notably the amygdala, specialized parts of the prefrontal cortex, and mirror neurons; and sympathetic nervous system activity that prepares the body for action (see Review 11.1).

Review 11.1

Emotion and the Body

Facial Expressions	Reflect internal feelings, influence internal feelings (facial feedback), communicate feelings, signal intentions, affect behavior and feelings of others (mood contagion), conceal or pretend an emotion (deception).
The Brain	Specific areas and circuits are involved in processing specific emotions (e.g., disgust) and in different aspects of emotional experience (e.g., recognizing facial expressions in others, expressing an emotion oneself).
Amygdala	Determines emotional importance of incoming sensory information; is responsible for the initial decision to approach or withdraw; is involved in learning, recognizing, and expressing fear.
Cortex	Appraises the significance of emotional information from the amygdala. The left prefrontal area is associated with "approach" emotions (e.g., happiness, anger); the right prefrontal area with "withdrawal" emotions (e.g., fear, sadness).
Mirror Neurons	Found in various parts of the brain, these cells fire in response to the actions or emotions of another person, possibly creating synchrony, promoting empathy, and generating mood contagion.
Autonomic Nervous System	Activates the hormones epinephrine and norepinephrine, which produce energy and alertness.

Interactive

BIOLOGY and *Lie Detection*

You've probably seen more than one television crime drama where a police officer or forensics expert said she could tell immediately whether a bad guy was lying. What a great skill! Wouldn't it be good to know for sure if a suspect committed the crime, is a spy, stole company assets, or is planning a terrorist strike? The problem is that justice depends not only on finding out who is guilty but also on protecting those who didn't do anything. The challenge for social scientists and for law enforcement is to better identify liars without falsely accusing truth tellers. Various ways of pursuing this goal are discussed in the video *Detecting Lies.*

invalid because no physiological patterns of autonomic arousal are specific to lying (Leo, 2008; Lykken, 1998; Meijer & Verschuere, 2015). Machines cannot tell whether you are feeling guilty, angry, nervous, amused, or revved up from an exciting day. Innocent people may be tense and nervous about the whole procedure. They may react to the word *bank*, not because they robbed a bank but because they recently bounced a check; in either case, the machine will signal a lie. The reverse mistake is also common: People who are motivated to escape detection can often beat the machine by tensing muscles or thinking about an exciting experience during neutral questions.

Unfortunately, the idea that some people have a "natural" ability to detect the lies of others is not supported by evidence. Even highly educated and trained individuals have only about a 54 percent chance of detecting a lie (Bond & DePaulo, 2008). (For the rest of us, the success rate is 50 percent, no better than flipping a coin.) People may speak hesitantly in telling a story, seem stressed in their speech, or avoid looking the interrogator in the eye for many reasons (DePaulo et al., 2003; Leo, 2008; Vrij, Granhag, & Porter, 2010). They may be frightened, not know what answers are expected, have nervous mannerisms, or come from a culture that regards direct eye contact as confrontational or rude.

For centuries, people have tried to determine when a person is lying by detecting physiological responses that cannot be controlled consciously. This is the idea behind the *polygraph machine* (lie detector), which was invented in 1915 by a Harvard professor named William Marston. (Marston went on to become famous for a *really* important creation: Wonder Woman.) The polygraph is based on the assumption that a lie generates emotional arousal. A person who is guilty and fearful of being found out will therefore have increased activity in the autonomic nervous system while responding to incriminating questions: a faster heart rate, increased respiration rate, and increased electrical conductance of the skin.

Law enforcement officers remain enthusiastic about the polygraph, but most psychological scientists regard polygraph tests as

The polygraph will correctly catch many liars and guilty people. The main problem is that it also falsely identifies many innocent people as having lied (see Figure 11.2). For this reason, polygraph results are inadmissible in most courts. But some government agencies and most police departments continue to use them, not for their accuracy but because they hope to scare people into telling the truth and induce suspects to confess—by telling them that they failed the test (Leo, 2008).

Because of the unreliability of the polygraph, researchers are trying to find other ways of measuring physiological signs of lying. The Computer Voice Stress Analyzer and Layered Voice Analysis are based on the assumption that the human voice contains telltale signals that betray a speaker's emotional state and intent to deceive. Its promoters claim high degrees of accuracy, but research has mostly yielded negative findings (Harnsberger et al., 2009; Leo, 2008). Like the polygraph, voice analyzers detect physiological changes that may indicate fear, anger, or other signs of stress rather than lying, and they often falsely label true statements as lies.

The hottest new effort at lie detection is brain imaging (Ganis, 2015). Some researchers are trying to find "brain fingerprints" by using fMRIs of brain activity to see whether they reveal that a person possesses guilty knowledge of a crime and is lying about it. Some companies are already advertising that they can predict with better than 90 percent certainty whether or not someone is telling the truth.

Figure 11.2 Misjudging the Innocent

This graph shows the average percentages across three studies of classifications by lie detectors. Nearly half of the innocent people were classified as guilty, and a significant number of guilty people were classified as innocent. The suspect's guilt or innocence had been independently confirmed by other means, such as by admissions by the actual perpetrators (Iacono & Lykken, 1997).

Don't buy it. Areas of the brain that light up on a fMRI when people are allegedly lying are also those involved with many other cognitive functions, including memory, self-awareness, and self-monitoring (Greely & Illes, 2007). And because of the normal variability among people in their autonomic and brain reactivity, innocent but highly reactive people are still likely to be mislabeled guilty by these tests (Stix, 2008). A 2011 report from the British Royal Society's committee on neuroscience and law concluded that using brain scanners to determine whether a witness is lying is premature because of their unreliability, and to date American courts have agreed.

More promising methods of lie detection are cognitive rather than biological. One approach increases the "cognitive load" on the suspect because liars have more things to keep straight in their minds—the truth, the lie they told, and the story they concocted to cover it up. When the interviewer increases that mental load, as by asking the suspect to tell the story backward, liars make more mistakes (Vrij et al., 2011).

But no method to date is foolproof at catching the guilty, and the main reason is that most methods rest on a faulty assumption: that universally identifiable biological or cognitive signs reveal with high accuracy when a person is lying. We're telling the truth!

Emotion and the Mind

LO 11.1.C Summarize the basic research findings indicating that cognitive appraisal plays a role in emotional experience.

Two friends of ours returned from a mountain-climbing trip to Nepal. One said, "I was ecstatic! The crystal-clear skies, the millions of stars, the friendly people, the majestic mountains, the harmony of the universe!" The other said, "I was miserable! The bedbugs and fleas, the lack of toilets, the yak-butter tea, the awful food, the unforgiving mountains!" Same trip, two different emotional reactions to it. Why? As the video *Theories of Emotion and Motivation* shows, understanding the processes involved in emotion can be complicated.

In the first century A.D., the Stoic philosophers suggested an answer: People do not become angry or sad or ecstatic because of actual events but because of their explanations of those events. Modern psychologists have verified the Stoics' ideas experimentally. Many years ago, Stanley Schachter and Jerome Singer (1962) argued that the experience of emotion depends both on physiological arousal and on how you interpret and explain that arousal. Your body may be churning away in high gear, but unless you can explain and label those changes, you will not feel a true emotion. This idea spurred other investigators to study how emotions are created and influenced by **appraisals**: beliefs, perceptions of the situation, expectations, goals, and attributions that people make to explain their own and other people's behavior (Fairholme et al., 2009; Lindquist & Barrett, 2008; Moors et al., 2013). Human beings, after all, are the only species that can say, "The more I thought about it, the madder I got." We think ourselves into an emotional state, and sometimes we think ourselves out of it.

The importance of appraisals in emotion explains why two people often have different emotional reactions to the same situation. Imagine that you get an A on your psychology midterm; how will you feel? Or perhaps you get a D on that midterm; how will you feel then? Most people assume that success brings happiness and failure brings unhappiness, but the emotions you feel will depend more on how you explain your grade than on what you actually get. Do you attribute your grade to your own efforts (or lack of them) or to the teacher, fate, or luck? In a series of experiments, students who believed they did well because of their own efforts tended to feel proud, competent, and satisfied. Those who believed they did well because of a lucky fluke tended to feel gratitude, surprise, or guilt ("I don't deserve this"). Those who believed their failures were their own fault tended to feel regretful, guilty, or resigned. And those who blamed others tended to feel angry (Weiner, 1986).

Those appraisal patterns also differ across cultures. Japanese and Americans tend to differ in their appraisals of the causes and responsibility for errors and for success. As a result, Japanese are more likely to blame themselves when something goes wrong and to experience shame, whereas Americans are more likely to blame others and experience anger. In the case of success, Americans are more likely to take credit and feel proud, whereas Japanese are more likely to regard their success as reflecting the situation and opportunity—and feel lucky (Imada & Ellsworth, 2011).

Most people assume that second-place winners feel happier about their performance than third-place winners do. Yet when psychologists questioned this assumption, they found that usually the opposite is true, as the text explains. In this European swimming competition, silver medalist Vitaly Romanovich of Russia (left) is clearly feeling a lot grumpier not only than the gold medalist Federico Colbertaldo of Italy (center) or bronze medalist Samuel Pizzetti of Italy—he can't even bring himself to display his medal!

Here is a more surprising example of how thoughts affect emotions. Of two Olympic finalists, one who wins a second-place silver medal and one who wins a third-place bronze medal, who will feel happier? Won't it be the silver medalist? Nope. In a study of athletes' reactions to placing second and third in the 1992 Olympics and the 1994 Empire State Games, the bronze medalists were happier than the silver medalists (Medvec, Madey, & Gilovich, 1995). Apparently, the athletes were comparing their performance to what might have been. The second-place winners, comparing themselves to the gold medalists, were unhappy that they didn't get the gold. But the third-place winners, comparing themselves to those who did worse than they, were happy that they earned a medal at all!

appraisals

A person's perceptions, beliefs, attributions, and goals, which determine which emotion he or she will feel in a given circumstance; they are a central component of emotion and the emotional experience.

Cognitions and physiology are inextricably linked in the experience of emotion. Thoughts affect emotions, and emotional states influence thoughts (Fairholme et al., 2009; Keltner, Ellsworth, & Edwards, 1993). Blaming others for your woes can make you feel angry, but because you are angry you may be more inclined to think the worst of other people's motives; when you are sad, you are more likely to feel that the rotten situation made them do what they did. The complicated mix of emotions that people feel when they have "disappointing wins" (outcomes that were not as good as they had expected) or "relieving losses" (bad outcomes that could have been worse) shows how powerfully thoughts affect emotional responses.

An infant's primitive emotions do not have much mental sophistication: "Hey, I'm mad because no one is feeding me!" As a child's cerebral cortex matures, however, appraisals become more complex, and so do emotions: "Hey, I'm mad because this situation is entirely unfair!" Some emotions, such as shame and guilt, depend completely on the maturation of higher cognitive capacities and do not occur until a child is 2 or 3 years old (and never in some people). These *self*-conscious emotions require the emergence of a sense of self and the ability to perceive that you have behaved badly or let down another person (Baumeister, Stillwell, & Heatherton, 1994; Conroy et al., 2015; Tangney et al., 1996).

Appraisals, therefore, are essential to the creation of most emotions. But when people decide that it is shameful for a man to dance on a table with a lampshade on his head, or for a woman to walk down a street with her arms and legs uncovered, where do their ideas

Children need to be old enough to have a sense of self before they can feel the moral emotions of shame, guilt, or remorse.

about shame originate? If you are a person who loudly curses others when you are angry, where did you learn that cursing is acceptable? To answer these questions, we turn to the role of culture.

Quiz for Module 11.1

1. The components of emotion are physiological changes, _____, action tendencies, and _____.

   a. Facial expressions / nonverbal behaviors

   b. Biological changes / cultural norms

   c. Internal feelings / external displays

   d. Cognitive processes / subjective feelings

2. Which of the following emotions does *not* have a universal facial expression?

   a. Surprise

   b. Anger

   c. Jealousy

   d. Disgust

3. Three-year-old Gricelda sees her dad dressed in a gorilla costume and runs away in fear. What brain structure is probably involved in her emotional reaction?

   a. Pons

   b. Amygdala

   c. Substantia nigra

   d. Pineal gland

4. Aldo is watching *The Bloodthirsty Butchers Meet the Maniac Madmen in 3D*. What cells in his brain are making him wince every time the main character is being attacked?

   a. Mirror neurons

   b. Pontine neurons

   c. Purkinje cells

   d. Thalamic extension

5. "There is nothing either good or bad, but thinking makes it so." This scene from William Shakespeare's play *Hamlet* (Act 2, Scene 2) is a simple summary of the role of _____ in the experience of emotion.

   a. Norepinephrine

   b. Facial expressions

   c. Appraisals

   d. The thalamus

Emotion and Culture

A young wife leaves her house one morning to draw water from the local well as her husband watches from the porch. On her way back from the well, a male stranger stops her and asks for some water. She gives him a cupful and then invites him home to dinner. He accepts. The husband, wife, and guest have a pleasant meal together. In a gesture of hospitality, the husband invites the guest to spend the night with his wife. The guest accepts. In the morning, the husband leaves early to bring home breakfast. When he returns, he finds his wife again in bed with the visitor.

At what point in this story will the husband feel angry? The answer depends on his culture (Hupka, 1981, 1991). A North American husband would feel rather angry at a wife who had an extramarital affair, and a wife would feel rather angry at being offered to a guest as if she were a lamb chop. But a Pawnee husband of the 19th century would be enraged at any man who dared ask his wife for water. An Ammassalik Inuit husband finds it perfectly honorable to offer his wife to a stranger, but only once; he would be angry to find his wife and the guest having a second encounter. And a century ago, a Toda husband in India would not have been angry at all because the Todas allowed both husband and wife to take lovers. Both spouses might feel angry, though, if one of them had a *sneaky* affair, without announcing it publicly.

In most cultures, people feel angry in response to insult and the violation of social rules, but as this story shows, they often disagree about what an insult or correct rule is. In this section, we will explore how culture influences the emotions we feel and the ways in which we express them.

How Culture Shapes Emotions

LO 11.2.A   Describe the ways emotional experience can differ across cultures, in terms of concepts, language, and expectations.

Are some emotions specific to particular cultures and not found elsewhere? What does it mean that some languages have words for subtle emotional states that other languages lack? The Germans have *schadenfreude*, a feeling of joy at another's misfortune. The Japanese speak of *hagaii*, helpless anguish tinged with frustration. Tahitians have *mehameha*, a trembling sensation that Tahitians feel when ordinary categories of perception are suspended—at twilight, in the brush, watching fires glow without heat. In the West, an event that cannot be identified is usually greeted with fear, yet *mehameha* does not describe what Westerners call fear or terror (Levy, 1984). Culture also shapes and labels the experience of blends of emotions, as in the English word *bittersweet* or the mixed emotions of pleasure and regret in *nostalgia*. But English lacks an emotion word that is central to inhabitants of the tiny Micronesian atoll of Ifaluk: *fago*, translated as "compassion/love/sadness," which reflects the sad feeling one has when a loved one is absent or in need, and the pleasurable sense of compassion in being able to care and help (Lutz, 1988).

Do these interesting linguistic differences mean that Germans are more likely than others actually to feel *schadenfreude*, the Japanese to feel *hagaii*, and the Tahitians to feel *mehameha*? Or are they just more willing to give these subtle emotions a name? Most people in all cultures are capable of feeling certain innate emotions, the ones that have physiological hallmarks in the brain and nervous system. But people in different cultures might indeed differ in their abilities to experience emotional blends and variations such as *schadenfreude*, *hagaii*, or *mehameha*.

The difference between innate emotions and more complex cultural variations seems to be reflected in languages all over the world (Hepper et al., 2014). A *prototype* is a typical representative of a class of things. People everywhere consider some emotions to be prototypical examples of the concept *emotion*: Thus, most people will say that *anger* and *sadness* are more representative of an emotion than *irritability* and *nostalgia* are. Prototypical emotions are reflected in the emotion words that young children learn first: *happy*, *sad*, *mad*, and *scared*. As children develop, they begin to draw emotional distinctions that are less prototypical and more specific to their language and culture, such as *ecstatic*, *depressed*, *hostile*, or *anxious* (Hupka, Lenton, & Hutchison, 1999; Shaver, Wu, & Schwartz, 1992). And their appraisals of a given situation or provocation will also vary—as we saw earlier in describing the difference between Americans and Japanese—depending on their culture's values, norms, and traditions. In this way, children and adults come to experience the nuances of emotional feeling that their cultures emphasize. The result is many varieties of emotion, some shading into one another, which have labels in some languages but not in others.

All emotions depend on the culture and context that produce them and shape their expression. Anger may be universal, but the way it is experienced will vary from culture to culture—whether it feels good or bad, useful or destructive. And cultures determine much of what people feel emotional *about*. For example, disgust is universal, but the content of what produces disgust changes as an infant matures, and it varies across cultures (Rozin, Lowery, & Ebert, 1994). People in some cultures learn to become disgusted by bugs (which other people find beautiful or tasty), unfamiliar sexual practices, dirt, death, contamination by a handshake with a stranger, or particular foods (e.g., meat if they are vegetarian, or pork if they are Muslims or Orthodox Jews).

Communicating Emotions

LO 11.2.B   Explain how display rules and emotion work influence the communication of emotion in a social and cultural context.

Suppose that someone who was dear to you died. Would you cry, and if so, would you do it alone or in public? Your answer will depend in part on your culture's **display rules** for emotion (Ekman et al., 1987; Gross, 1998; Hayashi & Shiomi, 2015). In some cultures, grief is

display rules

Social and cultural rules that regulate when, how, and where a person may express (or suppress) emotions.

What you feel about the idea of consuming this insect depends on the culture you are from.

emotion work

Expression of an emotion, often because of a role requirement, that a person does not really feel.

expressed by weeping; in others, by tearless resignation; and in still others, by dance, drink, and song. When you feel an emotion, how you express it is rarely a matter of "I say what I feel." You may be obliged to disguise what you feel. You may wish you could feel what you say.

Even the smile, which seems a straightforward signal of friendliness, has many meanings and uses that are not universal (LaFrance, 2011). Americans smile more frequently than Germans, not because Americans are inherently friendlier but because they differ in their notions of when a smile is appropriate. After a German–American business meeting, the Americans often complain that the Germans were cold and aloof, and the Germans often complain that the Americans were excessively cheerful, hiding their real feelings under the mask of a smile (Hall & Hall, 1990). The Japanese smile even more than Americans do, to disguise embarrassment, anger, or other negative emotions whose public display is considered rude and incorrect.

Display rules also govern *body language*, nonverbal signals of body movement, posture, gesture, and gaze (Birdwhistell, 1970). Many aspects of body language are specific to particular languages and cultures, which makes even the simplest gesture subject to misunderstanding and offense (Matsumoto & Hwang, 2013). The sign of the University of Texas at Austin football team, the Longhorns, is to extend the index finger and the pinkie. In Italy and other parts of Europe, it means you're saying a man's wife has been unfaithful to him—a serious insult.

Display rules tell us not only what to do when we are feeling an emotion, but also how and when to show an emotion we do *not* feel. Most people are expected to demonstrate sadness at funerals, happiness at weddings, and affection toward relatives. What if we don't actually feel sad, happy, or affectionate? Acting out an emotion we do not really feel because we believe it is socially appropriate is called **emotion work**. It is part of our efforts to regulate our emotions when we are with others (Gabriel et al., 2015; Gross, 1998). Sometimes emotion work is a job requirement. Flight attendants, waiters, and customer-service representatives must put on a happy face to convey cheerfulness, even if they are privately angry about a rude or drunken customer. Bill collectors must put on a stern face to convey threat, even if they feel sorry for the person they are collecting money from (Hochschild, 2003).

Gender and Emotion

LO 11.2.C   **Explain sex differences that appear to exist in emotional experience, and comment on the complex reasons for these differences.**

"Women are too emotional," men often complain. "Men are too uptight," women often reply. This is a familiar gender stereotype. Generally, when people say that women are "emotional,"

Around the world, the cultural rules for expressing emotions differ. The display rule for a formal Japanese wedding portrait is "no direct expressions of emotion," but not every member of this family has learned that rule yet.

they are not thinking of the overwhelming evidence that far more men than women "lose their cool" by getting into fistfights and killing each other. What, then, does "too emotional" mean? We need to define our terms and examine our assumptions. And we need to consider the larger culture in which men and women live, which shapes the rules and norms that govern how the sexes are supposed to behave.

Although women are more likely than men to suffer from clinical depression, neither sex feels any of the everyday emotions more often than the other, whether the emotion is anger, worry, embarrassment, anxiety, love, or grief (Archer, 2004; Deffenbacher et al., 2003; Fischer et al., 1993; G. Harris, 2003; Kring & Gordon, 1998; Shields, 2005). The major difference between the sexes has less to do with whether they feel emotions than with how and when their emotions are expressed, and how others perceive those expressions.

In Western cultures, both sexes unconsciously associate "angry" with male and "happy" with female. When researchers showed students a series of computer-generated, fairly sex-neutral faces with a range of angry to happy expressions, the students consistently rated the angry faces as being masculine and the happy faces as feminine (Becker et al., 2007). This stereotyped link between gender and emotion may explain why a man who expresses anger in a professional context is considered high status, but a professional woman who does exactly the same thing loses status. She's considered to be an angry person, someone "out of control" (Brescoll & Uhlmann, 2008). Powerful women thus often face a dilemma: express anger when a subordinate or adversary has done something illegal or incompetent (and risk being thought "overemotional") or behave calmly (and risk being seen as "cold and unemotional").

Conversely, women who don't smile when others expect them to are often disliked, even if they are actually smiling as often as men would. This may be why North American women, on average, smile more than men do, gaze at their listeners more, have more emotionally expressive faces, use more expressive hand and body movements, and touch others more (DePaulo, 1992; Kring & Gordon, 1998). Women smile more than men to pacify others, convey deference to someone of higher status, or smooth over conflicts (Hess, Adams, & Kleck, 2005; LaFrance, 2011; Shields, 2005).

American women also talk about their emotions more than men do. They are far more likely to cry and to acknowledge emotions that reveal vulnerability and weakness, such as "hurt feelings," fear, sadness, loneliness, shame, and guilt (Grossman & Wood, 1993; Timmers, Fischer, & Manstead, 1998). In contrast, most American men express only one emotion more freely than women do: anger toward strangers, especially other men. Otherwise, men are expected to control and mask negative feelings. When they are worried or afraid, they are more likely than women to use vague terms, saying that they feel moody, frustrated, or on edge (Fehr et al., 1999).

However, the influence of a particular situation often overrides gender rules. You won't find many gender differences in emotional expressiveness at a football game or the World Series! Furthermore, both sexes do similar emotion work when the situation or job requires it. A male flight attendant has to smile as much with passengers as a female attendant does, and a female FBI agent has to be as emotionally strong and controlled as a male agent. One of the most important situational constraints on emotional expression is the status of the participants, whatever their gender (Kenny et al., 2010; Snodgrass, 1992). A man is as likely as a woman to control his temper when the target of anger is someone with higher status or power; few people will readily sound off at a professor, police officer, or employer. As for empathy in judging other people's emotions, supposedly a "female" skill, a series of experiments found that working-class people of both sexes are more skilled in empathic accuracy—judging emotional expressions in others and reading the emotions of strangers in job interviews—than upper-class people are. Working-class women *and* men have a greater interest in being able to read the nonverbal cues of those who have higher status and more power than they (Kraus, Côté, & Keltner, 2010).

Even when gender differences exist, they are not universal. Italian, French, Spanish, and Middle Eastern men and women can have entire conversations using highly expressive

Both sexes feel emotionally attached to friends, but often they express their affections differently. From childhood on, girls tend to prefer "face-to-face" friendships based on shared feelings; boys tend to prefer "side-by-side" friendships based on shared activities.

hand gestures and facial expressions. In contrast, in Asian cultures, both sexes are taught to control emotional expression (Matsumoto, 1996; Mesquita & Frijda, 1992). Israeli and Italian men are more likely than women to mask feelings of sadness, but British, Spanish, Swiss, and German men are *less* likely than their female counterparts to inhibit this emotion (Wallbott, Ricci-Bitti, & Bänninger-Huber, 1986).

In sum, the answer to "Which sex is more emotional?" is sometimes men, sometimes women, and sometimes neither, depending on the circumstances and their culture—and how we define our terms.

JOURNAL PROMPT 11.2

Thinking Critically—Ask Questions, Be Willing to Wonder: What does it mean if one language has a term for an emotion that another language lacks, like schadenfreude or hagaii? Are people whose languages include these words actually more likely to feel the emotion, or just to have a term that describes it?

Quiz for Module 11.2

1. "*Saudade . . . .*" your Portuguese friend Beatriz sighs. "Saudade; I've got a melancholic feeling of incompleteness" she continues pedantically. "You wouldn't understand; there's not really an equivalent word in English." That is factually true, but how does it affect our understanding of culture and emotional experience?

   a. You and Beatriz might differ in your experience of saudade, but chances are good that both of you will understand and experience prototypical emotions similarly.

   b. If Beatriz explains the concept of saudade well enough, you should be able to "translate" some set of three or four English words that capture the same emotional meaning.

   c. You and Beatriz are likely to have very different emotions as you go through life; this example highlights the extraordinary cultural diversity in emotional experience.

   d. Emotion words have translatable counterparts across languages because emotions are universal; Beatriz needs to expand her vocabulary to capture what she's trying to convey.

2. Your Japanese friend Suki is told by her professor that she received a D on her exam. In response, Suki broke into a wide smile and thanked the professor profusely. When you received the same news about your lousy grade on the exam, you showed a mix of anger and disgust on your face, and skulked back to your seat. What can explain the difference in the outward signs of emotion between you and Suki?

   a. Culturally variable display rules

   b. Prototypical emotion families

   c. Universal facial expressions of emotion

   d. Mirror neurons

3. The ShinyBrite Corporation has instituted a new policy for its customer-service representatives. They are required to smile at the end of every sentence during their interaction with a customer, from "How are you?" to "Thanks for stopping by to see us today!" and each sentence in between. As you might imagine, customer-service representatives often deal with grumpy, dissatisfied customers, and therefore might not be inclined to feel happy themselves as they go through their business day. What is ShinyBrite asking its employees to do?

   a. Engage in emotion work

   b. Enact expression modulation

   c. Endure mood recovery

   d. Enable mood displacement

4. Compared to American men, American women tend to

   a. Talk about their emotions to a greater extent

   b. Express anger more freely

   c. Feel everyday emotions more frequently

   d. Express more negative emotions rather than positive emotions

5. Which emotion do men tend to express more freely than women?

   a. Anger

   b. Sadness

   c. Surprise

   d. Mirth

The Nature of Stress

As we have seen, emotions can take many forms, varying in complexity and intensity, depending on physiology, cognitive processes, and cultural rules. These same three factors can help us understand those difficult situations in which negative emotions become chronically stressful, and in which chronic stress can create negative emotions.

When people say they are "under stress," they mean all sorts of things: They are having recurring conflicts with a parent, are feeling frustrated and angry about their lives, are fighting with a partner, are overwhelmed with caring for a sick child, can't keep up with work obligations, or just lost a job. Are these stressors linked to illness—to migraines, stomachaches, flu, or more life-threatening diseases such as cancer? And do they affect everyone in the same way?

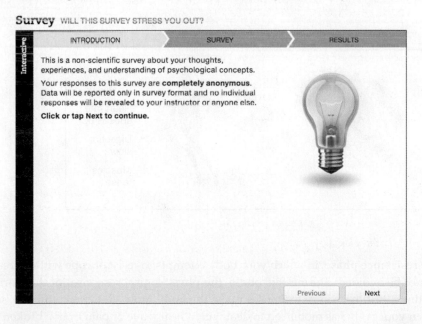

Survey WILL THIS SURVEY STRESS YOU OUT?

| INTRODUCTION | SURVEY | RESULTS |

This is a non-scientific survey about your thoughts, experiences, and understanding of psychological concepts.

Your responses to this survey are **completely anonymous**. Data will be reported only in survey format and no individual responses will be revealed to your instructor or anyone else.

Click or tap Next to continue.

Previous   Next

Stress and the Body

LO 11.3.A Describe the three phases of the general adaptation syndrome, and discuss how modern conceptualizations of the HPA axis and psychoneuroimmunology extend those ideas.

The modern era of stress research began in 1956, when physician Hans Selye published *The Stress of Life*. Environmental stressors such as heat, cold, toxins, and danger, Selye wrote, disrupt the body's equilibrium. The body then mobilizes its resources to fight off these stressors

general adaptation syndrome

According to Hans Selye, a series of physiological reactions to stress occurring in three phases: alarm, resistance, and exhaustion.

and restore normal functioning, as shown in the video *Fight or Flight*. Selye described the body's response to stressors of all kinds as a **general adaptation syndrome**, a set of physiological reactions that occur in three phases:

1. The **alarm phase**, in which the body mobilizes the sympathetic nervous system to meet the immediate threat. The threat could be anything from taking a test you haven't studied for to running from a rabid dog. As we saw earlier, the release of adrenal hormones, epinephrine and norepinephrine, occurs with any intense emotion. It boosts energy, tenses muscles, reduces sensitivity to pain, shuts down digestion (so that blood will flow more efficiently to the brain, muscles, and skin), and increases blood pressure. Decades before Selye, psychologist Walter Cannon (1929) described these changes as the "fight-or-flight" response, a phrase still in use.

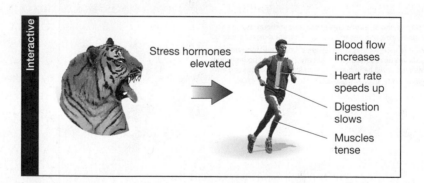

2. The **resistance phase**, in which your body attempts to resist or cope with a stressor that cannot be avoided. During this phase, the physiological responses of the alarm phase continue, but these very responses make the body more vulnerable to other stressors. When your body has mobilized to deal with a heat wave or pain from a broken leg, you may find you are more easily annoyed by minor frustrations. In most cases, the body will eventually adapt to the stressor and return to normal.

3. The **exhaustion phase**, in which persistent stress depletes the body of energy, thereby increasing vulnerability to physical problems and illness. The same reactions that allow the body to respond effectively in the alarm and resistance phases are unhealthy as long-range responses. Tense muscles can cause headache and neck pain. Increased blood pressure can become chronic hypertension. If normal digestive processes are interrupted or shut down for too long, digestive disorders may result.

Selye did not believe that people should aim for a stress-free life. Some stress, he said, is positive and productive, even if it also requires the body to produce short-term energy: competing in an athletic event, falling in love, working hard on a project you enjoy. And some negative stress is simply unavoidable; it's called life. To get an idea of what your body goes through during stress, watch the video *Stress and Your Health 1.*

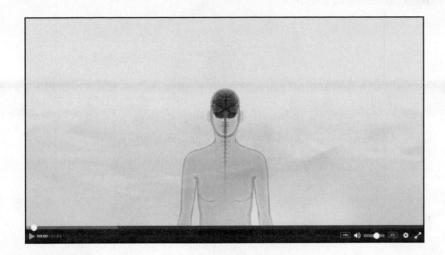

CURRENT APPROACHES   One of Selye's most important observations was that the very biological changes that are adaptive in the short run, because they permit the body to respond quickly to danger, can become hazardous in the long run (McEwen, 2007). Modern researchers are learning how this happens.

When you are under stress, your brain's hypothalamus sends messages to the endocrine glands along two major pathways. One, as Selye observed, activates the sympathetic division of the autonomic nervous system for "fight or flight," producing the release of epinephrine and norepinephrine from the inner part (medulla) of the adrenal glands. In addition, the hypothalamus initiates activity along the **HPA axis** (HPA stands for hypothalamus–pituitary–adrenal cortex). The hypothalamus releases chemical messengers that communicate with the pituitary gland, which in turn sends messages to the outer part (cortex) of the adrenal glands. The adrenal cortex secretes **cortisol** and other hormones that elevate blood sugar and protect the body's tissues from inflammation in case of injury (see Figure 11.3).

One result of HPA axis activation is increased energy, which is crucial for short-term responses to stress (Kemeny, 2003). But if cortisol and other stress hormones stay high too long, they can lead to hypertension, immune disorders, other physical ailments, and emotional problems such as depression (Ping et al., 2015). Elevated levels of cortisol also motivate animals (and presumably humans, too) to seek out rich comfort foods and store the extra calories as abdominal fat.

The cumulative effects of external sources of stress may help us to understand why people at the lower rungs of the socioeconomic ladder have worse health and higher mortality rates for almost every disease and medical condition than do those at the top (Adler & Snibbe, 2003). In addition to the obvious reasons of lack of access to good medical care and reliance on diets that lead to obesity and type 2 diabetes, low-income people often live with continuous environmental stressors: higher crime rates, discrimination, rundown housing, and greater exposure to hazards such as chemical contamination (Gallo & Matthews, 2003). These conditions affect urban blacks disproportionately and may help account for their higher incidence of hypertension (high blood pressure), which can lead to kidney disease, strokes, and heart attacks (Clark et al., 1999; Pascoe & Richman, 2009).

Children are particularly vulnerable to the stressors associated with poverty or maltreatment by parents: The more years they are exposed to family disruption, violence, and instability, the higher their cortisol levels and the greater the snowballing negative effect

HPA (hypothalamus–pituitary–adrenal cortex) axis

A system activated to energize the body to respond to stressors. The hypothalamus sends chemical messengers to the pituitary gland, which in turn prompts the adrenal cortex to produce cortisol and other hormones.

cortisol

A hormone secreted by the adrenal cortex that elevates blood sugar and protects the body's tissues in case of injury; if chronically elevated due to stress, it can lead to hypertension, immune disorders, other illnesses, and possibly depression.

Figure 11.3 The Brain and Body Under Stress

When a person is in danger or under stress, the hypothalamus sends messages to the endocrine glands along two major pathways. In one, the hypothalamus activates the sympathetic division of the autonomic nervous system, which stimulates the adrenal medulla to produce epinephrine and norepinephrine. The result is the many bodily changes associated with "fight or flight." In the other pathway, messages travel along the HPA axis to the adrenal cortex, which produces cortisol and other hormones. The result is increased energy and protection from tissue inflammation in case of injury.

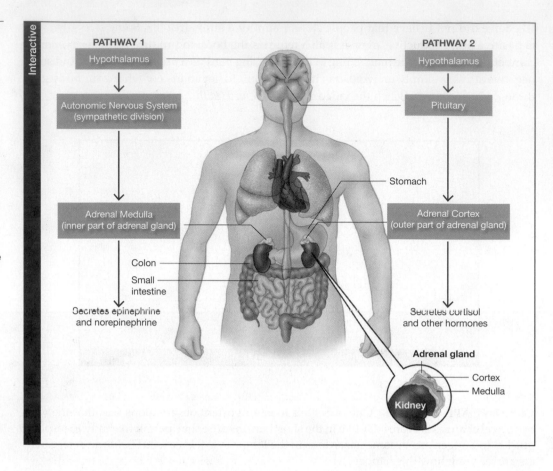

Figure 11.4 Stress and the Common Cold

Chronic stress lasting a month or more boosts the risk of catching a cold. The risk is increased among people undergoing problems with their friends or loved ones; it is highest among people who are out of work (Cohen et al., 1998).

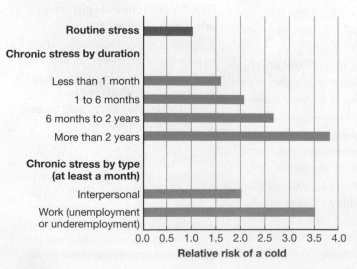

on their physical health, mental health, and cognitive abilities (especially working memory, the ability to hold items of information in memory for current use) in adolescence and adulthood. Persistent childhood stress takes its toll on health both through biological mechanisms, such as chronically elevated cortisol, and behavioral ones. Children living with chronic stress often become hypervigilant to danger, mistrust others, have poor relationships, are unable to regulate their emotions, abuse drugs, and don't eat healthy food. No wonder that by the time they are adults, they have an elevated risk of cardiovascular disease, autoimmune disorders, type 2 diabetes, and early mortality (Evans & Schamberg, 2009; Miller, Chen, & Parker, 2011).

Because work is central in most people's lives, the effects of persistent unemployment can threaten health for people at all income levels, even increasing their vulnerability to the common cold. In one study, heroic volunteers were given either ordinary nose drops or nose drops containing a cold virus, and then were quarantined for 5 days. The people most likely to get a cold's miserable symptoms were those who had been underemployed or unemployed for at least a month. As Figure 11.4 shows, the longer the work problems lasted, the greater the likelihood of illness (Cohen et al., 1998).

Nonetheless, the physiological changes caused by stress do not occur to the same extent in everyone. People's responses to stress vary according to their learning history, gender, preexisting medical conditions, and genetic predisposition for high blood pressure, heart disease, obesity, diabetes, or other health problems (Belsky & Pluess, 2013; McEwen, 2000, 2007). This is why some people respond to the same stressor with much greater increases in blood pressure, heart rate, and hormone levels than other individuals do, and their physical changes take longer to return to normal. These hyperresponsive individuals may be the ones most at risk for eventual illness. For some tips on how to lessen the impact of stress in your life, watch the video *Stress and Your Health 2*.

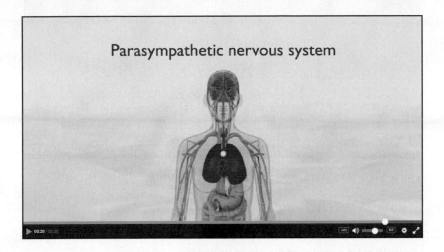

THE IMMUNE SYSTEM: PNI Researchers in the field of *health psychology* (and its medical relative, behavioral medicine) investigate all aspects of how mind and body affect each other to preserve wellness or cause illness. To investigate these interweaving factors, researchers have created an interdisciplinary specialty with the cumbersome name **psychoneuroimmunology**, or **PNI** for short. The "psycho" part stands for psychological processes such as emotions and perceptions; "neuro" for the nervous and endocrine systems; and "immunology" for the immune system, which enables the body to fight disease and infection.

PNI researchers are especially interested in the white blood cells of the immune system, which are designed to recognize foreign or harmful substances (*antigens*), such as flu viruses, bacteria, and tumor cells, and then destroy or deactivate them. The immune system deploys different kinds of white blood cells as weapons, depending on the nature of the enemy. Natural killer cells are important in tumor detection and rejection, and are involved in protection against the spread of cancer cells and viruses. Helper T cells enhance and regulate the immune response; they are the primary target of the HIV virus that causes AIDS. Chemicals produced by the immune cells are sent to the brain, and the brain in turn sends chemical signals to stimulate or restrain the immune system. Anything that disrupts this communication loop—whether drugs, surgery, or chronic stress—can weaken or suppress the immune system (Segerstrom & Miller, 2004).

Some PNI researchers have gotten down to the level of cell damage to see how stress can lead to illness, aging, and even premature death. At the end of every chromosome is a protein complex called a *telomere* that, in essence, tells the cell how long it has to live. Every time a cell divides, enzymes whittle away a tiny piece of the telomere; when it is reduced to almost nothing, the cell stops dividing and dies. Chronic stress, especially if it begins in childhood, appears to shorten the telomeres (Puterman et al., 2015). One team of researchers compared two groups of healthy 20- to 50-year-old women: 19 who had healthy children and 39 who were primary caregivers of a child chronically ill with a serious disease, such as cerebral palsy. Of course, the mothers of the sick children felt that they were under stress, but they also had significantly greater cell damage than did the mothers of healthy children. In fact, the cells of the highly stressed women looked like those of women at least 10 years older, and their telomeres were much shorter (Epel et al., 2004). To learn more about how biological factors interact with other factors to influence health, watch the video *Health Psychology*.

psychoneuroimmunology (PNI)

The study of the relationships among psychology, the nervous and endocrine systems, and the immune system.

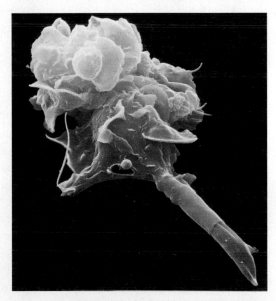

The immune system consists of fighter cells that look more fantastical than any alien creature Hollywood could design. This one is about to engulf and destroy a cigarette-shaped parasite that causes a tropical disease.

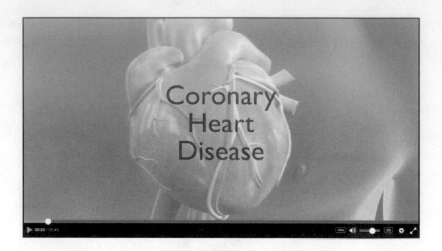

Stress and the Mind

LO 11.3.B Describe some of the contributions to health that result from optimism, conscientiousness, and a sense of control.

Before you try to persuade your instructors that the stress of constant studying is bad for your health, consider this mystery: The large majority of individuals who are living with stressors, even serious ones such as loss of a job or the death of a loved one, do not get sick (Bonanno, 2004; Taylor, Repetti, & Seeman, 1997). What protects them? What attitudes and qualities are most strongly related to health, well-being, and long life?

OPTIMISM When something bad happens to you, what is your first reaction? Do you tell yourself that you will somehow come through it okay, or do you gloomily mutter, "More proof that if something can go wrong for me, it will"? In a fundamental way, optimism—the general expectation that things will go well in spite of occasional setbacks—makes life possible. If people are in a jam but believe things will get better eventually, they will keep striving to make that prediction come true. Even despondent fans of the Chicago Cubs, who have not won the World Series in living memory, maintain a lunatic optimism that "there's always next year."

At first, studies of optimism reported (optimistically!) that optimism is better for health, well-being, and even longevity than pessimism is (Carver & Scheier, 2002; Maruta et al., 2000). You can see why popularizers in the media ran far with this ball, some claiming that having an optimistic outlook would prolong the life of people suffering from serious illnesses. Unfortunately, that hope proved false: A team of Australian researchers who followed 179 patients with lung cancer over a period of 8 years found that optimism made no difference in who lived or in how long they lived (Schofield et al., 2004). Indeed, for every study showing the benefits of optimism, another shows that it can actually be harmful: Among other things, optimists are more likely to keep gambling, even when they lose money, and they can be more vulnerable to depression when the hoped-for outcome does not occur (McNulty & Fincham, 2012). Optimism also backfires when it keeps people from preparing themselves for complications of surgery ("Oh, everything will be fine") or causes them to underestimate risks to their health (Friedman & Martin, 2011).

Pessimists naturally accuse optimists of being unrealistic, and often that is true! For optimism to reap its benefits, it must be grounded in reality, spurring people to take better care of themselves and to regard problems and bad news as difficulties they can overcome. Realistic optimists are more likely than pessimists to be active problem solvers, get support from friends, and seek information that can help them (Brissette, Scheier, & Carver, 2002; Geers, Wellman, & Lassiter, 2009). They keep their senses of humor, plan for the future, and reinterpret the situation in a positive light. Pessimists, in contrast, often do self-destructive

Is the glass half-empty or half-full? Optimists may be likely to see the benefits of this situation ("There's something more than nothing!"), whereas pessimists may be likely to see the downside ("It's not all that it could be").

things: They drink too much, smoke, fail to wear seat belts, drive too fast, and refuse to take medication for illness. So, however, do unrealistic optimists.

CONSCIENTIOUSNESS AND CONTROL   Thus, it is not optimism by itself that predicts health and well-being. You can recite "Everything is good! Everything will work out!" 20 times a day, but it won't get you much (except odd glances from your classmates). Optimism needs a behavioral partner.

In one of the longest longitudinal studies ever conducted in psychology—90 years!—researchers were able to follow the lives of more than 1,500 children originally studied by Lewis Terman, beginning in 1921. Terman followed these children, affectionately called the "Termites," long into their adulthood, and when he died in 1956, other researchers took up the project (Kern, Della Porta, & Friedman, 2014). Health psychologists Howard Friedman and Leslie Martin (2011) found that the secret to longevity for the Termites was *conscientiousness*, the ability to persist in pursuit of goals, get a good education, work hard but enjoy the work and its challenges, and be responsible. Conscientious people are optimists, in the sense that they believe their efforts will pay off, and they act in ways to make that expectation come true. The findings on the Termites, who were largely a homogeneous cohort that was white and middle class, have been replicated across more than 20 independent samples that differed in terms of ethnicity and social class (Deary, Weiss, & Batty, 2010).

Conscientiousness is related to another important cognitive ingredient in health: having an internal locus of control. **Locus of control** refers to your general expectation about whether you can control the things that happen to you (Rotter, 1990). People who have an *internal locus of control* ("internals") tend to believe that they are responsible for what happens to them. Those who have an *external locus of control* ("externals") tend to believe that their lives are controlled by luck, fate, or other people. Having an internal locus of control, especially concerning things you can do *right now* rather than vague future events, is associated with good health, academic achievement, political activism, and emotional well being (Frazier et al., 2011; Roepke & Grant, 2011; Strickland, 1989).

Most people can tolerate all kinds of stressors if they feel able to predict or control them. Consider crowding. Mice get really nasty when they're crowded, but many people love crowds, voluntarily getting squashed in New York's Times Square on New Year's Eve or at a rock concert. Human beings show signs of stress not when they are actually crowded but when they *feel* crowded (Evans, Lepore, & Allen, 2000). People who have the greatest control over their work pace and activities, such as executives and managers, have fewer illnesses and stress symptoms than do employees who have little control, who feel trapped doing repetitive tasks, and who have a low chance of promotion (Karasek & Theorell, 1990). People can usually cope better with continuous, predictable noise (such as the hum of a bustling city street) than with intermittent, loud, unpredictable noise (such as the racket of airplanes heard by people living near airports). This information has proven important in medical care because the high-decibel beeps and alarms going off in hospital rooms, at unpredictable intervals, is often very stressful to patients, elevating their blood pressure and cortisol (Stewart, 2011; Szalma & Hancock, 2011).

Feeling in control affects the immune system, which may be why it helps to speed up recovery from surgery and some diseases (E. Skinner, 1996). People who have an internal locus of control are better able than externals to resist infection by cold viruses and even the health-impairing effects of poverty and discrimination (Cohen, Tyrrell, & Smith, 1993; Krieger & Sidney, 1996; Lachman & Weaver, 1998). As with realistic optimism, feeling in control also makes people more likely to take action to improve their health when necessary. In studies of patients recovering from heart attacks, those who believed the heart attack occurred because they smoked, didn't exercise, or had a stressful job were more likely to change their bad habits and recover quickly. In contrast, those who thought their illness was due to bad luck or fate—factors outside their control—were less likely to generate plans for recovery and more likely to resume their old unhealthy habits (Affleck et al., 1987; Ewart, 1995).

locus of control
A general expectation about whether the results of your actions are under your own control (internal locus) or beyond your control (external locus).

CULTURE and *Control*

Eastern and Western cultures tend to hold different attitudes toward the ability and desirability of controlling one's own life. In general, Western cultures celebrate **primary control**, in which people try to influence events by trying to exert direct control over them: If you are in a bad situation, you change it, fix it, or fight it. The Eastern approach emphasizes **secondary control**, in which people try to accommodate to a bad situation by changing their own aspirations or desires: If you have a problem, you live with it or act in spite of it (Rothbaum, Weisz, & Snyder, 1982).

A Japanese psychologist once offered some examples of Japanese proverbs that teach the benefits of yielding to the inevitable (Azuma, 1984): *To lose is to win* (giving in, to protect the

What kind of control can you exert on a situation? The Japanese say that "willow trees do not get broken by piled up snow." Is it reasonable to think that you can change something that can't be changed, or is it healthier to accept a situation for what it is?

harmony of a relationship, demonstrates the superior trait of generosity); *willow trees do not get broken by piled-up snow* (no matter how many problems pile up in your life, flexibility will help you survive them); and *the true tolerance is to tolerate the intolerable* (some "intolerable" situations are facts of life that no amount of protest will change). You can imagine how long "To lose is to win" would survive on an American football field, or how long most Americans would be prepared to tolerate the intolerable! Yet an important part of coping, for any of us, is learning to accept limited resources, irrevocable losses, and circumstances over which we have little or no direct influence—all aspects of secondary control (E. Skinner, 2007).

People who are ill or under stress can reap the benefits of both Western and Eastern forms of control by avoiding either–or thinking: by taking responsibility for future actions while not blaming themselves unduly for past ones. Among first-year college students who are doing poorly in their classes, future success depends on maintaining enough primary control to keep working hard and learning to study better, *and* on the ability to come to terms with the fact that success is not going to drop into their laps without effort (Hall et al., 2006). Among women who are recovering from sexual assault or coping with cancer, adjustment is related to a woman's belief that she is not to blame for being raped or for getting sick but that she *is* in charge of taking care of herself from now on (Frazier, 2003; Taylor, Lichtman, & Wood, 1984). "I felt that I had lost control of my body somehow," said one cancer survivor, "and the way for me to get back some control was to find out as much as I could." This way of thinking allows people to avoid guilt and self-blame while retaining a belief that they can take steps to get better.

Many problems require us to decide what we can change and to accept what we cannot; perhaps the secret of healthy control lies in knowing the difference.

primary control

An effort to modify reality by changing other people, the situation, or events; a "fighting back" philosophy.

secondary control

An effort to accept reality by changing your own attitudes, goals, or emotions; a "learn to live with it" philosophy.

Overall, then, a sense of control is a good thing, but critical thinkers might want to ask: Control over what? It is surely not beneficial for people to believe they can control absolutely every aspect of their lives; some things, such as death, taxes, or being a random victim of a crime, are out of anyone's control. Health and well-being are not enhanced by self-blame ("Whatever goes wrong with my health is my fault") or the belief that all disease can be prevented by doing the right thing ("If I take vitamins and hold the right positive attitude, I'll never get sick").

JOURNAL PROMPT 11.3

Thinking Critically—Consider Other Interpretations: Most people think stress is something "out there" that just happens to them. However, there is another way of looking at stress—as something in you, something that depends on your thoughts and emotion. Do you see your work as an endless set of assignments you will never complete or as challenging tasks to master? The answer will affect how stressed you are.

Quiz for Module 11.3

1. Steve is unexpectedly called on in class to discuss a question. He hasn't the faintest idea of the answer, and he feels his heart pound and his palms sweat. According to Selye's general adaptation syndrome, Steve is in the _____ phase of his stress response.
   a. Adaptive
   b. Resistance
   c. Exhaustion
   d. Alarm

2. A hormone that elevates blood sugar and protects the body from tissue inflammation during injury is called
   a. Adrenalase
   b. Cortisol
   c. Pituitin
   d. Androsol

3. Marty, finishing his studies in medical school, mutters, "Illness is a product of the body!" Cleo, finishing her doctorate in clinical psychology, counters, "Illness is a product of the mind!" Boris, who is getting a PhD in biology, bellows, "Illness is a product of the body's natural defense systems!" Listening to all this, Petra pipes up: "Health and illness are a product of all three." What is Petra studying?
   a. Psychoneuroimmunology
   b. Neurotaxicendonology

   c. Biolucenteschatology
   d. Pharmalogicetricology

4. Which group of people would you predict might reap a variety of health benefits?
   a. Unrealistic optimists
   b. Optimists
   c. Realistic optimists
   d. Pessimists

5. Anika usually takes credit for doing well on her work assignments and blames her failures on lack of effort. Benicia attributes her successes to luck and blames her failures on the fact that she is an indecisive Gemini. Anika has an _____ locus of control, whereas Benicia has an _____ locus.
   a. External / internal
   b. Developed / undeveloped
   c. Undeveloped / developed
   d. Internal / external

Stress and Emotion

Perhaps you have heard people say things like "She was so depressed, it's no wonder she got sick" or "He's always so angry, he's going to give himself a heart attack one day." Are negative emotions, especially anger and depression, hazardous to your health?

First, we can eliminate the popular belief in a "cancer-prone" personality. (This notion was initially promoted by the tobacco industry to draw attention away from smoking as a leading cause of cancer.) Research has thoroughly discredited this belief; studies of thousands of people around the world, from Japan to Finland, have found no link between personality traits and risk of cancer (Nakaya et al., 2003).

Second, we need to separate the effects of negative emotions on healthy people from the effects of such emotions on people who are ill. After a person already has a virus or medical condition or is living in a chronically stressful situation, negative emotions such as anxiety and helplessness can indeed increase the risk of illness and affect the speed of recovery (Kiecolt-Glaser et al., 1998). People who become depressed after a heart attack are significantly more likely to die from cardiac causes in the succeeding year, even controlling for severity of the disease and other risk factors (Frasure-Smith et al., 1999). But can anger and depression be causes of illness on their own? Some answers are provided in the video *Stress Effects.*

Hostility and Depression: Do They Hurt?

LO 11.4.A Summarize the evidence that negative emotions (such as hostility and depression) detract from health.

One of the first modern efforts to link emotions and illness occurred in the 1970s, with research on the "Type A" personality, a set of qualities thought to be associated with heart disease: ambitiousness, impatience, anger, working hard, and having high standards for oneself. Later studies ruled out all of these factors except one: The toxic ingredient in the Type A personality turned out to be hostility (Myrtek, 2007). Indeed, working hard and having high standards proved to be important factors in good health and longevity, as the Termite study showed (Friedman & Martin, 2011).

By "hostility," we do not mean the irritability or anger that everyone feels on occasion, but *cynical* or *antagonistic hostility*, which characterizes people who are mistrustful of others and always ready to provoke mean, furious arguments. In a classic study of male physicians who had been interviewed as medical students 25 years earlier, those who were chronically angry and resentful were five times as likely as nonhostile men to get heart disease, even when other risk factors such as smoking and a poor diet were taken into account (Ewart & Kolodner, 1994; Williams, Barefoot, & Shekelle, 1985) (see Figure 11.5). These findings have been replicated in other large-scale studies, with African Americans and whites, and with women as well as men (Krantz et al., 2006; Williams et al., 2000). Proneness to anger is a significant risk factor all on its own for impairments of the immune system, elevated blood pressure, heart disease, and even slower healing of wounds (Chida & Hamer, 2008; Gouin et al., 2008; Suinn, 2001).

Clinical depression, too, is linked to at least a doubled risk of later heart attack and cardiovascular disease (Frasure-Smith & Lespérance, 2005; Gan et al., 2014). But what accounts for that link? A large prospective study found that depressed people were more likely to accumulate fat in the belly and midriff (perhaps because of the elevated cortisol that often occurs with depression), where it is more likely to increase the risk of diabetes and heart disease (Vogelzangs et al., 2008). Thus, one reason that depression might lead to heart disease over time would not be depression itself, but more likely the lethargy and overeating that depression can produce in some of its sufferers.

For some time, researchers thought that depression might also lead to cancer, but now it looks as though the reverse is true—that cancer can cause depression, and not just because the diagnosis is "depressing." Cancerous tumors, as well as the immune system that is fighting them, produce high levels of a chemical that can cause the emotional and behavioral symptoms of depression (Brüning et al., 2015). A study of cancer in rats, which after all are not aware of having the disease,

Figure 11.5 Hostility and Heart Disease

Anger is more hazardous to health than a heavy workload. Men who had the highest hostility scores as young medical students were the most likely to have coronary heart disease 25 years later (Williams, Barefoot, & Shekelle, 1985).

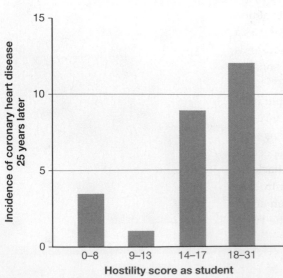

found that the animals would float passively in water instead of swimming for safety, and show other signs of anxiety and apathy (Pyter et al., 2009).

Positive Emotions: Do They Help?

LO 11.4.B   Summarize the evidence that positive emotions contribute to health.

Just as negative emotions can be unhealthful, positive emotions seem to be healthful, although it is difficult to separate cause and effect. Finding a group of very old people who are happy does not mean that happiness contributed to their longevity; as people age, they often become less angry and more content. They might have been really surly when they were age 20 or 50. Moreover, cheerfulness and health may coexist without one causing the other. A longitudinal study of Harvard men found that some life paths led the men to be happy *and* well and others to be sad *and* ill. Happiness did not cause wellness, and sadness did not cause illness (Vaillant, 2012).

Nonetheless, positive emotions could be physically beneficial because they soften or counteract the high arousal caused by negative emotions or chronic stressors. They may dispose people to think more creatively about their opportunities and choices and, as with optimism and internal locus of control, motivate people to take action to achieve their goals (Kok, Catalino, & Frederickson, 2008). People who express positive feelings are also more likely to attract friends and supporters than are people who are always bitter and brooding, and, as we will see, social support is one of the most powerful contributors to good health (Friedman & Martin, 2011; Ong, 2010; Pressman & Cohen, 2012).

If you don't feel bouncy and happy all the time, don't worry; everyone feels grumpy, irritable, and unhappy on occasion. But are negative emotions more typical of your life than positive ones? If so, what actions might you take to ensure a better ratio of positive to negative emotions? A pioneering researcher in the field of health psychology discusses some of these issues in the video *Personality and Health*.

Emotional Inhibition and Expression

LO 11.4.C   Discuss how confession, forgiveness, and other forms of "letting grievances go" contribute to health benefits.

If negative emotions are risky, you might assume that the safest thing to do when you feel angry, depressed, or worried is to try to suppress those feelings. For small problems and annoyances, suppression is usually just fine! But anyone who has tried to banish an unwelcome thought, a bitter memory, or pangs of longing for an ex-lover knows how hard it can be to do this (Wegner, 1994). When you are trying to avoid a thought, you are in fact processing the thought more frequently; you are rehearsing it. That is why, when you are obsessed with

Everyone has secrets and private moments of sad reflection. But when you feel sad or fearful for too long, keeping your feelings to yourself may increase your stress.

Figure 11.6 Heartfelt Forgiveness

Participants in a study were asked to think of someone who they felt had offended or hurt them. Then they were asked to imagine unforgiving reactions (such as rehearsing the hurt and harboring a grudge) and forgiving reactions (such as feeling empathy or forgiving the person). As you can see from the orange bars, people's heart rates increased much more sharply when their thoughts were unforgiving. The blue bars indicate the heart rates also took longer to return to normal in the unforgiving conditions.

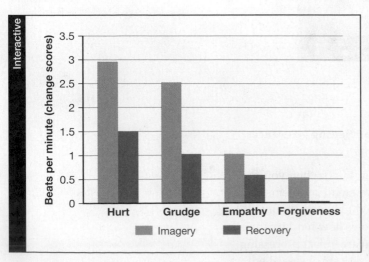

someone you were previously romantically involved with, trying not to think of the person actually prolongs your emotional responsiveness to him or her (Wegner & Gold, 1995).

The continued inhibition of thoughts and emotions actually requires physical effort that can be stressful to the body. People who are able to express matters of great emotional importance to them show elevated levels of disease-fighting white blood cells, whereas people who suppress such feelings tend to have decreased levels (Smyth, Pennebaker, & Arigo, 2012). Suppressing important feelings has a social cost, too. In a longitudinal study that followed first-year college students as they adjusted to being in a new environment, those who expressed their worries and fears openly with other students ended up with better relationships and greater satisfaction, compared to those who said they preferred to keep their emotions to themselves (Srivastava et al., 2009).

THE BENEFITS OF CONFESSION   Given the findings on the harmful effects of feeling negative emotions and also the difficulty and costs of suppressing them, what is a person supposed to do with them? One way to reduce the wear and tear of negative emotions comes from research on the benefits of confession: divulging (even if only to yourself) private thoughts and feelings that make you ashamed, worried, frightened, or sad (Pennebaker, 2002, 2011). A randomized controlled trial of 156 patients following their first heart attack found that those who wrote about their feelings about the heart attack fared better and improved more quickly than a control group who wrote about neutral daily activities (Willmott et al., 2011). And first-year college students who privately wrote down their "deepest thoughts and feelings" about coming to college reported greater short-term homesickness and anxiety, compared to students who wrote about trivial topics. But by the end of the school year, they had had fewer bouts of flu and fewer visits to the infirmary than the control group did (Pennebaker, Colder, & Sharp, 1990).

This method is especially powerful when people write about traumatic experiences. When a group of college students was asked to write about a personal, traumatic experience for 20 minutes a day for 4 days, many told stories of sexual coercion, physical beatings, humiliation, or parental abandonment. Yet most had never discussed these experiences with anyone. The researchers collected data on the students' physical symptoms, white blood cell counts, emotions, and visits to the health center. On every measure, the students who wrote about traumatic experiences were better off than those who wrote only about neutral topics (Pennebaker, Kiecolt-Glaser, & Glaser, 1988). Subsequent research has confirmed the benefits of expressing and working through memories of traumatic events head on, rather than trying to suppress intrusive, troubling thoughts (Dalgleish, Hauer, & Kuyken, 2008).

The benefits of writing occur primarily when the revelation produces insight and understanding, thereby fostering the ability to distance yourself from the bad experience and ending the stressful repetition of obsessive thoughts and unresolved feelings (Kross & Ayduk, 2011; Lepore, Ragan, & Jones, 2000). One young woman, who had been molested at the age of 9 by a boy a year older, at first wrote about her feelings of embarrassment and guilt. By the third day, she was writing about how angry she felt at the boy. By the last day, she had begun to see the whole event differently; he was a child too, after all. When the study was over, she said, "Before, when I thought about it, I'd lie to myself . . . . Now, I don't feel like I even have to think about it because I got it off my chest. I finally admitted that it happened."

THE BENEFITS OF LETTING GRIEVANCES GO   Another way of letting go of negative emotions is to give up the thoughts that produce them and adopt a perspective that might lead to forgiveness. When people rehearse their grievances and hold on to their grudges, their blood pressure, heart rate, and skin conductance rise. Forgiving thoughts (as in the preceding example—"He was a child too") reduce these signs of physiological arousal and restore feelings of control (Witvliet et al., 2015). (See Figure 11.6.) Forgiveness, like confession when it works, helps people see events in a new light. It promotes empathy, the ability to see the situation from another person's perspective. It strengthens and repairs ongoing relationships (Fehr, Gelfand, & Nag, 2010). But it is important not to oversimplify: Forgiveness is not a cure-all and not always a good thing; it depends on the context in which the conflict occurs (McNulty & Fincham, 2012). In a study of women at a domestic violence shelter, the women who forgave their abusive partners were more likely to return to them, and within marriage, forgiveness predicts continued psychological and physical violence (McNulty, 2011).

Forgiveness does *not* mean that the offended person denies, ignores, or excuses the offense, which might be serious. It does mean that the victim is able, finally, to come to terms with the injustice and let go of obsessive feelings of hurt, rage, and vengefulness. As the Chinese proverb says, "He who pursues revenge should dig two graves."

JOURNAL PROMPT 11.4

Thinking Critically—Avoid Emotional Reasoning: Confession and forgiveness are two powerful means of dealing with the burden of stressful emotions. Yet confession (divulging to yourself or to others some emotionally charged topic that's been weighing on you) and forgiveness (coming to terms with an injustice or letting go of a grudge) can often be the *last* thing that people are motivated to do. What advice would you give to someone who's been troubled by a stressful emotional event? How would you encourage a person to open up and let grievances go?

Quiz for Module 11.4

1. Which aspect of Type A behavior is most hazardous to the heart?
   a. Cynical hostility
   b. Working hard
   c. Being in a hurry
   d. Irritability in traffic

2. Clinical depression has been linked to heart attacks and cardiovascular disease. What's the probable mechanism that drives that link?
   a. Depressed people are likely to accumulate belly fat, which increases the risk of diabetes and heart disease.
   b. Depression causes a decrease in epinephrine production, which in turn makes the heart pump harder to maintain health.
   c. Lower HPA levels are associated with clinical depression, and HPA factor is one of the contributors to heart health.
   d. The phrase "a heavy heart" is just that; coping with depression itself is taxing on the heart.

3. What does the research evidence show is the link between personality traits and the risk of cancer?
   a. There is no link between personality traits and risk of cancer.
   b. Personality accounts for ٰpercent of the variability in cancer risk.

   c. Personality accounts for 12 percent of the variability in cancer risk.
   d. Personality accounts for approximately 8 percent of the variability in cancer risk.

4. Cameron is generally upbeat, positive, and has a good outlook on life. Cameron also has a clean bill of health and is feeling fit. What can we conclude about the relationship between Cameron's positive emotions and health status?
   a. Cameron experiences positive emotions and enjoys good health.
   b. Cameron's positive emotions caused good health outcomes.
   c. Cameron's good health outcomes caused an upbeat outlook on life.
   d. Cameron has had a positive outlook on life and enjoyed good health, and will continue to do so.

5. Amber has many worries about going to college, but she is afraid to tell anyone. What might be the healthiest solution for her?
   a. Writing down her feelings and then rereading and rethinking what she wrote.
   b. Tweeting her friends about her moods.
   c. Talking frequently to anyone who will listen.
   d. Trying not to think about her feelings.

Coping with Stress

We have noted that most people who are under stress, even those living in difficult situations, do not become ill. In addition to feeling optimistic and in control, and not wallowing around in negative emotions, how do they manage to cope?

The most immediate way to deal with the physiological tension of stress and negative emotions is to take time out and reduce the body's physical arousal. One successful method is the ancient Buddhist practice of *mindfulness meditation*, which fosters emotional tranquility. The goal is to learn to accept feelings of anger, sadness, or anxiety without judging them or trying to get rid of them (a form of secondary control) (Davidson et al., 2003). Many meditation practices exist; a common one is to focus on your breathing, and as thoughts intrude, acknowledge them but then send them away and return to your breaths. Doing this even in brief sessions over several weeks produces changes in brain activity associated with positive emotions and increases feelings of control. Over an extended time, meditation seems to stimulate greater activity of the enzymes involved in the length of telomeres and increases the longevity of key immune cells (Jacobs et al., 2011; Moyer et al., 2011). To learn more about the benefits of meditation, watch *Reducing Stress, Improving Health*.

Another central way of reducing negative emotions and lowering the risk of illness is exercise. Exercise is as beneficial for improving mood (especially depression and anxiety) as taking aspirin is for getting rid of a headache (Otto & Smits, 2011). People who are physically fit have improved cardiovascular health and cognitive function, and lower risk of type 2 diabetes, than people who are less fit even when all are under the same pressures. People who exercise regularly and moderately also show lower physiological arousal to stressors (Vita et al., 1998). Exercise even seems to slow the progression of degenerative diseases, such as Parkinson's (Gitler, 2011).

These activities, along with any others that calm your body and focus your mind—massage, prayer, music, dancing, baking bread—are all good for health. But if your house has burned down or you need a serious operation, other coping strategies will be necessary.

Solving the Problem

LO 11.5.A   Discuss how emotion-focused coping and problem-focused coping contribute to the problem-solving approach to dealing with stress.

Years ago, at the age of 23, a friend of ours named Simi Linton was struck by tragedy. Linton, her new husband, and her best friend were in a horrific car accident. When she awoke in a hospital room, with only a vague memory of the crash, she learned that her husband and friend had been killed and that she herself had permanent spinal injury and would never walk again.

How in the world does anyone recover from such a devastating event? Some people advise survivors of disaster or tragedy to "get it out of your system" or to "get in touch with your feelings." But survivors know they feel miserable. What should they *do*? This question gets to the heart of the difference between *emotion-focused* and *problem-focused coping* (Lazarus & Folkman, 1984). Emotion-focused coping concentrates on the emotions the problem has caused, whether anger, anxiety, or grief. For a period of time after any tragedy or disaster, it is normal to give in to these emotions and feel overwhelmed by them. In this stage, people often need to talk obsessively about the event so that they can come to terms with it, make sense of it, and decide what to do about it (Lepore, Ragan, & Jones, 2000).

Eventually, most people become ready to concentrate on solving the problem itself. The specific steps in problem-focused coping depend on the nature of the problem: whether it is a pressing but one-time decision; a continuing difficulty, such as living with a disability; or an anticipated event, such as having an operation. After the problem is identified, the coper can learn as much as possible about it from professionals and from others in the same predicament (Clarke & Evans, 1998). Becoming informed increases the feeling of control, which in turn can speed recovery (Doering et al., 2000). (But be wary of bad information, which is as prevalent on the Internet as the helpful kind.)

As for Simi Linton, she learned how to do just about everything in her wheelchair (including dancing!), and she went back to school. She got a PhD in psychology, remarried, and became a highly respected teacher, counselor, writer, and activist committed to improving conditions and opportunities for people with disabilities (Linton, 2006).

Television personality Robin Roberts faced a series of life-threatening illnesses but relied on a variety of coping strategies to persevere.

Rethinking the Problem

LO 11.5.B Describe three effective coping strategies that rely on rethinking the stressful problem at hand, and give an example of each.

Some problems cannot be solved; these are the unavoidable facts of life, such as an inability to have children, losing your job, or developing a chronic illness. Now what? Health psychologists have identified three effective cognitive coping methods:

1. **Reappraising the situation.** Although you may not be able to get rid of a stressor, you can choose to think about it differently, a process called *reappraisal*. Reappraisal can turn anger into sympathy, worry into determination, and feelings of loss into feelings of opportunity. Maybe that job you lost was dismal but you were too afraid to quit and look for another; now you can. Reappraisal improves well-being and reduces negative emotions (Moskowitz et al., 2009).

2. **Learning from the experience.** Many people emerge from adversity with newfound or newly acquired skills, having been forced to learn something they had not known before, such as how to cope with the medical system or how to manage a deceased parent's estate. Others discover sources of courage and strength they did not know they had. Those who draw lessons from the inescapable tragedies of life, and find meaning in them, thrive as a result of adversity instead of simply surviving it (Davis, Nolen-Hoeksema, & Larson, 1998; Folkman & Moskowitz, 2000). In fact, having a history of *some* experiences with loss, hardship, illness, or other stressors actually predicts better health outcomes over the years than having a life with *no* adversity (Seery et al., 2013). Facing life's stresses head on gives people the skills of mastery and control, which are keys to well-being and knowing how to cope with further problems.

3. **Making social comparisons.** In a difficult situation, successful copers often compare themselves to others who they feel are less fortunate. Even if they have fatal diseases, they find someone who is worse off (Taylor & Lobel, 1989; Wood, Michela, & Giordano, 2000). One patient with AIDS said in an interview, "I made a list of all the other diseases I would rather not have than AIDS. Lou Gehrig's disease; being in a wheelchair; rheumatoid arthritis, when you are in knots and in terrible pain." Sometimes successful copers

Social groups provide us with a sense of belonging and improve our health.

also compare themselves to those who are doing better than they are. They might say, "Look at her—she's had such family troubles and survived that awful bout with cancer, and she's happier than ever with her life. How did she do it?" or "He and I have the same kinds of problems. How come he's doing so much better in school than I am? What does he know that I don't?" Such comparisons are beneficial when they provide a person with information about ways of coping, managing an illness, or improving a stressful situation (Suls, Martin, & Wheeler, 2002).

Drawing on Social Support

LO 11.5.C Discuss the ways in which friends can help or hinder successful coping efforts.

A final way to deal with negative emotions and stress is to reach out to others. Your health depends not only on what is going on in your body and mind but also on what is going on in your relationships: what you take from them, and what you give to them. When social groups provide individuals with a sense of meaning, purpose, and belonging, they produce enormous benefits for their members' health and well-being (Haslam et al., 2009; Uchino, 2009). Being involved in social networks and a close community is one of the most powerful predictors of having a long and healthy life (Friedman & Martin, 2011). Why?

WHEN FRIENDS HELP YOU COPE . . . Think of all the ways in which family members, friends, neighbors, and coworkers can help you. They can offer concern and affection. They can help you evaluate problems and plan a course of action. They can offer resources and services such as lending you money or a car, or taking notes in class for you when you are sick. Most of all, they are sources of attachment and connection, which everyone needs throughout life.

Friends can even improve your health. In general, work-related stress and unemployment increase a person's vulnerability to the common cold, but having a lot of friends and social contacts helps to reduce that risk (Cohen et al., 2003). Social support is especially important for people who have stressful jobs that require high cardiovascular responsiveness day after day, such as firefighters. Having social support helps the heart rate and stress hormones return to normal more quickly after a stressful episode (Roy, Steptoe, & Kirschbaum, 1998).

When social support comes from a loving partner, its benefits on the immune system are especially powerful. In one study of 16 couples, the wives had to lie in an MRI machine, periodically receiving a mild but stressful electric shock on their ankle (Coan, Schaefer, & Davidson, 2006). During the procedure, some women received a touch on the hand from a stranger; others held hands with their husbands. The women's brain images showed activation in the hypothalamus and other regions involved with pain, physical arousal, and negative emotions. Yet, as you can see in Figure 11.7, the moment the women felt a husband's reassuring hand, their brain activation subsided in all the regions that had been revved up to cope with threat and fear. Holding hands with a stranger, although comforting, did not produce as great a decrease in brain activation as did a husband's touch.

When a touch is affectionate and welcome, it elevates some "therapeutic" hormones, especially *oxytocin*, the hormone that induces relaxation and is associated with mothering and attachment. In fact, human bodies may be designed not only for a "fight-or-flight" response to stress and challenge, but also a "tend-and-befriend" response—being friendly and conciliatory, seeking out a friend or loved one, taking care of others (Taylor & Master, 2011). Animal studies find that early nurturing by parents or other adults

Figure 11.7 Hugs and Health

Women had to lie in an MRI machine while receiving mild but stressful shocks on their ankle. Those who showed the highest activation of the hypothalamus and other regions of the brain involved in stress and anxiety went through the test alone. A stranger's calming touch reduced activation somewhat, and a husband's touch reduced it even more. The women in "super couples," those who felt the closest to their husbands (right bar), showed the lowest signs of stress (Coan, Schaefer, & Davidson, 2006).

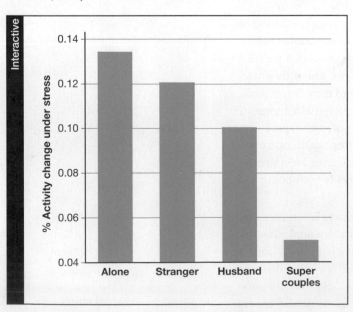

who "tend and befriend" the young can affect the sensitivity of the HPA axis, making the infants more resilient to later chronic stressors (Young et al., 2014). Such findings may help explain why children who lack nurturing become physically more vulnerable to illness, and why a significant minority of children who grow up under adverse conditions do not develop health problems: They have been protected by having warm, nurturing mothers (Miller et al., 2011).

However, once again it is important not to oversimplify, by concluding that people can defeat any illness if they just have the right amount and kind of social support. Some years ago, a psychiatrist claimed, on the basis of a preliminary study, that women with advanced breast cancer lived longer if they joined support groups, but the study has been discredited and was never replicated (Coyne et al., 2009; Coyne & Tennen, 2010). Therapy does not prolong survival, although it often is emotionally and socially beneficial to individual members.

Moreover, not all cultural groups define "social support" the same way or benefit from the same kind. Asians and Asian Americans are more reluctant than Anglo-Americans to ask for help explicitly from friends, colleagues, and family and to disclose feelings of distress to others. Being culturally attuned to the harmony of their relationships, many Asians are concerned about the potentially negative and embarrassing effects of self-disclosure or of seeking help. As a result, they often feel more stressed and have elevated stress hormones when they are required to ask for help or reveal their private feelings (Kim, Sherman, & Taylor, 2008). But Asians do not differ from Anglos in their reliance on, and need for, *implicit* social support—the knowledge that someone will be there to help if they need it.

. . . AND COPING WITH FRIENDS   Needless to say, sometimes other people aren't helpful. Sometimes they themselves are the source of unhappiness, stress, and anger. Even Facebook, which brings so much pleasure and feelings of connection to millions of people, has a dark side. "Everyone" seems so happy and successful, listing all their accomplishments, babies, promotions, great jobs, adorable new puppies, perfect batches of cookies, and super vacations, that many people feel worse about themselves after spending time scrolling through their friends' updates. After all, many students don't post that they are lonely or just got dumped; parents don't report the tedium of raising young children or their kids' tantrums, only the children's latest cute saying or photo. A series of studies of first-year college students found that most of them consistently underestimated their friends' and peers' moods and negative experiences, and overestimated how much fun their peers were having. (It's the "no one is as lonely as I am"/ "everyone else is going to parties" syndrome.) As a result of comparisons to allegedly happier Facebook friends, many came away feeling more lonely and dejected themselves; women were especially vulnerable to feelings of inadequacy (Jordan et al., 2011).

In close relationships, the same person who is a source of support can also become a source of stress, especially if the two parties are arguing all the time. Being in an unhappy, bitter, uncommunicative relationship can significantly impair health (Friedman & Martin, 2011). It makes the partners depressed and angry, affects their health habits, elevates stress hormones, and also directly influences their cardiovascular, endocrine, and immune systems (Kiecolt-Glaser & Newton, 2001). Couples who argue in a hostile fashion—criticizing, interrupting, or insulting each other, and becoming angry and defensive—show significant elevations of cortisol and poorer immune function afterward (Kiecolt-Glaser et al., 2005). Couples who argue in a positive fashion—trying to find common ground, compromising, listening to each other's concerns, and using humor to defuse tension—do not show these impairments.

In addition to being sources of conflict, friends and relatives may be unsupportive in times of trouble simply out of ignorance or awkwardness. They may abandon you or say

Friends can be our greatest source of warmth, support, and fun—and also sources of exasperation, anger, and misery.

Review 11.2

Factors That Increase the Risk of Illness

Factors	Examples
Environmental	Poverty, lack of access to health care, exposure to toxins, crime, discrimination
Experiential	Childhood neglect, traumatic events, chronic job stress, unemployment
Biological	Viral or bacterial infections, disease, genetic vulnerability, toxins
Psychological	Hostility, chronic major depression, emotional inhibition, low levels of conscientious-ness, external locus of control (fatalism), feeling powerless
Behavioral	Smoking, poor diet, lack of exercise, abuse of alcohol and other drugs, lack of sleep
Social	Lack of supportive friends, low involvement in meaningful groups, being in a hostile, bitter relationship

something stupid and hurtful. Sometimes they actively block your efforts to change bad health habits, such as binge drinking or smoking, or by making fun of you or pressuring you to conform to what "everyone" does. And sometimes, because they have never been in the same situation and do not know what to do to help, they offer the wrong kind of support. They may try to cheer you up, saying, "Everything will be fine," rather than let you talk about your fears or find solutions. Or they may try to press you to join a support group "for your own good" even if you regard disclosing your feelings in groups as culturally or personally inappropriate for you.

Finally, we should not forget the benefits of giving support, rather than always being on the receiving end. Julius Segal (1986), a psychologist who worked with Holocaust survivors, hostages, refugees, and other survivors of catastrophe, wrote that a key element in their recovery was compassion for others: "healing through helping." Why? The ability to look outside yourself is related to all of the successful coping mechanisms we have discussed. It encourages you to solve problems instead of blaming others or just venting your emotions, helps you reappraise the situation by seeing it from another person's perspective, fosters forgiveness, and allows you to gain perspective on your own problems (Brown et al., 2003). Healing through helping thus helps everyone to accept difficult situations that are facts of life.

As you can see in Review 11.2, the factors that affect health and illness range from those we can't do anything about to those that we can. Successful coping does not mean eliminating all sources of stress or all difficult emotions. It does not mean constant happiness or a life without anger, grief, and frustration. The healthy person faces problems, deals with them, learns from them, and gets beyond them. To wish for a life without stress, or a life without emotion, would be like wishing for a life without friends. The result might be calm, but it would be joyless. Chronic problems, difficult decisions, and occasional tragedies are inescapable. How we handle them is the test of our humanity.

JOURNAL PROMPT 11.5

Thinking Critically—Don't Oversimplify: Where and who are the sources of social support in your life? Your short list might include family, friends, or roommates, but who forms your extended support network? Are there religious or social groups you feel a part of and can count on in times of need? Would you include some professors in your support network? As you think about what you give to and take from those around you, also think about the kind of support that's offered and the effectiveness of the support in various coping situations.

Quiz for Module 11.5

1. Martin and Lewis had their home burglarized. At first they were both shaken, and told friends how scared they were by the break-in and how angry they felt at themselves for not being better prepared. Three weeks later Martin was still bemoaning their situation, while Lewis was comparing security companies and installing window locks. Martin was engaged in _____, whereas Lewis was practicing _____.

   a. Emotion-focused coping / problem-focused coping

   b. Social comparison / social support seeking

   c. Problem-focused coping / social comparison

   d. Social support seeking / emotion-focused coping

2. You accidentally broke your eyeglasses. Which response is an example of reappraisal?

   a. "What a shame, but I've been wanting new frames anyway."

   b. "I am such a stupid, clumsy idiot!"

   c. "I never do anything right."

   d. "I'll forget about it in aerobics class."

3. Olivia broke her thumb right in the middle of volleyball season, and had to miss the last six games. Although she was disappointed, she realized she was better off than Brianna, who broke her arm at the start of volleyball season and didn't play at all. What coping strategy is Olivia using?

   a. Social comparison

   b. Mindfulness

   c. Social support

   d. Learning from experience

4. What hormone is elevated when happy couples hug one another?

   a. Oxytocin

   b. Oxycontin

   c. Oxycodone

   d. Thimerosal

5. Angela knows that her roommate Sakura has been having a tough time lately. Wanting to help, she's told Sakura multiple times that she's available to hang out, to chat, or to offer whatever Sakura needs to help her cope. An equal number of times Angela's offers have been turned down, and she's starting to think she and Sakura aren't as close as she believed. What's another likely reason for Sakura's rebuffs?

   a. There are cultural differences in social support seeking and how providers of social support are defined.

   b. Sakura's problems are so massive that rumination and chastisement are the only effective coping mechanisms.

   c. Angela wants to offer emotion-focused coping, but Sakura is seeking problem-focused coping.

   d. Sakura has adopted a tend-and-befriend approach to her problems, but Angela's methods are consistent with a fight-or-flight response.

Taking Psychology with You

How Much Control Do We Have over Our Emotions and Our Health?

The prosecution called Dzhokhar Tsarnaev's crimes particularly "heinous, cruel, and depraved," but the defense argued that Dzhokhar was influenced by his extremist brother Tamerlan. Given these vastly different characterizations, could they have controlled themselves and controlled their feelings?

When we are feeling extreme emotions or when major stressors require the body to cope with threat, fear, or danger, the body whirls into action to give us the energy to respond. Just about everyone has had the unpleasant experience of a racing heart, sweaty palms, and other emotional symptoms upon seeing a former lover with a new partner. But does that mean we have no control over our emotions? That if we yell, scream, or become violent when we're angry, it's not our fault?

How about our health? People do have some control over the psychological and social factors involved in the onset and course of many illnesses, such as negative emotions, pessimism, and lack of supportive friends. And we can choose to do the three things that are the strongest behavioral predictors of longevity and health, which are not psychological at all: not smoking (or quitting), eating a healthful diet, and exercising regularly. But does that mean that if we become sick, it's our own fault?

Life is full of stressful experiences, emotional problems, and disastrous bolts out of the blue that we cannot predict or avoid. At such times, critical thinking becomes especially important because the temptation is great to slide into oversimplified, either–or thinking: For example, if you are angry about some injustice, *either* you try to squelch your feelings *or* you take them out on the nearest innocent target. If you become ill, *either* you accept traditional medical procedures *or* you use alternative psychological ones, such as visual imagery, meditation, and support groups. It seems easier to jump to one explanation or solution and stick with it, without examining the evidence (pro and con) for its effectiveness. In stressful times, everyone is inclined to let emotional reasoning cloud their good judgment.

Usually, though, solutions and ways of coping do not require either–or answers. People can accept traditional medical treatments while *also* appreciating the power of optimism, meditation, and social support in their recovery and well-being. In the case of managing anger, the Tsarnaev brothers could surely have found a course of action between suppressing their feelings completely and committing murder.

Hostile anger, as we have seen in this chapter, is particularly hazardous to health, but what should people do when they are enraged? When we examine the evidence, we find that the pop-psych advice to "ventilate your anger and get it out of your system" often backfires: Many people feel worse both physically and mentally after an angry confrontation. When people brood and ruminate about their anger, talk to others incessantly about how angry they are, or ventilate their feelings in hostile acts, their blood pressure shoots up, they often feel angrier, and they behave even *more* aggressively later than if they had just let their feelings of anger subside (Bushman et al., 2005;

Tavris, 1989). Conversely, when people learn to control their tempers and express anger constructively, they usually feel better, not worse; calmer, not angrier.

When people are feeling angry, they may not be able to control that racing heart or the emotion itself, but they can control what they do next: They can take five, calm down, and cool off rather than act impetuously and make matters worse. They can use their critical-thinking skills to avoid emotional reasoning and check their perceptions of the situation for accuracy. People who are quick to feel anger tend to interpret other people's actions as intentional offenses. People who are slow to anger tend to give others the benefit of the doubt, and they are not as focused on their own injured pride.

Critical thinkers might also learn to think carefully about how to express anger, and make a calm decision on how to proceed, so that they will get the results they want. Many people say harsh and hurtful things in anger simply to make the other person feel bad. But shouting "You moron! How could you be so stupid!" is not likely to get the person to apologize, let alone to change his or her behavior. If the goal is to improve a bad situation or achieve justice, learning how to express anger so the other person will listen is essential.

In short, we may not be able to control the stressors in our lives or the intensity of some emotions we feel after great loss, injustice, or tragedy, but we human beings have something almost better: the ability to think about our actions and to control what we do next.

Shared Writing Prompt

Folk wisdom abounds with advice for dealing with stress. "Take a deep breath." "Count to 10." "Think happy thoughts." Jot down four or five strategies that you commonly use to deal with stress in your life, then think critically about them. Based on what you've learned in this chapter, how effective are the techniques you rely on? Do some of your strategies work better for some forms of stress (e.g., deadlines, studying) whereas some are better suited to other situations (e.g., relationship issues, family matters)? What could you be doing differently to manage the stress in your life and become a better coper?

Summary

The Nature of Emotion

LO 11.1.A Explain the components that define an emotion, list the emotions that have a universal facial expression, and describe some of the limits affecting the ability to decode facial expressions of emotion.

Emotions evolved to bind people together, motivate them to achieve their goals, and help them make decisions and plans. The experience of *emotion* involves physiological changes, cognitive processes, action tendencies, and subjective feelings. Some facial expressions—anger, fear, sadness, happiness, disgust, surprise, contempt, and possibly pride—are widely recognized across cultures. But an accurate reading of others' facial expressions increases among members of the same ethnicity, and depends on the social context. Also, because people can and do disguise their emotions, their expressions do not always communicate accurately.

LO 11.1.B Discuss the brain structures involved in the experience of emotions, explain what mirror neurons do, and describe the primary chemicals involved in emotional experience.

The amygdala is responsible for initially evaluating the emotional importance of incoming sensory information and is especially involved in fear. The cerebral cortex provides the cognitive ability to override this initial appraisal. Regions of the *left* prefrontal cortex appear to be specialized for the motivation to approach others (as with happiness and anger), whereas regions of the *right* prefrontal region are specialized for withdrawal or escape (as with disgust and fear). *Mirror neurons* throughout the brain are activated when people observe others, especially other people of the same group or others they like. These neurons seem to be involved in empathy, imitation, synchrony, and *mood contagion*.

During the experience of any emotion, *epinephrine* and *norepinephrine* produce a state of physiological arousal to prepare the body for an output of energy.

LO 11.1.C Summarize the basic research findings indicating that cognitive appraisal plays a role in emotional experience.

Cognitive approaches to emotion emphasize the perceptions and *appraisals* that are involved in different emotions. Thoughts and emotions operate reciprocally, each influencing the other. Some emotions, such as shame and guilt, require complex cognitive capacities.

Emotion and Culture

LO 11.2.A Describe the ways emotional experience can differ across cultures, in terms of concepts, language, and expectations.

Many psychologists believe that all human beings share the ability to experience certain basic emotions. However, cultural differences in values, norms, and appraisals generate emotion blends and culture-specific emotional feelings. Culture affects almost every aspect of emotional experience, including which emotions are considered appropriate or wrong, and what people feel emotional about.

LO 11.2.B Explain how display rules and emotion work influence the communication of emotion in a social and cultural context.

Culture strongly influences *display rules*, including those governing nonverbal *body language*, that regulate how and whether people express their emotions. *Emotion work* is the effort a person makes to display an emotion he or she does not feel but feels obliged to convey.

LO 11.2.C Explain sex differences that appear to exist in emotional experience, and comment on the complex reasons for these differences.

Women and men are equally likely to feel all emotions, although gender rules shape differences in emotional expression. American women on average are more expressive than men, except when it comes to expressing anger at strangers. Both sexes are less expressive to a person of higher status than they, both sexes will do the emotion work their job requires, and some situations foster expressiveness in everybody.

The Nature of Stress

LO 11.3.A Describe the three phases of the general adaptation syndrome, and discuss how modern conceptualizations of the HPA axis and psychoneuroimmunology extend those ideas.

Hans Selye argued that environmental stressors produce a *general adaptation syndrome*, in which the body responds in three stages: *alarm*, *resistance*, and *exhaustion*. If a stressor persists, it may overwhelm the body's ability to cope, and illness may result. Modern research has added to Selye's work. When a person is under stress or in danger, the hypothalamus sends messages to the endocrine glands along two major pathways. One activates the sympathetic division of the autonomic nervous system, releasing adrenal hormones from the inner part of the adrenal glands. In the other, the hypothalamus initiates activity along the *HPA axis*. When the stressors of poverty and unemployment become chronic, they can increase people's stress levels and increase their chances of illness. But responses to stress differ across individuals, depending on the type of stressor and the individual's own genetic predispositions. Researchers in *psychoneuroimmunology (PNI)* are studying the interaction among psychological factors, the nervous and endocrine systems, and the immune system (particularly the white blood cells that destroy harmful foreign bodies, called *antigens*).

LO 11.3.B Describe some of the contributions to health that result from optimism, conscientiousness, and a sense of control.

Realistic optimism, conscientiousness, and having an *internal locus of control* improve immune function and also increase a person's ability to tolerate pain, live with ongoing problems, and recover from illness, possibly because they motivate people to take better care of themselves.

Stress and Emotion

LO 11.4.A Summarize the evidence that negative emotions (such as hostility and depression) detract from health.

Researchers have sought links between emotions, stress, and illness. There is no "cancer-prone personality," but chronic anger, especially in the form of *cynical* or *antagonistic* hostility, is a strong risk factor in heart disease. Major depression also increases the risk of later heart disease.

LO 11.4.B Summarize the evidence that positive emotions contribute to health.

People who consciously suppress their emotions (caused by serious matters) are at greater risk of illness than people who acknowledge and cope with negative emotions. The effort to suppress worries, secrets, and memories of upsetting experiences can become stressful to the body.

LO 11.4.C Discuss how confession, forgiveness, and other forms of "letting grievances go" contribute to health benefits.

Two ways of letting go of negative emotions include confession and forgiveness. The goal is to achieve insight and understanding, distance oneself from the bad experience, and let go of grudges. Forgiveness can be harmful, of course, if it keeps people in violent and abusive relationships.

Coping with Stress

LO 11.5.A Discuss how emotion-focused coping and problem-focused coping contribute to the problem-solving approach to dealing with stress.

An effective approach to coping is to focus on solving the problem (*problem-focused coping*) rather than on venting the emotions caused by the problem (*emotion-focused coping*).

LO 11.5.B   Describe three effective coping strategies that rely on rethinking the stressful problem at hand, and give an example of each.

Rethinking about a problem, which involves *reappraisal*, learning from the experience, and comparing oneself to others can provide new insights and a revised frame of mind.

LO 11.5.C   Discuss the ways in which friends can help or hinder successful coping efforts.

Social support is essential in maintaining physical health and emotional well-being; it even prolongs life and speeds recovery from illness. A touch or a hug from a supportive partner calms the alarm circuits of the brain and raises levels of *oxytocin*, which may result in reduced heart rate and blood pressure. However, friends and family can also be sources of stress. In close relationships, couples who fight in a hostile and negative way show impaired immune function.

Chapter 11 Quiz

1. Ada was feeling a little down in the dumps—sad, grumpy, just not herself. Her grandmother told her, "Smile, Ada; you'll feel better!" Which theory predicts that Grandma is correct?

   a. Cannon-Bard theory

   b. Circumplex model of emotions

   c. Cultural relativity

   d. Facial feedback

2. If you visited a strange, exotic land and carefully observed the facial expressions of the members of that culture, about which emotion would you most likely be mistaken?

   a. Jealousy

   b. Happiness

   c. Sadness

   d. Anger

3. During times of stress or intense emotion, the adrenal glands secrete _____ and _____ to heighten arousal and alertness.

   a. Cortisol / dopamine

   b. Serotonin / GABA

   c. Epinephrine / norepinephrine

   d. Insulin / betatine

4. Florian has to get an immunization shot during his upcoming visit to the doctor. The night before, on the drive there, and in the waiting room he keeps thinking about how much the shot is going to hurt, and how uncomfortable he'll be. When the time comes the doctor produces a needle 2 millimeters long that barely scratches the skin. Nonetheless, Florian screams in pain. What's going on here?

   a. Florian's appraisal of the situation led to an emotional reaction that was not consistent with the actual intensity or valence of the emotion-eliciting event.

   b. An emotional blend, rather than a primary emotion, led to Florian's outburst.

   c. Florian's elevated levels of glutamine, histine, and thychrosine caused the pain intensity to increase.

   d. Social comparison led Florian to respond as he thought he should to the average of most immunization experiences.

5. Hidalgo, Tomás, Mary, and Sonjî are all attending a variety show at the Student Union. Which emotion are they likely to experience in common?

   a. Schadenfraude

   b. Fago

   c. Happiness

   d. Hagaii

6. Culturally variable norms that dictate how, when, and to whom emotion is expressed are called _____; role requirements within a job that dictate how and when emotions should be expressed (even if they aren't experienced) are called _____.

   a. Mood management / mood contagion

   b. Emotion management / mood management

   c. Display rules / emotion work

   d. Emotion work / emotion management

7. Who is more emotional: women or men?

   a. It depends

   b. Women

   c. Men

   d. Men for happiness, women for contempt

8. Which of the following is *not* one of the phases of Hans Selye's general adaptation syndrome?

   a. Resistance

   b. Exhaustion

   c. Readiness

   d. Alarm

9. Ginny's motto is "I am the master of my fate." Frieda's motto is "Whatever will be, will be." Who would you predict has an internal locus of control?

   a. Neither Ginny nor Freida

   b. Frieda

   c. Both Ginny and Frieda

   d. Ginny

10. The characteristic in the cluster of Type A personality traits that's harmful to health is

    a. Impatience

    b. Hostility

    c. Ambitiousness

    d. Hard working

11. Will positive emotions, all by themselves, contribute to health and longevity?

    a. Yes for women; no for men.

    b. Yes; there is a direct relationship between the ratio of smiles-to-frowns per day and years of longevity.

    c. Possibly, but their effects are likely to be due (and be a result of) other mechanisms at work.

    d. No; there's no evidence that positive emotional experiences contribute to health, stress management, coping, or wellness.

12. What's an appropriate strategy for letting grievances go?

    a. Forgiveness needs to be mutual; both parties in a grievance need to forgive one another for any health benefits to result.

    b. Forgiveness of severe offenses should be pursued at all costs.

    c. Forgiveness produces minimal health benefits, although the forgiven will probably benefit more than the forgiver.

    d. Forgiveness that inspires empathy, frees the mind, and strengthens relationships can be beneficial to the forgiver.

13. Carlos wants to reduce stress in his life, so he makes a list of all the events that cause him stress, identifies three strategies for dealing with each item, and disciplines himself to pursue at least one strategy each day. What kind of coping scheme is Carlos using?

    a. Problem-focused coping

    b. Emotion-focused coping

    c. Regulatory shift

    d. Emotion management

14. "When life gives you lemons, make lemonade." This saying is an example of _____ as a coping strategy.

    a. Reappraising the situation

    b. Learning from experience

    c. Making social comparisons

    d. Drawing on social support

15. Social support networks present an opportunity for which type of stress reaction?

    a. Fight-or-flight

    b. Tend-and-befriend

    c. Here-and-gone

    d. Now-or-never

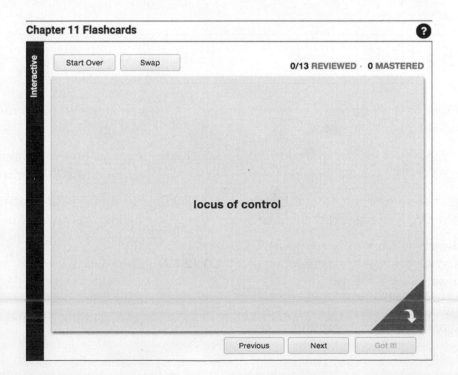

Chapter 12
Motivation

◀ Listen to the Audio

Learning Objectives

LO 12.1.A Define motivation, and distinguish between intrinsic and extrinsic motivation.

LO 12.1.B Discuss the biological factors that contribute to weight, and define what a *set point* is.

LO 12.1.C Discuss five major environmental influences on weight, and provide an example of each.

LO 12.1.D Distinguish between anorexia nervosa and bulimia nervosa, and discuss some factors that contribute to each disorder.

LO 12.2.A Describe how passionate love, compassionate love, social bonding, and the action of vasopressin and oxytocin all contribute to our understanding of the biology of love.

LO 12.2.B Explain how attachment theory can be applied to adult romantic relationships.

LO 12.2.C Summarize the research on gender differences and cultural differences in romantic relationships.

LO 12.3.A Summarize early research findings on sexuality, and describe how biology, hormones, and expectations might contribute to differences in the sexuality of women and men.

LO 12.3.B Discuss six motives for sex and contrast these with three motives for rape.

LO 12.3.C Explain the ways in which culture and gender contribute to both sexual behavior and expectations about that behavior.

LO 12.4.A Describe three conditions that make goal-setting successful, distinguish between performance goals and mastery goals, and discuss the self-fulfilling prophecy cycle.

LO 12.4.B Describe how working conditions affect motives to achieve.

LO 12.5.A Discuss how accurate people are at estimating the type, duration, and extent of their future emotions, and comment on what research indicates makes people happy.

LO 12.5.B Describe three types of motivational conflicts people often face, and give an example of each.

Ask questions . . . be willing to wonder

What accounts for the worldwide epidemic of obesity?

Why do we fall in love, and why with *that person*?

Why are some people straight and others gay?

After a setback, why do some people persist in their goals whereas others give up?

If you've ever looked closely at the walls of your elementary school, your dentist's office, or the lobby of any midsized corporation, you already understand everything you need to know about motivation. Chances are those locations have several posters featuring generic photos and a tidy inspirational message, such as "Believe you can, and you're halfway there," "The harder you work, the luckier you get," and the perennial standby, "There is no 'I' in 'TEAM'." Understanding motivation, it seems, is as simple as spending $9.99 and getting four thumbtacks.

But if that seems *too* simple, you might be willing to pay more for the advice of an "expert." Search the Internet for the phrase "hire a motivational speaker" and you'll get hundreds of thousands of results. There are numerous agencies and individuals ready to tell you about everything from the secrets of innovation to the keys to success to what the future holds, all for a fee, of course. If you'd rather not sit through a 45-minute presentation, many speakers will happily sell you an elaborate set of workbooks and videos to improve your motivation on your own time.

By now you're probably guessing that understanding motivation is not as simple and straightforward as poster manufacturers and well-meaning hucksters make it seem. Understanding a person's motives means answering a core question of psychology: Why do people do what they do? Your own experience tells you that the reasons for a behavior can be a varying and interactive set of biological, psychological, cultural, and interpersonal forces. What's more, the enormous range of people's thoughts and behaviors means that offering any single answer to the "why" question is likely to come up short.

For many decades, the study of motivation was dominated by a focus on biological *drives*, such as those to acquire food and water, to have sex, to seek novelty, and to avoid cold and pain. But drive theories do not account for the full complexity of human motivation, because people are conscious creatures who think and plan ahead, set goals for themselves, and plot strategies to reach those goals. People may have a drive to eat, for instance, but that information doesn't tell us why some individuals will go on hunger strikes to protest injustice.

In this chapter, we will examine four central areas of human motivation: food, love, sex, and achievement. We will also see how happiness and well-being are affected by the kinds of goals we set for ourselves.

Motivation and the Hungry Animal

Before we begin examining specific motives, it's important to understand what "motivation" means to psychologists in the first place.

Defining Motivation

motivation

An inferred process within a person or animal that causes movement either toward a goal or away from an unpleasant situation.

LO 12.1.A   Define motivation, and distinguish between intrinsic and extrinsic motivation.

Describing someone as "motivated" conjures up many possible definitions. Synonyms like *striving*, *craving*, *goal-oriented*, or *focused* come to mind, but those terms beg for definition as well. A scurrying cockroach appears motivated not to be eaten by a bird, but would you call the roach's behavior "craving"? A general definition of **motivation** seems necessary, and for most psychologists, it refers to a process within a person or animal that causes that organism to move toward a goal or away from an unpleasant situation.

intrinsic motivation

The pursuit of an activity for its own sake.

There are two main sources of motivation. **Intrinsic motivation** refers to the desire to do something for its own sake and the pleasure it brings. For example, a runner may be motivated to exercise simply because it makes her feel good and energized. A young child may be motivated to read purely because reading is a pleasurable activity. **Extrinsic motivation** refers to the desire to do something for external rewards, such as money, good grades, or other external enticement. A runner whose motive is to run farther than her next-door neighbor or to win a slew of medals is focused on something different than the intrinsic value of exercise. Similarly, a child who reads only to rack up Good Reader points or get a certificate from the local library may find little pleasure in the world of books. As we see throughout this chapter, whether your motives are intrinsic or extrinsic affects how readily you meet your goals, and how satisfied meeting them can make you feel. Before discussing that, however, let's examine a very basic motive that needs to be met in order to survive: eating.

extrinsic motivation

The pursuit of an activity for external rewards, such as money or fame.

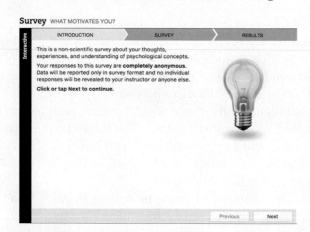

The Biology of Weight

LO 12.1.B   Discuss the biological factors that contribute to weight, and define what a *set point* is.

If you've ever been extremely hungry you know how powerful a motive food can be. You become focused only on satisfying your hunger, and accept the first edible morsels you can find rather than puzzling through which delicacy you really crave. But assuming you don't wait to arrive at the brink of starvation before you eat, on a day-to-day level, how much do genes, psychological processes, and the environment affect our motivation to eat, or shape what we choose to eat?

At one time, most psychologists thought that being overweight was a sign of emotional disturbance. If you were fat, it was because you hated your mother, feared intimacy, or were trying to fill an emotional hole in your psyche by loading up on rich desserts. The evidence for such psychological theories of overweight, however, came mainly from self-reports and from flawed studies that lacked control groups or objective measures of how much people were actually eating. When researchers performed controlled studies, they learned that fat people, on average, are no more and no less emotionally disturbed than average-weight people. Even more surprising, researchers found that heaviness is not always caused by overeating (Munsch & Jansen, 2014; Stunkard et al., 2004). Many heavy people do eat large quantities of food, but so do some thin people. In one early experiment, in which volunteers gorged themselves for months, it was as hard for slender people to gain weight as it was for most heavy people to lose weight. After the study was over, the slender people lost weight as fast as dieters gained it back (Sims, 1974). The video *Food Cravings and Preferences* offers some explanations for why it is easier to gain weight than to lose it.

set point
The genetically influenced weight range for an individual; it is maintained by biological mechanisms that regulate food intake, fat reserves, and metabolism.

GENETIC INFLUENCES ON WEIGHT AND BODY SHAPE   The explanation that emerged from such findings was that a biological mechanism keeps your body weight at a genetically influenced **set point**, the weight you stay at—plus or minus 10 percent—when you are not trying to gain or lose (Lissner et al., 1991). Set-point theory generated much research on how the body regulates appetite, eating, and weight gain and loss. Everyone has a genetically programmed *basal metabolism rate*, the rate at which the body burns calories for energy, and a fixed number of fat cells, which store fat for energy and can change in size. Obese people have about twice the number of fat cells as normal-weight adults do, and their fat cells are bigger (Kopelman, Caterson, & Dietz, 2009). When people lose weight, they don't lose the fat cells; the cells just get thinner, and easily plump up again.

A complex interaction of metabolism, fat cells, and hormones keeps people at the weight their bodies are designed to be, much in the way that a thermostat keeps a house at a constant temperature. When a heavy person diets, the body's metabolism slows down to conserve energy and fat reserves (Harrington et al., 2013). When a thin person overeats, metabolism speeds up, burning energy. In one study, in which 16 slender volunteers ate 1,000 extra

Body weight and shape are strongly affected by genetic factors. Set-point theory helps explain why the Pimas of the American Southwest gain weight easily but lose it slowly, whereas some people from other backgrounds can eat a lot of food yet remain slender.

Both of these mice have a mutation in the *ob* gene, which usually makes mice chubby, like the one on the right. But when leptin is injected daily, the mice eat less and burn more calories, becoming slim, like his friendly pal. Unfortunately, leptin injections have not had the same results in most human beings.

calories every day for 8 weeks, their metabolisms sped up to burn the excess calories. They were like hummingbirds, in constant movement: fidgeting, pacing, changing positions frequently while seated (Levine, Eberhardt, & Jensen, 1999).

What sets the set point? Genes, to start with. Pairs of adult identical twins who grow up in different families are just as similar in body weight and shape as twins raised together. And when identical twins gain weight, they gain it in the same place: Some pairs store extra pounds around their waists, others on their hips and thighs (Comuzzie & Allison, 1998; Horn et al., 2015). Genes also influence how much *brown fat* a person has in addition to the usual white fat. Brown fat is an energy-burning type of fat that seems important in regulating body weight and blood sugar. It is lacking in obese people, which may be one reason that fat people can't burn all the calories they consume (Cypess et al., 2009). However, production of brown fat is also triggered by cold and exercise, which, in mice at least, turns ordinary white fat brown (Ouellet et al., 2012). Brown fat cells are fascinating; when they run out of their own sources of energy, they suck fat out of the rest of the body to keep their proprietor warm. Sorry, you can't (yet!) order a brown-fat supplement online.

GENE MUTATIONS AND LEPTIN When a mutation occurs in the genes that regulate normal eating and weight control, the result may be obesity. One gene, called *obese*, or *ob* for short, causes fat cells to secrete a protein, which researchers have named *leptin* (from the Greek *leptos*, meaning "slender"). Leptin travels through the blood to the brain's hypothalamus, which is involved in the regulation of appetite. When leptin levels are normal, people eat just enough to maintain their weight. When a mutation of the *ob* gene causes leptin levels to be too low, however, the hypothalamus thinks the body lacks fat reserves and signals the individual to overeat. Injecting leptin into leptin-deficient mice reduces the animals' appetites, speeds up their metabolisms, and makes them more active; as a result, the animals shed weight. Alas, for most obese people, and for people who are merely overweight, taking leptin does not produce much weight loss (Comuzzie & Allison, 1998).

Studies of mice suggest that leptin plays its most crucial role early in life, by altering the brain chemistry that influences how much an animal or person later eats. More specifically, leptin helps regulate body weight by strengthening neural circuits in the hypothalamus that reduce appetite and by weakening circuits that stimulate it (Elmquist & Flier, 2004). During a critical period in infancy, leptin influences the formation of those neural connections, and the set point is, well, set (Bouret, Draper, & Simerly, 2004). Some researchers speculate that because of this early neural plasticity, overfeeding infants while the hypothalamus is developing may later produce childhood obesity.

OTHER FACTORS IN OBESITY Numerous other genes are linked to being overweight or obese (Farooqi & O'Rahilly, 2004; Frayling et al., 2007; Herbert et al., 2006; Stice et al., 2008). One gene modulates production of a protein that apparently converts excess calories into heat rather than fat. You have receptors in your nose and mouth that keep urging you to eat more ("The food is right there! It's good! Eat!"), receptors in your gut telling you to quit ("You've had enough already!"), and leptin and other chemicals telling you that you have stored enough fat or not enough. The hormone *ghrelin* makes you hungry and eager to eat more, and leptin turns off your appetite after a meal, making you eat less. This complex set-point system seems to explain why dieters who lose weight so rarely keep it off. Even a year after their weight loss, the bodies of dieters are still leptin deficient, sending out hormonal signals to eat more and restore the lost pounds (Kissileff et al., 2012).

As if all this weren't enough, your brain will get high on sugary foods even if your tongue can't taste them or enjoy their texture. Sweets increase pleasure-inducing dopamine levels in the brain, making you crave more rich food (de Araujo et al., 2008). (Forget about trying to fool your brain with artificial sweeteners; they just make you want the real thing.) Some obese individuals may have underactive reward circuitry, which leads them to overeat to boost their dopamine levels (Stice et al., 2008). When heavy people joke (or lament) that they are "addicted" to rich food, they may be right.

The complexity of the mechanisms governing appetite and weight explains why appetite-suppressing drugs inevitably fail in the long run: They target only one of the many factors that conspire to keep you the weight you are.

But efforts to sell weight-loss products, surgeries, and programs thrive because 69 percent of adults and at least 35 percent of children and teenagers in the United States are now overweight or obese, according to recent figures from the Centers for Disease Control and Prevention. Increases in obesity rates have occurred in both sexes, all social classes, and all age groups, and in many other countries (Popkin, 2009), including Mexico, Egypt, North Africa, Canada, Great Britain, Japan, and Australia, and even coastal China and Southeast Asia. Many health researchers are worried about this trend because obesity is considered a leading risk factor in type 2 diabetes, high blood pressure, heart disease, stroke, and other disorders. (Some experts, however, think that these health concerns have been exaggerated because many overweight people are otherwise fit and in good cardiovascular health, and many thin people are not [Wildman et al., 2008].) But a puzzle remains: If genes and all the chemical factors and fat cells they regulate are so strongly implicated in weight, why are so many people, all over the world, getting fatter?

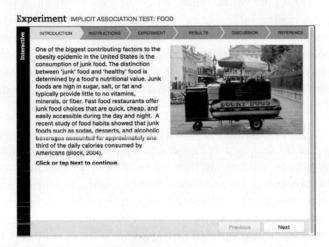

Experiment IMPLICIT ASSOCIATION TEST: FOOD

Environmental Influences on Weight

LO 12.1.C Discuss five major environmental influences on weight, and provide an example of each.

The leading culprits causing the worldwide rise in weight have to do with five big changes in the environment and several less obvious ones:

1. **The increased abundance of fast food and processed foods** that are inexpensive, readily available, and high in sugar, starch, and carbohydrates (Monteiro et al., 2013). Human beings are genetically predisposed to gain weight when rich food is abundant because, in our species' evolutionary past, starvation was all too often a real possibility. Therefore, a tendency to store calories in the form of fat provided a definite survival advantage. Unfortunately, evolution did not produce a comparable mechanism to prevent people who do not have hummingbird metabolisms from gaining weight when food is easily available, tasty, rich, varied, and cheap. That, of course, is precisely the situation today, surrounded as we are by 3/4-pound burgers, fries, chips, tacos, candy bars, pizza, and soda.

   One research team followed thousands of ninth-grade schoolchildren, before and after a new fast-food restaurant opened near their schools. Those whose schools were within a block of a burger or pizza outlet were more likely to become obese in the next year than students whose schools were a quarter of a mile or more away (Currie et al., 2009). Proximity to fast food seems to be a major cause of the "freshman 15" as well. In a study at two very different universities, one in the Midwest and the other on the East Coast, more than 70 percent of all first-year students gained significant amounts of weight (Lloyd-Richardson et al., 2009).

2. **The widespread consumption of high-sugar, high-calorie soft drinks.** Throughout most of human history, the proportion of calories consumed in beverages (milk, wine, fruit juice, and the like) was low, and thus the human body did not evolve a mechanism that would compensate for fluid intake by lowering food intake. Then, 50 years ago, soft

Many people believe that what they eat and how much they eat is regulated by how hungry they feel. But the motivation to eat is complicated, as Brian Wansink (2006) has demonstrated in a clever series of experiments. Here are some of the invisible external influences on your eating habits that he has identified:

- **Package size:** People eat more from a large container (say, of popcorn) than a small one.

- **Plate size:** People eat more when they serve themselves on large plates rather than small ones.

- **Cues to how much has been eaten:** People eat more from a buffet when waiters quickly replace their dirty dishes, thereby eliminating telltale signs of how much food has already been consumed.

- **Kitchen and table layouts:** People eat more when food and snacks are displayed prominently, are varied, and are easily accessible.

- **Distraction:** People eat more when they are being distracted by friends and the environment.

The next time you are out with friends, take notes on how much everyone is eating (including yourself) and notice whether any of these influences are at work. If you are trying to lose weight, how can you alter your own "food environment" to correct for these influences?

drinks, which are loaded with sugar and calories, began spreading across the globe. Putting sweeteners into drinks has led to a weight gain of up to 14 pounds per person in those who drink two to three sodas a day (Powell & Popkin, 2013).

3. **The sharp decline in exercise and other expenditures of energy** because of remote controls, a preference for sedentary activities such as watching television and playing video games, and the speed and convenience of driving rather than walking or biking.

4. **The increased portion sizes of food and drinks.** Servings of food and drinks have become supersized, double or triple what they were only one generation ago. Even babies and toddlers are being fed as much as 30 percent more calories than they need (Fox et al., 2004). In France, people eat rich food but much less of it than Americans do. Their notion of what a proper portion is—for yogurt, soda, a salad, a sandwich, anything—is much smaller than in the United States (Rozin et al., 2003).

5. **The abundance of highly varied foods.** When diets are predictable, people habituate to what they are eating and eat less of it. That is why all diets that restrict people to eating only a few kinds of foods (only watermelon, only protein, only whatever) are successful at first. As soon as food becomes more varied, however, people eat more and gain more weight (Remick, Polivy, & Pliner, 2009). In fact, people will even eat more M&Ms when they are available in a bowl containing 10 colors than when the same number of candies are in a bowl containing only seven colors (Wansink, 2006).

In addition to these obvious causes, researchers have identified other suspects in the mystery of increasing obesity. One is sleeplessness. Sleep plays an important role in regulating weight, and many infants, children, and adults are simply not getting enough of it (Bell & Zimmerman, 2010). Another is a woman's excessive weight gain during pregnancy—something at one time recommended but that is now known to produce infants of higher-than-normal birth weight, who then have a greater risk of becoming obese adults because of the metabolic changes we mentioned earlier (Ludwig & Currie, 2010). A third possibility is central heating and air conditioning, which keep people from shivering and burning brown fat in winter and sweltering (and therefore eating less) in summer. And yet another candidate is exposure to cold viruses: Children exposed to adenovirus-36 are more likely to become obese than children who are not infected, and this link has been found in adults in Korea and Italy as well as in the United States (Gabbert et al., 2010). The virus was first isolated in the late 1970s, when obesity rates began to climb. Obesity itself is not contagious—the virus is long gone after a person has gained the weight—but someone could catch the virus from a thin person who harbors it.

Ultimately, the obesity puzzle requires us to apply the critical-thinking guidelines "be willing to wonder," "tolerate uncertainty," and "consider other explanations." When David Allison, an obesity researcher, observed significant weight gain among a colony of research marmosets, with no obvious causes due to changes in exercise or amount of food, his curiosity was aroused. He and his colleagues examined 24 samples from eight species, domestic and wild, in different environments, totaling some 20,000 animals. Weight increases over a decade varied from 3 percent (in dogs) to 21 percent (in wild rats), but all species showed an average weight gain (Klimentidis et al., 2011). These animals aren't watching TV or drinking gallons of soda! Perhaps, however, they are eating more human junk food, provided by their human owners or found in the trash. Or perhaps some as-yet-undiscovered environmental factors that animals and humans share will one day provide the answer.

The Body as Battleground: Eating Disorders

LO 12.1.D **Distinguish between anorexia nervosa and bulimia nervosa, and discuss some factors that contribute to each disorder.**

Some people lose the battle between the body they have and the body they want, developing serious eating disorders that reflect an irrational terror of being fat. In **bulimia nervosa**, the person binges (eats vast quantities of rich food) and then purges by inducing vomiting or abusing laxatives. In **anorexia nervosa**, the person eats hardly anything and therefore becomes dangerously thin; people with anorexia typically have severely distorted body images, thinking they are fat even when they are emaciated. Anorexia has the highest mortality rate of all mental disorders; many of its sufferers die of heart or kidney failure or complications brought on by weakened bones. To learn more about these disorders, watch the video *Eating Disorders*.

bulimia nervosa
An eating disorder characterized by episodes of excessive eating (bingeing) followed by forced vomiting or use of laxatives (purging).

anorexia nervosa
An eating disorder characterized by fear of being fat, a distorted body image, radically reduced consumption of food, and emaciation.

Bulimia and anorexia are the most well-known eating disorders, and occur most often among young white women. But more than 40 percent of all cases of eating disorders occur among men, older adults, ethnic minority groups, young children, and athletes, and do not fit the diagnostic criteria for bulimia or anorexia (Thomas, Vartanian, & Brownell, 2009). People with *binge-eating disorder* binge without purging; others chew whatever food they want but spit it out without swallowing; others are normal weight but take no joy in eating because they worry obsessively about gaining a pound; some develop phobias about eating certain kinds of food. All of these disorders involve an unhealthy attitude toward food, weight, and the body.

Genes play a role in the development of some eating disorders, particularly anorexia nervosa, which has been found across cultures and throughout history (Striegel-Moore & Bulik, 2007). But most disorders are generated by psychological factors, including depression and anxiety, low self-esteem, perfectionism, and a distorted body image (Hilbert et al., 2014; Presnell, Bearman, & Stice, 2004; Sherry & Hall, 2009). Cultural factors can also generate dissatisfaction

Some argue that the increased prevalence of anorexia and other eating disorders is a product of girls and women seeing ultra-thin fashion models on the pages of magazines. Meanwhile, eating disorders and body image distortions among boys and men are increasing too, as the "ideal" male evolves into a more bulky, muscular shape. What do you think?

with one's body. Bulimia is rare to nonexistent in non-Western cultures and has only become a significant problem in Western cultures with the rise of the thin ideal for women (Keel & Klump, 2003). A meta-analysis of experimental and correlational studies found that women's exposure to the media ideal of impossibly thin women fosters the belief that "thin is beautiful" and increases the risk of disordered eating (Grabe, Ward, & Hyde, 2008; Slevec & Tiggemann, 2011). American culture is also rife with body snarking, the relentlessly critical and snide appraisals of other people's bodies that get posted on blogs, YouTube, Facebook, and Twitter, and are constant topics for entertainment magazines and talk shows (Boepple & Thompson, 2015).

So perhaps it is no wonder that in the United States, women's dissatisfaction with their bodies now crosses all ethnic lines; the levels among Asian American, African American, Hispanic, and Anglo women are virtually the same (Grabe & Hyde, 2006). Eating disorders and body image distortions among boys and men are increasing too, though they take different forms. Just as anorexic women see their gaunt bodies as being too fat, some men have the delusion that their muscular bodies are too puny, so they abuse steroids and exercise or pump iron compulsively (Thompson & Cafri, 2007). In contrast, Chinese men in Taiwan and pastoral nomads of northern Kenya do not think the heavily muscled male body is especially desirable or attractive, and their cultures do not promote media images of muscular males. Men in these cultures have fewer body image disorders than American men do and virtually no interest in muscle-building drugs (Campbell, Pope, & Filiault, 2005; Yang, Gray, & Pope, 2005).

In sum, within a given environment, genetic predispositions for a certain body weight and metabolism interact with psychological needs, cultural norms, and individual habits to shape, in this case quite literally, who we are.

JOURNAL WRITING PROMPT 12.1

Thinking Critically—Don't Oversimplify: When it comes to eating, people want everything right now: fast food, quick weight loss schemes, and even quick fixes for eating disorders. Based on what you've learned about the motives for hunger and eating, why would you predict that quick "anything" probably wouldn't be a solution?

Quiz for Module 12.1

1. Mary is asked why she loves to perform interpretive dance. "I enjoy it, and I want to express myself," she replies. Olivia is asked the same question. "I want to be noticed by a talent scout, and I want to get a performing contract from it." Mary is showing signs of _____, whereas Olivia is showing signs of _____.
   a. Extrinsic motivation / intrinsic motivation
   b. Psychological striving / genetic drift
   c. Genetic drift / psychological striving
   d. Intrinsic motivation / extrinsic motivation

2. The hormone that helps regulate appetite by telling the hypothalamus that the body has stored enough fat is called
   a. Mystin
   b. Ghrelin
   c. Leptin
   d. Obstin

3. Which of the following is *not* a leading environmental cause of worldwide weight gain?
   a. Competition for scarce resources
   b. Increases in portion size
   c. The availability of a wide variety of foods
   d. A steep decline in exercise

4. Americans' expectation of what constitutes "one portion of food" has _____ over the past several decades.
   a. Stayed the same
   b. Decreased
   c. Increased
   d. Shown an inverted-U trend

5. An eating disorder characterized by episodes of excessive eating followed by forced vomiting is called
   a. Anorexia nervosa
   b. Bulimia nervosa
   c. Purgative nervosa
   d. Bingeing

The Social Animal: Motives to Love

Katari Chand is 102 years old. That's pretty remarkable, although her husband has her beat; Karam Chand is 109. Longevity is a wonderful thing to celebrate, but the Chands have another claim to fame: They've been married for 90 years. They met as teenagers in India, wed in 1925, and have been together ever since. When asked the secret of their long relationship, Mr. Chand offered this advice: "It's important to have no secrets and not to argue." He also added, "I've never held back from enjoying life," as he took a puff from his nightly cigarette and a sip of his weekly whisky.

Alcohol and tobacco aside, what do the Chands know that so many others do not? What's kept them in love for 90 years, when so many other romantic passions die in 5 years, 5 weeks, or 5 hours? What *is* love, anyway—the crazy, passionate, heart-palpitating feeling of falling for another person, or the steady, stable feeling of deep and abiding attachment?

The Biology of Love

LO 12.2.A Describe how passionate love, compassionate love, social bonding, and the action of vasopressin and oxytocin all contribute to our understanding of the biology of love.

Psychologists who study love distinguish *passionate (romantic) love*, characterized by a whirlwind of intense emotions and sexual passion, from *companionate love*, characterized by affection and trust. Passionate love is the stuff of crushes, infatuations, "love at first sight," and the early stage of love affairs. It may burn out completely or evolve into companionate love. Passionate love is known in all cultures and has a long history. Wars and duels have been fought because of it, people have committed suicide because of it, great love affairs have begun and been torn apart because of it. Yet, although the experience of romantic love is universal, many cultures have not regarded it as the proper basis for anything serious—such as marriage (Hatfield & Rapson, 2008).

In this era of fMRI, it was inevitable that researchers would seek to explain passionate love by examining the brain. And if you think that what scientists are finding about diet and weight is complicated, their efforts to tease apart the links between romantic passion, sexual yearning, and long-term love make the problem of obesity seem like, well, a piece of cake. There are olfactory cues in a potential partner's scent that can turn you on (or off). There are physical cues in the potential partner's voice and body shape, and even in how similar his or her face is to yours. There is the dopamine jolt of reward, from the same dopamine that makes anticipation of a fabulous meal or an addictive drug so pleasurable, and there are the arousal and excitement provided by adrenaline (Aron et al., 2005; Cozolino, 2006; Ortigue et al., 2010). And there are hormones involved in attachment and bonding.

WHERE DOES LOVE BEGIN?   The neurological origins of passionate love may begin in infancy, in the baby's attachment to the mother. In the view of evolutionary psychologists, maternal and romantic love, the deepest of human attachments, share a common evolutionary purpose—preserving the species—and so they share common neural mechanisms, the ones that make attachment and pair-bonding feel good. Key neurotransmitters and hormones that are involved in pleasure and reward are activated in the mother–baby pair-bond and again later in the pair-bond of adult lovers (Diamond, 2004).

Two important hormones for social bonding are *vasopressin* and *oxytocin*, which play a crucial role in the attachment–caregiving system, influencing feelings and expressions of love, caring, and trust not only between mothers and babies but also between friends and between lovers (Poulin, Holman, & Buffone, 2012; Walum et al., 2008). In one study, volunteers who inhaled oxytocin in a nasal spray were later more likely than control subjects to trust one another in various risky interactions (Kosfeld et al., 2005). In another study, couples given oxytocin increased their nonverbal expressions of love for one another—gazing, smiling, and fondling—in contrast to couples given a placebo (Gonzaga et al., 2006). Conversely, when

The biology of the baby–mother bond may be the origin of adult romantic love, with its exchange of loving gazes and depth of attachment.

prairie voles, a monogamous species, are given a drug that blocks oxytocin, they continue to mate, but they don't get attached to their partners (Ross et al., 2009).

These findings have inspired some oversimplifiers to call oxytocin the "love" or "cuddle" hormone, or even "liquid trust." Cute, but if it really is such a spur to love and attachment, why are humans fighting so much? It turns out that giving people doses of oxytocin makes them more likely to favor their *own* group over other groups, and increases defensive aggression against outsiders (De Dreu et al., 2011). So perhaps oxytocin is the "cuddle your own kind and the hell with the rest of you" hormone. Moreover, high levels of oxytocin in women and of vasopressin in men are actually biological markers of relationship *distress* (Taylor, Saphire-Bernstein, & Seeman, 2010). Finally, people's love and attachment histories affect how they respond to oxytocin as well as the other way around (DeWall et al., 2014). After inhaling oxytocin, men who had had good attachments to their mothers remembered their moms as being unusually caring and supportive compared to men with good attachments who were given a placebo, whereas men who had troubled early home lives remembered their moms as being much less caring than similar men who received a placebo (Bartz et al., 2010).

THE ROLE OF ENDORPHINS   Some of the characteristic feelings and actions that occur during attachment are mediated by reward circuits in the brain and involve the release of *endorphins*, the brain's natural opiates. When baby mice and other animals are separated from their mothers, they cry out in distress, and the mother's touch (or lick) releases endorphins that soothe the infant. But when puppies, guinea pigs, and chicks are injected with low doses of either morphine or endorphins, the animals show much less distress than usual when separated from their mothers; the chemicals seem to be a biological replacement for mom (Panksepp et al., 1980). And when mice are genetically engineered to lack certain opioid receptors, they become less attached to their mothers and do not show signs of distress when separated from them. These findings suggest that endorphin-stimulated euphoria may be a child's initial motive for seeking affection and cuddling—that, in effect, a child attached to a parent is a child addicted to love. The addictive quality of adult passionate love, including the physical and emotional distress that new lovers feel when they are apart, may involve the same biochemistry (Diamond, 2004).

Using fMRI, neuroscientists have found other neurological similarities between infant–mother love and adult romantic love. Certain parts of the brain are activated when people look at images of their sweethearts, in contrast to other parts that are activated when they see pictures of friends or furniture. And these are the same areas that are activated when mothers see images of their own children as opposed to pictures of other children (Bartels & Zeki, 2004).

Clearly, then, the bonds of attachment are biologically based. Yet, as we saw with oxytocin, it is important to avoid oversimplifying, such as by concluding that "love is all in our hormones" or "love occurs in this corner of the brain but not that one." Human love affairs involve many other factors that affect whom we choose, how we get along with that person, and whether we stay with a partner over the years (perhaps even 90 years!).

The Psychology of Love

LO 12.2.B   **Explain how attachment theory can be applied to adult romantic relationships.**

Many romantics believe there is only one true love awaiting them. Considering the presence of 7 billion people on the planet, the odds of finding said person are a bit daunting. What if you're in Omaha and your true love is in Dubrovnik? You could wander for years and never cross paths. Fortunately, evolution has made it possible for human beings to form deep and lasting attachments without traveling the world. In fact, the first major predictor of whom we love is plain *proximity*: We tend to choose our friends and lovers from the set of people who live, study, or work near us. The second major predictor is *similarity*—in looks, attitudes, beliefs, values, personality, and interests (Berscheid & Reis, 1998; Montoya & Horton, 2013). Although it is commonly believed that opposites attract, the fact is that we tend to choose friends and loved ones who are most like us.

The Internet has made it possible to match people on all kinds of dimensions: age, political attitudes, religion or secularism, sexual orientation, disabilities, preferences for particular sexual activities, and preferences for pets. Matchmaking companies administer lengthy questionnaires and personality inventories, claiming to use scientific principles to pair up potential soul mates; one, called Chemistry, promises to match you according to your pattern of neurotransmitters and sex hormones, and GenePartner claims it will find you a DNA match (Finkel et al., 2012). However, these sites typically do not make public the studies on which they base their claims, and the premises of these sciency-sounding matchmaking sites may be faulty, especially those based on unvalidated personality or neurotransmitter types and anecdotal testimonials (King, Austin-Oden, & Lohr, 2009).

A review of the research on Internet dating found that these sites often don't deliver the love of your life (or even the love of your month), and they don't do better than old-fashioned methods of meeting people in generating *long-term* relationships (Finkel et al., 2012). Can you think why?

Internet services capitalize on the fact that like attracts like, and try to help people find their "perfect match." How well do these services work?

- Matching attitudes are important at first, but other things are more important for the long haul, such as how the two partners cope when faced with decisions and stresses, and how they handle conflict.

- People's self-reports are often inaccurate and distorted; they lie to themselves as well as on the questionnaire.

- Most people don't know why they are attracted to one person and not another. You can like the characteristics on a potential partner's profile, but that has little connection to whether you will like that person in person, so to speak. Similarly, many people think they know exactly what they "must have" in a partner, and then they meet someone who has few of those qualities but a whole bunch of others that suddenly become essential.

The latest trend in digital dating may circumvent some of these problems but create others. Smartphone apps such as Tinder, Zoosk, or Hinge allow people to make swift decisions about whether they are attracted to one another, and often set up equally swift dates. Although these apps bring back an important element of interpersonal attraction—the face-to-face exploration of rapport, interests, and chemistry that can't be gained from simply reading a carefully groomed online dating profile—they have also been criticized for encouraging casual sex or superficial relationships (Finkel, 2015). The video *The Dating Game* offers more insights into dating and mating.

THE ATTACHMENT THEORY OF LOVE After you find someone to love, *how* do you love? According to Phillip Shaver and Cindy Hazan (1993), adults, just like babies, can be *secure*, *anxious*, or *avoidant* in their attachments. Securely attached lovers are rarely jealous or worried about being abandoned. They are more compassionate and helpful than insecurely attached people and are quicker to understand and forgive their partners if the partner does something thoughtless or annoying (Konrath et al., 2014; Mikulincer & Shaver, 2007). Anxious lovers are always agitated about their relationships; they want to be close but worry that their partners will leave them. Other people often describe them as clingy, which may be why they are more likely than secure lovers to suffer from unrequited love. Avoidant people distrust and avoid intimate attachments.

Where do these differences come from? According to the *attachment theory of love*, people's attachment styles as adults derive in large part from how their parents cared for them (Simpson & Rholes, 2015). Children form internal "working models" of relationships: Can I trust others? Am I worthy of being loved? Will my parents leave me? If a child's parents are cold and rejecting and provide little or no emotional and physical comfort, the child learns to expect other relationships to be the same. In contrast, if children form secure attachments to trusted parents, they become more trusting of others, expecting to form other secure attachments with friends and lovers in adulthood (Feeney & Cassidy, 2003; Milan, Zona, & Snow, 2013). However, a child's own temperament and genetic predispositions could also help account for the consistency of attachment styles from childhood to adulthood, as well as for the working models of relationships that are formed during childhood (Fraley et al., 2011; Gillath et al., 2008). A child who is temperamentally fearful or difficult, or whose reward circuits do not function normally, may reject even the kindest parent's efforts to console. That child may therefore come to feel anxious or ambivalent in his or her adult relationships.

The Minnesota Longitudinal Study of Risk and Adaptation has followed a large sample of children from birth to adulthood, to see how early attachment styles can create cascading effects on adult relationships. People who are treated poorly early in life and lack secure attachments may end up on a pathway that makes committed relationships difficult. As children, they have trouble regulating negative emotions; as teenagers, they have trouble dealing with and recovering from conflict with their peers; as adults, they tend to "protect" themselves by becoming the less-committed partner in their relationships. If these individuals are lucky enough to get into a relationship with a securely attached partner, however, these vulnerabilities in maintaining a stable partnership can be overcome (Oriña et al., 2011; Simpson, Collins, & Salvatore, 2011; Simpson & Overall, 2014).

THE INGREDIENTS OF LOVE When people are asked to define the key ingredients of love, most agree that love is a mix of passion, intimacy, and commitment (Hutcherson, Seppala, & Gross, 2015; Lemieux & Hale, 2000). Intimacy is based on deep knowledge of the other person, which accumulates gradually, but passion is based on emotion, which is generated by novelty and change. That is why passion is usually highest at the beginning of a relationship, when two people begin to disclose things about themselves to each other, and lowest when knowledge of the other person's beliefs and habits is at its maximum, when it seems that they have nothing left to learn about the beloved. Nonetheless, according to an analysis of a large number of adult couples and a meta-analysis of 25 studies of couples in long- and short-term relationships, romantic love can persist for many years and is strongly associated with a couple's happiness. What diminishes among these happy couples is that part of romantic love we might call *obsessiveness*, constant thinking and worrying about the loved one and the relationship (Acevedo & Aron, 2009).

Biological factors such as the brain's opiate system may contribute to early passion, as we noted, but most psychologists believe that the ability to sustain a long and intimate love relationship has more to do with a couple's attitudes, values, and balance of power than with genes or hormones. One of the most important psychological predictors of satisfaction in long-term relationships is the perception, by both partners, that the relationship is fair, rewarding, and balanced. Partners who feel overbenefited (getting more than they are giving) tend to feel guilty; those who feel underbenefited (not getting what they feel they deserve) tend to feel resentful and angry (Galinsky & Sonenstein, 2013; Pillemer, Hatfield, & Sprecher, 2008). A couple may tootle along comfortably until a stressful event—such as the arrival of children, serious illness, unemployment, or retirement—evokes simmering displeasure over issues of "what's fair."

Another key psychological factor in couples' ability to sustain love is the nature of their primary motivation to maintain the relationship: Is it positive (to enjoy affection and intimacy) or negative (to avoid feeling insecure and lonely)? Couples motivated by the former goal tend to report more satisfaction with their partners (Gable & Poore, 2008). We will see that this difference in motivation—positive or negative—affects happiness and satisfaction in many different domains of life.

The critical-thinking guideline "define your terms" may never be more important than in matters of love. The way we define love deeply affects our satisfaction with relationships and whether our relationships last. After all, if you believe that the only real love is the kind defined by obsession, sexual passion, and hot emotion, then you may decide you are out of love when the initial phase of attraction fades, as it eventually must—and you will be repeatedly disappointed. Robert Solomon (1994) argued that "We conceive of [love] falsely . . . . We expect an explosion at the beginning powerful enough to fuel love through all of its ups and downs instead of viewing love as a process over which we have control, a process that tends to increase with time rather than wane." However, people fall in love in different ways: Some couples do so gradually, over time, after "falling in friendship" first; and couples in arranged marriages may come to love each other long after the wedding (Aron et al., 2008). All the fMRIs in the world can't capture the rich variety of how people grow to love one another. For more discussion of these and related topics, watch the video *Meeting Our Needs.*

Gender, Culture, and Love

LO 12.2.C Summarize the research on gender differences and cultural differences in romantic relationships.

Which sex is more romantic? Which sex truly understands true love? Which sex falls in love but won't commit? Pop-psych books are full of stereotyped answers, but in reality, neither sex loves more than the other (Dion & Dion, 1993; Hatfield & Rapson, 1996/2005). Men and women are equally likely to suffer the heart-crushing torments of unrequited love. They are equally likely to be securely or insecurely attached (Feeney & Cassidy, 2003). Both sexes suffer when a love relationship ends, assuming they did not want it to.

What might be the intrinsic and extrinsic motivators keeping this couple together?

However, women and men often do differ, on average, in how they *express* the fundamental motives for love and intimacy. Males in many cultures learn early that revelations of emotion can be construed as evidence of vulnerability and weakness, which are considered unmasculine. Thus, men in such cultures often develop ways of revealing love that are based on actions rather than words: doing things for the partner, supporting the family financially, or just sharing the same activity, such as watching TV or a football game together (Shields, 2002).

These gender differences reflect gender roles, which are in turn shaped by social, economic, and cultural forces. For most of human history, around the world, the idea that two people would marry for love was considered preposterous. ("Love? Whatever. We have alliances to make, work to do, and kids to produce.") Only in the 20th century did love come to be seen as the "normal" motive for marrying (Coontz, 2005). Even then, women remained far more pragmatic than men in choosing a partner until roughly the 1980s (Reis & Aron, 2008). One reason was that a woman did not just marry a man; she married a standard of living. Therefore, she could not afford to marry someone unsuitable or waste her time in a relationship that was not going anywhere, even if she loved the guy. She married, in short, for extrinsic reasons rather than intrinsic ones. In contrast, a man could afford to be sentimental and romantic in his choice of partner. Henry VIII married his six wives for as many motives, but the wives didn't have much say about it.

In the second half of the 20th century, as women entered the workforce and as two incomes became necessary in most families, the gender difference in romantic love faded, and so did economic motivations to marry, all over the world. Nowadays, most people marry for intrinsic motives, for the pleasure of being with the partner they chose—if they marry at all (DePaulo, 2006). Only tiny numbers of women and men would consider marrying someone they did not love. Pragmatic reasons for marriage persist only in countries with high rates of poverty or in which the extended family controls female sexuality and the financial terms of marriage (Coontz, 2005). Yet even in these countries, such as India and Pakistan, the tight rules governing marriage choices are loosening. So are the rules forbidding divorce, even in previously extremely traditional nations such as Japan, China, and South Korea (Rosin, 2012).

As you can see, our motivations to love may start with biology and the workings of the brain, but they are shaped and directed by our early experiences with parents, the culture we live in, the historical era that shapes us, and something as utterly unromantic as economic dependency or self-sufficiency.

JOURNAL WRITING PROMPT 12.2

Thinking Critically—Define Your Terms: Many people define love as an overwhelming romantic passion. What are the consequences of defining love that way? What other definitions might lead to greater satisfaction in a relationship over time?

Quiz for Module 12.2

1. Two important hormones that play a role in social bonding are _____ and _____.
   a. Vasopressin / oxytocin
   b. Melatonin / amyline
   c. Epinephrine / norepinephrine
   d. Ghrelin / leptin

2. Audrey feels a swell of emotion whenever Gina is nearby. She knows it's love at first sight, and she feels tingly and excited when she thinks of spending time with Gina. The kind of love Audrey is experiencing is called
   a. Companionate love
   b. Passionate love
   c. Extrinsic love
   d. Biological love

3. Dominic is somewhat uncomfortable being close to others and finds it difficult to trust them completely. He gets nervous when someone wants to get too close emotionally, and he finds it difficult to let himself depend on others. Which adult attachment style would describe Dominic's feelings and behavior?

   a. Dependent attachment

   b. Secure attachment

   c. Avoidant attachment

   d. Anxious attachment

4. Marcie's motivation to stay with Bruno is that she enjoys his company and feels close to him. Lydia's motivation to stay with Tim is that she doesn't like feeling lonely and is unsure if she can find another partner. Which relationship would you predict has the greatest satisfaction?

   a. Lydia and Tim

   b. Marcie and Bruno

   c. Both couples should be about equally satisfied

   d. Both couples should feel similar dissatisfaction

5. In many cultures, how do men learn to express love?

   a. By having children and starting a family

   b. By writing about their emotions

   c. By enacting considerate behaviors

   d. By communicating their feelings to their partners

The Erotic Animal: Motives for Sex

Most people believe that sex is a biological drive, merely a matter of doing what comes naturally. "What's there to discuss about sexual motivation?" they say. "Isn't it all inborn, inevitable, and inherently pleasurable?"

It is certainly true that in most other species, sexual behavior is genetically programmed. Without instruction, a male stickleback fish knows exactly what to do with a female stickleback, and a whooping crane knows when to whoop. But as sex researcher and therapist Leonore Tiefer (2004) has observed, for human beings "sex is not a natural act." Sex, she says, is more like dancing than digestion, something you learn rather than a simple physiological process. For one thing, the activities that one culture considers "natural"—such as mouth-to-mouth kissing or oral sex—are often considered unnatural in another culture or historical time. Second, people have to learn from experience and culture what they are supposed to do with their sexual desires and how they are expected to behave. And third, people's motivations for sexual activity are by no means always and only for intrinsic pleasure. Human sexuality is influenced by a blend of biological, psychological, and cultural factors.

The Biology of Desire

LO 12.3.A Summarize early research findings on sexuality, and describe how biology, hormones, and expectations might contribute to differences in the sexuality of women and men.

In the middle of the last century, Alfred Kinsey and his associates (1948, 1953) published two pioneering books on male and female sexuality. Kinsey's team surveyed thousands of Americans from 1938 to 1963 about their sexual attitudes and behavior, and they also reviewed the existing research on sexual physiology. At that time, many people believed that women were not as sexually motivated as men and that women cared more about affection than sexual satisfaction, notions soundly refuted by Kinsey's interviews.

Kinsey was attacked not only for his findings, but also for even daring to ask people about their sexual lives. The national hysteria that accompanied the Kinsey Reports seems hard to believe today: "Danger Lurks In Kinsey Book!" screamed one headline. Yet it is still difficult for social scientists to conduct serious, methodologically sound research on the development of human sexuality. As John Bancroft, a leading sexologist, has observed, because many American adults need to believe that young children have no sexual feelings, they interpret any evidence of normal sexual expression in childhood (such as masturbation or "playing doctor") as a symptom of sexual abuse. And because many adults are uncomfortable

The "Kinsey Report on American Women" (though the book was actually titled *Sexual Behavior in the Human Female*) was not exactly greeted with praise and acceptance—or clear thinking. Cartoonists made fun of its being a "bombshell," and in this 1953 photo, two famous jazz singers and an actress spoofed women's shock about the book—and their eagerness to read it.

about sexual activity among teenagers, they try to restrict or eliminate it by prohibiting sex education and promoting abstinence, both of which actually increase rates of teenage sexuality and pregnancy (Bancroft, 2006; J. Levine, 2003; Trenholm et al., 2007). For an overview of historical and recent attitudes toward sexuality, watch the video *The Power of Sex.*

Following Kinsey, the next wave of sex research began in the 1960s with the laboratory research of physician William Masters and his associate Virginia Johnson (1966). Masters and Johnson's research helped to sweep away cobwebs of superstition and ignorance about how the body works. In studies of physiological changes during sexual arousal and orgasm, they confirmed that male and female orgasms are remarkably similar and that all orgasms are physiologically the same, regardless of the source of stimulation.

If you have ever taken a sex education class, you may have had to memorize Masters and Johnson's description of the "four stages of the sexual response cycle": desire, arousal (excitement), orgasm, and resolution. Unfortunately, the impulse to treat these four stages as if they were like the cycles of a washing machine led to a mistaken inference of universality. Not everyone has an orgasm even following great excitement, and in many women, desire *follows* arousal (Laan & Both, 2008). Masters and Johnson's research was limited by the selection of a sample consisting only of men and women who were easily orgasmic, and they did not

investigate how people's physiological responses might vary according to age, experience, culture, and genetic predispositions (Tiefer, 2004). People vary not only in their propensity for sexual excitation and responsiveness, but also in their ability to inhibit and control that excitement (Bancroft et al., 2009). That is, some people are all accelerator and no brakes, and others are slow to accelerate but quick to brake.

FACTORS PROMOTING SEXUAL DESIRE   One biological factor that promotes sexual desire in both sexes is the hormone testosterone, an androgen (masculinizing hormone). This fact has created a market for the legal and illegal use of androgens. The assumption is that if the goal is to increase sexual desire in women and men who complain of low libido, testosterone should be increased, like adding fuel to your gas tank; if the goal is to reduce sexual desire in sex offenders, testosterone should be lowered, perhaps through chemical castration. Yet these efforts often fail to produce the expected results (Berlin, 2003; M. Anderson, 2005). Why? A primary reason is that in primates, unlike other mammals, sexual motivation requires more than hormones; it is also affected by social experience and context (Randolph et al., 2014; Wallen, 2001). That is why desire can persist in sex offenders who have lost testosterone, and why desire might remain low in people who have been given testosterone. Indeed, artificially administered testosterone does not do much more than a placebo to increase sexual satisfaction in healthy people, nor does a drop in testosterone invariably cause a loss of sexual motivation or enjoyment. In studies of women who had had their uteruses or ovaries surgically removed or who were going through menopause, use of a testosterone patch increased their sexual activity to only one more time a month over the placebo group (Buster et al., 2005).

MEN AND WOMEN: SAME OR DIFFERENT?   Despite the similarities in sexual response that Kinsey and then Masters and Johnson identified, the question of whether men and women are alike or different in some underlying, biologically based sex drive continues to provoke lively debate. Although women on average are certainly as capable as men of sexual pleasure, men do have higher rates of almost every kind of sexual behavior, including masturbation, erotic fantasies, casual sex, and orgasm (Peplau, 2003; Schmitt et al., 2012). These sex differences occur even when men are forbidden by cultural or religious rules to engage in sex at all; Catholic priests have more of these sexual experiences than Catholic nuns do (Baumeister, Catanese, & Vohs, 2001). Men are also more likely than women to admit to having sex because "the opportunity presented itself" (Meston & Buss, 2007).

Biological and evolutionary psychologists argue that these differences occur universally because the hormones and brain circuits involved in sexual behavior differ for men and women. They maintain that for men, the wiring for sex overlaps with that for dominance and aggression, which is why sex and aggression are more likely to be linked in men than in women. For women, the circuits and hormones governing sexuality and nurturance seem to overlap, which is why sex and love are more likely to be linked in women than in men (Diamond, 2008).

Other psychologists, however, believe that most gender differences in sexual behavior reflect women's and men's different roles and experiences in life (Ainsworth & Baumeister, 2012; Eagly & Wood, 1999; Tiefer, 2008). Women may have been more reluctant than men to have casual sex not because they have a lesser "drive" but because the experience is not as likely to be gratifying to them because of the greater risk of harm and risk of unwanted pregnancy, and because of the social stigma that may attach to women who have casual sex. Heterosexual women are just as likely as men to say they would accept a sexual offer from a great-looking person (or an unattractive *famous* person, which might explain some motives of groupies). And both sexes are equally likely to say they would accept sex with friends or casual hook-ups who they think will be great lovers and give them a "positive sexual experience" (Conley et al., 2011; Rosin, 2012).

Of course, both views could be correct. It is possible that men's sexual behavior is more biologically influenced than is women's, increasing men's interest in having frequent, casual sex, whereas women's sexual desires and responsiveness are more affected by circumstances, the specific relationship, and cultural norms (Baumeister, 2000; Farr, Diamond, & Boker, 2014; Schmitt et al., 2012).

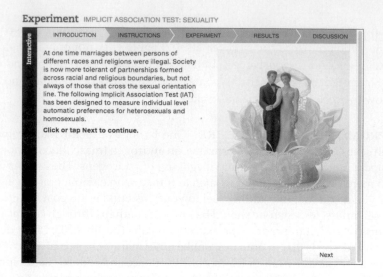

Experiment IMPLICIT ASSOCIATION TEST: SEXUALITY

| INTRODUCTION | INSTRUCTIONS | EXPERIMENT | RESULTS | DISCUSSION |

At one time marriages between persons of different races and religions were illegal. Society is now more tolerant of partnerships formed across racial and religious boundaries, but not always of those that cross the sexual orientation line. The following Implicit Association Test (IAT) has been designed to measure individual level automatic preferences for heterosexuals and homosexuals.

Click or tap Next to continue.

Next

The Psychology of Desire

LO 12.3.B   Discuss six motives for sex and contrast these with three motives for rape.

Psychologists are fond of observing that the sexiest sex organ is the brain, where perceptions begin. People's values, fantasies, and beliefs profoundly affect their sexual desire and behavior. That is why a touch on the knee by an exciting new date feels terrifically sexy, but the same touch by a creepy stranger on a bus feels disgusting. It is why a worried thought can kill sexual arousal in a second, and why a fantasy can be more erotic than reality.

THE MANY MOTIVES FOR SEX   To most people, the primary motives for sex are pretty obvious: to enjoy the pleasure of it, to express love and intimacy, or to make babies. But other motives are not so positive, including money or perks, duty or feelings of obligation, rebellion, power over the partner, and submission to the partner to avoid his or her anger or rejection.

One survey of nearly 2,000 people yielded 237 motives for having sex, and nearly every one of them had been rated as the *most* important motive by someone. Most men and women listed the same top 10, including attraction to the partner, love, fun, and physical pleasure. But some said, "I wanted to feel closer to God," "I was drunk," "to get rid of a headache" (that was #173), "to help me fall asleep," "to make my partner feel powerful," "to return a favor," "because someone dared me," or "to hurt an enemy or a rival" ("I wanted to make him pay so I slept with his girlfriend"; "I wanted someone else to suffer from herpes as I do"). In this survey, men were more likely than women to say they use sex to gain status, enhance their reputation (e.g., because the partner was normally "out of my league"), or get things (such as a promotion) (Meston & Buss, 2007).

Across the many studies of motives for sex, there appear to be several major categories (Cooper, Shapiro, & Powers, 1998; Meston & Buss, 2007):

- *Pleasure*: the satisfaction and physical pleasure of sex.
- *Intimacy*: emotional closeness with the partner, spiritual transcendence.
- *Insecurity*: reassurance that you are attractive or desirable.
- *Partner approval*: the desire to please or appease the partner; the desire to avoid the partner's anger or rejection.
- *Peer approval*: the wish to impress friends, be part of a group, and conform to what everyone else seems to be doing.
- *Attaining a goal*: to get status, money, revenge, or "even the score."

The many motivations for sex range from sex for profit to sex for fun.

People's motives for having sex affect many aspects of their sexual behavior, including whether they engage in sex in the first place, whether they enjoy it, whether they have unprotected or otherwise risky sex, and whether they have few or many partners (Browning et al., 2000; Muise, Impett, & Desmarais, 2013; Snapp et al., 2014). Extrinsic motives, such as having sex to gain approval from others or get some tangible benefit, are most strongly associated with risky sexual behavior, including having many partners, not using birth control, and pressuring a partner into sex (Hamby & Koss, 2003). For men, extrinsic motives include peer pressure, inexperience, a desire for popularity, or a fear of seeming unmasculine. Women's extrinsic motives include not wanting to lose the relationship; feeling obligated after the partner had spent time and money on them; feeling guilty about not doing what the partner demands; or wanting to avoid conflict and quarrels (Impett, Gable, & Peplau, 2005).

When one partner is feeling insecure about the relationship, he or she is also more likely to consent to unwanted sex. In a study of 125 college women, one-half to two-thirds of the Asian American, white, and Latina women had consented to having sex when they didn't really want to, and all of the African American women said they had. Do you remember the attachment theory of love discussed earlier? Anxiously attached women were the most willing to consent to unwanted sex, especially if they feared their partners were less committed than they were. They reported that they often had sex out of feelings of obligation and to prevent the partner from leaving. Securely attached women also occasionally had unwanted sex, but their reasons were different: to gain sexual experience, to satisfy their curiosity, or to actively please their partners and further the intimacy between them (Impett, Gable, & Peplau, 2005).

SEXUAL COERCION AND RAPE   One of the most persistent differences in the sexual experiences of women and men has to do with sexual coercion. A U.S. government survey of rape and domestic violence, based on a nationally representative sample of 16,507 adults, reported that nearly one in five women said they had been raped or experienced attempted rape at least once. (The researchers defined rape as completed or attempted forced penetration, including forced penetration enabled by alcohol or drugs.) The investigators also found high rates of aggression not usually measured in studies of rape, including coercive efforts to control the woman's reproductive and sexual health. Men also reported being victimized, but the numbers were much lower: One in seven said they had been severely beaten at the hands of a partner, and 1 to 2 percent said they had been raped, most when they were younger than age 11 (Black et al., 2011).

However, many women who report a sexual assault that meets the legal definition of rape—being forced to engage in sexual acts against their will—do not label it as such (McMullin & White, 2006; Peterson & Muehlenhard, 2011). Most women define "rape" as being forced into intercourse by an acquaintance or stranger, as an act that caused them to fight back, or as having been molested as a child. They are least likely to call their experience rape if they were sexually assaulted by a boyfriend, had previously had consensual sex with him, were drunk or otherwise drugged, or were forced to have oral sex or unwanted manual stimulation. Other women are motivated to avoid labeling the experience with such a charged word because they are embarrassed, or simply because they don't want to think of someone they know personally as being a "rapist" (Koss, 2011; Perilloux, Duntley, & Buss, 2014; Peterson & Muehlenhard, 2011).

What causes some men to rape? Evolutionary arguments—that rape stems from the male drive to fertilize as many females as possible, the better to distribute their genes—have not been supported (Buss & Schmitt, 2011). Among human beings, rape is often committed by high-status men, including sports heroes and other celebrities, who could easily find consenting sexual partners. All too frequently its victims are children or older adults, who do not reproduce. And sadistic rapists often injure or kill their victims, hardly a way to perpetuate one's genes. The human motives for rape thus appear to be primarily psychological, and include these:

- **Narcissism and hostility toward women.** Sexually aggressive males often are narcissistic, are unable to empathize with women, and feel entitled to have sexual relations with whatever woman they choose. They misperceive women's behavior in social situations, equate feelings of power with sexuality, and accuse women of provoking them (Bushman et al., 2003; Malamuth et al., 1995; Widman & McNulty, 2010).

- **A desire to dominate, humiliate, or punish the victim.** This motive is apparent among soldiers who rape captive women during war and then often kill them (Olujic, 1998). Similarly, reports of the systematic rapes of female cadets at the U.S. Air Force Academy suggest that the rapists' motives were to humiliate the women and get them to drop out. Aggressive motives also occur in the rape of men by other men, usually by anal penetration (King & Woollett, 1997). This form of rape typically occurs in youth gangs, where the intention is to humiliate rival gang members, and in prison, where again the motive is to conquer and degrade the victim.

- **Sadism.** A minority of rapists are violent criminals who get pleasure out of inflicting pain on their victims and who often murder them in planned, grotesque ways (Healey, Lussier, & Beauregard, 2013; Turvey, 2008).

You can see that the answer to the question "Why do people have sex?" is not a simple matter of "doing what's natural." In addition to the intrinsic motives of intimacy, pleasure, procreation, and love, extrinsic motives include intimidation, dominance, insecurity, appeasing the partner, approval from peers, and the wish to prove oneself a real man or a desirable woman.

Gender, Culture, and Sex

LO 12.3.C Explain the ways in which culture and gender contribute to sexual behavior and expectations about that behavior.

Think about kissing. Westerners like to think about kissing, and to do it, too. But if you think kissing is natural, try to remember your first serious kiss and all you had to learn about noses, breathing, and the position of teeth and tongue. The sexual kiss is so complicated that some cultures have never gotten around to it. They think that kissing another person's mouth—the very place that food enters!—is disgusting (Tiefer, 2004). Others have elevated the sexual kiss to high art; why do you suppose one version is called French kissing?

As the kiss illustrates, simply having the physical equipment to perform a sexual act is not enough to explain sexual motivation. People have to learn what is supposed to turn them on (or off), which parts of the body and what activities are erotic (or repulsive), and even how to have pleasurable sexual relations. In some cultures, oral sex is regarded as a bizarre sexual deviation; in others, it is considered not only normal but also supremely desirable. In many cultures, men believe that women who have experienced sexual pleasure of any kind will become unfaithful, so sexual relations are limited to quick intercourse; in other cultures, men's satisfaction and pride depend on knowing the woman is sexually satisfied too. In some cultures, sex itself is seen as something joyful and beautiful, an art to be cultivated as one might cultivate the skill of gourmet cooking. In others, it is considered ugly and dirty, something to be gotten through as rapidly as possible. These differences in perceptions are explored further in the video *Cultural Norms and Sexual Behavior*.

These teenagers are following the sexual scripts for their gender and culture—the boys by ogling and making sexual remarks about girls to impress their peers, and the girls by preening and wearing makeup to look attractive.

How do cultures transmit their rules and requirements about sex to their members? During childhood and adolescence, people learn their culture's *gender roles*, collections of rules that determine the proper attitudes and behavior for men and women. Like an actor in a play, a person following a gender role relies on a **sexual script** that provides instructions on how to behave in sexual situations (Gagnon & Simon, 1973; Sakaluk et al., 2014). If you are a teenage girl, are you supposed to be sexually adventurous and assertive or sexually modest and passive? What if you are a teenage boy? What if you are an older woman or man? The answers differ from culture to culture, as members act in accordance with the sexual scripts for their gender, age, sexual orientation, religion, social status, and peer group.

In many parts of the world, boys acquire their attitudes about sex in a competitive atmosphere where the goal is to impress other males, and they talk and joke about masturbation and other sexual experiences with their friends. Although their traditional sexual scripts are encouraging them to value physical sex, traditional scripts are teaching girls to value relationships and make themselves attractive (Matlin, 2012). At an early age, girls learn that the closer they match the cultural ideal of beauty, the greater their power, sexually and in other ways. They learn that they will be scrutinized and evaluated according to their looks, which of course is the meaning of being a "sex object" (Impett et al., 2011). What many girls and women may not realize is that the more sexualized their clothing, the more likely they are to be seen as incompetent and unintelligent (Graff, Murnen, & Smolak, 2012; Montemurro & Gillen, 2013).

Scripts can be powerful determinants of behavior, including the practice of safe sex to reduce the risk of unwanted pregnancy or sexually transmitted diseases. In interviews with black women ages 22 to 39, researchers found that a reduced likelihood of practicing safe sex was associated with scripts fostering the beliefs that *men control relationships; women sustain relationships; male infidelity is normal; men control sexual activity; women want to use condoms, but men control condom use* (Bowleg, Lucas, & Tschann, 2004). As one woman summarized, "The ball was always in his court." These scripts, the researchers noted, were rooted in African American history and the recurring scarcity of men available for long-term commitments. The scripts originated to preserve the stability of the family, but they encourage some women to maintain sexual relationships at the expense of their own needs and safety.

Today, however, the scripts are changing, largely as a result of women's improving economic status. The ball is no longer always in the man's court, and as a result, girls and young women increasingly feel free to control their own sexual lives (Rosin, 2012). Whenever women have needed marriage to ensure their social and financial security, they have regarded sex as a bargaining chip, an asset to be rationed rather than an activity to be enjoyed for its

sexual scripts

Sets of implicit rules that specify proper sexual behavior for a person in a given situation, varying with the person's gender, age, sexual orientation, religion, social status, and peer group.

BIOLOGY and *Sexual Orientation*

Why is it that most people are heterosexual, some homosexual, and others bisexual? Many psychological explanations for homosexuality have been proposed over the years, but none of them has been supported. Homosexuality is not a result of having a smothering mother, an absent father, or emotional problems. It is not caused by seduction by an older adult (Rind, Tromovitch, & Bauserman, 1998). It is not caused by parental practices or role models. Most gay men recall that they rejected the typical boy role and boys' toys and games from an early age, in spite of enormous pressures from their parents and peers to conform to the traditional male role (Bailey & Zucker, 1995). Conversely, the overwhelming majority of children of gay parents do not become gay, as a learning explanation would predict, although they are more likely than the children of straight parents to be open-minded about homosexuality and gender roles

(Bailey et al., 1995; Fedewa, Black, & Ahn, 2015; Sasnett, 2015). The video *Sexual Orientation* provides more information about the humans that other humans are attracted to.

Many researchers, therefore, have turned to biological explanations of sexual orientation. One line of supporting evidence is that homosexual behavior—including courtship displays, sexual activity, and rearing of young by two males or two females—has been documented in some 450 species, from bottlenose dolphins to penguins to chimpanzees (Volker & Vasey, 2006). Sexual orientation also seems to be moderately heritable, particularly in men (Bailey, Dunne, & Martin, 2000; Rahman & Wilson, 2003). But the large majority of gay men and lesbians do not have a close gay relative, and their siblings, including twins, are overwhelmingly likely to be heterosexual (Peplau et al., 2000).

The assumption that homosexual behavior is rare or "unnatural" is contradicted by the ample evidence of same-sex sexual activity in more than 450 nonhuman species. These young male penguins at a zoo in Germany entwine their necks, kiss, call to each other, and have sex—and they firmly reject females. Another male pair in another zoo, Silo and Roy, seemed so desperate to incubate an egg together that they put a rock in their nest and sat on it. Their human keeper was so touched that he gave them a fertile egg to hatch. Silo and Roy sat on it for the necessary 34 days until their chick, Tango, was born, and then they raised Tango beautifully. "They did a great job," said the zookeeper.

Credit: Nicole Bengiveno/The *New York Times*

Researchers have also examined the role of prenatal exposure to androgens and how this might affect brain organization and partner preference (McFadden, 2008; Rahman & Wilson, 2003). Female babies accidentally exposed in the womb to masculinizing hormones are more likely than other girls to become bisexual or lesbian and to prefer typical boys' toys and activities (Collaer & Hines, 1995). However, most androgenized girls do not become lesbians, and most lesbians were not exposed in the womb to atypical prenatal hormones (Peplau et al., 2000).

Other prenatal events might predispose a child toward a same-sex orientation. More than a dozen studies have found that the probability of a man's becoming gay rises significantly according to the number of older brothers he has, gay or not, when these brothers are born of the same mother. (The percentage of males who become exclusively homosexual is nonetheless low.) A study of 944 homosexual and heterosexual men suggests that this "brother effect" has nothing to do with family environment but rather with conditions within the womb before birth (Bogaert, 2006). The only factor that predicted sexual orientation was having older biological brothers; growing up with older stepbrothers or adoptive brothers (or sisters) had no influence at all. The increased chance of homosexuality occurred even when men had older brothers born to the same mother but raised in a different home. No one yet has any idea, however, what prenatal influence might account for these results.

Several other intriguing biological findings are also associated with sexual orientation. A team of Swedish scientists exposed

Phyllis Lyon and Del Martin (left) lived together for 56 years. In 2008, 2 months after they were finally legally allowed to marry, Del Martin died. Gay men, like this couple on the right, are increasingly likely to adopt children. Why does the issue of legalizing gay and lesbian marriage and the adoption of children evoke so much emotion and controversy?

people to two odors: a testosterone derivative found in men's sweat and an estrogen-like compound found in women's urine. It appears that when a hormone is from the sex you are *not* oriented toward, the olfactory system registers it, but the hypothalamus, which regulates sexual arousal and response, does not. Thus, the brain activity of lesbians in response to the odors was similar to that of heterosexual men, and the brain activity of gay men was similar to that of heterosexual women (Berglund, Lindström, & Savic, 2006; Savic, Berglund, & Lindström, 2005). But the researchers wisely noted that their study could not answer questions of cause and effect: whether the differences in orientation were caused by brain differences, or whether past sexual experiences affected their brains differently.

The basic problem with trying to find a single origin of sexual orientation is that sexual identity and behavior take different forms, and they don't correlate strongly (Savin-Williams, 2006). Some people are heterosexual in behavior but have homosexual fantasies and even define themselves as gay or lesbian. Some men, such as prisoners, are homosexual in behavior because they lack opportunities for heterosexual sex, but they do not define themselves as gay and prefer women as sexual partners. In some cultures, teenage boys go through a homosexual phase that they do not define as homosexual and that does not affect their future relations with women (Herdt, 1984). Similarly, in Lesotho, in South Africa, women have intimate relations with other women, including passionate kissing and oral sex,

but they do not define these acts as sexual, as they do when a man is the partner (Kendall, 1999). Some gay men are feminine in interests and manner, but many are not; some lesbians are "butch" (i.e., masculine in interests and manner), but most are not (Singh et al., 1999).

Moreover, although some lesbians have an exclusively same-sex orientation their whole lives, the majority have more fluid sexual orientations. A researcher interviewed 100 lesbian and bisexual women over a 10-year span and found that only one-third reported consistent attraction only to other women; two-thirds also felt attracted to men. For most of these women, love was truly blind as far as gender was concerned; their sexual behavior depended on whether they loved the partner, not what sex he or she was (Diamond, 2008). Similarly, when men and women watch erotic films, men are more influenced than women are by the gender of the people having sex, whereas women are more influenced than men are by the context in which the sex occurs. Thus, most straight men are turned off by watching gay male couples, most gay men are turned off by watching heterosexual couples, and most straight and lesbian women are turned on by watching anyone of either sex, as long as the context is erotic (Rupp & Wallen, 2008).

Biological factors cannot account for this diversity of sexual responses, cultural customs, or experience. At present, therefore, we must tolerate uncertainty about the origins of sexual orientation. Perhaps the origins will turn out to differ, on average, for males and females, and also differ among individuals, whatever their primary orientation.

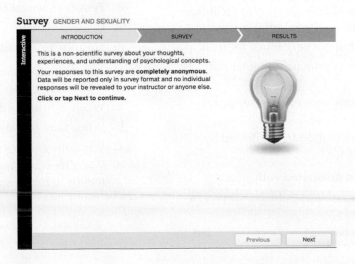

Survey GENDER AND SEXUALITY

| INTRODUCTION | SURVEY | RESULTS |

This is a non-scientific survey about your thoughts, experiences, and understanding of psychological concepts.

Your responses to this survey are **completely anonymous.** Data will be reported only in survey format and no individual responses will be revealed to your instructor or anyone else.

Click or tap Next to continue.

Previous   Next

In the TV series *Girls*, the friends include a virgin, a sexual adventurer, and a heroine looking for love and sex with one man. This rewriting of the traditional sexual script for women, and the easy, explicit way the girls talk about sex, has drawn both fans and critics.

own sake. After all, a woman with no economic resources of her own cannot afford to casually seek sexual pleasure if that means risking an unwanted pregnancy, the security of marriage, her reputation in society, her physical safety, or, in some cultures, her very life. When women become better educated, self-supporting, and able to control their own fertility—three major worldwide changes that began in the last half of the 20th century—they are more likely to want sex for pleasure rather than as a means to another goal.

In the United States, young people's sexual attitudes and behavior changed dramatically between 1943 and 1999: For example, approval of premarital sex leapt from 12 percent to 73 percent among young women, and from 40 percent to 79 percent among young men (Wells & Twenge, 2005). Conversely, when women are not financially dependent on men and have goals of economic self-sufficiency, it is easier for them to refuse sex as well as to leave an abusive relationship or situation. By 2010, the percentage of girls ages 15–17 who had had sexual intercourse dropped from 37.2 to 27; teen pregnancies and reports of acquaintance rape also reached a record low (Hamilton et al., 2015).

JOURNAL WRITING PROMPT 12.3

Thinking Critically—Don't Oversimplify: Given that a minimum level of testosterone is important in sexual desire, many people assume that adding testosterone will increase desire and removing it will lower desire. Why does this assumption oversimplify the issue?

Quiz for Module 12.3

1. William Masters and Virginia Johnson described four stages of the sexual response cycle. According to their original research, what is the correct order of those stages?

   a. Arousal, desire, resolution, orgasm

   b. Arousal, desire, orgasm, resolution

   c. Desire, arousal, orgasm, resolution

   d. Desire, arousal, resolution, orgasm

2. In primates (including humans), how does the mere introduction of increased testosterone affect sexual desire?

   a. A great deal for women, but not very much for men.

   b. A great deal; sexual desire is primarily a biological process.

   c. Not very much; testosterone does not contribute to sexual desire.

   d. Not very much; primate sexual desire is affected by many interacting processes.

3. Risky sexual behavior is often associated with

   a. Extrinsic motives, such as having sex to impress one's friends

   b. Intrinsic motives, such as having sex for pleasure and intimacy

   c. A pre-rapist profile, including drug use and minor legal infractions

   d. Mastery motives, such as competing with another for a potential mate

4. Research on the motives of rapists finds that rape is usually a result of

   a. Thwarted sexual desire

   b. Female provocation

   c. Crossed signals

   d. Hostility or a need for peer approval

5. Under what conditions are women most likely to use sex as a "bargaining chip"?

   a. When they are using birth control

   b. When they already have two children

   c. When they are financially dependent

   d. When they are employed and thus have their own money to bargain with

The Competent Animal: Motives to Achieve

Almost every adult works. Students work at studying. Homemakers work, often more hours than salaried employees, at running a household. Artists, poets, and actors work, even if they are paid erratically (or not at all). Most people are motivated to work in order to meet the needs for food and shelter. Yet survival does not explain why some people want to do their work well and others just want to get it done. And it does not explain why some people work to make a living and then put their passion for achievement into unpaid activities, such as learning to become an accomplished guitar player or traveling to Madagascar to catch sight of a rare bird for their bird-watching list. In this section we'll look at how motivation affects work, but also how work affects a person's motivations. Watch *Theories of Emotion and Motivation* for an overview of some of these issues.

The Effects of Motivation on Work

LO 12.4.A   Describe three conditions that make goal-setting successful, distinguish between performance goals and mastery goals, and discuss the self-fulfilling prophecy cycle.

Psychologists, particularly those in the field of *industrial/organizational psychology*, have measured the psychological qualities that spur achievement and success and also the environmental conditions that influence productivity and satisfaction.

THE IMPORTANCE OF GOALS   To understand the motivation to achieve, researchers today emphasize goals rather than inner drives: What you accomplish depends on the goals you set for yourself and the reasons you pursue them (Dweck & Grant, 2008). Not just any old goals will promote achievement, though. A goal is most likely to improve your motivation and performance when three conditions are met (Locke & Latham, 2002, 2006):

- **The goal is specific.** Defining a goal vaguely, such as "doing your best," is as ineffective as having no goal at all. You need to be specific about what you are going to do and when you are going to do it: "I will write four pages of this paper today."

- **The goal is challenging but achievable.** You are apt to work hardest for tough but realistic goals. The highest, most difficult goals produce the highest levels of motivation and performance, unless, of course, you choose impossible goals that you can never attain.

- **The goal is framed in terms of getting what you want rather than avoiding what you do not want. Approach goals** are positive experiences that you seek directly, such as getting a better grade or learning to scuba dive. **Avoidance goals** involve the effort to avoid unpleasant experiences, such as trying not to make a fool of yourself at parties or trying to avoid being dependent.

approach goals

Goals framed in terms of desired outcomes or experiences, such as learning to scuba dive.

avoidance goals

Goals framed in terms of avoiding unpleasant experiences, such as trying not to look foolish in public.

performance goals

Goals framed in terms of performing well in front of others, being judged favorably, and avoiding criticism.

mastery (learning) goals

Goals framed in terms of increasing one's competence and skills.

All of the motives discussed in this chapter are affected by approach versus avoidance goals. People who frame their goals in specific, achievable approach terms (e.g., "I'm going to lose weight by jogging three times a week") feel better about themselves, feel more competent, are more optimistic, and are less depressed than people who frame the same goals in avoidance terms (e.g., "I'm going to lose weight by cutting out rich foods") (Coats, Janoff-Bulman, & Alpert, 1996; Updegraff, Gable, & Taylor, 2004). Similarly, people who have sex for *approach* motives—to enjoy their own physical pleasure, to promote a partner's happiness, or to seek intimacy—tend to have happier and less conflicted relationships than those who have sex to *avoid* a partner's loss of interest or quarrels with the partner (Muise, Impett, & Desmarais, 2013). Can you guess why approach goals produce better results than avoidance goals? Approach goals allow you to focus on what you can actively do to accomplish them and on the intrinsic pleasure of the activity. Avoidance goals make you focus on what you have to give up.

In the case of work, defining your goals will move you along the road to success, but what happens when you hit a pothole? Some people give up when a goal becomes difficult or they are faced with a setback, whereas others become even more determined to succeed. The crucial difference between them is *why* they are working for that goal: to show off in front of others or learn the task for the satisfaction of it.

People who are motivated by **performance goals** are concerned primarily with being judged favorably and avoiding criticism. Those who are motivated by **mastery (learning) goals** are concerned with increasing their competence and skills and finding intrinsic pleasure in what they are learning (Grant & Dweck, 2003; Senko, Durik, & Harackiewicz, 2008). When people who are motivated by performance goals do poorly, they will often decide the fault is theirs and stop trying to improve. Because their goal is to demonstrate their abilities, they set themselves up for grief when they temporarily fail, as all of us must if we are to learn anything new. In contrast, people who are motivated to master new skills will generally regard failure and criticism as sources of useful information that will help them improve. They know that learning takes time. In business, education, and every other area of life, the lesson is clear: Failure is essential to eventual success.

Mastery goals are powerful intrinsic motivators at all levels of education and throughout life. Students who are in college primarily to master new areas of knowledge choose more challenging projects, persist in the face of difficulty, use deeper and more elaborate study strategies, are less likely than other students to cheat, and enjoy learning more than do students who are there only to get a degree and a meal ticket (Elliot & McGregor, 2001; Grant & Dweck, 2003). As usual, though, we should avoid oversimplifying: Olympic athletes, world-class musicians, and others who are determined to become the best in their field blend performance and mastery goals.

Another contributor to success is self-control (Duckworth & Gross, 2014). As the name suggests, self-control is the ability to regulate attention, emotion, and behavior in the presence of temptation. If you've been able to focus on your studying while the TV, telephone, Facebook, and text messages loom large, you've shown admirable self-control. In fact, you should keep it up. Researchers have demonstrated that higher levels of self-control early in life predict later academic achievement, enhanced physical health, better employment, and higher earnings (Duckworth & Carlson, 2013; Mischel, 2014; Moffitt et al., 2011).

More recent research also highlights the importance of *grit*, a sustained dedication to a passionate interest with determination and effort over a period of years (Duckworth & Gross, 2014). The performance of many experts from top violinists to chess masters to National Spelling Bee winners is often the result of thousands of hours of dedicated practice (Duckworth et al., 2011; Ericsson, 2001; Ericsson & Charness, 1994). That kind of grittiness, hanging in there over the long haul, contributes to success independent of the more focused efforts of self-control. In fact, grit predicts achievement outcomes such as graduating from high school on time, being an effective novice teacher, or making it through the grueling first year of West

Interactive

THE MANY MOTIVES OF ACCOMPLISHMENT

IMMORTALITY

William Faulkner (1897–1962), Novelist

"Really the writer doesn't want success . . . He wants to leave a scratch on that wall [of oblivion]—Kilroy was here—that somebody a hundred or a thousand years later will see."

KNOWLEDGE

Helen Keller (1880–1968), Blind/ deaf author and lecturer

"Knowledge is happiness, because to have knowledge—broad, deep knowledge—is to know true ends from false, and lofty things from low."

FREEDOM

Nelson Mandela (1918–2013), Former president of South Africa

"For to be free is not merely to cast off one's chains, but to live in a way that respects and enhances the freedom of others."

AUTONOMY

Georgia O'Keeffe (1887–1986), Artist

"[I] found myself saying to myself—I can't live where I want to, go where I want to, do what I want to . . . I decided I was a very stupid fool not to at least paint as I wanted to."

POWER

Henry Kissinger (b. 1923), Former secretary of state

"Power is the ultimate aphrodisiac."

DUTY

Eleanor Roosevelt (1884–1962), Humanitarian, lecturer, stateswoman

"As for accomplishments, I just did what I had to do as things came along."

EXCELLENCE

Florence Griffith Joyner (1959– 1998), Olympic gold medalist

"When you've been second best for so long, you can either accept it, or try to become the best. I made the decision to try and be the best."

GREED

Ivan Boesky (b. 1937), Financier, convicted of insider trading violations

"Greed is all right . . . . I think greed is healthy. You can be greedy and still feel good about yourself."

self-fulfilling prophecy

An expectation that comes true because of the tendency of the person holding it to act in ways that bring it about.

self-efficacy

A person's belief that he or she is capable of producing desired results, such as mastering new skills and reaching goals.

Point (Duckworth & Quinn, 2009; Eskreis-Winkler et al., 2014). Individuals who succeed in this task may show varying levels of self-control, but their grit carries them through to successful goal attainment.

EXPECTATIONS AND SELF-EFFICACY   How hard you work for something also depends on your expectations. If you are fairly certain of success, you will work harder to reach your goal than if you are fairly certain of failure.

A classic experiment showed how quickly experience affects these expectations. Young women were asked to solve 15 anagram puzzles. Before working on each one, they had to estimate their chances of solving it. Half of the women started off with very easy anagrams, but half began with insoluble ones. Sure enough, those who started with the easy ones increased their estimates of success on later ones. Those who began with the impossible ones decided they would all be impossible. These expectations, in turn, affected the young women's ability to actually solve the last 10 anagrams, which were the same for everyone. The higher the expectation of success, the more anagrams the women solved (Feather, 1966). After they are acquired, therefore, expectations can create a **self-fulfilling prophecy** (Merton, 1948): Your expectations make you behave in ways that cause the expectation to come true. You expect to succeed, so you work hard—and succeed. Or you expect to fail, so you don't do much work—and do poorly.

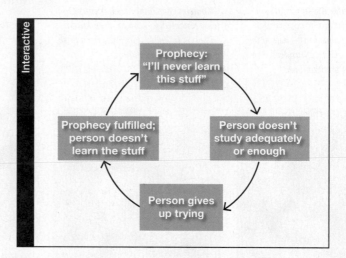

Your expectations are further influenced by your level of confidence in yourself and your abilities (Dweck & Grant, 2008; Judge, 2009). No one is born with a feeling of confidence, or **self-efficacy**. You acquire it through experience in mastering new skills, overcoming obstacles, and learning from occasional failures. Self-efficacy also comes from having successful role models who teach you that your ambitions are possible and from having people around to give you constructive feedback and encouragement (Bandura, 2013).

People who have a strong sense of self-efficacy are quick to cope with problems rather than stewing and brooding about them. Studies in North America, Europe, and Russia find that self-efficacy has a positive effect on just about every aspect of people's lives: how well they do on a task, the grades they earn, how persistently they pursue their goals, the kind of career choices they make, their ability to solve complex problems, their motivation to work for political and social goals, their health habits, and even their chances of recovery from a heart attack (Bandura et al., 2001; Maddux, 1995; Stajkovic & Luthans, 1998). Meta-analyses of decades of research find that self-efficacy and the setting of ambitious but achievable goals are indeed the strongest predictors of learning and accomplishment (Lanaj, Chang, & Johnson, 2012; Sitzmann & Ely, 2011).

The Effects of Work on Motivation

LO 12.4.B   Describe how working conditions affect motives to achieve.

Many people think the relationship between work and motivation runs in one direction: You are motivated, so you choose a career and you work hard to get it. But psychological scientists have also studied the reverse direction: how the availability of careers affects motivation. For example, one simple but powerful factor that affects many people's motivation to work in a particular field is the proportion of men and women in that occupation (Kanter, 2006). When occupations are segregated by gender, many people form gender stereotypes about the requirements of such careers: Female jobs require kindness and nurturance; male jobs require strength and smarts. These stereotypes, in turn, stifle many people's aspirations to enter a nontraditional career and also create self-fulfilling prejudices in employers (Agars, 2004; Cejka & Eagly, 1999; Eccles, 2011).

A natural experiment in India showed the powerful influence of role models on adolescents' educational and achievement ambitions (Beaman et al., 2012). In 1993, a law was passed reserving leadership positions for women in nearly 500 randomly selected villages. Years later, a survey of 8,453 adolescents (ages 11 to 15) found that in villages with the female leaders, the gender gap in educational aspirations had closed by nearly one-third. What you see, apparently, influences what you want—and what you think you can get.

In the United States, when law, veterinary medicine, pharmacy, and bartending were almost entirely male professions, and nursing, teaching, and childcare were almost entirely female, few women aspired to enter the "male" professions. When job segregation became illegal, however, people's career motivations changed. Today, it is common to see a female lawyer, veterinarian, pharmacist, and bartender. And although women are still a minority in engineering, math, and science, their numbers have been rising: In 1960, women earned only 0.4 percent of the doctorates in engineering, 5.2 percent of those in mathematics, and 8.8 percent of those in the life sciences. But by 2012, according to government statistics, the percentages had jumped to 22.2 percent, 25.2 percent, and 52.4 percent, respectively. As these numbers have increased, the old view that women are not "naturally" suited to engineering, math, and science has been fading fast.

As women attain greater numbers in fields that previously were closed to them, today it is men who are more likely to be suffering from dissatisfaction and low motivation to succeed; it is men who are more likely to reject college or drop out of school and training programs for the kinds of jobs that would be available to them. Women are far more likely than men to educate themselves for the careers of the future in service industries, health care, and education; men are still reluctant to go into "women's work." This gender shift is occurring in developing as well as developed nations, a result of changes in the global economy—the slow erosion of traditionally male jobs in construction, manufacturing, and high finance and the expanding need for people who are educated and have good communication and "people" skills. In 2010, young American women had a median income higher than that of their male peers in 1,997 out of 2,000 metropolitan regions. In Brazil, one-third of married women earn more than their husbands. Women are the majorities in colleges and professional schools on every continent except Africa; in Bahrain, Qatar, and Guyana, women are 70 percent of college graduates (Rosin, 2012).

WORKING CONDITIONS   Imagine that you live in a town that has one famous company, Boopsie's Biscuits & Buns. Everyone in the town is grateful for the 3B company and goes to work there with high hopes. Soon, however, an odd thing starts happening to many employees. They complain of fatigue and irritability. They are taking lots of sick leave. Productivity declines. What's going on at Boopsie's Biscuits & Buns? Is everybody suffering from sheer laziness?

Like employees, students can have poor working conditions that affect their motivation. They may have siblings who interrupt them, or they may need to study wherever and whenever they can, even under less than optimal circumstances.

Most observers would answer that something is wrong with those employees. But what if something is wrong with Boopsie's? Psychologists want to know how conditions at work nurture or crush our motivation to succeed. After people are in a job, what motivates some to do well? Why do others lose their motivation altogether?

To begin with, achievement depends on having the *opportunity* to achieve. When someone does not do well at work, others are apt to say it is the individual's own fault because he or she lacks the internal drive to make it. But what the person may really lack is a fair chance to make it, and this is especially true for those who have been subjected to systematic discrimination (Sabattini & Crosby, 2009). After they have entered a career, people may become more motivated to advance up the ladder or less so, depending on how many rungs they are permitted to climb. Women used to be rare in politics, but today it's not news that they are governors, senators, congresswomen, or presidential candidates.

Several other aspects of the work environment are likely to increase work motivation and satisfaction and reduce the chances of emotional burnout (Bakker, 2011; Maslach, Schaufeli, & Leiter, 2001; Rhoades & Eisenberger, 2002):

- The work feels meaningful and important to employees.

- Employees have control over many aspects of their work, such as setting their own hours and making decisions.

- Tasks are varied rather than repetitive.

- Employees have supportive relationships with their superiors and coworkers.

- Employees receive useful feedback about their work, so they know what they have accomplished and what they need to do to improve.

- The company offers opportunities for its employees to learn and advance.

Companies that foster these conditions tend to have more productive and satisfied employees. Workers become more creative in their thinking, more engaged in their work, and feel better about themselves than they do if they feel stuck in routine jobs that give them no control or flexibility over their daily tasks.

Conversely, when people are put in situations that frustrate their desire and ability to succeed, they often become dissatisfied, their motivation declines, and they may drop out. For example, a study of nearly 2,500 women and men in science, engineering, and technology explored the reasons that many of the women eventually left their jobs, with some abandoning science altogether. The women who lost their motivation to work in these fields reported feeling isolated (many said they were the only woman in their work group), and two-thirds said they had been sexually harassed (Hewlitt, Luce, & Servon, 2008). Other reasons included being paid less than men for the same work and having working conditions that did not allow them to handle their family obligations. Mothers are still more likely than fathers to reduce their work hours, modify their work schedules, and feel distracted on the job because of childcare concerns (Sabattini & Crosby, 2009). What do you think might be the "working conditions" today that are causing many men to lose their motivation to enter the careers they previously dominated, as well as creating the lopsided sex ratio on so many campuses?

In sum, as you can see, work motivation and satisfaction depend on the right fit between qualities of the individual and conditions of the work.

JOURNAL WRITING PROMPT 12.4

Thinking Critically—Define Your Terms: As the text discusses, people sometimes frame their goals in vague, unrealistic, or negative ways. Think of two goals you would like to accomplish. You might consider goals related to studying more efficiently, improving communication with a family member, solving problems in a particular relationship, or becoming more physically fit. Now phrase each of your two goals in a way that makes it (1) specific, (2) challenging but achievable, and (3) something to be approached rather than avoided. How can framing your goals in this way improve your motivation to reach them?

Quiz for Module 12.4

1. Horatio wants to earn a black belt in karate. Which way of thinking about this goal is most likely to help him reach it?

   a. "I should be sure not to lose many matches."

   b. "I should do the best I can."

   c. "I will set specific goals that are tough but attainable."

   d. "I will set specific goals that I know I can reach easily."

2. Miranda wants to learn to ice skate because it looks fun and she likes to try new things. Junko wants to learn to ice skate because she doesn't want to be embarrassed next winter in front of her friends and she's afraid of being left out of fun events. Miranda's motives are generally _____, whereas Junko's motives are primarily _____.

   a. Idiographic / nomothetic

   b. Accomplishment goals / attainment goals

   c. Approach goals / approach goals

   d. Approach goals / avoidance goals

3. Claude and Ingo are both studying for the bar exam to become lawyers. Claude feels a lot of pressure to pass the exam, so he can impress his friends and make his family proud. Ingo feels a lot of pressure as well because he wants to challenge himself and tackle a fair test of his learning and studying. Claude appears to be motivated by _____ goals, whereas Ingo is motivated by _____ goals.

   a. Approach / avoidance

   b. Mastery / learning

   c. Performance / mastery

   d. Nomographic / idiothetic

4. Monique was complaining to her roommate Jana, "I'll never learn all this psychology material; the course is too hard and I'm just not cut out for it." As Jana studies that night, she notices that Monique has her book open and her notes out, but she's spending the majority of her time playing on her phone and just glancing at the material. Jana received an A on her exam, whereas Monique got a D. "See, I told you," Monique said, "I'm just not cut out for this." Monique's behavior is showing all the signs of:

   a. Self-endowment

   b. A self-attainment cycle

   c. A self-fulfilling prophecy

   d. Self-efficacy

5. Which of these working conditions contributes to satisfaction and increased work motivation?

   a. Tasks that are repetitive rather than varied

   b. Tasks whose meaning or significance is unclear

   c. Supervisors who maintain a clear separation from workers

   d. Opportunities to learn and advance in the job

Motives, Values, and the Pursuit of Happiness

Life, liberty, and the pursuit of happiness. These values seem fundamental enough to be inalienable rights. You're on your own with the life and liberty part, but we can examine what psychological scientists know about what makes people happy, and what people *think* will make them happy.

Imagining and Attaining Happiness

LO 12.5.A Discuss how accurate people are at estimating the type, duration, and extent of their future emotions, and comment on what research indicates makes people happy.

When you think about setting goals for yourself, here is a crucial psychological finding to keep in mind: People are really bad at predicting what will make them happy and what will make them miserable, and at estimating how long those feelings will last (Wilson & Gilbert,

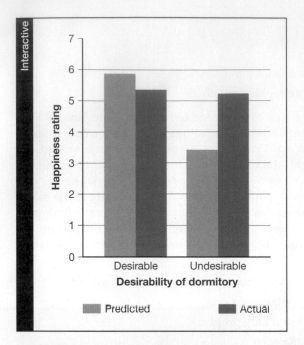

Figure 12.1 The Misprediction of Emotion

In a real-life longitudinal study, college students about to be randomly assigned to a dorm had to predict how happy or unhappy they would feel about being assigned to a house they had ranked as "desirable" or "undesirable." Most students thought that they would be much less happy in an "undesirable" dorm, but in fact, 1 year later, there was no difference between the two groups (Dunn, Wilson, & Gilbert, 2003).

2005). In one study, college students were asked how happy or unhappy they imagined they would feel after being randomly assigned to live in a dorm they thought was "desirable" or "undesirable" (Dunn, Wilson, & Gilbert, 2003). The students predicted that their dorm assignments would have a huge impact on their overall level of happiness and that being assigned to an undesirable dorm would essentially wreck their satisfaction for the whole year. In fact, as you can see from Figure 12.1, a year later, both groups had nearly identical levels of happiness no matter where they were living.

Perhaps the undesirable dorms turned out to be unexpectedly pleasant, with cool people living in them? No. The students had focused on the wrong factors when forecasting their future feelings of happiness in the houses; they had placed far more importance on what the house looked like and on its location than on its inhabitants. But in fact, it's people who make a place fun or unpleasant to live in, and all of the dorms had likable people in them. Because the students could not foresee this, or how much they would like their new roommates, they mispredicted their future happiness.

This result has been replicated in many different contexts: The good is rarely as good as we imagine it will be, and the bad is rarely as terrible. The reason is that people adjust quickly to happy changes—new relationships, a promotion, even winning the lottery—and fail to anticipate that they will cope with bad experiences just as quickly. They will make sense of unexpected events, cope with tragedies, and make excuses for loved ones who hurt them. Yet people make many decisions based on false assumptions about how they will feel in the future. Many spend more money than they can afford on a car or house because they think that *this* is what will make them truly happy.

What, then, *does* make people happy? In all the domains of human motivation that we have examined, a key conclusion emerges: People who are motivated by the intrinsic satisfaction of an activity are happier and more satisfied than those motivated solely by extrinsic rewards (Deci & Ryan, 1985; Kasser & Ryan, 2001). We also saw how intrinsic motivation in any domain will rise or fall depending on the goals we choose and the way we think of them. Goals, in turn, are determined by our values about what is important in life: freedom, religion, equality, wealth, fame, wisdom, serenity, sexual passion, the desire to improve the world, or anything else. Psychological research cannot tell us which values to choose, but it does help illuminate the consequences of our choices.

In the United States, many people are more motivated to make money than to find activities they enjoy. They imagine that greater wealth will bring greater happiness, yet after they are at a level that provides basic comfort and security, more isn't necessarily better. They adjust quickly to the greater wealth and then think they need even more of it to be happier (Dunn, Gilbert, & Wilson, 2011; Gilbert, 2006). Having great wealth even seems to impair people's ability to savor and enjoy small pleasures—sunny days, cold beers, and chocolate (Quoidbach et al., 2015). In addition, regardless of whether they live in the United States (an affluent nation) or Russia (a struggling nation), people who are primarily motivated to get rich have poorer psychological adjustment and lower well-being than do people whose primary values are self-acceptance, affiliation with others, or wanting to make the world a better place (Ryan et al., 1999). This is especially true when the reasons for striving for money are, again, extrinsic (e.g., you do it to impress others and show off your possessions) rather than intrinsic (e.g., you do it so you can afford to do the volunteer work you love) (Carver & Baird, 1998; Srivastava, Locke, & Bartol, 2001). In contrast, having positive, intrinsically enjoyable *experiences* makes most people happier than having *things*: Doing, in other words, is more satisfying than buying (Carter & Gilovich, 2012; Headey, 2008). Watch the video *Affective Forecasting* for more insights into how successful humans are at predicting what will make them happy . . . or miserable.

Should I Stay or Should I Go?

LO 12.5.B   Describe three types of motivational conflicts people often face, and give an example of each.

Whichever values and goals you choose, if they are in conflict, the discrepancy can produce emotional stress and unhappiness. Two motives conflict when the satisfaction of one leads to the inability to act on the other—that is, when you want to have your cake and eat it, too. The three major kinds of motivational conflicts are these (Lewin, 1948):

1. **Approach–approach conflicts** occur when you are equally attracted to two or more possible activities or goals: You would like to be a veterinarian *and* a rock singer; you would like to go out Tuesday night with friends *and* study like mad for an exam Wednesday.

2. **Avoidance–avoidance conflicts** require you to choose between the lesser of two evils because you dislike both alternatives. Novice parachute jumpers must choose between the fear of jumping and the fear of losing face if they don't jump.

3. **Approach–avoidance conflicts** occur when a single activity or goal has both a positive and a negative aspect. In culturally diverse nations, differing cultural values produce many approach–avoidance conflicts, as students have told us. A Chicano student says he wants to become a lawyer, but his parents, valuing family closeness, worry that if he goes to law school, he will become independent and feel superior to his working-class family. A black student from a poor neighborhood, in college on scholarship, is torn between wanting to leave his background behind him forever and returning to help his home community. And a white student wants to be a marine biologist, but her friends tell her that only nerdy guys and dweebs go into science.

Years ago, humanist psychologist Abraham Maslow (1970) envisioned people's motives as forming a pyramid. At the bottom level were basic survival needs for food, sleep, and water; at the next level were security needs, for shelter and safety; at the third level were social needs, for belonging and affection; at the fourth level were esteem needs, for self-respect and the respect of others; and at the top, when all other needs had been met, were those for self-actualization and self-transcendence. Maslow's theory became immensely popular, and motivational speakers still often refer to it, using colorful pictures of the pyramid. But the theory, which was based mostly on Maslow's observations of people he personally decided were "self-actualized," has had little empirical support (Sheldon, 2011; Sheldon et al., 2001). The main reason is that people have *simultaneous* needs for comfort and safety and for love, intimacy, and competence. Higher needs may even supersede lower ones. History is full of examples of people who would rather die of torture or starvation than sacrifice their convictions, or who would rather explore, risk, or create new art than be safe and secure.

As we have seen in this chapter, many motives spur us to action, but psychological well-being depends on finding activities and choosing goals that are intrinsically satisfying and consistent with our core values, and on developing the self-efficacy to achieve them. The motives and goals that inspire us, and the choices we make in their pursuit, are what give our lives passion, color, and meaning. Choose them wisely.

JOURNAL WRITING PROMPT 12.5

Thinking Critically—Avoid Emotional Reasoning: Write down either an event that you're really looking forward to (a concert, taking a trip, visiting friends) or that you're really dreading (a difficult course, a medical procedure, finding a job) that's about 4 to 6 months away. Regardless of the event you chose, write down the reasons why you think the event could be both good and bad; that is, if you chose something you're looking forward to, write about what's potentially good and potentially bad about that event. What are the amount and types of reasons you came up with in both the "good" and "bad" categories? How many of those reasons are based on how you're feeling right now, versus how you *think* you'll be feeling 4 to 6 months from now? Comment on how well you think you can predict your emotional reaction to your anticipated event.

Quiz for Module 12.5

1. "If I could just win the lottery, I'd be set for life," lamented Zane. "Winning the lottery would change everything, and I'd be happy every day." Based on what you know about predicting future emotional states, how accurate do you think Zane's prophecy is?

   a. Somewhat accurate; studies show that people can predict their future happiness correctly about 48 percent of the time, or a little less than half.

   b. Very accurate; research shows that the lifestyles of lottery winners become radically different after attaining their prizes.

   c. Not very accurate; he will probably be happy, but not as happy as he thinks, nor will his life change as dramatically as he anticipates.

   d. Not at all accurate; winning a lottery and receiving lots of money all at once are events that make most people unhappy.

2. Wayne is watching the sunset because he knows Cheryl generally likes nature, and he really likes Cheryl and wants Cheryl to really like him. Frank is watching the sunset because sunsets are a beautiful thing to watch. Who is likely to enjoy the sunset the most?

   a. Frank

   b. Wayne

   c. Cheryl

   d. Frank and Wayne

3. What tends to make people happy?

   a. Purchases

   b. Acquisitions

   c. Money

   d. Experiences

4. A Pakistani student desperately wants an education and a career as a pharmacist, but she also does not want to be disobedient to her parents, who have arranged a marriage for her back home. Which kind of conflict does she have?

   a. Approach / approach

   b. Double-approach / avoidance

   c. Approach / avoidance

   d. Avoidance / avoidance

5. Alan wants to go to the Motörhead concert (one of his favorite bands), but it's on the same night as the Rush concert (another of his favorite bands). He can't be in two places at the same time, and that's frustrating. It's also frustrating because this is a(n) _____ conflict.

   a. Double-approach / avoidance

   b. Approach / approach

   c. Approach / avoidance

   d. Avoidance / avoidance

Taking Psychology with You
How to Attain Your Goals

What are your values? What would you most like to achieve and accomplish in your life? Love, wealth, security, passion, freedom, fame, the desire to improve the world, being the best in a sport or other skill? Something else? What are your short-term goals: Would you like to improve your love life? Get better grades? Enjoy school more? Lose weight? Become a better tennis player?

A whole world of motivational speakers, books, and DVDs offer inspiration, enthusiasm, and a few magic steps to change your life, but we hope that by now you will apply critical thinking to their promises. Enthusiastic inspiration is fine as far as it goes, but it usually doesn't transfer into helping you make real-life changes. In contrast, think about some of the lessons that you have learned in this chapter:

- *Seek activities that are intrinsically pleasurable.* If you really, really want to study Swahili or Swedish even though these languages are not in your prelaw requirements, try to find a way to do it. As the great writer Ray Bradbury said at age 89, the secret to living to a grand old age is to "do what you love and love what you do." Or take advice from 109-year-old Karam Chand, whom you met earlier in this chapter: "I've never held back from enjoying life." If you are not enjoying your major or your job, consider finding a career that would be more intrinsically pleasurable, or

at least make sure you have other projects and activities that you do enjoy for their own sake.
- *Focus on learning goals, not only on performance goals.* In general, you will be better able to cope with setbacks if your goal is to learn rather than to show others how good you are. Regard failure as a chance to learn rather than as a sign of incompetence.
- *Assess your working conditions.* Everyone has working conditions. Whether you are a student, a self-employed writer, or a homemaker, if your motivation and well-being are starting to wilt, check out your environment. Are you getting support from others? Do you have opportunities to develop ideas and vary your routine, or are you expected to do the same thing day after day? Are there barriers that might limit your advancement in your chosen field?
- *Take steps to resolve motivational conflicts.* Are you torn between competing goals? For instance, are you unhappily stuck between the goal of achieving independence and a desire to be cared for by your parents? The reconciliation of conflicts like these is important for your well-being.

Most important, think critically about the goals you have chosen for yourself: Are they what *you* want to do or what someone else wants you to do? Do they reflect your values? If you are not happy with your body, your relationships, or your work, why not? Think about it.

Shared Writing Prompt

Throughout the chapter we've highlighted the role of genetics, psychology, culture, environmental factors, and other influences on motivated behavior. We've also distinguished between intrinsic motives and extrinsic motives in shaping someone's pursuit of a goal. But is it ever that simple? Think of something that you're motivated to accomplish: Achieve in school, excel at a sport, master a new language, change some unhealthy habits. Write down as

specifically as you can what your current behavior is and what your desired end goal should be. As you progress from Point A to Point B, what motivates you? Do you find that a combination of both intrinsic and extrinsic motives are driving your behavior? For the goal you've selected, do environmental factors outweigh genetic ones in attaining your outcomes? Comment on the specific and interacting forces that are driving your behavior in this situation.

Summary

Motivation and the Hungry Animal

LO 12.1.A   Define motivation, and distinguish between intrinsic and extrinsic motivation.

Motivation refers to a process within a person or animal that causes that organism to move toward a goal or away from an unpleasant situation. *Intrinsic motivation* refers to the desire to do something for its own sake and the pleasure it brings.

Extrinsic motivation refers to the desire to do something for external rewards, such as money and good grades.

LO 12.1.B   Discuss the biological factors that contribute to weight, and define what a *set point* is.

Overweight and obesity are not simply a result of failed willpower, emotional disturbance, or overeating. Hunger, weight, and eating are regulated by a set of bodily mechanisms, such as *basal metabolism rate* and number of fat cells, that keep people close to their genetically influenced *set point*. Genes influence body shape, distribution of fat, number of fat cells, and amount of *brown fat*, and whether the body will convert excess calories into fat. The *ob gene* regulates *leptin*, which enables the hypothalamus to regulate appetite and metabolism. The hormone *ghrelin* spurs appetite and leptin reduces it.

LO 12.1.C   Discuss five major environmental influences on weight, and provide an example of each.

Genetics alone cannot explain why rates of overweight and obesity are rising all over the world among all social classes, ethnicities, and ages. The major environmental reasons are (1) the increased abundance of inexpensive fast food and processed food; (2) the increased consumption of high-calorie sugary sodas; (3) the rise of sedentary lifestyles; (4) increased portion sizes; and (5) the availability of highly varied foods.

LO 12.1.D   Distinguish between anorexia nervosa and bulimia nervosa, and discuss some factors that contribute to each disorder.

Anorexia nervosa and *bulimia nervosa* are the best-known eating disorders, occurring mostly among young white women; however, a large percentage of all cases of eating disorders affect women and men of varying ages and ethnicities. Genetic and cultural factors influence eating disorders, but most are due to psychological causes, such as depression, anxiety, perfectionism, or a distorted body image.

The Social Animal: Motives to Love

LO 12.2.A   Describe how passionate love, compassionate love, social bonding, and the action of vasopressin and oxytocin all contribute to our understanding of the biology of love.

All human beings have a need for attachment and love. Psychologists distinguish *passionate (romantic) love* from *companionate love*. Various brain chemicals and hormones, including *vasopressin* and *oxytocin*, are associated with bonding and trust; *endorphins* and dopamine create the rushes of pleasure and reward associated with romantic passion.

LO 12.2.B   Explain how attachment theory can be applied to adult romantic relationships.

Two strong predictors of whom people will love are *proximity* and *similarity*. When in love, people form different kinds of attachments. *Attachment theory* views adult love relationships, like those of infants, as being *secure*, *avoidant*, or *anxious*.

LO 12.2.C   Summarize the research on gender differences and cultural differences in romantic relationships.

Men and women are equally likely to feel love and need attachment, but they differ, on average, in how they express feelings of love and how they define intimacy. A couple's attitudes, values, and perception that the relationship is fair and balanced are better predictors of long-term love than are genes or hormones.

The Erotic Animal: Motives for Sex

LO 12.3.A   Summarize early research findings on sexuality, and describe how biology, hormones, and expectations might contribute to differences in the sexuality of women and men.

Human sexuality is not simply a matter of "doing what comes naturally" because what is "natural" for one person or culture may not be so natural for others. The Kinsey surveys of male and female sexuality and the laboratory research of Masters and Johnson showed that physiologically, both sexes are capable of sexual arousal and response. However, individuals vary enormously in sexual excitement, response, and inhibition. The hormone testosterone promotes sexual desire in both sexes, although hormones do not cause sexual behavior in a simple, direct way.

LO 12.3.B   Discuss six motives for sex and three motives for rape.

A balanced view of sexuality is that male sexuality is more biologically influenced than is women's, whereas female sexuality is more governed by circumstances, relationships, and cultural norms. Men and women have sex to satisfy many different psychological motives, including pleasure, intimacy, security, the partner's approval, peer approval, or to attain a specific goal. People's motives for consenting to unwanted sex vary, depending on their feelings of security and commitment in the relationship. Men who rape do so for diverse reasons, including narcissism and hostility toward women; a desire to dominate, humiliate, or punish the victim; and sometimes sadism.

LO 12.3.C   Explain the ways in which culture and gender contribute to sexual behavior and expectations about that behavior.

Cultures transmit ideas about sexuality through *gender roles* and *sexual scripts*, which specify appropriate behavior during courtship and sex, depending on a person's gender, age, and sexual orientation. As in the case of love, gender differences (and similarities) in sexuality are strongly affected by cultural and economic factors. As gender roles have become more alike and women have become more economically independent, the sexual behavior of men and women has become more alike, with women wanting sex for pleasure rather than as a bargaining chip.

The Competent Animal: Motives to Achieve

LO 12.4.A   Describe three conditions that make goal-setting successful, distinguish between performance goals and mastery goals, and discuss the self-fulfilling prophecy cycle.

People achieve more when they have specific, focused goals; when they set high but achievable goals for themselves; and when they have *approach goals* (seeking a positive outcome) rather than *avoidance goals* (avoiding an unpleasant outcome). The motivation to achieve also depends on whether people set *mastery (learning) goals*, in which the focus is on learning the task well, or *performance goals*, in which the focus is on performing well for others. Self-confidence and grit both contribute to the attainment of goals. People's expectations can create *self-fulfilling prophecies* of success or failure. These expectations stem from one's level of *self-efficacy*.

LO 12.4.B   Describe how working conditions affect motives to achieve.

Work motivation also depends on conditions of the job itself. When jobs are highly gender segregated, people often stereotype the abilities of the women and men working in those fields. Working conditions that promote motivation and satisfaction are those that provide workers with a sense of meaningfulness, control, variation in tasks, supportive relationships, feedback, and opportunities for advancement.

Motives, Values, and the Pursuit of Happiness

LO 12.5.A   Discuss how accurate people are at estimating the type, duration, and extent of their future emotions, and comment on what research indicates makes people happy.

People are not good at predicting what will make them happy and what will make them miserable, and at estimating how long those feelings will last. Well-being increases when people enjoy the intrinsic satisfaction of an activity. Having intrinsically enjoyable experiences makes most people happier than having riches and possessions.

LO 12.5.B   Describe three types of motivational conflicts people often face, and give an example of each.

In an *approach–approach conflict*, a person is equally attracted to two goals. In an *avoidance–avoidance conflict*, a person is equally repelled by two goals. An *approach–avoidance conflict* is the most difficult to resolve because the person is both attracted to and repelled by the same goal. Abraham Maslow believed that human motives could be ranked from basic biological needs for survival to higher psychological needs for self-actualization, but this popular theory has not been supported empirically. Rather, psychological well-being depends on finding activities and choosing goals that are intrinsically satisfying and on developing the self-efficacy to achieve them.

Chapter 12 Quiz

1. Leonard thinks that if he gets good grades in school, girls will notice him, his friends will admire him, and his parents will be proud of him. Accordingly, he slogs through his coursework with little focus on understanding the material and an eye toward getting the highest grades he can. Leonard is showing all the signs of being _____ motivated.

   a. Hyper-
   b. Intrinsically
   c. Psychologically
   d. Extrinsically

2. Which gene causes fat cells to secrete the hormone leptin?

   a. Ghrelin
   b. Ob
   c. Leptos
   d. DC3

3. Why would you predict that people who visit buffet restaurants would tend to overeat compared to diners who patronize a more traditional restaurant?

   a. Buffets are attractive to large groups, and large groups tend to eat more than smaller parties.
   b. Buffet restaurants feature fattier foods than traditional restaurants or fast-food restaurants.
   c. The slowness of walking through a buffet line provides time for fat cells to build up.
   d. The abundance of highly varied foods generally inspires people to eat more.

4. The eating disorder with the highest mortality among all mental disorders is

   a. Bulimia nervosa
   b. Anorexia nervosa
   c. Binge-eating disorder
   d. Night eating syndrome

5. Peter and Austin have been in a healthy romantic relationship for 17 years. Chances are good that their relationship is characterized by

   a. Intense emotions
   b. Passionate love
   c. Companionate love
   d. Infatuation

6. Lola isn't jealous when her partner talks to other people at parties or spends a weekend with friends. She understands that couples like to do things together but also sometimes need to do things separately, and she's not worried that her partner will abandon her for someone he likes more. Lola's attachment style is no doubt

   a. Anxious
   b. Avoidant
   c. Assertive
   d. Secure

7. Emily is unable to sustain meaningful romantic relationships. She is distrustful of others and always ends a relationship when the other person wants to be committed. Her attachment style can best be described as

   a. Avoidant
   b. Regressive
   c. Secure
   d. Anxious

8. "Of course I want to marry George," said Linda. "His net worth is huge, and it's a good strategic move for both our families. Besides that, he owns a lot of land. And, given enough time, I may eventually come to love him." During what time period would Linda's attitudes be most representative of those of most women in her U.S. culture?

   a. 2010
   b. 1872
   c. 1966
   d. 1997

9. One of the first researchers to study sexual behavior was
   a. Agnes Stevens
   b. Tom Bartholomew
   c. Ronald Isaacson
   d. Alfred Kinsey

10. Madison agrees to unwanted sex with her partner, primarily because she is afraid her partner will leave her if she doesn't, and she also feels obligated to give him pleasure when he wants it. What kind of attachment style would you predict Madison has?
    a. Anxious
    b. Secure
    c. Ambivalent
    d. Hesitant

11. The implicit cultural and gender rules that specify proper sexual behavior for a person in a specific situation are called
    a. Sexual scripts
    b. Expectations
    c. Normative roles
    d. Gender schemes

12. Research on goal setting indicates that goals should be framed as approach goals that are _____ and _____.
    a. Specific / challenging
    b. Short term / optimistic
    c. Attainable / popular
    d. Distant / general

13. Which statement best summarizes the effects of the workplace on worker motivation?
    a. The properties of the workplace are more important than the internal motives of the worker; even lazy people can get ahead in the proper environment.
    b. Motivation affects work, but working conditions generally don't affect motivation.
    c. Intrinsic motivations to succeed are great, but people also need the opportunity and appropriate work conditions to be able to succeed.
    d. Research shows that working conditions account for approximately 18 percent of a person's achievement outcomes, with the other 82 percent due to personal factors.

14. Generally speaking, how bad are the future bad things that people anticipate will be bad?
    a. Even worse
    b. Not so bad
    c. About as bad as people think
    d. Twice as bad as people predict

15. Which of the following is *not* a reason why Abraham Maslow's pyramid model of hierarchical needs is not widely adopted as a general explanation of motivation?
    a. People often have simultaneous needs.
    b. It lacks empirical support.
    c. It was never very popular.
    d. People often pursue higher needs at the expense of lower needs.

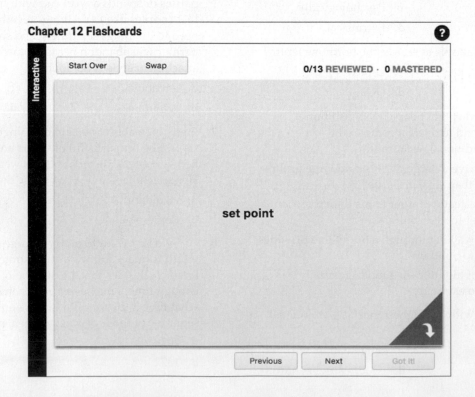

Chapter 12 Flashcards   ?

Start Over   Swap   0/13 REVIEWED · 0 MASTERED

Interactive

set point

Previous   Next   Got it!

Chapter 13
Development over the Lifespan

◀ Listen to the Audio

Learning Objectives

LO 13.1.A Outline the three stages of prenatal development, and list six factors that can adversely affect a woman's pregnancy.

LO 13.1.B Describe some inborn abilities that infants have, and summarize some cultural influences on physical and psychological development.

LO 13.1.C Discuss how contact comfort and separation anxiety contribute to feelings of attachment, and list four factors that contribute to insecure attachment.

LO 13.2.A List the milestones of language development that occur between the first 2 months and 6 years of life.

LO 13.2.B Describe the four stages of cognitive development proposed by Piaget, explain the defining characteristics of each stage, and discuss four modifications of Piaget's theory.

LO 13.3.A Discuss the evidence for and against the proposition that moral development occurs in distinct stages over time.

LO 13.3.B Compare the ways in which power assertion, inductive appeals, self-regulation, and conscience contribute to moral development.

LO 13.4.A Distinguish between biological sex, gender identity, gender typing, and intersex conditions.

LO 13.4.B Summarize the basic findings regarding biological, cognitive, and learning influences on gender identity and gender typing.

LO 13.5.A Outline the physiological changes that girls and boys experience during adolescence.

LO 13.5.B Outline the psychological and behavioral changes that girls and boys experience during adolescence.

LO 13.6.A List the eight "crises" of development proposed by Erik Erikson.

LO 13.6.B Outline the psychological and behavioral changes that women and men experience as they progress through emerging adulthood and middle age.

LO 13.6.C Summarize the findings regarding declines or improvements in cognitive functioning as people age, and distinguish between fluid intelligence and crystallized intelligence.

Ask questions . . . be willing to wonder

How does a baby's thinking differ from an adult's?

What makes the years from 18 to 25 unlike adolescence or adulthood?

Is mental decline inevitable in old age?

Do childhood experiences affect us for our entire lives?

Annegret Raunigk knows a thing or two about development over the lifespan. The 65-year-old schoolteacher, who lives in Berlin, has 13 children and seven grandchildren; to say "she's surrounded by kids" is no understatement. But her circle of offspring recently got larger. In 2015, she gave birth to quadruplets, aided by *in vitro* fertilization treatments she received in the Ukraine. (Both the eggs and sperm were donated, a procedure that is illegal in her native Germany.) Her motivation for having another child, she reported, was that her youngest daughter, a 9-year-old, wanted to have a younger sibling. Annegret didn't intend on having quadruplets: "At first, I only wanted one child. But then things happen. I am not a planner, but rather spontaneous." Addressing concerns that giving birth at her advanced age to infants who were born 14 weeks premature (all the quadruplets weighed 2 pounds or less at birth), she remarked, "No one who doesn't know me can criticize me. I am doing what I think is right."

When, if ever, is a human being "too old" to have a baby, whether by *in vitro* fertilization or adoption? Would it make any difference if the mother were "only" 55 years old? 50? Do you feel the same about older fathers as you do about older mothers? Is there a "right time" to become a parent? For that matter, is there a right time to do anything in life—go to school, get married, retire, . . . die?

The universal human journey from birth to death was once far more predictable than it is today. Going to college, choosing a job, starting a family, and advancing up the ladder to retirement were all events that tended to happen in sequence. But because of demographic changes, an unpredictable economy, advances in reproductive technology, and many other forces, millions of people are now doing things out of order, if they do them at all. Today, going to college, having children, changing careers, or starting a family may occur in almost any decade of adulthood.

Developmental psychologists study physiological and cognitive changes across the lifespan and how these are affected by a person's genetic predispositions, culture, circumstances, and experiences. Some focus on children's mental and social development, including *socialization*, the process by which children learn the rules and behavior expected of them by society. Others specialize in the study of adolescents, adults, or the very old. In this chapter, we will explore some of their major findings, starting at the very beginning of human development, with the period before birth, and continuing through adulthood into old age. The video *The Plastic Brain* gives you an overview of how some important aspects of physical development take place.

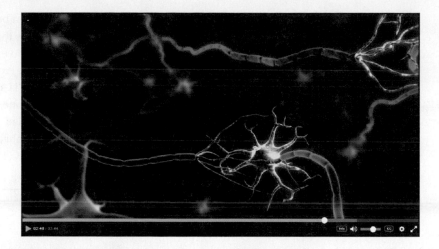

From Conception Through the First Year

A baby's development, before and after birth, is a marvel of *maturation*, the sequential unfolding of genetically influenced behavior and physical characteristics. In only 9 months of a mother's pregnancy, a cell grows from a dot this big (.) to a squealing bundle of energy who looks just like Aunt Norma. In another 15 months, that bundle of energy grows into a babbling toddler who is curious about everything. No other time in human development brings so many changes so fast.

Prenatal Development

LO 13.1.A Outline the three stages of prenatal development, and list six factors that can adversely affect a woman's pregnancy.

Prenatal development begins at fertilization, when the male sperm unites with the female ovum (egg) to form a single-celled egg called a *zygote*. The zygote soon begins to divide, and in 10 to 14 days, it has become a cluster of cells that attaches itself to the wall of the uterus. The outer portion of this cluster will form part of the placenta and umbilical cord, and when implantation

Development depends on the genetic hand you are dealt at birth, the resources and opportunities your parents provide for you, the experiences that happen to you, and the unexpected events of history. What futures might you imagine for these three children? At the end of this chapter, you'll see who they are.

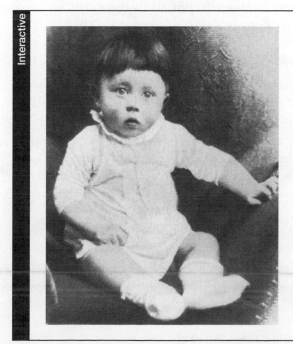

is completed about 2 weeks after fertilization, the inner portion becomes the *embryo*. The placenta, connected to the embryo by the umbilical cord, serves as the growing embryo's link for food from the mother. It allows nutrients to enter and wastes to exit, and it screens out some, but not all, harmful substances. At 8 weeks after conception, the embryo is only 1½ inches long. During the fourth to eighth weeks, the hormone testosterone is secreted by the rudimentary testes in embryos that are genetically male; without this hormone, the embryo will develop to be anatomically female. After 8 weeks, the organism, now called a *fetus*, further develops the organs and systems that existed in rudimentary form in the embryonic stage. Watch the video *Sex and Gender Differences 1* to learn more about how a fetus develops into a female or a male.

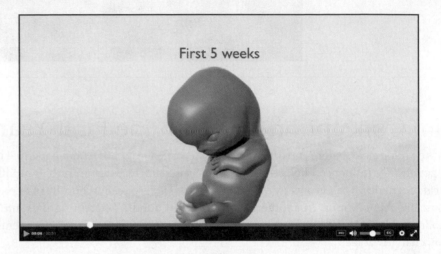

First 5 weeks

Although the womb is a fairly sturdy protector of the growing embryo or fetus, the prenatal environment—which is influenced by the mother's own health, genetic predispositions, allergies, and diet—can affect the course of development, as by predisposing an infant to later obesity or immune problems (Coe & Lubach, 2008). Most people don't realize it, but fathers play a role in prenatal development, too. Because of genetic mutations in sperm, fathers over age 50 have three times the risk of conceiving a child who develops schizophrenia as fathers under age 25 do (Goriely et al., 2013); teenage fathers have an increased risk that their babies will be born prematurely or have low birth weight; babies of men exposed to solvents and other chemicals in the workplace are more likely to be miscarried or stillborn, or to develop cancer later in life; and having an older father increases the probability that a child will have autism or bipolar disorder (Frans et al., 2008; Kong et al., 2012; Sandin et al., 2014).

During a woman's pregnancy, some harmful influences can cross the placental barrier and affect the fetus (O'Rahilly & Müller, 2001). These influences include:

1. **German measles** (rubella), especially early in the pregnancy, can affect the fetus's eyes, ears, and heart. The most common consequence is deafness. Rubella is preventable if the mother has been vaccinated, which can be done up to 3 months before pregnancy.

2. **X-rays or other radiation, pollutants, and toxic substances** can cause fetal deformities and cognitive abnormalities that can last throughout life. Exposure to lead is associated with attention problems and lower IQ scores, as is exposure to mercury (found most commonly in contaminated fish), pesticides, and high air pollution (Newland & Rasmussen, 2003; Perera et al., 2013; Raloff, 2011).

3. **Sexually transmitted diseases** can cause mental retardation, blindness, and other physical disorders. Genital herpes affects the fetus only if the mother has an outbreak at the time of delivery, which exposes the newborn to the virus as the baby passes through the birth canal. (This risk can be avoided by having a cesarean section.) HIV, the virus that causes AIDS, can also be transmitted to the fetus, especially if the mother has developed AIDS and has not been treated.

4. **Cigarette smoking** during pregnancy increases the likelihood of miscarriage, premature birth, an abnormal fetal heartbeat, and an underweight baby. The negative effects

may last long after birth, showing up in increased rates of infant sickness, sudden infant death syndrome (SIDS), and, in later childhood, hyperactivity, learning difficulties, asthma, and even antisocial behavior (Button, Thapar, & McGuffin, 2005; Chudal et al., 2015).

5. **Maternal stress** can affect the fetus, increasing the risk of later cognitive and emotional problems and vulnerability to adult diseases such as hypertension (Ping et al., 2015; Talge, Neal, & Glover, 2007). Babies of mothers who developed posttraumatic stress disorder in the aftermath of the World Trade Center attacks on 9/11 were more likely to have abnormal cortisol levels themselves at 1 year of age, and also to weigh less at birth, both indicators of future health problems (Yehuda et al., 2005).

6. **Drugs** can be harmful to the fetus, whether they are illicit ones such as cocaine and heroin, or legal substances such as alcohol, antibiotics, antidepressants, antihistamines, tranquilizers, acne medication, prescription opiate painkillers, and diet pills (Healy, 2012; Lester, LaGasse, & Seifer, 1998; Stanwood & Levitt, 2001). Regular consumption of alcohol can kill neurons throughout the fetus's developing brain and impair the child's later mental abilities, attention span, and academic achievement (Gautam et al., 2015; Streissguth, 2001). Having more than two drinks a day significantly increases the risk of *fetal alcohol syndrome (FAS)*, which is associated with low birth weight, a smaller brain, facial deformities, lack of coordination, and mental retardation.

In addition to avoiding these teratogens, a pregnant woman can do much to have a healthy baby. She can maintain a healthy weight, take prenatal vitamins (especially folic acid, which prevents neural defects in the brain and spinal cord), and get regular prenatal care (Abu-Saad & Fraser, 2010).

The Infant's World

LO 13.1.B Describe some inborn abilities that infants have, and summarize some cultural influences on physical and psychological development.

Newborn babies could never survive on their own, but they are far from being passive and inert. Many abilities, tendencies, and characteristics are universal in human beings and are present at birth or develop very early, given certain experiences. Newborns begin life with several *motor reflexes*, automatic behaviors that are necessary for survival. They will suck on anything suckable, such as a nipple or finger. They will grasp tightly a finger pressed on their tiny palms. They will turn their heads toward a touch on the cheek or corner of the mouth and search for something to suck on, a handy rooting reflex that allows them to find the breast or bottle. Many of these reflexes eventually disappear, but others—such as the knee-jerk, eyeblink, and sneeze reflexes—remain.

Babies are also equipped with a set of inborn perceptual abilities. They can see, hear, touch, smell, and taste (bananas and sugar water are in, rotten eggs are out; Steiner, 1973). A newborn's visual focus range is only about 8 inches, the average distance between the baby and the face of the person holding the baby, but visual ability develops rapidly. Newborns can distinguish contrasts, shadows, and edges. And they can discriminate their mother or other primary caregiver on the basis of smell, sight, or sound almost immediately. Even more impressive, babies are born with an interest in novelty and some basic cognitive skills, including a fundamental sense of number (they know that three things are more than two things) (Izard et al., 2009).

Experience, however, plays a crucial role in shaping an infant's mind, brain, and gene expression right from the get-go. Infants who get little touching will grow more slowly and release less growth hormone than their amply cuddled peers, and throughout their lives, they have stronger reactions to stress and are more prone to depression and its cognitive deficits (Diamond & Amso, 2008; Field, 2009). Although infants everywhere develop according to the same maturational sequence, many

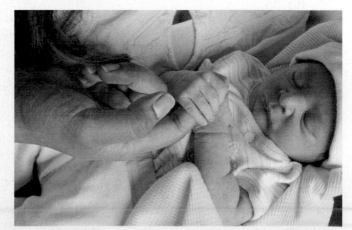

Infants are born with a grasping reflex; they will cling to any offered finger. And they need the comfort of touch, which their adult caregivers love to provide.

Cultural differences can affect the kinds of experiences newborns have, and influence their mind, brain, and gene expression.

aspects of their development depend on cultural customs that govern how their parents hold, touch, feed, and talk to them (Rogoff, 2003). In the United States, Canada, and most European countries, babies are expected to sleep for eight uninterrupted hours by the age of 4 or 5 months. This milestone is considered a sign of neurological maturity, although many babies wail when the parent puts them in the crib at night and leaves the room. But among Mayan Indians, rural Italians, African villagers, Indian Rajput villagers, and urban Japanese, this nightly clash of wills rarely occurs because the infant sleeps with the mother for the first few years of life, waking and nursing about every 4 hours. These differences in babies' sleep arrangements reflect cultural and parental values. Mothers in these cultures believe it is important to sleep with the baby so that both will forge a close bond; in contrast, many urban North American and German parents believe it is important to foster the child's independence as soon as possible (Super & Harkness, 2013).

Attachment

LO 13.1.C Discuss how contact comfort and separation anxiety contribute to feelings of attachment, and list four factors that contribute to insecure attachment.

Emotional attachment is a universal capacity of all primates and is crucial for health and survival all through life. The mother is usually the first and primary object of attachment for an infant, but in many cultures (and other species), babies become just as attached to their fathers, siblings, and grandparents (Hrdy, 1999; Shwalb & Shwalb, 2015).

Interest in the importance of early attachment began with the work of British psychiatrist John Bowlby (1969, 1973), who observed the devastating effects on babies raised in orphanages without touches or snuggling, and on other children raised in conditions of severe deprivation or neglect. The babies were physically healthy but emotionally despairing, remote, and listless. By becoming attached to their caregivers, Bowlby said, children gain a secure base from which they can explore the environment and a haven of safety to return to when they are afraid. Ideally, infants will find a balance between feeling securely attached to the caregiver and feeling free to explore and learn in new environments.

CONTACT COMFORT   Attachment begins with physical touching and cuddling between infant and parent. **Contact comfort**, the pleasure of being touched and held, is crucial not only for newborns, but also for everyone throughout life because it releases a flood of pleasure-producing and stress-reducing endorphins (Rilling & Young, 2014). In hospital settings, even the mildest touch by a nurse or physician on a patient's arm or forehead is reassuring psychologically and lowers blood pressure.

Margaret and Harry Harlow first demonstrated the importance of contact comfort by raising infant rhesus monkeys with two kinds of artificial mothers (Harlow, 1958; Harlow & Harlow, 1966). One, which they called the "wire mother," was a forbidding construction of wires and warming lights, with a milk bottle connected to it. The other, the "cloth mother," was constructed of wire but covered in foam rubber and cuddly terry cloth (see Figure 13.1). At the time, many psychologists thought that babies become attached to their mothers simply because mothers provide food (Blum, 2002). But the Harlows' baby monkeys ran to the terry-cloth mother when they were frightened or startled, and snuggling up to it calmed them down. Human children also seek contact comfort when they are in an unfamiliar situation, are scared by a nightmare, or fall and hurt themselves.

contact comfort

In primates, the innate pleasure derived from close physical contact; it is the basis of the infant's first attachment.

separation anxiety

The distress that most children develop, at about 6 to 8 months of age, when their primary caregivers temporarily leave them with strangers.

SEPARATION AND SECURITY   After babies have become emotionally attached to the mother or other caregiver, separation can be a wrenching experience. Between 6 and 8 months of age, babies become wary or fearful of strangers. They wail if they are put in an unfamiliar setting or are left with an unfamiliar person. And they show **separation anxiety** if the primary caregiver temporarily leaves them. This reaction usually continues until the middle of the second year, but many children show signs of distress until they are about 3 years old (Hrdy, 1999). All children go through this phase, although cultural childrearing practices

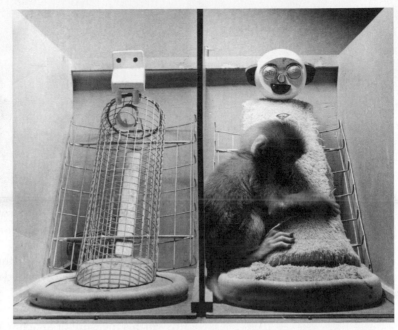

Figure 13.1 The Comfort of Contact

Infants need cuddling as much as they need food. In Margaret and Harry Harlow's studies, infant rhesus monkeys were reared with a cuddly terry-cloth "mother" and with a bare wire "mother" that provided milk. The infants would cling to the terry-cloth mother when they were not being fed. But when an unfamiliar and scary toy (a mechanical spider or a large teddy bear) was placed in the enclosure, the infant monkey would run to the terry-cloth mother for comfort. Only when reassured by that contact comfort would the infant venture back out to examine the toy.

influence how strongly the anxiety is felt and how long it lasts (see Figure 13.2). In cultures where babies are raised with lots of adults and other children, separation anxiety is not as intense or as long-lasting as it can be in cultures where babies form attachments primarily or exclusively with the mother (Rothbaum, Morelli, & Rusk, 2011).

To study the nature of the attachment between mothers and babies, Mary Ainsworth (1973, 1979) devised an experimental method called the *Strange Situation*. A mother brings her baby into an unfamiliar room containing lots of toys. After a while, a stranger comes in and attempts to play with the child. The mother leaves the baby with the stranger. She then returns and plays with the child, and the stranger leaves. Finally, the mother leaves the baby alone for 3 minutes and returns. In each case, observers note how the baby behaves with the mother, with the stranger, and when the baby is alone.

Ainsworth divided the children into categories on the basis of their reactions to the Strange Situation. Some babies were *securely attached*: They cried or protested when the parent left the room; they welcomed her back and then played happily again; they were clearly more attached to the mother than to the stranger. Other babies were *insecurely attached*, and this insecurity took one of two forms. Some children were *avoidant*, not caring if the mother left the room, making little effort to seek contact with her upon her return, and treating the stranger about the same as the mother. Other insecure children were *anxious* or *ambivalent*, resisting contact with the mother at reunion but protesting loudly if she left. Some anxious-ambivalent babies cried to be picked up and then demanded to be put down; others behaved as if they were angry with the mother and resisted her efforts to comfort them. Attachment theory is explored in more detail in the video *Attachment*.

WHAT CAUSES INSECURE ATTACHMENT? Ainsworth believed that the difference between secure, avoidant, and anxious-ambivalent attachment lies primarily in the way mothers treat their babies during the first year. Mothers who are sensitive and responsive to their babies' needs, she said, create securely attached infants; mothers who are

Figure 13.2 The Rise and Fall of Separation Anxiety

At around 6 months of age, many babies begin to show separation anxiety when the person who is their main source of attachment tries handing them over to someone else or leaves the room. This anxiety typically peaks at about a year of age and then steadily declines. But the proportion of children responding this way varies across cultures. It is high among rural African children and low among children raised in a communal Israeli kibbutz, where children become attached to many adults. (Data from Kagan, Kearsley, & Zelazo, 1978.)

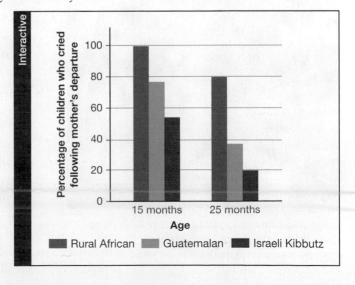

Interactive

Percentage of children who cried following mother's departure

Age

■ Rural African   ■ Guatemalan   ■ Israeli Kibbutz

uncomfortable with or insensitive to their babies create insecurely attached infants. To many, the implication was that babies needed exactly the right kind of mothering from the very start in order to become securely attached, and that putting a child in daycare would retard this development—notions that have caused considerable insecurity among mothers!

Ainsworth's measure of attachment, however, did not take the baby's experience into account. Babies who become attached to many adults, because they live in large extended families or have spent a lot of time with adults in daycare, may seem to be avoidant in the Strange Situation because they don't panic when their mothers leave. But perhaps they have simply learned to be comfortable with strangers. Moreover, although a small correlation exists between a mother's sensitivity to her child and the security of her child's attachment, this doesn't tell us which causes which, or whether something else causes both sensitivity and secure attachment. Programs designed to help new mothers become less anxious and more attuned to their babies do help some moms become more sensitive, but these programs only modestly affect the child's degree of secure attachment (Bakermans-Kranenburg et al., 2008).

The emphasis on maternal sensitivity also overlooks the fact that most children, all over the world, form a secure attachment to their mothers in spite of wide variations in childrearing practices (LeVine & Norman, 2008; Mercer, 2006). German babies are frequently left on their own for a few hours at a stretch by mothers who believe that even babies should become self-reliant. And among the Efe of Africa, babies spend about half their time away from their mothers in the care of older children and other adults (Tronick, Morelli, & Ivey, 1992). Yet German and Efe children are not insecure, and they develop as normally as children who spend more time with their mother. Likewise, time spent in daycare—10 hours a week to more than 30—has no effect on the security of a child's attachment (Oliviera et al., 2015; NICHD Early Child Care Research Network, 2006).

What factors, then, *do* promote insecure attachment?

Longitudinal studies find that good daycare does not affect the security of children's attachments and often produces many social and intellectual benefits.

- **Abandonment and deprivation in the first year or two of life.** Institutionalized babies are more likely than adopted children to have later problems with attachment, whereas babies adopted before age 1 or 2 eventually become as securely attached as any other children (Lionetti, Pastore, & Barone, 2015; van den Dries et al., 2009; Vorria et al., 2015).

- **Parenting that is abusive, neglectful, or erratic because the parent is chronically irresponsible or clinically depressed.** A South African research team observed 147 mothers with their 2-month-old infants and followed up when the babies were 18 months old. Many of the mothers who had suffered from postpartum depression became either too intrusive with their infants or too remote and insensitive. In turn, their babies were more likely to be insecurely attached at 18 months (Tomlinson, Cooper, & Murray, 2005).

- **The child's own genetically influenced temperament.** Babies who are fearful and prone to crying from birth are more likely to show insecure behavior in the Strange Situation, suggesting that their later insecure attachment may reflect a temperamental predisposition (Gillath et al., 2008; Khoury et al., 2015; Seifer et al., 1996).

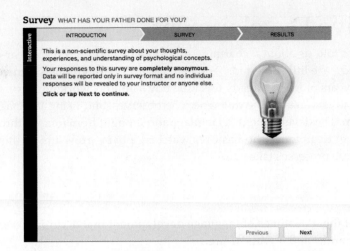

- **Stressful circumstances in the child's family.** Infants and young children may temporarily shift from secure to insecure attachment, becoming clingy and fearful of being left alone, if their families are undergoing a period of stress, as during parental divorce or a parent's chronic illness (Belsky et al., 1996; Mercer, 2006).

The bottom line, however, is that infants are biologically disposed to become attached to their caregivers. Normal, healthy attachment will occur within a wide range of cultural, family, and individual variations in childrearing customs. Although, sadly, things can go wrong in prenatal development and in the first year after birth, the plasticity of the brain and human resilience can often overcome early deprivation or even harm.

JOURNAL PROMPT 13.1

Thinking Critically—Analyze Assumptions and Biases: Think about people who live under a totalitarian regime. In most cases they can't do or say what they want (for fear of governmental reprisal), and their access to information is often limited (by state-run newspapers or censored Internet access). In contrast, people living in a free society can do as they please and learn what they want to. But what happens when those benefits collide? Suppose a pregnant woman wanted to exercise her right to continue smoking and drinking throughout her pregnancy, despite ample evidence that this is a really bad idea? Should she be arrested or fined? Would such a law be enforceable? Take a stand on this issue and present your arguments.

Quiz for Module 13.1

1. Which of the following is the correct sequence of prenatal development?

   a. Zygote, embryo, fetus

   b. Zygote, fetus, embryo

   c. Embryo, zygote, fetus

   d. Embryo, fetus, zygote

2. Which of the following does *not* cross the placental barrier during a woman's pregnancy?

   a. Heroin

   b. HIV

   c. Alcohol

   d. Insulin

3. How far is a typical newborn's visual focus range?

   a. 24 inches

   b. 8 inches

   c. 31 inches

   d. 5 feet

4. Seven-month-old Diego is left in the care of a nurturing, competent babysitter while his mother runs errands for a few hours. Even though both adults are attentive and responsive, Diego nonetheless cries and wails when his mother leaves. The baby is showing signs of

   a. Separation anxiety

   b. Maternal distress

   c. Developmental delay

   d. Response management

5. According to Mary Ainsworth's classification system, which of these is *not* a form of attachment?

   a. Anxious

   b. Avoidant

   c. Apprehensive

   d. Secure

language

A system that combines meaningless elements such as sounds or gestures to form structured utterances that convey meaning.

Cognitive Development

A friend of ours told us about a charming exchange he had with his 2-year-old grandson. "You're very old," the little boy said. "Yes, I am," said his grandfather. "I'm very new," said the child. Two years old, and already this little boy's mind is working away, making observations, trying to understand the differences he observes, and using language (creatively!) to describe them. The development of language and thought from infancy throughout childhood is a marvel to anyone who has ever watched a baby grow up. In this section we'll explore how these processes take place.

Language

LO 13.2.A List the milestones of language development that occur between the first 2 months and 6 years of life.

Try to read this sentence aloud:

Kamaunawezakusomamanenohayawewenimtuwamaanasana.

Can you tell where one word begins and another ends? Unless you know Swahili, the syllables of this sentence will sound like gibberish.[1]

Well, to a baby learning its native tongue, *every* sentence must be gibberish at first. How, then, does an infant pick out discrete syllables and words from the jumble of sounds in the environment, much less figure out what the words mean? And how is it that within a few years, children not only understand thousands of words but can also produce and understand an endless number of new word combinations?

To answer, we must first appreciate that a **language** is not just any old communication system; it is a set of rules for combining inherently meaningless elements into utterances that convey meaning. The elements are usually sounds, but they can also be the gestures of American Sign Language (ASL) and other manual languages that deaf and hearing-impaired people use. Because of language, we can refer not only to the here and now but also to past and future events, and to things or people who are not present. Furthermore, language, whether spoken or signed, allows human beings to express and comprehend an infinite number of novel utterances, created on the spot. This ability is critical; except for a few fixed phrases ("How are you?" "Get a life!"), most of the utterances we produce or hear over a lifetime are new. How in the world do we do this?

LANGUAGE: BUILT IN OR LEARNED?   Many psychological scientists believe that an innate facility for language evolved in human beings because it was extraordinarily beneficial (Pinker, 1994, 2013). It permitted our prehistoric ancestors to convey precise information about time, space, and events (as in "Honey, are you going on the mammoth hunt today?") and allowed them to negotiate alliances that were necessary for survival ("If you share your nuts and berries with us, we'll share our mammoth with you"). Language may also have developed because it provides the human equivalent of the mutual grooming that other primates rely on to forge social bonds (Dunbar, 2004; Tomasello, 2008). Just as other primates will clean, stroke, and groom one another for hours as a sign of affection and connection, human friends will sit for hours and chat over coffee.

At one time, the leading theory held that children acquired language by imitating adults and paying attention when adults corrected their mistakes. Then along came linguist Noam Chomsky (1957, 1980, 2015), who argued that language was far too complex to be learned bit by bit, as one might learn a list of world capitals. Because no one actually teaches us grammar when we are toddlers, said Chomsky, the human brain must contain an innate mental module—a *universal grammar*—that allows young children to develop

---

[1] *Kama unaweza kusoma maneno haya, wewe ni mtu wa maana sana*, in Swahili, means "If you can read these words, you are a remarkable person."

language if they are exposed to an adequate sampling of conversation. Their brains are sensitive to the core features common to all languages, such as nouns and verbs, subjects and objects, and negatives. These common features occur even in languages as seemingly different as Mohawk and English, or Okinawan and Bulgarian (Baker, 2001; Cinque, 1999; Nevins, Pesetsky, & Rodrigues, 2009). In English, even 2-year-olds use syntax to help them acquire new verbs in context: They understand that "Jane blicked the baby!" involves two people, but the use of the same verb in "Jane blicked!" involves only Jane (Dautriche et al., 2014; Yuan & Fisher, 2009).

Evidence for Chomsky's theory that humans have an innate mental module for language comes from several directions. Children in different cultures go through similar stages of linguistic development, and they combine words in ways that adults never would. They reduce a parent's sentences ("Let's go to the store!") to their own two-word versions ("Go store!") and make many charming errors that an adult would not ("The alligator goed kerplunk," "Hey, Horton heared a Who") (Ervin-Tripp, 1964; Marcus et al., 1992). Adults do not consistently correct their children's syntax, yet children learn to speak or sign correctly anyway. Parents may even reward children for syntactically incorrect or incomplete sentences: The 2-year-old who says "Want milk!" is likely to get it; most parents would not wait for a more grammatical (or polite) request.

Most compelling, deaf children who have never learned a standard language, either signed or spoken, have made up their own sign languages out of thin air, and these languages often show similarities in sentence structure across countries as varied as the United States, Taiwan, Spain, and Turkey (Fay et al., 2014; Goldin-Meadow, 2003). The most astounding case comes from Nicaragua, where a group of deaf children, attending special schools, created a homegrown but grammatically complex sign language that is unrelated to Spanish (Senghas, Kita, & Özyürek, 2004). Scientists have had a unique opportunity to observe the evolution of this language as it developed from a few simple signs to a full-blown linguistic system.

However, in the last decade, psycholinguists have taken aim at Chomsky's view, and many now believe that the assumption of a universal grammar is simply wrong (Dunn et al., 2011; Evans & Levinson, 2009; Hinzen, 2014; Tomasello, 2003). In spite of commonalities in language acquisition around the world, the world's 7,000 languages have some major differences that do not seem explainable by a universal grammar (Gopnik, Choi, & Bamberger, 1996). The language spoken by the remote Pirahã in the Amazon and the Wari' language of Brazil apparently lack key grammatical features that occur in other languages (Everett, 2012). One team constructed an evolutionary history for four major language groups and found that each group followed its own structural rules, suggesting that human language is driven by cultural requirements rather than an innate grammar (Dunn et al., 2011; Majid, Jordan, & Dunn, 2014). The anti-innate-module school argues that language is a cultural tool, comparable to the physical tools that people have invented in adapting to different physical and cultural environments. Culture, they say, is the primary determinant of a language's linguistic structure, not an innate grammar.

Experience and culture certainly play a large role in language development. Parents may not go around correcting their children's speech all day, but they do recast and expand their children's clumsy or ungrammatical sentences ("Monkey climbing!" "Yes, the monkey is climbing the tree"). Children, in turn, often imitate those recasts and expansions, indicating that they are learning from them (Bohannon & Symons, 1988).

Some scientists argue that instead of inferring grammatical rules because of an innate disposition to do so, children learn the *probability* that any given word or syllable will follow another, something infants as young as 8 months are able to do (Seidenberg,

These deaf Nicaraguan children have invented their own grammatically complex sign language, one that is unrelated to Spanish or to any conventional gestural language (Senghas, Kita, & Özyürek, 2004).

MacDonald, & Saffran, 2002). Because so many word combinations are used repeatedly ("Pick up your socks!" "Come to dinner!"), little kids seem able to track short word sequences and their frequencies, which in turn plays a role in teaching them not only vocabulary but syntax (Arnon & Clark, 2011). Eventually, children also learn how nonadjacent words co-occur (e.g., *the* and *ducky* in "the yellow ducky"), and are able to generalize their knowledge to learn syntactic categories (Gerken, Wilson, & Lewis, 2005; Lany & Gómez, 2008).

In this view, infants are more like statisticians than grammarians, and their "statistics" are based on experience. Using computers, these theorists have designed mathematical models of the brain that can acquire some aspects of language, such as regular and irregular past-tense verbs, without the help of a preexisting mental module or preprogrammed rules. These computer programs, called *computer neural networks*, simply adjust the connections among hypothetical neurons in response to incoming data, such as repetitions of a word in its past-tense form. The success of these computer models, say their designers, suggests that children, too, may be able to acquire linguistic features without getting a head start from inborn brain modules (Rodriguez, Wiles, & Elman, 1999; Tomasello, 2008).

Although the argument between the Chomsky school and the culture school continues, both sides agree that language development depends on both biological readiness and social experience. Children who are not exposed to language during their early years rarely speak normally or catch up grammatically. Such sad evidence suggests a critical period in language development during the first few years of life or possibly the first decade. During these years, children need exposure to language and opportunities to practice their emerging linguistic skills in conversation with others. Let's see how these skills develop.

FROM COOING TO COMMUNICATING   The acquisition of language may begin in the womb. Canadian psychologists tested newborn babies' preference for hearing English or Tagalog (a major language of the Philippines) by measuring the number of times the babies sucked on a rubber nipple—a measure of babies' interest in a stimulus—while hearing each language alternating during a 10-minute span. Those whose mothers spoke only English during pregnancy showed a clear preference for English by sucking more during the minutes when English was spoken. Those whose bilingual mothers spoke both languages showed equal preference for both languages (Byers-Heinlein, Burns, & Werker, 2010; Fennell & Byers-Heinlein, 2014).

Thus, infants are already responsive to the pitch, intensity, and sound of language, and they also react to the emotions and rhythms in voices. Adults take advantage of these infant abilities by speaking baby talk, called *parentese*. When most people speak to babies, their pitch is higher and more varied than usual and their intonation and emphasis on vowels are exaggerated. Parents all over the world do this. Adult members of the Shuar, a nonliterate hunter-gatherer culture in South America, can accurately distinguish American mothers' infant-directed speech from their adult-directed speech just by tone (Bryant & Barrett, 2007). Parentese helps babies learn the melody and rhythm of their native language.

In what has to have been one of the most adorable research projects ever, three investigators compared the way mothers spoke to their babies and to pets, which also tend to evoke baby talk. The mothers exaggerated vowel sounds for their babies but not for Noodles the poodle or Chubby the cat, suggesting that parentese is, indeed, a way of helping infants acquire language (Burnham, Kitamura, & Vollmer-Conna, 2002).

By 4 to 6 months of age, babies can often recognize their own names and other words that are regularly spoken with emotion, such as "mommy" and "daddy." They also know many of the key consonant and vowel sounds of their native language and can distinguish such sounds from those of other languages (Kuhl et al., 1992). Then, over time, exposure to the baby's native language reduces the child's ability to perceive speech sounds that do not exist in their own. Thus, Japanese infants can hear the difference between the English sounds

la and *ra*, but older Japanese children cannot. Because this contrast does not exist in their language, they become insensitive to it.

Between 6 months and 1 year, infants become increasingly familiar with the sound structure of their native language. They are able to distinguish words from the flow of speech. They will listen longer to words that violate their expectations of what words should sound like and even to sentences that violate their expectations of how sentences should be structured (Jusczyk, 2002). They start to babble, making many "ba-ba" and "goo-goo" sounds, endlessly repeating sounds and syllables. At 7 months, they begin to remember words they have heard, but because they are also attending to the speaker's intonation, speaking rate, and volume, they cannot always recognize the same word when different people speak it (Houston & Jusczyk, 2003). Then, by 10 months, they can suddenly do it—a remarkable leap forward in only 3 months. And at about 1 year of age, though the timing varies considerably, children take another giant step: They start to name things. They already have some concepts in their minds for familiar people and objects, and their first words represent these concepts ("mama," "doggie," "truck").

Also at the end of the first year, babies develop a repertoire of symbolic gestures. They gesture to refer to objects (e.g., sniffing to indicate "flower"), to request something (smacking the lips for "food"), to describe objects (raising the arms for "big"), and to reply to questions (opening the palms or shrugging the shoulders for "I don't know"). They clap in response to pictures of things they like. Children whose parents encourage them to use gestures acquire larger vocabularies, have better comprehension, are better listeners, and are less frustrated in their efforts to communicate than children who are not encouraged to use gestures (Goodwyn & Acredolo, 1998). When babies begin to speak, they continue to gesture along with their words, just as adults often gesture when talking. These gestures are not a substitute for language but are deeply related to its development, as well as to the development of thinking and problem solving (Fay et al, 2014; Goldin-Meadow, Cook, & Mitchell, 2009). Parents, in turn, use gesture (pointing, touching, tapping) to capture their babies' attention and teach them the meanings of words (Clark & Estigarribia, 2011).

One surprising discovery is that babies who are given infant "brain stimulation" videos to look at do not learn more words than a control group, and often they are actually *slower* at acquiring words than babies who do not watch videos. For every hour a day that 8- to 16-month-old babies watch one of these videos, they acquire six to eight fewer words than other children (DeLoache et al., 2010; Zimmerman, Christakis, & Meltzoff, 2007). However, the more that parents read and talk to their babies and infants, the larger the child's vocabulary at age 3 and the faster the child processes familiar words (Weisleder & Fernald, 2013).

Between the ages of 18 months and 2 years, toddlers begin to produce words in two- or three-word combinations ("Mama here," "go 'way bug," "my toy"). The child's first combinations of words have been described as **telegraphic speech**. When people had to pay for every word in a telegram, they quickly learned to drop unnecessary articles (*a, an,* or *the*) and auxiliary verbs (*is* or *are*). Similarly, the two-word sentences of toddlers omit articles, word endings, auxiliary verbs, and other parts of speech, yet these sentences are remarkably accurate in conveying meaning. Children use two-word sentences to locate things ("there toy"), make demands ("more milk"), negate actions ("no want," "all gone milk"), describe events ("Bambi go," "hit ball"), describe objects ("pretty dress"), show possession ("Mama dress"), and ask questions ("where Daddy?"). Pretty good for a little kid, don't you think?

By the age of 6, the average child has a vocabulary of between 8,000 and 14,000 words, meaning that children acquire several new words a day between the ages of 2 and 6. They absorb new words as they hear them, inferring their meaning from their knowledge of grammatical contexts and from the social contexts in which they hear the words used (Golinkoff & Hirsh-Pasek, 2006; Rice, 1990).

Symbolic gestures emerge early!

telegraphic speech
A child's first word combinations, which omit (as a telegram did) unnecessary words.

Thinking

LO 13.2.B Describe the four stages of cognitive development proposed by Piaget, explain the defining characteristics of each stage, and discuss four modifications of Piaget's theory.

Children do not think the way adults do. For most of the first year of life, if something is out of sight, it's out of mind: If you cover a baby's favorite rattle with a cloth, the baby thinks the rattle has vanished and stops looking for it. And a 4-year-old may protest that a sibling has more fruit juice when it is only the shapes of the glasses that differ, not the amount of juice. Some truths and myths regarding childhood cognition are explored in the video *Smart Babies by Design*

Yet children are smart in their own way. Like good little scientists, children are always testing their child-sized theories about how things work (Gopnik, Griffiths, & Lucas, 2015). When your toddler throws her spoon on the floor for the sixth time as you try to feed her, and you say, "That's enough! I will *not* pick up your spoon again!" the child will immediately test your claim. Are you serious? Are you angry? What will happen if she throws the spoon again? She is not doing this to drive you crazy; rather, she is learning that her desires and yours can differ, and that sometimes those differences are important and sometimes they are not.

How and why does children's thinking change? In the 1920s, Swiss psychologist Jean Piaget [Zhan Pee-ah-ZHAY] (1896–1980) proposed that children's cognitive abilities unfold naturally, like the blooming of a flower, almost independent of what else is happening in their lives. Although many of his specific conclusions have been rejected or modified over the years, his ideas inspired thousands of studies by investigators all over the world.

PIAGET'S THEORY OF COGNITIVE STAGES According to Piaget (1929/1960, 1984), as children develop, their minds constantly adapt to new situations and experiences. Sometimes they *assimilate* new information into their existing mental categories: A German shepherd and a terrier both fit the category *dogs*. At other times, however, children must change their mental categories to *accommodate* their new experiences: A cat does not belong to the category *dogs* and a new category is required, one for *cats*. Both processes are constantly interacting, Piaget said, as children go through four stages of cognitive development.

From birth to age 2, said Piaget, babies are in the *sensorimotor stage*. In this stage, the infant learns through concrete actions: looking, touching, putting things in the mouth, sucking, grasping. "Thinking" consists of coordinating sensory information with bodily movements. Gradually, these movements become more purposeful as the child explores the environment and learns that specific movements will produce specific results. Pulling a cloth away will reveal a hidden toy; letting go of a fuzzy toy duck will cause it to drop out of reach; banging on the table with a spoon will produce dinner (or Mom, taking the spoon away).

Like a good little scientist, this child is trying to figure out cause and effect: "If I throw this dish, what will happen? Will there be a noise? Will Mom come and give it back to me? How many times will she give it back to me?"

A major accomplishment at this stage, said Piaget, is **object permanence**, the understanding that something continues to exist even when you can't see it or touch it. In the first few months, infants will look intently at a little toy, but if you hide it behind a piece of paper they will not look behind the paper or make an effort to get the toy. By about 6 months of age, however, infants begin to grasp the idea that the toy exists whether or not they can see it. If a baby of this age drops a toy from her playpen, she will look for it; she also will look under a cloth for a toy that is partially hidden. By 1 year of age, most babies have developed an awareness of the permanence of objects; even if a toy is covered by a cloth, it must be under there. This is when they love to play peekaboo. Object permanence, said Piaget, represents the beginning of the child's capacity to use mental imagery and symbols. The child becomes able to hold a concept in mind, to learn that the word *fly* represents an annoying, buzzing creature and that *Daddy* represents a friendly, playful one.

From about ages 2 to 7, the child's use of symbols and language accelerates. Piaget called this the *preoperational stage* because he believed that children still lack the cognitive abilities necessary for understanding abstract principles. Piaget believed (mistakenly, as we will see) that preoperational children cannot take another person's point of view because their thinking is *egocentric*: They see the world only from their own frame of reference and cannot imagine that others see things differently. Furthermore, said Piaget, preoperational children cannot grasp the concept of **conservation**, the notion that physical properties do not change when their form or appearance changes. Children at this age do not understand that an amount of liquid or a number of blocks remains the same even if you pour the liquid from one glass to another of a different size or if you stack the blocks (see Figure 13.3). If you pour liquid from a short, fat glass into a tall, narrow glass, preoperational children will say there is more liquid in the second glass. They attend to the appearance of the liquid (its height in the glass) to judge its quantity, and so they are misled.

From the ages of 7 to about 12, Piaget said, children increasingly become able to take other people's perspectives and they make fewer logical errors. Piaget called this the *concrete operations* stage because he thought children's mental abilities are tied to information that is concrete, that is, to actual experiences that have happened or concepts that have a tangible meaning to them. Children at this stage make errors of reasoning when they are asked to think about abstract ideas such as "patriotism" or "future education." During these years,

object permanence

The understanding, which develops throughout the first year, that an object continues to exist even when you cannot see it or touch it.

conservation

The understanding that the physical properties of objects, such as the number of items in a cluster or the amount of liquid in a glass, can remain the same even when their form or appearance changes.

Figure 13.3 Piaget's Principle of Conservation

If you've got access to young children (through babysitting; as an aunt, uncle, or sibling; through a local daycare center; or as a parent yourself), you can examine some of Piaget's principles yourself. In one test for conservation of size (left), the child must say which is bigger—a round lump of clay or the same amount of clay pressed flat. Preoperational children think that the flattened clay is bigger because it seems to take up more space. In a test for conservation of quantity (right), the child is shown two short glasses with equal amounts of liquid. Then the contents of one glass are poured into a tall, narrower glass, and the child is asked whether one container now has more. Most preoperational children do not understand that pouring liquid from a short glass into a taller one leaves the amount of liquid unchanged. They judge only by the height of liquid in the glass.

nonetheless, children's cognitive abilities expand rapidly. They come to understand the principles of conservation and of cause and effect. They learn mental operations, such as basic arithmetic. They are able to categorize things (e.g., oaks as trees) and to order things serially from smallest to largest, lightest to darkest, and shortest to tallest.

Finally, said Piaget, beginning at about age 12 or 13 and continuing into adulthood, people become capable of abstract reasoning and enter the *formal operations* stage. They are able to reason about situations they have not experienced firsthand, and they can think about future possibilities. They are able to search systematically for answers to problems. They are able to draw logical conclusions from premises common to their culture and experience.

CURRENT VIEWS OF COGNITIVE DEVELOPMENT   Piaget's central idea has been well supported: New reasoning abilities depend on the emergence of previous ones. You cannot learn algebra before you can count, and you cannot learn philosophy before you understand logic. But since Piaget's original work, the field of developmental psychology has undergone an explosion of imaginative research that has allowed investigators to get into the minds of even the youngest infants. The result has been a modification of Piaget's ideas, and some developmental scientists go so far as to say that his ideas have been overturned. Here's why:

1. **Cognitive abilities develop in continuous, overlapping waves rather than discrete steps or stages.** If you observe children at different ages, as Piaget did, it will seem that they reason differently. But if you study the everyday learning of children at any given age, you will find that a child may use several different strategies to solve a problem, some more complex or accurate than others (Siegler, 2006). Learning occurs gradually, with retreats to former ways of thinking as well as advances to new ones. Children's reasoning ability also depends on the circumstances—who is asking them questions, the specific words used, the materials used, and what they are reasoning about—and not just on the stage they are in. In short, cognitive development is *continuous*; new abilities do not simply pop up when a child turns a certain age (Courage & Howe, 2002).

2. **Preschoolers are not as egocentric as Piaget thought.** Most 3- and 4-year-olds *can* take another person's perspective (Flavell, 1999). When 4-year-olds play with 2-year-olds, they modify and simplify their speech so the younger children will understand (Shatz & Gelman, 1973). One preschooler we know showed her teacher a picture she had drawn of a cat and an unidentifiable blob. "The cat is lovely," said the teacher, "but what is this thing here?" "That has nothing to do with you," said the child. "That's what the *cat* is looking at."

   By about ages 3 to 4, children also begin to understand that you cannot predict what a person will do just by observing a situation or knowing the facts. You also have to know what the person is feeling and thinking; the person might be mistaken or even be lying. They start asking why other people behave as they do ("Why is Johnny so mean?"). In short, they are developing a **theory of mind**, a system of beliefs about how their own and other people's minds work and how people are affected by their beliefs and emotions. They begin to use verbs like *think* and *know*, and by age 4, they understand that what another person thinks might not match their own knowledge. In one typical experiment, a child watched as another child placed a ball in the closet and left the room. An adult then entered and moved the ball into a basket. Three-year-olds predicted that when the other child returned, he would look for the ball in the basket because that is where the 3-year-old knew it was. But 4-year-olds said that the child would look in the closet, where the other child believed it was (Flavell, 1999; Wellman, Cross, & Watson, 2001).

   Remarkably, early aspects of a theory of mind are present in infancy: Babies aged 13 to 15 months are surprised when they realize that an adult has a false or pretend belief (Luo & Baillargeon, 2010). The ability to understand that people can have false beliefs

theory of mind

A system of beliefs about the way one's own mind and the minds of others work, and of how individuals are affected by their beliefs and feelings.

is a milestone because it means the child is beginning to question how we know things—the foundation for later higher-order thinking (Moll, Kane, & McGowan, 2015).

3. **Children, even infants, reveal cognitive abilities much earlier than Piaget believed possible.** Taking advantage of the fact that infants look longer at novel or surprising stimuli than at familiar ones, psychologists have designed delightfully innovative methods of testing what babies know. These methods reveal that babies may be born with mental modules or core knowledge systems for numbers, spatial relations, the properties of objects, and other features of the physical world (Kibbe & Leslie, 2011; Schultz & Tomasello, 2015; Scott & Baillargeon, 2013; Spelke & Kinzler, 2007).

Thus, at only 4 months of age, babies will look longer at a ball if it seems to roll through a solid barrier, leap between two platforms, or hang in midair than they do when the ball obeys the laws of physics. This suggests that the unusual event is surprising to them (see Figure 13.4). Infants as young as 2½ to 3½ months are aware that objects continue to exist even when masked by other objects, a form of object permanence that Piaget never imagined possible in babies so young (Baillargeon, 2004). And, most devastating to Piaget's notion of infant egocentrism, even 5-month-old infants are able to perceive other people's actions as being intentional; they detect the difference between a person who is reaching for a toy with her hand rather than accidentally touching it with a stick (Woodward, 2009). Even 3-month-old infants can learn this. At that tender age, they are obviously not yet skilled at intentionally reaching for objects. But when experimenters covered their little hands with "sticky mittens"—covered with Velcro—so that soft toys would stick to them, the babies actually learned from that experience to distinguish the intentional versus accidental reaches of others (Sommerville, Woodward, & Needham, 2005).

4. **Cognitive development is influenced by a child's culture.** One of Piaget's contemporaries, Russian psychologist Lev Vygotsky (1896–1934), had disagreed with Piaget by emphasizing the sociocultural influences on children's cognitive development. Vygotsky (1962) believed that children develop mental representations of the world through culture, language, and the environment, and that adults play a major role in this process by constantly guiding and teaching their children. As a result, he said, instead of going through invariant stages, a child's cognitive development may proceed in any number of directions. Vygotsky was correct. Culture—the world of tools, language, rituals, beliefs, games, and social institutions—shapes and structures children's cognitive development, fostering some abilities and not others (Tomasello, 2014). Thus, nomadic hunters excel in spatial abilities because spatial orientation is crucial for finding water holes and successful hunting routes. In contrast, children who live in settled agricultural communities, such as the Baoulé of the Ivory Coast, develop rapidly in the ability to quantify but much more slowly in spatial reasoning.

Despite these modifications, Piaget left an enduring legacy: the insight that children are not passive vessels into which education and experience are poured. Children actively interpret their worlds, using their developing abilities to assimilate new information and figure things out. As the video *How Thinking Develops* points out, these insights have shaped psychologists' own thinking about thinking.

JOURNAL PROMPT 13.2

Thinking Critically—Ask Questions, Be Willing to Wonder: In most psychological experiments, if researchers wanted to know someone's opinions, thoughts, or reactions, they would simply ask that person. That strategy is difficult to use with infants who haven't learned to talk yet; instructing a 10-month-old to "circle a number on a scale to give your response" or asking "which of these items do you prefer?" isn't going to get you very far. What behaviors could you measure to infer what an infant is thinking about, or even *that* an infant is thinking? How could you verify that your inferences are accurate?

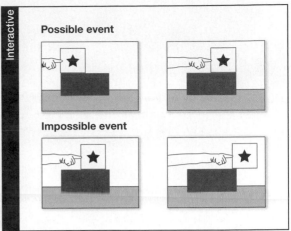

Possible event

Impossible event

Figure 13.4 Testing Infants' Knowledge

In this clever procedure, a baby watches as a box is pushed from left to right along a platform. The box is pushed until it reaches the end of the platform (a possible event) or until only a bit of it rests on the platform (an impossible event). Babies look longer at the impossible event, suggesting that it surprises them. Somehow they know that an object needs physical support and cannot just float on air (Baillargeon, 1994).

Experience and culture influence cognitive development. Children who work with clay, wood, and other materials, such as this young potter in India, tend to understand the concept of conservation sooner than children who have not had this kind of experience.

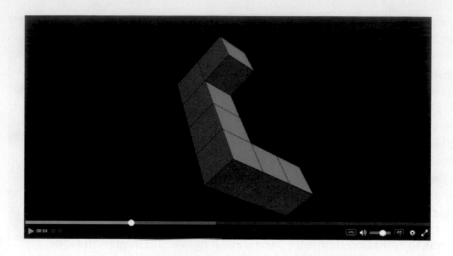

Quiz for Module 13.2

1. Noam Chomsky proposed that children learn language because of
   a. Formal education
   b. Trial and error
   c. Reinforcement from the environment
   d. A universal grammar

2. Children begin to produce words in two- or three-word combinations around the age of
   a. 1 year
   b. 20 months
   c. 3 years
   d. 8 months

3. According to Piaget, object permanence is a hallmark of the _____ stage of cognitive development.
   a. Concrete operations
   b. Preoperational
   c. Sensorimotor
   d. Formal operations

4. According to Piaget, children have difficulty grasping the principle of conservation of matter during the _____ stage of cognitive development.
   a. Preoperational
   b. Sensorimotor
   c. Concrete operations
   d. Formal operations

5. Which of the following represents a substantial departure from Piaget's original formulation of cognitive development?
   a. Cognitive abilities mature and change over time.
   b. Children don't enter the stage of formal operations until about 13 years old.
   c. Children are active learners who interpret their world.
   d. Cognitive abilities develop in overlapping waves, rather than discrete stages.

Moral Development

You've probably heard people refer to their child as "my little angel." But clearly, children quite often behave far from angelically! Like so much of our behavior, being good has to be learned. How do children learn to tell right from wrong, resist the temptation to behave selfishly, and obey the rules of social conduct? In this section, we'll discuss issues of moral development.

Early Views of Moral Development

LO 13.3.A   Discuss the evidence for and against the proposition that moral development occurs in distinct stages over time.

In the 1960s, Lawrence Kohlberg (1964), inspired by Piaget's work, argued that children's ability to understand right from wrong, and other forms of moral reasoning, evolved along with the rest of their cognitive abilities, progressing through three levels. Very young children obey rules because they fear being punished if they disobey, and later because they think it is in their best interest to obey. At about age 10, their moral judgments shift to ones based on conformity and loyalty to others, and then to an understanding of the rule of law. In adulthood, a few individuals go on to develop a moral standard based on universal human rights. Martin Luther King, Jr. fought against laws supporting segregation, Mohandas Gandhi advocated nonviolent solutions to injustice in India, and Susan B. Anthony fought for women's right to vote, all because those were right and just principles to endorse.

Kohlberg was right that moral reasoning skills increase during the school years, but unfortunately so do cheating, lying, cruelty, and the cognitive ability to rationalize these actions. Accordingly, developmental psychologists today place greater emphasis on how children learn to regulate their own emotions and behavior (Mischel, 2013). Most children learn to inhibit their wishes to beat up their younger siblings, steal a classmate's toy, or scream at the top of their lungs if they don't get their way. The child's emerging ability to understand right from wrong, and to behave accordingly, depends on the emergence of conscience and moral emotions such as shame, guilt, and empathy (Kochanska et al., 2005; Ongley & Malti, 2014).

As we saw in discussing criticisms of Piaget's theory, even very young children are capable of feeling empathy for others and taking another person's point of view. Children obey rules not only because they are afraid of what will happen to them if they disobey, but also because they understand right from wrong. By age 5, they know it is wrong to hurt someone even if a teacher tells them to (Turiel, 2014). The capacity for understanding right from wrong seems to be inborn. Evolutionary psychologists argue that this "moral sense" underlies the basic beliefs, judgments, and behavior that are considered moral almost everywhere, and that it originated in cooperative, altruistic strategies that permitted our forebears to resolve conflicts and get along (Delton et al., 2011; Krebs, 2008).

Can a moral sense and a desire to behave well with others be nurtured or extinguished by specific methods of childrearing? For decades, most developmental psychologists assumed that the answer was "Of course!" and they set about trying to pinpoint which parental techniques create well-behaved, kind, unselfish children. Then came a flood of behavioral-genetic studies that led to a very different assumption: The effects of the parents' methods depend (of course!) on the kind of child they have. Is it one who heeds discipline or one who is resistant and hostile?

Today, many researchers are seeking a middle ground by studying gene–environment interactions (Schmidt et al., 2009). Aggressive, antisocial adolescents often have a history of maltreatment and abuse in childhood *and* a gene variant linked to aggressive behavior. Good parenting, however, can help to override a genetic vulnerability. One provocative hypothesis suggests that infants and toddlers who show high levels of distress and irritability are actually more responsive to, and influenced by, styles of parenting than easygoing babies are. Easygoing babies are "dandelions"; they survive in almost any circumstances they encounter because they are, well, easygoing. "Orchid children," in contrast, are highly sensitive to their environments; under adversity, they wither (Kennedy, 2013). When such babies have impatient, rejecting, or coercive parents, they later tend to become aggressive and even more difficult and defiant. When they have patient, supportive, firm parents, they become better natured and happier—in a word, they bloom (Belsky, Bakermans-Kranenburg, & van IJzendoorn, 2007; Belsky & Pluess, 2009b).

Keeping the complexity of this issue in mind, let's look at how parental discipline methods interact with a child's temperament in the development of conscience and moral behavior.

How do children internalize moral rules? How do they learn that cheating, stealing, and grabbing a younger sibling's toy are wrong?

power assertion

A method of childrearing in which the parent uses punishment and authority to correct the child's misbehavior.

induction

A method of childrearing in which the parent appeals to the child's own abilities, sense of responsibility, and feelings for others in correcting the child's misbehavior.

Getting Children to Be Good

LO 13.4.A Compare the ways in which power assertion, inductive appeals, self-regulation, and conscience contribute to moral development.

When you did something wrong as a child, did the adults in your family spank you, shout at you, threaten you, or explain the error of your ways? To try to enforce moral standards and good behavior, many parents rely on **power assertion**, which includes threats, physical punishment, depriving the child of privileges, and generally taking advantage of being bigger, stronger, and more powerful. Of course, a parent may have no alternative other than "Do it because I say so!" if the child is too young to understand a rule or impishly keeps trying to break it. Moreover, the culture and context in which the discipline occurs makes an enormous difference. Is the parent–child relationship fundamentally loving and trusting or one full of hostility and fighting? Does the child interpret the parents' actions as being fair and caring, or unfair and cruel?

But when power assertion consists of sheer parental bullying, cruel insults ("You are so stupid, I wish you'd never been born"), and frequent physical punishment, it is associated with greater aggressiveness and reduced empathy in children (Alink et al., 2009; Kochanska et al., 2015; Moore & Pepler, 2006). Physical punishment often backfires, especially when it is used inappropriately or harshly; it spirals out of control, causing the child to become angry and resentful. Moreover, harsh but ineffective discipline methods are often transmitted to the next generation: Aggressive parents teach their children that the way to discipline children is by behaving aggressively (Capaldi et al., 2003).

What is the alternative? In contrast to power assertion, a parent can use **induction**, appealing to the child's own abilities, empathy, helpful nature, affection for others, and sense of responsibility ("You made Doug cry; it's not nice to bite"; "You must never poke anyone's eyes because that could really hurt them"). Or the parent might appeal to the child's own helpful inclinations ("I know you're a person who likes to be nice to others") rather than citing external reasons to be good ("You'd better be nice or you won't get dessert").

SELF-CONTROL AND CONSCIENCE   One of the most important social-emotional skills that children need to acquire is the ability to control their immediate impulses and wishes. In particular, they need to learn to *delay gratification* to gain later benefits. The original classic study of delayed gratification used a "marshmallow test": Preschoolers were offered a choice between eating one marshmallow right away or having two marshmallows if they could wait a few minutes while the experimenter stepped out of the room (Mischel, Shoda,

Power assertion is the use of physical force, threats, insults, or other kinds of power to get the child to obey ("Do it because I say so!" "Stop that right now!"). The child may obey, but only when the parent is present—and the child often feels resentful.

The parent who uses induction appeals to the child's good nature, empathy, love for the parent, and sense of responsibility to others and offers explanations of rules ("You're too grown up to behave like that"; "Fighting hurts your little brother"). The child tends to internalize reasons for good behavior.

& Rodriguez, 1989). Dozens of studies have been conducted since, including follow-ups on what became of the children in the first experiments, and the results are clear: Children who are able to resist the single marshmallow (or other prize) in favor of getting a larger reward later are better able to control negative emotions, pay attention to the task at hand, and do well in school. Indeed, the early ability to postpone gratification has effects on health, success, and well-being that last for *decades* (Casey et al., 2011; Eigsti et al., 2006; Mischel, 2014; Ponitz et al., 2009).

Where does this skill come from? Partly from temperament and personality because children who can control their emotions and impulses usually do so across situations (de Ridder et al., 2012; Raffaelli, Crockett, & Shen, 2005). Partly from learning: Children and young people can learn to improve their ability to delay gratification by focusing on the later benefits, by distracting themselves from focusing on the appealing prize, and by mentally "cooling" the hot, appealing features of the prize (e.g., by imagining the marshmallow as a cloud or a little cotton ball, rather than as a sweet treat). And partly from the way their parents treat them.

A longitudinal study of 106 preschool children explored the links between parental discipline, the child's self-control, and the emergence of conscience (Kochanska & Knaack, 2003). The children who were most able to regulate their impulses early in life were the least likely to get in trouble later by fighting or destroying things, and the most likely to have a high conscience score. In turn, their behavior was negatively correlated with the mother's use of power assertion, meaning that mothers who ordered their children to "behave" tended to have children who were impulsive and aggressive. However, cause and effect worked in both directions. Some mothers relied on power assertion *because* their children were impulsive, defiant, and aggressive and would not listen to them. This pattern of findings teaches us to avoid oversimplifying, by concluding that "It's all in what the mother does" or that "It's all in the child's personality." Mothers and children, it seems, raise each other.

Children's ability to regulate their impulses and delay gratification is a major milestone in the development of conscience and moral behavior.

JOURNAL PROMPT 13.3

Thinking Critically—Avoid Emotional Reasoning: Would you rather have $10 now or $20 in 2 weeks? If you want easy money, you can get a lesser amount right away, but if you're willing to delay gratification, you can get more in a little while. Regardless of the option you'd pick, explain your reasoning. What are your thoughts and motives driving the choice you'd make? Would it matter if the circumstances were changed; how about $100 right now or $200 in 2 weeks?

Quiz for Module 13.3

1. Early psychological theory and research on moral development considered it to be
   a. An innate quality of humans
   b. Overlapping waves of continuous improvement
   c. A series of stages
   d. Behavior that was learned through reinforcement

2. Lawrence Kohlberg argued that very young children obey rules because
   a. They understand the larger moral principles behind the rules
   b. They know it's the right thing to do
   c. They fear being punished
   d. They have an innate understanding of morality

3. "Why do I have to write a thank-you note to Grandma?" whined Morrie. "Because I told you to!" his mother replied. What parenting style is Morrie's mother using?
   a. Autonomous
   b. Induction
   c. Deduction
   d. Power assertion

4. "Why do I have to write a thank-you note to Grandma?" whined Morrie. "Because it's polite to thank someone for a gift, and you're a polite person," his mother replied. What parenting style is Morrie's mother using?
   a. Deduction
   b. Induction
   c. Power assertion
   d. Fiduciary

5. Henrietta is waiting with her father in the car while her sister finishes her dance lesson. It'll be a little while, so her father offers to take her to the candy store to get a small treat. However, Henrietta knows that if she waits patiently until her sister is finished, her father will take them to the ice cream shop for a bigger treat. "Thanks for the offer, Pop, but I'd rather wait until she's done," Henrietta decides. "No surprise," replied her father, "that's the choice you usually make." Based on what you know about delay of gratification, what do you predict for Henrietta's long-term future?

a. She has a predicted life expectancy of approximately 42 years.

b. She's likely to be a typical case of "burnout," shining brightly then fizzling fast.

c. She will probably be less successful than her sister at most endeavors.

d. She'll probably be happy in a successful career and enjoy many health benefits.

Gender Development

When they learned a baby girl was on the way, our two psychologist friends took a scientific approach to naming her. First they consulted lists of the 100 most popular names over the past several years and selected those between 51 and 100; popular, but not too popular. Then they chose names that were gender-neutral, such as Chris or Morgan, and asked a sample of friends to rate both the familiarity and femininity of a large set of names. When the data were analyzed (and the parents weighed in with their own preferences), their daughter Casey finally had her name.

But then something curious happened. Casey was born without a lot of hair, and her parents shied away from early ear-piercing, ribbons and bows, or garish pink clothing. Within the first year of her life, strangers would comment "What a darling little fellow!" or "Hi there, champ," assuming that this child, devoid of many typical gender markers, must be a boy. The efforts to give Casey a fair start in life, with a gender-neutral name that wouldn't immediately activate people's stereotypical assumptions about girls, didn't stop people from defaulting to a different stereotype: Males are normative, and females are the exception (Gilman, 1911).

Psychological scientists have increasingly turned their attention to understanding what it means to be a "girl" or a "boy," "female" or "male," and all that is bound up in those time-honored yet currently shifting conceptions of how to categorize people in the world. In terms of gender *development*, some of the primary questions are these: How soon do children notice that girls and boys are different sexes and understand which sex they themselves are? How do children learn the rules of femininity and masculinity, the things that girls do that are different from what boys do?

Gender Identity

LO 13.4.A Distinguish between biological sex, gender identity, gender typing, and intersex conditions.

gender identity

The fundamental sense of being male or female; it is independent of whether the person conforms to the social and cultural rules of gender.

gender typing

The process by which children learn the abilities, interests, and behaviors associated with being masculine or feminine in their culture.

Let's start by clarifying some terms. **Gender identity** refers to a child's sense of being male or female, of belonging to one sex and not the other. **Gender typing** is the process of socializing children into their gender roles, and thus reflects society's ideas about which abilities, interests, traits, and behaviors are appropriately masculine or feminine. A person can have a strong gender identity and not be gender typed: A man may be confident in his maleness and not feel threatened by doing "unmasculine" things such as needlepointing a pillow; a woman may be confident in her femaleness and not feel threatened by doing "unfeminine" things such as serving in combat. The factors that influence sex and gender are discussed in the video *Sex and Gender Differences 2*.

In the past, psychologists tried to distinguish the terms *sex* and *gender*, reserving "sex" for the physiological or anatomical attributes of males and females and "gender" for differences

that are learned. Thus, they might speak of a sex difference in the frequency of baldness but a gender difference in fondness for romance novels. Today, these two terms are often used interchangeably because, as we have noted repeatedly in this book, nature and nurture are inextricably linked (Roughgarden, 2004).

The complexity of sex and gender development is especially apparent in people who do not fit the familiar categories of male and female. Every year, thousands of babies are born with **intersex conditions**, formerly known as *hermaphroditism*. In these conditions, chromosomal or hormonal anomalies cause the child to be born with ambiguous genitals, or genitals that conflict with the infant's chromosomes. A child who is genetically female might be born with an enlarged clitoris that looks like a penis. A child who is genetically male might be born with androgen insensitivity, a condition that causes the external genitals to appear female.

As adults, many intersexed individuals call themselves *transgender*, a term describing a broad category of people who do not fit comfortably into the usual categories of male and female, masculine and feminine. Some transgender people are comfortable living with the physical attributes of both sexes, considering themselves to be "gender queer" and even refusing to be referred to as *he* or *she*. Some feel uncomfortable in their sex of rearing and wish to be considered a member of the other sex. You have probably also heard the term *transsexual*, describing people who are not intersexed yet who feel that they are male in a female body or vice versa; their gender identity is at odds with their

intersex conditions (intersexuality)
Conditions in which chromosomal or hormonal anomalies cause a child to be born with ambiguous genitals, or genitals that conflict with the infant's chromosomes.

Throughout history and across cultures, some people have broken out of conventional gender categories. Some women have lived as men, as did the 18th-century pirates Ann Bonny and Mary Read. Some men have lived as women: The Muxes (pronounced "moo-shays") of southern Mexico are males who consider themselves female, live as females, and are a socially accepted category (center). Caitlyn Jenner (formerly Bruce) attracted attention in 2015 by completing a gender transition.

anatomical sex or appearance. Many transsexuals try to make a full transition to the other sex through surgery or hormones. Intersexed people and transsexuals have lived in virtually all cultures throughout history (Denny, 1998; Roughgarden, 2004). Recently, Facebook acknowledged the diversity of people's conceptions of their gender identity by offering over 50 possibilities for gender identification, such as *gender fluid*, *nonbinary*, *two-spirit*, or *cisgender* (Ball, 2014).

Influences on Gender Development

LO 13.4.B   Summarize the basic findings regarding biological, cognitive, and learning influences on gender identity and gender typing.

To understand the typical course of gender development, as well as the variations, developmental psychologists study the interacting influences of biology, cognition, and learning on gender identity and gender typing.

BIOLOGICAL INFLUENCES   Starting in the preschool years, boys and girls congregate primarily with other children of their sex, and most prefer the toys and games of their own sex. They will play together if required to, but given their druthers, they usually choose to play with same-sex friends. The kind of play that young girls and boys enjoy also differs, on average. Little boys, like young males in all primate species, are more likely than females to go in for physical roughhousing, risk taking, and aggressive displays. These sex differences occur all over the world, almost regardless of whether adults encourage boys and girls to play together or separate them (Lytton & Romney, 1991; Maccoby, 1998, 2002). Many parents lament that although they try to give their children the same toys, it makes no difference; their sons want trucks and guns and their daughters want dolls.

Biological scientists believe that these play and toy preferences have a basis in prenatal hormones, particularly the presence or absence of prenatal androgens (masculinizing hormones). Girls who were exposed to higher-than-normal prenatal androgens in the womb are later more likely than nonexposed girls to prefer "boys' toys" such as cars and fire engines, and they are also more physically aggressive than other girls (Berenbaum & Bailey, 2003; Martin & Dinella, 2012). A study of more than 200 healthy children in the general population also found a relationship between fetal testosterone and play styles. (Testosterone is produced in fetuses of both sexes, although it is higher on average in males.) The higher the levels of fetal testosterone, as measured in the amniotic fluid of the children's mothers during pregnancy, the higher the children's later scores on a measure of male-typical play (Auyeung et al., 2009). In studies of rhesus monkeys, who of course are not influenced by their parents' possible gender biases, male monkeys, like human boys, consistently and strongly prefer to play with wheeled toys rather than cuddly plush toys, whereas female monkeys, like human girls, are more varied in their toy preferences (Hassett, Siebert, & Wallen, 2008).

Do these findings have anything to do with gender identity, the core sense of being female or male? A psychologist reviewed hundreds of cases of children whose sex of rearing was discrepant with their anatomical or genetic sex. He learned that the answer is enormously complex because a person's gender identity depends on the interactions of genes, prenatal hormones, anatomical structures, and experiences in life (Zucker, 1999). Consider a longitudinal study of 16 genetic males who had a rare condition that caused them to be born without a penis. The babies were otherwise normal males, with testicles and appropriate androgen levels. Two of the boys were raised as male and developed a male gender identity. Fourteen had been socially and surgically assigned to the female sex, according to the custom when they were born. Of those 14, eight eventually declared themselves male, five decided to live as females, and one had an unclear gender identity (Reiner & Gearheart, 2004).

Look familiar? In a scene typical of many homes and nursery schools, the boy likes to play with trucks and the girl with dolls. Whether or not such behavior is biologically based, the gender rigidity of the early years does not inevitably continue into adulthood unless cultural rules reinforce it.

COGNITIVE INFLUENCES   Cognitive psychologists explain the mystery of children's gender segregation and toy and play preferences by studying children's changing cognitive abilities. Even before babies can speak, they can discriminate two sexes. By the age of 9 months, most babies can discriminate female from male faces (Fagot & Leinbach, 1993), and they can match female faces with female voices (Poulin-Dubois et al., 1994). By the age of 18 to 20 months, most toddlers have a concept of gender labels. They can accurately identify their own gender and that of people in picture books and begin correctly using the words *boy, girl,* and *man* (interestingly, *lady* and *woman* come later) (Zosuls et al., 2009).

After children can label themselves and others consistently as being a boy or a girl, shortly before age 2, they change their behavior to conform to the category they belong to. Many begin to prefer same-sex playmates and sex-traditional toys without being explicitly taught to do so (Halim et al., 2014; Martin, Ruble, & Szkrybalo, 2002). They become more gender typed in their toy play, games, aggressiveness, and verbal skills than children who still cannot consistently label males and females. Most notably, girls stop behaving aggressively (Fagot, 1993). It is as if they go along behaving like boys until they know they are girls. At that moment, they seem to decide: "Girls don't do this. I'm a girl; I'd better not either."

By about age 5, most children have developed a stable gender identity, a sense of themselves as being male or female regardless of what they wear or how they behave. Only then do they understand that what girls and boys do does not necessarily indicate what sex they are: A girl remains a girl even if she can climb a tree, and a boy remains a boy even if he has long hair. At this age, children consolidate their knowledge, with all of its mistakes and misconceptions, into a **gender schema**, a mental network of beliefs and expectations about what it means to be male or female and about what each sex is supposed to wear, do, feel, and think (Bem, 1993; Martin & Ruble, 2004). Gender schemas are most rigid between ages 5 and 7; at this age, it's really hard to dislodge a child's notion of what boys and girls can do (Martin et al., 2002).

Gender schemas even include metaphors. After age 4, children of both sexes will usually say that rough, spiky, black, or mechanical things are male and that soft, pink, fuzzy, or flowery things are female; that black bears are male and pink poodles are female (Leinbach, Hort, & Fagot, 1997; Swinkels, 2009). But the content of these schemas is not innate. A hundred years ago, an article in *Ladies' Home Journal* advised: "The generally accepted rule is pink for the boys, and blue for the girls. The reason is that pink, being a more decided and stronger color, is more suitable for the boy, while blue, which is more delicate and dainty, is prettier for the girl" (Paoletti, 2012). The invention of gender-specific "rules" of clothing for babies and young children was a creation of late 20th-century marketing.

Many people retain inflexible gender schemas throughout their lives. They feel uncomfortable or angry with men or women who break out of traditional roles, not to mention with transgendered individuals who don't fit either category or want to change the one they grew up with. However, with experience and cognitive sophistication, older children often become more flexible in their gender schemas, especially if they have friends of the other sex and if their families and cultures encourage such flexibility (Martin & Ruble, 2004).

Cultures and religions, too, differ in their schemas for the roles of women and men. In all Western, industrialized nations, it is taken for granted that women and men alike should be educated; indeed, laws mandate a minimum education for both sexes. But in cultures where female education is prohibited in the name of religious law, many girls who attend school receive death threats and some have had acid thrown on their faces. Gender schemas can be powerful, and events that challenge their legitimacy can be enormously threatening.

LEARNING INFLUENCES   A third influence on gender development is the environment, which is full of subtle and not-so-subtle messages about what girls and boys are supposed to do. Behavioral and social-cognitive learning theorists study how the process of *gender socialization* instills these messages in children (Bussey & Bandura, 1999). They find that gender socialization begins at the moment of birth. Many parents are careful to dress their baby in outfits they consider to be the correct color and pattern for his or her sex. Clothes don't matter to the infant, of course, but they are signals to adults about how to treat the child;

gender schema
A cognitive schema (mental network) of knowledge, beliefs, metaphors, and expectations about what it means to be male or female.

Crystal Smith transcribed a number of commercials directed to "boys" or "girls," and made these "word clouds" out of the result. You can see at once how advertisers cater to exaggerated gender schemas.

remember the case of Casey, whom you read about earlier? Adults often respond to the same baby differently, depending on whether the child is dressed as a boy or a girl (Shakin, Shakin, & Sternglanz, 1985).

Parents, teachers, and other adults convey their beliefs and expectations about gender even when they are entirely unaware that they are doing so. When parents believe that boys are naturally better at math or sports and that girls are naturally better at English, they unwittingly communicate those beliefs by how they respond to a child's success or failure. They may tell a son who did well in math, "You're a natural math whiz, Johnny!" But if a daughter gets good grades, they may say, "Wow, you really worked hard in math, Joanie, and it shows!" The implication is that girls have to try hard but boys have a natural gift. Messages like these are not lost on children. Both sexes tend to lose interest in activities that are supposedly not natural for them, even when they all start out with equal abilities (Dweck, 2006; Frome & Eccles, 1998).

In today's fast-moving world, however, society's messages to women and men, and parents' messages to their children, keep evolving. As a result, gender development has become a lifelong process, in which gender schemas, attitudes, and behavior change as people have new experiences and as society itself changes (Rosin, 2012). Five-year-old children may behave like sexist piglets while they are trying to figure out what it means to be male or female. Their behavior is shaped by a combination of hormones, genetics, cognitive schemas, parental and social lessons, religious and cultural customs, and experiences. But their gender-typed behavior as 5-year-olds usually has little to do with how they will behave at 25 or 45. In fact, by early adulthood, women and men show virtually no average differences in cognitive abilities, personality traits, self-esteem, or psychological well-being (Hyde, 2007).

That is why children can grow up in an extremely gender-typed family and yet, as adults, find themselves in careers or relationships or identities they would never have imagined for themselves. If 5-year-olds are the gender police, many adults end up breaking the law.

JOURNAL PROMPT 13.4

Thinking Critically—Tolerate Uncertainty: Most people fall into the categories "male" or "female." This makes it difficult for parents and doctors to be certain about how best to treat infants who are born with intersex conditions. Should such infants be assigned surgically to one sex or the other, or should they be left alone until they are grown? In the absence of clear answers, how would you make this decision?

Quiz for Module 13.4

1. A child's sense of being female or male is called
   a. Gender expectancy
   b. Gender typing
   c. Gender socialization
   d. Gender identity

2. Some intersexed individuals consider themselves _____, whereas people who feel they are in the wrong body are often described as _____.
   a. Transgender / transsexual
   b. Gender-specific / gender-neutral
   c. Transsexual / transgender
   d. Transformative / transcendent

3. From a biological perspective, prenatal hormones, especially _____, may contribute to the play preferences and toy preferences shown by young girls and boys.
   a. Thymosins
   b. Teratogens
   c. Androgens
   d. Thyrogens

4. Nelda expects that boys will wear pants, not cry when punched, and spit in public if they feel like it. Nelda has developed a
   a. Gender identity
   b. Gender attribution
   c. Gender schema
   d. Sex role

5. Adults watch an unfamiliar baby dressed in a black hat, beige shirt, and white pants play with an assortment of toys. Some adults are told ahead of time that the child is a girl, whereas others are told it is a boy. All adults are later asked to rate how forcefully the child played. According to the learning perspective on gender development, which adults will think that the child was more forceful in its playing?

a. Those who thought the child was a girl

b. Those who thought the child was a boy

c. Both sets of adults should rate the child's play equally

d. Those adults who were parents themselves

Adolescence

Adolescence refers to the period of development between the age at which a person becomes capable of sexual reproduction and adulthood. For most of human history, this time span has been only a few months, and this is still true in some cultures, where a sexually mature boy or girl is expected to marry and assume adult tasks. In modern Western societies, however, teenagers are not considered emotionally mature enough to assume the full rights, responsibilities, and roles of adulthood. In this section we'll examine the ups and downs of adolescence, starting with changes in the body and then turning to changes in the mind.

The Physiology of Adolescence

LO 13.5.A Outline the physiological changes that girls and boys experience during adolescence.

In middle childhood (ages 6 to 12), children go through a period called **adrenarche** (a-DREN-ar-kee), when the adrenal glands begin pumping out hormones that affect brain development, most notably an androgen called DHEA (Campbell, 2011). These hormones divert glucose in the brain to foster the maturation of brain regions vital to interpreting social and emotional cues. Indeed, children's brains during these years are at their most flexible and responsive to learning. Children become able to control their impulses, reason better, focus and plan for the future, and understand mortality and death. As children typically approach the end of middle childhood they enter **puberty**, the age at which a person becomes capable of sexual reproduction.

Until puberty, boys and girls produce roughly the same levels of androgens (masculinizing hormones) and estrogens (feminizing hormones). But from puberty on, boys have a higher level of androgens than girls do, and girls have a higher level of estrogens than boys do. In boys, the reproductive glands are the testes (testicles), which produce sperm; in girls, the reproductive glands are the ovaries, which release eggs. During puberty, these organs mature and the individual becomes capable of reproduction. In girls, signs of sexual maturity are the development of breasts and **menarche**, the onset of menstruation. In boys, the signs are the onset of nocturnal emissions and the growth of the testes, scrotum, and penis. Hormones are also responsible for the emergence of *secondary sex characteristics*, such as a deepened voice and facial and chest hair in boys and pubic hair in both sexes.

The onset of puberty depends on both biological and environmental factors. Menarche depends on a female's having a critical level of body fat, which is necessary to sustain a pregnancy and which triggers the hormonal changes associated with puberty. An increase in body fat among children in developed countries may help explain why the average age of puberty declined in Europe and North America until the mid-20th century. The average age of menarche now occurs at about 12 years and 6 months in white girls and a few months earlier in black girls (Anderson, Dallal, & Must, 2003). However, other signs of puberty in girls, such as pubic hair and breast buds, have been appearing at younger and younger ages; boys, too, are entering puberty 6 months to 2 years sooner than previously estimated.

adrenarche [a-DREN-ur-kee]

A time in middle childhood when the adrenal glands begin producing the adrenal hormone DHEA and other hormones that affect cognitive and social development.

puberty

The age at which a person becomes capable of sexual reproduction.

menarche [men-AR-kee]

The onset of menstruation during puberty.

Children typically enter puberty around the end of middle childhood.

BIOLOGY and *the Adolescent Brain*

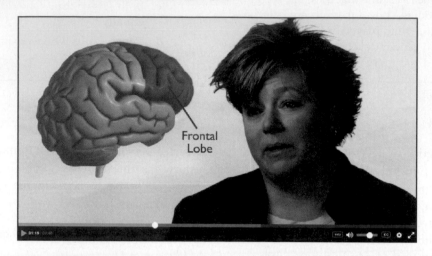

Frontal Lobe

When does a teenager become capable of thinking like an adult? This is not just an academic question; it can be a matter of life or death. In many U.S. states, teenage criminals are tried and sentenced as adults. In 2005, the Supreme Court banned the death penalty for juveniles as cruel and unusual punishment, and in 2012, it ruled that mandatory sentences of life without parole are likewise excessive (Bath et al., 2015). The Court based the death penalty decision in part on evidence showing that adolescents often get into trouble because their brains are neurologically immature (Albert, Chein, & Steinberg, 2013; Steinberg, 2007). Indeed, full neurological and cognitive maturity often does not occur until about age 25, much later than commonly believed. For that reason, Laurence Steinberg and Elizabeth Scott (2003) argued that many teenagers who commit crimes should be considered "less guilty by reason of adolescence." The developmental changes that occur in a person's brain are the subject of the video *Risky Behavior and Brain Development*.

When people think of physical changes in adolescence, they usually think of hormones and maturing bodies. But the adolescent brain undergoes significant developmental changes, notably a major pruning of synapses. This pruning occurs primarily in the prefrontal cortex, which is responsible for impulse control and planning, and the parts of the brain involved in emotional processing (Spear, 2000). Errors in the pruning process during adolescence may be involved in the onset of schizophrenia in vulnerable individuals.

Another change involves myelinization, which provides insulation for neurons and improves the efficiency of neural transmission, strengthening the connections between the emotional areas of the brain and the reasoning prefrontal cortex. This process may continue through the late teens or early 20s, which would help explain why the strong emotions of the adolescent years often overwhelm rational decision making and cause some teenagers to behave more impulsively than adults. It would explain why adolescents are more vulnerable to peer pressure that encourages them to try risky, dumb, or dangerous things—why taunts of "I dare you!" and "You're chicken!" have more power over a 15-year-old than a 25-year-old. Even when teenagers know they are doing the wrong thing, many lack the reasoning ability to foresee the consequences of their actions down the line (Reyna & Farley, 2006).

If adolescence is literally a state of diminished responsibility, how should the courts treat teenage offenders? To what extent should adolescents be held accountable for their actions? What do you think?

In Alabama, Colby Smith (left) and his friend Evan Miller, then ages 14 and 16, beat a 52-year-old man with a baseball bat and set his trailer home on fire, leaving him to die in the blaze. They were tried as adults on a charge of murder and sentenced to life imprisonment without the possibility of parole. Miller filed a motion for a new trial, arguing that the sentence constituted cruel and unusual punishment in violation of the Eighth Amendment. In 2012, the U.S. Supreme Court agreed, prohibiting mandatory sentences of life without parole for juveniles convicted of murder. The Court sided with developmental psychologists, who had argued that the brains of teenagers are a "work in progress." What does the evidence show?

The onset and length of puberty vary considerably. Some girls go through menarche at 9 or 10, or even earlier, and some boys are still growing in height after age 19. Early-maturing boys generally have a more positive view of their bodies than late-maturing boys do, and their relatively greater size and strength give them a boost in sports and the prestige that being a good athlete brings young men. But they are also more likely to smoke, drink alcohol, use other drugs, and break the law than later-maturing boys (Cota-Robles, Neiss, & Rowe, 2002; Rudolph et al., 2014). Some early-maturing girls have the prestige of being socially popular, but they are also more likely to fight with their parents, drop out of school, have a negative body image, abuse drugs, have poorer relationships, and be angry or depressed (Skoog, Özdemir, & Stattin, 2015; Westling, Andrews, & Peterson, 2012). Early menarche itself does not cause these problems; rather, it tends to accentuate existing behavioral problems and family conflicts. Girls who go through puberty relatively late, in contrast, have a more difficult time at first, but by the end of adolescence, many are happier with their appearance and are more popular than their early-maturing classmates (Beltz et al., 2014; Caspi & Moffitt, 1991; Stattin & Magnusson, 1990).

The Psychology of Adolescence

LO 13.5.B Outline the psychological and behavioral changes that girls and boys experience during adolescence.

The media love sensational stories about teenagers who are angry or violent, live in emotional turmoil, feel lonely, have low self-esteem, and are running wild sexually. Parents and prosecutors have become so alarmed about "sexting," the practice of emailing nude pictures to friends, that adolescents in the United States and Canada have been convicted on charges of creating and distributing child pornography. Yet in reality, overall feelings of self-esteem do not suddenly plummet after the age of 13 for boys or girls (Gentile et al., 2009), and the rate of violent crimes committed by adolescents has been dropping steadily since 1993. As for sex, according to the National Youth Risk Behavior Survey, today's high school students are actually more conservative than their parents were at their age; fewer are having sex, and among those who are, the number of partners has declined (Rosin, 2012).

Similarly, studies of representative samples of adolescents find that only a minority are seriously troubled, angry, or unhappy. Nevertheless, three kinds of problems are more common during adolescence than during childhood or adulthood: conflict with parents, mood swings and depression, and higher rates of reckless, rule-breaking, and risky behavior (Steinberg, 2007). Rule breaking often occurs because teenagers are developing their own standards and values by trying on the styles, actions, and attitudes of their peers, in contrast to those of their parents.

Peers become especially influential in adolescence because they represent the values and style of the generation that teenagers identify with, the generation that they will share experiences with as adults (Bukowski, 2001; Harris, 2009; Smith, Chein, & Steinberg, 2014). Many people report that feeling rejected by their peers when they were teenagers was more devastating than punitive treatment by parents. According to a government-sponsored review of whether and how online technologies affect child safety, the most frequent dangers that teenagers face on the Internet are not pornography or even predatory adults, and definitely not sexting. "Bullying and harassment, most often by peers, are the most frequent threats that minors face, both online and offline," the report found (Berkman Center for Internet & Society, 2008, 2012).

Adolescents who are lonely, depressed, anxious, or angry tend to express these concerns in ways characteristic of their sex. Boys are more likely than girls to externalize their problems in acts of aggression and other antisocial behavior. Girls are more likely to internalize their feelings and problems by becoming withdrawn, blaming themselves for whatever goes wrong, or developing eating disorders (Wicks-Nelson & Israel, 2003). In general, girls are more dissatisfied than boys with their bodies and general appearance; boys are more dissatisfied than girls with their social behavior at school and with friends (Gentile et al., 2009).

Keep in mind that the "psychology of adolescence" depends profoundly on the larger culture in which teenagers live. During the 1960s and early 1970s, a period of great social upheaval during which many teenagers rebelled against their parents' lives and values, some observers wrote as if teenage rebellion were a universal, biologically driven phase; today, most teenagers remain close to their parents and see no reason to rebel against them. In this light, consider the role of culture's influence on a particular personality trait, narcissism. Narcissism is not the same thing as self-esteem; it is a combination of excessive self-regard and a lack of empathy or interest in others (Twenge, 2013). And it is not the kind of understandable self-focus that is common among adolescents and young adults who are worried about their future relationships and work lives (Roberts, Edmonds, & Grijalva, 2010).

Jean Twenge and her colleagues (2008) have amassed considerable evidence that narcissism has been rising among today's cohort of college students and younger teenagers, to such a degree that they refer to this cohort as "Generation Me." American college students' scores on the Narcissistic Personality Inventory, which measures a grandiose sense of importance, entitlement, and cynicism (narcissists agree that "I wish somebody would someday write my biography" and "I find it easy to manipulate people"), have steadily increased between the years 1982 and 2008 (Twenge et al., 2008; Twenge & Foster, 2010). Why? One answer, they suggest, is that we live in a time in which American culture has become more self-focused and less other-directed. Consider, for example, the relatively recent "selfie" culture, and the popularity of the phrase, "Pics or it didn't happen!" There's a generation of people focused on documenting every aspect of their lives, with themselves as the center of attention. Do you think these research findings sound reflective of today's youth culture? Why or why not?

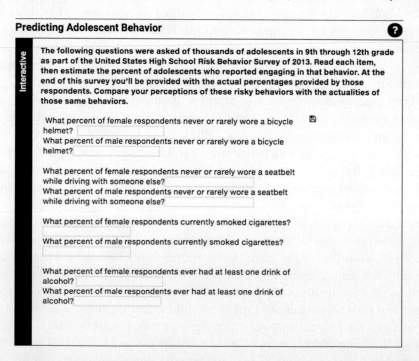

Predicting Adolescent Behavior

Interactive

The following questions were asked of thousands of adolescents in 9th through 12th grade as part of the United States High School Risk Behavior Survey of 2013. Read each item, then estimate the percent of adolescents who reported engaging in that behavior. At the end of this survey you'll be provided with the actual percentages provided by those respondents. Compare your perceptions of these risky behaviors with the actualities of those same behaviors.

What percent of female respondents never or rarely wore a bicycle helmet?

What percent of male respondents never or rarely wore a bicycle helmet?

What percent of female respondents never or rarely wore a seatbelt while driving with someone else?

What percent of male respondents never or rarely wore a seatbelt while driving with someone else?

What percent of female respondents currently smoked cigarettes?

What percent of male respondents currently smoked cigarettes?

What percent of female respondents ever had at least one drink of alcohol?

What percent of male respondents ever had at least one drink of alcohol?

JOURNAL PROMPT 13.5

Thinking Critically—Examine the Evidence: Adolescence is the period between puberty and adulthood. Fair enough. But we live in a culture that likes gradations and distinctions. People can't just listen to "heavy metal" music anymore; it seems crucial to identify whether it's black metal, death metal, grindcore, speed metal, or thrash. Similarly, the period formerly known as adolescence seems to have been replaced by "tweens," "preadolescence," "late adolescence," and so on. Do you think these distinctions are valid or important? Consider the cognitive, social, physical, and emotional development that takes place during adolescence. Would knowing that someone is in "early" or "late" adolescence influence your perceptions of that person?

Quiz for Module 13.5

1. The developmental period during which adrenal glands secrete hormones that affect brain development is called
   a. Puberty
   b. Menarche
   c. Adrenarche
   d. Meniscus

2. Charlie's voice is deepening and his armpits are getting hairy. Ana's breasts are developing and she is growing pubic hair. Both children are going through
   a. Adrenarche
   b. Menarche
   c. Puberty
   d. Rapprochement

3. Menarche refers to
   a. The time at which a person becomes capable of sexual reproduction
   b. A period of accelerated growth in adolescent boys

   c. The timespan between middle childhood and adrenarche
   d. The onset of menstruation in girls

4. Adolescents who are moody, violent, lonely, and sexually wild are
   a. The exception, rather than the rule
   b. Typical of most people in that age range
   c. Virtually nonexistent
   d. Late-maturing girls

5. Which of the following is *not* a problem typically seen with greater frequency during adolescence, compared to childhood or adulthood?
   a. Heroin addiction
   b. Reckless and risky behavior
   c. Mood swings and depression
   d. Conflicts with parents

Adulthood

According to ancient Greek legend, the Sphinx was a monster—half lion, half woman—who terrorized passersby on the road to Thebes. The Sphinx would ask each traveler a question and then murder those who failed to answer correctly. (The Sphinx was a pretty tough grader.) The question was this: What animal walks on four feet in the morning, two feet at noon, and three feet in the evening? Only one traveler, Oedipus, knew the solution to the riddle. The animal, he said, is Man, who crawls on all fours as a baby, walks upright as an adult, and limps in old age with the aid of a staff.

The Sphinx was the first lifespan theorist. Since then, many philosophers, writers, and scientists have speculated on the course of adult development. Are the changes of adulthood predictable, like those of childhood? What are the major psychological issues of adult life? Is mental and physical deterioration in old age inevitable? For some opinions on these and related questions, watch the video *Different Perspectives in the World.*

Stages and Ages

LO 13.6.A **List the eight "crises" of development proposed by Erik Erikson.**

One of the first modern theorists to propose a lifespan approach to psychological development was psychoanalyst Erik H. Erikson (1902–1994). Erikson (1950/1963, 1982) wrote that all individuals go through eight stages in their lives. Each stage is characterized by what he called a "crisis," a particular psychological challenge that ideally should be resolved before the individual moves on:

- **Trust versus mistrust** is the challenge that occurs during the baby's first year, when the baby depends on others to provide food, comfort, cuddling, and warmth. If these needs are not met, the child may never develop the essential trust of others necessary to get along in the world.

- **Autonomy (independence) versus shame and doubt** is the challenge that occurs when the child is a toddler. The young child is learning to be independent and must do so without feeling too ashamed or uncertain about his or her actions.

- **Initiative versus guilt** is the challenge that occurs as a preschooler develops. The child is acquiring new physical and mental skills, setting goals, and enjoying newfound talents, but must also learn to control impulses. The danger lies in developing too strong a sense of guilt over his or her wishes and fantasies.

- **Competence versus inferiority** is the challenge for school-age children, who are learning to make things, use tools, and acquire the skills for adult life. Children who fail these lessons of mastery and competence may come out of this stage feeling inadequate and inferior.

- **Identity versus role confusion** is the challenge of adolescence, when teenagers must decide who they are, what they are going to do, and what they hope to make of their lives. Erikson used the term *identity crisis* to describe what he considered to be the primary conflict of this stage. Those who resolve it will emerge with a strong identity, ready to plan for the future. Those who do not will sink into confusion, unable to make decisions.

- **Intimacy versus isolation** is the challenge of young adulthood. After you have decided who you are, said Erikson, you must share yourself with another and learn to make commitments. No matter how successful you are in your work, you are not complete until you are capable of intimacy.

- **Generativity versus stagnation** is the challenge of the middle years. Now that you know who you are and have an intimate relationship, will you sink into complacency and selfishness, or will you experience generativity—creativity and renewal? Parenthood is the most common route to generativity, but people can be productive, creative, and nurturant in other ways, in their work or their relationships with the younger generation.

- **Ego integrity versus despair** is the final challenge of late adulthood and old age. As they age, people strive to reach the ultimate goals of wisdom, spiritual tranquility, and acceptance of their lives. Just as the healthy child will not fear life, said Erikson, the healthy adult will not fear death.

Erikson recognized that cultural and economic factors affect people's progression through these stages. Some societies make the passages relatively easy. If you know you are going to be a farmer like your parents and you have no alternative, you are unlikely to have an adolescent identity crisis (unless you hate farming). If you have many choices, however, or if, on the contrary, the economy has made it difficult to find any good job, the transition can become prolonged (Schwartz, 2004). Similarly, cultures that place a high premium on independence and individualism will make it difficult for many of their members to resolve Erikson's sixth crisis, that of intimacy versus isolation.

According to Erik Erikson, children must master the crisis of competence and older adults must resolve the challenge of generativity, as this child and her grandmother are doing. But are the needs for competence and generativity significant at only one stage of life?

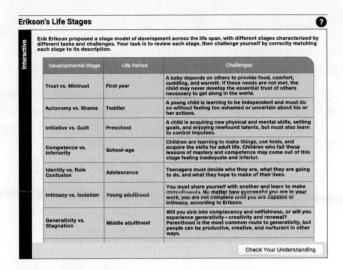

Erikson's Life Stages   ?

Erik Erikson proposed a stage model of development across the life span, with different stages characterized by different tasks and challenges. Your task is to review each stage, then challenge yourself by correctly matching each stage to its description.

Developmental Stage	Life Period	Challenges
Trust vs. Mistrust	First year	A baby depends on others to provide food, comfort, cuddling, and warmth. If these needs are not met, the child may never develop the essential trust of others necessary to get along in the world.
Autonomy vs. Shame	Toddler	A young child is learning to be independent and must do so without feeling too ashamed or uncertain about his or her actions.
Initiative vs. Guilt	Preschool	A child is acquiring new physical and mental skills, setting goals, and enjoying newfound talents, but must also learn to control impulses.
Competence vs. Inferiority	School-age	Children are learning to make things, use tools, and acquire the skills for adult life. Children who fail these lessons of mastery and competence may come out of this stage feeling inadequate and inferior.
Identity vs. Role Confusion	Adolescence	Teenagers must decide who they are, what they are going to do, and what they hope to make of their lives.
Intimacy vs. Isolation	Young adulthood	You must share yourself with another and learn to make commitments. No matter how successful you are in your work, you are not complete until you are capable of intimacy, according to Erikson.
Generativity vs. Stagnation	Middle adulthood	Will you sink into complacency and selfishness, or will you experience generativity—creativity and renewal? Parenthood is the most common route to generativity, but people can be productive, creative, and nurturant in other ways.

Check Your Understanding

Now that people's lives have become less predictable, these psychological issues may also occur in different orders or return even after having been resolved. For example, although adolescence in Western societies is often a time of confusion about identity and aspirations, an identity crisis is not limited to the teen years. A man who has worked in one job for 20 years, and then is laid off at age 45 and must find an entirely new career, may have an identity crisis too. Likewise, competence is not mastered once and for all in childhood. People learn new skills and lose old ones throughout their lives, and their sense of competence rises and falls accordingly. And people who are highly generative, in terms of being committed to helping their communities or the next generation, tend to do volunteer work or choose occupations that allow them to contribute to society throughout their lives (McAdams, 2006). As one psychologist observed many years ago, "There is not one process of aging, but many; there is not one life course followed, but multiple courses . . . . The variety is as rich as the historic conditions people have faced and the current circumstances they experience" (Pearlin, 1982).

Stage theories, therefore, do not adequately describe how adults grow and change, or remain the same, across the lifespan. Yet Erikson was right to show that development does not stop at adolescence or young adulthood; it is an ongoing process. His ideas were influential because he placed adult development in the context of family, work, and society, and he specified many of the essential concerns of adulthood: trust, competence, identity, generativity, and the ability to enjoy life and accept death. Collectively, they reflect the timeless and universal human concerns of adulthood (Dunkel & Sefcek, 2009; Schwartz et al., 2013).

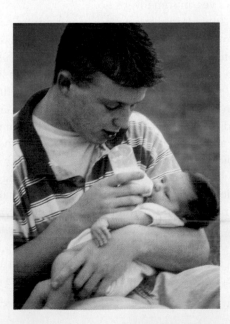

What is your reaction to these two first-time parents? Adriana Iliescu gave birth at age 66; the young man became a father at 15. Many people react negatively to individuals who they feel are "off time" for the transition to parenthood. How young is too young and how old is too old to become a parent?

The Transitions of Life

LO 13.6.B Outline the psychological and behavioral changes that women and men experience as they progress through emerging adulthood and middle age.

When nearly everyone your age goes through the same experience or enters a new role at the same time—going to college, having a baby, retiring—adjusting to these transitions is relatively easy. Similarly, if you aren't doing these things and hardly anyone you know is doing them either, you will not feel out of step. Today, however, most people will face unanticipated transitions—events that happen without warning, such as being fired from a job. And many people have to deal with changes that they expect to happen that do not: not getting a job after college, not getting married at the age they expected, not getting promoted, not being able to afford to retire, or realizing that they cannot have children (Schlossberg & Robinson, 1996). With this in mind, let's consider some of the major transitions of life. To begin, watch the video *Identity* for an overview of some major issues.

EMERGING ADULTHOOD   In industrialized nations, major demographic changes have postponed the timing of career decisions, marriage or cohabitation, and parenthood until a person's late 20s or even 30s, on the average. Many young people between the ages of 18 and 25 are in college and at least partly dependent financially on their parents. This phenomenon has created a phase of life that some call *emerging adulthood* (Arnett, 2014). When emerging adults are asked whether they feel they have reached adulthood, the majority answer: in some ways yes, in some ways no.

In certain respects, emerging adults have moved beyond adolescence into maturity, becoming more emotionally controlled, more confident, less dependent, and less angry and alienated (Azmitia, Syed, & Radmacher, 2008; Roberts, Caspi, & Moffitt, 2001). But they are also the group most likely to live unstable lives and feel unrooted. Emerging adults move more often than people in other demographic groups do—back to their parents' homes and then out again, from one city to another, from living with roommates to living on their own. And their rates of risky behavior (such as binge drinking, having unprotected sex, and driving at high speeds or while drunk) are higher than those of any other age group, including adolescents (Arnett, 2014).

Of course, not all young people in this age group are alike. Some groups within the larger society, such as Mormons, promote early marriage and parenthood. And young people who are poor, who have dropped out of school, who had a child at age 16, or who have few opportunities to get a good job will not have the income or leisure to explore many options. But the overall shift in all industrialized nations toward a global economy, increased education, and delayed career and family decisions means that emerging adulthood is likely to grow in importance as a distinct phase of prolonged exploration and freedom.

THE MIDDLE YEARS For most women and men, the midlife years between 35 and 65 are the prime of life (MacArthur Foundation, 1999; Mroczek & Sprio, 2005). Contrary to the many jokes about "midlife crises," in which a formerly conventional adult changes partner, job, and car and runs off to Tahiti, these years are typically a time of the greatest psychological well-being, good health, productivity, and community involvement. They are also often a time of reflection and reassessment. People look back on what they have accomplished, take stock of what they regret not having done, and think about what they want to do with their remaining years. When crises do occur, it is for reasons not related to aging but to specific life-changing events, such as illness or the loss of a job or partner (Robinson & Wright, 2013; Wethington, 2000).

But doesn't menopause make most midlife women depressed, irritable, and irrational? **Menopause**, which usually occurs between ages 45 and 55, is the cessation of menstruation after the ovaries stop producing estrogen and progesterone. Menopause does produce physical symptoms in many women, notably hot flashes, as the vascular system adjusts to the decrease in estrogen. But only about 10 percent of all women have unusually severe physical symptoms.

The negative view of menopause as a syndrome that causes depression and other negative emotional reactions is based on women who have undergone early menopause following a hysterectomy (removal of the uterus) or who have had a lifetime history of depression (Mauas, Kopala-Sibley, & Zuroff, 2014). But these women are not typical. According to many surveys of thousands of healthy, randomly chosen women in the general population, most women view menopause with relief that they no longer have to worry about pregnancy or menstrual periods. The vast majority have only a few physical symptoms (which can be annoying and bothersome but are temporary) and most do not become depressed; only 3 percent even report regret at having reached menopause (McKinlay, McKinlay, & Brambilla, 1987). In one study of 1,000 postmenopausal women, fewer than half reported physical symptoms and only 5 percent of those complained of mood symptoms (Ness, Aronow, & Beck, 2006).

Although women lose their fertility after menopause and men theoretically remain fertile throughout their lives, men have a biological clock too. Testosterone diminishes, although it never drops as sharply in men as estrogen does in women. The sperm count may also gradually drop, and the sperm that remain are more susceptible to genetic mutations that can increase the risk of certain diseases in children conceived by older fathers, as we saw earlier (Wyrobek et al., 2006).

The physical changes of midlife do not by themselves predict how people will feel about aging or how they will respond to it (Schaie & Willis, 2002). People's views of aging are influenced by the culture they live in and by the promises of technology to prolong life and health—some realistic, some still science fiction. Is aging something natural and inevitable, to be accepted gracefully? Or is it a process to be fought tooth and nail, with every chemical, surgical, and genetic weapon we can lay our hands on? If we can live to 100, why not have a baby at 65? To what extent should society pay for life-extending interventions? These issues will be hotly debated in the years to come.

menopause

The cessation of menstruation and of the production of ova; it is usually a gradual process lasting up to several years.

Old Age

LO 13.6.C Summarize the findings regarding declines or improvements in cognitive functioning as people age, and distinguish between fluid intelligence and crystallized intelligence.

When does old age start? A few decades ago, you would have been considered old in your 60s, but that has changed. The fastest-growing segment of the population in North America now consists of people over the age of 85. There were 5.8 million Americans age 85 or older in 2012, and the Census Bureau projects that there may be as many as 18 million by 2050 (Ortman, Velkoff, & Hogan, 2014). *Gerontologists*, researchers who study aging and the old, have been investigating the likely consequences of this massive demographic change.

More and more old people are living healthy, active, mentally stimulating lives.

One consequence is that the phase of retirement will change significantly. When people expected to live only until their early 70s, retirement at 65 was associated with loss—a withdrawal from work and fulfilling activities, with not much to look forward to but illness and old age. Today, thanks to the enormous cohort of healthy baby boomers, retirement might last 20 or 30 years. Thus, it is no longer simply a life transition from working to not working. People in the phase of what some psychologists are calling "positive retirement" often find a new career, volunteer work, or engrossing activities (Halpern, 2008).

Nonetheless, gerontologists are concerned about this trend because various aspects of intelligence, memory, decision making, and other forms of mental functioning decline significantly with age. After roughly age 65, adults start scoring lower on tests of reasoning, spatial ability, and complex problem solving than do younger adults. It takes them longer to retrieve words and names, dates, and other information; in fact, the speed of cognitive processing in general slows down. However, older people vary in this respect, with some declining significantly and others remaining sharp (Lövdén et al., 2010; Salthouse, 2012).

Fortunately, not all cognitive abilities worsen with age. **Fluid intelligence** is the capacity for deductive reasoning and the ability to use new information to solve problems. It reflects in part an inherited predisposition, and it parallels other biological capacities in its growth and later decline (Bosworth & Schaie, 1999; Li et al., 2004; Opitz et al., 2014). **Crystallized intelligence** consists of knowledge and skills built up over a lifetime, the kind of intelligence that gives us the ability to do arithmetic, define words, or take political positions. It depends heavily on education and experience, and it tends to remain stable or even improve over the lifespan. This is why physicians, lawyers, teachers, farmers, musicians, insurance agents, politicians, psychologists, and people in many other occupations can continue working well into old age (Halpern, 2008). Also, older adults are often able to compensate for age-related declines by recruiting parts of the brain that are not commonly activated when young people do the same tasks—an example of the brain's impressive plasticity (flexibility) (Huang et al., 2012).

Many of the physical and mental losses that do occur in old age are physiologically and genetically based and are seen in all societies, but others have to do with cultural, behavioral, and psychological factors (Park & Gutchess, 2006). Psychologists have made great strides in separating conditions previously thought to be an inevitable part of old age from those that are preventable or treatable:

- Apparent senility in older adults is often caused by malnutrition, prescription medications, harmful combinations of medications, and over-the-counter drugs (such as sleeping pills and antihistamines), all of which can be hazardous to older people.

- Weakness, frailty, and even many of the diseases associated with old age are often caused by being inactive and sedentary (Booth & Neufer, 2005).

- Depression, passivity, and memory problems may result from the loss of meaningful activity, intellectual stimulation, goals to pursue, and control over events (Hess, 2005; Schaie & Zuo, 2001).

Older people can profit from aerobic exercise and strength training, which maintain physical strength and flexibility, boost the brain's blood supply, and promote the development of new cells in the hippocampus and other areas of the brain. The result is improved functioning in memory, planning, concentration, and making schedules (Colcombe & Kramer, 2003; Erickson et al., 2011; Hertzog et al., 2008). Mental stimulation also fosters the growth of neural connections in the brain, even well into old age. Cognitive enrichment cannot prevent most cases of serious cognitive decline and dementia, but the declines may be delayed (Bozzali et al., 2015; Gatz, 2007; Hertzog et al., 2008).

Perhaps the best news is that as people get older, most become better able to regulate negative feelings and emphasize the positive. The frequency of intense negative emotions is highest among people aged 18 to 34, then drops sharply to age 65. After 65, it levels off, rising only slightly among old people facing crises of illness and bereavement (Charles & Carstensen, 2004; Opitz et al., 2014; Urry & Gross, 2010). Apparently, many people do grow wiser, or at least more tranquil, with age.

fluid intelligence

The capacity for deductive reasoning and the ability to use new information to solve problems; it is relatively independent of education and tends to decline in old age.

crystallized intelligence

Cognitive skills and specific knowledge of information acquired over a lifetime; it is heavily dependent on education and tends to remain stable over the lifetime.

Remember the ordinary children pictured at the beginning of the chapter? Each turned out to be not-so-ordinary in their later lives. They are Adolf Hitler, Queen Elizabeth, and Albert Einstein. Now that you have read this chapter, what kinds of genetic, familial, and historical influences can you think of that might explain what made these three famous people so remarkably different?

Some researchers who study aging are therefore optimistic. In their view, people who have challenging occupations and interests, who remain active mentally, who exercise regularly, and who adapt flexibly to change and loss are more likely than others to maintain their cognitive abilities and well-being. "Use it or lose it," they say, and they are hopeful that research into the brain's remarkable plasticity will one day produce successful interventions to prevent or delay cognitive decline (Lövdén et al., 2010). In a study of people who were 100 years old at the *start* of the investigation, fully 73 percent of them were free of dementia at the time of their deaths (in one case, at age 111) (Hagberg & Samuelsson, 2008). Why? Genome-wide association studies are beginning to identify the specific molecular circuits that are associated with good memory in some very old individuals such as these (Barnes, 2011). Other gerontologists are less upbeat. "When you've lost it, you can't use it," they reply. They are worried about the growing numbers of people living into their 90s and beyond, when rates of cognitive impairment and dementia rise dramatically (Salthouse, 2006). The challenge for society is to prepare for the many people who will be living into advanced old age, by helping as many as possible to keep using their brains instead of losing them.

JOURNAL PROMPT 13.6

Thinking Critically—Consider Other Explanations: People assume that aging inevitably produces senility, depression, weakness, and a decline in mental abilities. What else could be causing these problems?

Quiz for Module 13.6

1. Nels is examining his life. On the one hand, he could take it easy and settle into a comfortable complacency surrounded by the material possessions he's accumulated and the social standing he enjoys. On the other hand, he could challenge himself to make the world a better place, by helping others, sharing his talents, or contributing to his community. According to Erikson's stage theory of development, what stage is Nels in?

   a. Generativity versus stagnation

   b. Initiative versus guilt

   c. Autonomy versus shame

   d. Competence versus inferiority

2. According to Erikson's stage model, which of the following is *not* a crisis faced by people as they progress through the lifespan?

   a. Ego integrity versus despair

   b. Identity versus role confusion

   c. Criticality versus acceptance

   d. Trust versus mistrust

3. The period between 18 and 25 years of age after adolescence, partially after college, not quite to full-blown life responsibilities has been dubbed

   a. Post-adolescence

   b. Emerging adulthood

   c. Phenarche

   d. The "crisis years"

4. The termination of menstruation is called

   a. Andropause

   b. Adrenarche

   c. Menarche

   d. Menopause

5. Farley's grandfather is still pretty sharp for an 80-year-old. He's not as quick as he used to be when it comes to learning how to use Farley's technical gadgets, but he can still add a column of numbers in his head just fine, just like when he worked as an accountant. Grandpa is showing predictable deficits in _____ but not _____.

   a. Fluid intelligence / crystallized intelligence

   b. Inductive protocols / deductive protocols

   c. Deductive protocols / inductive protocols

   d. Crystallized intelligence / fluid intelligence

Taking Psychology with You
The Wellsprings of Resilience

Most people take it for granted that the path from childhood to adolescence to adulthood is a fairly straight one. We think of the lasting attitudes, habits, and values our parents taught us. We continue to have deep attachments to our families, even when we are fighting with them. And many people carry with them the scars of emotional wounds they suffered as children. Children who have been beaten, neglected, or constantly subjected to verbal or physical abuse by their parents are more likely than other children to have emotional problems, become delinquent and violent, commit crimes, drop out of school, and develop mental disorders and chronic stress-related illnesses (Emery & Laumann-Billings, 1998; Margolin & Gordis, 2004; Repetti, Taylor, & Seeman, 2002).

And yet when researchers began to question the entrenched assumption that early trauma always has long-lasting negative effects and considered the evidence for alternative views, they got quite a different picture. Most children, they discovered, are resilient, eventually overcoming even the effects of war, childhood illness, having abusive or alcoholic parents, early deprivation, or being sexually molested (Kaufman & Zigler, 1987; Nelson et al., 2007; Rutter et al., 2004; Werner, 1989; West & Prinz, 1987).

It is widely assumed that people who recover from adversity must be rare and have special qualities. But the surprising evidence shows that resilience is actually quite ordinary (Masten, 2001). Many of the children who outgrow early deprivation and trauma have easygoing temperaments or personality traits, such as self-efficacy and self-control, that help them roll with even severe punches. They have a secure attachment style, which helps them work through traumatic events in a way that heals their wounds and restores hope and emotional balance (Mikulincer, Shaver, & Horesh, 2006). If children lack secure attachments with their own parents, they may be rescued by love and attention from their siblings, peers, extended family members, or other caring adults. And some have experiences outside the family—in schools, places of worship, or other organizations—that give them a sense of competence, moral support, solace, religious faith, and self-esteem (Cowen et al., 1990; Garmezy, 1991).

Perhaps the most powerful reason for the resilience of so many children, and for the changes that all of us make throughout our lives, is that we are constantly interpreting our experiences. We can decide to repeat the mistakes our parents made or break free of them. We can decide to remain prisoners of childhood or to strike out in new directions at age 20, 50, or 70. As the world changes in unpredictable ways, the territory of adulthood will continue to expand, providing new frontiers as well as fewer signposts and road maps to guide us. Increasingly, age will be what we make of it.

So take these findings to heart. It may seem that the trials and tribulations, worries and woes, stresses and storms you're enduring at this stage in your life will be with you forever. Chances are they won't—life is a continuous process of change and adaptation—but even if they are, you're probably more resilient than you give yourself credit for.

Shared Writing Prompt

There are various strategies for coping with stressful events, such as engaging in problem-focused coping, maintaining optimism, rethinking the problem, or relying on social support. Think of a childhood event that has the potential to have a lasting negative impact on the course of development, for example, a death in the family, divorce, serious illness, or extreme deprivation. Now write your thoughts about how coping mechanisms could be used as a source of resilience to this event. Which mechanisms could be enacted by the person experiencing the event, and which could be provided by friends and loved ones? Which coping strategies would seem to be more or less effective for which kinds of events? What kinds of interventions, either early on or through the lifespan, could contribute to the wellsprings of resilience?

Summary

From Conception through the First Year

LO 13.1.A   Outline the three stages of prenatal development, and list six factors that can adversely affect a woman's pregnancy.

Prenatal development begins at fertilization, when the male sperm unites with the female ovum (egg) to form a single-celled egg called a *zygote*. During the first 8 weeks of prenatal development, the organism is called an *embryo*; after that, it is known as a *fetus*. Harmful influences that can adversely affect the fetus's development include German measles, toxic substances, some sexually transmitted diseases, cigarettes, alcohol, illegal drugs, over-the-counter medications, and chronic maternal stress. Fathers affect prenatal development too; the sperm of teenage boys and men over age 50 may have mutations that increase the risk of miscarriage, birth defects, and certain diseases in their offspring.

LO 13.1.B   Describe some inborn abilities that infants have, and also some cultural influences on physical and psychological development.

Babies are born with *motor reflexes*, perceptual abilities, and rudimentary cognitive skills. Cultural practices affect the timing of physical milestones.

LO 13.1.C   Discuss how contact comfort and separation anxiety contribute to feelings of attachment, and list four factors that contribute to insecure attachment.

Babies' innate need for *contact comfort* gives rise to emotional attachment to their caregivers, and by the age of 6 to 8 months, infants begin to feel *separation anxiety*. Studies of the *Strange Situation* have distinguished *secure* from *insecure* attachment; insecurity can take one of two forms, *avoidant* or *anxious-ambivalent* attachment. Styles of attachment are relatively unaffected by the normal range of childrearing practices, and also by whether or not babies spend time in daycare. Insecure attachment is promoted by parents' rejection, mistreatment, or abandonment of their infants; by a mother's postpartum depression, which can affect her ability to care for her baby; by the child's own fearful, insecure temperament; or by stressful family situations.

Cognitive Development

LO 13.2.A   List the milestones of language development that occur between the first 2 months and 6 years of life.

In support of the view that the human brain contains a mental module that is sensitive to a *universal grammar*, children from different cultures go through similar stages of language development; adults do not consistently correct their children's syntax; and groups of children who have never been exposed to adult language often invent their own. However, languages also vary around the world, suggesting that language is a cultural tool. It's also possible that children learn the statistical probability that any given word or syllable will follow another. At 4 to 6 months of age, babies begin to recognize the sounds of their own language. They go through a babbling phase from age 6 months to 1 year, and at about 1 year, they start saying single words and using symbolic gestures. At age 2, children speak in two- or three-word *telegraphic* sentences that convey a variety of messages.

LO 13.2.B   Describe the four stages of cognitive development proposed by Piaget, explain the defining characteristics of each stage, and discuss four modifications of Piaget's theory.

Jean Piaget argued that children's thinking changes and adapts through *assimilation* and *accommodation*. Piaget proposed four stages of cognitive development: *sensorimotor* (birth to age 2), during which the child learns *object permanence*; *preoperational* (ages 2 to 7), during which language and symbolic thought develop, although the child remains *egocentric* in reasoning; *concrete operations* (ages 7 to 12), during which the child comes to understand *conservation*; and *formal operations* (age 12 to adulthood), during which abstract reasoning develops. Today, we know that the changes from one stage to another are not as clear-cut as Piaget implied; development is more continuous and overlapping. Babies and young children have greater cognitive abilities, at earlier ages, than Piaget thought, and young children are not always egocentric.

Moral Development

LO 13.3.A   Discuss the evidence for and against the proposition that moral development occurs in distinct stages over time.

Lawrence Kohlberg proposed that as children mature cognitively, they go through three levels of moral reasoning. But people can reason morally without behaving morally. Developmental psychologists study how children learn to internalize standards of right and wrong and to behave accordingly. This ability depends on the emergence of conscience and the moral emotions of guilt, shame, and empathy.

LO 13.3.B   Compare the ways in which power assertion, inductive appeals, self-regulation, and conscience contribute to moral development.

As a strategy for teaching children to behave, a parent's use of *power assertion* is associated with a child's aggressiveness and lack of empathy. *Induction* is associated with children who develop empathy, internalize moral standards, and can resist temptation. The capacity of very young children to *delay gratification* and control their feelings is associated with the development of internalized moral standards and conscience.

Gender Development

LO 13.4.A   Distinguish between biological sex, gender identity, gender typing, and intersex conditions.

Gender development includes the emerging awareness of *gender identity*, the understanding that a person is biologically male or female regardless of what he or she does or wears, and *gender typing*, the process by which boys and girls learn what it means to be masculine or feminine in their culture. Some individuals are born with *intersex* physical conditions, living with the physical attributes of both sexes, and consider themselves to be *transgender*. *Transsexuals* feel that they are male in a female body or vice versa; their gender identity is at odds with their anatomical sex.

LO 13.4.B   Summarize the basic findings regarding biological, cognitive, and learning influences on gender identity and gender typing.

Universally, young children tend to prefer same-sex toys and playing with other children of their own sex. Biological psychologists account for this phenomenon in terms of genes and prenatal androgens. Cognitive psychologists study how children develop *gender schemas* for the categories "male" and "female," which in turn shape their gender-typed behavior. Learning theorists study the direct and subtle reinforcers and social messages that foster gender typing.

Adolescence

LO 13.5.A   Outline the physiological changes that girls and boys experience during adolescence.

During *adrenarche*, the adrenal glands begin releasing hormones that affect brain development. *Adolescence* begins with the physical changes of *puberty*. In girls, puberty is signaled by *menarche* and the development of breasts; in boys, it begins with the onset of nocturnal emissions and the development of the testes, scrotum, and penis. Hormones produce *secondary sex characteristics*, such as pubic hair in both sexes and a deeper voice in males.

LO 13.5.B   Outline the psychological and behavioral changes that girls and boys experience during adolescence.

Most American adolescents do not go through extreme emotional turmoil, anger, or rebellion. However, conflict with parents, mood swings and depression, and reckless or rule-breaking behavior increase.

Adulthood

LO 13.6.A   List the eight "crises" of development proposed by Erik Erikson.

Erik Erikson proposed that life consists of eight stages, each with a unique psychological challenge, or crisis, that must be resolved, such as an *identity crisis* in adolescence. Erikson identified many of the essential concerns of adulthood and showed that development is a lifelong process. However, psychological issues or crises are not confined to particular chronological periods or stages.

LO 13.6.B   Outline the psychological and behavioral changes that women and men experience as they progress through emerging adulthood and middle age.

Many people between the ages of 18 and 25, especially if they are not financially independent, find themselves in a life phase called *emerging adulthood*. The middle years are generally not a time of turmoil or crisis but the prime of most people's lives. In women, *menopause* begins in the late 40s or early 50s. In middle-aged men, hormone production slows down and sperm counts decline; fertility continues, but with increased risk of fetal abnormalities.

LO 13.6.C   Summarize the findings regarding declines or improvements in cognitive functioning as people age, and distinguish between fluid intelligence and crystallized intelligence.

The speed of cognitive processing slows down in old age, and *fluid intelligence* parallels other biological capacities in its eventual decline. *Crystallized intelligence*, in contrast, depends heavily on culture, education, and experience, and it tends to remain stable over the lifespan.

Many supposedly inevitable results of aging, such as senility, depression, and physical frailty, are often avoidable. Exercise and mental stimulation promote the growth of synapses in the human brain, even well into old age, although some mental losses are inevitable.

Chapter 13 Quiz

1. An embryo is formed
   a. About 3 days after fertilization
   b. About 4 weeks after fertilization
   c. Within 48 hours after fertilization
   d. About 2 weeks after fertilization

2. One cultural difference that affects newborn development is
   a. Whether the child sleeps independently or with the parents during the first several months of life
   b. The timing of when newborns exhibit a sucking response
   c. The delay between birth and the grasping response
   d. Whether the child has been exposed to natural environments or has been raised in relative isolation.

3. The Strange Situation refers to
   a. The first weeks of a newborn's life in a cultural context
   b. An experimental procedure for investigating attachment
   c. Conflicting sources of contact comfort
   d. An emo rock group

4. "Does baby want to play with the beads?! Do yooooooouuuu want to play with the beeeeeaaaaads? Yes you doooooo!! Yes you^{dooooooooo}, don't^{yooouuuuuuuuu}?!!" This style of speech is often referred to as
   a. Ipsative
   b. Telegraphic
   c. Singularity
   d. Parentese

5. Piaget observed that sometimes children _____ new information into their existing mental categories, whereas other times children need to change their mental categories to _____ their new experiences.
   a. Assimilate / accommodate
   b. Accommodate / assimilate
   c. Operationalize / externalize
   d. Externalize / operationalize

6. Edgar watches his mother pour some bourbon into a short, squatty glass. He then watches as she transfers the liquid from the short glass into a tall, slender one. "Now there's more!" concludes Edgar, looking at the tall glass. According to Piaget's stage theory of cognitive development, Edgar is probably about
   a. 10 years old
   b. 6 months old

   c. 4 years old
   d. 1 year old

7. During the 1960s, the theorist who proposed that moral development progressed through identifiable stages was
   a. Lawrence Kohlberg
   b. Jean Piaget
   c. Erik Erikson
   d. Douglas Colvin

8. What's an effective parenting strategy to get children to be good and shift their focus to internal norms of appropriate behavior?
   a. Induction
   b. Power assertion
   c. Production blocking
   d. Internalization

9. Hormonal or chromosomal anomalies can result in a child being born with ambiguous or conflicting genitals. This condition is known as
   a. Intersexuality
   b. Transvestism
   c. Transexualism
   d. Transubstantiation

10. Little males, both human and monkey, like to play with wheeled toys rather than cuddly dolls. Little females, both human and monkey, show a variety of toy preferences. Cross-species evidence such as this has led some researchers to conclude that _____ influences play a major role in gender development.
    a. Maternal
    b. Cognitive
    c. Learning
    d. Biological

11. Signs of sexual maturity in girls are the onset of menstruation and the development of _____. Signs of sexual maturity in boys are the growth of the genitals and the onset of _____.
    a. Androgens / testosterone
    b. Pubic hair / testosterone
    c. Breasts / nocturnal emissions
    d. Sexual attitudes / opposite-sex play

12. Adolescent boys who are lonely, anxious, or depressed tend to _____ these problems, whereas adolescent girls who feel the same way tend to _____ these problems.
    a. Write about / verbalize
    b. Communicate / write about

c. Internalize / externalize

d. Externalize / internalize

13. According to Erikson's stage model of development across the lifespan, the challenge faced during young adulthood is

   a. Identity versus role confusion

   b. Intimacy versus isolation

   c. Generativity versus stagnation

   d. Competence versus inferiority

14. What does the evidence suggest about the middle years of adulthood, between the ages of approximately 35 and 65?

   a. For most people this is a period of good health, well-being, productivity, and general reflection on life.

   b. For most people this is a time of turbulence and harsh reexamination of missed opportunities or failed endeavors.

   c. For most people this is a time of radical changes in attitudes, behaviors, and interests.

   d. For most men, this is a time when feelings of inadequacy and lack of fulfillment rise to the surface of consciousness.

15. Researchers who study aging and the older years of the lifespan are called

   a. Eschatologists

   b. Hoarologists

   c. Gerontologists

   d. Ontologists

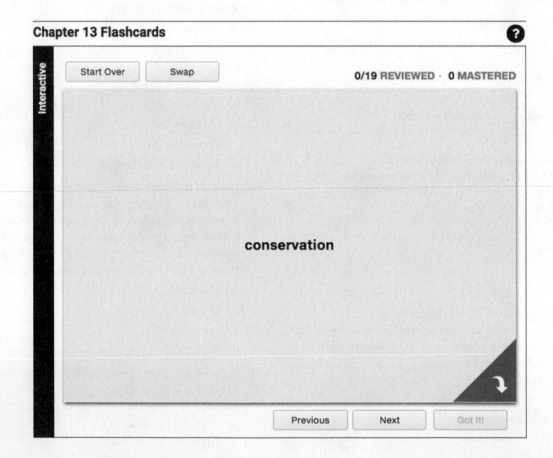

Chapter 14
Theories of Personality

◀ Listen to the Audio

Learning Objectives

LO 14.1.A Describe the structure of personality according to psychoanalysis, five psychological defense mechanisms, and five stages of psychosexual development.

LO 14.1.B Explain how the views of Carl Jung and the object-relations school differed from Sigmund Freud's approach to personality.

LO 14.1.C Summarize three ways in which psychodynamic theories falter under scientific scrutiny.

LO 14.2.A Outline some ways in which objective personality inventories differ from popular personality tests used in business, dating, or other areas.

LO 14.2.B List the Big Five personality dimensions, and describe the characteristics of each one.

LO 14.3.A Define what temperaments are, and discuss how they relate to personality traits.

LO 14.3.B Explain how twin studies can be used to estimate the heritability of personality traits.

LO 14.3.C Summarize the arguments for and against the conclusion that personality "is all in our genes."

LO 14.4.A Explain how reciprocal determinism and the nonshared environment contribute to our understanding of how traits and behavior can be shaped by the environment.

LO 14.4.B Summarize three lines of evidence that suggest parental influence over children's personality development is limited.

LO 14.4.C Discuss some ways in which peers influence the development of personality in children.

LO 14.5.A Compare individualist and collectivist cultures, describe some average personality differences between them, and describe three traits that show considerable cultural variability.

LO 14.5.B Evaluate some pros and cons of the cultural approach to understanding personality.

LO 14.6.A Describe the core humanist ideas advanced by Abraham Maslow, Carl Rogers, and Rollo May.

LO 14.6.B Discuss how the narrative approach to personality hinges on answering the central question, "Who am I?"

LO 14.6.C Summarize the shortcomings of the humanist approach to personality, and identify some areas of substantial contribution.

Ask questions . . . be willing to wonder

How accurate are those tests that tell you what "personality type" you are?

When people talk about "repressing" a memory or being "in denial," where does that language come from?

If you hear that shyness or another personality trait is "inherited," does that mean it can't be changed?

Why is the same person often so different with family, with friends, and in the classroom?

If you've ever had a friend set you up on a blind date, you might have heard that the mystery individual "has a great personality." What distinguishes a great personality from a "pretty good" personality? And where does personality come from in the first place?

In the world of dating, "personality" usually refers to a constellation of desirable attributes; the person is funny, warm, a good conversationalist, caring, quick-witted, and so on. But when psychologists talk about personality they usually mean some enduring pattern of thoughts and behaviors; funny or not, warm or cold, quick-witted or dull. In fact, the "person" part of "personality" implies that there's something deep-seated, stable, and far-reaching involved—something that gets right to the very core of what makes the person who she or he *is*.

In this chapter we will see how psychologists study personality, and how they explain where it comes from and what contributes to it. We will begin with the oldest theory of personality, the psychodynamic view, so that you will have a sense of how influential it was, why it continues to appeal to some, and why many of its ideas have become outdated. Next, we will consider evidence for the newest theory, the genetic view. Few scientists today think that babies are tiny lumps of clay, shaped entirely by their experiences, or that parents alone determine whether their infant becomes an adventurer, a sourpuss, or a worrywart. We will then examine leading approaches to personality that are neither psychodynamic nor biological: the environmental approach, which emphasizes the role of social learning, situations, parents, and peers; the cultural approach, which emphasizes cultural influences on traits and behavior; and the humanist and narrative approaches, which emphasize self-determination and people's own view of themselves. For an overview of these many approaches, watch the video *Personality Theories*.

Psychodynamic Theories of Personality

A man apologizes for "displacing" his frustrations at work onto his family. A woman suspects that she is "repressing" a childhood trauma. An alcoholic reveals that he is no longer "in denial" about his drinking. A teacher informs a divorcing couple that their 8-year-old child is "regressing" to immature behavior. All these notions about displacing, repressing, denying, and regressing have become commonplace in everyday language, but their usage in this context can be traced back to Sigmund Freud's views on personality.

Sigmund Freud (1856-1939)

Freud and Psychoanalysis

LO 14.1.A **Describe the structure of personality according to psychoanalysis, five psychological defense mechanisms, and five stages of psychosexual development.**

Like most of the theorists and researchers we'll discuss in this chapter, Freud viewed **personality** as a distinctive pattern of behavior, mannerisms, thoughts, motives, and emotions that characterize an individual over time and across situations. But to enter the world of Sigmund Freud is to enter a realm of unconscious motives, raging passions, guilty secrets, unspeakable yearnings, and conflicts between desire and duty. These unseen forces, Freud believed, have far more power over our personalities than our conscious intentions do. Freud's theory of **psychoanalysis** highlighted the role of these motives and conflicts in shaping personality.

Freud's theory is called **psychodynamic** because it emphasizes the movement of psychological energy within the person. (Freud did not use "dynamic" in today's sense, to mean "powerful" or "energetic." *Dynamics* is a term from physics that refers to the motion and balance of systems under the action of outside or internal forces.) Today's psychodynamic theories differ from Freudian theory and from one another, but they all share an emphasis on unconscious processes going on within the mind. They also share an assumption that adult personality and ongoing problems are formed primarily by experiences in early childhood. These experiences produce unconscious thoughts and feelings, which later form characteristic habits, conflicts, and often self-defeating behavior.

THE STRUCTURE OF PERSONALITY In Freud's theory, personality consists of three major systems: the id, the ego, and the superego. Any action we take or problem we have results from the interaction and degree of balance among these systems (Freud, 1905b, 1920/1960, 1923/1962).

The **id**, which is present at birth, is the reservoir of unconscious psychological energies and the motives to avoid pain and obtain pleasure. The id contains two competing instincts: the life, or sexual, instinct (fueled by psychic energy called the **libido**) and the death, or aggressive, instinct. As energy builds up in the id, tension results. The id may discharge this tension in the form of reflex actions, physical symptoms, or uncensored mental images and unbidden thoughts.

The **ego**, the second system to emerge, is a referee between the needs of instinct and the demands of society. It bows to the realities of life, putting a rein on the id's desire for sex and aggression until a suitable, socially appropriate outlet for them can be found. The ego, said Freud, is both conscious and unconscious, and it represents "reason and good sense."

The **superego**, the last system of personality to develop, is the voice of conscience, representing morality and parental authority. The superego judges the activities of the id, handing out good feelings of pride and satisfaction when you do something well and handing out miserable feelings of guilt and shame when you break the rules. The superego is partly conscious but largely unconscious.

According to Freud, the healthy personality must keep all three systems in balance. Someone who is too controlled by the id is governed by impulse and selfish desires. Someone who is too controlled by the superego is rigid, moralistic, and bossy. Someone who has a weak ego is unable to balance personal needs and wishes with social duties and realistic limitations.

personality

A distinctive and relatively stable pattern of behavior, thoughts, motives, and emotions that characterizes an individual.

psychoanalysis

A theory of personality and a method of psychotherapy developed by Sigmund Freud; it emphasizes unconscious motives and conflicts.

psychodynamic theories

Theories that explain behavior and personality in terms of unconscious energy dynamics within the individual.

id

In psychoanalysis, the part of personality containing inherited psychic energy, particularly sexual and aggressive instincts.

libido (li-BEE-do)

In psychoanalysis, the psychic energy that fuels the life or sexual instincts of the id.

ego

In psychoanalysis, the part of personality that represents reason, good sense, and rational self-control.

superego

In psychoanalysis, the part of personality that represents conscience, morality, and social standards.

defense mechanisms

Methods used by the ego to prevent unconscious anxiety or threatening thoughts from entering consciousness.

psychosexual stages

In Freud's theory, the idea that sexual energy takes different forms as the child matures; the stages are oral, anal, phallic (Oedipal), latency, and genital.

DEFENSE MECHANISMS   If a person feels anxious or threatened when the wishes of the id conflict with social rules, the ego has weapons at its command to relieve the tension. These unconscious strategies, called **defense mechanisms**, deny or distort reality, but they also protect us from conflict and anxiety. They become unhealthy only when they cause self-defeating behavior and emotional problems. Here are five primary defense mechanisms identified by Freud and later analysts (A. Freud, 1967; Perry & Metzger, 2014; Vaillant, 1992):

1. **Repression** occurs when a threatening idea, memory, or emotion is blocked from consciousness. A woman who had a frightening childhood experience that she cannot remember is said to be repressing her memory of it. Freud used the term *repression* to mean both unconscious expulsion of disturbing material from awareness and conscious suppression of such material. However, modern analysts tend to think of it only as an unconscious defense mechanism.

2. **Projection** occurs when a person's own unacceptable or threatening feelings are repressed and then attributed to someone else. A person who is embarrassed about having sexual feelings toward members of a different ethnic group may project this discomfort onto them, saying, "Those people are dirty-minded and oversexed."

3. **Displacement** occurs when people direct emotions that make them uncomfortable or conflicted—commonly, anger and lust—toward people, animals, or objects that are not the real object of their feelings. A boy who is forbidden to express anger toward his father may "take it out" on his toys or his younger sister. When displacement serves a higher cultural or socially useful purpose, as in the creation of art or inventions, it is called *sublimation*. Freud argued that society has a duty to help people sublimate their unacceptable sexual and aggressive impulses for the sake of civilization. Sexual passion may be sublimated into the creation of art or literature, and aggressive energy into sports.

4. **Regression** occurs when a person reverts to a previous phase of psychological development. An 8-year-old boy who is anxious about his parents' divorce may regress to earlier habits of thumb sucking or clinging. Adults may regress to immature behavior when they are under pressure—perhaps by having temper tantrums when they don't get their way.

5. **Denial** occurs when people refuse to admit that something unpleasant is happening, such as mistreatment by a partner; that they have a problem, such as drinking too much; or that they are feeling a forbidden emotion, such as anger. Denial protects a person's self-image and preserves the illusion of invulnerability: "It can't happen to me."

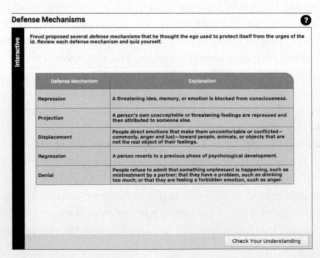

THE DEVELOPMENT OF PERSONALITY   Freud argued that personality develops in a series of **psychosexual stages**, in which sexual energy takes different forms as the child matures. Each new stage produces a certain amount of frustration, conflict, and anxiety. If these are not resolved properly, normal development may be interrupted, and the child may remain *fixated*, or stuck, at the current stage.

Freud thought that some people remain fixated at the *oral stage*, which occurs during the first year of life, when babies experience the world through their mouths. As adults, they will seek oral gratification in smoking, overeating, nail-biting, or pencil-chewing; some may become clinging and dependent, like a nursing child. Others remain fixated at the *anal stage*, at ages 2 to 3, when toilet training and control of bodily wastes are the key issues. They may become "anal retentive," holding everything in, obsessive about neatness and cleanliness. Or they may become just the opposite, "anal expulsive"—messy and disorganized.

For Freud, however, the most crucial stage for the formation of personality was the *phallic (Oedipal) stage*, which lasts roughly from age 3 to age 5 or 6. During this stage, said Freud, the child unconsciously wishes to possess the parent of the other sex and to get rid of the parent of the same sex. Children often proudly announce, "I'm going to marry Daddy (or Mommy) when I grow up," and they reject the same-sex "rival." Freud labeled this phenomenon the **Oedipus complex**, after the Greek legend of King Oedipus, who unwittingly killed his father and married his mother.

Boys and girls, Freud believed, go through the Oedipal stage differently. Boys are discovering the pleasure and pride of having a penis, so when they see a naked girl for the first time, they are horrified. Their unconscious exclaims (in effect), "Her penis has been cut off! Who could have done such a thing to her? Why, it must have been her father. And if he could do it to her, my father could do it to me!" This realization, said Freud, causes the boy to repress his desire for his mother and identify with his father. He accepts his father's authority and the father's standards of conscience and morality; the superego has emerged.

Freud admitted that he did not quite know what to make of girls, who, lacking the penis, could not go through the same steps. He speculated that a girl, upon discovering male anatomy, would panic that she had only a puny clitoris instead of a stately penis. She would conclude that she already had lost her penis. As a result, Freud said, girls do not have the motivating fear that boys do to give up their Oedipal feelings and develop a strong superego; they have only a lingering sense of "penis envy."

Freud believed that when the Oedipus complex is resolved, at about age 5 or 6, the child's personality is fundamentally formed. Unconscious conflicts with parents, unresolved fixations and guilts, and attitudes toward the same and the other sex will continue to replay themselves throughout life. The child settles into a supposedly nonsexual *latency stage*, in preparation for the *genital stage*, which begins at puberty and leads to adult sexuality.

In Freud's view, therefore, your adult personality is shaped by how you progressed through the early psychosexual stages, which defense mechanisms you developed to reduce anxiety, and whether your ego is strong enough to balance the conflict between the id (what you would like to do) and the superego (your conscience).

Oedipus complex

In psychoanalysis, a conflict occurring in the phallic (Oedipal) stage, in which a child desires the parent of the other sex and views the same-sex parent as a rival.

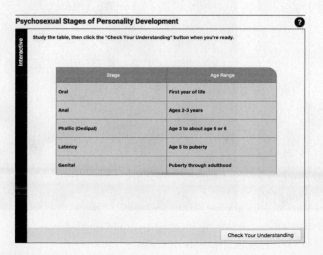

Psychosexual Stages of Personality Development   ❓

Study the table, then click the "Check Your Understanding" button when you're ready.

Stage	Age Range
Oral	First year of life
Anal	Ages 2-3 years
Phallic (Oedipal)	Age 3 to about age 5 or 6
Latency	Age 5 to puberty
Genital	Puberty through adulthood

Check Your Understanding

FREUD IN PERSPECTIVE   As you might imagine, Freud's ideas were not exactly received with yawns. Sexual feelings in 5-year-olds! Repressed longings in respectable adults! Unconscious meanings in dreams! Penis envy! This was strong stuff in the early years of the 20th century, and before long, psychoanalysis had captured the public imagination in Europe and the United States.

But psychoanalysis also produced a sharp rift with the emerging schools of empirical psychology because so many of Freud's ideas were scientifically untestable or failed to be supported when they were tested. Modern critics have discovered that Freud was not the theoretical genius, impartial scientist, or even successful clinician that he claimed to be. On the contrary, Freud often bullied his patients into accepting his explanations of their symptoms and, the greatest sin for anyone claiming to be a scientist, he ignored all evidence disconfirming his ideas (Borch-Jacobsen & Shamdasani, 2012; McNally, 2003; Powell & Boer, 1995; Samuel, 2013; Webster, 1995).

On the positive side, Freud welcomed women into the profession of psychoanalysis, wrote eloquently about the devastating results for women of society's suppression of their sexuality, and argued, ahead of his time, that homosexuality was neither a sin nor a perversion but a "variation of the sexual function" and "nothing to be ashamed of" (Freud, 1961). Freud was thus a mixture of intellectual vision and blindness, sensitivity and arrogance. His provocative ideas left a controversial legacy to psychology, one that others began to tinker with immediately.

Other Psychodynamic Approaches

LO 14.1.B   Explain how the views of Carl Jung and the object-relations school differed from Sigmund Freud's approach to personality.

Some of Freud's followers stayed in the psychoanalytic tradition and modified Freud's theories from within. Women, as you might imagine, were not too pleased about "penis envy." Clara Thompson (1943/1973) and Karen Horney [HORN-eye] (1926/1973) argued that it was insulting and unscientific to claim that half the human race is dissatisfied with its anatomy. When women feel inferior to men, they said, we should look for explanations in the disadvantages that women live with and their second-class status. Other psychoanalysts broke away from Freud, or were actively rejected by him, and went off to start their own schools.

JUNGIAN THEORY   Carl Jung (1875–1961) was originally one of Freud's closest friends and a member of his inner circle, but the friendship ended with a furious quarrel about the nature of the unconscious. In addition to the individual's own unconscious, said Jung (1967), all human beings share a vast **collective unconscious**, containing universal memories, stories, symbols, and images, which he called **archetypes**.

collective unconscious

In Jungian theory, the universal memories and experiences of humankind, represented in the symbols, stories, and images (archetypes) that occur across all cultures.

archetypes [AR-ki-tipes]

Universal, symbolic images that appear in myths, art, stories, and dreams; to Jungians, they reflect the collective unconscious.

In the Jungian view, Lord Voldemort is a modern archetype of evil, fighting the wise and kindly Hero archetype of Dumbledore.

An archetype can be an image, such as the "magic circle," called a *mandala* in Eastern religions, which Jung thought symbolizes the unity of life and "the totality of the self." Or it can be a figure found in fairy tales, legends, and popular stories, such as the Hero, the nurturing Earth Mother, the Strong Father, or the Wicked Witch. It can even be an aspect of the self; the *shadow* archetype reflects the prehistoric fear of wild animals and represents the bestial, evil side of human nature. Some basic archetypes, such as the Hero, the Earth Mother, and the evil Villain, do appear in the stories and images of virtually every society (Campbell, 1949/1968; Neher, 1996). Jungians would consider the Joker, Darth Vader, Dracula, the Dark Lord Sauron, and Harry Potter's tormentor Voldemort as expressions of the shadow archetype.

Although Jung shared with Freud a fascination with the darker aspects of the personality, he had more confidence in the positive, forward-moving strengths of the ego. He believed that people are motivated not only by past conflicts but also by their future goals and their desire to fulfill themselves. Jung was also among the first to identify extroversion/introversion as a basic dimension of personality. Nonetheless, many of Jung's ideas were more suited to mysticism and philosophy than to empirical psychology, which may be why so many Jungian ideas became popular with New Age and other spiritual movements.

THE OBJECT-RELATIONS SCHOOL   Freud essentially regarded the baby as if it were an independent, greedy little organism ruled by its own instinctive desires; other people were relevant only insofar as they gratified the infant's drives or blocked them. But by the 1950s, increased awareness of the importance of human attachments led to a different view of infancy, put forward by the **object-relations school**, which was developed in Great Britain by Melanie Klein, D. W. Winnicott, and others. To object-relations theorists, the central problem in life is to find a balance between the need for independence and the need for others. This balance requires constant adjustment to separations and losses: small ones that occur during quarrels, moderate ones such as leaving home for the first time, and major ones such as divorce or death. The way we react to these separations, according to object-relations analysts, is largely determined by our experiences in the first year or two of life (Orbach, 2009).

The reason for the clunky word *object* in object relations, instead of the warmer word *human* or *parent*, is that the infant's attachment is not only to a real person (usually the mother) but also to the infant's evolving perception of her. The child creates a *mental representation* of the mother—someone who is kind or fierce, protective or rejecting. The child's representations of significant adults, whether realistic or distorted, unconsciously affect personality throughout life, influencing whether the person relates to others with trust or suspicion, acceptance or criticism.

The object-relations school also departs from Freudian theory regarding the nature of male and female development (Sagan, 1988; Winnicott, 1957/1990). In the object-relations view, children of both sexes identify first with the mother. Girls, who are the same sex as the mother, do not need to separate from her; the mother treats a daughter as an extension of herself. But boys must break away from the mother in order to develop a masculine identity; the mother encourages a son to be independent and separate. Thus men, in this view, develop more rigid boundaries between themselves and other people than women do.

Evaluating Psychodynamic Theories

LO 14.1.C Summarize three ways in which psychodynamic theories falter under scientific scrutiny.

Psychodynamic psychology is the thumb on the hand of psychology—connected to the other fingers, but also set apart from them because it differs radically from empirical approaches in its language, methods, and standards of acceptable evidence. Many

object-relations school

A psychodynamic approach that emphasizes the importance of the infant's first 2 years of life and the baby's formative relationships, especially with the mother.

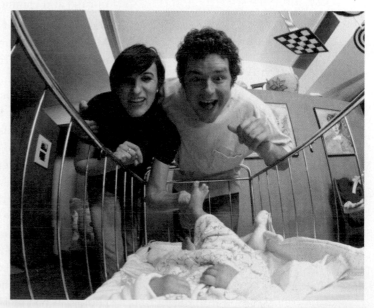

According to object-relations theory, a baby constructs unconscious representations of his or her parents that will influence the child's relations with others throughout life.

psychological scientists believe that psychodynamic approaches belong in philosophy or literature rather than in academic psychology. But some psychotherapists and laypeople remain attracted to the psychodynamic perspective's emphasis on the darker, less visible aspects of personality.

Although modern psychodynamic theorists differ in many ways, they share a general belief that to understand personality we must explore its unconscious dynamics and origins. They see the overall framework of Freud's theory as timeless and brilliant, even if many of his specific ideas have proved faulty (Westen, 1998; Westen, Gabbard, & Ortigo, 2008). The majority of psychological scientists, however, think that most of the assumptions of psycho-analytic theory are nonsense, best regarded as literary metaphors rather than as scientific explanations (Cioffi, 1998; Crews, 1998). Indeed, most of the cornerstone assumptions in psychoanalytic theory, such as the notion that the mind "represses" traumatic experiences, have not been supported scientifically (McNally, 2003; Rofé, 2008; Wegner, 2011). As for object-relations analysts, they make all kinds of assumptions about what an infant feels and wants, but how do they know?

Psychological scientists have shown that psychodynamic theories are guilty of three scientific failings:

1. **Violating the principle of falsifiability.** A theory that is impossible to disconfirm in principle is not scientific. Many psychodynamic concepts about unconscious motivations are, in fact, impossible to confirm or disconfirm. Followers often accept an idea because it seems intuitively right or their experience seems to support it. Anyone who doubts the idea or offers disconfirming evidence is then accused of being "defensive" or "in denial."

2. **Drawing universal principles from the experiences of a few atypical patients.** Freud and most of his followers generalized from a few individuals, often patients in therapy, to all human beings. Of course, sometimes case studies can generate valid insights about human behavior. The problem occurs when the observer fails to confirm his or her observations by studying larger, more representative samples and including appropriate control groups. For example, some psychodynamically oriented therapists, believing in Freud's notion of a childhood "latency" stage, have assumed that if a child masturbates or enjoys sex play, the child has probably been sexually molested. But research finds that masturbation and sexual curiosity are not found only in abused children; these are normal and common childhood behaviors (Bancroft, 2006; Friedrich et al., 1998).

3. **Basing theories of personality development on the retrospective accounts of adults.** Most psychodynamic theorists have not observed random samples of children at different ages, as modern child psychologists do, to construct their theories of development. Instead, they have worked backward, creating theories based on themes in adults' recollections of childhood. The analysis of memories can be an illuminating way to achieve insights about our lives; in fact, it is the only way we can think about our own lives! But memory is often inaccurate, influenced as much by what is going on in our lives now as by what happened in the past. If you are currently not getting along with your mother, you may remember all the times when she was hard on you and forget the counterexamples of her kindness.

   Retrospective analysis has another problem: It creates an *illusion of causality* between events. People often assume that if A came before B, then A must have caused B. If your mother spent 3 months in the hospital when you were 5 years old and today you feel shy and insecure in college, an object-relations analyst might draw a connection between the two facts. But a lot of other things could be causing your shyness and insecurity, such as being away from home for the first time, at a large and impersonal college. When psychologists conduct longitudinal studies, following people from childhood to adulthood, they often get a very different picture of causality from the one that emerges by looking backward.

Despite these serious problems, some psychodynamic concepts *have* been empirically tested and validated. Researchers have identified unconscious processes in thought, memory, and behavior. They have found evidence for the major defense mechanisms, such as projection, denial, and displacement (Baumeister, Dale, & Sommer, 1998; Cramer, 2000; Marcus-Newhall et al., 2000). One fascinating study suggests that homophobia may sometimes be an attempt to deal with unconscious but threatening homosexual feelings. When people were subliminally shown the word *me* or *other* before seeing pictures and words related to heterosexuality or homosexuality, and were asked to sort the pictures and words into the appropriate categories on a computer, most sorted the words and pictures associated with their own sexual orientation faster when *me* had been the subliminal cue. But a subset of self-identified straight people sorted the discrepant (homosexual) words and images faster when they had been exposed to *me*—and those people were more likely to favor antigay policies (Weinstein et al., 2012).

Finally, research has confirmed the psychodynamic idea that we are often unaware of the motives behind our own puzzling or self-defeating actions.

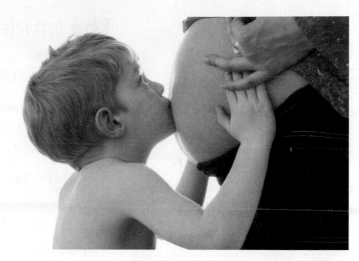

Freud claimed, without much empirical evidence, that all little girls suffer from 'penis envy.' But studies of preschool girls and boys find that young children of both sexes are curious about, and often imagine having, the reproductive abilities of the other sex (Linday, 1994).

JOURNAL PROMPT 14.1

Thinking Critically—Analyze Assumptions: Freud and his followers assumed they could derive general principles of personality by studying patients in therapy, that childhood traumas inevitably have lifelong emotional consequences, and that memories are reliable guides to the past. What is wrong with these assumptions?

Quiz for Module 14.1

1. According to Freud's theory of psychoanalysis, the part of personality that contains unconscious psychic energies related to sex and aggression is called the

    a. Ego

    b. Id

    c. Superego

    d. Collective unconscious

2. A 4-year-old girl wants to snuggle on Daddy's lap but refuses to kiss her mother. Which Freudian concept does that suggest?

    a. Repression

    b. Sublimation

    c. Oedipus complex

    d. Denial

3. Donny, a celibate priest, writes award-winning poetry about sexual passion and erotic encounters. Which Freudian concept does that suggest?

    a. Regression

    b. Denial

    c. Projection

    d. Sublimation

4. Carl Jung thought that all humans shared universal memories, symbols, and images, which he called _____, and that these were stored in the _____.

    a. Archetypes / collective unconscious

    b. Prototypes / superego

    c. Complexes / id

    d. Objects / personal unconscious

5. Which of the following is *not* a criticism of psychodynamic theories of personality?

    a. Many psychodynamic theorists reached universal conclusions about general principles based on the experiences of a few atypical patients in therapy.

    b. Psychodynamic theories violate the scientific principle of falsifiability.

    c. Although influential in psychology, these theories haven't received much attention from laypeople in society at large.

    d. Psychodynamic explanations for personality development are based on retrospective accounts offered by adults.

The Modern Study of Personality

People love to fit themselves and their friends into "types"; they have been doing it forever. Early Greek philosophers thought our personalities fell into four fundamental categories depending on mixes of body fluids. If you were an angry, irritable sort of person, you supposedly had an excess of choler, and even now the word *choleric* describes a hothead. And if you were sluggish and unemotional, you supposedly had an excess of phlegm, making you a "phlegmatic" type.

Popular Personality Tests

LO 14.2.A Outline some ways in which objective personality inventories differ from popular personality tests used in business, dating, or other areas.

That particular theory is long gone, but unscientific tests of personality types still exist, aimed at predicting how people will do at work, whether they will get along with others, or whether they will succeed as leaders. One such test, the Myers–Briggs Type Indicator, is hugely popular in business, at motivational seminars, and with matchmaking services; at least 2.5 million Americans take it each year (Gladwell, 2004). The test assigns people to one of 16 different types, depending on how an individual scores on the dimensions of introverted or extroverted, logical or intuitive. Unfortunately, the Myers–Briggs test is not much more reliable than measuring body fluids; one study found that fewer than half of the respondents scored as the same type a mere five weeks later. Worse, knowledge of a person's type does not reliably predict that person's behavior on the job or in relationships (Barbuto, 1997; Paul, 2004; Pittenger, 1993, 2005). Equally useless from a scientific point of view are many of the tests used by businesses and government to predict which "types" are apt to steal, take drugs, or be disloyal on the job (Ehrenreich, 2001).

Identifying broad personality "types" hasn't advanced the study of personality much, although the study of specific **traits** of an individual—habitual ways of behaving, thinking, and feeling—has produced many measures that *are* scientifically valid and useful in research. These **objective tests (inventories)** are standardized questionnaires requiring written responses, typically to multiple-choice or true–false items. They provide information about countless aspects of personality, including values, interests, self-esteem, emotional problems, and typical ways of responding to situations. Using well-constructed inventories, psychologists have identified hundreds of traits, ranging from sensation-seeking (the enjoyment of risk) to mood awareness (attention directed toward one's emotional states) to perfectionism (a striving for flawlessness). The hallmarks of a sound psychological test are reviewed in the video *Measuring Personality*.

trait
A characteristic of an individual, describing a habitual way of behaving, thinking, or feeling.

objective tests (inventories)
Standardized questionnaires requiring written responses; they typically include scales on which people are asked to rate themselves.

Core Personality Traits

LO 14.2.B **List the Big Five personality dimensions, and describe the characteristics of each one.**

Are some personality traits more important or central than others? Do some of them overlap or cluster together? For Gordon Allport, one of the most influential psychologists in the empirical study of personality, the answer to both questions was yes. Allport (1961) recognized that not all traits have equal weight and significance in people's lives. Most of us, he said, have five to ten *central traits* that reflect a characteristic way of behaving, dealing with others, and reacting to new situations. For instance, some people see the world as a hostile, dangerous place, whereas others see it as a place for fun and frolic. *Secondary traits*, in contrast, are more changeable aspects of personality, such as music preferences, habits, casual opinions, and the like.

Raymond B. Cattell (1973) advanced the study of this issue by applying a statistical method called **factor analysis**. Performing a factor analysis is like adding water to flour: It causes the material to clump up into little balls. When applied to traits, this procedure identifies clusters of correlated items that seem to be measuring some common, underlying factor. Today, hundreds of factor-analytic studies support the existence of a cluster of five central "robust factors," known informally as the *Big Five* (Chang, Connelly, & Geeza, 2012; Costa & McCrae 2011, 2014; McCrae et al., 2005; Paunonen, 2003; Roberts & Mroczek, 2008):

factor analysis
A statistical method for analyzing the intercorrelations among various measures or test scores; clusters of measures or scores that are highly correlated are assumed to measure the same underlying trait or ability (factor).

1. **Extroversion versus introversion** describes the extent to which people are outgoing or shy. It includes such traits as being sociable or reclusive, adventurous or cautious, socially dominant or more passive, eager to be in the limelight or inclined to stay in the shadows.

2. **Neuroticism (negative emotionality) versus emotional stability** describes the extent to which a person suffers from such traits as anxiety, an inability to control impulses, and a tendency to feel negative emotions such as anger, guilt, contempt, and resentment. Neurotic individuals are worriers, complainers, and defeatists, even when they have no major problems. They are always ready to see the sour side of life and none of its sweetness (Barlow et al., 2014).

3. **Agreeableness versus antagonism** describes the extent to which people are good-natured or irritable, cooperative or abrasive, secure or suspicious and jealous. It reflects the tendency to have friendly relationships or hostile ones.

4. **Conscientiousness versus impulsiveness** describes the degree to which people are responsible or undependable, persevering or quick to give up, steadfast or fickle, tidy or careless, self-disciplined or impulsive.

5. **Openness to experience versus resistance to new experience** describes the extent to which people are curious, imaginative, questioning, and creative or conforming, unimaginative, predictable, and uncomfortable with novelty.

In spite of some cultural variations, the Big Five have emerged as central personality dimensions throughout the world, in countries as diverse as Britain, Canada, the Czech Republic, China, Ethiopia, Turkey, the Netherlands, Japan, Spain, the Philippines, Germany, Portugal, Israel, Korea, Russia, and Australia (Digman & Shmelyov, 1996; Katigbak et al., 2002; McCrae et al., 2005; Somer & Goldberg, 1999). One monumental research venture gathered data from thousands of people across 50 cultures. In this massive project as in many smaller ones, the five personality factors emerged whether people were asked for self-reports or were assessed by others (McCrae et al., 2005; Terracciano & McCrae, 2006).

Although the Big Five are quite stable over a lifetime, they are influenced by universal processes of maturation and aging. Data from an enormous cross-sectional sample involving more than 1.2 million children, adolescents, and adults, ages 10 to 65, revealed that whereas adult trends are overwhelmingly in the direction of greater maturity and adjustment, maturity plummets between late childhood and adolescence (Soto et al., 2011). Another survey of

People's personalities are often reflected in how they arrange their workspaces.

thousands of people in 10 countries, and a meta-analysis of 92 longitudinal studies, found that young people, ages 16 to 21, are the most neurotic (emotionally negative) and the least agreeable and conscientious. But there is good news for crabby, irresponsible neurotics, especially young ones. As you can see in Figure 14.1, people tend to become more agreeable, conscientious, and emotionally stable between ages 30 and 40 (Bleidorn et al., 2013; Costa et al., 1999; Roberts, Walton, & Viechtbauer, 2006). The slow, steady rise of conscientiousness over the lifespan, a change that is found in many countries, suggests that this trait is associated with maturation. In their later years, people also tend to become less extroverted and less open to new experiences (Roberts & Mroczek, 2008; Specht, Eglott, & Schmukle, 2011).

Experience, too, shapes personality traits. For example, extroverts obviously seek out certain experiences that shy people might not, but after people are in a situation that brings out qualities they did not know they had, their traits may be modified accordingly (Specht et al., 2011). Those situations can change with social and economic conditions. A large group of women, graduates of Mills College, was followed from college until their 70s—quite an undertaking by investigators! When these women were young, in the 1960s, they led constrained lives that were highly gender stereotyped. As a result, at that time their personality traits did not predict their work or educational experiences—extroverts and introverts alike were behaving conventionally in their choices of family and work. But as gender roles changed and opportunities for women opened up in society at large, individual personality traits took on more power to predict the behavior of these women. In particular, the traits of extroversion, conscientiousness, and openness to experience came to be better predictors of the kind of work the women were doing and how satisfied they were feeling in their middle and later years (George, Helson, & John, 2011).

The Big Five do not provide a complete picture of personality, of course. Clinical psychologists note that various traits involved in mental disorders are missing, such as psychopathy (lack of remorse and empathy), self-absorption, impulsivity, and obsessiveness (Westen & Shedler, 1999). Personality researchers note that other significant traits are missing, such as religiosity, dishonesty, humorousness, independence, and conventionality (Abrahamson,

Figure 14.1 Consistency and Change in Personality over the Lifespan

Although the Big Five traits are fairly stable, changes do occur over the lifespan. As you can see, neuroticism (negative emotionality) is highest among young adults and then declines, whereas conscientiousness is lowest among young adults and then steadily increases (Costa et al., 1999).

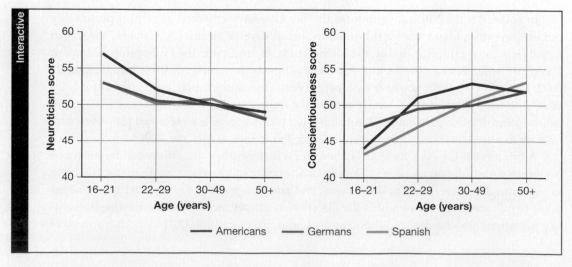

Interactive

Rate Your Traits

For each of the ten items that follow, write a number from 1 to 7 indicating the extent to which you see that trait as being characteristic of you, where 1 = "I *disagree* strongly that this trait describes me" to 7 = "I *agree* strongly that this trait describes me." Use the midpoint, 4, if you neither agree nor disagree that the trait describes you. (This self-test comes from Gosling, Rentfrow, & Swann, 2003.)

1. _____ Extroverted, enthusiastic
2. _____ Critical, quarrelsome
3. _____ Dependable, self-disciplined
4. _____ Anxious, easily upset
5. _____ Open to new experiences, complex
6. _____ Reserved, quiet
7. _____ Sympathetic, warm
8. _____ Disorganized, careless
9. _____ Calm, emotionally stable
10. _____ Conventional, uncreative

To score yourself on the Big Five traits, use this key:

|---|---|
Extroversion:	High on question 1, low on question 6
Emotional stability:	High on question 9, low on question 4
Agreeableness:	High on question 7, low on question 2
Conscientiousness:	High on question 3, low on question 8
Openness:	High on question 5, low on question 10

Now ask a friend or relative to rate you on each of the 10 items. How closely does that rating match your own? If you find a discrepancy, what might be the reason for it?

Baker, & Caspi, 2002, Paunonen & Ashton, 2001). But most agree that the Big Five do lie at the core of key personality variations among individuals, and not only human individuals, either, as we are about to see.

JOURNAL PROMPT 14.2

Thinking Critically—Define Your Terms. During the early history of psychology various *instinct theories* received attention. Someone who was combative was thought to have a strong "aggressive instinct," just as someone who was kind and generous was thought to have a well-developed "caring instinct." In fact, as you've just learned, Sigmund Freud wrote about the "life instinct" and the "death instinct" that he thought unconsciously drove much of our behavior. How is calling something a "trait" different from calling it an "instinct"? If your friend were highly extroverted, would you say she fell at the far end of that trait dimension, or would you say she had a strong "outgoing instinct"? Both terms refer to some relatively stable, unseen, internal force that produces behavior, so how can you distinguish traits from instincts, and why is that distinction important?

Quiz for Module 14.2

1. Scientifically valid measures of personality are called
   a. Objective tests
   b. Projective techniques
   c. Interest indicators
   d. Trait protocols

2. Raymond Cattell advanced the study of personality by
   a. Quantifying Jungian concepts
   b. Developing case-study analysis
   c. Devising the Myers-Briggs Type Indicator
   d. Using factor analysis

3. Which of the following is *not* one of the Big Five personality factors?
   a. Agreeableness
   b. Introversion
   c. Psychoticism
   d. Openness to experience

4. In the Big Five model of personality, which dimension provides an opposing endpoint to *conscientiousness*?
   a. Impulsiveness
   b. Neuroticism
   c. Openness to experience
   d. Introversion

5. Which one of the Big Five typically decreases by age 40?
   a. Agreeableness
   b. Neuroticism
   c. Extroversion
   d. Openness to experience

Genetic Influences on Personality

A mother we know was describing her two children: "My daughter has always been difficult, intense, and testy," she said, "but my son is the opposite, placid and good-natured. They came out of the womb that way." Was this mother right? Is it possible to be born touchy or good-natured? What aspects of personality might have an inherited component? Researchers measure genetic contributions to personality in three ways: by studying personality traits in other species, by studying the temperaments of human infants and children, and by conducting heritability studies of twins and adopted individuals. Let's examine each of these approaches in turn.

BIOLOGY and *Animal Traits*

In recent years, scientists have been drawing on research in physiology, genetics, ecology, and ethology (the study of animals in their natural habitats) to investigate the nature of "personality" in our fellow animals, in order to better understand the evolutionary and biological underpinnings of human personality traits. These investigators argue that just as it has been evolutionarily adaptive for human beings to vary in their ways of responding to the world and those around them, so it has been for animals. It would be beneficial for a species if some of its members were bold or impulsive enough to risk life and limb to confront a stranger or to experiment with a new food, and if other members were more cautious.

When we think of an individual who has a personality, we usually think of a human being. But bears, dogs, pigs, hyenas, goats, cats, and of course primates also have distinctive, characteristic ways of behaving that make them different from their fellows (Adams et al., 2015; Weinstein, Capitanio, & Gosling, 2008). At one time, scientists were reluctant to refer to those distinctive patterns as personality traits; attributing human qualities to nonhuman creatures seemed a sure sign of anthropomorphism. Even so, articles about the personalities of mice appeared in the 1950s and 1960s, and then, in 1993, an academic article described personality in a most unlikely species: the humble octopus. When the researchers dropped a crab into a tank of octopuses and had independent observers note what happened, some of the creatures would aggressively grab that dinner right away; others seemed more passive and waited for the crab to swim near them; and some waited and attacked the crab when no one was watching (Mather & Anderson, 1993). Apparently, you don't have to be a person to have a personality. You don't even have to be a mammal.

In another imaginative set of studies, Samuel D. Gosling and his colleagues (2003) recruited dog owners and their dogs in a local park. In the first study, the owners provided personality assessments of their dogs and filled out the same personality inventory for themselves. The owners then designated another person who knew them

Family portraits of dogs, as of people, often reveal different personalities: Someone is posing nicely, someone isn't paying attention, someone is distracted, and someone is goofing off by biting a neighbor's ear.

and their dogs, and who could judge the personalities of both. In a second study, the owners brought their dogs to an enclosed section of the park where three independent observers rated the dogs, so the researchers could compare the owners' judgments of their dogs' personalities with the observers' ratings. The dog owners, their friends, and the neutral observers all agreed strongly in their ratings of the dogs' personalities along four of the Big Five dimensions: extroversion, agreeableness, emotional reactivity (neuroticism), and openness to experience.

To date, most of the Big Five factors have been identified in 64 different species, including the squishy squid. These findings point to the evolutionary importance of the Big Five and their biological basis. So when you hear your dog- or horse- or cat-crazy friend say, "Pluto is such a shy and nervous guy, whereas Pepper is outgoing and sociable," your friend is probably being an accurate observer.

Heredity and Temperament

LO 14.3.A Define what temperaments are, and discuss how they relate to personality traits.

Let's turn now to human personalities. Even in the first weeks after birth, human babies differ in activity level, mood, responsiveness, heart rate, and attention span (Fox et al., 2005a). Some are irritable and cranky; others are placid and calm. Some will cuddle up in an adult's

Extreme shyness and fear of new situations tend to be biologically based, stable aspects of temperament, both in human beings and in monkeys. On the left, a timid infant rhesus monkey cowers behind a friend in the presence of an outgoing stranger.

arms and snuggle; others squirm and fidget, as if they cannot stand being held. Some smile easily; others fuss and cry. These differences appear even when you control for possible prenatal influences, such as the mother's nutrition, drug use, or problems with the pregnancy. Babies thus are born with genetically influenced **temperaments**, dispositions to respond to the environment in certain ways (Clark & Watson, 2008). Temperaments include *reactivity* (how excitable, arousable, or responsive a baby is), *soothability* (how easily the baby is calmed when upset), and positive and negative emotionality. Temperaments are quite stable over time and are the clay out of which later personality traits are molded (Clark & Watson, 2008; Dyson et al., 2015; Else-Quest et al., 2006).

Even at 4 months of age, highly reactive infants are excitable, nervous, and fearful; they overreact to any little thing, even a colorful picture placed in front of them. As toddlers, they tend to be wary and fearful of new things—toys that make noise, odd-looking robots—even when their moms are right there. At 5 years, many of these children are still timid and uncomfortable in new situations and with new people (Hill-Soderlund & Braungart-Rieker, 2008). At 7 years, many still have symptoms of anxiety, even if nothing traumatic has ever happened to them. They are afraid of being kidnapped, they need to sleep with the light on, and they are afraid of sleeping in an unfamiliar house. In contrast, nonreactive infants lie there without fussing, babbling happily; they rarely cry. As toddlers, they are outgoing and curious about new toys and events. They continue to be easygoing throughout childhood (Fox et al., 2005a; Kagan, 1997).

Children at these two extremes differ physiologically, too. During mildly stressful tasks, reactive children are more likely than nonreactive children to have increased heart rates, heightened brain activity, and high levels of stress hormones. You can see how biologically based temperaments might form the basis of the later personality traits we call extroversion, agreeableness, or neuroticism.

Heredity and Traits

LO 14.3.B Explain how twin studies can be used to estimate the heritability of personality traits.

A third way to study genetic contributions to personality is to estimate the **heritability** of specific traits within groups of children or adults. Heritability refers to the proportion of the total variation in a trait that is attributable to genetic variation within a group. Estimates of heritability come from behavioral-genetic studies of adopted children and of identical and fraternal twins reared apart and together.

temperaments

Physiological dispositions to respond to the environment in certain ways; they are present in infancy and in many non-human species and are assumed to be innate.

heritability

A statistical estimate of the proportion of the total variance in some trait that is attributable to genetic differences among individuals within a group.

Identical twins Gerald Levey (left) and Mark Newman were separated at birth and raised in different cities. When they were reunited at age 31, they discovered some astounding similarities. Both were volunteer firefighters, wore mustaches, and were unmarried. Both liked to hunt, watch old John Wayne movies, and eat Chinese food. They drank the same brand of beer, held the can with the little finger curled around it, and crushed the can when it was empty. It's tempting to conclude that all of these similarities are due to heredity, but we should also consider other explanations: Some could result from shared environmental factors such as social class and upbringing, and some could be due merely to chance. For any given set of twins, we can never know for sure.

Findings from adoption and twin studies have provided compelling support for a genetic contribution to personality. Identical twins reared apart will often have unnerving similarities in gestures, mannerisms, and moods; indeed, their personalities often seem as similar as their physical features. If one twin tends to be optimistic, glum, or excitable, the other will probably be that way too (Braungart et al., 1992; Plomin, DeFries, & Knopik, 2013). Behavioral-genetic findings have produced remarkably consistent results: For the Big Five and many other traits from aggressiveness to overall happiness, heritability is about .50 (Bartels, 2015; Bouchard, 1997a; Lykken & Tellegen, 1996; Vukasović & Bratko, 2015; Waller et al., 1990; Weiss, Bates, & Luciano, 2008). This means that within a group of people, about 50 percent of the variation in such traits is attributable to genetic differences among the individuals in the group. These findings have been replicated in many countries. For more information on heritability and personality, watch the video *Twins and Personality*.

Evaluating Genetic Theories

LO 14.3.C Summarize the arguments for and against the conclusion that personality "is all in our genes."

Behavioral-genetic research, to date, permits us only to *infer* the existence of relevant genes—just as, if you find a toddler covered in chocolate, it's pretty safe to infer that candy is somewhere close by. Scientists expect that the actual genes underlying key traits will one day be discovered, and dozens of possible associations between specific genes and personality traits have already been reported (Fox et al., 2005b; Plomin, DeFries, & Knopik, 2013). You will be hearing lots more about genetic discoveries in the coming years, so it is good to understand what they mean and don't mean.

Psychologists hope that one intelligent use of behavioral-genetic findings will be to help people become more accepting of themselves and their children. Although we can all learn to make improvements and modifications to our personalities, most of us probably will never be able to transform our personalities completely because of our genetic dispositions and temperaments. This realization might make people more realistic about what psychotherapy can do for them, and about what they can do for their children.

However, many people oversimplify this information and conclude "it's all in our genes." A judge in New York imposed a severe sentence on a man convicted of one count of possession of child pornography because the judge was sure the man had "an as-of-yet-un-discovered gene" that caused his behavior. (That judge needs to take an intro psych course.) Fortunately, the ruling was overturned. This judge not only knew nothing about genetics—there is no "porn gene"—but also failed to understand that even when genetics are involved in some behavior, having a genetic *predisposition* does not necessarily imply genetic *inevitability*. A person might have a genetic predisposition toward depression or anxiety, but without certain environmental stresses or circumstances, the person will probably not develop an emotional disorder.

As Robert Plomin (1989), a leading behavioral geneticist, observed, "The wave of acceptance of genetic influence on behavior is growing into a tidal wave that threatens to engulf the second message of this research: These same data provide the best available evidence for the importance of environmental influences." Let us now see what some of those influences might be.

JOURNAL PROMPT 14.3

Thinking Critically—Don't Oversimplify: Some personality traits, such as shyness, are highly heritable. Some people think that means "genes are everything"; a shy person can never learn to be comfortable in new situations, so there's no point trying to change. What is a more accurate way to think about the impact of heredity on personality?

Quiz for Module 14.3

1. Temperaments refer to
   a. Attachment styles that are acquired within the first year of life.
   b. Learned patterns of experience that shape the expression of personality traits.
   c. Physiological dispositions to respond to the environment in certain ways.
   d. Qualities of the environment that interact with traits of an individual in that environment.

2. Temperaments are expressed in terms of _____, _____, and _____.
   a. Happiness / sadness / anger
   b. Innateness / acquisition / learning
   c. Encoding / patterning / expression
   d. Reactivity / soothability / emotionality

3. Five-month-old Julia is excitable, nervous, and fearful. She would be described as having a(n) _____ temperament.
   a. Provoking
   b. Reactive
   c. Dispositional
   d. Orthographic

4. The proportion of the total variance in a trait that is attributable to genetic variation within a group is also known as
   a. Genetic shift
   b. Linkage
   c. Heritability
   d. Genetic constancy

5. What does it mean to have a genetic predisposition toward certain behaviors?
   a. Those behaviors may or may not be expressed within a given environment.
   b. The person with the predisposition will act in ways determined by that predisposition.
   c. The environment has little impact on modifying those behaviors.
   d. Eventually those behaviors will be observed, given a long enough lifespan.

Environmental Influences on Personality

reciprocal determinism

In social-cognitive learning theories, the two-way interaction between aspects of the environment and aspects of the individual in the shaping of personality traits.

The environment may exert an influence on variations in personality, but what *is* the environment, exactly? In this section, we will consider the relative influence of three aspects of the environment: the particular situations you find yourself in, how your parents treat you, and who your peers are.

Situations and Social Learning

LO 14.4.A **Explain how reciprocal determinism and the nonshared environment contribute to our understanding of how traits and behavior can be shaped by the environment.**

nonshared environment

Unique aspects of a person's environment and experience that are not shared with family members.

The very definition of a trait is that it is consistent across situations. But people often behave one way with their parents and a different way with their friends, one way at home and a different way in other settings. In learning terms, the reason for people's inconsistency is that different behaviors are rewarded, punished, or ignored in different contexts. You are more likely to be extroverted in an audience of screaming, cheering Taylor Swift fans than at home with relatives who would regard such noisy displays with alarm and condemnation. This is why some behaviorists think it does not even make much sense to talk about "personality."

Social-cognitive learning theorists, however, argue that people do acquire central personality traits from their learning history and their resulting expectations and beliefs. A child who studies hard and gets good grades, attention from teachers, admiration from friends, and praise from parents will come to expect that hard work in other situations will also pay off. That child will become, in terms of personality traits, "ambitious" and "motivated." A child who studies hard and gets poor grades, is ignored by teachers and parents, and is rejected by friends for being a grind will come to expect that working hard isn't worth it. That child will become, in terms of personality traits, "unambitious" or "unmotivated."

Today, most personality researchers recognize that people can have a core set of stable traits *and* that their behavior can vary across situations (Fleeson, 2004). Your particular qualities continually interact with the situation you are in. Your temperaments, habits, and beliefs influence how you respond to others, whom you hang out with, and the situations you seek (Bandura, 2001; Cervone & Shoda, 1999; Mischel & Shoda, 1995). In turn, the situation influences your behavior and beliefs, rewarding some and extinguishing others. In social-cognitive learning theory, this process is called **reciprocal determinism**.

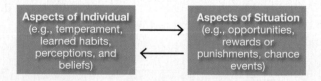

The two-way process of reciprocal determinism (as opposed to the one-way determinism of "genes determine everything" or "everything is learned") helps answer a question asked by everyone who has a sibling: What makes children who grow up in the same family so different, apart from their genes? The answer seems to be: an assortment of experiences that affect each child differently, chance events that cannot be predicted, situations that children find themselves in, and peer groups that the children belong to (Harris, 2006; Plomin, 2011; Rutter et al., 2001). Behavioral geneticists refer to these unique and chance experiences that are not shared with other family members as the **nonshared environment**: being in Mrs. Schmidt's class in the fourth grade (which might inspire you to become a scientist), winning the lead in the school play (which might push you toward an acting career), or being bullied at school (which might have caused you to see yourself as weak and powerless). All of these

Who is the "real" Beyoncé—doting mother or Sasha Fierce, the persona she used to put on in each performance? By understanding reciprocal determinism, we can avoid over-simplifying. Our genetic dispositions and personality traits cause us to choose some situations over others, but situations then influence which aspects of our personalities we express.

experiences work reciprocally with your own interpretation of them, your temperament, and your perceptions (Did Mrs. Schmidt's class excite you or bore you?).

Keeping the concept of reciprocal determinism in mind, let us look at two of the most important environmental influences in people's lives: their parents and their friends.

Parental Influence—and Its Limits

LO 14.4.B Summarize three lines of evidence that suggest parental influence over children's personality development is limited.

If you check out parenting books online or in a bookstore, you will find that in spite of the zillion different kinds of advice they offer, they share one entrenched belief: Parental child-drearing practices are the strongest influence, maybe even the *sole* influence, on children's personality development. For many decades, few psychologists thought to question this assumption, and many still accept it. Yet the belief that personality is primarily determined by how parents treat their children has begun to crumble under the weight of three kinds of evidence (Harris, 2006, 2009; Plomin, 2011):

1. **The shared environment of the home has relatively little influence on most personality traits.** In behavioral-genetic research, the "shared environment" includes the family you grew up with and the experiences and background you shared with your siblings and parents. If these had as strong an influence as commonly assumed, then studies should find a strong correlation between the personality traits of adopted children and those of their adoptive parents. In fact, the correlation is weak to nonexistent, indicating that the influence of childrearing practices and family life is very small compared to the influence of genetics (Cohen, 1999; Plomin, 2011). It is only the nonshared environment that has a strong impact.

2. **Few parents have a single childrearing style that is consistent over time and that they use with all their children.** Developmental psychologists have tried for many years to identify the effects of specific childrearing practices on children's personality traits. The problem is that parents are inconsistent from day to day and over the years. Their childrearing practices vary, depending on their own stresses, moods, and marital satis-faction (Holden & Miller, 1999). As one child we know said to her exasperated mother,

"Why are you so mean to me today, Mommy? I'm this naughty every day." Moreover, parents tend to adjust their methods of childrearing according to the temperament of the child; they are often more lenient with easygoing children and more punitive with difficult ones.

3. **Even when parents try to be consistent in the way they treat their children, there may be little relation between what they do and how the children turn out.** Some children of troubled and abusive parents are resilient and do not suffer lasting emotional damage, and some children of the kindest and most nurturing parents succumb to drugs, mental illness, or gangs.

Of course, parents do influence their children in lots of ways that are unrelated to the child's personality. They contribute to their children's religious beliefs, intellectual and occupational interests, motivation to succeed, skills, values, and adherence to traditional or modern notions of masculinity and femininity (Beer, Arnold, & Loehlin, 1998; Krueger, Hicks, & McGue, 2001). Above all, what parents do profoundly affects the quality of their relationship with their children—whether their children feel loved, secure, and valued or humiliated, frightened, and worthless (Harris, 2009).

Parents also have some influence even on traits in their children that are highly heritable. In one longitudinal study that followed children from age 3 to age 21, those who were impulsive, uncontrollable, and aggressive at age 3 were far more likely than calmer children to grow up to be impulsive, unreliable, and antisocial and more likely to commit crimes (Caspi, 2000). Early temperament was a strong and consistent predictor of these later personality traits. But not *every* child came out the same way. What protected some of those at risk, and helped them move in a healthier direction, was having parents who made sure they stayed in school, supervised them closely, and gave them consistent discipline.

Nevertheless, it is clear that, in general, parents have less influence on a child's personality than many people think. Because of reciprocal determinism, the relationship runs in both directions, with parents and children continually influencing one another. Moreover, as soon as children leave home, starting in preschool, parental influence on children's behavior *outside* the home begins to wane. The nonshared environment—peers, chance events, and circumstances—takes over.

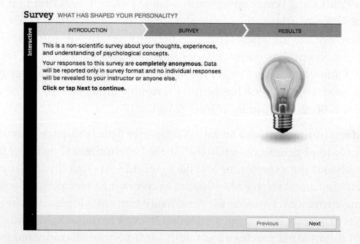

The Power of Peers

LO 14.4.C Discuss some ways in which peers influence the development of personality in children.

When two psychologists surveyed 275 freshmen at Cornell University, they found that most of them had secret lives and private selves that they never revealed to their parents (Garbarino & Bedard, 2001). On Facebook, many teenagers report having committed crimes, drinking, taking drugs, cheating in school, sexting, and having sex, all without their parents having a clue. (They assume, often incorrectly, that what they reveal is private and read only by their several hundred closest friends.) This phenomenon of showing only one facet of your personality to your parents and an entirely different one to your peers becomes especially apparent in adolescence.

Children, like adults, live in two environments: their homes and their world outside the home. At home, children learn how their parents want them to behave and what they can get away with; as soon as they go to school, however, they conform to the dress, habits, language, and rules of their peers. Most adults can remember how terrible they felt when their classmates laughed at them for pronouncing a word "the wrong way" or doing something "stupid" (i.e., not what the rest of the kids were doing), and many recall the pain of being excluded. To avoid being laughed at or rejected, most children will do what they can to conform to the norms and rules of their immediate peer group (Harris, 2009). Children who were law-abiding in the fifth grade may start breaking the law in high school, if that is what it takes—or what they think it takes—to win the respect of their peers.

It has been difficult to tease apart the effects of parents and peers because parents usually try to arrange things so that their children's environments duplicate their own values and customs. To see which has the stronger influence on personality and behavior, therefore, we must look at situations in which the peer group's values clash with the parents' values. When parents value academic achievement and their child's peers think that success in school is only for sellouts or geeks, whose view wins? The answer, typically, is peers (Arroyo & Zigler, 1995; Harris, 2009; Menting et al., 2015). Conversely, children whose parents gave them no encouragement or motivation to succeed may find themselves with peers who are working like mad to get into college, and start studying hard themselves.

Thus, peers play a tremendous role in shaping our personality traits and behavior, causing us to emphasize some attributes or abilities and downplay others. Of course, as the theory of reciprocal determinism would predict, our temperaments and dispositions also cause us to select particular peer groups (if they are available) instead of others, and our temperaments influence how we behave within the group. But when we are among peers, most of us go along with them, molding facets of our personalities to the pressures of the group.

In sum, core personality traits may stem from genetic dispositions, but they are profoundly shaped by learning, peers, situations, experience, and, as we will see next, the largest environment of all: the culture.

Interactive	Our peers can exert a strong influence on our behavior, for better or for worse. Sometimes we "go along with the crowd" for no reason other than that the crowd is doing the behavior in the first place. Listed below are some behaviors that adolescents in 9th to 12th grade reported performing during the 2013 U.S. High School Risk Behavior Survey. Thousands of students responded to the questions. Do any of these results surprise you by being either much higher or much lower than you would have predicted? What do these results say about the power of peers in influencing an individual's behavior?	
	Did not eat for 24 hours or more to lose weight	13%
	Sometimes, rarely, or never used sunscreen	90%
	Watched television 3 or more hours per day	33%
	Played video or computer games, or used a computer more than 3 hours per day	41%
	Were not physically active for 60 minutes on at least 1 day during the previous week	15%
	Were not physically active for 60 minutes on at least 5 days during the previous week	53%
	Did not eat breakfast on all 7 days of the preceding week	62%
	Drank soda one or more times per day	27%
	Drank alcohol or used drugs before sexual intercourse	22%
	Did not use any method to prevent pregnancy (if sexually active)	14%

JOURNAL PROMPT 14.4

Thinking Critically—Examine the Evidence: Think of a central trait that both you and those people close to you would agree really captures your personality; maybe you're particularly outgoing, or shy, or assertive, or funny. Now answer this question: What environmental forces shaped that trait? (No fair saying "I was just born shy.") What type of influence did your parents or other family members have on the development of the central trait you're examining? How did peers, friends, or teachers help to shape that aspect of your personality? Give examples of how the situations you've found yourself in and the people you've interacted with helped to hone your personality.

Quiz for Module 14.4

1. Behavior, habits, and beliefs influence whom you interact with and the situations you seek out. The people with whom you interact and the situations you find yourself in influence your behaviors, habits, and beliefs. Your behavior, habits, and beliefs in turn influence the situations you find yourself in. This cyclic process is known as

   a. Reciprocal determinism

   b. Shared identification

   c. Expressive integration

   d. The Moebius process

2. Which contributes most to the variation among siblings in their personality traits?

   a. The way their parents treat them

   b. The family environment that all of them share

   c. The unique experiences they have that are not shared with their families

   d. The length of time they are raised in the same household

3. How much influence do parents have on shaping a child's personality?

   a. 23 percent

   b. A great deal

   c. None

   d. Very little

4. Mona tries her best to treat all of her children the same and enforce her rules and standards equally, but she slips now and then: Sometimes she's a little more lenient toward Jerry, other times she's a little more strict with Willard, and still other times she lets Frieda get away with a transgression. Mona is concerned about the impact her parenting is having on her children's developing personalities, but why shouldn't she worry?

   a. Few parents have a single childrearing style that is maintained consistently over time.

   b. Temperament determines roughly 80 percent of personality, so there's little she could do to change that.

   c. Her archetypal "mother" status is acknowledged even when she slips up a little.

   d. Children react more strongly to an underlying parental style than they do to surface behaviors.

5. Fourteen-year-old Felicity is quiet and reserved around her parents. When she's with her friends, however, she is boisterous and a bit obnoxious. How common is this pattern of behavior among children and adolescents?

   a. Fairly uncommon; even young children show remarkable consistency in their behaviors across a variety of interaction partners.

   b. Fairly common; the way we behave in different environments reflects the differential impact of parents and peers in shaping behavior.

   c. Fairly common; "multiple identities theory" suggests that core personality traits do little to shape behavior.

   d. Very uncommon; personality traits and behavioral tendencies are solidified early in life.

Cultural Influences on Personality

If you get an invitation to come to a party at 7:00 P.M., what time are you actually likely to get there? If someone gives you the finger or calls you a rude name, are you more likely to become furious or laugh it off? Most Western psychologists regard conscientiousness about time and quickness to anger as personality traits that result partly from genetic dispositions and partly from experience. But *culture* also has a profound effect on people's behavior, attitudes, beliefs, and the traits they value or disdain.

Culture, Values, and Traits

LO 14.5.A   Compare individualist and collectivist cultures, describe some average personality differences between them, and describe three traits that show considerable cultural variability.

individualist cultures

Cultures in which the self is regarded as autonomous, and individual goals and wishes are prized above duty and relations with others.

Quick! Answer this question: "Who are you?"

Your answer will be influenced by your cultural background, and particularly by whether your culture emphasizes individualism or community (Hofstede & Bond, 1988; Kanagawa, Cross, & Markus, 2001; Markus & Kitayama, 1991; Triandis, 1996, 2007). In **individualist cultures**, the independence of the individual often takes precedence over the

Individualistic Americans exercise by biking, walking, or jogging, going in different directions and wearing different clothes while they do it. Collectivist Japanese employees at their hiring ceremony exercise in identical fashion.

needs of the group, and the self is often defined as a collection of personality traits ("I am outgoing, agreeable, and ambitious") or in occupational terms ("I am a psychologist"). In **collectivist cultures**, group harmony often takes precedence over the wishes of the individual, and the self is defined in the context of relationships and the community ("I am the son of a farmer, descended from three generations of storytellers on my mother's side and five generations of farmers on my father's side . . .") (see Table 14.1). In one fascinating study that showed how embedded this dimension is in language and how it shapes our thinking, bicultural individuals born in China tended to answer "Who am I?" in terms of their own individual attributes when they were writing in English. But they described themselves in terms of their relations to others when they were writing in Chinese (Ross, Xun, & Wilson, 2002).

CULTURE AND THE SELF   Individualist and collectivist ways of defining the self influence many aspects of life, including which personality traits we value, how and whether we express emotions, how much we value having relationships or maintaining freedom, and how freely we express angry or aggressive feelings (Forbes et al., 2009; Oyserman & Lee, 2008; Yamawaki, Spackman, & Parrott, 2015). These influences are subtle but powerful. In one study, Chinese and American pairs had to play a communication game that required each partner to be able to take the other's perspective. Eye-gaze measures showed that the Chinese players were almost always able to look at the target from their partner's perspective, whereas the American players often completely failed at this task (Wu & Keysar, 2007). Of course, members of both cultures understand the difference between their own view of things and that of another person's, but the collectivist-oriented Chinese pay closer attention to other people's nonverbal expressions, the better to monitor and modify their own responses.

Because people from collectivist cultures are concerned with adjusting their own behavior depending on the social context, they tend to regard personality and the sense of self as being more flexible than people from individualist cultures do. In a study comparing Japanese

collectivist cultures

Cultures in which the self is regarded as embedded in relationships, and harmony with one's group is prized above individual goals and wishes.

Table 14.1 Some Average Differences between Individualist and Collectivist Cultures

Members of Individualist Cultures	Members of Collectivist Cultures
Define the self as autonomous, independent of groups.	Define the self as an interdependent part of groups.
Give priority to individual, personal goals.	Give priority to the needs and goals of the group.
Value independence, leadership, achievement, self-fulfillment.	Value group harmony, duty, obligation, security.
Give more weight to an individual's attitudes and preferences than to group norms as explanations of behavior.	Give more weight to group norms than to individual attitudes as explanations of behavior.
Attend to the benefits and costs of relationships; if costs exceed advantages, a person is likely to drop the relationship.	Attend to the needs of group members; if a relationship is beneficial to the group but costly to the individual, the individual is likely to stay in the relationship.

Source: Triandis (1996).

and Americans, the Americans reported that their sense of self changes only 5 to 10 percent in different situations, whereas the Japanese said that 90 to 99 percent of their sense of self changes (de Rivera, 1989). The group-oriented Japanese believe it is important to enact *tachiba*, to perform your social roles correctly so that there will be harmony with others. Americans, in contrast, tend to value "being true to your self" and having a "core identity." Americans often value "self"-enhancement even at the expense of others, but the Japanese way of being a "good self" is through constant self-criticism in the context of maintaining face with others (Hamamura & Heine, 2008).

To further separate universal from culture-specific aspects of personality, a group of cross-cultural psychologists conducted in-depth research with Chinese (in Hong Kong and mainland China) and South Africans, administering Western personality inventories but also developing indigenous measures to capture cultural variations (Cheung, van de Vijver, & Leong, 2011). In China, they found evidence for a personality factor they call "interpersonal relatedness." This trait occurs universally, just as the Big Five do, but Asians, and Asian Americans who are less acculturated to American society, score higher on it than do European Americans or highly acculturated Asian Americans. In South Africa, where a personality inventory has been developed in the nine official Bantu languages, Afrikaans, and English, the researchers found the familiar Big Five, but also a few other central factors, including "relationship harmony" (approachability vs. distance, conflict seeking vs. resolving, etc.), "soft-heartedness," and "facilitating" (providing guidance to others).

CULTURE AND TRAITS   When people fail to understand the influence of culture on behavior, they often attribute another person's mysterious or annoying actions to individual personality traits when they are really due to cultural norms. Take cleanliness. How often do you bathe? Once a day, once a week? Do you regard baths as healthy and invigorating or as a disgusting wallow in dirty water? How often, and where, do you wash your hands—or feet? A person who would seem obsessively clean in one culture might seem an appalling slob in another (Fernea & Fernea, 1994).

Or consider helpfulness. Many years ago, in a classic cross-cultural study of children in Kenya, India, Mexico, the Philippines, Okinawa, the United States, and five other societies, researchers measured how often children behaved altruistically (offering help, support, or unselfish suggestions) or egoistically (seeking help and attention or wanting to dominate others) (Whiting & Edwards, 1988; Whiting & Whiting, 1975). American children were the least altruistic on all measures and the most egoistic. The most altruistic children came from societies in which children are assigned many tasks, such as caring for younger children and gathering and preparing food. These children knew that their work made a genuine contribution to the well-being or economic survival of the family. In cultures that value individual achievement and self-advancement, taking care of others has less importance, and altruism as a personality trait is not cultivated to the same extent (de Guzman, Do, & Kok, 2014).

Or consider tardiness. Individuals differ in whether they try to be places "on time" or are always late, but cultural norms affect how individuals regard time in the first place. In northern Europe, Canada, the United States, and most other individualistic cultures, time is organized into linear segments in which people do one thing "at a time" (Hall, 1983; Hall & Hall, 1990; Leonard, 2008). The day is divided into appointments, schedules, and routines, and because time is a precious commodity, people don't like to "waste" time or "spend" too much time on any one activity. In such cultures, being on time is taken as a sign of conscientiousness or thoughtfulness and being late as a sign of indifference or intentional disrespect. Therefore, it is considered the height of rudeness (or high status) to keep someone waiting. But in Mexico, southern Europe, the Middle East, South America, and Africa, time is organized along parallel lines. People do many things at once, and the needs of friends and family supersede mere appointments; they think nothing of waiting for hours or days to see someone. The idea of having to be somewhere "on time," as if time mattered more than a person, is unthinkable.

In many cultures, children are expected to contribute to the family income and to take care of their younger siblings. These experiences encourage helpfulness over independence.

CULTURE and *Violence*

Many people think that men are more violent than women because men have higher levels of testosterone. But if that is so, then why, given that men everywhere have testosterone, do rates of male aggressiveness vary enormously across cultures and throughout history? Why are rates of violence higher in some regions of the United States than in others?

To answer these questions, Richard Nisbett (1993) began by examining the historical record. He found that the American South, along with some western regions of the country originally settled by Southerners, have much higher rates of white homicide and other violence than the rest of the country has—but only particular kinds of violence: the use of fists or guns to protect a man's sense of honor, protect his property, or respond to perceived insults. Nisbett considered various explanations, such as poverty or racial tensions. But when he controlled for regional differences in poverty and the percentage of blacks in the population, by county, "Southernness" remained an independent predictor of homicide. Nisbett also ruled out a history of slavery as an explanation: Regions of the South that had the highest concentrations of slaves in the past have the lowest white homicide rates today.

Nisbett hypothesized that the higher rates of violence in the South derive from economic causes: Higher rates occur in cultures that were originally based on herding, in contrast to cultures based on agriculture. Why would this be so? People who depend economically on agriculture tend to develop cooperative strategies for survival. But people who depend on their herds are extremely vulnerable; their livelihoods can be lost in an instant by the theft of their animals. To reduce the likelihood of theft, Nisbett theorized, herders learn to be hyperalert to any threatening act (real or perceived) and respond to it immediately with force. This would explain why cattle rustling and horse thievery were capital crimes in the Old West, and why Mediterranean and Middle Eastern herding cultures even today place a high value on male aggressiveness. And indeed, when Nisbett looked at agricultural practices *within* the South, he found that homicide rates were more than twice as high in the hills and dry plains areas (where herding occurs) as in farming regions.

The emphasis on aggressiveness and vigilance in herding communities, in turn, fosters a *culture of honor*, in which even small disputes and trivial insults (trivial to people from other cultures, that is) put a man's reputation for toughness on the line, requiring him to respond with violence to restore his status (Cohen, 1998). Although the herding economy has become much less prevalent in the South and West, the legacy of its culture of honor remains. These regions have rates of honor-related homicides (such as murder to avenge a perceived insult to one's family) that are *five times higher* than in other regions of the country. Cultures of honor also have higher rates of domestic violence. Both sexes in such cultures believe it is appropriate for a man to physically assault a woman if he believes she is threatening his honor and reputation by being unfaithful or by leaving him (Vandello & Cohen, 2008).

Why do these practices continue long after they have served their original purpose, considering that most young Southern men aren't out herding cattle? In a series of experiments, Southern men were more likely than Northern men to assume that their male peers believe that aggressive action is *required* to restore honor. Thus, the cultural practice is perpetuated because "everyone else" seems to demand it (Vandello, Cohen, & Ransom, 2008).

Nisbett and his colleagues also wanted to demonstrate how these external cultural norms literally "get under the skin" to affect physiology and personality. They brought 173 Northern and Southern male students into their lab and conducted three experiments to measure how these students would respond psychologically and physiologically to being insulted (Cohen et al., 1996). They explained that the experiment would assess the students' performance on various

Many people assume that men can't help being violent because of their biology. Yet, on average, men in agricultural economies are far more cooperative and nonviolent than men in herding economies. Amish farmers have always had very low rates of violence, whereas in the Old West, the cattle-herding cowboy culture was a violent one. (Fortunately, the shootout here is a reenactment.)

tasks and that the experimenter would be taking saliva samples to measure everyone's blood sugar levels throughout the procedure. Actually, the saliva samples were used to measure levels of cortisol, a hormone associated with high levels of stress, and testosterone, which is associated with dominance and aggression. At one point in the experiment, a confederate of the experimenter, who seemed to be another student participant, bumped into each man and called him an insulting name (a seven-letter word beginning with "a," if you want to know).

As you can see in Figure 14.2, Northerners responded calmly to the insult; if anything, they thought it was funny. But many Southerners were immediately inflamed and their levels of cortisol and testosterone shot up. They were more likely to feel that their masculinity had been threatened, and they were more likely to retaliate aggressively than Northerners were. Southerners and Northerners who were not insulted were alike on most measures, with the exception that the Southerners were actually more polite and deferential. It appears that they have more obliging manners than Northerners—until they are insulted. Then, look out.

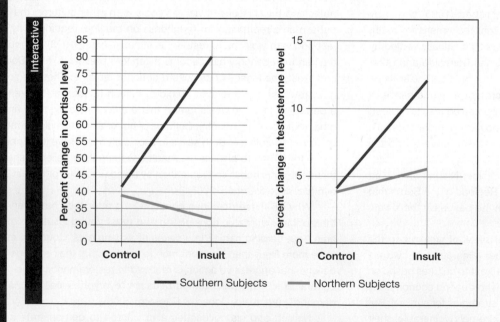

Figure 14.2 Aggression and Cultures of Honor

As these two graphs show, when young men from Northern states were insulted in an experiment, they shrugged it off, thinking it was funny or trivial. But for young Southern men, levels of the stress hormone cortisol and of testosterone shot up, and they were more likely to retaliate aggressively (Cohen et al., 1996).

Evaluating Cultural Approaches

LO 14.5.B Evaluate some pros and cons of the cultural approach to understanding personality.

A woman we know, originally from England, married a Lebanese man. They were happy together but had the usual number of marital misunderstandings and squabbles. After a few years, they visited his family home in Lebanon, where she had never been before. "I was stunned," she told us. "All the things I thought he did because of his *personality* turned out to be because he's *Lebanese*! Everyone there was just like him!"

Our friend's reaction illustrates both the contributions and the limitations of cultural studies of personality. She was right in recognizing that some of her husband's behavior was attributable to his culture; his Lebanese notions of time were indeed very different from her English notions. But she was wrong to infer that the Lebanese are all "like him": Individuals are affected by their culture, but they vary within it.

Cultural psychologists face the problem of how to describe cultural influences on personality without oversimplifying or stereotyping (Church & Lonner, 1998). As one student of ours put it, "How come when we students speak of 'the' Japanese or 'the' blacks or 'the' whites or 'the' Latinos, it's called stereotyping, and when you do it, it's called 'cross-cultural psychology'?" This question shows excellent critical thinking! The study of culture does not rest on the assumption that all members of a culture behave the same way or have the same personality traits. People vary according to their temperaments, beliefs, and learning histories, and this variation occurs within every culture.

Moreover, culture itself may have variations within every society. The United States has an individualist culture overall, but the South, with its history of strong regional identity, is more collectivist than the rugged, independent West (Vandello & Cohen, 1999). The collectivist Chinese and the Japanese both value group harmony, but the Chinese are more likely to *also* promote individual achievement, whereas the Japanese are more likely to strive for group consensus (Dien, 1999; Lu, 2008). And African Americans are more likely than white Americans to blend elements of American individualism and African collectivism. Thus, an individualist philosophy predicts grade point average for white students, but collectivist values are a better predictor for black students (Komarraju & Cokley, 2008). Average cross-cultural differences, even in a dimension as influential as individualist–collectivist, are not rigidly fixed or applicable to all groups within a society (Oyserman & Lee, 2008).

Finally, in spite of their differences, cultures share many human concerns and needs for love, attachment, family, work, and religious or communal tradition. Nonetheless, cultural rules are what, *on average*, make Swedes different from Bedouins, and Cambodians different from Italians. The traits that we value, our sense of self versus community, and our notions of the right way to behave—all key aspects of personality—begin with the culture in which we are raised. And our self-esteem and well-being are deeply influenced by feeling that our own personal traits match the cultural norm: Extroverts are happiest in a culture that values individual success and self-promotion; conscientious people are happiest in a tidy, rule-governed country such as Switzerland. When an individual's personality traits clash with those endorsed by the larger culture, as travelers and immigrants know, people can feel oddly out of sync with the world around them (Fulmer et al., 2010).

JOURNAL PROMPT 14.5

Thinking Critically—Don't Oversimplify: People often speak of "the" German personality or "the" British character. How can we think about the cultural factors that influence personality traits without stereotyping?

Quiz for Module 14.5

1. Cultures that value group harmony and group norms are called _____ cultures.
   a. Concentric
   b. Collectivist
   c. Communal
   d. Socialist

2. Audrey defines herself as a unique individual striving for the things she wants for herself. Her extroversion makes her stand out from the crowd, and she likes it that way. Audrey thinks she has a unique personality that sets her apart from her family and friends. What is Audrey's most likely country of origin?
   a. Indonesia
   b. South Korea
   c. Costa Rica
   d. United States

3. Himari was born and raised in Japan. If asked to describe herself, what would she be most likely to say?
   a. "I am my parents' daughter and a hard-working team member at my job."
   b. "I'm ambitious and outgoing, and I like to stand out in a crowd."
   c. "I can't really describe myself; my sense of self is always changing."
   d. "I'm 5'7", I have light brown eyes, and I love horses."

4. Chrissie is hanging out with her college friends: Mario (who's from Mexico), Nunzio (who's from Italy), and Felix (who's from Canada). They agree to meet for dinner the next evening at 7:00 P.M. "Wait," asked Felix. "Is that a *North American* 7:00 P.M.? When is everybody actually going to show up?" Why would Felix feel the need to ask that question?
   a. Mario, Nunzio, and Felix are all likely to show up within 10 minutes of one another, whereas Chrissie will probably be 45 minutes late.
   b. Felix himself is likely to be late, given his cultural background.
   c. Cultures differ in terms of how well their members understand directions and instructions.
   d. There is cultural variability in the value placed on timeliness and tardiness.

5. Why is it difficult to evaluate the utility of cultural explanations of personality?
   a. Inequities of resources and differences in experiences make it impossible to understand the effects of culture on an individual without having lived in that culture.
   b. "Culture" cannot be defined adequately.
   c. There's a fine balance between describing broad cultural tendencies without stereotyping people or ignoring universal human experiences.
   d. The evidence for cultural differences in personality has been largely anecdotal, rather than based on detailed scientific studies.

The Inner Experience

A final way to look at personality starts from each person's own point of view, from the inside out. Biology may hand us temperamental dispositions that benefit or limit us, the environment may deal us some tough or fortunate experiences, our parents may treat us as we would or would not have wished, but the sum total of our personality is how we, individually, weave all of these elements together. Watch *What Is Personality?* to appreciate the many ways personality might be defined.

Humanist Approaches

LO 14.6.A   Describe the core humanist ideas advanced by Abraham Maslow, Carl Rogers, and Rollo May.

One such approach to personality comes from **humanist psychology**, which was launched as a movement in the early 1960s. The movement's chief leaders—Abraham Maslow (1908–1970), Carl Rogers (1902–1987), and Rollo May (1909–1994)—argued that it was time to replace psychoanalysis and behaviorism with a "third force" in psychology, one that would draw a fuller picture of human potential and personality. Psychologists who take a humanist approach to personality emphasize our uniquely human capacity to determine our own actions and futures

ABRAHAM MASLOW   The trouble with psychology, said Maslow (1970, 1971), was that it had ignored many of the positive aspects of life, such as joy, laughter, love, happiness, and *peak experiences*, rare moments of rapture caused by the attainment of excellence or the experience of beauty. The traits that Maslow thought most central to personality were not the Big Five, but rather the qualities of the *self-actualized person*—the person who strives for a life that is meaningful, challenging, and satisfying.

For Maslow, personality development could be viewed as a gradual progression toward self-actualization. Most psychologists, he argued, had a lopsided view of human nature, a result of their emphasis on studying emotional problems and negative traits such as neuroticism or insecurity. As Maslow (1971) wrote, "When you select out for careful study very fine and healthy people, strong people, creative people . . . then you get a very different view of mankind. You are asking how tall can people grow, what can a human being become?"

CARL ROGERS   As a clinician, Carl Rogers (1951, 1961) was interested not only in why some people cannot function well but also in what he called the "fully functioning individual." How you behave, he said, depends on your subjective reality, not on the external reality around you. Fully functioning people experience *congruence*, or harmony, between the image they project to others and their true feelings and wishes. They are trusting, warm, and open, rather than defensive or intolerant. Their beliefs about themselves are realistic.

To become fully functioning people, Rogers maintained, we all need **unconditional positive regard**, love and support for the people we are, without strings (conditions) attached. This doesn't mean that Winifred should be allowed to kick her brother when she is angry with him or that Wilbur may throw his dinner out the window because he doesn't like pot roast. In these cases, a parent can correct the child's behavior without withdrawing love from the child. The child can learn that the behavior, not the child, is what is bad. "The rule in our house is 'no violence,' children" is a very different message from "You are horrible children for behaving so badly."

Unfortunately, Rogers observed, many children are raised with *conditional positive regard*: "I will love you if you behave well, and I won't love you if you behave badly." Adults often treat each other this way, too. People treated with conditional regard begin to suppress or deny feelings or actions that they believe are unacceptable to those they love. The result, said Rogers, is incongruence, a sense of being out of touch with your feelings, of not being true to your real self, which in turn produces low self-regard, defensiveness, and unhappiness. A person experiencing incongruence scores high on neuroticism, becoming bitter and negative.

ROLLO MAY   May shared with the humanists a belief in free will. But he also emphasized some of the inherently difficult and tragic aspects of the human condition, including loneliness, anxiety, and alienation. May brought to American psychology elements of the European philosophy of **existentialism**, which emphasizes such inevitable challenges of human existence as the search for the meaning of life, the need to confront death, and the necessity of taking responsibility for our actions.

You are never too old for self-actualization. Hulda Crooks, shown here at age 91 climbing Mt. Fuji, took up mountain climbing at age 54. "It's been a great inspiration for me," she said. "When I come down from the mountain I feel like I can battle in the valley again." She died at the age of 101.

humanist psychology

A psychological approach that emphasizes personal growth, resilience, and the achievement of human potential.

unconditional positive regard

To Carl Rogers, love or support given to another person with no conditions attached.

existentialism

A philosophical approach that emphasizes the inevitable dilemmas and challenges of human existence.

Existential psychologists remind us of the inevitable struggles of human existence, such as the fight against loneliness and alienation.

Free will, wrote May, carries a price in anxiety and despair, which is why so many people try to escape from freedom into narrow certainties and blame others for their misfortunes. For May, our personalities reflect the ways we cope with the struggles to find meaning in existence, to use our freedom wisely, and to face suffering and death bravely. May popularized the humanist idea that we can choose to make the best of ourselves by drawing on inner resources such as love and courage, but he added that we can never escape the harsh realities of life and loss.

Narrative Approaches

LO 14.6.B Discuss how the narrative approach to personality hinges on answering the central question, "Who am I?"

In the past two decades, another approach to personality has focused on the importance of the *life narrative*, the story that each of us develops over time to explain ourselves and make meaning of everything that has happened to us (Bruner, 1990; McAdams & Guo, 2015; McAdams & Manczak, 2015; Sarbin, 1997). In the narrative view, your distinctive personality rests on the story you tell to answer the question, "Who am I?"

Because the narrative approach emphasizes how the stories we tell give us an identity, shape our behavior, and motivate us to pursue or abandon our goals, it integrates the many diverse influences on personality that we have discussed in this chapter. Do you believe you are a victim of bad childhood experiences or a survivor of them? Do you believe that your mood swings are caused by a biochemical imbalance or an imbalanced love affair? When you tell about your life to others, do you play the hero or the passive bystander?

The life narrative you create for yourself reflects your needs and justifies the actions you take, or fail to take, to solve your problems. It affects whether you even feel that you can solve your problems and transform your life (McAdams & Manczak, 2015). Psychotherapist David Epston worked with an immigrant woman named Marisa, who had been abused and rejected all her life. "To tell a story about your life turns it into a history," he told her, "one that can be left behind, and makes it easier for you to create a future of your own design" (quoted in O'Hanlon, 1994). Marisa came to see that she could tell a new story about her experiences, one that did not emphasize the tragedies that had befallen her but rather her triumphs in overcoming them. "My life has a future now," she told Epston. "It will never be the same again."

In the narrative view, your stories about how you see and explain yourself are the essence of your personality, capturing everything that has happened to you and all the factors that affect your biology, psychology, and relationships. They are what make you unique in all the world.

Evaluating Humanist and Narrative Approaches

LO 14.6.C **Summarize the shortcomings of the humanist approach to personality, and identify some areas of substantial contribution.**

As with psychodynamic theories, the major scientific criticism of humanist psychology is that many of its assumptions are untestable. Freud looked at humanity and saw destructive drives, selfishness, and lust. Maslow and Rogers looked at humanity and saw cooperation, selflessness, and love. May looked at humanity and saw fear of freedom, loneliness, and the struggle for meaning. These differences, say critics, may tell us more about the observers than about the observed.

Many humanist concepts, although intuitively appealing, are difficult to define operationally. How can we know whether a person is self-fulfilled or self-actualized? How can we tell whether a woman's decision to quit her job and become a professional rodeo rider represents an "escape from freedom" or a freely made choice? And what exactly is unconditional positive regard? If it is defined as unquestioned support of a child's efforts at mastering a new skill, or as assurance that the child is loved in spite of her or his mistakes, then it is clearly a good idea. But in the popular culture, it has often been interpreted as an unwillingness ever to say "no" to a child or to offer constructive criticism and set limits, which children need.

Despite such concerns, humanist psychologists have brought balance to the study of personality. A specialty known as "positive psychology" follows in the footsteps of humanism by focusing on the qualities that enable people to be optimistic and resilient in times of stress (Donaldson, Dollwet, & Rao, 2015; Gable & Haidt, 2005; Seligman & Csikszentmihaly, 2000). Influenced in part by the humanists, psychologists are studying many positive human traits, such as courage, altruism, the motivation to excel, and self-confidence. Developmental psychologists are studying ways to foster children's empathy and creativity. And some researchers are studying the emotional and existential effects of the fear of death.

As for narrative approaches, research is flourishing, showing how the stories that we tell about ourselves play a crucial role in shaping our distinctive personalities (McAdams & Manczak, 2015). Cognitive psychologists emphasize how our stories shape and distort our memories. Psychotherapists are exploring the ways in which clients who tell self-defeating life stories might turn them around, creating more hopeful and positive ones. Social and cultural psychologists examine how a culture or society's dominant myths and shared stories influence people's ambitions and expectations, political views, and beliefs that the world can be improved or will never change.

The humanist, existential, and narrative views of personality share one central message: We have the power to choose our own destinies, even when fate delivers us into tragedy. Across psychology, this message has fostered an appreciation of resilience in the face of adversity.

Now that you have read about the major influences on personality (see Review 14.1), how would you explain your own personality or those of your best friends?

Thinking Critically—Define Your Terms: Unconditional positive regard sounds like a good thing, but what does it mean, exactly? Does it mean giving loved ones your total support and approval, no matter what they do? Does it permit setting limits and offering constructive criticism? What situations can you think of where telling someone an unpleasant truth about themselves or putting boundaries on their behavior might be the most loving thing to do?

Review 14.1

The Major Influences on Personality

Psychodynamic	Unconscious dynamics shape human motives, guilt, conflicts, and defenses.
Genetic	Children are born with particular temperaments, and most traits are highly influenced by genes.
Environmental	Learning, situations, and unique experiences affect which traits are encouraged and which genes are expressed.
Parents	Modify and shape a child's temperament and genetic predispositions; affect gender roles, attitudes, and self-concept; affect the quality of the relationship with the child.
Peer group	Influences an individual's values, behavior, ambitions, goals, etc.
Situation	Determines which behaviors are rewarded and which are punished or ignored, thereby shaping the expression or suppression of particular traits.
Chance events	May influence a person's experiences and choices in unexpected ways, thus encouraging the development of some traits over others.
Cultural	Cultural norms specify which traits are valued, affect basic notions of the self and personality, and shape behaviors from aggressiveness to altruism.
Humanist	Despite genetic, environmental, cultural, and psychodynamic influences, people can exercise free will to become the kind of person they want to be.
Narrative	Personality rests on the stories people create to explain their lives (e.g., whether they see themselves as victims or survivors); these stories can change.

Quiz for Module 14.6

1. Which theorist is *not* usually associated with the humanist movement in psychology?

   a. Carl Rogers

   b. Rollo May

   c. Abraham Maslow

   d. Carl Hovland

2. According to Carl Rogers, _____ individuals experience congruence or harmony between the image they project to others and the way they feel inside. They are warm and open, and they hold realistic beliefs about themselves.

   a. Autonomous

   b. Fully functioning

   c. Unconditional

   d. Self-complete

3. There are inevitable dilemmas and challenges associated with living life. We all need to confront the fear of death and explore the meaning of life, and we must take responsibility for our actions as we do so. The way we cope with these struggles helps to shape who we are as an individual. This three-sentence lesson is a good summary of

   a. Logical positivism

   b. Stoicism

   c. Fideism

   d. Existentialism

4. Delia is given a tough assignment in her psychology class: "Describe who you are." Those four words open up so many possibilities: a physical description, a list of traits, the genetic inheritance her parents contributed, the social and cultural groups that define her as a person. To complete the assignment, Delia decides to simply write the story of her life, noting the highs and lows, triumphs and tragedies she has experienced so far. Which approach to understanding personality has Delia adopted?

   a. Narrative

   b. Psychodynamic

   c. Trait

   d. Hypothetico-deductive

5. Which of the following is *not* a criticism of humanistic theories of personality?

   a. Humanistic theories contain concepts that are difficult to define operationally.

   b. Although influential in psychology, these theories haven't received much attention from laypeople in society at large.

   c. Humanistic theories contain concepts that are vague and open to interpretation.

   d. Humanistic explanations for personality contain assumptions that are untestable.

Taking Psychology with You

How to Avoid the "Barnum Effect"

How well does the following paragraph describe you?

Some of your aspirations tend to be pretty unrealistic. At times you are extroverted, affable, and sociable, while at other times you are introverted, wary, and reserved. You pride yourself on being an independent thinker and do not accept others' opinions without satisfactory proof. You prefer a certain amount of change and variety, and you become dissatisfied when hemmed in by restrictions and limitations. At times you have serious doubts as to whether you have made the right decision or done the right thing.

When people believe that this description was written just for them, as the result of a personalized horoscope or handwriting analysis, they all say the same thing: "It describes me *exactly*!" Everyone thinks this description is accurate because it is vague enough to apply to almost everyone and it is flattering. Don't we all consider ourselves to be "independent thinkers"?

This is why many psychologists worry about the "Barnum effect" (Snyder & Shenkel, 1975). P. T. Barnum was the great circus showman who said, "There's a sucker born every minute." He knew that the formula for success was to "have a little something for everybody," which is just what unscientific personality profiles, horoscopes, and handwriting analysis (graphology) have in common. They have "a little something for everyone" and are therefore nonfalsifiable.

For example, graphologists claim that they can identify your personality traits from the form and distribution of your handwritten letters. Wide spacing between words means you feel isolated and lonely. If your lines drift upward, you are an "uplifting" optimist, and if your lines droop downward, you are a pessimist who feels you are being "dragged down." If you make large capital *I*'s, you have a large ego.

Graphologists are not the same as handwriting experts, who are trained to determine, say, whether a document is a forgery. Graphologists, like astrologers, usually know little or nothing about the scientific method, how to correct for their biases, or how to empirically test their claims. That is why the many different graphological approaches usually conflict. According to one system, a certain way of crossing *t*'s reveals someone who is vicious and sadistic; according to another, it reveals a practical joker (Beyerstein, 1996).

Whenever graphology *has* been tested empirically, it has failed. A meta-analysis of 200 published studies found no validity or reliability to graphology in predicting work performance, aptitudes, or personality. No school of graphology fared better than any other, and no graphologist was able to perform better than untrained amateurs making guesses from the same writing samples (Dean, 1992; Klimoski, 1992).

If graphology were just an amusing game, no one would worry about it, but unfortunately it can have harmful consequences. Graphologists have been hired by companies to predict a person's leadership ability, attention to detail, willingness to be a good team player, and more. They pass judgment on people's honesty, generosity, and even supposed criminal tendencies (Tang, 2012). How would you feel if you were turned down for a job because some graphologist branded you a potential thief on the basis of your alleged "desire-for-possession hooks" on your *S*'s?

If you do not want to be a victim of the Barnum effect, research offers this advice to help you think critically about graphology and its many cousins:

- *Beware of all-purpose descriptions that could apply to anyone.* Sometimes you doubt your decisions; who among us has not? Sometimes you feel outgoing and sometimes shy; who does not? Do you "have sexual secrets that you are afraid of confessing"? Just about everybody does.

- *Beware of your own selective perceptions.* Most of us are so impressed when an astrologer, psychic, or graphologist gets something right that we overlook all the descriptions that are plain wrong. Be aware of the confirmation bias—the tendency to explain away all the descriptions that don't fit.

- *Resist flattery and emotional reasoning.* This is a hard one! It is easy to reject a profile that describes you as selfish or stupid. Watch out for the ones that make you feel good by telling you how wonderful and smart you are, what a great leader you will be, or how modest you are about your exceptional abilities.

If you keep your ability to think critically with you, you won't end up paying hard cash for soft answers or taking a job you dislike because it fits your "personality type." In other words, you'll have proved Barnum wrong.

Shared Writing Prompt

Which one of these statements presumably doesn't belong with the others?

1. "Your slanted k's reveal a dominant personality."
2. "Some of your aspirations tend to be pretty unrealistic."
3. "You are less extroverted than most test takers who've taken this personality test."
4. "You will meet a dark, mysterious stranger who will change your life."

These are examples of, respectively, handwriting analysis, the Barnum effect, feedback from a personality measure, and fortune-telling. At first glance they all seem to have the same tone; revealing some deep secret about an individual. But what sets the scientific study of personality apart from the rest of the pack? What critical-thinking guidelines can you apply to answer this question?

Summary

Psychodynamic Theories of Personality

LO 14.1.A Describe the structure of personality according to psychoanalysis, five psychological defense mechanisms, and five stages of psychosexual development.

Sigmund Freud was the founder of *psychoanalysis*, which was the first *psychodynamic* theory, emphasizing unconscious processes and a belief in the formative role of childhood experiences and early unconscious conflicts.

To Freud, the personality consists of the *id*, the *ego*, and the *superego*. *Defense mechanisms* protect the ego from unconscious anxiety, and include repression, projection, displacement (one form of which is sublimation), regression, and denial. Freud believed that personality develops in a series of *psychosexual stages*, with the *phallic (Oedipal) stage* most crucial.

LO 14.1.B Explain how the views of Carl Jung and the object-relations school differed from Sigmund Freud's approach to personality.

Several thinkers splintered from Freud's original psychodynamic views. Carl Jung believed that people share a *collective unconscious* that contains universal memories and images, called *archetypes*. The *object-relations school* emphasizes the importance of the first 2 years of life rather than the Oedipal phase; the infant's representations of important figures, especially the mother, rather than sexual needs and drives; and the problem in male development of breaking away from the mother.

LO 14.1.C Summarize three ways in which psychodynamic theories falter under scientific scrutiny.

Psychodynamic approaches have been criticized for violating the principle of falsifiability; for overgeneralizing from atypical patients to everyone; and for basing theories on the unreliable memories and retrospective accounts of adults, which can create an *illusion of causality*. However, some psychodynamic ideas have received empirical support, including the existence of nonconscious processes and defenses.

The Modern Study of Personality

LO 14.2.A Outline some ways in which objective personality inventories differ from popular personality tests used in business, dating, or other areas.

Most popular tests that divide personality into "types" are not valid or reliable. In research, psychologists typically rely on *objective tests (inventories)* to identify and study personality traits and disorders.

LO 14.2.B List the Big Five personality dimensions, and describe the characteristics of each one.

Gordon Allport argued that people have a few *central traits* that are key to their personalities and a greater number of *secondary traits* that are less fundamental. Raymond Cattell used *factor analysis* to identify clusters of traits that he considered the basic components of personality. Studies around the world provide strong evidence for the *Big Five* dimensions of personality: extroversion versus introversion, neuroticism (negative emotionality) versus emotional stability, agreeableness versus antagonism, conscientiousness versus impulsiveness, and openness to experience versus resistance to new experience. Although these dimensions are quite stable, some of them do change over the lifespan, reflecting maturational development, societal events, and adult responsibilities.

Genetic Influences on Personality

LO 14.3.A Define what temperaments are, and discuss how they relate to personality traits.

In human beings, individual differences in *temperaments*, such as reactivity, soothability, and positive or negative emotionality, emerge at birth or early in life and influence subsequent personality development.

LO 14.3.B   Explain how twin studies can be used to estimate the heritability of personality traits.

Behavioral-genetic data from twin and adoption studies suggest that the *heritability* of many adult personality traits is about .50. Genetic influences create dispositions and set limits on the expression of specific traits.

LO 14.3.C   Summarize the arguments for and against the conclusion that personality "is all in our genes."

Even traits that are highly heritable are often modified throughout life by circumstances, chance, and learning. Conclusions that "biology is destiny" or our fates are controlled by our genes are not warranted.

Environmental Influences on Personality

LO 14.4.A   Explain how reciprocal determinism and the nonshared environment contribute to our understanding of how traits and behavior can be shaped by the environment.

People often behave inconsistently in different circumstances when behaviors that are rewarded in one situation are punished or ignored in another. According to *social-cognitive learning theory*, personality results from the interaction of the environment and aspects of the individual, in a pattern of *reciprocal determinism*.

LO 14.4.B   Summarize three lines of evidence that suggest parental influence over children's personality development is limited.

Three lines of evidence challenge the popular assumption that parents have the greatest impact on their children's personalities and behavior: (1) Behavioral-genetic studies find that the major environmental influence is from the *nonshared environment*; (2) few parents have a consistent childrearing style over time and with all their children; and (3) even when parents try to be consistent, there may be little relation between what they do and how the children turn out. However, parents can modify their children's temperaments, prevent children at risk of delinquency from choosing a path of antisocial behavior, and influence many of their children's values and attitudes.

LO 14.4.C   Discuss some ways in which peers influence the development of personality in children.

One major environmental influence on personality comes from a person's peer groups, which can be more powerful than parents. Most children and teenagers behave differently with their parents than with their peers.

Cultural Influences on Personality

LO 14.5.A   Compare individualist and collectivist cultures, describe some average personality differences between them, and describe three traits that show considerable cultural variability.

Many qualities that Western psychologists treat as individual personality traits are heavily influenced by *culture*. People from *individualist cultures* define themselves in different terms than those from *collectivist cultures*, and they perceive their "selves" as more stable across situations. Cultures vary in their norms for many behaviors, such as cleanliness and notions of time.

LO 14.5.B   Evaluate some pros and cons of the cultural approach to understanding personality.

Cultural theories of personality face the problem of describing broad cultural differences and their influences on personality without promoting stereotypes or overlooking universal human needs.

The Inner Experience

LO 14.6.A   Describe the core humanist ideas advanced by Abraham Maslow, Carl Rogers, and Rollo May.

Humanist psychologists focus on a person's subjective sense of self and the free will to change. They emphasize human potential and the strengths of human nature, as in Abraham Maslow's concepts of *peak experiences* and *self-actualization*. Carl Rogers stressed the importance of *unconditional positive regard* in creating a fully functioning person. Rollo May brought *existentialism* into psychology, emphasizing some of the inherent challenges of human existence that result from having free will, such as the search for meaning in life.

LO 14.6.B   Discuss how the narrative approach to personality hinges on answering the central question, "Who am I?"

As another way of understanding personality from the "inside," some personality psychologists study *life narratives*, the stories people create to explain themselves and make sense of their lives. These stories may serve to suppress changes in our lives or encourage them.

LO 14.6.C   Summarize the shortcomings of the humanist approach to personality, and identify some areas of substantial contribution.

Some ideas from humanist psychology are subjective and difficult to measure, but others have fostered research on positive aspects of personality, such as optimism and resilience under adversity, and the importance of life narratives.

Chapter 14 Quiz

1. According to Freud's psychodynamic theory, what is the correct sequence of psychosexual stages in the development of personality?

   a. Id, ego, superego

   b. Oral, anal, phallic, latency, genital

   c. Oral, anal, latency, genital, phallic

   d. Anal, oral, latency, phallic, genital

2. An image of a cross (a horizontal line bisected by a vertical line) can be found in cultures, nations, religions, and other groups around the world. Carl Jung would take this as evidence that the cross is

   a. An object relation

   b. A "familiarizer"

   c. An archetype

   d. A psychodynamic mandala

3. "The reason why people can't remember childhood trauma and infantile sexual urges is because they've been repressed into unconsciousness, where they remain hidden from the conscious mind. When they're adults, we can ask people about their dreams, and piece together from there the symbolic dream content that reveals the unconscious truth from experiences that happened 30 years earlier." How much of a basis does this theorizing provide for scientific testing?

   a. Much

   b. A great deal

   c. Virtually none

   d. A moderate amount

4. Mauricio says, "I took a personality test online, and it told me that I was a high mood regulator with empathic tendencies. I guess I am!" Cleo says, "I took an online personality test and it showed that I was high in sociality; now I know!" Marty says, "Ever since my online personality test told me I was an intuito-deductive-sympathist, I've understood myself so much better!" Cassandra says, "I took an online personality test, and it was fun. Now I'm going back to studying legitimate scientific psychology." Who has reached the correct conclusions from her or his experience?

   a. Marty

   b. Cleo

   c. Mauricio

   d. Cassandra

5. The Big Five personality dimensions include extroversion versus _____, agreeableness versus _____, and _____ versus impulsiveness.

   a. Introversion / antagonism / conscientiousness

   b. Neuroticism / openness to experience / emotional stability

   c. Conscientiousness / neuroticism / antagonism

   d. Resistance / introversion / openness to experience

6. Nona is describing her 4-month-old daughter, Laurel. "She startles at every little sound. She always seems nervous and fearful, and she overreacts to the littlest inconvenience. At the playground the other day a friendly dog licked her shoulder, and we had to go home because she started crying and screaming so much!" How would you describe Laurel's temperament?

   a. Distractible

   b. Slow to warm up

   c. Highly reactive

   d. Flexible

7. Suppose you learned that a particular trait had a heritability of 0.35. What does this mean?

   a. Thirty-five percent of your behaviors regulated by the trait in question is determined by your genetic inheritance.

   b. Thirty-five percent of your particular personality makeup is due to genetic factors.

   c. Thirty-five percent of your particular personality makeup is due to environmental factors.

   d. Thirty-five percent of the trait in question is attributable to genetic variation within the group under consideration.

8. Harlan was born with a genetic predisposition to speak Icelandic. Yet he lived his entire life in Marrowbone, Kentucky, and never encountered a person from Iceland, never heard Icelandic being spoken, and really never had any exposure to anything having to do with Iceland or its language. How much did his genetic predisposition benefit him in life?

   a. Very much; having a gene such as that illustrates that he had a rich and varied genetic makeup.

   b. Not at all; genes only account for 20 percent of the variability in most behaviors.

   c. Not at all; genes are expressed in an appropriate environmental context.

   d. Very much; he will pass on his Icelandic genes to his children, who are likely to make better use of them.

9. Wally is a rather shy and retiring type. As such, he seeks out situations that fit his introverted temperament, such as libraries, lone mountaintops, and movie theaters in the afternoon. Finding himself in these environments reinforces for him that he is a shy and retiring type. Wally's case is an example of

a. Reciprocal determinism

b. The nonshared environment

c. Attributional drift

d. Attributional shift

10. What's one reason why parents have less influence over shaping their children's personalities than most people assume?

a. Personality traits are largely genetic—about 62 percent—so the parental influence is already present in a child's genetic makeup.

b. Parenting styles tend to be consistent across children; as such, one would expect the personalities of siblings raised in the same home to be similar, and they're not.

c. The shared environment of the home exerts little influence on personality development; the nonshared environment has a stronger impact.

d. Parents typically spend the majority of their time interacting with one another, rather than with their children; as such, the opportunities for influence are rare.

11. When Isabella leaves the house to go to middle school each morning, she is dressed in the conservative style that her mother prefers. As she waits for the bus, however, she unbuttons an extra button on her shirt, pulls her skirt a little higher above her knees, and applies a small amount of eye shadow and lipstick, all to match the style and dress of her friends. How unusual is her behavior?

a. Highly unusual; adolescence is typically a time of confusion, especially for young girls, so they tend to follow the rules and examples set by their parents.

b. Fairly unusual; Isabella is making a conscious decision to reject the standards of her mother, so she is demonstrating a psychodynamic shift.

c. Not that unusual; adolescents inhabit an environment of parental influence and an environment of peer influence, and those influences are not always the same.

d. Fairly unusual; Isabella's cultural standards, reinforced in the home environment, should still be in place throughout her school day.

12. Carl values independence, achievement, and self-fulfillment. If push comes to shove, he's not afraid to defy the will of the group and make his own decisions in his own best interests. Carl's cultural background is most likely

a. Individualist

b. Collectivist

c. Existentialist

d. Venezuelan

13. "It figures," muttered Lydia. "Jeroen won't loan me $20, 'on principle,' he says. The Dutch are so stubborn! I've got a better chance of getting $20 from Umberto; those Italians are a soft touch . . . so emotional. I'm glad 'culture is destiny,' like I learned in my psychology class." What mistake, of many, is Lydia making in her reasoning?

a. That there are cultural differences between groups.

b. That culture exerts an impact on people's personalities.

c. That examining cultural differences can lead to stereotypical thinking.

d. That cultural influences are the same as cultural truths.

14. When Jerry traveled to Nepal last summer, he felt a strange sensation while sitting on a mountaintop. It was kind of an inner peace, and he sort of felt as one with the universe. He couldn't describe it clearly, but it was like a transcendent awakening of the untapped potential of his inner self. According to Abraham Maslow, Jerry had a _____, and furthermore, he is probably _____.

a. Existential breakthrough / harmoniously attuned

b. Disconnection / a thetan

c. Peak experience / self-actualized

d. Unconditional moment / fully functioning

15. An approach to understanding personality that integrates genetic, cultural, environmental, and inner experience perspectives on personality is the _____ approach.

a. Psychodynamic

b. Narrative

c. Thelemic

d. Collectivist

16. The primary evidence for having a peak experience seems to be the feeling that you think you've had a peak experience. What does this faulty reasoning indicate?

    a. Psychodynamic theory is a better predictor of human behavior than humanism is.

    b. The basic tenets of humanism are difficult to define, operationalize, or measure.

    c. The uniqueness of human experience means we can't formulate general principles of behavior.

    d. People are different, simple as that; no use trying to explain what they do.

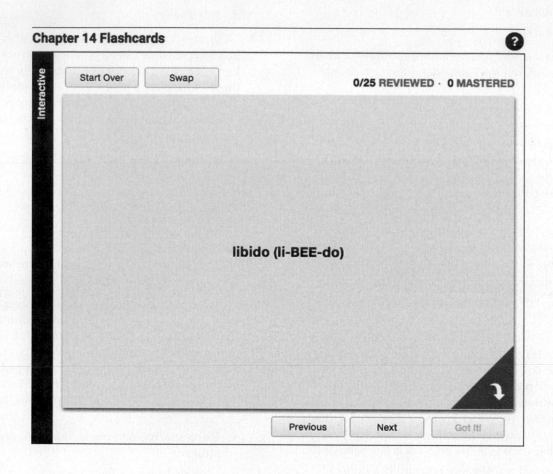

Chapter 14 Flashcards ?

Interactive

| Start Over | Swap |

0/25 REVIEWED · 0 MASTERED

libido (li-BEE-do)

| Previous | Next | Got It! |

Chapter 15
Psychological Disorders

◀ Listen to the Audio

⌄ Learning Objectives

LO 15.1.A Consider why it is difficult to obtain a universally agreed-upon definition of "mental disorder."

LO 15.1.B Describe four dangers associated with using the DSM for diagnosis of mental disorders, and give an example of each.

LO 15.1.C Explain the theoretical basis of projective tests, and identify the problems associated with these techniques.

LO 15.2.A Differentiate the major symptoms of generalized anxiety disorder and panic disorder.

LO 15.2.B Describe the characteristics of a phobia, and explain why agoraphobia can be so disabling.

LO 15.3.A Define posttraumatic stress disorder, and discuss its symptoms and origins.

LO 15.3.B Distinguish between obsessions and compulsions, and discuss the defining elements of obsessive–compulsive disorder.

LO 15.4.A Describe how major depression differs from normal feelings of sadness or loneliness.

LO 15.4.B Explain the main features of bipolar disorder.

LO 15.4.C Discuss the four major factors that contribute to the onset of depression.

LO 15.5.A Explain the main features of borderline personality disorder.

LO 15.5.B Distinguish between the terms *psychopathy* and *antisocial personality disorder*, and note the common elements of each.

LO 15.5.C List and explain the major factors that contribute to the central features of psychopathy.

LO 15.6.A Discuss how the biological model of addiction would explain drug abuse and alcoholism.

LO 15.6.B Discuss how the learning model of addiction would explain drug abuse and alcoholism.

LO 15.6.C Explain the different predictions that the biological model and learning model would make regarding the benefits of total abstinence from versus moderate intake of alcohol.

LO 15.7.A Discuss the factors that make dissociative identity disorder a controversial diagnosis.

LO 15.7.B Evaluate the likely explanations for dissociative personality disorder.

LO 15.8.A Describe the five major symptoms of schizophrenia, and give an example of each.

LO 15.8.B Describe the three main contributing factors to the origin of schizophrenia.

Ask questions . . . be willing to wonder

Are mental disorders the same in every culture?

Why do some people get over a traumatic experience fairly quickly, yet others develop posttraumatic stress disorder?

Why do some people get depressed for no reason, and others have reason, but don't get depressed?

What's the matter with psychopaths that makes them capable of such heartless deception and cruelty?

Can problem drinkers ever learn to drink moderately?

Syd Barrett was the founding member of the multiplatinum rock group Pink Floyd. John Nash was a Nobel Prize–winning mathematician, whose life and work formed the basis for the movie *A Beautiful Mind*. Howard Hughes was a billionaire whose career included producing Hollywood movies, shaping the aviation industry, and acquiring multiple parcels of prime real estate. J. D. Salinger wrote a classic of American fiction, *The Catcher in the Rye*. Ricky Williams won the Heisman Trophy as a running back at the University of Texas at Austin, then went on to play for the New Orleans Saints, Miami Dolphins, and Baltimore Ravens. Catherine Zeta-Jones has enjoyed fame and acclaim for her many acting roles and modeling career. Robin Williams was heralded as a comedic genius who won an Academy Award for his acting talents. Astronaut Buzz Aldrin walked on the surface of the Moon, an accomplishment only a handful of humans can claim. And if author J. K. Rowling never published another word of her writing, her fame would still be cemented by her *Harry Potter* novels.

What do these people share in common besides their celebrity and notable achievements? Each of them suffered from some form of mental illness that impacted their lives to a greater or lesser extent. Syd Barrett and John Nash both battled schizophrenia, a brain disorder that can lead to erratic behavior and strained interpersonal relationships. Howard Hughes showed classic signs of obsessive–compulsive disorder, often micromanaging details of his and others' lives to the smallest degree. Hughes also lived as a recluse, something that J. D. Salinger did for the last 60 of his 91 years on this planet. Ricky Williams also sought isolation as the effects of his social anxiety disorder grew worse. Catherine Zeta-Jones has struggled with bipolar disorder, a condition that involves periods of both agitated excitement and deep depression. Robin Williams and Buzz Aldrin wrestled with both substance abuse and, as did J. K. Rowling, bouts of depression. In fact, Rowling's depiction of the Dementors is reportedly based on her experience with depression: sucking the life out of victims who feel they'll never be happy again.

Most psychological problems are far less newsworthy and far more common than the public's impression of them. Some people go through episodes of complete inability to function yet get along fine between those episodes. Some people function adequately every day yet suffer constant melancholy, always feeling below par. And some people cannot control their worries or tempers. In this chapter, you will learn about the many psychological problems that cause people unhappiness and anguish, as well as about the severe disorders that make people unable to control their behavior. But be forewarned: One of the most common worries that people have is "Am I normal?" It is normal to fear being abnormal, especially when you are reading about psychological problems! But it is also normal to have problems. All of us occasionally have difficulties that seem too much to handle, and it is often unclear precisely when "normal" problems shade into "abnormal" ones.

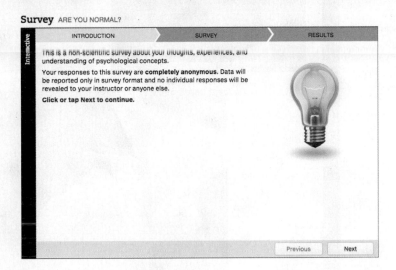

Survey ARE YOU NORMAL?

| INTRODUCTION | SURVEY | RESULTS |

This is a non-scientific survey about your thoughts, experiences, and understanding of psychological concepts.

Your responses to this survey are **completely anonymous**. Data will be reported only in survey format and no individual responses will be revealed to your instructor or anyone else.

Click or tap Next to continue.

Previous   Next

Diagnosing Mental Disorders

Many people confuse unusual behavior—behavior that deviates from the norm—with mental disorder, but the two are not the same. A person may behave in ways that are statistically rare (collecting ceramic dolphins, being a genius at math, committing murder) without having a mental illness. Conversely, some mental disorders, such as depression and anxiety, are extremely common. People also confuse mental disorder and insanity. In the law, the definition of insanity rests primarily on whether a person is aware of the consequences of his or her actions and can control his or her behavior. But *insanity* is a legal term only; a person may have a mental illness and yet be considered sane by the court.

Dilemmas of Definition

LO 15.1.A Consider why it is difficult to obtain a universally agreed-upon definition of "mental disorder."

If frequency of the problem is not a guide, and if insanity reflects only one extreme kind of mental illness, how then should we define a "mental disorder"? Diagnosing mental problems is not as straightforward as diagnosing medical problems such as diabetes or appendicitis. One leading definition, which takes evolutionary factors and social values into account, is that a mental disorder is a "harmful dysfunction." That is, it involves behavior or an emotional state that is (1) *harmful* to oneself or others, as judged by the community or culture in which it occurs, and (2) *dysfunctional* because it is not performing its evolutionary function (Wakefield, 2006, 2011). Evolution has prepared us to feel afraid when we are in danger, so that we can escape; dysfunction occurs when this normal alarm mechanism fails to turn off after the danger is past. If the behavior is not troubling to the individual or harmful to society, it is not a mental disorder. Conversely, if the behavior *is* harmful or undesirable, such as illiteracy and delinquency, it is still not necessarily a mental disorder if an evolutionary function isn't involved.

What is a mental disorder? In Papua New Guinea, young men go through an initiation rite in which small, deep cuts are made on their backs to create permanent scars that signify a crocodile's scales (top left). This common cultural practice would not be defined as a disorder. In contrast, most people would agree that a woman who mutilates herself for the sole purpose of inflicting injury and pain, as the patient in the upper right photo has done, has a mental disorder. But what about the scars on the arm of the 23-year-old woman (bottom center) who had them made by a "body artist"? She also has scars on her leg and her stomach, along with 29 piercings. Does she have a mental disorder?

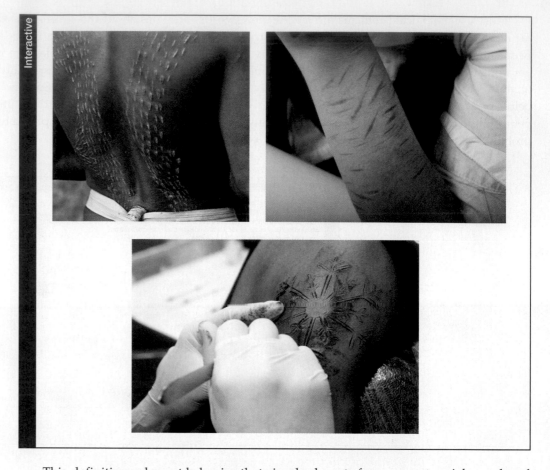

mental disorder

Any behavior or emotional state that causes an individual great suffering, is self-destructive, seriously impairs the person's ability to work or get along with others, or makes a person unable to control the impulse to endanger others.

This definition rules out behavior that simply departs from current social or cultural notions of what is healthy or normal: A student might think that getting tattoos all over his body is totally cool, but if his parents disagree, they don't get to accuse him of having a mental disorder! However, the definition does include the behavior of people who think they are perfectly fine yet who cause enormous harm to themselves or others, such as a child who is unable to control the desire to set fires, compulsive gamblers who lose the family's savings, or people who hear voices telling them to stalk a celebrity day and night.

The main criticism of defining mental disorder as "harmful dysfunction" is that it is often unclear what the evolutionary function or underlying pathology of a particular harmful behavior or emotional state might be. In this chapter, therefore, we define **mental disorder** as any condition that causes a person to suffer, is self-destructive, seriously impairs a person's ability to work or get along with others, or makes a person unable to control the impulse to endanger others. By this definition, many people will have some mental health problem in the course of their lives. To find out how psychologists define a mental disorder, watch the video *What Does It Mean to Have a Mental Disorder?*

Dilemmas of Diagnosis

LO 15.1.B Describe four dangers associated with using the DSM for diagnosis of mental disorders, and give an example of each.

Even with a general definition of mental disorder, classifying mental disorders into distinct categories is not an easy job. In this section, we will see why this is so.

CLASSIFYING DISORDERS: THE DSM   The standard reference manual used to diagnose mental disorders is the *Diagnostic and Statistical Manual of Mental Disorders (DSM)*, published by the American Psychiatric Association (2013). The DSM's primary aim is *descriptive*: to provide clear diagnostic categories so that clinicians and researchers can agree on which disorders they are talking about and then can study and treat these disorders. Its diverse diagnostic categories include attention-deficit disorders, disorders due to brain damage from disease or drugs, eating disorders, problems with sexual identity or behavior, impulse-control disorders (such as violent rages and pathological gambling or stealing), personality disorders, and sleep–wake disorders, along with other major disorders we will discuss in this chapter.

The DSM lists the symptoms of each disorder and, wherever possible, gives information about the typical age of onset, predisposing factors, course of the disorder, prevalence of the disorder, sex ratio of those affected, and cultural issues that might affect diagnosis. In making a diagnosis, clinicians are encouraged to take into account many factors, such as the client's personality traits, medical conditions, stresses at work or home, and the duration and severity of the problem (Caspi et al., 2014; Galatzer-Levy & Bryant, 2013).

The DSM has had an extraordinary impact worldwide. Virtually all textbooks in psychiatry and psychology base their discussions of mental disorders on the DSM. With each new edition of the manual, the number of mental disorders has grown. The first edition, published in 1952, was only 86 pages long and contained about 100 diagnoses. The DSM-IV, published in 1994 and slightly revised in 2000, is 900 pages long and contains nearly 400 diagnoses of mental disorder. The DSM-5, published in 2013, is 947 pages and contains about the same number of diagnoses.

What is the reason for this explosion of mental disorders? A primary reason is economic: Insurance companies require clinicians to assign their clients an appropriate DSM code number for whatever the client's problem is, which puts pressure on compilers of the manual to add more diagnoses so that physicians and psychologists will be compensated and patients will be covered (Zur & Nordmarken, 2008).

The DSM affects you in ways you probably can't imagine. Its influence is reflected in the casual way that people today talk of someone's being "bipolar," having "a touch of Asperger's," "being a borderline," or suffering from posttraumatic stress disorder (PTSD). As we will see, some of its diagnostic categories became cultural fads that spread like wildfire, causing much harm before the fires were extinguished. Because of the DSM's powerful influence, therefore, we want you to understand its limitations and some of the problems that are built into the effort to classify and label mental disorders.

1. **The danger of overdiagnosis.** If you give a young child a hammer, the old saying goes, it will turn out that everything he runs into needs pounding. Likewise, say critics, if you give mental health professionals a diagnostic label, it will turn out that everyone they run into has the symptoms of the new disorder.

    Consider attention-deficit/hyperactivity disorder (ADHD), a diagnosis given to children and adults who are impulsive, messy, restless, and easily frustrated and who have trouble concentrating. Since ADHD was added to the DSM, the number of cases has skyrocketed in the United States, where it is diagnosed at least 10 times as often as it is in Europe. Critics fear that parents, teachers, and mental health professionals are overdiagnosing this condition, especially in boys, who make up 80–90 percent of all ADHD cases. The critics argue that normal boyish behavior—being rambunctious, refusing to nap, being playful, not listening to teachers in school—has been turned into a psychological problem (Cummings & O'Donohue, 2008; Panksepp, 1998). A longitudinal study of more than a hundred 4- to 6-year-olds found that the number of children who met the criteria for ADHD declined as the children got older (Lahey et al., 2005). Those who

If you've ever watched a group of boys, you know that they can often be impulsive, messy, and restless. Those qualities are also part of the diagnosis of ADHD. How would you distinguish between normal boisterous boy behavior and a clinical diagnosis? Does having a diagnostic label available make it easier to apply a diagnosis when one might not be called for?

truly had the disorder remained highly impulsive and unable to concentrate, but others simply matured. Now ADHD is being overdiagnosed in adults as well. Have trouble concentrating? Bored? You could get diagnosed with ADHD (Frances, 2013).

In children, an alarming example of overdiagnosis involves bipolar disorder, which occurs primarily in adolescents and adults. Childhood bipolar disorder (CBD), a diagnosis that was based on small, inconclusive studies, was promoted by one psychiatrist who received multimillion-dollar payments from a pharmaceutical company that makes a powerful, risky antipsychotic drug often prescribed for the disorder (Greenberg, 2008). As soon as "childhood bipolar disorder" had a name, the number of diagnoses rose from 20,000 to 800,000 in just 1 year (Leibenluft & Rich, 2008; Moreno et al., 2007). "The CBD fad is the most shameful episode in my forty-five years of observing psychiatry," wrote Allen Frances (2013), an eminent psychiatrist who directed revision of the DSM-IV; the DSM-5 removed this diagnosis.

2. **The power of diagnostic labels.** After a person has been given a diagnosis, other people begin to see that person primarily in terms of the label and overlook other possible explanations. When a rebellious, disobedient teenager is diagnosed as having "oppositional-defiant disorder" or a child is labeled as having "disruptive mood dysregulation disorder," people tend to regard those problems as being inherent in the individual. But maybe the teenager is "defiant" because he has been mistreated or his parents don't listen to him, and maybe the child has "disruptive" temper outbursts because his parents are not setting limits. And after a teenager or child is labeled, observers tend to ignore changes in his or her behavior, all the times the teenager is not being defiant or the child is getting along fine without having tantrums.

On the other hand, many people welcome having a diagnostic label applied to them. Being given a diagnosis reassures those who are seeking an explanation for their emotional symptoms or those of their children ("Whew! So *that's* what it is!"). Some people even come to identify themselves according to a diagnosis and make it a central focus of their lives. Many people with Asperger's syndrome have established websites and support groups and have even adopted a nickname ("Aspies"). What happens, then, when the label vanishes? The DSM-5 has removed Asperger's as a specific diagnosis, enfolding it into the spectrum of autism disorders, over the protests of many people who want the label.

3. **The confusion of serious mental disorders with normal problems.** The DSM is not called "The Diagnostic and Statistical Manual of Mental Disorders and a Whole Bunch of Everyday Problems." Yet each edition of the DSM has added more everyday problems, including, in DSM-5, "caffeine intoxication" and "parent–child relational problem." Some critics fear that by lumping together normal difficulties with true mental illnesses, such as schizophrenia and major depression, the DSM implies that everyday problems are comparable to serious mental disorders (Houts, 2002).

A related concern is that the DSM-5 has loosened the criteria needed for making a diagnosis, thereby increasing the number of people who can be labeled with a disorder. The DSM-5 has added binge-eating disorder, whose symptoms include "eating until feeling uncomfortably full" or "when not feeling physically hungry." Who would not receive this diagnosis on occasion? One of the most vehement protests regarding DSM-5 changes was on just this issue of moving the goalposts for a diagnosis. In the past, people who were grieving over the death of a loved one were not considered to have clinical depression unless the grief became prolonged or incapacitating. However, the DSM-5 removed the "bereavement exemption" from diagnoses of major depression. This change outraged many mental health professionals, who objected to the blurring of the symptoms of normal bereavement with those of severe depression (Greenberg, 2008). To the editors of the DSM-5, depression is depression, whatever generates it. To the protesters, this change turns an understandable and universal reason for human sorrow into a mental disorder (Horwitz & Wakefield, 2007).

4. **The illusion of objectivity.** Finally, some psychologists argue that the whole enterprise of the DSM is a vain attempt to impose a veneer of science on an inherently subjective process (Gomory et al., 2011; Horwitz & Grob, 2011; Houts, 2002; Kutchins & Kirk, 1997;

Tiefer, 2004). Many decisions about what to include as a disorder, say these critics, are based not on empirical evidence but on group consensus. The problem is that group consensus often reflects prevailing attitudes and prejudices rather than objective evidence. It is easy to see how prejudice operated in the past. In the early years of the 19th century, a physician argued that many slaves were suffering from *drapetomania*, an urge to escape from slavery (Landrine, 1988). (He made up the word from *drapetes*, the Latin word for "runaway slave," and *mania*, meaning "mad" or "crazy.") Thus, doctors could assure slave owners that a mental illness, not the intolerable condition of slavery, made slaves seek freedom. This diagnosis was very convenient for slave owners. Today, of course, we know that "drapetomania" was foolish and cruel.

Harriet Tubman (on the left) poses with some of the people she helped to escape from slavery on her "Underground Railroad." Slaveholders welcomed the idea that Tubman and others who insisted on their freedom had a mental disorder called "drapetomania."

Over the years, psychiatrists have quite properly rejected many other "disorders" that reflected cultural prejudices, such as lack of vaginal orgasm, childhood masturbation disorder, and homosexuality. But critics argue that some DSM diagnoses continue to be affected by prejudices and values, as when clinicians try to decide if wanting to have sex "too often"

CULTURE and *Mental Illness*

Researchers are making great progress in separating mental disorders that are universal—usually involving genetic vulnerabilities, brain disease, or brain damage—from those that are specific to particular cultural contexts, norms, and traditions. In response to critics who argue that almost all diagnoses of mental disorder are matters of consensus, clinicians point out that certain disorders occur everywhere. From the Inuit of Alaska to the Pacific Islanders to the Yoruba of Nigeria, some individuals have schizophrenic delusions, are severely depressed, cannot control their aggressive behavior, or have panic attacks (Butcher, Lim, & Nezami, 1998; Kleinman, 1988).

However, culture does influence and shape the particular symptoms a sufferer of these disorders will have. In Latin America and southern Europe, a person having a panic attack may report feelings of choking, being smothered, and fear of dying. In the United States, the fear of "going crazy" is a more common symptom than elsewhere. In Greenland, some fishermen suffer from "kayak-angst," a sudden attack of dizziness and fear that occurs while they are fishing in small, one-person kayaks (Amering & Katschnig, 1990). The symptoms of posttraumatic stress disorder have taken different forms in the aftermath of wars and disasters all over the world. Although some physiological symptoms of stress are universal, soldiers respond to cultural expectations of how they should feel during and after a war. Sometimes the stress is expressed as "shell shock" (World War I), physical illness such as paralysis or the feeling of having a weak heart (the Civil War), or emotional distress such as uncontrollable anxiety (the Vietnam and Iraq wars) (Watters, 2011). Depression also occurs all over the world, but members of various ethnic groups differ in what symptoms they express (e.g., drinking, crying, withdrawing), in their willingness to talk about their feelings and seek help, and in the likelihood of committing suicide. In the United States, a group among the highest risk of suicide is American Indian men, and the group at lowest risk is African American women (Goldston et al., 2008).

The DSM-IV and DSM-5 both made a concerted effort to recognize the influence of culture on mental disorders and their diagnoses. The DSM-5 discusses three culture-related concepts:

- *Cultural syndrome*, a set of symptoms specific to the culture in which they occur. For example, Latinos may experience an *ataque de nervios*, an episode of uncontrollable screaming, crying, and agitation. In Japan, *taijin kyofusho* describes an intense fear that the body, its parts, or its functions displease, embarrass, or are offensive to others.

- *Cultural idiom of distress*, a linguistic term or way of talking about suffering among people in a cultural group. For example, the Shona of Zimbabwe have *kufungisisa*, "thinking too much"—ruminating on upsetting thoughts and worries.

- *Cultural explanation of symptoms*, something like a culture's own diagnostic system. For example, in Haiti, *maladi moun* ("humanly caused illness") is used to explain various medical and psychological disturbances: Illness is caused by other people's envy and malice.

By comparing mental and emotional symptoms across different times and places, researchers can distinguish universal disorders from those that are cultural syndromes. One meta-analysis found that bulimia nervosa, involving cycles of binge eating and vomiting to maintain weight, is a cultural syndrome that occurs primarily in the United States and is unknown in most other parts of the world. Yet anorexia nervosa, a body image disorder in which the sufferer usually feels "too fat" even at the point of starving to death, has been found throughout history and across cultures (Keel & Klump, 2003).

projective tests

Psychological tests used to infer a person's motives, conflicts, and unconscious dynamics on the basis of the person's interpretations of ambiguous stimuli.

or "not often enough" indicates a mental disorder (Wakefield, 2011). Emotional problems allegedly associated with menstruation remain in the DSM-5, but behavioral problems associated with testosterone have never been considered for inclusion. In short, critics maintain, many diagnoses continue to stem from cultural biases about what constitutes normal or appropriate behavior.

Supporters of the DSM maintain that it is important to help clinicians distinguish among disorders that share certain symptoms, such as anxiety, irritability, or delusions, so they can be diagnosed reliably and treated properly. And they fully acknowledge that the boundaries between "normal problems" and "mental disorders" are fuzzy and often difficult to determine (Helzer et al., 2008; McNally, 2011). That is why the DSM-5 editors decided to classify many disorders along a spectrum of symptoms, and in degrees from mild to severe, rather than as discrete categories.

Dilemmas of Determination

LO 15.1.C Explain the theoretical basis of projective tests, and identify the problems associated with these techniques.

Clinical psychologists and psychiatrists usually arrive at a diagnosis by interviewing a patient and observing the person's behavior when he or she arrives at the office, hospital, or clinic. But many also use psychological tests to help them determine a diagnosis. Such tests are also commonly used in schools (e.g., to determine whether a child has a learning disorder) and in court settings (e.g., to try to determine which parent should have custody in a divorce case, whether a child has been sexually abused, or whether a defendant is mentally competent).

PROJECTIVE TESTS **Projective tests** consist of ambiguous pictures, sentences, or stories that the test taker interprets or completes. A child or adult may be asked to draw a person, a house, or some other object, or to finish a sentence (such as "My father . . . " or "Women are . . . "). The psychodynamic assumption behind projective tests is that the person's unconscious feelings will be "projected" onto the test and revealed in the person's responses.

Projective tests can help clinicians establish rapport with their clients and can encourage clients to open up about anxieties and conflicts they might be ashamed to discuss. But the evidence is overwhelming that these tests lack reliability and validity, which makes them inappropriate for their most common uses—assessing personality traits or diagnosing mental disorders. They lack reliability because different clinicians often interpret the same person's scores differently, perhaps projecting their own beliefs and assumptions when they decide what a specific response means. The tests have low validity because they fail to measure what they are supposed to measure (Hunsley, Lee, & Wood, 2015). One reason is that responses to a projective test are significantly affected by sleepiness, hunger, medication, worry, verbal ability, the clinician's instructions, the clinician's personality (friendly and warm, or cool and remote), and other events occurring that day.

One of the most popular projectives is the *Rorschach inkblot test*, which was devised by Swiss psychiatrist Hermann Rorschach in 1921. It consists of 10 cards with symmetrical abstract patterns, originally formed by spilling ink on a piece of paper and folding it in half. The test taker reports what she or he sees in the inkblots, and the clinician interprets the answers according to the symbolic meanings emphasized by psychodynamic theories. Although the Rorschach is widely used among clinicians, efforts to confirm its reliability and validity have repeatedly failed. The Rorschach does not reliably diagnose depression, post-traumatic stress reactions, personality disorders, or serious mental disorders. Claims of the Rorschach's success often come from testimonials at workshops where clinicians are taught how to use the test, which is hardly an impartial way of assessing it (Wood et al., 2003).

Many psychotherapists and clinical social workers use projective tests with young children to help them express feelings they cannot reveal verbally. But during the 1980s, some of them began using projective methods for another purpose: to determine whether a child had been sexually abused. They claimed they could identify a child who had been abused by

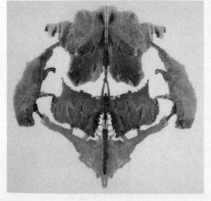
A Rorschach inkblot. What do you see in it?

observing how the child played with "anatomically detailed" dolls (dolls with realistic genitals), and that is how many of them testified in hundreds of court cases (Ceci & Bruck, 1995).

Unfortunately, these therapists had not tested their beliefs by using a fundamental scientific procedure: comparison with a control group. They had not asked, "How do *nonabused* children play with these dolls?" When psychological scientists conducted controlled research to answer this question, they found that large percentages of nonabused children are also fascinated with the doll's genitals. They will poke at them, grab them, pound sticks into a female doll's vagina, and do other things that alarm adults. The crucial conclusion was that you cannot reliably diagnose sexual abuse on the basis of children's doll play (Bruck, Ceci, & Francoeur, 2000; Hunsley, Lee, & Wood, 2015; Koocher et al., 1995). Over the years, clinicians have therefore devised other kinds of "props" and toys that they hope will facilitate children's reporting of having been molested. Unfortunately, studies involving alleged abuse victims, children who have been through medical exams, and children who have participated in lab experiments have failed to find consistent evidence that props improve young children's ability to make accurate reports. On the contrary, these props actually elevate the risk of false reports of touch (Poole, Bruck, & Pipe, 2011). You can see how someone who does not understand the problems with projective tests, or who lacks an understanding of children's cognitive limitations, might make inferences about a child's behavior that are dangerously wrong.

Another situation in which projective tests are used widely but often inappropriately is in child custody assessments because judges long for an objective way to determine which parent is better suited to have custody. But when a panel of psychological scientists impartially examined the leading psychological assessment measures, most of which are projective tests, they found that "these measures assess ill-defined constructs, and they do so poorly, leaving no scientific justification for their use in child custody evaluations" (Emery, Otto, & O'Donohue, 2005).

For years, many therapists used anatomically detailed dolls as a projective test to determine whether a child had been sexually abused. But the empirical evidence, including studies of nonabused children in a control group, shows that this practice is simply not valid. It can lead to false allegations because it often misidentifies nonabused children who are merely fascinated with the dolls' genitals.

OBJECTIVE TESTS   Many clinicians use **objective tests (inventories)**, standardized questionnaires that ask about the test taker's behavior and feelings. Inventories are generally more reliable and valid than either projective methods or subjective clinical judgments (Dawes, 1994; Meyer et al., 2001). The leading objective test of major depression is the Beck Depression Inventory and the most widely used diagnostic assessment for personality and emotional disorders is the *Minnesota Multiphasic Personality Inventory (MMPI)*. The MMPI is organized into 10 categories, or *scales*, covering such problems as depression, paranoia, schizophrenia, and introversion. Four additional *validity scales* indicate whether a test taker is likely to be lying, defensive, or evasive while answering the items.

Inventories are only as good as their questions and how knowledgeably they are interpreted. Some test items on the MMPI fail to consider differences among cultural, regional, and socioeconomic groups. For instance, Mexican, Puerto Rican, and Argentine respondents score differently from non–Hispanic Americans, on average, on the Masculinity–Femininity Scale. This difference does not reflect emotional problems but traditional Latino attitudes toward sex roles (Cabiya et al., 2000). Also, the MMPI sometimes labels a person's responses as evidence of mental disorder when they are a result of understandable stresses and conflicts, such as during divorce or other legal disputes, when participants are upset and angry (Guthrie & Mobley, 1994; Leib, 2008). However, testing experts continue to improve the reliability and validity of the MMPI in clinical assessment, restructuring the clinical scales to reflect current research on mental disorders and personality traits (Butcher & Perry, 2008; Sellbom, Ben-Porath, & Bagby, 2008).

We turn now to a closer examination of some of the disorders described in the DSM. Because we cannot cover all of them in one chapter, we have singled out several that illustrate the range of psychological problems that afflict humanity, from the common to the very rare.

objective tests (inventories)
Standardized objective questionnaires requiring written responses; they typically include scales on which people are asked to rate themselves.

JOURNAL PROMPT 15.1

Thinking Critically—Define Your Terms: The study of psychological disorders is often called abnormal psychology, which literally means "deviating from what is normal or usual." Why is the term "abnormal psychology" insufficient to capture what's included in this area of study? Can a person behave abnormally yet not be disordered? Can you think of examples from your own behavior when you've "deviated from what is normal or usual," without feeling you were in danger of being clinically diagnosed?

Quiz for Module 15.1

1. According to the authors' definition of a mental disorder, which of these features is *not* a defining element?

   a. The condition seriously impairs the person's ability to work or get along with others.

   b. The condition is unusual or atypical for that person's reference group.

   c. The condition is self-destructive.

   d. The condition causes the person to suffer.

2. The primary purpose of the DSM is to

   a. Keep the number of diagnostic categories of mental disorders to a minimum

   b. Help psychologists assess normal as well as abnormal behavior

   c. Describe the causes of common disorders

   d. Provide descriptive criteria for diagnosing mental disorders

3. Which of the following is a potential limitation associated with using the DSM?

   a. A lack of descriptive information for identifying disorders

   b. Lacking general acceptance within the field of psychology

   c. Underdiagnosing the prevalence of mental disorders

   d. Confusing serious mental disorders with normal problems

4. Emily was diagnosed with a serious mental illness. What is an appropriate way to describe her condition, being mindful of the pitfalls and promises of the DSM?

   a. Emily is a person with schizophrenia.

   b. Emily is a schizophrenic.

   c. Emily is insane.

   d. Emily is a mental patient.

5. Giovanni is shown a series of ambiguous figures made from splotches of ink, and he's asked to identify what he sees in each one. "The first one is an elephant," replied Giovanni. "The next one is a picture of an elephant. That one? An elephant. This one is an elephant, too. Here . . . I see an elephant, from the rear. And this last one looks a little like an elephant." "Ah," murmured the therapist, "Plainly this man has issues with dominance, superiority, and hierarchy. He rebels against authority and is likely to injure animals if given a chance." What are the therapist's conclusions based on?

   a. Giovanni's responses to a standardized inventory of objective questions.

   b. Empirically based psychodynamic theory.

   c. Giovanni's responses to an unreliable and invalid projective test.

   d. The reliable measurement of hidden inner conflicts; in this case, proboscidean angst.

Anxiety Disorders

Anyone who is waiting for important news or living in an unpredictable situation quite sensibly feels anxiety, a general state of apprehension or psychological tension. And anyone who is in a dangerous and unfamiliar situation, such as making a first parachute jump or facing a peevish python, quite sensibly feels flat-out fear. In the short run, these emotions are adaptive because they energize us to cope with danger. They ensure that we don't make that first jump without knowing how to operate the parachute, and that we get away from that snake as fast as we can.

But sometimes fear and anxiety become detached from any actual danger, or these feelings continue even when danger and uncertainty are past. The result may be *generalized anxiety disorder*, marked by long-lasting feelings of apprehension and doom; *panic attacks*, short-lived but intense feelings of anxiety; or *phobias*, excessive fears of specific things or situations.

Anxiety and Panic

LO 15.2.A Differentiate the major symptoms of generalized anxiety disorder and panic disorder.

The chief characteristic of **generalized anxiety disorder** is excessive, uncontrollable anxiety or worry—a feeling of foreboding and dread—that occurs on a majority of days during a 6-month period and that is not brought on by physical causes such as disease, drugs, or drinking too much coffee.

Some people suffer from generalized anxiety disorder without having lived through any specific anxiety-producing event. They may have a genetic predisposition to experience its symptoms—sweaty palms, a racing heart, shortness of breath—when they are in unfamiliar or uncontrollable situations. Genes may also be involved in causing abnormalities in the amygdala, the core structure for the acquisition of fear, and in the prefrontal cortex, which is associated with the ability to realize when danger has passed (Lonsdorf et al., 2009). But anxiety disorders may also stem from experience: Some chronically anxious people have a history, starting in childhood, of being unable to control or predict their environments (Barlow, 2000; Mineka & Zinbarg, 2006). Whatever the origin of generalized anxiety disorder, its sufferers have mental biases in the way they attend to and process threatening information. They perceive everything as an opportunity for disaster, a cognitive habit that fuels their anxiety and keeps it bubbling along (Boswell et al., 2013; Mitte, 2008). Learn more about anxiety disorders by watching the video *Living With a Disorder 1*.

generalized anxiety disorder

A continuous state of anxiety marked by feelings of worry and dread, apprehension, difficulties in concentration, and signs of motor tension.

panic disorder

An anxiety disorder in which a person experiences recurring panic attacks, periods of intense fear, and feelings of impending doom or death, accompanied by physiological symptoms such as rapid heart rate and dizziness.

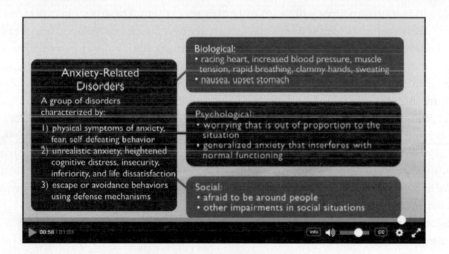

PANIC DISORDER   Another kind of anxiety disorder is **panic disorder**, in which a person has recurring attacks of intense fear or panic, often with feelings of impending doom or death. Panic attacks may last from a few minutes to (more rarely) several hours. Symptoms include trembling and shaking, dizziness, chest pain or discomfort, rapid heart rate, feelings of unreality, hot and cold flashes, sweating, and—as a result of all these scary physical reactions—a fear of dying, going crazy, or losing control. Many sufferers fear they are having a heart attack.

Although panic attacks seem to come out of nowhere, they in fact usually occur in the aftermath of stress, prolonged emotion, specific worries, or frightening experiences. A friend of ours was on a plane that was a target of a bomb threat while airborne at 33,000 feet. He coped beautifully at the time, but 2 weeks later, seemingly out of nowhere, he had a panic attack. Such delayed attacks after life-threatening scares are common.

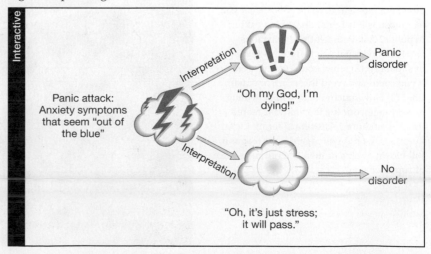

phobia

An exaggerated, unrealistic fear of a specific situation, activity, or object.

agoraphobia

A set of phobias, often set off by a panic attack, involving the basic fear of being away from a safe place or person.

The essential difference between people who develop panic disorder and those who do not lies in how they *interpret* their bodily reactions (Barlow, 2000; Bentley et al., 2013). Healthy people who have occasional panic attacks see them correctly as a result of a passing crisis or period of stress, comparable to another person's migraines. But people who develop panic disorder regard the attack as a sign of illness or impending death, and they begin to live their lives in restrictive ways, trying to avoid future attacks.

Fears and Phobias

LO 15.2.B Describe the characteristics of a phobia, and explain why agoraphobia can be so disabling.

Are you afraid of bugs, snakes, or dogs? Are you vaguely uncomfortable or so afraid that you can't stand to be around one? A **phobia** is an exaggerated fear of a specific situation, activity, or thing. Some common phobias—such as fear of snakes, insects, heights (acrophobia), or being trapped in enclosed spaces (claustrophobia)—may have evolved to be easily acquired in human beings because these fears reflected real dangers for the species. Some fears, as of the number 13 (triskaidekaphobia), may reflect idiosyncratic experiences or cultural traditions. Whatever its source, a true *phobia* is frightening and often incapacitating for its sufferer. It is not just a tendency to say "ugh" at tarantulas or skip the snake display at the zoo.

People who have a *social phobia* become extremely anxious in situations in which they will be observed by others—eating in a restaurant, speaking in public, having to perform for an audience. They worry that they will do or say something that will be excruciatingly embarrassing and that other people will laugh at them or reject them. These phobias are more severe forms of the occasional shyness and social anxiety that everyone experiences. For people with a social phobia, the mere thought of being in a new situation with unfamiliar people is scary enough to cause sweating, trembling, nausea, and an overwhelming feeling of inadequacy. So they don't go, increasing their isolation and imagined fears.

By far the most disabling fear disorder is **agoraphobia**. In ancient Greece, the *agora* was the social, political, business, and religious center of town, the public meeting place away from home. The fundamental fear in agoraphobia is panic and its imagined disastrous consequences—being trapped in a public place, where escape might be difficult or where help might be unavailable. Individuals with agoraphobia report many specific fears—of being in a crowded movie theater, driving in traffic or tunnels, or going to parties—but the underlying fear is of being away from a safe place, usually home, or a safe person, usually a parent or partner.

Agoraphobia typically begins with a panic attack that seems to have no cause. The attack is so unexpected and scary that the agoraphobic-to-be begins to avoid situations that he or she thinks may provoke another one. A woman we know had a panic attack while driving on a

What scares you? Everyone fears something. Stop for a moment to think about what you fear most. Is it heights? Snakes? Speaking in public? Ask yourself these questions: (1) How long have you feared this thing or situation? (2) How would you respond if you could not avoid this thing or situation? (3) How much would you be willing to rearrange your life to avoid this feared thing or situation? After considering these questions, would you regard your fear as a full-blown phobia or merely a normal source of apprehension?

freeway. This was a perfectly normal posttraumatic response to the suicide of her husband a few weeks earlier. But thereafter she avoided freeways, as if the freeway, and not the suicide, had caused the attack. Because so many of the actions associated with agoraphobia arise as a mistaken effort to avoid a panic attack, psychologists regard agoraphobia as a "fear of fear" rather than simply a fear of places.

JOURNAL PROMPT 15.2

Thinking Critically—Define Your Terms: There are many scary and/or aversive situations in life, such as being stuck in a pit full of rattlesnakes, hearing the pilot say, "Folks, thanks for flying with us on your very final trip," or making a visit to the dentist's office. But what separates reasonable fear from a debilitating phobia? Sometimes fearing the thing you fear is exactly the correct response; the thing you fear might kill you. In other cases, the thing you fear has no fearful properties whatsoever. So where's the dividing line between a normal and expected response, and a phobic one?

Quiz for Module 15.2

1. A continuous state of dread, apprehension, motor tension, and difficulties concentrating is characteristic of
   a. Panic attacks
   b. Generalized anxiety disorder
   c. Panic disorder
   d. Major depression

2. Bo was relaxing with friends one night when he suddenly felt sweaty, clammy, and as though his heart was going to beat right out of his chest. As a young man he was shocked to think he was having a heart attack, and his friends called 911 straight away. The paramedics conducted a thorough battery of tests and assured him his heart was in perfect shape. What diagnosis did they offer instead?
   a. Generalized anxiety disorder
   b. Narcissistic personality disorder
   c. Seizure disorder
   d. Panic attack

3. What is a key factor in the development of panic disorder?
   a. Cultural differences in the value placed on regular mental health checks
   b. How people interpret their bodily reactions associated with stress and anxiety
   c. A predisposition to mood disorders
   d. Whether the individual experienced significant childhood trauma

4. Georgette has an intense fear of cheese. It's not that she doesn't like the taste, and it's not as though she ever has to eat any; her diet can be varied and balanced without ever ingesting cheese. Yet she's really afraid of cheese—pictures of cheese, the sight and smell of cheese, and she hates when photographers cue her to smile. It's pretty clear that Georgette is suffering from
   a. Generalized anxiety disorder
   b. A phobia
   c. Panic attacks
   d. Panic disorder

5. Franklin Delano Roosevelt once famously intoned, "The only thing we have to fear is fear itself." He was speaking on the subject of current conditions in the United States during his first inaugural address as president, but inadvertently he could have also been describing the conditions surrounding
   a. Agoraphobia
   b. Bipolar disorder
   c. Generalized anxiety disorder
   d. Obsessive–compulsive disorder

Trauma and Obsessive–Compulsive Disorders

Stress symptoms are entirely normal in response to the usual problems and conflicts of life, and even in response to life's tragedies. Likewise, it's normal to go through times of being "obsessed" with some person or goal, and to follow small superstitious rituals. But sometimes these behaviors cross the line into disorders that affect a person's ability to function.

Posttraumatic Stress Disorder

LO 15.3.A Define posttraumatic stress disorder, and discuss its symptoms and origins.

posttraumatic stress disorder (PTSD)

A disorder in which a person who has experienced a traumatic or life-threatening event has symptoms such as nightmares, flashbacks, insomnia, reliving of the trauma, and increased physiological arousal.

Insomnia, flashbacks, agitation, and other signs of distress are understandable reactions to going through a crisis or trauma, such as war, rape, torture, natural disasters, sudden bereavement, or terrorist attacks. But if the symptoms persist for 1 month or longer and begin to impair a person's functioning, the sufferer may have **posttraumatic stress disorder (PTSD)**. Symptoms of PTSD include reliving the trauma in recurrent, intrusive thoughts, flashbacks, or nightmares; a sense of detachment from others and a loss of interest in familiar activities; and increased physiological arousal, reflected in insomnia, irritability, and impaired concentration. The video *Memories We Don't Want* provides more information about PTSD.

For years after the 9/11 attacks on the World Trade Center and Pentagon, many people have suffered PTSD symptoms, especially if they lost loved ones, were first responders, or lived or worked nearby (C. Maslow et al., 2015; Neria, DiGrande, & Adams, 2011). Yet most people who live through a traumatic experience eventually recover without developing PTSD, and the epidemic of PTSD that many experts predicted after 9/11 never materialized (Bonanno et al., 2010). Why, then, if most people recover, do some continue to have PTSD symptoms for years, sometimes for decades?

One answer, again, involves a genetic predisposition. Behavioral-genetic studies of twins in the general population and of combat veterans have found that PTSD symptoms have a heritable component (Stein et al., 2002; Yehuda et al., 2009). PTSD has also been linked to certain personality and mental characteristics that have a heritable component (Almli et al., 2015). A prospective study that followed children from their early years to about age 17 found that people who develop PTSD after a traumatic experience often have a prior history of psychological problems, such as anxiety and impulsive aggression. And some lack the social, psychological, and neurological resources to avoid having preventable traumatic experiences in the first place or to cope with unavoidable ones. In this study, the children with above-average IQs were less likely to develop PTSD after a trauma than the average-IQ children were, apparently because the high-IQ kids had better cognitive coping skills (Breslau, Lucia, & Alvarado, 2006).

Interestingly, in many PTSD sufferers, the hippocampus is smaller than average (O'Doherty et al., 2015). The hippocampus is crucially involved in autobiographical memory. An abnormally small one may figure in the difficulty of some trauma survivors to react to their memories as events from their past, which may be why they keep reliving them in the present. An MRI study of identical twins, only one of whom in each pair had been in combat in Vietnam, showed that two things were necessary for a veteran to develop chronic PTSD: serving in combat *and* having a smaller hippocampus than normal. Twins who had smaller hippocampi but no military service did not develop PTSD, and neither did the twins who *did* experience combat but who had normal-sized hippocampi (Gilbertson et al., 2002).

In sum, many cases of long-lasting PTSD seem to be a result of impaired cognitive and neurological functioning that existed before the trauma took place, making it more likely that the trauma will trigger persistent, long-lasting symptoms.

Obsessions and Compulsions

LO 15.3.B **Distinguish between obsessions and compulsions, and discuss the defining elements of obsessive–compulsive disorder.**

Obsessive–compulsive disorder (OCD) is characterized by recurrent, persistent, unwished-for thoughts or images (*obsessions*) and by repetitive, ritualized behaviors that the person feels must be carried out to avoid disaster (*compulsions*). Of course, many people have trivial compulsions and practice superstitious rituals. Baseball players are famous for them; one won't change his socks and another insists on eating chicken every day while he is on a hitting streak. Obsessions and compulsions become a disorder when they become uncontrollable and interfere with a person's life.

People who have obsessive thoughts often find them frightening or repugnant: thoughts of killing a child, of becoming contaminated by a handshake, or of having unknowingly hurt someone in a traffic accident. Obsessive thoughts take many forms, but they are alike in reflecting impaired ways of reasoning and processing information.

As for compulsions, the most common are handwashing, counting, touching, and checking. A woman *must* check the furnace, lights, locks, and oven three times before she can sleep; a man *must* run up and down the stairs 60 times in 10 minutes or else start over from the beginning. OCD sufferers usually realize that their behavior is senseless, and they are often tormented by their rituals. But if they try to resist the compulsion, they feel mounting anxiety that is relieved only by giving in to it. However, not all OCD patients can specify a disaster that they believe their rituals prevent; some develop rituals to reduce general feelings of distress.

In many people with OCD, abnormalities in an area of the prefrontal cortex create a kind of cognitive rigidity, an inability to let go of intrusive thoughts, and behavioral rigidity, an inability to alter compulsive behavior after getting negative feedback (Snyder et al., 2015). Normally, after danger has passed or a person realizes that there is no cause for fear, the brain's alarm signal turns off. In people with OCD, however, false alarms keep clanging and the emotional networks keep sending out mistaken fear messages (Schwartz et al., 1996). The sufferer feels in a constant state of danger and tries repeatedly to reduce the resulting anxiety.

The DSM-5 includes *hoarding disorder* in the larger category of obsessive–compulsive disorders (Slyne & Tolin, 2014). Pathological hoarders fill their homes with newspapers, bags of old clothing, used tissue boxes—all kinds of junk. They are tormented by fears of throwing out something they may need later. A PET-scan study that compared obsessive hoarders with other people with obsessive symptoms found that hoarders had less activity in parts of the brain involved in decision making, problem solving, spatial orientation, and memory (Saxena et al., 2004). Perhaps these deficits help explain why hoarders keep things (their inability to decide what to throw away creates a constant worry) and why they often keep their papers and junk in the living room, kitchen, or even on the bed (they have trouble remembering where things are and thus feel the need to have them in sight).

This grief-stricken soldier has just learned that the body bag on the flight with him contains the remains of a close friend who was killed in action. Understandably, many soldiers suffer posttraumatic stress symptoms. But why do most eventually recover, whereas others have PTSD for many years?

obsessive–compulsive disorder (OCD)

An anxiety disorder in which a person feels trapped in repetitive, persistent thoughts (*obsessions*) and repetitive, ritualized behaviors (*compulsions*).

JOURNAL PROMPT 15.3

Thinking Critically—Ask Questions; Be Willing to Wonder: Here's a curious finding: Most people who suffer through a significant trauma won't develop posttraumatic stress disorder. Why is that? In your answer be sure to address genetic, situational, personality, and cultural contributions to developing or not developing PTSD.

Quiz for Module 15.3

1. Randy was physically and emotionally abused as a child. He received unpredictable and vicious beatings at the hands of various relatives, and was made to spend long hours locked in a dark closet for alleged "crimes against God" in the eyes of his parents. Sadly, Randy developed a psychological disorder later in life, namely,

   a. PTSD

   b. Schizophrenia

   c. OCD

   d. Narcissistic personality disorder

2. What anatomical difference do many PTSD sufferers have compared to non-PTSD sufferers?

   a. A thinner occipital lobe

   b. A larger occipital lobe

   c. A larger hippocampus

   d. A smaller hippocampus

3. Musician Joey Ramone was well known to have many superstitions and rituals throughout his life: Having to walk up and down a flight of stairs multiple times before continuing to his destination; touching each doorknob three times before opening a door; having to walk in and out of doorways repeatedly upon entering a room. He was diagnosed with

   a. Borderline personality disorder

   b. Posttraumatic stress disorder

   c. Obsessive–compulsive disorder

   d. Generalized anxiety disorder

4. Fritz can't stop washing his hands; he does it 23 times a day. Violet can't stop thinking about when and how she's going to die; these thoughts plague her 18 times every hour. Fritz suffers from _____, whereas Violet suffers from _____.

   a. A personality disorder / a mood disorder

   b. An obsession / a compulsion

   c. A mood disorder / a personality disorder

   d. A compulsion / an obsession

5. Hoarding disorder is recognized in the DSM-5 as a subcategory of

   a. Obsessive–compulsive disorder

   b. Mood disorders

   c. Personality disorders

   d. Dissociative disorder

Depressive and Bipolar Disorders

In the DSM-5, *depressive disorders* include a number of conditions that can cause persistent sad, empty, or irritable moods, accompanied by physical and cognitive changes that affect the person's ability to function in everyday life. People often speak of feeling "depressed," and of course everyone feels sad from time to time. These feelings, however, are a far cry from serious clinical depression.

Depression

LO 15.4.A   Describe how major depression differs from normal feelings of sadness or loneliness.

Major depression involves emotional, behavioral, cognitive, and physical changes severe enough to disrupt a person's ordinary functioning. Some episodes can last as long as 20 weeks, subside, and later recur. People with major depression feel despairing and worthless. They feel unable to get up and do things; it takes an enormous effort even to get dressed. They may overeat or stop eating, have difficulty falling asleep or sleeping through the night, have trouble concentrating, and feel tired all the time. They lose interest in activities that usually give them satisfaction and pleasure.

One symptom of major depression is recurring thoughts of death, leading some sufferers to try to commit suicide. In the United States, suicide is the second leading cause of death among people ages 15 to 24, after accidents (Centers for Disease Control and Prevention, 2013). Most people with suicidal thoughts do not really want to die; they want relief from the terrible pain of feeling that nobody cares, that life is not worth living, that they have been failures to their families, and that they are a burden on those they love. One team of psychologists looked up the "warning signs of suicide" that can be found on the Internet. Of the 75

Long before she became famous for writing the *Harry Potter* books, J. K. Rowling suffered incapacitating depression. She contemplated suicide, but the need to remain alive for her infant daughter kept her from killing herself. Later, she told an interviewer that she was never ashamed of having been depressed. On the contrary, she said, she was proud of herself for getting through that difficult time.

supposed indicators they found, only two are central: feelings of hopelessness and perceived burdensomeness (Mandrusiak et al., 2006; van Orden et al., 2006).

Major depression occurs at least twice as often among women as among men, all over the world. However, because women are more likely than men to talk about their feelings and more likely to seek help, depression in males (who are more likely to commit suicide) is probably underdiagnosed. Men who are depressed often try to mask their feelings by withdrawing, abusing alcohol or other drugs, driving recklessly, or behaving violently (Canetto & Cleary, 2012). As Susan Nolen-Hoeksema, a leading depression researcher, put it, "Women think and men drink." The biological underpinnings of depression are discussed in the video *Depression*.

major depression

A disorder involving disturbances in emotion (excessive sadness), behavior (loss of interest in one's usual activities), cognition (thoughts of hopelessness), and body function (fatigue and loss of appetite).

bipolar disorder

A mood disorder in which episodes of both depression and mania (excessive euphoria) occur.

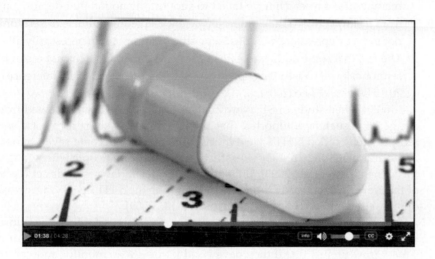

Bipolar Disorder

LO 15.4.B Explain the main features of bipolar disorder.

At the opposite pole from depression is *mania*, an abnormally high state of exhilaration. Mania is not the normal joy of being in love or winning the Pulitzer Prize. Instead of feeling fatigued and listless, a manic person is excessively wired and often irritable when thwarted. Instead of feeling hopeless and powerless, the person feels powerful and is full of plans; but these plans are usually based on delusional ideas, such as thinking that she or he has invented something that will solve the world's energy problems. People in a state of mania often get into terrible trouble, for example, by going on extravagant spending sprees or making rash decisions.

When people experience at least one episode of mania, typically alternating with episodes of depression, they are said to have **bipolar disorder** (formerly called *manic-depressive disorder*). The great humorist Mark Twain had bipolar disorder, which he described as "periodical and sudden changes of mood . . . from deep melancholy to half-insane tempests and cyclones." Other writers, artists, musicians, and scientists have also suffered from this disorder (Jamison, 1992). During the highs, many of these creative people produce their best work, but the price of the lows is disastrous relationships, bankruptcy, and sometimes suicide.

The DSM-5 has put bipolar disorders into their own category, as a bridge between depressive disorders and schizophrenia. The reason, as research is finding, is that symptoms and causes of bipolar disorder can overlap with those of depression and schizophrenia (and other disorders as well).

Origins of Depression

LO 15.4.C Discuss the four major factors that contribute to the onset of depression.

One of the great mysteries of depression is that most people who undergo a "depressing" experience do not become clinically depressed, and many people who are clinically depressed have not had objectively "depressing" experiences (Monroe & Reid, 2009). Most researchers thus emphasize a **vulnerability–stress model** of depression: how a person's vulnerabilities

vulnerability–stress model

Approaches that emphasize how individual vulnerabilities interact with external stresses or circumstances to produce specific mental disorders, such as depression.

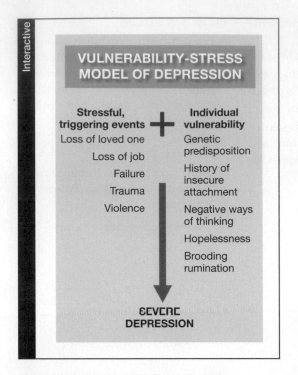

Figure 15.1 The Vulnerability–Stress Model of Depression

The vulnerability–stress model highlights the interplay between individual differences (in genetics, personality, or cognitive styles) and eliciting situations (stressful life events). The vulnerabilities by themselves may not lead to a diagnosable disorder, just as the stressful events may not be perceived as such by some individuals. But for some people with some vulnerabilities in some stressful situations, the outcome may be a disordered reaction, such as depression.

(genetic predispositions, personality traits, or habits of thinking) may interact with stressful events (e.g., violence, abuse, death of a loved one, or losing a job) to produce a given case (see Figure 15.1).

Let's consider the evidence for the central contributing factors to depression:

1. **Genetic predispositions.** Major depression is a moderately heritable disorder, so genes must be involved for some individuals. But so far the search for specific genes has been unsuccessful. One focus of investigation has been the genes that regulate serotonin, a neurotransmitter involved in mood. An early theory held that depression results from abnormally low levels of this neurotransmitter. However, many years of research have failed to support the notion that depression results from a simple neurotransmitter deficiency. Depleting animals of serotonin does not induce depression, nor does increasing brain serotonin necessarily alleviate it. The fact that some antidepressants raise serotonin levels does not mean that low serotonin levels caused the depression—a common but mistaken inference (Kirsch, 2010; Lacasse & Leo, 2005).

   In 2003, in a study of 847 New Zealanders who had been followed from birth to age 26, researchers reported that those who had a short form of a serotonin receptor gene called 5-HTT were much more likely to become severely depressed in the aftermath of extremely stressful events than were people with a long form of this gene (Caspi et al., 2003). But subsequent meta-analyses of direct replications of the New Zealand study found no links among the 5-HTT gene, life stresses, and depression (Duncan & Keller, 2011; Risch et al., 2009).

   Nonetheless, research into gene–environment interactions continues. Children who are at high genetic risk for developing depression (or aggressive disorders or alcohol abuse) may grow up just fine if they have good parents who monitor and control their children's vulnerabilities to these disorders (Dick et al., 2011; Dougherty et al., 2011). Moreover, the relative influence of genetic and environmental factors varies over the lifespan. A review of eight studies of identical twins found that although genetic predispositions predicted the twins' levels of depression and anxiety in childhood and young adulthood, by middle adulthood environmental factors and life experiences had become more powerful influences (Kendler et al., 2011).

2. **Violence, childhood physical abuse, and parental neglect.** One of the most powerful environmental factors associated with clinical depression is repeated experience with violence. Inner-city adolescents of both sexes who are exposed to high rates of violence in their families or communities report higher levels of depression and more attempts to commit suicide than those who are not subjected to constant violence (Mazza & Reynolds, 1999). The World Health Organization conducted a massive international research project in 21 countries, involving more than 100,000 people over age 18. In rich and poor countries alike, the strongest predictors of suicide and attempted suicide were repeated experiences of sexual abuse and violence in childhood and adolescence (Stein et al., 2010).

   The effects of maltreatment in childhood on later depression are independent of all other childhood and adult risk factors (Brown & Harris, 2008; Widom, DuMont, & Czaja, 2007). A mechanism that might explain this increased risk is that prolonged stress in childhood puts the body's responses to stress in overdrive, so that it overproduces the stress hormone cortisol (Gotlib et al., 2008). People who are depressed tend to have high levels of cortisol, which can affect the hippocampus and amygdala, causing mood and memory abnormalities.

   Among adults, domestic violence takes a particular toll on women. A longitudinal study that followed men and women from ages 18 to 26 compared those in physically abusive relationships with those in nonabusive ones. Although depressed women were more likely to enter abusive relationships to begin with, involvement in a violent relationship independently increased their rates of depression and anxiety—but, interestingly, not men's (Ehrensaft, Moffitt, & Caspi, 2006).

3. **Losses of important relationships.** A third line of investigation emphasizes the loss of important relationships in setting off depression in vulnerable individuals. When an

infant is separated from a primary attachment figure, the result is not only despair and passivity, but also harm to the immune system, which can later lead to depressive illness (Hennessy, Schiml-Webb, & Deak, 2009). Many people suffering from depression have a history of separations, losses, rejections, and impaired, insecure attachments (Cruwys et al., 2014; Hammen, 2009; Nolan, Flynn, & Garber, 2003; Weissman, Markowitz, & Klerman, 2000).

4. **Cognitive habits.** Finally, depression involves specific, negative ways of thinking about one's situation (Beck, 2005; Mathews & MacLeod, 2005). Depressed people typically believe that their situation is *permanent* ("Nothing good will ever happen to me") and *uncontrollable* ("I'm depressed because I'm ugly and horrible and I can't do anything about it"). Expecting nothing to get better, they do nothing to improve their lives and therefore remain unhappy. When depressed and nondepressed people are put into a sad mood and given a choice between looking at sad faces or happy faces, depressed people choose the sad faces—a metaphor for how they process the world in general, attending to everything that confirms the gloominess of life rather than any of its joys (Joormann & Gotlib, 2007). And when asked to recall happier times, nondepressed people cheer up, but depressed people feel even worse, as if the happy memory makes them feel that they will never be happy again (Joormann, Siemer, & Gotlib, 2007).

The cognitive biases associated with depression are not just correlates of the disorder. Longitudinal studies show that they play a causal role, interacting with severe life stresses to generate further depressive episodes (Hallion & Ruscio, 2011; Monroe et al., 2007). Depressed people, especially if they also have low self-esteem, tend to *ruminate*—brooding about everything that is wrong in their lives, persuading themselves that no one cares about them, and dwelling on reasons to feel hopeless. They have trouble preventing these thoughts from entering and remaining in their memory, which keeps them stewing in negative perceptions and unhappy past events (Joormann, Levens, & Gotlib, 2011; Kuster, Orth, & Meier, 2012; Moore et al., 2013). In contrast, nondepressed people who undergo stressful events are usually able to distract themselves, look outward, and seek solutions. Beginning in adolescence, women are much more likely than men to develop a ruminating, introspective style, which contributes both to longer-lasting depressions in women and to the sex difference in reported rates (Nolen-Hoeksema, 2004).

The factors we have described—genetics, violence, loss of important relationships, and cognitive habits and biases—combine in different ways to produce any given case of depression. That is why the same sad event—such as flunking a course, being dumped by a lover, or losing a job—can affect two people entirely differently: One rolls with the punch and another is knocked flat.

JOURNAL PROMPT 15.4

Thinking Critically—Consider Other Interpretations: A news headline announces that a gene has been identified as a cause of depression. Does this mean that everyone with the gene will become depressed? How should critical thinkers interpret this research?

Quiz for Module 15.4

1. Major depression is much more likely to be diagnosed among

   a. Children

   b. Men

   c. Pacific Islanders

   d. Women

2. Episodes of _____ and _____ characterize bipolar disorder.

   a. Depression / anxiety

   b. Mania / depression

   c. Obsession / compulsion

   d. Anger / sadness

3. Which of the following factors is *not* a common contributor to depression?

   a. Psychological weakness

   b. Losses of important relationships

   c. Cognitive habits

   d. Genetic predispositions

4. Biological researchers find that depressed people have unusually high levels of the stress hormone

   a. Anbesol

   b. Pinesol

   c. Thimerisol

   d. Cortisol

5. Depressed people tend to believe that the reasons for their unhappiness are

   a. Temporary

   b. Caused by the situation

   c. Out of their hands

   d. Controllable

Personality Disorders

Personality disorders involve impairments in personality that cause great distress to an individual or impair his or her ability to get along with others, *and* the presence of pathological traits such as excessive hostility or callousness.

Borderline Personality Disorder

LO 15.5.A Explain the main features of borderline personality disorder.

Borderline personality disorder characterizes people who have the personality trait of extremely negative emotionality and who are unable to regulate their emotions. They have a history of intense but unstable relationships in which they alternate between idealizing the partner and then devaluing the partner. They frantically try to avoid real or imagined abandonment by others, even if the "abandonment" is only a friend's brief vacation. They are self-destructive and impulsive, suffer chronic feelings of emptiness, and often threaten to commit suicide (which about 10 percent of them do). They are emotionally volatile, careening from anger to euphoria to anxiety (Crowell, Beauchaine, & Linehan, 2009; Schulze, Schmahl, & Niedtfeld, 2015). They love and hate intensely, sometimes simultaneously. (The term *borderline* comes from the original psychodynamic view of the disorder, as one thought to fall on the border between mild and severe mental illnesses, thereby creating an inconsistent ability to function in the world.)

Many people with borderline disorder deliberately injure themselves in repeated acts of cutting and self-mutilation. This form of "nonsuicidal self-injury" has been known for thousands of years and is found around the world; it is most prevalent among adolescents and young adults. Self-injury has two functions: It reduces stress and arousal within the individual, and it often produces social support or relieves the person of unwanted social obligations (Nock, 2010).

Although there has not been much empirical research on the development of borderline personality disorder, a leading theory is based on a "biosocial" model proposed by Marsha Linehan, who suffers from the disorder herself (and has developed one of the most successful treatments for it). In this view, a child is born with a genetic vulnerability that produces abnormalities in the frontal lobes and brain areas involved in emotion, and a disposition toward negative emotionality as a personality trait. As a result, the young child behaves impulsively and has heightened emotional sensitivity, which in turn are worsened by what Linehan calls an "invalidating environment": The child's parents do not acknowledge or tolerate the child's emotions and their expression, telling the child that those feelings are

borderline personality disorder

A disorder characterized by extreme negative emotionality and an inability to regulate emotions; it often results in intense but unstable relationships, impulsiveness, self-mutilating behavior, feelings of emptiness, and a fear of abandonment by others.

unjustified and the child should cope with them alone. At the same time, the parents intermittently reinforce the child's extreme emotional outbursts with their attention. As a result of getting these mixed messages, the child doesn't learn to understand and label what he or she is feeling, or how to regulate those feelings calmly. Instead, the child veers helplessly between trying to inhibit any sign of emotion and giving in to extreme expressions of it (Crowell, Beauchaine, & Linehan, 2009).

Antisocial Personality Disorder

LO 15.5.B Distinguish between the terms *psychopathy* and *antisocial personality disorder*, and note the common elements of each.

For several editions, the DSM has defined **antisocial personality disorder (APD)** in terms of behavior, describing people who repeatedly break the law and violate the rights of others; are impulsive and seek quick thrills; show reckless disregard for their own safety or that of others; often get into physical fights or assault others; and are irresponsible, failing to hold jobs or meet obligations. The problem with this definition is that it covers a grab-bag set of behaviors without specifying what the underlying mental disorder might be. Moreover, it could apply both to people who fall in with a bad crowd for a few years and to others who, as one researcher describes them, are "lifetime persistent offenders." For the latter, rule-breaking and irresponsibility start in early childhood and take different forms at different ages: "biting and hitting at age 4, shoplifting and truancy at age 10, selling drugs and stealing cars at age 16, robbery and rape at age 22, and fraud and child abuse at age 30" (Moffitt, 1993, 2005). Individual differences in aggressiveness are eerily apparent by an infant's first birthday, virtually as soon as a baby has the motor skills to hit or exert force, and seem to be an early predictor of later violence (Baker et al., 2013; Hay et al., 2011).

Many people with APD don't do as well as other individuals on neuropsychological tests of frontal lobe functioning, and they have less gray matter in the frontal lobes than other people do (Dinn & Harris, 2000; Raine, 2008). The frontal lobes are responsible for planning and impulse control, and impairments in this area can lead to an inability to control responses to frustration and provocation, to regulate emotions, and to understand the long-term consequences of indulging in immediate gratifications (Fairchild et al., 2013). One PET-scan study found that cold-blooded, predatory murderers had less brain activity in the frontal lobe than did men who murdered in the heat of passion or a control group of criminals who had not murdered anybody (Raine et al., 1998). Frontal lobe damage can be inherited or result from disease, accident, or physical abuse (Milner & McCanne, 1991), or perhaps from a genetic predisposition: In a longitudinal study of boys who had been physically abused in childhood, those who had a variation in a crucial gene later had far more arrests for violent crimes than did abused boys who had a normal gene (Caspi et al., 2002). Although only 12 percent of the abused boys had this variant, they accounted for nearly half of all later convictions for violent crimes.

As we keep reminding you, however, genes are not destiny. In the study we just described, boys who had the genetic variant but whose parents treated them lovingly did not grow up to be violent. Genes may affect the brain, in turn predisposing a child to rule-breaking and violent behavior, but many environmental influences can disrupt that pathway and alter the ways that genes express themselves. One is poor nutrition in the first 3 years of life, which has been linked with antisocial behavior up through adolescence; so has early separation from the mother; and so has brain damage caused by parental cruelty (Raine, 2008).

Over the objections of many clinical scientists, the DSM does not use the term *psychopathy*, which the DSM regards as one form of APD. The DSM-5, however, added another criterion for the diagnosis: lacking remorse for harms inflicted on others. This is the key symptom of psychopathy, which we describe next.

antisocial personality disorder (APD)

A personality disorder characterized by a lifelong pattern of irresponsible, antisocial behavior such as law-breaking, violence, and other impulsive, reckless acts.

Psychopathy: Myths and Evidence

LO 15.5.C List and explain the major factors that contribute to the central features of psychopathy.

psychopathy

A personality disorder characterized by fearlessness; lack of empathy, guilt, and remorse; the use of deceit; and coldheartedness.

Decades ago, Hervey Cleckley (1976) popularized the term **psychopathy** ["sigh CAW pa thee"], which he used to describe individuals who are heartless, utterly lack conscience, and are unable to feel normal emotions. Psychopaths are incapable not only of remorse but also of fear of punishment and of shame, guilt, and empathy for those they hurt. If caught in a lie or a crime, psychopaths may seem sincerely sorry and promise to make amends, but it is all an act. Some psychopaths are violent and sadistic, able to kill a pet, a child, or a random adult without a twinge of regret, but others are charming and manipulative, able to direct their energies into con games or career advancement, abusing other people emotionally or economically rather than physically (Skeem et al., 2011). One researcher in this field, Robert Hare, calls corporate psychopaths "snakes in suits" (Babiak & Hare, 2007).

Although psychopaths are probably more prevalent in individualistic Western societies, they are believed to exist in all cultures and throughout history. Even a close-knit culture such as the Yupik in Canada has a word for them, *kunlangeta* (Seabrook, 2008). An anthropologist once asked a member of the tribe what the group would do with a *kunlangeta*, and he said, "Somebody would have pushed him off the ice when nobody else was looking." Psychopaths are feared and detested everywhere.

In the popular imagination, and in plenty of horror movies and thrillers, psychopaths come in four varieties: corporate villains like Bernie Madoff, who swindled people out of billions of dollars in a Ponzi scheme that lasted many years; con artists, who are charming and charismatic hucksters; serial killers; and lifelong criminal offenders. In a thorough review for the journal *Psychological Science in the Public Interest*, a blue-ribbon team of investigators has separated myths about psychopaths from what the evidence shows (Skeem et al., 2011).

First, they reported what psychopathy is *not*: (1) It is not the same as being violent and sadistic. Many psychopaths have no criminal record or history of violence, and many criminals and rule violators are not psychopaths (Poythress et al., 2010). (2) It is not the same as being "psychotic." Psychopaths are not delusional, irrational, out of touch with reality, or unaware of the consequences of their actions; they just don't care about those consequences. (3) The belief that psychopaths are "born, not made," appears to be wrong. There seem to be several routes to psychopathy and any genetic predispositions interact with environmental influences. (4) The belief that "psychopaths cannot change their spots" is, surprisingly, also

In the popular imagination, psychopaths are sadistic and violent. Gary L. Ridgway, the deadliest convicted serial killer in U.S. history (known as the Green River Killer), strangled 48 women, placing their bodies in clusters around the country so he could "keep track of them." But most psychopaths are not murderers. Lacking empathy and conscience, they use charm and elaborate scams to deceive and defraud. Bernie Madoff swindled investors out of $17 billion in a Ponzi scheme (a kind of "shell game" where investors are paid from other people's investments, rather than from any actual gains accrued from the investments). Madoff used his charm and reputation in the industry to commit his crimes.

wrong. Some children and adults who score high on measures of psychopathy can indeed change with intensive treatment (Polaschek, 2014).

Moreover, psychopathy itself is not a single entity, like appendicitis; it involves a cluster of characteristics (Patrick, Fowles, & Krueger, 2009). Of these, two are central: First, psychopaths are fearless, unconcerned about being caught and punished for their misdeeds; this gives them a high tolerance for danger, risk, and thrill-seeking. Second, they lack empathy for others and remorse for their harmful acts. As a result, they often behave irresponsibly and treat animals and other people with great cruelty. They exploit and deceive others without flinching, and are callous and coldhearted.

Something certainly seems to be amiss in the emotional wiring of psychopaths, the wiring that allows all primates, not just human beings, to feel connected to others of their kind. The psychopath's reduced ability to feel emotional arousal suggests some aberration in the central nervous system (Hare, 1965, 1996; Lykken, 1995; Raine et al., 2000). Most psychopaths do not respond physiologically to the threat of punishment the way other people do, which may be why they can behave fearlessly in situations that would scare others to death. Normally, when a person is anticipating danger, pain, or punishment, the electrical conductance of the skin changes, a classically conditioned response that indicates anxiety or fear. But psychopaths are slow to develop such responses, which suggests that they have difficulty feeling the anxiety necessary for learning that their actions will have unpleasant consequences (Lorber, 2004; see Figure 15.2). Their lack of empathy for others also seems to have a physiological basis. When psychopaths are shown pictures of people crying and in distress, their skin conductance barely shifts, in contrast to that of nonpsychopaths, which shoots up (Blair et al., 1997).

Psychopaths also have difficulty identifying expressions of fear. Recently, clinical scientists have developed ways of measuring callousness and unemotionality in children, central dispositions that can develop into adult psychopathy (Bedford et al., 2015; Frick & Viding, 2009). Young children with these traits cannot correctly decode fear expressions in the faces, voices, or gestures of other people. They don't feel fear themselves or "get" fear in others, and as a result they may fail to respond to efforts by their parents and other adults to socialize them—and thus fail to develop a conscience (Sylvers, Brennan, & Lilienfeld, 2011).

No one yet knows for sure the origins of psychopathy. Whatever the possible genetic or biological reasons for the flaws in their "emotional wiring," the world they live in plays a big role also. A culture that rewards ruthless behavior in work and politics will generate many "snakes in suits," and a culture that rewards the slaughter of innocents for purposes of political or religious genocide will generate many cases of heartlessness and lack of empathy.

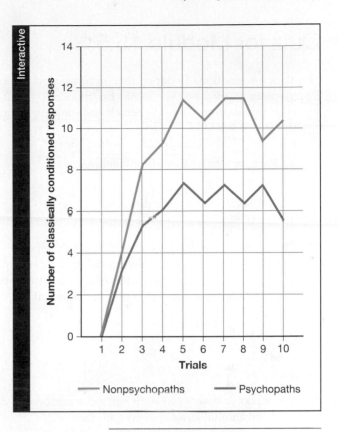

Figure 15.2 Emotions and Psychopathy

In several experiments, people diagnosed as psychopaths were slow to develop classically conditioned responses to anticipated danger, pain, or shock—responses that indicate normal anxiety. This deficit may be related to the ability of psychopaths to behave in destructive ways without remorse or regard for the consequences (Hare, 1965, 1993).

JOURNAL PROMPT 15.5

Thinking Critically—Define Your Terms: Chances are good that, at some point in your life, you've described someone as "psycho." Chances are also good that you used that term incorrectly for whatever intended meaning you had. First, briefly describe an instance when you've used that descriptor for someone else (if you've never used that word in this context, then think of a film, television show, or book you've encountered where the term has been used). What were the circumstances that led you to that utterance? What was it about the person's behavior that prompted you to use that descriptor? Next, think about the definitions of borderline personality disorder, antisocial personality disorder, psychopathy, and personality disorders in general. Assuming the person you were addressing wasn't actually diagnosable, what features of these disorders come closest to what you thought you had in mind when you used the term?

Quiz for Module 15.5

1. Nancy is emotionally dependent on others and panics or becomes angry when she thinks her friends have left her, even for vacation. She cuts herself and frequently threatens to commit suicide if she doesn't get what she wants. What diagnosis would you make regarding Nancy?

   a. Psychopathy with adjutant features

   b. Psychopathy

   c. Antisocial personality disorder

   d. Borderline personality disorder

2. Charles has a lifelong pattern of irresponsible behavior, including acts of violence, law-breaking, impulsivity, and reckless actions. A clinician interviewing him in his prison cell concluded that Charles could be diagnosed with

   a. OCD

   b. APD

   c. PTSD

   d. DID

3. Many people diagnosed with antisocial personality disorder have anomalies associated with the

   a. Occipital lobe

   b. Frontal lobe

   c. Substantia nigra

   d. Basal ganglia

4. When Jeffrey was a child, he liked to torture and kill small animals—the neighbors' pets, rabbits he trapped in the woods, really any living thing that was helpless and defenseless. Rather than feeling especially good or bad about his actions, Jeffrey tended to not feel anything in particular, certainly not guilt or regret. Jeffrey manifested signs associated with

   a. Psychopathy

   b. Borderline personality disorder

   c. Major depression

   d. Schizotypal disorder

5. "Psychopathy" is psychology's fancy name for describing someone who has

   a. Delusional thoughts or perceptions

   b. Violent tendencies

   c. A cluster of enduring personality attributes

   d. Sadistic urges to harm others

Drug Abuse and Addiction

The DSM-5 category of *substance-related and addictive disorders* covers the abuse of 10 classes of drugs, including alcohol, caffeine, hallucinogens, inhalants, cocaine, and tobacco, and adds "other (or unknown) substances," in case as-yet-unidentified ways of getting high turn up. All drugs that are used in a way that is self-destructive or impairs a person's ability to hold a job, care for children, get along with others, or complete schoolwork are alike in activating the brain's reward system. The DSM-5 has also added "gambling disorder" in this category, on the grounds that compulsive gambling activates the brain's reward mechanisms just as drugs do. But it relegated "Internet gaming disorder" to the appendix, as a condition warranting further study, and decided not to include excessive behavioral patterns popularly called "sex addiction," "shopping addiction," or "exercise addiction" because, as the manual explains, there is little evidence that these constitute mental disorders.

In this section, focusing primarily on the example of alcoholism, we will consider the two dominant approaches to understanding addiction and drug abuse—the biological model and the learning model—and then see how they might be reconciled.

Biology and Addiction

LO 15.6.A Discuss how the biological model of addiction would explain drug abuse and alcoholism.

The *biological model*, also called the *disease model*, holds that addiction, whether to alcohol or any other drug, is due primarily to a person's neurology and genetic predisposition. The clearest example of the biology of addiction is nicotine. Although smoking rates have declined over the past 50 years, nicotine addiction remains one of the most serious health problems worldwide. Unlike other addictions, it can begin quickly, within a month after the first cigarette—and for some teenagers, after only one cigarette—because nicotine almost immediately changes neuron receptors in the brain that react chemically to the drug (DiFranza, 2008). Genes produce variation in these nicotine receptors, which is one reason that some people are especially vulnerable to becoming addicted to cigarettes and have tremendous withdrawal symptoms when they try to give them up, whereas other people, even if they have been heavy smokers, can quit cold turkey (Bierut et al., 2008).

For alcoholism, the picture is more complicated. Genes are involved in some kinds of alcoholism but not all. There is a heritable component in the kind of alcoholism that begins in early adolescence and is linked to impulsivity, antisocial behavior, and criminality (Dick, 2007; Dick et al., 2008; Schuckit et al., 2007; Verhulst, Neale, & Kendler, 2015), but not in the kind of alcoholism that begins in adulthood and is unrelated to other disorders. Genes also affect alcohol "sensitivity"—how quickly people respond to alcohol, whether they tolerate it, and how much they need to drink before feeling high (Hu et al., 2008). In an ongoing longitudinal study of 450 young men, those who at age 20 had to drink more than others to feel any reaction were at increased risk of becoming alcoholic within the decade. This was true regardless of their initial drinking habits or family history of alcoholism (Schuckit, 1998; Schuckit et al., 2011).

In contrast, people who have a high sensitivity to alcohol are less likely to drink to excess, and this may partly account for ethnic differences in alcoholism rates. One genetic factor causes low activity of an enzyme involved in the metabolism of alcohol. People who lack this enzyme respond to alcohol with unpleasant symptoms, such as flushing and nausea. This genetic protection is common among Asians but rare among Europeans, which may be one reason that rates of alcoholism are much lower in Asian than in Caucasian populations; the Asian sensitivity to alcohol discourages them from drinking a lot (Heath et al., 2003). Not all Asians are the same in this regard, however. Korean American college students have higher rates of alcohol-use disorders and family histories of alcoholism than do Chinese American students (Duranceaux et al., 2008). And Native Americans have the same genetic protection that Asians do, yet they have much higher rates of alcoholism.

For years, the usual way of looking at biological factors and addiction was to assume that the first causes the second. However, the relationship also works the other way: *Addictions can result from the abuse of drugs* (Crombag & Robinson, 2004; Lewis, 2011). Many people become addicted not because their brains have led them to abuse drugs, but because the abuse of drugs has changed their brains. Over time, the repeated jolts of pleasure-producing dopamine modify brain structures in ways that maximize the appeal of the drug (or of other addictive experiences such as gambling), minimize the appeal of other rewards, and disrupt cognitive functions such as working memory, self-control, and decision making, which is why addictive behavior comes to feel automatic (Houben, Wiers, & Jansen, 2011; Lewis, 2011). Heavy use of cocaine, alcohol, and other drugs reduces the number of receptors for dopamine and creates the feeling of having a compulsion to keep using the drug (Volkow et al., 2001; see Figure 15.3). In the case of alcoholism, heavy drinking also reduces the level of painkilling endorphins, produces nerve damage, and shrinks the cerebral cortex. These changes can then create a craving for more liquor, and the person stays intoxicated for longer and longer times, drinking not for pleasure at all but simply to appease the craving (Heilig, 2008). Even after addicts have gone through detox and remained drug-free, their dopamine circuits remain blunted.

Thus, drug abuse, which begins as a voluntary action, can turn into drug addiction, a compulsive behavior that addicts find exceedingly difficult to control.

Philip Seymour Hoffman was a talented actor who received critical acclaim in films such as *The Big Lebowski, Capote*, and *Hunger Games*. Sadly, he also struggled with drug addiction throughout his life, going through periods of sobriety and abuse since young adulthood. Hoffman died in 2014 from "acute mixed drug intoxication." Heroin, cocaine, amphetamines, and benzodiazepines were found in his system.

Figure 15.3 The Addicted Brain

PET studies show that the brains of cocaine addicts have fewer receptors for dopamine, a neurotransmitter involved in pleasurable sensations. (The more yellow and red in the brain image, the more receptors.) The brains of people addicted to methamphetamine, alcohol, and even food show a similar dopamine deficiency.

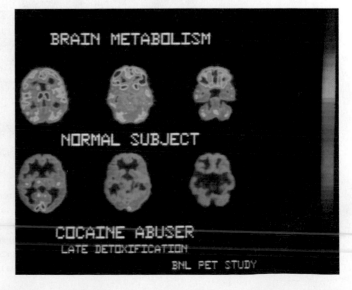

Learning, Culture, and Addiction

LO 15.6.B Discuss how the learning model of addiction would explain drug abuse and alcoholism.

Many people assume that if abnormalities are discovered in the brains of addicts, perhaps because of genetic reasons, nothing can be done about it. Yet consider the results from a team of scientists who studied the brains of people addicted to stimulants and their biological siblings who had no history of chronic drug abuse (Ersche et al., 2012). The addicts *and* their siblings revealed abnormalities in the parts of the brain involved in self-control. Indeed, impulsiveness, an inability to control one's immediate craving for something, is characteristic of addicts (and others who cannot control eating, gambling, texting, or other behaviors). But what enables their equally vulnerable siblings to resist temptation and addiction? Likely candidates include resilience, experience, peer groups, the ability to manage frustration, and strong coping skills (Volkow & Baler, 2012). The *learning model* examines the role of the environment, learning, and culture in encouraging or discouraging these factors and others involved in addiction. Four lines of research support the learning model:

1. **Addiction patterns vary according to cultural practices.** Alcoholism is much more likely to occur in societies that forbid children to drink but condone drunkenness in adults (as in Ireland) than in societies that teach children how to drink responsibly and moderately but condemn adult drunkenness (as in Italy, Greece, and France). In cultures with low rates of alcoholism (except for those committed to a religious rule that forbids use of all psychoactive drugs), adults demonstrate correct drinking habits to their children, gradually introducing them to alcohol in safe family settings. Alcohol is not used as a rite of passage into adulthood. Abstainers are not sneered at, and drunkenness is not considered charming, comical, or manly; it is considered stupid and obnoxious (Peele, 2010; Peele & Brodsky, 1991; Zapolsky et al., 2014).

   The cultural environment may be especially crucial for the development of alcoholism among young people with a genetic vulnerability to alcohol (Schuckit et al., 2008). In one such group of 401 American Indian youths, those who later developed drinking problems lived in a community in which heavy drinking was encouraged and modeled by their parents and peers. But those who felt a cultural and spiritual pride in being Native American, and who were strongly attached to their religious traditions, were less likely to develop drinking problems, even when their parents and peers were encouraging them to drink (Yu & Stiffman, 2007).

The disease model assumes that if children are given even a taste of a drink or a drug, they are more likely to become addicted or a drug abuser. The learning model assumes that the cultural context is crucial in determining whether people will become addicted or learn to use drugs moderately. In fact, when children learn the rules of social drinking with their families, as at Jewish Passover seders (left), alcoholism rates are much lower than in cultures in which drinking occurs mainly in bars or in privacy. Similarly, when marijuana is used as part of a religious tradition, as it is by members of the Rastafarian church in Jamaica, use of the "wisdom weed" does not lead to addiction or harder drugs.

Addiction rates can rise or fall rapidly as a culture changes. In colonial America, the average person drank two to three times the amount of liquor consumed today, yet alcoholism was not a serious problem. Drinking was a universally accepted social activity; families drank and ate together. Alcohol was believed to produce pleasant feelings and relaxation, and Puritan ministers endorsed its use (Critchlow, 1986). Then, between 1790 and 1830, when the American frontier was expanding, drinking came to symbolize masculine independence and toughness. The saloon became the place for drinking away from home. As people stopped drinking in moderation with their families, alcoholism rates shot up, as the learning model would predict.

Substance abuse and addiction problems also increase when people move from their culture of origin into another that has different drinking rules (Westermeyer, 1995). In most Latino cultures, such as those of Mexico and Puerto Rico, drinking and drunkenness are considered male activities. Latina women tend to drink rarely, if at all; they have few drinking problems until they move into an Anglo environment, when their rates of alcoholism rise (Canino, 1994). Likewise, when norms within a culture change, so may drinking habits and addiction rates. The cultural norm for American college women was previously low to moderate drinking; today, they are more likely to abuse alcohol than they ever used to. One reason is that the culture of many college campuses encourages drinking games, binge drinking (having at least four to five drinks in a 2-hour session), and getting drunk, especially among members of fraternities and sororities (Courtney & Polich, 2009). When everyone around you is downing shots one after another or playing Beer Pong, it's hard to say, "I'd really rather just have one drink."

2. **Policies of total abstinence tend to increase rates of addiction rather than reduce them.** In the United States, the temperance movement of the early 20th century held that drinking inevitably leads to drunkenness, and drunkenness to crime. The solution it won for the Prohibition years (1920–1933) was national abstinence. But this victory backfired: Again in accordance with the learning model, Prohibition reduced rates of drinking overall, but it *increased* rates of alcoholism among those who did drink. Because people were denied the opportunity to learn to drink moderately, they drank excessively when given the chance (McCord, 1989). And, of course, when a substance is forbidden, it becomes more attractive to some people. Most schools in the United States have zero-tolerance policies regarding marijuana and alcohol, but large numbers of students have tried them or use them regularly. In fact, rates of binge drinking have increased the most among underage students, who are legally forbidden to drink until age 21.

3. **Not all addicts have withdrawal symptoms when they stop taking a drug.** When heavy users of a drug stop taking it, they often suffer such unpleasant symptoms as nausea, abdominal cramps, depression, and sleep problems, depending on the drug. But these symptoms are far from universal. During the Vietnam War, nearly 30 percent of U.S. soldiers were taking heroin in doses far stronger than those available on the streets of American cities. These men believed themselves to be addicted, and experts predicted a drug-withdrawal disaster among the returning veterans. It never materialized; over 90 percent of the men simply gave up the drug, without significant withdrawal pain, when they came home to new circumstances (Robins, Davis, & Goodwin, 1974). Subsequent studies over the years find that this response is the *norm*, not the exception (Heyman, 2009, 2011), which is strong evidence against the idea that addiction is always a chronic disease. The majority of people who are dependent on cigarettes, tranquilizers, or painkillers are able to stop taking these drugs without outside help and without severe withdrawal symptoms (Prochaska, Norcross, & DiClemente, 1994). Many people find this information startling, even unbelievable. That is because people who can quit without help aren't entering programs to help them quit, so they are invisible to the general public and to the medical world. But they have been identified in random-sample community surveys.

Interactive

Test Your Motives for Drinking

If you drink, why do you do so? Check all of the motives that apply to you:

_____ To relax   _____ To cope with depression

_____ To escape from worries   _____ To get drunk and lose control

_____ To enhance a good meal   _____ To rebel against authority

_____ To conform to peers   _____ To relieve boredom

_____ To express anger   _____ To have sex

_____ To be sociable   _____ Other (specify)

Do your reasons promote abuse or responsible use? How do you respond physically to alcohol? What have you learned about drinking from your family, your friends, and cultural messages? What do your answers tell you about your own vulnerability to addiction?

One reason that many people are able to quit abusing drugs is that the environment in which a drug is used (the setting) and a person's expectations (mental set) have a powerful influence on the drug's *physiological* effects as well as its psychological ones. You might think a lethal dose of, say, amphetamines would be the same wherever the drug was taken. But studies of mice have found that the lethal dose varies depending on the mice's environment—whether they are in a large or small test cage, or whether they are alone or with other mice. The physiological response of human addicts to certain drugs also changes, depending on whether the addicts are in a "druggy" environment, such as a crack house, or an unfamiliar one (Crombag & Robinson, 2004; Siegel, 2005). This is the primary reason that addicts need to change environments if they are going to kick their habits. It's not just to get away from a peer group that might be encouraging them, but also to literally change and rewire their brain's response to the drug.

4. **Addiction does not depend on properties of the drug alone but also on the reasons for taking it.** For decades, doctors were afraid to treat people with chronic pain by giving them narcotics, fearing they would become addicted. As a result of this belief, millions of people were condemned to live with chronic suffering from back pain, arthritis, nerve disorders, and other conditions—and pain impedes healing. But then researchers learned that the great majority of pain sufferers use morphine and other opiates not to escape from the world but to function in the world, and they do not become addicted (Portenoy, 1994; Raja, 2008). (Of course, powerful opiates should not be prescribed for mild pain, and they must be carefully monitored.)

In the case of alcohol, people who drink simply to be sociable or to relax when they have had a rough day are unlikely to become addicted. *Problem* drinking occurs when people drink to disguise or suppress their anxiety or depression, when they drink alone to drown their sorrows and worries, or when they want an excuse to abandon inhibitions (Cooper et al., 1995; Mohr et al., 2001). College students who feel alienated and uninvolved with their studies are more likely than their happier peers to go out drinking with the conscious intention of getting drunk.

In many cases, then, the decision to start abusing drugs depends more on people's motives, and on the norms of their peer group and culture, than on the chemical properties of the drug itself.

Debating the Causes of Addiction

LO 15.6.C **Explain the different predictions that the biological model and learning model would make regarding the benefits of total abstinence from versus moderate intake of alcohol.**

The biological and learning models both contribute to our understanding of drug use and addiction. Yet, among many researchers and public health professionals, these views are quite polarized, especially when it comes to thinking about treatment (see Review 15.1). Such

Review 15.1

Biological and Learning Models of Addiction Contrasted

The biological and learning models of addiction differ in how they explain drug abuse and the solutions they propose:

The Biological Model	The Learning Model
Addiction is genetic, biological, or a chronic relapsing disease caused by changes in the brain produced by drug abuse.	Addiction is a way of coping, and people can learn to make better choices.
Once an addict, always an addict.	A person can grow beyond the need for alcohol or other drugs.
An addict must abstain from the drug forever.	Most problem drinkers can learn to drink in moderation.
A person is either addicted or not.	The degree of addiction will vary depending on the situation.
The solution is medical treatment and membership in groups that reinforce one's permanent identity as a recovering addict.	The solution involves learning new coping skills and changing one's environment.
An addict needs the same treatment and group support forever.	Treatment lasts only until the person no longer abuses the drug.

Source: *Based on Peele and Brodsky (1991); see also Heyman (2011) and Lewis (2011).*

polarization often leads to either–or thinking on a national scale: Either complete abstinence is the solution, or it is the problem. For example, those who advocate the biological (disease) model say that alcoholics and problem drinkers must abstain completely, and that young people should not be permitted to drink, even at home with their parents, until they are 21. Those who champion the learning model argue that most problem drinkers can learn to drink moderately if they learn safe drinking skills, acquire better ways of coping with stress, avoid situations that evoke conditioned responses to using drugs, and avoid friends who pressure them to drink excessively. Besides, they ask, how are young people going to learn to drink safely and moderately if they don't first do so at home or in other safe environments (Denning, Little, & Glickman, 2004; Glaser, 2014; Rosenberg, 1993)?

How can we assess these two positions critically? Because alcoholism, problem drinking, and other kinds of substance abuse occur for many reasons, neither model offers the only solution. In the case of alcohol, many problem drinkers cannot learn to drink moderately, especially if they have been drinking heavily for many years, by which time, as we saw earlier, physiological changes in their brains and bodies may have turned them from abusers into addicts. Unfortunately, total-abstinence groups such as Alcoholics Anonymous (AA) are ineffective for many people. According to its own surveys and those conducted independently, one-third to one-half of all people who join AA drop out. Many of these dropouts benefit from programs such as Harm Reduction, which teach people how to drink moderately and keep their drinking under control (Witkiewitz, Walthers, & Marlatt, 2013).

So instead of asking, "Can problem drinkers learn to drink moderately?" perhaps we should ask, "What are the factors that make it more or less likely that someone can learn to control problem drinking?" Problem drinkers who are most likely to become moderate drinkers have a history of less severe dependence on the drug. They lead more stable lives and have jobs and families. In contrast, those who are at greater risk of alcoholism (or other drug abuse) have these risk factors: (1) They have a genetic vulnerability to the drug or have been using it long enough for it to have damaged or changed their brains; (2) they believe that they have no control over their drinking or drug use; (3) they live in a culture or a peer group that promotes and rewards binge drinking or discourages moderate drug use; and (4) they have come to rely on the drug as a way of avoiding problems, suppressing anger or fear, or coping with stress.

JOURNAL PROMPT 15.6

Thinking Critically—Avoid Emotional Reasoning: People disagree passionately about whether alcoholics can learn to drink moderately. How can we move beyond emotional reasoning on this contentious issue?

Quiz for Module 15.6

1. A heritable component seems to play a role in alcoholism that
   a. Develops later in life, during adulthood
   b. Affects both Asian and African American men
   c. Affects women but not men
   d. Begins in early adolescence and is linked to other undesirable activities

2. What is the most reasonable conclusion about the role of genes in alcoholism?
   a. Without a key gene, a person cannot become an alcoholic.
   b. The presence of a key gene will almost always cause a person to become an alcoholic.
   c. Genes may increase a person's vulnerability to some kinds of alcoholism.
   d. "Addictive genes" have increasingly received research scrutiny.

3. Which cultural practice is associated with *low* rates of alcoholism?
   a. A gradual introduction to drinking in family settings
   b. Infrequent binge drinking
   c. Drinking as a rite of passage into adulthood
   d. Policies of prohibition

4. Which of the following is *not* an argument that would support the learning model of addiction?
   a. Addiction patterns vary according to cultural practices.
   b. Abstinence policies tend to increase rates of addiction rather than reduce them.
   c. Not all addicts have withdrawal symptoms when they stop taking a drug.
   d. Chemically manipulating brain regions causes the onset of addiction in laboratory animals.

5. If a solely biological explanation for addiction were correct, which of the following conclusions would follow?
   a. Total abstinence programs should show the highest rates of success for treating addiction.
   b. Moderate drinking programs would have a high success rate in treating addiction.
   c. Cultural variability in patterns of addiction would be expected.
   d. Setting, motives, and previous substance history should moderate reactions to a substance.

Dissociative Identity Disorder

When most people say "I'm just not myself today," it usually means they're in a bad mood, tired, or otherwise preoccupied. As a clinical diagnosis, "not being yourself" might imply a condition that has captured the public's imagination, yet left most psychological scientists highly skeptical.

Can You See the Real Me?

LO 15.7A Discuss the factors that make dissociative identity disorder a controversial diagnosis.

One of the most controversial diagnoses ever to arise in psychiatry and psychology is **dissociative identity disorder (DID)**, formerly and still popularly called *multiple personality disorder (MPD)*. This label describes the apparent emergence, within one person, of two or more distinct identities, each with its own name, memories, and personality traits. Cases of multiple personality portrayed on TV, in books, and in films such as *The Three Faces of Eve* and *Sybil* have captivated the public for years, and they still do. In 2009, Showtime televised *The United States of Tara*, a series in which a woman with a *very* tolerant husband and two teenagers keeps breaking into one of her three identities—a sex-and-shopping-mad teenage girl, a gun-loving redneck male, and a 1950s-style homemaker.

Some psychiatrists and clinical psychologists take dissociative identity disorder very seriously, believing that it originates in childhood as a means of coping with sexual abuse

dissociative identity disorder (DID)

A controversial disorder marked by the apparent appearance within one person of two or more distinct personalities, each with its own name and traits; formerly known as *multiple personality disorder (MPD)*.

or other traumatic experiences (Gleaves, 1996). In their view, the trauma produces a mental "splitting" (*dissociation*): One personality emerges to handle everyday experiences, and another personality (called an "alter") to cope with the bad ones. During the 1980s and 1990s, clinicians who believed a client had a "multiple personality" often used highly suggestive techniques to "bring out the alters," such as hypnosis, drugs, and even outright coercion (McHugh, 2008; Rieber, 2006; Spanos, 1996). Psychiatrist Richard Kluft (1987) wrote that efforts to determine the presence of alters may require "between 2½ and 4 hours of continuous interviewing. Interviewees must be prevented from taking breaks to regain composure . . . . In one recent case of singular difficulty, the first sign of dissociation was noted in the 6th hour, and a definitive spontaneous switching of personalities occurred in the 8th hour."

Mercy! After 8 hours of "continuous interviewing" without a single break, how many of us wouldn't do what the interviewer wanted? Clinicians who conducted such interrogations argued that they were merely *permitting* other personalities to reveal themselves, but skeptical psychological scientists countered that they were actively *creating* other personalities through suggestion and sometimes even intimidation with vulnerable clients who had other psychological problems (Lilienfeld & Lynn, 2015).

Psychological scientists have shown that "dissociative amnesia," the mechanism that supposedly causes traumatized children to repress their ordeal and develop several identities as a result, lacks historical and empirical support (Lynn et al., 2012). For one thing, truly traumatic experiences are remembered all too long and all too well (McNally, 2003; Pope et al., 2007). For another, scientific studies, as opposed to subjective case studies, have failed to confirm that the alleged personalities in DID have amnesia for what the others have done. In a study that compared nine DID patients with healthy controls and with another group of actors simulating DID, the patients were just as likely as the others to transfer autobiographical memories between identities when this information was needed as part of a task. Although patients *said* that they could not recall the autobiographical details of their alters, the results indicated that they could (Huntjens, Verschuere, & McNally, 2012).

Putting the Pieces Together

LO 15.7.B Evaluate the likely explanations for dissociative personality disorder.

So what is DID? The evidence suggests that it is a homegrown culture-bound syndrome. Only a handful of multiple personality cases had ever been diagnosed anywhere in the world before 1980; yet by the mid-1990s, tens of thousands of cases had been reported, mostly in the United States and Canada. MPD became a lucrative business, benefiting hospitals that opened MPD clinics, therapists who had a new disorder to treat, and psychiatrists and patients who wrote best-selling books. Then, in the 1990s, as a result of numerous malpractice cases across the country, courts ruled, on the basis of the testimony of scientific experts in psychiatry and psychology, that MPD was being generated by the clinicians who believed in it. The MPD clinics in hospitals closed, psychiatrists became more wary, and the number of cases dropped sharply almost overnight. But the promoters of the diagnosis have never admitted they were mistaken; they continue to treat patients for it, and it remains in the DSM-5.

No one disputes that some troubled, highly imaginative individuals can produce many different "personalities" when asked. But the *sociocognitive explanation* of DID holds that this phenomenon is simply an extreme form of the ability we all have to present different aspects of our personalities to others (Lilienfeld et al., 1999; Lynn et al., 2012). The disorder may seem very real to clinicians and their patients who believe in it, but in the sociocognitive view, it results from pressure and suggestion by clinicians, interacting with acceptance by vulnerable patients who find the idea that they have separate personalities a plausible explanation

Why did the number of "alters" reported by people with DID increase over the years? In the earliest cases, multiple personalities came only in pairs. In the 1886 story of *Dr. Jekyll and Mr. Hyde*, the kindly Dr. Jekyll turned into the murderous Mr. Hyde. At the height of the epidemic in North America in the 1990s, people were claiming to have several dozen, even hundreds, of alters, including demons, children, extraterrestrials, and animals.

for their problems. The diagnosis of DID also allows some people to account for past sexual or criminal behavior that they now regret or find intolerably embarrassing; they can claim their "other personality did it." In turn, therapists who believe in the diagnosis reward such patients with attention and praise for revealing more and more personalities—and a culture-bound syndrome is born (Hacking, 1995; Piper & Merskey, 2004). When Canadian psychiatrist Harold Merskey (1992) reviewed the published cases of MPD, he was unable to find a single one in which a patient had not been influenced by the therapist's suggestions or reports about the disorder in the media.

Even the famous case of "Sybil," a huge hit as a book and television special, was a hoax. Sybil never had a traumatic childhood of sexual abuse, she did not have multiple personality disorder, and her "symptoms" were generated by pressure from her psychiatrist, Cornelia Wilbur, who injected her with heavy-duty drugs to get her to reveal other "personalities" (Borch-Jacobsen, 2009; Nathan, 2011). Yet, despite this pressure, even after several years Sybil failed to recall a traumatic childhood memory and was not producing many alters. Finally, she wrote to Wilbur, admitting she was "none of the things I have pretended to be . . . . I do not have any multiple personalities . . . . I do not even have a 'double.' . . . I am all of them. I have been essentially lying." Wilbur replied that Sybil was merely experiencing massive denial and resistance, and threatened to withhold the drugs that Sybil had become addicted to. Sybil continued with therapy, and the two eventually produced the book that Wilber hoped would make her famous and wealthy. It did.

The story of MPD/DID offers a good lesson in critical thinking because it teaches us to be cautious about new diagnoses and previously rare disorders that suddenly catch fire in popular culture: to consider other explanations, examine assumptions and biases, and demand good evidence instead of simply accepting unskeptical media coverage.

JOURNAL PROMPT 15.7

Thinking Critically—Consider Other Interpretations: You've learned about a range of disorders in this chapter (such as depressive disorders, anxiety disorders, addiction), many of which affect vast numbers of people and can have devastating consequences. Consider substance abuse and addiction; there are untold millions of people worldwide grappling with some form of this disorder that holds the potential to ruin lives, destroy families, and kill people. Given that, why do you think dissociative identity disorder captures the public attention to so great an extent? It doesn't affect very many people, no one's ever died from it, and it may not even be reliably diagnosed. What are the qualities associated with DID that make it "appealing," for lack of a better word, compared to something like depression or alcoholism?

Quiz for Module 15.7

1. The "dissociative" part of dissociative identity disorder refers to

   a. A separation from reality

   b. A "splitting" of consciousness and identity

   c. An amnesiac response to a single traumatic incident

   d. A genetic precursor of schizophrenia

2. In a person diagnosed with dissociative identity disorder, one main "personality" interacts with the world on a regular basis, but other personalities called _____ are lurking in the recesses of consciousness.

   a. Others

   b. Alters

   c. Lessers

   d. Leroy and Marcie

3. Bitsy suffered through a prolonged series of traumatic events throughout her childhood. What prediction is most likely to be true as she progresses through adulthood?

   a. She'll have difficulty remembering those traumatic events without age-regression therapy.

   b. She'll develop dissociative identity disorder as a means of coping with those memories.

   c. She'll have difficulty forgetting those traumatic events.

   d. She'll have difficulty remembering those traumatic events without the aid of hypnosis.

4. What evidence suggests that dissociative identity disorder is a culture-bound syndrome?

   a. A person's alters often speak with accents or in a foreign language.

   b. A suspected genetic marker of dissociative identity disorder has received increased research attention within the past decade.

   c. Only a small number of DID cases had been diagnosed worldwide, yet tens of thousands of cases in the United States and Canada were diagnosed after the diagnosis became lucrative.

   d. Cases of true dissociative identity disorder have only been identified in Gabon, Equatorial Guinea, and Cameroon.

5. One promising explanation for the characteristics seen in dissociative identity disorder is

   a. The sociocognitive explanation

   b. The alternative hypothesis

   c. The dissociocognitive explanation

   d. The Omega hypothesis

Schizophrenia

We turn now to a last major category of psychological disorders, and one that has attracted a range of explanations since it was first given a name in the late 1800s (Kraepelin, 1896). Causes ranging from "a conflict between instincts" to "toxins in the endocrine system" to social conditions to "the frustration of basic urges" have been proposed for what we now know is a brain disease (Brown & Menninger, 1940; Hunt, 1938; Lazell & Prince, 1929; Meyer, 1910–1911). To gain more insight into schizophrenic disorders, watch the video *Living With a Disorder 2*.

Symptoms of Schizophrenia

LO 15.8.A Describe the five major symptoms of schizophrenia, and give an example of each.

In 1911, Swiss psychiatrist Eugen Bleuler coined the term *schizophrenia* to describe cases in which the personality loses its unity. Contrary to popular belief, people with schizophrenia do not have a "split" or "multiple" personality. Schizophrenia is a fragmented condition in which words are split from meaning, actions from motives, perceptions from reality. It is an example of a **psychosis**, a mental condition that involves distorted perceptions of reality and an inability to function in most aspects of life. The DSM-5's category is *schizophrenia spectrum and other psychotic disorders*, which includes conditions that vary in severity and duration.

schizophrenia

A psychotic disorder marked by delusions, hallucinations, disorganized and incoherent speech, inappropriate behavior, and cognitive impairments.

psychosis

An extreme mental disturbance involving distorted perceptions and irrational behavior; it may have psychological or organic causes. (Plural: *psychoses*.)

Schizophrenia is the cancer of mental illness: elusive, complex, and varying in form. The DSM-5 criteria for the disorder list five core abnormalities:

1. **Bizarre delusions.** Some people with schizophrenia have delusions of identity, believing that they are Moses, Jesus, or another famous person. Some have paranoid delusions, taking innocent events—a stranger's cough, a helicopter overhead—as evidence that everyone is plotting against them. They may insist that their thoughts have been inserted into their heads by someone controlling them or are being broadcast on television. Some believe that ordinary objects or people are really something or someone else, perhaps extraterrestrials in disguise. Some have delusional beliefs; that a celebrity loves them, or that they have the secret plan for world peace, for example.

2. **Hallucinations.** People with schizophrenia suffer from false sensory experiences that seem intensely real, such as feeling insects crawling on their bodies or seeing snakes coming through walls. By far the most common hallucination is hearing voices; it is virtually a hallmark of the disease. Some sufferers are so tormented by these voices that they commit suicide to escape them. One man described how he heard as many as 50 voices cursing him, urging him to steal other people's brain cells, or ordering him to kill himself. Once he picked up a ringing telephone and heard them screaming, "You're guilty!" over and over. They yelled "as loud as humans with megaphones," he told a reporter. "It was utter despair. I felt scared. They were always around" (Goode, 2003).

3. **Disorganized, incoherent speech.** People with schizophrenia often speak in an illogical jumble of ideas and symbols, linked by meaningless rhyming words or by remote associations called "word salads." A patient of Bleuler's wrote, "Olive oil is an Arabian liquor-sauce which the Afghans, Moors and Moslems use in ostrich farming. The Indian plantain tree is the whiskey of the Parsees and Arabs. Barley, rice and sugar cane, called artichoke, grow remarkably well in India. The Brahmins live as castes in Baluchistan. The Circassians occupy Manchuria and China. China is the Eldorado of the Pawnees" (Bleuler, 1911/1950). Others make only brief, empty replies in conversation because of diminished thought rather than an unwillingness to speak.

4. **Grossly disorganized or catatonic behavior.** Such behavior may range from childlike silliness to unpredictable and violent agitation. The person may wear three overcoats and gloves on a hot day, start collecting garbage, or hoard scraps of food. Some completely withdraw into a private world, sitting for hours without moving, a condition called *catatonic stupor*. Catatonic states can also produce frenzied, purposeless behavior that goes on for hours.

5. **Negative symptoms.** Many people with schizophrenia lose the motivation and ability to take care of themselves and interact with others; they may stop working or bathing, and become isolated and withdrawn. They lose expressiveness and thus seem emotionally flat; their facial expressions are unresponsive and they make poor eye contact. These symptoms are called "negative" because they involve the absence of normal behaviors or emotions.

Some signs of schizophrenia emerge early, in late childhood or early adolescence (Tarbox & Pogue-Geile, 2008), but the first full-blown psychotic episode typically occurs in late adolescence or early adulthood. In some individuals, the breakdown occurs suddenly; in others, it is more gradual, a slow change in personality. The more breakdowns and relapses the individual has had, the poorer the chances for recovery. Yet, contrary to stereotype, over 40 percent of people with schizophrenia *do* have one or more periods of recovery and go on to hold good jobs and have successful relationships, especially if they have strong family support and community programs (Harding, 2005; Hopper et al., 2007; Jobe & Harrow, 2010). What kind of mysterious disease could produce such a variety of symptoms and outcomes?

Interactive

Bryan Charnley painted 17 self-portraits, with comments, reflecting his battle with schizophrenia. He painted this one in March 1991, when his mind was clear. In June, he committed suicide.

April 20: "[I am feeling] paranoid. The person upstairs was reading my mind and speaking back to me to keep me in a sort of ego crucifixion. . . . I felt this was because I was discharging very strong vibrations."

May 6: "I had no tongue, no real tongue, and could only flatter. . . . The nail in the mouth expresses this. The people around me cannot understand how I was so stupid and cannot forgive me. . . . Thus I am a target. The nails in my eyes express that I cannot see whereas other people seem to have extrasensory perception and I am blind in this respect."

May 18: "My mind seemed to be thought broadcasting [and] it was beyond my will to do anything about it. I summed this up by painting my brain as an enormous mouth. . . . The trouble seemed to stem from a broken heart so I painted a great mass of gore there. . . . I feel I am giving off strong personality vibrations, hence the wavy lines emanating from my head."

Origins of Schizophrenia

LO 15.8.B Describe the three main contributing factors to the origin of schizophrenia.

Schizophrenia is clearly a brain disease. It involves reduced volumes of gray matter in the prefrontal cortex and temporal lobes; abnormalities in the hippocampus; and abnormalities in neurotransmitters, neural activity, and disrupted communication between neurons in areas involving cognitive functioning, such as memory, decision making, and emotional processing (Karlsgodt, Sun, & Cannon, 2010). Most individuals with schizophrenia also show enlargement of the *ventricles*, spaces in the brain that are filled with cerebrospinal fluid (see Figure 15.4) (Dazzan et al., 2015). And they are more likely than nonschizophrenic individuals

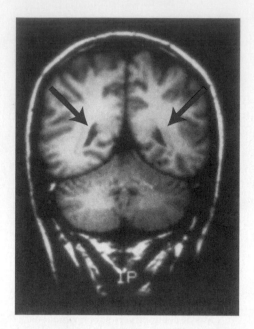
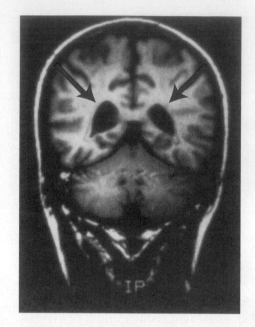

Figure 15.4 Schizophrenia and the Brain

People with schizophrenia are more likely to have enlarged ventricles (spaces) in the brain. These MRI scans of 28-year-old male identical twins show the difference in the size of ventricles between the twin without schizophrenia (left) and the one with schizophrenia (right).

to have abnormalities in the thalamus, the traffic-control center that filters sensations and focuses attention (Andreasen et al., 1994; Gur et al., 1998). Many have deficiencies in the auditory cortex and Broca's and Wernicke's areas, all involved in speech perception and processing; these might explain the nightmare of voice hallucinations.

Currently, researchers have identified three contributing factors in this disorder:

1. **Genetic predispositions.** Schizophrenia is highly heritable. A person has a much greater risk of developing the disorder if an identical twin develops it, even if the twins are reared apart (Gottesman, 1991; Gottesman et al., 2010; Heinrichs, 2005). Children with one schizophrenic parent have a lifetime risk of 7 to 12 percent, and children with two schizophrenic parents have a lifetime risk of 27 to 46 percent, compared to a risk in the general population of only about 1 percent (see Figure 15.5). Researchers all over the world are trying to identify the genes that might be involved in specific symptoms, such as hallucinations, sensitivity to sounds, cognitive impairments, and social withdrawal (Desbonnet, Waddington, & O'Tuathaigh, 2009; Tomppo et al., 2009). However, efforts to find the critical genes in schizophrenia have been difficult because

Figure 15.5 Genetic Vulnerability to Schizophrenia

This graph, based on combined data from 40 European twin and adoption studies conducted over seven decades, shows that the closer the genetic relationship to a person with schizophrenia, the higher the risk of developing the disorder. (Based on Gottesman, 1991; see also Gottesman et al., 2010.)

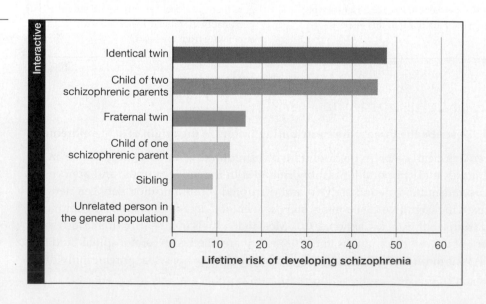

Lifetime risk of developing schizophrenia

several appear to be involved, and those are linked not only to schizophrenia but also to a range of other mental disorders, including autism, attention-deficit/hyperactivity disorder, bipolar disorder, and even dyslexia (Fromer et al., 2014; Walker & Tessner, 2008; Williams et al., 2011).

2. **Prenatal problems or birth complications.** Damage to the fetal brain significantly increases the likelihood of schizophrenia later in life. Such damage may occur if the mother suffers from malnutrition; schizophrenia rates rise during times of famine, as happened in China and elsewhere (St. Clair et al., 2005). Damage may also occur if the mother gets the flu virus during the first 4 months of prenatal development, which triples the risk of schizophrenia (Brown et al., 2004). And it may occur if complications during birth injure the baby's brain or deprive it of oxygen (Cannon et al., 2000). Other nongenetic prenatal factors that increase the child's risk of schizophrenia, especially if they combine with each other, include maternal diabetes and emotional stress, having a father over age 55, birth during the winter months, and very low birth weight (King, St-Hilaire, & Heidkamp, 2010).

3. **Biological events during adolescence.** In adolescence, the brain undergoes a natural pruning-away of synapses. Normally, this pruning helps make the brain more efficient in handling the new challenges of adulthood. But it appears that schizophrenic brains aggressively prune away too many synapses, which may explain why the first full-blown schizophrenic episode typically occurs in adolescence or early adulthood. Healthy teenagers lose about 1 percent of the brain's gray matter between ages 13 and 18. But as you can see in Figure 15.6, in a study that tracked the loss of gray matter in the brain over 5 years, adolescents with schizophrenia showed much more extensive and rapid tissue loss, primarily in the sensory and motor regions (Thompson et al., 2001b). "We were stunned to see a spreading wave of tissue loss that began in a small region of the brain," said Paul Thompson, who headed the study. "It moved across the brain like a forest fire, destroying more tissue as the disease progressed."

Thus, the developmental pathway of schizophrenia is something of a relay. It starts with genetic predispositions, which may combine with prenatal risk factors or birth complications that affect brain development. The resulting vulnerability then awaits the next stage, synaptic pruning within the brain during adolescence (Walker & Tessner, 2008). Then, according to the vulnerability–stress model of schizophrenia, these biological changes usually interact with environmental stressors to trigger the disease. This model explains why one identical twin may develop schizophrenia but not the other: Both may have a genetic susceptibility, but only one may have been exposed to other risk factors in the womb, birth complications, or stressful life events. These and other aspects of this disorder are discussed in the video *Schizophrenia*.

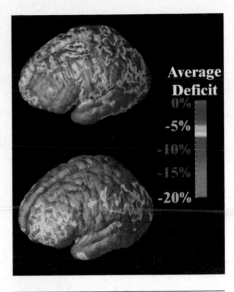

Average Deficit
0%
-5%
-10%
-15%
-20%

Figure 15.6 The Adolescent Brain and Schizophrenia

These dramatic images highlight areas of brain-tissue loss in adolescents with schizophrenia over a 5-year span. The areas of greatest tissue loss (regions that control memory, hearing, motor functions, and attention) are shown in red and magenta. The brain of a person without schizophrenia (top) looks almost entirely blue (P. Thompson et al., 2001b).

00:02 / 04:03

We have come to the end of a long walk along the spectrum of psychological problems—from those that cause temporary difficulty, such as occasional anxiety or "caffeine intoxication," to others that are severely disabling, such as major depression and schizophrenia. Psychologists strive to learn how biology, thought processes, culture, and experiences interact to produce these problems—the better to alleviate the suffering they cause.

JOURNAL PROMPT 15.8

Thinking Critically—Examine the Evidence: As you've no doubt seen on many police dramas, many psychological disorders can be faked. Even in real life criminals have feigned mental illness to get sympathy, negotiate reduced sentences, or avoid culpability. Schizophrenia would seem to be an easy disorder to fake: "Just act crazy." But if you were tasked with determining the validity of someone's diagnosis of schizophrenia, what evidence would you consult? What key indicators would you use to separate a false diagnosis from a true one? In your opinion, what would be the *best* evidence to determine whether someone had a legitimate diagnosis or not?

Quiz for Module 15.8

1. Which of the following is *not* a symptom of schizophrenia?
   a. Disorganized speech
   b. Hallucinations
   c. Delusional thinking
   d. Split personality

2. Jezebel has distorted perceptions of reality—she thinks her cat is controlling her thoughts and shows a general inability to function in most aspects of her life; she can't hold a job, she lives in isolation, and she rarely bathes. Jezebel is showing classic signs of
   a. Depression
   b. Neurosis
   c. Psychosis
   d. Dissociation

3. Hugh says he hears voices saying the same thing over and over: "Empty. Hollow. Thud." Yet objectively there is no one around and no one who is speaking. Hugh is suffering from
   a. Hallucinations
   b. Delusions
   c. Paranoiac disorder
   d. Dissociative personality disorder

4. Which of the following people is most likely to show a genetic vulnerability to developing schizophrenia?
   a. A fraternal twin of a person with schizophrenia
   b. The child of one schizophrenic parent
   c. An identical twin of a person with schizophrenia
   d. A sibling of a person with schizophrenia

5. A person's first full-blown schizophrenic episodes tend to occur in
   a. Adolescence or early adulthood
   b. Middle age
   c. Private
   d. The preoperational stage of cognitive development

Taking Psychology with You

Mental Disorder and Personal Responsibility

Romance writer Janet Dailey was once caught having plagiarized whole passages from another writer's work, and in self-defense she said she was suffering from "a psychological problem that I never even suspected I had." We wonder if it was in the DSM—but would it matter if it were? What "psychological problem" would absolve a person of responsibility for cheating?

One of the great questions generated by all diagnoses of mental disorder concerns personal responsibility, a topic that requires us to ask the right questions, examine the best evidence, and sometimes live with uncertainty. In law and in everyday life, many people reach for a psychological reason to exonerate themselves of responsibility for their actions. Many people—as an excuse for some habit that is immoral, illegal, or fattening—claim they are addicted to the behavior, whether it is having sex, shoplifting, or eating chocolate. Is their behavior really an "addiction" in the same way that drug addiction is? What about the behavior of a student who spends hours on end on the Internet? Some psychologists would call this an addiction if the student constantly goes online as a way of coping with depression, anxiety, or another emotional problem. But others believe that the student is probably no different from those in previous generations, who also found plenty of ways to avoid the common problems facing students everywhere: insecurity, worry about grades, a disappointing social life. This is not a mental disorder, they say, it's a normal problem, called Learning To Pass Courses and Figure Out Life.

This photo of Jared Lee Loughner was taken by the sheriff's office on the day he was arrested. In 2012, he was sentenced to life in prison without possibility of parole.

In criminal cases, where a defendant with a severe mental disorder has committed murder, debates about appropriate penalties continue. (The insanity defense is used in less than 1 percent of all criminal cases, and in those, 9 out of 10 defendants end up in mental hospitals, usually for far longer than they would have served with a criminal conviction.) In January 2011, Jared Lee Loughner went to a mall in Tucson, where he killed six people and wounded 14 more, including Congresswoman Gabrielle Giffords. His Internet postings were full of incoherent, hostile themes, including paranoid distrust of the government and his college. His friends, classmates, and own writings revealed that he had been undergoing a slow downward spiral in the preceding 2 years. Loughner's trial was suspended while he underwent psychiatric treatment for schizophrenia, and in the ensuing year, the courts struggled to decide whether he should be forcibly medicated with antipsychotics, which would make him seem "normal" in the courtroom, or whether he had the right to refuse.

Or consider Andrea Yates, a Texas woman who killed her five young children. Yates had suffered from clinical depression and psychotic episodes for years, and had tried to kill herself twice. Yates was overwhelmed by raising and homeschooling all of her children by herself, with no help from her reportedly domineering husband, who permitted her 2 hours a week of personal time. Although she suffered a postpartum psychotic episode after the birth of their fourth child and a clinical psychologist warned against her having another baby, her husband refused to consider birth control, although not for religious reasons. Yates was convicted of murder and sentenced to life in prison. On appeal 4 years later, another jury found her not guilty by reason of insanity and she was sent to a mental institution.

Do Jared Loughner and Andrea Yates deserve our pity, along with our condemnation for their horrible acts of murder? Interestingly, many observers feel angrier and less sympathetic toward people whose mental illnesses conform to gender stereotypes: men, like Jared Loughner, who are schizophrenic or alcoholic, and women, like Andrea Yates, who are depressed. They are more sympathetic to people whose illnesses do not conform to the stereotype: alcoholic or schizophrenic women and depressed men (Wirth & Bodenhausen, 2009). Apparently, many people think that gender-typical mental disorders are less likely to be "real."

What about murderers who understand right from wrong, who are not legally insane but cannot control themselves? If we learn that their behavior might be a result of brain damage, should that affect the punishment they receive? In some jurisdictions, a defendant may claim to have diminished responsibility for a crime. This claim does not exonerate the defendant, but it may result in reduced charges, perhaps from premeditated first-degree murder to manslaughter, or a milder sentence if the defendant is found guilty. A diminished-capacity defense holds that the defendant lacked the mental capacity to form a calculated and malicious plan but instead was impaired by mental illness or the great provocation of the situation.

When thinking about the relationship of mental disorder to personal responsibility, we face a dilemma, one that requires us to tolerate uncertainty. The law recognizes, rightly, that people who are mentally incompetent, delusional, or disturbed should not be judged by the same standards as mentally healthy individuals. At the same time, society has an obligation to protect its citizens from harm and to reject easy excuses for violations of the law. To balance these two positions, we need to find ways to ensure that people who commit crimes or behave reprehensibly face the consequences of their behavior, and also that people who are suffering from psychological problems have the compassionate support of society in their search for help. After all, psychological problems of one kind or another are challenges that all of us will face at some time in our lives.

Shared Writing Prompt

Scott Panetti's execution in the state of Texas was halted just 12 hours before it was to take place. Panetti has been on death row since 1995 for killing his in-laws while his wife and daughter watched. There's no dispute that he committed the crime or that he had his day in court. In fact, Panetti served as his own counsel, calling the Pope, J.F.K., and Jesus Christ to the witness stand on his behalf. You see, Scott Panetti has suffered from schizophrenia for the past 30 years, and it is unclear whether he understands the reasons for his impending execution (he thinks Satan is working through the state of Texas to punish him for his biblical preaching). What do you think? Should a demonstrably mentally ill person, judged by a jury, guilty of a capital offense, be put to death for his crime? Or are there extenuating circumstances that should mitigate his punishment?

Summary

Diagnosing Mental Disorders

LO 15.1.A Consider why it is difficult to obtain a universally agreed-upon definition of "mental disorder."

When defining *mental disorder*, mental health professionals emphasize the emotional suffering caused by the behavior, whether the behavior is harmful to others or society, and its degree of "harmful dysfunction."

LO 15.1.B Describe four dangers associated with using the DSM for diagnosis of mental disorders, and give an example of each.

The *Diagnostic and Statistical Manual of Mental Disorders (DSM)* is designed to provide objective criteria and categories for diagnosing mental disorder. Critics argue that the diagnosis of mental disorders, unlike those of medical diseases, is inherently a subjective process. They believe the DSM fosters overdiagnosis; overlooks the negative consequences of being given a diagnostic label; confuses serious mental disorders with everyday problems in living; and creates an illusion of objectivity. Supporters of the DSM believe that when the DSM criteria are used correctly and when empirically validated objective tests are used, reliability in diagnosis improves.

LO 15.1.C Explain the theoretical basis of projective tests, and identify the problems associated with these techniques.

In diagnosing psychological disorders, clinicians often use *projective tests* such as the *Rorschach inkblot test* or, with children, anatomically detailed dolls. These methods have low reliability and validity, creating problems when they are used in the legal arena, as in custody disputes, or in diagnosing disorders. In general, *objective tests (inventories)*, such as the *MMPI*, are more reliable and valid than projective ones.

Anxiety Disorders

LO 15.2.A Differentiate the major symptoms of generalized anxiety disorder and panic disorder.

Generalized anxiety disorder involves continuous, chronic anxiety and worry that interferes with daily functioning. *Panic disorder* involves sudden, intense attacks of profound fear. Panic attacks are common in the aftermath of stress or frightening experiences; those who go on to develop a disorder tend to interpret the attacks as a sign of impending disaster.

LO 15.2.B Describe the characteristics of a phobia, and explain why agoraphobia can be so disabling.

Phobias are unrealistic fears of specific situations, activities, or things. Common *social phobias* include fears of speaking in public, eating in a restaurant, or having to perform for an audience. *Agoraphobia*, the fear of being away from a safe place or person, is the most disabling phobia—a "fear of fear." It often begins with a panic attack, which the person tries to avoid in the future by staying close to "safe" places or people.

Trauma and Obsessive-Compulsive Disorders

LO 15.3.A Define posttraumatic stress disorder, and discuss its symptoms and origins.

Most people who live through a traumatic experience eventually recover, but a minority develop *posttraumatic stress disorder (PTSD)*, which involves such symptoms as nightmares, flashbacks, insomnia, and increased physiological arousal. The reasons for their increased vulnerability to traumatic events include genetic vulnerability; a history of psychological problems; a lack of social and cognitive resources; and having a smaller hippocampus than normal.

LO 15.3.B Distinguish between obsessions and compulsions, and discuss the defining elements of obsessive–compulsive disorder.

Obsessive–compulsive disorder (OCD) involves recurrent, unwished-for thoughts or images (obsessions) and repetitive, ritualized behaviors (compulsions) that a person feels unable to control. Some people with OCD have abnormalities in an area of the prefrontal cortex, which may contribute to their cognitive and behavioral rigidity. Parts of the brain involved in fear and responses to threat are also more active than normal in people with OCD.

Depressive and Bipolar Disorders

LO 15.4.A   Describe how major depression differs from normal feelings of sadness or loneliness.

Symptoms of *major depression* include distorted thinking patterns, feelings of worthlessness and despair, physical ailments such as fatigue and loss of appetite, and loss of interest in formerly pleasurable activities. Women are twice as likely as men to suffer from major depression, but depression in men may be underdiagnosed.

LO 15.4.B   Explain the main features of bipolar disorder.

In *bipolar disorder*, a person experiences episodes of both depression and *mania* (excessive euphoria), typically alternating between the two. It is equally common in both sexes.

LO 15.4.C   Discuss the four major factors that contribute to the onset of depression.

Vulnerability–stress models of depression (or any other disorder) highlight interactions between individual vulnerabilities and stressful experiences. Because depression is moderately heritable, the search for specific genes continues. For some vulnerable individuals, repeated losses of close relationships can set off episodes of major depression. Experiences with violence and parental neglect, especially in childhood, increase the risk of developing major depression in adulthood. Cognitive habits also play a role: believing that the origin of one's unhappiness is permanent and uncontrollable; feeling hopeless and pessimistic; and brooding or *ruminating* about one's problems.

Personality Disorders

LO 15.5.A   Explain the main features of borderline personality disorder.

Personality disorders are characterized by pathological personality traits that cause distress or an inability to get along with others. One is *borderline personality disorder*, characterized by extreme negative emotionality and an inability to regulate emotions, often resulting in intense but unstable relationships, self-mutilating behavior, feelings of emptiness, and a fear of abandonment by others.

LO 15.5.B   Distinguish between the terms *psychopathy* and *antisocial personality disorder*, and note the common elements of each.

Antisocial personality disorder describes people with a pattern of aggressive, reckless, impulsive, and often criminal behavior. Some people with APD have abnormalities in the prefrontal cortex, which can be a result of genetics, disease, or physical abuse.

LO 15.5.C   List and explain the major factors that contribute to the central features of psychopathy.

The term *psychopath* describes people who lack conscience and empathy; they are fearless and have trouble recognizing signs of fear in others, which makes normal socialization difficult. They do not feel remorse, shame, guilt, or anxiety over wrongdoing, and they can con others with ease. Contrary to stereotype, most psychopaths are not violent criminals, and many criminals are not psychopaths.

Drug Abuse and Addiction

LO 15.6.A   Discuss how the biological model of addiction would explain drug abuse and alcoholism.

According to the *biological (disease) model* of addiction, some people have a genetic vulnerability to the kind of alcoholism that begins in early adolescence and is linked to impulsivity, antisocial behavior, and criminality. Genes also affect sensitivity to alcohol, which varies across ethnic groups as well as among individuals. But heavy drug abuse also changes the brain in ways that make addiction more likely.

LO 15.6.B   Discuss how the learning model of addiction would explain drug abuse and alcoholism.

Advocates of the *learning model* of addiction point out that addiction patterns vary according to cultural practices and values; that policies of total abstinence tend to increase addiction rates and abuse because people who want to drink fail to learn how to drink in moderation; that many people can stop taking drugs without experiencing withdrawal symptoms; and that drug abuse depends on the reasons for taking a drug.

LO 15.6.C   Explain the different predictions that the biological model and learning model would make regarding the benefits of total abstinence from versus moderate intake of alcohol.

The biological and learning models are polarized on many issues, notably that of abstinence versus moderation. People who are most likely to abuse alcohol and other drugs have a genetic vulnerability or prolonged drug use has damaged their brains; they believe that they have no control over the drug; their culture or peer group promotes drug abuse; and they rely on the drug to cope with problems.

Dissociative Identity Disorder

LO 15.7.A   Discuss the factors that make dissociative identity disorder a controversial diagnosis.

In *dissociative identity disorder (DID)*, formerly called *multiple personality disorder (MPD)*, two or more distinct personalities and identities appear to split off (*dissociate*) within one person. Media coverage of sensational alleged cases of multiple personality, including the fraudulent case of "Sybil," greatly contributed to the rise in cases after 1980.

LO 15.7.B   Evaluate the likely explanations for dissociative personality disorder.

Some clinicians think DID is legitimate and originates in childhood trauma. But psychological scientists hold a *sociocognitive* explanation; namely, that DID is an extreme form of the ability to present different aspects of our personalities to others. In this view, the disorder emerges from pressure and suggestion by clinicians who believe in its prevalence, interacting with vulnerable patients who find the diagnosis a plausible explanation for their problems, thereby creating a culture-bound syndrome.

Schizophrenia

LO 15.8.A Describe the five major symptoms of schizophrenia, and give an example of each.

Schizophrenia is a psychotic disorder involving delusions, hallucinations, disorganized speech, inappropriate behavior, and negative symptoms, such as loss of motivation to take care of oneself and emotional flatness. Contrary to stereotype, however, many people with schizophrenia recover.

LO 15.8.B Describe the three main contributing factors to the origin of schizophrenia.

Schizophrenia is a brain disease that involves certain structural brain abnormalities, such as enlarged ventricles and neurotransmitter abnormalities. In the "relay" that produces the disorder, genetic predispositions interact with prenatal problems or birth complications, and excessive pruning of synapses during adolescence, all interacting with environmental stressors.

Chapter 15 Quiz

1. Patsy is plagued by troubling thoughts and actions that cause her a great deal of distress. She has difficulty holding a job for longer than a few weeks due to her condition. She has impaired social relations and is estranged from her family and former friends. According to the definition of mental disorder used in this chapter, what additional question would you want answered before concluding Patsy suffers from a psychological disorder?
   a. "Is the behavior self-destructive?"
   b. "Is the behavior abnormal?"
   c. "Does the behavior meet the definition of 'insanity'?"
   d. "Is the condition treatable?"

2. The main reference book used to aid in the clinical diagnosis of mental illness is called
   a. DMSO
   b. IPV
   c. ICBM
   d. DSM

3. Which of the following is *not* a concern associated with using projective tests as a primary means of diagnosing mental disorders?
   a. They haven't been available for very long, so their utility isn't yet known.
   b. They are unreliable, often leading to different interpretations of client responses.
   c. They are invalid, being based on untestable psychodynamic theories.
   d. Support comes primarily from anecdotal endorsements rather than experimental tests.

4. Barlow feels nervous and worried pretty much all the time, despite any obvious external circumstances that would justify his feelings. He has difficulty concentrating, and the tension in his jaw and muscles are noticeable, even to a casual observer. When asked how he feels, his typical response is "Dreadful," which is literally and figuratively true. What diagnosis would you make for Barlow's condition?
   a. Panic disorder
   b. Generalized anxiety disorder
   c. Panic disorder with catatonic ideology
   d. Splinophobia

5. Sophia once found herself in a busy restaurant when she had a panic attack, brought on by stress she felt over recent health problems and deaths of her friends and loved ones. A few weeks later she experienced another attack, this time in a grocery store. Over time Sophia gradually reduced her contact with the outside world, fearful that an attack might strike at any moment, and worried that she might find herself helpless, stricken, and embarrassed in a public place. Sophia's initial troubles have developed into
   a. Anthrophobia
   b. Agoraphobia
   c. A personality disorder
   d. Claustrophobia

6. Which of the following statements best characterizes what we know about the origins and development of posttraumatic stress disorder?
   a. PTSD is caused by a genetic variant that makes the peripheral nervous system hyper-responsive to troubling or traumatic situations
   b. Combat veterans who experienced the horrors of war and the traumas associated with it are likely to develop PTSD in the majority of cases.
   c. Childhood trauma accounts for the majority of cases (about 60 percent) of PTSD.
   d. Cases of long-lasting PTSD seem to be the result of impaired cognitive functioning or neurological functioning that was present prior to the trauma, and triggered by the traumatic event.

7. Micah feels the need to wash his feet multiple times a day. He scrubs them with prescription-strength disinfectant using a stiff-bristled brush, rinses them in scalding hot water, then applies a sequence of mechanic's grease remover, Dove bodywash, and harsh lye soap. He repeats this ritual every 4 hours throughout a 12-hour period. Micah is showing classic signs of:

   a. Insanity

   b. Obsession

   c. Compulsion

   d. A personality disorder

8. Alfie increasingly feels listless, worthless, hopeless, and very, very sad. Activities that used to give him pleasure hold no interest for him now, and he has to force himself to eat from time to time. Alfie would most likely be diagnosed with

   a. Generalized anxiety disorder

   b. Major depression

   c. Ataxia

   d. Bipolar disorder

9. Connie has been living with her college roommate, Stephanie, for a little over 2 months. They're becoming good friends, yet Connie is growing increasingly disturbed by Stephanie's behavior. For 3 days at a time Stephanie will lay in bed with the lights off, uncommunicative and disinterested in her friends and classes. However, one day Connie returned home to find Stephanie piling all the furniture in the middle of the room, talking excitedly about painting the ceiling with a toothbrush, and breathlessly describing how she'd worked out a plan to triple-major in Art, Biochemistry, and Political Science. Connie escorted Stephanie to the campus health center, where Stephanie received an initial diagnosis of

   a. Bipolar disorder

   b. Obsessive–compulsive disorder

   c. Borderline personality disorder

   d. Major depression

10. Depressed people typically have the cognitive habit of believing their situation is _____ and

    _____ .

    a. Dire / transitory

    b. Exogenous / endogenous

    c. Undiagnosed / treatable

    d. Permanent / uncontrollable

11. Which of the following is *not* a primary characteristic involved in the diagnosis of borderline personality disorder?

    a. Extreme negative emotionality

    b. Unstable relationships

    c. Lack of remorse

    d. Inability to regulate emotions

12. Antisocial personality disorder can be distinguished from psychopathy on the basis of _____. This characteristic is present in psychopathy but not necessarily in antisocial personality disorder.

    a. Impulsive actions

    b. Irresponsible behavior

    c. Lack of remorse

    d. Law-breaking

13. Two central features of psychopathy are _____ and _____ .

    a. Fearlessness / lack of empathy

    b. Unstable relationships / social discomfort

    c. Attention-seeking / need for admiration

    d. High IQ / careful planning

14. "Alcoholics can't change who they are; once an alcoholic, always an alcoholic." This sentiment would be consistent with:

    a. The detachment model of addiction

    b. The associative model of addiction

    c. The learning model of addiction

    d. The biological model of addiction

15. "The degree to which a person is addicted to a substance depends on the situation the person finds him- or herself in; solutions to addiction should emphasize modifying environments and teaching better life skills." This sentiment would be consistent with

    a. The learning model of addiction

    b. The attachment model of addiction

    c. The biological model of addiction

    d. The rapprochement model of addiction

16. Abstinence programs would tend to be encouraged by those who adopt a _____ model of addiction, whereas moderated intake programs would tend to be encouraged by those who adopt a _____ model of addiction.

    a. Detachment / attachment

    b. Learning / biological

    c. Attachment / detachment

    d. Biological / learning

17. Which of the following statements is damaging evidence against the traditional clinical view of dissociative identity disorder?

    a. The separate personalities within a DID patient typically remain hidden from one another.

    b. Different "alters" may adopt different mannerisms and speech patterns from one another.

    c. The autobiographical memories of DID patients can be transferred between their identities.

    d. DID patients may have more than one other "alter" or identifiable personality.

18. What seems to be a likely explanation for the explosion in diagnoses of dissociative identity disorder?

   a. The stigma associated with DID has been lifted, and patients have been more willing to seek treatment than in the past.

   b. Better tests and refined diagnostic categories have made the diagnosis of DID more accurate.

   c. Therapeutic suggestions and influence may be creating the appearance of identities where none exist.

   d. Improvements in clinical training have allowed practitioners to identify cases of DID in their client populations.

19. Which of the following is *not* an example of a negative symptom in schizophrenia?

   a. Decreased social interaction

   b. Lack of personal care

   c. Delusions

   d. Emotional flatness

20. Which of the following brain structures is enlarged among people with schizophrenia?

   a. Ventricles

   b. Prefrontal cortex gray matter

   c. Temporal lobe gray matter

   d. Cerebellum

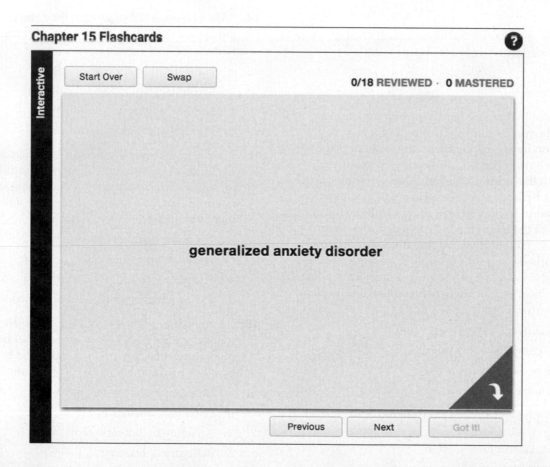

Chapter 15 Flashcards

Interactive

Start Over   Swap   0/18 REVIEWED · 0 MASTERED

generalized anxiety disorder

Previous   Next   Got It!

Chapter 16
Approaches to Treatment and Therapy

◀ Listen to the Audio

∨ Learning Objectives

LO 16.1.A Describe the four main categories of drugs commonly prescribed for the treatment of mental disorders, and discuss five major cautions associated with drug treatment.

LO 16.1.B Identify four forms of direct brain intervention used in treating mental disorders, and discuss the limitations of each.

LO 16.2.A Summarize the main elements of psychodynamic therapy.

LO 16.2.B Describe four methods of behavior therapy, and discuss the main techniques used in cognitive therapy.

LO 16.2.C Summarize the similarities and differences between client-centered therapy and existential therapy.

LO 16.2.D List the hallmarks of the family-systems perspective, and describe how they apply to family and couples therapy.

LO 16.3.A Define the *scientist–practitioner gap*, and identify some of the problems associated with assessing the effectiveness of therapy.

LO 16.3.B Provide examples of areas in which cognitive and behavior therapies have shown themselves to be particularly effective.

LO 16.3.C Discuss four ways in which therapy has the potential to harm clients, and give an example of each.

Ask questions . . . be willing to wonder

Why are there so many kinds of therapies, and how do they differ?

Should a client see a therapist of the same ethnicity?

What kind of therapy works best, and for which problems?

Can therapy ever be harmful?

Have you ever survived a traumatic event—war, violence in your family or neighborhood, the unexpected death of a loved one, or a natural disaster such as an earthquake or hurricane? Have you ever had to move away from the country or ethnic group you grew up in, to find yourself lonely and struggling in a new world? How about the pressures of being in college; do they ever make you feel depressed, worried, or perhaps even panicky?

For most of the emotional problems that all of us suffer on occasion, the two greatest healers are time and the support of friends. For some people, though, time and friends are not enough, and they continue to be troubled by normal life difficulties, such as family quarrels or fear of public speaking, or by a mental disorder: depression, generalized anxiety disorder, phobias, posttraumatic stress disorder, or schizophrenia. What kind of therapy might help them?

To become a licensed clinical psychologist, a person must have an advanced degree and a period of supervised training. However, the title *psychotherapist* is unregulated; anyone can set up any kind of program and call it "therapy"—and, by the thousands, they do! Across the United States and Canada, people can get credentialed as "experts" in some new fad simply by attending a weekend seminar or a training program lasting a week or two. To get the right treatment for whatever problem concerns you, you need to know what to look for and what to avoid.

In this chapter, we will evaluate (1) *biological treatments*, which are primarily provided by psychiatrists or other physicians, and which include medications or intervention in brain function; and (2) *psychotherapy*, specifically these major schools: psychodynamic therapies, cognitive and behavior therapies, humanist therapies, and family or couples therapy. We will assess which kinds of medication and psychotherapy work best for which problems, which ones are not helpful, and which ones might even be harmful.

Biological Treatments for Mental Disorders

For hundreds of years, people have tried to identify the origins of mental illness, attributing the causes at various times to evil spirits, pressure in the skull, disease, or bad environments. Today, biological explanations and treatments are dominant, partly because of evidence that some disorders have a genetic component or involve a biochemical or neurological abnormality, and partly because physicians and pharmaceutical companies have been aggressively promoting biomedical solutions.

The Question of Drugs

LO 16.1.A Describe the four main categories of drugs commonly prescribed for the treatment of mental disorders, and discuss five major cautions associated with drug treatment.

The most commonly used biological treatment is medication that alters the production of or response to neurotransmitters in the brain. Because drugs are so widely advertised and prescribed these days, both for severe disorders such as schizophrenia and for more common problems such as anxiety and depression, consumers need to understand what these drugs are, how they can best be used, and their limitations. Biomedical therapies are discussed in more detail in the video *Therapies in Action 1*.

In the years before the advent of antipsychotic medication, patients with severe mental disorders were often put in straitjackets or chained to their beds to keep them from harming themselves or others.

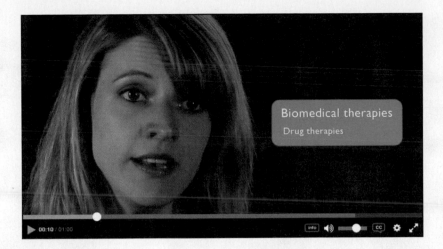

DRUGS COMMONLY PRESCRIBED FOR MENTAL DISORDERS The main classes of drugs used in the treatment of mental and emotional disorders are:

1. **Antipsychotic drugs**, also called *neuroleptics*—older ones such as Thorazine and Haldol and second-generation ones such as Clozaril, Risperdal, Zyprexa, and Seroquel—are used primarily in the treatment of schizophrenia and other psychoses. However, antipsychotic drugs are increasingly being prescribed "off label" for people with nonpsychotic disorders, such as major depression, bipolar disorder, posttraumatic stress disorder (PTSD), autism, attention-deficit disorder, and dementia.

   Most antipsychotic drugs are designed to block or reduce the sensitivity of brain receptors that respond to dopamine; some also block serotonin. Antipsychotic drugs can reduce agitation, delusions, and hallucinations, and they can shorten schizophrenic episodes. But they offer little relief from other symptoms of schizophrenia, such as jumbled thoughts, difficulty concentrating, apathy, emotional flatness, or inability to interact with others. This is why medication by itself is rarely sufficient to help people with schizophrenia manage their symptoms.

   Antipsychotics often cause troubling side effects, especially muscle rigidity, hand tremors, and other involuntary muscle movements, which can develop into a neurological disorder called *tardive* (late-appearing) *dyskinesia*. In addition, Zyprexa, Risperdal, and other antipsychotics, which manufacturers have been targeting for children and older adults, often carry unacceptable risks for these very groups. The immediate side effect is extreme weight gain—anywhere from 24 to 100 extra pounds a year—which has led to the development of thousands of cases of diabetes; other risks include stroke and death from sudden heart failure (Masand, 2000; Suzuki & Uchida, 2014; Wallace-Wells, 2009).

   Although the newer drugs now comprise 90 percent of the market for antipsychotics, a large federally funded study found that they are not significantly safer or more effective than the older, less expensive medications for schizophrenia, the only disorder for which they were originally approved (Lieberman et al., 2005; Swartz et al., 2007). And although antipsychotics are sometimes used to treat impulsive aggressiveness associated with attention-deficit disorder, dementia, and other mental problems, they are ineffective for these disorders. One study followed 86 people, ages 18 to 65, who were given Risperdal, Haldol, or a placebo to treat their aggressive outbursts (Tyrer et al., 2008). The placebo group improved the most. Antipsychotics, which are being given to about one-fifth of combat veterans suffering from PTSD, are also ineffective in reducing symptoms of this disorder (Krystal et al., 2011).

2. **Antidepressant drugs** are used primarily in the treatment of depression, anxiety, phobias, and obsessive–compulsive disorder. *Monoamine oxidase inhibitors (MAOIs)*, such as Nardil, elevate the levels of norepinephrine and serotonin in the brain by blocking or inhibiting an enzyme that deactivates these neurotransmitters. *Tricyclic antidepressants*, such as Elavil and Tofranil, boost norepinephrine and serotonin levels by preventing the normal reabsorption, or "reuptake," of these substances by the cells that have released

antipsychotic drugs

Drugs used primarily in the treatment of schizophrenia and other psychotic disorders; they are often used off label and inappropriately for other disorders such as dementia and impulsive aggressiveness.

antidepressant drugs

Drugs used primarily in the treatment of mood disorders, especially depression and anxiety.

Antipsychotic drugs can help some people with schizophrenia live normal lives. At left, Danny Dunn (seated) poses with her mother. Danny was diagnosed as having schizophrenia and bipolar disorder when she was 17, but medication, therapy, and family support help her function. "I still have challenges and problems," Danny says, "but life is so much better than it used to be." The photo on the right shows USC law professor Elyn Saks, who also benefited from medication and therapy, and wrote a memoir of her "journey through madness." She received a MacArthur Foundation "genius grant" for her contributions to mental health law.

them. These older antidepressants are usually more effective for severe depression than the more recent and popular ones, called *selective serotonin reuptake inhibitors (SSRIs)*, such as Prozac, Zoloft, Lexapro, Paxil, and Celexa (Healy, 2012). SSRIs work on the same principle as the tricyclics but specifically target serotonin; Cymbalta and Remeron target both serotonin and norepinephrine. Wellbutrin is chemically unrelated to the other antidepressants but is often prescribed for depression and sometimes as an aid to quit smoking.

All antidepressants tend to produce some unpleasant physical reactions, including dry mouth, headaches, constipation, nausea, restlessness, gastrointestinal problems, weight gain, and, in as many as one-third of all patients, decreased sexual desire and blocked or delayed orgasm (Hollon, Thase, & Markowitz, 2002). The specific side effects may vary with the particular drug. MAOIs interact with certain foods (such as cheese) and they can elevate blood pressure in some individuals to dangerously high levels, so they have to be carefully monitored. Some MAOIs and SSRIs can also produce tardive dyskinesia, although the risk is less than that associated with antipsychotic medications.

Although antidepressants are said to be nonaddictive, all of them, especially the SSRIs, can produce physical dependence, which may feel the same as an addiction to the person taking them. These medications should not be stopped abruptly without supervision by a physician because physical and emotional withdrawal symptoms may occur—including depression and anxiety, which can be mistaken for a relapse, and even mania, which can then cause the sufferer to be misdiagnosed as having bipolar disorder (Kirsch, 2010; Whitaker, 2010).

Antidepressants and most other psychotropic drugs (i.e., those that influence a person's mental state) now carry strong warnings about the risks of inducing suicide and violence. Of course, some severely depressed people are suicidal, and these drugs can be helpful in alleviating that impulse. But the warnings mean that the clinician and the patient need to be aware that a person on these medications may get worse; if that happens, medication should immediately be reassessed (Healy, 2012).

3. **Anti-anxiety drugs (tranquilizers)**—such as Valium, Xanax, Ativan, and Klonopin—increase the activity of the neurotransmitter gamma-aminobutyric acid (GABA). Tranquilizers may temporarily help individuals who are having an acute anxiety attack, but they are not considered the treatment of choice over time. Symptoms often return if the medication is stopped, and a significant percentage of people who take tranquilizers overuse them and develop problems with withdrawal and tolerance (i.e., they need larger and larger doses to get the same effect). *Beta blockers*, a class of drugs primarily used to manage heart irregularities and hypertension, are sometimes prescribed to relieve acute

tranquilizers

Drugs commonly prescribed for patients who complain of unhappiness, anxiety, or worry.

Review 16.1

Drugs Commonly Used in the Treatment of Psychological Disorders

	Antipsychotics (Neuroleptics)	Antidepressants	Anti-Anxiety Drugs	Lithium Carbonate
Examples	Thorazine Haldol Clozaril Risperdal Coroquol	Prozac (SSRI) Nardil (MAOI) Elavil (tricyclic) Paxil (SSRI) Wellbutrin (other) Cymbalta (other) Remeron (other)	Valium Xanax Klonapin Beta blockers	
Primarily used for	Schizophrenia Other psychoses Impulsive anger Bipolar disorder	Depression Anxiety disorders Panic disorder Obsessive–compulsive disorder	Mood disorders Panic disorder Acute anxiety (e.g., stage fright)	Bipolar disorder

anxiety—for example, caused by stage fright or athletic competition—which they do by slowing the heart rate and lowering blood pressure. But beta blockers are not approved for anxiety disorders.

4. A special category of drug, a salt called **lithium carbonate**, often helps people who suffer from bipolar disorder, although how it produces its effects is unknown. Lithium must be given in exactly the right dose, and bloodstream levels of the drug must be carefully monitored because too little will not help and too much is toxic; in some people, lithium produces short-term side effects (tremors) and long-term problems (kidney damage) (Kemp, 2014). Other drugs commonly prescribed for people with bipolar disorder include Depakote and Tegretol.

For a review of these drugs and their uses, see Review 16.1

SOME CAUTIONS ABOUT DRUG TREATMENTS Without question, drugs have rescued some people from emotional despair and helped countless others live with chronic problems such as schizophrenia, obsessive–compulsive disorder, and panic attacks. They have enabled people suffering from severe depression or mental disturbances to be released from hospitals, to function in the world, and to respond to psychotherapy. Yet many psychiatrists and drug companies are trumpeting the benefits of medication without informing the public of its limitations.

Most people are unaware of how a *publication bias*—the tendency for journals to publish positive findings but not negative or ambiguous ones—affects what we know. Independent researchers were able to obtain unpublished data submitted to the U.S. Food and Drug Administration (FDA) on 12 popular antidepressants, and you can see the surprising results they uncovered in Figure 16.1. Of the 38 studies that reported positive results, 37 were later published. Of the 36 studies with negative or mixed results, only 14 were published (Turner et al., 2008). Even more worrisome for the prospects of impartial research, the majority of researchers who are studying the effectiveness of medication have financial ties to the pharmaceutical industry, in the form of lucrative consulting fees, funding for their clinical trials, stock investments, and patents. Studies that are independently funded often do not get the positive results that industry-funded drug trials do (Angell, 2004; Healy, 2002; Krimsky, 2003). In this section, therefore, we want to give you an idea of what you are not hearing from the drug companies.

1. **The placebo effect.** New drugs often promise quick and effective cures. But the **placebo effect** ensures that many people will respond positively to a new drug just because of the enthusiasm surrounding it and because of their own expectations that the drug will make

lithium carbonate
A drug frequently given to people suffering from bipolar disorder.

placebo effect
The apparent success of a medication or treatment due to the patient's expectations or hopes rather than to the drug or treatment itself.

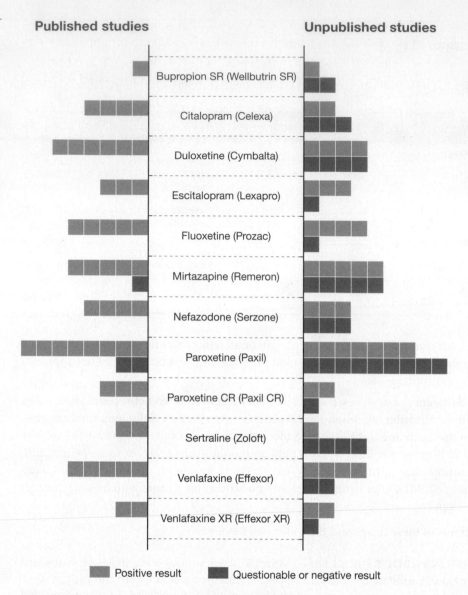

Figure 16.1 Drugs and Publication Bias

To get FDA approval for a new medication, a pharmaceutical company must present evidence of the drug's effectiveness. On the bars in this figure, each box represents one study. On the left side, you can see that most of the published studies supported the effectiveness of 12 antidepressants. But when independent researchers got hold of all of the data submitted to the FDA, they found that many unpublished studies had questionable or negative results (right). (Based on Turner et al., 2008.)

Published studies   **Unpublished studies**

Bupropion SR (Wellbutrin SR)
Citalopram (Celexa)
Duloxetine (Cymbalta)
Escitalopram (Lexapro)
Fluoxetine (Prozac)
Mirtazapine (Remeron)
Nefazodone (Serzone)
Paroxetine (Paxil)
Paroxetine CR (Paxil CR)
Sertraline (Zoloft)
Venlafaxine (Effexor)
Venlafaxine XR (Effexor XR)

■ Positive result   ■ Questionable or negative result

them feel better. After a while, when placebo effects decline, many drugs turn out to be neither as effective as promised nor as widely applicable. This has happened repeatedly with each new generation of tranquilizer and each new "miracle" antipsychotic drug and antidepressant (Healy, 2012; Moncrieff, 2001, 2013).

In fact, considerable evidence shows that much of the effectiveness of antidepressants, especially for people who are only mildly depressed, is due to a placebo effect (Khan et al., 2003; Kirsch, 2010). Overall, only about half of all depressed patients respond positively to any given antidepressant medication, and of those, fewer than half are actually responding to the specific biological effects of the drug (Hollon, Thase, & Markowitz, 2002). A meta-analysis of more than 5,000 patients in 47 clinical trials revealed that the placebo effect was "exceptionally large," accounting for more than 80 percent of the alleviation of symptoms. The drugs were most effective for patients with severe depression (Kirsch et al., 2008). The psychological expectation of improvement by taking a placebo actually produces some of the same brain changes that medication does (Benedetti et al., 2005).

Another line of evidence supports the argument that, for most people, the benefits of antidepressants are unrelated to their chemical action: Higher doses of the drugs do not produce greater reductions in depressive symptoms, only more side effects (Kirsch, 2010). But when the drug isn't working, its manufacturer generally advises the prescribing physician to increase the dose.

2. **High relapse and dropout rates.** A person may have short-term success with antipsychotic or antidepressant drugs. However, in part because of these drugs' unpleasant side effects, anywhere from one-half to two-thirds of people stop taking them. When they do, they are likely to relapse, especially if they have not learned how to cope with their disorders (Hollon et al., 2002).

   One reason some patients may stop taking a drug is that they have been given the wrong dose. The same dose may be metabolized differently in men and women, old people and young people, and Asians and African Americans or Anglos (Lin, Poland, & Chien, 1990; Strickland et al., 1995). Groups may differ in the dosages they can tolerate because of variations in metabolic rates, amount of body fat, the number or type of drug receptors in the brain, or cultural differences in smoking and diet.

3. **Disregard for effective, possibly better nonmedical treatments.** The popularity of drugs has been fueled by pressure from managed-care organizations, which prefer to pay for one patient visit for a prescription rather than 10 visits for psychotherapy, and by drug company marketing and advertising. In 1997, the FDA permitted pharmaceutical companies to advertise directly to the public, a practice still forbidden in most of the rest of the world; sales of new drugs skyrocketed as consumers began to request them. Because ads promise such wonderful results, medication often seems the best way to deal with an emotional or behavioral problem; yet nonmedical treatments may work just as well or better. Consider this study of more than 168,000 children who had been referred to a behavioral-care facility to be treated for attention-deficit disorder. More than 60 percent of the boys and 23 percent of the girls were on Ritalin or another drug. But after six sessions of behavior therapy for the children and 10 sessions for the parent, only 11 percent of the boys and 2 percent of the girls remained on medication (Cummings & Wiggins, 2001; see also March, 2011).

4. **Unknown risks over time and drug interactions.** The effects of taking antidepressants indefinitely are still unknown, especially for vulnerable groups such as children, pregnant women, and older adults—or for the generation of young adults who have been taking them since childhood or adolescence, when the brain is still developing. After British drug authorities reported that nine unpublished studies of Paxil found that it tripled the risk of suicidal thoughts and suicide attempts in adolescents who were taking the drug compared to those given a placebo, the FDA now warns against prescribing SSRIs to anyone under age 18.

   The reason we don't know about long-term effects until a drug has been on the market for years is that new drugs are initially tested clinically on just a few hundred people for just a few weeks or months, even when the drug is one that a person might take indefinitely (Angell, 2004). (The cost of bringing most new drugs to market is very high, and manufacturers feel they cannot afford to wait years to determine whether there might be long-term hazards.) Nonetheless, many psychiatrists, understandably frustrated by the failure of existing antipsychotics and antidepressants to help all of their patients, are prescribing "cocktails" of medications—this one for anxiety, plus this one for depression, plus another to manage the side effects. They report anecdotal success in some cases, but as yet there has been virtually no research on the benefits and risks of these combination approaches.

5. **Untested off-label uses.** Most consumers do not realize that after the FDA approves a drug, doctors are permitted to prescribe it for other conditions and to populations other than those on which it was originally tested. As already noted, antipsychotics such as Risperdal are being used for nonpsychotic disorders. Likewise, antidepressants are being marketed for "social phobias"; Prozac, when its patent expired, was renamed Sarafem and marketed to women for "premenstrual dysphoric disorder"; and Ritalin, widely given to school-aged children, is being prescribed for 2- and 3-year-olds.

In coming years, you will be hearing about many "promising medications" for such common psychological problems as memory loss, eating disorders, smoking, and alcoholism.

Every large pharmaceutical company is working on one or more of these. But we hope you will resist the impulse to jump on any new drug bandwagon. Critical thinkers must weigh the benefits and limitations of any medication for psychological problems; wait for the data on safety and effectiveness; and resist the temptation to oversimplify.

Direct Brain Intervention

LO 16.1.B **Identify four forms of direct brain intervention used in treating mental disorders, and discuss the limitations of each.**

For most of human history, a person suffering from mental illness often got a rather extreme form of "help." A well-meaning tribal healer or, in later centuries, a doctor, would try to release the "psychic pressures" believed to be causing the symptoms by drilling holes in the victim's skull. It didn't work! To learn more about the history of therapeutic "cures," watch the video *Assessing Treatment Effectiveness.*

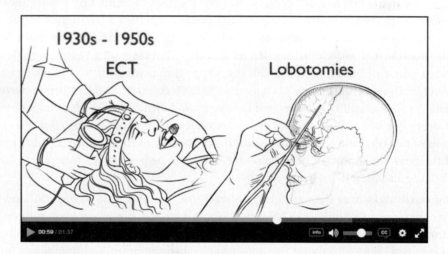

The most famous modern effort to cure mental illness through *psychosurgery*—intervening directly in the brain—was invented in 1935, when a Portuguese neurologist, António Egas Moniz, drilled two holes into the skull of a mental patient and used an instrument to crush nerve fibers running from the prefrontal lobes to other areas. (Later, some doctors just used an ice pick.) This operation, called a *prefrontal lobotomy*, was supposed to reduce the patient's emotional symptoms without impairing intellectual ability. The procedure—which, incredibly, was never assessed or validated scientifically—was performed on more than 40,000 people in the United States, including President John F. Kennedy's sister Rosemary. Tragically, lobotomies left many patients apathetic, withdrawn, and unable to care for themselves (Dully, 2008; Raz, 2013; Valenstein, 1986). Yet, Moniz won a Nobel Prize for his work.

In contrast to surgical intervention, some psychiatrists now attempt to alter brain function by stimulating the brain externally. The oldest method is **electroconvulsive therapy (ECT)**, or "shock therapy," which is used for the treatment of severe depression, although no one knows how or why it works. An electrode is placed on one side of the head and a brief current is turned on. The current triggers a seizure that typically lasts 1 minute, causing the body to convulse. In the past, there were many horror stories about the misuse of ECT and its dire effects on memory. Today, however, patients are given muscle relaxants and anesthesia, so they sleep through the procedure and their convulsions are minimized. The World Psychiatric Association and the FDA have endorsed ECT as safe and effective, especially for people with episodes of crippling depression and suicidal impulses and for those who have not responded to other treatments (Shorter & Healy, 2008). About 100,000 Americans receive ECT every year. However, the mood-improving effect of ECT is usually short-lived, and the depression almost always returns within a few weeks or months (Hollon, Thase, & Markowitz, 2002; U.S. Food and Drug Administration, 2011). And ECT is *ineffective* with other disorders, such as schizophrenia or alcoholism, though it is occasionally misused for these conditions.

electroconvulsive therapy (ECT)

A procedure used in cases of prolonged and severe major depression, in which a brief brain seizure is induced.

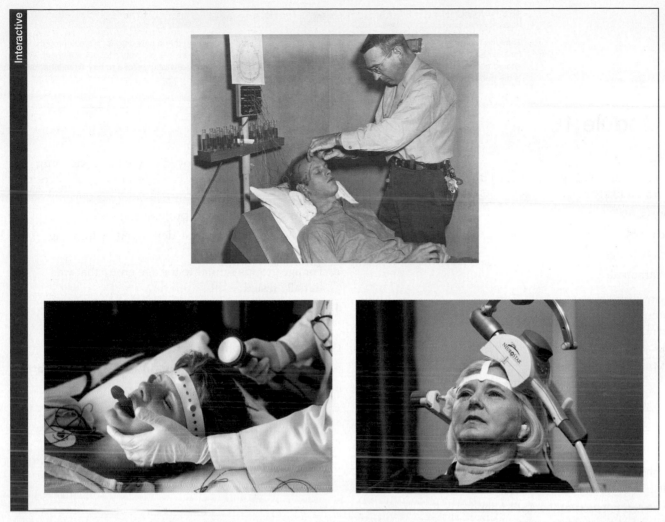

Someone getting a lobotomy (top), a man receiving electroconvulsive therapy (lower left), and a researcher demonstrating transcranial magnetic stimulation (lower right).

Neuroscientists are investigating other ways of electrically stimulating the brains of severely depressed individuals (Nieudworp et al., 2015; Nitsche et al., 2009). One is *transcranial magnetic stimulation (TMS)*, which involves the use of a pulsing magnetic coil held to a person's skull over the left prefrontal cortex, an area of the brain that is less active in people with depression. As with ECT, the benefits of TMS, when they occur, are short-lived, but it can be effective with some patients and has fewer side effects than ECT (George & Post, 2011; Prasser et al., 2015).

In recent years, psychosurgery has returned, with neurologists experimenting with procedures on parts of the brain thought to be involved in various disorders that have not responded to any other treatments (Brunoni et al., 2011). One approach is *deep brain stimulation (DBS)*, which originally was approved for patients with Parkinson's disease and epilepsy; now it is being used for a variety of mental disorders, such as obsessive–compulsive disorder, though again no one knows how or why it might be helpful (Sharma et al., 2015). DBS requires surgery to implant electrodes into the brain and to embed a small box, similar to a pacemaker, under the collarbone. But it also is experimental and risky, and claims of its success are based only on patients' self-reports, so the powerful placebo effect of surgery cannot be ruled out (Lozano et al., 2008). The company that developed this expensive device has hired psychiatrists to lobby for it and mounted a vigorous marketing campaign to get it approved, but critics are concerned that the method has not been adequately tested, its effectiveness and side effects are unknown, and it promises more than it delivers (Barglow, 2008; Fins et al., 2011).

JOURNAL PROMPT 16.1

Thinking Critically—Avoid Emotional Reasoning: You hear a researcher claiming that a new drug is "a breakthrough drug" for depression, or for anxiety, or for some other problem. Such announcements always generate a lot of excitement. Why should people be cautious before concluding that a new drug is the miracle they are longing for it to be? What information is the public often *not* getting from the company that makes the drug?

Quiz for Module 16.1

1. Karl suffers from hallucinations, delusions, and general agitation associated with his psychological disorder. What medication would likely be prescribed to offer some relief?

   a. Antidepressants

   b. Antipsychotics

   c. Anti-anxiety drugs

   d. Lithium carbonate

2. Antidepressant drugs generally known as _____ have been around longer than _____; the first group also tends to be more effective for severe depression than the latter group.

   a. OBEs / MBEs

   b. Omega7s / OCDs

   c. TMSs / DBSs

   d. MAOIs / SSRIs

3. How does lithium carbonate work to treat bipolar disorder?

   a. It lowers the production of anhydrase type 6 in the callosum.

   b. It alters the composition of the ASPM gene.

   c. No one is entirely certain.

   d. It raises the levels of DHO-3 in serotonin receptors.

4. After a drug has been approved by the Food and Drug Administration (FDA), how can it be prescribed by competent medical professionals?

   a. In any way the medical professional sees fit

   b. Only for the intended use developed by the drug manufacturer

   c. For age groups similar to the age group that was initially tested

   d. For groups older than, but not younger than, the intended population

5. How does electroconvulsive therapy (ECT) work?

   a. It realigns axonic connections in an affected brain area.

   b. No one is entirely certain.

   c. It causes the electrical activity throughout the body to be momentarily depolarized.

   d. It stimulates the formation of neural plasticity.

Major Schools of Psychotherapy

All good psychotherapists want to help clients think about their lives in new ways and find solutions to the problems that plague them. In this section, we will consider the major schools of psychotherapy. To illustrate the philosophy and methods of each one, we will focus on a fictional fellow named Murray. Murray is a smart guy whose problem is all too familiar to many students: He procrastinates. He just can't seem to settle down and write his term papers. He keeps getting incompletes, and before long the incompletes turn to Fs. Why does Murray procrastinate, manufacturing his own misery? What kind of therapy might help him? Watch *Therapies in Action 2* for an overview of techniques that are available to mental health professionals.

psychoanalysis

A theory of personality and a method of psychotherapy, developed by Sigmund Freud, that emphasizes the exploration of unconscious motives and conflicts; modern *psychodynamic therapies* share this emphasis but differ from Freudian analysis in various ways.

Psychodynamic Therapy

LO 16.2.A Summarize the main elements of psychodynamic therapy.

Sigmund Freud was the father of the "talking cure," as one of his patients called it. In his method of **psychoanalysis**, which required patients to come for treatment several days a week, often for years, patients talked not about their immediate problems but about their dreams and their memories of childhood. Freud believed that intensive analysis of these

dreams and memories would give patients insight into the unconscious reasons for their symptoms. With insight and emotional release, he believed, the person's symptoms would disappear.

Freud's psychoanalytic method has since evolved into many different forms of *psychodynamic therapy*, all of which share the goal of exploring the unconscious dynamics of personality, such as defenses and conflicts. Proponents of these therapies often refer to them as "depth" therapies because the purpose is to delve into the deep, unconscious processes believed to be the source of the patient's problems rather than to concentrate on "superficial" symptoms and conscious beliefs. One modern psychodynamic approach is based on *object-relations theory*, which emphasizes the unconscious influence of people's earliest mental representations of their parents and how these affect reactions to separations and losses throughout life.

A major element of most psychodynamic therapies is **transference**, the client's transfer (displacement) of emotional elements of his or her inner life—usually feelings about the client's parents—outward onto the analyst. Have you ever responded to a new acquaintance with unusually quick affection or dislike, and later realized it was because the person reminded you of a relative whom you loved or loathed? That experience is similar to transference. In therapy, a woman might transfer her love for her father to the analyst, believing that she has fallen in love with the analyst. A man who is unconsciously angry at his mother for rejecting him might become furious with his analyst for going on vacation. Through analysis of transference in the therapy setting, psychodynamic therapists believe that clients can see their emotional conflicts in action and work through them (Schafer, 1992; Westen, 1998).

transference

In psychodynamic therapies, a critical process in which the client transfers unconscious emotions or reactions, such as emotional feelings about his or her parents, onto the therapist.

Psychodynamic therapists emphasize the clinical importance of transference, the process by which the client transfers emotional feelings toward other important people in his or her life (usually the parents) onto the therapist. They know that "love's arrow" isn't really intended for them!

behavior therapy

A form of therapy that applies principles of classical and operant conditioning to help people change self-defeating or problematic behaviors.

graduated exposure

In behavior therapy, a method in which a person suffering from a phobia or panic attacks is gradually taken into the feared situation or exposed to a traumatic memory until the anxiety subsides.

flooding

In behavior therapy, a form of exposure treatment in which the client is taken directly into a feared situation until his or her panic subsides.

systematic desensitization

In behavior therapy, a step-by-step process of desensitizing a client to a feared object or experience; it is based on the classical-conditioning procedure of counter-conditioning.

Today, most psychodynamic therapists borrow methods from other forms of therapy. They are more concerned with helping clients solve their problems and ease their emotional symptoms than traditional analysts were, and they tend to limit therapy to a specific number of sessions, say, 10 or 20. Perhaps they might help our friend Murray gain the insight that he procrastinates as a way of expressing anger toward his parents. He might realize that he is angry because they insist he study for a career he dislikes. Ideally, Murray will come to this insight by himself. If the analyst suggests it, Murray might feel too defensive to accept it.

Behavior and Cognitive Therapy

LO 16.2.B Describe four methods of behavior therapy, and discuss the main techniques used in cognitive therapy.

Clinical psychologists who practice behavior therapy would get right to the problem: What are the reinforcers in Murray's environment that are maintaining his behavior? "Mur," they would say, "forget about insight. You have lousy study habits." Clinicians who practice cognitive therapy would focus on helping Murray understand how his beliefs about studying, writing papers, and success are woefully unrealistic. Often these two approaches are combined.

BEHAVIORAL TECHNIQUES   **Behavior therapy** is based on principles of classical and operant conditioning. Here are some of these methods (Martin & Pear, 2014):

1. **Exposure.** The most widely used behavioral approach for treating fears and panic is **graduated exposure**. When people are afraid of some situation, object, or upsetting memory, they usually do everything they can to avoid confronting or thinking of it. Unfortunately, this seemingly logical response only makes the fear worse. Exposure treatments, either in the client's imagination or in actual situations, are aimed at reversing this tendency. In graduated exposure, the client controls the degree of confrontation with the source of the fear. Someone who is trying to avoid thinking of a traumatic event might be asked to imagine the event over and over, until it no longer evokes the same degree of panic. A more dramatic form of exposure is **flooding**, in which the therapist takes the client directly into the feared situation and remains there until the client's panic and anxiety decline. Thus a person suffering from agoraphobia might be taken into a department store or a subway, an action that would normally be terrifying to contemplate.

2. **Systematic desensitization.** Systematic desensitization is an older behavioral method, a step-by-step process of breaking down a client's conditioned associations with a feared object or experience (Wolpe, 1958). It is based on the classical-conditioning procedure of *counterconditioning*, in which a stimulus (such as a dog) for an unwanted response (such as fear) is paired with some other stimulus or situation that elicits a response incompatible with the undesirable one. In this case, the incompatible response is usually relaxation. The client learns to relax deeply while imagining or looking at a sequence of feared stimuli, arranged in a hierarchy from the least frightening to the most frightening. The hierarchy itself is provided by the client. The sequence for a person who is terrified of spiders might be to read the classic children's story *Charlotte's Web*, then look at pictures of small, cute spiders, then look at pictures of taran-

In this virtual reality version of systematic desensitization, a man uses technology to overcome his fear of heights.

tulas, then move on to observing a real spider, and so on. At each step, the person must become relaxed before going on. Eventually, the fear responses are extinguished.

In a growing specialty called *cybertherapy*, some behavior therapists have developed virtual reality (VR) programs to desensitize clients to various phobias, notably of flying, heights, spiders, and public speaking, and to help clients reduce anxiety (Gregg & Tarrier, 2007; Jacob & Storch, 2015; Wiederhold & Wiederhold, 2000.) Others are experimenting with VR to treat combat veterans who are suffering from intractable posttraumatic stress symptoms. In a program called Virtual Iraq/Afghanistan, vets get a combination of exposure and desensitization (Rizzo et al., 2015b). They wear a helmet with video goggles and earphones to hear the sounds of war, and then play a modified version of the VR game *Full Spectrum Warrior* adapted to the Iraq experience (S. Halpern, 2008; Rizzo et al., 2015a).

3. **Behavioral self-monitoring.** Before you can change your behavior, it helps to identify the reinforcers that are supporting your unwanted habits: attention from others, temporary relief from tension or unhappiness, or tangible rewards such as money or a good meal. One way to do this is to keep a record of the behavior that you would like to change. Would you like to cut back on eating sweets? You may not be aware of how much you are eating throughout the day to relieve tension, to boost your energy, or just to be sociable when you are hanging out; a behavioral record will show just how much and when you eat. A mother might complain that her child "always" has temper tantrums; a behavioral record will show when, where, and with whom those tantrums occur. After the unwanted behavior is identified, along with the reinforcers that have been maintaining it, a treatment program can be designed to change it. For instance, you might find other ways to reduce stress besides eating, and make sure that you are nowhere near junk food in the late afternoon, when your energy is low. The mother can learn to respond to her child's tantrum not with her attention (or a cookie to buy silence) but with a time-out, banishing the child to a corner where no positive reinforcers are available.

4. **Skills training.** It is not enough to tell someone "Don't be shy" if the person does not know how to make small talk with others, or "Don't yell!" if the person does not know how to express feelings calmly. Therefore, some behavior therapists use operant-conditioning techniques, modeling, and role-playing to teach the skills a client might lack. A shy person might learn how to converse in social settings by focusing on other people rather than on his or her own insecurity. Skills-training programs have been designed for all kinds of behavioral problems: to teach parents how to discipline their children, impulsive adults how to manage anger, autistic children how to behave appropriately, and people with schizophrenia how to hold a job. These skills are also being taught in virtual worlds, such as *Second Life*. After face-to-face sessions with a therapist, the client creates an avatar to explore a virtual environment and experiment with new behaviors; the therapist can monitor the client's psychological and even physiological reactions at the same time.

A behaviorist would treat Murray's procrastination in several ways. Monitoring his own behavior with a diary would let Murray know exactly how he spends his time, and how much time he should realistically allot to a project. Instead of having a vague, impossibly huge goal, such as "I'm going to reorganize my life," Murray would establish specific small goals, such as reading the two books necessary for an English paper and writing one page of an assignment. If Murray does not know how to write clearly, however, even writing one page might feel overwhelming; he might also need some skills training, such as a basic composition class. Most of all, the therapist would change the reinforcers that are maintaining Murray's "procrastination behavior"—perhaps the immediate gratification of partying with friends—and replace them with reinforcers for getting the work done.

COGNITIVE TECHNIQUES Gloomy thoughts can generate an array of negative emotions and self-defeating behavior. The underlying premise of **cognitive therapy** is that constructive thinking can do the opposite, reducing or dispelling anger, fear, and depression. Cognitive therapists help clients identify the beliefs and expectations that might be unnecessarily prolonging their unhappiness, conflicts, and other problems (J. Beck, 2011). They ask clients to examine the evidence for their beliefs that everyone is mean and selfish, that ambition is hopeless, or that love is doomed. Clients learn to consider other explanations for the behavior

behavioral self-monitoring

In behavior therapy, a method of keeping careful data on the frequency and consequences of the behavior to be changed.

skills training

In behavior therapy, an effort to teach the client skills that he or she may lack, as well as new constructive behaviors to replace self-defeating ones.

cognitive therapy

A form of therapy designed to identify and change irrational, unproductive ways of thinking and, hence, to reduce negative emotions.

Can you cure your fears? Write down a list of situations that evoke your fear, starting with one that produces little anxiety (e.g., seeing a photo of a tiny spider) and ending with the most frightening one possible (e.g., looking at live tarantulas at the pet store). Then find a quiet room where you will have no distractions or interruptions, sit in a comfortable reclining chair, and relax all the muscles of your body. Breathe slowly and deeply. Imagine the first, easiest scene, remaining as relaxed as possible. Do this until you can confront the image without becoming the least bit anxious. When that happens, go on to the next scene in your hierarchy. Do not try this all at once; space out your sessions over time. Does it work?

rational emotive behavior therapy (REBT)

A form of cognitive therapy devised by Albert Ellis, designed to challenge the client's unrealistic thoughts.

of people who annoy them: Was my father's strict discipline an attempt to control me, as I have always believed? What if he was really trying to protect and care for me? By requiring people to identify their assumptions and biases, examine the evidence, and consider other interpretations, cognitive therapy, as you can see, teaches critical thinking.

Aaron Beck pioneered the application of cognitive therapy for depression (Beck, 1976; Beck & Dozois, 2011). Depression often arises from specific pessimistic thoughts that the sources of your misery are permanent and that nothing good will ever happen to you again. For Beck, these beliefs are not "irrational"; rather, they are unproductive or based on misinformation. A therapist using Beck's approach would ask you to test your beliefs against the evidence. If you say, "But I *know* no one likes me," the therapist might say, "Oh, yes? How do you know? Do you really not have a single friend? Has anyone in the past year been nice to you?"

Another school of cognitive therapy is Albert Ellis's **rational emotive behavior therapy (REBT)** (Ellis, 1993; Ellis & Ellis, 2011). In this approach, the therapist uses rational arguments to directly challenge a client's unrealistic beliefs or expectations. Ellis pointed out that people who are emotionally upset often *overgeneralize*: They decide that one annoying act by someone means that person is bad in every way, or that a normal mistake they made is evidence that they are rotten to the core. Many people also *catastrophize*, transforming a small problem into disaster: "I failed this test, and now I'll flunk out of school, and no one will ever like me, and even my cat will hate me, and I'll never get a job." Many people drive themselves crazy with notions of what they "must" do. The therapist challenges these thoughts directly, showing the client why they are irrational and misguided.

A cognitive therapist might treat Murray's procrastination by having Murray write down his thoughts about work, read the thoughts as if someone else had said them, and then write a rational response to each one. This technique would encourage Murray to examine the validity of his assumptions and beliefs. Many procrastinators are perfectionists; if they cannot do something perfectly, they will not do it at all. Unable to accept their limitations, they set impossible standards and catastrophize:

Negative Thought	Rational Response
If I don't get an A+ on this paper, my life will be ruined.	My life will be a lot worse if I keep getting incompletes. It's better to get a B or even a C than to do nothing.
My professor is going to think I'm an idiot when he reads this. I'll feel humiliated by his criticism.	He hasn't accused me of being an idiot yet. If he makes some criticisms, I can learn from them and do better next time.

In the past, behavioral and cognitive therapists debated whether it is most helpful to work on changing clients' thoughts or changing their behavior. But today, most of them believe that thoughts and behavior influence each other, which is why *cognitive-behavioral therapy (CBT)* is more common than either cognitive or behavior therapy alone.

A new wave of CBT practitioners, inspired by Eastern philosophies such as Buddhism, has begun to question the goal of changing a client's self-defeating thoughts. They argue that it is difficult to completely eliminate unwanted thoughts and feelings, especially when people have been rehearsing them for years. They therefore propose a form of CBT based on "mindfulness" and "acceptance": Clients learn to explicitly identify and accept whatever negative thoughts and feelings arise, without trying to eradicate them or letting them derail healthy behavior (Khoury et al., 2013; Norton et al., 2015). Instead of trying to persuade a client who is afraid of making public speeches that her fear is irrational, therapists who adopt this approach would encourage her to accept the anxious thoughts and feelings without judging them—or herself—harshly. Then she can focus on coping techniques and ways of giving speeches *despite* her anxiety. Another effective version of mindfulness-based cognitive therapy adds the Eastern tradition of "attentional breathing," which a client practices when he or she is in a low mood or beginning a downward spiral of negative, depressive thoughts (Coelho, Canter, & Ernst, 2007; Segal, Teasdale, & Williams, 2004). By sitting quietly and focusing attention on the present moment, especially on awareness of one's breath, a person can interrupt the spiral of negative thinking. Health psychologists advise this technique for reducing stress and improving daily well-being. You can learn more about this technique and its applications by watching the video *Cognitive-Behavioral Therapy*.

Humanist and Existential Therapy

LO 16.2.C **Summarize the similarities and differences between client-centered therapy and existential therapy.**

In the 1960s, *humanist psychologists* rejected the two dominant psychological approaches of the time, psychoanalysis and behaviorism. Humanists regarded psychoanalysis, with its emphasis on dangerous sexual and aggressive impulses, as too pessimistic a view of human nature, one that overlooked human resilience and the capacity for joy. And humanists regarded behaviorism, with its emphasis on observable acts, as too mechanistic and "mindless" a view of human nature, one that ignored what really matters to most people—their uniquely human hopes and aspirations. In the humanists' view, human behavior is not completely determined by either unconscious conflicts or the environment. People are capable of free will and therefore have the ability to make more of themselves than either psychoanalysts or behaviorists would predict. The goal of humanist psychology was, and still is, to help people express themselves creatively and achieve their full potential.

Humanist therapy, like its parent philosophy humanism, starts from the assumption that human nature is basically good and that people behave badly or develop problems when they have been warped by self-imposed limits. Humanist therapists, therefore, want to know how clients subjectively see their own situations and how they construe the world around them. They explore what is going on "here and now," not past issues of "why and how."

In **client-centered (nondirective) therapy**, developed by Carl Rogers, the therapist's role is to listen to the client's needs in an accepting, nonjudgmental way and to offer what Rogers called *unconditional positive regard*. Whatever the client's specific complaint is, the goal is to build the client's self-esteem and self-acceptance and help the client find a more productive way of seeing his or her problems. Thus, a Rogerian might assume that Murray's procrastination masks his low self-regard and that Murray is out of touch with his real feelings and wishes. Perhaps he is not passing his courses because he is trying to please his parents by majoring in prelaw when he would secretly rather become an artist. Rogers (1951, 1961) believed that effective therapists must be warm and genuine. For Rogerians, *empathy*, the therapist's ability to understand what the client says and identify the client's feelings, is the crucial ingredient of successful therapy: "I understand

humanist therapy

A form of psychotherapy based on the philosophy of humanism, which emphasizes personal growth, resilience, the achievement of human potential, and the client's ability to change rather than being destined to repeat past conflicts.

client-centered (nondirective) therapy

A humanist approach, devised by Carl Rogers, which emphasizes the therapist's empathy with the client and the use of unconditional positive regard.

Humanist therapists emphasize the importance of warmth, concern, and empathic listening to the client.

existential therapy

A form of therapy designed to help clients explore the meaning of existence and face the great questions of life, such as death, freedom, alienation, and loneliness.

how frustrated you must be feeling, Murray, because no matter how hard you try, you don't succeed." The client will eventually internalize the therapist's support and become more self-accepting.

Existential therapy helps clients face the great questions of existence, such as death, freedom, loneliness, and meaninglessness. Existential therapists, like humanist therapists, believe that our lives are not inevitably determined by our pasts or our circumstances; we have the free will to choose our own destinies. As Irvin Yalom (1989) explained, "The crucial first step in therapy is the patient's assumption of responsibility for his or her life predicament. As long as one believes that one's problems are caused by some force or agency outside oneself, there is no leverage in therapy." Yalom argues that the goal of therapy is to help clients cope with the inescapable realities of life and death and the struggle for meaning. However grim our experiences may be, he believes, "they contain the seeds of wisdom and redemption." Perhaps the most remarkable example of a man able to find seeds of wisdom in a barren landscape was Viktor Frankl (1905–1997), who developed a form of existential therapy after surviving a Nazi concentration camp. In that pit of horror, Frankl (1955) observed, some people maintained their sanity because they were able to find meaning in the experience, shattering though it was.

Some observers believe that all therapies are ultimately existential. In different ways, therapy helps people determine what matters to them, what values guide them, and what changes they will have the courage to make. A humanist or existential therapist might help Murray think about the significance of his procrastination, what his ultimate goals in life are, and how he might find the strength to reach them.

Family and Couples Therapy

LO 16.2.D List the hallmarks of the family-systems perspective, and describe how they apply to family and couples therapy.

Murray's situation is getting worse. His father has begun to call him Tomorrow Man, which upsets his mother, and his younger brother, the math major, has been calculating how much tuition money Murray's incompletes are costing. His older sister, Isabel, the biochemist who never took an incomplete grade in her life, now proposes that all of them go to a family therapist. "Murray's not the only one in this family with complaints," she says.

Family therapists would maintain that Murray's problem developed in the context of his family, that it is sustained by the dynamics of his family, and that any change he makes will affect all members of his family (Nichols, 2012). One of the most famous early family therapists, Salvador Minuchin (1984), compared the family to a kaleidoscope, a changing pattern of mosaics in which the pattern is larger than any one piece. In this view, efforts to isolate and treat one member of the family without the others are doomed. Only if all family members reveal their differing perceptions of each other can mistakes and misperceptions be identified. A teenager, for instance, may see his mother as crabby and nagging when actually she is tired and worried. A parent may see a child as rebellious when in fact the child is lonely and desperate for attention.

Family members are usually unaware of how they influence one another. By observing the entire family, the family therapist hopes to discover tensions and imbalances in power and communication. A child may have a chronic illness or a psychological problem, such as anorexia, that affects the workings of the whole family. One parent may become overinvolved with the sick child whereas the other parent retreats, and each may start blaming the other. The child, in turn, may cling to the illness or disorder as a way of expressing anger, keeping the parents together, getting the parents' attention, or asserting control (Cummings & Davies, 2011).

Even when it is not possible to treat the whole family, some therapists will treat individuals in a **family-systems perspective**, which recognizes that people's behavior in a family is as interconnected as that of two dancers (Bowen, 1978; Cox & Paley, 2003; Ram et al., 2014). Clients learn that if they change in any way, even for the better, their families may protest noisily or may send subtle messages that read, "Change back!" Why? Because when one family member changes, each of the others must change too. As the saying goes, it takes two to tango, and if one dancer stops, so must the other. But most people do not like change. They are comfortable with old patterns and habits, even those that cause them trouble. They want to keep dancing the same old dance, even if their feet hurt.

When a couple is arguing frequently about issues that never seem to get resolved, they may be helped by going together to *couples therapy*, which is designed to help couples manage the inevitable conflicts that occur in all relationships. One of the most common problems that couples complain about is the "demand–withdraw" pattern, in which one partner badgers the other about some perceived failing, demanding that he or she change. The more the badgering partner demands, the more the target withdraws, sulks, or avoids the subject (Baucom et al., 2011; Christensen & Jacobson, 2000). Couples therapists generally insist on seeing both partners, so that they will hear both sides of the story. They cut through the blaming and attacking ("She never listens to me!" "He never does anything!"), and instead focus on helping the couple resolve their differences, get over hurt and blame, and make specific behavioral changes to reduce anger and conflict.

Many couples therapists, like some cognitive therapists, are moving away from the "fix all the differences" approach. Instead, they are helping couples learn to accept and live with qualities in both partners that aren't going to change much (Baucom et al., 2011; Hayes, 2004). A wife can stop trying to turn her calm, steady husband into a spontaneous adventurer ("After all, that's what I originally loved about him; he's as steady as a rock"), and a husband can stop trying to make his shy wife more assertive ("I have always loved her remarkable serenity").

Family and couples therapists may use psychodynamic, behavioral, cognitive, or humanist approaches in their work; they share only a focus on the family or the couple. In Murray's case, a family therapist would observe how Murray's procrastination fits his family dynamics. Perhaps it allows Murray to get his father's attention and his mother's sympathy. Perhaps it keeps Murray from facing his greatest fear: If he does finish his work, it will not measure up to his father's impossibly high standards. The therapist will not only help Murray change his work habits, but will also help his family deal with a changed Murray.

family-systems perspective

An approach to doing therapy with individuals or families by identifying how each family member forms part of a larger interacting system.

Some Features Associated with Types of Psychotherapy

Different approaches to therapy emphasize different aspects of thought and behavior. Review the list below, then quiz yourself by matching the type of therapy with the features that characterize it.

Type of Therapy	Features
Psychodynamic Therapy	transference
Behavior Therapy	systematic desensitization
Existential Therapy	facing the fear of death
Cognitive Therapy	reappraisal of thoughts
Humanist Therapy	unconditional positive regard
Family Therapy	assessment of interactions among relatives

Check Your Understanding

The kinds of psychotherapy that we have discussed are all quite different in theory, and so are their techniques (see Review 16.2). Yet in practice, many psychotherapists take an *integrative approach*, drawing on methods and ideas from various schools and avoiding strong allegiances to any one theory. This flexibility enables them to treat clients with whatever methods are most appropriate and effective. In an Internet-based survey of more than 2,400 psychotherapists, two-thirds said they practice cognitive-behavioral therapy *and* that the single most influential therapist they followed was Carl Rogers *and* that they often incorporate ideas of mindfulness and acceptance (Cook, Biyanova, & Coyne, 2009).

Interactive

Review 16.2

The Major Schools of Therapy Compared

	Primary Goal	Methods
Psychodynamic	Insight into unconscious motives and feelings that prolong symptoms	Probing unconscious motives, examining the process of transference, exploring childhood experiences
Cognitive-Behavioral Behavioral	Modification of self-defeating behaviors	Graduated exposure (flooding), systematic desensitization, behavioral records, skills training
Cognitive	Modification of irrational or unvalidated beliefs	Prompting the client to test beliefs against evidence; exposing the faulty reasoning in catastrophizing and mind-reading; sometimes helping the client accept unpleasant thoughts and feelings and live with them
Humanist and Existential Humanist	Insight; self-acceptance and self-fulfillment; new, optimistic perceptions of oneself and the world	Providing a nonjudgmental setting in which to discuss issues; use of empathy and unconditional positive regard by the therapist
Existential	Finding meaning in life and accepting inevitable losses	Varies with the therapist; philosophic discussions about the meaning of life, the client's goals, finding the courage to survive loss and suffering
Family and Couples Family	Modification of family patterns	May use any of the preceding methods to change family patterns that perpetuate problems and conflicts
Couples	Resolution of conflicts, breaking out of destructive habits	May use any of the preceding methods to help couples communicate better, resolve conflicts, or accept what cannot be changed

The life narrative, the story that each of us develops to explain who we are and how we got that way, is important (McAdams & McLean, 2013). All successful therapies share two key elements: They are able to motivate the client into wanting to change, and they replace a client's pessimistic or unrealistic narrative with one that is more hopeful and attainable (Howard, 1991; Schafer, 1992).

JOURNAL PROMPT 16.2

Thinking Critically—Analyze Assumptions and Biases: Many psychotherapists assume that therapy is an art, an exchange between therapist and client whose essence cannot be captured by research. How valid is this assumption? Should consumers assume they can rely on the testimonials of satisfied clients as a basis for choosing an effective and appropriate type of therapy for their specific needs?

Quiz for Module 16.2

1. Consuela has been in psychodynamic therapy for 4 months. She feels like she really connects with her therapist and that he really understands her true "inner self" in a way no one has before. Consuela tells her friends about how helpful, compassionate, and caring her therapist is, and how she looks forward to their sessions together. When her therapist asked her during one session, "Are you ready to do some hard work today?" Consuela replied, "Yes, Daddy." Consuela is showing many signs of _____ during the psychodynamic process.

   a. Id dilation

   b. Reaction formation

   c. Destabilization

   d. Transference

2. Many a parent over the decades has believed that the way to teach a child to swim is to row the child to the middle of a lake and toss the child overboard. This "sink-or-swim" philosophy is based on the notion that the child will quickly learn the desired behavior (swimming) to avoid the undesired behavior (drowning). In a way, this approach also mirrors the behavior therapy technique of

   a. Flooding

   b. Behavioral self-monitoring

   c. Graduated exposure

   d. Systematic desensitization

3. "I just can't lose weight!" moaned a frustrated Lucy. "I know I'm eating more fruits and vegetables every day, and I'm cutting back on sweets and snacks. But the pounds won't come off!" "Have you considered keeping a record of your food intake?" asked her sympathetic friend Diana. "That way you could objectively see what you're actually eating, and use that to shape your behavioral goals." Diana is intuitively recommending _____ as an approach to weight-loss therapy for Lucy.
   a. Skills training
   b. Desensitization
   c. Behavioral self-monitoring
   d. Flooding

4. "I just feel so frustrated with my life," Willie complained. "Life can seem meaningless and empty," Dr. Molay replied. "Does God have some kind of plan for me?" Willie asked, expectantly. "It's a cold and random universe . . . " Molay answered. "I know that someday I'm going to die, and then I'll be forgotten, and in the meantime I'll wade through a sea of loneliness," Willie whispered. "Yes. Yes, that's likely to be true," replied Dr. Molay. "So what's the point of it all?!" demanded Willie.

"Your grim reality must fuel your desires for self-fulfillment and personal responsibility in shaping your world, your way," proclaimed Dr. Molay. What kind of therapy does Dr. Molay appear to subscribe to?
   a. Cognitive-behavioral therapy
   b. Exposure therapy
   c. Cognitive therapy
   d. Existential therapy

5. Dr. Selpuoc is explaining her approach to her job: "The unit is made up of several individual, interacting parts. If the unit is failing, there's likely to be trouble with the constituent elements. But fixing the individual parts doesn't necessarily mean the unit will work effectively. Both the individual elements and the unit as a whole need to be tinkered with to make the entire system work efficiently again." What specialization does Dr. Selpuoc endorse?
   a. HVAC restoration
   b. DID restitution
   c. Psychodynamic mending
   d. Family-systems therapy

Evaluating Psychotherapy

Poor Murray! He is getting a little baffled by all these therapies. He wants to make a choice soon; no sense in procrastinating about that, too! Is there any scientific evidence, he wonders, that might help him decide which therapy or therapist will be best for him?

The Scientist–Practitioner Gap

LO 16.3.A Define the *scientist–practitioner gap*, and identify some of the problems associated with assessing the effectiveness of therapy.

Psychotherapy is, first and foremost, a relationship. Its success depends in part on the bond between the therapist and client, called the **therapeutic alliance**. When both parties respect and understand each other and agree on the goals of treatment, the client is more likely to improve (Klein et al., 2003). Now suppose that Murray has met a nice psychotherapist who seems smart and friendly, who he respects and understands, and who respects and understands Murray in return. Is a good alliance enough? How important is the *kind* of therapy that an individual practices?

These questions have generated a huge debate among clinical practitioners and psychological scientists. Many psychotherapists believe that trying to evaluate psychotherapy using standard empirical methods is an exercise in futility: Numbers and graphs, they say, cannot possibly capture the complex exchange that takes place between a therapist and a client. Psychotherapy, they maintain, is an art that you acquire from clinical experience; it is not a science. That's why almost any method will work for some people (Laska, Gurman, & Wampold, 2014; Lilienfeld, 2014). Other clinicians argue that efforts to measure the effectiveness of psychotherapy ignore the fact that many patients have an assortment of emotional problems and need therapy for a longer time than research can reasonably allow (Marcus et al., 2014; Westen, Novotny, & Thompson-Brenner, 2004).

For their part, psychological scientists agree that therapy is often a complex process. But that is no reason, they argue, that it cannot be scientifically investigated just like any other complex psychological process, such as the development of language or personality

therapeutic alliance

The bond of confidence and mutual understanding established between therapist and client, which allows them to work together to solve the client's problems.

randomized controlled trials
Research designed to determine the effectiveness of a new medication or form of therapy, in which people with a given problem or disorder are randomly assigned to one or more treatment groups or to a control group.

(Crits-Christoph, Wilson, & Hollon, 2005; Kazdin, 2008). Moreover, they are concerned that when therapists fail to keep up with empirical findings in the field, their clients may suffer. It is crucial, scientists say, for therapists to be aware of research on the most beneficial methods for particular problems, on ineffective or potentially harmful techniques, and on topics relevant to their practice, such as memory and child development (Lilienfeld, Lynn, & Lohr, 2015).

Over the years, the breach between scientists and therapists has widened, creating what is commonly called the *scientist–practitioner gap*. One reason for the growing split has been the rise of professional schools that are not connected to academic psychology departments and that train students solely to do therapy. Graduates of these schools sometimes know little about research methods or even about research assessing different therapy techniques.

The scientist–practitioner gap has also widened because of the proliferation of unvalidated therapies in a crowded market. Some repackage established techniques under a new name; some are based on a therapist's name and charisma. A blue-ribbon panel of clinical scientists, convened to assess the problem of the scientist–practitioner gap for the journal *Psychological Science in the Public Interest*, reported that the current state of clinical psychology is comparable to that of medicine in the early 1900s, when physicians typically valued personal experience over scientific research. The authors concluded that it is time for "a new accreditation system that demands high-quality science training as a central feature of doctoral training in clinical psychology" (Baker, McFall, & Shoham, 2008). The Academy of Psychological Clinical Science, an alliance of 49 clinical science graduate programs and nine clinical science internships, is making a concerted effort to institute just such a system (Bootzin, 2009).

PROBLEMS IN ASSESSING THERAPY   Because so many therapies all claim to be successful, and because of economic pressures on insurers and rising health costs, clinical psychologists are increasingly being called on to provide empirical assessments of therapy. Why can't you just ask people if the therapy helped them? The answer is that no matter what kind of therapy is involved, clients are motivated to tell you it worked. "Dr. Blitznik is a genius!" they will exclaim. "I would *never* have taken that job (or moved to Cincinnati, or found my true love) if it hadn't been for Dr. Blitznik!" Every kind of therapy ever devised produces enthusiastic testimonials from people who feel it saved their lives.

The first problem with testimonials is that none of us can be our own control group. How do people know they wouldn't have taken the job, moved to Cincinnati, or found true love anyway—maybe even sooner, if Dr. Blitznik had not kept them in treatment? Second, Dr. Blitznik's success could be due to the placebo effect: The client's anticipation of success and the buzz about Dr. B.'s fabulous new method might be the active ingredients, rather than Dr. B.'s therapy itself. Third, notice that you never hear testimonials from the people who dropped out, who weren't helped, or who actually got worse. So researchers cannot be satisfied with testimonials, no matter how glowing. They know that thanks to the *justification of effort* effect, people who have put time, money, and effort into something will tell you it was worth it. No one wants to say, "Yeah, I saw Dr. Blitznik for 5 years, and boy, was it ever a waste of time."

To guard against these problems, some clinical researchers conduct **randomized controlled trials**, in which people with a given problem or disorder are randomly assigned to one or more treatment groups or to a control group. Sometimes the results of randomized controlled trials have been startling. After natural or human-caused disasters, therapists often arrive on the scene to treat survivors for symptoms of trauma. In an intervention called critical incident stress debriefing (CISD), survivors gather in a group for "debriefing," which generally lasts from 1 to 3 hours. Participants are expected to disclose their thoughts and emotions about the traumatic experience, and the group leader warns members about possible traumatic symptoms that might develop.

Two young women comfort each other at a makeshift memorial for the victims of a shooting spree that left 12 dead and 58 wounded at a movie theater in Aurora, Colorado. It is widely believed that most survivors of any disaster will need the help of therapists to avoid developing posttraumatic stress disorder. Does the evidence support this belief? What do randomized controlled studies show?

CULTURE and *Psychotherapy*

Many therapists and clients establish successful therapeutic alliances in spite of coming from different backgrounds. But sometimes cultural differences cause misunderstandings that result from ignorance or prejudice (Comas-Díaz, 2006; Draguns, 2013; Sue et al., 2007). A lifetime of experience with racism and a general cultural distrust may keep some African Americans from revealing feelings that they believe a white therapist would not understand or accept (Whaley & Davis, 2007). Misunderstandings and prejudice may be one reason Asian American, Latino, and African American clients are more likely to stay in therapy when their therapists' ethnicity matches their own. When clients and psychotherapists are culturally matched, they are more likely to share perceptions of what the client's problem is, agree on the best way of coping, and have the same expectations about what therapy can accomplish (Hwang, 2006; Zone et al., 2005).

Understanding a culture's particular traditions can also help clinicians design more effective interventions for individual and community problems. In the Pacific Northwest, where substance abuse among Native Americans and Alaska Natives has widespread and devastating effects, successful approaches combine bicultural skills training with community involvement, which plays an essential role in native life (Hawkins, Cummins, & Marlatt, 2004; Smith et al., 2014).

In establishing a bond with clients, therapists must distinguish normal cultural patterns from individual psychological problems. An Irish American family therapist, Monica McGoldrick (2005), described some problems that are typical of Irish American families. These problems arise from Irish history and religious beliefs. "In general, the therapist cannot expect the family to turn into a physically affectionate, emotionally intimate group, or to enjoy being in therapy very much," she observed. "The notion of Original Sin—that you are guilty before you are born—leaves them with a heavy sense of burden. Someone not sensitized to these issues may see this as pathological. It is not. But it is also not likely to change and the therapist should help the family tolerate this inner guilt rather than try to get rid of it." (Did you notice the link between her observation and acceptance-based forms of cognitive therapy?)

More and more psychotherapists are becoming "sensitized to the issues" caused by cultural differences (Arredondo et al., 2005; Sue et al., 2007). Many Latino and Asian clients are likely to react to a formal interview with a therapist with relative passivity and deference, leading some therapists to misdiagnose this cultural norm as a problem with shyness. In Latin American cultures, *susto*, or "loss of the soul," is a common response to extreme grief or fright; the person believes that his or her soul has departed along with that of the deceased relative. A psychotherapist unfamiliar with this culturally determined response might conclude that the sufferer was delusional or psychotic. Latino clients are also more likely than Anglos to value harmony in their relationships, which often translates into an unwillingness to express negative emotions or confront family members or friends directly, so therapists need to help such clients find ways to communicate better within that cultural context (Arredondo et al., 2014). Latino clinicians, being aware of the stigma associated with psychotherapy in their culture, are also developing ways to help their clients overcome ambivalence about seeking psychological help (Añez et al., 2008).

Being aware of cultural differences, however, does not mean that therapists should stereotype clients. After all, some Asians do have problems with excessive shyness, some Latinos do have psychoses, and some Irish do not carry burdens of guilt! It does mean that therapists must ensure that their clients find them to be trustworthy and effective; and it means that clients must be aware of their own prejudices too.

Native Americans from various tribes in Washington State have been renewing their cultural tradition of canoe journeys. "The way to teach culture is to live it," said Terri Tavenner, a former cultural director of one of the tribes. "You have to know where you've been and where you're going." In Seattle, a program designed to prevent drug abuse and other problems among urban Indian adolescents uses canoe journeys as a metaphor for the journey of life. The youths learn the psychological and practical skills, along with the cultural values, that they need to undertake a canoe journey—skills they will also need to navigate throughout life (Hawkins, Cummins, & Marlatt, 2004).

Figure 16.2 Do Posttraumatic Interventions Help—or Harm?

Victims of serious car accidents were assessed at the time of the event, 4 months later, and 3 years later. Half received a form of posttraumatic intervention called critical incident stress debriefing (CISD); half received no treatment. As you can see, almost everyone had recovered within 4 months, but one group had higher stress symptoms than everyone else, even after 3 years: the people who were the most emotionally distressed right after the accident *and* who received CISD. The therapy actually impeded their recovery (Mayou et al., 2000).

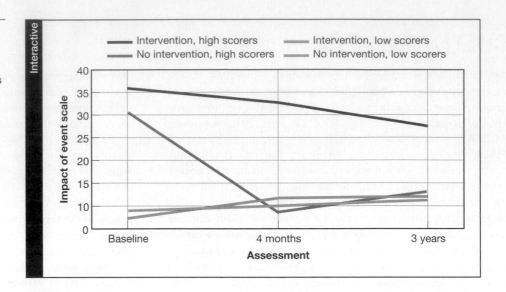

Yet randomized controlled studies with people who have been through terrible experiences—including burns, accidents, miscarriages, violent crimes, and combat—find that posttraumatic interventions can actually *delay* recovery in some people (van Emmerik et al., 2002; McNally, Bryant, & Ehlers, 2003; Paterson, Whittle, & Kemp, 2015). In one study, victims of serious car accidents were followed for 3 years; some had received the CISD intervention and some had not. As you can see in Figure 16.2, almost everyone had recovered in only 4 months and remained fine after 3 years. The researchers then divided the survivors into two groups: those who had had a highly emotional reaction to the accident at the outset ("high scorers"), and those who had not. For the latter group, the intervention made no difference; they improved quickly.

Now look at what happened to the people who had been the most traumatized by the accident: If they did *not* get CISD, they were fine in 4 months, too, like everyone else. But for those who *did* get the intervention, CISD actually blocked improvement, and they had higher stress symptoms than all the others in the study even after 3 years. The researchers concluded that "psychological debriefing is ineffective and has adverse long-term effects. It is not an appropriate treatment for trauma victims" (Mayou et al., 2000). The World Health Organization, which deals with survivors of trauma around the world, has officially endorsed this conclusion.

You can see, then, why the scientific assessment of psychotherapeutic claims and methods is so important.

When Therapy Helps

LO 16.3.B **Provide examples of areas in which cognitive and behavior therapies have shown themselves to be particularly effective.**

We turn now to the evidence showing the benefits of psychotherapy and which therapies work best in general, and for which disorders in particular (e.g., Chambless & Ollendick, 2001). For many problems and most emotional disorders, cognitive and behavior therapies have emerged as the method of choice (Hofmann et al., 2012):

- *Depression.* Cognitive therapy's greatest success has been in the treatment of mood disorders, especially depression (Beck, 2005), and people in cognitive therapy are less likely than those on drugs to relapse when the treatment is over. The reason may be that the lessons learned in cognitive therapy last a long time after treatment, according to follow-ups done from 15 months to many years later (Hayes et al., 2004; Hollon, Thase, & Markowitz, 2002; Seligman et al., 1999; Watts et al., 2015).

- *Suicide attempts.* In a randomized, controlled study of 120 adults who had attempted suicide and had been sent to a hospital emergency room, those who were given 10 sessions of cognitive therapy, in comparison to those who were simply given the usual follow-up care (being tracked and given referrals for help), were only about half as likely to attempt suicide again in the next 18 months. They also scored significantly lower on tests of depressive mood and hopelessness (Brown et al., 2005; Ougrin et al., 2015).

- *Anxiety disorders.* Exposure techniques are more effective than any other treatment for posttraumatic stress disorder, agoraphobia, and specific phobias such as fear of dogs or flying. Cognitive-behavioral therapy is often more effective than medication for panic disorder, generalized anxiety disorder, and obsessive–compulsive disorder (Adams et al., 2015; Mitte, 2005; Otto et al., 2009; Watts et al., 2015).

- *Anger and impulsive violence.* Cognitive therapy is often successful in reducing chronic anger, abusiveness, and hostility, and it also teaches people how to express anger more calmly and constructively (Deffenbacher et al., 2003; Hoogsteder et al., 2015).

- *Health problems.* Cognitive and behavior therapies are highly successful in helping people cope with pain, chronic fatigue syndrome, headaches, and irritable bowel syndrome; quit smoking or overcome other addictions; recover from eating disorders such as bulimia and binge eating; overcome insomnia and improve their sleeping patterns; and manage other health problems (Butler et al., 1991; Crits-Christoph, Wilson, & Hollon, 2005; Davis et al., 2015; Stepanski & Perlis, 2000).

- *Childhood and adolescent behavior problems.* Behavior therapy is the most effective treatment for behavior problems that range from bed-wetting to impulsive anger, and even for problems that have biological origins, such as autism (Hoogsteder et al., 2015; Scarpa, Williams, & Attwood, 2013; Sukhodolsky et al., 2013).

- *Relapses.* Cognitive-behavioral approaches have also been highly effective in reducing the rate of relapse among people with problems such as substance abuse, depression, or sexual offending, and even schizophrenia (Hutton et al., 2014; Witkiewitz & Marlatt, 2004).

However, no single type of therapy can help everyone. In spite of their many successes, behavior and cognitive therapies have had failures, especially with people who are unmotivated to carry out a behavioral or cognitive program or who have ingrained personality disorders and psychoses. Also, cognitive-behavioral therapies are designed for specific, identifiable problems, but sometimes people seek therapy for less clearly defined reasons, such as wishing to introspect about their feelings or explore moral issues.

There is also no simple rule for how long therapy needs to last. Sometimes a single session of treatment is enough to bring improvement, if it is based on sound psychotherapeutic principles. A therapy called *motivational interviewing*, which focuses specifically on increasing a client's motivation to overcome problems such as drinking, smoking, and binge eating, has been shown to be effective in as few as one or two sessions (Burke et al., 2003; Cassin et al., 2008; Miller & Rollnick, 2002). The therapist essentially puts the client into a state of cognitive dissonance: "I want to be healthy and I see myself as a smart, competent person, but here I am doing something stupid and self-defeating. Do I want to feel better or not?" The therapist then offers the client a cognitive and behavioral strategy of improvement (Wagner & Ingersoll, 2008). Some problems, however, are chronic or particularly difficult to treat and respond better to longer therapy. According to one meta-analysis that included eight randomized, controlled studies, long-term psychodynamic therapy (lasting a year or more) can be more effective than short-term approaches for complex mental problems and chronic personality disorders (Leichsenring & Rabung, 2008).

Furthermore, some people and problems require combined approaches. Young adults with schizophrenia are best helped by combining medication with family-intervention therapies that teach parents behavioral skills for dealing with their troubled children, and that

The use of animals in rehabilitation therapy, to help people with a variety of mental and physical problems, has been growing.

educate the family about how to cope with the illness constructively (Elis, Caponigro, & Kring, 2013; Goldstein & Miklowitz, 1995). In studies over a 2-year period, only 30 percent of the patients with schizophrenia in such family interventions relapsed compared to 65 percent of those whose families were not involved. The same combined approach—medication and family-focused therapy—also reduces the severity of symptoms in adolescents with bipolar disorder and delays relapses (Miklowitz, 2007).

SPECIAL PROBLEMS AND POPULATIONS   Some therapies are targeted for the problems of particular populations. *Rehabilitation psychologists* are concerned with the assessment and treatment of people who are physically disabled, temporarily or permanently, because of chronic pain, physical injuries, epilepsy, addictions, or other conditions. They conduct research to find the best ways to teach disabled people to live independently, improve their motivation, enjoy sex, and follow healthy regimens. Because more people are surviving traumatic injuries and living long enough to develop chronic medical conditions, rehabilitation psychology is one of the fastest-growing areas of health care.

Other problems require more than one-on-one help from a psychotherapist. *Community psychologists* set up programs at a community level, often coordinating outpatient services at local clinics with support from family and friends. Some community programs help people who have severe mental disorders, such as schizophrenia, by setting up group homes that provide counseling, job and skills training, and a support network. Without such community support, many people with mental illness are treated at hospitals, released to the streets, and stop taking their medications. Their psychotic symptoms return, they are rehospitalized, and a revolving-door cycle is established.

A community intervention called *multisystemic therapy (MST)* has been highly successful in reducing teenage violence, criminal activity, drug abuse, and school problems in troubled inner-city communities. Its practitioners combine family-systems techniques with behavioral

BIOLOGY and *Psychotherapy*

One of the longest debates in the history of treating mental disorders has been over which kind of treatment is better: medical or psychological. This debate rests on a common but mistaken assumption: If a disorder appears to have biological origins or involve biochemical abnormalities, then biological treatments must be most appropriate. In fact, however, changing your behavior and thoughts through psychotherapy or simply by having other new experiences can also change the way your brain functions, just as the expectations associated with a placebo can.

This fascinating link between mind and brain was first illustrated dramatically in PET-scan studies of people with obsessive–compulsive disorder. Among those who were taking the SSRI Prozac, the metabolism of glucose in a critical part of the brain decreased, suggesting that the drug was having a beneficial effect by "calming" that area. But exactly the *same* brain changes occurred in patients who were getting cognitive-behavioral therapy and no medication (Schwartz et al., 1996). Other studies have shown that CBT produces predictable EEG changes in neural activity in the brains of people undergoing this form of therapy,

changes associated with the reduction of symptoms of depression and anxiety (Miskovic et al., 2011).

Moreover, even when medications are beneficial, they are rarely sufficient as "cures." People who are depressed because of difficulties in their lives may get a lift from an antidepressant, but the pill will not teach them how to manage those difficulties. In recent years, prominent people have "come out," admitting that they suffer from severe mental disorders and describing what it took for them to survive (see Temple Grandin's [2010] account of her autism and Elyn Saks's [2007] riveting story of learning to live with schizophrenia). What these accounts reveal is that even when medication helps, it is a relatively small part of the program of activities, support, and therapy needed for functioning in the world. One man with bipolar disorder told his psychotherapist: "Lithium cuts out the highs as well as the lows. I don't miss the lows, but I gotta admit that there were some aspects of the highs that I do miss. It took me a while to accept that I had to give up those highs. Wanting to keep my job and my marriage helped!" (quoted in Kring et al., 2010). The drug alone could not have helped this man learn to live with his illness.

methods, but apply them in the context of forming "neighborhood partnerships" with local leaders, residents, parents, and teachers (Henggeler et al., 1998; Swenson et al., 2005; Tiernan et al., 2015). The premise of multisystemic therapy is that because aggressiveness and drug abuse are often reinforced or caused by the adolescent's family, classroom, peers, and local culture, you cannot successfully treat the adolescent without also "treating" his or her environment. Indeed, MST has been shown to be more effective than other methods on their own (Schaeffer & Borduin, 2005).

When Therapy Harms

LO 16.3.C Discuss four ways in which therapy has the potential to harm clients, and give an example of each.

In a tragic case that made news around the world, police arrested four people on charges of recklessly causing the death of 10-year-old Candace Newmaker during a session of "rebirthing" therapy. (The procedure supposedly helps adopted children form attachments to their adoptive parents by "reliving" birth.) The child was completely wrapped in a blanket (the "womb") and was surrounded by large pillows. The therapists then pressed in on the pillows to simulate contractions and told the girl to push her way out of the blanket over her head. Candace repeatedly said that she could not breathe and felt she was going to die. But instead of unwrapping her, the therapists said, "You've got to push hard if you want to be born—or do you want to stay in there and die?" Candace lost consciousness and was rushed to a local hospital, where she died. Connell Watkins and Julie Ponder, unlicensed social workers who operated the counseling center, went to prison for reckless child abuse resulting in death.

Candace's tragic story is an extreme example, but every treatment and intervention carries some risks, and that includes psychotherapy (Koocher, McMann, & Stout, 2014). In a small percentage of cases, a person's symptoms may actually worsen, the client may become too dependent on the therapist, or the client's outside relationships may deteriorate (Lilienfeld, 2007). The risks to clients increase with any of the following:

1. **The use of empirically unsupported, potentially dangerous techniques.** "Rebirthing" therapy was born (so to speak) in the 1970s, when its founder claimed that, while taking a bath, he had reexperienced his own traumatic birth. But the basic assumptions of this method—that people can recover from trauma, insecure attachment, or other psychological problems by "reliving" their emergence from the womb—are contradicted by the vast research on infancy, attachment, memory, and posttraumatic stress disorder and its treatment. Besides, why should anyone assume that being born is traumatic? Isn't it pretty nice to be let out of cramped quarters and see daylight and beaming parental faces?

Troubled teens attend a boot camp designed as an intervention for delinquent behavior. Results from carefully controlled studies indicate the success of such interventions is questionable, at best.

Table 16.1 Potentially Harmful Therapies

Intervention	Potential Harm
Critical incident stress debriefing (CISD)	Heightened risk of emotional symptoms
Scared Straight interventions	Worsening of conduct problems
Facilitated communication	False allegations of sexual and child abuse
Attachment therapies	Death and serious injury to children
Recovered-memory techniques (e.g., dream analysis)	Induction of false memories of trauma, family breakups
"Multiple personality disorder"–oriented therapy	Induction of "multiple" personalities
Grief counseling for people with normal bereavement reactions	Increased depressive symptoms
Expressive-experiential therapies	Worsening and prolonging painful emotions
Boot-camp interventions for conduct disorder	Worsening of aggression and conduct problems
DARE (Drug Abuse and Resistance Education)	Increased use of alcohol and other drugs

Source: Based on Lilienfeld (2007).

Rebirthing is one of a variety of practices, collectively referred to as "attachment therapy," that are based on the use of harsh tactics that allegedly will help children bond with their parents. These techniques include withholding food, isolating the children for extended periods, humiliating them, pressing great weights upon them, and requiring them to exercise to exhaustion (Mercer, Sarner, & Rosa, 2003). However, abusive techniques are ineffective in treating behavior problems and often backfire, making the child angry, resentful, and withdrawn. They are hardly a way to help an adopted or emotionally troubled child feel more attached to his or her parents.

Table 16.1 lists a number of therapies that have been shown, through randomized controlled trials or meta-analysis, to have a significant risk of harming clients.

2. **Inappropriate or coercive influence, which can create new problems for the client.** In any successful therapy, the therapist and client come to agree on an explanation for the client's problems. Of course, the therapist will influence this explanation, according to his or her training and philosophy. Some therapists, however, cross the line. They so zealously believe in the prevalence of certain problems or disorders that they actually induce the client to produce the symptoms they are looking for (Mazzoni, Loftus, & Kirsch, 2001; McHugh, 2008; Nathan, 2011). Therapist influence, and sometimes outright coercion, is a likely reason for the huge numbers of people who were diagnosed with multiple personality disorder in the 1980s and 1990s and for an epidemic of recovered memories of sexual abuse during this period.

3. **Prejudice or cultural ignorance on the part of the therapist.** Some therapists may be prejudiced against some clients because of the client's gender, culture, religion, or sexual orientation. They may be unaware of their prejudices, yet express them in nonverbal ways that make the client feel ignored, disrespected, and devalued (Sue et al., 2007). A therapist may also try to induce a client to conform to the therapist's standards and values, even if they are not appropriate for the client or in the client's best interest. For many years, gay men and lesbians who entered therapy were told that homosexuality was a mental illness that could be cured. Some of the so-called treatments were harsh, such as electric shock for "inappropriate" arousal. Although these methods were discredited decades ago (Davison, 1976), other "reparative" therapies (whose practitioners claim they can turn gay men and lesbians into heterosexuals) continue to surface. But there is no reliable empirical evidence supporting these claims, and both the American Psychological Association and the American Psychiatric Association oppose reparative therapies on ethical and scientific grounds. The former organization has issued "Guidelines for Psychological Practice with Lesbian, Gay, and Bisexual Clients" (2012).

4. **Sexual intimacies or other unethical behavior on the part of the therapist.** The ethical guidelines of both APAs prohibit therapists from having any sexual intimacies with their

clients or violating other professional boundaries. Occasionally, some therapists behave like cult leaders, persuading their clients that their mental health depends on staying in therapy and severing their connections to their "toxic" families (Watters & Ofshe, 1999). Such psychotherapy cults are created by the therapist's use of techniques that foster the client's isolation, prevent the client from terminating therapy, and reduce the client's ability to think critically.

To avoid these risks and benefit from what good, effective psychotherapy has to offer, people looking for the right therapy must become educated consumers, willing to use the critical-thinking skills we have emphasized throughout this book.

Modern psychotherapy has been of enormous value to many people. But psychotherapists themselves have raised some provocative questions about the values inherent in what they do. How much personal change is possible? Does psychotherapy promote unrealistic notions of endless happiness and complete self-fulfillment? Many Americans have an optimistic, let's-fix-this-fast attitude toward all problems. In contrast, Eastern cultures have a less optimistic view of change, and they tend to be more tolerant of events they regard as being outside of human control. And, as we saw earlier in this chapter, some Western psychotherapists teach techniques of mindfulness and greater self-acceptance instead of self-improvement (Hayes et al., 2004; Kabat-Zinn, 1994).

In the hands of an empathic and knowledgeable practitioner, psychotherapy can help you make decisions and clarify your values and goals. It can teach you new skills and new ways of thinking. It can help you get along better with your family and break out of destructive family patterns. It can get you through bad times when no one seems to care or to understand what you are feeling. It can teach you how to manage depression, anxiety, and anger.

However, despite its many benefits, psychotherapy cannot transform you into someone you're not. It cannot turn an introvert into an extrovert. It cannot cure an emotional disorder overnight. It cannot provide a life without problems. And it is not intended to substitute for experience—for work that is satisfying, relationships that are sustaining, activities that are enjoyable. As Socrates knew, the unexamined life is not worth living. Yet, as we would add, the unlived life is not worth examining.

JOURNAL PROMPT 16.3

Thinking Critically—Examine the Evidence: New therapies are often established on the basis of notions that someone thought sounded plausible, such as that accurate memories can be "uprooted" through hypnosis or that emotional problems stem from the "trauma" of childbirth. What is wrong with basing a new form of therapy on an untested hunch instead of on evidence that it works?

Quiz for Module 16.3

1. Ann is rather cold and unemotional, likes to get her way, and is impatient when others don't provide what she wants exactly when she wants it. She entered into therapy with Dr. Baldwin, who is warm and nurturing, likes to consider many perspectives on a problem, and works methodically to craft effective solutions. Predictably, a _____ was never really formed between the clinician and the client.

   a. Beneficence link

   b. Therapeutic alliance

   c. Mental health parity

   d. Practitioner bond

2. Carl insists that he has all the "evidence" he needs to do his job effectively. "I've been a therapist for 40 years," he crowed. "I know what works for my clients and what doesn't. I can tell my methods are effective because my clients are quick to tell me how much better they feel, every time I ask them at the end of each session." What do Carl's attitudes illustrate?

   a. The therapeutic alliance

   b. The psychodynamic allegiance

   c. The humanistic federation

   d. The scientist–practitioner gap

3. Lakisha wants to pursue therapy to help with her feelings of depression. Based on what you know about the effectiveness of different types of treatments, what type of therapy would you recommend to her?

   a. Psychodynamic therapy

   b. Cognitive-behavioral therapy

   c. Psychoanalysis

   d. Humanistic therapy

4. _____ psychologists assess and treat people who are physically disabled.

   a. Recusative

   b. Restorative

   c. Rehabilitation

   d. Reparative

5. Dr. Lechstein insists that any new clients he takes on in therapy agree to first attend a weekend retreat that involves his proprietary 28-step program of Sensual Touching®, Erotic Reawakening®, and Intimate Exploration®. The cost of the $2,500 weekend must be paid in full up front, and in return Dr. Lechstein commits to participating in all 28 steps with each client. His policy is that this is a required first step for those seeking treatment at his smoking-cessation clinic. When would Dr. Lechstein's policies be allowed by any governing board of psychology?

   a. Never

   b. If he required only a $500 deposit before proceeding

   c. If clients could be reimbursed by their insurance companies

   d. If the 28-step program could be paid in 28 installments

Taking Psychology with You

Becoming a Smart Consumer of Psychological Treatments

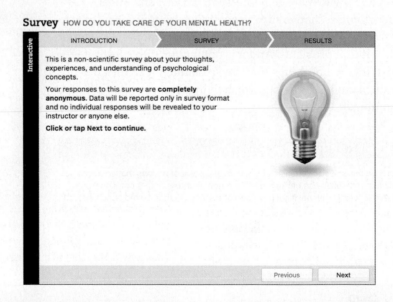

If you have a persistent problem that you do not know how to solve, one that causes you considerable unhappiness and that has lasted 6 months or more, it may be time to look for help. To take the lessons of this chapter with you, you might want to consider these suggestions:

Take all ads and Internet promotions for prescription drugs with a large grain of salt: Be skeptical! Currently, the United States and New Zealand are the only countries that allow pharmaceutical companies to advertise prescription drugs directly to consumers. (Pay close attention to the commercials during the next hour of television you watch, and count how many ads you see for some kind of drug.) Remember that ads are not about educating you; they are about selling you a product. "New" is not necessarily better; many "me too" drugs simply tinker with a blockbuster drug's formula in the smallest

way, and are then legally (if not medically) entitled to claim it is "new and improved." Consult a pharmacist or the FDA's website, and check out any drug you are about to take; go to reliable sources that are not funded by the pharmaceutical industry. The Public Citizen's Health Research Group continues to revise its excellent consumer guide, *Worst Pills, Best Pills.*

Make an informed decision when you choose a therapist. Make sure you are dealing with a reputable individual with appropriate credentials and training. Your school counseling center is a good place to start. You might also seek out a university psychology clinic, where you may be able to get therapy with a graduate student in training; these students are closely supervised, and the fees will be lower.

Choose a therapy or treatment most likely to help you. If possible, begin by talking to a competent psychotherapist or counselor about your problems and what intervention might help you. But don't forget that not all therapies are equally effective for all problems. You should not spend 4 years in psychodynamic therapy for panic attacks, which can generally be helped in a few sessions of cognitive-behavioral therapy. Likewise, if you have a specific emotional problem—such as depression, anger, or anxiety—or if you are coping with chronic health problems, look for a cognitive or behavior therapist. However, if you just want to discuss your life with a wise and empathic counselor, the kind of therapy may not matter so much.

Consider, but be wary of, online therapy delivered by video, smartphone, or email. Many people are unwilling to seek help in a one-on-one therapy session or are unable to do so because of where they live or other obstacles. Clinical scientists have been studying and promoting the use of technologies to reach such individuals (Kazdin, 2015). Randomized controlled studies have demonstrated the effectiveness of some Internet programs, such as one designed to help people quit smoking (Muñoz et al., 2006) and others that deliver monitored, validated CBT instructions. Telephone therapy—sometimes called "telemental psychotherapy"—can also be helpful, as evidenced by the success of "quitlines" to help people stop smoking (Lichtenstein, Zhu, & Tedeschi, 2010; Toll et al., 2015). Many people are actually more likely to stay with a program of therapy-by-telephone than with face-to-face therapies. One company, Lantern, hopes that their subscription smartphone app linking clients and therapists will fill the gap between questionable self-help books and pricey extended therapy sessions (Carrns, 2014). However, if you start any kind of therapy with a professional therapist via email, smartphone, or video, be sure the therapist is using an "HIPAA-compliant" method, that is, following government guidelines to protect your privacy. Although therapy by email may seem to be easiest, it has serious limitations as a form of therapy because the therapist cannot see a client's nonverbal cues, and vice versa.

Consider a self-help group. Not all psychological problems require the aid of a professional. In the United States, an estimated 7 to 15 million adults belong to self-help groups (online and in person) for every possible problem—for alcoholics and relatives of alcoholics; people suffering from depression, anorexia, or schizophrenia; women with breast cancer; parents of murdered children; people with diabetes; rape victims; stepparents; relatives of patients with Alzheimer's disease; and people with just about any other concern you can think of. Self-help groups can be reassuring and supportive in ways that family, friends, and psychotherapists sometimes may not be. For example, people with disabilities face unique challenges that involve coping not only with physical problems but also with the condescension, hostility, and prejudice of many nondisabled people (Linton, 1998). Other disabled people, who share these challenges, can offer the right kind of empathy and useful advice.

However, keep your critical-thinking skills with you: Self-help groups are not regulated by law or by professional standards, and they vary widely in their philosophies and methods. Some are accepting and tolerant, offering support and spiritual guidance. Others are confrontational and coercive, and members who disagree with the premises of the group may be made to feel deviant, crazy, or "in denial."

Choose self-help books that are scientifically based and promote realistic goals. You can find a self-help book for every problem, from how to toilet-train your children to how to find happiness. Critical thinkers can learn how to distinguish good ones from useless ones. To begin with, good self-help books do not promise the impossible. This rules out books that promise perfect sex, total love, or high self-esteem in 30 days. (Sorry.) Truly helpful books are not based on the author's pseudoscientific theories, armchair observations, or personal accounts. People who have survived difficulties can tell inspirational stories, of course, but an author's own experience and vague advice to, say, "find love in your heart" or "take charge of your life" won't get you far. In contrast, when self-help books propose a specific, step-by-step, empirically supported program for the reader to follow, they can actually be as effective as treatment administered by a therapist—*if* the reader follows through with the program (Rosen et al., 2015). One such book is *Changing for Good* (Prochaska, Norcross, & DiClemente, 1994), which describes the ingredients of effective change that apply to people in and out of therapy.

Because the world is full of therapies that lack empirical support, it takes knowledge and critical thinking to tell the good ones from the harmful ones, the real from the phony, and the phony from the fraudulent. But as long as people yearn for a magic bullet to cure their problems—medical, psychological, or technological—quick-fix solutions will find a ready audience. If you or someone you know is thinking about getting help with a problem, the video *Finding a Therapist If You Need One* offers some useful guidelines.

Shared Writing Prompt

The benefits of psychotherapy are well documented, but we can ask questions about its implicit message. Does psychotherapy foster unrealistic expectations of personal change? When should clients think about living with problems or situations they cannot change?

Epilogue
TAKING THIS BOOK WITH YOU

You've come a long way since you began this book. As your course draws to a close, we invite you to stand back and ask yourself what you have learned from all the topics, studies, and controversies you've been studying. Can you identify some fundamental principles and findings that you can apply to your own experiences? If the theories and findings in this book are to be of long-lasting value to you, they must jump off the printed page and into your daily life.

The four general perspectives introduced way back in Chapter 1 suggest some questions to ask when considering an issue or problem that matters to you. When you are distressed, the *biological perspective* directs you to ask what is going on in your body. Do you have a physical condition that could be affecting you psychologically? Are alcohol or other drugs altering your ability to make decisions or act as you would like? The *learning perspective* directs you to focus on the reinforcers and punishers in your environment. What consequences are maintaining behavior you would like to change (your own or someone else's)? The *sociocultural perspective* reminds you to analyze how friends and relatives support or hinder you in achieving your goals. Are you comfortable with the role you are playing as a man or a woman, romantic partner, family member, student, or employee? The *cognitive perspective* directs you to analyze your thoughts about your situation. Are you brooding too much, rehearsing negative thoughts? Can you accept information that challenges your beliefs, or is the "confirmation bias" getting in the way?

A good way to start applying specific psychological concepts is to review the key terms at the ends of each chapter in this book—say, cognitive dissonance, positive reinforcement, or locus of control—and think of ways they apply in your own life. As you've learned in this course, psychological findings can also be applied to larger social issues, such as disputes between neighbors and nations, prejudice and cross-cultural relations, improving children's school achievement, or reducing crime.

Most of all, we hope you'll realize that the best way to take this book with you is to practice the principles of critical and scientific thinking it emphasizes. Old theories may give way to new ones, findings may be modified by new evidence, but the methods of psychology continue, and their hallmark is critical thinking.

—The Authors

Summary

Biological Treatments for Mental Disorders

LO 16.1.A   Describe the four main categories of drugs commonly prescribed for the treatment of mental disorders, and discuss five major cautions associated with drug treatment.

Biological treatments for mental disorders are in the ascendance because of research findings on the genetic and biological causes of some disorders and because of economic and social factors. The medications most commonly prescribed for mental disorders include *antipsychotic drugs*, *antidepressants*, tranquilizers, and *lithium carbonate*. Drawbacks of drug treatment include the *placebo effect*; high dropout and relapse rates among people who take medications without also learning how to cope with their problems; the difficulty of finding the correct dose for each individual; and the long-term risks of medication and of possible drug interactions when several are being taken. Medication should not be prescribed uncritically and routinely, especially when psychological therapies can work as well for many mood and behavioral problems.

LO 16.1.B   Identify four forms of direct brain intervention used in treating mental disorders, and discuss the limitations of each.

When drugs and psychotherapy have failed to help seriously disturbed people, some psychiatrists have intervened directly in the brain (*psychosurgery*). *Prefrontal lobotomy* never had any scientific validation, yet was performed on many thousands of people. *Electroconvulsive therapy (ECT)*, has been used successfully to treat acute episodes of suicidal depression, although its benefits rarely last. A newer method, *transcranial magnetic stimulation (TMS)*, is being studied as a way of treating severe depression. *Deep brain stimulation (DBS)* requires the surgical implantation of electrodes and a stimulation device.

Major Schools of Psychotherapy

LO 16.2.A Summarize the main elements of psychodynamic therapy.

Psychodynamic ("depth") therapies include Freudian *psychoanalysis* and its modern variations, such as approaches based on *object-relations theory*. These therapies explore unconscious dynamics by focusing on the process of *transference* to break through the patient's defenses and by examining childhood issues and past experiences.

LO 16.2.B Describe four methods of behavior therapy, and discuss the main techniques used in cognitive therapy.

Behavior therapists draw on classical and operant principles of learning. They use such methods as *graduated exposure* and *flooding*; *systematic desensitization*; *behavioral self-monitoring*; and *skills training*. *Cognitive therapists* aim to change the irrational thoughts involved in negative emotions and self-defeating actions. Aaron Beck's *cognitive therapy* and Albert Ellis's *rational emotive behavior therapy (REBT)* are two leading approaches. *Cognitive-behavioral therapy (CBT)* is now the most common approach.

LO 16.2.C Summarize the similarities and differences between client-centered therapy and existential therapy.

Humanist therapy holds that human nature is essentially good and attempts to help people feel better about themselves by focusing on here and-now issues and on their capacity for change. Carl Rogers's *client-centered (nondirective) therapy* emphasizes the importance of the therapist's empathy and ability to provide *unconditional positive regard*. *Existential therapy* helps people cope with the dilemmas of existence, such as the meaning of life and the fear of death.

LO 16.2.D List the hallmarks of the family-systems perspective, and describe how they apply to family and couples therapy.

Family therapies are based on the view that individual problems develop in the context of the whole family. They share a *family-systems perspective*, the understanding that any one person's behavior in the family affects everyone else. In *couples therapy*, the therapist usually sees both partners in a relationship.

Evaluating Psychotherapy

LO 16.3.A Define the *scientist–practitioner gap*, and identify some of the problems associated with assessing the effectiveness of therapy.

Successful therapy often requires a *therapeutic alliance* between the therapist and the client, so that they understand each other and can work together. A *scientist–practitioner gap* has developed because researchers and many clinicians hold different assumptions about the value of empirical research for doing psychotherapy and for assessing its effectiveness. In assessing the effectiveness of psychotherapy, researchers need to control for the placebo effect and the *justification of effort* effect. They rely on *randomized controlled trials* to determine which therapies are empirically supported.

LO 16.3.B Provide examples of areas in which cognitive and behavior therapies have shown themselves to be particularly effective.

Some psychotherapies are better than others for specific problems. Behavior therapy and cognitive-behavioral therapy are often the most effective for depression, anxiety disorders, anger problems, certain health problems (such as pain, insomnia, and eating disorders), and childhood and adolescent behavior problems. Family-systems therapies, especially when combined with behavioral techniques as in *multisystemic therapy*, are especially helpful for children, young adults with schizophrenia, and aggressive adolescents. The length of time needed for successful therapy depends on the problem and the individual. Some methods, such as *motivational interviewing*, produce benefits in only a session or two; long-term psychodynamic therapy can be helpful for people with severe disorders and personality problems.

LO 16.3.C Discuss four ways in which therapy has the potential to harm clients, and give an example of each.

In some cases, therapy is harmful. The therapist may use empirically unsupported and potentially harmful techniques, such as "rebirthing"; inadvertently create new disorders in the client through undue influence or suggestion; hold a prejudice about the client's gender, ethnicity, religion, or sexual orientation; or behave unethically, for example by permitting a sexual relationship with the client.

Chapter 16 Quiz

1. Drugs commonly used to treat mental disorders fall into the classes of _____, tranquilizers, _____, and antidepressant drugs.
   a. Leptokurtics / platykurtics
   b. Antipsychotics / lithium carbonate
   c. Anticonvulsive / antitrophic
   d. MAOIs / SSRIs

2. People who suffer from bipolar disorder might be prescribed
   a. Anti-anxiety drugs
   b. Tranquilizers
   c. Lithium carbonate
   d. Beta blockers

3. Anti-anxiety drugs, otherwise known as tranquilizers, work by increasing the activity of
   a. GABA
   b. Lithium
   c. Glutamate
   d. The sympathetic nervous system

4. Dr. Nichopoulos prescribes aspirin to treat Aaron's depression, yet he tells Aaron that the medication is a powerful new antidepressant drug. After a month of taking the drug, Aaron reports that his symptoms have lessened, his outlook has brightened, and his mood has improved. What's going on here?
   a. Aaron has been coerced.
   b. A new psychotropic use for aspirin has been discovered.
   c. GABA receptors have been activated in Aaron's central nervous system.
   d. The placebo effect is at work.

5. A procedure that involves severing or otherwise destroying the connections between the prefrontal lobes and the rest of the brain is called
   a. Freemanotomy
   b. Keseyotomy
   c. Lobotomy
   d. Egastomy

6. Both ECT and TMS tend to be used primarily in the treatment of
   a. Depression
   b. Anxiety
   c. Eating disorders
   d. Panic disorder

7. Sigmund Freud's method of psychotherapy is called
   a. Holism
   b. Object relations
   c. Psychodrama
   d. Psychoanalysis

8. Rico is afraid of tigers. His therapist suggests a technique in which Rico first learns some relaxation exercises. After Rico has mastered ways of calming himself, his therapist shows him a photo of a tiger taken from a far distance, while Rico practices relaxing. After this step has been mastered, the therapist asks Rico to hold a stuffed tiger toy while practicing his skills. Eventually he experiences, in sequence, a slide show on tigers, close-up photos of tigers, a documentary on the majestic beasts, and finally a trip to the zoo. What therapeutic technique was Rico's therapist using?
   a. Flooding
   b. Systematic desensitization
   c. Behavioral self-monitoring
   d. Rational-promotive assistance

9. Francesca wishes she were more patient with other people and more relaxed in work settings. She's smart enough to know that wishing won't make it so! A therapist helps her by teaching techniques that foster patience and cooperation, such as counting to three silently before responding to a question, setting a timer to establish 10-minute break periods every 2 hours, and an exercise to learn all her coworkers' names and hobbies. The therapist is providing Francesca with
   a. Skills training
   b. Behavioral self-monitoring
   c. Transference
   d. Graduated exposure

10. "If I don't get into a good college, I'll never be able to get a good job!" wailed Doug to his therapist. "Think about that," challenged his therapist. "Is that really what will happen, or are you just catastrophizing?" "But . . . but . . . if I don't get into a good college, my parents will hate me and my girlfriend will dump me!" protested Doug. "Not getting into a good college doesn't rob you of all the fine qualities you have that make people love you," snapped his therapist. "Not getting into a good college means you didn't get into a good college; it's not the end of the world and it doesn't mean the sky will fall down on you." What kind of therapy does Doug's therapist seem to be practicing?
    a. Psychodynamic therapy
    b. Rational-emotive therapy
    c. Psychoanalytic therapy
    d. Behavioral control therapy

11. "If I don't get into a good college, I'll never be able to get a good job!" wailed Doug to his therapist. "That can really be upsetting; most people would be upset by that experience, and that's a natural feeling to have," replied his therapist. "Can you tell me more about how that makes you feel?" "If I don't get into a good college, my parents will hate me and my girlfriend will dump me!" continued Doug. "It sure would be disappointing to miss a significant goal in your life, but people who truly love you will continue to love you for who you are," Doug's therapist said, soothingly. "This is just my opinion, but I think it's important to remember that you're a person of worth, and that you can aspire to and achieve many things in your life." What kind of therapy does Doug's therapist seem to be practicing?
    a. Cognitive-behavioral
    b. Object relations
    c. Primal
    d. Humanist

12. Lisa and Allison are having trouble in their relationship. They seem to squabble about money (Lisa likes to spend and Allison doesn't) and their communication patterns on this issue aren't very good. In most other ways their relationship is quite solid, and they definitely love and respect

one another. What therapeutic approach might be good for them?

a. Couples therapy

b. Behavioral therapy for Allison

c. Behavioral therapy for Lisa

d. Gestalt therapy

13. How does a randomized controlled trial work in assessing the effectiveness of therapy?

a. Clinicians' case notes, representing different perspectives on a single case, are reviewed by a panel of qualified mental health professionals to judge the best outcomes.

b. Best clinical practices are codified in a kind of "handbook," and clinicians who adopt that therapeutic perspective are encouraged to follow that guide.

c. Psychological scientists review a random selection of case notes on an anonymous client, where the parameters of a disorder have been carefully controlled ahead of time.

d. People with a given disorder are randomly assigned to one or more treatment groups or to a control group.

14. Ingo wants help to quit smoking. What kind of therapy should he pursue?

a. Cognitive-behavioral therapy, to learn techniques to modify his behavior and extinguish his undesirable habits

b. Psychodynamic therapy, to explore his oral fixation and address the unconscious sexual significance cigarettes have in his life

c. Humanist therapy, so he can feel good about the choices he's already made in his life and accept the fact that he is a smoker—a *good* smoker

d. Existential therapy, so he can realize that smoking is symbolic of the end we all must face, and that cancer represents the pain of survival

15. Which of the following is *not* a risk to clients undergoing therapy?

a. Devaluation of a client's customs or cultural clues by a therapist

b. An intractable problem that doesn't respond well to therapy

c. Empirically unsupported therapeutic techniques

d. Coercive influence exerted by the therapist over the client

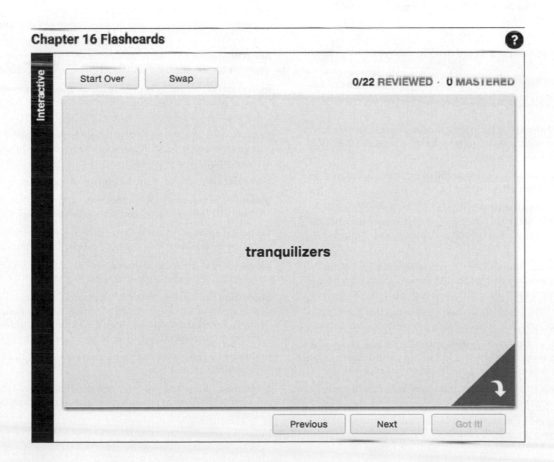

Chapter 16 Flashcards   ?

Start Over   Swap   0/22 REVIEWED · 0 MASTERED

tranquilizers

Previous   Next   Got It!

Glossary

absolute threshold The smallest quantity of physical energy that can be reliably detected by an observer.

acculturation The process by which members of minority groups come to identify with and feel part of the mainstream culture.

action potential A brief change in electrical voltage that occurs between the inside and the outside of an axon when a neuron is stimulated; it serves to produce an electrical impulse.

activation–synthesis theory The theory that dreaming results from the cortical synthesis and interpretation of neural signals triggered by activity in the lower part of the brain.

adrenal hormones Hormones that are produced by the adrenal glands and that are involved in emotion and stress.

adrenarche [a-DREN-ar-kee] A time in middle childhood when the adrenal glands begin producing the adrenal hormone DHEA and other hormones that affect cognitive and social development.

affect heuristic The tendency to consult one's emotions instead of estimating probabilities objectively.

agoraphobia A set of phobias, often set off by a panic attack, involving the basic fear of being away from a safe place or person.

algorithm A problem-solving strategy guaranteed to produce a solution even if the user does not know how it works.

alternative hypothesis An assertion that the independent variable in a study will have a certain predictable effect on the dependent variable; also called an *experimental or research hypothesis*.

amnesia The partial or complete loss of memory for important personal information.

anorexia nervosa An eating disorder characterized by fear of being fat, a distorted body image, radically reduced consumption of food, and emaciation.

amygdala [uh-MIG-dul-uh] A brain structure involved in the arousal and regulation of emotion and the initial emotional response to sensory information.

antidepressant drugs Drugs used primarily in the treatment of mood disorders, especially depression and anxiety.

antipsychotic drugs Drugs used primarily in the treatment of schizophrenia and other psychotic disorders; they are often used off label and inappropriately for other disorders such as dementia and impulsive aggressiveness.

antisocial personality disorder (APD) A personality disorder characterized by a lifelong pattern of irresponsible, antisocial behavior such as law-breaking, violence, and other impulsive, reckless acts.

applied psychology The study of psychological issues that have direct practical significance; also, the application of psychological findings.

appraisals A person's perceptions, beliefs, attributions, and goals, which determine which emotion he or she will feel in a given circumstance; they are a central component of emotion and the emotional experience.

approach goals Goals framed in terms of desired outcomes or experiences, such as learning to scuba dive.

archetypes [AR-ki-tipes] Universal, symbolic images that appear in myths, art, stories, and dreams; to Jungians, they reflect the collective unconscious.

arithmetic mean An average that is calculated by adding up a set of quantities and dividing the sum by the total number of quantities in the set.

attribution theory The theory that people are motivated to explain their own and other people's behavior by attributing causes of that behavior to a situation or a disposition.

autonomic nervous system The subdivision of the peripheral nervous system that regulates the internal organs and glands.

availability heuristic The tendency to judge the probability of a type of event by how easy it is to think of examples or instances.

avoidance goals Goals framed in terms of avoiding unpleasant experiences, such as trying not to look foolish in public.

axon A neuron's extending fiber that conducts impulses away from the cell body and transmits them to other neurons.

basic concepts Concepts that have a moderate number of instances and that are easier to acquire than those having few or many instances.

basic psychology The study of psychological issues for the sake of knowledge rather than for its practical application.

Bayesian statistics Statistics that involve a formula for calculating the likelihood of a hypothesis being true and meaningful, taking into account relevant prior knowledge.

behavior modification The application of operant-conditioning techniques to teach new responses or to reduce or eliminate maladaptive or problematic behavior; also called *applied behavior analysis*.

behavior therapy A form of therapy that applies principles of classical and operant conditioning to help people change self-defeating or problematic behaviors.

behavioral genetics An interdisciplinary field of study concerned with genetic contributions to individual differences in behavior and personality.

behavioral self-monitoring In behavior therapy, a method of keeping careful data on the frequency and consequences of the behavior to be changed.

behaviorism An approach to psychology that emphasizes the study of observable behavior and the role of the environment and prior experience as determinants of behavior.

binocular cues Visual cues to depth or distance requiring two eyes.

biological perspective A psychological approach that emphasizes bodily events and changes associated with actions, feelings, and thoughts.

biological rhythm A periodic, more or less regular fluctuation in a biological system; it may or may not have psychological implications.

bipolar disorder A mood disorder in which episodes of both depression and mania (excessive euphoria) occur.

borderline personality disorder A disorder characterized by extreme negative emotionality and an inability to regulate emotions; it often results in intense but unstable relationships, impulsiveness, self-mutilating behavior, feelings of emptiness, and a fear of abandonment by others.

brain stem The part of the brain at the top of the spinal cord, consisting of the medulla and the pons.

brightness Lightness or luminance; the dimension of visual experience related to the amount (intensity) of light emitted from or reflected by an object.

bulimia nervosa An eating disorder characterized by episodes of excessive eating (bingeing) followed by forced vomiting or use of laxatives (purging).

case study A detailed description of a particular individual being studied or treated.

cell body The part of the neuron that keeps it alive and determines whether or not it will fire.

central nervous system (CNS) The portion of the nervous system consisting of the brain and spinal cord.

cerebellum A brain structure that regulates movement and balance, is involved in remembering simple skills and acquired reflexes, and plays a role in cognitive and emotional learning.

cerebral cortex A collection of several thin layers of cells covering the cerebrum; it is largely responsible for higher mental functions. *Cortex* is Latin for "bark" or "rind."

cerebral hemispheres The two halves of the cerebrum.

cerebrum [suh-REE-brum] The largest brain structure, consisting of the upper part of the brain; divided into two hemispheres, it is in charge of most sensory, motor, and cognitive processes. From the Latin for "brain."

childhood amnesia The inability to remember events and experiences that occurred during the first 2 or 3 years of life.

chromosomes Within every cell, rod-shaped structures that carry the genes.

chunk A meaningful unit of information; it may be composed of smaller units.

circadian [sur-CAY-dee-un] rhythm A biological rhythm with a period (from peak to peak or trough to trough) of about 24 hours; from the Latin *circa*, "about," and *dies*, "a day."

classical conditioning The process by which a previously neutral stimulus becomes associated with a stimulus that already elicits a response and, in turn, acquires the capacity to elicit a similar or related response. Also called *Pavlovian* or *respondent conditioning*.

client-centered (nondirective) therapy A humanist approach, devised by Carl Rogers, which emphasizes the therapist's empathy with the client and the use of unconditional positive regard.

cochlea [KOCK-lee-uh] A snail-shaped, fluid-filled organ in the inner ear, containing the organ of Corti, where the receptors for hearing are located.

cognitive dissonance A state of tension that occurs when a person simultaneously holds two cognitions that are psychologically inconsistent or when a person's belief is incongruent with his or her behavior.

cognitive dissonance A state of tension that occurs when a person holds two cognitions that are psychologically inconsistent, or when a person's belief is incongruent with his or her behavior.

cognitive ethology The study of cognitive processes in nonhuman animals.

cognitive perspective A psychological approach that emphasizes mental processes in perception, memory, language, problem solving, and other areas of behavior.

cognitive schema An integrated mental network of knowledge, beliefs, and expectations concerning a particular topic or aspect of the world.

cognitive therapy A form of therapy designed to identify and change irrational, unproductive ways of thinking and, hence, to reduce negative emotions.

collective unconscious In Jungian theory, the universal memories and experiences of humankind, represented in the symbols, stories, and images (archetypes) that occur across all cultures.

collectivist cultures Cultures in which the self is regarded as embedded in relationships, and harmony with one's group is prized above individual goals and wishes.

concept A mental category that groups objects, relations, activities, abstractions, or qualities having common properties.

conditioned response (CR) The classical-conditioning term for a response that is elicited by a conditioned stimulus; it occurs after the conditioned stimulus is associated with an unconditioned stimulus.

conditioned stimulus (CS) The classical-conditioning term for an initially neutral stimulus that comes to elicit a conditioned response after being associated with an unconditioned stimulus.

conditioning A basic kind of learning that involves associations among environmental stimuli and an organism's behavior.

cones Visual receptors involved in color vision.

confabulation Confusion of an event that happened to someone else with one that happened to you, or a belief that you remember something when it never actually happened.

confidence interval A statistical measure that provides, with a specified probability, a range of values within which a population mean is likely to lie.

confirmation bias The tendency to look for or pay attention only to information that confirms one's own belief.

confirmation bias The tendency to look for or pay attention only to information that confirms one's own belief.

conservation The understanding that the physical properties of objects, such as the number of items in a cluster or the amount of liquid in a glass, can remain the same even when their form or appearance changes.

consolidation The process by which a long-term memory becomes durable and relatively stable.

consolidation The process by which a memory becomes durable and stable.

contact comfort In primates, the innate pleasure derived from close physical contact; it is the basis of the infant's first attachment.

continuous reinforcement A reinforcement schedule in which a particular response is always reinforced.

control condition In an experiment, a comparison condition in which participants are not exposed to the same treatment as in the experimental condition.

convergence The turning inward of the eyes, which occurs when they focus on a nearby object.

corpus callosum The bundle of nerve fibers connecting the two cerebral hemispheres.

correlation coefficient A measure of correlation that ranges in value from −1.00 to +1.00.

correlation A measure of how strongly two variables are related to one another.

correlational study A descriptive study that looks for a consistent relationship between two phenomena.

cortisol A hormone secreted by the adrenal cortex that elevates blood sugar and protects the body's tissues in case of injury; if chronically elevated due to stress, it can lead to hypertension, immune disorders, other illnesses, and possibly depression.

counterconditioning In classical conditioning, the process of pairing a conditioned stimulus with a stimulus that elicits a response that is incompatible with an unwanted conditioned response.

critical thinking The ability and willingness to assess claims and make judgments on the basis of well-supported reasons and evidence rather than emotion or anecdote.

cross-sectional study A study in which people (or animals) of different ages are compared at a given time.

crystallized intelligence Cognitive skills and specific knowledge acquired over a lifetime; it is heavily dependent on education and tends to remain stable over time.

crystallized intelligence Cognitive skills and specific knowledge of information acquired over a lifetime; it is heavily dependent on education and tends to remain stable over the lifetime.

cue-dependent forgetting The inability to retrieve information stored in memory because of insufficient cues for recall.

culture A program of shared rules that govern the behavior of people in a community or society, and a set of values, beliefs, and customs shared by most members of that community.

dark adaptation A process by which visual receptors become maximally sensitive to dim light.

decay theory The theory that information in memory eventually disappears if it is not accessed; it applies better to short-term than to long-term memory.

declarative memories Memories of facts, rules, concepts, and events ("knowing that"); they include semantic and episodic memories.

deep processing In the encoding of information, the processing of meaning rather than simply the physical or sensory features of a stimulus.

defense mechanisms Methods used by the ego to prevent unconscious anxiety or threatening thoughts from entering consciousness.

deindividuation In groups or crowds, the loss of awareness of one's own individuality.

dendrites A neuron's branches that receive information from other neurons and transmit it toward the cell body.

dependent variable A variable that an experimenter predicts will be affected by manipulations of the independent variable.

depressants Drugs that slow activity in the central nervous system.

descriptive methods Methods that yield descriptions of behavior but not necessarily causal explanations.

descriptive statistics Statistical procedures that organize and summarize research data.

dialectical reasoning A process in which opposing facts or ideas are weighed and compared, with a view to determining the best solution or resolving differences.

difference threshold The smallest difference in stimulation that can be reliably detected by an observer when two stimuli are compared; also called *just noticeable difference (jnd)*.

diffusion of responsibility In groups, the tendency of members to avoid taking action because they assume that others will.

discriminative stimulus A stimulus that signals when a particular response is likely to be followed by a certain type of consequence.

display rules Social and cultural rules that regulate when, how, and where a person may express (or suppress) emotions.

dissociation A split in consciousness in which one part of the mind operates independently of others.

dissociative identity disorder (DID) A controversial disorder marked by the apparent appearance within one person of two or more distinct personalities, each with its own name and traits; formerly known as *multiple personality disorder (MPD)*.

DNA (deoxyribonucleic acid) The chromosomal molecule that transfers genetic characteristics by way of coded instructions for the structure of proteins.

doctrine of specific nerve energies The principle that different sensory modalities exist because signals received by the sense organs stimulate different nerve pathways leading to different areas of the brain.

double-blind study An experiment in which neither the people being studied nor the individuals running the study know who is in the control group and who is in the experimental group until after the results are tallied.

effect size An objective, standardized way of describing the strength of the independent variable's influence on the dependent variable.

ego In psychoanalysis, the part of personality that represents reason, good sense, and rational self-control.

elaborative rehearsal Association of new information with already stored knowledge and analysis of the new information to make it memorable.

electroconvulsive therapy (ECT) A procedure used in cases of prolonged and severe major depression, in which a brief brain seizure is induced.

electroencephalogram (EEG) A recording of neural activity detected by electrodes.

emotion A state of arousal involving facial and bodily changes, brain activation, cognitive appraisals, subjective feelings, and tendencies toward action.

emotion work Expression of an emotion, often because of a role requirement, that a person does not really feel.

emotional intelligence The ability to identify your own and other people's emotions accurately, express your emotions clearly, and regulate emotions in yourself and others.

empirical Relying on or derived from observation, experimentation, or measurement.

endocrine glands Internal organs that produce hormones and release them into the bloodstream.

endogenous Generated from within rather than by external cues.

endorphins [en-DOR-fins] Chemical substances in the nervous system that are similar in structure and action to opiates; they are involved in pain reduction, pleasure, and memory and are known technically as *endogenous opioid peptides*.

entrapment A gradual process in which individuals escalate their commitment to a course of action to justify their investment of time, money, or effort.

epigenetics The study of stable changes in the expression of a particular gene that occur without changes in DNA base sequences; the Greek prefix *epi*- means "on top of" or "in addition to."

episodic memories Memories of personally experienced events and the contexts in which they occurred.

equilibrium The sense of balance.

ethnic identity A person's identification with a racial or ethnic group.

ethnocentrism The belief that one's own ethnic group, nation, or religion is superior to all others.

event-related potentials (ERP) A technique that isolates the neural activity associated with a specific stimulus ("event").

evolution A change in gene frequencies within a population over many generations; a mechanism by which genetically influenced characteristics of a population may change.

evolutionary psychology A field of psychology emphasizing evolutionary mechanisms that may help explain human commonalities in cognition, development, emotion, social practices, and other areas of behavior.

evolutionary psychology A field of psychology emphasizing evolutionary mechanisms that may help explain human commonalities in social practices, perception, emotional responses, and other areas of behavior.

existential therapy A form of therapy designed to help clients explore the meaning of existence and face the great questions of life, such as death, freedom, alienation, and loneliness.

existentialism A philosophical approach that emphasizes the inevitable dilemmas and challenges of human existence.

experiment A controlled test of a hypothesis in which the researcher manipulates one variable to discover its effect on another.

experimenter effects Unintended changes in study participants' behavior due to cues that the experimenter inadvertently conveys.

explicit memory Conscious, intentional recollection of an event or of an item of information.

extinction The weakening and eventual disappearance of a learned response; in classical conditioning, it occurs when the conditioned stimulus is no longer paired with the unconditioned stimulus.

extinction The weakening and eventual disappearance of a learned response; in operant conditioning, it occurs when a response is no longer followed by a reinforcer.

extrinsic motivation The pursuit of an activity for external rewards, such as money or fame.

extrinsic reinforcers Reinforcers that are not inherently related to the activity being reinforced.

facial feedback The process by which the facial muscles send messages to the brain about the basic emotion being expressed.

factor analysis A statistical method for analyzing the intercorrelations among various measures or test scores; clusters of measures or scores that are highly correlated are assumed to measure the same underlying trait or ability (factor).

factor analysis A statistical method for analyzing the intercorrelations among various measures or test scores; clusters of measures or scores that are highly correlated are assumed to measure the same underlying trait, ability, or aptitude (factor).

familiarity effect The tendency of people to feel more positive toward a person, item, product, or other stimulus the more familiar they are with it.

family-systems perspective An approach to doing therapy with individuals or families by identifying how each family member forms part of a larger interacting system.

feature detectors Cells in the visual cortex that are sensitive to specific features of the environment.

feminist psychology A psychological approach that analyzes the influence of social inequities on gender relations and on the behavior of the two sexes.

field research Descriptive or experimental research conducted in a natural setting outside the laboratory.

flooding In behavior therapy, a form of exposure treatment in which the client is taken directly into a feared situation until his or her panic subsides.

fluid intelligence The capacity for deductive reasoning and the ability to use new information to solve problems; it is relatively independent of education and tends to decline in old age.

fluid intelligence The capacity to reason and use information to solve problems; it is relatively independent of education.

fMRI (functional magnetic resonance imaging) A type of magnetic resonance imaging used to study brain activity associated with specific thoughts and behaviors.

framing effect The tendency for people's choices to be affected by how a choice is presented, or framed, such as whether it is worded in terms of potential losses or gains.

fraternal (dizygotic) twins Twins that develop from two separate eggs fertilized by different sperm; they are no more alike genetically than are any other pair of siblings.

frequency distribution A summary of how frequently each score in a set occurred.

frequency polygon (line graph) A graph showing a set of points obtained by plotting score values against score frequencies; adjacent points are joined by straight lines.

frontal lobes Lobes at the front of the brain's cerebral cortex; they contain areas involved in short-term memory, higher-order thinking, initiative, social judgment, and (in the left lobe, typically) speech production.

functionalism An early psychological approach that emphasized the function or purpose of behavior and consciousness.

fundamental attribution error The tendency, in explaining other people's behavior, to overestimate personality factors and underestimate the influence of the situation.

g factor A general intellectual ability assumed by many theorists to underlie specific mental abilities and talents.

ganglion cells Neurons in the retina of the eye, which gather information from receptor cells (by way of intermediate bipolar cells); their axons make up the optic nerve.

gate control theory The theory that the experience of pain depends in part on whether pain impulses get past a neurological "gate" in the spinal cord and thus reach the brain.

gender identity The fundamental sense of being male or female; it is independent of whether the person conforms to the social and cultural rules of gender.

gender schema A cognitive schema (mental network) of knowledge, beliefs, metaphors, and expectations about what it means to be male or female.

gender typing The process by which children learn the abilities, interests, and behaviors associated with being masculine or feminine in their culture.

general adaptation syndrome According to Hans Selye, a series of physiological reactions to stress occurring in three phases: alarm, resistance, and exhaustion.

generalized anxiety disorder A continuous state of anxiety marked by feelings of worry and dread, apprehension, difficulties in concentration, and signs of motor tension.

genes The functional units of heredity; they are composed of DNA and specify the structure of proteins

genetic marker A segment of DNA that varies among individuals, has a known location on a chromosome, and can function as a genetic landmark for a gene involved in a physical or mental condition.

genome The full set of genes in each cell of an organism (with the exception of sperm and egg cells), together with noncoding DNA located outside the genes.

Gestalt principles Principles that describe the brain's organization of sensory information into meaningful units and patterns.

glia [GLY-uh or GLEE-uh] Cells that support, nurture, and insulate neurons, remove debris when neurons die, enhance the formation and maintenance of neural connections, and modify neuronal functioning.

graduated exposure In behavior therapy, a method in which a person suffering from a phobia or panic attacks is gradually taken into the feared situation or exposed to a traumatic memory until the anxiety subsides.

graph A drawing that depicts numerical relationships.

groupthink The tendency for all members of a group to think alike for the sake of harmony and to suppress disagreement.

heritability A statistical estimate of the proportion of the total variance in some trait that is attributable to genetic differences among individuals within a group.

heuristic A rule of thumb that suggests a course of action or guides problem solving but does not guarantee an optimal solution.

higher-order conditioning In classical conditioning, a procedure in which a neutral stimulus becomes a conditioned stimulus through association with an already established conditioned stimulus.

hindsight bias The tendency to overestimate one's ability to have predicted an event after the outcome is known; the "I knew it all along" phenomenon.

hippocampus A brain structure involved in the storage of new information in memory.

histogram (bar graph) A graph in which the heights (or lengths) of bars are proportional to the frequencies of individual scores or classes of scores in a distribution.

hormones Chemical substances, secreted by organs called *glands*, that affect the functioning of other organs.

HPA (hypothalamus–pituitary–adrenal cortex) axis A system activated to energize the body to respond to stressors. The hypothalamus sends chemical messengers to the pituitary gland, which in turn prompts the adrenal cortex to produce cortisol and other hormones.

hue The dimension of visual experience specified by color names and related to the wavelength of light.

humanist psychology A psychological approach that emphasizes personal growth, resilience, and the achievement of human potential.

humanist therapy A form of psychotherapy based on the philosophy of humanism, which emphasizes personal growth, resilience, the achievement of human potential, and the client's ability to change rather than being destined to repeat past conflicts.

hypnosis A procedure in which the practitioner suggests changes in a subject's sensations, perceptions, thoughts, feelings, or behavior.

hypothalamus A brain structure involved in emotions and drives vital to survival; it regulates the autonomic nervous system.

hypothesis A statement that attempts to predict or to account for a set of phenomena; scientific hypotheses specify relationships among events or variables and are empirically tested.

id In psychoanalysis, the part of personality containing inherited psychic energy, particularly sexual and aggressive instincts.

identical (monozygotic) twins Twins that develop when a fertilized egg divides into two parts that develop into separate embryos.

implicit learning Learning that occurs when you acquire knowledge about something without being aware of how you did so and without being able to state exactly what it is you have learned.

implicit memory Unconscious retention in memory, as evidenced by the effect of a previous experience or previously encountered information on current thoughts or actions.

inattentional blindness Failure to consciously perceive something you are looking at because you are not attending to it.

independent variable A variable that an experimenter manipulates.

individualist cultures Cultures in which the self is regarded as autonomous, and individual goals and wishes are prized above duty and relations with others.

induction A method of childrearing in which the parent appeals to the child's own abilities, sense of responsibility, and feelings for others in correcting the child's misbehavior.

inferential statistics Statistical procedures that allow researchers to draw inferences about how statistically meaningful a study's results are.

informed consent The doctrine that anyone who participates in human research must do so voluntarily and must know enough about the study to make an intelligent decision about whether to take part.

instinctive drift During operant learning, the tendency for an organism to revert to instinctive behavior.

intelligence An inferred characteristic of an individual, usually defined as the ability to profit from experience, acquire knowledge, think abstractly, act purposefully, or adapt to changes in the environment.

intelligence quotient (IQ) A measure of intelligence originally computed by dividing a person's mental age by his or her chronological age and multiplying by 100; it is now derived from norms provided for standardized intelligence tests.

intermittent (partial) schedule of reinforcement A reinforcement schedule in which a particular response is sometimes but not always reinforced.

internal desynchronization A state in which biological rhythms are not in phase with one another.

intersex conditions (intersexuality) Conditions in which chromosomal or hormonal anomalies cause a child to be born with ambiguous genitals, or genitals that conflict with the infant's chromosomes.

intrinsic motivation The pursuit of an activity for its own sake.

intrinsic reinforcers Reinforcers that are inherently related to the activity being reinforced.

justification of effort The tendency of individuals to increase their liking for something that they have worked hard or suffered to attain; a common form of dissonance reduction.

just-world hypothesis The notion that many people need to believe that the world is fair and that justice is served, that bad people are punished and good people are rewarded.

kinesthesis [KIN-es-THEE-sis] The sense of body position and movement of body parts; also called *kinesthesia*.

language A system that combines meaningless elements such as sounds or gestures to form structured utterances that convey meaning.

latent learning A form of learning that is not immediately expressed in an overt response; it occurs without obvious reinforcement.

lateralization Specialization of the two cerebral hemispheres for particular operations.

learning A relatively permanent change in behavior (or behavioral potential) due to experience.

learning perspective A psychological approach that emphasizes how the environment and experience affect a person's or animal's actions; it includes *behaviorism* and *social-cognitive learning theories*.

lesion method The removal or disabling of a brain structure to gain better understanding of its function; this method is used only in animals.

libido (li-BEE-do) In psychoanalysis, the psychic energy that fuels the life or sexual instincts of the id.

lithium carbonate A drug frequently given to people suffering from bipolar disorder.

localization of function Specialization of particular brain areas for particular functions.

locus of control A general expectation about whether the results of your actions are under your own control (internal locus) or beyond your control (external locus).

longitudinal study A study in which people (or animals) are followed and periodically reassessed over a period of time.

long-term memory (LTM) In the three-box model of memory, the memory system involved in the long-term storage of information.

long-term potentiation A long-lasting increase in the strength of synaptic responsiveness, thought to be a biological mechanism of long-term memory.

loudness The dimension of auditory experience related to the intensity of a pressure wave.

lucid dreams Dreams in which the dreamer is aware of dreaming

maintenance rehearsal Rote repetition of material in order to maintain its availability in memory.

major depression A disorder involving disturbances in emotion (excessive sadness), behavior (loss of interest in one's usual activities), cognition (thoughts of hopelessness), and body function (fatigue and loss of appetite).

mastery (learning) goals Goals framed in terms of increasing one's competence and skills.

mean *See* arithmetic mean.

measure of central tendency A number intended to characterize an entire set of data.

measure of variability A number that indicates how dispersed scores are around the mean of the distribution.

median A measure of central tendency; the value at the midpoint of a distribution of scores when the scores are ordered from highest to lowest.

medulla [muh-DUL-uh] A structure in the brain stem responsible for certain automatic functions, such as breathing and heart rate.

melatonin A hormone, secreted by the pineal gland, that is involved in the regulation of daily biological rhythms.

menarche [men-AR-kee] The onset of menstruation during puberty.

menopause The cessation of menstruation and of the production of ova; it is usually a gradual process lasting up to several years.

mental age (MA) A measure of mental development expressed in terms of the average mental ability at a given age.

mental disorder Any behavior or emotional state that causes an individual great suffering, is self-destructive, seriously impairs the person's ability to work or get along with others, or makes a person unable to control the impulse to endanger others.

mental image A mental representation that mirrors or resembles the thing it represents; mental images occur in many and perhaps all sensory modalities.

mental set A tendency to solve problems using procedures that worked before on similar problems.

meta-analysis A set of techniques for combining data from a number of related studies to determine the explanatory strength of a particular independent variable.

metacognition The knowledge or awareness of one's own cognitive processes, and the ability to monitor and control those processes.

mirror neurons Brain cells that fire when a person or animal observes another carrying out an action; these neurons appear to be involved in empathy, language comprehension, imitation, and reading emotions.

mnemonics Strategies and tricks for improving memory, such as the use of a verse or a formula.

mode A measure of central tendency; the most frequently occurring score in a distribution.

monocular cues Visual cues to depth or distance, which can be used by one eye alone.

mood-congruent memory The tendency to remember experiences that are consistent with one's current mood and overlook or forget experiences that are not.

motivation An inferred process within a person or animal that causes movement either toward a goal or away from an unpleasant situation.

MRI (magnetic resonance imaging) A method for studying body and brain tissue, using magnetic fields and special radio receivers.

myelin sheath A fatty insulation that may surround the axon of a neuron.

multiple intelligences theory A theory of intelligence that emphasizes many different ways of processing information.

narcolepsy A disorder involving sudden and unpredictable daytime attacks of sleepiness or lapses into REM sleep.

natural selection The evolutionary process in which individuals with genetically influenced traits that are adaptive in a particular environment tend to survive and to reproduce in greater numbers than do other individuals; as a result, their traits become more common in the population.

negative correlation An association between increases in one variable and decreases in another.

negative reinforcement A reinforcement procedure in which a response is followed by the removal, delay, or decrease in intensity of an unpleasant stimulus; as a result, the response becomes stronger or more likely to occur.

nerve A bundle of nerve fibers (axons and sometimes dendrites) in the peripheral nervous system.

neurogenesis The production of new neurons from immature stem cells.

neuromodulators Neurochemicals that modulate the functioning of neurons and neurotransmitters.

neuron A cell that conducts electrochemical signals; the basic unit of the nervous system; also called a *nerve cell*.

neurotransmitter A chemical substance that is released by a transmitting neuron at the synapse and that alters the activity of a receiving neuron.

nonconscious processes Mental processes occurring outside of and not available to conscious awareness.

nonshared environment Unique aspects of a person's environment and experience that are not shared with family members.

normal curve A symmetrical, bell-shaped frequency polygon representing a normal distribution.

normal distribution A theoretical frequency distribution having certain special characteristics. For example, the distribution is symmetrical; the mean, mode, and median all have the same value; and the farther a score is from the mean, the less the likelihood of obtaining it.

norms In test construction, established standards of performance.

norms (social) Rules that regulate social life, including explicit laws and implicit cultural conventions.

null hypothesis An assertion that the independent variable in a study will have no effect on the dependent variable.

object permanence The understanding, which develops throughout the first year, that an object continues to exist even when you cannot see it or touch it.

objective tests (inventories) Standardized questionnaires requiring written responses; they typically include scales on which people are asked to rate themselves.

object-relations school A psychodynamic approach that emphasizes the importance of the infant's first 2 years of life and the baby's formative relationships, especially with the mother.

observational learning A process in which an individual learns new responses by observing the behavior of another (a model) rather than through direct experience; sometimes called *vicarious conditioning*.

observational study A study in which a researcher carefully and systematically observes and records behavior without interfering with the behavior; it may involve either naturalistic or laboratory observation.

obsessive–compulsive disorder (OCD) An anxiety disorder in which a person feels trapped in repetitive, persistent thoughts (*obsessions*) and repetitive, ritualized behaviors (*compulsions*).

occipital [ahk-SIP-uh-tuhl] lobes Lobes at the lower back part of the brain's cerebral cortex; they contain areas that receive visual information.

Oedipus complex In psychoanalysis, a conflict occurring in the phallic (Oedipal) stage, in which a child desires the parent of the other sex and views the same-sex parent as a rival.

operant conditioning The process by which a response becomes more likely to occur or less so, depending on its consequences.

operational definition A precise definition of a term in a hypothesis, which specifies the operations for observing and measuring the process or phenomenon being defined.

opiates Drugs, derived from the opium poppy, that relieve pain and commonly produce euphoria.

opponent-process theory A theory of color perception that assumes that the visual system treats pairs of colors as opposing or antagonistic.

organ of Corti [core-tee] A structure in the cochlea containing hair cells that serve as the receptors for hearing.

oxytocin A hormone, secreted by the pituitary gland, that stimulates uterine contractions during childbirth, facilitates the ejection of milk during nursing, and seems to promote, in both sexes, attachment and trust in relationships.

panic disorder An anxiety disorder in which a person experiences recurring panic attacks, periods of intense fear, and feelings of impending doom or death, accompanied by physiological symptoms such as rapid heart rate and dizziness.

papillae [pa-PILL-ee] Knoblike elevations on the tongue, containing the taste buds. (Singular: *papilla*.)

parallel distributed processing (PDP) model A model of memory in which knowledge is represented as connections among thousands of interacting processing units, distributed in a vast network, and all operating in parallel. Also called a *connectionist model*.

parasympathetic nervous system The subdivision of the autonomic nervous system that operates during relaxed states and that conserves energy.

parietal [puh-RYE-uh-tuhl] lobes Lobes at the top of the brain's cerebral cortex; they contain areas that receive information on pressure, pain, touch, and temperature as well as handle attention and awareness of spatial relationships.

percentile score   A score that indicates the percentage of people who scored at or below a given raw score; also called *centile rank*.

perception   The process by which the brain organizes and interprets sensory information.

perceptual constancy   The accurate perception of objects as stable or unchanged despite changes in the sensory patterns they produce.

perceptual set   A habitual way of perceiving, based on expectations.

performance goals   Goals framed in terms of performing well in front of others, being judged favorably, and avoiding criticism.

peripheral nervous system (PNS)   All portions of the nervous system outside the brain and spinal cord; it includes sensory and motor nerves.

personality   A distinctive and relatively stable pattern of behavior, thoughts, motives, and emotions that characterizes an individual.

PET scan (positron-emission tomography)   A method for analyzing biochemical activity in the brain, for example by using injections of a glucose-like substance containing a radioactive element.

phantom pain   The experience of pain in a missing limb or other body part.

phobia   An exaggerated, unrealistic fear of a specific situation, activity, or object.

phrenology   The now-discredited theory that different brain areas account for specific character and personality traits, which can be "read" from bumps on the skull.

pitch   The dimension of auditory experience related to the frequency of a pressure wave; the height or depth of a tone.

pituitary gland   A small endocrine gland at the base of the brain that releases many hormones and regulates other endocrine glands.

placebo   An inactive substance or fake treatment used as a control in an experiment or given by a medical practitioner to a patient.

placebo effect   The apparent success of a medication or treatment due to the patient's expectations or hopes rather than to the drug or treatment itself.

plasticity   The brain's ability to change and adapt in response to experience, through neurogenesis, or by reorganizing or growing new neural connections.

pons   A structure in the brain stem involved in, among other things, sleeping, waking, and dreaming.

positive correlation   An association between increases in one variable and increases in another—or between decreases in one and in another.

positive reinforcement   A reinforcement procedure in which a response is followed by the presentation of, or increase in intensity of, a reinforcing stimulus; as a result, the response becomes stronger or more likely to occur.

postdecision dissonance   In the theory of cognitive dissonance, tension that occurs when you believe you may have made a bad decision.

posttraumatic stress disorder (PTSD)   A disorder in which a person who has experienced a traumatic or life-threatening event has symptoms such as nightmares, flashbacks, insomnia, reliving of the trauma, and increased physiological arousal.

power assertion   A method of childrearing in which the parent uses punishment and authority to correct the child's misbehavior.

prejudice   A strong, unreasonable dislike or hatred of a group, based on a negative stereotype.

primary control   An effort to modify reality by changing other people, the situation, or events; a "fighting back" philosophy.

primary punisher   A stimulus that is inherently punishing; an example is electric shock.

primary reinforcer   A stimulus that is inherently reinforcing, typically satisfying a physiological need; an example is food.

priming   A method for measuring implicit memory in which a person reads or listens to information and is later tested to see whether the information affects performance on another type of task.

principle of falsifiability   The principle that a scientific theory must make predictions that are specific enough to expose the theory to the possibility of disconfirmation; that is, the theory must predict not only what will happen but also what will *not* happen.

proactive interference   Forgetting that occurs when previously stored material interferes with the ability to remember similar, more recently learned material.

procedural memories   Memories for the performance of actions or skills ("knowing how").

projective tests   Psychological tests used to infer a person's motives, conflicts, and unconscious dynamics on the basis of the person's interpretations of ambiguous stimuli.

proposition   A unit of meaning that is made up of concepts and expresses a single idea.

prototype   An especially representative example of a concept.

psychedelic drugs   Consciousness-altering drugs that produce hallucinations, change thought processes, or disrupt the normal perception of time and space.

psychoactive drugs   Drugs capable of influencing perception, mood, cognition, or behavior.

psychoanalysis   A theory of personality and a method of psychotherapy, originally formulated by Sigmund Freud, that emphasizes unconscious motives and conflicts.

psychoanalysis   A theory of personality and a method of psychotherapy, developed by Sigmund Freud, that emphasizes the exploration of unconscious motives and conflicts; modern *psychodynamic therapies* share this emphasis but differ from Freudian analysis in various ways.

psychodynamic theories   Theories that explain behavior and personality in terms of unconscious energy dynamics within the individual.

psychological tests   Procedures used to measure and evaluate personality traits, emotional states, aptitudes, interests, abilities, and values.

psychology   The discipline concerned with behavior and mental processes and how they are affected by an organism's physical state, mental state, and external environment; the term is often represented by Ψ, the Greek letter psi (usually pronounced "sy").

psychometrics   The measurement of mental abilities, traits, and processes.

psychoneuroimmunology (PNI)   The study of the relationships among psychology, the nervous and endocrine systems, and the immune system.

psychopathy   A personality disorder characterized by fearlessness; lack of empathy, guilt, and remorse; the use of deceit; and coldheartedness.

psychosexual stages   In Freud's theory, the idea that sexual energy takes different forms as the child matures; the stages are oral, anal, phallic (Oedipal), latency, and genital.

psychosis   An extreme mental disturbance involving distorted perceptions and irrational behavior; it may have psychological or organic causes. (Plural: *psychoses*.)

puberty   The age at which a person becomes capable of sexual reproduction.

punishment   The process by which a stimulus or event weakens or reduces the probability of the response that it follows.

random assignment   A procedure for assigning people to experimental and control groups in which each individual has the same probability as any other of being assigned to a given group.

randomized controlled trials   Research designed to determine the effectiveness of a new medication or form of therapy, in which people with a given problem or disorder are randomly assigned to one or more treatment groups or to a control group.

range   A measure of the spread of scores, calculated by subtracting the lowest score from the highest score.

rapid eye movement (REM) sleep Sleep periods characterized by eye movement, loss of muscle tone, and vivid dreams.

rational emotive behavior therapy (REBT) A form of cognitive therapy devised by Albert Ellis, designed to challenge the client's unrealistic thoughts.

reasoning The drawing of conclusions or inferences from observations, facts, or assumptions.

recall The ability to retrieve and reproduce from memory previously encountered material.

reciprocal determinism In social-cognitive learning theories, the two-way interaction between aspects of the environment and aspects of the individual in the shaping of personality traits.

recognition The ability to identify previously encountered material.

reinforcement The process by which a stimulus or event strengthens or increases the probability of the response that it follows.

relearning method A method for measuring retention that compares the time required to relearn material with the time used in the initial learning of the material.

reliability In test construction, the consistency of scores derived from a test, from one time and place to another.

REM behavior disorder A disorder in which the muscle paralysis that normally occurs during REM sleep is absent or incomplete, and the sleeper is able to act out his or her dreams.

representative sample A group of individuals, selected from a population for study, which matches the population on important characteristics such as age and sex.

repression In psychoanalytic theory, the selective, involuntary pushing of threatening or upsetting information into the unconscious.

reticular activating system (RAS) A dense network of neurons found in the core of the brain stem; it arouses the cortex and screens incoming information.

retina Neural tissue lining the back of the eyeball's interior, which contains the receptors for vision.

retinal disparity The slight difference in lateral separation between two objects as seen by the left eye and the right eye.

retroactive interference Forgetting that occurs when recently learned material interferes with the ability to remember similar material stored previously.

rods Visual receptors that respond to dim light.

role A given social position that is governed by a set of norms for proper behavior.

saturation Vividness or purity of color; the dimension of visual experience related to the complexity of light waves.

schizophrenia A psychotic disorder marked by delusions, hallucinations, disorganized and incoherent speech, inappropriate behavior, and cognitive impairments.

seasonal affective disorder (SAD) A controversial disorder in which a person experiences depression during the winter and an improvement of mood in the spring.

secondary control An effort to accept reality by changing your own attitudes, goals, or emotions; a "learn to live with it" philosophy.

secondary punisher A stimulus that has acquired punishing properties through association with other punishers.

secondary reinforcer A stimulus that has acquired reinforcing properties through association with other reinforcers.

selective attention The focusing of attention on selected aspects of the environment and the blocking out of others.

self-efficacy A person's belief that he or she is capable of producing desired results, such as mastering new skills and reaching goals.

self-fulfilling prophecy An expectation that comes true because of the tendency of the person holding it to act in ways that bring it about.

semantic memories Memories of general knowledge, including facts, rules, concepts, and propositions.

semicircular canals Sense organs in the inner ear that contribute to equilibrium by responding to rotation of the head.

sensation The detection, by sense organs, of physical energy emitted or reflected by physical objects.

sense receptors Specialized cells that convert physical energy in the environment or the body to electrical energy that can be transmitted as nerve impulses to the brain.

sensory adaptation The reduction or disappearance of sensory responsiveness when stimulation is unchanging or repetitious.

sensory deprivation The absence of normal levels of sensory stimulation.

sensory register A memory system that momentarily preserves extremely accurate images of sensory information.

separation anxiety The distress that most children develop, at about 6 to 8 months of age, when their primary caregivers temporarily leave them with strangers.

serial-position effect The tendency for recall of the first and last items on a list to surpass recall of items in the middle of the list.

set point The genetically influenced weight range for an individual; it is maintained by biological mechanisms that regulate food intake, fat reserves, and metabolism.

sex hormones Hormones that regulate the development and functioning of reproductive organs and that stimulate the development of male and female sexual characteristics; they include androgens, estrogens, and progesterone.

sexual scripts Sets of implicit rules that specify proper sexual behavior for a person in a given situation, varying with the person's gender, age, sexual orientation, religion, social status, and peer group.

shaping An operant-conditioning procedure in which successive approximations of a desired response are reinforced.

short-term memory (STM) In the three-box model of memory, a limited-capacity memory system involved in the retention of information for brief periods; it is also used to hold information retrieved from long-term memory for temporary use.

signal-detection theory A psychophysical theory that divides the detection of a sensory signal into a sensory process and a decision process.

significance tests Statistical tests that show how likely it is that a study's results occurred merely by chance.

single-blind study An experiment in which participants do not know whether they are in an experimental or a control group.

skills training In behavior therapy, an effort to teach the client skills that he or she may lack, as well as new constructive behaviors to replace self-defeating ones.

sleep apnea A disorder in which breathing briefly stops during sleep, causing the person to choke and gasp and momentarily awaken.

social cognition An area in social psychology concerned with social influences on thought, memory, perception, and beliefs.

social identity The part of a person's self-concept that is based on his or her identification with a nation, religious or political group, occupation, or other social affiliation.

social-cognitive theories Theories that emphasize how behavior is learned and maintained through observation and imitation of others, positive consequences, and cognitive processes such as plans, expectations, and beliefs.

socialization The process by which children learn the behaviors, attitudes, and expectations required of them by their society or culture.

sociobiology   An interdisciplinary field that emphasizes evolutionary explanations of social behavior in animals, including human beings.

sociocultural perspective   A psychological approach that emphasizes social and cultural influences on behavior.

somatic nervous system   The subdivision of the peripheral nervous system that connects to sensory receptors and to skeletal muscles; sometimes called the *skeletal nervous system*.

source misattribution   The inability to distinguish an actual memory of an event from information you learned about the event elsewhere.

spinal cord   A collection of neurons and supportive tissue running from the base of the brain down the center of the back, protected by a column of bones (the spinal column).

spontaneous recovery   The reappearance of a learned response after its apparent extinction.

standard deviation   A commonly used measure of variability that indicates the average difference between scores in a distribution and their mean.

standardize   In test construction, to develop uniform procedures for giving and scoring a test.

state-dependent memory   The tendency to remember something when the remainder is in the same physical or mental state as during the original learning or experience.

stem cells   Immature cells that renew themselves and have the potential to develop into mature cells; given encouraging environments, stem cells from early embryos can develop into any cell type.

stereotype   A summary impression of a group, in which a person believes that all members of the group share a common trait or traits (positive, negative, or neutral).

stereotype threat   A burden of doubt a person feels about his or her performance, due to negative stereotypes about his or her group's abilities.

stimulants   Drugs that speed up activity in the central nervous system.

stimulus discrimination   In operant conditioning, the tendency of a response to occur in the presence of one stimulus but not in the presence of other similar stimuli that differ from it on some dimension.

stimulus discrimination   The tendency to respond differently to two or more similar stimuli; in classical conditioning, it occurs when a stimulus similar to the CS fails to evoke the CR.

stimulus generalization   After conditioning, the tendency to respond to a stimulus that resembles one involved in the original conditioning; in classical conditioning, it occurs when a stimulus that resembles the CS elicits the CR.

stimulus generalization   In operant conditioning, the tendency for a response that has been reinforced (or punished) in the presence of one stimulus to occur (or be suppressed) in the presence of other similar stimuli.

structuralism   An early psychological approach that emphasized the analysis of immediate experience into basic elements.

subconscious processes   Mental processes occurring outside of conscious awareness but accessible to consciousness when necessary.

successive approximations   In the operant-conditioning procedure of shaping, behaviors that are ordered in terms of increasing similarity or closeness to the desired response.

superego   In psychoanalysis, the part of personality that represents conscience, morality, and social standards.

suprachiasmatic [soo-pruh-kye-az-MAT-ick] nucleus (SCN)   An area of the brain containing a biological clock that governs circadian rhythms.

surveys   Questionnaires and interviews that ask people directly about their experiences, attitudes, or opinions.

sympathetic nervous system   The subdivision of the autonomic nervous system that mobilizes bodily resources and increases the output of energy during emotion and stress.

synapse   The site where transmission of a nerve impulse from one nerve cell to another occurs; it includes the axon terminal, the synaptic cleft, and receptor sites in the membrane of the receiving cell.

synesthesia   A condition in which stimulation of one sense also evokes another.

systematic desensitization   In behavior therapy, a step-by-step process of desensitizing a client to a feared object or experience; it is based on the classical-conditioning procedure of counterconditioning.

tacit knowledge   Strategies for success that are not explicitly taught but that instead must be inferred.

taste buds   Nests of taste receptor cells.

telegraphic speech   A child's first word combinations, which omit (as a telegram did) unnecessary words.

temperaments   Physiological dispositions to respond to the environment in certain ways; they are present in infancy and in many nonhuman species and are assumed to be innate.

temporal lobes   Lobes at the sides of the brain's cerebral cortex; they contain areas involved in hearing, memory, perception, emotion, and (in the left lobe, typically) language comprehension

thalamus   A brain structure that relays sensory messages to the cerebral cortex.

theory   An organized system of assumptions and principles that purports to explain a specified set of phenomena and their interrelationships.

theory of mind   A system of beliefs about the way one's own mind and the minds of others work, and of how individuals are affected by their beliefs and feelings.

therapeutic alliance   The bond of confidence and mutual understanding established between therapist and client, which allows them to work together to solve the client's problems.

timbre   The distinguishing quality of a sound; the dimension of auditory experience related to the complexity of the pressure wave.

tolerance   Increased resistance to a drug's effects accompanying continued use.

trait   A characteristic of an individual, describing a habitual way of behaving, thinking, or feeling.

tranquilizers   Drugs commonly prescribed for patients who complain of unhappiness, anxiety, or worry.

transcranial direct current stimulation (tDCS)   A technique that applies a very small electric current to stimulate or suppress activity in parts of the cortex; it enables researchers to identify the functions of a particular area.

transcranial magnetic stimulation (TMS)   A method of stimulating brain cells, using a powerful magnetic field produced by a wire coil placed on a person's head; it can be used by researchers to temporarily inactivate neural circuits.

transference   In psychodynamic therapies, a critical process in which the client transfers unconscious emotions or reactions, such as emotional feelings about his or her parents, onto the therapist.

triarchic [try-ARE-kick] theory of intelligence   A theory of intelligence that emphasizes analytic, creative, and practical abilities.

trichromatic theory   A theory of color perception that proposes three mechanisms in the visual system, each sensitive to a certain range of wavelengths; their interaction is assumed to produce all the different experiences of hue.

unconditional positive regard   To Carl Rogers, love or support given to another person with no conditions attached.

unconditioned response (UR)   The classical-conditioning term for a response elicited by an unconditioned stimulus.

unconditioned stimulus (US)   The classical-conditioning term for a stimulus that already elicits a certain response without additional learning.

validity   The ability of a test to measure what it was designed to measure.

validity effect   The tendency of people to believe that a statement is true or valid simply because it has been repeated many times.

variables   Characteristics of behavior or experience that can be measured or described by a numeric scale.

volunteer bias   A shortcoming of findings derived from a sample of volunteers instead of a representative sample; the volunteers may differ from those who did not volunteer.

vulnerability–stress model   Approaches that emphasize how individual vulnerabilities interact with external stresses or circumstances to produce specific mental disorders, such as depression.

withdrawal   Physical and psychological symptoms that occur when someone addicted to a drug stops taking it.

working memory   In many models of memory, a cognitively complex form of short-term memory; it involves active mental processes that control retrieval of information from long-term memory and interpret that information appropriately for a given task.

z-score (standard score)   A number that indicates how far a given raw score is above or below the mean, using the standard deviation of the distribution as the unit of measurement.

References

Abbott, Jacenta D., Wijeratne, Tissa, Hughes, Andrew, Perre, Diana, & Lindell, Annukka K. (2014). The influence of left and right hemisphere brain damage on configural and featural processing of affective faces. *Laterality: Asymmetries of Body, Brain and Cognition, 19*(4), 455–472.

Abrahamson, Amy C., Baker, Laura A., & Caspi, Avshalom. (2002). Rebellious teens? Genetic and environmental influences on the social attitudes of adolescents. *Journal of Personality and Social Psychology, 83,* 1392–1408.

Abrams, David B., & Wilson, G. Terence. (1983). Alcohol, sexual arousal, and self-control. *Journal of Personality and Social Psychology, 45,* 188–198.

Abrams, Dominic. (2015). Social identity and intergroup relations. In Mario Mikulincer; Phillip R. Shaver; John F. Dovidio; & Jeffry A. Simpson (Eds.), *APA handbook of personality and social psychology: Volume 2. Group processes* (pp. 203–228). Washington, DC: American Psychological Association.

Abu-Saad, K., & Fraser, D. (2010). Maternal nutrition and birth outcomes. *Journal of Epidemiologic Reviews, 32*(1), 5–25.

Acevedo, Bianca P., & Aron, Arthur. (2009). Does a long-term relationship kill romantic love? *Review of General Psychology, 13,* 59–65.

Adams, Mark James, Majolo, Bonaventura, Ostner, Julia, Schülke, Oliver, De Marco, Arianna, Thierry, Bernard, et al. (2015). Personality structure and social style in macaques. *Journal of Personality and Social Psychology*, electronic preview.

Adams, Thomas G., Brady, Robert E., Lohr, Jeffrey M., & Jacobs, W. Jake. (2015). A meta-analysis of CBT components for anxiety disorders. *The Behavior Therapist, 38*(4), 87–97.

Addis, Donna R., Wong, Alana T, & Schacter, Daniel L. (2007). Remembering the past and imagining the future: Common and distinct neural substrates during event construction and elaboration. *Neuropsychologia, 45,* 1363–1377.

Ader, Robert. (2000). True or false: The placebo effect as seen in drug studies is definitive proof that the mind can bring about clinically relevant changes in the body: The placebo effect: If it's all in your head, does that mean you only think you feel better? *Advances in Mind-Body Medicine, 16,* 7–11.

Adler, Nancy E., & Snibbe, Alana C. (2003). The role of psychosocial processes in explaining the gradient between socioeconomic status and health. *Current Directions in Psychological Science, 12,* 119–123.

Adolph, Karen E. (2000). Specificity of learning: Why infants fall over a veritable cliff. *Psychological Science, 11,* 290–295.

Adolph, Karen E., & Kretch, Kari S. (2012). Infants on the edge: Beyond the visual cliff. In Alan M. Slater & Paul C. Quinn (Eds.), *Developmental psychology: Revisiting the classic studies* (pp. 36–55). London: Sage.

Adolph, Karen E., Kretch, Kari S., & LoBue, Vanessa. (2014). Fear of heights in infants? *Current Directions in Psychological Science, 23*(1), 60–66.

Affleck, Glenn, Tennen, Howard, Croog, Sydney, & Levine, Sol. (1987). Causal attribution, perceived control, and recovery from a heart attack. *Journal of Social and Clinical Psychology, 5,* 339–355.

Agars, Mark D. (2004). Reconsidering the impact of gender stereotypes on the advancement of women in organizations. *Psychology of Women Quarterly, 28,* 103–111.

Aggarwal, Sunil K., Carter Gregory T., Sullivan Mark D., et al. (2009). Medicinal use of cannabis in the United States: Historical perspectives, current trends, and future directions. *Journal of Opioid Management, 5,* 153–168.

Agrawal, Yuri, Platz, Elizabeth A., & Niparko, John K. (2008). Prevalence of hearing loss and differences by demographic characteristics among US adults. *Archives of Internal Medicine, 168,* 1522–1530.

Aguiar, Patrícia, Vala, Jorge, Correia, Isabel, & Pereira, Cícero. (2008). Justice in our world and in that of others: Belief in a just world and reactions to victims. *Social Justice Research, 21,* 50–68.

Ahn, Sun Joo (Grace), Le, Amanda Minh Tran, & Bailenson, Jeremy. (2013). The effect of embodied experiences on self–other merging, attitude, and helping behavior. *Media Psychology, 16*(1), 7–38.

Ainsworth, Mary D. S. (1973). The development of infant–mother attachment. In B. M. Caldwell & H. N. Ricciuti (Eds.), *Review of child development research* (Vol. 3). Chicago: University of Chicago Press.

Ainsworth, Mary D. S. (1979). Infant–mother attachment. *American Psychologist, 34,* 932–937.

Ainsworth, Sarah E., & Baumeister, Roy F. (2012). Changes in sexuality: How sexuality changes across time, across relationships, and across sociocultural contexts. *Clinical Neuropsychiatry: Journal of Treatment Evaluation, 9*(1), 32–38.

Albert, Dustin, Chein, Jason, & Steinberg, Laurence. (2013). The teenage brain: Peer influences on adolescent decision making. *Current Directions in Psychological Science, 22*(2), 114–120.

Alcock, James E. (2011, March/April). Back from the future: Parapsychology and the Bem affair. *Skeptical Inquirer,* 31–39.

Alink, Lenneke R. A., Mesman, Judi, van Zeijl, Jantien, et al. (2009). Maternal sensitivity moderates the relation between negative discipline and aggression in early childhood. *Social Development, 18,* 99–120.

Allport, Gordon W. (1954/1979). *The nature of prejudice.* Reading, MA: Addison-Wesley.

Allport, Gordon W. (1961). *Pattern and growth in personality.* New York: Holt, Rinehart & Winston.

Almli, Lynn M., Stevens, Jennifer S., Smith, Alicia K., Kilaru, Varun, Meng, Qian, Flory, Janine, et al. (2015). A genome-wide identified risk variant for PTSD is a methylation quantitative trait locus and confers decreased cortical activation to fearful faces. *American Journal of Medical Genetics Part B: Neuropsychiatric Genetics, 168*(5), 327–336.

Amabile, Teresa M. (1983). *The social psychology of creativity.* New York: Springer-Verlag.

Amabile, Teresa M., & Khaire, Mukti. (2008). Creativity and the role of the leader. *Harvard Business Review, 86.* Online at http://hbr.harvardbusiness.org/2008/10/creativity-and-the-role-of-the-leader/ar/1.

Ambady, Nalini. (2011, May/June). The mind in the world: Culture and the brain. *APS Observer, 24.*

Amedi, Amir, Merabet, Lotfi, Bermpohl, Felix, & Pascual-Leone, Alvaro. (2005). The occipital cortex in the blind: Lessons about plasticity and vision. *Current Directions in Psychological Science, 14,* 306–311.

American Psychiatric Association. (2013). *Diagnostic and statistical manual of mental disorders* (5th ed.) Arlington, VA: Author.

American Psychological Association. (2012). Guidelines for psychological practice with lesbian, gay, and bisexual clients. *American Psychologist, 67,* 10–42.

Amering, Michaela, & Katschnig, Heinz. (1990). Panic attacks and panic disorder in cross-cultural perspective. *Psychiatric Annals, 20,* 511–516.

Anastasi, Anne, & Urbina, Susan. (1997). *Psychological testing* (7th ed.). Upper Saddle River, NJ: Prentice-Hall.

Anderson, Amanda. (2005). *The way we argue now: A study in the cultures of theory.* Princeton, NJ: Princeton University Press.

Anderson, Craig A., Berkowitz, Leonard, Donnerstein, Edward, et al. (2003). The influence of media violence on youth. *Psychological Science in the Public Interest, 4*(3) [whole issue].

Anderson, Craig A., Shibuya, Akiko, Ihori, Nobuko, et al. (2010). Violent video game effects on aggression, empathy, and prosocial behavior in eastern and western countries: A meta-analytic review. *Psychological Bulletin, 136,* 151–173.

Anderson, John R. (1990). *The adaptive nature of thought.* Hillsdale, NJ: Erlbaum.

Anderson, Matthew. (2005). Is lack of sexual desire a disease? Is testosterone the cure? *Medscape Ob/Gyn & Women's Health.* Available at www.medscape.com/viewarticle/512218.

Anderson, Sarah E., Dallal, Gerard E., & Must, Aviva. (2003). Relative weight and race influence average age at menarche: Results from two nationally representative surveys of U.S. girls studied 25 years apart. *Pediatrics, 111,* 844–850.

Anderson-Barnes, Victoria C., McAuliffe, Caitlin, Swanberg, Kelly M., & Tsao, Jack W. (2009, October). Phantom limb pain: A phenomenon of proprioceptive memory? *Medical Hypotheses, 73,* 555–558.

Andrade, Julio A. (2015). Reconceptualising whistleblowing in a complex world. *Journal of Business Ethics, 128,* 321–335.

Andreano, Joseph M., & Cahill, Larry. (2006). Glucocorticoid release and memory consolidation in men and women. *Psychological Science, 17,* 466–470.

Andreasen, Nancy C., Arndt, Stephan, Swayze, Victor, II, et al. (1994). Thalamic abnormalities in schizophrenia visualized through magnetic resonance image averaging. *Science, 266,* 294–298.

Añez, Luis M., Silva, Michelle A., Paris Jr., Manuel, & Bedregal, Luis E. (2008). Engaging Latinos through the integration of cultural values and motivational interviewing principles. *Professional Psychology: Research and Practice, 39,* 153–159.

Angell, Marcia. (2004). *The truth about the drug companies: How they deceive us and what to do about it.* New York: Random House.

Antrobus, John. (1991). Dreaming: Cognitive processes during cortical activation and high afferent thresholds. *Psychological Review, 98,* 96–121.

Antrobus, John. (2000). How does the dreaming brain explain the dreaming mind? *Behavioral and Brain Sciences, 23,* 904–907.

Archer, John. (2004). Sex differences in aggression in real-world settings: A meta-analytic review. *Review of General Psychology, 8,* 291–322.

Arendt, Hannah. (1963). *Eichmann in Jerusalem: A report on the banality of evil.* New York: Viking.

Arkes, Hal R. (1993). Some practical judgment and decision-making research. In N. J. Castellan, Jr., et al. (Eds.), *Individual and group decision making: Current issues.* Hillsdale, NJ: Erlbaum.

Arkes, Hal R., Boehm, Lawrence E., & Xu, Gang. (1991). The determinants of judged validity. *Journal of Experimental Social Psychology, 27,* 576–605.

Arnett, Jeffrey J. (2014). *Emerging adulthood: The winding road from the late teens through the twenties.* (2nd ed.) New York: Oxford University Press.

Arnon, Inbal, & Clark, Eve V. (2011). Why *"on your feet"* is better than *"feet"*: Children's word production is facilitated in familiar sentence-frames. *Language Learning & Development, 7,* 107–129.

Aron, Arthur, Fisher, Helen, Mashek, Debra J., et al. (2005). Reward, motivation, and emotion systems associated with early-stage intense romantic love. *Journal of Neurophysiology, 94,* 327–337.

Aron, Arthur, Fisher, Helen E., Strong, Greg, et al. (2008). Falling in love. In S. Sprecher, A. Wenzel, & J. Harvey (Eds.), *Handbook of relationship initiation.* New York: Psychology Press.

Aronson, Elliot. (2000). *Nobody left to hate.* New York: Freeman.

Aronson, Elliot. (2010). *Not by chance alone: My life as a social psychologist.* New York: Basic Books.

Aronson, Elliot. (2012). *The social animal* (11th ed.). New York: Worth.

Aronson, Elliot, & Mills, Judson. (1959). The effect of severity of initiation on liking for a group. *Journal of Abnormal and Social Psychology, 59,* 177–181.

Aronson, Joshua. (2010). Jigsaw and the nurture of human intelligence. In M. H. Gonzales, C. Tavris, & J. Aronson (Eds.), *The scientist and the humanist: A festschrift in honor of Elliot Aronson.* New York: Psychology Press.

Arredondo, Patricia, Gallardo-Cooper, Maritza, Delgado-Romero, Edward A., & Zapata, Angela L. (2014). *Culturally responsive counseling with Latinas/os.* New York: American Counseling Association.

Arredondo, Patricia, Rosen, Daniel C., Rice, Tiffany, Perez, Patricia, & Tovar-Gamero, Zoila G. (2005). Multicultural counseling: A 10-year content analysis of the *Journal of Counseling and Development. Journal of Counseling and Development, 83,* 155–161.

Arroyo, Carmen G., & Zigler, Edward. (1995). Racial identity, academic achievement, and the psychological well-being of economically disadvantaged adolescents. *Journal of Personality and Social Psychology, 69,* 903–914.

Arum, Richard, & Josipa Roksa. (2011). *Academically adrift: Limited learning on college campuses.* Chicago: University of Chicago Press.

Asch, Solomon E. (1952). *Social psychology.* Englewood Cliffs, NJ: Prentice-Hall.

Asch, Solomon E. (1965). Effects of group pressure upon the modification and distortion of judgments. In H. Proshansky & B. Seidenberg

(Eds.), *Basic studies in social psychology*. New York: Holt, Rinehart & Winston.

Aserinsky, Eugene, & Kleitman, Nathaniel. (1955). Two types of ocular motility occurring in sleep. *Journal of Applied Physiology, 8,* 1–10.

Atkinson, Richard C., & Shiffrin, Richard M. (1968). Human memory: A proposed system and its control processes. In K. W. Spence & J. T. Spence (Eds.), *The psychology of learning and motivation: Vol. 2. Advances in research and theory*. New York: Academic Press.

Atkinson, Richard C., & Shiffrin, Richard M. (1971, August). The control of short-term memory. *Scientific American, 225*(2), 82–90.

Atran, Scott. (2010). *Talking to the enemy*. New York: HarperCollins.

AuBuchon, Peter G., & Calhoun, Karen S. (1985). Menstrual cycle symptomatology: The role of social expectancy and experimental demand characteristics. *Psychosomatic Medicine, 47,* 35–45.

Auyeung, Bonnie, Baron-Cohen, Simon, Ashwin, Emma, et al. (2009). Fetal testosterone predicts sexually differentiated childhood behavior in girls and in boys. *Psychological Science, 20,* 144–148.

Aviczer, Hillel, Hassin, Ran R., Ryan, Jennifer, et al. (2008). Angry, disgusted, or afraid? Studies on the malleability of emotion perception. *Psychological Science, 19,* 724–732.

Axel, Richard. (1995, October). The molecular logic of smell. *Scientific American,* 154–159.

Azmitia, Margarita, Syed, Moin, & Radmacher, Kimberly. (2008). On the intersection of personal and social identities: Introduction and evidence from a longitudinal study of emerging adults. In M. Azmitia, M. Syed, & K. Radmacher (Eds.), *The intersections of personal and social identities. New Directions for Child and Adolescent Development, 120,* 1–16. San Francisco: Jossey-Bass.

Azuma, Hiroshi. (1984). Secondary control as a heterogeneous category. *American Psychologist, 39,* 970–971.

Baas, Matthijs, De Dreu, Carsten K. W., & Nijstad, Bernard A. (2008). A meta-analysis of 25 years of mood-creativity research: Hedonic tone, activation, or regulatory focus? *Psychological Bulletin, 134,* 779–806.

Babiak, Paul, & Hare, Robert. (2007). *Snakes in suits*. New York: Collins Business.

Baddeley, Alan D. (1992). Working memory. *Science, 255,* 556–559.

Baddeley, Alan D. (2007). *Working memory, thought, and action*. New York: Oxford University Press.

Bahrick, Harry P., Bahrick, Phyllis O., & Wittlinger, Roy P. (1975). Fifty years of memory for names and faces: A cross-sectional approach. *Journal of Experimental Psychology: General, 104,* 54–75.

Bailey, J. Michael, Bobrow, David, Wolfe, Marilyn, & Mikach, Sarah. (1995). Sexual orientation of adult sons of gay fathers. *Developmental Psychology, 31,* 124–129.

Bailey, J. Michael, Dunne, Michael P., & Martin, Nicholas G. (2000). Genetic and environmental influences on sexual orientation and its correlates in an Australian twin sample. *Journal of Personality and Social Psychology, 78,* 524–536.

Bailey, J. Michael, & Zucker, Kenneth J. (1995). Childhood sex-typed behavior and sexual orientation: A conceptual analysis and quantitative review. *Developmental Psychology, 31,* 43–55.

Baillargeon, Renée. (2004). Infants' physical world. *Current Directions in Psychological Science, 13,* 89–94.

Baker, Erika, Shelton, Katherine H., Baibazarova, Eugenia, Hay, Dale F., & van Goozen, Stephanie H. M. (2013). Low skin conductance activity in infancy predicts aggression in toddlers 2 years later. *Psychological Science, 24*(6), 1051–1056.

Baker, Mark C. (2001). *The atoms of language: The mind's hidden rules of grammar*. New York: Basic Books.

Baker, Timothy B., McFall, Richard M., & Shoham, Varda. (2008). Current status and future prospects of clinical psychology: Toward a scientifically principled approach to mental and behavioral health care. *Psychological Science in the Public Interest, 9.*

Bakermans-Kranenburg, Marian J., Breddels-van Baardewijk, Philomeen, Juffer, Femmie, et al. (2008). Insecure mothers with temperamentally reactive infants: A chance for intervention. In F. Juffer, M. J. Bakermans-Kranenburg, & M. H. van IJzendoorn (Eds.), *Promoting positive parenting: An attachment-based intervention*. New York: Taylor & Francis.

Bakker, Arnold B. (2011). An evidence-based model of work engagement. *Current Directions in Psychological Science, 20,* 265–269.

Balcetis, Emily, & Dunning, David. (2010). Wishful seeing: More desired objects are seen as closer. *Psychological Science, 21,* 147–152.

Balcetis, Emily, Dunning, David, & Miller, Richard L. (2008). Do collectivists know themselves better than individualists? Cross-cultural studies of the holier than thou phenomenon. *Journal of Personality and Social Psychology, 95,* 1252–1267.

Ball, Aimee Lee. (2014, April 6). Who are you on Facebook now? *New York Times,* p. ST16.

Balter, Michael. (2012). "Killjoys" challenge claims of clever animals. *Science, 335,* 1036–1037.

Bancroft, John. (2006). Normal sexual development. In H. E. Barbaree & W. L. Marshall (Eds.), *The juvenile sex offender* (2nd ed.). New York: Guilford Press.

Bancroft, John, Graham, Cynthia A., Janssen, Erick, & Sanders, Stephanie A. (2009). The dual control model: Current status and future directions. *Journal of Sex Research, 46,* 121–142.

Bandura, Albert. (1977). *Social learning theory*. Englewood Cliffs, NJ: Prentice-Hall.

Bandura, Albert. (1986). *Social foundations of thought and action: A social cognitive theory*. Englewood Cliffs, NJ: Prentice-Hall.

Bandura, Albert. (1999). Moral disengagement in the perpetration of inhumanities. *Personality and Social Psychology Review, 3,* 193–209.

Bandura, Albert. (2001). Social cognitive theory: An agentic perspective. *Annual Review of Psychology, 52,* 1–26. Palo Alto, CA: Annual Reviews.

Bandura, Albert. (2012). Social cognitive theory. In Paul A. M. van Lange, Arie W. Kruglanski, & E. Tory Higgins (Eds.), *Handbook of theories in social psychology* (Vol. 1, pp. 349–373). Thousand Oaks, CA: Sage.

Bandura, Albert. (2013). The role of self-efficacy in goal-based motivation. In Edwin A. Locke; & Gary P. Latham (Eds.), *New developments in goal setting and task performance*. New York: Routledge/ Taylor & Francis Group.

Bandura, Albert, Caprara, Gian Vittorio, Barbaranelli, Claudio, et al. (2001). Sociocognitive self-regulatory mechanisms governing transgressive behavior. *Journal of Personality and Social Psychology, 80,* 125–135.

Bandura, Albert, Ross, Dorothea, & Ross, Sheila A. (1963). Vicarious reinforcement and imitative learning. *Journal of Abnormal and Social Psychology, 67,* 601–607.

Barash, David P., & Lipton, Judith Eve. (2001). *The myth of monogamy: Fidelity and infidelity in animals and people.* New York: W. H. Freeman.

Barbuto, J. E. (1997). A critique of the Myers-Briggs Type Indicator and its operationalization of Carl Jung's psychological types. *Psychological Reports, 80,* 611–625.

Bargary, Gary, & Mitchell, Kevin J. (2008). Synaesthesia and cortical connectivity. *Trends in Neurosciences, 31,* 335–342.

Darglow, Peter. (2008, September/October). Corporate self interest and vague nerve stimulation for depression. *Skeptical Inquirer,* 35–40.

Barlow, David H. (2000). Unraveling the mysteries of anxiety and its disorders from the perspective of emotion theory. *American Psychologist, 55,* 1247–1263.

Barlow, David H., Ellard, Kristen K., Sauer-Zavala, Shannon, Bullis, Jacqueline R., & Carl, Jenna R. (2014). The origins of neuroticism. *Perspectives on Psychological Science, 9*(5), 481–496.

Barnes, Carol. (2011, September 1). Secrets of aging. *The Scientist.* Available at http://the-scientist.com/2011/09/01/secrets-of-aging/.

Barnier, Amanda J., Cox, Rochelle E., & McConkey, Kevin M. (2014). The province of "highs": The high hypnotizable person in the science of hypnosis and in psychological science. *Psychology of Consciousness: Theory, Research, and Practice, 1*(2), 168–183.

Barnsley, N., McAuley, J. H., Mohan, et al. (2011). The rubber hand illusion increases histamine reactivity in the real arm. *Current Biology, 21,* R945–6.

Barrett, Lisa F., Mesquita, Batja, & Gendron, Maria. (2011). Context in emotion perception. *Current Directions in Psychological Science, 20,* 286–290.

Barsky, S. H., Roth, M. D., Kleerup, E. C., Simmons, M., & Tashkin, D. P. (1998). Histopathologic and molecular alterations in bronchial epithelium in habitual smokers of marijuana, cocaine, and/or tobacco. *Journal of the National Cancer Institute, 90,* 1198–1205.

Bartels, Andreas, & Zeki, Semir. (2004). The neural correlates of material and romantic love. *NeuroImage, 21,* 1155–1166.

Bartels, Meike. (2015). Genetics of wellbeing and its components satisfaction with life, happiness, and quality of life: A review and meta-analysis of heritability studies. *Behavior Genetics, 45*(2), 137–156.

Bartlett, Frederic C. (1932). *Remembering.* Cambridge, UK: Cambridge University Press.

Bartoshuk, Linda M., Duffy, V. B., Lucchina, L. A., et al. (1998). PROP (6-n-propylthiouracil) supertasters and the saltiness of NaCl. *Annals of the New York Academy of Sciences, 855,* 793–796.

Bartoshuk, Linda M. (1998). Born to burn: Genetic variation in taste. Paper presented at the annual meeting of the American Psychological Association, San Francisco.

Bartoshuk, Linda M. (2009). Taste. In J. M. Wolfe, K. R. Kluender, D. M. Levi, et al., *Sensation and perception* (2nd ed.). Sunderland, MA: Sinauer Associates.

Bartoshuk, Linda M., & Snyder, Derek J. (2012). The biology and psychology of taste. In Kelly D. Brownell & Mark S. Gold (Eds.), *Food and addiction: A comprehensive handbook* (pp. 126–130). New York: Oxford University Press.

Bartz, Jennifer A., Zaki, Jamil, Ochsner, Kevin N., et al. (2010, December 14). Effects of oxytocin on recollections of maternal care and closeness. *Proceedings of the National Academy of Sciences, 107,* 21371–21375.

Bath, Eraka, Pope, Kayla, Ijadi-Maghsoodi, Roya, & Thomas, Christopher. (2015). Juvenile life without parole: Updates on legislative and judicial trends and on facilitating fair sentencing. *Journal of the American Academy of Child and Adolescent Psychiatry, 54*(5), 343–347.

Battaglia, Francesco P., Benchenane, Karim, Sirota, Anton, et al. (2011). The hippocampus: hub of brain network communication for memory. *Trends in Cognitive Sciences, 15,* 310–318.

Baucom, Katherine J. W., Sevier, Mia, Eldridge, Kathleen A., et al. (2011). Observed communication in couples two years after integrative and traditional behavioral couple therapy: Outcome and link with five-year follow-up. *Journal of Consulting and Clinical Psychology 79,* 565–576.

Bauer, Patricia. (2002). Long-term recall memory: Behavioral and neuro-developmental changes in the first 2 years of life. *Current Directions in Psychological Science, 11,* 137–141.

Bauer, Patricia. (2015). A complementary processes account of the development of childhood amnesia and a personal past. *Psychological Review, 122*(2), 204–231.

Baumann, Christian R., Mignot, Emmanuel, Lammers, Gert Jan, Overeem, Sebastiaan, Arnulf, Isabelle, Rye, David, et al. (2014). Challenges in diagnosing narcolepsy without cataplexy: A consensus statement. *Sleep: Journal of Sleep and Sleep Disorders Research, 37*(6), 1035–1042.

Baumeister, Roy F. (2000). Gender differences in erotic plasticity: The female sex drive as socially flexible and responsive. *Psychological Bulletin, 126,* 347–374.

Baumeister, Roy F., Campbell, Jennifer D., Krueger, Joachim I., & Vohs, Kathleen D. (2003). Does high self-esteem cause better performance, interpersonal success, happiness, or healthier lifestyles? *Psychological Science in the Public Interest, 4*(1)[whole issue].

Baumeister, Roy F., Catanese, Kathleen R., & Vohs, Kathleen D. (2001). Is there a gender difference in strength of sex drive? Theoretical views, conceptual distinctions, and a review of relevant evidence. *Personality and Social Psychology Review, 5,* 242–273.

Baumeister, Roy F., Dale, Karen, & Sommer, Kristin L. (1998). Freudian defense mechanisms and empirical findings in modern social psychology: Reaction formation, projection, displacement, undoing, isolation, sublimation, and denial. *Journal of Personality, 66,* 1081–1124.

Baumeister, Roy F., Stillwell, Arlene M., & Heatherton, Todd F. (1994). Guilt: An interpersonal approach. *Psychological Bulletin, 115,* 243–267.

Beaman, Lori, Duflo, Esther, Pande, Rohini, & Topalova, Petia. (2012, February 3). Female leadership raises aspirations and educational attainment for girls: A policy experiment in India. *Science, 335,* 582–586.

Beauchamp, Gary K., & Mennella, Julie A. (2011). Flavor perception in human infants: Development and functional significance. *Digestion, 83,* 1–6.

Bechara, Antoine, Dermas, Hanna, Tranel, Daniel, & Damasio, Antonio R. (1997). Deciding advantageously before knowing the advantageous strategy. *Science, 275,* 1293–1294.

Beck, Aaron T. (1976). *Cognitive therapy and the emotional disorders*. New York: International Universities Press.

Beck, Aaron T. (2005). The current state of cognitive therapy: A 40-year retrospective. *Archives of General Psychiatry, 62*, 953–959.

Beck, Aaron T., & Dozois, D. J. A. (2011). Cognitive therapy: Current status and future directions. *Annual Review of Medicine, 62*(2).

Beck, Diane M. (2010). The appeal of the brain in the popular press. *Perspectives on Psychological Science, 5*, 762–766.

Beck, Hall P., & Irons, Gary. (2011). Finding Little Albert: A seven-year search for psychology's lost boy. *The Psychologist, 24*, 392–395.

Beck, Judith S. (2011). *Cognitive behavior therapy: Basics and beyond* (2nd ed.). New York:Guilford Press.

Becker, D. Vaughn, Kenrick, Douglas T., Neuberg, Steven L., et al. (2007). The confounded nature of angry men and happy women. *Journal of Personality and Social Psychology, 92*, 179–190.

Beckett, Katherine, Nyrop, Kris, & Pfingst, Lori. (2006). Race, drugs, and policing: Understanding disparities in drug delivery arrests. *Criminology, 44*, 105–137.

Bedford, Rachael, Pickles, Andrew, Sharp, Helen, Wright, Nicola, & Hill, Jonathan. (2015). Reduced face preference in infancy: A developmental precursor to callous-unemotional traits? *Biological Psychiatry, 78*(2), 144–150.

Beer, Jeremy M., Arnold, Richard D., & Loehlin, John C. (1998). Genetic and environmental influences on MMPI factor scales: Joint model fitting to twin and adoption data. *Journal of Personality and Social Psychology, 74*, 818–827.

Bell, Janice F., & Zimmerman, Frederick J. (2010). Shortened nighttime sleep duration in early life and subsequent childhood obesity. *Archives of Pediatric and Adolescent Medicine, 164*, 840–845.

Belsky, Jay, Bakermans-Kranenburg, Marian J., & van IJzendoorn, Marinus H. (2007). For better *and* for worse: Differential susceptibility to environmental influences. *Current Directions in Psychological Science, 16*, 300–304.

Belsky, Jay, Campbell, Susan B., Cohn, Jeffrey F., & Moore, Ginger. (1996). Instability of infant-parent attachment security. *Developmental Psychology, 32*, 921–924.

Belsky, Jay, & Pluess, Michael. (2009a). Beyond diathesis stress: Differential susceptibility to environmental influences. *Psychological Bulletin, 135*, 885–908.

Belsky, Jay, & Pluess, Michael. (2009b). The nature (and nurture?) of plasticity in early human development. *Perspectives on Psychological Science, 4*, 345–351.

Belsky, Jay, & Pluess, Michael. (2013). Beyond risk, resilience, and dysregulation: Phenotypic plasticity and human development. *Development and Psychopathology, 25*(4, Pt. 2), 1243–1261.

Beltz, Adriene M., Corley, Robin P., Bricker, Josh B., Wadsworth, Sally J., & Berenbaum, Sheri A. (2014). Modeling pubertal timing and tempo and examining links to behavior problems. *Developmental Psychology, 50*(12), 2715–2726.

Bem, Daryl. (2011). Feeling the future: Experimental evidence for anomalous retroactive influences on cognition and affect. *Journal of Personality and Social Psychology, 100*, 407–425.

Bem, Daryl, & Honorton, Charles. (1994). Does psi exist? Replicable evidence for an anomalous process of information transfer. *Psychological Bulletin, 115*, 4–18.

Bem, Sandra L. (1993). *The lenses of gender*. New Haven, CT: Yale University Press.

Ben Amar, Mohammed. (2005). Cannabinoids in medicine: A review of their therapeutic potential. *Journal of Ethnopharmacology, 105*, 1–25.

Benedetti, Fabrizio, & Levi-Montalcini, Rita. (2001). Opioid and non-opioid mechanisms of placebo analgesia. Paper presented at the annual meeting of the American Psychological Society, Toronto.

Benedetti, Fabrizio, Mayberg, Helen S., Wager, Tor D., et al. (2005, November 9). Neurobiological mechanisms of the placebo effect. *The Journal of Neuroscience, 45*, 10390–10402.

Benjamin, Ludy T., Jr. (1998). Why Gorgeous George, and not Wilhelm Wundt, was the founder of psychology: A history of popular psychology in America. Invited address presented at the National Institute on the Teaching of Psychology, St. Petersburg Beach.

Benjamin, Ludy T., Jr. (2003). Why can't psychology get a stamp? *Journal of Applied Psychoanalytic Studies, 5*, 443–454.

Bennett, Craig M., Baird, Abigail A., Miller, Michael B., & Wolford, George L. (2010). Neural correlates of interspecies perspective taking in the post-mortem Atlantic Salmon: An argument for multiple comparisons correction. *Journal of Serendipitous and Unexpected Results. 1*, 1–5.

Bentley, Kate H., Gallagher, Matthew W., Boswell, James F., Gorman, Jack M., Shear, M. Katherine, Woods, Scott W., et al. (2013). The interactive contributions of perceived control and anxiety sensitivity in panic disorder: A triple vulnerabilities perspective. *Journal of Psychopathology and Behavioral Assessment, 35*(1), 57–64.

Beran, Michael J., & Beran, Mary M. (2004). Chimpanzees remember the results of one-by-one addition of food items to sets over extended time periods. *Psychological Science, 15*, 94–99.

Berenbaum, Sheri A., & Bailey, J. Michael. (2003). Effects on gender identity of prenatal androgens and genital appearance: Evidence from girls with congenital adrenal hyperplasia. *Journal of Clinical Endocrinology and Metabolism, 88*, 1102–1106.

Berger, F., Gage, F. H., & Vijayaraghavan, S. (1998). Nicotinic receptor-induced apoptotic cell death of hippocampal progenitor cells. *Journal of Neuroscience, 18*, 6871–6881.

Berger, Shelley L., Kouzarides, Tony, Shiekhattar, Ramin, & Shilatifard, Ali. (2009). An operational definition of epigenetics. *Genes and Development, 23*, 781–783.

Berglund, Hans, Lindström, Per, & Savic, Ivanka. (2006). Brain response to putative pheromones in lesbian women. *Proceedings of the National Academy of Sciences, 103*, 8269–8274.

Berkman Center for Internet & Society. (2008, December 31). Enhancing child safety and online technologies: Final report of the Internet Safety Task Force. Final report available at http://cyber.law.harvard.edu/sites/cyber.law.harvard.edu/files/ISTTF_Final_Report.pdf.

Berkman Center for Internet & Society. (2012, September 17). Bullying in a networked era: A literature review. Authored by Nathaniel Levy; Sandra Cortesi; Urs Gasser; Edward Crowley; Meredith Beaton; June Casey; & Caroline Nolan. Available at http://papers.ssrn.com/sol3/papers.cfm?abstract_id=2146877.

Berlin, Fred S. (2003). Sex offender treatment and legislation. *Journal of the American Academy of Psychiatry and the Law, 31*, 510–513.

Bernstein, Daniel M., & Loftus, Elizabeth F. (2009). How to tell if a particular memory is true or false. *Perspectives on Psychological Science, 4*, 370–374.

Berntsen, Dorthe, & Thomsen, Dorthe K. (2005). Personal memories for remote historical events: Accuracy and clarity of flashbulb memories related to World War II. *Journal of Experimental Psychology: General, 134,* 242–257.

Berscheid, Ellen, & Reis, Harry T. (1998). Attraction and close relationships. In D. T. Gilbert, S. T. Fiske, & G. Lindzey (Eds.), *The handbook of social psychology, Vol. 2* (4th ed.). New York: McGraw-Hill.

Best, Joel. (2012). *Damned lies and statistics: Untangling numbers from the media, politicians, and activists* (updated ed.). Berkeley and Los Angeles: University of California Press.

Beyerstein, Barry L. (1996). Graphology. In G. Stein (Ed.), *The encyclopedia of the paranormal.* Amherst, NY: Prometheus Books.

Bhatarah, Parveen, Ward, Geoff, & Tan, Lydia. (2008). Examining the relationship between free recall and immediate serial recall: The serial nature of recall and the effect of test expectancy. *Memory and Cognition, 36,* 20–34.

Bierut, Laura Jean, Stitzel, Jerry A., Wang, Jen C., et al. (2008). Variants in nicotinic receptors and risk for nicotine dependence. *American Journal of Psychiatry, 165,* 1163–1171.

Binder, Jens, Zagefka, Hanna, Brown, Rupert, et al. (2009). Does contact reduce prejudice or does prejudice reduce contact? A longitudinal test of the contact hypothesis among majority and minority groups in three European countries. *Journal of Personality and Social Psychology, 96,* 843–856.

Birdwhistell, Ray L. (1970). *Kinesics and context: Essays on body motion communication.* Philadelphia: University of Pennsylvania Press.

Birkhead, Tim. (2001). *Promiscuity: An evolutionary history of sperm competition.* Cambridge, MA: Harvard University Press.

Bischof, Matthias, & Bassetti, Claudio L. (2004). Total dream loss: A distinct neuropsychological dysfunction after bilateral PCA stroke. *Annals of Neurology, 56*(4), 583–586.

Biss, Renée K., & Hasher, Lynn. (2012). Happy as a lark: Morning-type younger and older adults are higher in positive affect. *Emotion, 12,* 437–441.

Biswal, Bharat B., Mennes, Maarten, Zuo, Xi-nian, et al. (2010). Toward discovery science of human brain function. *Proceedings of the National Academy of Sciences of the United States of America, 107,* 4734–4739.

Bjork, Elizabeth L., & Bjork, Robert A. (2011). Making things hard on yourself, but in a good way: Creating desirable difficulties to enhance learning. In M. A. Gernsbacher, R. W. Pew, L. M. Hough, & J. R. Pomerantz (Eds.), *Psychology and the real world: Essays illustrating fundamental contributions to society.* New York: Worth.

Black, Michele C., Basile, Kathleen C., Breiding, Matthew J., et al. (2011). The national intimate partner and sexual violence survey: Summary report. National Center for Injury Prevention and Control, Centers for Disease Control and Prevention, Atlanta, Georgia.

Blackmore, Susan. (2001, March/April). Giving up the ghosts: End of a personal quest. *Skeptical Inquirer, 25.*

Blagrove, Mark. (1996). Problems with the cognitive psychological modeling of dreaming. *Journal of Mind and Behavior, 17,* 99–134.

Blair, R. D. J., Jones, L., Clark, F., & Smith, M. (1997). The psychopathic individual: A lack of responsiveness to distress cues? *Psychophysiology, 45,* 192–198.

Blakemore, Colin, & Cooper, Grahame F. (1970). Development of the brain depends on the visual environment. *Nature, 228,* 477–478.

Blass, Thomas (Ed.). (2000). *Obedience to authority: Current perspectives on the Milgram paradigm.* Mahwah, NJ: Erlbaum.

Bleidorn, Wiebke, Klimstra, Theo A., Denissen, Jaap J. A., Rentfrow, Peter J., Potter, Jeff, & Gosling, Samuel D. (2013). Personality maturation around the world: A cross-cultural examination of social-investment theory. *Psychological Science, 24*(12), 2530–2540.

Bleuler, Eugen. (1911/1950). *Dementia praecox or the group of schizophrenias.* New York: International Universities Press.

Bliss, T. V., & Collingridge, G. L. (1993). A synaptic model of memory: Long-term potentiation in the hippocampus. *Nature, 361,* 31–39.

Bloom, Mia. (2005). *Dying to kill: The allure of suicide terror.* New York: Columbia University Press.

Blum, Deborah. (2002). *Love at Goon Park: Harry Harlow and the science of affection.* Cambridge, MA: Perseus Books.

Blumberg, Mark S., Gall, Andrew J., & Todd, William D. (2014). The development of sleep–wake rhythms and the search for elemental circuits in the infant brain. *Behavioral Neuroscience, 128*(3), 250–263.

Bluming, Avrum, & Tavris, Carol. (2009, April 22). Hormone replacement therapy: Real concerns and false alarms. *The Cancer Journal, 15,* 93–104.

Bock, Jeorg, Poeggel, Gerd, Gruss, Michael, Wingenfeld, Katharina, & Braun, Katharina. (2014). Infant cognitive training preshapes learning-relevant prefrontal circuits for adult learning: Learning-induced tagging of dendritic spines. *Cerebral Cortex, 24*(11), 2920–2930.

Boepple, Leah, & Thompson, J. Kevin. (2015). A content analytic comparison of fitspiration and thinspiration websites. *International Journal of Eating Disorders,* electronic preview.

Boesch, Cristophe. (1991). Teaching among wild chimpanzees. *Animal Behavior, 41,* 530–532.

Bogaert, Anthony F. (2006, June 28). Biological versus nonbiological older brothers and men's sexual orientation. *Proceedings of the National Academy of Sciences, 103,* 10771–10774.

Bohannon, John N., & Symons, Victoria. (1988). Conversational conditions of children's imitation. Paper presented at the biennial Conference on Human Development, Charleston, South Carolina.

Bolshakov, Vadim Y., & Siegelbaum, Steven A. (1994). Postsynaptic induction and presynaptic expression of hippocampal long-term depression. *Science, 264,* 1148–1152.

Bonanno, George A. (2004). Loss, trauma, and human resilience. *American Psychologist, 59,* 20–28.

Bonanno, George A., Brewin, Chris R., Kaniasty Krzysztof, & La Greca, Annette M. (2010). Weighing the costs of disaster: Individuals, families, and communities. *Psychological Science in the Public Interest, 11,* 1–49.

Bond, Charles F., & DePaulo, Bella M. (2008). Individual differences in judging deception: Accuracy and bias. *Psychological Bulletin, 134,* 477–492.

Bond, Rod, & Smith, Peter B. (1996). Culture and conformity: A meta-analysis of studies using Asch's (1952b, 1956) line judgment task. *Psychological Bulletin, 119,* 111–137.

Boot, Walter R., Blakely, Daniel P., & Simons, Daniel J. (2011, September 13). Do action video games improve perception and cognition? *Frontiers in Psychology, 2,* 226.

Booth, Frank W., & Neufer, P. Darrell. (2005). Exercise controls gene expression. *American Scientist, 93,* 28–35.

Bootzin, Richard R. (2009, March). Update on the psychological science accreditation system. *The Observer,* 20–21.

Borch-Jacobsen, Mikkel. (2009). *Making minds and madness: From hysteria to depression.* Cambridge, UK: Cambridge University Press.

Borch-Jacobsen, Mikkel, & Shamdasani, Sonu. (2012). *The Freud files: An inquiry into the history of psychoanalysis.* New York: Cambridge University Press.

Boring, Edwin G. (1953). A history of introspection. *Psychological Bulletin, 50,* 169–187.

Born, Jan, & Wilhelm, Ines. (2012). System consolidation of memory during sleep. *Psychological Research, 76,* 192–203.

Bornstein, Robert F., Leone, Dean R., & Galley, Donna J. (1987). The generalizability of subliminal mere exposure effects: Influence of stimuli perceived without awareness on social behavior. *Journal of Personality and Social Psychology, 53,* 1070–1079.

Boroditsky, Lera. (2003). Linguistic relativity. In L. Nadel (Ed.), *Encyclopedia of cognitive science.* London: Nature Publishing Group.

Boroditsky, Lera, Schmidt, Lauren, & Phillips, Webb. (2003). Sex, syntax, and semantics. In D. Gentner & S. Goldin-Meadow (Eds.), *Language in mind: Advances in the study of language and thought.* Cambridge: MIT Press.

Boswell, James F., Thompson-Hollands, Johanna, Farchione, Todd J., & Barlow, David H. (2013). Intolerance of uncertainty: A common factor in the treatment of emotional disorders. *Journal of Clinical Psychology, 69*(6), 630–645.

Bosworth, Hayden B., & Schaie, K. Warner. (1999). Survival effects in cognitive function, cognitive style, and sociodemographic variables in the Seattle Longitudinal Study. *Experimental Aging Research, 25,* 121–139.

Botvinick, Matthew, & Cohen, Jonathan. (1998). Rubber hands feel touch that eyes can see. *Nature, 391,* 756.

Bouchard, Thomas. (1995). Nature's twice-told tale: Identical twins reared apart—what they tell us about human individuality. Paper presented at the annual meeting of the Western Psychological Association, Los Angeles.

Bouchard, Thomas. (1997a). The genetics of personality. In K. Blum & E. P. Noble (Eds.), *Handbook of psychiatric genetics.* Boca Raton, FL: CRC Press.

Bouchard, Thomas. (1997b). IQ similarity in twins reared apart: Findings and responses to critics. In R. J. Sternberg & E. Grigorenko (Eds.), *Intelligence: Heredity and environment.* New York: Cambridge University Press.

Bouchard, Thomas. (2004). Genetic influence on human psychological traits: A survey. *Current Directions in Psychological Science, 13,* 148–151.

Bouchard, Thomas. (2014). Genes, evolution, and intelligence. *Behavior Genetics, 44*(6), 549–577.

Bouret, Sebastien G., Draper, Shin J., & Simerly, Richard B. (2004). Trophic action of leptin on hypothalamic neurons that regulate feeding. *Science, 304,* 108–110.

Bousfield, W. A. (1953). The occurrence of clustering in the recall of randomly arranged associates. *Journal of General Psychology, 49,* 229–240.

Bowen, Murray. (1978). *Family therapy in clinical practice.* New York: Jason Aronson.

Bower, Gordon H., & Forgas, Joseph P. (2000). Affect, memory, and social cognition. In E. Eich et al. (Eds.), *Cognition and emotion.* New York: Oxford University Press.

Bowers, Kenneth S., Regehr, Glenn, Balthazard, Claude, & Parker, Kevin. (1990). Intuition in the context of discovery. *Cognitive Psychology, 22,* 72–110.

Bowlby, John. (1969). *Attachment and loss. Vol. 1. Attachment.* New York: Basic Books.

Bowlby, John. (1973). *Attachment and loss: Vol. 2. Separation.* New York: Basic Books.

Bowleg, Lisa, Lucas, Kenya J., & Tschann, Jeanne M. (2004). "The ball was always in his court": An exploratory analysis of relationship scripts, sexual scripts, and condom use among African American women. *Psychology of Women Quarterly, 28,* 70–82.

Bowles, Samuel. (2008). Policies designed for self-interested citizens may undermine "the moral sentiments": Evidence from economic experiments. *Science, 320,* 1605–1609.

Bozzali, Marco, Dowling, Claire, Serra, Laura, Spanò, Barbara, Torso, Mario, Marra, Camillo, et al. (2015). The impact of cognitive reserve on brain functional connectivity in Alzheimer's disease. *Journal of Alzheimer's Disease, 44*(1), 243–250.

Brand-Miller, Jennie C., Fatima, Kaniz, Middlemiss, Christopher, et al. (2007). Effect of alcoholic beverages on postprandial glycemia and insulinemia in lean, young, healthy adults. *American Journal of Clinical Nutrition, 85,* 1545–1551.

Brandt, Mark J. (2011). Sexism and gender inequality across 57 societies. *Psychological Science, 22,* 1413–1418.

Braun, Kathryn A., Ellis, Rhiannon, & Loftus, Elizabeth F. (2002). Make my memory: How advertising can change our memories of the past. *Psychology and Marketing, 19,* 1–23.

Braungart, J. M., Plomin, Robert, DeFries, J. C., & Fulker, D. W. (1992). Genetic influence on tester-rated infant temperament as assessed by Bayley's Infant Behavior Record: Nonadoptive and adoptive siblings and twins. *Developmental Psychology, 28,* 40–47.

Breland, Keller, & Breland, Marian. (1961). The misbehavior of organisms. *American Psychologist, 16,* 681–684.

Brennan, Patricia A., & Mednick, Sarnoff A. (1994). Learning theory approach to the deterrence of criminal recidivism. *Journal of Abnormal Psychology, 103,* 430–440.

Brescoll, Victoria L., & Uhlmann, Eric L. (2008). Can an angry woman get ahead? Status conferral, gender, and expression of emotion in the workplace. *Psychological Science, 19,* 268–275.

Breslau, Naomi, Lucia, Victoria C., & Alvarado, German F. (2006). Intelligence and other predisposing factors in exposure to trauma and posttraumatic stress disorder. *Archives of General Psychiatry, 63,* 1238–1245.

Brezina, V. (2010). Beyond the wiring diagram: Signaling through complex neuromodulator networks. *Philosophical Transactions of the Royal Society of London B: Biological Sciences, 365,* 2363–2374.

Briggs, Gemma, Hole, Graham J., & Land, Michael G. (2011). Emotional involving telephone conversations lead to driver error and visual tunnelling. *Transportation Research Part F: Traffic Psychology and Behaviour, 14*(4), 313–323.

Brissette, Ian, Scheier, Michael F., & Carver, Charles S. (2002). The role of optimism in social network development, coping, and psychological adjustment during a life transition. *Journal of Personality and Social Psychology, 82,* 102–111.

Broadway, James M., & Engle, Randall W. (2011). Lapsed attention to elapsed time? Individual differences in working memory capacity and temporal reproduction. *Acta Psychologica, 137,* 115–126.

Brockner, Joel, & Rubin, Jeffrey Z. (1985). *Entrapment in escalating conflicts: A social psychological analysis.* New York: Springer-Verlag.

Broks, Paul. (2004). *Into the silent land: Travels in neuropsychology.* New York: Grove Press.

Brooks-Gunn, Jeanne. (1986). Differentiating premenstrual symptoms and syndromes. *Psychosomatic Medicine, 48,* 385–387.

Brosnan, Sarah F., & de Waal, Frans B. M. (2003). Monkeys reject unequal pay. *Nature, 425,* 297–299.

Brown, Alan S. (2004). *The déjà vu experience: Essays in cognitive psychology.* New York: Psychology Press.

Brown, Alan S. (2012). *The tip of the tongue state.* New York: Psychology Press.

Brown, Alan S., Begg, M. D., Gravenstein, S., et al. (2004). Serologic evidence of prenatal influenza in the etiology of schizophrenia. *Archives of General Psychiatry, 61,* 774–780.

Brown, Daniel, Scheflin, Alan W., & Whitfield, Charles L. (1999). Recovered memories: The current weight of the evidence in science and in the courts. *Journal of Psychiatry and Law, 27,* 5–156.

Brown, G. W., & Harris, T. O. (2008). Depression and the serotonin transporter 5-HTTLPR polymorphism: A review and a hypothesis concerning gene-environment interaction. *Journal of Affective Disorders, 111,* 1–12.

Brown, Gillian R., Laland, Keven N., & Mulder, Monique B. (2009). Bateman's principles and human sex roles. *Trends in Ecology and Evolution, 24,* 297–304.

Brown, Gregory K., Ten Have, Thomas, Henriques, Gregg R., et al. (2005, August 3). Cognitive therapy for the prevention of suicide attempts. *Journal of the American Medical Association, 294,* 563–570.

Brown, J. F., & Menninger, Karl A. (1940). The psychoses primarily functional in origin. In J. F. Brown & Karl A. Menninger (Eds.), *The psychodynamics of abnormal behavior* (pp. 316–336). New York: McGraw-Hill.

Brown, Jonathon D. (2012). Understanding the better than average effect: Motives (still) matter. *Personality and Social Psychology Bulletin, 38,* 209–219.

Brown, Peter C., Roediger, Henry L., III, & McDaniel, Mark A. (2014). *Make it stick: The science of successful learning.* Cambridge, MA: Belknap Press of Harvard University Press.

Brown, Roger. (1986). *Social psychology* (2nd ed.). New York: Free Press.

Brown, Roger, & Kulik, James. (1977). Flashbulb memories. *Cognition, 5,* 73–99.

Brown, Roger, & McNeill, David. (1966). The "tip of the tongue" phenomenon. *Journal of Verbal Learning and Verbal Behavior, 5,* 325–337.

Brown, Ryan P., & Josephs, Robert A. (1999). A burden of proof: Stereotype relevance and gender differences in math performance. *Journal of Personality and Social Psychology, 76,* 246–257.

Brown, Stephanie L., Nesse, Randolph M., Vinokur, Amiram D., & Smith, Dylan M. (2003). Providing social support may be more beneficial than receiving it. Results from a prospective study of mortality. *Psychological Science, 14,* 320–327.

Browning, James R., Hatfield, Elaine, Kessler, Debra, & Levine, Tim. (2000). Sexual motives, gender, and sexual behavior. *Archives of Sexual Behavior, 29,* 135–153.

Bruck, Maggie. (2003). Effects of suggestion on the reliability and credibility of children's reports. Invited address at the annual meeting of the American Psychological Society, Atlanta.

Bruck, Maggie, Ceci, Stephen J., & Francoeur, Emmett. (2000). Children's use of anatomically detailed dolls to report genital touching in a medical examination: Developmental and gender comparisons. *Journal of Experimental Psychology: Applied, 6,* 74–83.

Bruder, Carl E. G. E., Piotrowski, Arkadjusz, Gijsbers, Antoinet A., et al. (2008). Phenotypically concordant and discordant monozygotic twins display different DNA copy-number-variation profiles. *American Journal of Human Genetics, 82,* 763–771.

Bruinius, Harry. (2006). *Better for all the world: The secret history of forced sterilization and America's quest for racial purity.* New York: Knopf.

Bruner, Jerome S. (1990). *Acts of meaning.* Cambridge, MA: Harvard University Press.

Brüning, César Augusto, Martini, Franciele, Soares, Suelen Mendonça, Savegnago, Lucielli, Sampaio, Tuane Bazanella, & Nogueira, Cristina Wayne. (2015). Depressive-like behavior induced by tumor necrosis factor-α is attenuated by m-trifluoromethyl-diphenyldiselenide in mice. *Journal of Psychiatric Research,* published online May 5, 2015.

Brunoni, André R., Teng, Chei Tung, Correa, Claudio, et al. (2011, December 31). Neuromodulation approaches for the treatment of major depression: challenges and recommendations from a working group meeting. *Arq. Neuro-Psiquiatr, 68.* Available (in English) from http://www.scielo.br/scielo.php?script=sci_arttext&pid=S0004-282X2010000300021&lng=en&nrm=iso>. doi.org/10.1590/S0004-282X2010000300021.

Bryant, Gregory A., & Barrett, H. Clark. (2007). Recognizing intentions in infant-directed speech. *Psychological Science, 18,* 746–751.

Buchanan, Tony W. (2007). Retrieval of emotional memories. *Psychological Bulletin, 133,* 761–779.

Buck, Linda, & Axel, Richard. (1991). A novel multigene family may encode odorant receptors: A molecular basis for odor recognition. *Cell, 65,* 175–187.

Buhrmester, Michael, Kwang, Tracy, & Gosling, Samuel D. (2011). Amazon's Mechanical Turk: A new source of inexpensive, yet high-quality, data? *Perspectives on Psychological Science, 6*(1), 3–5.

Bukowski, William M. (2001). Friendship and the worlds of childhood. In D. W. Nangle & C. A. Erdley (Eds.), The role of friendship in psychological adjustment. *New directions for child and adolescent development, No. 91.* San Francisco, CA: Jossey-Bass.

Bulatov, Aleksandr, Bulatova, Natalija, Loginovich, Yelena, & Surkys, Tadas. (2015). Illusion of extent evoked by closed two-dimensional shapes. *Biological Cybernetics, 109*(2), 163–178.

Buller, David J. (2005). *Adapting minds: Evolutionary psychology and the persistent quest for human nature.* Cambridge MA: MIT Press.

Burgaleta, Miguel, Head, Kevin, Álvarez-Linera, Juan, Martínez, Kenia, et al. (2012). Sex differences in brain volume are related to specific skills, not to general intelligence. *Intelligence, 40,* 60–68.

Burger, Jerry M. (2009). Replicating Milgram: Would people still obey today? *American Psychologist, 64,* 1–11.

Burger, Jerry M. (2014). Situational features in Milgram's experiment that kept his participants shocking. *Journal of Social Issues, 70*(3), 489–500.

Burke, Brian L., Arkowitz, Hal, & Menchola, Marisa. (2003). The efficacy of motivational interviewing: A meta-analysis of controlled clinical trials. *Journal of Consulting and Clinical Psycholology, 71,* 843–861.

Burnham, Denis, Kitamura, Christine, & Vollmer-Conna, Uté. (2002, May 24). What's new, pussycat? On talking to babies and animals. *Science, 296,* 1435.

Bushman, Brad J., & Anderson, Craig A. (2009). Comfortably numb: Desensitizing effects of violent media on helping others. *Psychological Science, 20,* 273–277.

Bushman, Brad J., Bonacci, Angelica M., Pedersen William C., et al. (2005). Chewing on it can chew you up: Effects of rumination on triggered displaced aggression. *Journal of Personality and Social Psychology, 88,* 969–983.

Bushman, Brad J., Bonacci, Angelica M., van Dijk, Mirjam, & Baumeister, Roy F. (2003). Narcissism, sexual refusal, and aggression: Testing a narcissistic reactance model of sexual coercion. *Journal of Personality and Social Psychology, 84,* 1027–1040.

Bushman, Brad J., Ridge, Robert D., Das, Enny, et al. (2007). When God sanctions killing. *Psychological Science, 18,* 204–207.

Buss, David M. (1994). *The evolution of desire: Strategies of human mating.* New York: Basic Books.

Buss, David M. (1995). Evolutionary psychology: A new paradigm for psychological science. *Psychological Inquiry, 6,* 1–30.

Buss, David M. (1999). *Evolutionary psychology: The new science of the mind.* Boston: Allyn & Bacon.

Buss, David M., & Schmitt, David P. (2011). Evolutionary psychology and feminism. *Sex Roles, 64,* 768–787.

Bussey, Kay, & Bandura, Albert. (1999). Social-cognitive theory of gender development and differentiation. *Psychological Review, 106,* 676–713.

Buster, J. E., Kingsberg, S. A., Aguirre, O., et al. (2005). Testosterone patch for low sexual desire in surgically menopausal women: a randomized trial. *Obstetrics and Gynecology, 105* (Pt 1), 944–952.

Butcher, James N., Lim, Jeeyoung, & Nezami, Elahe. (1998). Objective study of abnormal personality in cross-cultural settings: The MMPI-2. *Journal of Cross-Cultural Psychology, 29,* 189–211.

Butcher, James N., & Perry, Julia N. (2008). *Personality assessment in treatment planning: Use of the MMPI-2 and BTPI.* New York: Oxford University Press.

Butler, S., Chalder, T., Ron, M., et al. (1991). Cognitive behaviour therapy in chronic fatigue syndrome. *Journal of Neurology, Neurosurgery and Psychiatry, 54,* 153–158.

Button, T. M. M., Thapar, A., & McGuffin, P. (2005). Relationship between antisocial behaviour, attention-deficit hyperactivity disorder and maternal prenatal smoking. *British Journal of Psychiatry, 187,* 155–160.

Byers-Heinlein, Krista, Burns, Tracey C., & Werker, Janet F. (2010). The roots of bilingualism in newborns. *Psychological Science, 21,* 343–348.

Cabiya, Jose J., Lucio, Emilia, Chavira, Denise A., et al. (2000). MMPI-2 scores of Puerto Rican, Mexican, and U.S. Latino college students: A research note. *Psychological Reports, 87,* 266–268.

Cacioppo, John T., Berntson, Gary G., Lorig, Tyler S., et al. (2003). Just because you're imaging the brain doesn't mean you can stop using your head: A primer and set of first principles. *Journal of Personality and Social Psychology, 85,* 650–661.

Cacioppo, Stephanie, Grippo, Angela J., London, Sarah, Goossens, Luc, & Cacioppo, John T. (2015). Loneliness: Clinical import and interventions. *Perspectives on Psychological Science, 10*(2), 238–249.

Cahill, Larry. (2012). A half-truth is a whole lie: On the necessity of investigating sex influences on the brain. *Endocrinology, 153*(6), 2541–2543.

Cahill, Larry, Prins, Bruce, Weber, Michael, & McGaugh, James L. (1994). ß-adrenergic activation and memory for emotional events. *Nature, 371,* 702–704.

Cahill, Larry, Uncapher, Melina, Kilpatrick, Lisa, et al. (2004). Sex-Related hemispheric lateralization of amygdala function in emotionally influenced memory: An FMRI investigation. *Learning and Memory, 11,* 261–266.

Calder, A. J., Keane, J., Manes, F., Antoun, N., & Young, A. W. (2000). Impaired recognition and experience of disgust following brain injury. *Nature Neuroscience, 3,* 1077–1078.

Callaghan, Glenn M., Chacon, Cynthia, Coles, Cameron, et al. (2009). An empirical evaluation of the diagnostic criteria for premenstrual dysphoric disorder: Problems with sex specificity and validity. *Women and Therapy, 32,* 1–21.

Camerer, Colin F. (2003). Strategizing in the brain. *Science, 300,* 1673–1675.

Cameron, Judy, Banko, Katherine M., & Pierce, W. David. (2001). Pervasive negative effects of rewards on intrinsic motivation: The myth continues. *Behavior Analyst, 24,* 1–44.

Campbell, Benjamin C. (2011). Adrenarche and middle childhood. *Human Nature, 22,* 327–349.

Campbell, Benjamin C., Pope, Harrison G., & Filiault, Shaun. (2005). Body image among Ariaal men from Northern Kenya. *Journal of Cross-Cultural Psychology, 36,* 371–379.

Campbell, Frances A., & Ramey, Craig T. (1995). Cognitive and school outcomes for high risk students at middle adolescence: Positive effects of early intervention. *American Educational Research Journal, 32,* 743–772.

Campbell, Joseph. (1949/1968). *The hero with 1,000 faces* (2nd ed.). Princeton, NJ: Princeton University Press.

Canetto, Silvia Sara, & Cleary, Anne. (2012). Men, masculinities, and suicidal behavior. *Social Science and Medicine, 74*(4), 461–465.

Canino, Glorisa. (1994). Alcohol use and misuse among Hispanic women: Selected factors, processes, and studies. *International Journal of the Addictions, 29,* 1083–1100.

Cannon, Tyrone D., Huttunen, Matti O., Loennqvist, Jouko, et al. (2000). The inheritance of neuropsychological dysfunction in twins discordant for schizophrenia. *American Journal of Human Genetics, 67,* 369–382.

Cannon, Walter B. (1929). *Bodily changes in pain, hunger, fear and rage* (2nd ed.). New York: Appleton.

Capaldi, Deborah M., Pears, Katherine C., Patterson, Gerald R., & Owen, Lee D. (2003). Continuity of parenting practices across generations in an at-risk sample: A prospective comparison of direct and mediated associations. *Journal of Abnormal Child Psychology, 31,* 127–142.

Carey, Benedict. (2011, January 11). You might already know this . . . *New York Times,* pp. D1, 3.

Carnagey, Nicholas L., & Anderson, Craig A. (2005). The effects of reward and punishment in violent video games on aggressive affect, cognition, and behavior. *Psychological Science, 16,* 882–889.

Carnahan, Thomas, & McFarland, Sam. (2007). Revisiting the Stanford prison experiment: Could participant self selection have led to the cruelty? *Personality and Social Psychology Bulletin, 33*(5), 603–614.

Carrns, Ann. (2014, October 25). Lantern, a start-up, offers online therapy for anxiety and more. *New York Times,* p. B5.

Carter, Travis J., & Gilovich, Thomas. (2012). I am what I do, not what I have. The differential centrality of experiential and material purchases to the self. *Journal of Personality and Social Psychology, 102*(6), 1304–1317.

Cartwright, Rosalind D. (1977). *Night life: Explorations in dreaming.* Englewood Cliffs, NJ: Prentice-Hall.

Cartwright, Rosalind D. (2010). *The twenty-four hour mind: The role of sleep and dreaming in our emotional lives.* New York: Oxford University Press.

Cartwright, Rosalind D., Young, Michael A., Mercer, Patricia, & Bears, Michael. (1998). Role of REM sleep and dream variables in the prediction of remission from depression. *Psychiatry Research, 80,* 249–255.

Carver, Charles S., & Baird, Eryn. (1998). The American dream revisited: Is it what you want or why you want it that matters? *Psychological Science, 9,* 289–292.

Carver, Charles S., & Scheier, Michael F. (2002). Optimism. In C. R. Snyder & S. J. Lopes (Eds.), *The handbook of positive psychology.* New York: Oxford University Press.

Casey, B. J., Somerville, Leah H., Gotlib, Ian H., et al. (2011). Behavioral and neural correlates of delay of gratification 40 years later. *Proceedings of the National Academy of Science, 108,* 14998–15003.

Caspi, Avshalom. (2000). The child is father of the man: Personality continuities from childhood to adulthood. *Journal of Personality and Social Psychology, 78,* 158–172.

Caspi, Avshalom, Houts, Renate M., Belsky, Daniel W., Goldman-Mellor, Sidra J., Harrington, HonaLee, Israel, Salomon, et al. (2014). The *p* factor: One general psychopathology factor in the structure of psychiatric disorders? *Clinical Psychological Science, 2*(2), 119–137.

Caspi, Avshalom, McClay, Joseph, Moffitt, Terrie E., et al. (2002, August 2). Role of genotype in the cycle of violence in maltreated children. *Science, 297,* 851–857.

Caspi, Avshalom, & Moffitt, Terrie E. (1991). Individual differences are accentuated during periods of social change: The sample case of girls at puberty. *Journal of Personality and Social Psychology, 61,* 157–168.

Caspi, Avshalom, Sugden, Karen, Moffitt, Terrie E., et al. (2003). Influence of life stress on depression: Moderation by a polymorphism in the 5-HTT gene. *Science, 301,* 386–389.

Cassin, Stephanie E., von Ranson, Kristin M., Heng, Kenneth, et al. (2008). Adapted motivational interviewing for women with bing eating disorder: A randomized controlled trial. *Psychology of Addictive Behaviors, 22,* 417–425.

Cattell, Raymond B. (1973). *Personality and mood by questionnaire.* San Francisco: Jossey-Bass.

Ceci, Stephen J., & Bruck, Maggie. (1995). *Jeopardy in the courtroom: A scientific analysis of children's testimony.* Washington, DC: American Psychological Association.

Cejka, Mary Ann, & Eagly, Alice H. (1999). Gender-stereotypic images of occupations correspond to the sex segregation of employment. *Personality and Social Psychology Bulletin, 25,* 413–423.

Centers for Disease Control & Prevention. (2013). National Vital Statistics System, National Center for Health Statistics, CDC. Available at www.cdc.gov/injury/wisqars/pdf/leading_causes_of_death_by_age_group_2013-a.pdf.

Cermak, Laird S., & Craik, Fergus I. M. (Eds.). (1979). *Levels of processing in human memory.* Hillsdale, NJ. Erlbaum.

Cervenka, Mackenzie C., Boatman-Reich, Dana F., Ward, Julianna, et al. (2011). Language mapping in multilingual patients: Electrocorticography and cortical stimulation during naming. *Frontiers in Human Neuroscience, 5,* 13.

Cervone, Daniel, & Shoda, Yuichi. (1999). Beyond traits in the study of personality coherence. *Current Directions in Psychological Science, 8,* 27–32.

Chabris, Christopher F., Hebert, Benjamin M., Benjamin, Daniel J., et al. (2012). Most reported genetic associations with general intelligence are probably false positives. *Psychological Science, 23*(11), 1314–1323.

Chabris, Christopher F., & Simons, Daniel. (1999). Gorillas in our midst: Sustained inattentional blindness for dynamic events. *Perception, 28,* 1059–1974.

Chabris, Christopher F., & Simons, Daniel. (2009). *The invisible gorilla, and other ways our intuitions deceive us.* New York: Crown.

Chambless, Dianne L., & Ollendick, T. H. (2001). Empirically supported psychological interventions: Controversies and evidence. *Annual Review of Psychology, 52,* 685–716.

Chan, Brenda L., Witt, Richard, Charrow, Alexandra P., et al. (2007). Mirror therapy for phantom limb pain [correspondence]. *New England Journal of Medicine, 357,* 2206–2207.

Chang, Anne-Marie, Buch, Alison M., Bradstreet, Dayna S., et al. (2011). Human diurnal preference and circadian rhythmicity are not associated with the CLOCK 3111C/T gene polymorphism. *Biological Rhythms, 26*, 276–279.

Chang, Luye, Connelly, Brian S., & Geeza, Alexis A. (2012). Separating method factors and higher order traits of the big five: A meta-analytic multitrait–multimethod approach. *Journal of Personality and Social Psychology, 102*, 408–426.

Charles, Susan T., & Carstensen, Laura L. (2004). A life-span view of emotional functioning in adulthood and old age. In P. Costa (Ed.), *Recent advances in psychology and aging* (Vol. 15). Amsterdam: Elsevier.

Chatelle, C., Thibaut, A., Gosseries, O., Bruno, M.A., Demertzi, A., Bernard, C., et al. (2014). Changes in cerebral metabolism in patients with a minimally conscious state responding to zolpidem. *Frontiers of Human Neuroscience, 2(8)*, 917.

Chaves, J. F. (1989). Hypnotic control of clinical pain. In N. P. Spanos & J. F. Chaves (Eds.), *Hypnosis: The cognitive-behavioral perspective.* Buffalo, NY: Prometheus Books.

Chebat, Daniel-Robert, Schneider, Fabien C., Kupers, Ron, & Ptito, Maurice. (2011). Navigation with a sensory substitution device in congenitally blind individuals. *Neuroreport, 22*, 342–347.

Chen, Zhansheng, Williams, Kipling D., Fitness, Julie, & Newton, Nicola C. (2008). When hurt will not heal. *Psychological Science, 19*, 789–795.

Cheney, Dorothy L., & Seyfarth, Robert M. (1985). Vervet monkey alarm calls: Manipulation through shared information? *Behavior, 94*, 150–166.

Cheon, Bobby K., Linvingston, Robert W., Chiao, Joan Y., & Hong, Ying-Yi. (2015). Contribution of serotonin transporter polymorphism (5-HTTLPR) to automatic racial bias. *Personality and Individual Differences, 79*, 35–38.

Cheung, Benjamin Y., Chudek, Maciej, & Heine, Steven J. (2011). Evidence for a sensitive period for acculturation: Younger immigrants report acculturating at a faster rate. *Psychological Science, 22*, 147–152.

Cheung, Fanny M., van de Vijver, Fons J. R., & Leong, Frederick T. L. (2011). Toward a new approach to the study of personality in culture. *American Psychologist, 66*, 593–603.

Chiarello, Christine, Welcome, Suzanne E., Halderman, Laura K., et al. (2009). A large-scale investigation of lateralization in cortical anatomy and word reading: Are there sex differences? *Neuropsychology, 23*, 210–222.

Chida, Yoichi, & Hamer, Mark. (2008). Chronic psychosocial factors and acute physiological responses to laboratory-induced stress in healthy populations: A quantitative review of 30 years of investigations. *Psychological Bulletin, 134*, 829–885.

Chipuer, Heather M., Rovine, Michael J., & Plomin, Robert. (1990). LISREL modeling: Genetic and environmental influences on IQ revisited. *Intelligence, 14*, 11–29.

Choi, Incheol, Dalal, Reeshad, Kim-Prieto, Chu, & Park, Hyekyung. (2003). Culture and judgment of causal relevance. *Journal of Personality and Social Psychology, 84*, 46–59.

Chomsky, Noam. (1957). *Syntactic structures.* The Hague, Netherlands: Mouton.

Chomsky, Noam. (1980). Initial states and steady states. In M. Piatelli-Palmerini (Ed.), *Language and learning: The debate between Jean Piaget and Noam Chomsky.* Cambridge, MA: Harvard University Press.

Chomsky, Noam. (2015). Some core contested concepts. *Journal of Psycholinguistic Research, 44*, 91–104.

Chrisler, Joan C. (2000). PMS as a culture-bound syndrome. In J. C. Chrisler, C. Golden, & P. D. Rozee (Eds.), *Lectures on the psychology of women* (2nd ed.). New York: McGraw-Hill.

Chrisler, Joan C., & Caplan, Paula. (2002). The strange case of Dr. Jekyll and Ms. Hyde: How PMS became a cultural phenomenon and psychiatric disorder. *Annual Review of Sex Research, 13*, 274–306.

Christakis, Dimitri A., Zimmerman, Frederick J., DiGiuseppe, David L., & McCarty, Carolyn A. (2004). Early television exposure and subsequent attentional problems in children. *Pediatrics, 113*, 708–713.

Christopher, Andrew N., & Wojda, Mark R. (2008). Social dominance orientation, right-wing authoritarianism, sexism, and prejudice toward women in the workforce. *Psychology of Women Quarterly, 32*, 65–73.

Chudal, Roshan, Brown, Alan S., Gissler, Mika, Suominen, Auli, & Sourander, Andre. (2015). Is maternal smoking during pregnancy associated with bipolar disorder in offspring? *Journal of Affective Disorders, 171*, 132–136.

Church, A. Timothy, & Lonner, Walter J. (1998). The cross-cultural perspective in the study of personality: Rationale and current research. *Journal of Cross-Cultural Psychology, 29*, 32–62.

Cialdini, Robert B. (2009). We have to break up. *Perspectives on Psychological Science, 4*, 5–6.

Cinque, Guglielmo. (1999). *Adverbs and functional heads: A cross-linguistic approach.* New York: Oxford University Press.

Cioffi, Frank. (1998). *Freud and the question of pseudoscience.* Chicago: Open Court.

Claidière, Nicolas, & Whiten, Andrew. (2012). Integrating the study of conformity and culture in humans and nonhuman animals. *Psychological Bulletin 138*, 126–145.

Clancy, Susan A. (2005). *Abducted: How people come to believe they were kidnapped by aliens.* Cambridge, MA: Harvard University Press.

Clark, Eve V., & Estigarribia, Bruno. (2011). Using speech and gesture to inform young children about unfamiliar word meanings. *Gesture, 11*, 1–23.

Clark, Lee Anna, & Watson, David. (2008). Temperament: An organizing paradigm for trait psychology. In O. P. John, R.W. Robbins, & L. A. Pervin (Eds.), *Handbook of personality: Theory and research* (3rd ed.). New York: Guilford Press.

Clark, Rodney, Anderson, Norman B., Clark, Vernessa R., & Williams, David R. (1999). Racism as a stressor for African Americans: A biopsychosocial model. *American Psychologist, 54*, 805–816.

Clarke, Peter, & Evans, Susan H. (1998). *Surviving modern medicine.* Rutgers, NJ: Rutgers University Press.

Cleary, Anne M. (2008). Recognition memory, familiarity, and déjà vu experiences. *Current Directions in Psychological Science, 17*, 353–357.

Cleckley, Hervey. (1976). *The mask of sanity* (5th ed.). St. Louis, MO: Mosby.

Cloninger, C. Robert. (1990). *The genetics and biology of alcoholism.* Cold Springs Harbor, ME: Cold Springs Harbor Press.

Coan, James A., Schaefer, Hillary, & Davidson, Richard J. (2006). Lending a hand: Social regulation of the neural response to threat. *Psychological Science, 17.*

Coats, Erik J., Janoff-Bulman, Ronnie, & Alpert, Nancy. (1996). Approach versus avoidance goals: Differences in self-evaluation and well-being. *Personality and Social Psychology Bulletin, 22,* 1057–1067.

Coe, Christopher L., & Lubach, Gabriele R. (2008). Fetal programming: Prenatal origins of health and illness. *Current Directions in Psychological Science, 17,* 36–41.

Coelho, Helen F., Canter, Peter H., & Ernst, Edzard. (2007). Mindfulness-based cognitive therapy: Evaluating current evidence and informing future research. *Journal of Consulting and Clinical Psychology, 75,* 1000–1005.

Cohen, David B. (1999). *Stranger in the nest: Do parents really shape their child's personality, intelligence, or character?* New York: Wiley.

Cohen, Dov. (1998). Culture, social organization, and patterns of violence. *Journal of Personality and Social Psychology, 75,* 408–419.

Cohen, Dov, Nisbett, Richard E., Bowdle, Brian F., & Schwarz, Norbert. (1996). Insult, aggression, and the Southern culture of honor: An "experimental ethnography." *Journal of Personality and Social Psychology, 70,* 945–960.

Cohen, Sheldon, Doyle, William J., Turner, Ronald, et al. (2003). Sociability and susceptibility to the common cold. *Psychological Science, 14,* 389–395.

Cohen, Sheldon, Frank, Ellen, Doyle, William J., et al. (1998). Types of stressors that increase susceptibility to the common cold in healthy adults. *Health Psychology, 17,* 214–223.

Cohen, Sheldon, Tyrrell, David A., & Smith, Andrew P. (1993). Negative life events, perceived stress, negative affect, and susceptibility to the common cold. *Journal of Personality and Social Psychology, 64,* 131–140.

Cohen Kadosh, Roi. (2015). Modulating and enhancing cognition using brain stimulation: Science and fiction. *Journal of Cognitive Psychology, 27*(2), 141–163.

Colcombe, Stanley, & Kramer, Arthur F. (2003). Fitness effects on the cognitive function of older adults: A meta-analytic study. *Psychological Science, 14,* 125–130.

Cole, Michael, & Scribner, Sylvia. (1974). *Culture and thought.* New York: Wiley.

Collaer, Marcia L., & Hines, Melissa. (1995). Human behavioral sex differences: A role for gonadal hormones during early development? *Psychological Bulletin, 118,* 55–107.

Collins, Allan M., & Loftus, Elizabeth F. (1975). A spreading-activation theory of semantic processing. *Psychological Review, 82,* 407–428.

Collins, Barry E., & Brief, Diana E. (1995). Using person-perception vignette methodologies to uncover the symbolic meanings of teacher behaviors in the Milgram paradigm. *Journal of Social Issues, 51,* 89–106.

Collins, Francis S. (2010). *The language of life: DNA and the revolution in personalized medicine.* New York: HarperCollins.

Coltman, David W., O'Donoghue, Paul, Jorgenson, Jon T., et al. (2003). Undesirable evolutionary consequences of trophy hunting. *Nature, 426,* 655–658.

Comas-Díaz, Lillian. (2006). Latino healing: The integration of ethnic psychology into psychotherapy. *Psychotherapy: Theory, Research, Practice, Training, 43,* 436–453.

Comuzzie, Anthony G., & Allison, David B. (1998). The search for human obesity genes. *Science, 280,* 1374–1377.

Conley, Terri D., Moors, Amy C., Matsick, Jes L., et al. (2011). Women, men, and the bedroom: Methodological and conceptual insights that narrow, reframe, and eliminate gender differences in sexuality. *Current Directions in Psychological Science, 20,* 296–300.

Conroy, David E., Ram, Nilam, Pincus, Aaron, & Rebar, Amanda L. (2015). Bursts of self-conscious emotions in the daily lives of emerging adults. *Self and Identity, 14*(3), 290–313.

Conroy, John. (2000). *Unspeakable acts, ordinary people: The dynamics of torture.* New York: Knopf.

Cook, Joan M., Biyanova, Tatyana, & Coyne, James C. (2009). Influential psychotherapy figures, authors, and books: An Internet survey of over 2,000 psychotherapists. *Psychotherapy: Theory, Research, Practice, Training, 46,* 42–51.

Coontz, Stephanie. (2005). *Marriage, a history: How love conquered marriage.* New York: Penguin.

Cooper, M. Lynne, Frone, Michael R., Russell, Marcia, & Mudar, Pamela. (1995). Drinking to regulate positive and negative emotions: A motivational model of alcohol use. *Journal of Personality and Social Psychology, 69,* 990–1005.

Cooper, M. Lynne, Shapiro, Cheryl M., & Powers, Anne M. (1998). Motivations for sex and risky sexual behavior among adolescents and young adults: A functional perspective. *Journal of Personality and Social Psychology, 75,* 1528–1558.

Corkin, Suzanne. (1984). Lasting consequences of bilateral medial temporal lobectomy: Clinical course and experimental findings in H. M. *Seminars in Neurology, 4,* 249–259.

Corkin, Suzanne. (2013). *Permanent present tense: The unforgettable life of the amnesic patient, H. M.* New York: Basic Books.

Corkin, Suzanne, Amaral, David G., Gonzalez, R. Gilberto, et al. (1997). H. M.'s medial temporal lobe lesion: Findings from magnetic resonance imaging. *Journal of Neuroscience, 17,* 3964–3979.

Corriveau, Kathleen H., Fusaro, Maria, & Harris, Paul L. (2009). Going with the flow: Preschoolers prefer nondissenters as informants. *Psychological Science, 20,* 372–377.

Cosmides, Leda, Tooby, John, & Barkow, Jerome H. (1992). Introduction: Evolutionary psychology and conceptual integration. In J. H. Barkow, L. Cosmides, & J. Tooby (Eds.), *The adapted mind: Evolutionary psychology and the generation of culture.* New York: Oxford University Press.

Costa, Paul T. Jr., & McCrae, Robert R. (2011). The Five-Factor Model, Five-Factor Theory, and interpersonal psychology. In Leonard M. Horowitz & Stephen Strack (Eds.), *Handbook of interpersonal psychology: Theory, research, assessment, and therapeutic interventions* (pp. 91–104). New York: Wiley.

Costa, Paul T. Jr., & McCrae, Robert R. (2014). The NEO inventories. In Robert P. Archer & Steven R. Smith (Eds.), *Personality assessment* (2nd ed., pp. 229–260). New York: Routledge/Taylor & Francis Group.

Costa, Paul T., Jr., McCrae, Robert R., Martin, Thomas A., et al. (1999). Personality development from adolescence through adulthood: Further cross-cultural comparisons of age differences. In V. J. Molfese & D. Molfese (Eds.), *Temperament and personality development across the life span*. Hillsdale, NJ: Erlbaum.

Cota-Robles, Sonia, Neiss, Michelle, & Rowe, David C. (2002). The role of puberty in violent and nonviolent delinquency among Anglo American, Mexican American, and African American boys. *Journal of Adolescent Research, 17*, 364–376.

Council, James R., Kirsch, Irving, & Grant, D. L. (1996). Imagination, expectancy and hypnotic responding. In R. G. Kunzendorf, N. K. Spanos, & B. J. Wallace (Eds.), *Hypnosis and imagination*. Amityville, NY: Baywood.

Courage, Mary L., & Howe, Mark L. (2002). From infant to child: The dynamics of cognitive change in the second year of life. *Psychological Bulletin, 128*, 250–277.

Courtney, Kelly E., & Polich, John. (2009). Binge drinking in young adults: Data, definitions, and determinants. *Psychological Bulletin, 135*, 142–156.

Cowan, Nelson. (2001). The magical number 4 in short-term memory: A reconsideration of mental storage capacity. *Behavioral and Brain Sciences, 24*, 87–185.

Cowan, Nelson, Morey, Candice C., Chen, Zhijian, et al. (2008) Theory and measurement of working memory capacity limits. In B. H. Ross (Ed.), *The psychology of learning and motivation*. San Diego: Elsevier.

Cowan, Ruth Schwarz. (2008). *Heredity and hope: The case for genetic screening*. Cambridge, MA: Harvard University Press.

Cowen, Emory L., Wyman, Peter A., Work, William C., & Parker, Gayle R. (1990). The Rochester Child Resilience Project (RCRP): Overview and summary of first year findings. *Development and Psychopathology, 2*, 193–212.

Cox, Martha J., & Paley, Blair. (2003). Understanding families as systems. *Current Directions in Psychological Science, 12*, 193–196.

Coyne, James C., & Tennen, Howard. (2010). Positive psychology in cancer care: Bad science, exaggerated claims, and unproven medicine. *Annals of Behavioral Medicine, 39*(1), 16–26.

Coyne, James C., Thombs, Brett D., Stefanek, Michael, & Palmer, Steven C. (2009). Time to let go of the illusion that psychotherapy extends the survival of cancer patients. *Psychological Bulletin, 135*, 179–182.

Cozolino, Louis. (2006). *The neuroscience of human relationships: Attachment and the developing social brain*. New York: Norton.

Craik, Fergus I. M., & Lockhart, Robert. (1972). Levels of processing: A framework for memory research. *Journal of Verbal Learning and Verbal Behavior, 11*, 671–684.

Craik, Fergus I. M., & Tulving, Endel. (1975). Depth of processing and the retention of words in episodic memory. *Journal of Experimental Psychology: General, 104*, 268–294.

Crair, Michael C., Gillespie, Deda C., & Stryker, Michael P. (1998). The role of visual experience in the development of columns in cat visual cortex. *Science, 279*, 566–570.

Cramer, Phebe. (2000). Defense mechanisms in psychology today: Further processes for adaptation. *American Psychologist, 55*, 637–646.

Crawford, Mary, & Marecek, Jeanne. (1989). Psychology constructs the female: 1968–1988. *Psychology of Women Quarterly, 13*, 147–165.

Crews, Frederick (Ed.). (1998). *Unauthorized Freud: Doubters confront a legend*. New York: Viking.

Critchlow, Barbara. (1986). The powers of John Barleycorn: Beliefs about the effects of alcohol on social behavior. *American Psychologist, 41*, 751–764.

Crits-Christoph, Paul, Wilson, G. Terence, & Hollon, Steven D. (2005). Empirically supported psychotherapies: Comment on Westen, Novotny, and Thompson-Brenner (2004). *Psychological Bulletin, 131*, 412–417.

Crombag, Hans S., & Robinson, Terry E. (2004). Drugs, environment, brain, and behavior. *Current Directions in Psychological Science, 13*, 107–111.

Crowell, Sheila E., Beauchaine, Theodore P., & Linehan, Marsha M. (2009). A biosocial developmental model of borderline personality: Elaborating and extending Linehan's theory. *Psychological Bulletin, 135*, 495–510.

Crozier, W. Ray, & de Jong, Peter J. (2013). *The psychological significance of the blush*. New York: Cambridge University Press.

Cruwys, Tegan, Haslam, S. Alexander, Dingle, Genevieve A., Haslam, Catherine, & Jetten, Jolanda. (2014). Depression and social identity: An integrative review. *Personality and Social Psychology Review, 18*(3), 215–238.

Cruz, Vitor Tedim, Nunes, Belina, Reis, Ana Mafalda, & Pereira, Jorge Resende. (2005). Cortical remapping in amputees and dysmelic patients: A functional MRI study. *NeuroRehabilitation, 18*, 299–305.

Cummings, E. Mark, & Davies, Patrick T. (2011). *Marital conflict and children: An emotional security perspective*. New York: Guilford Press.

Cumming, Geoff. (2014). The new statistics: Why and how. *Psychological Science, 25*(1), 7–29.

Cumming, Geoff, Fidler, Fiona, Leonard, Martine, et al. (2007). Statistical reform in psychology: Is anything changing? *Psychological Science, 18*, 230–232.

Cummings, Nicholas A., & O'Donohue, William T. (2008). *Eleven blunders that cripple psychotherapy in America*. New York: Routledge/Taylor & Francis.

Cummings, Nicholas A., & Wiggins, Jack G. (2001). A collaborative primary care/behavioral health model for the use of psychotropic medication with children and adolescents. *Issues in Interdisciplinary Care, 3*, 121–128.

Cunningham, William A., & Brosch, Tobias. (2012). Motivational salience: Amygdala tuning from traits, needs, values, and goals. *Current Directions in Psychological Science, 21*, 54–59.

Currie, Janet, DellaVigna, Stefano, Moretti, Enrico, & Pathania, Vikram. (2009, April). The effect of fast food restaurants on obesity. Unpublished paper. Available at www.econ.berkeley.edu/~moretti/obesity.pdf.

Curtiss, Susan. (1977). *Genie: A psycholinguistic study of a modern-day "wild child."* New York: Academic Press.

Cypess, A. M., Lehman, S., Williams, G., et al. (2009, April 9). Identification and importance of brown adipose tissue in adult humans. *New England Journal of Medicine, 360*, 1509–1517.

Czeipel, Marcin, Boddeke, Erik, & Copray, Sjef. (2015). Human oligodendrocytes in remyelination research. *Glia, 63*(4), 513–530.

Dadds, Mark R., Bovbjerg, Dana H., Redd, William H., & Cutmore, Tim R. H. (1997). Imagery in human classical conditioning. *Psychological Bulletin, 122,* 89–103.

Daley, Tamara C., Whaley, Shannon E., Sigman, Marian D., et al. (2003). IQ on the rise: The Flynn Effect in rural Kenyan children. *Psychological Science, 14,* 215–219.

Dalgliesh, Tim, Hauer, Beatrijs, & Kuyken, Willem. (2008). The mental regulation of autobiographical recollection in the aftermath of trauma. *Current Directions in Psychological Science, 17,* 259–263.

Dalton, K. S., Morris, D. L., Delanoy, D. I., et al. (1996). Security measures in an automated ganzfeld system. *Journal of Parapsychology, 60,* 129–147.

Damasio, Antonio R. (2003). *Looking for Spinoza: Joy, sorrow, and the feeling brain.* San Diego: Harcourt.

Damasio, Hanna, Grabowski, Thomas J., Frank, Randall, et al. (1994). The return of Phineas Gage: Clues about the brain from the skull of a famous patient. *Science, 264,* 1102–1105.

Damon, William. (1995). *Greater expectations.* New York: Free Press.

D'Antonio, Michael. (2004, May 2). How we think. *Los Angeles Times Magazine,* pp. 18–20, 30–32.

Darley, John M. (1995). Constructive and destructive obedience: A taxonomy of principal agent relationships. In A. G. Miller, B. E. Collins, & D. E. Brief (Eds.), Perspectives on obedience to authority: The legacy of the Milgram experiments. *Journal of Social Issues, 51*(3), 125–154.

Darley, John M., & Latane, Bibb. (1968). Bystander intervention in emergencies: Diffusion of responsibility. *Journal of Personality and Social Psychology, 8,* 377–383.

Darwin, Charles. (1859/1964). *On the origin of species.* [A facsimile of the first edition, edited by Ernst Mayer, 1964.] Cambridge, MA: Harvard University Press.

Darwin, Charles. (1872/1965). *The expression of the emotions in man and animals.* Chicago: University of Chicago Press.

Daum, Irene, & Schugens, Markus M. (1996). On the cerebellum and classical conditioning. *Psychological Science, 5,* 58–61.

Dautriche, Isabelle, Cristia, Alejandrina, Brusini, Perrine, Yuan, Sylvia, Fisher, Cynthia, & Christophe, Anne. (2014). Toddlers default to canonical surface-to-meaning mapping when learning verbs. *Child Development, 85*(3), 1168–1180.

Davelaar, Eddy J., Goshen-Gottstein, Yonatan, Ashkenazi, Amir, et al. (2004). The demise of short-term memory revisited: Empirical and computational investigations of recency effects. *Psychological Review, 112,* 3–42.

Davey Smith, George. (2011). Epigenetics for the masses: More than Audrey Hepburn and yellow mice? *International Journal of Epidemiology, 40,* 303–308.

Davey Smith, George. (2012). Epidemiology, epigenetics and the "gloomy prospect": Embracing randomness in population research and practice. *International Journal of Epidemiology, 40,* 537–562.

Davidson, Richard J. (1992). Anterior cerebral asymmetry and the nature of emotion. *Brain and Cognition, 20,* 125–151.

Davidson, Richard J., Kabat-Zinn, Jon, Schumacher, J., et al. (2003). Alterations in brain and immune function produced by mindfulness meditation. *Psychosomatic Medicine, 65,* 564–570.

Davis, Christopher G., Nolen-Hoeksema, Susan, & Larson, Judith. (1998). Making sense of loss and benefiting from the experience: Two construals of meaning. *Journal of Personality and Social Psychology, 75,* 561–574.

Davis, Michael, Myers, Karyn M., Ressler, Kerry J., & Rothbaum, Barbara O. (2005). Facilitation of extinction of conditioning fear by D-cycloserine. *Current Directions in Psychological Science, 14,* 214–219.

Davis, Michelle L., Powers, Mark B., Handelsman, Pamela, Medina, Johnna L., Zvolensky, Michael, & Smits, Jasper A. J. (2015). Behavioral therapies for treatment-seeking cannabis users: A meta-analysis of randomized controlled trials. *Evaluation and the Health Professions, 38*(1), 94–114.

Davison, Gerald C. (1976). Homosexuality: The ethical challenge. *Journal of Consulting and Clinical Psychology, 44,* 157–162.

Dawes, Robyn M. (1994). *House of cards: Psychology and psychotherapy built on myth.* New York: Free Press.

Dazzan, Paola, Arango, Celso, Fleischacker, Wolfgang, Galderisi, Silvana, Glenthøj, Birte, Leucht, Stephan, et al. (2015). Magnetic resonance imaging and the prediction of outcome in first-episode schizophrenia: A review of current evidence and directions for future research. *Schizophrenia Bulletin, 41*(3), 574–583.

Dean, Geoffrey. (1992). The bottom line: Effect size. In B. Beyerstein & D. Beyerstein (Eds.), *The write stuff: Evaluations of graphology—The study of handwriting analysis.* Buffalo, NY: Prometheus Books.

de Araujo, Ivan E., Oliveira-Maia, A. J., Sotnikova, T. D., et al. (2008, March 27). Food reward in the absence of taste receptor signaling. *Neuron, 57,* 930–941.

Deary, Ian J., Weiss, Alexander, & Batty, G. David. (2010). Intelligence, personality, and health outcomes. *Psychological Science in the Public Interest, 11,* 53–80.

de Bono, Edward. (1985). *De Bono's thinking course.* New York: Facts on File.

Deci, Edward L., Koestner, Richard, & Ryan, Richard M. (1999). A meta-analytic review of experiments examining the effects of extrinsic rewards on intrinsic motivation. *Psychological Bulletin, 125,* 627–668.

Deci, Edward L., & Ryan, Richard M. (1985). *Intrinsic motivation and self-determination of human behavior.* New York: Plenum Press.

De Dreu, Carsten K. W., Greer, Lindred L., Van Kleef, Gerben A., et al. (2011). Oxytocin promotes human ethnocentrism. *Proceedings of the National Academy of Sciences, 108,* 1262–1266.

Deffenbacher, Jerry L., Deffenbacher, David M., Lynch, Rebekah S., & Richards, Tracy L. (2003). Anger, aggression, and risky behavior: A comparison of high and low anger drives. *Behaviour Research and Therapy, 41,* 701–718.

de Guzman, Maria Rosario T., Do, Kieu Anh, & Kok, Car Mun. (2014). The cultural contexts of children's prosocial behaviors. In Laura M. Padilla-Walker & Gustavo Carlo (Eds.), *Prosocial development: A multidimensional approach* (pp. 221–241). New York: Oxford University Press.

De Houwer, Jan, Teige-Mocigemba, Sarah, Spruyt, Adriaan, & Moors, Agnes. (2009). Implicit measures: A normative analysis and review. *Psychological Bulletin, 135,* 347–368.

DeLoache, Judy S., Chiong, Cynthia, Sherman, Kathleen, et al. (2010). Do babies learn from baby media? *Psychological Science, 21,* 1570–1574.

Delton, Andrew W., Krasnow, Max M., Cosmides, Leda, & Tooby, John. (2011). Evolution of direct reciprocity under uncertainty can explain human generosity in one-shot encounters. *Proceedings of the National Academy of Sciences, 108,* 13335–13340.

Dement, William. (1978). *Some must watch while some must sleep.* New York: Norton.

Dement, William. (1992). *The sleepwatchers.* Stanford, CA: Stanford Alumni Association.

Dement, William. (2005). History of sleep medicine. *Neurologic Clinics, 23*(4), 945–965.

Denning, Patt, Little, Jeannie, & Glickman, Adina. (2004). *Over the influence: The harm reduction guide for managing drugs and alcohol.* New York: Guilford Press.

Denny, Dallas (Ed.). (1998). *Current concepts in transgender identity.* New York: Garland Press.

DePaulo, Bella M. (1992). Nonverbal behavior and self-presentation. *Psychological Bulletin, 111,* 203–243.

DePaulo, Bella M. (2006). *Singled out: How singles are stereotyped, stigmatized, and ignored, and still live happily ever after.* New York: St. Martin's Press.

DePaulo, Bella M., Lindsay, James J., Malone, Brian E., et al. (2003). Cues to deception. *Psychological Bulletin, 129,* 74–118.

de Ridder, Denise T. D., Lensvelt-Mulders, Gerty, Finkenauer, Catrin, et al. (2012). Taking stock of self-control: A meta-analysis of how trait self-control relates to a wide range of behaviors. *Personality and Social Psychology Review, 16,* 76–99.

de Rivera, Joseph. (1989). Comparing experiences across cultures: Shame and guilt in America and Japan. *Hiroshima Forum for Psychology, 14,* 13–20.

Des Roches, Simone, Torresdal, Jack, Morgan, Travis W., Harmon, Luke J., & Rosenblum, Erica B. (2013). Beyond black and white: Divergent behavior and performance in three rapidly evolving lizard species at White Sands. *Biological Journal of the Linnean Society, 111*(1), 169–182.

Desbonnet, L., Waddington, J. L., & O'Tuathaigh, C. M. (2009). Mutant models for genes associated with schizophrenia. *Biochemical Society Transactions, 37*(Pt 1), 308–312.

de Schotten, Michel Thiebaut, Cohen, Laurent, Amemiya, Eduardo, Braga, Lucia W., & Dehaene, Stanislas. (2014). Learning to read improves the structure of the arcuate fasciculus. *Cerebral Cortex, 24*(4), 989–995.

DeValois, Russell L., & DeValois, Karen K. (1975). Neural coding of color. In E. C. Carterette & M. P. Friedman (Eds.), *Handbook of perception* (Vol. 5). New York: Academic Press.

Devlin, B., Daniels, Michael, & Roeder, Kathryn. (1997). The heritability of IQ. *Nature, 388,* 468–471.

de Waal, Frans. (2001). *The ape and the sushi master: Cultural reflections by a primatologist.* New York: Basic Books.

de Waal, Frans. (2002). Evolutionary psychology: The wheat and the chaff. *Current Directions in Psychological Science, 11,* 187–191.

DeWall, C. Nathan, & Bushman, Brad J. (2011). Social acceptance and rejection: The sweet and the bitter. *Current Directions in Psychological Science, 20,* 256–260.

DeWall, C. Nathan, Gillath, Omri, Pressman, Sarah D., Black, Lora L., Bartz, Jennifer A., Moskovitz, Jackob, et al. (2014). When the love hormone leads to violence: Oxytocin increases intimate partner violence inclinations among high trait aggressive people. *Social Psychological and Personality Science, 5*(6), 691–697.

Diamond, Adele, & Amso, Dima. (2008). Contributions of neuroscience to our understanding of cognitive development. *Current Directions in Psychological Science, 17,* 136–141.

Diamond, Lisa M. (2004). Emerging perspectives on distinctions between romantic love and sexual desire. *Current Directions in Psychological Science, 13,* 116–119.

Dick, Danielle M. (2007). Identification of genes influencing a spectrum of externalizing psychopathology. *Current Directions in Psychological Science, 16,* 331–335.

Dick, Danielle M., Aliev, Fazil, Wang, Jen C., et al. (2008). A systematic single nucleotide polymorphism screen to fine-map alcohol dependence genes on chromosome 7 identifies association with a novel susceptibility gene ACN9. *Biological Psychiatry, 63,* 1047–1053.

Dick, Danielle M., Meyers, Jacquelyn L., Latendresse, Shawn J., et al. (2011). CHRM2, parental monitoring, and adolescent externalizing behavior: Evidence for gene-environment interaction. *Psychological Science, 22,* 481–489.

Dien, Dora S. (1999). Chinese authority-directed orientation and Japanese peer-group orientation: Questioning the notion of collectivism. *Review of General Psychology, 3,* 372–385.

Dienes, Zoltan. (2011). Bayesian versus orthodox statistics: Which side are you on? *Perspectives on Psychological Science, 6,* 274–290.

DiFranza, Joseph R. (2008, May). Hooked from the first cigarette. *Scientific American,* 82–87.

Digman, John M., & Shmelyov, Alexander G. (1996). The structure of temperament and personality in Russian children. *Journal of Personality and Social Psychology, 71,* 341–351.

Dimberg, Ulf, Thunberg, Monika, & Elmehed, Kurt. (2000). Unconscious facial reactions to emotional facial expressions. *Psychological Science, 11,* 86–89.

Dinges, David F., Whitehouse, Wayne G., Orne, Emily C., et al. (1992). Evaluating hypnotic memory enhancement (hypermnesia and reminiscence) using multitrial forced recall. *Journal of Experimental Psychology: Learning, Memory, and Cognition, 18,* 1139–1147.

Dingfelder, Sadie F. (2010, November). A second chance for the Mexican wolf. *APA Monitor, 41,* 20.

Dinn, W. M., & Harris, C. L. (2000). Neurocognitive function in antisocial personality disorder. *Psychiatry Research, 97,* 173–190.

Dion, Kenneth L., & Dion, Karen K. (1993). Gender and ethnocultural comparisons in styles of love. *Psychology of Women Quarterly, 17,* 463–474.

Doering, Stephan, Katzlberger, Florian, Rumpold, Gerhard, et al. (2000). Videotape preparation of patients before hip replacement surgery reduces stress. *Psychosomatic Medicine, 62,* 365–373.

Dolnick, Edward. (1990, July). What dreams are (really) made of. *The Atlantic Monthly, 226,* 41–45, 48–53, 56–58, 60–61.

Domhoff, G. William. (1996). *Finding meaning in dreams: A quantitative approach.* New York: Plenum Press.

Domhoff, G. William. (2003). *The scientific study of dreams: Neural networks, cognitive development, and content analysis.* Washington, DC: American Psychological Association.

Domhoff, G. William. (2011). Dreams are embodied simulations that dramatize conceptions and concerns: the continuity hypothesis in empirical, theoretical, historical context. *International Journal of Dream Research, 4,* 50–62.

Donaldson, Stewart I., Dollwet, Maren, & Rao, Meghana A. (2015). Happiness, excellence, and optimal human functioning revisited: Examining the peer-reviewed literature linked topositive psychology. *Journal of Positive Psychology, 10*(3), 185–195.

Donlea, Jeffrey M., Ramanan, Narendrakumar, & Shaw, Paul J. (2009). Use-dependent plasticity in clock neurons regulates sleep need in *Drosophila. Science, 324,* 105–108.

Dougherty, Lea R., Klein, Daniel N., Rose, Suzanne, & Laptook, Rebecca S. (2011). Hypothalamic-pituitary-adrenal axis reactivity in the preschool-age offspring of depressed parents: Moderation by early parenting. *Psychological Science, 22,* 650–658.

Dovidio, John F., & Gaertner, Samuel L. (2008). New directions in aversive racism research: Persistence and pervasiveness. In C. Willis-Esqueda (Ed.), *Motivational aspects of prejudice and racism.* Nebraska Symposium on Motivation. New York: Springer Science + Business Media.

Dovidio, John F., & Gaertner, Samuel L. (2010). Intergroup bias. In Fiske, S. T., Gilbert, D. T., & Lindzey, G. (Eds.), *Handbook of social psychology* (Vol. 2, 5th ed.). Hoboken, NJ: Wiley.

Dovidio, John F., Pagotto, L., & Hebl, M. R. (2011). Implicit attitudes and discrimination against people with physical disabilities. In R. L. Wiener & S. L. Willborn (Eds.), *Disability and aging discrimination: Perspectives in law and psychology,* pp. 157–183. New York: Springer Science + Business Media.

Downing, P. E., Chan, A. W.-Y., Peelen, M. V., et al. (2006). Domain specificity in visual cortex. *Cerebral Cortex, 16,* 1453–1461.

Draguns, Juris G. (2013). Cross-cultural and international extensions of evidence-based psychotherapy: Toward more effective and sensitive psychological services everywhere. *Psychologia: An International Journal of Psychological Sciences, 56*(2), 74–88.

Duckworth, Angela Lee, & Carlson, S. M. (2013). Self-regulation and school success. In B. M. Sokol; M. E. Grouzet; & U. Mulller (Eds.), *Self-regulation and autonomy: Social and developmental dimensions of human conduct* (pp. 208–230). New York: Cambridge University Press.

Duckworth, Angela Lee, & Gross, James J. (2014). Self-control and grit: Related but separable determinants of success. *Current Directions in Psychological Science, 23*(5), 319–325.

Duckworth, Angela Lee, Kirby, Teri A., Tsukayama, Eli, Berstein, Heather, & Ericsson, K. Anders. (2011). Deliberate practice spells success. Why grittier competitors triumph at the National Spelling Bee. *Social Psychological and Personality Science, 2*(2), 174–181.

Duckworth, Angela Lee, & Quinn, P. D. (2009). Development and validation of the Short Grit Scale (Grit-S). *Journal of Personality Assessment, 91,* 166–174.

Duckworth, Angela L., & Seligman, Martin E. P. (2005, Dec.) Self-discipline outdoes IQ in predicting academic performance of adolescents. *Psychological Science, 16* (12), 939–944.

Duffy, Jeanne, F., Cain, Sean W., Change, Anne-Marie, et al. (2011). Sex difference in the near-24-hour intrinsic period of the human circadian timing system. *Proceedings of the National Academy of Science, 108,* 15602–15608.

Dully, Howard. (2008). *My lobotomy.* New York: Broadway Books.

Dumit, Joseph. (2004). *Picturing personhood: Brain scans and biomedical identity.* Princeton, NJ: Princeton University Press.

Duncan, Laramie E., & Keller, Matthew C. (2011). A critical review of the first 10 years of candidate gene by-environment interaction research in psychiatry. *American Journal of Psychiatry, 168,* 1041–1049.

Dunkel, Curtis S., & Sefcek, Jon A. (2009). Eriksonian lifespan theory and life history theory: An integration using the example of identity formation. *Review of General Psychology, 13,* 13–23.

Dunlosky, John, & Lipko, Amanda R. (2007). Metacomprehension: A brief history and how to improve its accuracy. *Current Directions in Psychological Science, 16,* 228–232.

Dunn, Barnaby D., Stefanovitch, Iolanta, Evans, Davy, et al. (2010). Can you feel the beat? Interoceptive awareness is an interactive function of anxiety- and depression-specific symptom dimensions. *Behaviour Research and Therapy, 48,* 1133–1138.

Dunn, Elizabeth W., Gilbert, Daniel T., & Wilson, Timothy D. (2011). If money doesn't make you happy, then you probably aren't spending it right. *Journal of Consumer Psychology, 21*(2), 115–125.

Dunn, Elizabeth W., Wilson, Timothy D., & Gilbert, Daniel T. (2003). Location, location, location: The misprediction of satisfaction in housing lotteries. *Personality and Social Psychology Bulletin, 29,* 1421–1432.

Dunn, Michael, Greenhill, Simon J., Levinson, Stephen C., et al. (2011, April 13). Evolved structure of language shows lineage-specific trends in word-order universals. *Nature, 473,* 79–92.

Dunning, David. (2005). *Self-insight: Roadblocks and detours on the path to knowing thyself.* New York: Psychology Press.

Dunning, David, Johnson, Kerri, Ehrlinger, Joyce, & Kruger, Justin. (2003). Why people fail to recognize their own incompetence. *Current Directions in Psychological Science, 12,* 83–87.

Durisko, C., & Fiez, Julie A. (2010). Functional activation in the cerebellum during working memory and simple speech tasks. *Cortex, 46*(7), 896–906.

Durrant, Joan, & Ensom, Ron. (2012). Physical punishment of children: Lessons from 20 years of research. *Canadian Medical Association Journal,* published ahead of print February 6, 2012. www.cmaj.ca/content/early/2012/02/06/cmaj.101314.short.

Dweck, Carol S. (2006). *Mindset: The new psychology of success.* New York: Random House.

Dweck, Carol S., & Grant, Heidi. (2008). Self-theories, goals, and meaning. In J. Y. Shah & W. L. Gardner (Eds.), *Handbook of motivation science.* New York: Guilford.

Dyson, Margaret W., Olino, Thomas M., Durbin, C. Emily, Goldsmith, H. Hill, Bufferd, Sara J., Miller, Anna R., et al. (2015). The structural and rank-order stability of temperamentin young children based on a laboratory-observational measure. *Psychological Assessment,* electronic preview.

Eagly, Alice H., Eaton, Asia, Rose, Suzanna M., et al. (2012). Feminism and psychology: Analysis of a half-century of research on women and gender. *American Psychologist, 67*, 211–230.

Eagly, Alice H., & Wood, Wendy. (1999). The origins of sex differences in human behavior: Evolved dispositions versus social roles. *American Psychologist, 54*, 408–423.

Earl-Novell, Sarah L., & Jessup, Donna C. (2005). The relationship between perceptions of premenstrual syndrome and degree performance. *Assessment and Evaluation in Higher Education, 30*, 343–352.

Ebbinghaus, Hermann M. (1885/1913). *Memory: A contribution to experimental psychology* (H. A. Ruger & C. E. Bussenius, Trans.). New York: Teachers College Press, Columbia University.

Eccles, Jacqueline S. (2011). Understanding women's achievement choices: Looking back and looking forward. *Psychology of Women Quarterly, 35*, 520–516.

Edwards, Kari, & Smith, Edward E. (1996). A disconfirmation bias in the evaluation of arguments. *Journal of Personality and Social Psychology, 71*, 5–24.

Ehrenreich, Barbara. (2001, June 4). What are they probing for? [Essay.] *Time*, p. 86.

Ehrensaft, Miriam K., Moffitt, Terrie E., & Caspi, Avshalom. (2006). Is domestic violence followed by an increased risk of psychiatric disorders among women but not among men? A longitudinal cohort study. *American Journal of Psychiatry, 163*, 885–892.

Eich, Eric, & Hyman, Ray. (1992). Subliminal self-help. In D. Druckman & R. A. Bjork (Eds.), *In the mind's eye: Enhancing human performance*. Washington, DC: National Academy Press.

Eigsti, Inge-Marie, Zayas, Vivian, Mischel, Walter, Shoda, Yuichi, et al. (2006). Predicting cognitive control from preschool to late adolescence and young adulthood. *Psychological Science, 17*, 478–484.

Eisenberger, Naomi I., Lieberman, Matthew D., & Williams, Kipling D. (2003). Does rejection hurt? An fMRI study of social exclusion. *Science, 302*, 290–292.

Ekman, Paul. (2003). *Emotions revealed*. New York: Times Books.

Ekman, Paul, & Friesen, Wallace V. (1969). The repertoire of nonverbal behavior: Categories, origins, usage, and coding. *Semiotica, 1*(1), 49–98.

Ekman, Paul, Friesen, Wallace V., & O'Sullivan, Maureen. (1988). Smiles when lying. *Journal of Personality and Social Psychology, 54*, 414–420.

Ekman, Paul, Friesen, Wallace V., O'Sullivan, Maureen, et al. (1987). Universals and cultural differences in the judgments of facial expression of emotion. *Journal of Personality and Social Psychology, 53*, 712–717.

Elfenbein, Hilary Anger. (2013). Nonverbal dialects and accents in facial expressions of emotion. *Emotion Review, 5*(1), 90–96.

Elis, Ori, Caponigro, Janelle M., & Kring, Ann M. (2013). Psychosocial treatments for negative symptoms in schizophrenia: Current practices and future directions. *Clinical Psychology Review, 33*(8), 914–928.

Elliot, Andrew J., & McGregor, Holly A. (2001). A 2 x 2 achievement goal framework. *Journal of Personality and Social Psychology, 80*, 501–519.

Ellis, Albert. (1993). Changing rational-emotive therapy (RET) to rational emotive behavior therapy (REBT). *Behavior Therapist, 16*, 257–258.

Ellis, Albert, & Ellis, Debbie Joffee. (2011). *Rational emotive behavior therapy*. Washington, DC: American Psychological Association.

Else-Quest, Nicole M., Hyde, Janet S., Goldsmith, H. Hill, & Can Hulle, Carol A. (2006). Gender differences in temperament: A meta-analysis. *Psychological Bulletin, 132*, 33–72.

Else-Quest, Nicole M., Hyde, Janet S., & Linn, Marcia C. (2010). Cross-national patterns of gender differences in mathematics: A meta-analysis. *Psychological Bulletin, 136*, 103–127.

Emberson, Lauren L., Lupyan, Gary, Goldstein, Michael H., & Spivey, Michael J. (2010). Overheard cell-phone conversations: When less speech is more distracting. *Psychological Science, 21*, 1383–1388.

Emery, Robert E., & Laumann-Billings, Lisa. (1998). An overview of the nature, causes, and consequences of abusive family relationships. *American Psychologist, 53*, 121–135.

Emery, Robert E., Otto, Randy K., & O'Donohue, William T. (2005). A critical assessment of child custody evaluations: Limited science and a flawed system. *Psychological Science in the Public Interest, 6*, 1–29.

Engle, Randall W. (2002). Working memory capacity as executive attention. *Current Directions in Psychological Science, 11*, 19–23.

Epel, Elissa S., Blackburn, Elizabeth H., Lin, Jue, et al. (2004, December 7). Accelerated telomere shortening in response to life stress. *Proceedings of the National Academy of Science, 101*, 17312–17315.

Epley, Nicholas, Schroeder, Juliana, & Waytz, Adam. (2013). Motivated mind perception: Treating pets as people and people as animals. In Sarah J. Gervais (Ed.), *Nebraska Symposium on Motivation, 60*, 127–152.

Erceg-Hurn, David M., & Miosevich, Vikki M. (2008). Modern robust statistical methods. *American Psychologist, 63*, 591–601.

Erickson, Kirk I., Voss, Michelle W., Prakash, Ruchika S., et al. (2011). Exercise training increases size of hippocampus and improves memory. *Proceedings of the National Academy of Sciences, 108*, 3017–3022.

Ericsson, K. Anders. (2001). Attaining excellence through deliberate practice: Insights from the study of expert performance. In M. Ferrari (Ed.), *The pursuit of excellence in education*. Hillsdale, NJ: Erlbaum.

Ericsson, K. Anders, & Charness, N. (1994). Expert performance: Its structure and acquisition. *American Psychologist, 49*, 725–747.

Erikson, Erik H. (1950/1963). *Childhood and society* (2nd ed.). New York: Norton.

Erikson, Erik H. (1982). *The life cycle completed*. New York: Norton.

Ersche, Karen D., Jones, Simon, Williams, Guy B., et al. (2012, February 3). Abnormal brain structure implicated in stimulant drug addiction. *Science, 335*, 601–604.

Ervin-Tripp, Susan. (1964). Imitation and structural change in children's language. In E. H. Lenneberg (Ed.), *New directions in the study of language*. Cambridge, MA: MIT Press.

Escera, Carles, Cilveti, Robert, & Grau, Carles. (1992). Ultradian rhythms in cognitive operations: Evidence from the P300 component of the event-related potentials. *Medical Science Research, 20*, 137–138.

Eskreis-Winkler, Lauren, Shulman, Elizabeth P., Beale, Scott A., & Duckworth, Angela Lee. (2014). The grit effect: Predicting retention in the military, the workplace, school and marriage. *Frontiers in Psychology, 5,* 36.

Evans, Christopher. (1984). *Landscapes of the night* (edited and completed by Peter Evans). New York: Viking.

Evans, Gary W., Lepore, Stephen J., & Allen, Karen Mata. (2000). Cross-cultural differences in tolerance for crowding: Fact or fiction? *Journal of Personality and Social Psychology, 79,* 204–210.

Evans, Gary W., & Schamberg, Michelle A. (2009, March 30). Childhood poverty, chronic stress, and adult working memory. *Proceedings of the National Academy of Sciences, 106.*

Evans, Nicholas, & Stephen C. Levinson. (2009). The myth of language universals: Language diversity and its importance for cognitive science. *Behavioral and Brain Sciences, 32,* 429–492.

Everett, Daniel L. (2012). *Language: The cultural tool.* New York: Pantheon.

Ewart, Craig K. (1995). Self-efficacy and recovery from heart attack. In J. E. Maddux (ed.), *Self-efficacy, adaptation, and adjustment: Theory, research, and application.* New York: Plenum Press.

Ewart, Craig K., & Kolodner, Kenneth B. (1994). Negative affect, gender, and expressive style predict elevated ambulatory blood pressure in adolescents. *Journal of Personality and Social Psychology, 66,* 596–605.

Eyferth, Klaus. (1961). [The performance of different groups of the children of occupation forces on the Hamburg-Wechsler Intelligence Test for Children] *Archiv für die Gesamte Psychologie, 113,* 222–241.

Fagot, Beverly I. (1993, June). Gender role development in early childhood: Environmental input, internal construction. Invited address presented at the annual meeting of the International Academy of Sex Research, Monterey, CA.

Fagot, Beverly I., & Leinbach, Mary D. (1993). Gender-role development in young children: From discrimination to labeling. *Developmental Review, 13,* 205–224.

Fairchild, Graeme, van Goozen, Stephanie H. M., Calder, Andrew J., & Goodyer, Ian M. (2013). Research review: Evaluating and reformulating the developmental taxonomic theory of antisocial behaviour. *Journal of Child Psychology and Psychiatry, 54*(9), 924–940.

Fairholme, C. P., Boisseau, C. L., Ellard, K. K., et al. (2009). Emotions, emotion regulation, and psychological treatment: A unified perspective. In A. M. Kring & D. M. Sloan (Eds.), *Emotion regulation and psychopathology.* New York: Guilford Press.

Fallon, James H., Keator, David B., Mbogori, James, et al. (2004). Hostility differentiates the brain metabolic effects of nicotine. *Cognitive Brain Research, 18,* 142–148.

Fallone, Gahan, Acebo, Christine, Seifer, Ronald, & Carskadon, Mary A. (2005). Experimental restriction of sleep opportunity in children: Effects on teacher ratings. *Sleep, 28,* 1280–1286.

Farooqi, I. Sadaf, & O'Rahilly, Stephen. (2004). Monogenic human obesity syndromes. *Recent Progress in Hormone Research, 59,* 409–124.

Farr, Rachel H., Diamond, Lisa M., & Boker, Stephen M. (2014). Female same-sex sexuality from a dynamical systems perspective: Sexual desire, motivation, and behavior. *Archives of Sexual Behavior, 43*(8), 1477–1490.

Fausto-Sterling, Anne. (1997). Beyond difference: A biologist's perspective. *Journal of Social Issues, 53,* 233–258.

Fay, Nicolas, Lister, Casey J., Ellison, T. Mark, & Goldin-Meadow, Susan. (2014). Creating a communication system from scratch: Gesture beats vocalization hands down. *Frontiers in Psychology, 5.*

Feather, N. T. (1966). Effects of prior success and failure on expectations of success and subsequent performance. *Journal of Personality and Social Psychology, 3,* 287–298.

Fedewa, Alicia L., Black, Whitney W., & Ahn, Soyeon. (2015). Children and adolescents with same-gender parents: A meta-analytic approach in assessing outcomes. *Journal of GLBT Family Studies, 11*(1), 1–34.

Feeney, Brooke C., & Cassidy, Jude. (2003). Reconstructive memory related to adolescent-parent conflict interactions. *Journal of Personality and Social Psychology, 85,* 945–955.

Fehr, Beverley, Baldwin, Mark, Collins, Lois, et al. (1999). Anger in close relationships: An interpersonal script analysis. *Personality and Social Psychology Bulletin, 25,* 299–312.

Fehr, Ernest, & Fischbacher, Urs. (2003). The nature of human altruism. *Nature, 425,* 785–791.

Fehr, Ryan, Gelfand, Michele J., & Nag, Monisha. (2010). The road to forgiveness: A meta-analytic synthesis of its situational and dispositional correlates. *Psychological Bulletin, 136,* 894–914.

Fein, Steven, & Spencer, Steven J. (1997). Prejudice as self-image maintenance: Affirming the self through derogating others. *Journal of Personality and Social Psychology, 73,* 31–44.

Feinberg, Andrew P. (2008). Epigenetics at the epicenter of modern medicine. *Journal of the American Medical Association, 299,* 1345–1350.

Feinberg, Matthew, Willer, Robb, & Keltner, Dacher. (2012). Flustered and faithful: Embarrassment as a signal of prosociality. *Journal of Personality and Social Psychology, 102,* 81–97.

Feinstein, Justin S., Adolphs, Ralph, Damasio, Antonio, & Tranel, Daniel. (2011). The human amygdala and the induction and experience of fear. *Current Biology, 21,* 34–38.

Fellner, Jamie. (2009, June 19). Race, drugs, and law enforcement in the United States. *Stanford Law and Policy Review, 20,* 257–291.

Fennell, Christopher, & Byers-Heinlein, Krista. (2014). You sound like mommy: Bilingual and monolingual infants learn words best from speakers typical of their language environments. *International Journal of Behavioral Development, 38*(4), 309–316.

Ferguson, Christopher J. (2007). The good, the bad and the ugly: A meta-analytic review of positive and negative effects of violent video games. *Psychiatric Quarterly, 78,* 309–316.

Ferguson, Christopher J. (2009). Media violence effects: Confirmed truth or just another X-file? *Journal of Forensic Psychology Practice, 9,* 103–126.

Ferguson, Christopher J. (2013). *Adolescents, crime, and the media: A critical analysis.* New York: Springer.

Ferguson, Christopher J., & Kilburn, John. (2010). Much ado about nothing: The misestimation and overinterpretation of violent video game effects in eastern and western nations: Comment on Anderson et al. *Psychological Bulletin, 136,* 174–178.

Fernea, Elizabeth, & Fernea, Robert. (1994). Cleanliness and culture. In W. J. Lonner & Roy Malpass (Eds.), *Psychology and culture.* Boston: Allyn & Bacon.

Ferri, S., Peeters, R., Nelissen, K., Vanduffel, W., Rizzolatti, G., & Orban, G. A. (2015). A human homologue of monkey f5c. *NeuroImage, 111*, 251–266.

Feshbach, Seymour, & Tangney, June. (2008). Television viewing and aggression: Some alternative perspectives. *Perspectives on Psychological Science, 3*, 387–389.

Festinger, Leon. (1957). *A theory of cognitive dissonance.* Evanston, IL: Row, Peterson.

Festinger, Leon, Pepitone, Albert, & Newcomb, Theodore. (1952). Some consequences of deindividuation in a group. *Journal of Abnormal and Social Psychology, 47*, 382–389.

Festinger, Leon, Riecken, Henry W., & Schachter, Stanley. (1956). *When prophecy fails.* Minneapolis: University of Minnesota Press.

Fidler, Fiona, & Loftus, Geoffrey R. (2009). Why figures with error bars should replace *p* values: Some conceptual arguments and empirical demonstrations. *Journal of Psychology, 217*, 27–37.

Field, Tiffany. (2009). The effects of newborn massage: United States. In T. Field et al. (Eds.), *The newborn as a person: Enabling healthy infant development worldwide.* Hoboken, NJ: Wiley.

Fields, Chris. (2011). From "Oh, OK" to "Ah, yes" to "Aha!": Hyper-systemizing and the rewards of insight. *Personality and Individual Differences, 50*(8), 1159–1167.

Fields, R. Douglas. (2004, April). The other half of the brain. *Scientific American*, pp. 54–61.

Fine, Cordelia. (2010). From scanner to sound bite: Issues in interpreting and reporting sex differences in the brain. *Current Directions in Psychological Science, 19*, 280–283.

Fine, Ione, Wade, A. R., Brewer, A. A., et al. (2003). Long-term deprivation affects visual perception and cortex. *Nature Neuroscience, 6*, 915–916.

Finkel, Eli J. (2015, February 8). In defense of Tinder. *New York Times*, p. SR9.

Finkel, Eli J., Eastwick, Paul W., Karney, Benjamin R., et al. (2012). Online dating: A critical analysis from the perspective of psychological science. *Psychological Science in the Public Interest, 13*, 3–66.

Finney, Eva M., Fine, Ione, & Dobkins, Karen R. (2001). Visual stimuli activate auditory cortex in the deaf. *Nature Neuroscience, 4*, 1171–1173.

Fins, Joseph J., Mayberg, Helen S., Nuttin, Bart, et al. (2011). Misuse of the FDA's humanitarian device exemption in deep brain stimulation for obsessive-compulsive disorder. *Health Affairs, 30*, 302–311.

Fischer, Pamela C., Smith, Randy J., Leonard, Elizabeth, et al. (1993). Sex differences on affective dimensions: Continuing examination. *Journal of Counseling and Development, 71*, 440–443.

Fischer, Peter, Krueger, Joachim I., Greitemeyer, Tobias, et al. (2011). The bystander-effect: A meta-analytic review on bystander intervention in dangerous and non-dangerous emergencies. *Psychological Bulletin, 137*, 517–537.

Fischhoff, Baruch. (1975). Hindsight is not equal to foresight: The effect of outcome knowledge on judgment under uncertainty. *Journal of Experimental Psychology: Human Perception and Performance, 1*, 288–299.

Fitzgerald, Daniel A., Arnold, Jennifer F., Becker, Eni S., et al. (2011). How mood challenges emotional memory formation: An fMRI investigation. *NeuroImage, 56*, 1783–1790.

Fitzgerald, Ryan J., Oriet, Chris, & Price, Heather L. (2015). Suspect filler similarity in eyewitness lineups: A literature review and a novel methodology. *Law and Human Behavior, 39*(1), 62–74.

Fivush, Robyn, & Nelson, Katherine. (2004). Culture and language in the emergence of autobiographical memory. *Psychological Science, 15*, 573–582.

Flavell, John H. (1999). Cognitive development: Children's knowledge about the mind. *Annual Review of Psychology, 50*, 21–45.

Fleeson, William. (2004). Moving personality beyond the person-situation debate. *Current Directions in Psychological Science, 13*, 83–87.

Flynn, James R. (1987). Massive IQ gains in 14 nations: What IQ tests really measure. *Psychological Bulletin, 95*, 29–51.

Flynn, James R. (2013). The "Flynn Effect" and Flynn's paradox. *Intelligence, 41*(6), 851–857.

Flynn-Evans, Erin E., Tabandeh, Homayoun, Skene, Debra J., & Lockley, Steven W. (2014). Circadian rhythm disorders and melatonin production in 127 blindwomen with and without light perception. *Journal of Biological Rhythms, 29*(3), 215–224.

Fogassi, Leonardo, & Ferrari, Pier Francesco. (2007). Mirror neurons and the evolution of embodied language. *Current Directions in Psychological Science, 16*, 136–141.

Folkman, Susan, & Moskowitz, Judith T. (2000). Positive affect and the other side of coping. *American Psychologist, 55*, 647–654.

Forbes, Gordon, Zhang, Xiaoying, Doroszewicz, Krystyna, & Haas, Kelly. (2009). Relationships between individualism-collectivism, gender, and direct or indirect aggression: A study in China, Poland, and the US. *Aggressive Behavior, 35*, 24–30.

Forgas, Joseph P. (1998). On being happy and mistaken: Mood effects on the fundamental attribution error. *Journal of Personality and Social Psychology, 75*, 318–331.

Forgas, Joseph P., & Bond, Michael H. (1985). Cultural influences on the perception of interaction episodes. *Personality and Social Psychology Bulletin, 11*, 75–88.

Foster, Jeffrey L., Huthwaite, Thomas, Yesberg, Julia A., et al. (2012). Repetition, not number of sources, increases both susceptibility to misinformation and confidence in the accuracy of eyewitnesses. *Acta Psychologica, 139*, 320–326.

Foulkes, David. (1962). Dream reports from different states of sleep. *Journal of Abnormal and Social Psychology, 65*, 14–25.

Foulkes, David. (1999). *Children's dreaming and the development of consciousness.* Cambridge, MA: Harvard University Press.

Foulkes, David, & Domhoff, G. William. (2014). Bottom-up or top-down in dream neuroscience?: A top-down critique of two bottom-up studies. *Consciousness and Cognition: An International Journal, 27*, 168–171.

Fouts, Roger S., & Rigby, Randall L. (1977). Man–chimpanzee communication. In T. A. Seboek (Ed.), *How animals communicate.* Bloomington: University of Indiana Press.

Fouts, Roger S. (with Stephen T. Mills). (1997). *Next of kin: What chimpanzees have taught me about who we are.* New York: Morrow.

Fox, Mary Kay, Pac, Susan, Devaney, Barbara, & Jankowski, Linda. (2004). Feeding Infants and Toddlers Study: What foods are infants and toddlers eating? *Journal of the American Dietetic Association, 104*, 22–30.

Fox, Nathan A., Henderson, Heather A., Marshall, Peter J., et al. (2005a). Behavioral inhibition: Linking biology and behavior within a developmental framework. *Annual Review of Psychology, 56,* 235–262.

Fox, Nathan A., Nichols, Kate E., Henderson, Heather A., et al. (2005b). Evidence for a gene-environment interaction in predicting behavioral inhibition in middle childhood. *Psychological Science, 16,* 921–926.

Fréchette, Sabrina, Zoratti, Michael, & Romano, Elisa. (2015). What is the link between corporal punishment and child physical abuse? *Journal of Family Violence, 30*(2), 135–148.

Fraga, Mario F., Ballestar, Esteban, Paz, Maria F., et al. (2005). Epigenetic differences arise during the lifetime of monozygotic twins. *Proceedings of the National Academy of Sciences, 102,* 10604–10609.

Fraley, R. Chris, Vicary, Amanda M., Brumbaugh, Claudia C., & Roisman, Glenn I. (2011). Patterns of stability in adult attachment: An empirical test of two models of continuity and change. *Journal of Personality and Social Psychology, 101,* 974–992.

Frances, Allen. (2013). The new crisis of confidence in psychiatric diagnosis. *Annals of Internal Medicine, 159*(3), 221–222.

Frankl, Viktor E. (1955). *The doctor and the soul: An introduction to logotherapy.* New York: Knopf.

Frans, Emma M., Sandin, Sven, Reichenberg, Abraham, et al. (2008). Advancing paternal age and bipolar disorder. *Archives of General Psychiatry, 65,* 1034–1040.

Frasure-Smith, Nancy, & Lespérance, Francois. (2005). Depression and coronary heart disease: Complex synergism of mind, body, and environment. *Current Directions in Psychological Science, 14,* 39–43.

Frasure-Smith, Nancy, Lespérance, Francois, Juneau, M., Talajic, M., & Bourassa, M. G. (1999). Gender, depression, and one-year prognosis after myocardial infarction. *Psychosomatic Medicine, 61,* 26–37.

Frayling, Timothy M., Timpson, Nicholas J., Weedon, Michael N., et al. (2007, May 11). A common variant in the *FTO* gene is associated with body mass index and predisposes to childhood and adult obesity. *Science, 316,* 889–894.

Frazier, Patricia. (2003). Perceived control and distress following sexual assault: A longitudinal test of a new model. *Journal of Personality and Social Psychology, 84,* 1257–1269.

Frazier, Patricia, Keenan, Nora, Anders, Samantha, et al. (2011). Perceived past, present, and future control and adjustment to stressful life events. *Journal of Personality and Social Psychology, 100,* 749–765.

Frensch, Peter A., & Rünger, Dennis. (2003). Implicit learning. *Current Directions in Psychological Science, 12,* 13–18.

Freud, Anna. (1967). *Ego and the mechanisms of defense* (The writings of Anna Freud, Vol. 2) (rev. ed.). New York: International Universities Press.

Freud, Sigmund. (1900/1953). The interpretation of dreams. In J. Strachey (Ed.), *The standard edition of the complete psychological works of Sigmund Freud* (Vols. 4 and 5). London: Hogarth Press.

Freud, Sigmund. (1905a). Fragment of an analysis of a case of hysteria. In J. Strachey (Ed. and Trans.), *Standard edition of the complete psychological works of Sigmund Freud* (Vol. 7). London: Hogarth Press.

Freud, Sigmund. (1905b). Three essays on the theory of sexuality. In J. Strachey (Ed.), *Standard edition* (Vol. 7). London: Hogarth Press.

Freud, Sigmund. (1920/1960). *A general introduction to psychoanalysis* (Joan Riviere, trans.). New York: Washington Square Press.

Freud, Sigmund. (1923/1962). *The ego and the id* (Joan Riviere, trans.). New York: Norton.

Freud, Sigmund. (1961). *Letters of Sigmund Freud, 1873–1939.* Edited by Ernst L. Freud. London: Hogarth Press.

Frick, Paul J., & Viding, Essi. (2009). Antisocial behavior from a developmental psychopathology perspective. *Development and Psychopathology, 21,* 1111–1131.

Fridlund, Alan J. (1994). *Human facial expression: An evolutionary view.* San Diego: Academic Press.

Fridlund, Alan J., Beck, Hall P., Goldie, William D., & Irons, Gary. (2012). Little Albert: A neurologically impaired child. *History of Psychology, 15,* 302–327.

Friedler, Brett, Crapser, Joshua, & McCullough, Louise. (2015). One is the deadliest number: The detrimental effects of social isolation on cerebrovascular diseases and cognition. *Acta Neuropathologica, 129*(4), 493–509.

Friedman, Howard S., & Martin, Leslie R. (2011). *The longevity project.* New York: Hudson Street Press.

Friedrich, William, Fisher, Jennifer, Broughton, Daniel, et al. (1998). Normative sexual behavior in children: A contemporary sample. *Pediatrics, 101,* 1–8. See also www.pediatrics.org/cgi/content/full/101/4/e9.

Frijda, Nico H., Kuipers, Peter, & ter Schure, Elisabeth. (1989). Relations among emotion, appraisal, and emotional action readiness. *Journal of Personality and Social Psychology, 57,* 212–228.

Frome, Pamela M., & Eccles, Jacquelynne S. (1998). Parents' influence on children's achievement-related perceptions. *Journal of Personality and Social Psychology, 74,* 435–452.

Fromer, Menachem, Pocklington, Andrew J., Kavanagh, David H., Williams, Hywel J., Dwyer, Sarah, Gormle, Padhraig, et al. (2014). *De novo* mutations in schizophrenia implicate synaptic networks. *Nature, 506,* 179–184.

Frye, Richard E., Schwartz, B. S., & Doty, Richard L. (1990). Dose-related effects of cigarette smoking on olfactory function. *Journal of the American Medical Association, 263,* 1233–1236.

Fryer, Roland G. (2011). Financial incentives and student achievement: Evidence from randomized trials. *Quarterly Journal of Economics, 126,* 1755–1798.

Fuchs, C. S., Stampfer, M. J., Colditz, G. A., et al. (1995, May 11). Alcohol consumption and mortality among women. *New England Journal of Medicine, 332,* 1245–1250.

Fulmer, C. Ashley, Gelfand, Michele J., Kruglanski, Arie W., et al. (2010). On "feeling right" in cultural contexts: How person-culture match affects self-esteem and subjective well-being. *Psychological Science, 21,* 1563–1569.

Gabbert, Charles, Donohue, Michael, Arnold, John, & Schwimmer, Jeffrey B. (2010, September 20). Adenovirus 36 and obesity in children and adolescents. *Pediatrics,* published online at http://pediatrics.aappublications.org/content/early/2010/09/20/peds.2009-3362.

Gable, Shelly L., & Haidt, Jonathan. (2005). What (and why) is positive psychology? *Review of General Psychology, 9,* 103–110.

Gable, Shelly L., & Poore, Joshua. (2008). Which thoughts count? Algorithms for evaluating satisfaction in relationships. *Psychological Science, 19,* 1030–1036.

Gabriel, Allison S., Daniels, Michael A., Diefendorff, James M., & Greguras, Gary J. (2015). Emotional labor actors: A latent profile analysis of emotional labor strategies. *Journal of Applied Psychology, 100*(3), 863–879.

Gaddy, Melinda A., & Ingram, Rick E. (2014). A meta-analytic review of mood-congruent implicit memory in depressed mood. *Clinical Psychology Review, 34*(5), 402–416.

Gaertner, Samuel L., Mann, Jeffrey A., Dovidio, John F., et al. (1990). How does cooperation reduce intergroup bias? *Journal of Personality and Social Psychology, 59*, 692–704.

Gagnon, John, & Simon, William. (1973). *Sexual conduct: The social sources of human sexuality*. Chicago: Aldine.

Gal, David, & Rucker, Derek D. (2010). When in doubt, shout! Paradoxical influences of doubt on proselytizing. *Psychological Science, 21*, 1701–1707.

Galanter, Eugene. (1962). Contemporary psychophysics. In R. Brown, E. Galanter, H. Hess, & G. Mandler (Eds.), *New directions in psychology*. New York: Holt, Rinehart & Winston.

Galatzer-Levy, Isaac R., & Bryant, Richard A. (2013).636, 120 ways to have a posttraumatic stress disorder. *Perspectives on Psychological Science, 8*(6), 651–662.

Galinsky, Adena M., & Sonenstein, Freya Lund. (2013). Relationship commitment, perceived equity, and sexual enjoyment among young adults in the United States. *Archives of Sexual Behavior, 42*(1), 93–104.

Gallant, Sheryle J., Hamilton, Jean A., Popiel, Debra A., et al. (1991). Daily moods and symptoms: Effects of awareness of study focus, gender, menstrual-cycle phase, and day of the week. *Health Psychology, 10*, 180–189.

Gallese, Vittorio, Gernsbacher, Morton Ann, Heyes, Cecilia, et al. (2011). Mirror neuron forum. *Perspectives on Psychological Science, 6*, 369–407.

Gallo, Linda C., & Matthews, Karen A. (2003). Understanding the association between socioeconomic status and physical health: Do negative emotions play a role? *Psychological Bulletin, 129*, 10–51.

Galotti, Kathleen M. (2007). Decision structuring in important real-life choices. *Psychological Science, 18*, 320–325.

Galotti, Kathleen M., Wiener, Hillary J. D., & Tandler, Jane M. (2014). Real-life decision making in college students I: Consistency across specific decisions. *The American Journal of Psychology, 127*(1), 19–31.

Gan, Yong, Gong, Y., Tong, X., Sun, H., Cong, Y., Dong, X., et al. (2014). Depression and the risk of coronary heart disease: A meta-analysis of prospective cohort studies. *BMC Psychiatry, 14*, 371.

Ganis, Giorgio. (2015). Deception detection using neuroimaging. In Pär Anders Granhag; Aldert Vrij; & Bruno Verschuere (Eds.), Detecting deception: Current challenges and cognitive approaches (pp. 105-121). New York: Wiley-Blackwell.

Garbarino, James, & Bedard, Claire. (2001). *Parents under siege*. New York: Free Press.

Garcia, John, & Gustavson, Carl R. (1997, January). Carl R. Gustavson (1946–1996): Pioneering wildlife psychologist. *APS Observer*, pp. 34–35.

Garcia, John, & Koelling, Robert A. (1966). Relation of cue to consequence in avoidance learning. *Psychonomic Science, 4*, 23–124.

Garcia-Sierra, Adrian, Rivera-Gaxiola, Maritza, Percaccio, Cherie R., et al. (2011). Bilingual language learning: An ERP study relating early brain responses to speech, language input, and later word production. *Journal of Phonetics, 39*, 546–557.

Gardner, Howard. (1983). *Frames of mind: The theory of multiple intelligences*. New York: Basic Books.

Gardner, Howard. (2011). The theory of multiple intelligences. In Morton Ann Gernsbacher, R.W. Pew, L.M. Hough, & J.R. Pomerantz (Eds.), *Psychology and the real world: Essays illustrating fundamental contributions to society* (pp. 122–130). New York: Worth.

Gardner, R. Allen, & Gardner, Beatrice T. (1969). Teaching sign language to a chimpanzee. *Science, 165*, 664–672.

Garmezy, Norman. (1991). Resilience and vulnerability to adverse developmental outcomes associated with poverty. *American Behavioral Scientist, 34*, 416–430.

Garry, Maryanne, Manning, Charles G., Loftus, Elizabeth F., & Sherman, Steven J. (1996). Imagination inflation: Imagining a childhood event inflates confidence that it occurred. *Psychonomic Bulletin and Review, 3*, 208–214.

Garry, Maryanne, & Polaschek, Devon L. L. (2000). Imagination and memory. *Current Directions in Psychological Science, 9*, 6–10.

Garven, Sena, Wood, James M., Malpass, Roy S., & Shaw, John S., III. (1998). More than suggestion: The effect of interviewing techniques from the McMartin Preschool case. *Journal of Applied Psychology, 83*, 347–359.

Gasser, Peter, Kirchner, Katharina, & Passie, Torsten. (2015). LSD-assisted psychotherapy for anxiety associated with a life-threatening disease: A qualitative study of acute and sustained subjective effects. *Journal of Psychopharmacology, 29*(1), 57–68.

Gatz, Margaret. (2007). Genetics, dementia, and the elderly. *Current Directions in Psychological Science, 16*, 123–127.

Gautam, Prapti, Lebel, Catherine, Narr, Katherine L., Mattson, Sarah N., May, Philip A., Adnams, Colleen M., et al. (2015). Volume changes and brain-behavior relationships in white matter and subcortical gray matter in children with prenatalalcohol exposure. *Human Brain Mapping, 36*(6), 2318–2329.

Gauthier, Irene, Skudlarksi, P., Gore, J. C., & Anderson, A. W. (2000). Expertise for cars and birds recruits brain areas involved in face recognition. *Nature Neuroscience, 3*, 191–197.

Gawande, Atul. (1998, September 21). The pain perplex. *The New Yorker*, pp. 86, 88, 90, 92–94.

Gawande, Atul. (2009, March 30). Hellhole. *The New Yorker*, pp. 36–45.

Gazzaniga, Michael S. (1967). The split brain in man. *Scientific American, 217*(2), 24–29.

Gazzaniga, Michael S. (1988). *Mind matters*. Boston: Houghton-Mifflin.

Gazzaniga, Michael S. (1989). Organization of the human brain. *Science, 245*, 947–952.

Gazzaniga, Michael S. (2005). *The ethical brain*. Washington, DC: Dana Press.

Gazzaniga, Michael S. (2008). *Human: The science behind what makes us unique*. New York: Ecco/Harper Collins.

Geers, Andrew L., Wellman, Justin A., & Lassiter, G. Daniel. (2009). Dispositional optimism and engagement: The moderating influence of goal prioritization. *Journal of Personality and Social Psychology, 96,* 913–932.

Gelbard-Sagiv, H., Mukamel, R., Harel, M., et al. (2008, October 3). Internally generated reactivation of single neurons in human hippocampus during free recall. *Science, 322,* 96–101.

Gentile, Brittany, Grabe, Shleey, Dolan-Pascoe, Brenda, et al. (2009). Gender differences in domain-specific self-esteem: A meta-analysis. *Review of General Psychology, 13,* 34–45.

Gentner, Dedre, & Goldin-Meadow, Susan (Eds.). (2003). *Language in mind: Advances in the study of language and thought.* Cambridge: MIT Press.

Gentner, Dedre, Özyürek, Asli, Gürcanli, Özge, & Goldin-Meadow, Susan. (2013). Spatial language facilitates spatial cognition: Evidence from children who lack language input. *Cognition, 127*(3), 318–330.

George, Linda G., Helson, Ravenna, & John, Oliver P. (2011). The "CEO" of women's work lives: How Big Five conscientiousness, extraversion, and openness predict 50 years of work experiences in a changing sociocultural context. *Journal of Personality and Social Psychology, 101,* 812–830.

George, Mark S., & Post, Robert M. (2011). Daily left prefrontal repetitive transcranial magnetic stimulation for acute treatment of medication-resistant depression. *The American Journal of Psychiatry, 168,* 356–364.

Gerken, Louann A., Wilson, Rachel, & Lewis, William. (2005). Infants can use distributional cues to form syntactic categories. *Journal of Child Language, 32,* 249–268.

Gershoff, Elizabeth T. (2002). Parental corporal punishment and associated child behaviors and experiences: A meta-analytic and theoretical review. *Psychological Bulletin, 128,* 539–579.

Gibbs, Robert B. (2010). Estrogen therapy and cognition: A review of the cholinergic hypothesis. *Endocrine Review, 31,* 224–253.

Gibson, Eleanor, & Walk, Richard. (1960). The "visual cliff." *Scientific American, 202,* 80–92.

Giesbrecht, Timo, Lynn, Steven Jay, Lilienfeld, Scott O., & Merckelbach, Harald. (2008). Cognitive processes in dissociation: An analysis of core theoretical assumptions. *Psychological Bulletin, 134,* 617–647.

Gigerenzer, Gerd, Gaissmaier, Wolfgang, Kurz-Milcke, Elke, et al. (2008) Helping doctors and patients make sense of health statistics. *Psychological Science in the Public Interest, 8,* 53–96.

Gilbert, Daniel T. (2006a, July 2). If only gay sex caused global warming. *Los Angeles Times,* Comment section, M1, M6.

Gilbert, Daniel T. (2006b). *Stumbling on happiness.* New York: Knopf.

Gilbert, Daniel T., & Malone, Patrick S. (1995). The correspondence bias. *Psychological Bulletin, 117*(1), 21–38.

Gilbertson, Mark W., Shenton, Martha E., Ciszewski, Aleksandra, et al. (2002). Hippocampal volume predicts pathologic vulnerability to psychological trauma. *Nature Neuroscience, 5,* 1242–1247.

Gilchrist, Amanda L., & Cowan, Nelson. (2012). Chunking. In V. Ramachandran (Ed.), *Encyclopedia of human behavior* (Vol. 1). San Diego: Academic Press.

Gilestro, Giorgio F., Tononi, Giulio, & Cirelli, Chiara. (2009). Widespread changes in synaptic markers as a function of sleep and wakefulness in *Drosophila. Science, 324,* 109–112.

Gillath, Omri, Shaver, Phillip R., Baek, Jong-Min, & Chun, David S. (2008). Genetic correlates of adult attachment style. *Personality and Social Psychology Bulletin, 34,* 1396–1405.

Gilman, Charlotte Perkins. (1911). *The man-made world; or, our androcentric culture.* New York: Charlton.

Ginges, Jeremy, & Atran, Scott. (2011). Psychology out of the laboratory: The challenge of violent extremism. *American Psychologist, 66,* 507–519.

Ginty, Annie T., & Conklin, Sarah M. (2012). Preliminary evidence that acute long-chain omega-3 supplementation reduces cardiovascular reactivity to mental stress: A randomized and placebo controlled trial. *Biological Psychology, 89,* 269–272.

Gitler, Aaron D. (2011, November 4). Another reason to exercise. *Science, 334,* 606–607.

Gladwell, Malcolm. (2004, September 20). Personality plus. *The New Yorker,* pp. 42–48.

Glaser, Gabrielle. (2014, July 6). A different way to tame a constant adversary. *New York Times,* p. MB1.

Gleaves, David H. (1996). The sociocognitive model of dissociative identity disorder: A reexamination of the evidence. *Psychological Bulletin, 120,* 42–59.

Glick, Peter, & Fiske, Susan T. (2012). An ambivalent alliance: Hostile and benevolent sexism as complementary justifications for gender inequality. In John Dixon & Mark Levine (Eds.), *Beyond prejudice: Extending the social psychology of conflict, inequality and social change* (pp. 70–88). New York: Cambridge University Press.

Glick, Peter, Fiske, Susan T., Mladinic, Antonio, et al. (2000). Beyond prejudice as simple antipathy: Hostile and benevolent sexism across cultures. *Journal of Personality and Social Psychology, 79,* 763–775.

Glick, Peter, Lameiras, Maria, Fiske, Susan T., et al. (2004). Bad but bold: Ambivalent attitudes toward men predict gender inequality in sixteen nations. *Journal of Personality and Social Psychology, 86,* 713–728.

Golden, Robert M., Gaynes, Bradley N., Ekstrom, R. David, et al. (2005). The efficacy of light therapy in the treatment of mood disorders: A review and meta-analysis of the evidence. *American Journal of Psychiatry, 162,* 656–662.

Golder, Scott A., & Macy, Michael W. (2011). Diurnal and seasonal mood vary with work, sleep, and daylength across diverse cultures. *Science, 333,* 1878–1881.

Goldin-Meadow, Susan. (2003). *The resilience of language.* New York: Psychology Press.

Goldin-Meadow, Susan, Cook, Susan W., & Mitchell, Zachary A. (2009). Gesturing gives children new ideas about math. *Psychological Science, 20,* 267–272.

Goldman-Rakic, Patricia S. (1996). Opening the mind through neurobiology. Invited address at the annual meeting of the American Psychological Association, Toronto, Canada.

Goldstein, Jill M., Seidman, Larry J., Horton, Nicholas J., et al. (2001). Normal sexual dimorphism of the adult human brain assessed by in vivo magnetic resonance imaging. *Cerebral Cortex, 11,* 490–497.

Goldstein, Michael, & Miklowitz, David. (1995). The effectiveness of psychoeducational family therapy in the treatment of schizophrenic disorders. *Journal of Marital and Family Therapy, 21,* 361–376.

Goldstein, Noah J., Cialdini, Robert B., & Griskevicius, Vladas. (2008). A room with a viewpoint: Using social norms to motivate environmental conservation in hotels. *Journal of Consumer Research, 35,* 472–482.

Goldston, David B., Molock, Sherry D., Whitbeck, Leslie B., et al. (2008). Cultural considerations in adolescent suicide prevention and psychosocial treatment. *American Psychologist, 63,* 14–31.

Golinkoff, Roberta M., & Hirsh-Pasek, Kathy. (2006). Baby wordsmith: From associationist to social sophisticate. *Current Directions in Psychological Science, 15,* 30–33.

Golub, Sharon. (1992). *Periods: From menarche to menopause.* Newbury Park, CA: Sage.

Gomory, Tomi, Wong, Stephen E., Cohen, David, & Lacasse, Jeffrey R. (2011, December). Clinical social work and the biomedical industrial complex. *Journal of Sociology and Social Welfare, 38.* Available at www.wmich.edu/hhs/newsletters_journals/jssw/38-4.html.

Gonsalves, Brian D., & Cohen, Neal J. (2010) Brain imaging, cognitive processes, and brain networks. *Perspectives on Psychological Science, 5,* 744–752.

Gonzaga, Gian C., Turner, Rebecca A., Keltner, Dacher, et al. (2006). Romantic love and sexual desire in close relationships. *Emotion, 6,* 163–179.

Good, Catherine, Aronson, Joshua, & Harder, Jayne A. (2008). Problems in the pipeline: Stereotype threat and women's achievement in high-level math courses. *Journal of Applied Developmental Psychology, 29,* 17–28.

Goode, Erica. (2003, May 6). Experts see mind's voices in new light. *The New York Times,* Science Times, pp. D1, D4.

Gopnik, Alison. (2009). *The philosophical baby.* New York: Farrar, Straus & Giroux.

Gopnik, Alison, Griffiths, Thomas L., & Lucas, Christopher G. (2015). When younger learners can be better (or at least more open-minded) than older ones. *Current Directions in Psychological Science, 24*(2), 87–92.

Gopnik, Myrna, Choi, Sooja, & Baumberger, Therese. (1996). Cross-linguistic differences in early semantic and cognitive development. *Cognitive Development, 11,* 197–227.

Goriely, Anne, McGrath, John J., Hultman, Christina M., Wilkie, Andrew O. M., & Malaspina, Dolores. (2013)."Selfish spermatogonial selection": A novel mechanism for the association between advanced paternal age and neurodevelopmental disorders. *American Journal of Psychiatry, 170*(6), 599–608.

Gosling, Samuel D. (2009). *Snoop: What your stuff says about you.* New York: Basic Books.

Gosling, Samuel D., Kwan, Virginia S. Y., & John, Oliver P. (2003). A dog's got personality: A cross-species comparative approach to personality judgments in dogs and humans. *Journal of Personality and Social Psychology, 85,* 1161–1169.

Gosling, Samuel D., Rentfrow, P. J., & Swann, William B., Jr. (2003). A very brief measure of the Big Five personality domains. *Journal of Research in Personality, 37,* 504–528.

Gosling, Samuel D., Vazire, Simine, Srivatava, Sanjay, & John, Oliver P. (2004). Should we trust web-based studies? A comparative analysis of six preconceptions about Internet questionnaires. *American Psychologist, 59,* 93–104.

Gotlib, Ian H., Joormann, Jutta, Minor, Kelly L., & Hallmayer, Joachim. (2008). HPA axis reactivity: A mechanism underlying the associations among 5-HTTLPR, stress, and depression. *Biological Psychiatry, 63,* 847–851.

Gottesman, Irving. (1991). *Schizophrenia genesis: The origins of madness.* New York: Freeman.

Gottesman, Irving, Laursen, Thomas M., Bertelsen, Aksel, & Mortensen, Preben B. (2010). Severe mental disorders in offspring with 2 psychiatrically ill parents. *Archives of General Psychiatry, 67,* 252–257.

Gottfredson, Linda S. (2002). g: Highly general and highly practical. In R. J. Sternberg & E. L. Grigorenko (Eds.), *The general intelligence factor: How general is it?* Mahwah, NJ: Erlbaum.

Gougoux, Frederic, Zatorre, Robert J., Lassonde, Maryse, et al. (2005). A functional neuroimaging study of sound localization: Visual cortex activity predicts performance in early-blind individuals. *PloS Biology, 3,* 324–333.

Gould, Stephen Jay. (1987). *An urchin in the storm.* New York: W. W. Norton.

Gould, Stephen Jay. (1994, November 28). Curveball. [Review of *The Bell Curve,* by Richard J. Herrnstein and Charles Murray.] *The New Yorker,* 139–149.

Grabe, Shelly, & Hyde, Janet S. (2006). Ethnicity and body dissatisfaction among women in the United States: A meta-analysis. *Psychological Bulletin, 132,* 622–640.

Grabe, Shelly, Ward, L. Monique, & Hyde, Janet S. (2008). The role of the media in body image concerns among women: A meta-analysis of experimental and correlational studies. *Psychological Bulletin, 134,* 460–476.

Graeber, Manuel B., & Streit, Wolfgang J. (2010). Microglia: Biology and pathology. *Acta Neuropathologica, 119,* 89–105.

Graff, Kaitlin, Murnen, Sarah K., & Smolak, Linda. (2012). Too sexualized to be taken seriously? Perceptions of a girl in childlike vs. sexualizing clothing. *Sex Roles, 66*(11–12), 764–775.

Graham, Jesse, Haidt, Jonathan, & Nosek, Brian A. (2009). Liberals and conservatives rely on different sets of moral foundations. *Journal of Personality and Social Psychology, 96,* 1029–1046.

Graham, Jill W. (1986). Principled organizational dissent: A theoretical essay. *Research in Organizational Behavior, 8,* 1–52.

Grandin, Temple. (2010). *Thinking in pictures: My life with autism* (Rev. ed.). New York: Vintage.

Grant, Heidi, & Dweck, Carol S. (2003). Clarifying achievement goals and their impact. *Journal of Personality and Social Psychology, 85,* 541–553.

Grant, Igor, Gonzalez, Raul, Carey, Catherine L., et al. (2003). Nonacute (residual) neurocognitive effects of cannabis use: A meta-analytic study. *Journal of the International Neuropsychological Society, 9,* 679–689.

Gray, Kurt, & Wegner, Daniel M. (2008). The sting of intentional pain. *Psychological Science, 19*, 1260–1261.

Greely, Henry, & Illes, Judy. (2007). Neuroscience-based lie detection: The urgent need for regulation. *American Journal of Law and Medicine, 35*.

Greely, Henry, Sahakian, Barbara, Harris, John, et al. (2008). Towards responsible use of cognitive-enhancing drugs by the healthy. *Nature, 455*, 702–705.

Green, Joseph P., & Lynn, Steven J. (2010). Hypnotic responsiveness: Expectancy, attitudes, fantasy proneness, absorption, and gender. *Clinical and Experimental Hypnosis, 59*, 103–121.

Greenberg, Rosalie. (2008). *Bipolar kids: Helping your child find calm in the mood storm*. Boston: Da Capo Press.

Greenberger, Ellen, Lessard, Jared, Chen, Chuansheng, & Farruggia, Susan P. (2008). Self-entitled college students: Contributions of personality, parenting, and motivational factors. *Journal of Youth and Adolescence, 37*, 1193–1204.

Greenough, William T. (1984). Structural correlates of information storage in the mammalian brain: A review and hypothesis. *Trends in Neurosciences, 7*, 229–233.

Greenough, William T., & Black, James E. (1992). Induction of brain structure by experience: Substrates for cognitive development. In M. Gunnar & C. A. Nelson (Eds.), *Behavioral developmental neuroscience: Vol. 24. Minnesota Symposia on Child Psychology*. Hillsdale, NJ: Erlbaum.

Greenwald, Anthony G., McGhee, Debbie E., & Schwartz, Jordan L. K. (1998). Measuring individual differences in implicit cognition: The Implicit Association Test. *Journal of Personality and Social Psychology, 74*, 1464–1480.

Greenwald, Anthony G., Poehlman, T. Andrew, Uhlmann, Eric L., & Banaji, Mahzarin R. (2009). Understanding and using the Implicit Association Test: III. Meta-analysis of predictive validity. *Journal of Personality and Social Psychology, 97*, 17–41.

Greenwald, Anthony G., Spangenberg, Eric R., Pratkanis, Anthony R., & Eskenazi, Jay. (1991). Double-blind tests of subliminal self-help audiotapes. *Psychological Science, 2*, 119–122.

Gregg, L., & Tarrier, N. (2007). Virtual reality in mental health: A review of the literature. *Social Psychiatry and Psychiatric Epidemiology, 42*, 343–54.

Gregory, Richard L. (1963). Distortion of visual space as inappropriate constancy scaling. *Nature, 199*, 678–679.

Greitemeyer, Tobias. (2015). When bystanders increase rather than decrease intentions to help. *Social Psychology, 46*(2), 116–119.

Griffin, Donald R. (2001). *Animal minds: Beyond cognition to consciousness*. Chicago: University of Chicago Press.

Griffiths, R. R., Richards, W. A., Johnson, M. W., et al. (2008). Mystical-type experiences occasioned by psilocybin mediate the attribution of personal meaning and spiritual significance fourteen months later. *Journal of Psychopharmacology, 22*, 621–632.

Grimshaw, Gina M., Kwasny, Kristin M., Covell, Ed, & Johnson, Ryan A. (2003). The dynamic nature of language lateralization: Effects of lexical and prosodic factors. *Neuropsychologia, 41*, 1008–1019.

Grinspoon, Lester, & Bakalar, James B. (1993). *Marihuana, the forbidden medicine*. New Haven, CT: Yale University Press.

Griskevicius, Vladas, Haselton, Martie G., & Ackerman, Joshua M. (2015). Evolution and close relationships. In Mario Miculincer, Philip R. Shaver, Jeffrey A. Simpson, & John F. Dovidio (Eds.), *APA handbook of personality and social psychology: Volume 3.Interpersonal relations* (pp. 3–32). Washington, DC: American Psychological Association.

Grob, Charles S., Danfroth, Alicia L., Chopra, Gurpreet S., et al. (2011). Pilot study of psilocybin treatment for anxiety in patients with advanced-stage cancer. *Archives General Psychiatry, 68*, 71–78.

Gross, James J. (1998). The emerging field of emotion regulation: An integrative review. *Review of General Psychology, 2*, 271–299.

Grossman, Michele, & Wood, Wendy. (1993). Sex differences in intensity of emotional experience: A social role interpretation. *Journal of Personality and Social Psychology, 65*, 1010–1022.

Groves, R. M., Mosher, W. D., Lepkowski, J., & Kirgis, N. G. (2009). Planning and development of the continuous National Survey of Family Growth. National Center for Health Statistics. *Vital Health Statistics, 1*(48). Available from www.cdc.gov/nchs/data/series/sr_01/sr01_048.pdf.

Guilford, J. P. (1988). Some changes in the structure-of-intellect model. *Educational and Psychological Measurement, 48*, 1–4.

Gur, R. E., Maany, V., Mozley, P. D., et al. (1998). Subcortical MRI volumes in neuroleptic-naive and treated patients with schizophrenia. *American Journal of Psychiatry, 155*, 1711–1717.

Gur, Ruben C., Gunning-Dixon, Faith, Bilker, Wareen B., & Gur, Raquel E. (2002). Sex differences in temporo-limbic and frontal brain volumes of healthy adults. *Cerebral Cortex, 12*, 998–1003.

Gustavson, Carl R., Garcia, John, Hankins, Walter G., & Rusiniak, Kenneth W. (1974). Coyote predation control by aversive conditioning. *Science, 184*, 581–583.

Güth, Werner, & Kocher, Martin G. (2014). More than thirty years of ultimatum bargaining experiments: Motives, variations, and a survey of the recent literature. *Journal of Economic Behavior and Organization, 108*, 396–409.

Guthrie, Paul C., & Mobley, Brenda D. (1994). A comparison of the differential diagnostic efficiency of three personality disorder inventories. *Journal of Clinical Psychology, 50*, 656–665.

Guthrie, Robert. (1976). *Even the rat was white: A historical view of psychology*. New York: Harper & Row.

Guzman-Marin, Ruben, Suntsova, Natalia, Methippara, Melvi, et al. (2005). Sleep deprivation suppresses neurogenesis in the adult hippocampus of rats. *European Journal of Neuroscience, 22*, 2111–2116.

Haber, Ralph N. (1970, May). How we remember what we see. *Scientific American, 222*, 104–112.

Hacking, Ian. (1995). *Rewriting the soul: Multiple personality and the sciences of memory*. Princeton, NJ: Princeton University Press.

Hafer, Caorlyn L., & Rubel, Alicia N. (2015). Long-term focus and prosocial–antisocial tendencies interact to predict belief in just world. *Personality and Individual Differences, 75*, 121–124.

Hagberg, B., & Samuelsson, G. (2008). Survival after 100 years of age: A multivariate model of exceptional survival in Swedish centenarians. *Journals of Gerontology. Series A (Biological Sciences and Medical Sciences), 63*, 1219–1226.

Hager, Joseph C., & Ekman, Paul. (1979). Long-distance transmission of facial affect signals. *Ethology and Sociobiology, 1*, 77–82.

Hahn, Robert, Fuqua-Whitley, Dawna, Wethington, Holly, et al. (2008). Effectiveness of universal school-based programs to prevent violent and aggressive behaviour: A systematic review. *Child: Care, Health, and Development, 34*, 139.

Haidt, Jonathan. (2012). *The righteous mind: Why good people are divided by politics and religion.* New York: Pantheon Books.

Haier, Richard J., Jung, Rex E., Yeo, Ronald A., et al. (2005). The neuroanatomy of general intelligence: sex matters. *NeuroImage, 25*, 320–327.

Haimov, Iris, & Lavie, Peretz. (1996). Melatonin—A soporific hormone. *Current Directions in Psychological Science, 5*, 106–111.

Hale, Joanna, Thompson, Jacqueline M., Morgan, Helen M., Cappelletti, Marinella, & Cohen Kadosh, Roi. (2014). Better together?: The cognitive advantages of synaesthesia for time, numbers, and space. *Cognitive Neuropsychology, 31*(7–8), 545–564.

Halim, May Ling, Ruble, Diane N., Tamis-LeMonda, Catherine S., Zosuls, Kristina M., Lurye, Leah E., & Greulich, Faith K. (2014). Pink frilly dresses and the avoidance of all things "girly": Children's appearance rigidity and cognitive theories of gender development. *Developmental Psychology, 50*(4), 1091–1101.

Hall, Calvin. (1953a). A cognitive theory of dreams. *Journal of General Psychology, 49*, 273–282.

Hall, Calvin. (1953b). *The meaning of dreams.* New York: McGraw-Hill.

Hall, Edward T. (1959). *The silent language.* Garden City, NY: Doubleday.

Hall, Edward T. (1976). *Beyond culture.* New York: Anchor.

Hall, Edward T. (1983). *The dance of life: The other dimension of time.* Garden City, NY: Anchor Press/Doubleday.

Hall, Edward T., & Hall, Mildred R. (1987). *Hidden differences: Doing business with the Japanese.* Garden City, NY: Anchor Press/Doubleday.

Hall, Edward T., & Hall, Mildred R. (1990). *Understanding cultural differences.* Yarmouth, ME: Intercultural Press.

Hall, G. Stanley. (1899). A study of anger. *American Journal of Psychology, 10*, 516–591.

Hall, Nathan C., Perry, Raymond P., Ruthig, Joelle C., et al. (2006). Primary and secondary control in achievement settings: A longitudinal field study of academic motivation, emotions, and performance. *Journal of Applied Social Psychology, 36*, 1430–1470.

Hallion, Lauren S., & Ruscio, Ayelet M. (2011). A meta-analysis of the effect of cognitive bias modification on anxiety and depression. *Psychological Bulletin, 137*, 940–958.

Halpern, Diane F. (2014). *Thought and knowledge: An introduction to critical thinking.* New York: Psychology Press.

Halpern, Sue. (2008, May 19). Virtual Iraq. *The New Yorker*, pp. 32–37.

Hamamura, Takeshi, & Heine, Steven J. (2008). The role of self-criticism in self-improvement and face maintenance among Japanese. In E. C. Chang (Ed.), *Self-criticism and self-enhancement: Theory, research, and clinical implications.* Washington, DC, US: American Psychological Association.

Hamby, Sherry L., & Koss, Mary P. (2003). Shades of gray: A qualitative study of terms used in the measurement of sexual victimization. *Psychology of Women Quarterly, 27*, 243–255.

Hamilton, B.E., Martin, J.A., Osterman, M.J.K., & Curtin, S. C. (2015). *Births: Final data for 2013.* Hyattsville, MD: National Center for Health Statistics.

Hammen, Constance. (2009). Adolescent depression. *Current Directions in Psychological Science, 18*, 200–204.

Haney, Craig, Banks, Curtis, & Zimbardo, Philip. (1973). Interpersonal dynamics in a simulated prison. *International Journal of Criminology and Penology, 1*, 69–97.

Haney, Craig, & Zimbardo, Philip. (1998). The past and future of U.S. prison policy: Twenty-five years after the Stanford Prison Experiment. *American Psychologist, 53*, 709–727.

Hardie, Elizabeth A. (1997). PMS in the workplace: Dispelling the myth of cyclic function. *Journal of Occupational and Organizational Psychology, 70*, 97–102.

Harding, Courtenay M. (2005). Changes in schizophrenia across time: Paradoxes, patterns, and predictors. In L. Davidson, C. Harding, & L. Spaniol (Eds.), *Recovery from severe mental illnesses: Research evidence and implications for practice* (Vol. 1). Boston: Center for Psychiatric Rehabilitation/Boston University.

Hardy, John, & Singleton, Andrew. (2009). Genome wide association studies and human disease. *New England Journal of Medicine, 360*, 1759–1768.

Hare, Robert D. (1965). Temporal gradient of fear arousal in psychopaths. *Journal of Abnormal Psychology, 70*, 442–445.

Hare, Robert D. (1996). Psychopathy: A clinical construct whose time has come. *Criminal Justice and Behavior, 23*, 24–54.

Hare, William. (2009, March/April). What open-mindedness requires. *Skeptical Inquirer, 33*, 36–39.

Haritos-Fatouros, Mika. (1988). The official torturer: A learning model for obedience to the authority of violence. *Journal of Applied Social Psychology, 18*, 1107–1120.

Harlow, Harry F. (1958). The nature of love. *American Psychologist, 13*, 673–685.

Harlow, Harry F., & Harlow, Margaret K. (1966). Learning to love. *American Scientist, 54*, 244–272.

Harlow, Harry F., Harlow, Margaret K., & Meyer, D. R. (1950). Learning motivated by a manipulation drive. *Journal of Experimental Psychology, 40*, 228–234.

Harmon-Jones, Eddie, & Harmon-Jones, Cindy. (2015). Neural foundations of motivational orientations. In Guido H. Gendolla; Mattie Tops; & Sander L. Koole (Eds.), *Handbook of biobehavioral approaches to self-regulation* (pp. 175–187). New York: Springer.

Harnsberger, James D., Hollien, Harry, Martin Camilo A., & Hollien, Kevin A. (2009). Stress and deception in speech: Evaluating Layered Voice Analysis. *Journal of Forensic Sciences, 54*, 642–650.

Harrington, D. M., Martin, C. K., Ravussin, E., & Katzmarzyk, P. T. (2013). Activity related energy expenditure, appetite and energy intake: Potential implications for weight management. *Appetite, 67*, 1–7.

Harris, Christine. (2003). Factors associated with jealousy over real and imagined infidelity: An examination of the social-cognitive and evolutionary psychology perspectives. *Psychology of Women Quarterly, 27*, 319–329.

Harris, Gardiner. (2003, August 7). Debate resumes on the safety of depression's wonder drugs. *New York Times*, pp. A1, C4.

Harris, Judith R. (2006). *No two alike: Human nature and human individuality.* New York: Norton.

Harris, Judith R. (2009). *The nurture assumption* (2nd ed.). New York: Free Press.

Harris, Lasana T., & Fiske, Susan T. (2006). Dehumanizing the lowest of the low: Neuro-imaging responses to extreme outgroups. *Psychological Science, 17,* 847–853.

Hart, A. J., Whalen, P. J., Shin, L. M., et al. (2000). Differential response in the human amygdala to racial outgroup vs. ingroup face stimuli. *NeuroReport, 11,* 2351–2355.

Hart, John, Jr., Berndt, Rita S., & Caramazza, Alfonso. (1985, August 1). Category-specific naming deficit following cerebral infarction. *Nature, 316,* 339–340.

Haruno, Masahiko, Kimura, Minoru, & Frith, Christopher D. (2014). Activity in the nucleus accumbens and amygdala underlies individual differences in prosocial and individualistic economic choices. *Journal of Cognitive Neuroscience, 26*(8), 1861–1870.

Haslam, S. Alexander, Jetten, Jolanda, Postmes, Tom, & Haslam, Catherine. (2009). Social identity, health and well-being: An emerging agenda for applied psychology. *Applied Psychology: An International Review, 58,* 1–23.

Haslam, S. Alexander, & Reicher, Stephen. (2003, Spring). Beyond Stanford: Questioning a role-based explanation of tyranny. *Society for Experimental Social Psychology Dialogue, 18,* 22–25.

Hassett, Janice M., Siebert, Erin R., Wallen, Kim. (2008). Sex differences in rhesus monkey toy preferences parallel those of children. *Hormones and Behavior, 54,* 359–364.

Hatfield, Elaine, & Rapson, Richard L. (1996/2005). *Love and sex: Cross-cultural perspectives.* Boston: University Press of America.

Hatfield, Elaine, & Rapson, Richard L. (2008). Passionate love and sexual desire: Multidisciplinary perspectives. In J. P. Forgas & J. Fitness (Eds.), *Social relationships: Cognitive, affective, and motivational processes.* New York: Psychology Press.

Haut, Jennifer S., Beckwith, Bill E., Petros, Thomas V., & Russell, Sue. (1989). Gender differences in retrieval from long-term memory following acute intoxication with ethanol. *Physiology and Behavior, 45,* 1161–1165.

Häuser, Winfried, Bartram-Wunn, Eva, Bartram, Claas, et al. (2011). Systematic review: Placebo response in drug trials of fibromyalgia syndrome and painful peripheral diabetic neuropathy-magnitude and patient-related predictors. *Pain, 152,* 1709–1717.

Havas, David A., Glenberg, Arthur M., Gutowski, Karol A., et al. (2010). Cosmetic use of botulinum toxin-A affects processing of emotional language. *Psychological Science, 21,* 895–900.

Hawkins, Elizabeth H., Cummins, Lillian H., & Marlatt, G. Alan. (2004). Preventing substance abuse in American Indian and Alaska Native Youth: Promising strategies for healthier communities. *Psychological Bulletin, 130,* 304–323.

Hawkins, Scott A., & Hastie, Reid. (1990). Hindsight: Biased judgments of past events after the outcomes are known. *Psychological Bulletin, 107,* 311–327.

Hay, Dale F., Mundy, Lisa, Roberts, Siwan, et al. (2011). Known risk factors for violence predict 12-month-old infants' aggressiveness with peers. *Psychological Science, 22,* 1205–1211.

Hayashi, Hajimu, & Shiomi, Yuki. (2015). Do children understand that people selectively conceal or express emotion? *International Journal of Behavioral Development, 39*(1), 1–8.

Hayes, Steven C. (2004). Acceptance and commitment therapy and the new behavior therapies: Mindfulness, acceptance, and relaitonship. In S. C. Hayes, V. M. Follette, & M. M. Linehan (2004). *Mindfulness and acceptance: Expanding the cognitive-behavioral tradition.* New York: Guilford Press.

Hayes, Steven C., Follette, Victoria M., & Linehan, Marsha M. (Eds.). (2004). *Mindfulness and acceptance: Expanding the cognitive-behavioral tradition.* New York: Guilford Press.

Headey, Bruce. (2008). Life goals matter to happiness: A revision of set-point theory. *Social Indicators Research, 86,* 213–231.

Healey, Jay, Lussier, Patrick, & Beauregard, Eric. (2013). Sexual sadism in the context of rape and sexual homicide: An examination of crime scene indicators. *International Journal of Offender Therapy and Comparative Criminology, 57*(4), 402–424.

Healy, David. (2002). *The creation of psychopharmacology.* Cambridge, MA: Harvard University Press.

Healy, David. (2012). *Pharmageddon.* Berkeley: University of California Press.

Heath, A. C., Madden, P. A. F., Bucholz, K. K., et al. (2003). Genetic and genotype x environment interaction effects on risk of dependence on alcohol, tobacco, and other drugs: New research. In R. Plomin et al. (Eds.), *Behavioral genetics in the postgenomic era.* Washington, DC: APA Books.

Hébert, Richard. (2001, September). Code overload: Doing a number on memory. *APS Observer, 14,* 1, 7–11.

Hedden, Trey, Ketay, Sarah, Aron, Arthur, Markus, Hazel Rose, & Gabrieli, John D. E. (2008). Cultural influences on neural substrates of attentional control. *Psychological Science, 19*(1), 12–17.

Hegarty, Mary, & Waller, David. (2005). Individual differences in spatial abilities. In P. Shah & A. Miyake (Eds.), *The Cambridge handbook of visuospatial thinking.* New York: Cambridge University Press.

Heijmans, Bastiaan T., & Mill, Jonathan. (2012). Commentary: The seven plagues of epigenetic epidemiology. *International Journal of Epidemiology, 41,* 74–78.

Heilig, Markus. (2008, December 1). Molecular biology teases out two distinct forms of alcoholism. *The Scientist, 22.* Available at www.the-scientist.com/article/display/55237/.

Heinrichs, R. Walter. (2005). The primacy of cognition in schizophrenia. *American Psychologist, 60,* 229–242.

Held, Suzanne, D. E., & Spinka, Marek. (2011). Animal play and animal welfare. *Animal Behaviour, 81,* 891–899.

Helson, Ravenna, Roberts, Brent, & Agronick, Gail. (1995). Enduringness and change in creative personality and the prediction of occupational creativity. *Journal of Personality and Social Psychology, 6,* 1173–1183.

Helzer, John E., Wittchen, Hans-Ulrich, Krueger, Robert F., & Kraemer, Helena C. (2008). Dimensional options for DSM-V: The way forward. In J. E. Helzer, H. C. Kramer, & R. F. Krueger (Eds.), *Dimensional approaches in diagnostic classification: Refining the research agenda for DSM-V.* Washington, DC. American Psychiatric Association.

Henderlong, Jennifer, & Lepper, Mark. (2002). The effects of praise on children's intrinsic motivation: A review and synthesis. *Psychological Bulletin, 128,* 774–795.

Henggeler, Scott W., Schoenwald, Sonya K., Borduin, Charles M., et al. (1998). *Multisystemic treatment of antisocial behavior in children and adolescents.* New York: Guilford Press.

Hennessy, Michael B., Schiml-Webb, Patricia A., & Deak, Terrence. (2009). Separation, sickness, and depression. *Current Directions in Psychological Science, 18,* 227–231.

Henrich, Joseph, Boyd, Robert, Bowles, Samuel, et al. (2001). In search of Homo Economicus: Behavioral experiments in 15 small scale societies. *American Economics Review, 91,* 73–78.

Henrich, Joseph, Heine, Steven J., & Norenzayan, Ara. (2010, June 15). The weirdest people in the world? *Behavioral and Brain Sciences, 33,* 61–83.

Hepper, Erica G., Wildschut, T., Sedikides, C., Ritchie, T. D., Yung, Y. F., Hansen, N., et al. (2014). Pancultural nostalgia: Prototypical conceptions across cultures. *Emotion, 14*(4), 733–747.

Herbert, Alan, Gerry, Norman P., McQueen, Matthew B., et al. (2006, April 14). A common genetic variant is associated with adult and childhood obesity. *Science, 312,* 279–283.

Herculano-Houzel, Suzana. (2009). The human brain in numbers: A linearly scaled-up primate brain. *Frontiers of Human Neuroscience, 3,* 31.

Herdt, Gilbert. (1984). *Ritualized homosexuality in Melanesia.* Berkeley: University of California Press.

Herek, Gregory M., & Capitanio, John P. (1996). "Some of my best friends": Intergroup contact, concealable stigma, and heterosexuals' attitudes toward gay men and lesbians. *Personality and Social Psychology Bulletin, 22,* 412–424.

Herman, Judith. (1992). *Trauma and recovery.* New York: Basic Books.

Herman, Louis M., Kuczaj, Stan A., & Holder, Mark D. (1993). Responses to anomalous gestural sequences by a language-trained dolphin: Evidence for processing of semantic relations and syntactic information. *Journal of Experimental Psychology: General, 122,* 184–194.

Herman, Louis M., & Morrel-Samuels, Palmer. (1996). Knowledge acquisition and asymmetry between language comprehension and production: Dolphins and apes as general models for animals. In M. Bekoff & D. Jamieson (Eds.), *Readings in animal cognition.* Cambridge, MA: MIT Press.

Heron, Woodburn. (1957). The pathology of boredom. *Scientific American, 196*(1), 52–56.

Hertzog, Christopher, Kramer, Arthur F., Wilson, Robert S., & Lindenberger, Ulman. (2008). Enrichment effects on adult cognitive development: Can the functional capacity of older adults be preserved and enhanced? *Psychological Science in the Public Interest, 9,* 1–65.

Herz, Rachel S., & Cupchik, Gerald C. (1995). The emotional distinctiveness of odor-evoked memories. *Chemical Senses, 20,* 517–528.

Hess, Thomas M. (2005). Memory and aging in context. *Psychological Bulletin, 131,* 383–406.

Hess, Ursula, Adams, Reginald B., Jr., & Kleck, Robert. (2005). Who may frown and who should smile? Dominance, affiliation, and the display of happiness and anger. *Cognition and Emotion, 19,* 515–536.

Hess, Ursula, & Thibault, Pascal. (2009). Darwin and emotional expression. *American Psychologist, 64,* 120–128.

Hewlett, Sylvia Ann, Luce, Carolyn B., & Servon, Lisa J. (2008, June). Stopping the exodus of women in science. *Harvard Business Review.* Available at https://hbr.org/2008/06/stopping-the-exodus-of-women-in-science.

Heyman, Gene M. (2009). *Addiction: A disorder of choice.* Cambridge, MA: Harvard University Press.

Heyman, Gene M. (2011). Received wisdom regarding the roles of craving and dopamine in addiction. *Perspectives on Psychological Science, 6,* 156–160.

Hibbing, John R. (2005). Are political orientations genetically transmitted? *American Political Science Review, 99,* 153–167.

Hilbert, Anja, Pike, Kathleen M., Goldschmidt, Andrea B., Wilfley, Denise E., Fairburn, Christopher G., Dohm, Faith-Anne, et al. (2014). Risk factors across the eating disorders. *Psychiatry Research, 220*(1–2), 500–506.

Hilgard, Ernest R. (1977). *Divided consciousness: Multiple controls in human thought and action.* New York: Wiley-Interscience.

Hilgard, Ernest R. (1986). *Divided consciousness: Multiple controls in human thought and action* (2nd ed.). New York: Wiley.

Hill-Soderlund, Ashley L., & Braungart-Rieker, Julia M. (2008). Early individual differences in temperamental reactivity and regulation: Implications for effortful control in early childood. *Infant Behavior and Development, 31,* 386–397.

Hilts, Philip J. (1995). *Memory's ghost: The strange tale of Mr. M. and the nature of memory.* New York: Simon & Schuster.

Hinzen, Wolfram. (2014). The future of universal grammar research. *Language Sciences, 46* (Part B), 97–99.

Hirsch, Helmut V. B., & Spinelli, Nico. (1970). Visual experience modifies distribution of horizontally and vertically oriented receptive fields in cats. *Science, 168,* 869–871.

Hirsh, Jacob B., Galinsky, Adam D., & Zhong, Chen-Bo. (2011). Drunk, powerful, and in the dark: How general processes of disinhibition produce both prosocial and antisocial behavior. *Perspectives on Psychological Science, 6,* 415–427.

Hirst, W., Phelps, E. A., Meksin, R., Vaidya, C. J., Johnson, M. K., Mitchell, K. J., et al. (2015). A ten-year follow-up of a study of memory for the attack of September 11, 2001: Flashbulb memories and memories for flashbulb events. *Journal of Experimental Psychology: General, 144*(3), 604–623.

Hobson, J. Allan. (1988). *The dreaming brain.* New York: Basic Books.

Hobson, J. Allan. (1990). Activation, input source, and modulation: A neurocognitive model of the state of the brain mind. In R. R. Bootzin, J. F. Kihlstrom, & D. L. Schacter (Eds.), *Sleep and cognition.* Washington, DC: American Psychological Association.

Hobson, J. Allan. (2002). *Dreaming: An introduction to the science of sleep.* New York: Oxford University Press.

Hobson, J. Allan, Pace-Schott, Edward F., & Stickgold, Robert. (2000). Dreaming and the brain: Toward a cognitive neuroscience of consicous states. *Behavioral and Brain Sciences, 23,* 793–842, 904–1018, 1083–1121.

Hobson, J. Allan, Sangsanguan, Suchada, Arantes, Henry, & Kahn, David. (2011). Dream logic: The inferential reasoning paradigm. *Dreaming, 21,* 1–15.

Hochschild, Arlie R. (2003). *The Managed Heart: Commercialization of human feeling* (2nd ed.). Berkeley: University of California Press.

Hodson, Gordon. (2011). Do ideologically intolerant people benefit from intergroup contact? *Current Directions in Psychological Science, 20,* 154–159.

Hoekstra, Hopi E., Hirschmann, Rachel J., & Bundey, Richard A., et al. (2006). A single amino acid mutation contributes to adaptive color pattern in beach mice. *Science 313,* 101–104.

Hofmann, Stefan G., Asnaani, Anu, Vonk, Imke J. J., Sawyer, Alice T., & Fang, Angela. (2012). The efficacy of cognitive behavioral therapy: A review of meta-analyses. *Cognitive Therapy and Research, 36*(5), 427–440.

Hofstede, Geert, & Bond, Michael H. (1988). The Confucius connection: From cultural roots to economic growth. *Organizational Dynamics*, 5–21.

Holden, George W., Brown, Alan S., Baldwin, Austin S., & Croft Caderao, Kathryn. (2014). Research findings can change attitudes about corporal punishment. *Child Abuse and Neglect, 38*(5), 902–908.

Holden, George W., & Miller, Pamela C. (1999). Enduring and different: A meta-analysis of the similarity in parents' child rearing. *Psychological Bulletin, 125*, 223–254.

Hollon, Steven D., Thase, Michael E., & Markowitz, John C. (2002). Treatment and prevention of depression. *Psychological Science in the Public Interest, 3*, 39–77.

Hoogsteder, Larissa M., Stams, Geert Jan J. M., Figge, Mariska A., Changoe, Kareshma, van Horn, Joan E., Hendriks, Jan, et al. (2015). A meta-analysis of the effectiveness of individually oriented cognitive behavioral treatment (CBT) for severe aggressive behavior in adolescents. *Journal of Forensic Psychiatry and Psychology, 26*(1), 22–37.

Hopper, Kim, Harrison, Glynn, Janca, Aleksandar, & Sartorius, Norman. (Eds.) (2007). *Recovery from schizophrenia: An international investigation*. New York: Oxford University Press.

Horn, Erin E., Turkheimer, Eric, Strachan, Eric, & Duncan, Glen E. (2015). Behavioral and environmental modification of the genetic influence on body mass index: A twin study. *Behavior Genetics, 45*(4), 409–426.

Horn, John L., & Cattell, Raymond B. (1966). Refinement and test of the theory of fluid and crystallized general intelligences. *Journal of Educational Psychology, 57*, 253–270.

Hornung, Richard W., Lanphear, Bruce P., & Dietrich, Kim N. (2009). Age of greatest susceptibility to childhood lead exposure: A new statistical approach. *Environmental Health Perspectives, 117*, 1309–1312.

Horwitz, Allan V., & Grob, Gerald N. (2011). The checkered history of American psychiatric epidemiology. *The Milbank Quarterly, 89*, 628–657.

Houben, Katrijn, Wiers, Reinout W., & Jansen, Anita. (2011). Getting a grip on drinking behavior: Training working memory to reduce alcohol abuse. *Psychological Science, 22*, 968–975.

Houdek, Pavel, Polidarová, Lenka, Nováková, Marta, Matějů, Kristýna, Kubík, _těpán, & Sumová, Alena. (2015). Melatonin administered during the fetal stage affects circadian clock in the suprachiasmatic nucleus but not in the liver. *Developmental Neurobiology, 75*(2), 131–144.

Houston, Derek M., & Jusczyk, Peter W. (2003). Infants' long-term memory for the sound patterns of words and voices. *Journal of Experimental Psychology: Human Perception & Performance, 29*, 1143–1154.

Houts, Arthur C. (2002). Discovery, invention, and the expansion of the modern Diagnostic and Statistical Manuals of Mental Disorders. In L. E. Beutler & M. L. Malik (Eds.), *Rethinking the DSM: A psychological perspective*. Washington, DC: American Psychological Association.

Howard, George S. (1991). Culture tales: A narrative approach to thinking, cross-cultural psychology, and psychotherapy. *American Psychologist, 46*, 187–197.

Howe, Mark L. (2000). *The fate of early memories: Developmental science and the retention of childhood experiences*. Washington, DC: American Psychological Association.

Howe, Mark L., Courage, Mary L., & Peterson, Carole. (1994). How can I remember when "I" wasn't there? Long-term retention of traumatic experiences and emergence of the cognitive self. *Consciousness and Cognition, 3*, 327–355.

Hrdy, Sarah B. (1994). What do women want? In T. A. Bass (Ed.), *Reinventing the future: Conversations with the world's leading scientists*. Reading, MA: Addison-Wesley.

Hrdy, Sarah B. (1999). *Mother nature*. New York: Pantheon.

Hrdy, Sarah B. (2009). *Mothers and others*. Cambridge, MA: Belknap Press of Harvard University Press.

Hu, H., Real, E., Takamiya, K., et al. (2007). Emotion enhances learning via norepinephrine regulation of AMPA-receptor trafficking. *Cell, 131*, 160–173.

Hu, Wei, Saba, Laura, Kechris, Katherina, et al. (2008). Genomic insights into acute alcohol tolerance. *Journal of Pharmacology and Experimental Therapeutics, 326*, 792–800.

Huang, C. M., Polk, T. A., Goh, J. O., & Park, D. C. (2012). Both left and right posterior parietal activations contribute to compensatory processes in normal aging. *Neuropsychologia, 50*, 55–66.

Hubel, David H., & Wiesel, Torsten N. (1962). Receptive fields, binocular interaction and functional architecture in the cat's visual cortex. *Journal of Physiology (London), 160*, 106–154.

Hubel, David H., & Wiesel, Torsten N. (1968). Receptive fields and functional architecture of monkey striate cortex. *Journal of Physiology (London), 195*, 215–243.

Hugdahl, Kenneth, & Westerhausen, René. (2010). *The two halves of the brain: Information processing in the cerebral hemispheres*. New York: MIT Press.

Huggins, Martha K., Haritos-Fatouros, Mika, & Zimbardo, Philip G. (2003). *Violence workers: Police torturers and murderers reconstruct Brazilian atrocities*. Berkeley, CA: University of California Press.

Hunsley, John, Lee, Catherine M., & Wood, James. (2015). Controversial and questionable assessment techniques. In S. O. Lilienfeld, S. J. Lynn, & J. M. Lohr (Eds.), *Science and pseudoscience in clinical psychology*. (2nd ed., pp. 42–82) New York: Guilford Press.

Hunt, J. McV. (1938). An instance of the social origin of conflict resulting in psychoses. *American Journal of Orthopsychiatry, 8*(1), 158–164.

Huntjens, Rafaële J. C., Verschuere, Bruno, & McNally, Richard J. (2012). Inter-identity autobiographical amnesia in patients with dissociative identity disorder. *PloS One, 7*(7), e40580.

Hupka, Ralph B. (1981). Cultural determinants of jealousy. *Alternative Lifestyles, 4*, 310–356.

Hupka, Ralph B. (1991). The motive for the arousal of romantic jealousy. In P. Salovey (Ed.), *The psychology of jealousy and envy*. New York: Guilford Press.

Hupka, Ralph B., Lenton, Alison P., & Hutchison, Keith A. (1999). Universal development of emotion categories in natural language. *Journal of Personality and Social Psychology, 77*, 247–278.

Hutcherson, Cendri A., Seppala, Emma M., & Gross, James J. (2015). The neural correlates of social connection. *Cognitive, Affective and Behavioral Neuroscience, 15*(1), 1–14.

Hutton, Paul, Wood, Lisa, Taylor, Peter J., Irving, Kerry, & Morrison, Anthony P. (2014). Cognitive behavioural therapy for psychosis: Rationale and protocol for a systematic review and meta-analysis. *Psychosis: Psychological, Social and Integrative Approaches, 6*(3), 220–230.

Hwang, Hyisung, & Matsumoto, David. (2015). Evidence for the universality of facial expressions of emotion. In Avinash Awasthi (Ed.), *Understanding facial expressions in communication: Cross-cultural and multidisplinary perspectives* (pp. 41–56). New York: Springer.

Hwang, Wei-Chin. (2006). The psychotherapy adaptation and modification framework: Application to Asian Americans. *American Psychologist, 61*, 702–715.

Hyde, Janet S. (2007). New directions in the study of gender similarities and differences. *Current Directions in Psychological Science, 16*, 259–263.

Hyman, Ira E., Boss, Matthew, Wise, Breanne M., et al. (2010). Did you see the unicycling clown? Inattentional blindness while walking and talking on a cell phone. *Applied Cognitive Psychology, 24*, 597–607.

Hyman, Ira E., Jr., & Pentland, Joel. (1996). The role of mental imagery in the creation of false childhood memories. *Journal of Memory and Language, 35*, 101–117.

Iacoboni, Marco. (2008). *Mirroring people: The new science of how we connect with others.* New York: Farrar, Strauss & Giroux.

Iber, Conrad, Ancoli-Israel, Sonia, Chesson, Andrew L., & Quan, Stuart F. (2007). The AASM *Manual for the scoring of sleep and associated events: Rules, terminology and technical specifications.* Westchester, IL: American Academy of Sleep Medicine.

Imada, Toshie, & Ellsworth, Phoebe C. (2011). Proud Americans and lucky Japanese: Cultural differences in appraisal and corresponding emotion. *Emotion, 11*, 329–345.

Impett, Emily A., Gable, Shelly, & Peplau, Letitia A. (2005). Giving up and giving in: The costs and benefits of daily sacrifice in intimate relationships. *Journal of Personality and Social Psychology, 89*, 327–344.

Impett, Emily A., Henson, James M., Breines, Juliana G., et al. (2011). Embodiment feels better: Girls' body objectification and well-being across adolescence. *Psychology of Women Quarterly, 35*, 46–58.

Innocenti, Giorgio M., & Price, David J. (2005). Exuberance in the development of cortical networks. *Nature Reviews Neuroscience, 6*, 955–965.

Inzlicht, Michael, & Ben-Zeev, Talia. (2000). A threatening intellectual environment: Why females are susceptible to experiencing problem-solving deficits in the presence of males. *Psychological Science, 11*, 365–371.

Islam, Mir Rabiul, & Hewstone, Miles. (1993). Intergroup attributions and affective consequences in majority and minority groups. *Journal of Personality and Social Psychology, 64*, 936–950.

Ito, Tiffany A., & Urland, Geoffrey R. (2003). Race and gender on the brain: Electrocortical measures of attention to the race and gender of multiply categorizable individuals. *Journal of Personality and Social Psychology, 85*, 616–626.

Izard, Carroll E. (1994). Innate and universal facial expressions: Evidence from developmental and cross-cultural research. *Psychological Bulletin, 115*, 288–299.

Izard, Véronique, Sann, Coralie, Spelke, Elizabeth S., & Streri, Arlette. (2009). Newborn infants perceive abstract numbers. *Proceedings of the National Academy of Sciences, 106*, 10382–10385.

Jack, Fiona, & Hayne, Harlene. (2010). Childhood amnesia: Empirical evidence for a two-stage phenomenon. *Memory, 18*, 831–844.

Jack, Rachel E., Garrod, O.G.B., Yu, H., Caldara, R., & Schyns, P.G. (2012) Facial expressions of emotion are not culturally universal. *Proceedings of the National Academy of Sciences of the United States of America, 109*(19), 7241–7244.

Jackson, Daren C., Mueller, Corrina J., Dolski, Isa, et al. (2003). Now you feel it, now you don't: Frontal brain electrical asymmetry and individual differences in emotion regulation. *Psychological Science, 14*, 612–617.

Jacob, Marni L., & Storch, Eric A. (2015). Computer-aided psychotherapy technologies. In Naakesh A. Dewan; John S. Luo; & Nancy M. Lorenzi (Eds.), *Mental health practice in a digital world: A clinician's guide* (pp. 57–80). New York: Springer.

Jacobs, Tonya L., Epel, Elissa S., Lin, Jue, et al. (2011). Intensive meditation training, immune cell telomerase activity, and psychological mediators. *Psychoneuroendocrinology, 36*, 664–681.

Jacobsen, Paul B, Bovbjerg, Dana H., Schwartz, Marc D., et al. (1995). Conditioned emotional distress in women receiving chemotherapy for breast cancer. *Journal of Consulting & Clinical Psychology, 63*, 108–114.

James, William. (1890/1950). *Principles of psychology* (Vol. 1). New York: Dover.

James, William. (1902/1936). *The varieties of religious experience.* New York: Modern Library.

Jamison, Kay. (1992). *Touched with fire: Manic depressive illness and the artistic temperament.* New York: Free Press.

Janis, Irving L. (1982). *Groupthink: Psychological studies of policy decisions and fiascoes* (2nd ed.). Boston: Houghton-Mifflin.

Janis, Irving L. (1989). *Crucial decisions: Leadership in policymaking and crisis management.* New York: Free Press.

Jenkins, John G., & Dallenbach, Karl M. (1924). Obliviscence during sleep and waking. *American Journal of Psychology, 35*, 605–612.

Jensen, Arthur R. (1998). *The g factor: The science of mental ability.* Westport, CT: Praeger/Greenwood.

Jeon, Lieny, Buettner, Cynthia K., & Hur, Eunhye. (2014). Family and neighborhood disadvantage, home environment, and children's school readiness. *Journal of Family Psychology, 28*(5), 718–727.

Jin, Wenfei, Xu, Shuhua, Wang, Haifeng, et al. (2012). Genome-wide detection of natural selection in African Americans pre- and post-admixture. *Genome Research, 22*, 519–527.

Jobe, Thomas H., & Harrow, Martin. (2010). Schizophrenia course, long-term outcome, recovery, and prognosis. *Current Directions in Psychological Science, 19*, 220–225.

Johanek, Lisa M., Meyer, Richard A., Friedman, Robert M., et al. (2008). A role for polymodal C-fiber afferents in nonhistaminergic itch. *Journal of Neuroscience, 28*, 7659–7669.

Johns, Michael, Schmader, Toni, & Martens, Andy. (2005). Knowing is half the battle: Teaching stereotype threat as a means of improving women's math performance. *Psychological Science, 16*, 175–179.

Johnson, Marcia K., Hashtroudi, Shahin, & Lindsay, D. Stephen. (1993). Source monitoring. *Psychological Bulletin, 114*, 3–28.

Johnson, Marcia K., Mitchell, Karen J., & Ankudowich, Elizabeth. (2012). The cognitive neuroscience of the true and false memories. In Robert F. Belli (Ed.), *True and false recovered memories: Toward a reconciliation of the debate* (Nebraska Symposium on Motivation, Vol. 58, pp. 15–52). New York: Springer.

Johnson, Marcia K., Raye, Carol L., Mitchell, Karen J., & Ankudowich, Elizabeth. (2011). The cognitive neuroscience of true and false memories. In R. F. Belli (Ed.), *True and false recovered memories: Toward a reconciliation of the debate* (Vol. 58). New York: Springer.

Jones, Edward E. (1990). *Interpersonal perception.* New York: Macmillan.

Jones, Jo, & Mosher, William D. (2013, December). Fathers' involvement with their children: United States, 2006–2010. *National Health Statistics Reports, 71.*

Jones, Mary Cover. (1924). A laboratory study of fear: The case of Peter. *Pedagogical Seminary, 31*, 308–315.

Joormann, Jutta, & Gotlib, Ian H. (2007). Selective attention to emotional faces following recovery from depression. *Journal of Abnormal Psychology, 116*, 80–85.

Joormann, Jutta, Levens, Sara M., & Gotlib, Ian H. (2011). Sticky thoughts: Depression and rumination are associated with difficulties manipulating emotional material in working memory. *Psychological Science, 22*, 979–983.

Joormann, Jutta, Siemer, Matthias, & Gotlib, Ian H. (2007). Mood regulation in depression: Differential effects of distraction and recall of happy memories on sad mood. *Journal of Abnormal Psychology, 116*, 484–490.

Jordan, Alexander H., Monin, Benoît, Dweck, Carol S., et al. (2011). Misery has more company than people think: Underestimating the prevalence of others' negative emotions. *Personality and Social Psychology Bulletin, 37*, 120–135.

Jordan-Young, Rebecca M. (2010). *Brainstorm: The flaws in the science of sex differences.* Cambridge, MA: Harvard University Press.

Jost, John T. (2006). The end of the end of ideology. *American Psychologist, 61*, 651–670.

Jost, John T., Glaser, Jack, Kruglanski, Arie W., & Sulloway, Frank J. (2003). Political conservatism as motivated social cognition. *Psychological Bulletin, 129*, 339–375.

Jost, John T., Nosek, Brian A., & Gosling, Samuel D. (2008). Ideology: Its resurgence in social, personality, and political psychology. *Perspectives on Psychological Science, 3*, 126–136.

Judd, Charles M., Park, Bernadette, Ryan, Carey S., et al. (1995). Stereotypes and ethnocentrism: Diverging interethnic perceptions of African American and white American youth. *Journal of Personality and Social Psychology, 69*, 460–481.

Judge, Timothy A. (2009). Core self-evaluations and work success. *Current Directions, 18*, 18–22.

Jung, Carl. (1967). *Collected works.* Princeton, NJ: Princeton University Press.

Jusczyk, Peter W. (2002). How infants adapt speech-processing capacities to native-language structure. *Current Directions in Psychological Science, 11*, 15–18.

Kabat-Zinn, Jon. (1994). *Wherever you go, there you are: Mindfulness meditation in everyday life.* New York: Hyperion.

Kagan, Jerome. (1989). *Unstable ideas: Temperament, cognition, and self.* Cambridge, MA: Harvard University Press.

Kagan, Jerome. (1997). Temperament and the reactions to unfamiliarity. *Child Development, 68*, 139–143.

Kahneman, Daniel. (2003). A perspective on judgment and choice: Mapping bounded rationality. *American Psychologist, 58*, 697–720.

Kahneman, Daniel. (2011). *Thinking, fast and slow.* New York: Farrar, Straus & Giroux.

Kaminski, Juliane, Call, Josep, & Fisher, Julia. (2004). Word learning in a domestic dog: Evidence for "fast mapping." *Science, 304*, 1682–1683.

Kammers, M. P. M., de Vignemont, L., Verhagen, L., & Dijkerman, H. C. (2009). The rubber hand illusion in action. *Neuropsychologia, 47*, 204–211.

Kanagawa, Chie, Cross, Susan E., & Markus, Hazel R. (2001). "Who am I?" The cultural psychology of the conceptual self. *Personality and Social Psychology Bulletin, 27*, 90–103.

Kandel, Eric R. (2001). The molecular biology of memory storage: A dialogue between genes and synapses. *Science, 294*, 1030–1038.

Kandel, Eric R., & Schwartz, James H. (1982). Molecular biology of learning: Modulation of transmitter release. *Science, 218*, 433–443.

Kane, Michael J., Brown, Leslie H., McVay, Jennifer C., et al. (2007). For whom the mind wanders, and when: An experience-sampling study of working memory and executive control in daily life. *Psychological Science, 18*, 614–621.

Kanter, Rosabeth M. (2006). Some effects of proportions on group life: Skewed sex ratios and responses to token women. In J. N. Levine & R. L. Moreland (Eds.), *Small groups. Key Readings in Social Psychology.* New York: Psychology Press.

Karasek, Robert, & Theorell, Tores. (1990). *Healthy work: Stress, productivity, and the reconstruction of working life.* New York: Basic Books.

Karlsgodt, Katherine H., Sun, Daqiang, & Cannon, Tyrone D. (2010). Structural and functional brain abnormalities in schizophrenia. *Current Directions in Psychological Science, 19*, 226–231.

Karney, Benjamin, & Bradbury, Thomas N. (2000). Attributions in marriage: State or trait? A growth curve analysis. *Journal of Personality and Social Psychology, 78*, 295–309.

Karni, Avi, Tanne, David, Rubenstein, Barton S., et al. (1994). Dependence on REM sleep of overnight improvement of a perceptual skill. *Science, 265*, 679–682.

Karpicke, Jeffrey D. (2012). Retrieval-based learning: Active retrieval promotes meaningful learning. *Current Directions in Psychological Science, 21*, 157–163.

Karpicke, Jeffrey D., Butler, Andrew C., & Roediger, Henry L. III. (2009). Metacognitive strategies in student learning: Do students practise retrieval when they study on their own? *Memory, 17*, 471–479.

Karpicke, Jeffrey D., & Roediger, Henry L. III. (2007). Repeated retrieval during learning is the key to long-term retention. *Journal of Memory and Language, 57*, 151–162.

Karpicke, Jeffrey D., & Roediger, Henry L. III. (2008, February 15). The critical importance of retrieval for learning. *Science, 319*, 966–968.

Kaschak, Michael P., Kutta, Timothy J., & Jones, John L. (2011). Structural priming as implicit learning: Cumulative priming effects and individual differences. *Psychonomic Bulletin & Review, 18,* 1133–1139.

Kasser, Tim, & Ryan, Richard M. (2001). Be careful what you wish for: Optimal functioning and the relative attainment of intrinsic and extrinsic goals. In P. Schmuck & K. M. Sheldon (Eds.), *Life goals and well-being.* Lengerich, Germany: Pabst Science.

Katigbak, Marcia S., Church, A. Timothy, Guanzon-Lapeña, Ma. Angeles, et al. (2002). Are indigenous personality dimensions culture specific? Philippine inventories and the Five-Factor model. *Journal of Personality and Social Psychology, 82,* 89–101.

Kato, Tsukasa. (2014). A reconsideration of sex differences in response to sexual and emotional infidelity. *Archive of Sexual Behavior, 43*(7), 1281–1288.

Kaufman, Joan, & Zigler, Edward. (1987). Do abused children become abusive parents? *American Journal of Orthopsychiatry, 57,* 186–192.

Kazdin, Alan E. (2008). Evidence-based treatment and practice: New opportunities to bridge clinical research and practice, enhance the knowledge base, and improve patient care. *American Psychologist, 63,* 146–150.

Kazdin, Alan E. (2012). *Behavior modification in applied settings* (7th ed.). Longrove, IL: Waveland Press.

Kazdin, Alan E. (2015). Technology-based interventions and reducing the burdens of mental illness: Perspectives and comments on the special series. Cognitive and Behavioral Practice, electronic preview.

Keating, Caroline F. (1994). World without words: Messages from face and body. In W. J. Lonner & R. Malpass (Eds.), *Psychology and culture.* Needham Heights, MA: Allyn & Bacon.

Keel, Pamela K., & Klump, Kelly L. (2003). Are eating disorders culture-bound syndromes? Implications for conceptualizing their etiology. *Psychological Bulletin, 129,* 747–769.

Keen, Sam. (1986). *Faces of the enemy: Reflections of the hostile imagination.* San Francisco: Harper & Row.

Keizer, Kees, Lindenberg, Siegwart, & Steg, Linda. (2008, December 12). The spreading of disorder. *Science, 322,* 1681–1685.

Kelman, Herbert C., & Hamilton, V. Lee. (1989). *Crimes of obedience: Toward a social psychology of authority and responsibility.* New Haven, CT: Yale University Press.

Keltner, Dacher, Ellsworth, Phoebe C., & Edwards, Kari. (1993). Beyond simple pessimism: Effects of sadness and anger on social perception. *Journal of Personality and Social Psychology, 64,* 740–752.

Kemeny, Margaret E. (2003). The psychobiology of stress. *Current Directions in Psychological Science, 12,* 124–129.

Kemp, David E. (2014). Managing the side effects associated with commonly used treatments for bipolar depression. *Journal of Affective Disorders, 169* (Suppl. 1), S34–S44.

Kendall, K. Limakatso. (1999). Women in Lesotho and the (Western) construction of homophobia. In E. Blackwood & S. E. Wieringa (Eds.), *Female desires: Same-sex relations and transgender practices across cultures.* New York: Columbia University Press.

Kendler, Kenneth S., Eaves, Lindon J., Loken, Erik K., et al. (2011). The impact of environmental experiences on symptoms of anxiety and depression across the life span. *Psychological Science, 22,* 1343–1352.

Kennedy, Eilis. (2013). Orchids and dandelions: How some children are more susceptible to environmental influences for better or worse and the implications for child development. *Clinical Child Psychology and Psychiatry, 18*(3), 319–321.

Kenny, David A., Snook, Amanda, Boucher, Eliane, & Hancock, Jeffrey T. (2010). Interpersonal sensitivity, status, and stereotype accuracy. *Psychological Science, 21,* 1735–1739.

Kenrick, Douglas T., Sundie, Jill M., Nicastle, Lionel D., & Stone, Gregory O. (2001). Can one ever be too wealthy or too chaste? Searching for nonlinearities in mate judgment. *Journal of Personality and Social Psychology, 80,* 462–471.

Kenrick, Douglas T., & Trost, Melanie R. (1993). The evolutionary perspective. In A. E. Beall & R. J. Sternberg (Eds.), *The psychology of gender.* New York: Guilford Press.

Kern, Margaret L., Della Porta, Serenity S., & Friedman, Howard S. (2014). Lifelong pathways to longevity: Personality, relationships, flourishing, and health. *Journal of Personality, 82*(6), 472–484.

Khan, A., Detke, M., Khan, S. R., & Mallinckrodt, C. (2003). Placebo response and antidepressant clinical trial outcome. *Journal of Nervous and Mental Diseases, 191,* 211–218.

Khan, Cynthia M., Rini, Christine, Bernhardt, Barbara A., Roberts, J. Scott, Christensen, Kurt D., Evans, James P., et al. (2014). How can psychological science inform research about genetic counseling for clinical genomic sequencing? *Journal of Genetic Counseling.*

Khoury, Bassam, Lecomte, Tania, Fortin, Guillaume, Masse, Marjolaine, Therien, Phillip, Bouchard, Vanessa, et al. (2013). Mindfulness-based therapy: A comprehensive meta-analysis. *Clinical Psychology Review, 33*(6), 763–771.

Khoury, Jennifer E., Gonzalez, Andrea, Levitan, Robert, Masellis, Mario, Basile, Vincenzo, & Atkinson, Leslie. (2015). Infant emotion regulation strategy moderates relations between self-reported maternal depressive symptoms and infant hpa activity. Infant and Child Development, electronic preview.

Kibbe, Melissa M., & Leslie, Alan M. (2011). What do infants remember when they forget? Location and identity in 6-month-olds' memory for objects. *Psychological Science, 22,* 1500–1505.

Kida, Thomas. (2006). *Don't believe everything you think: The 6 basic mistakes we make in thinking.* Amherst, NY: Prometheus Books.

Kiecolt-Glaser, Janice K., Loving, Timothy J., Stowell, Jeffrey R., et al. (2005). Hostile marital interactions, proinflammatory cytokine production, and wound healing. *Archives of General Psychiatry, 62,* 1377–1384.

Kiecolt-Glaser, Janice K., & Newton, Tamara L. (2001). Marriage and health: His and hers. *Psychological Bulletin, 127,* 472–503.

Kiecolt-Glaser, Janice K., Page, Gayle G., Marucha, Phillip T., et al. (1998). Psychological influences on surgical recovery: Perspectives from psychoneuroimmunology. *American Psychologist, 53,* 1209–1218.

Kihlstrom, John F. (1994). Hypnosis, delayed recall, and the principles of memory. *International Journal of Clinical and Experimental Hypnosis, 40,* 337–345.

Kim, Heejung S., Sherman, David K., & Taylor, Shelley E. (2008). Culture and social support. *American Psychologist, 63,* 518–526.

Kim, Hengjun J., Kim, Namkug, Kim, Sehyun, Hong, Seokjun, Park, Kyungmo, Lim, Sabina, et al. (2012). Sex differences in amygdala subregions: Evidence from subregional shape analysis. *NeuroImage, 60*(4), 2054–2061.

King, Aimee E., Austin-Oden, Deena, & Lohr, Jeffrey M. (2009, January). Browsing for love in all the wrong places. *Skeptic, 15,* 48–55.

King, M., & Woollett, E. (1997). Sexually assaulted males: 115 men consulting a counseling service. *Archives of Sexual Behavior, 26,* 579–588.

King, Patricia M., & Kitchener, Karen S. (1994). *Developing reflective judgment: Understanding and promoting intellectual growth and critical thinking in adolescents and adults.* San Francisco: Jossey Bass.

King, Patricia M., & Kitchener, Karen S. (2002). The reflective judgment model: Twenty years of research on epistemic cognition. In B. K. Hofer & P. R. Pintrich (Eds.), *Personal epistemology: The psychology of beliefs about knowledge and knowing.* Mahwah, NJ: Erlbaum.

King, Patricia M., & Kitchener, Karen S. (2004). Reflective judgment: Theory and research on the development of epistemic assumptions through adulthood. *Educational Psychologist, 39,* 5–18.

King, Ryan S., Mauer, Marc, & Young, Malcolm C. (2005). *Incarceration and crime: A complex relationship.* Washington, D.C.: The Sentencing Project.

King, Suzanne, St-Hilaire, Annie, & Heidkamp, David. (2010). Prenatal factors in schizophrenia. *Current Directions in Psychological Science, 19,* 209–213.

Kinoshita, Sachiko, & Peek-O'Leary, Marie. (2005). Does the compatibility effect in the race Implicit Association Test reflect familiarity or affect? *Psychonomic Bulletin and Review, 12,* 442–452.

Kinsey, Alfred C., Pomeroy, Wardell B., & Martin, Clyde E. (1948). *Sexual behavior in the human male.* Philadelphia: Saunders.

Kinsey, Alfred C., Pomeroy, Wardell B., Martin, Clyde E., & Gebhard, Paul H. (1953). *Sexual behavior in the human female.* Philadelphia: Saunders.

Kirsch, Irving. (1997). Response expectancy theory and application: A decennial review. *Applied and Preventive Psychology, 6,* 69–70.

Kirsch, Irving. (2004). Conditioning, expectancy, and the placebo effect: Comment on Stewart-Williams and Podd (2004). *Psychological Bulletin, 130,* 341–343.

Kirsch, Irving. (2010). *The emperor's new drugs: Exploding the antidepressant myth.* New York: Basic Books.

Kirsch, Irving, Deacon, B. J., Huedo-Medina, T. B., et al. (2008). Initial severity and antidepressant benefits: A meta-analysis of data submitted to the Food and Drug Administration. *PLoS Medicine, 5,* e45.

Kirsch, Irving, & Lynn, Steven J. (1995). The altered state of hypnosis: Changes in the theoretical landscape. *American Psychologist, 50,* 846–858.

Kirsch, Irving, Silva, Christopher E., Carone, James E., et al. (1989). The surreptitious observation design: An experimental paradigm for distinguishing artifact from essence in hypnosis. *Journal of Abnormal Psychology, 98,* 132–136.

Kissileff, H. R., Thornton, J. C., Torres M. I., et al. (2012). Leptin reverses declines in satiation in weight-reduced obese humans. *American Journal of Clinical Nutrition, 95,* 309–317.

Kitchener, Karen S., Lynch, Cindy L., Fischer, Kurt W., & Wood, Phillip K. (1993). Developmental range of reflective judgment: The effect of contextual support and practice on developmental stage. *Developmental Psychology, 29,* 893–906.

Klauer, Sheila G., Dingus, Thomas A., Neale, Vicki L., et al. (2006). *The impact of driver inattention on near-crash/crash risk: An analysis using the 100-car naturalistic driving study data* [pdf]. Performed by Virginia Tech Transportation Institute, Blacksburg, VA, sponsored by National Highway Traffic Safety Administration, Washington, DC DOT HS 810 594.

Klein, Daniel N., Schwartz, Joseph E., Santiago, Neil J., et al. (2003). Therapeutic alliance in depression treatment: Controlling for prior change and patient characteristics. *Journal of Consulting and Clinical Psychology, 71,* 997–1006.

Klein, Raymond, & Armitage, Roseanne. (1979). Rhythms in human performance: 1 1/2-hour oscillations in cognitive style. *Science, 204,* 1326–1328.

Kleinke, Chris L., Peterson, Thomas R., & Rutledge, Thomas R. (1998). Effects of self-generated facial expressions on mood. *Journal of Personality and Social Psychology, 74,* 272–279.

Kleinman, Arthur. (1988). *Rethinking psychiatry: From cultural category to personal experience.* New York: Free Press.

Klimentidis, Yann C., Beasley, T. Mark, Lin, Hui-Yi, et al. (2011). Canaries in the coal mine: A cross-species analysis of the plurality of obesity epidemics. *Proceedings of the Royal Society B, 278,* 1626–1632.

Klimoski, Richard J. (1992). Graphology and personnel selection. In B. Beyerstein & D. Beyerstein (Eds.), *The write stuff: Evaluations of graphology—The Study of handwriting analysis.* Buffalo, NY: Prometheus Books.

Klingberg, Torkel. (2010). Training and plasticity of working memory. *Trends in Cognitive Sciences, 14,* 317–324.

Kluft, Richard P. (1987). The simulation and dissimulation of multiple personality disorder. *American Journal of Clinical Hypnosis, 30,* 104–118.

Knapp, Mark L., Hall, Judith A., & Horgan, Terrence G. (2014). *Nonverbal communication in human interaction* (8th ed.). Belmont, CA: Wadsworth.

Knuycky, Leslie R., Kleider, Heather M., & Cavrak, Sarah E. (2014). Line-up misidentifications: When being "prototypically black" is perceived as criminal. *Applied Cognitive Psychology, 28*(1), 39–46.

Kochanska, Grazyna, Brock, Rebecca L., Chen, Kuan-Hua, Aksan, Nazan, & Anderson, Steven W. (2015). Paths from mother–child and father–child relationships to externalizing behavior problems in children differing in electrodermal reactivity: A longitudinal study from infancy to age 10. *Journal of Abnormal Child Psychology, 43*(4), 721–734.

Kochanska, Grazyna, Forman, David R., Aksan, Nazan, & Dunbar, Stephen B. (2005). Pathways to conscience: Early mother–child mutually responsive orientation and children's moral emotion, conduct, and cognition. *Journal of Child Psychology and Psychiatry, 46,* 19–34.

Kochanska, Grazyna, & Knaack, Amy. (2003). Effortful control as a personality characteristic of young children: Antecedents, correlates, and consequences. *Journal of Personality, 71,* 1087–1112.

Kohlberg, Lawrence. (1964). Development of moral character and moral ideology. In M. Hoffman & L. W. Hoffman (Eds.), *Review of child development research.* New York: Russell Sage Foundation.

Köhler, Wolfgang. (1925). *The mentality of apes.* New York: Harcourt, Brace.

Köhler, Wolfgang. (1929). *Gestalt psychology.* New York: Horace Liveright.

Köhler, Wolfgang. (1959). Gestalt psychology today. Presidential address to the American Psychological Association, Cincinnati. Reprinted in E. R. Hilgard (Ed.), *American psychology in historical perspective: Addresses of the presidents of the American Psychological Association, 1892–1977.* Washington, DC: American Psychological Association, 1978.

Kok, Bethany E., Catalino, Lahnna I., & Fredrickson, Barbara L. (2008). The broadening, building, buffering effects of positive emotions. In S. J. Lopez (Ed.), *Positive psychology: Exploring the best in people* (Vol 2). Westport, CT: Praeger/Greenwood.

Kok, Bethany E., Coffey, Kimberly A., Cohn, Michael A., Catalino, Lahnna I., Vacharkulksemsuk, Tanya, Algoe, Sara B., et al. (2013). How positive emotions build physical health: Perceived positive social connections account for the upward spiral between positive emotions and vagal tone. *Psychological Science, 24(7),* 1123–1132.

Kolla, Bhanu, P., & Auger, R. Robert. (2011). Jet lag and shift work sleep disorders: How to help reset the internal clock. *Cleveland Clinic Journal of Medicine, 78,* 675–684.

Koller, Karin, Brown, Terry, Spurgeon, Anne, & Levy, Len. (2004). Recent developments in low-level lead exposure and intellectual impairment in children. *Environmental Health Perspectives, 112,* 987–994.

Komarraju, Meera, & Cokley, Kevin O. (2008). Horizontal and vertical dimensions of individualism-collectivism: A comparison of African Americans and European Americans. *Cultural Diversity and Ethnic Minority Psychology, 14,* 336–343.

Kong, Augustine, Frigge, Michael L., Masson, Gisli, et al. (2012, August 22). Rate of de novo mutations and the importance of father's age to disease risk. *Nature, 48,* 471–475.

Konrath, Sara H., Chopik, William J., Hsing, Courtney K., & O'Brien, Ed. (2014). Changes in adult attachment styles in American college students over time: A meta-analysis. *Personality and Social Psychology Review, 18(4),* 326–348.

Koocher, Gerald P., Goodman, Gail S., White, C. Sue, et al. (1995). Psychological science and the use of anatomically detailed dolls in child sexual-abuse assessments. *Psychological Bulletin, 118,* 199–222.

Koocher, Gerald P., McMann, Madeline R., & Stout, Annika O. (2014). Controversial therapies for children. In Candice A. Alfano &Deborah C. Beidel (Eds.), *Comprehensive evidence based interventions for children and adolescents* (pp. 31–42). New York: Wiley.

Kopelman, Peter G., Caterson, Ian D., & Dietz, William H. (Eds.). (2009). *Clinical obesity in adults and children* (3rd ed.). New York: Wiley-Blackwell.

Kornell, Nate. (2009). Metacognition in humans and animals. *Current Directions in Psychological Science, 18,* 11–15.

Kornell, Nate, & Bjork, Robert A. (2007). The promise and perils of self-regulated study. *Psychonomic Bulletin and Review, 14,* 219–224.

Kornum, Birgitte R., Faraco, Juliette, & Mignot, Emmanuel. (2011). Narcolepsy with hypocretin/orexin deficiency, infections and auto-immunity of the brain. *Current Opinion in Neurobiology, 21,* 897–903.

Kosfeld, Michael, Heinrichs, Markus, Zak, Paul J., et al. (2005). Oxytocin increases trust in humans. *Nature, 435,* 673–676.

Koss, Mary. (2011). Hidden, unacknowledged, acquaintance, and date rape: Looking back, looking forward. *Psychology of Women Quarterly, 35,* 348–354.

Kosslyn, Stephen M. (1980). *Image and mind.* Cambridge, MA: Harvard University Press.

Kosslyn, Stephen M., Thompson, William L., Costantini-Ferrando, Maria F., et al. (2000). Hypnotic visual illusion alters color processing in the brain. *American Journal of Psychiatry, 157,* 1279–1284.

Kostović, Ivica, & Judaš, Miloš. (2009). Early development of neuronal circuitry of the human prefrontal cortex. In M. Gazzaniga et al. (Eds.), The cognitive neurosciences (4th ed., pp. 29–47).

Kounios, John, & Beeman, Mark. (2009). The *aha!* moment: The cognitive neuroscience of insight. *Current Directions in Psychological Science, 18,* 210–216.

Koyama, Tetsua, McHaffie, John G., Laurienti, Paul J., & Coghill, Robert C. (2005). The subjective experience of pain: Where expectations become reality. *Proceedings of the National Academy of Sciences, 102,* 12950–12955.

Kraepelin, Emil. (1896). *Psychiatrie: Einlehrbuch fur studeirende und aertze.* Funfte, vollstndig umgearbeitete auflage. Leipzig.

Krantz, David S., Olson, Marian B., Francis, Jennifer L., et al. (2006). Anger, hostility, and cardiac symptoms in women with suspected coronary artery disease: The women's ischemia syndrome evaluation (WISE) study. *Journal of Women's Health, 15,* 1214–1223.

Kraus, Michael W., Côté, Stéphane, & Keltner, Dacher. (2010). Social class, contextualism, and empathic accuracy. *Psychological Science, 21,* 1716–1723.

Krebs, Dennis L. (2008). Morality: An evolutionary account. *Perspectives on Psychological Science, 3,* 149–172.

Krieger, Nancy, & Sidney, S. (1996). Racial discrimination and blood pressure: The CARDIA study of young black and white adults. *American Journal of Public Health, 86,* 1370–1378.

Krimsky, Sheldon. (2003). *Science in the private interest.* Lanham, MD: Rowman & Littlefield.

Kring, Ann, & Gordon, Albert H. (1998). Sex differences in emotion: Expression, experience, and physiology. *Journal of Personality and Social Psychology, 74,* 686–703.

Kring, Ann, Johnson, Sheri, Davison, Gerald C., & Neale, John M. (2010). *Abnormal psychology* (11th ed.). New York: Wiley.

Kross, Ethan, & Ayduk, Ozlem. (2011). Making meaning out of negative experiences by self-distancing. *Current Directions in Psychological Science, 20(3),* 187–191.

Krueger, Alan B. (2007). *What makes a terrorist: Economics and the roots of terrorism.* Princeton, NJ: Princeton University Press.

Krueger, Robert F., Hicks, Brian M., & McGue, Matt. (2001). Altruism and antisocial behavior: Independent tendencies, unique personality correlates, distinct etiologies. *Psychological Science, 12,* 397–402.

Krupa, David J., Thompson, Judith K., & Thompson, Richard F. (1993). Localization of a memory trace in the mammalian brain. *Science, 260,* 989–991.

Krützen, Michael, Mann, Janet, Heithaus, Michael R., et al. (2005). Cultural transmission of tool use in bottlenose dolphins. *Proceedings of the National Academy of Sciences, 102,* 8939–8943.

Krystal, J. H., Rosenheck, Robert A., Kramer, Joyce A., et al. (2011, August 3). Adjunctive risperidone treatment for antidepressant-resistant symptoms of chronic military service–related PTSD: A randomized trial. *Journal of the American Medical Association, 306,* 493.

Kuhl, Patricia K., Williams, Karen A., Lacerda, Francisco, et al. (1992, January 31). Linguistic experience alters phonetic perception in infants by 6 months of age. *Science, 255,* 606–608.

Kuhn, Deanna, Weinstock, Michael, & Flaton, Robin. (1994). How well do jurors reason? Competence dimensions of individual variation in a juror reasoning task. *Psychological Science, 5,* 289–296.

Kuncel, Nathan R., Hezlett, Sarah A., & Ones, Deniz S. (2004). Academic performance, career potential, creativity, and job performance: Can one construct predict them all? *Journal of Personality and Social Psychology, 86,* 148–161.

Kuster, Farah, Orth, Ulrich, & Meier, Laurenz L. (2012). Rumination mediates the prospective effect of low self-esteem on depression: A five-wave longitudinal study. *Personality and Social Psychology Bulletin, 38,* 747–759.

Kutchins, Herb, & Kirk, Stuart A. (1997). *Making us crazy: DSM. The psychiatric bible and the creation of mental disorders.* New York: Free Press.

Laan, Ellen, & Both, Stephanie. (2008). What makes women experience desire? In L. Tiefer (Ed.), The New View campaign against the medicalization of sex (Special Issue). *Feminism and Psychology, 18,* 505–514.

LaBerge, Stephen. (2014). Lucid dreaming: Paradoxes of dreaming consciousness. In Etzel Cardeña, Steven Jay Lynn, & Stanley Krippner (Eds.), *Varieties of anomalous experience: Examining the scientific evidence* (2nd ed., pp. 145–173). Washington, DC: American Psychological Association.

Lacasse, Jeffrey R., & Leo, Jonathan. (2005, December). Serotonin and depression: A disconnect between the advertisements and the scientific literature. *PLoS Medicine,* 2(12): e392.

Lachman, Margie E., & Weaver, Suzanne L. (1998). The sense of control as a moderator of social class differences in health and well-being. *Journal of Personality and Social Psychology, 74,* 763–773.

LaFrance, Marianne. (2011). *Lip service.* New York: Norton.

Lai, Vicky Tzuyin, & Boroditsky, Lera. (2013). The immediate and chronic influence of spatio-temporal metaphors on the mental representations of time in English, Mandarin, and Mandarin-English speakers. *Frontiers in Psychology, 4,* 142.

Lamont, Ruth, Swift, Hannah, & Abrams, Dominic. (electronic preview). A review and meta-analysis of age-based stereotype threat: Negativestereotypes, not facts, do the damage. *Psychology and Aging.*

Lanaj, Klodiana, Chang, Chu-Hsiang, & Johnson, Russell E. (2012). Regulatory focus and work-related outcomes: A review and meta-analysis. *Psychological Bulletin, 138,* 998–1034.

Landrigan, C. P., Fahrenkopf, A. M., Lewin, D., et al. (2008). Effects of the Accreditation Council for Graduate Medical Education duty hour limits on sleep, work hours, and safety. *Pediatrics, 122,* 250–258.

Landrine, Hope. (1988). Revising the framework of abnormal psychology. In P. Bronstein & K. Quina (Eds.), *Teaching a psychology of people.* Washington, DC: American Psychological Association.

Lang, Ariel J., Craske, Michelle G., Brown, Matt, & Ghaneian, Atousa. (2001). Fear-related state dependent memory. *Cognition and Emotion, 15,* 695–703.

Langer, Ellen J., Blank, Arthur, & Chanowitz, Benzion. (1978). The mindlessness of ostensibly thoughtful action: The role of placebic information in interpersonal interaction. *Journal of Personality and Social Psychology, 36,* 635–642.

Lany, Jill, & Gómez, Rebecca L. (2008). Twelve-month-old infants benefit from prior experience in statistical learning. *Psychological Science, 19,* 1247–1252.

Laska, Kevin M., Gurman, Alan S., & Wampold, Bruce E. (2014). Expanding the lens of evidence-based practice in psychotherapy: A common factors perspective. *Psychotherapy,* 51(4), 467–481.

Latremoliere, Alban, & Woolf, Clifford J. (2009). Central sensitization: A generator of pain hypersensitivity by central neural plasticity. *Journal of Pain, 10,* 895–926.

Lau, Hiuyan, Alger, Sara E., & Fishbein, William. (2011). Relational memory: A daytime nap facilitates the abstraction of general concepts. *PloS One, 6,* e27139.

Lavie, Peretz. (1976). Ultradian rhythms in the perception of two apparent motions. *Chronobiologia, 3,* 21–218.

Lavie, Peretz. (2001). Sleep-wake as a biological rhythm. *Annual Review of Psychology, 52,* 277–303.

Lazarus, Richard S., & Folkman, Susan. (1984). *Stress, appraisal, and coping.* New York: Springer.

Lazell, E. W., & Prince, L. H. (1929). A study of the causative factors in dementia praecox. The influence of the blood and serum on embryological cells. A preliminary communication. *U.S. Veterans Bureau Medical Bulletin, 5,* 40–41.

LeDoux, Joseph E. (1996). *The emotional brain.* New York: Simon & Schuster.

Lee, Joowon, Ahn, Jae-Hyeon, & Park, Byungho. (2015). The effect of repetition in Internet banner ads and the moderating role of animation. *Computers in Human Behavior, 46,* 202–209.

Lee, Susan J., & McEwen, Bruce S. (2001). Neurotrophic and neuroprotective actions of estrogens and their therapeutic implications. *Annual Review of Pharmacology & Pharmacological Toxicology, 41,* 569–591.

Lee, Yueh-Ting, McCauley, Clark, & Jussim, Lee. (2013). Stereotypes as valid categories of knowledge and human perceptions of group differences. *Social and Personality Psychology Compass,* 7(7), 470–486.

Legrenzi, Paolo, & Umiltà, Carlo. (2011). *Neuromania: On the limits of brain science.* New York: Oxford University Press.

Leib, Rebecca. (2008). MMPI-2 family problems scales in child-custody litigants. *Dissertation Abstracts International:* Section B: The Sciences and Engineering. 68(7-B), 4879.

Leibenluft, Ellen, & Rich, Brendan A. (2008). Pediatric bipolar disorder. *Annual Review of Clinical Psychology, 4,* 163–187.

Leichsenring, Falk, & Rabung, Sven. (2008). Effectiveness of long-term psychodynamic therapy: A meta-analysis. *Journal of the American Medical Association,* 300(13), 1551–1565.

Leinbach, Mary D., Hort, Barbara E., & Fagot, Beverly I. (1997). Bears are for boys: Metaphorical associations in young children's gender stereotypes. *Cognitive Development, 12,* 107–130.

Lemieux, Robert, & Hale, Jerold L. (2000). Intimacy, passion, and commitment among married individuals: Further testing of the Triangular Theory of Love. *Psychological Reports, 87,* 941–948.

Lent, Roberto, Azevedo, Frederico A. C., Andrade-Moraes, Carlos H., & Pinto, Ana V. O. (2012). How many neurons do you have? Some dogmas of quantitative neuroscience under revision. *European Journal of Neuroscience, 35,* 1–9.

Leo, Richard A. (2008). *Police interrogation and American justice.* Cambridge, MA: Harvard University Press.

Leonard, Karen M. (2008). A cross-cultural investigation of temporal orientation in work organizations: A differentiation matching approach. *International Journal of Intercultural Relations, 32,* 479–492.

Lepore, Stephen J., Ragan, Jennifer D., & Jones, Scott. (2000). Talking facilitates cognitive-emotional processes of adaptation to an acute stressor. *Journal of Personality and Social Psychology, 78,* 499–508.

Leppänen, Jukka, & Nelson, Charles A. (2012). Early development of fear processing. *Current Directions in Psychological Science, 21,* 200–204.

Lepper, Mark R., Greene, David, & Nisbett, Richard E. (1973). Undermining children's intrinsic interest with extrinsic rewards. *Journal of Personality and Social Psychology, 28,* 129–137.

Leproult, Rachel, Van Reeth, Olivier, Byrne, Maria M., et al. (1997). Sleepiness, performance, and neuroendocrine function during sleep deprivation: Effects of exposure to bright light or exercise. *Journal of Biological Rhythms, 12,* 245–258.

Lerner, Melvin J. (1980). *The belief in a just world: A fundamental delusion.* New York: Plenum Press.

Lester, Barry M., LaGasse, Linda L., & Seifer, Ronald. (1998, October 23). Cocaine exposure and children: The meaning of subtle effects. *Science, 282,* 633–634.

Levenson, Robert W., & Miller, Bruce L. (2007). Loss of cells—loss of self. *Current Directions in Psychological Science, 16,* 289–294.

Levenson, Robert W., Ekman, Paul, & Friesen, Wallace V. (1990). Voluntary facial action generates emotion-specific autonomic nervous system activity. *Psychophysiology, 27,* 363–384.

Levine, James A., Eberhardt, Norman L., & Jensen, Michael D. (1999, January 8). Role of nonexercise activity thermogenesis in resistance to fat gain in humans. *Science, 283,* 212–214.

Levine, Judith. (2003). *Harmful to minors.* Minneapolis: University of Minnesota Press.

LeVine, Robert A., & Norman, Karin. (2008). Attachment in anthropological perspective. In R. A. LeVine & R. S. New (Eds.), *Anthropology and child development: A cross-cultural reader.* Malden, MA: Blackwell.

Levine, Robert V. (2003, May–June). The kindness of strangers. *American Scientist, 91,* 227–233.

Levine, Robert V., Norenzayan, Ara, & Philbrick, Karen. (2001). Cross-cultural differences in helping strangers. *Journal of Cross-Cultural Psychology, 32,* 543–560.

Levy, Becca. (1996). Improving memory in old age through implicit self-stereotyping. *Journal of Personality and Social Psychology, 71,* 1092–1107.

Levy, David A. (2010). *Tools of critical thinking: Metathoughts for psychology* (2nd ed.). Long Grove, IL: Waveland.

Levy, Jerre, Trevarthen, Colwyn, & Sperry, Roger W. (1972). Perception of bilateral chimeric figures following hemispheric deconnection. *Brain, 95,* 61–78.

Levy, Robert I. (1984). The emotions in comparative perspective. In K. R. Scherer & P. Ekman (Eds.), *Approaches to emotion.* Hillsdale, NJ: Erlbaum.

Lewin, Kurt. (1948). *Resolving social conflicts.* New York: Harper.

Lewis, Marc D. (2011). Dopamine and the neural "now": Essay and review of *Addiction: A disorder of choice. Perspectives on Psychological Science, 6,* 150–155.

Lewontin, Richard C. (1970). Race and intelligence. *Bulletin of the Atomic Scientists, 26*(3), 2–8.

Lewontin, Richard C. (2001, March 5). Genomania: A disorder of modern biology and medicine. Invited address at the University of California, Los Angeles.

Lewontin, Richard C., Rose, Steven, & Kamin, Leon J. (1984). *Not in our genes: Biology, ideology, and human nature.* New York: Pantheon.

Lewy, Alfred J., Lefler, Bryan J., Emens, Jonathan S., & Bauer, Vance K. (2006). The circadian basis of winter depression. *Proceedings of the National Academy of Sciences, 103,* 7414–7419.

Li, Shu-Chen, Lindenberger, Ulman, Hommel, Bernhard, et al. (2004). Transformations in the couplings among intellectual abilities and constituent cognitive processes across the life span. *Psychological Science, 15,* 155–163.

Lichtenstein, Edward, Zhu, Shu-Hong, & Tedeschi, Gary J. (2010). Smoking cessation quitlines: An underrecognized intervention success story. *American Psychologist, 65,* 252–261.

Lieberman, J. A., Stroup, T. S., McEvoy, J. P., et al. (2005, September 22). Effectiveness of antipsychotic drugs in patients with chronic schizophrenia. *New England Journal of Medicine, 353,* 1209–1223.

Lieberman, Matthew. (2000). Intuition: A social cognitive neuroscience approach. *Psychological Bulletin, 126,* 109–137.

Lien, Mei-Ching, Ruthruff, Eric, & Johnston, James C. (2006). Attentional limitations in doing two tasks at once: The search for exceptions. *Current Directions in Psychological Science, 16,* 89–93.

Liepert, J., Bauder, H., Miltner, W. H., et al. (2000). Treatment-induced cortical reorganization after stroke in humans. *Stroke, 31,* 1210–1216.

Lilienfeld, Scott O. (2007). Psychological treatments that cause harm. *Perspectives on Psychological Science, 2,* 53–70.

Lilienfeld, Scott O. (2014). The Dodo Bird verdict: Status in 2014. *The Behavior Therapist, 37*(4), 91–95.

Lilienfeld, Scott O., & Lynn, Steven Jay. (2015). Dissociative identity disorder: A contemporary scientific perspective. In Scott O. Lilienfeld; Steven Jay Lynn; & Jeffry M. Lohr (Eds.), *Science and pseudoscience in clinical psychology* (2nd ed., pp. 113–152). New York: Guilford Press.

Lilienfeld, Scott O., Lynn, Steven Jay, Kirsch, Irving, et al. (1999). Dissociative identity disorder and the sociocognitive model: Recalling the lessons of the past. *Psychological Bulletin, 125,* 507–523.

Lilienfeld, Scott O., Lynn, Steven Jay, & Lohr, Jeffrey M. (Eds.). (2015). *Science and pseudoscience in clinical psychology.* (2nd ed.) New York: Guilford Press.

Lin, Keh-Ming, Poland, Russell E., & Chien, C. P. (1990). Ethnicity and psychopharmacology: Recent findings and future research directions. In E. Sorel (Ed.), *Family, culture, and psychobiology.* New York: Legas.

Lindquist, Kristen A., & Barrett, Lisa F. (2008). Constructing emotion. *Psychological Science, 19,* 898–903.

Lindsay, D. Stephen, Hagen, Lisa, Read, J. Don, et al. (2004). True photographs and false memories. *Psychological Science, 15,* 149–154.

Lindsay, D. Stephen, & Read, J. Don. (1994). Psychotherapy and memories of childhood sexual abuse: A cognitive perspective. *Applied Cognitive Psychology, 8,* 281–338.

Linton, Simi. (1998). *Claiming disability: Knowledge and identity.* New York: New York University Press.

Linton, Simi. (2006). *My body politic.* Ann Arbor, University of Michigan Press.

Linville, P. W., Fischer, G. W., & Fischhoff, B. (1992). AIDS risk perceptions and decision biases. In J. B. Pryor & G. D. Reeder (Eds.), *The social psychology of HIV infection.* Hillsdale, NJ: Erlbaum.

Lionetti, Francesca, Pastore, Massimiliano, & Barone, Lavinia. (2015). Attachment in institutionalized children: A review and meta-analysis. *Child Abuse and Neglect, 42,* 135–145.

Lisman, John, Yasuda, Ryohei, & Raghavachari, Stridhar. (2012). Mechanisms of CaMKII action in long-term potentiation. *Nature Reviews Neuroscience, 13,* 169–182.

Lissner, L., Odell, P. M., D'Agostino, R. B., et al. (1991, June 27). Variability of body weight and health outcomes in the Framingham population. *New England Journal of Medicine, 324,* 1839–1844.

Liu, Ke, Chen, DaiShi, Guo, WeiWei, Yu, Ning, Wang, Xiao Yu, Ji, Fei, et al. (2014). Spontaneous and partial repair of ribbon synapse in cochlear inner haircells after ototoxic withdrawal. *Molecular Neurobiology.*

Lloyd-Richardson, E. E., Bailey, S., Fava, J. L., Wing, R., Tobacco Etiology Research Network (TERN). (2009). A prospective study of weight gain during the college freshman and sophomore years. *Preventive Medicine, 48,* 256–261.

LoBue, Vanessa, & DeLoache, Judy S. (2008). Detecting the snake in the grass. *Psychological Science, 19,* 284–289.

LoBue, Vanessa, & DeLoache, Judy S. (2011). What's so special about slithering serpents? Children and adults rapidly detect snakes based on their simple features. *Visual Cognition, 19*(1), 129–143.

Locke, Edwin A., & Latham, Gary P. (2002). Building a practically useful theory of goal setting and task motivation. *American Psychologist, 57,* 705–717.

Locke, Edwin A., & Latham, Gary P. (2006). New directions in goal-setting theory. *Current Directions in Psychological Science, 15,* 265–268.

Loehlin, John C., Horn, J. M., & Willerman, L. (1996). Heredity, environment, and IQ in the Texas adoption study. In R. J. Sternberg & E. Grigorenko (Eds.), *Intelligence: Heredity and environment.* New York: Cambridge University Press.

Loftus, Elizabeth F. (2011). Intelligence gathering post-9/11. *American Psychologist, 66,* 532–541.

Loftus, Elizabeth F., & Greene, Edith. (1980). Warning: Even memory for faces may be contagious. *Law and Human Behavior, 4,* 323–334.

Loftus, Elizabeth, & Guyer, Melvin J. (2002). Who abused Jane Doe? *Skeptical Inquirer.* Part 1: May/June, 24–32. Part 2: July/August, 37–40.

Loftus, Elizabeth F., Miller, David G., & Burns, Helen J. (1978). Semantic integration of verbal information into a visual memory. *Journal of Experimental Psychology: Human Learning and Memory, 4,* 19–31.

Loftus, Elizabeth F., & Palmer, John C. (1974). Reconstruction of automobile destruction: An example of the interaction between language and memory. *Journal of Verbal Learning and Verbal Behavior, 13,* 585–589.

Loftus, Elizabeth F., & Pickrell, Jacqueline E. (1995). The formation of false memories. *Psychiatric Annals, 25,* 720–725.

Longo, Matthew R., & Haggard, Patrick. (2012). What is it like to have a body? *Current Directions in Psychological Science, 21,* 140–145.

Lonner, Walter J. (1995). Culture and human diversity. In E. Trickett, R. Watts, & D. Birman (Eds.), *Human diversity: Perspectives on people in context.* San Francisco: Jossey-Bass.

Lonner, Walter J., & Malpass, Roy. (Eds.) (1994). *Psychology and culture.* Needham Heights, MA: Allyn & Bacon.

Lonsdorf, Tina B., Weike, Almut I., Nikamo, Pernilla, et al. (2009). Genetic gating of human fear learning and extinction: Possible implications for gene-environment interaction in anxiety disorder. *Psychological Science, 20,* 198–206.

López, Steven R. (1995). Testing ethnic minority children. In B. B. Wolman (Ed.), *The encyclopedia of psychology, psychiatry, and psychoanalysis.* New York: Holt.

Lorber, Michael F. (2004). Psychophysiology of aggression, psychopathy, and conduct problems: A meta-analysis. *Psychological Bulletin, 130,* 531–552.

Lövdén, Martin, Bächman, Lars, Lindenberger, Ulman, et al. (2010). A theoretical framework for the study of adult cognitive plasticity. *Psychological Bulletin, 136,* 659–676.

Loughnan, Steve, Kuppens, Peter, Allik, Jüri, et al. (2011). Economic inequality is linked to biased self-perception. *Psychological Science, 22,* 1254–1258.

Löw, Andreas, Lang, Peter J., Smith, J. Carson, & Bradley, Margaret M. (2008). Both predator and prey: Emotional arousal in threat and reward. *Psychological Science, 19,* 865–873.

Lozano, A. M., Mayberg, H. S., Giacobbe, P., et al. (2008). Subcallosal cingulate gyrus deep brain stimulation for treatment-resistant depression. *Biological Psychiatry, 64,* 461–467.

Lu, Luo. (2008). The individual-oriented and social-oriented Chinese bicultural self: Testing the theory. *Journal of Social Psychology, 148,* 347–373.

Lubinski, David. (2004). Introduction to the special section on cognitive abilities: 100 years after Spearman's (1904) "'General Intelligence,' objectively determined and measured." *Journal of Personality and Social Psychology, 86,* 96–111.

Lucchina, L. A., Curtis, O. F., Putnam, P., et al. (1998). Psychophysical measurement of 6-n-propylthiouracil (PROP) taste perception. *Annals of the New York Academy of Sciences, 855,* 816–819.

Ludeke, Steven, Johnson, Wendy, & Bouchard, Thomas J. Jr. (2013). "Obedience to traditional authority": A heritable factor underlying authoritarianism, conservatism and religiousness. *Personality and Individual Differences, 55*(4), 375–380.

Luders, Eileen, Narr, Katherine L., Thompson, Paul M., et al. (2004). Gender differences in cortical complexity. *Nature Neuroscience, 7,* 799–800.

Ludwig, David S., & Currie, Janet. (2010). The association between pregnancy weight gain and birthweight: A within-family comparison. *The Lancet, 376,* 984–990.

Lugaresi, Elio, Medori, R., Montagna, P., et al. (1986, October 16). Fatal familial insomnia and dysautonomia with selective degeneration of thalamic nuclei. *New England Journal of Medicine, 315,* 997–1003.

Luhrmann, T. M. (2000). *Of two minds: The growing disorder in American psychiatry.* New York: Knopf.

Luo, Yuyan, & Baillargeon, Renée. (2010). Toward a mentalistic account of early psychological reasoning. *Current Directions in Psychological Science, 19,* 301–307.

Luria, Alexander R. (1980). *Higher cortical functions in man* (2nd rev. ed.). New York: Basic Books.

Lutz, Catherine. (1988). *Unnatural emotions.* Chicago: University of Chicago Press.

Lykken, David T. (1995). *The antisocial personalities.* Hillsdale, NJ: Erlbaum.

Lykken, David T. (1998). *A tremor in the blood: Uses and abuses of the lie detector.* New York: Plenum Press.

Lykken, David T., & Tellegen, Auke. (1996). Happiness is a stochastic phenomenon. *Psychological Science, 7,* 186–189.

Lynn, Steven Jay, & Green, Joseph P. (2011). The sociocognitive and dissociation theories of hypnosis: Toward a rapprochement. *Clinical and Experimental Hypnosis, 59,* 277–293.

Lynn, Steven Jay, & Kirsch, Irving. (2015). Hypnosis, suggestion, and suggestibility: An integrative model. *American Journal of Clinical Hypnosis, 57*(3), 314–329.

Lynn, Steven Jay, Krackow, Elisa, Loftus, Elizabeth F., Locke, Timothy G., & Lilienfeld, Scott O. (2015). Constructing the past: Problematic memory recovery techniques in psychotherapy. In Scott O. Lilienfeld; Steven Jay Lynn; & Jeffrey M. Lohr (Eds.), *Science and pseudoscience in clinical psychology* (2nd ed., pp. 210–244). New York: Guilford Press.

Lynn, Steven Jay, Lilienfeld, Scott O., Merckelbach, Harald, et al. (2012). Dissociation and dissociative disorders: Challenging conventional wisdom. *Current Directions in Psychological Science, 21,* 48–53.

Lynn, Steven Jay, Rhue, Judith W., & Weekes, John R. (1990). Hypnotic involuntariness: A social cognitive analysis. *Psychological Review, 97,* 69–184.

Lytton, Hugh, & Romney, David M. (1991). Parents' differential socialization of boys and girls: A meta-analysis. *Psychological Bulletin, 109,* 267–296.

Müller, Christian P., & Homberg, Judith R. (2015). The role of serotonin in drug use and addiction. *Behavioural Brain Research, 277,* 146–192.

Ma, Wei Ji, Husain, Masud, & Bays, Paul M. (2014). Changing concepts of working memory. *Nature Neuroscience, 17*(3), 347–356.

Maass, Anne, Cadinu, Mara, Guarnieri, Gaia, & Grasselli, Annalisa. (2003). Sexual harassment under social identity threat: The computer harassment paradigm. *Journal of Personality and Social Psychology, 85,* 853–870.

MacArthur Foundation Research Network on Successful Midlife Development. (1999). Report of latest findings. Available at http://midmac.med.harvard.edu/.

Maccoby, Eleanor E. (1998). *The two sexes: Growing up apart, coming together.* Cambridge, MA: Belknap Press/Harvard University Press.

Maccoby, Eleanor E. (2002). Gender and group process: A developmental perspective. *Current Directions in Psychological Science, 11,* 54–58.

Mack, Arien. (2003). Inattentional blindness: Looking without seeing. *Current Directions in Psychological Science, 12,* 180–184.

Macrae, C. Neil, & Bodenhausen, Galen V. (2000). Social cognition: Thinking categorically about others. *Annual Review of Psychology, 51,* 93–120.

Maddux, James E. (Ed.). (1995). *Self-efficacy, adaptation, and adjustment: Theory, research, and application.* New York: Plenum Press.

Madsen, Kreesten M., Hviid, Anders, Vestergaard, Mogens, et al. (2002). A population-based study of measles, mumps, and rubella vaccination and autism. *New England Journal of Medicine, 347,* 1477–1482.

Maia, Tiago V. (2009). Fear conditioning and social groups: Statistics, not genetics. *Cognitive Science, 33*(7), 1232–1251.

Majid, Asifa, Jordan, Fiona, Dunn, Michael. (2014). Semantic systems in closely related languages. *Language Sciences, 49,* 1–18.

Malamuth, Neil M., Linz, Daniel, Heavey, Christopher L., et al. (1995). Using the confluence model of sexual aggression to predict men's conflict with women: A 10-year follow-up study. *Journal of Personality and Social Psychology, 69,* 353–369.

Mandrusiak, Michael, Rudd, M. David, Joiner Jr., Thomas E., et al. (2006). Warning signs for suicide on the Internet: A descriptive study. *Suicide and Life-Threatening Behavior, 36,* 263–271.

Manning, Carol A., Hall, J. L., & Gold, Paul E. (1990). Glucose effects on memory and other neuropsychological tests in elderly humans. *Psychological Science, 1,* 307–311.

March, J. S. (2011). The preschool ADHD Treatment Study (PATS) as the culmination of twenty years of clinical trials in pediatric psychopharmacology. *Journal of the American Academy of Child and Adolescent Psychiatry, 50,* 427–430.

Marcus, David K., O'Connell, Debra, Norris, Alyssa L., & Sawaqdeh, Abere. (2014). Is the dodo bird endangered in the 21st century?: A meta-analysis of treatment comparison studies. *Clinical Psychology Review, 34*(7), 519–530.

Marcus, Gary. (2004). *The birth of the mind: How a tiny number of genes creates the complexities of human thought.* New York: Basic Books.

Marcus, Gary, Pinker, Steven, Ullman, Michael, et al. (1992). Overregularization in language acquisition. *Monographs of the Society for Research in Child Development, 57* (Serial No. 228), 1–182.

Marcus-Newhall, Amy, Pedersen, William C., Carlson, Mike, & Miller, Norman. (2000). Displaced aggression is alive and well: A meta-analytic review. *Journal of Personality and Social Psychology, 78,* 670–689.

Margolin, Gayla, & Gordis, Elana B. (2004). Children's exposure to violence in the family and community. *Current Directions in Psychological Science, 13,* 152–155.

Mariën, Peter, Ackermann, Herman, Adamaszek, Michael, Barwood, Caroline H. S., Beaton, Alan, Desmond, John, et al. (2014). Consensus paper: Language and the cerebellum: An ongoing enigma. *The Cerebellum, 13*(3), 386–410.

Mariotti, Paolo, Di Giacopo, Raffaella, Mazza, Marianna, Martini, Annalisa, & Canestri, Jorge. (2015). Rapid eye movement sleep behavior disorder: A window on the emotional world of Parkinson disease. *Sleep: Journal of Sleep and Sleep Disorders Research, 38*(2), 287–294.

Markus, Hazel R., & Kitayama, Shinobu. (1991). Culture and the self: Implications for cognition, emotion, and motivation. *Psychological Review, 98,* 224–253.

Marlatt, G. Alan, & Rohsenow, Damaris J. (1980). Cognitive processes in alcohol use: Expectancy and the balanced placebo design. In N. K. Mello (Ed.), *Advances in substance abuse* (Vol. 1). Greenwich, CT: JAI Press.

Marsh, Elizabeth J., & Tversky, Barbara. (2004). Spinning the stories of our lives. *Applied Cognitive Psychology, 18,* 491–503.

Martin, Carol Lynn, & Dinella, Lisa M. (2012). Congruence between gender stereotypes and activity preference in self-identified tomboys and non-tomboys. *Archives of Sexual Behavior, 41*(3), 599–610.

Martin, Carol Lynn, & Ruble, Diane. (2004). Children's search for gender cues. *Current Directions in Psychological Science, 13,* 67–70.

Martin, Carol Lynn, Ruble, Diane, & Szkrybalo, Joel. (2002). Cognitive theories of early gender development. *Psychological Bulletin, 128,* 903–933.

Martin, Garry, & Pear, Joseph. (2014). *Behavior modification: What it is and how to do it* (10th ed.). New York: Psychology Press.

Maruta, T., Colligan R. C., Malinchoc, M., & Offord, K. P. (2000). Optimists vs. pessimists: Survival rate among medical patients over a 30-year period. *Mayo Clinic Proceedings, 75,* 140–143.

Marvan, M. L., Diaz-Erosa, M., & Montesinos, A. (1998). Premenstrual symptoms in Mexican women with different educational levels. *Journal of Psychology, 132,* 517–526.

Masand, P. S. (2000). Side effects of antipsychotics in the elderly. *Journal of Clinical Psychiatry, 61*(Suppl. 8), 43–49.

Maslach, Christina, Schaufeli, Wilmar B., & Leiter, Michael P. (2001). Job burnout. *Annual Review of Psychology, 52,* 397–422.

Maslow, Abraham H. (1970) *Motivation and personality* (2nd ed.). New York: Harper & Row.

Maslow, Abraham H. (1971). *The farther reaches of human nature.* New York: Viking.

Maslow, Carey B., Caramanica, Kimberly, Welch, Alice E., Stellman, Steven D., Brackbill, Robert M., & Farfel, Mark R. (2015). Trajectories of scores on a screening instrument for PTSD among world trade center rescue, recovery, and clean-up workers. *Journal of Traumatic Stress, 28*(3), 198–205.

Mason, Michael P. (2008). *Head cases: Stories of brain injury and its aftermath.* New York: Farrar, Straus, & Giroux.

Masten, Ann S. (2001). Ordinary magic: Resilience processes in development. *American Psychologist, 56,* 227–238.

Masters, William H., & Johnson, Virginia E. (1966). *Human sexual response.* Boston: Little, Brown.

Masuda, Takahiko, & Nisbett, Richard E. (2001). Attending holistically versus analytically: Comparing the context sensitivity of Japanese and Americans. *Journal of Personality and Social Psychology, 81,* 922–934.

Mather, Jennifer A., & Anderson, Roland C. (1993). Personalities of octopuses (Octopus rubescens). *Journal of Comparative Psychology, 197,* 336–340.

Mather, Mara, Shafir, Eldar, & Johnson, Marcia K. (2000). Misremembrance of options past: Source monitoring and choice. *Psychological Science, 11,* 132–138.

Mathews, Andrew, & MacLeod, Colin. (2005). Cognitive vulnerability to emotional disorders. *Annual Review of Clinical Psychology, I,* 167–195.

Mathy, Fabien, & Feldman, Jacob. (2012). What's magic about magic numbers?: Chunking and data compression inshort-term memory. *Cognition, 122*(3), 346–362.

Matlin, Margaret. (2012). *The psychology of women* (7th ed.). Belmont, CA: Cengage.

Matsumoto, David. (1996). *Culture and psychology.* Pacific Grove, CA: Brooks-Cole.

Matsumoto, David, & Hwang, Hyisung. (2013). Cultural similarities and differences in emblematic gestures. *Journal of Nonverbal Behavior, 37*(1), 1–27.

Matsumoto, David, & Yoo, Seung Hee. (2006). Toward a new generation of cross-cultural research. *Perspectives on Psychological Science, 1,* 234–250.

Matthews, Gerald, Zeidner, Moshe, & Roberts, Richard D. (2003) *Emotional intelligence: Science and myth.* Cambridge, MA: MIT Press/Bradford Books.

Matthews, Gerald, Zeidner, Moshe, & Roberts, Richard D. (2012). Emotional intelligence: A promise unfulfilled? *Japanese Psychological Research, 54*(2), 105–127.

Mauas, Viviana, Kopala-Sibley, Daniel C., & Zuroff, David C. (2014). Depressive symptoms in the transition to menopause: The roles of irritability, personality vulnerability, and self-regulation. *Archives of Women's Mental Health, 17*(4), 279–289.

Mayer, Jane. (2009). *The dark side: The inside story of how the war on terror turned into a war on American ideals* (reprint edition). New York: Anchor.

Mayer, John D., & Salovey, Peter. (1997). What is emotional intelligence? In P. Salovey & D. Sluyter (Eds.), *Emotional development and emotional intelligence: Implications for educators.* New York: Basic Books.

Mayou, R. A., Ehlers, A., & Hobbs, M. (2000). Psychological debriefing for road traffic accident victims. *British Journal of Psychiatry, 176,* 589–593.

Mazza, James J., & Reynolds, William M. (1999). Exposure to violence in young inner-city adolescents: Relationships with suicidal ideation, depression, and PTSD symptomatology. *Journal of Abnormal Child Psychology, 27,* 203–213.

Mazzoni, Giuliana A., Loftus, Elizabeth F., & Kirsch, Irving. (2001). Changing beliefs about implausible autobiographical events: A little plausibility goes a long way. *Journal of Experimental Psychology: Applied, 7,* 51–59.

Mazzoni, Giuliana A., Loftus, Elizabeth F., Seitz, Aaron, & Lynn, Steven J. (1999). Changing beliefs and memories through dream interpretation. *Applied Cognitive Psychology, 13,* 125–144.

McAdams, Dan P. (2006). *The redemptive self: Stories Americans live by.* New York: Oxford University Press.

McAdams, Dan P., & Guo, Jen. (2015). Narrating the generative life. *Psychological Science, 26*(4), 475–483.

McAdams, Dan P., & Manczak, Erika. (2015). Personality and the life story. In Mario Mikulincer; Phillip R. Shaver; Lynne M. Cooper; & Randy J. Larsen (Eds.), *APA handbook of personality and social psychology: Volume 4. Personality processes and individual differences* (pp. 425–446). Washington, DC: American Psychological Association.

McAdams, Dan P., & McLean, Kate C. (2013). Narrative identity. *Current Directions in Psychological Science, 22*(3), 233–238.

McCabe, David P., & Castel, Alan D. (2008). Seeing is believing: The effect of brain images on judgments of scientific reasonsing. *Cognition, 107,* 343–352.

McClearn, Gerald E., Johanson, Boo, Berg, Stig, et al. (1997). Substantial genetic influence on cognitive abilities in twins 80 or more years old. *Science, 176,* 1560–1563.

McClelland, James L. (1994). The organization of memory: A parallel distributed processing perspective. *Revue Neurologique, 150,* 570–579.

McClelland, James L. (2011). Memory as a constructive process: The parallel-distributed processing approach. In S. Nalbantian, P. Matthews, & J. L. McClelland (Eds.), *The memory process: Neuroscientific and humanistic perspectives.* Cambridge, MA: MIT Press.

McCord, Joan. (1989). Another time, another drug. Paper presented at a conference on Vulnerability to the Transition from Drug Use to Abuse and Dependence, Rockville, MD.

McCrae, Robert R. (1987). Creativity, divergent thinking, and openness to experience. *Journal of Personality and Social Psychology, 52,* 1258–1265.

McCrae, Robert R., Terracciano, Antonio, & members of the Personality Profiles of Cultures Project. (2005). Universal features of personality traits from the observer's perspective: Data from 50 cultures. *Journal of Personality and Social Psychology, 88,* 547–561.

McDaniel, Mark A., Argarwal, Pooja K., Huelser, Barbie J., McDermott, Kathleen B., & Roediger, Henry L. III. (2011). Test-enhanced learning in a middle school science classroom: The effects of quiz frequency and placement. *Journal of Educational Psychology, 103,* 199–414.

McDaniel, Mark A., Howard, Daniel C., & Einstein, Gilles O. (2009). The Read-Recite-Review study strategy: Effective and portable. *Psychological Science, 20,* 516–522.

McDonough, Laraine, & Mandler, Jean M. (1994). Very long-term recall in infancy. *Memory, 2,* 339–352.

McEwen, Bruce S. (2007). Physiology and neurobiology of stress and adaptation: Central role of the brain. *Physiological Review, 87,* 873–904.

McFadden, Dennis. (2008). What do sex, twins, spotted hyenas, ADHD, and sexual orientation have in common? *Perspectives on Psychological Science, 3,* 309–322.

McFarlane, Jessica, Martin, Carol L., & Williams, Tannis M. (1988). Mood fluctuations: Women versus men and menstrual versus other cycles. *Psychology of Women Quarterly, 12,* 201–223.

McFarlane, Jessica M., & Williams, Tannis M. (1994). Placing premenstrual syndrome in perspective. *Psychology of Women Quarterly, 18,* 339–373.

McGaugh, James L. (1990). Significance and remembrance: The role of neuromodulatory systems. *Psychological Science, 1,* 15–25.

McGee, Harold. (2010, April 13). Cilantro haters, it's not your fault. *New York Times.* Available at www.nytimes.com/2010/04/14/dining/14curious.html.

McGeown, William J., Venneri, Annalena, Kirsch, Irving, et al. (2012). Suggested visual hallucination without hypnosis enhances activity in visual areas of the brain. *Consciousness and Cognition, 21,* 100–116.

McGoldrick, Monica. (2005). Irish families. In M. McGoldrick, J. Giordano, & N. Garcia-Preto (Eds.), *Ethnicity and family therapy* (3rd ed.). New York: Guilford.

McGrayne, Sharon B. (2011). *The theory that would not die: How Bayes' rule cracked the Enigma code, hunted down Russian submarines and emerged triumphant from two centuries of controversy.* New Haven, CT: Yale University Press.

McGregor, Ian, & Holmes, John G. (1999). How storytelling shapes memory and impressions of relationship events over time. *Journal of Personality and Social Psychology, 76,* 403–419.

McGue, Matt, Bouchard, Thomas J., Jr., Iacono, William G., & Lykken, David T. (1993). Behavioral genetics of cognitive ability: A life-span perspective. In R. Plomin & G. E. McClearn (Eds.), *Nature, nurture, and psychology.* Washington, DC: American Psychological Association.

McHugh, Paul R. (2008). *Try to remember: Psychiatry's clash over meaning, memory, and mind.* New York: Dana Press.

McHugh, Paul R., Lief, Harold I., Freyd, Pamela P., & Fetkewicz, Janet M. (2004). From refusal to reconciliation: Family relationships after an accusation based on recovered memories. *Journal of Nervous and Mental Disease, 192,* 525–531.

McKee, Richard D., & Squire, Larry R. (1992). Equivalent forgetting rates in long-term memory for diencephalic and medial temporal lobe amnesia. *Journal of Neuroscience, 12,* 3765–3772.

McKemy, D. D., Neuhausser, W. M., Julius, D. (2002). Identification of a cold receptor reveals a general role for TRP channels in thermosensation. *Nature, 416,* 52–58.

McKinlay, John B., McKinlay, Sonja M., & Brambilla, Donald. (1987). The relative contributions of endocrine changes and social circumstances to depression in mid-aged women. *Journal of Health and Social Behavior, 28,* 345–363.

McNally, Richard J. (2003). *Remembering trauma.* Cambridge, MA: Harvard University Press.

McNally, Richard J. (2011). *What is mental illness?* Cambridge, MA: Harvard University Press.

McNally, Richard J., Bryant, Richard A., & Ehlers, Anke. (2003). Does early psychological intervention promote recovery from post-traumatic stress? *Psychological Science in the Public Interest, 4,* 45–79.

McNulty, James K. (2011). The dark side of forgiveness: The tendency to forgive predicts continued psychological and physical aggression in marriage. *Journal of Family Psychology, 24,* 787–790.

McNulty, James K., & Fincham, Frank D. (2012). Beyond positive psychology? Toward a contextual view of psychological processes and well-being. *American Psychologist, 67,* 101–110.

Medawar, Peter B. (1979). *Advice to a young scientist.* New York: Harper & Row.

Mednick, Sara C., Cai, Denise J., Shuman, Tristan, et al. (2011). An opportunistic theory of cellular and systems consolidation. *Trends in Neuroscience, 34,* 504–514.

Mednick, Sara C., Nakayama, Ken, Cantero, Jose L., et al. (2002). The restorative effect of naps on perceptual deterioration. *Nature Neuroscience, 5,* 677–681.

Mednick, Sarnoff A. (1962). The associative basis of the creative process. *Psychological Review, 69,* 220–232.

Medvec, Victoria H., Madey, Scott F., & Gilovich, Thomas. (1995). When less is more: Counterfactual thinking and satisfaction among Olympic medalists. *Journal of Personality and Social Psychology, 69,* 603–610.

Meeus, Wim H. J., & Raaijmakers, Quinten A. W. (1995). Obedience in modern society: The Utrecht studies. In A. G. Miller, B. E. Collins, & D. E. Brief (Eds.), Perspectives on obedience to authority: The legacy of the Milgram experiments (Special Issue). *Journal of Social Issues, 51,*155–175.

Mehl, Matthias R., Vazire, Simine, Ramírez-Esparza, Nairán, & Pennebacker, James W. (2007). Are women really more talkative than men? *Science, 317,* 82.

Meijer, Ewout H., & Verschuere, Bruno. (2015). The polygraph: Current practice and new approaches. In Pär Anders Granhag; Aldert Vrij; & Bruno Verschuere (Eds.), *Detecting deception: Current challenges and cognitive approaches* (pp. 59–80). New York: Wiley-Blackwell.

Meindl, James R., & Lerner, Melvin J. (1985). Exacerbation of extreme responses to an out-group. *Journal of Personality and Social Psychology, 47,* 71–84.

Meltzoff, Andrew N., & Gopnik, Alison. (1993). The role of imitation in understanding persons and developing a theory of mind. In S. Baron-Cohen, H. Tager-Flusberg, & D. Cohen (Eds.), *Understanding other minds.* New York: Oxford University Press.

Melzack, Ronald. (1992, April). Phantom limbs. *Scientific American, 266,* 120–126. Reprinted in the special issue, Mysteries of the Mind, 1997.

Melzack, Ronald. (1993). Pain: Past, present and future. *Canadian Journal of Experimental Psychology, 47,* 615–629.

Melzack, Ronald, & Wall, Patrick D. (1965). Pain mechanisms: A new theory. *Science, 13,* 971–979.

Mendell, Lorne M. (2014). Constructing and deconstructing the gate theory of pain. *Pain, 155*(2), 210–216.

Mendoza-Denton, Rodolfo, & Page-Gould, Elizabeth. (2008). Can cross-group friendships influence minority students' well-being at historically white universities? *Psychological Science, 19,* 933–939.

Mennella, Julie A., Lukasewycz, Laura D., Castor, Sara M., & Beauchamp, Gary K. (2011). The timing and duration of a sensitive period in human flavor learning: A randomized trial. *American Journal of Clinical Nutrition, 93,* 1019–1024.

Menting, Barbara, Van Lier, Pol A. C., Koot, Hans M., Pardini, Dustin, & Loeber, Rolf. (2015). Cognitive impulsivity and the development of delinquency from late childhood to early adulthood: Moderating effects of parenting behavior and peer relationships. *Development and Psychopathology,* electronic preview.

Mercer, Jean. (2006). *Understanding attachment.* Westport, CT: Praeger.

Mercer, Jean, Sarner, Larry, and Rosa, Linda. (2003). *Attachment therapy on trial.* Westport, CT: Praeger.

Merikle, Philip M., & Skanes, Heather E. (1992). Subliminal self-help audiotapes: A search for placebo effects. *Journal of Applied Psychology, 77,* 772–776.

Merskey, Harold. (1992). The manufacture of personalities: The production of MPD. *British Journal of Psychiatry, 160,* 327–340.

Merton, Robert K. (1948). The self-fulfilling prophecy. *Antioch Review, 8,* 193–210.

Mesquita, Batja, & Frijda, Nico H. (1992). Cultural variations in emotions: A review. *Psychological Bulletin, 112,* 179–204.

Messerli, Franz H. (2012). Chocolate consumption, cognitive function, and Nobel laureates. *New England Journal of Medicine, 367,* 1562–1564.

Meston, Cindy M., & Buss, David M. (2007). Why humans have sex. *Archives of Sexual Behavior, 36,* 477–507.

Metcalfe, Janet. (2009). Metacognitive judgments and control of study. *Current Directions in Psychological Science, 18,* 159–163.

Meyer, Adolf. (1910–1911). The nature and conception of dementia praecox. *Journal of Abnormal Psychology, 5*(5), 274–285.

Meyer, Gregory J., Finn, Stephen E., Eyde, Lorraine D., et al. (2001). Psychological testing and psychological assessment. *American Psychologist, 56,* 128–165.

Mezulis, Amy H., Abramson, Lyn Y., Hyde, Janet S., & Hankin, Benjamin L. (2004). Is there a positivity bias in attributions? *Psychological Bulletin, 130,* 711–747.

Mgode, Georgies F., Wetjens, Bart J., Nwrath, Thorben, et al. (2012). Diagnosis of tuberculosis by trained african giant pouched rats and confounding impact of pathogens and microflora of the respiratory tract. *Journal of Clinical Microbiology, 50,* 274–280.

Michael, Robert B., Garry, Maryanne, & Kirsch, Irving. (2012). Suggestion, cognition, and behavior. *Current Directions in Psychological Science, 21,* 151–156.

Michel, Maximilian, & Lyons, Lisa C. (2014). Unraveling the complexities of circadian and sleep interactions with memory formation through invertebrate research. *Frontiers in Systems Neuroscience, 8.*

Mieda, Michihiro, Willie, Jon T., Hara, Junko, et al. (2004). Orexin peptides prevent cataplexy and improve wakefulness in an orexin neuron-ablated model of narcolepsy in mice. *Proceedings of the National Academy of Science, 101,* 4649–4654.

Miklowitz, David J. (2007). The role of the family in the course and treatment of bipolar disorder. *Current Directions in Psychological Science, 16,* 192–196.

Mikulincer, Mario, & Shaver, Philip R. (2007). *Attachment in adulthood: Structure, dynamics, and change.* New York: Guilford Press.

Mikulincer, Mario, Shaver, Phillip R., & Horesh, Nita. (2006). Attachment bases of emotion regulation and posttraumatic adjustment. In D. K. Snyder, J. A. Simpson, & J. N. Hughes (Eds.), *Emotion regulation in couples and families: Pathways to dysfunction and health.* Washington, DC: American Psychological Association.

Milan, Stephanie, Zona, Kate, & Snow, Stephanie. (2013). Pathways to adolescent internalizing: Early attachment insecurity as a lasting source of vulnerability. *Journal of Clinical Child and Adolescent Psychology, 42*(3), 371–383.

Milgram, Stanley. (1963). Behavioral study of obedience. *Journal of Abnormal and Social Psychology, 67,* 371–378.

Milgram, Stanley. (1974). *Obedience to authority: An experimental view.* New York: Harper & Row.

Miller, George A. (1956). The magical number seven, plus or minus two: Some limits on our capacity for processing information. *Psychological Review, 63,* 81–97.

Miller, Greg. (2011, January 21). ESP paper rekindles discussion about statistics. *Science, 331,* 272–273.

Miller, Gregory E., Chen, Edith, & Parker, Karen J. (2011). Psychological stress in childhood and susceptibility to the chronic diseases of aging: Moving toward a model of behavioral and biological mechanisms. *Psychological Bulletin, 137,* 959–997.

Miller, Gregory E., Lachman, Margie E., Chen, Edith, et al. (2011). Pathways to resilience: Maternal nurturance as a buffer against the effects of childhood poverty on metabolic syndrome. *Psychological Science, 22,* 1591–1599.

Miller, Inglis J., & Reedy, Frank E. (1990). Variations in human taste bud density and taste intensity perception. *Physiology and Behavior, 47,* 1213–1219.

Miller, William R., & Rollnick, Stephen. (2002). *Motivational interviewing: Preparing people for change* (2nd ed.). New York: Guilford Press.

Miller-Jones, Dalton. (1989). Culture and testing. *American Psychologist, 44,* 360–366.

Milner, Brenda. (1970). Memory and the temporal regions of the brain. In K. H. Pribram & D. E. Broadbent (Eds.), *Biology of memory.* New York: Academic Press.

Milner, J. S., & McCanne, T. R. (1991). Neuropsychological correlates of physical child abuse. In J. S. Milner (Ed.), *Neuropsychology of aggression.* Norwell, MA: Kluwer Academic.

Milton, Julie, & Wiseman, Richard. (1999). Does Psi exist? Lack of replication of an anomalous process of information transfer. *Psychological Bulletin, 125,* 387–391.

Milton, Julie, & Wiseman, Richard. (2001). Does Psi exist? Reply to Storm and Ertel (2001). *Psychological Bulletin, 127,* 434–438.

Mineka, Susan, & Zinbarg, Richard. (2006). A contemporary learning theory perspective on the etiology of anxiety disorders: It's not what you thought it was. *American Psychologist, 61,* 10–26.

Minkel, Jared, Moreta, Marisa, Muto, Julianne, Htaik, Oo, Jones, Christopher, Basner, Mathias, et al. (2014). Sleep deprivation potentiates HPA axis stress reactivity in healthy adults. *Health Psychology, 33*(11), 1430–1434.

Minuchin, Salvador. (1984). *Family kaleidoscope.* Cambridge, MA: Harvard University Press.

Mischel, Walter. (1973). Toward a cognitive social learning reconceptualization of personality. *Psychological Review, 80,* 252–253.

Mischel, Walter. (2009, May). The new genetics and what it means for psychological science. Introduction to the presidential symposium at the annual meeting of the Association for Psychological Science, San Francisco.

Mischel, Walter. (2013). *The marshmallow test: Mastering self-control.* New York: Little, Brown.

Mischel, Walter. (2014). *The marshmallow test: Mastering self-control.* New York: Little, Brown.

Mischel, Walter, & Shoda, Yuichi. (1995). A cognitive affective system theory of personality: Reconceptualizing situations, dispositions, dynamics, and invariance in personality structures. *Psychological Review, 102,* 246–268.

Mischel, Walter, Shoda, Yuichi, & Rodriguez, Monica L. (1989). Delay of gratification in children. *Science, 244,* 933–938.

Miskovic, Vladimir, Moscovitch, David A., Santesso, Diane L., et al. (2011). Changes in EEG cross-frequency coupling during cognitive behavioral therapy for social anxiety disorder. *Psychological Science, 22,* 507–516.

Mistry, Jayanthi, & Rogoff, Barbara. (1994). Remembering in cultural context. In W. J. Lonner & R. Malpass (Eds.), *Psychology and culture.* Needham Heights, MA: Allyn & Bacon.

Mitchell, David B. (2006). Nonconscious priming after 17 years: Invulnerable implicit memory? *Psychological Science, 17,* 925–929.

Mitchell, Karen J., & Johnson, Marcia K. (2009). Source monitoring 15 years later: What have we learned from fMRI about the neural mechanisms of source memory? *Psychological Bulletin, 135,* 638–677.

Mitte, Kristin. (2005). Meta-analysis of cognitive-behavioral treatments for generalized anxiety disorder: A comparison with pharmacotherapy. *Psychological Bulletin, 131,* 785–795.

Mitte, Kristin. (2008). Memory bias for threatening information in anxiety and anxiety disorders: A meta-analytic review. *Psychological Bulletin, 134,* 886–911.

Mitterer, Holger, & de Ruiter, Jan Peter. (2008). Recalibrating color categories using world knowledge. *Psychological Science, 19,* 629–634.

Miyamoto, Yuri, Nisbett, Richard E., & Masuda, Takahiko. (2006). Culture and the physical environment: Holistic versus analytic perceptual affordances. *Psychological Science, 17,* 113–119.

Mnookin, Seth. (2011). *The panic virus: A true story of medicine, science, and fear.* New York: Simon & Schuster.

Modigliani, Andre, & Rochat, François. (1995). The role of interaction sequences and the timing of resistance in shaping obedience and defiance to authority. In A. G. Miller, B. E. Collins, & D. E. Brief (Eds.), Perspectives on obedience to authority: The legacy of the Milgram experiments (Special Issue). *Journal of Social Issues, 51*(3), 107–125.

Moffitt, Terrie E. (1993). Adolescence-limited and life-course-persistent antisocial behavior: A developmental taxonomy. *Psychological Review, 100,* 674–701.

Moffitt, Terrie E. (2005). The new look of behavioral genetics in developmental psychopathology: Gene–environment interplay in antisocial behaviors. *Psychological Bulletin, 131,* 533–554.

Moffitt, Terrie E., Arseneault, Louise, Belsky, Daniel, Dickson, Nigel, Hancox, Robert J., Harrington, HonaLee, et al. (2011). A gradient of childhood self-control predicts health, wealth, and public safety. *Proceedings of the National Academy of Sciences of the United States of America, 108*(7), 2693–2698.

Moghaddam, Fathali M. (2005). The staircase to terrorism: A psychological exploration. *American Psychologist, 60,* 161–169.

Mohr, Cynthia, Armeli, Stephen, Tennen, Howard, et al. (2001). Daily interpersonal experiences, context, and alcohol consumption: Crying in your beer and toasting good times. *Journal of Personality and Social Psychology, 80,* 489–500.

Moll, Henrike, Kane, Sarah, & McGowan, Luke. (2015). Three-year-olds express suspense when an agent approaches a scene with a false belief. *Developmental Science,* electronic preview.

Monahan, Jennifer L., Murphy, Sheila T., & Zajonc, R. B. (2000). Subliminal mere exposure: Specific, general, and diffuse effects. *Psychological Science, 11,* 462–466.

Moncrieff, Joanna. (2001). Are antidepressants overrated? A review of methodological problems in antidepressant trials. *Journal of Nervous and Mental Disease, 189,* 288–295.

Moncrieff, Joanna. (2013). *The bitterest pills: The troubling story of antipsychotic drugs.* New York: Palgrave Macmillan.

Monroe, Scott M., & Reed, Mark W. (2009). Life stress and major depression. *Current Directions in Psychological Science, 18,* 68–72.

Monteiro, C.A., Moubarac, J.C., Cannon, G., Ng, S.W., & Popkin, B. (2013). Ultra-processed products are becoming dominant in the global food system. *Obesity Reviews, 14,* 21–28.

Montemurro, Beth, & Gillen, Meghan M. (2013). How clothes make the woman immoral: Impressions given off bysexualized clothing. *Clothing and Textiles Research Journal, 31*(3), 167–181.

Montoya, R. Matthew, & Horton, Robert S. (2013). A meta-analytic investigation of the processes underlying the similarity-attraction effect. *Journal of Social and Personal Relationships, 30*(1), 64–94.

Moore, Mollie N., Salk, Rachel H., Van Hulle, Carol A., Abramson, Lyn Y., Hyde, Janet S., Lemery-Chalfant, Kathryn, et al. (2013). Genetic and environmental influences on rumination, distraction, and depressed mood in adolescence. *Clinical Psychological Science, 1*(3), 316–322.

Moore, Timothy E. (1992, Spring). Subliminal perception: Facts and fallacies. *Skeptical Inquirer, 16,* 273–281.

Moore, Timothy E. (1995). Subliminal self-help auditory tapes: An empirical test of perceptual consequences. *Canadian Journal of Behavioural Science, 27,* 9–20.

Moore, Timothy E., & Pepler, Debra J. (2006). Wounding words: Maternal verbal aggression and children's adjustment., *Journal of Family Violence 21,* 89–93.

Moors, Agnes, Ellsworth, Phoebe C., Scherer, Klaus, & Frijda, Nico. (2013). Appraisal theories of emotion: State of the art and future development. *Emotion Review, 5*(2), 119–124.

Morell, Virginia. (2008, March). Minds of their own. *National Geographic, 213,* 36–61.

Moreno, Carmen, Laje, Gonzalo, Blanco, Carlos, et al. (2007). National trends in the outpatient diagnosis and treatment of bipolar disorder in youth. *Archives of General Psychiatry, 64,* 1032–1039.

Morewedge, Carey K., & Norton, Michael I. (2009). When dreaming is believing: The (motivated) interpretation of dreams. *Journal of Personality and Social Psychology, 96,* 249–264.

Morgan, Charles A., Hazlett, Gary, Baranoski, Madelon, et al. (2007). Accuracy of eyewitness identification is significantly associated with performance on a standardized test of face recognition. *International Journal of Law and Psychiatry, 30,* 213–223.

Morton, Thomas A., Postmes, Tom, Haslam, S. Alexander, & Hornsey, Matthew J. (2009). Theorizing gender in the face of social change: Is there anything essential about essentialism? *Journal of Personality and Social Psychology, 96,* 653–664.

Moskowitz, Judith T., Hult, Jen R., Bussolari, Cori, & Acree, Michael. (2009). What works in coping with HIV? A meta-analysis with implications for coping with serious illness. *Psychological Bulletin, 135,* 121–141.

Most, Steven B., Simons, Daniel J., Scholl, Brian J., et al. (2001). How not to be seen: The contribution of similarity and selective ignoring to sustained inattentional blindness. *Psychological Science, 12,* 9–17.

Moyer, Christopher A., Donnelly, Michael P. W., Anderson, Jane C., et al. (2011). Frontal electroencephalographic asymmetry associated with positive emotion is produced by brief meditation training. *Psychological Science, 22,* 1277–1279.

Mroczek, Daniel K., & Spiro, Avron. (2005). Changes in life satisfaction during adulthood: Findings from the veterans affairs normative aging study. *Journal of Personality and Social Psychology, 88,* 189–202.

Muise, Amy, Impett, Emily A., & Desmarais, Serge. (2013). Getting it on versus getting it over with: Sexual motivation, desire, and satisfaction in intimate bonds. *Personality and Social Psychology Bulletin, 39*(10), 1320–1332.

Mukamal, Kenneth J., Conigrave, Katherine M, Mittleman, Murray A., et al. (2003). Roles of drinking pattern and type of alcohol consumed in coronary heart disease in men. *New England Journal of Medicine, 348,* 109–118.

Müller, Christian P., & Schumann, Gunter. (2011). Drugs as instruments: A new framework for non-addictive psychoactive drug use. *Behavioral and Brain Sciences, 34,* 293–310.

Muñoz, Ricardo F., Lenert, Leslie L., Delucchi, Kevin, et al. (2006). Toward evidence-based Internet interventions: A Spanish/English Web site for international smoking cessation trials. *Nicotine and Tobacco Research, 8,* 77–87.

Munsch, Simone, & Jansen, Anita. (2014). Obesity. In Stefan G. Hofman; David J. Dozois; Winfried Rief; & Jasper A. Smits (Eds.), *The Wiley handbook of cognitive behavioral therapy* (pp. 593–617). New York: Wiley-Blackwell.

Murray, Charles. (2008). Real education: Four simple truths for bringing America's schools back to reality. New York: Crown Forum.

Myrtek, Michael. (2007). Type A behavior and hostility as independent risk factors for coronary heart disease. In J. Jordan et al. (Eds.), *Contributions toward evidence-based psychocardiology: A systematic review of the literature.* Washington, DC. American Psychological Association.

Na, Jinkyung, & Kitayama, Shinobu. (2011). Spontaneous trait inference is culture-specific: Behavioral and neural evidence. *Psychological Science, 22,* 1025–1032.

Nadal, Kevin, Griffin, Katie E., Vargas, Vivian M., et al. (2011). Processes and struggles with racial microaggressions from the white American perspective: Recommendations for workplace settings. In M. A. Paludi, C. A. Paludi, & E. R. DeSouza (Eds.), *Praeger handbook on understanding and preventing workplace discrimination.* Santa Barbara, CA: Praeger/ABC-CLIO.

Nakamoto, Takamichi. (2015). Olfactory interfaces. In Robert R. Hoffman; Peter A. Hancock; Mark W. Scerbo; Raja Parasuraman; & James L. Szalma (Eds.),*The Cambridge handbook of applied perception research* (Vol. I, pp. 408–423). New York: Cambridge University Press.

Nakaya, Naoki, Tsubono, Yoshitaka, Hosokawa, Toru, et al. (2003). Personality and the risk of cancer. *Journal of the National Cancer Institute, 95,* 799–805.

Nash, Michael R. (1987). What, if anything, is regressed about hypnotic age regression? A review of the empirical literature. *Psychological Bulletin, 102,* 42–52.

Nash, Michael R. (2001, July). The truth and the hype of hypnosis. *Scientific American, 285,* 46–49, 52–55.

Nash, Michael R., & Barnier, Amanda J. (2007). *The Oxford handbook of hypnosis*. Oxford, UK: Oxford University Press.

Nash, Michael R., & Nadon, Robert. (1997). Hypnosis. In D. L. Faigman, D. Kaye, M. J. Saks, & J. Sanders (Eds.), *Modern scientific evidence: The law and science of expert testimony*. St. Paul, MN: West.

Nathan, Debbie. (2011). *Sybil exposed: The extraordinary story behind the famous multiple personality case*. New York: Free Press.

Navarrete, Carlos David, Olsson, Andreas, Ho, Arnold K, et al. (2009). Fear extinction to an out-group face: The role of target gender. *Psychological Science, 20*, 155–158.

Neal, David T., & Chartrand, Tanya L. (2011). Embodied emotion perception: Amplifying and dampening facial feedback modulates emotion perception accuracy. *Social Psychological and Personality Science, 2*, 673–678.

Neher, Andrew. (1996). Jung's theory of archetypes: A critique. *Journal of Humanistic Psychology, 36*, 61–91.

Neisser, Ulric, & Harsch, Nicole. (1992). Phantom flashbulbs: False recollections of hearing the news about Challenger. In E. Winograd & U. Neisser (Eds.), *Affect and accuracy in recall: Studies of "flashbulb memories."* New York: Cambridge University Press.

Nelson, Charles A., Zeanah, Charles H., Fox, Nathan A., et al. (2007, December 21). Cognitive recovery in socially deprived young children: The Bucharest early intervention project. *Science, 318*, 1937–1940.

Neria, Yuval, DiGrande, Laura, & Adams, Ben G. (2011). Posttraumatic stress disorder following the September 11, 2001, terrorist attacks. *American Psychologist, 66*, 429–446.

Ness, Jose, Aronow, Wilbert S., & Beck, Gwen. (2006). Menopausal symptoms after cessation of hormone replacement therapy. *Maturitas, 53*, 356–361.

Nesse, Randolph M., & Ellsworth, Phoebe C. (2009). Evolution, emotion, and emotional disorders. *American Psychologist, 64*, 129–139.

Nevins, Andrew, David Pesetsky, and Cilene Rodrigues. (2009). Pirahã exceptionality: A reassessment. *Language, 85*(2), 355–404.

Newcombe, Nora S., Lloyd, Marianne E., & Balcomb, Frances. (2012). Contextualizing the development of recollection: Episodic memory and binding in young children. In S. Ghetti & P. J. Bauer (Eds.), *Origins and development of recollection: Perspectives from psychology and Neuroscience*. New York: Oxford University Press.

Newland, M. Christopher, & Rasmussen, Erin B. (2003). Behavior in adulthood and during aging is affected by contaminant exposure in utero. *Current Directions in Psychological Science, 12*, 212–217.

NICHD Early Child Care Research Network. (2006). Infant–mother attachment classification: Risk and protection in relation to changing maternal caregiving quality. *Developmental Psychology, 42*, 38–58.

Nichols, Michael P. (2012). *Family therapy: Concepts and methods* (10th ed.). Upper Saddle River, NJ: Pearson.

Nickerson, Raymond S. (1998). Confirmation bias: A ubiquitous phenomenon in many guises. *Review of General Psychology, 2*, 175–220.

Nieuwdorp, Wendy, Koops, Sanne, Somers, Metten, & Sommer, Iris E. C. (2015). Transcranial magnetic stimulation, transcranial direct current stimulation and electroconvulsive therapy for medication-resistant psychosis of schizophrenia. *Current Opinion in Psychiatry, 28*(3), 222–228.

Nisbett, Richard E. (1993). Violence and U.S. regional culture. *American Psychologist, 48*, 441–449.

Nisbett, Richard E. (2009). *Intelligence and how to get it: Why schools and culture count*. New York: Norton.

Nisbett, Richard E., Aronson, Joshua, Blair, Clancy, et al. (2012). Intelligence: New findings and theoretical developments. *American Psychologist, 67*, 130–159.

Nisbett, Richard E., & Ross, Lee. (1980). *Human inference: Strategies and shortcomings of social judgment*. Englewood Cliffs, NJ: Prentice-Hall.

Nishimoto, Shinji, Vu, An T., Naselaris, Thomas, et al. (2011). Reconstructing visual experiences from brain activity evoked by natural movies. *Current Biology, 21*, 1641–1646.

Nitsche, Michael A., Cohen, Leonardo G., Wassermann, Eric M., et al. (2008). Transcranial direct current stimulation: State of the art 2008. *Brain Stimulation, 1*, 206–223.

Nivet, Emmanuel, Vignes, Michel, Girard, Stéphane D., et al. (2011). Engraftment of human nasal olfactory stem cells restores neuroplasticity in mice with hippocampal lesions. *Journal of Clinical Investigation, 121*, 2808–2820.

Noble, Mark, Mayer-Pröschel, Margot, Davies, Jeannette E., et al. (2011). Cell therapies for the central nervous system: How do we identify the best candidates? *Current Opinion in Neurology, 24*, 570–576.

Nock, Matthew K. (2010). Self-injury. *Annual Review of Clinical Psychology, 6*, 339–363.

Nolan, Susan A., Flynn, Cynthia, & Garber, Judy. (2003). Prospective relations between rejection and depression in young adolescents. *Journal of Personality and Social Psychology, 85*, 745–755.

Nolen-Hoeksema, Susan. (2004). Lost in thought: Rumination and depression. Paper presented at the National Institute on the Teaching of Psychology, St. Petersburg, Florida.

Norman, Donald A. (1988). *The psychology of everyday things*. New York: Basic.

Norman, Donald A. (2004). *Emotional design: Why we love (or hate) everyday things*. New York: Basic Books.

Norton, Alice R., Abbott, Maree J., Norberg, Melissa M., & Hunt, Caroline. (2015). A systematic review of mindfulness and acceptance-based treatments for social anxiety disorder. *Journal of Clinical Psychology, 71*(4), 283–301.

Nosek, Brian A., Greenwald, Anthony G., & Banaji, Mahzarin R. (2007). The Implicit Association Test at 7: A methodological and conceptual review. In J. A. Bargh (Ed.), *Social psychology and the unconscious*. New York: Psychology Press.

Nyberg, Lars, Habib, Reza, McIntosh, Anthony R., & Tulving, Endel. (2000). Reactivation of encoding-related brain activity during memory retrieval. *Proceedings of the National Academy of Sciences, 97*, 11120–11124.

Odgers, Candice L., Caspi, Avshalom, Nagin, Daniel S., et al. (2008). Is it important to prevent early exposure to drugs and alcohol among adolescents? *Psychological Science, 19*, 1037–1044.

O'Doherty, Daniel C. M., Chitty, Kate M., Saddiqui, Sonia, Bennett, Maxwell R., & Lagopoulos, Jim. (2015). A systematic review and meta-analysis of magnetic resonance imaging measurement of structural volumes inposttraumatic stress disorder. *Psychiatry Research: Neuroimaging, 232*(1), 1–33.

Offit, Paul A. (2008). Autism's false prophets: Bad science, risky medicine, and the search for a cure. New York Columbia University Press.

Ofshe, Richard J., & Watters, Ethan. (1994). *Making monsters: False memory, psychotherapy, and sexual hysteria.* New York: Scribners.

Ogden, Jenni A., & Corkin, Suzanne. (1991). Memories of H. M. In W. C. Abraham, M. C. Corballis, & K. G. White (Eds.), *Memory mechanisms: A tribute to G. V. Goddard.* Hillsdale, NJ: Erlbaum.

Ogden, Jenni. (2012). *Trouble in mind: Stories from a neuropsychologist's casebook.* New York: Oxford University Press.

O'Hanlon, Bill. (1994, November/December). The third wave. *Family Therapy Networker,* pp. 18–29.

Öhman, Arne, & Mineka, Susan. (2001). Fears, phobias, and preparedness: Toward an evolved module of fear and fear learning. *Psychological Review, 108,* 483–522.

Oliveira, Paula Salgado, Fearon, R. M. Pasco, Belsky, Jay, Fachada, Inês, & Soares, Isabel. (2015). Quality of institutional care and early childhood development. *International Journal of Behavioral Development, 39*(2), 161–170.

Olson, James M., Vernon, Philip A., Harris, Julie Aitken, & Jang, Kerry L. (2001). The heritability of attitudes: A study of twins. *Journal of Personality and Social Psychology, 80,* 845–850.

Olson, Michael A. (2009). Measures of prejudice. In T. Nelson (Ed.), *The handbook of prejudice, stereotyping, and discrimination.* New York: Psychology Press.

Olsson, Andreas, Ebert, Jeffrey, Banaji, Mahzarin, & Phelps, Elizabeth A. (2005). The role of social groups in the persistence of learned fear. *Science, 309,* 785–787.

Olsson, Andreas, & Phelps, Elizabeth. (2004). Learned fear of "unseen" faces after Pavlovian, observational, and instructed fear. *Psychological Science, 15,* 822–828.

Olujic, M. B. (1998). Embodiment of terror: Gendered violence in peacetime and wartime in Croatia and Bosnia-Herzegovina. *Medical Anthropology Quarterly, 12,* 31–50.

O'Neill, Sarah, & Zajac, Rachel. (2012). The role of repeated interviewing in children's responses to cross-examination-style questioning. *British Journal of Psychology, 104*(1), 14–38.

Ong, Anthony D. (2010). Pathways linking positive emotion and health in later life. *Current Directions in Psychological Science, 19,* 358–362.

Ongley, Sophia F., & Malti, Tina. (2014). The role of moral emotions in the development of children's sharing behavior. *Developmental Psychology, 50*(4), 1148–1159.

Opitz, Philipp C., Lee, Ihno A., Gross, James J., Urry, & Heather L. (2014). Fluid cognitive ability is a resource for successful emotion regulation in older and younger adults. *Frontiers in Psychology, 5.*

O'Rahilly, Ronan, & Müller, Fabiola. (2001). *Human embryology and teratology.* New York: Wiley.

Orbach, Susie. (2009). *Bodies,* London: Profile Books.

Oriña, M. Minda, Collins, W. Andrew, Simpson, Jeffry A., et al. (2011). Developmental and dyadic perspectives on commitment in adult romantic relationships. *Psychological Science, 22,* 908–915.

Ortigue, Stephanie, Bianchi-Demicheli, Francesco, Patel, Nisa, Frum, Chris, & Lewis, James W. (2010). Neuroimaging of love: fMRI meta-analysis evidence toward new perspectives in sexual medicine. *Journal of Sexual Medicine, 7*(11), 3541–3552.

Ortman, Jennifer M., Velkoff, Victoria A., & Hogan, Howard. (2014, May 14). An aging nation: The older population in the United States. Population Estimates and Projections Current Population Reports, U.S. Census Bureau. Available at www.census.gov/prod/2014pubs/p25-1140.pdf.

Osland, Teresa M., Bjorvatn, Bjørn, Steen, Vidar M., & Pallesen, Ståle. (2011). Association study of a variable-number tandem repeat polymorphism in the clock gene PERIOD3 and chronotype in Norwegian university students. *Chronobiology International, 28,* 764–770.

Ostrovsky, Yuri, Andalman, Aaron, & Sinha, Pawan. (2006). Vision following extended congenital blindness. *Psychological Science, 12,* 1009–1014.

Ostrovsky, Yuri, Meyers, Ethan, Ganesh, Suma, et al. (2009). Visual parsing after recovery from blindness. *Psychological Science, 20,* 1484–1491.

Oswald, Frederick L., Mitchell, Gregory, Blanton, Hart, Jaccard, James, & Tetlock, Philip E. (2013). Predicting ethnic and racial discrimination: A meta-analysis of IAT criterion studies. *Journal of Personality and Social Psychology, 105*(2), 171–192.

Otto, Michael, Behar, E., Smits, Jasper A. J., & Hoffmann, S. G. (2009). Combining pharmacological and cognitive behavioral therapy in the treatment of anxiety disorders. In M. M. Antony & M.B. Stein (Eds.), *Oxford handbook of anxiety and related disorders.* New York: Oxford University Press.

Otto, Michael, & Smits, Jasper A. J. (2012). *Exercise for mood and anxiety.* New York: Oxford University Press.

Ouellet, Véronique; Labbé, Sébastien M., Blondin, Denis P., et al. (2012). Brown adipose tissue oxidative metabolism contributes to energy expenditure during acute cold exposure in humans. *The Journal of Clinical Investigation, 122,* 545–552.

Ougrin, Dennis, Tranah, Troy, Stahl, Daniel, Moran, Paul, & Asarnow, Joan Rosenbaum. (2015). Therapeutic interventions for suicide attempts and self-harm in adolescents: Systematic review and meta-analysis. *Journal of the American Academy of Child and Adolescent Psychiatry, 54*(2), 97–107.

Overeem, Sebastiaan, van Nues, Soffie J., van der Zande, Wendy L., et al. (2011). The clinical features of cataplexy: A questionnaire study in narcolepsy patients with and without hypocretin-1 deficiency. *Sleep Medicine, 12,* 12–18.

Oyserman, Daphna, & Lee, Spike W. S. (2008). Does culture influence what and how we think? Effects of priming individualism and collectivism. *Psychological Bulletin, 134,* 311–342.

Özgen, Emre. (2004). Language, learning, and color perception. *Current Directions in Psychological Science, 13,* 95–98.

Packer, Dominic J. (2008). Identifying systematic disobedience in Milgram's obedience experiments: A meta-analytic review. *Perspectives on Psychological Science, 3,* 301–304.

Packer, Dominic J. (2009). Avoiding groupthink: Whereas weakly identified members remain silent, strongly identified members dissent about collective problems. *Psychological Science, 20,* 619–626.

Pagel, James F. (2003). Non-dreamers. *Sleep Medicine, 4,* 235–241.

Pail, Gerald, Huf, Wolfgang, Pjrek, Edda, et al. (2011). Bright-light therapy in the treatment of mood disorders. *Neuropsychobiology, 64*, 152–162.

Pan, Bing, Hembrooke, Helene, Joachims, Thorsten, et al. (2007). In Google we trust: Users' decisions on rank, position, and relevance. *Journal of Computer-Mediated Communication, 12*, 3.

Panksepp, Jaak. (1998). Attention deficit hyperactivity disorders, psychostimulants, and intolerance of childhood playfulness: A tragedy in the making? *Current Directions in Psychological Science, 7*, 91–98.

Panksepp, Jaak, Herman, B. H., Vilberg, T., et al. (1980). Endogenous opioids and social behavior. *Neuroscience and Biobehavioral Reviews, 4*, 473–487.

Paoletti, Jo. (2012). *Pink and blue: Telling the girls from the boys in America.* Bloomington: University of Indiana Press.

Parada, Maria, Corral, Montserrat, Mota, Nayara, et al. (2012). Executive functioning and alcohol binge drinking in university students. *Addictive Behaviors, 37*, 167–172.

Park, Denise, & Gutchess, Angela. (2006). The cognitive neuroscience of aging and culture. *Current Directions in Psychological Science, 15*, 105–108.

Parker, Elizabeth S., Cahill, Larry, & McGaugh, James L. (2006). A case of unusual autobiographical remembering. *Neurocase, 12*, 35–49.

Parlee, Mary B. (1982). Changes in moods and activation levels during the menstrual cycle in experimentally naive subjects. *Psychology of Women Quarterly, 7*, 119–131.

Parlee, Mary B. (1994). The social construction of premenstrual syndrome: A case study of scientific discourse as cultural contestation. In M. G. Winkler & L. B. Cole (Eds.), *The good body: Asceticism in contemporary culture.* New Haven, CT: Yale University Press.

Parrish, Audrey E., Evans, Theodore A., & Beran, Michael J. (2014). Defining value through quantity and quality—chimpanzees (*pan troglodytes*) undervalue food quantities when items are broken. *Behavioural Processes.*

Parry, Marc. (2011, October 9). Raymond Tallis takes out the "neurotrash." *Chronicle of Higher Education.* Available at http://chronicle.com/article/Raymond-Tallis-Takes-Out-the/129279/.

Pascoe, Elizabeth A., & Richman, Laura S. (2009). Perceived discrimination and health: A meta-analytic review. *Psychological Bulletin, 135*, 531–554.

Pascual-Leone, Alvaro, Amedi, Amir, Fregni, Felipe, & Merabet, Lofte B. (2005). The plastic human brain cortex. *Annual Review of Neuroscience, 28*, 377–401.

Pashler, Harold, McDaniel, Mark, Rohrer, Doug, & Bjork, Robert. (2008). Learning styles: Concepts and evidence. *Psychological Science in the Public Interest, 9*, 105–119.

Pastalkova, Eva, Itskov, Vladimir, Amarasingham, Asohan, & Buzsáki, György. (2008, September 5). Internally generated cell assembly sequences in the rat hippocampus. *Science, 321*, 1322–1327.

Paterson, Helen M., Whittle, Keenan, & Kemp, Richard I. (2015). Detrimental effects of post-incident debriefing on memory and psychological responses. *Journal of Police and Criminal Psychology, 30*(1), 27–37.

Patrick, Christopher J., Fowles, Don C., & Krueger, Robert F. (2009). Triarchic conceptualization of psychopathy: Developmental origins of disinhibition, boldness, and meanness. *Development and Psychopathology, 21*, 913–938.

Patterson, David R., & Jensen, Mark P. (2003). Hypnosis and clinical pain. *Psychological Bulletin, 129*, 495–521.

Patterson, Francine, & Linden, Eugene. (1981). *The education of Koko.* New York: Holt, Rinehart & Winston.

Paul, Annie M. (2004). *The cult of personality.* New York: The Free Press.

Paul, Annie M. (2011, September 11). The trouble with homework. *New York Times,* Sunday Review, p. 6.

Paul, Richard. (1984, September). Critical thinking: Fundamental to education for a free society. *Educational Leadership,* 4–14.

Paunonen, Sampo V. (2003). Big Five factors or personality and replicated predictions of behavior. *Journal of Personality & Social Psychology, 84*, 411–422.

Paunonen, Sampo V., & Ashton, Michael C. (2001). Big Five factors and facets and the prediction of behavior. *Journal of Personality and Social Psychology, 81*, 524–539.

Pavlov, Ivan P. (1927). *Conditioned reflexes* (G. V. Anrep, trans.). London: Oxford University Press.

Pearlin, Leonard. (1982). Discontinuities in the study of aging. In T. K. Hareven & K. J. Adams (Eds.), *Aging and life course transitions: An interdisciplinary perspective.* New York: Guilford.

Peele, Stanton. (2010). Alcohol as evil – Temperance and policy. *Addiction Research and Theory, 18*(4), 374–382.

Peele, Stanton, & Brodsky, Archie (with Mary Arnold). (1991). *The truth about addiction and recovery.* New York: Simon & Schuster.

Peier, A. M., Moqrich, A., Hergarden, A. C., et al. (2002). A TRP channel that senses cold stimuli and menthol. *Cell, 108*, 705–715.

Pennebaker, James W. (2002). Writing, social processes, and psychotherapy: From past to future. In S. J. Lepore & J. M. Smyth (Eds.), *The writing cure: How expressive writing promotes health and emotional well-being.* Washington, DC: American Psychological Association.

Pennebaker, James W. (2011). *The secret life of pronouns: What our words say about us.* New York: Bloomsbury.

Pennebaker, James W., Colder, Michelle, & Sharp, Lisa K. (1990). Accelerating the coping process. *Journal of Personality and Social Psychology, 58*, 528–527.

Pennebaker, James W., Kiecolt-Glaser, Janice, & Glaser, Ronald. (1988). Disclosure of traumas and immune function: Health implications for psychotherapy. *Journal of Consulting and Clinical Psychology, 56*, 239–245.

Peplau, Letitia Anne. (2003). Human sexuality: How do men and women differ? *Current Directions in Psychological Science, 12*, 37–40.

Peplau, Letitia Anne, Spalding, Leah R., Conley, Terri D., & Veniegas, Rosemary C. (2000). The development of sexual orientation in women. *Annual Review of Sex Research, 10*, 70–99.

Pepperberg, Irene M. (2000). *The Alex studies: Cognitive and communicative abilities of grey parrots.* Cambridge, MA: Harvard University Press.

Pepperberg, Irene M. (2002). Cognitive and communicative abilities of grey parrots. *Current Directions in Psychological Science, 11*, 83–87.

Pepperberg, Irene M. (2008). *Alex and me.* New York: HarperCollins.

Perera, Frederica P., Wang, Shuang, Rauh, Virginia, Zhou Hui, et al. (2013). Prenatal exposure to air pollution, maternal psychological distress, and child behavior. *Pediatrics, 132*(5), e1284–e1294.

Perilloux, Carin, Duntley, Joshua D., & Buss, David M. (2014). Blame attribution in sexual victimization. *Personality and Individual Differences, 63,* 81–86.

Perry, J. Christopher, & Metzger, Jesse. (2014). Introduction to "Defense mechanisms in psychotherapy." *Journal of Clinical Psychology, 70*(5), 405.

Peterson, Donald R. (2003). Unintended consequences: Ventures and misadventures in the education of professional psychologists. *American Psychologist, 58,* 791–800.

Peterson, Lloyd R., & Peterson, Margaret J. (1959). Short-term retention of individual verbal items. *Journal of Experimental Psychology, 58,* 193–198.

Peterson, Zoë D., & Muehlenhard, Charlene L. (2011). A match-and-motivation model of how women label their nonconsensual sexual experiences. *Psychology of Women Quarterly, 35,* 558–570.

Petkova, Valeria I., & Ehrsson, H. Henrik. (2008). If I were you: Perceptual illusion of body swapping. *PLoS One, 3:* e3832.

Pettigrew, Thomas T., & Tropp, Linda R. (2006). A meta-analytic test of intergroup contact theory. *Journal of Personality and Social Psychology, 90,* 751–783.

Pfungst, Oskar. (1911/1965). *Clever Hans (the horse of Mr. Von Osten), a contribution to experimental animal and human psychology.* New York: Henry Holt.

Phinney, Jean S. (2006). Acculturation is not an independent variable: Approaches to studying acculturation as a complex process. In Marc H. Bornstein & Linda R. Cote (Eds.), *Acculturation and parent–child relationships: Measurement and development* (pp. 79–95). Mahwah, NJ: Erlbaum.

Piaget, Jean. (1929/1960). *The child's conception of the world.* Paterson, NJ: Littlefield, Adams.

Piaget, Jean. (1952). *Play, dreams, and imitation in childhood.* New York: Norton.

Piaget, Jean. (1984). Piaget's theory. In P. Mussen (Series Ed.) & W. Kessen (Vol. Ed.), *Handbook of child psychology: Vol. 1. History, theory, and methods* (4th ed.). New York: Wiley.

Pierce, W. David, Cameron, Judy, Banko, Katherine M., & So, Sylvia. (2003). Positive effects of rewards and performance standards on intrinsic motivation. *Psychological Record, 53,* 561–579.

Pika, Simone, & Mitani, John. (2006). Referential gesture communication in wild chimpanzees (*Pan troglodytes*). *Current Biology, 16,* 191–192.

Pillemer, Jane, Hatfield, Elaine, & Sprecher, Susan. (2008). The importance of fairness and equity for the marital satisfaction of older women. *Journal of Women and Aging, 20,* 215–229.

Pilley, John W. (2013). Border collie comprehends sentences containing a prepositional object, verb, and direct object. *Learning and Motivation, 11*(1), 229–240.

Ping, Erin Yong, Laplante, David P., Elgbeili, Guillaume, Hillerer, Katharina M., Brunet, Alain, O'Hara, Michael W., et al. (2015). Prenatal maternal stress predicts stress reactivity at 2½ years of age: The Iowa Flood Study. *Psychoneuroendocrinology, 56,* 62–78.

Pinker, Steven. (1994). *The language instinct: How the mind creates language.* New York: Morrow.

Pinker, Steven. (2002). *The blank slate: The modern denial of human nature.* New York: Viking.

Pinker, Steven. (2013). *Language, cognition, and human nature: Selected articles.* New York: Oxford University Press.

Piper, August, & Merskey, Harold. (2004). The persistence of folly: A critical examination of dissociative identity disorder. Part I: The excesses of an improbable concept. *Canadian Journal of Psychiatry, 49,* 592–600. [Note: Part II (The defence and decline of multiple personality or dissociative identity disorder) appeared in the *Canadian Journal of Psychiatry, 49,* 678–683.]

Pitcher, David, Goldhaber, Tanya, Duchaine, Bradley, Walsh, Vincent, Kanwisher, Nancy. (2012). Two critical and functionally distinct stages of face and body perception. *Journal of Neuroscience, 32*(45), 15877–15885.

Pittenger, David J. (1993). The utility of the Myers-Briggs Type Indicator. *Review of Educational Research, 63,* 467–488.

Pittenger, David J. (2005). Cautionary comments regarding the Myers-Briggs Type Indicator. *Consulting Psychology Journal: Practice and Research, 57,* 210–221.

Plomin, Robert. (1989). Environment and genes: Determinants of behavior. *American Psychologist, 44,* 105–111.

Plomin, Robert. (2011). Commentary: Why are children in the same family so different? Non-shared environment three decades later. *International Journal of Epidemiology, 40,* 582–592.

Plomin, Robert. (2013). Child development and molecular genetics: 14 years later. *Child Development, (84)*(1), 104–120.

Plomin, Robert, DeFries, John C., & Knopik, Valerie S. (2013). *Behavioral Genetics* (6th ed.). New York: Worth.

Plotnik, Joshua M., de Waal, Frans B. M., & Reiss, Diana. (2006). Self-recognition in an Asian elephant. *Proceedings of the National Academy of Sciences, 103,* 17053–17057.

Pobric, Gorana, Mashal, Nira, Faust, Miriam, & Lavidor, Michal. (2008). The role of the right cerebral hemisphere in processing novel metaphoric expressions: A transcranial magnetic stimulation study. *Journal of Cognitive Neuroscience, 20,* 170–181.

Polaschek, Devon L. L. (2014). Adult criminals with psychopathy: Common beliefs about treatability and change have little empirical support. *Current Directions in Psychological Science, 23*(4), 296–301.

Ponitz, Claire C., McClelland, Megan M., Matthews, J. S., & Morrison, Frederick J. (2009). A structured observation of behavioral self-regulation and its contribution to kindergarten outcomes. *Developmental Psychology, 45,* 605–619.

Poole, Debra, Bruck, Maggie, & Pipe, Margaret-Ellen. (2011). Forensic interviewing aids: Do props help children answer questions about touching? *Current Directions in Psychological Science, 20,* 11–15.

Poole, Debra, Lamb, Michael E. (1998). *Investigative interviews of children.* Washington, DC: American Psychological Association.

Pope, Harrison G., Jr., Poliakoff, Michael B., Parker, Michael P., et al. (2007). Is dissociative amnesia a culture-bound syndrome? Findings from a survey of historical literature. *Psychological Medicine, 37,* 22533.

Popkin, Barry M. (2009). *The world is fat: The fads, trends, policies, and products that are fattening the human race.* New York: Avery (Penguin).

Portenoy, Russell K. (1994). Opioid therapy for chronic nonmalignant pain: Current status. In H. L. Fields & J. C. Liebeskind (Eds.), *Progress in pain research and management. Pharmacological approaches to the treatment of chronic pain: Vol. 1.* Seattle: International Association for the Study of Pain.

Posner, Michael I., & Rothbart, Mary K. (2011). Brain states and hypnosis research. *Consciousness and Cognition, 20,* 325–327.

Posthuma, Danielle, De Gues, Eco J., Baare, W. F., et al. (2002). The association between brain volume and intelligence is of genetic origin. *Nature Neuroscience, 5,* 83–84.

Postmes, Tom, & Spears, Russell. (1998). Deindividuation and antinormative behavior: A meta-analysis. *Psychological Bulletin, 123,* 238–259.

Poulin, Michael J., Holman, E. Alison, & Buffone, Anneke. (2012). The neurogenetics of nice: Receptor genes for oxytocin and vasopressin interact with threat to produce prosocial behavior. *Psychological Science, 23,* 446–452.

Poulin-Dubois, Diane, Serbin, Lisa A., Kenyon, Brenda, & Derbyshire, Alison. (1994). Infants' intermodal knowledge about gender. *Developmental Psychology, 30,* 436–442.

Powell, Elyse, & Popkin, Barry, M. (2013). Trends in intakes of added sugars in the United States, 1977–2010. *American Journal of Clinical Nutrition, 97.*

Powell, Russell A., & Boer, Douglas P. (1995). Did Freud misinterpret reported memories of sexual abuse as fantasies? *Psychological Reports, 77,* 563–570.

Powell, Russell A., Digdon, Nancy, Harris, Ben, & Smithson, Christopher. (2014). Correctingthe record on Watson, Rayner and Little Albert: Albert Barger as "Psychology's Lost Boy." *American Psychologist, 69,* 600–611.

Poythress, Norman G., Edens, John F., Skeem, Jennifer L., Lilienfeld, Scott O., et al. (2010). Identifying subtypes among offenders with antisocial personality disorder: A cluster-analytic study. *Journal of Abnormal Psychology, 119,* 389–400.

Prasser, Julia, Schecklmann, Martin, Poeppl, Timm B., Frank, Elmar, Kreuzer, Peter M., Hajak, Goeran, et al. (2015). Bilateral prefrontal rTMS and theta burst TMS as an add-on treatment for depression: A randomized placebo controlled trial. *World Journal of Biological Psychiatry, 16*(1), 57–65.

Premack, David, & Premack, Ann J. (1983). *The mind of an ape.* New York: Norton.

Presnell, Katherine, Bearman, Sarah Kate, & Stice, Eric. (2004). Risk factors for body dissatisfaction in adolescent boys and girls: A prospective study. *International Journal of Eating Disorders, 36,* 389–401.

Pressman, Sarah D., & Cohen, Sheldon. (2012). Positive emotion word use and longevity in famous deceased psychologists. *Health Psychology, 31*(3), 297–305.

Prete, Giulia, Laeng, Bruno, Fabri, Mara, Foschi, Nicoletta, & Tomassi, Luca. (2015). Right hemisphere or valence hypothesis, or both?: The processing of hybrid faces in the intact and callosotomized brain. *Neuropsychologia, 68,* 94–106.

Price, Donald D., Finniss, Damien G., & Benedetti, Fabrizio. (2008). A comprehensive review of the placebo effect: Recent advances and current thought. *Annual Review of Psychology, 59,* 565–590.

Primack, Brian A., Silk, Jennifer S., DeLozier, Christian R., et al. (2011). Using ecological momentary assessment to determine media use by individuals with and without major depressive disorder. *Archives of Pediatrics and Adolescent Medicine, 165,* 360–365.

Principe, Gabrielle, Kanaya, Tamoe, Ceci, Stephen J., & Singh, Mona. (2006). Believing is seeing: How rumors can engender false memories in preschoolers. *American Psychologist, 17,* 243–248.

Prochaska, James O., Norcross, John C., & DiClemente, Carlo C. (1994). *Changing for good.* New York: Morrow.

Pronin, Emily. (2008, May 30). How we see ourselves and how we see others. *Science, 320,* 1177–1180.

Pronin, Emily, Gilovich, Thomas, & Ross, Lee. (2004). Objectivity in the eye of the beholder: Divergent perceptions of bias in self versus others. *Psychological Review, 111,* 781–799.

Proulx, Michael J., Ptito, Maurice, & Amedi, Amir. (2014). Multisensory integration, sensory substitution and visual rehabilitation. *Neuroscience and Biobehavioral Reviews, 41,* 1–2.

Punamaeki, Raija-Leena, & Joustie, Marja. (1998). The role of culture, violence, and personal factors affecting dream content. *Journal of Cross-Cultural Psychology, 29,* 320–342.

Puterman, E., Lin, J., Krauss, J., Blackburn, E. H., & Epel, E. S. (2015). Determinants of telomere attrition over 1 year in healthy older women: Stress and health behaviors matter. *Molecular Psychiatry, 20*(4), 529–535.

Pynoos, R. S., & Nader, K. (1989). Children's memory and proximity to violence. *Journal of the American Academy of Child and Adolescent Psychiatry, 28,* 236–241.

Pyter, L. M., Pineros, V., Galang, J. A., et al. (2009, June 2). Peripheral tumors induce depressive-like behaviors and cytokine production and alter hypothalamic-pituitary-adrenal axis regulation. *Proceedings of the National Academy of Sciences, 106,* 9069–9074.

Qin, Yu, Zhang, Wen, & Yang, Ping. (2015). Current states of enndogenous stem cells in adult spinal cord. *Journal of Neuroscience Research, 93*(3), 391–398.

Quinn, Diane M., & Spencer, Steven J. (2001). The interference of stereotype threat with women's generation of mathematical problem-solving strategies. *Journal of Social Issues, 57,* 55–71.

Quinn, Paul C., & Bhatt, Ramesh S. (2012). Grouping by form in young infants: Only relevant variability promotes perceptual learning. *Perception, 41*(12), 1468–1476.

Quoidbach, Jordi, Dunn, Elizabeth W., Hansenne, Michel, & Bustin, Gaelle. (2015). The price of abundance: How a wealth of experiences impoverishes savoring. *Personality and Social Psychology Bulletin, 41*(3), 393–404.

Radel, Rémi, & Clément-Guillotin, Corentin. (2012). Evidence of motivational influences in early visual perception: Hunger modulates conscious access. Psychological Science, 23, 232–234.

Radford, Benjamin. (2010, March/April). The psychic and the serial killer. *Skeptical Inquirer, 34,* 32–37.

Radford, Benjamin. (2011, September/October). Holly Bobo still missing: Psychics hurt investigation. *Skeptical Inquirer, 35,* 9.

Raffaelli, Marcela, Crockett, Lisa J., & Shen, Yuh-ling. (2005). Developmental stability and change in self-regulation from childhood to adolescence. *Journal of Genetic Psychology, 166*, 54–75.

Rahman, Qazi, & Wilson, Glenn D. (2003). Born gay? The psychobiology of human sexual orientation. *Personality and Individual Differences, 34*, 1337–1382.

Raine, Adrian. (2008). From genes to brain to antisocial behavior. *Current Directions in Psychological Science, 17*, 323–328.

Raine, Adrian, Lencz, Todd, Bihrle, Susan, et al. (2000). Reduced prefrontal gray matter volume and reduced autonomic activity in antisocial personality disorder. *Archives of General Psychiatry, 57*, 119–127.

Raine, Adrian, Meloy, J. Reid, Bihrle, Susan, et al. (1998). Reduced prefrontal and increased subcortical brain functioning assessed using positron emission tomography in predatory and affective murderers. *Behavioral Science and Law, 16*, 319–332.

Raja, Srinivasa. (2008, May 8). From poppies to pill-popping: Is there a "middle way?" Paper presented at the annual meeting of the American Pain Society, Tampa, FL.

Raley, Sara, Bianchi, Suzanne M., & Wang, Wendy. (2012). When do fathers care?: Mothers' economic contribute and fathers' involvement in child care. *American Journal of Sociology, 117*(5), 1422–1459.

Raloff, Janet. (2011). Environment: Chemicals linked to kids' lower IQs: Studies identify effects from pesticides still used on farms. *Science News, 179*, 15.

Ram, Nilam, Shiyko, Mariya, Lunkenheimer, Erika S., Doerksen, Shawna, Conroy, David. (2014). Families as coordinated symbiotic systems: Making use of nonlinear dynamic models. In Susan M. McHale; Paul Amato; & Alan Booth (Eds.), *Emerging methods in family research* (pp. 19–37). New York: Springer.

Ramachandran, Vilayanur S., & Altschuler, Eric L. (2009). The use of visual feedback, in particular mirror visual feedback, in restoring brain function. *Brain, 132*, 1693–1710.

Ramachandran, Vilayanur S., & Blakeslee, Sandra. (1998). *Phantoms in the brain*. New York: William Morrow.

Ramachandran, Vilayanur S., Krause, Beatrix, & Case, Laura K. (2011). The phantom head. *Perception, 40*(3), 367–370.

Randall, David K. (2012). *Dreamland: Adventures in the strange world of sleep*. New York: Norton.

Randolph, John F., Zheng, Huiyong, Harlow, Sioban D., Avis, Nancy E., & Greendale, Gail A. (2014). Masturbation frequency and sexual function domains are associated with serum reproductive hormone levels across the menopausal transition. *Journal of Clinical Endocrinology and Metabolism, 99*.

Rasch, Björn, Büchel, Christian, Gais, Steffen, & Born, Jan. (2007). Odor cues during slow-wave sleep prompt declarative memory consolidation. *Science, 315*, 1426–1429.

Raser, Jonathan M., & O'Shea, Erin K. (2005). Noise in gene expression: Origins, consequences, and control. *Science, 309*, 2010–2013.

Rasheed, Parveen, & Al-Sowielem, Latifa S. (2003). Prevalence and predictors of premenstrual syndrome among college-aged women in Saudi Arabia. *Annals of Saudi Medicine, 23*, 381–387.

Rauschecker, Josef P. (1999). Making brain circuits listen. *Science, 285*, 1686–1687.

Raz, Amir, Fan, Jin, & Posner, Michael I. (2005). Hypnotic suggestion reduces conflict in the human brain. *Proceedings of the National Academy of Science, 102*, 9978–9983.

Raz, Amir, Kirsch, Irving, Pollard, Jessica, & Nitkin-Kamer, Yael. (2006). Suggestion reduces the Stroop effect. *Psychological Science, 17*, 91–95.

Raz, Mical. (2013). *The lobotomy letters: The making of American psychosurgery*. Rochester, NY: University of Rochester Press.

Reber, Paul J., Stark, Craig E. L., & Squire, Larry R. (1998). Contrasting cortical activity associated with category memory and recognition memory. *Learning and Memory, 5*, 420–428.

Redd, W. H., Dadds, M. R., Futterman, A. D., Taylor, K., & Bovbjerg, D. (1993). Nausea induced by mental images of chemotherapy. *Cancer, 72*, 629–636.

Redelmeier, Donald A., & Tversky, Amos. (1996). On the belief that arthritis pain is related to the weather. *Proceedings of the National Academy of Sciences, 93*, 2895–2896.

Redick, Thomas S., Shipstead, Zach, Harrison, Tyler L., et al. (2012, June 18). No evidence of intelligence improvement after working memory training: A randomized, placebo-controlled study. *Journal of Experimental Psychology: General*. doi: 10.1037/a0029082.

Reedy, F. E., Bartoshuk, L. M., Miller, I. J., et al. (1993). Relationships among papillae, taste pores, and 6-n-propylthiouracil (PROP) suprathreshold taste sensitivity. *Chemical Senses, 18*, 618–619.

Reese, Elaine, Jack, Fiona, & White, Naomi. (2010). Origins of adolescents' autobiographical memories. *Cognitive Development, 25*, 352–367.

Regard, Marianne, & Landis, Theodor. (1997). "Gourmand syndrome": Eating passion associated with right anterior lesions. *Neurology, 48*, 1185–1190.

Reiner, William G., & Gearhart, John P. (2004, January 22). Discordant sexual identity in some genetic males with cloacal exstrophy assigned to female sex at birth. *New England Journal of Medicine, 350*, 333–341.

Reis, Harry T., & Aron, Arthur. (2008). Love: What is it, why does it matter, and how does it operate? *Perspectives on Psychological Science, 3*, 80–86.

Remick, Abigail K., Polivy, Janet, & Pliner, Patricia. (2009). Internal and external moderators of the effect of variety on food intake. *Psychological Bulletin, 135*, 434–451.

Rensink, Ronald. (2004). Visual sensing without seeing. *Psychological Science, 15*, 27–32.

Repantis, Dimitris, Schlattmann, Peter, Laisney, Oona, & Heuser, Isabella. (2010). Modafinil and methylphenidate for neuroenhancement in healthy individuals. A systematic review. *Pharmacological Research, 62*, 187–206.

Repetti, Rena L., Taylor, Shelley E., & Seeman, Teresa E. (2002). Risky families: Family social environments and the mental and physical health of offspring. *Psychological Bulletin, 128*, 330–366.

Rescorla, Robert A. (1988). Pavlovian conditioning: It's not what you think It Is. *American Psychologist, 43*, 151–160.

Rescorla, Robert A. (2008). Evaluating conditioning of related and unrelated stimuli using a compound test. *Learning and Behavior, 36*(2), 67–74.

Resnik, Karmen, Bradbury, David, Barnes, Gareth R., & Leff, Alex P. (2014). Between thought and expression, a magnetoencephalography study of the "tip-of-the-tongue" phenomenon. *Journal of Cognitive Neuroscience, 26*(10), 2210–2223.

Reuter, Christoph, & Oehler, Michael. (2011). Psychoacoustics of chalkboard squeaking. *Journal of the Acoustical Society of America, 130,* 2545.

Reyna, Valerie, & Farley, Frank. (2006). Risk and rationality in adolescent decision making. *Psychological Science in the Public Interest, 7,* 1–44.

Reynolds, Arthur J., Temple, Judy A., Ou, Suh-Ruu, et al. (2011). School-based early childhood education and age 28 well-being: Effects by timing, dosage, and subgroups. *Science, 333,* 360–364.

Reynolds, Brent A., & Weiss, Samuel. (1992). Generation of neurons and astrocytes from isolated cells of the adult mammalian central nervous system. *Science, 255,* 1707–1710.

Reynolds, Kristi, Lewis, L. Brian, Nolen, John David L., et al. (2003). Alcohol consumption and risk of stroke: A meta-analysis. *Journal of the American Medical Association, 289,* 579–588.

Rhoades, Linda, & Eisenberger, Robert. (2002). Perceived organizational support: A review of the literature. *Journal of Applied Psychology, 87,* 698–714.

Rice, Mabel L. (1990). Preschoolers' QUIL: Quick incidental learning of words. In G. Conti-Ramsden & C. E. Snow (Eds.), *Children's language* (Vol. 7). Hillsdale, NJ: Erlbaum.

Richardson, John T. E. (Ed.). (1992). *Cognition and the menstrual cycle.* New York: Springer-Verlag.

Richardson-Klavehn, Alan, & Bjork, Robert A. (1988). Measures of memory. *Annual Review of Psychology, 39,* 475–543.

Ridley-Johnson, Robyn, Cooper, Harris, & Chance, June. (1983). The relation of children's television viewing to school achievement and I.Q. *Journal of Educational Research, 76,* 294–297.

Rieber, Robert W. (2006). *The bifurcation of the self.* New York: Springer.

Rietveld, Cornelius A., Esko, Tõnu, Davies, Gail, et al. (2014). Common genetic variants associated with cognitive performance identified using the proxy-phenotype method. *Proceedings of the National Academy of Sciences of the United States of America, 111*(38), 13790–13794.

Rilling, James K, & Young, Larry J. (2014). The biology of mammalian parenting and its effect on offspring social development. *Science, 345,* 771–776.

Rind, Bruce, Tromovitch, Philip, & Bauserman, Robert. (1998). A meta-analytic examination of assumed properties of child sexual abuse using college samples. *Psychological Bulletin, 124,* 22–53.

Risch, N., Herrell, R., Lehner, T., et al. (2009). Interaction between the serotonin transporter gene (5-HTTLPR), stressful life events, and risk of depression: A meta-analysis. *Journal of the American Medical Association, 301,* 2462–2471.

Rizzo, Albert, Cukor, Judith, Gerardi, Maryrose, Alley, Stephanie, Reist, Chris, Roy, Mike, et al. (2015a). Virtual reality exposure for PTSD due to military combat and terrorist attacks. *Journal of Contemporary Psychotherapy,* electronic preview.

Rizzo, Albert, Difede, JoAnn, Rothbaum, Barbara Olasov, Buckwalter, J. Galen, Daughtry, J. Martin, & Reger, Greg M. (2015b). Update and expansion of the virtual Iraq/Afghanistan PTSD exposure therapy system. In Marilyn P. Safir; Helene S. Wallach; & Albert Rizzo (Eds.), *Future directions in post-traumatic stress disorder: Prevention, diagnosis, and treatment* (pp. 303–328). New York: Springer Science + Business Media.

Rizzolatti, G., & Sinigaglia, C. (2010). The functional role of the parieto-frontal mirror circuit: Interpretations and misinterpretations. *Nature Reviews Neuroscience, 11,* 264–274.

Ro, Tony, Farnè, Alessandro, Johnson, Ruth, et al. (2007). Feeling sounds after a thalamic lesion. *Annals of Neurology, 62,* 433–441.

Roberson, Debi, Davidoff, Jules, Davies, Ian R. L., & Shapiro, Laura R. (2005). Color categories: Evidence for the cultural relativity hypothesis. *Cognitive Psychology, 50*(4), 378–411.

Roberson, Debi, Davies, Ian, & Davidoff, Jules. (2000). Color categories are not universal: Replications and new evidence in favor of linguistic relativity. *Journal of Experimental Psychology: General, 129,* 369–398.

Roberts, Adam. (2015). Terrorism research: Past, present, and future. *Studies in Conflict & Terrorism, 38*(1), 62–74.

Roberts, Brent W., Caspi, Avshalom, & Moffitt, Terrie E. (2001). The kids are alright: Growth and stability in personality development from adolescence to adulthood. *Journal of Personality and Social Psychology, 81,* 670–683.

Roberts, Brent W., Edmonds, Grant, & Grijalva, Emily. (2010). It is developmental me, not generation me: Developmental changes are more important than generational changes in narcissism. *Perspectives on Psychological Science, 5,* 97–102.

Roberts, Brent W., & Mroczek, Daniel. (2008). Personality trait change in adulthood. *Current Directions in Psychological Science, 17,* 31–35.

Roberts, Brent W., Walton, Kate E., & Viechtbauer, Wolfgang. (2006). Patterns of mean-level change in personality traits across the life course: A meta-analysis of longitudinal studies. *Psychological Bulletin, 132,* 1–25.

Roberts, Julian V. (2000). Changing public attitudes towards corporal punishment: The effects of statutory reform in Sweden. *Child Abuse and Neglect, 24,* 1027–1035.

Robertson, Lynn C., Lamb, Marvin R., & Knight, Robert T. (1988). Effects of lesions of temporal-parietal junction on perceptual and attentional processing in humans. *Journal of Neuroscience, 8,* 3757–3769.

Robins, Lee N., Davis, Darlene H., & Goodwin, Donald W. (1974). Drug use by U.S. Army enlisted men in Vietnam: A follow-up on their return home. *American Journal of Epidemiology, 99,* 235–249.

Robinson, Oliver C., & Wright, Gordon R. T. (2013). The prevalence, types and perceived outcomes of crisisepisodes in early adulthood and midlife: A structured retrospective-autobiographical study. *International Journal of Behavioral Development, 37*(5), 407–416.

Robinson, Thomas, Wilde, M. L., Navracruz, L. C., et al. (2001). Effects of reducing children's television and video game use on aggressive behavior: A randomized controlled trial. *Archives of Pediatric and Adolescent Medicine, 155,* 13–14.

Rodriguez, Paul, Wiles, Janet, & Elman, Jeffrey L. (1999). A recurrent neural network that learns to count. *Connection Science, 11,* 5–40.

Roediger, Henry L., III, McDermott, Kathleen B., & McDaniel, Mark A. (2011). Using testing to improve learning and memory. In M. A. Gernsbacher, R. Pew, L. Hough, & J. R. Pomerantz (Eds.), Psychology and the real world: Essays illustrating fundamental contributions to society (pp. 65–74). New York: Worth.

Roediger, Henry L., III, Putnam, Adam L., & Smith, Megan A. (2011). Ten benefits of testing and their applications to educational practice. In J. Mestre & B. Ross (Eds.), *Psychology of learning and motivation: Cognition in education.* Oxford, UK: Elsevier.

Roepke, Susan K., & Grant, Igor. (2011). Toward a more complete understanding of the effects of personal mastery on cardiometabolic health. *Health Psychology, 30,* 615–632.

Rofé, Yacov. (2008). Does repression exist? Memory, pathogenic, unconscious and clinical evidence. *Review of General Psychology, 12,* 63–85.

Rogers, Carl. (1951). *Client-centered therapy: Its current practice, implications, and theory.* Boston: Houghton-Mifflin.

Rogers, Carl. (1961). *On becoming a person.* Boston: Houghton-Mifflin.

Rogers, Ronald W., & Prentice-Dunn, Steven. (1981). Deindividuation and anger-mediated interracial aggression: Unmasking regressive racism. *Journal of Personality and Social Psychology, 41,* 63–73.

Rogers, Timothy T., & McClelland, James L. (2014). Parallel distributed processing at 25: Further explorations in the microstructure of cognition. *Cognitive Science, 38*(6), 1024–1077.

Rogoff, Barbara. (2003). *The cultural nature of human development.* New York: Oxford University Press.

Rojstaczer, Stuart, & Healy, Christopher. (2012). Where A is ordinary: The evolution of American college and university grading, 1940–2009. *Teachers College Record, 114,* 7. www.tcrecord.org/library, ID Number: 16473.

Romanczyk, Raymond G., Arnstein, Laura, Soorya, Latha V., & Gillis, Jennifer. (2003). The myriad of controversial treatments for autism: A critical evaluation of efficacy. In S.O. Lilienfeld, S. J. Lynn, & J. M. Lohr (Eds.), *Science and pseudoscience in clinical psychology.* New York: Guilford Press.

Romans, Sarah E., Kreindler, David, Asllani, Eriola, Einstein, Gillian, Laredo, Sheila, Levitt, Anthony, et al. (2012). Mood and the menstrual cycle. *Psychotherapy and Psychosomatics, 82*(1), 53–60.

Rosa, Linda, Rosa, Emily, Sarner, Larry, & Barrett, Stephen. (1998). A close look at therapeutic touch. *Journal of the American Medical Association, 279*(13), 1005–1010.

Rosch, Eleanor H. (1973). Natural categories. *Cognitive Psychology, 4,* 328–350.

Rosen, Gerald M., Glasgow, Russell E., Moore, Timothy E., Barrera, Manuel Jr. (2015). Self-help therapy: Recent developments in the science and business of giving psychology away. In Scott O. Lilienfeld; Steven Jay Lynn; & Jeffrey M. Lohr (Eds.), *Science and pseudoscience in clinical psychology* (2nd ed., pp. 245–274). New York: Guilford Press.

Rosenberg, Harold. (1993). Prediction of controlled drinking by alcoholics and problem drinkers. *Psychological Bulletin, 113,* 129–139.

Rosenthal, Robert. (1966). *Experimenter effects in behavioral research.* New York: Appleton-Century-Crofts.

Rosenthal, Robert. (1994). Interpersonal expectancy effects: A 30-year perspective. *Current Directions in Psychological Science, 3,* 176–179.

Rosenzweig, Mark R. (1984). Experience, memory, and the brain. *American Psychologist, 39,* 365–376.

Rosin, Hanna. (2012). *The end of men: And the rise of women.* New York: Riverhead Books.

Rosnow, Ralph, & Rosenthal, Robert. (2011). *Beginning behavioral research: A conceptual primer* (7th ed.). Upper Sadddle River, NJ: Pearson.

Ross, Heather E., Freeman, Sara M., Spiegel, Lauren L., et al. (2009). Variation in oxytocin receptor density in the nucleus accumbens has differential effects on affiliative behaviors in monogamous and polygamous voles. *Journal of Neuroscience, 29,* 1312–1318.

Ross, Lee. (2010). Dealing with conflict: Experiences and experiments. In M. H. Gonzales, C. Tavris, & J. Aronson (Eds.), *The scientist and the humanist: A festschrift in honor of Elliot Aronson.* New York: Psychology Press.

Ross, Michael, Xun, W. Q. Elaine, & Wilson, Anne E. (2002). Language and the bicultural self. *Personality and Social Psychology Bulletin, 28,* 1040–1050.

Rothbaum, Fred, Morelli, Gilda, & Rusk, Natalie. (2011). Attachment, learning, and coping: The interplay of cultural similarities and differences. In Michele J. Gelfand; Chi-yue Chiu; & Ying-yi Hong (Eds.), Advances in culture and psychology (Vol. 1, pp. 153–215). New York: Oxford University Press.

Rothbaum, Fred, Weisz, John, Pott, Martha, et al. (2000). Attachment and culture: Security in the United States and Japan. *American Psychologist, 55,* 1093–1104.

Rothermund, Klaus, & Wentura, Dirk. (2004). Underlying processes in the Implicit Association Test: Dissociating salience from associations. *Journal of Experimental Psychology: General, 133,* 139–165.

Rotter, Julian B. (1990). Internal versus external control of reinforcement: A case history of a variable. *American Psychologist, 45,* 489–493.

Roughgarden, Joan. (2004). *Evolution's rainbow: Diversity, gender, and sexuality in nature and people.* Berkeley: University of California Press.

Rouw, Romke, & Scholte, Steven S. (2007). Increased structural connectivity in grapheme-color synesthesia. *Nature Neuroscience, 10,* 792–797.

Rowatt, Wade C., Ottenbreit, Alison, Nesselroade Jr., K. Paul, & Cunningham, Paige A. (2002). On being holier-than-thou or humbler-than-thee: A social-psychological perspective on religiousness and humility. *Journal for the Scientific Study of Religion, 41,* 227–237.

Roy, Mark P., Steptoe, Andrew, & Kirschbaum, Clemens. (1998). Life events and social support as moderators of individual differences in cardiovascular and cortisol reactivity. *Journal of Personality and Social Psychology, 75,* 1273–1281.

Rozin, Paul, Kabnick, Kimberly, Pete, Erin, et al. (2003). The ecology of eating: Smaller portion sizes in France than in the United States help explain the French paradox. *Psychological Science, 14,* 450–454.

Rozin, Paul, Lowery, Laura, & Ebert, Rhonda. (1994). Varieties of disgust faces and the structure of disgust. *Journal of Personality and Social Psychology, 66,* 870–881.

Rudolph, Karen D., Troop-Gordon, Wendy, Lambert, Sharon F., & Natsuaki, Misaki N. (2014). Long-term consequences of pubertal timing for youth depression: Identifying personal and contextual pathways of risk. *Development and Psychopathology, 26*(4, Pt. 2), 1423–1444.

Ruggerio, Vincent. (2011). *Beyond feelings: A guide to critical thinking* (9th ed.). New York: McGraw-Hill.

Rumbaugh, Duane M. (1977). *Language learning by a chimpanzee: The Lana project.* New York: Academic Press.

Rumbaugh, Duane M., Savage-Rumbaugh, E. Sue, & Pate, James L. (1988). Addendum to "Summation in the chimpanzee (Pan troglodytes)." *Journal of Experimental Psychology: Animal Behavior Processes, 14,* 118–120.

Rumelhart, David E., McClelland, James L., & the PDP Research Group. (1986). *Parallel distributed processing: Explorations in the microstructure of cognition* (Vols. 1 and 2). Cambridge, MA: MIT Press.

Rupp, Heather A., & Wallen, Kim. (2008). Sex differences in response to visual sexual stimuli: A review. *Archives of Sexual Behavior, 37,* 206–218.

Ruse, Michael. (2010). Is Darwinism past its "sell-by" date? The origin of species at 150. *European Review, 18,* 311–327.

Rushton, J. Philippe, & Jensen, Arthur R. (2005). Thirty years of research on race differences in cognitive ability. *Psychology, Public Policy, and Law, 11,* 235–294.

Rutter, Michael, O'Connor, Thomas G., & the English and Romanian Adoptees (ERA) Study Team. (2004). Are there biological programming effects for psychological development? Findings from a study of Romanian adoptees. *Developmental Psychology, 40,* 81–94.

Rutter, Michael, Pickles, Andrew, Murray, Robin, & Eaves, Lindon. (2001). Testing hypotheses on specific environmental causal effects on behavior. *Psychological Bulletin, 127,* 291–324.

Ryan, Richard M., Chirkov, Valery I., Little, Todd D., et al. (1999). The American dream in Russia: Extrinsic aspirations and well-being in two cultures. *Personality and Social Psychology Bulletin, 25,* 1509–1524.

Rymer, Russ. (1993). *Genie: An abused child's flight from silence.* New York: HarperCollins.

Sabattini, Laura, & Crosby, Faye. (2009). Work ceilings and walls: Work-life and "family-friendly" policies. In M. Barreto, M. Ryan, & M. Schmitt (Eds.), *The glass ceiling in the 21st century: Understanding barriers to gender equality.* Washington, DC: American Psychological Association.

Sack, Robert L. (2010). Jet lag. *The New England Journal of Medicine, 362,* 440–447.

Sackett, Paul R., Borneman, Matthew J., & Connelly, Brian S. (2008). High-stakes testing in higher education and employment: Appraising the evidence for validity and fairness. *American Psychologist, 63,* 215–227.

Sackett, Paul R., Hardison, Chaitra M., & Cullen, Michael J. (2004). On interpreting stereotype threat as accounting for African American-White differences on cognitive tests. *American Psychologist, 59,* 7–13.

Sacks, Oliver. (1985). *The man who mistook his wife for a hat and other clinical tales.* New York: Simon & Schuster.

Sageman, Marc. (2008). *Leaderless jihad: Terror networks in the twenty-first century.* Philadelphia: University of Pennsylvania Press.

Sahley, Christie L., Rudy, Jerry W., & Gelperin, Alan. (1981). An analysis of associative learning in a terrestrial mollusk: 1. Higher-order conditioning, blocking, and a transient US preexposure effect. *Journal of Comparative Physiology, 144,* 1–8.

Sakai, Kiyoshi, Yamamoto, Akihito, Matsubara, Kohki, et al. (2012). Human dental pulp-derived stem cells promote locomotor recovery after complete transection of the rat spinal cord by multiple neuro-regenerative mechanisms. *The Journal of Clinical Investigation, 122,* 80–90.

Sakaluk, John K., Todd, Leah M., Milhausen, Robin, & Lachowsky, Nathan J. (2014). Dominant heterosexual sexual scripts in emerging adulthood: Conceptualization and measurement. *Journal of Sex Research, 51*(5), 516–531.

Saks, Elyn. (2007). *The center cannot hold: My journey through madness.* New York: Hyperion.

Saletan, William. (2011, November). Sex on the brain: Are boys' brains different from girls' brains? Scientists debate the question. *Slate.* Available at www.slate.com/articles/health_and_science/human_nature/2011/11/boys_brains_girls_brains_how_to_think_about_sex_differences_in_psychology_.html.

Salovey, Peter, & Grewal, Daisy. (2005). The science of emotional intelligence. *Current Directions in Psychological Science, 14,* 281–285.

Salthouse, Timothy A. (2006). Mental exercise and mental aging: Evaluating the validity of the "use it or lose it" hypothesis. *Perspectives on Psychological Science, 1,* 68–87.

Salthouse, Timothy A. (2012). Does the level at which cognitive change occurs change with age? *Psychological Science, 23,* 18–23.

Sameroff, Arnold J., Seifer, Ronald, Barocas, Ralph, et al. (1987). Intelligence quotient scores of 4-year-old children: Social-environmental risk factors. *Pediatrics, 79,* 343–350.

Sampson, Robert J, Sharkey, Patrick, & Raudenbush, Stephen W. (2008). Durable effects of concentrated disadvantage among verbal ability of African-American children. *Proceedings of the National Academy of Sciences, 105,* 845–853.

Samuel, Lawrence R. (2013). *Shrinkn: A cultural history of psychoanalysis in America.* Lincoln: University of Nebraska Press.

Sandin, Sven, Lichtenstein, Paul, Kuja-Halkola, Ralf, Larsson, Henrik, Hultman, Christina M., & Reichenberg, Abraham. (2014). The familial risk of autism. *Journal of the American Medical Association, 311*(17), 1770–1777.

Sarbin, Theodore R. (1991). Hypnosis: A fifty-year perspective. *Contemporary Hypnosis, 8,* 1–15.

Sarbin, Theodore R. (1997). The power of believed-in imaginings. *Psychological Inquiry, 8,* 322–325.

Sasnett, Sherri. (2015). Are the kids all right?: A qualitative study of adults with gay and lesbianparents. *Journal of Contemporary Ethnography, 44*(2), 196–222.

Saucier, Deborah M., & Kimura, Doreen. (1998). Intrapersonal motor but not extrapersonal targeting skill is enhanced during the midluteal phase of the menstrual cycle. *Developmental Neuropsychology, 14,* 385–398.

Saucier, Gerard. (2000). Isms and the structure of social attitudes. *Journal of Personality and Social Psychology, 78,* 366–385.

Savage-Rumbaugh, Sue, & Lewin, Roger. (1994). *Kanzi: The ape at the brink of the human mind.* New York: Wiley.

Savage-Rumbaugh, Sue, Shanker, Stuart, & Taylor, Talbot. (1998). *Apes, language and the human mind.* New York: Oxford University Press.

Savic, Ivanka, Berglund, Hans, & Lindström, Per. (2005, May 17). Brain response to putative pheromones in homosexual men. *Proceedings of the National Academy of Sciences, 102,* 7356–7361.

Savin-Williams, Ritch C. (2006). Who's gay? Does it matter? *Current Directions in Psychological Science, 15,* 40–44.

Saxena, Sanjaya, Brody, Arthur L., Maidment, Karron M., et al. (2004). Cerebral glucose metabolism in obsessive-compulsive hoarding. *American Journal of Psychiatry, 161,* 1038–1048.

Scarpa, Angela, Williams White, Susan, & Attwood, Tony. (Eds.). (2013). *CBT for children and adolescents with high-functioning autism spectrum disorders.* New York: Guilford Press.

Scarr, Sandra. (1993). Biological and cultural diversity: The legacy of Darwin for development. *Child Development, 64,* 1333–1353.

Scarr, Sandra, Pakstis, Andrew J., Katz, Soloman H., & Barker, William B. (1977). Absence of a relationship between degree of white ancestry and intellectual skill in a black population. *Human Genetics, 39,* 69–86.

Scarr, Sandra, & Weinberg, Robert A. (1994). Educational and occupational achievement of brothers and sisters in adoptive and biologically related families. *Behavioral Genetics, 24,* 301–325.

Schachter, Stanley, & Singer, Jerome E. (1962). Cognitive, social, and physiological determinants of emotional state. *Psychological Review, 69,* 379–399.

Schacter, Daniel L. (2001). *The seven sins of memory: How the mind forgets and remembers.* Boston: Houghton-Mifflin.

Schacter, Daniel L., Benoit, Roland G., De Brigard, Felipe, & Szpunar, Karl K. (2015). Episodic future thinking and episodic counterfactual thinking: Intersections between memory and decisions. *Neurobiology of Learning and Memory, 117,* 14–21.

Schacter, Daniel L., Chiu, Chi-yue, & Ochsner, Kevin N. (1993). Implicit memory: A selective review. *Annual Review of Neuroscience, 16,* 159–182.

Schaeffer, Cindy M., & Borduin, Charles M. (2005). Long-term follow-up to a randomized clinical trial of multisystemic therapy with serious and violent juvenile offenders. *Journal of Consulting and Clinical Psychology, 73,* 445–453.

Schafer, Roy. (1992). *Retelling a life: Narration and dialogue in psychoanalysis.* New York: Basic Books.

Schaie, K. Warner, & Willis, Sherry L. (2002). *Adult development and aging* (5th ed.). Upper Saddle River, NJ: Prentice Hall.

Schaie, K. Warner, & Zuo, Yan-Ling. (2001). Family environments and cognitive functioning. In R. J. Sternberg & E. Grigorenko (Eds.), *Cognitive development in context.* Hillsdale, NJ: Erlbaum.

Schank, Roger (with Peter Childers). (1988). *The creative attitude.* New York: Macmillan.

Schellenberg, E. Glenn. (2004). Music lessons enhance IQ. *Psychological Science 15,* 511–514.

Schenck, Carlos H., & Mahowald, Mark W. (2002). REM sleep behavior disorder: Clinical, developmental, and neuroscience perspectives 16 years after its formal identification in SLEEP. *Sleep, 25,* 120–138.

Schiller, Daniela, & Phelps, Elizabeth A. (2011). Does reconsolidation occur in humans? *Frontiers in Behavioral Neuroscience, 5,* 1–12.

Schlossberg, Nancy K., & Robinson, Susan P. (1996). *Going to plan B.* New York: Simon & Schuster/Fireside.

Schlosser, Ralf W., Balandin, Susan, Hemsley, Bronwyn, Iacono, Teresa, Probst, Paul, & von Tetzchner, Stephen. (2014). Facilitated communication and authorship: A systematic review. *AAC: Augmentative and Alternative Communication, 30*(4), 359–368.

Schlösser, Thomas, Dunning, David, Johnson, Kerri L., & Kruger, Justin. (2013). How unaware are the unskilled? Empirical tests of the "signal extraction" counterexplanation for the Dunning–Kruger effect in self-evaluation of performance. *Journal of Economic Psychology, 39,* 85–100.

Schmelz, M., Schmidt, R., Bickel, A., et al. (1997). Specific C-receptors for itch in human skin. *Journal of Neuroscience, 17,* 8003–8008.

Schmidt, Frank L., & Hunter, John. (2004). General mental ability in the world of work: Occupational attainment and job performance. *Journal of Personality and Social Psychology, 86,* 162–173.

Schmidt, Louis A., Fox, Nathan A., Perez-Edgar, Koraly, & Hamer, Dean H. (2009). Linking gene, brain, and behavior: DRD4, frontal asymmetry, and temperament. *Psychological Science, 20,* 831–837.

Schmidt, S. D., Myskiw, J. C., Furini, C. R. G., Schmidt, B. E., Cavalcante, L. E., & Izquierdo, I. (2015). PACAP modulates the consolidation and extinction of the contextual fear conditioning through NMDA receptors. *Neurobiology of Learning and Memory, 118,* 120–124.

Schmitt, David P. (2003). Universal sex differences in the desire for sexual variety: Tests from 52 nations, 6 continents, and 13 islands. *Journal of Personality and Social Psychology, 85,* 85–104.

Schmitt, David P., Jonason, Peter K., Byerley, Garrett J., et al. (2012). A reexamination of sex differences in sexuality: New studies reveal old truths. *Current Directions in Psychological Science, 21,* 135–139.

Schnable, Patrick S., Ware, Doreen, Fulton, Robert S., et al. (2009). The B73 maize genome: Complexity, diversity, and dynamics. *Science, 326,* 1112–1115.

Schnell, Lisa, & Schwab, Martin E. (1990, January 18). Axonal regeneration in the rat spinal cord produced by an antibody against myelin-associated neurite growth inhibitors. *Nature, 343,* 269–272.

Schofield, P., Ball, D., Smith, J. G., et al. (2004). Optimism and survival in lung carcinoma patients. *Cancer, 100,* 1276–1282.

Schuckit, Marc A. (1998). Relationship among genetic, environmental, and psychological variables in predicting alcoholism. Invited address presented at the annual meeting of the American Psychological Association, San Francisco.

Schuckit, Marc A., Smith, Tom L., Pierson, Juliann, et al. (2007). Patterns and correlates of drinking in offspring from the San Diego Prospective Study. *Alcoholism: Clinical and Experimental Research, 31,* 1681–1691.

Schuckit, Marc A., Smith, Tom L., Trim, Ryan, et al. (2008). The performance of elements of a "level of response to alcohol"-based model of drinking behaviors in 13-year-olds. *Addiction, 103,* 1786–1792.

Schuckit, Marc A., Smith, Tom L., Trim, Ryan S., Allen, Rhonda C., Fukukura, Tsutomu, Knight, Emily E., et al. (2011). A prospective evaluation of how a low level of response to alcohol predicts later heavy drinking and alcohol problems. *American Journal of Drug and Alcohol Abuse, 37*(6), 479–486.

Schulze, Cornelia, & Tomasello, Michael. (2015). 18-month-olds comprehend indirect communicative acts. *Cognition, 136,* 91–98.

Schulze, Lars, Schmahl, Christian, & Niedtfeld, Inga. (2015). Neural correlates of disturbed emotion processing in borderline personality disorder: A multimodal meta-analysis. *Biological Psychiatry,* electronic preview.

Schwartz, Barry. (2004). *The paradox of choice: Why more is less.* New York: Ecco Press.

Schwartz, Jeffrey, Stoessel, Paula W., Baxter, Lewis R., et al. (1996). Systematic changes in cerebral glucose metabolic rate after successful behavior modification treatment of obsessive–compulsive disorder. *Archives of General Psychiatry, 53,* 109–113.

Schwartz, Seth J., Unger, Jennifer B., Zamboanga, Byron L., & Szapocznik, José. (2010). Rethinking the concept of acculturation. *American Psychologist, 65,* 237–251.

Schwartz, Seth J., Zamboanga, Byron L., Luyckx, Koen, Meca, Alan, & Ritchie, Rachel A. (2013). Identity in emerging adulthood: Reviewing the field and looking forward. *Emerging Adulthood, 1*(2), 96–113.

Scott, Rose M., & Baillargeon, Renée. (2013). Do infants really expect agents to act efficiently?: A critical test of the rationality principle. *Psychological Science, 24*(4), 466–474.

Seabrook, John. (2008, November 10). Suffering souls: The search for the roots of psychopathy. *The New Yorker,* pp. 64–73.

Sears, Pauline, & Barbee, Ann H. (1977). Career and life satisfactions among Terman's gifted women. In J. C. Stanley, W. C. George, & C. H. Solano (Eds.), *The gifted and the creative: A fifty-year perspective.* Baltimore Johns Hopkins University Press.

Seery, Mark D., Leo, Raphael J., Lupien, Shannon P., Kondrak, Cheryl L., & Almonte, Jessica L. (2013). An upside to adversity?: Moderate cumulative lifetime adversity is associated with resilient responses in the face of controlled stressors. *Psychological Science, 24*(7), 1181–1189.

Segal, Julius. (1986). *Winning life's toughest battles.* New York: McGraw-Hill.

Segal, Zindel V., Teasdale, John D., & Williams, J. Mark G. (2004). Mindfulness based cognitive therapy: Theoretical rationale and empirical status. In S. C. Hayes, V. M. Follette, & M. Linehan (Eds.), *Mindfulness and acceptance: Expanding the cognitive-behavioral tradition.* New York: Guilford Press.

Segall, Marshall H., Campbell, Donald T., & Herskovits, Melville J. (1966). *The influence of culture on visual perception.* Indianapolis, IN: Bobbs-Merrill.

Segall, Marshall H., Dasen, Pierre P., Berry, John W., & Poortinga, Ype H. (1999). *Human behavior in global perspective* (2nd ed.). Boston: Allyn & Bacon.

Segerstrom, Suzanne C., & Miller, Gregory E. (2004). Psychological stress and the human immune system: A meta-analytic study of 30 years of inquiry. *Psychological Bulletin, 130,* 601–630.

Seidenberg, Mark S., MacDonald, Maryellen C., & Saffran, Jenny R. (2002). Does grammar start where statistics stop? *Science, 298,* 553–554.

Seifer, Ronald, Schiller, Masha, Sameroff, Arnold, et al. (1996). Attachment, maternal sensitivity, and infant temperament during the first year of life. *Developmental Psychology, 32,* 12–25.

Sekuler, Robert, & Blake, Randolph. (1994). *Perception* (3rd ed.). New York: Knopf.

Seligman, Martin E. P., & Csikszentmihaly, Mihaly. (2000). Positive psychology: An introduction. *American Psychologist, 55,* 5–14.

Seligman, Martin E. P., & Hager, Joanne L. (1972, August). Biological boundaries of learning: The sauce-béarnaise syndrome. *Psychology Today,* 59–61, 84–87.

Seligman, Martin E. P., Schulman, Peter, DeRubeis, Robert J., & Hollon, Steven D. (1999, December 21). The prevention of depression and anxiety. *Prevention and Treatment, 2,* ArtID 8a.

Sellbom, Martin, Ben-Porath, Yossef S., & *Bagby, R. Michael* (2008). Personality and psychopathology: Mapping the MMPI-2 Restructured Clinical (RC) Scales onto the Five Factor Model of Personality. *Journal of Personality Disorders, 22,* 291–312.

Senghas, Ann, Kita, Sotaro, & Özyürek, Asli. (2004). Children creating core properties of language: Evidence from an emerging sign language in Nicaragua. *Science, 305,* 1779–1782.

Senko, Corwin, Durik, Amanda M., & Harackiewicz, Judith M. (2008). Historical perspectives and new directions in achievement goal theory: Understanding the effects of mastery and performance-approach goals. In J. Y. Shah, & W. L. Gardner (Eds.), *Handbook of motivation science.* New York: Guilford Press.

Serpell, Robert, & Haynes, Brenda Pitts. (2004). The cultural practice of intelligence testing: Problems of international export. In Robert J. Sternberg & Elena L. Grigorenko (Eds.), *Culture and competence: Contexts of life success* (pp. 163–185). Washington, DC: American Psychological Association.

Shaffer, Ryan, & Jadwiszczok, Agatha. (2010, March/April). Psychic defective: Sylvia Browne's history of failure. *Skeptical Inquirer, 34,* 38–42.

Shakin, M., Shakin, D., & Sternglanz, S. H. (1985). Infant clothing: Sex labeling for strangers. *Sex Roles, 12,* 955–964.

Shariff, Azim F., & Tracy, Jessica L. (2011). What are emotion expressions for? *Current Directions in Psychological Science, 20,* 395–399.

Sharma, Mayur, Saleh, Emam, Deogaonkar, Milind, & Rezai, Ali. (2015). DBS for obsessive–compulsive disorder. In Bomin Sun & Antonio De Salles (Eds.), *Neurosurgical treatments for psychiatric disorders* (pp. 113–123). New York: Springer Science + Business Media.

Sharman, Stephanie J., Manning, Charles G., & Garry, Maryanne. (2005). Explain this: Explaining childhood events inflates confidence for those events. *Applied Cognitive Psychology, 19,* 16–74.

Shatz, Marilyn, & Gelman, Rochel. (1973). The development of communication skills: Modifications in the speech of young children as a function of the listener. *Monographs of the Society for Research in Child Development, 38.*

Shaver, Phillip R., & Hazan, Cindy. (1993). Adult romantic attachment: Theory and evidence. In D. Perlman & W. H. Jones (Eds.), *Advances in personal relationships* (Vol. 4). London: Kingsley.

Shaver, Phillip R., Wu, Shelley, & Schwartz, Judith C. (1992). Cross-cultural similarities and differences in emotion and its representation: A prototype approach. In M. S. Clark (Ed.), *Review of Personality and Social Psychology* (Vol. 13). Newbury Park, CA: Sage.

Shaw, Philip, Greenstein, Dede, Lerch, Jason, et al. (2006). Intellectual ability and cortical development in children and adolescents. *Nature, 440,* 676–679.

Sheldon, Kennon M. (2011). Integrating behavioral-motive and experiential-requirement perspectives on psychological needs: A two process model. *Psychological Review, 118*(4), 552–569.

Sheldon, Kennon M., Elliot, Andrew J., Kim, Youngmee, & Kasser, Tim. (2001). What is satisfying about satisfying events? Testing 10 candidate psychological needs. *Journal of Personality and Social Psychology, 80,* 325–339.

Shepard, Roger N., & Metzler, Jacqueline. (1971). Mental rotation of three-dimensional objects. *Science, 171,* 701–703.

Sherif, Muzafer, Harvey, O. J., White, B. J., et al. (1961). *Intergroup conflict and cooperation: The Robbers Cave experiment.* Norman: University of Oklahoma Institute of Intergroup Relations.

Sherif, Muzafer. (1958). Superordinate goals in the reduction of intergroup conflicts. *American Journal of Sociology, 63,* 349–356.

Sherry, John L. (2001). The effects of violent video games on aggression: A meta-analysis. *Human Communication Research, 27,* 409–431.

Sherry, Simon B., & Hall, Peter A. (2009). The perfectionism model of binge eating: Tests of an integrative model. *Journal of Personality and Social Psychology, 96,* 690–709.

Sherwin, Barbara B. (1998). Estrogen and cognitive functioning in women. *Proceedings of the Society for Experimental Biological Medicine, 217,* 17–22.

Shields, Stephanie A. (2002). *Speaking from the heart: Gender and the social meaning of emotion.* New York: Cambridge University Press.

Shields, Stephanie A. (2005). The politics of emotion in everyday life: "Appropriate" emotion and claims on identity. *Review of General Psychology, 9,* 3–15.

Shields, Stephanie A., & Dicicco, Elaine C. (2011). The social psychology of sex and gender: From gender differences to doing gender. *Psychology of Women Quarterly, 35,* 491–499.

Shors, Tracey J. (2009, March). Saving new brain cells. *Scientific American,* pp. 46–54.

Shwalb, David W., & Shwalb, Barbara J. (2015). Fathering diversity within societies. In Lene Arnett Jensen (Ed.), *The Oxford handbook of human development and culture: An interdisciplinary perspective* (pp. 602–661). New York: Oxford University Press.

Sidanius, Jim, Pratto, Felicia, & Bobo, Lawrence. (1996). Racism, conservatism, affirmative action, and intellectual sophistication: A matter of principled conservatism or group dominance? *Journal of Personality and Social Psychology, 70,* 476–490.

Sidanius, Jim, Van Laar, Colette, Levin, Shana, & Sinclair, Stacey. (2004). Ethnic enclaves and the dynamics of social identity on the college campus: The good, the bad, and the ugly. *Journal of Personality and Social Psychology, 87,* 96–110.

Siegel, Ronald K. (1989). *Intoxication: Life in pursuit of artificial paradise.* New York: Dutton.

Siegel, Shepard. (2005). Drug tolerance, drug addiction, and drug anticipation. *Current Directions in Psychological Science, 14,* 296–300.

Siegler, Robert S. (2006). Microgenetic analyses of learning. In D. Kuhn & R. S. Siegler (Eds.), *Handbook of child psychology: Vol. 2. Cognition, perception, and language* (6th ed.). New York: Wiley.

Silke, Andrew (Ed.). (2003). *Terrorists, victims, and society: Psychological perspectives on terrorism and its consequences.* New York: Wiley.

Simcock, Gabrielle, & Hayne, Harlene. (2002). Breaking the barrier: Children fail to translate their preverbal memories into language. *Psychological Science, 13,* 225–231.

Simonton, Dean Keith, & Song, Anna. (2009). Eminence, IQ, physical and mental health, and achievement domain. *Psychological Science, 20,* 429–434.

Simpson, Jeffry A., Collins, W. Andrew, & Salvatore, Jessica E. (2011). The impact of early interpersonal experience on adult romantic relationship functioning: Recent findings from the Minnesota Longitudinal Study of Risk and Adaptation. *Current Directions in Psychological Science, 20,* 355–359.

Simpson, Jeffry A., & Overall, Nickola C. (2014). Partner buffering of attachment insecurity. *Current Directions in Psychological Science, 23*(1), 54–59.

Simpson, Jeffry A., & Rholes, W. Steven. (2015). *Attachment theory and research: New directions and emerging themes.* New York: Guilfrod Press.

Sims, Ethan A. (1974). Studies in human hyperphagia. In G. Bray & J. Bethune (Eds.), *Treatment and management of obesity.* New York: Harper & Row.

Sinaceur, Marwan, Heath, Chip, & Cole, Steve. (2005). Emotional and deliberative reactions to a public crisis: Mad cow disease in France. *Psychological Science, 16,* 247–254.

Singer, Margaret T. (2003). *Cults in our midst* (rev. ed.). New York: Wiley.

Singh, Devendra, Vidaurri, Melody, Zambarano, Robert J., & Dabbs, James M., Jr. (1999). Lesbian erotic role identification: Behavioral, morphological, and hormonal correlates. *Journal of Personality and Social Psychology, 76,* 1035–1049.

Šikl, Radovan, Šimeček, Michal, Porubanová-Norquist, Michaela, Bezdíček, Ondřej, Kremláček, Jan, Stoůlka, Pavel, et al. (2013). Vision after 53 years of blindness. *i-Perception, 4,* 498–507.

Sitzmann, Traci, & Ely, Katherine. (2011). A meta-analysis of self-regulated learning in work-related training and educational attainment: What we know and where we need to go. *Psychological Bulletin, 137,* 421–442.

Skeem, Jennifer L., Polaschek, Devon L. L., Patrick, Christopher, & Lilienfeld, Scott O. (2011). Psychopathic personality: Bridging the gap between scientific evidence and public policy. *Psychological Science in the Public Interest, 12,* 95–162.

Skinner, B. F. (1938). *The behavior of organisms: An experimental analysis.* New York: Appleton-Century-Crofts.

Skinner, B. F. (1948/1976). *Walden Two.* New York: Macmillan.

Skinner, B. F. (1956). A case history in the scientific method. *American Psychologist, 11,* 221–233.

Skinner, B. F. (1972). The operational analysis of psychological terms. In *B. F. Skinner, Cumulative record* (3rd ed.). New York: Appleton-Century-Crofts.

Skinner, B. F. (1990). Can psychology be a science of mind? *American Psychologist, 45,* 1206–1210.

Skinner, Ellen A. (1996). A guide to constructs of control. *Journal of Personality and Social Psychology, 71,* 549–570.

Skinner, Ellen A. (2007). Secondary control critiqued: Is it secondary? Is it control? *Psychological Bulletin, 133,* 911–916.

Skoog, Thérése, Özdemir, Sevgi Bayram, & Stattin, Håkan. (2015). Understanding the link between pubertal timing in girls and the development of depressive symptoms: The role of sexual harassment. *Journal of Youth and Adolescence,* electronic preview.

Slade, Pauline. (1984). Premenstrual emotional changes in normal women: Fact or fiction? *Journal of Psychosomatic Research, 28,* 1–7.

Slater, Mel, Antley, Angus, Davison, Adam, et al. (2006). A virtual reprise of the Stanley Milgram obedience experiments. *PLoS One* 1(1), e39.

Slavin, Robert E., & Cooper, Robert. (1999). Improving intergroup relations: Lessons learned from cooperative learning programs. *Journal of Social Issues, 55,* 647–663.

Slevec, Julie, & Tiggemann, Marika. (2011). Media exposure, body dissatisfaction, and disordered eating in middle-aged women: A test of the sociocultural model of disordered eating. *Psychology of Women Quarterly, 35,* 617–627.

Sloane, Stephanie, Baillargeon, Renée, & Premack, David. (2012). Do infants have a sense of fairness? *Psychological Science, 23,* 196–204.

Slovic, Paul, Finucane, Melissa L., Peters, Ellen., & MacGregor, Donald G. (2002). The affect heuristic. In T. Gilovich, D. Griffin, & D. Kahneman (Eds.), *Heuristics and biases: The psychology of intuitive judgment.* New York: Cambridge University Press.

Slovic, Paul, & Peters, Ellen. (2006). Risk perception and affect. *Current Directions in Psychological Science, 15,* 322–325.

Slyne, Kristin, & Tolin, David F. (2014). The neurobiology of hoarding disorder. In Randy O. Frost & Gail Steketee (Eds), *The Oxford handbook of hoarding and acquiring* (pp. 177–186). New York: Oxford University Press.

Small, Gary. (2008). iBrain: Surviving the technological alteration of the modern mind. New York: Collins Living.

Smith, Ashley R., Chein, Jason, & Steinberg, Laurence. (2014). Peers increase adolescent risk taking even when the probabilities of negative outcomes are known. *Developmental Psychology, 50*(5), 1564–1568.

Smith, David N. (1998). The psychocultural roots of genocide: Legitimacy and crisis in Rwanda. *American Psychologist, 53,* 743–753.

Smith, James F., & Kida, Thomas. (1991). Heuristics and biases: Expertise and task realism in auditing. *Psychological Bulletin, 109,* 472–489.

Smith, M. Elizabeth, & Farah, Martha J. (2011). Are prescription stimulants "smart pills"? The epidemiology and cognitive neuroscience of prescription stimulant use by normal healthy individuals. *Psychological Bulletin, 137,* 717–741.

Smith, Peter B., & Bond, Michael H. (1994). *Social psychology across cultures: Analysis and perspectives.* Boston: Allyn & Bacon.

Smith, Stevens S., Rouse, Leah M., Caskey, Mark, Fossum, Jodi, Strickland, Rick, Culhane, J. Kevin, et al. (2014). Culturally tailored smoking cessation for adult American Indian smokers: A clinical trial. *The Counseling Psychologist, 42*(6), 852–886.

Smyth, Joshua M., Pennebaker, James W., & Arigo, Danielle. (2012). What are the health effects of disclosure? In Andrew Baum; Tracey A. Revenson; & Jerome Singer (Eds.), *Handbook of health psychology* (2nd ed., pp. 175–191). New York: Psychology Press.

Snapp, Shannon, Lento, Rene, Ryu, Ehri, & Rosen, Karen S. (2014). Why do they hook up?: Attachment style and motives of college students. *Personal Relationships, 21*(3), 468–481.

Snodgrass, Sara E. (1992). Further effects of role versus gender on interpersonal sensitivity. *Journal of Personality and Social Psychology, 62,* 154–158.

Snowdon, Charles T. (1997). The "nature" of sex differences: Myths of male and female. In P.A. Gowaty (Ed.), *Feminism and evolutionary biology.* New York: Chapman and Hall.

Snyder, C. R., & Shenkel, Randee J. (1975, March). The P. T. Barnum effect. *Psychology Today,* 52–54.

Snyder, Hannah R., Kaiser, Roselinde H., Warren, Stacie L., & Heller, Wendy. (2015). Obsessive–compulsive disorder is associated with broad impairments in executive function: A meta-analysis. *Clinical Psychological Science, 3*(2), 301–330.

Sobraske, Katherine Hanson, Boster, James S., & Gaulin, Steven J. (2013). Mapping the conceptual space of jealousy. *Ethos, 41*(3), 249–270.

Solms, Mark. (1997). *The neuropsychology of dreams.* Mahwah, NJ: Erlbaum.

Solomon, Robert C. (1994). *About love.* Lanham, MD: Littlefield Adams.

Somer, Oya, & Goldberg, Lewis R. (1999). The structure of Turkish trait-descriptive adjectives. *Journal of Personality and Social Psychology, 76,* 431–450.

Sommer, Iris E. C., Aleman, André, Bouma, Anke, & Kahn, René S. (2004). Do women really have more bilateral language representation than men? A meta-analysis of functional imaging studies. *Brain: A Journal of Neurology, 127,* 1845–1852.

Sommer, Iris E. C., Aleman, André, Somers, Metten, et al. (2008). Sex differences in handedness, asymmetry of the planum temporale and functional language lateralization. *Brain Research, 1206,* 76–88.

Sommer, Robert. (1969). *Personal space: The behavioral basis of design.* Englewood Cliffs, NJ: Prentice-Hall.

Sommer, Robert. (1977, January). Toward a psychology of natural behavior. *APA Monitor.* Reprinted in *Readings in psychology 78/79.* Guilford, CT: Dushkin, 1978.

Sommerville, Jessica A., Woodward, Amanda L., & Needham, Amy. (2005). Action experience alters 3-month-old infants' perception of others' actions. *Cognition, 96,* B1–B11.

Sonoda, Hideto, Kohnoe, Shunji, Yamazato, Tetsuro, et al. (2011). Colorectal cancer screening with odour material by canine scent detection. *Gut, 60,* 814–819.

Soto, Christopher J., John, Oliver P., Gosling, Samuel D., & Potter, Jeff. (2011). Age differences in personality traits from 10 to 65: Big Five domains and facets in a large cross-sectional sample. *Journal of Personality and Social Psychology 100,* 330–348.

Spanos, Nicholas P. (1991). A sociocognitive approach to hypnosis. In S. J. Lynn & J. W. Rhue (Eds.), *Theories of hypnosis: Current models and perspectives.* New York: Guilford Press.

Spanos, Nicholas P. (1996). *Multiple identities and false memories: A sociocognitive perspective.* Washington, DC: American Psychological Association.

Spanos, Nicholas P., Burgess, Cheryl A., Roncon, Vera, et al. (1993). Surreptitiously observed hypnotic responding in simulators and in skill-trained and untrained high hypnotizables. *Journal of Personality and Social Psychology, 65,* 391–398.

Spanos, Nicholas P., Menary, Evelyn, Gabora, Natalie J., et al. (1991). Secondary identity enactments during hypnotic past-life regression: A sociocognitive perspective. *Journal of Personality and Social Psychology, 61,* 308–320.

Spanos, Nicholas P., Stenstrom, Robert J., & Johnson, Joseph C. (1988). Hypnosis, placebo, and suggestion in the treatment of warts. *Psychosomatic Medicine, 50,* 245–260.

Spear, Linda P. (2000). The adolescent brain and age-related behavioral manifestations. *Neuroscience and Biobehavioral Review, 24,* 417–463.

Spearman, Charles. (1927). *The abilities of man.* London: Macmillan.

Specht, Jule, Egloff, Boris, & Schmukle, Stefan C. (2011). Stability and change of personality across the life course. *Journal of Personality and Social Psychology, 101,* 862–882.

Spelke, Elizabeth S., & Kinzler, Katherine D. (2007). Core knowledge. *Developmental Science, 10,* 89–96.

Sperling, George. (1960). The information available in brief visual presentations. *Psychological Monographs, 74*(498).

Sperry, Roger W. (1964). The great cerebral commissure. *Scientific American, 210*(1), 42–52.

Sperry, Roger W. (1982). Some effects of disconnecting the cerebral hemispheres. *Science, 217,* 1223–1226.

Spitz, Herman H. (1997). *Nonconscious movements: From mystical messages to facilitated communication.* Mahwah, NJ: Erlbaum.

Spring, Bonnie, Chiodo, June, & Bowen, Deborah J. (1987). Carbohydrates, tryptophan, and behavior: A methodological review. *Psychological Bulletin, 102,* 234–256.

Squier, Leslie H., & Domhoff, G. William. (1998). The presentation of dreaming and dreams in introductory psychology textbooks: A critical examination with suggestions for textbook authors and course instructors. *Dreaming, 8,* 149–168.

Squire, Larry R., Ojemann, Jeffrey G., Miezin, Francis M., et al. (1992). Activation of the hippocampus in normal humans: A functional anatomical study of memory. *Proceedings of the National Academy of Science, 89,* 1837–1841.

Squire, Larry R., & Zola-Morgan, Stuart. (1991). The medial temporal lobe memory system. *Science, 253,* 1380–1386.

Srivastava, Abhishek, Locke, Edwin A., & Bartol, Kathryn M. (2001). Money and subjective well-being: It's not the money, it's the motives. *Journal of Personality and Social Psychology, 80,* 959–971.

Srivastava, Sanjay, Tamir, Maya, McGonigal, Kelly M., et al. (2009). The social costs of emotional suppression: A prospective study of the transition to college. *Journal of Personality and Social Psychology, 96,* 883–897.

Staats, Carolyn K., & Staats, Arthur W. (1957). Meaning established by classical conditioning. *Journal of Experimental Psychology, 54,* 74–80.

Stajkovic, Alexander D., & Luthans, Fred. (1998). Self-efficacy and work-related performance: A meta-analysis. *Psychological Bulletin, 124,* 240–261.

Stanley, Damian, Phelps, Elizabeth, & Banaji, Mahzarin. (2008). The neural basis of implicit attitudes. *Current Directions in Psychological Science, 17,* 164–170.

Stanovich, Keith. (2010). *How to think straight about psychology* (9th ed.). Boston: Allyn & Bacon.

Stanton, Stephen J., Mullette-Gillman, O'Dhaniel A., & Huettel, Scott A. (2011). Seasonal variation of salivary testosterone in men, normally cycling women, and women using hormonal contraceptives. *Physiology and Behavior, 104,* 804–808.

Stanwood, Gregg D., & Levitt, Pat. (2001). *The effects of cocaine on the developing nervous system.* In C. A. Nelson & M. Luciana (Eds.), *Handbook of developmental cognitive neuroscience.* Cambridge, MA: MIT Press.

Stattin, Haken, & Magnusson, David. (1990). *Pubertal maturation in female development.* Hillsdale, NJ: Erlbaum.

Staub, Ervin. (1999). The roots of evil: Social conditions, culture, personality, and basic human needs. *Personality and Social Psychology Review, 3,* 179–192.

Steele, Claude. (2010). *Whistling Vivaldi: How stereotypes affect us and what we can do.* New York: W.W. Norton.

Steele, Claude, & Aronson, Joshua. (1995). Stereotype threat and the intellectual test performance of African-Americans. *Journal of Personality and Social Psychology, 69,* 797–811.

Steffens, Sabine, Veillard, Niels R., Arnaud Claire, et al. (2005). Low dose oral cannabinoid therapy reduces progression of atherosclerosis in mice. *Nature 434,* 782–786.

Stein, Dan J., Chiu, Wai Tat, Hwang, Irving, et al. (2010, May 13). Cross-national analysis of the associations between traumatic events and suicidal behavior: Finding from the WHO World Mental Health surveys. *PLoS One, 5,* Article e10574.

Stein, Leslie J., Cowart, Beverly J., & Beauchamp, Gary K. (2012). The development of salty taste acceptance is related to dietary experience in human infants: A perspective study. *American Journal of Clinical Nutrition, 95,* 123–129.

Stein, M. B., Jang, K. L., Taylor, S., et al. (2002). Genetic and environmental influences on trauma exposure and posttraumatic stress disorder symptoms: A general population twin study. *American Journal of Psychiatry, 159,* 1675–1681.

Steinberg, Laurence. (2007). Risk taking in adolescence. *Current Directions in Psychological Science, 16,* 55–59.

Steinberg, Laurence, & Scott, Elizabeth S. (2003). Less guilty by reason of adolescence. *American Psychologist, 58,* 1009–1018.

Steiner, Jacob E. (1973). The gustofacial response: Observation on normal and anencephalic newborn infants. *Symposium on Oral and Sensory Perception, 4,* 254–278.

Steiner, Robert A. (1989). *Don't get taken!* El Cerrito, CA: Wide-Awake Books.

Stel, Mariëlle, Blascovich, Jim, McCall, Cade, et al. (2010). Mimicking disliked others: Effects of a priori liking on the mimicry-liking link. *European Journal of Social Psychology, 40,* 867–880.

Stenberg, Craig R., & Campos, Joseph. (1990). The development of anger expressions in infancy. In N. Stein, B. Leventhal, & T. Trabasso (Eds.), *Psychological and biological approaches to emotion.* Hillsdale, NJ: Erlbaum.

Stepanski, Edward, & Perlis, Michael. (2000). Behavioral sleep medicine: An emerging subspecialty in health psychology. *Journal of Psychosomatic Research, 49,* 343–347.

Stephan, Walter G., Ageyev, Vladimir, Coates-Shrider, Lisa, et al. (1994). On the relationship between stereotypes and prejudice: An international study. *Personality and Social Psychology Bulletin, 20,* 277–284.

Sternberg, Robert J. (1988). *The triarchic mind: A new theory of human intelligence.* New York: Viking.

Sternberg, Robert J. (2004). Culture and intelligence. *American Psychologist, 59*, 325–338.

Sternberg, Robert J. (2012). The triarchic theory of successful intelligence. In D. P. Flanagan & P. L. Harrison (Eds.), *Contemporary intellectual assessment: Theories, tests, and issues* (3rd ed.). New York: Guilford Press.

Sternberg, Robert J., Forsythe, George B., Hedlund, Jennifer, et al. (2000). *Practical intelligence in everyday life.* New York: Cambridge University Press.

Sternberg, Robert J., Wagner, Richard K., Williams, Wendy M., & Horvath, Joseph A. (1995). Testing common sense. *American Psychologist, 50*, 912–927.

Stevenson, Harold W., Chen, Chuansheng, & Lee, Shin-ying. (1993, January 1). Mathematics achievement of Chinese, Japanese, and American children: Ten years later. *Science, 259*, 53–58.

Stevenson, Harold W., & Stigler, James W. (1992). *The learning gap.* New York: Summit.

Stevenson, Richard, Oaten, Megan, Case, Trevor, & Repacholi, Betty. (2014). Is disgust prepared?: A preliminary examination in young children. *Journal of General Psychology, 141*(4), 326–347.

Stewart, John. (2011). *Why noise matters.* Oxford, UK: Routledge.

Stewart-Williams, Steve, & Podd, John. (2004). The placebo effect: Dissolving the expectancy versus conditioning debate. *Psychological Bulletin, 130*, 324–340.

Stice, Eric, Spoor, S., Bohon, C., & Small, D. M. (2008, October 17). Relation between obesity and blunted striatal response to food is moderated by *TaqIA* A1 allele. *Science, 322*, 449–452.

Stiles, Carol, Murray, Susan, & Kentish-Barnes, Cosmo. (2011, October 28). *Udderly Robotic* [Radio Broadcast]. Country Life. Wellington: Radio New Zealand National.

Stillman, Tyler F., & Baumeister, Roy F. (2013). Social rejection reduces intelligent thought and self-regulation. In C. Nathan DeWall (Ed.), *The Oxford handbook of social exclusion* (pp. 132–139). New York: Oxford University Press.

Stix, Gary. (2008, August). Lighting up the lies. *Scientific American,* pp. 18–19.

Stoch, M. B., Smythe, P. M., Moody, A. D., & Bradshaw, D. (1982). Psychosocial outcome and CT findings after gross undernourishment during infancy: A 20-year developmental study. *Developmental Medicine and Child Neurology, 24*(4), 419–436.

Strack, Fritz, Martin, Leonard L., & Stepper, Sabine. (1988). Inhibiting and facilitating conditions of the human smile: A nonobtrusive test of the facial feedback hypothesis. *Journal of Personality and Social Psychology, 54*(5), 768–777.

Strahan, Erin J., Spencer, Steven J., & Zanna, Mark P. (2002). Subliminal priming and persuasion: Striking while the iron is hot. *Journal of Experimental Social Psychology.*

Stratford, Jennifer M., & Finger, Thomas E. (2011). Central representation of postingestive chemosensory cues in mice that lack the ability to taste. *The Journal of Neuroscience, 31*, 9101–9110.

Straus, Murray A. (2005). Children should never, ever, be spanked no matter what the circumstances. In D. R. Loseke, R. J. Gelles, & M. M. Cavanaugh (Eds.), *Current controversies about family violence* (2nd ed.). Thousand Oaks, CA: Sage.

Strayer, David L., & Drews, Frank A. (2007). Cell-phone-induced driver distraction. *Current Directions in Psychology, 16*, 128–131.

Strayer, David L., Drews, Frank A., & Crouch, Dennis J. (2006). A comparison of the cell phone driver and the drunk driver. *Human Factors, 48*, 381–391.

Streissguth, Ann P. (2001). Recent advances in fetal alcohol syndrome and alcohol use in pregnancy. In D. P. Agarwal & H. K. Seitz (Eds.), *Alcohol in health and disease.* New York: Marcel Dekker.

Streyffeler, Lisa L., & McNally, Richard J. (1998). Fundamentalists and liberals: Personality characteristics of Protestant Christians. *Personality and Individual Differences, 24*, 579–580.

Strickland, Bonnie R. (1989). Internal–external control expectancies: From contingency to creativity. *American Psychologist, 44*, 1–12.

Striegel-Moore, Ruth H., & Bulik, Cynthia M. (2007). Risk factors for eating disorders. *American Psychologist, 62*, 181–198.

Stunkard Albert J., Berkowitz, R. I., Schoeller, D., Maislin, G., & Stallings, V. A. (2004). Predictors of body size in the first 2y of life: A high-risk study of human obesity. *International Journal of Obesity, 28*, 503–513.

Suddendorf, Thomas, & Whiten, Andrew. (2001). Mental evolution and development: Evidence for secondary representation in children, great apes, and other animals. *Psychological Bulletin, 127*, 629–650.

Sue, Derald W. (2010). *Microaggressions in everyday life: Race, gender, and sexual orientation.* Hoboken, NJ: Wiley.

Sue, Derald W., Capodilupo, Christina M., Torino, Gina C., et al. (2007). Racial microaggressions in everyday life: Implications for clinical practice. *American Psychologist, 62*, 271–286.

Suedfeld, Peter. (1975). The benefits of boredom: Sensory deprivation reconsidered. *American Scientist, 63*(1), 60–69.

Suinn, Richard M. (2001). The terrible twos—Anger and anxiety. *American Psychologist, 56*, 27–36.

Sukhodolsky, Denis G., Bloch, Michael H., Panza, Kaitlyn E., & Reichow, Brian. (2013). Cognitive-behavioral therapy for anxiety in children with high-functioning autism: A meta-analysis. *Pediatrics, 132*(5), e1341–e1350.

Suls, Jerry, Martin, René, & Wheeler, Ladd. (2002). Social comparison: Why, with whom, and with what effect? *Current Directions in Psychological Science, 11*, 159–163.

Super, Charles M., & Harkness, Sara. (2013). Culture and children's sleep. In Amy R. Wolfson & Hawley E. Montgomery-Downs (Eds.), *The Oxford handbook of infant, child, and adolescent sleep and behavior* (pp. 81–98). New York: Oxford University Press.

Surowiecki, James. (2004). *The wisdom of crowds.* New York: Doubleday.

Suzuki, Takefumi, & Uchida, Hiroyuki. (2014). Successful withdrawal from antipsychotic treatment in elderly male inpatients with schizophrenia—Description of four cases and review of the literature. *Psychiatry Research, 220*(1–2), 152–157.

Swartz, Marvin S., Perkins, Diana O., Stroup, T. Scott, et al., & CATIE Investigators. (2007). Effects of antipsychotic medications on psychosocial functioning in patients with chronic schizophrenia: Findings from the NIMH CATIE study. *American Journal of Psychiatry, 164*, 428–36.

Swenson, Cynthia C., Henggeler, Scott W., Taylor, Ida S., & Addison, Oliver W. (2005). *Multisystemic therapy and neighborhood partnerships: Reducing adolescent violence and substance abuse.* New York: Guilford Press.

Swinkels, Alan. (2009, August). *Man's best friend is a good boy: Sexist language in pet books.* Paper presented at the annual convention of the American Psychological Association, Toronto.

Sylvers, Patrick D., Brennan, Patricia A., & Lilienfeld, Scott O. (2011). Psychopathic traits and preattentive threat processing in children: A novel test of the fearlessness hypothesis. *Psychological Science, 22,* 1280–1287.

Symons, Donald. (1979). *The evolution of human sexuality.* New York: Oxford University Press.

Szalma, James L., & Hancock, Peter A. (2011). Noise effects on human performance: A meta-analytic synthesis. *Psychological Bulletin, 1137,* 682–707.

Szpunar, Karl K., Addis, Donna R., & Schacter, Daniel L. (2012). Memory for emotional simulations: Remembering a rosy future. *Psychological Science, 23,* 24–29.

Tajfel, Henri, Billig, M. G., Bundy, R. P., & Flament, C. (1971). Social categorization and intergroup behavior. *European Journal of Social Psychology, 1,* 149–178.

Tajfel, Henri, & Turner, John C. (1986). The social identity theory of intergroup behavior. In S. Worchel & W. G. Austin (Eds.), *Psychology of intergroup relations.* Chicago: Nelson-Hall.

Takahashi, Kazutoshi, Tanabe, Koji, Ohnuki, Mari, et al. (2007). Induction of pluripotent stem cells from adult human fibroblasts by defined factors. *Cell, 131,* 861–872.

Talarico, Jennifer M. (2009). Freshman flashbulbs: Memories of unique and first-time evens in starting college. *Memory, 17,* 256–265.

Talarico, Jennifer M., & Rubin, David C. (2003). Confidence, not consistency, characterizes flashbulb memories. *Psychological Science, 14,* 455–461.

Talbot, Margaret. (2008, May 12). Birdbrain: The woman behind the world's chattiest parrots. *The New Yorker,* on line archive.

Talbot, Margaret. (2009, April 27). Brain gain: The underground world of neuroenhancing drugs. *The New Yorker,* pp. 32–43.

Talge, N. M., Neal, C., & Glover, V. (2007). Antenatal maternal stress and long-term effects on child neurodevelopment: how and why? *Journal of Child Psychology and Psychiatry, 48,* 245–261.

Tallis, Raymond. (2011). *Aping mankind: Neuromania, Darwinitis, and the misrepresentation of humanity.* Durham, UK: Acumen.

Talmi, Deborah, Grady, Cheryl L., Goshen-Gottstein, Yonatan, & Moscovitch, Morris. (2005). Neuroimaging the serial position curve: A test of single-store versus dual-store models. *Psychological Science, 16,* 716–723.

Tang, Thomas Li-Ping. (2012). Detecting honest people's lies in handwriting: The power of the ten commandments and internalized ethical values. *Journal of Business Ethics, 106*(4), 389–400.

Tang, Yiyuan, Zhang, Wutian, Chen, Kewei, et al. (2006). Arithmetic processing in the brain shaped by cultures. *Proceedings of the National Academy of Sciences, 103,* 10775–10780.

Tangney, June P., Wagner, Patricia E., Hill-Barlow, Deborah, et al. (1996). Relation of shame and guilt to constructive versus destructive responses to anger across the lifespan. *Journal of Personality and Social Psychology, 70,* 797–809.

Tanner, Wilson P., Jr., & Swets, John A. (1954). A decision-making theory of visual detection. *Psychological Review, 61*(6), 401–409.

Tarbox, Sarah I., & Pogue-Geile, Michael F. (2008). Development of social functioning in preschizophrenia children and adolescents: A systematic review. *Psychological Bulletin, 34,* 561–583.

Tavris, Carol. (1989). *Anger: The misunderstood emotion* (rev. ed.). New York: Simon & Schuster/Touchstone.

Tavris, Carol, & Aronson, Elliot. (2007). *Mistakes were made (but not by me).* Orlando, FL: Houghton Mifflin Harcourt.

Taylor, Annette Kujawski, & Kowalski, Patricia. (2004). Naïve psychological science: The prevalence, strength, and sources of misconceptions. *Psychological Record, 54,* 15–25.

Taylor, Shelley E., Lichtman, Rosemary R., & Wood, Joanne V. (1984). Attributions, beliefs about control, and adjustment to breast cancer. *Journal of Personality and Social Psychology, 46,* 489–502.

Taylor, Shelley E., & Lobel, Marci. (1989). Social comparison activity under threat: Downward evaluation and upward contacts. *Psychological Review, 96,* 569–575.

Taylor, Shelley E., & Master, Sarah L. (2011). Social responses to stress: The tend-and-befriend model. In Contrada, R. J. & Baum, A. (Eds.). *The handbook of stress science: Biology, psychology, and health* (pp. 101–109). New York: Springer.

Taylor, Shelley E., Repetti, Rena, & Seeman, Teresa. (1997). Health psychology: What is an unhealthy environment and how does it get under the skin? *Annual Review of Psychology* (Vol. 48). Palo Alto, CA: Annual Reviews.

Taylor, Shelley E., Saphire-Bernstein, Shimon, & Seeman, Teresa E. (2010). Are plasma oxytocin in women and plasma vasopressin in men biomarkers of distressed pair-bond relationships? *Psychological Science, 21,* 3–7.

Terhune, Devin B., Tai, Sarah, Cowey, Alan, et al. (2011). Enhanced cortical excitability in grapheme-color synesthesia and its modulation. *Current Biology, 21,* 2006–2009.

Terman, Lewis M., & Oden, Melita H. (1959). *Genetic studies of genius: Vol. 5. The gifted group at mid-life.* Stanford, CA: Stanford University Press.

Terracciano, Antonio, & McCrae, Robert R. (2006, February). "National character does not reflect mean personality traits levels in 49 cultures": Reply. *Science, 311,* 777–779.

Thaler, Lore, Arnott, Stephen R., & Goodale, Melvyn A. (2011). Neural correlates of natural human echolocation in early and late blind echolocation experts. *PLoS One, 6,* 1–16.

Thomas, Ayanna K., & Dubois, Stacey J. (2011). Reducing the burden of stereotype threat eliminates age differences in memory distortion. *Psychological Science, 12,* 1515–1517.

Thomas, Jennifer J., Vartanian, Lenny R., & Brownell, Kelly D. (2009). The relationship between eating disorder not otherwise specified (EDNOS) and officially recognized eating disorders: Meta-analysis and implications for DSM. *Psychological Bulletin, 135,* 407–433.

Thompson, Clara. (1943/1973). Penis envy in women. *Psychiatry, 6,* 123–125. Reprinted in J. B. Miller (Ed.), *Psychoanalysis and women.* New York: Brunner/Mazel.

Thompson, Clive. (2011, November 1). Why kids can't search. *Wired.* www.wired.com/magazine/2011/11/st_thompson_searchresults/.

Thompson, J. Kevin, & Cafri, Guy (Eds.). (2007). *The muscular ideal: Psychological, social, and medical perspectives.* Washington, DC: American Psychological Association.

Thompson, Paul M., Cannon, T. D., Narr, K. L., et al. (2001). Genetic influences on brain structure. *Nature Neuroscience, 4,* 1253–1258.

Thompson, Paul M., Vidal, Christine N., Giedd, Jay N., et al. (2001). Mapping adolescent brain change reveals dynamic wave of accelerated gray matter loss in very early-onset schizophrenia. *Proceedings of the National Academy of Sciences, 98,* 11650–11655.

Thompson, Richard F. (1983). Neuronal substrates of simple associative learning: Classical conditioning. *Trends in Neurosciences, 6,* 270–275.

Thompson, Richard F. (1986). The neurobiology of learning and memory. *Science, 233,* 941–947.

Thompson, Richard F., & Kosslyn, Stephen M. (2000). Neural systems activated during visual mental imagery: A review and meta-analyses. In A. W. Toga & J. C. Mazziotta (Eds.), *Brain mapping: The systems.* San Diego: Academic Press.

Thompson, Robin, Emmorey, Karen, & Gollan, Tamar H. (2005). "Tip of the fingers" experiences by deaf signers. *Psychological Science, 16,* 856–860.

Thorndike, Edward L. (1898). Animal intelligence: An experimental study of the associative processes in animals. *Psychological Review Monograph Supplement, 2* (Whole No. 8).

Thorndike, Edward L. (1903). *Educational psychology.* New York: Columbia University Teachers College.

Tiefer, Leonore. (2004). *Sex is not a natural act, and other essays* (rev. ed.). Boulder, CO: Westview.

Tiernan, Kristine, Foster, Sharon L., Cunningham, Phillippe B., Brennan, Patricia, & Whitmore, Elizabeth. (2015). Predicting early positive change inmultisystemic therapy with youth exhibiting antisocial behaviors. *Psychotherapy, 52*(1), 93–102.

Timmers, Monique, Fischer, Agneta H., & Manstead, Antony S. R. (1998). Gender differences in motives for regulating emotions. *Personality and Social Psychology Bulletin, 24,* 974–985.

Tinti, Carla, Schmidt, Susanna, Sotgiu, Igor, et al. (2009). The role of importance/consequentiality appraisal in flashbulb memory formation: The case of the death of Pope John Paul III. *Applied Cognitive Psychology, 23,* 236–253.

Toll, Benjamin A., Martino, Steve, O'Malley, Stephanie S., Fucito, Lisa M., McKee, Sherry A., Kahler, Christopher W., et al. (2015). A randomized trial for hazardous drinking and smoking cessation for callers to a quitline. *Journal of Consulting and Clinical Psychology, 83*(3), 445–454.

Tolman, Edward C. (1938). The determiners of behavior at a choice point. *Psychological Review, 45,* 1–35.

Tolman, Edward C., & Honzik, Chase H. (1930). Introduction and removal of reward and maze performance in rats. *University of California Publications in Psychology, 4,* 257–275.

Tomasello, Michael. (2003). *Constructing a language: A usage-based theory of language acquisition.* Cambridge, MA: Harvard University Press.

Tomasello, Michael. (2008). *Origins of human communication.* Cambridge, MA: MIT Press.

Tomasello, Michael. (2014). *A natural history of human thinking.* Cambridge, MA: Harvard University Press.

Tomlinson, Mark, Cooper, Peter, & Murray, Lynne. (2005). The mother–infant relationship and infant attachment in a South African peri-urban settlement. *Child Development, 76,* 1044–1054.

Tomppo, L., Hennah, W., Miettunen, J., et al. (2009). Association of variants in DISC1 with psychosis-related traits in a large population cohort. *Archives of General Psychiatry, 66,* 134–141.

Tourangeau, Roger, & Yan, Ting. (2007). Sensitive questions in surveys. *Psychological Bulletin, 133,* 859–883.

Tracy, Jessica L., & Robins, Richard W. (2007). Emerging insights into the nature and function of pride. *Current Directions in Psychological Science, 16,* 147–151.

Tracy, Jessica L., & Robins, Richard W. (2008). The nonverbal expression of pride: Evidence for cross-cultural recognition. *Journal of Personality and Social Psychology, 94,* 516–530.

Tranquillo, Nicholas. (Ed.). (2014). *Dream consciousness: Allan Hobson's new approach to the brain and its mind.* Cham, Switzerland: Springer.

Trenholm, Christopher, Devaney, Barbara, Fortson, Ken, Quay, Lisa, Wheeler, Justin, & Clark, Melissa. (2007). Impacts of Four Title V, Section 510 Abstinence Education Programs Final Report. Mathematica Policy Research, Princeton, NJ.

Triandis, Harry C. (1996). The psychological measurement of cultural syndromes. *American Psychologist, 51,* 407–415.

Triandis, Harry C. (2007). Culture and psychology: A history of the study of their relationship. In S. Kitayama & D. Cohen (Eds.), *Handbook of cultural psychology.* New York: Guilford Press.

Trivers, Robert. (1972). Parental investment and sexual selection. In B. Campbell (Ed.), *Sexual selection and the descent of man.* New York: Aldine de Gruyter.

Trivers, Robert. (2004). Mutual benefits at all levels of life. [Book review.] *Science, 304,* 965.

Tronick, Edward Z., Morelli, Gilda A., & Ivey, Paula K. (1992). The Efe forager infant and toddler's pattern of social relationships: Multiple and simultaneous. *Developmental Psychology, 28,* 568–577.

Tucker-Drob, Elliot M. (2012). Preschools reduce early academic-achievement gaps: A longitudinal twin approach. *Psychological Science, 23,* 310–319.

Tulving, Endel. (1985). How many memory systems are there? *American Psychologist, 40,* 385–398.

Turiel, Elliot. (2014). Morality: Epistemology, development, and social opposition. In Melanie Killen & Judith G. Smetana (Eds.), *Handbook of moral development* (2nd ed., pp. 3–22). New York: Psychology Press.

Turkheimer, Eric, & Horn, Erin E. (2014). Interactions between socioeconomic status and components of variation in cognitive ability. In Deborah Finkel & Chandra A. Reynolds (Eds.), *Behavior genetics of cognition across the lifespan* (pp. 41–68). New York: Springer Science + Business Media.

Turner, C. F., Ku, L., Rogers, S. M., et al. (1998). Adolescent sexual behavior, drug use, and violence: Increased reporting with computer survey technology. *Science, 280,* 867–873.

Turner, E. H., Matthews, A. M., Linardatos, E., et al. (2008). Selective publication of antidepressant trials and its influence on apparent efficacy. *New England Journal of Medicine, 358,* 252–60.

Turner, Marlene E., Pratkanis, Anthony R., & Samuels, Tara. (2003). Identity metamorphosis and groupthink prevention: Examining Intel's departure from the DRAM industry. In A. Haslam, D. van Knippenberg, M. Platow, & N. Ellemers (Eds.), *Social identity at work: Developing theory for organizational practice.* Philadelphia: Psychology Press.

Turvey, Brent E. (2008). Serial crime. In B. E. Turvey (Ed.), *Criminal profiling: An introduction to behavioral evidence analysis* (3rd ed.). San Diego: Elsevier Academic Press.

Tustin, Karen, & Hayne, Harlene. (2010). Defining the boundary: Age-related changes in childhood amnesia. *Developmental Psychology, 46*, 1049–1061.

Tversky, Amos, & Kahneman, Daniel. (1973). Availability: A heuristic for judging frequency and probability. *Cognitive Psychology, 5*, 207–232.

Tversky, Amos, & Kahneman, Daniel. (1981). The framing of decisions and the psychology of choice. *Science, 211*, 453–458.

Twenge, Jean M. (2009). Change over time in obedience: The jury's still out, but it might be decreasing. *American Psychologist, 64*, 28–31.

Twenge, Jean M. (2013). The evidence for Generation Me and against Generation We. *Emerging Adulthood, 1*(1), 11–16.

Twenge, Jean M., & Foster, Joshua D. (2010). Birth cohort increases in narcissistic personality traits among American college students, 1982–2009. *Social Psychological and Personality Science, 1*, 99–106.

Twenge, Jean M., Konrath, Sara, Foster, Joshua D., Campbell, W. Keith, & Bushman, Brad J. (2008). Egos inflating over time: A cross-temporal meta-analysis of the Narcissistic Personality Inventory. *Journal of Personality, 76*, 875–901.

Tyrer, P., Oliver-Africano, P. C., Ahmed, Z., et al. (2008, January 5). Risperidone, haloperidol, and placebo in the treatment of aggressive challenging behaviour in patients with intellectual disability: a randomised controlled trial. *Lancet, 371*, 57–63.

U. S. Food and Drug Administration. (2011). Executive Summary Prepared for the January 27–28, 2011 meeting of the neurological devices panel to discuss the classification of electroconvulsive therapy devices (ECT). Available online at www.fda.gov/downloads/AdvisoryCommittees/CommitteesMeetingMaterials/MedicalDevicesAdvisoryCommittee/neurologicalDevicesPanel/UCM240933.pdf.

Uchino, Bert N. (2009). Understanding the links between social support and physical health: A life-span perspective with emphasis on the separability of perceived and received support. *Perspectives on Psychological Science, 4*(3), 236–255.

Ullian, E. M., Chrisopherson, K. S., & Barres, B. A. (2004). Role for glia in synaptogenesis. *Glia, 47*, 209–216.

Updegraff, John A., Gable, Shelly L., & Taylor, Shelley E. (2004). What makes experiences satisfying? The interaction of approach-avoidance motivations and emotions in well-being. *Journal of Personality and Social Psychology, 86*, 496–504.

Urry, Heather L., & Gross, James J. (2010). Emotion regulation in older age. *Current Directions in Psychological Science, 19*, 352–357.

Urry, Heather L., Nitschke, Jack B., Dolski, Isa, et al. (2004). Making a life worth living: Neural correlates of well-being. *Psychological Science, 15*, 367–372.

Usher, JoNell A., & Neisser, Ulric. (1993). Childhood amnesia and the beginnings of memory for four early life events. *Journal of Experimental Psychology: General, 122*, 155–165.

Uttall, William R. (2001). *The new phrenology: The limits of localizing cognitive processes in the brain.* Cambridge, MA: MIT Press/Bradford Books.

Vaillant, George E. (Ed.). (1992). *Ego mechanisms of defense.* Washington, DC: American Psychiatric Press.

Vaillant, George E. (2012) *Triumphs of experience: The men of the Harvard grant study.* Cambridge, MA: Belknap Press of Harvard University Press.

Valenstein, Elliot. (1986). *Great and desperate cures: The rise and decline of psychosurgery and other radical treatments for mental illness.* New York: Basic Books.

Valentine, Tim, & Mesout, Jan. (2009). Eyewitness identification under stress in the London dungeon. *Applied Cognitive Psychology, 23*, 151–161.

Van Baaren, Rick, Janssen, L., Chartrand, T. L., & Dijksterhuis, A. (2009). Where is the love? The social aspects of mimicry. *Philosophical Transactions of the Royal Society of London, B: Biological Sciences, 364*, 2381–2389.

Van Cantfort, Thomas E., & Rimpau, James B. (1982). Sign language studies with children and chimpanzees. *Sign Language Studies, 34*, 15–72.

Vandello, Joseph A., & Bosson, Jennifer K. (2013). Hard won and easily lost: A review and synthesis of theory and research on precarious manhood. *Psychology of Men and Masculinity, 14*(2), 101–113.

Vandello, Joseph A., & Cohen, Dov. (1999). Patterns of individualism and collectivism across the United States. *Journal of Personality and Social Psychology, 77*, 279–292.

Vandello, Joseph A., & Cohen, Dov. (2008). U.S. Southern and Northern differences in perceptions of norms about agression: Mechanisms for the perpetuation of a culture of honor. *Social and Personality Psychology Compass, 2*, 652–667.

Vandello, Joseph A., Cohen, Dov, & Ransom, Sean. (2008). U.S. Southern and Northern differences in perceptions of norms about aggression: Mechanisms for the perpetuation of a culture of honor. *Journal of Cross-Cultural Psychology, 39*, 162–177.

Vandenberg, Brian. (1985). Beyond the ethology of play. In A. Gottfried & C. C. Brown (Eds.), *Play interactions.* Lexington, MA: Lexington Books.

van den Dries, Linda, Juffer, Femmie, van IJzendoorn, Marinus H., & Bakermans-Kranenburg, Marian J. (2009). Fostering security? A meta-analysis of attachment in adopted children. *Children and Youth Services Review, 31*, 410–421.

van der Toorn, Jojanneke, Tyler, Tom R., & Jost, John T. (2011). More than fair: Outcome dependence, system justification, and the perceived legitimacy of authority figures. *Journal of Experimental Social Psychology, 47*, 127–138.

van deRuit, Mark, Perenboom, Matthijs, & Grey, Michael J. (2015). TMS brain mapping in less than two minutes. *Brain Stimulation, 8*(2), 231–239.

van de Werken, Maan, Giménez, Marina C., de Vries, Bonnie, Beersma, Domien G. M., & Gordijn, Marijke C. M. (2013). Short-wavelength attenuated polychromatic white light during work at night: Limited melatonin suppression without substantial decline of alertness. *Chronobiology International, 30*(7), 843–854.

Van Emmerik, Arnold A., Kamphuis, Jan H., Hulsbosch, Alexander M., & Emmelkamp, Paul M. G. (2002, September 7). Single session debriefing after psychological trauma: A meta-analysis. *The Lancet, 360*, 766–771.

Van Horn, J. D., Irimia, A., Torgerson, C. M., et al. (2012) Mapping connectivity damage in the case of Phineas Gage. *PLoS One 7*(5), e37454.

van IJzendoorn, Marinus H., Juffer, Femmie, & Klein Poelhuis, Caroline W. (2005). Adoption and cognitive development: A meta-analytic comparison of adopted and nonadopted children's IQ and school performance. *Psychological Bulletin, 131,* 301–316.

Van Laar, Colette, Levin, Shana, & Sidanius, Jim. (2008). Ingroup and outgroup contact: A longitudinal study of the effects of cross-ethnic friendships, dates, roommate relationships and participation in segregated organizations. In U. Wagner, L. R. Tropp, G. Finchilescu, & C. Tredoux (Eds.), *Improving intergroup relations: Building on the legacy of Thomas F. Pettigrew.* Malden, MA: Blackwell.

Van Orden, Kimberly A., Lynam, Meredith E., Hollar, Daniel, & Joiner Jr., Thomas E. (2006). Perceived burdensomeness as an indicator of suicidal symptoms. *Cognitive Therapy and Research, 30,* 457–467.

van Schaik, Carel. (2006, April). Why are some animals so smart? *Scientific American,* pp. 64–71.

van Tilburg, Miranda A. L., Becht, Marleen C., & Vingerhoets, Ad J. J. M. (2003). Self-reported crying during the menstrual cycle: Sign of discomfort and emotional turmoil or erroneous beliefs? *Journal of Psychosomatic Obstetrics and Gynecology, 24,* 247–255.

Västfjäll, Daniel, Peters, Ellen, & Slovic, Paul. (2014). The affect heuristic, mortality salience, and risk: Domain-specific effects of a natural disaster on risk-benefit perception. *Scandinavian Journal of Psychology, 55*(6), 527–532.

Vedaa, Øystein, West Saxvig, Ingvild, Wilhelmsen-Langeland, Ane, et al. (2012). School start time, sleepiness and functioning in Norwegian adolescents. *Scandinavian Journal of Educational Research, 56,* 55–67.

Verhulst, B., Neale, M. C., & Kendler, K. S. (2015). The heritability of alcohol use disorders: A meta-analysis of twin and adoption studies. *Psychological Medicine, 45*(5), 1061–1072.

Vita, A. J., Terry, R. B., Hubert, H. B., & Fries, J. F. (1998). Aging, health risks, and cumulative disability. *New England Journal of Medicine, 338,* 1035–1041.

Vogelzangs, N., Kritchevsky, S. B., Beekman, A. T., et al. (2008). Depressive symptoms and change in abdominal obesity in older persons. *Archives of General Psychiatry, 65,* 1386–1393.

Voigt, Benjamin F., Kudaravalli, Sridhar, Wen, Xiaoquan, & Pritchard, Jonathan K. (2006). A map of recent positive selection in the human genome. *PLoS Biology, 4,* e72.

Volker, Sommer, & Vasey, Paul L. (Eds.). (2006). *Homosexual behaviour in animals: An evolutionary perspective.* New York: Cambridge University Press.

Volkow, Nora D., & Baler, Ruben D. (2012, February 3). To stop or not to stop? *Science, 335,* 546–548.

Volkow, Nora D., Chang, Linda, Wang, Gene-Jack, et al. (2001). Association of dopamine transporter reduction with psychomotor impairment in methamphetamine abusers. *American Journal of Psychiatry, 158,* 377–382.

Vorona, Robert D., Szklo-Coxe, Mariana, Wu, Andrew, et al. (2011). Dissimilar teen crash rates in two neighboring southeastern Virginia cities with different high school start times. *Journal of Clinical Sleep Medicine, 7,* 145.

Vorria, Panayiota, Ntouma, Maria, & Rutter, Michael. (2015). Vulnerability and resilience after early institutional care: The Greek Metera Study. *Development and Psychopathology,* electronic preview.

Vorria, Panayiota, Ntouma, Maria, Vairami, Maria, & Rutter, Michael. (2015). Attachment relationships of adolescents who spent their infancy in residential group care: The Greek Metera study. *Attachment and Human Development, 17*(3), 257–271.

Vrij, Aldert, Granhag, Pär Anders, Mann, Samantha, & Leal, Sharon. (2011). Outsmarting the liars: Toward a cognitive lie detection approach. *Current Directions in Psychological Science, 20,* 28–32.

Vrij, Aldert, Granhag, Pär Anders, & Porter, Stephen. (2010). Pitfalls and opportunities in nonverbal and verbal lie detection. *Psychological Science in the Public Interest, 11,* 89–121.

Vroon, Piet. (1997). *Smell: The secret seducer* (Paul Vincent, trans.). New York: Farrar, Straus & Giroux.

Vukasović, Tena, & Bratko, Denis. (2015). heritability of personality. A meta-analysis of behavior genetic studies. *Psychological Bulletin, 141*(4), 769–785.

Vul, Edward, Harris, Christine, Winkielman, Piotr, & Pashler, Harold. (2009). Puzzlingly high correlations in fMRI studies of emotion, personality, and social cognition. *Perspectives on Psychological Science, 4,* 274–290.

Vul, Edward, & Pashler, Harold. (2008). Measuring the crowd within. *Psychological Science, 19,* 645–647.

Vygotsky, Lev. (1962). *Thought and language.* Cambridge, MA: MIT Press.

Waber, Rebecca L., Shiv, Baba, Carmon, Ziv, & Ariely, Dan. (2008). Commercial features of placebo and therapeutic efficacy. *Journal of the American Medical Association, 299,* 1016–1017.

Wade, Carole. (2006). Some cautions about jumping on the brain-scan bandwagon. *APS Observer,* pp. 19, 23–24.

Wagenaar, Willem A. (1986). My memory: A study of autobiographical memory over six years. *Cognitive Psychology, 18,* 225–252.

Wagenmakers, Eric-Jan, Wetzels, Ruud, Borsboom, D., & van der Maas, H. (2011). Why psychologists must change the way they analyze their data: The case of psi. *Journal of Personality and Social Psychology, 100,* 426–432.

Wager, Tor D., Rilling, James K., Smith, Edward E., et al. (2004). Placebo-induced changes in fMRI in the anticipation and experience of pain. *Science, 303,* 1162–1167.

Wagner, Christopher C., & Ingersoll, Karen S. (2008). Beyond cognition: Broadening the emotional base of motivational interviewing. *Journal of Psychotherapy Integration, 18,* 191–206.

Wagner, Ullrich, Gais, Steffen, Haider, Hilde, et al. (2004). Sleep inspires insight. *Nature, 427,* 352–355.

Wahlstrom, Kyla. (2010). School start time and sleepy teens. *Archives of Pediatrics & Adolescent Medicine, 164,* 676–677.

Wai, Jonathan, & Putallaz, Martha. (2011). The Flynn Effect puzzle: A 30-year examination from the right tail of the ability distribution provides some missing pieces. *Intelligence, 39,* 443–455.

Wakefield, Jerome. (2006). Are there relational disorders? A harmful dysfunction perspective: Comment on the special section. *Journal of Family Psychology, 20,* 423–427.

Wakefield, Jerome. (2012). The DSM-5's proposed new categories of sexual disorder: The problem of false positives in sexual diagnosis. *Journal of Clinical Social Work, 40*(2), 213–223.

Walker, Anne. (1994). Mood and well-being in consecutive menstrual cycles: Methodological and theoretical implications. *Psychology of Women Quarterly, 18,* 271–290.

Walker, David L., Ressler, Kerry J., Lu, Kwok-Tung, & Davis, Michael. (2002). Facilitation of conditioned fear extinction by systemic administration or intra-amygdala infusions of D-cycloserine as assessed with fear-potentiated startle in rats. *Journal of Neuroscience, 22,* 2343–2351.

Walker, Elaine, & Tessner, Kevin. (2008). Schizophrenia. *Perspectives on Psychological Science, 3,* 30–37.

Wallace-Wells, Ben. (2009, February 5). Bitter pill. *Rolling Stone,* pp. 56–63, 74–76.

Wallbott, Harald G., Ricci-Bitti, Pio, & Bänninger-Huber, Eva. (1986). Non-verbal reactions to emotional experiences. In K. R. Scherer, H. G. Wallbott, & A. B. Summerfield (Eds.), *Experiencing emotion: A cross-cultural study.* Cambridge, UK: Cambridge University Press.

Wallen, Kim. (2001). Sex and context: Hormones and primate sexual motivation. *Hormones and Behavior, 40,* 339–357.

Waller, Niels G., Kojetin, Brian A., Bouchard, Thomas J., Jr., et al. (1990). Genetic and environmental influences on religious interests, attitudes, and values: A study of twins reared apart and together. *Psychological Science, 1,* 138–142.

Walton, Gregory M., & Cohen, Geoffrey L. (2011, March 18). A brief social-belonging intervention improves academic and health outcomes of minority students. *Science, 331,* 1447–1451.

Walum, Hasse, Westberg, Lars, Henningsson, Susanne, et al. (2008). Genetic variation in the vasopressin receptor 1a gene (AVPR1A) associates with pair-bonding behavior in humans. *Proceedings of the National Academy of Sciences, 105,* 14153–14156.

Wang, Alvin Y., Thomas, Margaret H., & Ouellette, Judith A. (1992). The keyword mnemonic and retention of second-language vocabulary words. *Journal of Educational Psychology, 84,* 520–528.

Wang, Qi. (2008). Being American, being Asian: The bicultural self and autobiographical memory in Asian Americans. *Cognition, 107,* 743–751.

Wang, Rong, & Bianchi, Suzanne. (2009). ATUS fathers' involvement in childcare. *Social Indicator Research, 93,* 141–145.

Wansink, Brian (2006). *Mindless eating.* New York: Bantam.

Warren, Gayle H., & Raynes, Anthony E. (1972). Mood changes during three conditions of alcohol intake. *Quarterly Journal of Studies on Alcohol, 33,* 979–989.

Watanabe, Shigeru. (2001). Van Gogh, Chagall and pigeons: Picture discrimination in pigeons and humans. *Animal Cognition, 4,* 1435–9448.

Watanabe, Shigeru. (2010). Pigeons can discriminate "good" and "bad" paintings by children. *Animal Cognition, 13,* 75–85.

Watkins, Linda R., & Maier, Steven F. (2003). When good pain turns bad. *Current Directions In Psychological Science, 12,* 232–236.

Watson, John B. (1925). *Behaviorism.* New York: Norton.

Watson, John B., & Rayner, Rosalie. (1920). Conditioned emotional reactions. *Journal of Experimental Psychology, 3,* 1–14. Reprinted in *American Psychologist, 55,* 2000, 313–317.

Watters, Ethan. (2011). *Crazy like us: The globalization of the American psyche.* New York: Basic Books.

Watters, Ethan, & Ofshe, Richard. (1999). *Therapy's delusions.* New York: Scribner.

Watts, Sarah E., Turnell, Adrienne, Kladnitski, Natalie, Newby, Jill M., & Andrews, Gavin. (2015). Treatment-as-usual (TAU) is anything but usual: A meta-analysis of CBT versus TAU for anxiety and depression. *Journal of Affective Disorders, 175,* 152–167.

Weaver, Charles N. (2008) Social distance as a measure of prejudice among ethnic groups in the United States. *Journal of Applied Social Psychology, 38,* 778–795.

Wechsler, David. (1955). *Manual for the Wechsler Adult Intelligence Scale.* New York: Psychological Corporation.

Wegner, Daniel M. (1986). Transactive memory: A contemporary analysis of the group mind. In Brian Mullen & George R. Goethals (Eds.), *Theories of group behavior* (pp. 185–208). New York: Springer-Verlag.

Wegner, Daniel M. (1994). Ironic processes of mental control. *Psychological Review, 101*(1), 34–52.

Wegner, Daniel M. (2011). Setting free the bears: Escape from thought suppression *American Psychologist, 66*(8), 671–680.

Wegner, Daniel M., Fuller, Valeria A., & Sparrow, Betsy. (2003). Clever hands: Uncontrolled intelligence in facilitated communication. *Journal of Personality and Social Psychology, 85,* 5–19.

Wegner, Daniel M., & Gold, Daniel B. (1995). Fanning old flames: Emotional and cognitive effects of suppressing thoughts of a past relationship. *Journal of Personality and Social Psychology, 68,* 782–792.

Wehr, Thomas A., Duncan, Wallace C., Sher, Leo, et al. (2001). A circadian signal of change of season in patients with seasonal affective disorder. *Archives of General Psychiatry, 58,* 1108–1114.

Weil, Andrew T. (1974a, June). Parapsychology: Andrew Weil's search for the true Geller. *Psychology Today,* pp. 45–50.

Weil, Andrew T. (1974b, July). Parapsychology: Andrew Weil's search for the true Geller: Part II. The letdown. *Psychology Today,* pp. 74–78, 82.

Weiner, Bernard. (1986). *An attributional theory of motivation and emotion.* New York: Springer-Verlag.

Weinstein, Netta, Ryan, William S., DeHaan, Cody R., et al. (2012). Parental autonomy support and discrepancies between implicit and explicit sexual identities: Dynamics of self-acceptance and defense. *Journal of Personality and Social Psychology, 102,* 815–832.

Weinstein, Tamara A., Capitanio, John P., & Gosling, Samuel D. (2008). Personality in animals. In O.P. John, R.W. Robbins, & L.A. Pervin (Eds.), *Handbook of personality: Theory and research.* New York: Guilford Press.

Weisleder, Adriana, & Fernald, Anne. (2013). Talking to children matters: Early language experience strengthens processing and builds vocabulary. *Psychological Science, 24*(11), 2143–2152.

Weiss, Alexander, Bates, Timothy C., & Luciano, Michelle. (2008). Happiness is a personal(ity) thing. *Psychological Science, 19,* 205–210.

Weissman, Myrna M., Markowitz, John C., & Klerman, Gerald L. (2000). *Comprehensive guide to interpersonal psychotherapy.* New York: Basic Books.

Wellman, Henry M., Cross, David, & Watson, Julanne. (2001). Meta-analysis of theory-of-mind development: The truth about false belief. *Child Development, 72,* 655–684.

Wells, Brooke E., & Twenge, Jean. (2005). Changes in young people's sexual behavior and attitudes, 1943–1999: A cross-temporal meta-analysis. *Review of General Psychology, 9,* 249–261.

Wells, Gary L., & Olson, Elisabeth A. (2003). Eyewitness testimony. *Annual Review of Psychology, 54,* 277–295.

Werner, Emmy E. (1989). High-risk children in young adulthood: A longitudinal study from birth to 32 years. *American Journal of Orthopsychiatry, 59,* 72–81.

Wertheimer, Michael. (1923/1958). Principles of perceptual organization. In D. C. Beardslee & M. Wertheimer (Eds.), *Readings in perception.* Princeton, NJ: Van Nostrand.

West, Melissa O., & Prinz, Ronald J. (1987). Parental alcoholism and childhood psychopathology. *Psychological Bulletin, 102,* 204–218.

Westen, Drew. (1998). The scientific legacy of Sigmund Freud: Toward a psychodynamically informed psychological science. *Psychological Bulletin, 124,* 333–371.

Westen, Drew, Gabbard, Glen O., & Ortigo, Kile M. (2008) Psychoanalytic approaches to personality. In Oliver P. John; Richard W. Robins; & Lawrence Pervin (Eds.), *Handbook of personality: Theory and research* (3rd ed., pp. 61–113). New York: Guilford Press.

Westen, Drew, Novotny, Catherine M., & Thompson-Brenner, Heather. (2004). The empirical status of empirically supported psychotherapies: Assumptions, findings, and reporting in controlled clinical trials. *Psychological Bulletin, 130,* 631–663.

Westen, Drew, & Shedler, Jonathan. (1999). Revising and assessing axis II, Part II: Toward an empirically based and clinically useful classification of personality disorders. *American Journal of Psychiatry, 156,* 273–285.

Westermeyer, Joseph. (1995). Cultural aspects of substance abuse and alcoholism: Assessment and management. *Psychiatric Clinics of North America, 18,* 589–605.

Westling, Erika, Andrews, Judy A., & Peterson, Missy. (2012). Gender differences in puberty timing, social competence, and cigarette use: A test of the early maturation hypothesis. *Journal of Adolescent Health, 51,* 150–155.

Wethington, Elaine. (2000). Expecting stress: Americans and the "midlife crisis." *Motivation and Emotion, 24,* 85–103.

Wetzels, Ruud, Matzke, Dora, Lee, Michael D., et al. (2011). Statistical evidence in experimental psychology: An empirical comparison using 855 *t* tests. *Perspectives on Psychological Science, 6,* 291–298.

Whaley, Arthur L., & Davis, King E. (2007). Cultural competence and evidence-based practice in mental health services. *American Psychologist, 62,* 563–574.

Wheeler, Mary E., & Fiske, Susan T. (2005). Controlling racial prejudice: Social-cognitive goals affect amygdala and stereotype activation. *Psychological Science, 16,* 56–63.

Whitaker, Robert. (2010). *Anatomy of an epidemic.* New York: Crown.

Whiting, Beatrice B., & Edwards, Carolyn P. (1988). *Children of different worlds: The formation of social behavior.* Cambridge, MA: Harvard University Press.

Whiting, Beatrice, & Whiting, John. (1975). *Children of six cultures.* Cambridge, MA: Harvard University Press.

Whitlock, Jonathan R., Heynen, Arnold J., Shuler, Marshall G., & Bear, Mark F. (2006, August 25). Learning induces long-term potentiation in the hippocampus. *Science, 313,* 1093–1098.

Whorf, Benjamin L. (1956). *Language, thought and reality.* Cambridge, MA: MIT Press. (Original work published 1940.)

Wicks-Nelson, Rita, & Israel, Allen C. (2003). *Behavior disorders of childhood* (5th ed.). Upper Saddle River, NJ: Prentice Hall.

Widen, Sherri C., & Russell, James A. (2010). Differentiation in preschooler's categories of emotion. *Emotion, 10,* 651–661.

Widman, Laura, & McNulty, James K. (2010). Sexual narcissism and the perpetration of sexual aggression. *Archives of Sexual Behavior, 39*(4), 926–939.

Widom, Cathy Spatz, DuMont, Kimberly, & Czaja, Sally J. (2007). A prospective investigation of major depressive disorder and comorbidity in abused and neglected children grown up. *Archives of General Psychiatry, 64,* 49–56.

Wiederhold, Brenda K., & Wiederhold, Mark D. (2000). Lessons learned from 600 virtual reality sessions. *CyberPsychology and Behavior, 3,* 393–400.

Wildman, R. P., Muntner, P., Reynolds, K., et al. (2008, August 11). The obese without cardiometabolic risk factor clustering and the normal weight with cardiometabolic risk factor clustering: prevalence and correlates of 2 phenotypes among the US population. *Archives of Internal Medicine, 168,* 1617–1624.

Wilhelm, Ines, Diekelmann, Susanne, Molzow, Ina, et al. (2011). Sleep selectively enhances memory expected to be of future relevance. *Journal of Neuroscience, 31,* 1563–1569.

Williams, Janice E., Paton, Catherine C., Siegler, Ilene C., et al. (2000). Anger proneness predicts coronary heart disease risk. *Circulation, 101,* 2034–2039.

Williams, Kipling D. (2009). Ostracism: Effects of being excluded and ignored. *Advances in Experimental Social Psychology, 41,* 279–314.

Williams, Lisa A., & DeSteno, David. (2009). Pride: Adaptive social emotion or seventh sin? *Psychological Science, 20,* 284–288.

Williams, Nigel M., Franke, Barbara, Mick, Eric, et al. (2011). Genome-wide analysis of copy number variants in attention deficit hyperactivity disorder: the role of rare variants and duplications at 15q13.3. *American Journal of Psychiatry, 169,* 195–204.

Williams, Redford B., Jr., Barefoot, John C., & Shekelle, Richard B. (1985). The health consequences of hostility. In M. A. Chesney & R. H. Rosenman (Eds.), *Anger and hostility in cardiovascular and behavioral disorders.* New York: Hemisphere.

Willmott, Lynn, Harris, Peter, Gellaitry, Grace, et al. (2011). The effects of expressive writing following first myocardial infarction: A randomized controlled trial. *Health Psychology, 30*(5), 642–650.

Wilner, Daniel, Walkley, Rosabelle, & Cook, Stuart. (1955). *Human relations in interracial housing.* Minneapolis: University of Minnesota Press.

Wilson, Edward O. (1975). *Sociobiology: The new synthesis.* Cambridge, MA: Belknap/Harvard University Press.

Wilson, Edward O. (1978). *On human nature.* Cambridge, MA: Harvard University Press.

Wilson, John Paul, Hugenberg, Kurt, & Bernstein, Michael J. (2013). The cross-race effect and eyewitness identification: How to improve recognition and reduce decision errors in eyewitness situations. *Social Issues and Policy Review, 7*(1), 83–113.

Wilson, Sandra Jo, & Lipsey, Mark W. (2007). School-based interventions for aggressive and disruptive behavior: Update of a meta-analysis. *American Journal of Preventive Medicine, 33*, S130–S143.

Wilson, Timothy. (2011). *Redirect: The surprising new science of psychological change.* New York: Little, Brown.

Wilson, Timothy, & Gilbert, Daniel. (2005). Affective forecasting: Knowing what to want. *Current Directions in Psychological Science, 14,* 131–134.

Wiltermuth, Scott S., & Heath, Chip. (2009). Synchrony and cooperation. *Psychological Science, 20,* 1–5.

Winick, Myron, Meyer, Knarig Katchadurian, & Harris, Ruth C. (1975). Malnutrition and environmental enrichment by early adoption. *Science, 190,* 1173–1175.

Winnicott, D. W. (1957/1990). *Home is where we start from.* New York: Norton.

Wirth, James H., & Bodenhausen, Galen V. (2009). The role of gender in mental-illness stigma: A national experiment. *Psychological Science, 20,* 169–173.

Wispé, Lauren G., & Drambarean, Nicholas C. (1953). Physiological need, word frequency, and visual duration thresholds. *Journal of Experimental Psychology, 46,* 25–31.

Witkiewitz, Katie, & Marlatt, G. Alan. (2004). Relapse prevention for alcohol and drug problems: That was Zen, this is Tao. *American Psychologist, 59,* 224–235.

Witkiewitz, Katie, Walthers, Justin, & Marlatt, G. Alan. (2013). Harm reduction in mental health practice. In Vikki L. Vandiver (Ed.), *Best practices in community mental health: A pocket guide* (pp. 65–82). Chicago: Lyceum Books.

Witvliet, Charlotte vanOyen, Mohr, Alicia J. Hofelich, Hinman, Nova G., & Knoll, Ross W. (2015). Transforming or restraining rumination: The impact of compassionate reappraisal versus emotion suppression on empathy, forgiveness, and affective psychophysiology. *Journal of Positive Psychology, 10*(3), 248–261.

Wolf, S. A., Melnik, A., & Kempermann, G. (2011). Physical exercise increases adult neurogenesis and telomerase activity, and improves behavioral deficits in a mouse model of schizophrenia. *Brain, Behavior, and Immunology, 25*(5), 971–980.

Wollen, Keith A., Weber, Andrea, & Lowry, Douglas H. (1972). Bizarreness versus interaction of mental images as determinants of learning. *Cognitive Psychology, 3,* 518–523.

Wood, James M., Nezworski, M. Teresa, Lilienfeld, Scott O., & Garb, Howard N. (2003). *What's wrong with the Rorschach?* San Francisco: Jossey-Bass.

Wood, Joanne V., Michela, John L., & Giordano, Caterina. (2000). Downward comparison in everyday life: Reconciling self-enhancement models with the mood-cognition priming model. *Journal of Personality and Social Psychology, 79,* 563–579.

Wood, Wendy, Lundgren, Sharon, Ouellette, Judith A., et al. (1994). Minority influence: A meta-analytic review of social influence processes. *Psychological Bulletin, 115,* 323–345.

Woodward, Amanda L. (2009). Infants' grasp of others' intentions. *Current Directions in Psychological Science, 18,* 53–57.

Woody, Erik Z., & Bowers, Kenneth S. (1994). A frontal assault on dissociated control. In S. J. Lynn & J. W. Rhue (Eds.), *Dissociation: Clinical, theoretical and research perspectives.* New York: Guilford Press.

Woody, Erik Z., & Sadler, Pamela. (2012). Dissociation theories of hypnosis. In M. R. Nash, M. Nash, & A. Barnier (Eds.), *The Oxford handbook of hypnosis: Theory, research, and Practice.* New York: Oxford University Press.

World Health Organization. (2011). *WHO report on the global tobacco epidemic, 2011: Warning about the dangers of tobacco.* Geneva: Author.

Wu, Shali, & Keysar, Boaz. (2007). The effect of culture on perspective taking. *Psychological Science, 18,* 600–606.

Wynne, Clive D. L. (2004). *Do animals think?* Princeton, NJ: Princeton University Press.

Wyrobek, A. J., Eskenazi, B., Young, S., et al. (2006, June 9). Advancing age has differential effects on DNA damage, chromatin integrity, gene mutations, and aneuploidies in sperm. *Proceedings of the National Academy of Sciences, 103,* 9601–9606.

Xu, Jinghong, Yu, Liping, Stanford, Terrence R., Rowland, Benjamin A., & Stein, Barry E. (2015). What does a neuron learn from multisensory experience? *Journal of Neurophysiology, 113*(3), 883–889.

Yalom, Irvin D. (1989). *Love's executioner and other tales of psychotherapy.* New York: Basic Books.

Yamawaki, Niwako, Spackman, Matthew P., Parrott, W. Gerrod. (2015). A cross-cultural comparison of American and Japanese experiences of personal and vicarious shame. *Journal of Cognition and Culture, 15*(1–2), 64–86.

Yang, Chi-Fu Jeffrey, Gray, Peter, & Pope, Harrison G. Jr. (2005). Male body image in Taiwan versus the West: Yanggang Zhiqi meets the Adonis Complex. *American Journal of Psychiatry, 162,* 263–269.

Yapko, Michael. (1994). *Suggestions of abuse: True and false memories of childhood sexual trauma.* New York: Simon & Schuster.

Yehuda, Rachel, Cai, Guiqing, Golier, Julia A., et al. (2009). Gene expression patterns associated with posttraumatic stress disorder following exposure to the World Trade Center attacks. *Biological Psychiatry, 66,* 708–711.

Yehuda, Rachel, Engel, Stephanie M., Brand, Sarah R., et al. (2005). Transgenerational effects of posttraumatic stress disorder in babies of mothers exposed to the World Trade Center attacks during pregnancy. *The Journal of Clinical Endocrinology and Metabolism, 90,* 4115–4118.

Young, Christopher, Majolo, Bonaventura, Heistermann, Michael, Schülke, Oliver, & Ostner, Julia. (2014). Responses to social and environmental stress are attenuated by strong male bonds in wild macaques. *Proceedings of the National Academy of Sciences of the United States of America, 111*(51), 18195–18200.

Young, Terry, Finn, Laurel, Peppard, Paul E., et al. (2008). Sleep-disordered breathing and mortality: Eighteen-year follow-up of the Wisconsin Sleep Cohort. *Sleep, 31,* 1071–1078.

Yu, Junying, Vodyanik, Maxim A., Smuga-Otto, Kim, et al. (2007). Induced pluripotent stem cell lines derived from human somatic cells. *Science, 318,* 1917–1920.

Yu, M., Zhu, X., Li, J., et al. (1996). Perimenstrual symptoms among Chinese women in an urban area of China. *Health Care for Women International, 17*, 161–172.

Yu, ManSoo, & Stiffman, Arlene R. (2007). Culture and environment as predictors of alcohol abuse/dependence symptoms in American Indian youths. *Addictive Behaviors, 32*, 2253–2259.

Yuan, Sylvia, & Fisher, Cynthia. (2009). "Really? She blicked the baby?" Two-year-olds learn combinatorial facts about verbs by listening. *Psychological Science, 20*, 619–626.

Yzerbyt, Vincent Y., Corneille, Olivier, Dumont, Muriel, & Hahn, Kirstin. (2001). The dispositional inference strikes back: Situational focus and dispositional suppression in causal attribution. *Journal of Personality and Social Psychology, 81*, 365–376.

Zadra, Antonio, Desautels, Alex, Petit, Dominique, & Montplaisir, Jacques. (2013). Somnambulism: Clinical aspects and pathophysiological hypotheses. *Lancet Neurology, 12*(3), 285–294.

Zaehle, Tino, Sandmann, Pascale, Thorne, Jeremy D., et al. (2011). Transcranial direct current stimulation of the prefrontal cortex modulates working memory performance: Combined behavioural and electrophysiological evidence. *BMC Neuroscience, 12*, 1–11.

Zajac, Rachel, & Henderson, Nicola. (2009). Don't it make my brown eyes blue: Co-witness misinformation about a target's appearance can impair target-absent line-up performance. *Memory, 17*, 266–278.

Zajonc, R. B. (1968). Attitudinal effects of mere exposure. *Journal of Personality and Social Psychology, 9*, Monograph Supplement 2, 1–27.

Zapolski, Tamika C. B., Pedersen, Sarah L., McCarthy, Denis M., & Smith, Gregory T. (2014). Less drinking, yet more problems: Understanding African American drinking and related problems. *Psychological Bulletin, 140*(1), 188–223.

Zhang, Tie-Yuan, & Meaney, Michael J. (2010). Epigenetics and the environmental regulation of the genome and its function. *Annual Review of Psychology, 61*, 439–466.

Zhu, L. X., Sharma, S., Stolina, M., et al. (2000). Delta-9-tetrahydrocannabinol inhibits antitumor immunity by a CB2 receptor-mediated, cytokine-dependent pathway. *Journal of Immunology, 165*, 373–380.

Zimmerman, Frederick J., Christakis, Dimitri A., & Meltzoff, Andrew N. (2007). Associations between media viewing and language development in children under age 2 years. *Journal of Pediatrics, 151*, 364–368.

Zone, Nolon, Sue, Stanley, Chang, Janer, et al. (2005). Beyond ethnic match: Effects of client–therapist cognitive match in problem perception, coping orientation, and therapy goals on treatment outcomes. *Journal of Community Psychology, 33*, 569–585.

Zosuls, Kristina M., Ruble, Diane N., Tamis-LeMonda, Catherine S., et al. (2009). The acquisition of gender labels in infancy: Implications for gender-typed play. *Developmental Psychology, 45*, 688–701.

Zou, Zhihua, & Buck, Linda. (2006). Combinatorial effects of odorant mixes in olfactory cortex. *Science, 311*, 1477–1481.

Zubieta, Jon-Kar, Bueller, Joshua A., Jackson, Lisa R., et al. (2005). Placebo effects mediated by endogenous opioid activity on m-opioid receptors. *Journal of Neuroscience, 25*, 7754–7762.

Zucker, Kenneth J. (1999). Intersexuality and gender identity differentiation. *Annual Review of Sex Research, 10*, 1–69.

Zur, Ofer, & Nordmarken, M. A. (2008, May/June). DSM: Diagnosing for status and money. *National Psychologist*, p. 15.

Credits

Text

Chapter 1   *Page 5:* Radford, Benjamin (2011, September/October). Holly Bobo still missing: Psychics hurt investigation. Skeptical Inquirer, 35, 9; *Page 7:* Vincent Ruggiero (1988) Teaching Thinking Across the Curriculum. Harper & Row; *Pages 7-8:* Paul, Annie M. (2011). The trouble with homework. The New York Times, September 11, Sunday Review, 6; *Page 9:* de Bono, Edward (1985). De Bono's thinking course. New York: Facts on File; *Page 11:* Steiner, Robert A. (1989). Don't get taken! El Cerrito, CA. Wide Awake Books; *Page 13:* Based on Steiner, Robert A. (1989). Don't get taken! El Cerrito, CA: Wide-Awake Books.; *Page 16:* Köhler, Wolfgang (1959). Gestalt psychology today. Presidential address to the American Psychological Association, Cincinnati. Reprinted in E. R. Hilgard (Ed.), American psychology in historical perspective: Addresses of the presidents of the American Psychological Association, 1892–1977. Washington, DC: American Psychological Association, 1978.; *Pages 16-17:* James, William (1890/1950). Principles of psychology (Vol. 1). New York: Dover; *Page 17:* Freud, Sigmund (1905a). Fragment of an analysis of a case of hysteria. In J. Strachey (ed. and trans.), Standard edition of the complete psychological works of Sigmund Freud (Vol. 7).; *Page 23:* Benjamin, Ludy T., Jr. (2003). Why can't psychology get a stamp? Journal of Applied Psychoanalytic Studies, 5, 443–454.; *Page 24:* Luhrmann, T. M. (2000). Of two minds: The growing disorder in American psychiatry. New York: Knopf.; *Page 28:* Aronson, Elliot (2010). Not by chance alone: My life as a social psychologist. New York: Basic.; *Pages 28-29:* Aronson, Elliot (2010). Not by chance alone: My life as a social psychologist. New York: Basic.

Chapter 2   *Page 36:* Medawar, Peter B. (1979). Advice to a young scientist. New York: Harper & Row.; *Page 41:* Henrich, Joseph; Heine, Steven J.; & Norenzayan, Ara (2010, June 15). The weirdest people in the world? Behavioral and Brain Sciences, 33, 61–83.; *Page 45:* Basson, Rosemary; McInnis, Rosemary; Smith, Mike D.; et al. (2002). Efficacy and safety of sildenafil citrate in women with sexual dysfunction associated with female sexual arousal disorder. Journal of Women's Health and Gender Based Medicine, 11, 367–377.; *Page 53:* Basson, Rosemary; McInnis, Rosemary; Smith, Mike D.; et al. (2002). Efficacy and safety of sildenafil citrate in women with sexual dysfunction associated with female sexual arousal disorder. Journal of Women's Health and Gender Based Medicine, 11, 367–377.; *Page 64:* Thomas Huxley. (September 23, 1860). Letter of Reply to Charles Kingsley.; *Page 65:* Best, Joel (2012). Damned lies and statistics: Untangling numbers from the media, politicians, and activists (updated ed.). Berkeley and Los Angeles: University of California Press. *Page 65:* Children's Defense Fund (CDF), 1994.

Chapter 3   *Page 72:* Thorndike, Edward L. (1903). Educational psychology. New York: Columbia University Teachers College.; *Page 72:* Watson, John B. (1925). Behaviorism. New York: Norton.; *Page 76:* Davey Smith, George (2012). Epidemiology, epigenetics and the "gloomy prospect": Embracing randomness in population research and practice. International Journal of Epidemiology, 40, 537–562.; *Page 76:* Davey Smith, George (2011). Epigenetics for the masses: More than Audrey Hepburn and yellow mice? International Journal of Epidemiology, 40, 303–308.; *Page 83:* Based on Buss, David M. (1995). Evolutionary psychology: A new paradigm for psychological science. Psychological Inquiry, 6, 1–30.; *Page 84:* Buss, David M. (1995). Evolutionary psychology: A new paradigm for psychological science. Psychological Inquiry, 6, 1–30.; *Page 85:* Buller, David J. (2005). Adapting minds: Evolutionary psychology and the persistent quest for human nature. Cambridge MA: MIT Press.; *Page 90:* Graph based on data from Bouchard, Thomas J., Jr., & McGue, Matthew (1981). Familial studies of intelligence: A review. Science, 212, 1055–1058.; *Page 94:* Data from Horgan, John (1995, November). Get smart, take a test: A long-term rise in IQ scores baffles intelligence experts. Scientific American, 273, 12, 14.

Chapter 4   *Page 102:* Regard, Marianne, & Landis, Theodor (1997). "Gourmand syndrome": Eating passion associated with right anterior lesions. Neurology, 48, 1185–1190.; *Page 107:* http://etc.usf.edu/clipart/53100/53184/53184_purkinje_lg.gif; *Page 118:* Cacioppo, John T.; Berntson, Gary G.; Lorig, Tyler S.; et al. (2003). Just because you're imaging the brain doesn't mean you can stop using your head: A primer and set of first principles. Journal of Personality and Social Psychology, 85, 650–661.; *Page 118:* Parry, Marc (2011, October 9). Raymond Tallis takes out the "neurotrash." Chronicle of Higher Education. http://chronicle.com/article/Raymond-Tallis-Takes-Out-the/129279/.; *Page 129:* Sperry, Roger W. (1982). Some effects of disconnecting the cerebral hemispheres. Science, 217, 1223–1226.; *Page 131:* Adapted from Gougoux, Frederic; Zatorre, Robert J.; Lassonde, Maryse; et al. (2005). A functional neuroimaging study of sound localization: Visual cortex activity predicts performance in early-blind individuals. PLoS Biology, 3, 324–333.; *Page 132:* Ambady, Nalini (2011, May/June). The mind in the world: Culture and the brain. APS Observer, 24.; *Page 132:* Fine, Cordelia (2010). From scanner to sound bite: Issues in interpreting and reporting sex differences in the brain. Current Directions in Psychological Science, 19, 280–283.; *Page 136:* Talbot, Margaret (2008, May 12). Birdbrain: The woman behind the world's chattiest parrots. The New Yorker, on line archive.; *Page 136:* Greely, Henry; Sahakian, Barbara; Harris, John; et al. (2008). Towards responsible use of cognitive-enhancing drugs by the healthy. Nature, 455, 702–705. doi:10.1038/456702a.

Chapter 5   *Page 145:* Ecclesiastes 3:2, King James Version; *Page 147:* McFarlane, Jessica; Martin, Carol L.; & Williams, Tannis M. (1988). Mood fluctuations: Women versus men and menstrual versus other cycles. Psychology of Women Quarterly, 12, 201–223.; *Page 149:* Evans, Christopher (1984). Landscapes of the night (edited and completed by Peter Evans). New York: Viking. *Page 150:* http://www.helpguide.org/images/harvard/brain-wave-patterns-during-sleep.jpg; *Page 149:* Zadra, Antonio; Desautels, Alex; Petit, Dominique; & Montplaisir, Jacques (2013). Somnambulism: Clinical aspects and pathophysiological hypotheses. The Lancet Neurology, 12(3), 285–294. *Page 151:* http://www.howsleepworks.com/images/hypnogram.jpg; *Page 153:* Wahlstrom, Kyla (2010). School start time and sleepy teens. Archives of Pediatrics & Adolescent Medicine, 164, 676–677.; *Page 154:* Payne, Jessica D.; Stickgold, Robert; Swanberg, Kelley; & Kensinger, Elizabeth A. (2008). Sleep preferentially enhances memory for emotional components of scenes. Psychological Science, 19, 781–788.; *Page 156:* Freud; *Page 156:* Freud; *Page 156:* Freud; *Page 157:* Dolnick, Edward (1990, July). What dreams are (really) made of. The Atlantic Monthly, 226, 41–45, 48–53, 56–58, 60–61.; *Page 157:* Cartwright, Rosalind D.; Young, Michael A.; Mercer, Patricia; & Bears, Michael (1998). Role of REM sleep and dream variables in the prediction of remission from depression. Psychiatry Research, 80, 249–255; *Page 158:* Hobson, J. Allan (1988). The dreaming brain. New York: Basic.; *Page 159:* Hobson, J. Allan (2002). Dreaming: An introduction to the science of sleep. New York: Oxford University Press.; *Page 159:* Hobson, J. Allan (1988). The dreaming brain. New York: Basic.; *Page 166:* James, William (1902/1936). The varieties of religious experience. New York: Modern Library.

Chapter 6   *Page 183:* © Pearson Education, Inc.; *Page 197:* © Pearson Education, Inc.; *Page 205:* Mozell, Maxwell M.; Smith, Bruce P.; Smith, Paul E.; et al. (1969). Nasal chemoreception in flavor identification. Archives of Otolaryngology, 90, 367–373.; *Page 216:* Blackmore, Susan (2001, March/April). Giving up the ghosts: End of a personal quest. Skeptical Inquirer, 25.; *Page 217:* Andrew Weil, The Marriage of the Sun and Moon: Dispatches from the Frontiers of Consciousness, Houghton Mifflin Harcourt, 11-Nov-2004.

Chapter 7   *Page 227:* Robert A. Rescorla. Pavlovian Conditioning It's Not What You Think It Is. American Psychologist, 43(3), 151-160; *Page 248:* Lepper, Mark R.; Greene, David; & Nisbett, Richard E. (1973). Undermining children's intrinsic interest with extrinsic rewards. Journal of Personality and Social Psychology, 28, 129–137.; *Page 248:* Deci, Edward L.; Koestner, Richard; & Ryan, Richard M. (1999). A meta-analytic review of experiments examining the effects of extrinsic rewards on intrinsic motivation. Psychological Bulletin, 125, 627–668.; *Page 250:* Tolman, Edward C., & Honzik, Chase H. (1930). Introduction and removal Of reward and maze performance in rats. University of California Publications in Psychology, 4, 257–275.; *Page 254:* Anderson, Sarah E.; Dallal, Gerard E.; & Must, Aviva (2003). Relative weight and race influence average age at menarche: Results from two nationally representative surveys of U.S. girls studied 25 years apart. Pediatrics, 111, 844–850.

Chapter 8 *Page 260:* Brown, Roger (1986). Social psychology (2nd ed.). New York: Free Press.; *Page 261:* Stanley Milgram; *Page 263:* Milgram, Stanley (1974). Obedience to authority: An experimental view. New York: Harper & Row.; *Page 264:* Milgram, Stanley (1974). Obedience to authority: An experimental view. New York: Harper & Row.; *Page 265:* Darley, John M. (1995). Constructive and destructive obedience: A taxonomy of principal agent relationships. In A. G. Miller, B. E. Collins, & D. E. Brief (Eds.), Perspectives on obedience to authority: The legacy of the Milgram experiments. Journal of Social Issues, 51(3), 125–154.; *Page 265:* Haslam, S. Alexander, & Reicher, Stephen (2003, Spring). "Beyond Stanford: Questioning a role-based explanation of tyranny." Society for Experimental Social Psychology Dialogue, 18, 22–25.; *Page 265:* Haney, Craig; Banks, Curtis; & Zimbardo, Philip (1973). Interpersonal dynamics in a simulated prison. International Journal of Criminology and Penology, 1, 69–97.; *Page 266:* C. P. Snow quoted in Obedience to authority : an experimental view by Stanley Milgram, New York : Harper & Row, ©1974.; *Page 266:* Milgram, Stanley (1974). Obedience to authority: An experimental view. New York: Harper & Row.; *Page 269:* Milgram, Stanley (1974). Obedience to authority: An experimental view. New York: Harper & Row.; *Page 271:* Gal, David, & Rucker, Derek D. (2010). When in doubt, shout! Paradoxical influences of doubt on proselytizing. Psychological Science, 21, 1701–1707.; *Page 272:* Arkes, Hal R. (1993). Some practical judgment and decision-making research. In N. J. Castellan, Jr., et al. (Eds.), Individual and group decision making: Current issues.Hillsdale, NJ: Erlbaum.; *Page 273:* Alford, John R.; Funk, Carolyn L.; & Hibbing, John R. (2005). Are political orientations genetically transmitted? American Political Science Review, 99, 153–167.; *Page 273:* Graham, Jesse; Haidt, Jonathon; & Nosek, Brian A. (2009). Liberals and conservatives rely on different sets of moral foundations. Journal of Personality and Social Psychology, 96, 1029–1046.; *Page 285:* Sherif, Muzafer; Harvey, O.J.; White, B.J.; Hood, William; & Sherif, Carolyn (1961). Intergroup conflict and cooperation: The Robbers Cave Experiment. Norman: University of Oklahoma Institute of Intergroup Relations."; *Page 289:* Allport, Gordon W. (1954/1979). The nature of prejudice. Reading, MA: Addison-Wesley.; *Page 291:* Fellner, Jamie (2009, June 19). Race, drugs, and law enforcement in the United States. Stanford Law and Policy Review, 20, 257–291.; *Page 294:* Mendoza-Denton, Rodolfo, & Page-Gould, Elizabeth (2008). Can cross-group friendships influence minority students' well-being at historically white universities? Psychological Science,19, 933–939.; *Page 296:* Hall, Edward T., & Hall, Mildred R. (1987). Hidden differences: Doing business with the Japanese. Garden City, NY: Anchor Press/Doubleday.; *Page 296:* MICHAEL SLACKMAN, The Fine Art of Hiding What You Mean to Say, August 6, 2006.

Chapter 9 *Page 312:* D'Antonio, Michael (2004, May 2). How we think. Los Angeles Times Magazine, 18–20, 30–32.; *Page 323:* Dunning, David; Johnson, Kerri; Ehrlinger, Joyce; & Kruger, Justin (2003). Why people fail to recognize their own incompetence. Current Directions in Psychological Science, 12, 83–87.; *Page 324:* Sternberg, Robert J. (1988). The triarchic mind: A new theory of human intelligence. New York: Viking.; *Page 326:* Duckworth, Angela L.; Seligman, Martin E. P. (2005, Dec.) Self-discipline outdoes IQ in predicting academic performance of adolescents. Psychological Science,16 (12), 939–944.; *Page 327:* Stevenson, Harold W.; Chen, Chuansheng; & Lee, Shin-ying (1993, January 1). Mathematics achievement of Chinese, Japanese, and American children: Ten years later. Science, 259, 53–58.; *Page 333:* Based on Helson, Ravenna; Roberts, Brent; & Agronick, Gail (1995). Enduringness and change in creative personality and the prediction of occupational creativity. Journal of Personality and Social Psychology, 6, 1173–1183; McCrae, Robert R. (1987). Creativity, divergent thinking, and openness to experience. Journal of Personality and Social Psychology, 52, 1258–1265.; Schank, Roger (with Peter Childers) (1988). The creative attitude. New York: Macmillan.

Chapter 10 *Page 340:* Parker, Elizabeth S.; Cahill, Larry; & McGaugh, James L. (2006). A case of unusual autobiographical remembering. Neurocase, 12, 35–49.; *Page 348:* Garven, Sena; Wood, James M.; Malpass, Roy S.; & Shaw, John S., III (1998). More than suggestion: The effect of interviewing techniques from the McMartin Preschool case. Journal of Applied Psychology, 83, 347–359.; *Page 357:* Hassabis, Demis, & Maguire, Eleanor A. (2007). Deconstructing episodic memory with construction. Trends in Cognitive Sciences, 11, 299–306.; *Page 367:* Linton, Marigold (1978), "Real World Memory After Six Years: An In Vivo Study of Very Long Term Memory," in Practical Aspects of Memory, eds., Michael M. Gruneberg, Peter E. Morris and Robert N. Sykes, New York, NY: Academic Press/Elsevier, 77–83.; *Page 370:* McNally, Richard J. (2003). Remembering trauma. Cambridge, MA: Harvard University Press.; *Page 372:* Piaget, Jean (1952). Play, dreams, and imitation in childhood. New York: W. W. Norton.

Chapter 11 *Page 384:* Shakespeare's, History of Henry VI, Part III, Act III, Scene 2 London. The palace; *Page 388:* Iacono, William G., & Lykken, David T. (1997). The scientific status of research on polygraph techniques: The case against polygraph tests. In D. L. Faigman, D. Kaye, M. J. Saks, & J. Sanders (eds.), Modern scientific evidence: The law and science of expert testimony. St. Paul, MN: West.; *Page 393:* Brescoll, Victoria L., & Uhlmann, Eric L. (2008). Can an angry woman get ahead? Status conferral, gender, and expression of emotion in the workplace. Psychological Science, 19, 268–275.; *Page 398:* Cohen, Dov (1998). Culture, social organization, and patterns of violence. Journal of Personality and Social Psychology, 75, 408–419.; *Page 404:* Williams, Redford B., Jr.; Barefoot, John C.; & Shekelle, Richard B. (1985). The health consequences of hostility. In M. A. Chesney & R. H. Rosenman (Eds.), Anger and hostility in cardiovascular and behavioral disorders. New York: Hemisphere.; *Page 410:* Coan, James A.; Schaefer, Hillary; & Davidson, Richard J. (2006). Lending a hand: Social regulation of the neural response to threat. Psychological Science, 17.

Chapter 12 *Page 431:* Solomon, Robert C. (1994). About love. Lanham, MD: Littlefeld Adams.; *Page 433:* Tiefer, Leonore (2004). Sex is not a natural act, and other essays (rev. ed.). Boulder, CO: Westview. *Page 435:* Meston, Cindy M., & Buss, David M. (2007). Why humans have sex. Archives of Sexual Behavior, 36, 477–507.; *Page 435:* Conley, Terri D.; Moors, Amy C.; Matsick, Jes L.; et al. (2011). Women, men, and the bedroom: Methodological and conceptual insights that narrow, ref rame, and eliminate gender differences in sexuality. Current Directions in Psychological Science, 20, 296–300.; *Page 436:* Based on Cooper, M. Lynne; Shapiro, Cheryl M.; & Powers, Anne M. (1998). Motivations for sex and risky sexual behavior among adolescents and young adults: A functional perspective. Journal of Personality and Social Psychology, 75, 1528–1558; Meston, Cindy M., & Buss, David M. (2007). Why humans have sex. Archives of Sexual Behavior, 36, 477–507.; *Page 439:* Bowleg, Lisa; Lucas, Kenya J.; & Tschann, Jeanne M. (2004). "The ball was always in his court": An exploratory analysis of relationship scripts, sexual scripts, and condom use among African American women. Psychology of Women Quarterly, 28, 70–82.; *Page 443:* Sources: Locke, Edwin A., & Latham, Gary P. (2002). Building a practically useful theory of goal setting and task motivation. American Psychologist, 57, 705–717.; Locke, Edwin A., & Latham, Gary P. (2006). New directions in goal-setting theory. Current Directions in Psychological Science, 15, 265–268.; *Page 445:* William Faulkner, The sound and the fury, Harmondsworth : Penguin, 1900; *Page 445:* Helen Keller, Annie Sullivan, John Albert Macy, The story of my life, London : Doubleday, Page & Company, 1903; *Page 445:* Nelson Mandela, Long walk to freedom : the autobiography of Nelson Mandela, London : Little Brown, 1994.; *Page 445:* Jan Garden Castro and Georgia O'Keeffe, The art & life of Georgia O'Keeffe, New York : Crown, ©1985.; *Page 445:* Quoted in Kissinger: A Biography, Walter Isaacson by Walter Isaacson, Simon and Schuster, May-2013 - Biography & Autobiography; *Page 445:* Eleanor Roosevelt Quoted in Russell Freedman, Eleanor Roosevelt: A Life of Discovery by Russell Freedman, Houghton Mifflin Harcourt, 1993; *Page 445:* Florence Griffith Joyner Quoted in African-American Sports Greats: A Biographical Dictionary by David L. Porter, ABC-CLIO, 01-Jan-1995; *Page 445:* Ivan Boesky, Commencement address at university of California, Berkeley, School of Business Administration, May 18, 1986.; *Page 448:* Sources: Based on Bakker, Arnold B. (2011). An evidence-based model of work engagement. Current Directions in Psychological Science, 20, 265–269.; Maslach, Christina; Schaufeli, Wilmar B.; & Leiter, Michael P. (2001). Job burnout. Annual Review of Psychology, 52, 397–422.; Rhoades, Linda, & Eisenberger, Robert (2002). Perceived organizational support: A review of the literature. Journal of Applied Psychology, 87, 698–714.; *Page 450:* Dunn, Elizabeth W.; Wilson, Timothy D.; & Gilbert, Daniel T. (2003). Location, location, location: The misprediction of satisfaction in housing lotteries. Personality and Social Psychology Bulletin, 29, 1421–1432.; *Page 451:* Lewin, Kurt (1948). Resolving social conflicts. New York: Harper. *Page 453:* Ray Bradbury and Sam Weller, Ray Bradbury : the last interview and other conversations, Brooklyn : Melville House, (2014).

Chapter 13 *Page 463:* Data from Kagan, Jerome; Kearsley, Richard B.; & Zelazo, Philip R. (1978). Infancy: Its place in human development. Cambridge, MA: Harvard University Press.; *Page 473:* Data from Baillargeon, Renée (1994). How do infants learn about the physical world? Current Directions in Psychological Science, 5, 133–140.; *Page 481:* Paoletti, Jo (2012). Pink and blue: Telling the girls from the boys in America. Bloomington, IN: University of Indiana Press.; *Page 485:* Berkman Center for Internet & Society (2008, December 31). Enhancing child safety and online technologies: Final report of the Internet Safety Task Force. Final report available at http://cyber.law.harvard.edu/sites/cyber.law.harvard.edu/files/ISTTF_Final_Report.pdf.; *Page 489:* Pearlin, Leonard (1982). Discontinuities in the study of aging.

In T. K. Hareven & K. J. Adams (Eds.), Aging and life course transitions: An interdisciplinary perspective. New York: Guilford.

Chapter 14 *Page 502:* Based on Freud, Anna (1967). Ego and the mechanisms of defense (The writings of Anna Freud, Vol. 2) (rev. ed.). New York: International Universities Press.; Perry & Metzger, 2014; Vaillant, George E. (Ed.) (1992). Ego mechanisms of defense. Washington, DC: American Psychiatric Press.; *Page 504:* Freud, Sigmund (1961). Letters of Sigmund Freud, 1873–1939. Edited by Ernst L. Freud. London: Hogarth Press.; *Page 509:* Based on Chang, Luye; Connelly, Brian S.; & Geeza, Alexis A. (2012). Separating method factors and higher order traits of the big five: A meta-analytic multitrait–multimethod approach. Journal of Personality and Social Psychology,102, 408–426; Costa & McCrae 2011, 2014; McCrae, Robert R.; Terracciano, Antonio; & members of the Personality Profiles of Cultures Project (2005). Universal features of personality traits from the observer's perspective: Data from 50 cultures. Journal of Personality and Social Psychology, 88, 547–561; Paunonen, Sampo V. (2003). Big Five factors or personality and replicated predictions of behavior. Journal of Personality & Social Psychology, 84, 411–422.; Roberts, Brent W., & Mroczek, Daniel (2008). Personality trait change in adulthood. Current Directions in Psychological Science, 17, 31–35.; *Page 510:* Costa, Paul T., Jr.; McCrae, Robert R.; Martin, Thomas A.; et al. (1999). Personality development from adolescence through adulthood. Further cross cultural comparisons of age differences. In V. J. Molfese & D. Molfese (Eds.), Temperament and personality development across the life span. Hillsdale, NJ: Erlbaum.; *Page 511:* This self-test comes from Gosling, Samuel D.; Rentfrow, P. J.; & Swann, William B., Jr. (2003). A very brief measure of the Big Five personality domains. Journal of Research in Personality, 37, 504–528.; *Page 515:* Plomin, Robert (1989). Environment and genes: Determinants of behavior. American Psychologist, 44, 105–111.; *Page 517:* Based on Harris, Judith R. (2006). No two alike: Human nature and human individuality. New York: Norton.; Harris, Judith R. (2009). The nurture assumption (2nd ed.). New York: Free Press; Plomin, Robert (2011). Commentary: Why are children in the same family so different? Non-shared environment three decades later. International Journal of Epidemiology, 40, 582–592.; *Page 521:* Triandis, Harry C. (1996). The psychological measurement of cultural syndromes. American Psychologist, 51, 407–415.; *Page 524:* Cohen, Dov; Nisbett, Richard E.; Bowdle, Brian F.; & Schwarz, Norbert (1996). Insult, aggression, and the Southern culture of honor: An "experimental ethnography." Journal of Personality and Social Psychology, 70, 945–960.; *Page 527:* Maslow, Abraham H. (1971). The farther reaches of human nature. New York: Viking.; *Page 528:* Quoted in O'Hanlon, Bill (1994, November/December). The third wave. Family Therapy Networker, 18–29.; *Page 531:* Snyder, C. R., & Shenkel, Randee J. (1975, March). The P. T. Barnum effect. Psychology Today, 52–54.

Chapter 15 *Page 542:* Frances, Allen (2013). Saving normal. New York: William Morrow.; *Page 543:* Diagnostic and Statistical Manual of Mental Disorders, 5th Edition: DSM-5; *Page 545:* Emery, Robert E.; Otto, Randy K.; & O'Donohue, William T. (2005). A critical assessment of child custody evaluations: Limited science and a fawed system. Psychological Science in the Public Interest, 6, 1–29.; *Page 553:* Nolen-Hoeksema, Susan (2004). Lost in thought: Rumination and depression. Paper presented at the National Institute on the Teaching of Psychology, St. Petersburg, Florida.; *Page 553:* Mark Twain, Autobiography of Mark Twain, Volume 1: The Complete and Authoritative Edition, University of California Press, 2010.; *Page 557:* Moffitt, Terrie E. (1993). Adolescence-limited and life-course-persistent anti-social behavior: A developmental taxonomy. Psychological Review, 100, 674–701. p.679.; *Page 559:* Based on Hare, Robert D. (1965). Temporal gradient of fear arousal in psychopaths. Journal of Abnormal Psychology, 70, 442–445.; Hare, Robert D. (1993). Without conscience: The disturbing world of the psychopaths among us. New York: Pocket Books.; *Page 565:* Based on Peele, Stanton, & Brodsky, Archie (with Mary Arnold) (1991). The truth about addiction and recovery. New York: Simon & Schuster.; *Page 567:* Kluft, Richard P. (1987). The simulation and dissimulation of multiple personality disorder. American Journal of Clinical Hypnosis, 30, 104–118.; *Page 568:* Nathan, Debbie (2011). Sybil exposed: The extraordinary story behind the famous multiple personality case. New York: Free Press.; *Page 570:* Goode, Erica (2003, May 6). Experts see mind's voices in new light. The New York Times, Science Times, D1, D4.; *Page 570:* Bleuler, Eugen (1911/1950). Dementia praecox or the group of schizophrenias. New York: International Universities Press.; *Page 572:* Based on Gottesman, Irving I. (1991). Schizophrenia genesis: The origins of madness. New York: Freeman.; *Page 573:* Thompson, Paul M.; Vidal, Christine N.; Giedd, Jay N.; et al. (2001b). Mapping adolescent brain change reveals dynamic wave of accelerated gray matter loss in very early-onset schizophrenia. Proceedings of the National Academy of Sciences, 98, 11650–11655.

Chapter 16 *Page 586:* Based on Turner, E. H.; Matthews, A. M.; Linardatos, E.; et al. (2008). Selective publication of antidepressant trials and its infuence on apparent efficacy. New England Journal of Medicine, 358, 252–60.; *Page 592:* Martin, Garry, & Pear, Joseph (2014). Behavior modification: What it is and how to do it (10th ed.). New York: Psychology Press.; *Page 596:* Yalom, Irvin D. (1989). Love's executioner and other tales of psychotherapy. New York: Basic.; *Page 600:* Baker, Timothy B.; McFall, Richard M.; & Shoham, Varda (2008). Current status and future prospects of clinical psychology: Toward a scientifically principled approach to mental and behavioral health care. Psychological Science in the Public Interest, 9, entire issue.; *Page 601:* McGoldrick, Monica (2005). Irish families. In M. McGoldrick, J. Giordano, & N. Garcia-Preto (Eds.), Ethnicity and family therapy (3rd ed.). New York: Guilford.; *Page 602:* Mayou, R. A.; Ehlers, A.; & Hobbs, M. (2000). Psychological debriefing for road traffic accident victims. British Journal of Psychiatry, 176, 589–593.; *Page 602:* Mayou, R. A.; Ehlers, A.; & Hobbs, M. (2000). Psychological debriefing for road traffic accident victims. British Journal of Psychiatry, 176, 589–593.; *Page 604:* Quoted in Kring, Ann; Johnson, Sheri; Davison, Gerald C.; & Neale, John M. (2010). Abnormal psychology (11th Ed.). New York: Wiley.; *Page 606:* Based on Lilienfeld, Scott O. (2007). Psychological treatments that cause harm. Perspectives on Psychological Science, 2, 53–70.; *Page 610:* The authors.

Photographs

Chapter 1 *Page 1:* Rawpixel/Shutterstock, *Page 3:* 2Happy/Shutterstock, *Page 3:* Justin Sullivan/Getty Images, *Page 7:* Biehler Michael/Shutterstock, *Page 9:* Racorn/Shutterstock, *Page 10:* Digital N/Shutterstock, *Page 11:* Tom Williams/CQ Roll Call/Newscom, *Page 11:* Fayaz Aziz/Reuters, *Page 11:* Sergey Mironov/Alamy, *Page 11:* Daniel Lainé/Corbis, *Page 12:* Jonathan Larsen/Diadem Images/Alamy, *Page 12:* Lisa F. Young/Fotolia, *Page 12:* WavebreakmediaMicro/Fotolia, *Page 12:* Eric Fowke/PhotoEdit, *Page 15:* North Wind Picture Archives/Alamy, *Page 16:* Pictorial Press Ltd/Alamy, *Page 16:* Library of Congress Prints and Photographs Division, *Page 17:* Library of Congress Prints and Photographs Division[LC-USZ62-72266], *Page 23:* Goodluz/Shutterstock, *Page 24:* Wavebreakmedia/Shutterstock, *Page 26:* Mark Bowden/Getty Images, *Page 26:* Miguel Medina/Getty Images.

Chapter 2 *Page 34:* Bill Greene/The Boston/Getty Images, *Page 42:* Bettmann/Corbis, *Page 42:* NASA Images, *Page 42:* DHA/Reuters, *Page 43:* Dangubic/Fotolia, *Page 49:* Peter Dazeley/Getty Images, *Page 59:* Robert Crum/Shutterstock, *Page 63:* Frank Kiernan

Chapter 3 *Page 71:* Jodi Cobb/National Geographic Image Collection/Alamy, *Page 72:* Shannon LeMay-Finn, *Page 73:* Science Source, *Page 74:* Africa Studio/Fotolia, *Page 77:* Eric Isselee/Shutterstock, *Page 80:* Karen H. Ilagan/Shutterstock, *Page 80:* Nils Jorgensen/Rex Features/Presselect/Alamy, *Page 84:* David Tipling/Alamy, *Page 85:* Pictorial Press Ltd/Alamy, *Page 93:* Anadolu Agency/Getty Images, *Page 94:* BestPhotoStudio/Shutterstock, *Page 96:* Science Photo Library/Alamy.

Chapter 4 *Page 101:* Kolvenbach/Alamy, *Page 103:* Johns Hopkins University Applied Physics Laboratory, *Page 107:* Science Source, *Page 110:* Steve Gschmeissner/Science Photo Library/Alamy, *Page 113:* Samuel Borges/Fotolia, *Page 116:* Jochen Tack/Glow Images, *Page 116:* Phanie/SuperStock, *Page 118:* Pearson Education, *Page 118:* Pearson Education, *Page 126:* Science Source, *Page 128:* Pearson Education, *Page 129:* WavebreakMediaMicro/Fotolia.

Chapter 5 *Page 141:* Art Kowalsky/Alamy, *Page 143:* BSIP SA/Alamy, *Page 145:* Maridav/Shutterstock, *Page 145:* Brainsil/Fotolia, *Page 146:* B. Boissonnet/BSIP/AGE Fotostock, *Page 150:* Amana Images inc./Alamy, *Page 150:* Vera Kailova/Shutterstock, *Page 152:* TheFinalMiracle/Shutterstock, *Page 158:* Science Source, *Page 158:* Science Source, *Page 158:* Science Source, *Page 158:* Uckyo/Fotolia, *Page 162:* Bookstaver/AP Images, *Page 163:* BSIP SA/Alamy, *Page 167:* Images & Stories/Alamy, *Page 167:* Science Source, *Page 167:* Hemis/Doizer Marc/Alamy, *Page 169:* David Pollack/Fine Art/Corbis, *Page 171:* Sylvie Bouchard/Fotolia, *Page 171:* Oneinchpunch/Fotolia.

Chapter 6 *Page 177:* Hektor2/Fotolia, *Page 181:* Wicab, Inc., *Page 181:* Joe Giddens/ZUMA Press/Newscom, *Page 183:* Hwongcc/Shutterstock, *Page 183:* Thomas Males/Alamy, *Page 186:* Ashok Saxena/Alamy, *Page 190:* Erich

Name Index

Subject Index

A

Abecedarian Project, 93
Absolute numbers, 65
Absolute threshold, 181–182
Acculturation, 283
Acetylcholine, 112, 114
Achievement, motivation and, 443–449
  effects of work on motivation, 447–448
  at work, 443–446
Action potential, 110
Activation-synthesis theory, 157–158, 159
Addiction, 560–566
  biological model of, 560–561, 565
  causes of, debating, 564–565
  learning model of, 562–564, 565
Adenine, 74
Adolescence, 483–487
  physiology of, 483–485
  psychology of, 485–486
Adoptees, heritability studies on, 88
Adrenal glands, 113, 114
Adrenal hormones, 114
Adrenalin, 114
Adrenarche, 483
Adulthood, 487–494
  old age, 491–493
  stages and ages, 488–489
  transitions of life, 490–491
    emerging adulthood, 490
    middle years, 491
Affect heuristic, 310
Affective neuroscientists, 103
Alarm phase, 396
Alcohol, 168, 169, 170
Algorithm, 306–307
Alice's Adventures in Wonderland (Carroll), 142
Alpha waves, 149, 150, 151, 165
Altered states of consciousness, 166–167
Alternate-forms reliability, 44–45
Altruism, 281–282
Alzheimer's disease, 96, 112, 609
American Psychiatric Association (APA), 541
Diagnostic and Statistical Manual of Mental Disorders (DSM), 541–543, 544

American Psychological Association
  code of ethics, 62–63
American Sign Language (ASL), 199
Amnesia, 370–371
  childhood, 372–373
Amphetamines, 168
Amygdala, 121, 126, 231
  emotions and, 384–385, 386
  memory and, 360, 362
Analytical intelligence, 324
Anatomical code, 180
Androgens, 114
Anger
  measuring, 292
  therapy for, effectiveness of, 602
Animal minds, 328–332
  animal intelligence, 328–329
  animals and language, 330–331
  anthropomorphism and anthropodenial for understanding, 331–332
Animal research
  ethics in, 63–64
  reasons for, 63
Anorexia nervosa, 425–426
Anthropodenial, 331–332
Anthropomorphism, 331–332
Antisocial personality disorder (APD), 557
Anvil, 200, 201
Anxiety disorders, 546–549
  fears, 548–549
  generalized anxiety disorder, 547
  panic disorder, 547–548
  phobias, 548–549
  therapy for, effectiveness of, 603
Applied behavior analysis. *See* Behavior modification
Applied psychology, 22
Appraisals, 389
Approach-approach conflicts, 451
Approach-avoidance conflicts, 451
Arithmetic means, 57
Asch line-judging study, 277
Assessment instruments. *See* Psychological tests
Association cortex, 123–124
Association for Psychological Science (APS), 25
Assumptions, analyzing, 8–9, 11
Astrologers, 5

Attachment, 462–465
  contact comfort, 462
  insecure, 463–465
  separation and security, 462–463
Attachment theory of love, 430
Attachment therapies, 606
Attitudes, 270–272
  cognitive dissonance, 270–271
  familiarity effect, 272
  implicit, measuring, 292
  validity effect, 272
Attributions, 268–270
Attribution theory, 268–270
Audition. *See* Hearing
Auditory cortex, 123
Auditory nerve, 201
Autonomic nervous system, 105, 386
Availability heuristic, 310
Avoidance-avoidance conflicts, 451
Axon, 107–108, 110–111
Axon terminals, 108, 110, 111

B

Balance, sense of, 209–210
Barbiturates, 168
Barnum effect, 531
Base rates, 65
Basic concepts, 303
Basic psychology, 22
Basilar membrane, 201
Behavior, 259–300
  consequences of, 235–238, 244–247
  group identity, 283–286
  individuals in groups, 276–282
  prejudice, 287–295
  social forces, 261–267
  social influences on, 268–275
Behavioral geneticists, 26, 86–87, 88, 274, 516
Behavioral genetics, 72, 73, 90, 273
Behavioral neuroscientists, 103
Behavioral self-monitoring, 593
Behaviorism, 222, 228
Behaviorists, 19
Behavior modification, 244
Behavior therapy, 592–593, 598
  behavioral self-monitoring in, 593
  exposure in, 592
  skills training in, 593
  systematic desensitization in, 592–593